THE WORLD

A History   Second Edition

Felipe Fernández-Armesto

UNIVERSITY OF NOTRE DAME

Volume Two: Since 1300

MAPS BY

DORLING KINDERSLEY

PRENTICE HALL
Upper Saddle River   London   Singapore
Toronto   Tokyo   Sydney   Hong Kong
Mexico City

Executive Editor: Charles Cavaliere
Editorial Assistant: Lauren Aylward
Production Project Manager: Lynn Savino Wendel
Senior Development Editor: Gerald Lombardi
Editor in Chief, History: Priscilla McGeehon
Editor in Chief, Development: Rochelle Diogenes
Editorial Director: Leah Jewell
Associate Supplements Editor: Emsal Hasan
Director of Marketing: Brandy Dawson
Executive Marketing Manager: Sue Westmoreland
Senior Marketing Manager: Laura Lee Manley
Marketing Assistant: Ashley Fallon
AV Project Manager: Mirella Signoretto
Manager, Rights and Permissions: Zina Arabia

Manager, Visual Research: Beth Brenzel
Image Permission Coordinator: Craig A. Jones
Cover Image Specialist: Karan Sanatar
Photo Researcher: Francelle Carapetyan
Composition/Full Service Project Management: Rebecca Dunn, Prepare, Inc.
Director, Media & Assessment: Brian Hyland
Media Editor: Sarah Kinney
Media Project Manager: Tina Rudowski
Senior Operations Specialist: Mary Ann Gloriande
Senior Art Director: Maria Lange
Interior and Cover Designer: QT Design
Printer/Binder: Courier Kendallville
Cover Printer: Lehigh-Phoenix Color/Hagerstown

DK DK Maps designed and produced by DK Education, a division of Dorling Kindersley Limited, 80 Strand, London WC2R ORL. DK and the DK logo are registered trademarks of Dorling Kindersley Limited.

This book was set in 11/13 Minion.
Credits and acknowledgments borrowed from other sources and reproduced, with permission, in this textbook appear on appropriate page within text or on page C-1.

Library of Congress Cataloging-in-Publication Data
Fernández-Armesto, Felipe.
  The world : a history / Felipe Fernandez-Armesto. -- Combined vol., 2nd ed.
    p. cm.
  Maps by Dorling Kindersley.
  Includes index.
  ISBN 978-0-13-606147-2 (combined)—ISBN 978-0-205-65501-4 (exam)—ISBN 978-0-13-606148-9 (v. 1)—
  ISBN 978-0-13-606149-6 (v. 2)—ISBN 978-0-205-68347-5 (v. a)—ISBN 978-0-13-608757-1 (v. b)—ISBN 978-0-13-606150-2 (v. c)
    1. Civilization--History. 2. Human ecology. I. Title.
  CB151.F48 2007
  909—dc22   2008050926

10 9 8 7 6 5 4 3 2 1

Prentice Hall
is an imprint of

www.pearsonhighered.com

ISBN 10:   0-13-606149-4
ISBN 13: 978-0-13-606149-6

Contents

"So far, we know of nowhere else in the cosmos where so much has happened and is happening today. By galactic standards, global history is a small story—but it is a good one"   xvii

PART 6

The Crucible: The Eurasian Crises of the Thirteenth and Fourteenth Centuries   409

"Without the Mongol peace, it is hard to imagine any of the rest of world history working out quite as it did, for these were the roads that carried Chinese ideas and transmitted technology westward and opened up European minds to the vastness of the world."   437

"Climate and microbes belong to two rebellious realms of nature that resist human power."   444

> *"The world did not wait passively for European outreach to transform it, as if touched by a magic wand. Other societies were already working magic of their own, turning states into empires and cultures into civilizations."*   484

PART 7   Convergence and Divergence to ca. 1700   529

> *"...from the period from the sixteenth century to the eighteenth, when the unprecedented growth of empires was one of the most dramatic features of the history of the world, empires spread as much by collaboration as by conquest...."*   531

"*A divergent pattern of evolution had made the life forms of the various continents ever more different from one another from the moment, perhaps 150 million years ago or more, when Pangaea—the unified world landmass—split and the continents began to drift apart. Relatively suddenly, by the scale of the long preceding period, the Columbian Exchange reversed that pattern.*" 568

18 Mental Revolutions: Religion and Science in the Sixteenth and Seventeenth Centuries 600

"*Despite the shortcomings of their missionaries or of their congregations, the enormous extensions of the frontiers of Islam, Buddhism, and Christianity remains one of the most conspicuous features of the world of the sixteenth and seventeenth centuries.*" 631

19 States and Societies: Political and Social Change in the Sixteenth and Seventeenth Centuries 634

"For the first time, a single–if small scale–system of trade encircled the Earth. Some regions were still outside this system: Australia and most of the South Pacific, parts of inland Africa, the far interiors of the Americas. But they were unlikely to be left outside for long." 666

PART 8 Global Enlightenments, 1700–1800 673

"The New Europes made the West big. A culture crammed, for most of its history, into a small, remote, and beleaguered corner of Eurasia now had much of the western hemisphere and important parts of the Pacific and of Africa at its disposal." 702

"Painstakingly recruited, thinly spread, colonists began to extend the limits of the inhabited world. At the edges of empires to which they belonged, where they reached out to touch the outposts of other expanding peoples, they helped to mesh the world together." 706

22 The Exchange of Enlightenments: Eighteenth-Century Thought   738

"Like all topics in the history of thought, the Enlightenment is complex and elusive. We had better begin by admitting that and relishing the challenge."   740

PART 9   The Frustrations of Progress to ca. 1900   773

23 Replacing Muscle: The Energy Revolutions   774

Contents

24 The Social Mold: Work and Society in the Nineteenth Century   810

25 Western Dominance in the Nineteenth Century: The Westward Shift of Power and the Rise of Global Empires   844

"For the contemporaries who took part in it, the appeal of industry was a form of enchantment. Like magic, or like today's information technology, which seems to have similar effects on many people, it multiplied power and effected dazzling transformations."   788

"As the pace of commerce speeded up, and its reach broadened, so did the range of economic opportunities and rewards, and so did the numbers of people worldwide who were left behind or left out."   812

" Meanwhile, even under imperialism, people continued to make their own history, thanks to systems of indirect rule and the empires' reliance on collaborators. Still, the nineteenth century remains a century of a "European miracle": the sudden, startling climax of a long, faltering commercial outthrust, imperial initiatives, and scientific progress."   875

"All the transformations of nineteenth-century states need to be understood against a common background: the declining credibility of traditional forms of authority, as conflicts overthrew old supremacies and economic change enriched new aspirants to power." *909*

PART 10 Chaos and Complexity: The World in the Twentieth Century 915

"Science, in most people's judgment, soared and failed. It sought to penetrate the heavens, and it ended by contaminating the Earth." *947*

"War dominated and can almost be said to have determined global politics in the twentieth century. War strained the empires the Europeans had constructed so laboriously in the nineteenth century. In the first half of the twentieth century, those empires barely endured, and in the second half, they all collapsed." 987

"It is tempting to characterize the twentieth century as a century of paradox. Frustrated hopes coincided with unprecedented progress. Utopias nourished moral sickness, suicide, and crime. The century of democracy was the century of dictators." 1022

"What are we going to do with our world? It is, so far, the only one we have to live in." 1051

Projection
A map projection is used to portray all or part of the round Earth on a flat surface, which cannot be done without some distortion. The projections in *The World* show the Earth at global, continental, country, and city scale and vary with each map. The map shown here uses a Robinson projection, which uses curvature to provide a good balance between the size and shape of the lands being depicted. As any number of projections could have been selected for each map in *The World*, great care was shown in choosing projections that best serve the goals of the author.

M aps use a unique visual language to convey a great deal of information in a relatively simple form. The maps in this book use a variety of different projections—techniques used to show the Earth's curved surface on a flat map—to trace the history of humans from about 150,000 years ago to the present. This brief guide explains the different features on the maps in *The World*, Second Edition and how to interpret the different layers of information embedded in them.

Inset Map and Global Locator Several of the maps in *The World* include inset maps that show in greater size and detail a region depicted on the main map. Many of the maps in *The World* also include global locators that highlight that portion of the Earth's surface that is being shown.

The Middle East and the Mediterranean, ca. 1000–500 B.C.E.

▦	Assyrian Empire at its greatest extent
▦	Babylonian Empire at its peak under Nebuchadnezzar II
▦	Phoenicia and Phoenician colonies
▦	Areas frequented or settled by Greeks
▦	Etruria
●	Greek colony
●	Phoenician colony
SLOVENIA	modern country
▣	copper
▣	gold
▣	tin
——	Greek trade route
——	Phoenician trade route
---	ancient coastline

Timeline
Many of the maps featured in *The World* are accompanied by timelines. Various important events and developments are plotted along a historical line, which shows the order in which they occurred during a certain period in history.

Topography
Many maps show relief—the contours of mountains and valleys. Topography is an important element in reading maps, because the size and scale of the physical terrain has served as a critical factor in shaping human history.

Map Key
Maps use symbols to both show the location of a feature and to give information about that feature. The symbols are explained in the key that accompanies each map.

Scalebar
When using a map to work out what distances are in reality, it is necessary to refer to the scale of that particular map. Many of the maps in *The World* (such as the one shown here) use a linear scale. This only works on equal-area maps, where distances are true. On maps with projections that are heavily curved, a special "perspective-scale graphic" is used to show distance.

KEY TO MAP FEATURES IN *THE WORLD*, SECOND EDITION

PHYSICAL FEATURES

——	coastline		glacier	
-----	ancient coastline		ancient lake	
——	river		marshland	
········	ancient river course		ice cap / sheet	
——	canal		ice shelf	

△ elevation above sea level (mountain height)

⌂ volcano

)(pass

LATITUDE/LONGITUDE

——	equator
——	lines of latitude / longitude
-----	tropics / polar circles
45°	degrees of longitude / latitude

BORDERS

——	international border
··········	undefined border
------	maritime border
——	internal border
·········	disputed border

COMMUNICATIONS

=====	major road
——	minor road
⋈⋈⋈⋈	major railway

SETTLEMENT / POSSESSION

○ settlement symbol

◇ colonial possession

TYPOGRAPHIC KEY

REGIONS

state / political region..... LAOS

administrative region within a state...................... HENAN

cultural / undefined region / group.................... FERGHANA

SETTLEMENTS

settlement / symbol location / definition...... Farnham

MISCELLANEOUS

tropics / polar circles.......... Antarctic Circle

people / cultural group..... Samoyeds

annotation............................. **1914** British protectorate

PHYSICAL FEATURES

continent / ocean..... AFRICA

INDIAN OCEAN

landscape features.....Mekong

Lake Rudolf

Tien Shan

Sahara

Major land borders are shown using a solid line.

Annotations provide additional explanatory information.

Political control is identified by color.

Broad arrows indicate general movement or spread of ideas, crops, or goods.

Thin arrows indicate journeys, trade routes, or campaigns.

Diffused colors are used to show a general region.

About Felipe Fernández-Armesto

Felipe Fernández-Armesto holds the William P. Reynolds Chair of History at the University of Notre Dame. He has master's and doctoral degrees from the University of Oxford, where he spent most of his teaching career, before taking up the Chair of Global Environmental History at Queen Mary College, University of London, in 2000, and the Prince of Asturias Chair at Tufts University (2005–2009). He is on the editorial boards of the History of Cartography for the University of Chicago Press, Studies in Overseas History (Leiden University), *Comparative Studies in Society and History, Journeys,* and *Journal of Global History.* Recent awards include the World History Association Book Prize (2007), Spain's Premio Nacional de Gastronomía (2005, for his work on the history of food), and the Premio Nacional de Investigación (Sociedad Geográfica Española, 2004). He has had many distinguished visiting appointments, including a Fellowship of the Netherlands Institute of Advanced Study in the Humanities and Social Sciences and a Union Pacific Visiting Professorship at the University of Minnesota. He won the Caird Medal of the National Maritime Museum in 1995 and the John Carter Brown Medal in 1999 and has honorary doctorates from

La Trobe University and the Universidad de los Andes. He has served on the Council of the Hakluyt Society, on the Committee of English PEN, and as Chairman of the PEN Literary Foundation. His work in journalism includes regular columns in the British and Spanish press, and, among his many contributions to broadcasting, he is the longest-serving presenter of BBC radio's flagship current affairs program, *Analysis.* He has been short-listed for the most valuable literary prize in the United Kingdom.

Fernández-Armesto is the author, coauthor, or editor of 30 books and numerous papers and scholarly articles. His work has been translated into 25 languages. His books include *Before Columbus; The Times Illustrated History of Europe; Columbus; Millennium: A History of the Last Thousand Years* (the subject of a ten-part series on CNN); *Civilizations: Culture, Ambition, and the Transformation of Nature; Near a Thousand Tables; The Americas; Humankind: A Brief History; Ideas that Changed the World; The Times Atlas of World Exploration; The Times Guide to the Peoples of Europe; Amerigo: The Man Who Gave His Name to America;* and *Pathfinders: A Global History of Exploration.*

Dear Reader,

History is stories. There are hundreds of tales in this book about real, flesh-and-blood people—commoners and kings, sons and mothers, heroes and villains, the famous and the failed. I try to combine them in two narratives that crisscross throughout the book. One is the story of how people connect and separate, as cultures take shape and influence and change one another. Alongside this story, there is another one of how humans interact with the rest of nature—other species, the unstable natural environment, the dynamic planet.

History is global. The whole world stays in view in almost every chapter. Readers can compare and connect what was happening in every region and every continent in every period—like observers from another galaxy, gazing at the world from outer space and seeing it whole.

History is universal. This book tries to say something about every sphere of life—including science and art, suffering and pleasure, thought and imagination.

History is a problem-posing discipline. This book is full of provocations, contested claims, debated speculations, open horizons, and questions too complex and too interesting to answer easily. I employ facts not just for their own sake but also to make my readers—and myself—think.

History is evidence. Readers of this book confront the sources on every page—the words, images, and objects people really used in the past—to reveal vivid pictures of what history looked like and what it felt like to live in the past.

History enhances life. I believe that a textbook can be entertaining, even amusing, as well as instructive and accessible; challenging without being hostile; friendly without being cloying.

History isn't over. This book is about how the world got to be the way it is, confronting present problems and perspectives for the future—which is, after all, only the past that hasn't yet happened.

Felipe Fernández-Armesto

INTRODUCING THE WORLD

By the standards of astronauts, say, or science fiction writers, historians seem timid, unadventurous creatures who are only interested in one puny species—our species, the human species—on one tiny planet—our planet, Earth. But Earth is special. So far, we know of nowhere else in the cosmos where so much has happened and is happening today. By galactic standards, global history is a small story—but it's a good one.

Humans, moreover, compared with other animals, seem outward looking. Our concerns range over the universe, and beyond it, to unseen worlds, vividly imagined or mysteriously revealed. Not just everything we do but also everything that occurs to our minds is part of our history and, therefore, is part of this book, including science and art, fun and philosophy, speculations and dreams. We continually generate stories—new stories—at an amazing rate.

But the present passes instantly into the past. The present is always over, transformed into history. And the past is always with us, tugging at our memories, shaping our thoughts, launching and limiting our lives. Human history may seem narrowly self-interested, but it focuses on an undeniably riveting subject that is also our favorite subject—ourselves.

THE WAY OF HUMANKIND

Although the story of this book is a human story, it can never be merely human because, in isolation humankind does not make perfect sense. Humans are animals, and to understand ourselves thoroughly and to know what, if anything, makes us unique, we have to compare ourselves with other animals. As with other animals, we are best studied in our habitats. We cannot begin to comprehend our own history except in context. Our story is inseparable from the climates where it takes place and the other life forms that we depend on or compete with. We lord it over other species, but we remain linked to them by the food chain. We transform our environment, but we can never escape from it. We differentiate ourselves from nature—we speak loosely, for instance, of nature as if we were not natural creatures ourselves. We distance ourselves from our fellow-animals by adopting what we think are unnatural behaviors—wearing clothes, for instance, cooking food, replacing nature with culture. In short, we do what is natural to us, and all the elaborate culture we produce generates new, intimate relationships with the environment we refashion and the life forms we exploit.

We are exceptionally ambitious compared to other animals, consciously remodeling environments to suit our own purposes. We carve out fields, turn prairies into wheat lands, deserts into gardens, and gardens into deserts. We fell forests where we find them and plant them where none exist; we dam rivers, wall seas, cultivate plants, breed creatures, extinguish some species, and call others into being by selection and hybridization. Sometimes we smother terrain with environments we build for ourselves. Yet none of these practices liberates us from nature. As we shall see, one of the paradoxes of the human story is that the more we change the environment, the more vulnerable we become to ecological lurches and unpredictable disasters. Failure to establish the right balance between exploitation and conservation has often left civilizations in ruins. History becomes a path picked across the wreckage. This does not mean that the environment determines our behavior or our lives, but it does set the framework in which we act.

We are an exceptionally successful species in terms of our ability to survive in a wide range of diverse climates and landscapes—more so than just about any other creature, except for the microbes we carry around with us. But even we are still explorers of our planet, engaged in an ongoing effort to change it. Indeed, we have barely begun to change planet Earth, though, as we shall see, some human societies have devoted the last ten thousand years to trying to do it. We call ourselves lords, or, more modestly, caretakers of creation, but about 90 percent of the biosphere is too far underwater or too deep below the Earth for us to inhabit with the technology we have at present: These are environments that humans have only recently begun to invade and that we still do not dominate.

If we humans are peculiarly ambitious creatures, who are always intruding in the life of the planet, we are also odd compared to other animals in the way we generate change among ourselves. We are an unpredictable, unstable species. Lots of other animals live social lives and construct societies. But those societies are remarkably stable compared to ours. As far as we know, ants and elephants have the same lifeways and the same kinds of relationships that they have had since their species first appeared. That is not to say animals never change their cultures. One of the fascinating discoveries in primatology is that apes and monkeys develop cultural differences from one another, even between groups living in similar and sometimes adjacent environments. In one forest region of Gabon in West Africa, chimpanzees have developed a termite-catching technology. They "fish" with stripped branches that they plunge into termite nests but do not use tools to break open nuts. Chimps in a neighboring region ignore the termites but are experts in nut cracking, using rocks like hammers and anvils. In Sumatra in Indonesia, orangutans play a game—jumping from falling trees—that is unknown to their cousins in nearby Borneo. In Ethiopia in East Africa, males in some baboon groups control harems while others nearby have one mate after another. In some chimpanzee societies, hunting and meat eating seem to have increased dramatically in recent times.

These are amazing facts, but the societies of nonhuman animals still change little compared with ours. So, alongside the theme of human interaction with the rest of nature is another great theme of our history: the ways our societies have changed, grown apart from one another, reestablished contact, and influenced one another in their turn.

THE WAY OF THIS BOOK

This book, then, interweaves two stories—stories of our interactions with nature and stories of our interactions with each other. The environment-centered story is about humans distancing themselves from the rest of nature and searching for a relationship that strikes a balance between constructive and destructive exploitation. The culture-centered story is of how human cultures have become mutually influential and yet mutually differentiating. Both stories have been going on for thousands of years. We do not know whether they will end in triumph or disaster.

There is no prospect of covering all of world history in one book. Rather, the fabric of this book is woven from selected strands. Readers will see these at every turn, twisted together into yarn, stretched into stories. Human-focused historical ecology—the environmental theme—will drive readers back, again and again, to the same concepts: sustenance, shelter, disease, energy, technology, art. (The last is a vital category for historians, not only because it is part of our interface with the rest of the world, but also because it forms a record of how we see reality and of how the way we see it changes.) In the global story of human interactions—the cultural theme—we return constantly to the ways people make contact with each another: migration, trade, war, imperialism, pilgrimage, gift exchange, diplomacy, travel—and to their social frameworks: the economic and political arenas, the human groups and groupings, the states and civilizations, the sexes and generations, the classes and clusters of identity.

The stories that stretch before us are full of human experience. "The stork feeds on snakes," said the ancient Greek sage, Agathon, "the pig on acorns, and history on human lives." The only way to build up our picture of human societies and ecosystems of the past is to start with the evidence people have left. Then we reassemble it bit by bit, with the help of imagination disciplined by the sources. Anyone reading a history book needs to bear in mind that interpreting evidence is a challenge—half burden and half opportunity. The subject matter of history is not the past directly because the past is never available to our senses. We have only the evidence about it. This makes history an art, not a science, an art disciplined by respect for the sources, just as patterns impose discipline on poets or as the limitations of stagecraft discipline a play.

For a book like this, the sources set the limits of my imagination. Sometimes these are concrete clues to what people really did—footprints of their wanderings, debris of their meals, fragments of their technologies, wreckage of their homes, traces of diseases in their bones. Usually, however, the sources do not reflect the way things were but the way people wished to represent them in their arts and crafts and writings. In short, most sources are evidence of what happened only in the minds of those who made them. This means, in turn, that our picture of what went on in the world beyond human minds is always tentative and open to reinterpretation. The historian's job is not—cannot be—to say what the past was like, but rather, what it felt like to live in it because that is what the evidence tends to reveal.

One of the most admirable historians of the twentieth century, R. G. Collingwood, who was also a professor of philosophy at Oxford, said that "all history is intellectual history." He was right. History—even the environmental and cultural history that is the subject of this book—is largely about what people perceived rather than what they really saw, what they thought or felt rather than what happened outwardly, what they represented rather than what was real. The nineteenth-century philosopher Arthur Schopenhauer, one of the most pessimistic thinkers ever, who drew on Hindu and Buddhist writings for his inspiration, said that history's only subject was "humankind's oppressive, muddlesome dream." He thought that made history pointless. I think the dream makes it intriguing.

Because the evidence is always incomplete, history is not so much a matter of describing or narrating or question-answering as it is a matter of problem-posing. No one reading this book should expect to be instructed in straightforward facts or to acquire proven knowledge. The thrill of history is asking the right question, not getting the right answer. Most of the time, the most we can hope for is to identify interesting problems that stimulate debate. And we have to accept that the debate is worthwhile for its own sake, even if we have insufficient knowledge to reach conclusions.

There is no agreement among historians even about what are the right sorts of questions to ask. Some—including me—are interested in huge philosophical questions, such as how does history happen? What makes change? Is it random or is it subject to scientific laws? Do impersonal forces beyond human control—environmental factors or economics or some world force called fate or evolution or God or progress—determine it? Or is change the externalization of

ideas, which arise in minds and are projected onto the world through human action? And if it's a mixture, what's the balance?

At a slightly lower level of analysis, some historians ask questions about how human societies function. How and why do societies grow and fragment and take different forms? How do some people get power over others? How and why do revolutions happen and states and civilizations rise and fall?

Other historians like to pose problems about the present. How did we get into the mess we're in? Can we trace the causes of present dilemmas back into the past and, if so, how far? Why do we have a globally connected world without global governance? Why is peace always precarious? Why does ecological overkill menace our global environment? Having accounted—or failed to account—for the present, some historians like to focus on the future. They demand lessons from history about how to change our behavior or cope with recurrences of past difficulties. Others, again, search to make sense of the past, to find an overall way of characterizing it or narrating it that makes us feel we understand it.

Yet others—the majority, in the current state of historical fashion, and again including me—like to study the past for its own sake and try to identify the questions that mattered to people at the time they first asked them. This does not mean that the sort of history found in this book is useless (although I do not necessarily think it would be a bad thing if it were). For to penetrate the minds of people of the past—especially the remote past of cultures other than your own—you have to make a supreme effort of understanding. The effort has dividends for the person who practices it. It enhances life by sharpening responses to the streetscapes and landscapes, art and artifacts, laws and letters we have inherited from the past. And understanding is what we need most today in our multicultural societies and multicivilizational world.

HOW THIS BOOK IS ARRANGED

After finding the time, accumulating the knowledge, posing the questions, stiffening the sinews, and summoning the blood, the big problem for the writer of a global history textbook is organizing the material. The big problem for the reader is navigating it. It is tempting to divide the world up into regions or cultures or even—as I did in a previous book—into biomes and devote successive chapters to each. You could call that "world history," if you genuinely managed to cover the world. But "global history" is different: an attempt to see the planet whole, as if from an immense, astral height, and discern themes that truly transcend geographical and cultural boundaries. In this book, therefore, I try to look at every continent in just about every chapter (there are a couple of chapters that, for reasons described in their place, focus only on part of the world). Each chapter concentrates on themes from the two great global stories: how human societies diverge and converge, and how they interact with the rest of nature.

Because history is a story in which the order of events matters, the chapters are grouped into 10 parts, arranged chronologically. There are 30 chapters—one for each week in a typical U.S. academic year (though of course, every reader or group of readers will go at their own pace)—and 10 parts. I hope there is plenty to surprise readers without making the parts perversely defiant of the "periods" historians conventionally speak of. Part I runs from roughly 150,000 to roughly 20,000 years ago, and, on the whole, the periods covered get shorter as sources accumulate, cultures diverge, data multiply, and readers' interests quicken. Of course, no one should be misled into thinking the parts are more than devices of convenience. Events that happened in, say, 1850, are in a different part of this book from those that happened in, say 1750. But the story is continuous, and the parts could equally well be recrafted to start and end at different moments.

At every stage, some parts of the world are more prominent than others because they are more influential, more populous, more world-shaping. For great stretches of the book, China occupies relatively more space; this is not for reasons of political correctness, but because China has, for much of the past, been immensely rich in globally influential initiatives. In the coverage of the last couple of hundred years, Europe and the United States get a lot of attention: this is not "Eurocentrism" or "Westocentrism" (if there is such a word), but an honest reflection of how history happened. But I have tried not to neglect the peoples and parts of the world that historians usually undervalue: poor and peripheral communities sometimes have a stunning impact on the world. The margins and frontiers of the world are often where world-changing events happen—the fault lines of civilizations, which radiate seismic effects.

Learning Features for the Second Edition of *The World*

The pedagogical program for the Second Edition of *The World* has been carefully devised to complement the narrative, reinforce important concepts, and prompt students to ask questions and formulate arguments.

Chapter-opening vignettes use dramatic and unusual stories to put the main themes of each chapter in relief. One-third of the chapter-opening vignettes in the Second Edition are new.

Focus Questions open each chapter and encourage students to think critically about the key questions raised in each chapter.

Making Connections tables throughout the text help students see the global linkages behind important historical developments. Praised by users of *The World,* every chapter in the Second Edition now includes at least one, and in some cases, as many as three, Making Connections tables. New Making Connections tables have been added to Chapters 9, 13, 15, 20, 21, 22, and 26. To further improve their visual efficacy, locator maps showing the regions examined in each Making Connections table have been added to the Second Edition.

A Closer Look sections, one per chapter, provide in-depth visual analysis of a specific cultural artifact. Praised by users for the way in which they connect the macro with the micro, detailed notes and tie lines draw the reader into close contact with the object, providing opportunities to pose larger questions. Users of *The World* have consistently cited the Closer Look sections as effective learning tools for their students. One-third of the Closer Look sections in the Second Edition are new. See page xxvii for a complete listing.

Maps Widely hailed by users of the First Edition, the maps in *The World* employ innovative perspectives to help the reader see world history in a fresh and dynamic way. A range of different maps—from two-page thematic maps to spot maps that pinpoint specific events—connect with the discussion on a variety of different levels. Each map in the Second Edition has been extensively checked for accuracy and/or re-drafted to improve its graphical presentation. The Second Edition includes 35 new full-size maps and 102 new locater maps. See page xxi for a listing of the maps in the Second Edition.

NEW The Big Picture Building on the success of the map program for the First Edition, each of the 10 parts in *The World* now ends with "The Big Picture," a two-page map of the world that graphically highlights an important, pivotal development in global history. Accompanied by text and questions, each Big Picture map provides the reader with a visual snapshot of what the world looked like at key intervals in human history. Interactive versions of the Big Picture maps can be found on MyHistoryLab. Short video clips of the author discussing developments in global history related to the Big Picture maps are also available on the MyHistoryLab that accompanies the text.

Visual Sources Users of *The World* consistently rank its photo program as the best found in any textbook available today. Intimately connected to the narrative, each photo provides a compelling visual record, from mammoth huts to satellite images of the Earth from space. Detailed captions, crafted by the author, explicate the meaning behind each visual source. There are over 100 new photos in the Second Edition of *The World.*

In Perspective sections conclude each chapter and do much more than summarize the preceding discussion. They put the developments covered in the chapter into historical perspective, and they make explicit for the student the process by which historians interpret the past.

Chronologies throughout each chapter arrange key historical developments in the order in which they occurred.

Key Terms are defined in the Glossary and set in boldface type in the text.

In-text Pronunciation Guides, embedded directly in the text, provide phonetic spellings for unfamiliar words.

CHANGES TO THE SECOND EDITION

The many helpful readers' reports and reviews of the First Edition by both users and non-users formed the basis for preparing the Second Edition. Every chapter was either updated with new and accepted scholarship or reorganized to clarify its presentation. In many chapters, more substantive changes were made in response to feedback and advice from teachers.

Chapters 1–15

Chapter 1 now begins with a discussion of Imo, the famous Japanese macaque. Chapter 2 examines the archaeological remains of an ancient feast to highlight the main problems of the chapter. Chapter 3 now begins with a discussion of Queen Hatshepsut's expedition to Punt. In Chapter 5, coverage of Babylon and classical Greece has been expanded. Chapter 6 now includes a new section on the Israelites and more discussion of Buddhism. Discussion of Rome has been increased in Chapter 7. Chapter 8 includes fuller treatment of Tang China. Chapter 9 now provides an overview of the main tenets of the major world religions. Chapter 10 opens with a story of Queen Gudit of Ethiopia. Both the Crusades and Ghana are examined in more depth in Chapter 12. The Renaissance receives more discussion in Chapter 15.

Chapters 16–30

The "In Perspective" section in Chapter 16 has been extensively revised and enhanced. The opening vignette for Chapter 17 now tells the story of Charles Ledger and quinine; the "In Perspective" section for this chapter has also been expanded. Chapter 18 now opens with a vignette about the experience of Siamese ambassadors in eighteenth-century France, and it examines the Protestant Reformation in more depth. The "In Perspective" sections in Chapters 19 and 20 have been expanded significantly. Chapter 21 provides more extensive treatment of the wars for independence in Latin America. Chapter 22 now includes more coverage of the French Revolution and the Napoleonic wars. Chapter 24 provides a new discussion of feminism in both Egypt and the United States. Chapter 25 has increased coverage of the Scramble for Africa. Chapter 26 includes new discussion of nationalism and state formation in Japan, Germany, Italy, and the United States. Chapter 29 now opens with the story of Dolores Jimenez and her role in the Mexican Revolution. Chapters 28 and 30 have been updated with important new information pertaining to the history of the twentieth century and the first decade of the twenty-first century: political and social developments, financial crises, and global warming.

SUPPORT MATERIALS

The World, Second Edition, comes with an extensive package of support materials for teachers and students.

For Instructors

◆ **The Instructor's Manual/Test-Item File** includes chapter outlines, overviews, key concepts, discussion questions, teaching notes, map quizzes, and suggestions for audiovisual resources, as well as approximately 1,500 test items. Particular emphasis is placed on essay questions that test students' understanding of concepts across chapters.

◆ **Test Manager** is a computerized test management program for Windows and Macintosh environments. The program allows instructors to select items from the test-item file to create tests. It also allows for online testing.

◆ **The Instructor's Resource Center** (*www.pearsonhighered.com*) Text-specific materials, such as the instructor's manual, the test-item file, map files, digital transparencies and PowerPoint™ presentations, are available for downloading by adopters.

For Instructors and Students

◆ *http://www.myhistorylab.com* MyHistoryLab for *The World* offers students and instructors a state-of-the-art, interactive learning tool for world history. Organized by the main subtopics of *The World*, and delivered within a course-management platform, MyHistoryLab supplements and enriches the classroom experience and can form the basis for an online course. New interactive Big Picture Maps and videos of the author outlining key developments in world history now enrich the MyHistoryLab for *The World*. Audio summaries of the main concepts in each chapter are also available for downloading to MP3 players. Please contact your Pearson representative for details.

◆ **NEW** *Around the World in Sixty Minutes Video Series.* In response to overwhelming requests from instructors and students around the country, Pearson Prentice Hall and Felipe Fernández-Armesto have teamed up to produce a ten-part video series that covers key, transformative develop-

ments in world history from the beginnings of agriculture to the world we inhabit today. Each segment in the Series is approximately 4-6 minutes in length and features Fernández-Armesto discussing pivotal changes in human history: the beginnings of agriculture, the axial age, the rise of world religions, the tensions between pastoralists and settled societies, the age of the plague, human transplantations, the Enlightenment, the Industrial Revolution, and the paradoxes of the twentieth century. Shot in various locations, and interspersed with photos and historical footage, each video in the Series can serve as an ideal lecture launcher in the classroom or as a self-directed review opportunity for students. Questions at the end of each segment allow students to respond with short essays and submit electronically via MyHistoryLab. A demo video clip can be viewed at www.pearsonhighered.com/theworld

As a further enrichment to the Series, each video is part of an integrated "learning zone" that also includes an interactive version of the Big Picture map that ends each of the ten Parts in *The World*.

◆ **NEW** **Interactive Big Picture Maps** feature the same maps as those in the text, rendered as globes that can be spun. Interactive icons on the globe allow students to explore visual and textual sources, which are linked to the e-book that accompanies *The World*.

The result is a rich, dynamic, and integrated learning experience that combines video, audio, visual sources, and text documents to reinforce the inquiry-based approach that sets *The World* apart from other books. A demonstration map can be viewed at www.pearsonhighered.com/theworld.

POPULAR VALUEPACKS FOR *THE WORLD*

◆ Titles from the renowned **Penguin Classics** series can be bundled with *The World* for a nominal charge. Please contact your Pearson Arts and Sciences sales representative for details.

◆ **Connections: Key Themes in World History**. Series Editor Alfred J. Andrea. Concise and tightly focused, the titles in the popular Connections Series are designed to place the latest research on selected topics of global significance, such as disease, trade, slavery, exploration, and modernization, into an accessible format for students. Available at a 50% discount when bundled with *The World*. For more information go to www.pearsonhighered.com.

◆ Getz/Hoffman/Rodriguez, *Exchanges: A Global History Reader* introduces students to the discipline of world history. Unlike other source collections, *Exchanges* helps students look beyond strictly delineated regionalism and chronological structures to understand history as a series of ongoing debates. Available at a 50% discount when bundled with *The World*.

Clark, *A Guide to Your History Course: What Every Student Needs to Know.* This concise, spiral-bound guidebook orients students to the issues and problems they will face in the history classroom. Available at a 50% discount when bundled with *The World*.

◆ **The Prentice Hall Atlas of World History, Second Edition** includes over 100 full-color maps in world history, drawn by Dorling Kindersley, one of the world's most respected cartographic publishers. Copies of the Atlas can be bundled with *The World* for a nominal charge. Contact your Pearson sales representative for details.

For Students

◆ Extensively revised and updated, the **Primary Source: Documents in Global History DVD** is both a rich collection of textual and visual documents in world history and an indispensable tool for working with sources. Extensively developed with the guidance of historians and teachers, the revised and updated DVD version includes over 800 sources in world history—from cave art to satellite images of the Earth from space. More sources from Africa, Latin America, and Southeast. Asia have been added to this revised and updated DVD version. All sources are accompanied by headnotes and focus questions, and are searchable by topic, region, or time period.

◆ **World History Study Site** (*www.pearsonhighered.com*) This course-based, open-access online companion provides a wealth of resources for both students and professors, including test questions, flash cards, links for further research, and Web-based assignments.

◆ **CourseSmart Textbooks Online** is an exciting new choice for students looking to save money. As an alternative to purchasing the print textbook, students can subscribe to the same content online and save up to 50% off the suggested list price of the print text. With a CourseSmart eTextbook, students can search the text, make notes online, print out reading assignments that incorporate lecture notes, and bookmark important passages for later review. For more information, or to subscribe to the CourseSmart eTextbook, visit *www.coursesmart.com*.

ACKNOWLEDGMENTS

Without being intrusive, I have tried not to suppress my presence—my voice, my views—in the text because no book is objective, other than by pretense, and the reader is entitled to get to know the writer's foibles and failures. In overcoming mine, I have had a lot of help (though there are sure still to be errors and shortcomings through my fault alone). Textbooks are teamwork, and I have learned an immense amount from my friends and helpers at Pearson Prentice Hall, especially my editors, Charles Cavaliere and Gerald Lombardi, whose indefatigability and forbearance made the book better at every turn. Laura Lee Manley, senior marketing manager, and Sue Westmoreland, Executive Marketing Manager, for their creativity. I also thank the picture researcher Francelle Carapetyan, and the members of the production and cartographic sections of the team who performed Herculean labors: Ann Marie McCarthy, senior managing editor; Lynn Savino Wendel, production project manager; Mirella Signoretto, map project manager; and David Roberts, cartographer.

I also owe a debt of gratitude to the senior management team at Pearson Prentice Hall who supported this endeavor every step of the way: Bill Barke, CEO, Pearson Arts & Sciences, Yolanda de Rooy, president of the Humanities and Social Sciences division; Leah Jewell, editorial director; Priscilla McGeehon, editor-in-chief for history; Rochelle Diogenes, editor-in-chief for development; and Brandy Dawson, director of marketing.

I could not have gotten through the work without the help and support of my wonderful colleagues at Queen Mary, University of London; the Institute of Historical Research, University of London; and the History Department of Tufts University. I owe special thanks to the many scholars who share and still share their knowledge of global history at the Pearson Prentice Hall Seminar Series in Global History, and through the World History Association, the *Journal of Global History,* the *Journal of World History,* and H-NET. David Ringrose of University of California, San Diego, was a constant guide, whose interest never flagged and whose wisdom never failed. Many colleagues and counterparts advised me on their fields of expertise or performed heroic self-sacrifice in putting all of the many pieces of the book together: Natia Chakvetadze, Shannon Corliss, Maria Guarascio, Anita Castro, Conchita Ordonez, Sandra Garcia, Maria Garcia, Hector Grillone, the late Jack Betterley, Jeremy Greene, Jai Kharbanda, Ernest Tucker (United States Naval Academy), Steve Ortega (Simmons College), David Way (British Library), Antony Eastmond (Courtland Institute), Morris Rossabi (Columbia University), David Atwill and Jade Atwill (Pennsylvania State University), Stephen Morillo (Wabash College), Peter Carey (Oxford University), Jim Mallory (Queens University, Belfast), Matthew Restall (Pennsylvania State University), Roderick Whitfield (School of Oriental and African Studies, University of London), Barry Powell (University of Wisconsin), Leonard Blussé (Harvard University), Guolong Lai (University of Florida), Frank Karpiel (The Citadel), George Kosar (Tufts University), David Kalivas and Eric Martin of H-NET and the many subscribers to their service who commented on the book or posted or e-mailed queries and suggestions, and the faculty, staff, and students of the many colleges where I got the chance to discuss the book (Boston College, Colorado State University, Essex Community College, Georgetown University, Jackson State University, Northern Kentucky University, Ohio State University, Penn State University, St John's University [New York], Salem State University, San José State University, Simmons College, U.S. Air Force Academy, U.S. Naval Academy, University at Buffalo, University of California [San Diego], San Diego State University, University of Arkansas [Little Rock], and University of Memphis) as well as the many good people whose assistance I may have failed to acknowledge.

Felipe Fernández-Armesto
Somerville, Massachusett

DEVELOPING *THE WORLD*

Developing a project like *The World* required the input and counsel of hundreds of individuals. David Ringrose, from the University of California at San Diego served as *The World*'s editorial consultant, closely reading and commenting on every draft of the book. His experience and understanding of classroom issues were invaluable to the development of *The World*. Nearly 100 reviewers critiqued portions of the manuscript from the first to the final draft. In addition, the manuscript was class-tested with over 1,000 students across the country who provided invaluable feedback and advice. Additionally, fifteen focus groups were held with teachers of world history to gather feedback and test ideas. An additional 75 reviewers of critiqued portions of *The World* to help prepare the Second Edition. We thank all those who shared their time and effort to make *The World* a better book.

Reviewers of the First Edition

Donald R. Abbott, San Diego Mesa College
Wayne Ackerson, Salisbury University
Roger Adelson, Arizona State University
Alfred J. Andrea, University of Vermont (Emeritus)
David G. Atwill, Pennsylvania State University
Leonard Blussé, Harvard University
Mauricio Borrero, St. John's University
John Brackett, University of Cincinnati
Gayle K. Brunelle, California State University—Fullerton
Fred Burkhard, Maryland University College
Antoinette Burton, University of Illinois
Jorge Cañizares-Esguerra, University of Texas—Austin
Elaine Carey, St. John's University
Tim Carmichael, College of Charleston
Douglas Chambers, University of Southern Mississippi
Nupur Chaudhuri, Texas Southern University
David Christian, San Diego State University
Duane Corpis, Georgia State University
Dale Crandall-Bear, Solano Community College
Touraj Daryaee, University of California, Irvine
Jeffrey M. Diamond, College of Charleston
Brian Fagan, University of California—Santa Barbara
Nancy Fitch, California State University—Fullerton
Alison Fletcher, Kent State University
Patricia Gajda, The University of Texas at Tyler
Richard Golden, University of North Texas
Stephen S. Gosch, University of Wisconsin—Eau Claire
Jonathan Grant, Florida State University
Mary Halavais, Sonoma State University

Shah M. Hanifi, James Madison University
Russell A. Hart, Hawaii Pacific University
Phyllis G. Jestice, University of Southern Mississippi
Amy J. Johnson, Berry College
Deborah Smith Johnston, Lexington High School
Eric A. Jones, Northern Illinois University
Ravi Kalia, City College of New York
David M. Kalivas, Middlesex Community College
Frank Karpiel, College of Charleston
David Kenley, Marshall University
Andrew J. Kirkendall, Texas A&M University
Dennis Laumann, The University of Memphis
Donald Leech, University of Minnesota
Jennifer M. Lloyd, SUNY—Brockport
Aran MacKinnon, University of West Georgia
Moria Maguire, University of Arkansas—Little Rock
Susan Maneck, Jackson State University
Anthony Martin, Wellesley College
Dorothea Martin, Appalachian State University
Adam McKeown, Columbia University
Ian McNeely, University of Oregon
Margaret E. Menninger, Texas State University—San Marcos
Stephen Morillo, Wabash College
William Morison, Grand Valley State University
Laura Neitzel, Brookdale Community College
Kenneth J. Orosz, University of Maine—Farmington
Michael Pavkovic, Hawaii Pacific University
Phyllis E. Pobst, Arkansas State University
Kenneth Pomeranz, University of California—Irvine

Sara B. Pritchard, Montana State University
Norman Raiford, Greenville Technical College
Stephen Rapp, Georgia State University
Vera Blinn Reber, Shippensburg University
Matthew Redinger, Montana State University—Billings
Matthew Restall, Pennsylvania State University
Jonathan Reynolds, Arkansas State University
Richard Rice, University of Tennessee—Chattanooga
Peter Rietbergen, Catholic University (Nijmegen)
David Ringrose, University of California—San Diego
Patricia Romero, Towson University
Morris Rossabi, Queens College
David G. Rowley, University of Wisconsin—Platteville
Sharlene Sayegh, California State University—Long Beach
William Schell, Murray State University
Linda Bregstein Scherr, Mercer County Community College
Patricia Seed, University of California, Irvine
Lawrence Sondhaus, University of Indianapolis
Richard Steigmann-Gall, Kent State University
John Thornton, Boston University
Ann Tschetter, University of Nebraska—Lincoln
Deborah Vess, Georgia College & State University
Stephen Vinson, SUNY—New Paltz
Joanna Waley-Cohen, New York University
Anne M. Will, Skagit Valley College
John Wills, University of Southern California
Theodore Jun Yoo, University of Hawaii—Manoa

Reviewers of the Second Edition

Jeffrey Alexander, Douglas College/The University of British Columbia
Emma Alexander-Mudaliar, University of Winnipeg
Gerald D. Anderson, North Dakota State University
Ellen Arnold, Macalester College
Daniel Ayana, Youngstown State University
Lt. David Bachler, United States Air Force Academy
Alan Baumler, Indiana University of Pennsylvania
Cynthia Bisson, Belmont University
Robert Blackey, California State University—San Bernardino

Robert Bond, Youngstown State University
Connie Brand, Meridian Community College
Tanya Brown, Pittsburgh State University
Byron Canner, University of Utah
Robert Carriedo, United States Air Force Academy
Carole R. Carter, University of Central Arkansas
Martin Scott Catino, University of South Carolina—Aiken
Yuan-ling Chao, Middle Tennessee State University
Gregory Crider, Wingate University
Eric Cunningham, Gonzaga University

Shawn Dry, Oakland Community College
Jeffrey Dym, California State University—Sacramento
Lisa Edwards, University of Massachusetts—Lowell
Jari Eloranta, Appalachian State University
Ken Faunce, Washington State University
Jeffrey Gaab, SUNY College at Farmingdale
Trevor Getz, San Francisco State University
Peter H. Griffin, Lindenwood University
William W. Haddad, California State University—Fullerton

Laura J. Hilton, Muskingum College

Matt Hopper, California Polytechnic State University

Ahmed H. Ibrahim, Missouri State University

Robert Irwin, Grant MacEwan College

Eric Johnson, Pennsylvania State University

Lisa Kazmier, Drexel University

Keith P. Knuuti, University of Hawaii—Windward Community College

Stephen Laffer, Florida State University

Eugene Larson, Los Angeles Pierce College

Paul Lococo Jr., Leeward Community College

David Longfellow, Baylor University

M. Lois Lucas, West Virginia State University

David McCarter, Indiana State University

Tom McCarthy, United States Naval Academy

Emerson Thomas McMullen, Georgia Southern University

Gerald Mills, University of Oklahoma

Ruma Niyogi, Saint Xavier University

Bradley Parker, University of Utah

Charles Parker, St. Louis University

Robert W. Patch, University of California, Riverside

Alice K. Pate, Columbus State University

Patrick Patterson, Honolulu Community College

Patricia M. Pelley, Texas Tech University

Wendy Pojmann, Sienna College

Timothy Pytell, California State University—San Bernardino

Scott S. Reese, Northern Arizona University

Jeremy Rich, Middle Tennessee State University

Paul Richgruber, Minneapolis Community and Tech College; Inver Hills Community College

William S. Rodner, Tidewater Community College

Anthony R. Santoro, Christopher Newport University

Adam R. Seipp, Texas A & M University

Elizabeth Sharpe, Jackson State University

Jeffrey M. Shumway, Brigham Young University

James J. Simon, Genesee Community College

Phillip Luke Sinitiere, University of Houston

Timothy G. Sistrunk, California State University—Chico

Rachel Stocking, Southern Illinois University—Carbondale

Jacky Swansinger, SUNY at Fredonia

Michael Tarver, Arkansas Tech University

Patricia L. Thompson, University of Texas at San Antonio

Kate Transchel, California State University

Mary A. Valante, Appalachian State University

Gilmar Visoni, Queensborough Community College

Paul Voisey, University of Alberta

Rick Warner, Wabash College

Joshua Weiner, American River College

Claude Welch, University at Buffalo, State University of New York

Scott N. West, University of Dayton

Kristina Wilson, Morehead State University

A NOTE ON DATES AND SPELLINGS

In keeping with common practice among historians of global history, we have used B.C.E. (before the common era) and C.E. (common era) to date events. For developments deep in the past, we have employed the phrase "years ago" to convey to the reader a clear sense of time. Specific dates are only given when necessary and when doing so improves the context of the narrative.

Recognizing that almost every non-English word can be transliterated in any number of ways, we have adopted the most widely used and simplest systems for spelling names and terms. The *pinyin* system of Chinese spelling is used for all Chinese words with the exception of such words as *Yangtze*, which are still widely referred to in its Wade-Giles form. Following common usage, we have avoided using apostrophes in the spelling of Arabic and Persian words, as well as words from other languages—thus, *Quran* and *Kaaba* instead of *Qu'ran* and *Ka'ba*, and *Tbilisi* instead of *T'bilisi*. Diacritical marks, accents, and other specialized symbols are used only if the most common variant of a name or term employs such devices (such as *Çatalhüyük*), if they are part of a personal noun (such as *Nicolás*), or if the inclusion of such markings in the spelling of a word makes pronouncing it easier (*Teotihuacán*).

Throughout the text the first appearance of important non-English words whose pronuciation may be unclear for the reader are followed by phonetic spellings in parentheses, with the syllable that is stressed spelled in capital letters. So, for example *Ugarit* is spelled phonetically as "OO-gah-riht." Chinese words are not stressed, so each syllable is spelled in lowercase letters. Thus, the city of Hangzhou in China is rendered phonetically as "hahngjoh." For monosyllabic words, the phonetic spelling is in lowercase letters. So *Rus* is spelled as "roos." The table below provides a guide for how the vowel sounds in *The World* are represented phonetically.

a	as in *cat, bat*
ah	as in *car, father*
aw	as in *law, paw*
ay	as in *fate, same*
eh	as in *bet, met*
ee	as in *beet, ease*
eye	as in *dine, mine*
ih	as in *if, sniff*
o	as in *more, door*
oh	as in *row, slow*
oo	as in *loop, moo*
ow	as in *cow, mouse*
uh	as in *but, rul*

PART 6

ENVIRONMENT

1300–1800
Little Ice Age

since mid-1200s
Lenses and clocks in Europe

CULTURE

1206–1360s
Mongol hegemony

The Crucible: The Eurasian Crises of the Thirteenth and Fourteenth Centuries

◀ **This Korean world map,** from about 1402, known as the Kangnido, is the earliest known map of the world from East Asia. It is also the oldest surviving Korean map. Based on Chinese maps from the fourteenth century, the Kangnido clearly shows Africa (with an enormous lake in the middle of the continent) and Arabia on the lower left. The Indian subcontinent, however, has been merged into a gigantic landmass that represents China. The Korean peninsula, on the upper right, is shown as much bigger than it actually is, while Japan, on the lower right, is placed much farther south than where it is actually located.

1330s–mid-1400s (and sporadically to 1700s)
Plague in Eurasia

since mid-1400s
Growth of Atlantic navigation

from 1350s
Rise of the Ottomans

1368–1644
Ming dynasty (China)

from 1440s
Rise of Muscovy

from mid-1400s
Rise of Incas, Aztecs
Beginnings of oceanic imperialism

CHAPTER 13

The World the Mongols Made

FRONT

BACK

FRONT

BACK

Two coins lie alongside each other in the British Museum in London. One, minted in 1230, is stamped with the name of the queen of Georgia, Rusudan, and the words, "Queen of Queens, Glory of the World and Faith, Champion of the Messiah." Beside it, another Georgian coin, minted only 17 years later, shows a figure on horseback, named as "King David, slave of the empire of the Great Khan Kuyuk." A lot had happened in Georgia in a short time. The changes the coins reflect were important not just for Georgia but for the world, for they were huge in scale, reshaping the politics, communications, and culture of Eurasia.

Georgia, protected by the high Caucasus Mountains, had been remarkably successful in resisting the nomad armies of the eleventh and twelfth centuries. Though the Seljuk Turks (see Chapter 12) had briefly terrorized the kingdom and exacted tribute, the Georgians fought back. They refused to pay tribute, recovered their lost territories, and extended their frontiers over parts of neighboring Armenia. In the early thirteenth century, Georgia was a formidable state, capable of imposing rulers as far afield as the Byzantine city of Trebizond on the Black Sea coast of Anatolia and the Muslim city of Ahar in Azerbaijan on the Caspian. In the 1220s, James of Vitry, a Catholic bishop and historian of his own times, admired Georgian pilgrims he saw in Jerusalem, who "march into the holy city with banners displayed, without paying tribute to anyone, for the Muslims dare in no way molest them."

As James of Vitry noted, Georgia was "surrounded by infidels on all sides". That did not seem to matter. The Georgians even promised the pope that they would assist in a new crusade. Suddenly, however, in 1224, letters from Georgia arrived in Rome, withdrawing the promise. "A savage people of hellish aspect have invaded my realm," wrote Rusudan, "as voracious as wolves in their hunger for spoils, and as brave as lions." In the next decade, her letters got increasingly desperate. The Mongols were coming. The world would never be the same again.

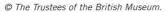 **The Mongols arrive in Georgia.** Two coins from the kingdom of Georgia, minted less than two decades apart, show that the Mongols had conquered that Caucasian state. The front of the top coin, minted by Queen Rusudan of Georgia in 1230, features a bust of a bearded Jesus Christ, draped in a mantle and backed by a cross-shaped halo. The Greek abbreviations for the words "Jesus" and "Christ" flank his right and left shoulders respectively. A Georgian inscription runs along the border. The back of the coin shows inscriptions in both Georgian and Arabic. In contrast, on the bottom coin, minted by King David in 1247, a figure on horse back has replaced the image of Jesus Christ (front), while the inscription on the back of the coin is exclusively in Arabic and identifies the king as "the slave of the Great Khan."

The effects of the events of the rest of the thirteenth century refashioned Eurasia, destroying old states, creating new ones, disrupting existing communications and reforging stronger, wider-ranging links. Eurasian civilizations benefited from enhanced contacts the Mongols fostered. Mongol methods were at first pitilessly bloody. They used terror and massacres to overawe their enemies. They razed cities, destroyed crops, slaughtered elites, and depleted peoples. Yet it looked as if a safer, richer, more interconnected, more dynamic, more expanding, and more enlightened world might emerge—as if something precious were to form in an alchemist's crucible, out of conflicting ingredients, flung at random and stirred with violence. Then a century of environmental disasters arrested these changes in most of Eurasia. Catastrophes reversed the growth of populations and prosperity. But previously marginal regions began to be drawn more closely into a widening pattern of contacts and cultural exchange. Some peoples, in Africa and Southeast Asia, for example, looked outward because they escaped disaster. Others, especially in Europe, did so because their reverses were so enormous that there was nothing else they could do.

THE MONGOLS: RESHAPING EURASIA

The earliest records of Mongol peoples occur in Chinese annals of the seventh century. At that time, the Mongols emerged onto the steppes of the Central Asian land now called Mongolia, from the forests to the north, where they seem to have been hunters and small-scale pig breeders. On the steppes they adopted a pastoral way of life. They became horse-borne nomads and sheepherders. Chinese and Khitan writers used versions of the names "Mongols" and "Tatars" for many different communities, with various religions and competing leaderships. One thing they had in common was that they spoke languages of common origins that were different from those of the Turks. In the early twelfth century, the bands or alliances they formed got bigger, and their raids against neighboring sedentary peoples became more menacing. In part, this was the effect of the growing preponderance of some Mongol groups over others. In part, it was the result of slow economic change.

Genghis Khan

Contact with richer neighbors gave Mongol chiefs opportunities for enrichment as mercenaries or raiders. Economic inequalities greater than the Mongols had ever known arose in a society in which blood relationships and seniority in age had formerly settled every person's position. Prowess in war enabled leaders to build up followers in parallel with—and sometimes in defiance of—the old social order. They called this process "crane catching"—comparing it to caging valuable birds. The most successful leaders enticed or forced rival groups into submission. The process spread to involve peoples who were not strictly Mongols, though the same name continued to be used—we use it still—for a confederation of many peoples, including many who spoke Turkic languages. In 1206, Temujin (TEH-moo-jeen), the most dynamic leader, proclaimed himself ruler (**khan**) "of all those who live in felt tents"—staking a claim to a steppe-wide empire. He was acclaimed by a title of obscure meaning, perhaps signifying "Ocean-King" and therefore, by implication, king of everything the ocean encloses. The title is traditionally rendered in the Roman alphabet as "Genghis Khan" (GEHN-gihs hahn).

We know maddeningly little about Temujin. Today, his memory is twisted between myths. When Mongolia was a communist state between 1921 and 1990, he was an almost unmentionable figure, inconsistent with the "peace-loving" image the communists tried to project. Now he is Mongolia's national hero. In his own day, he toyed with similarly contradictory images: a warlord who intimidated enemies into submission by massacre; an avenger of insults to his dynasty and tribe; an embodiment of Mongol convictions of superiority over sedentary peoples; a scourge of heaven, divinely appointed to chastise a wicked world; a lawgiver and architect of enduring empire.

In surviving documents, Genghis Khan addressed different audiences with conflicting messages. To Muslims, he was an instrument of God, sent to punish them for their sins. To Chinese, he was a candidate for the mandate of heaven. To Mongols, he was a giver of victory and of the treasure it brought. When he addressed monks and hermits, he stressed his own asceticism. "Heaven is weary of the inordinate luxury of China," he declared. "I have the same rags and the same food as cowherds and grooms, and I treat the soldiers as my brothers."

The violence endemic in the steppes now turned outward to challenge neighboring civilizations. Historians have been tempted to speculate about the reasons for the Mongols' expansion. One explanation is environmental. Temperatures in the steppe seem to have fallen during the relevant period. People farther west on the Russian plains complained that a cold spell in the early thirteenth century caused crops to fail. So declining pastures might have driven the Mongols to expand from the steppes. Population in the region seems to have been relatively high, and the pastoral way of life demands large amounts of grazing land to feed relatively few people. It is not a particularly energy-efficient way to provide food because it relies on animals eating plants and people eating animals, whereas farming produces humanly edible crops and cuts out animals as a wasteful intermediate stage of production. So perhaps the Mongol outthrust was a consequence of having more mouths to feed. Yet the Mongols were doing what steppelanders had always sought to do: dominate and exploit sedentary peoples. The difference was that they did it with greater ambition and greater efficiency than any of their predecessors.

Genghis Khan enforced or induced unity over almost the entire steppeland. The confederation of tribes he put together really did represent a combined effort of the steppe dwellers against the sedentary peoples who surrounded them. A single ideology came to animate, or perhaps reflect, that effort: the God-given terror-enforced right of the Mongols to conquer the world. The way events were recorded at the Mongol court in the next generation, it seemed as if from the moment of Genghis Khan's election as supreme ruler, "eternal heaven" had decreed that his conquests would encompass the world. The ruler is depicted as a constant devotee of **Tengri** (tehng-REE)—the sky, conceived as a supreme deity. The early Mongol-

Genghis Khan. Rashid al-Din (1247–1318) was a former Jewish rabbi, converted to Islam, who became the chief minister of the Mongol rulers of what is now Iran. His Compendium of Chronicles was propaganda that depicted Mongol rulers in Persian style. This is the image of Genghis Khan his successors liked to project—a lone, simple tent-dweller who was the arbitrator and lawgiver to petitioners from many nations.

"Exceptionally adaptable warmongers." This fourteenth-century Muslim painting shows the Mongols capturing Baghdad in 1258, with the help of siege craft and specialist engineers as well as their traditional cavalry. The last caliph appears behind a screen in his palace in the left background. In the center background, he emerges on a white horse to meet the Mongol leader, Hülegü. The painting seems to show the Mongols respecting the sacredness of the city and its ruler. Indeed, they showed their respect by putting the caliph to death without spilling his blood—a sign of reverence for the condemned in their culture.

inspired sources constantly insist on an analogy between the overarching unity of the sky and God's evident desire for the Earth to echo that unity through submission to one ruler.

It is more likely, however, that the sky cult was invented during the Mongol conquests to explain Genghis Khan's uniformly successful fortunes in war. The khan's imperial vision probably grew on him only gradually, as he felt his way from raiding, tribute gathering, and exacting ransom to constructing an empire, with permanent institutions of rule. Tradition alleges a turning point. When one of his generals proposed to exterminate ten million Chinese subjects and convert their fields into pasture for Mongol herds, Genghis Khan realized that he could profit more by sparing the peasants and taxing them to the tune of 500,000 ounces of silver, 400,000 sacks of grain, and 80,000 bolts of silk a year. The process, however, that turned the khan from destroyer to builder was tentative. He may have been only dimly aware of it.

Genghis Khan's initially limited ambitions are clear from the oath the Mongol chiefs swore to him at his election as khan, recorded in the earliest surviving Mongol record of the events. "If you will be our khan, we will go as your vanguard against the multitude of your enemies. All the beautiful girls and married women that we capture and all the fine horses we will bring to you." The khan acquired an unequaled reputation for lust and bloodlust. "My greatest joy," he was remembered for saying, "is to shed my enemies' blood, wring tears from their womenfolk and take their daughters for bedding." Meanwhile, he made the streets of Beijing—according to an admittedly imaginative eyewitness—"greasy with the fat of the slain." His tally of victims in Persia amounted, believably, to millions. When his army captured the city of Herat (heh-RAHT) in Afghanistan, it killed the entire population. Even after Genghis Khan had introduced more constructive policies, terror remained an instrument of empire. Mongol sieges routinely culminated in massacre. When the Mongols captured Baghdad in 1258, the last **caliph** and his sons were trampled to death—a ritual form of death reserved for rulers, which was designed to demoralize the enemy.

Wherever the Mongol armies went, their reputation preceded them. Armenian sources warned Westerners of the approach of "precursors of Antichrist . . . of hideous aspect and without pity in their bowels, . . . who rush with joy to carnage as if to a wedding feast or orgy." Rumors piled up in Germany, France, Burgundy, Hungary, and even in Spain and England, where Mongols had never been heard of before. The invaders looked like monkeys, it was said, barked like dogs, ate raw flesh, drank their horses' urine, knew no laws, and showed no mercy. Matthew Paris, the thirteenth-century English monk who, in his day, probably knew as much about the rest of the world as any of his countrymen, summed up the Mongols' image: "They are inhuman and beastly, rather monsters than men, thirsting for and drinking blood, tearing and devouring the flesh of

Chronology: The Rise of the Mongols

Seventh century	Earliest records of the Mongol people
Early twelfth century	Larger Mongol bands attack sedentary peoples
1206	Temujin proclaims himself khan

Mongol defeat. Japanese screen painters recorded the defeat of Mongol invaders. Though the Mongols adapted successfully to every kind of terrain, they were unable to continue their conquests overseas. The "divine winds"—kamikaze, as the Japanese called them—protected Japan by making it impossible for the Mongols adequately to supply or reinforce their task force.

dogs and men. . . .And so they come, with the swiftness of lightning to the confines of Christendom, ravaging and slaughtering, striking everyone with terror and with incomparable horror."

The Mongol conquests reached farther and lasted longer than those of any previous nomad empire (see Map 13.1). After Genghis Khan's death, the energy that the conquests generated took Mongol armies to the banks of the Elbe River in eastern Germany and the Adriatic Sea. Invasions of Syria, India, and Japan failed, and the Mongols withdrew from Europe without attempting to set up a permanent presence west of Russia. They completed the conquest of China, however, in 1279. At its fullest extent, therefore, the empire covered the region from the Volga River to the Pacific, encompassing the whole of Russia, Persia, China, the Silk Roads, and the steppes. This made it by a big margin the largest empire, in terms of territorial extent, the world had seen.

Efforts to explain this unique success appeal to Genghis Khan's military genius, the cunning with which the Mongols practiced feigned retreats only to encircle and destroy their advancing enemies, the effectiveness of their curved bows, the demoralizing psychological impact of their ruthless practices. Of course, they had the usual steppelander advantages of superior horsemanship and unrivaled mobility. It is likely that they succeeded, in part, through sheer numbers. Though we call it a Mongol army, Genghis Khan's was the widest alliance of steppelander peoples ever. And it is probable—though the sources are not good enough for certainty—that, relatively speaking, the steppeland was more populous in his day than ever before.

Above all, the Mongols were exceptionally adaptable warmongers. They triumphed not only in cavalry country, but also in environments where previous steppelander armies had failed, pressing into service huge forces of foot soldiers, mobilizing complex logistical support, organizing siege trains and fleets, appropriating the full potential of sedentary economies to finance further wars. The mountains of Georgia could not stop them. The Mongols captured the Georgian capital, Tbilisi (t-BEE-lee-see), in 1234, turning Georgia into a puppet kingdom. Nor, in the long run, could the rice paddies and rivers of southern China where the Mongols destroyed the Song dynasty in the 1270s. Toward the end of the century, when another supreme khan wanted to conquer Java and Japan, they were even willing to take to the sea. But both attempts failed.

"Though we call it a Mongol army, Genghis Khan's was the widest alliance of steppelander peoples ever."

HOLY
ROMAN
EMPIRE
Venice

POLISH
STATES
Esztergom
Pest
Cracow   Sandomierz
Vladimir
HUNGARY   Galich   Kamenets
SERBIA
BULGARIA

LATIN EMPIRE
Constantinople
EMPIRE OF
NICAEA
Anatolia
SELJUK
SULTANATE
OF RUM
CILICIA   Sivas
Kayseri
CRUSADER
STATES
Alexandria   Aleppo
Cairo   Homs
Jerusalem   Damascus
EGYPT
(MAMLUKS)   Ain Jalut
Mosul   Maragheh
IRAQ
Baghdad   Hamadan
ABBASID
CALIPHATE
Red Sea

Lithuanians

Novgorod

RUSSIAN
PRINCIPALITIES

Torzhok
Tver'
Yaroslavl'
Pereyaslavl'   Suzdal
Moscow   Vladimir
Chernigov   Kolomna
Kiev   Ryazan'
Pereyaslav

VOLGA
BULGARIA

Bulgar

Black Sea
Soldaia
EMPIRE OF TREBIZOND
Caucasus
GEORGIA
Thilisi
Derbent
AZERBAIJAN
Tabriz
Qazvin   Alamut
Amol
Qum   Rayy
Nishapur

Ural Mountains

Saray
Astrakhan

Volga

Don

Ural

Caspian Sea

S   t   e   p   p   e

Aral
Sea
Urgench
TRANSOXIANA
Amu Darya

Yanikant
Jand
Signak
Syr Darya

Zarnuq
Nur   Otrar
Bukhara   Tashkent
Banakat
Samarkand
Balkh
Herat   Hindu Kush

Lake
Balkhash   Ili

Balasaghun
Kashgaria
Kashgar
Pamirs

TURKESTAN

Ob

Irtysh

Issyk-Kul
Tien

PERSIA
(IRAN)
Iranian
Plateau

AFGHANISTAN   Parwan
Ghazni   Kabul

Mediterranean Sea

Euphrates   Tigris

Persian
Gulf

Arabian
Peninsula

OMAN

Arabian
Sea

Multan
PUNJAB   Delhi
Indus

INDI

Scale:
4,445 km
(2,774 miles)
N
8,372 km
(5,224 miles)
Scale varies with perspective

N

INDI

1200: Cold spell throughout Eurasian steppe

1211: First invasion of northern China

1237: Beginning of conquest of Russia

1242: Mongols reach Elbe River (Germany)

1260: Battle of Ain Jalut; Mongols invasion of Egypt repulsed

1276: Conquest of Song China complete

1292: Mongols raid Java

1206: Mongols united under Genghis Khan

1227: Death of Genghis Khan

1240: Kiev sacked

1258: Sack of Baghdad; last Caliph put to death

1274: First failed attempt at invading Japan

1281: Second failed invasion of Japan

1295: il-Khans adopt Islam

1200   1220   1240   1260   1280   1300

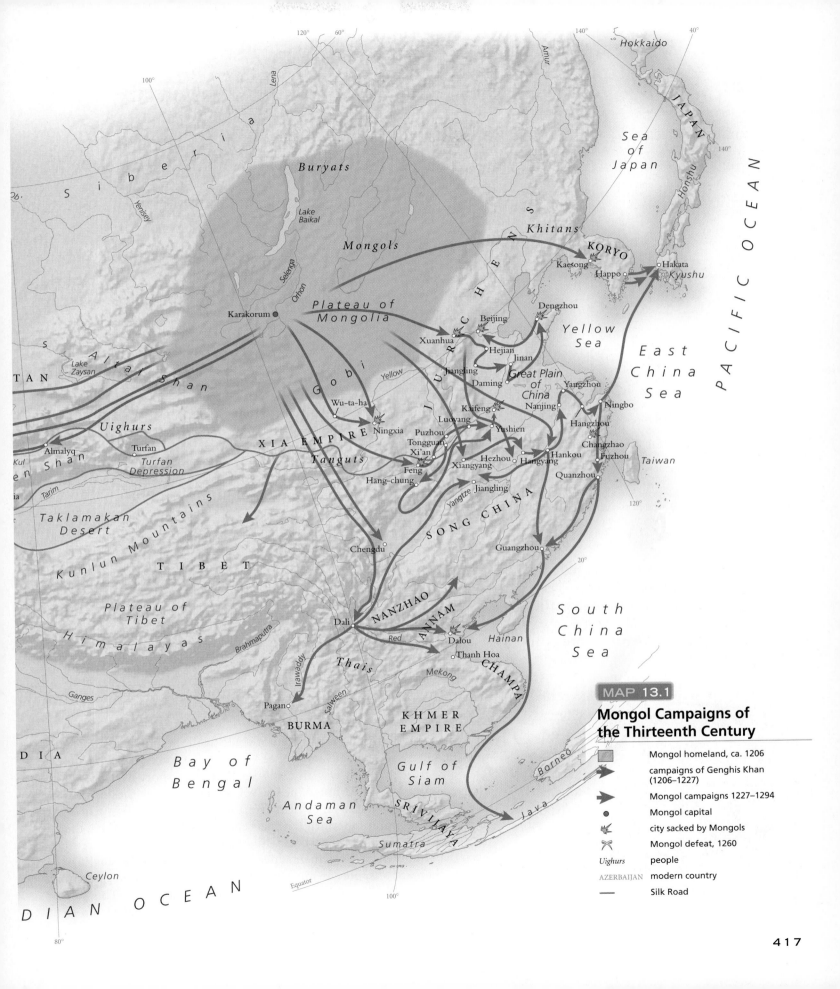

MAP 13.1

Mongol Campaigns of the Thirteenth Century

- ▢ Mongol homeland, ca. 1206
- ➤ campaigns of Genghis Khan (1206–1227)
- ➤ Mongol campaigns 1227–1294
- ● Mongol capital
- ✺ city sacked by Mongols
- ✖ Mongol defeat, 1260
- *Uighurs* people
- AZERBAIJAN modern country
- — Silk Road

Making Connections | REASONS FOR MONGOL MILITARY SUCCESS

TACTICS/STRATEGIES	TECHNOLOGIES	PRACTICES
Psychological warfare; feigned retreats; unrivaled mobility	Superior horsemanship; curved bows; siegecraft	Ability to adapt to different environments and to overcome complex logistical obstacles; alliance formation with other steppeland peoples; recruitment of workers and administrators without favoritism

William of Rubruck. "He shall pass into the country of strange peoples. He shall try good and evil in all things." In the only surviving illumination that illustrates his report, Friar William of Rubruck looks alarmed at the instructions from King Louis IX of France to go on a mission to the Mongols. William's journey of 1253–1255 took him as far as the Mongol capital of Karakorum and generated an account full of vivid and faithful detail. The text illustrates how Western Europeans were becoming more aware of the wider Eurasian world.

As well as for extent, the Mongol Empire was remarkable, by steppelander standards, for longevity. As his career progressed, Genghis Khan became a visionary lawgiver, a patron of letters, an architect of enduring empire. His first steps toward acquiring a bureaucracy and a judicial system more or less coincided with his election as khan. He then turned to lawmaking. Gradually, a code took shape, regulating hunting, army discipline, behavior at feasts, and social relationships, with death the penalty for murder, serious theft, conspiracy, adultery, sodomy, and witchcraft. Initially, the khan relied on Uighurs (see Chapter 9) for his administrators and ordered the adoption of the Uighur script for the Mongols' language. But he recruited as and where he conquered, without favoritism for any community or creed. His closest ministers included Muslims, Christians, and Buddhists.

In 1219, a Chinese Daoist sage, Changchun (chahng-chwuhn), answered the khan's call for wise experts. At the age of 71, he undertook an arduous three-year journey from China to meet the khan at the foot of the Hindu Kush Mountains in Afghanistan. There were sacrifices of principle Changchun would not make. He would not travel with recruits for the imperial harem, or venture "into a land where vegetables were unavailable"—by which he meant the steppe. Yet he crossed the Gobi Desert, climbed "mountains of huge cold," and braved wildernesses where his escort smeared their horses with blood to ward off demons. Admittedly, Changchun's meeting with the khan was disappointing. The question the conqueror was most eager to put was not about the art of government, but about a potion to confer longevity on himself.

The Mongol Steppe

Still, many lettered and experienced officials from the Jurchen, Khitan, and Tangut (THAN-goot) states (see Chapter 12) took service at the khan's court. The result was an exceptional, though short-lived, era in steppeland history: the **Mongol peace**. A European, who witnessed it in the 1240s, described it in an evident effort to reproach his fellow Christians with the moral superiority of their enemies: "The Mongols are the most obedient people in the world with regard to their leaders, more so even than our own clergy to their superiors. . . . There are no wranglings among them, no disputes or murders." This was obviously exaggerated, but Mongol rule did make the steppeland safe for outsiders. This was new. A previously inaccessible road through the steppes opened across

MAP 13.2

European Travelers of the Mongol Roads, 1245–1295

➤ John of Piano Carpini 1245–1247 and William of Rubruck 1253–1254

➤ Marco Polo 1271–1275

➤ Marco Polo 1275–1295

▨ Khanate of the Golden Horde

▨ Il-Khanate

▨ Chagatai Khanate

▨ Empire of the Great Khan

— Silk Road

Eurasia north of the Silk Road. Once they had learned the benefits of peace along the steppeland road, the Mongols became its highway police. Teams of Mongol horses, for instance, took the pope's ambassador, John of Piano Carpini, 3,000 miles in 106 days in 1246. Missionaries, spies, and craftsmen in search of work at the Mongol court also made the journey in an attempt to forge friendship between the Mongols and the Christian West, or, at least, to gather intelligence (see Map 13.2).

William of Rubruck—a Franciscan envoy recorded vivid details of his mission to Mongke Khan (MOHNG-keh hahn), Genghis Khan's grandson in 1253. As well as describing the road, William also described the Mongol way of life more accurately and completely than any Western visitor until the late nineteenth century.

After taking leave of the king of France, who hoped for an alliance with the Mongols against the Muslims, William crossed the Black Sea in May and set out across the steppe by wagon, bound for Karakorum (kah-rah-KOH-ruhm), the new city in Mongolia where the khan held court. "After three days," he recorded, "we found the Mongols and I really felt as if I were entering another world." By November, he was in the middle of Transoxiana, "famished, thirsty, frozen, and exhausted." In December, he was high in the dreaded Altai Shan (AHL-tay shahn), the mountain barrier that guarded the road to Karakorum. Here he "chanted the creed, among dreadful crags, to put the demons to flight." At last, on Palm Sunday, 1254, he entered the Mongol capital.

Friar William always insisted that he was a simple missionary, but he was treated as an ambassador and behaved like a master spy. And, indeed, he had more than one objective. The Mongols might be amenable to Christianity or at least to an alliance against common enemies in the Muslim world. On the other hand, they were potential enemies, who had already invaded the fringes of Europe and might do so again. Intelligence about them was precious. William realized that the seasonal migrations of Mongol life had a scientific basis and were calculated for military efficiency. "Every commander," he noted, "according to whether he has a greater or smaller number of men under him, is familiar with the limits of his pasture lands and where he ought to graze in summer and winter, spring and autumn."

Little useful intelligence escaped William. But he also showed interest in the culture he tried unsuccessfully to convert to Christianity. His description of a Mongol tent dwelling still holds good. The layout, social space, and way of life William saw have not changed much since his day. A frame of interlaced branches stretched between supports made of branches, converging at the top. The covering was of white felt, "and they decorate the felt with various fine designs." Up to 22 oxen hauled houses on wagons 20 feet broad.

Each wife of the master of the household had her own tent, where the master had a bench facing the entrance. In an inversion of Chinese rules of precedence, the women sat on the east side, the men to the right of the master, who sat at the north end. Ancestral spirits resided in felt bags arrayed around the walls. One each hung over the heads of master and mistress, with a guardian image between them. Others hung on the women's and men's sides of the tent, adorned with the udders of a cow and a mare, symbols of the sources of life for people who relied on dairy products for their diet. The household would gather to drink in the tent of the chosen wife of the night. "I should have drawn everything for you," William assured his readers, "had I known how to draw."

Shamans' trances released the spirits from the bags that held them. Frenzied drumming, dancing, and drinking induced the shamans' ecstasies. The power of speaking with the ancestors' voices gave **shamans** enormous authority in Mongol decision making, including the opportunity to interfere in making and unmaking khans. This was a point William missed. The Mongols leaders' interest in foreign religions, and their investment in the cult of heaven, were, in part at least, strategies to offset the power of the native priests.

Outside the tent, William vividly captured the nature of the terrain—so smooth that one woman could pilot 30 wagons, linked by trailing ropes. He described a way of life that reflected steppeland ecology. The Mongols had mixed flocks of various kinds of sheep and cattle. Mixed pastoralism is essential in an environment in which no other source of food is available. Different species have different cycles of lactation and fertility. Variety therefore ensures a reliable food supply.

The horse was the dominant partner of life on the steppe. Mare's milk was the Mongols' summer food. The intestines and dried flesh of horses provided cured meat and sausages for winter. By drawing blood from the living

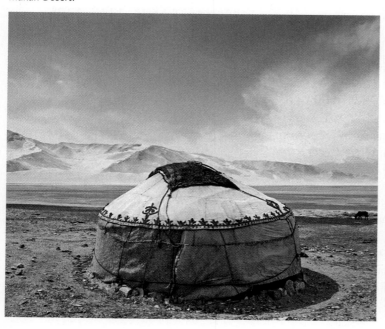

Yurt. The shape and decoration of a Mongol tent dwelling—known as a *yurt* or *ger*—has not changed since William of Rubruck described those he saw in the thirteenth century. In the background of this photograph are the Pamir Mountains, which travelers westward on the Silk Roads had to cross when they emerged from the Taklamakan Desert.

creatures, Mongols on campaign could refresh themselves without significantly slowing the herds. This was the basis of their reputation for blood-sucking savagery among their sedentary neighbors. They made, said William, "very fine shoes from the hind part of a horse's hide." Fermented mare's milk was the favorite intoxicating drink. The Mongols revered drunkenness and hallowed it by rites: offerings sprinkled over the bags of ancestral spirits, or poured out toward the quarters of the globe. Challenges to drinking bouts were a part of nightly entertainment. To the accompaniment of singing and clapping, the victim would be seized by the ears, with a vigorous tug "to make him open his gullet."

William related in detail his conversations with the habitually drunken Möngke Khan. Despite the khan's bluster and self-righteousness, the conversations revealed some of the qualities that made the Mongols of his era great: tolerance, adaptability, respect for tradition. "We Mongols believe," Möngke said, if we can trust William's understanding of his words, "that there is but one God, in Whom we live and in Whom we die, and towards him we have an upright heart." Spreading his hand, he added, "But just as God has given different fingers to the hand, so He has given different religions to people." Later in the thirteenth century, Kubilai Khan, another of Genghis Khan's grandsons, expressed himself to the Venetian traveler, Marco Polo, in similar terms. So this was genuinely a Mongol saying.

THE MONGOL WORLD BEYOND THE STEPPES: THE SILK ROADS, CHINA, PERSIA, AND RUSSIA

The steppeland route was ideal for horseborne travelers. Trading caravans, however, still favored the traditional **Silk Roads,** which crossed Eurasia to the south of the steppe through the Taklamakan (tahk-lah-mah-KAHN) Desert. These routes had developed over centuries, precisely because high mountains protected them from steppeland raiders. But they had never been totally secure before the Mongol peace. The new security boosted the amount of traffic the roads carried. Mongol partiality for merchants also helped. Mongols encouraged Chinese trade, uninhibited by any of the traditional Confucian prejudices against commerce as an ignoble occupation. In 1299, after the Mongol Empire had been divided among several rulers, a Persian merchant was made the ambassador of the Supreme Khan to the court of the subordinate Mongol **Il-khan** (EEL-hahn) in Persia—an elevation unthinkable under a native Chinese dynasty, which would have reserved such a post for an official educated in the Confucian classics. The khans gave low-cost loans to Chinese trading companies. Chinese goods—and with them, patterns and styles—flowed to Persian markets as never before. Chinese arts, under Mongol patronage, became more open to foreign influences.

Geography still made the Silk Roads hard to travel. Marco Polo was a young Venetian who accompanied his father and uncle on a trading mission to Mongol-ruled China in the early 1270s. "They were hard put to it to complete the journey in three and a half years," Marco Polo reported at the start of his own account, first "because of

The Silk Roads. Cresques Abraham was the finest mapmaker of his day. He painted this image of a caravan on the Silk Roads in the late 1370s or early 1380s in an atlas probably commissioned for the king of France. By that date, the Mongols no longer controlled the whole of the route, though the lances of an armed escort, presumably of Mongols, are visible behind the merchants. The caption says the caravan is bound for China, but it is heading in the opposite direction.

A Mongol Passport

Although they were in use in China before the Mongols arrived, documents called *paizi*, such as the one depicted here, were used as passports to regulate communication and administration in the vast Mongol Empire. Their use, the way they were designed, and the language in which they were written help us understand the massive movements of people and the rapid exchange of ideas and technology that occurred across Eurasia during the thirteenth and fourteenth centuries when Mongol rule was at its height. William of Rubruck and Marco Polo would have carried one of these passports on their return journeys to Europe from Mongol courts in Asia.

This passport is made of iron. Thick silver bands on it form characters in the script that the Tibetan monk Phagspa, a close adviser to Kubilai Khan (r. 1260–1294), devised for writing the Mongol language in 1269.

Most *paizi* were circular or rectangular and were either fastened on clothing or suspended from a person's neck, so that customs officers could easily see them.

Above the inscription is a handle with a silver lion mask inlaid on it that shows the influence of Tibetan and Indian art.

The inscription reads: "By the strength of Eternal Heaven, an edict of the Khan. He who has no respect [for the edict] shall be guilty."

The Metropolitan Museum of Art, Purchase, Bequest of Dorothy Graham Bennet, 1993 (1993.256) Photograph © The Metropolitan Museum of Art.

What does this passport reveal about the Mongol peace?

the snow and rain and flooded rivers and violent storms in the countries through which they had to pass, and because they could not ride so well in winter as in summer." The Taklamakan Desert was the great obstacle. The normal rule for caravans was the bigger the safer. But the modest water sources of the desert could not sustain many more than 50 men at a time with their beasts. The key to exploiting the desert routes was the distribution of water, which drains inland from the surrounding mountains and finds its way below the desert floor by underground channels. It was normal to go for 30 days without finding water, though there might be an occasional salt-marsh oasis or an unreliable river of shifting course, among featureless dunes. The worst danger was getting lost—"lured from the path by demon-spirits." "Yes," said Marco,

Demons. In Chinese and Mongol art, images of demons personify the torments of the desert—thirst, glare, sandstorms, extremes of heat and cold, the perils of being lost or attacked. William of Rubruck sang to drive away demons. Other travelers rang bells or deterred the demons with blood. In this fourteenth-century painting produced under Mongol patronage, the demon's dance evokes the swirling, stinging desert winds.

and even by daylight men hear these spirit-voices and often you fancy you are listening to the strains of many instruments, especially drums, and the clash of arms. For this reason bands of travelers make a point of keeping very close together. Before they go to sleep they set up a sign pointing in the direction in which they have to travel. And round the necks of their beasts they fasten little bells, so that by listening to the sound they may prevent them straying off the path.

As a fourteenth-century painter at Persia's Mongol court imagined them, the demons were black, athletic, and ruthless, waving the dismembered limbs of horses as they danced. As Friar William had seen, the Mongols recommended warding them off by smearing a horse's neck with blood.

A fourteenth-century guide included handy tips for Italian merchants who headed for East Asia to extend the reach of the commerce of their cities. At the port of Tana, on the Black Sea, you should furnish yourself with a good guide, regardless of expense. "And if the merchant likes to take a woman with him from Tana, he can do so." On departure from Tana, 25 days' supply of flour and salt fish were needed—"other things you will find in sufficiency and especially meat." The road was "safe by day and night," protected by Mongol police. But it was important to take a close relative for company. Otherwise, should a merchant die, his property would be forfeit. The text specified rates of exchange at each stop and recommended suitable conveyances for each stage of the journey: oxcart or horse-drawn wagon to the city of Astrakhan where the Don River runs into the Caspian Sea, depending on how fast the traveler wanted to go and how much he wanted to pay. Thereafter camel train or pack mule was best, until you arrived at the river system of China. Silver was the currency of the road, but the Chinese authorities would exchange it for paper money, which—Westerners were assured—they could use throughout China.

After the deserts, the next obstacles were the mountains on their rims. The Tian Shan, which screens the Taklamakan Desert, is one of the most formidable mountain ranges in the world: 1,800 miles long, up to 300 miles wide, and rising to 24,000 feet. The extraordinary environment these mountains enclose is odder still because of the deep depressions that punctuate them. That of Turfan (toor-FAHN) drops to more than 500 feet below sea level. Farther north, the Altai Shan Mountains guard

Chronology: Travelers during the Mongol Peace	
1245–1247	John of Piano Carpini
1253–1254	William of Rubruck
1271–1275; 1275–1295	Marco Polo
1275–1288	Rabban Bar Sauma

MAP 13.3

The Travels of Rabban Bar Sauma, 1275–1288

—— Silk Road

—— travels of Rabban Bar Sauma, 1275–1288

✝ Nestorian see

the Mongolian heartlands. "Before the days of the Mongols," wrote the bishop of the missionary diocese the Franciscans had established in China, "nobody believed that the Earth was habitable beyond these mountains, . . . but by God's leave and wonderful exertion the Mongols crossed them, and . . . so did I."

Europeans frequently made the journey to China. That reflects the balance of wealth and power at the time. China was rich and productive, Europe a needy backwater. We know of only one subject of the Chinese emperor who found it worthwhile to make the journey in the opposite direction. Rabban Bar Sauma was a Nestorian— a follower, that is, of a Christian tradition that had long flourished in Central Asia but the West had regarded as heretical since the fifth century (see Chapter 9).

When making a pilgrimage to Jerusalem, Bar Sauma planned a route between Nestorian monasteries, heading initially for Maragha (ma-rah-GEH) in what is now Azerbaijan, where the most respected bishop of the Nestorian church had his see. Maragha was a suitable way station: the intellectual capital of the western Mongol world, with a library reputedly of 400,000 books and a new astronomical observatory. There, Bar Sauma took service, first with the bishop, and later with the Mongol ruler of Persia, the Il-khan. He never completed his pilgrimage. In 1286, however, Bar Sauma did resume his travels. He was appointed the Mongols' ambassador to the kingdoms of the Christian West, to negotiate an alliance against Muslim Egypt (see Map 13.3).

When he got to Rome, Bar Sauma was accorded a signal honor: reception by the cardinals who had assembled to elect a pope. In Paris, he recognized the university there as an intellectual powerhouse reminiscent of Maragha, with schools of mathematics, astronomy, medicine, and philosophy. Persian was the only language in which Bar Sauma could communicate with Western interpreters. From the errors he makes in describing Western manners and politics, a lot evidently got lost in translation. He mistook diplomatic evasions for assent and vague expressions of Christian fellowship for doctrinal agreement. He returned to Persia with many assurances of friendship and exhortations to the Il-khan to convert to Christianity. The fact that he completed the journey at all shows how the Mongols made it possible to cross Eurasia.

China

The Mongols never ran their dominions as a centralized state. Nor did they apply consistent methods to govern territories as vast and diverse as theirs. Three main areas of conquest beyond the steppeland—in China, Persia, and Russia—were added after Genghis Khan's death. All were exploited in different ways, specific to the Mongols' needs and the peculiarities of each region.

The conquest of Song China was long and difficult for two reasons. It was a more powerful state than any the Mongols faced elsewhere, and it was highly defensible: compact, so that its armies could maneuver on interior lines of communication, and scored by terrain inhospitable to Mongol horsemen. But, fueled by resources from the Mongols' other conquests, and pursued with unfailing tenacity, the conquest unfolded relentlessly bit by bit. Letters from the Chinese court seeped desperation as the Mongols closed in for the kill. In 1274, the Chinese empress mother, Xie Qiao (shay chow), reflected on where the blame lay.

> The empire's descent into peril is due, I regret, to the instability of our moral virtue. . . . The sound of woeful lament reverberated through the countryside, yet we failed to investigate. The pall of hunger and cold enveloped the armed forces, yet we failed to console.

The real reasons for China's collapse lay in the superiority of the Mongols' war machine. Unlike previous steppelander invaders, the Mongols spared no resources to pursue all-out victory and hired the troops and equipment needed to subdue a country of cities, rice paddies, and rivers. Clearly, the size of the Mongols' existing empire helped. Persian engineers built the siege engines that helped overcome southern Chinese cities. The last battle was at Changzhao (chahng-jeeow) in 1275. The Chinese poet Yi Tinggao (yee teen-gow) was there, "smelling the acrid dust of the field," spying "the green irridescence of the dead." The human misery could be measured in the grief-stricken literature that survives: the suicide notes, the cries of longing for loved ones who disappeared in the chaos, massacred or enslaved. Years later, Ni Bozhuang (nee-bwo-chwang), bailiff of a Daoist monastery, recalled the loss of his wife: "I still do not know if you were taken because of your beauty, or if, surrounded by horses, you can still buy cosmetics." In 1276, with his advisers fleeing and his mother packed for

Kubilai Khan. Liu Guandao was Kubilai Khan's favorite painter. So we can be fairly sure that this is how the khan would like to be remembered: not just in the traditional inert Chinese pose (which Liu also painted), but also active, dressed and horsed like a Mongol ruler, engaged in the hunt. A woman, presumably his influential consort, Chabi, is at his side. The blank silk background evokes the featurelessness of the steppe, while also highlighting the human figures.

flight, the young Song emperor wrote his abdication letter to the Mongol khan. "The **Mandate of Heaven** having shifted, your Servant chooses to change with it, . . . yet my heart is full of emotions and these cannot countenance the prospect of the abrupt annihilation of the . . . altars of my ancestors. Whether they be misguidedly abandoned or specially preserved intact rests solely with the revitalized moral virtue you bring to the throne."

For the Mongols, the conquest of China was a logical continuation of the policies of Genghis Khan and a stage in fulfilling the destiny of world conquest heaven supposedly envisaged. But it was also the personal project and passion of Kubilai Khan (1214–1294), Genghis's grandson, who became so immersed in China that he never asserted his supremacy against those Mongol leaders in the extreme west of the Mongol world who resisted his claims. Some of his Chinese subjects resented Kubilai's foreign ways: the libations of fermented mare's milk with which he honored his gods, his barbarous banquets of meat, the officials he chose with great freedom from outside the Confucian elite and even from outside China. Marco Polo reported that all the Chinese "hated the government of the Great Khan, because he set over them steppelanders, most of whom were Muslims, and . . . it made them feel no more than slaves." In this respect, the khan indeed broke with Chinese tradition, which was to confine administrative positions to a meritocracy, whose members were selected by examination in the Confucian classics. Kubilai showed his reverence for Confucius by building a shrine in his honor, but he needed to recruit, as Genghis Khan had, from the full range of talent the Mongol Empire supplied.

Kubilai, indeed, remained a Mongol khan. In some respects, he flouted Chinese conventions. He showed traditional steppelander respect for the abilities of women, giving them court posts and, in one case, a provincial governorship. His wife, Chabi, was one of his closest political advisers. He introduced a separate tier of administration for Mongols, who became a privileged minority in China, ruled by their own laws, and resented for it by most Chinese. In defiance of Confucian teachings, Kubilai felt obliged to fulfill the vision of world conquest he inherited from Genghis Khan. But beyond China, he registered only fleeting success. In Java, the Mongols replaced one native prince with another, without making permanent gains. In Vietnam, the Mongols were only able to levy tribute at a rate too low to meet the cost of their campaigns there. So-called *kamikaze* winds—divine typhoons that wrecked the Mongol fleets—drove Kubilai's armies back from Japan.

While upholding Mongol traditions, Kubilai also sought, emphatically, to be a Chinese emperor who performed the due rites, dressed in the Chinese manner, learned the language, patronized the arts, protected the traditions, and promoted the interests of his Chinese subjects. Marco Polo, who seems to have served him as a sort of professional storyteller, called him "the most powerful master of men, lands, and treasures there has been in the world from the time of Adam until today."

Persia

In Persia, meanwhile, the Mongol rulers were like chameleons, gradually taking on the hues of the culture they conquered. But, as in China, they were anxious to maintain a distinct identity and to preserve their own traditions. The court tended to stay in the north, where there was grazing for the kinds of herds their

---

"For the Mongols, the conquest of China was a logical continuation of the policies of Genghis Khan and a stage in fulfilling the destiny of world conquest heaven supposedly envisaged."

followers brought with them from the steppe. The Il-khans—"subordinate rulers," so called in deference to Kubilai Khan's nominal superiority—retained nomadic habits, migrating every summer and winter to new camps with palatial tents. At the end of the thirteenth century, Gazan Khan's tent took three years to make, and 200 men took 20 days to erect it. In southern Iran and Iraq, the Il-khans tended to entrust power to local dynasties, securing their loyalty by marriages with the ruling family or court nobility. In effect, this gave them hostages for the good conduct of provincial rulers.

Eventually in 1295, the Il-khans adopted Islam, after flirtations with Nestorianism and Buddhism. This marked an important departure from the tradition of religious pluralism Genghis Khan had begun and Kubilai upheld. From the moment the Il-khan Ghazan (r. 1295–1304) declared his conversion to Islam, the state began to take on a militantly religious character, excluding the Christians, Zoroastrians, Buddhists, and Jews formerly admitted to the khan's service. Moreover, the form of Islam the Il-khans finally adopted was Shiism, the prevailing tradition in Iran. Shiites (see Chapter 9) embraced doctrines most Muslims rejected: that Muhammad's authority descended by heredity from his nephew Ali; that a divinely selected leader or imam would perfect the Prophet's message; and that in the meantime the clergy had the right to interpret Islam. The Il-khan's option for Shiism ensured that eventually Persia would remain an exceptional region in the Muslim world as the only officially Shiite state.

Indeed, the religious art of the Il-khanate is strikingly unlike that of any other Muslim country. The painters freely painted human figures, especially those of Muhammad and his nephew, and even copied Christian nativity scenes to produce versions of the Prophet's birth. The Il-khans' Persia, however, was not isolated from neighboring states. On the contrary, as was usual in the Mongol world, the presence of rulers descended from Genghis Khan promoted trans-Eurasian contacts and exchanges of goods, personnel, and ideas. Persia supplied China, for instance, with engineers, astronomers, and mathematicians, while Persia received Chinese porcelain and paper money, which, however, did not take root in Persia before the twentieth century. Chinese designs influenced Persian weavers, and Chinese dragons appeared on the tiles with which Persian buildings of the time were decorated. Mongol rule ended in Persia in 1343 when the last Il-khan died without an heir.

Russia

Meanwhile, the Mongols who remained in their Central Asian heartlands continued to lead their traditional, unreconstructed way of life. So did those who formed the elite in the remaining areas the heirs of Genghis Khan inherited: in Turkestan and Kashgaria in Central Asia, and the steppes of the lower Volga River. From the last of these areas, where the Mongols were known as the Golden Horde, they exercised a form of overlordship over Russia, where they practiced a kind of imperialism different from those in China and Persia. The Mongols left the Christian Russian principalities and city-states to run their own affairs. But their rulers had to receive charters from the khan's court at Saray (sah-REYE) on the lower Volga, where they had to make regular appearances, loaded with tribute and subject to ritual humiliations. The population had to pay taxes

Il-Khan art. When Mongols converted to Islam, they did not necessarily accept all the beliefs and conventions of orthodox religion. In this fourteenth-century painting from what is now Iran, the white rooster symbolizes the Muslim call to prayer—but the rooster was also a traditional Zoroastrian symbol of dawn. The prophet Muhammad, moreover, is realistically depicted at bottom right—something most Muslim painters would regard as impious today. The other figures are of angels.

Novgorod. The cathedral of St. Sophia in Novgorod in Russia would have presented essentially the same outline in the thirteenth century that it does today. At the time, it was one of relatively few buildings in that mercantile city-state built of stone rather than wood. The tallest gilded dome shows the position of the sanctuary at the heart of the church.

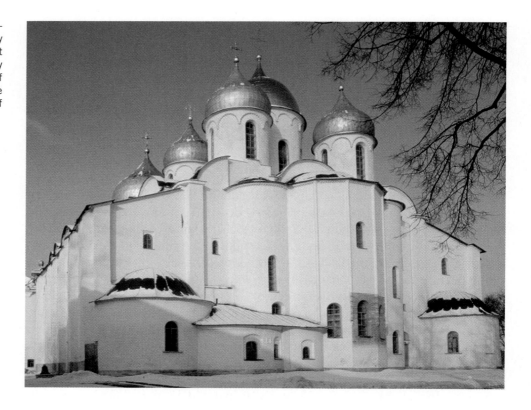

directly to Mongol-appointed tax gatherers—though as time went on, the Mongols assigned the tax gathering to native Russian princes and civic authorities.

The Russians tolerated this situation—albeit unhappily, and with many revolts—partly because the Mongols intimidated them by terror. When the Mongols took the great city of Kiev in 1240, it was said, they left only 200 houses standing and strewed the fields "with countless heads and bones of the dead." Partly, however, the Russians were responding to a milder Mongol policy. In most of Russia, the invaders came to exploit rather than to destroy. According to one chronicler, the Mongols spared Russia's peasants to ensure that farming would continue. Ryazan, a Russian principality on the Volga, southeast of Moscow, seems to have borne the brunt of the Mongol invasion. Yet there, if the local chronicle can be believed, "the pious Grand Prince Ingvary Ingvarevitch sat on his father's throne and renewed the land and built churches and monasteries and consoled newcomers and gathered together the people. And there was joy among the Christians whom God had saved from the godless and impious khan." Many cities escaped lightly by capitulating at once. Novgorod, that hugely rich city (see Chapter 11), which the Mongols might have coveted, they bypassed altogether.

Moreover, the Russian princes were even more fearful of enemies to the west, where the Swedes, Poles, and Lithuanians had constructed strong, unitary monarchies, capable of sweeping the princes away if they ever succeed in expanding into Russian territory. Equally menacing were groups of mainly German adventurers, organized into crusading "orders" of warriors, such as the Teutonic Knights and the Brothers of the Sword, who took monastic-style vows but dedicated themselves to waging holy war against pagans and heretics. In practice, these orders were self-enriching companies of professional fighters, who built up territorial domains along the Baltic coast by conquest. In campaigns between 1242 and 1245, Russian coalitions fought off invaders on the western front, but they could not sustain war on two fronts. The experience made them submissive to the Mongols.

THE LIMITS OF CONQUEST: MAMLUK EGYPT AND MUSLIM INDIA

Mamluk Egypt

In the 1200s, Egypt was in chaos because of rebellions by pastoralists from the southern desert and revolt by the Mamluks, the slaves who formed the elite fighting force. It seems counterintuitive to arm slaves. But for most of the thirteenth century, the policy worked well for the heirs of Saladin who had ruled Egypt since 1192. The rulers handpicked their slave army. The slaves came overwhelmingly from Turkic peoples that Mongol rebels displaced or captured and sold. These slaves had nowhere else to go and no future except in the Egyptian sultan's service. They were acquired young. They trained in barracks, which became their substitutes for families and the source of their pride and strong sense of comradeship. They seemed, from the ruler's point of view, ideally reliable: a dependent class. Increasingly, however, the Mamluks came to know their own strength. In the 1250s, they rebelled. Their own later propaganda cites the sultan's failure to reward them fairly for their services in repelling a crusader attack on Egypt, and their outrage at the promotion of a black slave to one of the highest offices in the court. The Mamluks "threw themselves upon him like the onrush of an unleashed torrent." In 1254, the Mamluks replaced the last heir of Saladin with rulers from their own ranks.

The rebels, however, while contending with internal enemies, perceived the Mongols as a greater threat and turned to face them. In September 1260, they turned back the Mongol armies at one of the decisive battles of the world at Ain Jalut in Syria. It was the first serious reversal the Mongols had experienced since Genghis Khan united them. And it gave the Mamluk commander, Baybars (BEYE-bahrs), the chance to take over Egypt and Syria. He boasted that he could play polo in Cairo and Damascus within the space of a single week. The Mamluks mopped up the last small crusader states on the coast of Syria and Palestine between 1268 and 1291. In combination with the effects of the internal politics of the Mongol world, which inhibited armies from getting too far from the centers of power, the Mamluk victory kept the Mongols out of Africa.

Mamluk victory also marked a further stage in the Islamization of Africa. The Mamluks levied tribute on the Christian kingdoms of Nubia (see Chapter 9). Then, in the next century, they imposed Islam there. Cairo, as we shall see in the next chapter, became a normal stopping place on the pilgrimage route to Mecca for Muslim kings and dignitaries from West Africa. Islam percolated through the region of Lake Chad and into Hausaland in what is today Nigeria.

"It seems counterintuitive to arm slaves. But for most of the thirteenth century, the policy worked well for the heirs of Saladin who had ruled Egypt since 1192."

Muslim India: The Delhi Sultanate

After the disruptions caused by the violent Turkic migrations of the twelfth century, it took a long time for a state in the mold of Mahmud's (mah-MOOD) to reemerge in Ghazna (GAHZ-nah) (see Chapter 12). By the 1190s, however, a Muslim Turkic dynasty and people, the Ghurids

Chronology: Rise of the Mamluks	
1254	Mamluks depose sultan of Egypt
1260	Mamluk army victorious at the battle of Ain Jalut in Syria
1268–1291	Mamluks overthrow last of the crusader states

MAP 13.4

The Delhi Sultanate

- Delhi Sultanate 1236
- area subject to sporadic influence by Delhi Sultanate
- border of Ghaznavid Empire 1186

(GOO-rids), had resumed the habit of raiding into Hindu India. As their victories accumulated, they began to levy fixed tribute in the Punjab and even established permanent garrisons in the Ganges valley. One of their most far-flung outposts—and therefore one of the strongest—was at the city of Delhi in northern India. The adventurer Iltutmish (eel-TOOT-mihsh) took command there in 1211. He was a former slave who had risen to general and received his freedom from his Ghurid masters. He avoided war with Hindus—which was, in essence, his job—in favor of building up his own resources. In 1216, exhibiting to his subordinates the letters that had granted him his freedom, he effectively declared himself independent. Over the next 12 years, he played the power game with skill, exploiting the rivalries of Muslim commanders to construct a state from the Indus River to the Bay of Bengal. Meanwhile, the effects of the Mongol conquests on Central Asia protected this new realm, which became known as the Sultanate of Delhi, against outside attack (see Map 13.4). The Mongols effectively eliminated any possible invader and drove many refugees to take service with Iltutmish. As one of the early chroniclers of the sultanate said, "Rulers and governors, . . . and many administrators and notables came to Iltutmish's court from fear of the slaughter and terror of the accursed Mongol, Genghis Khan."

There was no consistent form of administration. In most of the more remote territories, the Delhi sultan was an overlord, mediating between small, autonomous states, many of which Hindus ruled. Bengal was exceptional—a forest frontier, in which governors tried to promote Muslim settlement by making land grants to pioneering holy men and religious communities. But a core of lands was the sultan's personal property, exploited to benefit his treasury and run by administrators he appointed. Lands the sultan granted to warriors in exchange for military service ringed this core. For most of the rest of the century, the sultanate had a volatile history, punctuated by succession wars that were resolved at great oath-taking ceremonies, when the aristocracy of the realm—encompassing a great diversity of effectively freelance warriors and local rulers whom it was difficult or impossible for the sultan to dismiss—would make emotional but often short-lived declarations of loyalty.

Iltutmish's personal choice of successor set the tone on his deathbed in 1236. As an ex-slave, Iltutmish was no respecter of conventional ideas of hierarchy. Denouncing his sons for incompetence, he chose his daughter, Radiyya (rah-DEE-ah), as his successor. In the steppes, women often handled important jobs. In the Islamic world, a woman ruler was a form of impiety and a subversion of what was thought to be the natural order of the world. When, in 1250, a little before the Mamluks took over in Egypt, a woman had seized the throne there and applied to Baghdad for legitimation by the caliph, he is supposed to have replied that he could supply capable men, if no more existed in Egypt. Radiyya had to contend both with a brother who briefly ousted her—she had him put to death—and, what was harder, with male mistrust. Some of her coins emphasize claims to unique feminine virtues as "pillar of women." Others have modest inscriptions, in which all the glorious epithets are reserved for her father and the caliph in Baghdad. Her best strategy was to behave like a man. She dressed in male clothing, refused to cover her face, and, according to a slightly late source, "mounted horse like men, armed with bow and quiver." To conventional minds, these were provocations. She was ousted on grounds that—true or false—reflect male prejudices about female behavior. Accused of taking a black slave as a lover, she was deposed in 1240 in favor of a brother. Her real offense was self-assertion. Those modest coin inscriptions suggest that power brokers in the army and the court were willing to accept her, but only as a figurehead representative of her father, not as an active leader of men.

The sultanate had to cope not only with the turbulence of its own elite, but with its Hindu subjects and neighbors. Dominion by any state over the entire Indian subcontinent remained, at best, a dream. Frontier expansion was slow. Deforestation was an act of state, because, as a Muslim writer of the fourteenth century complained, "the infidels live in these forests, which for them are as good as city walls, and inside them they have their cattle and grain supplies of water collected from the rains, so that they cannot be overcome except by strong armies of men who go into these forests and cut down those reeds." In Bengal, the eastward shift of the Ganges River made Islamization easier. Charismatic **Sufis**, with tax-free grants of forest land for mosques and shrines, led the way.

For most of the thirteenth century, the Mongol menace overshadowed the sultanate. The internal politics of the dynasty of Genghis Khan caused dissensions and hesitancies that protected Delhi. Mongol dynastic disputes cut short periodic invasions. Moreover, a buffer state that dissident Mongols created in Delhi's western territories diminished the sultanate but also absorbed most of the khans' attacks. In the 1290s, however, the buffer collapsed. By what writers in Delhi considered a miracle, the subsequent Mongol attacks failed, faltered, or were driven off.

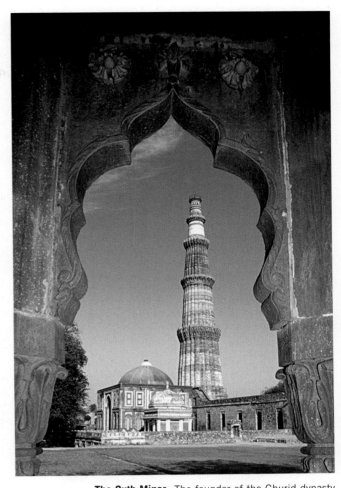

The Qutb Minar. The founder of the Ghurid dynasty began the Qutb Minar, near Delhi, as a monument to his own prowess in battle, toward the end of the twelfth century. Successors continued the project until, by the late fourteenth century, it was the tallest tower in India—much bigger than any minaret designed to hoist the call to prayer. The ridged form and decorative use of sandstone are typical of the stylistic traditions the Ghurids brought to India from Afghanistan.

EUROPE

With the scare the Mongol invasions caused and the loss of the last crusader states in Syria to the Mamluks, Latin Christendom looked vulnerable. Attempts were made to revitalize the crusading movement—especially by Louis IX, the king of France (r. 1226–1270) who became a model monarch for the Western world. But they all failed. A further reversal was the loss of Constantinople by its Latin rulers to a Byzantine revival. The Mongols destroyed or dominated most of the successor states that claimed Byzantium's legacy, but at the city of Nicaea in western Anatolia, rulers who continued to call themselves "Roman emperors" maintained the court rituals and art of Byzantine greatness. In 1261, they recaptured the old capital from the crusaders "after many failures," as the ruler at the time, Michael VIII, admitted, "because God wished us to know that the possession of the city was a grace dependent on his bounty."

Nevertheless, Latin Christendom grew on other fronts, extending the frontier deep into formerly pagan worlds along the Baltic in Livonia, Estonia, Prussia, and Finland. Between the 1220s and the 1260s, Christian kingdoms seized most of the Mediterranean seaboard of Spain and the Balearic Islands from the

MAP 13.5

Latin Christendom, 1200–1300

- ▨ predominantly pagan lands
- ▥ university/cathedral schools with date of foundation
- ✚ important churches with stained glass
- → reconquest of Spain in thirteenth century
- ➔ campaigns of Teutonic Knights and Sword Brothers

Maritime Trade Routes

—— Venetian

—— Genoese

—— Catalan

hands of Muslim rulers. Here the existing economy and population were not much disturbed. Conquests Castile and Portugal made over the same period in the Iberian southwest became a sort of Wild West of sparse settlements, tough frontiersmen, and vast cattle and sheep ranches. Meanwhile, traders of the western Mediterranean increased their commerce with northern Europe along the coasts the Spaniards conquered, through the Strait of Gibraltar (see Map 13.5). Toward the end of the century, as they became accustomed to Atlantic sailing conditions, some of them began to think of exploring the ocean for new routes and resources. In 1291, an expedition set off from the Italian city of Genoa to try to find "the regions of India by way of the ocean." The voyagers were never heard of again, but their voyage marked the beginning of a long, faltering effort by maritime communities of Western Europe to exploit the ocean at their feet.

The transforming influences, however, came from the east. The Mongol peace policing the routes that linked the extremities of Eurasia—ended Europe's relative isolation and stimulated trade and travel between Europe and China. The thirteenth century was the most intense period ever in trans-Eurasian communications, and European traditions were rechanneled as a result or, at least, guided more securely in directions they might have taken anyway. Paper, for instance, a Chinese invention that had already reached the West through Arab intermediaries, was a former luxury that came into general use in late-thirteenth-century Europe as a major contribution to what we would now call **information technology**, making written communication cheap, easy, and prolific. European maritime technology—a prerequisite of the prosperity borne by long-range trade and of the reach of most long-range imperialism—was especially primitive by non-European standards up to this time. The compass was first recorded in Europe in about 1190 in a text that explained the marvels of a pin well rubbed "with an ugly brown stone that draws iron to itself." As far as we know, the West had as yet no maritime charts. The earliest reference to such a device dates only from 1270. Gunpowder and the blast furnace were among the magical-seeming technologies that first reached Europe from China in the thirteenth and fourteenth centuries.

Meanwhile, with consequences for the future that can hardly be overestimated, Western science grew more **empirical**, more reliant on the reality of sense perceptions, more committed to the observation of nature. The renewal of this classical tradition in the West coincided with renewed contact with China, where empiricism had never been lost. At the University of Paris, which the Nestorian Rabban Bar Sauma so admired, scholars cultivated a genuinely scientific way of understanding the world. The end products were the marvelously comprehensive schemes of faith the encyclopedists of thirteenth-century Paris elaborated, especially in the work of the greatest intellect of the age, Thomas Aquinas (1225–1274), who arrayed in precise categories everything known by experience or report. In northwest Spain, an unknown, probably French artist of the thirteenth century depicted a similar vision of the whole cosmos in the stained glass windows of León Cathedral. The cosmos was measurable, portrayed between the dividers of Christ the geometer, like a ball of fluff trapped between tweezers (see page 434).

In the third quarter of the thirteenth century, Parisian teachers, of whom the most insistent was Siger of Brabant, pointed out that the doctrines of the church on the creation and the nature of the soul conflicted with classical philosophy and empirical evidence. "Every disputable question," they argued, "must be determined by rational arguments." Some thinkers took refuge in an evasive idea of "double truth," according to which things true in faith could be false in science and vice versa. The church condemned this doctrine in 1277 (along with a miscellany of magic and superstition).

Meanwhile, another professor in the thirteenth century at the University of Paris, Roger Bacon, stated that excessive deference to authority—including ancestral wisdom, custom, and consensus—was a cause of ignorance. He insisted that scientific observations could help to validate holy writ and that medical

Astrolabe. The Syrian instrument maker, al-Sarraj engraved his signature on this fine astrolabe in 1230–1231. The purpose of the astrolabe is to assist in astronomy—one of the many sciences in which the Islamic world excelled at the time. By suspending the instrument at eye level and swiveling a narrow central bar until it aligned with any observed star, the user could read the star's elevation above the horizon, as well as such additional information as the latitude, the date, and even the time of day from the engraved discs.
© National Maritime Museum Picture Library, London, England. Neg. #E5555–3

The measurable cosmos. This thirteenth-century illustrator of the creation of the world shows God as a well-equipped designer, measuring creation with an architect's or mathematician's dividers. The Earth is not the center of the cosmos, but a tiny blob in the corner, surrounded by chaos and dwarfed by God.

experiments could increase knowledge and save life. He also claimed—citing the lenses with which Archimedes reputedly set fire to a Roman fleet during the siege of the Greek city of Syracuse in Sicily in 212 B.C.E.—that science could cow and convert infidels. It was part of a modest scientific revolution in Western Christendom. The most relentless experimenter of the age was the German emperor and king of Sicily, Frederick II (r. 1212–1250). He was said to have had two men disemboweled to show the varying effects of sleep and exercise on the digestion, and to have brought up children in silence "in order to settle the question" of what language human beings "naturally" speak. "But he labored in vain, for all the children died."

Bacon was a Franciscan friar, a follower of Francis of Assisi (1181–1226), and his enthusiasm for science seems to have owed something to Francis's rehabilitation of nature: because the world made God manifest, it was worth observing. Francis was a witness and maker of the new European imagination. He was a rich man's son inspired by Jesus' advice to a rich youth ("Go, sell what thou hast and give to the poor. Then take up thy cross and follow me.") to seek a life of total dependence on God. In anyone less committed and charismatic, his behavior might have been considered insane or heretical. He launched his mission by stripping naked in the public square of his native city of Assisi in northern Italy, as a sign that he was throwing himself, unprotected, on God's mercy. He relied for sustenance on what people gave him. He attracted a following and modeled his followers' way of life on the way he thought Christ and the apostles lived, refusing to accept property, sharing everything the brethren received by way of alms.

The Franciscans became the spearhead of the church's mission to the poor and inspired other orders of friars—clergy who combined religious vows of poverty, chastity, and obedience with work in the world. In an age of urbanization, this was a particularly important mission, because friars could establish bonds of sympathy with the rootless masses who gathered in towns and faced the problem of adjusting to life away from the familiar companionship of rural parishes. Friars were also a valuable counterforce to heretics who denounced the church for worldliness. Friars, if they stayed true to their vocations, could match these enemies in holiness of life and in strict self-denial.

In his attitude toward nature, Francis was representative of his time and of the convergence of Western and Chinese attitudes to nature. In China, nature was the object of reverence and the subject of art. The same values now appeared in the West. Partly to rebut heretics repelled by the disorder of creation, Francis insisted on the goodness of God's creation, which was all "bright and beautiful." Even its conflicts and cruelties were there to elicit human love. He tried to enfold the whole of nature in love. He preached to ravens and called creatures, landscapes, sun, and moon his brothers and sisters, eventually welcoming "Sister Death." He communicated his sensibilities to his followers. As a result, Franciscans were prominent in scientific thinking in the West. Love of nature made them observe it more closely and keenly and scrutinize it for good uses.

Franciscans also became patrons of increasingly naturalistic art. The art they commissioned for their churches drew the onlooker into sacred spaces, as if in eyewitness of the lives of Jesus and the saints. The devotion of the rosary, introduced early in the thirteenth century, encouraged the faithful to imagine sacred mysteries, while praying, with the vividness of scenes of everyday life, as if witnessed in person. Franciscan art stirred the emotions of the devout by unprecedented realism—looking at the world with eyes as unblinking as those of the new scientific thinkers. Considered from one point of view, the realism Western painting increasingly favored was a tribute to the enhanced prestige of the senses. To paint what one's eyes could see was to confer dignity on a subject not previously thought worthy of art. So art linked the science and piety of the age.

It is hard to resist the impression that the revolutionary experiences of the West at the time—the technical progress, the innovations in art, the readjustment of notions of reality through the eyes of a new kind of science—were owed in part to influences transmitted along the routes the Mongols maintained. None of this experimentation and imagination put Western science abreast of that of China, where observation and experiment had been continuous in scientific tradition since the first millennium B.C.E. (see Chapter 6). In two technologies, however—key technologies, as they later proved to be, for their influence on world history—Western Europe came to house the world's leading centers of development and production.

The first technology was glass making. In the thirteenth century, demand for fine glassware leaped in the West because of the growing taste for using church windows made of stained glass, penetrated by light, to illuminate sacred stories and to exhibit glowingly the wonders of creation as the windows at Chartres Cathedral did. Simultaneously, glassmakers adapted their skills to meet domestic demand for glass mirrors and optical lenses. These objects were not manufactured on a significant scale anywhere else in the world, though for centuries scholars writing in Arabic had known how to make them and use them as aids to scientific observation. Now Western savants could make the same experiments themselves and even improve on them. In the thirteenth century, Robert Grosseteste, the first chancellor of the University of Oxford in England, explained the geometry of the way lenses operate. "It is obvious," he concluded, "that they can make very large objects appear very small, and contrariwise very small and remote objects as if they were large and easily discernible by sight."

Second, the West drew ahead in the technology of clockwork. Mechanical clocks had a long history in China and the Islamic world. But clockwork never caught on except in Europe. This is a hard fact to explain. Clockwork is too regular to match the movements of the heavens. It divides the day into arbitrary hours of equal length that do not match those of the sun. But this way of organizing life suited Western monasteries, where, apart from the prayers prescribed for the dawn and nightfall, the services of prayer were best arranged at regular intervals, independently of the sun. For city churches in an age of urban growth, regular

Making Connections | EUROPEAN TRANSFORMATIONS AND INNOVATIONS, THIRTEENTH AND EARLY FOURTEENTH CENTURIES

TRADE AND TRANSPORTATION	TECHNOLOGY AND SCIENCE	POLITICS	RELIGION
Increased communication across Eurasia leads to introduction of Chinese and Arabic technology, medicine, and inventions	Imported inventions such as paper, magnetic compasses, gunpowder, and blast furnace combine with focus on empiricism	Christian kingdoms seize Muslim lands in Spain, Mediterranean islands; revival of Crusades, extension of frontier north to the Baltics, Finland, and Scandinavia	Francis and his religious order place new emphasis on observing nature, serving the poor, and renouncing wealth; increased emphasis on sacred mysteries
Increased transportation and trade links within Europe aided by new infrastructure (roads, canals); growth of towns; economic and political stability leads to larger towns and cities; more productive industry	Better maritime technology expands range of sea voyages; demand for elaborate church windows spurs glassmaking and innovation in glass lenses; clocks provide regularized timekeeping for monasteries and cities; availability of paper multiplies books and empowers states with a medium for their messages	Bigger, richer states with more scope to communicate and enforce commands; more church-state competition and conflict	Mendicants prominent in scientific thinking in West; spearhead Church's mission to poor in growing towns

timekeeping was also convenient. Clockwork suited the rhythms of urban life. Civic authorities began to invest heavily in town clocks in the thirteenth and fourteenth centuries. This was the beginning of the still-familiar Western convention of an urban skyline dominated by the town hall clock tower.

The combination of lenses and clockwork mattered in the long run because eventually—not until the seventeenth century, when telescopes were combined with accurate chronometry—they gave Western astronomers an advantage over Muslim and Chinese competitors. This in turn gave Western scientists the respect of their counterparts and secured the patronage of rulers all over the world in societies interested in astronomy either for its own sake or—more often—because of astrology—the belief that events on Earth reflected the movements of the heavenly spheres.

"The importance of the Mongols' passage through world history does not stop at the frontiers of their empire. It resonated across Eurasia."

In Perspective
The Uniqueness of the Mongols

In the thirteenth century, a state arose that embraced the whole of the steppe. Like many great revolutions, the episode started bloodily and became constructive. When the Mongol alliance first challenged its neighbors, it seemed to threaten civilization with destruction—slaughtering settled peoples, razing cities, despising art and learning. Yet the Mongols came to play a unique and constructive role in the history of Eurasia. First, fear of the most devastating conquerors the interior had yet bred linked the peoples beyond the steppe, from Christendom to Japan. Then a peace that those same conquerors imposed connected them. For 100 years after the initial horror of the Mongol conquests, the steppe became a highway of fast communication, linking the extremities of the landmass and helping transfer culture across two continents. Without the Mongol peace, it is hard to imagine any of the rest of world history working out as it did, for these were the roads that carried Chinese ideas and technology westward and opened up European minds to the vastness of the world. The importance of the Mongols' passage through world history does not stop at the frontiers of their empire. It resonated across Eurasia.

The Eurasian experience was unique. Why did nothing like it happen in Africa or the Americas? Cultural exchanges across the grasslands of prairie, pampa, and Sahel never spread far until the nineteenth century. None of those regions saw conquerors like the Mongols, able to unify the entire region and turn it into a causeway of civilizations, shuttling ideas and techniques across a continent.

In the Americas, geography was an inhibiting influence. The North American prairie is aligned on a north–south axis, across climatic zones, whereas the

Chronology

1181–1226	Life of Francis of Assisi
1190	First European recorded reference to a compass
1206	Temujin proclaims himself khan
1211–1236	Reign of Iltutmish, sultan of Delhi
1225–1274	Life of Thomas Aquinas
1234	Mongols conquer Georgia
1241–1242	Mongol armies reach Elbe River, Germany
1253–1254	Mission of William of Rubruck to Mongolian court
1258	Mongols capture Baghdad, last caliph put to death
1260	Mamluks defeat Mongols at battle of Ain Jalut
1261	Byzantine Empire regains Constantinople
1268–1291	Mamluks overthrow last crusader states on coast of Palestine
1270	Earliest European reference to maritime charts
1271–1275	Marco Polo's first journey to China
1274, 1281	Failed Mongol attempts to invade Japan
1279	Mongol conquest of China completed
1286	Rabban Bar Sauma appointed Mongol ambassador to Christian West

North American prairie is aligned on a North–South axis, making transmissions of crops and culture difficult

Civilizations of Mesoamerica and Andes are not linked by grasslands or other easily traveled routes

Although the Sahel is aligned east–west, it never became a conduit of cultural exchange until the nineteenth century

MAP 13.6

Grassland Environments Compared

steppe stretches from east to west. Plants and animals can cross the steppe without encountering impenetrable environments. Seeds can survive the journey without perishing and without finding, at the end of the road, an environment too sunless or cold to thrive in. In North America, it took centuries longer to achieve comparable exchanges. As we have seen repeatedly—almost whenever the Americas have entered our story—transmissions of culture across latitudes are much harder to effect than those that occur within latitudes, which have relatively narrow boundaries, where climate and conditions are familiar.

Moreover, to function, an avenue of communications needs people at either end of it who want to be in touch. The Eurasian steppe was like a dumbbell, with densely populated zones and productive economies at either end of it (see Map 13.6). For people in Europe, Southwest Asia, and North Africa, access to the products of South, Southeast, and East Asia was highly desirable. For the suppliers of spices, drugs, fine textiles, and luxury products in the east, it was good to have customers who paid in silver. In the Americas, there was no chance to reproduce such relationships. The concentrations of wealth and population were in two regions—Mesoamerica and the Andes—that neither grasslands nor any other easily traveled routes linked. Though societies in other parts of the hemisphere drew lessons, models of life, technologies, and types of food from those areas, the results,

Eurasia is shaped like a dumbbell, with densely populated zones and productive economies at either end. The east–west axis of steppe facilitates transmission of crops, culture, and trade.

as we have seen (see Chapter 11) were hard to sustain because communications between these areas and outlying regions were difficult to keep up. Without the horse—extinct in the Americas for 10,000 years—the chances of an imperial people arising in the prairie or the pampa to do the sort of job the Mongols did in Europe were virtually zero. (Much later, as we shall see in Chapter 21, when European invaders reintroduced the horse in the Americas in the 1500s, experiments in grassland imperialism by peoples such as the Sioux followed.)

In Africa, the constraints were different. The **Sahel** might have played a role similar to that of the steppes in Eurasian history. There was a viable corridor of communication between the Nile and Niger valleys. In theory, an imperial people might have been able to open communications across the continent between the civilizations of East Africa, which were in touch with the world of the Indian Ocean, and those of West Africa, which the trade routes of the Sahara linked to the Mediterranean. But it never happened. For long-range empire building, the Sahel was, paradoxically, too rich compared with the Eurasian steppe. The environment of the Sahel was more diverse. Agrarian or partly agrarian states had more opportunity to develop, obstructing the formation of a Sahel-wide empire. Although pastoral peoples of the western Sahel often built up powerful empires, they always tended to run into either or both of two problems. First, as we have seen, and shall

"The Mongol peace lasted less than 150 years. The age of plague that was now about to begin would influence the history of Eurasia, and therefore of the world, for centuries."

see again, invaders from the desert always challenged and sometimes crushed them (see Chapter 12).

Second, while they lasted, the empires of the Sahel never reached east of the region of Lake Chad. Here states grew up, strong enough to resist conquest from outside, but not strong enough to expand to imperial dimensions themselves: states like Kanem and Bornu—which were sometimes separate, sometimes united. The accounts of early Muslim visitors reviled the region for its "reed huts . . . not towns" and people clad only in loin cloths. But by the twelfth and thirteenth centuries, Kanem and Bornu commanded respect in Arab geography. Lakeshore floodplains for agriculture enriched them, together with the gold they obtained from selling their surplus millet. Around 1300, according to Arab sources, the region enclosed 12 "kingdoms."

The Mongols, after their initial bout of extreme destructiveness, brought peace and, in the wake of that peace, wealth and learning. But with increased travel, it was not only goods and ideas that circulated with increased freedom. The steppeland also became a highway to communicate disease. The Mongol peace lasted less than 150 years. The age of plague that was now about to begin would influence the history of Eurasia, and therefore of the world, for centuries.

PROBLEMS AND PARALLELS

1. How did the Mongols transform Eurasia in the thirteenth century? What techniques did the Mongols use to rule neighboring civilizations, and how successful were they?

2. How did the steppelanders' spiritual and religious life differ from that of their settled neighbors? Why did Genghis Khan believe that his empire should encompass the entire world?

3. How did the Mongol peace enable traders and travelers like Marco Polo and Rabban Bar Sauma to journey along the Silk Roads? How did Europe benefit from Chinese inventions in technology during the thirteenth century?

4. How did the civilizations of China and Persia affect the Mongols? How did Kubilai Khan combine Mongol and Chinese traditions of rulership? Why was the conversion of the Il-khans in Persia to Shiite Islam so important?

5. What were the consequences of the Mamluk victory over the Mongols at Ain Jalut? Why was the Delhi Sultanate able to survive in north India for so long?

6. How did Francis of Assisi and the Franciscan order remedy some of the social problems that medieval Europe faced? How did the Franciscans' interest in nature influence European culture?

7. What was the impact of empirical-based learning on European thinking at this time? Why were European advances in glassmaking and clockmaking so important?

8. How did geography hinder the development of continent-wide empires in Africa and the Americas? Why was it easier for ideas and trade to cross Eurasia than to cross the Americas or Africa?

READ ON ▶ ▶ ▶

D. Morgan, *The Mongols* (1986) is the best history of the Mongols: concise, readable, reliable. R. Grousset, *The Empire of the Steppes* (1970) is a translation of the unsurpassed classic history of steppeland peoples in antiquity and the Middle Ages. Samuel Adshead, *Central Asia in World History* (1993) is also helpful on this period.

P. Jackson, ed., *The Travels of Friar William of Rubruck* (1990) is an outstanding and informative edition of the most vivid of sources. Extracts from sources of the same kind are in I. de Rachewiltz, ed., *Papal Envoys to the Great Khan* (1971) and C. Dawson, ed., *Mission to Asia* (1980). A. Waley, ed., *The Secret History of the Mongols* (2002) collects some Mongol sources in lively translation. There is a scholarly edition by U. Onon (2001).

M. Rossabi, *Voyager from Xanadu: Rabban Sauma and the First Journey from China to the West* (1992), and *Kubilai Khan* (1989) are the best books on their respective subjects. On the voyage of Chang Chun, J. Mirsky, *Chinese Travellers in the Middle Ages* (2000) translates the main texts.

On the Silk Roads, the exhibition catalog edited by S. Whitfield, *The Silk Roads* (2004) is the best work. R. Latham, ed., *The Travels of Marco Polo* (1958) is a convenient and accessible abridgment in translation.

On China, R. Davis, *Wind against the Mountain: The Crisis of Politics and Culture in Thirteenth-century China* (1996) is an outstanding account written with close reference to the sources. The exhibition catalog edited by M. Rossabi, *The Legacy of Genghis Khan* (1996) is the best guide to the art of the Ilkhanate and other Mongol successor-states. M. Ipsiroglu, *Painting and Culture of the Mongols* (1966) is indispensable.

J.A. Boyle, ed., *The History of the World Conqueror* (1997) and *The Successors of Genghis Khan* (1971) translates some of the most important sources on the Ilkhanate.

On the Mamluks, R.Irwin, *The Middle East in the Middle Ages: The Early Mamluk Sultanate* (1986) is the best account of the their rise, and R. Amitai-Preiss, *Mongols and Mamluks* (2005) is a superb study of the wars against the Mongols, S.A. El-Banasi, ed., *Mamluk Art* (2001) covers a wide range of revealing objects.

P. Jackson, *The Delhi Sultanate* (2003) is a splendid introduction to the subject. The best edition of Ibn Battuta is by H.W. Gibb and C.F. Beckingham for the Hakluyt Society, *The Travels of Ibn Battuta* (1956).

On the transmission of Chinese technology westward, J. Needham, *Science and Civilisation in China* (1956) is fundamental–but it is a vast work still in progress. An abridged version in two volumes–*The Shorter Science and Civilisation in China* (1980)–is available. For Western science in the period, A. Crombie, *Robert Grosseteste and the Origins of Experimental Science* (1971) is controversial and stimulating. D.C. Lindberg, *The Beginnings of Western Science* (1992) gives an efficient and comprehensive account.

Of many studies of St Francis none is entirely satisfactory, but J.H.R. Moorman, *St Francis of Assisi* (1976) and A Mockler, *Francis of Assisi* (1976) can be recommended, the first for its scholarship and brevity, the second for its vivacity. K.B.Wolf, *The Poverty of Riches* (2003) is good on St Francis's theology.

On glassmaking see G. Martin and A. MacFarlane, *The Glass Bathyscape* (2003) and, on clockwork, D. Landes, *Revolution in Time: Clocks and the Making of the Modern World* (1983). On the general background of the thirteenth-century West, D. Abulafia, ed., *The New Cambridge Medieval History*, vol. 5, (1999) is as close as one can get to a comprehensive guide.

The Revenge of Nature: Plague, Cold, and the Limits of Disaster in the Fourteenth Century

▲ **City of the dead.** The fourteenth-century Arab traveler Ibn Battuta described Cairo's Southern Cemetery as "a place of peculiar sanctity" that "contains the graves of innumerable scholars and pious believers." The Mamluk domes and minarets visible here form part of the Sultaniyyah tomb complex that was built around 1360, a little over 10 years after the plague known as the Black Death had struck the city.

"The people of Cairo are fond of pleasure and amusement," wrote Ibn Battuta, when he first visited the Egyptian city in 1325. Wanderlust had made this Muslim pilgrim the world's most traveled man. Yet he had never seen, and would never see again, a city so big. Cairo had—so Ibn Battuta was told—12,000 water carriers, 30,000 donkey-rental businesses, and 36,000 river craft transporting food and goods. Among sources of pleasure he noted were "boys and maids with lustrous eyes" and the park and promenade along the Nile River, "containing many beautiful gardens." "Mother of cities, . . . mistress of broad provinces and fruitful lands, boundless in multitude of buildings, peerless in splendor. . . ." There seemed no end to Ibn Battuta's praise. The next time he visited Cairo, 23 years later in 1348, plague raged in the city, and corpses were piled in its streets. "I was told that during the plague the number of deaths there had risen to twenty-one thousand a day. I found that all the sheikhs I had known were dead. May God Most High have mercy upon them!"

CAIRO

Ibn Battuta was witnessing the most devastating natural catastrophe ever to have hit Eurasia: the so-called **Black Death.** This visitation of disease was not an isolated episode, but part of an enormous change, the consequences of which overtook the world. In the fourteenth century, Eurasia entered an age of plague (which would later spread worldwide), while the world entered an age of cold, as the climate got cooler. This combination of environmental disasters killed millions of people, disrupted states, and checked expansion. Themes of the story of global history, familiar from the last few chapters of this book, halted or were reversed as Eurasia's densely populated zone contracted. The growth of populations, trades, and states in Eurasia slowed or stopped. Cultural transmissions across the landmass diminished. Isolation from the main routes of trade and travel suddenly became, in some respects, an advantage.

Among the hardest-hit societies were the most ambitious—those with the longest and most active records in challenging their environments to suit themselves. Peoples that suffered most included those who had succeeded best in exploiting nature by turning land and energy sources to their own uses: those at and around the edges of Eurasia—in east, southwest, and south Asia; in Europe; and North Africa. Their contacts with each other, which had formerly enriched them with the benefits of cultural exchange, now communicated unprecedented deadly disease.

FOCUS questions

How did climate change globally in the fourteenth century?

Which parts of the world suffered most from the plagues of the fourteenth century?

What were the social and political effects of the plague in China, the Islamic world, and Europe?

Why did some parts of the world escape plague?

How did the absence of plague affect Japan, Java, India, Mali, and the cultures around the Pacific Ocean?

It was as if nature had struck back. Indeed, that was, more or less, how many Europeans and Muslims saw it. The weather, they thought, was a whiplash and the plague a scourge that God wielded to humble human arrogance and remind people of the unshakable power of death. One school of Muslim theologians accepted plague as God's punishment for sins, while others argued that plague, when Muslims suffered it, was "a martyrdom and a mercy from God," but "a punishment for an infidel." In China, too, conventional wisdom understood natural disasters as examples of what historian Mark Elvin calls "moral meteorology"—the corrections of heaven, unleashed to restore the balance of nature disturbed by human wickedness.

In history books, human agency tends to crowd out the rest of nature. Nonhuman life gets into the picture only as a source of analogies for human behavior, or as the means of human strategies—part of an Eden or an enemy to be used or abused. It is easy to forget that humans inhabit only a fraction of the biosphere, most of which is still outside our dominion. Currents in the ocean and the atmosphere change climate and shape our world despite us. Nor do we even control the whole of the ecosystem of which we form part. Our own bodies host microorganisms that feed on us whether we like it or not, sometimes benefiting us, sometimes doing us harm. Disease bearers can change their habits and patterns of attack with bewildering speed, leaving us unsure how to respond. Viruses, for example, are a part of the ecosystem that is largely beyond our control.

Climate and microbes belong to two rebellious realms of nature that resist human power. What happens when they combine—when sudden, unpredictable changes in both realms threaten humans simultaneously? To find out, we need only look back 700 years.

The fourteenth century was exceptional in human history because, in parts of the world, climate change and disease coincided to menace or undermine human activities. Procreation could make up the loss of life—eventually. The empires we shall see shaken and the states overthrown in this chapter and the next were restored or replaced. The regions and classes that profited from disaster—for there were some, as there are in every disaster—did not always retain their advantage for long. But the social shake-up that accompanied the changes had, for some of the people affected, irreversible effects. And it was impossible to undo the jarring psychological impact on societies that had accumulated self-confidence over a long period of expansion.

The best—or even, because of the evidence available, the only—way to approach the changes of the fourteenth century is to start in those parts of the northern hemisphere, especially in Eurasia and North Africa, where the effects of cold and plague combined. We can then turn to areas that escaped plagues, or escaped their worst consequences, in India, sub-Saharan Africa, Japan, and southeast Asia. Finally, we shall turn to far-away and out-of-touch societies in and around the Pacific to appreciate how isolation—which usually retards change—acted as a form of quarantine against disease. This should help us see some of the difference plagues made. As plagues affected some of the planet's previously most dynamic regions, other parts of the world leaped into the sight lines of global history, drawing our attention.

Readers should be aware that the distribution of material in the pages that follow reflects the distribution of sources and of scholarship. Most of what we know about the ecological disasters of the era comes from Eurasia, and, within that area, most relates to Europe. For some other areas, only scattered archaeological studies help us trace the course and character of the diseases of the time. Legal records of the kinds that help us establish the social consequences of ecological change in Europe are, at present, unavailable for most other places.

CLIMATE CHANGE

In the fourteenth century, temperatures fell. Broadly speaking, over the preceding four centuries or so, global temperatures had been relatively warm. The warm spell had been a period of expansion for most societies, with much erosion of natural environments as people converted previously underexploited land for farming or grazing (see Chapter 10). Peoples overcome by ecological disasters in the past had been victims of droughts or of their own over-exploitation of the land. Now a cool period—of fluctuating but relatively low temperatures—would last for about 500 years more. During the intense phases of the cool period, a fall in average temperatures of two or three degrees could reverse expansion, forcing people to abandon high ground, remote settlements, and northerly latitudes (such as, in the fourteenth century, parts of Greenland and of what are now Norway and Finland).

Though meteorologists scour tree rings and glaciers for evidence of weather cycles, hot and cold spells seem to alternate unpredictably. If a common cause—some cosmic rhythm—underlies all of them, we do not know what it is. Short-term fluctuations are sometimes traceable to particular causes. The middle of the second decade of the fourteenth century, for instance, was a cold period all over the Northern Hemisphere, probably because of a sudden, localized occurrence: the explosion of Indonesian volcanoes, pumping ash into the atmosphere and clouding the sun. But the fall in temperatures was not confined to a few exceptional years. It was part of a general, long-term trend.

The trend began in the Arctic in the thirteenth century. The ice cap crept southward. Glaciers disrupted shipping. From the fourteenth century, indicators of falling temperatures in the North Atlantic and parts of Eurasia are abundant, and it is fair to suppose that the Northern Hemisphere generally was registering the effects. Mean annual temperatures in China, which had stayed above 32 degrees Fahrenheit from the seventh century to the eleventh, remained below freezing from the thirteenth century—a period of abrupt fluctuations—until late in the eighteenth. Evidence of marginal glacier growth suggests that North America, too, felt the cold in the fourteenth century. Other indicators for the same century include the persistence of pack ice in summer in the seas around Greenland and the disappearance of water-demanding plants from the hinterland of Lake Chad in Central Africa from about 1300 onward. This is important, because glacier growth affects precipitation. When water ices over, less of it evaporates, and less therefore falls as rain. Weakening winds may also have contributed to changes in rainfall patterns and to the lack of moisture in deep interior regions with continental climates.

Worldwide effects—it is worth adding—of the continuing trend are detectable in glacier levels from the sixteenth century onward. A particularly marked period of glacier growth, even in low latitudes and in the Southern Hemisphere, occurred in

"The fourteenth century was exceptional in human history because, in parts of the world, climate change and disease coincided to menace or undermine human activities."

FIGURE 14.1 GLOBAL TEMPERATURE CHANGE, 1000–1900
Source: Hidore, John E. Global Environment Change: Its Nature and Impact, © 1996. Electronically reproduced by permission of Pearson Education, Inc., Upper Saddle River, New Jersey.

the seventeenth century. The cold therefore remained dominant, with some fluctuations, and intensified in the seventeenth century. Warming resumed gradually in the eighteenth and early nineteenth centuries, and, after a mid–nineteenth-century cold spell, has now been a constant and consistent feature of global climate probably for about the past 150 years (see Figure 14.1).

It is important to stress that the rhythms of climate change are full of fluctuating and conflicting shifts and contrasts of pace. Three levels are detectable. At one level, there is a long-term alternation between ice ages, which periodically smother great parts of the globe, and global warming, when some glacier-covered areas reemerge. We are between ice ages now. Historians, perhaps rather overdramatically, have adopted the **Little Ice Age** as a name for the protracted period of relative cold that began in the fourteenth century, but this term is misleading if it encourages readers to think of huge ice sheets spreading over the globe. All the fluctuations of the period this book covers have happened in a relatively warm era of the history of the planet.

Meanwhile, at another level, periods of a few hundred years of relative cold and warmth alternate within eras of global warming. But even within these periods, sudden changes in the winds and ocean currents can reverse the overall trend, producing spells, lasting from 10 to 50 years or so, of warmer or cooler temperatures.

Finally, there are sudden interruptions of normal conditions—occurring irregularly and, in the present state of our knowledge, unpredictably—when the normal distribution of atmospheric pressure is disturbed for unknown reasons. This produces the notorious **El Niño** effect in the tropics and the Southern Hemisphere (see Chapter 4). In Europe, reversals of normal patterns of atmospheric pressure in the North Atlantic produce longer spells, often of a decade or so, of extremely cold weather. And of course, above the deep and various rhythms of climate, the irregular lurches of the weather continue all the time.

Climate change is usually slow but can become perceptible suddenly. Contemporary descriptions show that people in Europe began to feel the cold, along with other unaccustomed weather, in the early fourteenth century. Of course, people felt the cold, and it affected their lives, because temperatures were lower than previously, not because it was cold in any absolute sense. Even after the intense global warming we have experienced recently, global temperatures have probably only recently returned to where they were when the Little Ice Age began. And European summers were probably, on average, hotter in the fourteenth century than in the twentieth.

The weather of the early fourteenth century, however, seemed hostile to people who had to endure it (see Map 14.1). In 1309–1310, the Thames River, which flows through London, froze and, wrote a chronicler, "bread wrapped in straw or other covering froze and could not be eaten unless it was warmed." Colder weather forced farmers to abandon formerly productive land above 1,300 feet in the southwest of England and 1,000 feet in the north. The cold was, an English poet wrote, "a new kind of affliction, . . . not known for a thousand years . . . . No horror left us e'er so like a ghost." Encroaching glaciers forced farmers into retreat in Norway.

During the prolonged cold of 1315–1316, before the icebergs grew sufficiently to disrupt rainfall, heavy rains were reported all over northern Europe, wrecking the crops, inflicting famine. Grain "could not ripen, nor had bread such power or essential virtue as it usually has," complained an English chronicler. A chronicler in Austria likened the rains to Noah's flood in the Bible. Fifteen or 16 people usually died each month in Bruges and Ypres in what is today Belgium. During 1316, the figure rose to 150 each month in Ypres and 190 in Bruges. From May to October, while these cities ran out of food, they lost over 5 percent and 10 percent of their population respectively. Calamitous flooding and coastal erosion became common around the North Sea, culminating in the "Great Drowning" of 1362, when the sea swallowed vast areas of Holland and 60 parishes in Denmark. On the North Sea coast of England, divers can still visit drowned villages, victims of the rips the floods of the era tore in the coastline.

Far from the sea, cooling in the Northern Hemisphere brought droughts and famines. In Central Asia, the accumulated abundance that fueled Mongol conquests in the previous century seems to have run out. The Mongol world began to contract. According to official chronicles, China experienced exceptionally severe winters for 36 of the fourteenth century's 100 years. In partial consequence, famines struck some part of China in every year of the reign of the Shun Ti emperor (r. 1333–1368).

Though the evidence is too slight for certainty, climate change at about the same time seems to have helped to destroy an impressive regional system of agriculture and urban life deep in the North American interior, between the Gila and San Juan Rivers and in the neighborhood of present-day Phoenix, Arizona. First the Hohokam (hoh–HOH–kahm) people—as archaeologists called them—re-located, from their scattered villages and small dwellings and sought for closer collaboration in relatively few, dense settlements with huge multistorey adobe houses. At Paquimé they huddled in a city with all the traditional amenities of earlier indigenous civilizations (see Chapter 11): ball courts, carved facades for temples and palaces, wells and irrigation works, workshops for copper workers and jewelsmiths. There was even a macaw hatchery to produce the ornamental feathers the elite coveted. It was a splendid effort, but it was clearly a response to stress. Every indicator shows severe population loss throughout the Southwest in the thirteenth and

"The Frozen Thames," 1677. The Thames River with old London Bridge in the middle distance and Southwark Cathedral on the right. People amuse themselves on the ice. Some shoot, and others skate. The river froze solid ten times in the seventeenth century.

Casa Grande. In the fourteenth century, Casa Grande—as this adobe structure is now called—stood five stories high. Massive outer walls and clusters of small dwellings surrounded it. It was part of the last phase of a long effort to raise monumental architecture and concentrate dense populations in what is now desert in Arizona, Colorado, and New Mexico.

PACIFIC
OCEAN

Lack of rainfall
leads to population
loss throughout the
American Southwest

North American
glaciers increase

Polar ice cap begins
to creep southward in
the thirteenth century

Phoenix ARIZONA
Casa Grande ●Paquimé
Rocky Mountains

MEXICO

NORTH
AMERICA

Mississippi

Hudson
Bay

Greenland

Falling temperatures
force abandonment of
settlements in northerly
latitudes and on high ground

Iceland

Persistence of pack
ice in summer off
coast of Greenland

Thames River
freezes during
the winter of
1309–1310

Caribbean Sea

NORWAY
SWEDEN
FINLAND

RUSSIA

North
Sea
ENGLAND
London● ●Bruges
Ypres

DEN.
GERMANY
POLAND

Cold, heavy rain and
flooding destroy crops
and erode coastlines
in northern Europe

FRANCE
Salzburg
● AUSTRIA
ITALY

Steppe

Black Sea

Anatolia

Andes

SPAIN

ATLANTIC

OCEAN

Mediterranean Sea

Euphra

Andes

Amazon

SOUTH
AMERICA

MOROCCO
North Africa

EGYPT

Sahara

Niger

Nile

1,000 km
1,000 miles
scale varies with perspective

Lake Chad

N

Water-demanding
plants disappear from
the Lake Chad region

AFRICA

Danube

Tropic of Cancer

Equator

Cooling in Northern Hemisphere reduces food abundance, forcing Mongol world to contract

Severe winters and famines strike China throughout the fourteenth century

Between 1310 and 1315 Indonesian volcanoes pump ash into the atmosphere, clouding the sun.

MAP **14.1**

Climate Change in the Fourteenth Century

- ⌂ ice pack
- ▭ polar ice pack
- ▲ major volcanic eruptions
- ➤ prevailing current, South Pacific (Humboldt Current)
- ➤ El Niño current
- *ARIZONA* modern state or country
- ● city mentioned on pages 447–450

Making Connections | CLIMATE CHANGE IN EURASIA, AFRICA, AND THE AMERICAS

REGION/PERIOD		EVIDENCE AND ENVIRONMENTAL EFFECTS		EFFECTS ON HUMAN SOCIETY
Arctic / 1200s		Polar ice cap in Northern Hemisphere creeps southward		Glaciers disrupt shipping
North Atlantic, Arctic Ocean / 1300s		Falling temperatures, glaciation		Pack ice in summer around Greenland disrupts sea routes
Central Africa / 1300s		Disappearance of water-demanding plants near Lake Chad		Less rainfall reduces crop yields
Europe / 1300s		Thames River freezes; glaciers encroach in Norway; flooding and coastal erosion around North Sea		Formerly productive agricultural land abandoned in England; famine and mortality increase throughout northern Europe; flooding drowns many coastal villages in Holland, Denmark, England
Central Asia, China / 1300s		More severe winters		Abundance of food that fueled Mongol advances runs out; Mongol world contracts; famines strike China
American Southwest / 1300s		Less rainfall and water		Relocation of Hohokam villages in Arizona; severe population loss; major population centers abandoned

fourteenth centuries. By around 1400, even the new settlements were abandoned. Ruins remain. Casa Grande, in Pinal County, Arizona, leaves onlookers amazed at the ambition of the builders and clueless about what befell them. Some scholars have speculated that the conditions that crushed the Hohokam may also have driven migrants southward to colonize central Mexico and found the state that later became the kernel of the Aztec world (see Chapter 15). But the only evidence for this is in later, untrustworthy legends.

THE COMING OF THE AGE OF PLAGUE

In Eurasia the cold spell coincided with the beginning of an age of plague. Starting in the 1320s, unprecedented bouts of pestilence spread over much of Eurasia, culminating, in the late 1340s, in the disaster known to Europeans as the Black Death, which, in terms of the proportion of the population it wiped out, was probably the most lethal event ever experienced in human history up to that time. Recurrences—less widespread and less intense—of similar or identical diseases remained common and frequent in Eurasia until the eighteenth century. The age of plague was so unusual and significant that we want to know what the disease was, where it came from, what caused it, and how much damage it did. All these questions are hard to answer.

Most attempts to write the history of disease have foundered on a false assumption: that we can recognize past visitations of identifiable diseases, known to modern medical science, from symptoms historical sources describe. For two reasons, this is an unrealistic expectation.

First, people in the past looked at disease with perceptions different from ours. The symptoms they spotted would not necessarily be those an observer today would note, nor would they use the same sort of language we would to describe them. The signs we look for change as culture changes. From time to time, literary and scientific literature introduces new paradigms of disease and discards or displaces old ones.

Second, diseases themselves change. They change, perhaps, more than any other aspect of history because many of the microorganisms that cause disease are subject to rapid mutations. They evolve fast because they reproduce rapidly. They respond quickly to changing environments. The plagues of the age of plague need not all have been visitations of a single disease. They could have been "cocktails" of different diseases. They may have included some diseases that today's medical handbooks identify. But we must be open to the likelihood—it is stronger than a possibility—that some of the diseases that devastated Eurasia in the age of plague were peculiar to that period. They did not exist previously in the same forms and have ceased to exist since. New pathogens are deadly because they are unfamiliar. When they strike, no one has built up immunity to them.

So what can we say about the pathology of the Black Death? Of diseases now known to medical science, bubonic plague—not, perhaps, of the same variety we know today—most likely played a part in the age of plague. Bubonic plague is a rat-borne disease. Fleas that live on rats transmit it to humans. When they bite, fleas regurgitate the bacillus, ingested from rats' blood, into the bloodstream of human victims, or communicate infection by defecating into their bites. In cases of septicemic plague (a systemic, blood-poisoning disease), one of the first symptoms is generally death. Otherwise, swellings appear—small like Brazil nuts or big and ridged like grapefruit—over the neck and groin or behind the ears. Jitters, vomiting, dizziness, and pain might follow, often accompanied by an inability to tolerate light.

Fourteenth-century sources describe all these symptoms, together with sudden fainting, before victims, as one observer explained, "almost sleeping and with a great stench eased into death." The trouble is that during the first hundred years of the age of plague, of all the sources that describe the symptoms, fewer than one in six lists symptoms of this kind. Moreover, almost everyone at the time was convinced that plague spread by infection or contagion. Rats—the normal agent for the spread of bubonic plague—play no part in the accounts in the sources. The black rat, the culprit species in the transmission of bubonic plague, seems not to have existed at the time in plague-stricken Iceland, and was rare or absent in other afflicted places. Finally, it seems most unlikely that the frequent epidemics reported in China from the 1320s to the 1360s can have been of bubonic plague in the form now familiar to us, which, as we shall see, hit an unimmunized China in the late eighteenth century. The suddenness and virulence of the visitations that afflicted China suggest the arrival of a new and previously unexperienced pathogen. For the Chinese, with their long experience in farming and animal domestication, enjoyed highly developed natural immunities to the familiar diseases that breed in farming environments.

"The age of plague was so unusual and significant that we want to know what the disease was, where it came from, what caused it, and how much damage it did. All these questions are hard to answer."

Plague victims. The illustrator of an early fifteenth-century German chronicle imagined the plague of Egypt—sent by God, according to the Book of Exodus in the Bible, to make Pharaoh "let my people go"—with the same symptoms as the Black Death. In the background, Moses brings the plague down on Egypt by prayer. By implication, prayer and obedience to the will of God could also be remedies for plague.

Many accounts of the Black Death include a bewildering variety of symptoms that are not associated with bubonic plague: complications in the lungs, spitting blood, headaches, rapid breathing, discolored urine. The emphasis of some sources on lung disorders suggests a mixture of bubonic and pneumonic plague, which primarily attacks the lungs. To judge from other surviving descriptions, outbreaks of typhus, smallpox, various kinds of influenza, and hemorrhagic fevers coincided with some visitations of plague. In the Mediterranean, the plague usually struck in summer, while in northern Europe, autumn seems to have been the deadliest season. But, looked at as a whole, the plagues of the period had no seasonal pattern and no obvious connection with any particular weather systems or atmospheric conditions. This again points to the involvement of more than one pathogen.

Anthrax may have been a contributing factor. A form of anthrax certainly existed among cattle in Europe at the time. Whether or not anthrax was a factor, domestic animals were probably an essential part of the background—as carriers of disease, as a reservoir of infection, and even as sufferers. One of the curious features about the way some early plague victims described the disease is that they were sure that their domestic animals suffered from it, just as they did themselves. A chronicler in the city of Florence in Italy listed "dogs, cats, chickens, oxen, donkeys, and sheep" among the sufferers, with the same symptoms as human victims, including swellings in the groin and armpits. At the port of Salona on the Adriatic coast, the Black Death's first victims were "horses, oxen, sheep, and goats." The Egyptian chronicler, al-Maqrizi, who was among the most observant and thoughtful witnesses, believed that the disease started, like so many others, among animals before transferring to human hosts. It had spread from grazing flocks on the steppe in 1341, after which "the wind transmitted their stench around the world." Al-Maqrizi and other Muslim commentators thought wild animals caught it, too. If any of these sources are correct, the Black Death must have been—or included—a disease unknown today.

An unresolved question is, *How, if at all, were changes in climate and disease patterns linked?* The plague pathogens, as we have seen, were remarkably indifferent to weather, striking at different seasons and in climatically different regions of Eurasia, from the cold environment of Scandinavia and rain-drenched Western Europe to the hot, dry lands of the Middle East. The plagues were less penetrative, however, in hot, moist regions and do not seem to have gotten across the Sahara to tropical Africa, even though many potential disease carriers crossed that desert to trade. It is worth bearing in mind that the plague pathogens seem to have included new arrivals in the microbial world that remained active for as long as global cooling lasted.

The Course and Impact of Plague

The nature of the plague is hard to define, but the routes by which it traveled are easier to describe (see Map 14.2). The Italian chronicler Matteo Villani said the plague came "from China and upper India," by which he meant Central Asia, for which "India" at the time was a synonym, "then through their surrounding lands and then to coastal places across the ocean." Broadly speaking, Arabic sources specify the same, or a similar, path.

The age of plague indeed seems to have started in China. But that is not the same as saying that subsequent outbreaks elsewhere were the result of communication from China, or even that they were necessarily outbreaks of the same disease or diseases. Repeated occurrences—or, perhaps, a continuous visitation—of massively lethal maladies were recorded in southwest China, and over much of central China, north of the Yangtze River, in the early 1320s. In 1331, mortality rates in parts of northeast China that had endured five reported outbreaks of plague in the previous two decades reputedly reached 90 percent. Two years later, a plague claimed 400,000 lives in the Yangtze and Huai (hway) valleys. In 1353–1354, chroniclers reported that around two-thirds of the population perished from pestilence in eight distinct Chinese districts. Most of those areas experienced repeated bouts of disease of the same sort in the late 1350s or early 1360s.

Doubt persists, however, over whether the diseases rampant in China were the cause of—or even the same as—those found farther west. From the perspective of most commentators at the time in Europe and the Middle East, plague, like the Mongols, seemed to be an invader from the steppeland. Many observers at the time noted that the Mongols transmitted plague. A lawyer in northern Italy wrote one of the most detailed and doom-laden accounts of the arrival of plague in Europe. In 1346, by his account, "countless numbers of Tatars," as he called the Mongols, and Muslims "were struck down by a mysterious illness that brought sudden death." At the time, a Mongol army was laying siege to the Genoese trading colony of Kaffa on the nothern shore of Black Sea, where Italian merchants made contact with two great trade routes: those of the Silk Roads and the Volga valley. "But behold!" he continued, "the whole army was affected by a disease. . . which killed thousands every day. . . . But they ordered corpses to be placed in catapults and lobbed into the city in the hope that the intolerable stench would kill everyone inside."

The besiegers' stratagem worked. The disease proved highly contagious. "As it happened," the account went on, "among those who escaped from Kaffa by boat, there were a few sailors who had been infected with the poisonous disease. Some boats were bound for Genoa, others went to Venice and to other Christian areas. When the sailors reached these places and mixed with the people there, it was as if they had brought evil spirits with them."

Of course, there were multiple points of entry, as the same author acknowledged:

> Almost everyone who had been in the East, or in the regions to the south and north, fell victim to sudden death after contracting this pestilential disease. . . . The scale of the mortality and the form which it took persuaded those who lived, weeping and lamenting, . . . the Chinese, Indians, Medes, Kurds, Armenians, Cilicians, Georgians, Mesopotamians, Nubians, Ethiopians, Turks, Egyptians, Arabs, Saracens and Greeks (for almost all the East had been affected)—that the last judgement has come.

A pandemic on this scale was unprecedented. The pathogens responsible had found an eco-niche as wide as Eurasia.

Chroniclers' estimates of mortality are notoriously unreliable. Historians have been reluctant to believe claims that the plague wiped out half or more—sometimes much more—of the population where it struck, but verifiable evidence bears out some of the most shocking assessments of the damage. In Barcelona on the Mediterranean coast of Spain, 60 percent of jobs in the church fell vacant. Records of the archdiocese of York in northern England suggest the first visitation of the

"From the perspective of most commentators at the time in Europe and the Middle East, plague, like the Mongols, seemed to be an invader from the steppeland."

MAP 14.2

The Black Death, 1320–1355

▢ area of outbreak of plague

☺ recorded outbreak of plague

UZBEKISTAN modern country

Trade Routes

—— land route

—— Silk Roads

plague killed 40 percent of clergy there. Clergy were, perhaps, members of a high-risk profession, exceptionally exposed to infection by the need to minister to the sick. But the laity suffered just as much. In some manors in England, up to 70 percent of tenants died. Some villages in southern France lost 80 percent of their population. Towns ran out of cemetery space. The living had to pile the dead in pits with quicklime to speed decomposition and minimize rot. Half the villages of Sicily were abandoned, as were a third of those around Rome.

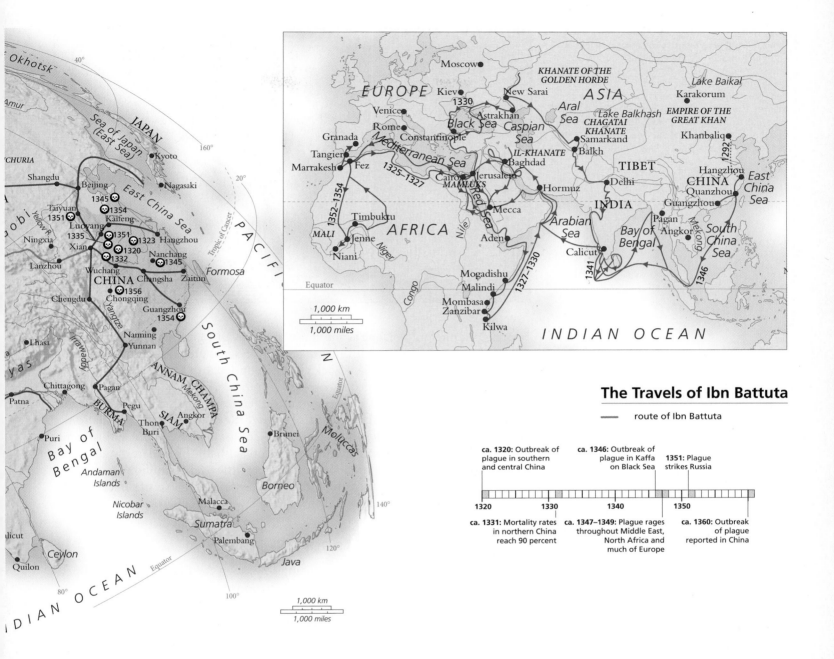

The Travels of Ibn Battuta

—— route of Ibn Battuta

ca. 1320: Outbreak of plague in southern and central China

ca. 1346: Outbreak of plague in Kaffa on Black Sea

1351: Plague strikes Russia

1320   1330   1340   1350

ca. 1331: Mortality rates in northern China reach 90 percent

ca. 1347–1349: Plague rages throughout Middle East, North Africa and much of Europe

ca. 1360: Outbreak of plague reported in China

When the plague reached the Middle East, the tireless traveler, Ibn Battuta, was there to observe it, on his way back to Cairo. Arriving in Syria in May 1348, he found that deaths in the city of Damascus reached 2,400 a day. In one town, three-quarters of the public officials had died. A sheikh delayed a banquet for Ibn Battuta until a day arrived when "I did not pray over a corpse." The plague spread along the coast of North Africa, causing—so people claimed—1,000 deaths a day at its height in Tunis, and reaching Morocco, where Ibn Battuta's own mother was among the victims.

In Central Asia, where plagues bred or where microorganisms traveled between the densely populated ends of Eurasia, we can also find indications of mortality. Arab sources reported that many steppeland dynasties and Mongol warriors succumbed to plague. Nestorian headstones at Chwolson in what is now

Flagellants. In 1349, the Black Death inspired thousands of penitents to organize processions and cults of self-flagellation across Europe in an attempt to deflect God's wrath. Like many others, the Flemish chronicler whose work is depicted here denounced the flagellants for claiming that their penance was a kind of baptism, that it could wipe out sin, and that it was a sacrifice akin to Christ's death on the cross. The king of France banned flagellation, and the pope outlawed it.

Turkmenistan refer to plague as the cause of deaths in 1338 and 1339. In 1345 and 1346, according to Russian chronicles, pestilence devastated cities in the Mongol-ruled parts of southern Russia. Uzbek villages emptied. In 1346–1347, an official in Crimea reputedly counted 85,000 corpses.

In China, too little work has been done on the demographic impact of plagues to make firm assertions. In general, there seems little doubt that the population of the empire fell in the relevant period. The census of 1393, with adjustments demographers made to compensate for the official habit of underestimating the numbers, suggests a total population of perhaps a little over 80 million—compared with about 120 million in the mid–fourteenth century. The loss of people was by no means uniform. Some regions even seem to have made slight gains.

Moral and Social Effects

Natural disasters always inspire moralizing. Although the Black Death killed people indiscriminately—the vicious and the virtuous alike—it was tempting, especially for Christians, to see it as a moral agent, even a divine instrument to call the world to repentance and make people good. The plague was a leveler, attacking all sorts and conditions. For many who experienced it, the plague was a test of faith, first eliciting selfish reactions of terror and flight, profiteering and despair, then, as Matteo Villani observed, "people . . . began to help one another, so that many were cured, and people felt safe in helping others." Dice makers, claimed an abbot in northern France, turned to making rosary beads. In China, as we shall see, plague, combined with other natural disasters, helped to stir up religious movements that over spilled into political revolution (see Chapter 15). In the Islamic world, fear of plague stimulated a revival of features of popular religion the clergy normally condemned: summoning spirits, magical spells, and charms.

"Although the Black Death killed people indiscriminately—the vicious and the virtuous alike—it was tempting, especially for Christians, to see it as a moral agent, even a divine instrument to call the world to repentance and make people good."

Medicine and Morals

As well as to prayer, penance, and superstition, plague was a stimulus to science as people searched for a cure. It was normal to speak of sin as if it were the cause of the plague. But most people did not take such talk literally. Moralistic explanations of

Treating the plague. In the mid–fifteenth century, a patron who was probably a plague survivor endowed a chapel in the high Alps at Lanslevillard. The chapel was dedicated to St. Sebastian, adopted by plague victims, perhaps because his arrow wounds resembled the pockmarks and pustules of so many diseases. The scene reproduced here shows the underarm buboes that are also a symptom of bubonic plague, the indiscriminate nature of the disease, its supposed origin as a punishment from God, and physicians' efforts to cure it by lancing pustules.

disease were hardly more convincing in the fourteenth century then they are today, and scientific inquiry soon replaced lamentations. The University of Paris medical faculty blamed "a year of many fogs and damps. . . . We must not overlook the fact that pestilence proceeds from divine will, . . . but this does not mean forsaking doctors." Astrologers produced fatalistic explanations. "Corrupt air" was widely blamed, perhaps caused by polluted wells, perhaps by earthquakes. In the Islamic world, too, religious interpretations of the origin of plague never inhibited scientific inquiry into its causes and possible cures. Muslim physicians also blamed corrupt air, caused in its turn by irregular weather, decaying matter, and astrological influences.

As for how to treat plague, practices were wildly different. In Cairo, healers smeared the swellings on the bodies of the afflicted with Armenian clay. In Muslim Spain, the physician Ibn Khatib advised abstention from grains, cheese, mushrooms, and garlic. Barley water and syrup of basil were widely prescribed as remedies or ways to prevent becoming ill. Gentile of Foligno in central Italy, who died of the plague in 1348, recommended dried snake's flesh, at least a year old. This was not as silly as it sounds. Snakes, whose venom can be beneficial in measured quantities, had a long and honorable therapeutic record with the medical profession. Another Italian, Gabriele de' Mussis, favored bloodlettings and plasters made of mallow leaves. Turks sliced off the heads of the boils on the bodies of the sick and supposedly extracted "green glands."

The overwhelming medical consensus among both Christians and Muslims saw infection and contagion as the main threats to the population. Where the authorities responded accordingly in time by imposing quarantine, lives were spared. Quarantine worked in places as busy as the great city of Milan in northern Italy.

Where it could not be averted, plague shattered morale. A poet in Cairo, al-Sallah al-Safadi, described the psychological effect of the disease. Those it spared were maddened. It "spread fear and misery in the hearts of women" and convinced even the mighty of their mortality. It entered houses "like bands of thieves," dispelling people's sense of security. "God has not just subdued Egypt,"

Burying the dead. "How come you feel no sadness when you bury a fellow-creature . . . that you remain unready for your own graves . . . that you pay no heed when warnings of death reach your ears?" The twelfth-century Muslim writer al Hariri asked this question in his *Maqamat*, a collection of moralistic stories. Al Hariri had no doubt that sickness, besides being a physical affliction, also served a moral purpose. God sent it to test human virtue and compassion. When the Black Death struck in the 1300s, many Muslims and Christians also saw the plague this way and tried to minister to the sick and dying. Yet the number of deaths could overwhelm the living, and many of the dead were dumped in mass graves.

al-Safadi concluded, "he has made her crawl on her knees." The Florentine poet, Petrarch, felt the guilt of survival among the corpses. He saw "just one comfort: that we shall follow those who went before." He raged at his fellow survivors: "Go, mortals, sweat, pant, toil, range the lands and seas to pile up riches you cannot keep. . . . The life we lead is a sleep; whatever we do are dreams. Only death breaks the sleep and wakes us from dreaming. I wish I could have woken before this."

The Jews

Plague had winners and losers. In Europe, Jews were among the losers. A skeptical German Franciscan reported the common opinion that Jews started the plague by poisoning wells "and many Jews confessed as much under torture: that they had bred spiders and toads in pots and pans, and had obtained poison from overseas. . . . Throughout Germany, and in all places, they were burnt. For fear of that punishment many accepted baptism and their lives were spared." The massacres that ensued, especially in Germany, were nearly always the result of outbreaks of mob violence, which the authorities tried to restrain. In July 1348, Pope Clement VI declared the Jews innocent of the charge of well poisoning and excommunicated anyone who harmed them. In January 1349, the city council of Cologne in the Rhineland warned authorities in other cities that anti-Jewish riots could ignite popular revolt. "Accordingly we intend to forbid any harrassment of the Jews in our city because of these flying rumors, but to defend them and keep them safe, as our predecessors did—and we are convinced that you ought to do the same." Not all authorities, however, were equally vigilant, equally effective, or equally committed to the defense of the Jews, and massacres continued.

Why did some people in Europe victimize Jews? Jewish communities had existed all over the Mediterranean since Roman times (see Map 14.3). Like other migrants from the east, such as Greeks, Syrians, and Arabs, Jews were an urban and often a commercial people. The itinerary of the twelfth-century Jewish merchant, Benjamin of Tudela, whose description of Constantinople we quoted in Chapter 12, describes their close-knit world, in which a structure of family firms and the fellow feeling of co-religionists gave Jews a commercial advantage and helped them to trade between the Christian and Muslim worlds. An isolated reference to Jews in Cologne occurs as early as 321 C.E. when the Rhineland was part of the Roman Empire, but Mediterranean communities were probably the springboard for Jewish colonization of northern European cities between the sixth and eleventh centuries.

Wherever they went, Jews were alternately privileged and persecuted: privileged, because rulers who needed productive settlers were prepared to reward them with legal immunities; persecuted, because host communities resented intruders who were given special advantages. Some scholars trace **anti-Semitism** to the influence of Christianity. Indeed, medieval anti-Semitism did exploit Christian prejudices. Gospel texts could be read—as they were, for example, at the time of the First Crusade (see Chapter 12)—to saddle Jews with collective responsibility for the death of Jesus. And Holy Week, when Christians prepare to commemorate Christ's death, was at best an expensive and at worst a fatal time for Jewish communities, who had to buy security from bloody reprisals.

MAP 14.3

Jews in Medieval Europe and the Middle East, 1100–1400

- ● major centers of Jewish resettlement, 1200–1500
- ☻ massacres of Jews, ca. 1100–1400
- **1290** date of expulsion of Jews
- ➤ travels of Benjamin of Tuleda, ca. 1160–1173
- ▶ presumed route of Benjamin of Tuleda
- ☆ Jewish communities in Muslim world

In the Greek and Roman world, however, anti-Semitism was older than Christianity. Medieval anti-Semitism, moreover, was just one aspect of a wider phenomenon: society's antipathy for groups it could not assimilate—comparable, for instance, to the treatment of lepers, Muslims, and, later, Gypsies. Outbreaks of anti-Jewish hatred are intelligible, in part, as examples of the prejudice outsiders commonly attract. At the time of the Black Death, lepers were also accused of well poisoning. So were random strangers and individuals unpopular in their communities. We can find similar phenomena in almost every culture. The case of the Jews in Europe demands attention not because it is unique, but because it is surprising, given Western society's indebtedness to Jewish traditions, and to the individual genius of many Jews.

The increasing pace and intensity of persecution in the fourteenth century drove Jews to new centers. England had already expelled those Jews who did not convert to Christianity in 1290. The Jews were forced out of most of France in the early fourteenth century, and from many areas of western Germany in the early fifteenth century. (Spain and Portugal followed suit in the 1490s.) The effect was to shift Jewish settlement toward the central and eastern Mediterranean, Poland, and Lithuania (which first admitted Jews in 1321).

Christianity's Supremacy over Judaism. Church and Synagogue are clearly sisters, but the Church is crowned and upright, while the Synagogue is blindfold, with bare, inclined head. These examples are from Bamberg Cathedral in Germany but the pairing of Church and Synagogue appears, with remarkable consistency, all over Europe. Typically, the Synagogue has a broken staff, while the tablets of the law slip from her other hand. If the sculpture of the Church shown here were undamaged, she would almost certainly hold a cross and a chalice.

Distribution of Wealth

Though the evidence relates almost entirely to Europe, there were also people—whole groups of people—who benefited from the effects of plague. In Western Europe, propertied women were certainly among them. The aristocratic marriage market could be fatal to women who married young and faced repeated pregnancies, but it also left many young widows—the last wives of aging, dying husbands. So property law had to provide for widows by ensuring them an adequate share in their dead husbands' estates and reversion of the property the women had brought to their marriages as dowries. More widows burying more husbands could shift the balance of property ownership between the sexes.

Chroniclers, insisting on death as a leveler, often remarked that the plague carried off men and women alike. But, after the terrible devastations of 1348, contemporaries who noticed a difference in mortality rates between the sexes all saw men as the main victims. The plagues of the fourteenth century, taken as a whole, seem to have hit men harder than women, presumably because women led relatively more secluded, and therefore protected, lives than men. Rich widows, often accumulating property from successive marriages, wielded power in their own right. To some extent, the same considerations applied lower down the ranks of society. For instance, during the period of high mortality associated with cold and famine in the second decade of the fourteenth century, more than half the weddings among the peasants of the manor of Taunton in southwest England involved rich widows. After the Black Death, the lords of the manor introduced massive license fees for anyone who wanted to make such marriages, ostensibly to protect widows from predatory Romeos. In unprecedented numbers, widows became the administrators of estates. Women of leisure, education, and power played a bigger part in Western society after this. The increased prominence of women in political, literary, and religious life from the fifteenth century onward might not have been possible without the damage plague did to men.

In Western Europe peasants, if they survived the plague, also benefited from it. In the long run, owners could only keep great properties viable after plague had scythed the labor force by splitting the proceeds with their workers, or by breaking the estates up and letting peasants farm the parcels as tenants. Instead of taking orders from the lord's agent or bailiff, tenants paid rent and could manage their landholdings to their own best advantage. The trend toward "free" peasantries started long before the Black Death struck because in many cases it suited landowners, too. Peasants often made the land more productive. It made economic sense to allow them the initiative to improve their holdings. In England, where the royal courts encouraged peasant freedom to expand their own jurisdiction at aristocrats' expense, about half the peasants in the south of the country were already free when the plague arrived.

Lords wrote off their rights to labor services because, as a steward on an English estate admitted in 1351, "the lord's interest made it necessary." The contract peasant dependants of an English abbey renegotiated is revealing. "At the time of the mortality or pestilence which occurred in 1349, scarcely two peasants remained on the manor." They threatened to leave unless the abbey made a new contract. Most of their former services—including plowing, weeding, carting, and preparing soil for planting—were commuted for rent "as long as it pleases the lord—and would that it might please the lord for ever," added the scribe, "since the aforesaid services were not worth very much." It is remarkable, however, that the growth of leaseholding and the relaxation of lordly controls over peasant farmers happened on a large scale in the late fourteenth and fifteenth centuries in the parts of Western Europe plague affected. In areas the Black Death bypassed—such as Poland, much of Russia, and what is now the Czech Republic and Slovakia—the opposite happened. Peasants became tied to their lords' land and subject to the landholders' jurisdiction.

Were the effects on the European peasantry duplicated in other plague-ridden lands? Certainly, the rural population became more restive and mobile in Egypt and Syria, where, in 1370, one jurist railed against the laws that obliged justices to return peasant refugees to the places from where they had fled. Villages in Egypt often had their tax burdens reduced in acknowledgment of the loss of population. The cost of labor services rose as population fell, creating opportunities for economic mobility among peasants and urban workers, and stimulating a further decline in rural population levels as peasants migrated to towns. But these changes did not disturb landowners' grip on their holdings. Peasants and landowners seem to have suffered together the effects of declining rural productivity.

Peasant Millenarianism

Where peasants benefited, improved conditions took a long time to take effect. Combined with the effects of climate change, the immediate consequences of the plague disturbed, even subverted, the sense of security and stability associated with a traditional way of life. Moreover, most governments responded to the demographic disaster, loss of revenue, and loss of labor by raising taxes and trying to limit labor mobility. In previous centuries, ecological disasters and political oppression had often driven peasants into religious extremism or rebellion. Now, popular revolt took on a new agenda: revolutionary **millenarianism**—the doctrine that in an imminent, divinely contrived relaunch of history, God would empower the poor. This happened independently but in strikingly similar ways, in both Europe and China. A popular preacher who incited peasant rebels in England in 1381, expressed the doctrine of egalitarianism:

> How can the lords say or prove that they are more lords than we—save that they make us dig and till the ground so that they can squander what we produce? . . . They have beautiful residences and manors, while we have the trouble and the work, always in the fields and under the snow. But it is from us and our labor that everything comes with which they maintain their pomp. . . . Good folk, things cannot go well in England, nor ever shall until all things are in common and there is neither villein nor noble, but all of us are of one condition.

Prophecies helped nourish revolt. Some Franciscans (see Chapter 13), with their special vocation to serve the poor, excited expectations that the end of the world could not be far off, and that a new age was at hand when God would release riches from the bowels of the Earth and eliminate inequality. In China, a similar doctrine inspired peasant rebels in the 1350s. A new Buddha would inaugurate a golden age and give his followers power over their oppressors (see Chapter 15).

The Wife of Bath. "Thanks be to God, who is for aye alive, / Of husbands at Church door have I had five." "The Wife of Bath" was a fictional character of about 1400—shown here in a contemporary illustration to the English writer Geoffrey Chaucer's verses about her. But, like all good satire, she was representative of the society of her times: sexually shameless, irrepressibly bossy, and determined to exert "power, during all my life" over any husband "who shall be both my debtor and my slave."
"Facsimile of Ellesnere Chaucher, The Life of Bath" 1400–1410. VdA Museum, London. Picture Desk, Inc./Kobal Collection

According to both movements, a divinely appointed hero would put a bloody end to the struggle of good and evil.

The next chapter describes the politics of the ensuing revolt in China. According to popular traditions dating from soon after the time, the leader of the rebellion, the founder of the Ming dynasty, who claimed to be the prophesied hero, experienced the effects of ecological crisis himself. In one story, he rose to prominence by inventing a medicine that could cure a devastating new plague "which killed half the people and which no known medicine could combat." In another version, the plague and the great Yellow River flood of 1344 reduced him to beggary, and eventually he joined the rebellion that brought him to supreme power.

In addition to contributing to revolution and a change of dynasty in China, and to instability in Europe, the plagues helped transform the Mongol world. The region the Mongols dominated spanned the plague's trans-Eurasian corridors of transmission. Though the evidence comes from European observers, it is a safe assumption that Mongol manpower suffered and that population levels in some regions from which the Mongols levied recruits and collected taxes also fell. The loss of China in 1368 was, of course, the Mongols' most spectacular forfeiture of power. But the effects went further. Mongol control slackened in other dominions, and, on the Chinese front, it never recovered.

In general, plague-stricken societies showed more of what we now call social mobility. The ranks of aristocracies, which were always subject to rapid turnover as families died out, thinned and refilled faster than ever. This seems to have applied as much to China's scholar elite, whose hold on power lapsed and was not fully reasserted until well into the fifteenth century, as to Western European nobilities, whose composition changed. In Western Europe, the increase in the number of free peasants and tenants created a form of rural capitalism. Families formerly restricted to modest social ambitions could accumulate wealth and bid for higher status, buying education or business opportunities or more land.

THE LIMITS OF DISASTER: BEYOND THE PLAGUE ZONE

How far did the plagues of the fourteenth century reach? In terms of effects, the plague was a regional phenomenon, changing the history of China, Western Europe, the Middle East, and the steppeland empires. But much of Central and Eastern Europe escaped. So did areas that ought to have been vulnerable to a disease spread by contagion or infection, such as southeast Asia, and the parts of Africa that were in touch, by way of the Indian Ocean or the Saharan caravan routes, with affected regions. Its relative isolation protected Japan. Apart from a pestilence in the capital Kyoto in 1342, which chroniclers were inclined to attribute to the vengeful spirit of a former emperor, Japan suffered no visitations of any disease on a scale resembling that of the Black Death. The principalities and city-states of central and northern Russia suffered relatively little and late—not before 1350, which is surprising in view of Russia's openness to the steppeland and close contact with the Mongols. India was relatively little affected—references to pestilence are not much more frequent in fourteenth-century sources than for other periods, and recorded outbreaks were localized.

Beyond the reach of the plagues—or, at least, beyond the zone of their most severe effects—the fourteenth century was an era of opportunity in Eurasia. The Mongols were now troubled giants, from whom states in India, Japan, and

"Beyond the reach of the plagues—or, at least, beyond the zone of their most severe effects—the fourteenth century was an era of opportunity in Eurasia."

southeast Asia were at last safe. We can look at those regions first, before turning to sub-Saharan Africa and the Pacific where, as far as we know, the plagues never penetrated.

India

In India, the sultanate of Delhi profited from the Mongols' decline. Sultan Muhammad Ibn Tughluq (r. 1325–1351) was the driving force of a policy of conquest that almost covered the subcontinent with campaigns (see Map 14.4). Ibn Battuta, who knew the sultan well, called him "of all men the most addicted to the making of gifts and the shedding of blood. His gate is never without some poor man enriched or some living man executed." Emphasis on the sultan's generosity reflects Ibn Battuta's own priorities. He was always on the lookout for rich patrons. But the key facts about Ibn Tughluq's methods are clear. He ran his court and army by balancing lavish gifts with intimidating displays of wrath.

Ibn Tughluq's administration was a machine for recycling wealth. Ibn Battuta describes the regular arrival of revenue collectors from villages, casting gold coins into a golden basin: "These contributions amount in all to a vast sum which the sultan gives to anyone he pleases." Annually, "the daughters of the infidel kings and who have been taken as captives in war during that year" were distributed among the sultan's chief supporters, after performing a sort of audition—singing and dancing, presumably to establish which girls were the most valuable.

MAP 14.4

South and Southeast Asia, ca. 1350

- region where Majapahit claimed tribute
- Delhi sultanate at its greatest extent, ca. 1335
- area subject to sporadic influence by Delhi Sultanate
- — main trade route
- • important trade centers

Traded Goods

- pepper
- cinnamon
- sandalwood
- nutmeg
- cloves
- mace

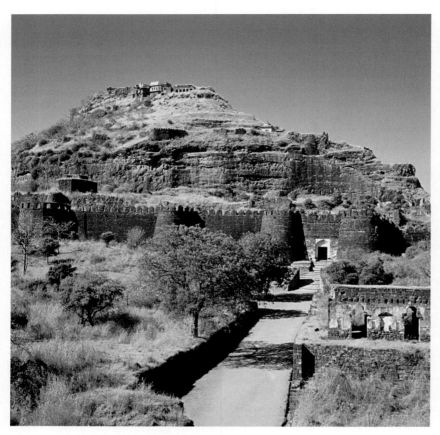

Daulatabad. The Delhi Sultan Ibn Tughluq (r. 1325–1351) transferred his court to the strongest fortress in India, which he called Daulatabad, or "City of Riches," near the frontier of his campaigns against Hindu kingdoms in the south. He planned to relocate the entire population of the city of Delhi to the surrounding slopes. The steep ascent made the place defensible. A narrow gangway was the only approach to the palace complex.

While praising Ibn Tughluq's sense of justice, Ibn Battuta indicts him for the use of terror, abuses of power, and judicial murder. "The Sultan was far too free in shedding blood. . . . Every day there are brought to the audience hall hundreds of people, chained, beaten and fettered, and those who are for execution are executed, those for torture tortured, and those for beating beaten." He put one of his brothers to death on a charge of rebellion, which Ibn Battuta clearly felt was trumped up—the first of many judicial murders. On one occasion, the sultan executed 350 alleged deserters at once. A sheikh who accused him of tyranny was fed with excrement and beheaded. Twice, Ibn Tughluq dealt with suspected conspiracies in Delhi by expelling the classes of Muslim notables whom he suspected of disaffection.

Ibn Tughluq's was a personal empire. His own dynamism and reputation, and a policy of religious toleration held it together—the only policy workable for a Muslim elite in a largely Hindu country. But Ibn Tughluq's state was not built to last. It relied on conquest to fuel the system. The Turkic elite, who provided the muscle for revenue collection at home and for war on the frontiers, demanded constant rewards. When they did not get them, they seceded from the state. This began to happen on a large scale toward the end of Ibn Tughluq's life. Conquest is, in any case, a gambler's game. Military fortunes change, and military systems, even of the most crushing superiority, can fail unpredictably. Disaster struck Ibn Tughluq, for instance, when a plague devastated his army. "The provinces withdrew their allegiance," Ibn Battuta reported, "and the outer regions broke away."

Moreover, the Delhi sultans were under constant pressure from the Muslim establishment to impose Islam by force, launch holy war, and ease the tax burden on Muslims at the expense of "infidels." The discontent evident among sheikhs and some Muslim notables during Ibn Tughluq's reign owed something, no doubt, to fear of the sultan's arbitrary measures. But frustration with his policies of toleration also inspired much of it. Ibn Tughluq's successor succumbed to these pressures. He forfeited Hindu allegiance. Beyond the frontier, Hindu states adopted a counter ideology of resistance to Islam—at least at the level of rhetoric, since religion rarely took priority over politics. In southern India, a Hindu state with imperial ambitions arose at Vijayanagar. The conquest juggernaut of the sultanate of Delhi stopped rolling, and provincial elites in outlying regions in Gujarat and Bengal dropped out of the empire. Again, as so often happened in Indian history, both the difficulties of and the capacity for an India-wide empire had been demonstrated. But again, the problems of maintaining such a large and diverse state were obvious. Future attempts would run into the same kinds of difficulties as those that caused the sultanate's control of the outer edges of the state to unravel and its expansion to come to a halt.

Southeast Asia

Rather as Delhi did in India, a native kingdom in Java, (the main island of what is today Indonesia), exploited the opportunity that emerged as the Mongol threat waned. The offshore world of Southeast Asia produced goods the Chinese market wanted. Some states in the region were in a position to threaten or control the passage of those goods by sea: pepper and cinnamon from southern India and Sri Lanka; sandalwood from Timor; timber and aromatic spices—nutmeg, cloves, and mace—from Borneo and the Moluccas. Control of the strait between Malaya, Java, and Sumatra was strategically vital for China-bound trade, and the shipping of Java made an important contribution to the commerce of the region. That is why Kubilai Khan focused on Java when he tried to extend his empire into Southeast Asia (see Chapter 15).

The establishment of a powerful state on Java, centered on the secure, inland city of Majapahit (Mah-jah-PAH-heet), was the achievement of Kertanagara, who died in 1292. Chroniclers credited him with magic powers or saintly virtues, according to their own prejudices. In fact, he seems to have balanced the rituals of Buddhist, Hindu, and indigenous religions to keep a diverse array of followers together. Kertanagara repulsed Kubilai Khan's Mongol invasion.

The king who launched Majapahit on its own imperial career in the mid–fourteenth century was Hayan Wuruk (died 1389). He had dazzling ambitions. We know this because his childhood playmate, who became one of his chief ministers, wrote a poem in his praise. The verses reveal what the king wanted people to think of him. The poem lovingly describes the royal palace at Majapahit, which had gates of iron and a "diamond-plastered" watchtower. Majapahit was like the sun and moon, while the villages of the rest of the kingdom are "of the aspect of stars." When Hayan Wuruk traveled the country, his court filled numberless carts. Through the streets of his capital, he paraded, clad in gold, borne on a throne carved with supporting lions, to the music of lutes and drums, conches and trumpets, and singers. Ambassadors from foreign courts brought him praises in Sanskrit verse.

Hayan Wuruk was both "Buddha in the body" and "Shiva incarnate"—worshipful to Buddhist and Hindu subjects alike. He was also a master of native rituals, skilled in the theater, dance, and song. "The king's song put them under a spell," the poet assures us, "like the cries of a peacock." Hayan Wuruk's realm, according to the poet, was more famous than any country in the world except India. In reality, the kingdom occupied little more than half the island of Java. The king, however, aimed to make it bigger. The poet listed tributaries in many islands in what is today Indonesia, and "protectorates" in northern Malaya, Thailand, and Indochina. Even China and India, he claimed, defer to Hayan Wuruk. "Already the other continents," he boasts, "are getting ready to show obedience to the illustrious prince" and a state "renowned for its purifying power in the world."

That was all the exaggeration of propaganda. But a disinterested chronicler, from Samudra-Pasai, a pepper-exporting port beyond the Strait of Malacca to the west, left a description of Majapahit that confirms much of the picture:

> The empire grew prosperous. People in vast numbers thronged the city. At this time every kind of food was in great abundance. There was a ceaseless coming and going of people from the territories overseas which had submitted to the king. . . . The land of Majapahit was supporting a large population. Everywhere one went there were gongs and drums being beaten, people dancing to the strains of all kinds of loud music, entertainments of all kinds like the living theater. . . . These were the commonest sights and went on day and night in the land of Majapahit.

"When Hayan Wuruk traveled the country, his court filled numberless carts. Through the streets of his capital, he paraded, clad in gold, borne on a throne carved with supporting lions, to the music of lutes and drums, conches and trumpets, and singers."

A CLOSER LOOK

A Javanese Queen

This fourteenth-century sculpture, carved before Islam had begun to dominate the culture of Java, depicts a Javanese queen as an incarnation of the Hindu goddess Parvati. Parvati is the wife of the supreme god Shiva, who is associated with destruction and transformation, and like him she has both benign and violent attributes.

The blooming lotus is one of the benign attributes of Parvati.

One of Parvati's sons, the elephant-headed god Ganesha, is depicted executing a dance step influenced by yoga.

Kartikkeya, another of Parvati's sons, is a god of war.

Parvati is often shown riding a lion, but here she rests on Nandi, the divine bull, whom Shiva rode.

Posthumous Portrait of a Queen as Parvati. Eastern Javanese period, 14th century. Indonesia. Andesite, H. 6 ft. 8 in. (203.2 cm); W. 3 ft. 3 in. (99.1 cm). The Metropolitan Museum of Art, New York, NY, U.S.A. Image copyright ∞© The Metropolitan Museum of Art / Art Resource, NY.

How does this sculpture reflect ideals of kingship in Java at this time?

Surviving temple reliefs show what the Java of Hayan Wuruk was like. Wooden houses, perched on pillars over stone terraces, formed neat villages. Peasants grew paddy rice, or coaxed water buffalo over dry fields to break up the soil. Women did the harvesting and cooking. Orchestras, beating gongs with sticks, accompanied masked dancers. Royal charters fill out the picture of economic activities. Industrial processes included salt making by evaporation, sugar refining, processing cured water-buffalo meat, oil pressing from seeds, making rice noodles, ironmaking, rattan weaving, and dyeing cloth. More sophisticated ceramics and textiles were imported from China. The same charters reveal the extension of royal power and impact into the hinterland. They establish direct relationships between the royal court and members of local elites. They favor the foundations of new temples and encourage the spread of communications, the building of bridges, the commissioning of ferries, and the erection of "rest houses, pious foundations, and hospitals" mentioned in the king's praise poem.

Majapahit was an expanding realm. As Mongol vigilance in the region relaxed, Majapahit's power increased. In the 1340s, a network of ports in the hands of Majapahit garrisons spread over the islands of Bali and Sumatra. Majapahit indeed seems to have annihilated commercial rivals in Sumatra and to have maintained fortified outposts on the coast of that island. In 1377, Hayan Wuruk launched an apparently successful expedition against Palembang, the major way station on the route from India to China. A struggle was on to profit from Southeast Asia's trade (see Map 14.4).

Japan

Japan, like Java, was a region that the plagues spared and the Mongols failed to conquer. Here, however, security from the Mongol menace had a contrasting effect. As the threat from the Mongols receded, so did pressure to stay united and serve the state. Potential rebels could now raise armies with increasing ease. Fourteenth-century Japan began to experience unprecedented instability. Familiar patterns in politics and social life were shaken like the contents of a kaleidoscope. Since the beginning of the rule of the shoguns, the hereditary chief ministers who controlled the government (see Chapter 11), Japan had enjoyed more than a century of stability. The warrior class had been pacified—maintained by grants of estates and their revenues. Now people at all social levels were accumulating wealth. Social status, which was supposedly protected by complicated standards of eligibility for different ranks, was up for grabs. Warriors began to diversify into new occupations, to sell or break up their estate rights, and, in increasing numbers, to resort to violence as a way of life.

At the top of this volatile society, rival branches of the imperial family contested the throne. The Emperor Godaigo (r. 1318–1339) fought to exclude family competitors and to take back the power the shoguns exercised in the emperor's name. He accused them of "drawing water from a stream and forgetting its source." Godaigo had his portrait painted showing himself with a sword—an accessory normally considered too active for an emperor, but one that signified his intentions to recover real power and keep hold of the symbols of imperial authority, which included a sacred sword.

Godaigo found, however, that he could not simply take up the reins of power himself. Traditional methods could no longer govern the country. Loyalty, though much talked of by writers at the time, became an unpredictable commodity, liable to change hands as circumstances changed. An oath the members of a warband took

"Fourteenth-century Japan began to experience unprecedented instability. Familiar patterns in politics and social life were shaken like the contents of a kaleidoscope."

A Shogun's Armor. This armor is believed to have belonged to Ashikaga Takauji who was shogun from 1338 to 1358. The quality and costliness of the gilt copper breastplate and helmet mountings show that the armor belonged to a person of high status. Stenciled in lacquered doeskin, an image of Fudo Myo-o—the god who personified the samurai virtues of outward ferocity and inner calm—adorns the breastplate.
The Metropolitan Museum of Art, Gift of Bashford Dean, 1914 (14.100.121) Photograph © 1991 The Metropolitan Museum of Art.

in 1336 declared, "Let there be no differences of opinion. Everything shall be discussed at a council. If some disobey this, they shall suffer the punishment of all the middling, small, and great gods of the country of Japan in Heaven, Earth and Hell." "Then was then," proclaimed a saying of the time. "Now is now: rewards are lord!"

Godaigo's army deserted in dissatisfaction over the rewards he could provide. "How," complained one of the officials who worked for his party, "can those who tend to have the outlook of a merchant be of use to the court?" Clearly, the new disorder was, for some, a kind of social revolution: the result of violations of the proper boundaries of class and rank.

In 1335, the most powerful of the warlords, Ashikaga Takauji, seized the position of supreme power as **shogun** in defiance of Godaigo's wishes. The Ashikaga dynasty emerged with the greatest share of authority because they promised the most rewards. They survived as shoguns almost until 1573 by accepting the realities of the changed world, withdrawing into a role as the greatest of a number of regional powers, and attempting only modest interventions in the spheres of other major warlords. The Ashikaga also restored the old relationship between shogun and emperor, in which pieties smothered the real displacement of power into the shogun's hands. "There is heaven," declared Ashikaga Takauji in his testament of 1357, "there is the sovereign, there is the earth, and there is the minister. . . . If the joint path of sovereign and subject is reversed, then there will be neither heaven nor earth, sovereign nor subject."

In 1336, the Ashikaga overwhelmed Godaigo's remaining supporters at the Battle of Minato River (see Map 14.5). Godaigo and his heirs, however, did not give up. Ashikaga victories confined them to a small enclave in the south of the country, but they resisted until the 1380s.

The chaos of the fourteenth century favored the rise of **Zen,** a tradition of Buddhism that valued personal extinction as a part of mystical experience. A twelfth-century Japanese text defined it: "a special transmission outside the scriptures, not founded on words or letters, which allows one to penetrate the nature of things by pointing directly to the mind." Zen made progress partly because of the influx of monks from China who were escaping from the Mongols, and partly because Zen ideas suited the warriors and warlords who now effectively ruled Japan. Discipline, self-denial, and willingness to die are martial virtues. The warriors recognized Zen monks as kindred spirits. Warrior families made Zen practitioners the custodians of their ancestral temples and tombs.

For the women of families of warrior and aristocratic rank, the changes of the period were oppressive. Women could attain responsible positions in the emperor's court. Hino Meishi, for instance, was in charge of the sacred imperial symbols in 1331, when the shogun tried to depose Godaigo. But changing marriage customs were unfavorable to women's personal independence. Until the fourteenth century, marriage in Japan was predominantly a private, essentially sexual relationship. Now it became increasingly formalized, as a union of two families. Wives moved into the homes of their husbands' families, instead of remaining in their own homes. Hino Meishi, for instance, started her experience of married life in 1333 in traditional manner, when her lover started visiting her openly. This publicly acknowledged the relationship as a permanent one. She worried, not because the arrangement was informal, but because her husband's family was of higher rank than her own. In the confused conditions of the civil war then raging, Meishi was forced to move house, but she ended up in her husband's home.

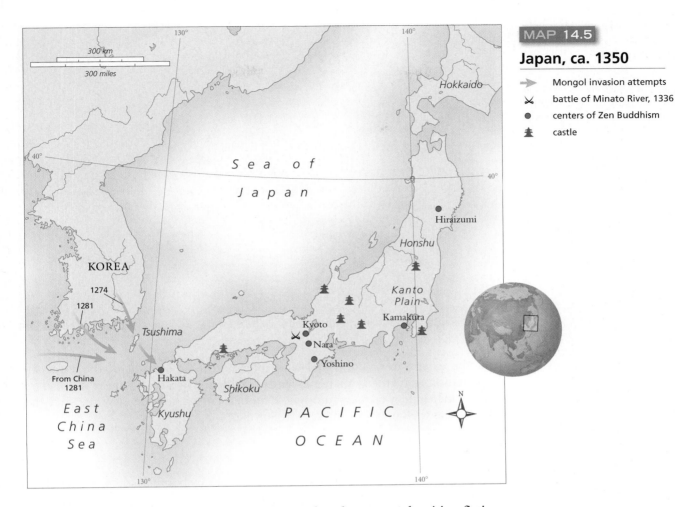

MAP 14.5

Japan, ca. 1350

→ Mongol invasion attempts

⚔ battle of Minato River, 1336

● centers of Zen Buddhism

🏯 castle

A sign of women's changed circumstances is that they stopped writing fiction and the kind of personal diaries familiar from earlier periods. Hino Meishi herself was the author of the last autobiographical memoir by a woman—which is why we know so much about her life. Self-expression was now considered inappropriate for the female sex. Wives came to be thought of as their husbands' property. In the same period, following changes in the practices of the imperial family, it became common for women aristocrats to receive a life interest in a share of family property, rather than inheriting property outright. Property rights were steered toward a single male heir. Among commoners, however, this practice failed to take hold, and women held growing amounts of property and engaged in more business in their own right.

The changes that were transforming the warrior class do not seem to have affected peasant prosperity. On the contrary, the peasants profited. Relaxation of central authority freed villagers from intrusive legislation. They could get on with improving crop yields as they saw fit. The new regime of rewards for military service meant that the landlords were always changing—dispossessed and replaced as the fortunes of war shifted. The rapid turnover of lords, who were usually absentees, also allowed the peasants to get on with their business. There were no epidemics in the fourteenth-century countryside in Japan, and serious crop failures were rare. Nor were population growth

Chronology: The Ashikaga Shogunate	
Fourteenth century	Changing marriage customs diminish women's independence
1318–1339	Emperor Godaigo seeks to regain imperial power
1335	Ashikaga Takauji defies Godaigo and seizes shogunate
1336	Godaigo's supporters defeated at Battle of Minato River

Zen garden. Zuiho-in is one of 24 temples within the temple complex of Daitokuji in Kyoto, one of the Japan's biggest Zen communities. Most temples have a garden of meditation designed to be observed from a single viewpoint to encourage solitude. The hallmarks of these gardens are the expanses of gravel raked to resemble waves, and rocks arranged like islands within it. Greenery is not a normal part of most Zen garden designs, perhaps because living plants are mutable—they change too easily with the passing seasons, whereas rocks are deceptively unchanging. But to ask what a Zen garden "means" is to invite an evasive answer.

and the extension of cultivated land interrupted. As a result of the successful exploitation of formerly marginal lands outside the great estates, the numbers of small independent farmers multiplied, though not on anything like the scale that occurred at the same time in Western Europe.

Mali

Just as Java and Japan seemed to grow in stature by comparison with the afflictions of China and the Mongols, so parts of West Africa projected an image of abundance toward the devastated Mediterranean world. A conspicuous piece of evidence for West African prosperity is the Catalan Atlas, made in the studio of the finest mapmaker in Europe, Cresques Abraham, on the Mediterranean island of Majorca, in the 1370s or 1380s. The map is smothered with gold paint, scattered with bright images in costly pigments, like the contents of a spilled jewel box. In the part of the map devoted to West Africa, a black king appears—bearded, crowned, enthroned, surrounded by depictions of rich cities of many turrets—holding a huge nugget of pure gold. "This is the richest king in all the land," says a caption.

His kingdom, Mali, occupied the Sahel region of grassland and mixed savanna between the Sahara Desert and the tropical forest. The desert sealed it from the effects of plague (see Map 14.6). According to tradition, a hero known as **Sundiata** founded the kingdom in the early thirteenth century. His story has obviously mythical features. He was a cripple, mocked and exiled, who returned home as a conqueror and avenger. The strength of his army, and those of his successors, was horsemen. Terracotta sculptures show us what they were like. Helmed and armed, with round shields and breastplates over slashed leather jackets, they kept their heads haughtily tilted and their horses on short rein, with elaborately braided bridles. Their great age of conquest came in the 1260s and 1270s when, according to the Muslim historian Ibn Khaldun, "their dominions expanded and they overcame the neighboring peoples . . . and all nations of the land of the blacks stood in awe of them."

The Kingdom of Mali, ca. 1350

Kingdom of Mali, ca. 1350

travels of Ibn Battuta, 1352–1354

gold mine

salt mine

alluvial gold

trade route

city

The "mansas," as the kings of Mali were titled, made pilgrimages to the Muslim holy city of Mecca via Cairo at intervals from the late thirteenth century, spreading the fame of their land. Although all Muslims are supposed to make the *hajj*, as the pigrimage to Mecca is called, at least once in their life if possible, the mere fact that the mansas could leave their country for the year-long journey shows how stable the state must have been. In about 1324, Mansa Musa stayed in Egypt for about three months on his way to Mecca. He gave 50,000 gold coins to the Mamluk sultan and distributed ingots of raw gold to officials. He endowed so many mosques and shrines that he caused inflation. By various accounts, the value of gold in Egypt fell 10 to 25 percent as a result of his stay. On his homeward journey, he raised loans that, it was said, he repaid at the rate of 700 coins for every 300 of the same value.

The location of West Africa's gold mines was a closely guarded commercial secret, but it was probably in Bure (BOO–ray), around the upper reaches of the

Mansa. "All the peoples of the land of the Blacks stood in awe of them," wrote Ibn Khaldun of the mounted warriors of the Mansas of Mali. Many fired-clay representations of these soldiers survive from the thirteenth to the fifteenth centuries. Nearly all show the same erect posture, proudly uptilted head, and elaborate helmets and bridles.

Niger River and the headwaters of the Gambia and Senegal rivers. The Volta River valley also had some gold. The merchants of Mali handled the gold trade but never controlled its production. When they tried to take over the mines, the miners refused to work. But the gold had to pass through the mansa's lands to get to trading cities, such as Walata and Timbuktu (tihm-buhk-TOO) near the edge of the Sahara. The mansa took nuggets for tribute—hence the image on Cresques Abraham's map.

In 1352, Ibn Battuta—that relentless traveler—set off to find the kingdom of Mali. He journeyed south from his home in Morocco to Taghaza, the salt-mining town on the edge of the Sahara, where "houses and mosques are built with blocks of salt." There he joined one of the merchant camel caravans that regularly crossed the desert, trading salt for gold. Mali was so rich in gold and so short of salt that the price of salt reputedly tripled or quadrupled in the kingdom's markets. Ibn Battuta and his companions crossed the desert by night marches. They ate "desert truffles swarming with lice" in a land "haunted by demons. . . . There is no visible road or track in these parts," Ibn Battuta recorded, "nothing but sand blown hither and thither by the wind." Water sources were sparse—ten days' journey apart.

Ibn Battuta reached the frontier of Mali at Walata. "It was then," he complained, "that I repented of having come to their country because of their lack of manners and their contempt for white men." He found the food disgusting, not appreciating how lucky he was to be served expensive millet at the desert's edge. Outraged to find himself watched when he relieved himself in the Niger, he failed, at first, to realize that the spectator was there to guard him from crocodiles. He found the sexual freedom of the women alarming, but approved of the way children were chained until they learned the Quran. He praised the "abhorrence of injustice" he found among black people.

The mansa's court impressed him, as it impressed other visitors in the same period. This consensus is striking, because North African Muslims rarely praised black achievements. The mansa, according to Ibn Battuta, commanded more devotion from his subjects than any other ruler in the world, though most of the court ceremonial was traditional among black kingdoms in West Africa. The mansa, for instance, spoke only through an intermediary, for to raise his voice was beneath his dignity. Supplicants had to prostrate themselves and sprinkle dust on their heads as they addressed him. When his words were relayed to the people, guards strummed their bowstrings, and everyone else hummed appreciatively. Sneezing in the mansa's presence was punishable by death. Hundreds of servants attended him with gilded rods. Court poets and scholars came to serve the mansa from Muslim Spain and North Africa.

Meanwhile, the gold of West Africa inspired heroic European efforts to get to its source. Western Europe produced only small amounts of silver, and its economies were permanently short of precious metals with which to trade. There was a longstanding adverse trade balance with more productive Silk-Road economies. To keep it going, this trade always needed infusions of cash. So, as Mali's reputation grew, the search for African gold obsessed European adventurers. Cresques Abraham depicted the fate of one of them, the Spaniard Jaume Ferrer, lost to shipwreck off the West African coast in 1346 in an attempt to find a sea route to Mali. The endeavor was hopeless. Mali was landlocked, and the African coasts had little gold until well into the fifteenth century.

Mansa Musa. "Lord of the blacks of Guinea," reads the legend accompanying the portrait of Mansa Musa (r. ca. 1312–1327), the king of Mali in West Africa, on the fourteenth-century Catalan Atlas. "This lord is the richest and most noble lord of all this region owing to the abundance of gold which is gathered in this land." The Mansa's wealth was said to exceed that of all other kings. His European-style crown and ample beard are compliments bestowed by an artist who had not learned, as Europeans were to do in later centuries, to despise black African kingship.

THE PACIFIC: SOCIETIES OF ISOLATION

Beyond the world that escaped the worst of the Black Death lay regions contagion did not threaten. Isolation, which had arresting effects in so many cases already familiar to readers of this book, was a privilege in the fourteenth century. To understand this unaccustomed reversal of what can only be called the normal pattern of global history, we need to look at some relatively isolated societies. The vastness of the Pacific—which the technology of the time could not cross—ensured that exceptionally isolated cultures lay scattered around and about that ocean.

Easter Island

No part of the inhabited globe was more isolated than Easter Island, which lay, at the time, more than 2,000 miles away from any other human habitation. The island covers only 64 square miles of the Pacific Ocean, way off the usual routes of navigation and the usual course of the winds. It is hard to believe that the Polynesian navigators who first colonized the island, possibly over 1,500 years ago, would have stayed if they had been able to continue their journey or turn around and go home. Most of the soil is poor. Nowadays, there are no nearby fisheries, though native traditions recall a time when the island's elite feasted on porpoise and dolphin. The first settlers brought chickens and the starchy plant called taro. But not much that was edible was available to them when they arrived. Migrant birds were their renewable source of food. The oldest art on the island shows a birdman. Feasts of fowl and egg-stealing competitions greeted the annual arrival of flocks of sooty terns.

Moais. Monumental statue making on Easter Island was probably at its most intense in the fourteenth century. For a small population on a poorly provided and remote island, the investment of energy the practice required seems astounding. The images are similar to those of ancestor cults elsewhere in Polynesia, but they are exceptional in being carved from stone, rather than wood, huge, and numerous. Isolation apparently made Easter Island culture distinctive, but still recognizably like that of other Polynesian colonies.

MAP 14.7

Easter Island (Rapa Nui)

⬚	main area of statues
◇	restored statue site
●	ceremonial center
●	settlement
◉	quarry for red topknots
◉	quarry for statues

Despite the natural poverty of the island and its isolation from other societies, in the fourteenth century it housed a people at the height of their ambition. Probably late in the first millennium, they had begun to erect monumental statues for reasons we can no longer determine. The statues, called *Moais*, resemble those other Polynesian peoples erected: tall, elongated, stylized faces hewn of stone. They were originally adorned with red topknots—sitting hatlike on their heads—and white coral eyes, looking out with a fixed stare. The Easter Island statues are unique compared with other Polynesian works of the same sort only because they are so big and there are so many of them—878 in all, including those abandoned, incomplete, in the quarries. Some 600 finished examples survive, most of them more than 20 feet tall (see Map 14.7).

It took real communal effort to make and erect the statues, each carved from a pillar of rock weighing between 30 and 40 tons. A single extended family—say, about 400 people—joining together to provide the labor and feed the workers, would have taken more than a year to complete the task. As time went on, the statues got bigger—a clear case of competition, driving up the costs of the culture, and, perhaps, condemning it to collapse, a century or two later. So an enterprising community could buck the effects of isolation, and even turn isolation to advantage—but, in an extreme case like that of Easter Island, the effort was evidently hard to sustain. Statue building slowed and, in the sixteenth or seventeenth century, stopped.

New Zealand

New Zealand was another, almost equally remote outpost of the Polynesian world, but with infinitely more resources than Easter Island, and therefore with better prospects of sustainable development. Although the date of the first settlement of New Zealand is disputed (see Chapter 11), fairly secure dates are possible for changes that were under way by the fourteenth century. Population increased. Hunting resources diminished in populated areas as the fur seal and moa began to get scarce, for the moa, a huge, flightless bird, with eggs as big as a hundred hen's eggs, was among the early settlers' main sources of food. Human overexploitation was almost certainly responsible for the moa's extinction. Its meat was processed in immense butcheries. At the biggest butchery, at the mouth of the Waitako River in South Island, up to 90,000 birds were dismembered with blades made of obsidian, a volcanic stone that can be honed to a razor-sharp edge. The same region had over 300 smaller sites, each handling at least 5,000 moa.

As the balance of the way of life shifted from hunting toward farming, mobile colonies settled down. The kind of wear the teeth of people buried in this period shows is different from that of their predecessors: fibrous foods and gritty mollusks ground their dental bites, which show fewer traces of the effects of a meat-rich diet. The results included stronger community identification with land and, therefore, more competition for cultivable resources. Part of the farming surplus was invested in war. From the fifteenth century, the number of places where weapons were made grew enormously. So did the number of fortified villages, especially in the North Island. War was only one of many forms of new or newly intensive activity that favored the power of chiefs. Farming required strong centers of power to organize collective activity and regulate the distribution of food. So did new fishing technologies with gigantic nets that needed many hands to operate them.

Ozette

Meanwhile, on the Pacific rim of the New World, people experimented with contrasting responses to isolation (see Map 14.8). Good evidence has survived for two different communities. One body of evidence comes from a community of hunters in the north of the hemisphere. Exact dates are hard to assign, but probably toward the end of the fifteenth century, a mudslide at Ozette, in Washington State, buried the homes of a community of whalers and seal fishers. The mud perfectly preserved the site. Archaeologists have revealed layers of sediment that show that ways of life had not changed here significantly for centuries before the disaster. The mud of Ozette gives us a unique glimpse into the lives of a hunting culture in what we think of in European terms as the late Middle Ages.

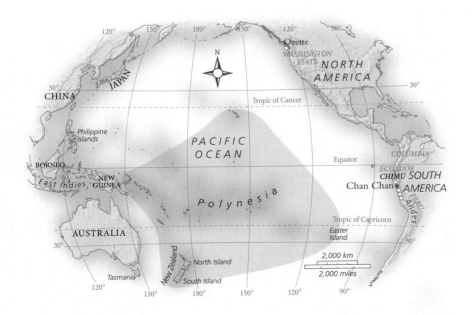

MAP 14.8

Societies of the Pacific, ca.1400

area of Polynesian settlement

PERU modern country or state

The victims of the mudslide lived in big cedarwood buildings, each more than 50 feet long and 30 feet wide. Each building housed about 40 people, divided typically by partitions into half a dozen smaller family units with their own hearths. Hanging mats helped insulate the walls. The Ozette people ate almost no vegetable matter except wild berries. Though they hunted land animals and birds, the sea was their main hunting ground. Fur seals provided nearly 90 percent of their meat. For cooking, they filled watertight cedarwood boxes with hot water and boiled or steamed their food. They hunted and fished in dugouts. Whale images dominated their art, probably because the art had a ritual or magical function in bringing good fortune to the whale hunt. Carvers also made bowls in the shape of men, depicted realistically except for big cavities, where the belly should be, to hold food or offerings. Their way of life was, broadly speaking, similar to that of the Thule Inuit centuries earlier (see Chapter 11).

Chan Chan

On the Pacific's South American edge, we can trace new activity to roughly the same period. Of course, this was not a region as isolated as New Zealand, Easter Island, or even Ozette. As we have seen many times in this book, the coasts of what are now Peru, Ecuador, and Pacific-side Colombia were always in touch with the cultures of the high Andes and, through them, with the lowlands beyond. In South America, in and around the fourteenth century, the latest experiment in state-building, intensive agriculture, and city life was under way at Chan Chan. This city was in the coastal desert region of Peru where the Moche had formerly built complex irrigation works and prosperous cities in defiance of a hostile environment (see Chapter 10). The methods of the Chimú (chee-MOO) people of Chan Chan were different. They concentrated agriculture around the city, where 30,000 people lived. The population of Chan Chan's hinterland was thinly distributed and not much greater than that of the city itself.

Cotton production was a major economic activity. Fishing seems to have mattered little. For protein, the people of Chan Chan—or, perhaps, just the elite—

Huaca del Dragón. The date of the stacked platforms of Huaca del Dragón, near the site of Chan Chan in Peru, is much disputed, but the adobe reliefs—of which a recently restored section is depicted here—are probably of Chimú workmanship. Below a frieze of warriors, a divine feast is shown. A double-headed serpent, with a rainbow-like body surrounded by clouds, devours curl-nosed victims, framing similar scenes shown in profile. Food-storage areas were built into the structure, which seems to have been both temple and warehouse—a repository, perhaps, for food of the gods.

relied on llamas. Pasture was limited, so the llamas were farmed in corrals in and around the city. Fodder supplemented grazing.

The city of Chan Chan covered almost 7 square miles. Spaces in Chan Chan served as the tombs of kings, dwellings for elites, and warehouses to store and distribute food. The layout shows that the Chimú state was oppressive, with a security-obsessed elite. High walls, fortified gateways and dog-leg corridors, designed with sharp turns to delay attackers and favor defenders, protected the rulers' quarters from their own people.

The warehouses were the most important buildings. Access to them was through chambers where costly ceremonies unfolded: sacrifices of llamas and men, deposits of precious objects. The storerooms were vital—the most vital part of the state—because El Niño periodically and unpredictably washed away the irrigation works. Stockpiling enabled the Chimú to recover when disaster struck.

The rulers' tombs were so rich that colonial-era Spaniards spoke of "mining" them. The Chimú elite favored gold for their precious ornaments and ritual objects. But gold did not occur naturally in this part of Peru. Trade or tribute must have brought it to Chimú, which was evidently an expansionist state. Perhaps it had to be to boost its resources in a difficult and depleted environment. Sites of towns built in the style of Chan Chan stretch between the Sana and Supe Rivers.

In Perspective
The Aftershock

Ibn Khaldun left an often-quoted but unforgettable description of the effects of the Black Death on the Muslim world:

> Civilization shrank with the decrease of mankind. Cities and buildings were bared, roads and signposts were abandoned, villages and palaces were deserted. Tribes and dynasties were expunged. It was as if the voice of existence in the world had called out for oblivion, and the world had responded to the call.

But how serious and enduring were the consequences? For Latin Christendom in Western Europe, the picture looked bleak. After the achievements of the previous century, and the benefits of a long period of enhanced contacts with the Islamic world and China, the West seemed poised for a great age of expansion. Now many promising initiatives of the preceding period ended. North Atlantic navigation, which Norse seafarers had developed so heroically in previous centuries, dwindled. The last Icelandic voyage to mainland America was in 1347. The Norse Greenland colonies became increasingly isolated. When a bishop's representative sailed to the more northerly of them in the 1340s, he "found nobody, either Christians or heathens, only some wild cattle and sheep, and they slaughtered the wild cattle for food, as much as the ships would carry, and then sailed home therewith themselves." When the Greenland colony was finally extinguished in the fifteenth century, it was by mysterious raiders of savage ferocity known to the Norse as Skraelingar—presumably, the Thule Inuit with whom the Norse had long shared the island. Exploration of other parts of the Atlantic virtually stopped at the time of the Black Death. In the half century preceding the onset of the plague, explorers from maritime communities in Western Europe had made considerable progress. Mapping of the African Atlantic had begun, with the Canary and Madeira Islands, and navigators had begun to investigate the pattern of the

"After the achievements of the previous century, and the benefits of a long period of enhanced contacts with the Islamic world and China, the West seemed poised for a great age of expansion. Now many promising initiatives of the preceding period ended."

Making Connections | BEYOND THE PLAGUE ZONE

REGION	⇨	TENTATIVE REASON FOR ABSENCE OF PLAGUE	⇨	CONSEQUENCES
Japan	⇨	Protected by relative isolation	⇨	Protected from Mongols; new threats emerge from prosperous provincial warlords; the imperial family divides into rival factions; new dynasty of shoguns emerges; Zen Buddhism becomes influential
Northern Russia	⇨	Unknown—interaction with Mongols should have made Russians vulnerable	⇨	Grand Duchy of Moscow begins to throw off Mongol rule in late 1300s
India	⇨	Unknown—although Silk Roads and sea trade connected it to other parts of Eurasia and Africa	⇨	Sultanate of Delhi profits from Mongols' decline, initiating policy of conquest; Turkic elite responsible for war and revenue collecting eventually secedes; Hindu/Muslim relations are always problematic
Southeast Asia	⇨	Unknown—trade routes from China, Europe, Africa should have made the region vulnerable	⇨	Establishment of powerful state on Java (Majapahit), to control trade with China and India, creating stable and prosperous society
Pacific	⇨	Isolation	⇨	Existing societies expand; shift from hunting to agriculture in New Zealand; Chimú state (Chan Chan) flourishes in Peru
Sub-Saharan West Africa	⇨	Unclear— trans-Saharan trade routes should have carried plague	⇨	Mali becomes rich and powerful from control over gold trade; European need for gold creates obsession with reaching Mali

northeast trade winds. Jaume Ferrer's shipwreck was symbolic. Few similar voyages were recorded in the second half of the fourteenth century.

Human foes supplemented the plague, famine, and cold. In 1354, an earthquake demolished the walls of the Byzantine city of Gallipoli at the entrance to the Dardanelles, which divides Europe from Anatolia. Ottoman Turks were waiting to take over the ruins, inaugurating a history of European anxiety about the defensibility of Christendom's eastern Mediterranean frontier – anxiety that would last, with fluctuations, for over 200 years. In the northeast, pagan Lithuanians eroded the conquests of the Teutonic Knights along the Baltic (see Chapter 13). To some extent, the gradual diffusion of Catholic faith, under Polish influence, into Lithuania made good these losses—for Christendom, if not for the Germans. Meanwhile, in parts of Eastern Europe, state-building continued, under rulers whose longevity helped bring stability. The period of the Black Death was spanned by the reigns of Charles the Great in Bohemia (r. 1346–1378), Casimir the Great in Poland (r. 1333–1370) and Louis the Great of Hungary (r. 1342–1382). On the whole, even in Western Europe, the effects of plague favored the state, because afflicted populations turned to monarchs as potential saviors and were willing to trust them with enhanced powers. Even peasant rebels tended to focus their resentments on the rest of the elite and appealed for aid directly—albeit, usually, unsuccessfully—to monarchs.

In the Mongol dominions, the case was different. Mongol expansion ceased. Russian principalities began to pry themselves free of Mongol control. The Mongol state in Persia fragmented, and the last Il-khan died in 1343. From the ruins of Mongol domination, a new state arose in Anatolia, under a Turkish dynasty, known as the Ottomans, whose center of operations from 1326 was at the formerly Byzantine city of Bursa, in what is now western Turkey, from where they were able to profit from the dislocation the Black Death caused (see Map 14.9). They gradually came to dominate Byzantium, invaded the Balkans, and established a close trading relationship with the Italian city of Genoa. Toward the end of the fourteenth century, they began to construct a navy, to extend their power into the Mediterranean. In China, as we shall see in the next chapter, the strain of the ecological crisis of the mid–fourteenth century contributed to the dissolution of the Mongol state and its replacement by a new regime of native Chinese rulers, under the Ming dynasty.

At a deeper level than that of the rise and fall of states and political elites, the coming of the age of plagues, made worse by unpredictable changes in climate, affected the balance of population—and therefore of power—among Eurasian civilizations. Natural disasters do not usually affect population trends for long. Population can recover with surprising speed. Recovery was harder in the wake of the Black Death because, although plagues became less ferocious, and populations built up immunity, pestilence affected the same regions for centuries to come, at a rate too rapid to enumerate. In Egypt, for instance, visitations of plague struck more than once, on average, every four years in the two centuries following the Black Death. The population of Eurasia probably remained static during the late fourteenth century and for most of the fifteenth. In the long run, of the three culture areas that suffered most, it appears that the Islamic world may have been more affected than Christendom or China, both of which seem to have recovered faster and resisted better. This can only be a tentative conclusion, because the evidence is unreliable. It does seem,

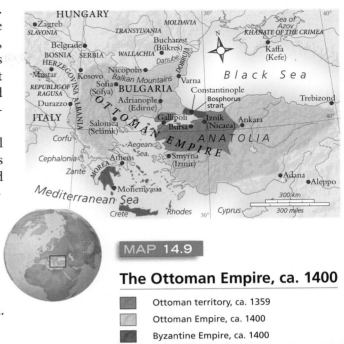

MAP 14.9

The Ottoman Empire, ca. 1400

■ Ottoman territory, ca. 1359
□ Ottoman Empire, ca. 1400
■ Byzantine Empire, ca. 1400

Chronology

1290	England expels Jews
Thirteenth and fourteenth centuries	Climate change in Northern Hemisphere; population rises in New Zealand and agriculture replaces hunting as way of life; rise of Chimú state (Chan Chan) in Peru
1309–1310	Thames River freezes (London)
1315–1316	Heavy rains in northern Europe
1320s	Plague epidemics in southwest and central China
1324	Mansa Musa makes *hajj* to Mecca
1325–1351	Reign of Ibn Tughluq (Delhi Sultanate, India)
1330s	Mortality rates in northeast China reach 90 percent
1335	Ashikaga Tokauji seizes shogunate (Japan)
1343	Last Il-khan dies in Persia
1346	Plague reported in Crimea (Black Sea)
1347	Last Icelandic voyage to America
1347–1349	Plague rages in Western Europe, Middle East, and North Africa
1350s	Peasant rebellions spread in China
1351	Plague strikes southern Russia
1352	Ibn Battuta sets off for Mali
1354	Ottoman Turks cross Dardanelles to occupy Byzantine city of Gallipoli
1360	Plague in China
1389	Death of Hayan Wuruk (Majapahit in Java)
ca.1400	Settlements in American Southwest abandoned

FIGURE 14.2 THE POPULATION OF EUROPE, CHINA, AND THE ISLAMIC WORLD COMPARED

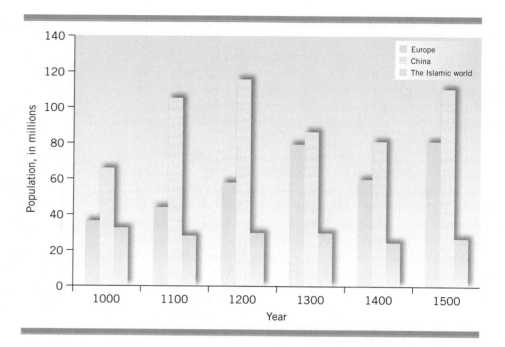

however, that the populations of Christendom and China recovered to preplague levels by the end of the fifteenth century, whereas in Egypt, Syria and, perhaps, other parts of the Islamic world, the recovery did not even begin until then. The increase of population thereafter was generally slower in the Islamic world than in Christendom and China until the twentieth century (see Figure 14.2). If correct, this conclusion may help to explain one of history's great shifts in wealth, power, and every kind of dynamism—away from the Islamic world. Whereas in what we call the Middle Ages, the Islamic world had contributed enormously— far more than Christendom—to cultural exchange in Eurasia, and had tended to win out in conflicts with Christendom, Muslim power dwindled over the succeeding centuries. The relative eclipse of the Islamic world and the relative ascent of Europe are major themes of the age of plague and, therefore, of the next two parts of this book.

PROBLEMS AND PARALLELS

1. How might Mongol rule have spread plague during the fourteenth century? How did rulers like Hayan Wuruk in Java and Ibn Tughluq in India profit from the decline of Mongol power? Why did the fading of the Mongol threat lead to political instability in Japan?

2. How did the climate change and age of plagues that began during the fourteenth century affect Western Europe, China, and the Islamic world? Why did peasants in China and Europe embrace millenarian ideas?

3. In what parts of the globe did plague and climate cause the most harm during the fourteenth century? Why was geographic isolation an advantage during the age of plague? Why was Mali under Mansa Musa so rich and powerful?

4. How was climate change related to plague? How did the onset of the Little Ice Age affect agriculture and settlement in Western Europe? How did climate change affect the people of the American Southwest?

5. Why is it difficult or impossible to understand the medical causes of the Black Death? What did West Europeans and Muslims believe caused the plague, and how did they try to treat it?

6. Who were the "winners" and "losers" in the plague years (other than the immediate survivors and victims)? Why did many Europeans blame the Jews for the Black Death? How did the status of upper-class women change in Western Europe and Japan during the fourteenth century?

READ ON ▶ ▶ ▶

H. Lamb, *Climate, History and the Modern World* (1995) is the classic work on its subject, complemented by B. Fagan's *The Little Ice Age* (2000). Classic works—now superseded on many points—on the global history of disease are H. Zinsser, *Rats, Lice, and History* (1996), and W. H. McNeill, *Plagues and Peoples* (1998). S. Cohn, *The Black Death* (2003) is indispensable for the plagues in Europe and for the epidemiology of the Black Death. N. Cantor, *In the Wake of the Plague* (2001) has some interesting material on social effects. R. Horrox, *The Black Death* (1994) is a valuable anthology of source material. M. W. Dols, *The Black Death in the Middle East* (1977)—though corrected in some respects by Cohn's work—is invaluable on its subject. As so often, the edition by H. Gibb and C. Beckingham of *The Travels of Ibn Battuta* (1994) is an indispensable guide.

On China, the *Cambridge History of China,* vols. 6–8, is fundamental, and the collection of essays edited by P. J. Smith and R. von Glahn, *The Song-Yuan-Ming Transition in Chinese History* (2003) crackles with revisionism. For Europe, M. Jones, ed., *The New Cambridge Medieval History* vi, (2000) is a comprehensive survey. On the problems of the status of women, G. Duby and M. Perrot, eds., *A History of Women* (2000) is the leading work; particularly useful work on the subjects touched in this chapter includes R. Smith, "Coping with Uncertainty: Women's Tenure of Customary Land in England," in J. Kermode, ed., *Enterprise and Individual in Fifteenth-Century England* (1997), and L. Mirrer, ed., *Upon My Husband's Death* (1992).

For Hohokam, the article by P. Crown, "The Hohokam of the American Southwest," *Journal of World History*, vol.iv (1990) is a good introduction. G. J. Gumerman, ed., *Themes in Southwest Prehistory* (1994) contains some important contributions.

On the Jews, N. Cohn, *Europe's Inner Demons* (2001) is a controversial but gripping attempt to trace the origins of anti-Semitism. P. Johnson, *History of the Jews* (1988)—though superseded in its coverage of the early period—remains the best general history. L. Kochan, *The Jew and his History* (1985) is a good introduction.

On peasant millenarianism, N. Cohn, *The Pursuit of the Millennium* (1970) remains unsurpassed. On Japan, J. Mass, ed., *Origins of Japan's Medieval World* (1997) amounts to a fine history of the fourteenth century. The Delhi sultanate is covered in R. Majumdar, *The History and Culture of the Indian People*, vol.4 (1951) and P. Jackson, *The Delhi Sultanate* (1999). On Java, T. Pigeaud, ed., *Java in the Fourteenth Century* (1960) is a marvelous edition of the poem I cite about Hayan Wuruk. D. G. Hall in N. Tarling, ed., *The Cambridge History of Southeast Asia*, vol.I (1992), provides further help. On Mali, N. Levtzion, *Ancient Ghana and Mali* (1986) is highly accessible, and D. T. Niane covers the subject expertly in *UNESCO History of Africa*, vol.iv (1998), but the classic work by E. W. R. Bovill, *The Golden Trade of the Moors* (1995), can still be read with pleasure. For the Pacific, J. van Tilburg, *Easter Island* (1995) is the only fully reliable work on that island. J. Belich, *Making Peoples* (2002) is insuperable on New Zealand. On Ozette, see R. Kirk and R. D. Dougherty, *Hunters of the Whale* (1998). On the Chimú, R. Keatinge, *Peruvian Prehistory* (1988) is standard.

CHAPTER 15

Expanding Worlds: Recovery in the Late Fourteenth and Fifteenth Centuries

▲ **Claudius Ptolemy's Geography,** written in Alexandria, Egypt in the second century, was still the standard source for how educated Europeans saw the world in the fifteenth century. Printed editions, like this one of 1482, usually included attempts to map the world as Ptolemy described it. Common features include a grid of lines of latitude and longitude—the system Ptolemy devised for locating places in relation to one another; the exaggerated size and prominence of Sri Lanka; locating the source of the Nile in mountains beyond large lakes deep in Africa; and showing the Indian Ocean as landlocked, which undermined navigators' confidence that they could reach India and Asia by sea.

· CECIAS APELIOTES ·

· SVBSOLANVS ·

Abd-ar-Razzak was a landlubber. The stories he knew about navigation on the Indian Ocean presented the sea as God's arena, where luck changed with the wind and storms fell like divine arrows. Every story ended with a shipwreck. The thought of a voyage terrified Abd-ar-Razzak. But he had a journey to face that he could only make by sea. In 1417, he was appointed Persian ambassador to Vijayanagar (vee-jeh-yeh-NAH-gar), a powerful state in southern India, and there were too many hostile kingdoms between it and Persia for him to cross by land. But his ship sailed late,

INDIAN OCEAN

> so that the favorable time for departing by sea, that is to say the beginning or
> middle of the monsoon, was allowed to pass, and we came to the end of the
> monsoon, which is the season when tempests and attacks from pirates are to be
> dreaded. . . . As soon as I caught the smell of the vessel, and all the terrors of the
> sea presented themselves before me, I fell into so deep a faint that for three days
> breathing alone indicated that life remained within me. When I came a little to myself, the mer-
> chants, who were my intimate friends, cried with one voice that the time for navigation was
> past, and that everyone who put to sea at this season was alone responsible for his death.

Abd-ar-Razzak's predicament, however, had a positive side. The late monsoon is so fierce that ships speed before it. He made the journey in only 19 days, about two-thirds of the time one might normally expect.

Abd-ar-Razzak's voyage demonstrates the crucial importance of winds in world history. Most of the Earth's surface area is sea. Long-range communications have to traverse wide waters. Throughout the age of sail—that is, for almost the entire history of travel—winds and currents set the limits of what was possible: the routes, the rates, the mutually accessible cultures. More particularly, Abd-ar-Razzak's experience illustrates the paradox of Indian Ocean navigation in his day. The monsoon winds made travel speedy, but the Indian Ocean was stormy, unsafe, and hard to get into and out of. Access from the east was barely possible in summer, when typhoons tore into the shores. Fierce storms guarded the southern approaches. No one who knew the reputation of these waters cared to venture between about 10 and 30 degrees south and 60 or 90 degrees east during the hurricane season. Arab legends claimed the region was impassable. Many European maps of the fifteenth century depicted the Indian Ocean as landlocked—literally inaccessible by sea. Yet it was the biggest and richest zone of long-range commerce in the world.

FOCUS questions

Why were some African empires able to expand on such an impressive scale during this period?

What role did geographic diversity play in the Inca and Aztec Empires?

What strong new empires arose on the Eurasian borderlands?

Why did China turn away from overseas expansion in the fifteenth century?

Why did Europe begin to reach out across the oceans in the late 1400s?

By the end of the fifteenth century, European navigators had found a way to penetrate it. Meanwhile, the Atlantic was developing into a rival zone, with transoceanic routes ready to be exploited. Indeed, seafaring on the Atlantic would transform the world by bringing cultures that had been torn apart into contact, conflict, commerce, and cultural and ecological exchange. The divergent, isolated worlds of ancient and medieval times were coming together to form the interconnected world we inhabit today.

How did it happen? How did the world rebound from the plagues and climate changes of the fourteenth century? For one thing, populations gradually acquired immunity against plague, as susceptible people died and those who were naturally most resistant passed on their genes. As for worsening climates, survivors relocated or just got used to colder, wetter conditions. To some extent, technological advance made up for—indeed, was a response to—decreased population. As we have seen, across Eurasia, and in parts of Africa that were in contact with Eurasia, the long period of accelerated exchange in the Song and Mongol eras had equipped expanding economies with improved technology (see Chapter 13). In regions that escaped the catastrophes of the fourteenth century, long-term population growth continued to strengthen states and economies. So it is not surprising that the world of the late fourteenth and fifteenth centuries was a world in recovery and even a world of resumed expansion.

Toward the end of the period, from about 1460 on, in states in widely separated parts of the world, expansion speeded up like springs uncoiling. An age of expansion really did begin, but the phenomenon was of an expanding world, not, as some historians say, of European expansion. The world did not wait passively for European outreach to transform it, as if touched by a magic wand. Other societies were already working magic of their own, turning states into empires and cultures into civilizations. Beyond the reach of the recurring plagues that stopped demographic growth in much of Eurasia, some of the most dynamic and rapidly expanding societies of the fifteenth century were in the Americas and sub-Saharan Africa. Indeed, in terms of territorial expansion and military effectiveness against opponents, African and American empires outclassed any state in Western Europe until the sixteenth century.

As we shall see, some European communities played big and growing roles. And their expansion did have unique features—exceptional range, above all, which enabled people from Western Europe to cross unprecedented distances on previously unexplored routes. But to appreciate what was special about Europe, we have to see it in global context and acknowledge that expansion was a worldwide phenomenon. If we start in Africa and approach Europe only after looking at the Americas and following Abd-ar-Razzak's route in Asia, we can begin to make sense of the peculiar features of the history of Atlantic-side European peoples, as they launched empires that will take up more and more space in the rest of the book.

FRAGILE EMPIRES IN AFRICA
East Africa

Ethiopia emerged relatively early from its period of quiescence following the rise and stagnation of the Solomid dynasty in the thirteenth century (see Chapter 11). In the late fourteenth century, the highland realm again began to reach beyond its mountains to dominate surrounding regions. Monasteries became schools of missionaries whose task was to consolidate Ethiopian power in the conquered pagan lands of Shoa and Gojam. Rulers, meanwhile, concentrated on reopening their ancient outlet to the Red Sea and thereby the Indian Ocean. This they accomplished by conquering the hostile lowlanders and recapturing the port of Massaweh in 1403. By then, Ethiopian rule stretched into the Great Rift valley. Trade northward along the valley was in slaves, ivory, gold, and ingredients of perfumes. Ethiopia largely controlled it. The resulting wealth funded defense of the empire and fueled expansionist ambitions. European visitors multiplied, as Ethiopia's Massaweh road became a standard route to reach the Indian Ocean.

Although Ethiopia conquered no more territory after 1469, the lives of saints, which are a major source for Ethiopian history in this period, tell of internal expansion. Wasteland was converted to farmland and settled by monks. In 1481, the Ethiopian church resumed contact with Rome, where the pope provided a church to house visiting Ethiopian monks. When Portuguese diplomatic missions began to arrive in Ethiopia—the first in the 1490s, a second in 1520—"men and gold and provisions like the sands of the sea and the stars in the sky" impressed them. As we shall see in the next chapter, however, they overestimated the empire's stability. Ethiopia had probably already overreached its resources.

> *"The world did not wait passively for European outreach to transform it, as if touched by a magic wand. Other societies were already working magic of their own, turning states into empires and cultures into civilizations."*

Virgin and Child. In the dynamic reign of Emperor Zara Yacob (1434–1468), Ethiopia conquered an outlet to the sea, extended and fortified its land frontier, pacified and Christianized pagan peoples, and made contact with Europe. But the enforcement of religious orthodoxy was perhaps closest to the emperor's heart. He commissioned many paintings of the Virgin and Child, often shown guarded, as here, by armed angels and worshipped by warrior saints.

Chronology: The Reemergence of Ethiopia

Late fourteenth century	Ethiopia expands into surrounding regions
1403	Recapture of port of Massaweh
1469	End of period of conquest
1481	Ethiopian church resumes contact with Rome
1490s	First Portuguese diplomatic missions arrive in Ethiopia

Southward from Ethiopia, at the far end of the Rift valley, lay the gold-rich Zambezi valley and the productive plateau beyond, which stretched to the south as far as the Limpopo River, and was rich in salt, gold, and elephants. Like Ethiopia, these areas looked toward the Indian Ocean for long-range trade with the economies of maritime Asia.

Unlike Ethiopia, communities in the Zambezi valley had ready access to the ocean, but they faced a potentially more difficult problem. Their outlets to the sea lay below the reach of the monsoon system and, therefore, beyond the reach of the normal routes of trade. Still, adventurous merchants—most of them, probably, from southern Arabia—risked the voyage to bring manufactured goods from Asia in trade for gold and ivory. Some of the most vivid evidence comes from the mosque in Kilwa (Kil-WAH), in modern Tanzania, where fifteenth-century Chinese porcelain bowls line the inside of the dome.

Further evidence of the effects of trade lie inland between the Zambezi and the Limpopo Rivers, where fortified, stone-built administrative centers—called **zimbabwes**—had been common for centuries. Now, in the late fourteenth and fifteenth centuries, the zimbabwes entered their greatest age. The most famous, Great Zimbabwe, included a formidable citadel on a hill 350 feet high, but remains of other citadels are scattered over the land (see Map 15.1). Near stone buildings, the beef-fed elite were buried with gifts: gold, jewelery, jeweled ironwork, large copper ingots, and Chinese porcelain that Arab traders brought across the Indian Ocean to Kilwa and Sofala, another great coastal city.

In the second quarter of the fifteenth century, the center of power shifted northward to the Zambezi valley, with the expansion of a new regional power. Mwene Mutapa (MWEH-nee MOO-TAH-pah), as it was called, arose during the northward migration of bands of warriors from what are now parts of Mozambique and KwaZulu-Natal. When one of their leaders conquered the middle Zambezi valley—a land rich in cloth, salt, and elephants—he took the title Mwene Mutapa, or "lord of the tribute payers," a name that became extended to the state. From about the mid–fifteenth century, the pattern of trade routes altered as Mwene Mutapa's conquests spread eastward toward the coast. But Mwene Mutapa never reached the ocean. Native merchants, who traded at inland fairs, had no interest in a direct outlet to the sea. They did well enough using middlemen on the coast and had no incentive for or experience of ocean trade. Like Mali (see Chapter 14), Mwene Mutapa was a landlocked empire, sustained by trade in gold and salt. The colonists were drawn, not driven, northward, though a decline in the navigability of the Sabi River may have stimulated the move.

Outer wall 820 feet long, 30 feet high, and 16 feet thick.

25 yards
25 meters

MAP 15.1

Great Zimbabwe

- ■ stone construction
- ⋯ walls in ruin
- — drain

West Africa

New states emerged in West Africa, too, but here the opportunities were the result, at least in part, of the decline of the old regional power, Mali (see Map 15.2). Like many empires of promise in out-of-the-way places, Mali became a victim of its relative isolation. From about 1360, a power struggle pitted the descendants of Mansa Musa against those of his brother, Mansa Sulayman. At

The turreted walls of Great Zimbabwe surround a 350-foot-high hill, crowned by a formidable citadel, which housed the elite, who ate beef and were buried with gifts of gold, copper, jewels, and Chinese porcelain. Though it was the biggest of the stone-built settlements of the period, Great Zimbabwe was typical, in style and substance, of other buildings in the region south of the Zambezi River during what we think of as the late Middle Ages.

about the end of the century, the Songhay, a people from lower down the Niger River, broke away and Mali lost Gao (gow). This was disastrous for Mali, because Gao was one of the great trading cities between the rain forest and the desert. Traders could now outflank Mali's trading monopoly. Mali was further weakened in the 1430s when invaders from the Sahara seized its northernmost towns.

Two decades later, in the 1450s, when Portuguese expeditions, pushing up the river Gambia, made the first recorded European contact with Mali, the Mansa's power was virtually confined to the original heartland. The result was a tragedy for the history of the world, for the absence of a strong African state undermined Europeans' view of black Africans as equals. The Portuguese expected to find a great, rich empire. Instead, they found Mali a ramshackle wreck. Their disappointment prejudiced them, and they wondered if black Africans had any capacity for political greatness. Thus, in maps, instead of the magnificent depictions of the Mansa of Mali typical of the fourteenth century—bearded and costumed in European fashion—the ruler of Mali became a figure of fun. Though some Europeans continued to treat black Africans as equals—and the Portuguese crown, in particular, maintained the affectation that black kings were fellow monarchs on a par with those of Europe—from now on, white people in Africa could nourish convictions of superiority. Although, as we shall see, other African realms or regions replaced Mali in European esteem and became famous for wealth or as places of opportunity for European adventurers, their elites never again commanded the same prestige in Europe.

A European view of the King of Mali, ca. 1480. By the 1430s, familiarity with the West African kingdom of Mali had caused disillusionment among European visitors, who expected magnificence of the sort depicted in the previous century in the Catalan Atlas (see Chapter 14). But Mali had declined, and its ruler appeared in this map by Gabriel Vallseca of Majorca, and others of the time, as a comically dressed and even laughable figure.

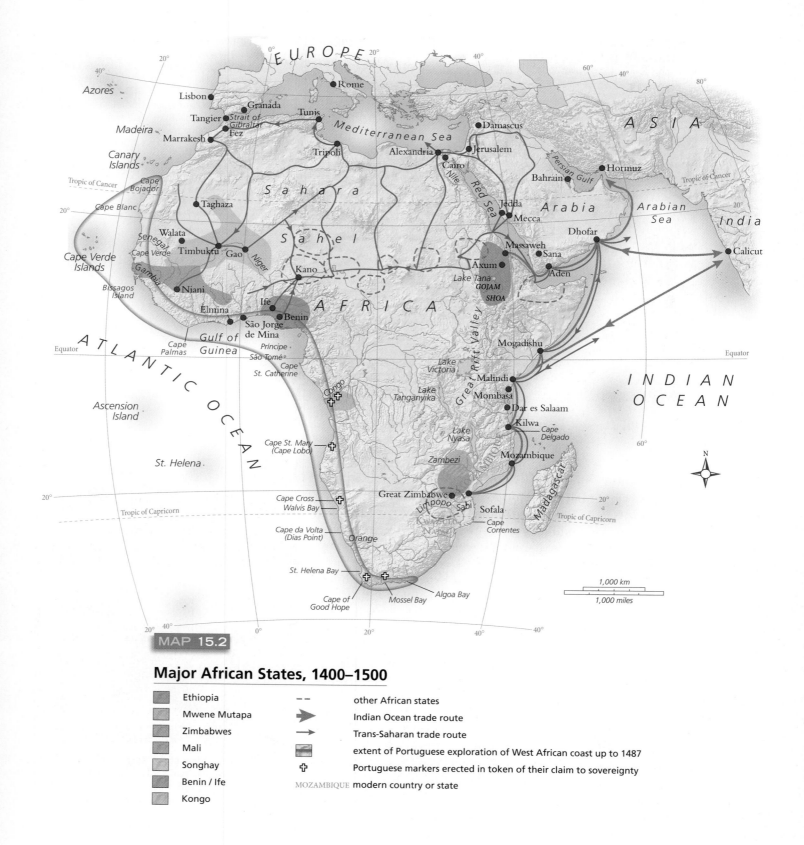

Major African States, 1400–1500

▨ Ethiopia	– –	other African states
▨ Mwene Mutapa	➤	Indian Ocean trade route
▨ Zimbabwes	→	Trans-Saharan trade route
▨ Mali	▨	extent of Portuguese exploration of West African coast up to 1487
▨ Songhay	✚	Portuguese markers erected in token of their claim to sovereignty
▨ Benin / Ife	MOZAMBIQUE	modern country or state
▨ Kongo		

Songhay (SOHNG-eye) gradually succeeded Mali as the most powerful state in the region, but it never controlled as much of the Saharan trade as Mali had. At first, isolated areas were converted to Islam, but Muhammad Touray Askia, an upstart general who used Islam to justify seizing the throne, wrenched Songhay into the Islamic mainstream in the late fifteenth century. In 1497, he undertook a pilgrimage to Mecca on a scale of magnificence calculated to echo that of Mansa Musa in 1324–1325 (see Chapter 14). Askia's ascent to power represented the triumph of Islam over the pagan magic that some of his predecessors and opponents claimed to wield. His victory also ensured that Sahelian Africa—the band of dry grasslands south of the Sahara—would be predominantly Muslim. His alliance with the Muslim intelligentsia made Songhay a state "favored by God" in the eyes of religious Muslims—the class on which the state depended for administrators. He stimulated trade by imposing peace and so increasing Saharan merchants' sense of security. He promoted a modest sort of capitalism by concentrating resources in the hands of religious foundations, which had the personnel and range of contacts to maximize their holdings' potential. New canals, wells, dikes, and reservoirs scored the land. Cultivated terrain was extended, especially for rice, which had long been known in the region but never previously farmed on a large scale.

Songhay, like Mali before it, benefited from the trade routes of the Sahara, which linked the Mediterranean coast to the Niger valley. The Niger River is navigable for almost its entire length, providing access to rich goldfields and the best national communications system in Africa. At the same time, the Atlantic's adverse winds and currents limited opportunities for long-range communications by sea. The states and cultures of the tropical forest and coast in the African "bulge" were therefore limited to contending for strictly regional power and wealth. Nevertheless, they have left plenty of evidence of economic expansion and of the growing wealth and power of their kings in the fifteenth century. There are, for instance, the fortifications of the city-state of Benin and the splendid metal weapons, adornments and courtly furnishings of Benin and the Ife.

The whole African coast from Senegambia to the mouth of the Niger impressed Europeans at the time. In 1486, the Portuguese crown celebrated the baptism of a Senegambian chief in Lisbon with a lavish display. The trading post that Portugal opened at São Jorge da Mina, on the underside of the African bulge, in 1482, appeared on maps as a fantasy city. It suited the purposes of the Portuguese monarchs to exaggerate the grandeur, but their propaganda reflected the reality of a region of rich kingdoms, busy commerce, and patches of urban life.

Farther south, too, in the Congo Basin, the opportunities for states to reach out by sea were limited. The Kingdom of Kongo dominated the Congo River's navigable lower reaches, probably from the mid–fourteenth century. The ambitions of its rulers became evident when Portuguese

Chronology: The Portuguese in West Africa and the Congo	
1450s	First reported Portuguese contact with Mali
1480s	Portuguese make contact with kingdom of Kongo
1482	West African trading post of São Jorge da Mina established
1486	Senegambian chief baptized in Lisbon

The fort of São Jorge da Mina, founded by the Portuguese in 1482 on the underside of West Africa's bulge, never really looked like this depiction on a richly decorated world map sold to an Italian ambassador in Lisbon in 1502. The turrets and spires are fanciful, but convey the image the mapmaker wanted to show: of exotic grandeur and financial success, since the fort attracted much of the region's trade in gold and slaves.

A CLOSER LOOK

A West African view of the Portuguese

The court art of Benin, in the Niger Delta of West Africa, preserves precious images of Portuguese visitors, as native artists saw them in the sixteenth century. The Obas, as the rulers of Benin were called, frequently asked for Portuguese military help, sometimes offering to adopt Christianity in exchange.

The Portuguese soldier, carved in ivory, is supporting the Oba's saltcellar. Salt was a precious commodity in Benin.

The soldier's short spear, feathered straw hat, and sweatband are local touches, but the rest of his clothes, his beard, his sword, and his pectoral cross were exotic emblems to the African artist who carved them.

African, Nigeria, Edo peoples, court of Benin, Salt-cellar: Portuguese Figure, 15th-16th century, Ivory; H. 7–1/8 in. (18.1 cm). The Metropolitan Museum of Art, Louis V. Bell and Rogers Funds, 1972. (1972.63ab) Photograph by Stan Reis. Photograph © 1984, The Metropolitan Museum of Art

How is this ivory carving evidence of West African expansion in the fifteenth century?

explorers established contact in the 1480s. Kongo enthusiastically adopted the religion and technology of the visitors. The kingdom became host to Portuguese missionaries, craftsmen, and mercenaries. The royal residence was rebuilt in Portuguese style. The kings issued documents in Portuguese, and members of the royal family went to Portugal for their education. One prince became an archbishop, and the kings continued to have Portuguese baptismal names for centuries thereafter. In emulating Portugal, the kings of Kongo were, of course, serving their own self-interest. Equipping their armies with European firepower, for example, gave the kings a military advantage over their neighbors. They gained territory and, more importantly, slaves, many of whom they sold to the Portuguese for export.

The Portuguese connection made Kongo the best-documented kingdom in West Africa in the sixteenth century. Missionary reports extolled the zeal of the "angelic" ruler Affonso I (r. 1506–1545) and commended him for "burning idolaters along with their idols," but the monarch's own letters to the king of Portugal reveal tensions with white slavers, who infringed the royal monopoly of European trade goods and seized slaves indiscriminately.

Although Ethiopia, Mwene Mutapa, Songhay, and Kongo were all formidable regional powers, and although many small states of the West African coast expanded commercially and territorially, little of this activity was on an unprecedented scale (see Map 15.2). Ethiopia's resumed rise was part of a sequence of expansion and decline that had been going on for centuries. Songhay was the latest in a series of empires in the Sahel. Trading states had long studded the underside of the West African bulge. Mwene Mutapa was the successor state of the builders of the zimbabwes. If there was something new out of the Africa at this time, it was part of a wider phenomenon. The empires grew at impressive rates and to impressive extents because they were in touch with other phenomena of commercial and political expansion: Songhay across the Sahara, Ethiopia and Mwene Mutapa across the Indian Ocean, the coastal trading cities and Kongo with the Portuguese. In the Americas, however, in the late fifteenth century, even states that had to contend with isolation could expand on a new scale.

"If there was something new out of the Africa at this time, it was part of a wider phenomenon. The empires grew at impressive rates and to impressive extents because they were in touch with other phenomena of commercial and political expansion . . ."

ECOLOGICAL IMPERIALISM IN THE AMERICAS

Since the inventive historian, Alfred Crosby, coined the term **ecological imperialism** in 1972, historians have used it to refer to the sweeping environmental changes European imperialists introduced in regions they colonized. The term also suits Native American empires, especially in mountainous regions of Mesoamerica and the Andes, where, as we have seen, the key to success in large-scale state-building lay in combining diverse regions and exploiting the complementary products of contrasting ecosystems.

The Inca Empire

In the late fifteenth century, the world's fastest-growing empire was the Inca Empire of Peru. Inca chronology is always uncertain because until the 1530s, the Incas made records in forms that are now indecipherable. Nonetheless, evidence suggests that they built their empire within a concentrated period—all during the reigns of three rulers in the late fifteenth and early sixteenth centuries.

FIGURE 15.1 MICROCLIMATES OF THE ANDES. The Andean environment packs tremendous ecological diversity into a small space, with various climatic zones at different altitudes, contrasting microclimates in the valleys, and tropical forest and the ocean close at hand.

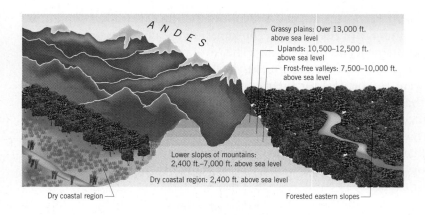

ANDES

Grassy plains: Over 13,000 ft. above sea level

Uplands: 10,500–12,500 ft. above sea level

Frost-free valleys: 7,500–10,000 ft. above sea level

Lower slopes of mountains: 2,400 ft.–7,000 ft. above sea level

Dry coastal region: 2,400 ft. above sea level

Dry coastal region

Forested eastern slopes

"The Inca realm encompassed coastal lowlands and the fringes of the Amazonian rain forest. The tribute system was based on the exchange of products between contrasting zones, as a form of insurance against disaster."

Probably early in the second half of the fifteenth century, the founders of the Inca state descended from the highlands to find fertile land. They occupied Cuzco in what is today Peru, which became their biggest city, and began subjugating their neighbors. Their story was typically Andean. They gathered many diverse environments into one state to facilitate exchanging and stockpiling a wide range of products. It was the story of Chavín de Huántar in 1000 B.C.E. (see Chapter 4). The Incas, however, took this well-established practice to new lengths. Theirs was one of the most environmentally diverse empires of the time. It was long and thin, with the Andes forming its spine and creating valleys and microclimates. Abrupt mountains multiplied microclimates, where sun, wind, and rain hit different slopes in different ways (see Figure 15.1). The Inca realm encompassed coastal lowlands and the fringes of the Amazonian rain forest. The tribute system was based on the exchange of products between contrasting zones, as a form of insurance against disaster. When the maize of the lowlands failed, for instance, potatoes from the highlands might still be abundant. The Inca uprooted populations and transferred them to new locations according to the needs of the system.

Economic security, however, came at a political price. To maintain the state, the Incas had to acquire new territories, leading to hectic and, in the long run, perhaps, unsustainable expansion. Moreover, their methods of subjugation were extreme. For example, they extinguished the coastal civilization of Chimú (see Chapter 14), razing its capital at Chan Chan almost to the ground and deporting its entire population. An Inca ruler was said to have drowned 20,000 enemy warriors when he conquered the Cañaris. The survivors became irreconcilable opponents. Many subject-peoples harbored grievances arising from memories of massacred warriors and forced migrations. Even the Incas' allies and elites were dissatisfied. The Checa, for instance, a people important to the Inca system of control, because their homeland straddled the route from Cuzco to the coast, never forgave the Inca for breaking his promise to perform ritual dances at their principal shrine in acknowledgment of their alliance. The Inca never seemed to have enough rewards to go around. The cults of dead leaders—who lay, mummified, in expensive shrines maintained by huge payrolls—existed to appease key Inca clans and factions, whose resources they boosted at the state's expense because tribute had to be diverted to meet the costs. Toward the end of the fifteenth century, the Inca Empire approached its greatest extent, from Quito (KEE-toh) in what is today Ecuador in the north, to the Valle Central in what is today Chile in the south. But at its core, the empire was shaky.

The Aztec Empire

In the same period, rapid expansion and environmental diversity characterized Mesoamerica. Here, an exceptionally dynamic state grew from the city of Tenochtitlán (teh-noch-teet-LAHN) in the valley of Mexico (and some neighboring, allied cities). Tenochtitlán stood in the middle of a lake, some 5,000 feet above sea level. It could not grow some of the staples of Mesoamerican life or any of the luxuries elites demanded for social or ritual purposes. The ground was swampy, and there was too little cultivable soil to grow enough maize and beans to feed the city. Tenochtitlán was too high and the climate too severe for cacao and cotton. Its people, whom we have traditionally called Aztecs, had only two options: poverty or warfare. They chose the latter.

Aztec expansion, like Inca expansion, was largely a late fifteenth- and early sixteenth-century phenomenon (see Map 15.3). At its peak, the Aztec Empire stretched from the Pánuco River in the north to what is now the Mexican-Guatemalan border on the Pacific coast, covering nearly 100,000 square miles and including hundreds of tributary communities.

The tribute collected demonstrated the power and reach and the ecological diversity of the regions from which the Aztecs extorted tribute. The Aztec bureaucracy meticulously listed and depicted it. From the "hot countries" in the south came ornamental feathers and jaguar pelts, jade, amber, gold, rubber for ritual ball games, and resin for incense. Overlapping regions supplied cacao, the essential ingredient of the addictive, high-status drink essential at Aztec ceremonies and parties. Ornamental shells arrived from the Gulf Coast and live eagles, deerskins, and tobacco from the mountain lands that fringed the valley of Mexico. For war and for the ball game, which was a form of mock warfare and an aristocratic exercise, Aztec nobles and priests dressed as gods, So on almost every folio of the tribute roll appear magnificent ritual garments and divine disguises. The tribute system brought necessities as well as luxuries: hundreds of thousands of bushels of maize and beans every year, with hundreds of thousands of cotton garments and quilted cotton suits of armor. Finally, there was the product that best expressed Aztec power and—perhaps in Aztec minds—supplied the blood that fueled the universe: human-sacrifice victims, captured in war or tendered in tribute. In 1487, for instance, at the dedication of a temple in Tenochtitlán, thousands of captives were said to have been slaughtered at once.

The Aztec system was complex, in the sense that tributary networks linked hundreds of communities. Some communities exchanged tribute, often collecting it from some tributaries to pass part of it on to others. Tenochtitlán was at the summit of the system, but it left most communities to govern themselves as long as they paid tribute. This was contrary to the highly interventionist politics of the Incas. According to records copied in the sixteenth century, Tenochtitlán only garrisoned or directly ruled 22 communities. The Aztecs did,

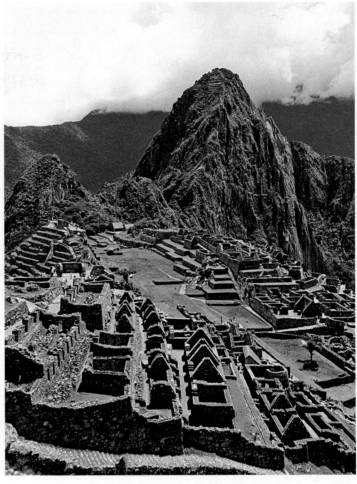

The Inca city of Machu Picchu in Peru is a miracle of urban engineering. It was built on a sharp 2,000-foot rise in the high Andes. Unrecorded in colonial times, it was discovered early in the twentieth century when the eccentric and adventurous American archaeologist, Hiram Bingham, was searching for another lost Inca city, Vilcamba. Unknown to Bingham, however, Vilcamba was in the tropical lowlands of Peru. The vast difference in climate between the two cities is stunning evidence of the environmental diversity of the Inca world.

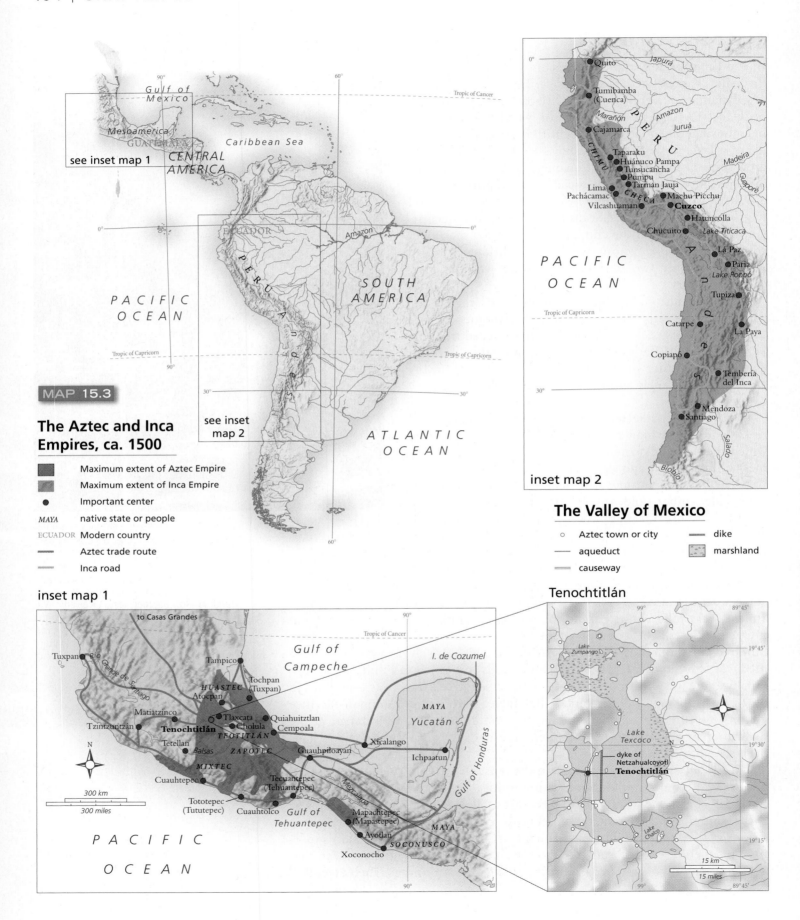

MAP 15.3

The Aztec and Inca Empires, ca. 1500

- Maximum extent of Aztec Empire
- Maximum extent of Inca Empire
- Important center
- *MAYA* native state or people
- ECUADOR Modern country
- Aztec trade route
- Inca road

inset map 2

The Valley of Mexico

- ○ Aztec town or city
- aqueduct
- causeway
- dike
- marshland

Tenochtitlán

inset map 1

however, share some of the same problems that afflicted the Incas. They relied on fragile alliances, bore the resentment of tributary peoples, and expanded so rapidly that their reach always threatened to outrun the available manpower and technology.

The Aztecs and Incas saw themselves as continuing the traditions of earlier empires. They recalled ruined supremacies of the past: Tula and Teotihuacán in the Aztec case, Tiahuanaco for the Incas. The reach of their power seems, however, to have exceeded anything either region had witnessed before. So how did they do it? Long-range exchanges with other cultures helped to propel empires in Eurasia and Africa into expansion, but these advantages did not apply in the Americas. Indeed, the Andean and Mesoamerican worlds were so isolated that they do not even seem to have been in touch with each other. They did not benefit from new technology. Nor, as far as we know, were people in either region bouncing back from anything resembling the demographic catastrophe of parts of the Old World in the previous century. There was no momentum of recovery behind the enormous extensions of Aztec and Inca power. The most likely explanation is that demographic growth crossed a critical threshold in both areas. Probably, only imperial solutions could command the resources and compel the exchanges of goods needed to sustain the growing cities in which the Aztecs and Incas lived. In any case, both empires, as we shall see in the next chapter, were short lived. Essentially they were empires of types traditional in the region and overreached the realistic limits of their potential.

Tribute. Early colonial Spanish administrators were careful to copy tribute records from the archives of the preconquest Aztec state. The records show both the complexity if the tributary networks that linked the Aztec world and the amazing environmental diversity of the regions from which tribute flowed. This folio, from the Codex Mendoza, shows the tribute due to Tenochtitlán—the Aztec capital in central Mexico—from the "hot country" near what is now the Mexican-Guatemalan border. Among the items depicted are ornamental feathers, bird skins, jaguar pelts, and jade beads.

NEW EURASIAN EMPIRES

The expanding states of fifteenth-century Africa and the Americas were conspicuous in their day. However, they proved relatively fragile. Sixteenth-century European conquerors swallowed the Aztec and Inca states almost at a gulp. Ethiopia barely survived in the sixteenth century, eroded by Muslim invaders and waves of pagan, pastoralist immigrants. Songhay fell to invaders from Morocco in the late sixteenth century. Finally, though Mwene Mutapa survived into the seventeenth century, having fought off would-be conquerors from Europe, it then dissolved gradually and ingloriously into numerous petty states. It was the borderlands that straddle Europe and Asia that nurtured the really big, really enduring new or resumed empires of the age, those of the Turks and Russians.

The Russian Empire

The rise of a powerful Russian state was without precedent. Previously, the geography of the region produced volatile and therefore usually short-lived empires. Its

Chronology: Incas and Aztecs	
ca. 1325	Aztecs found city of Tenochtitlán
ca. Mid-fifteenth century	Inca begin period of conquest and expansion
ca. Late-fifteenth century	Inca Empire approaches greatest extent
ca. Early sixteenth century	Aztec Empire reaches its peak

Making Connections | EXPANSION AND ITS LIMITS: AFRICA AND THE AMERICAS IN THE FIFTEENTH CENTURY

REGION/STATE OR EMPIRE	CAUSES FOR EXPANSION	EVIDENCE/EFFECTS OF EXPANSION	LIMITATIONS
East Africa / Ethiopia	Access to long-range trading routes to Indian Ocean via Red Sea ports	Recapture of coastal cities in 1400s, increased trade in slaves, ivory, gold, incense; creation of main access road to Indian Ocean	Limited agricultural land; need to control mountainous and lowland areas to access trade routes; major river systems to south and east with large populations; gradually encroaching Portuguese and Muslim influence by sixteenth century
East/Central Africa / Zambezi River Valley, Great Zimbabwe	Difficult access to Indian Ocean seaports; large populations with ivory, gold, metal resources	Manufactured goods from Asia (porcelain, silk, etc.) traded for gold, ivory; increasingly large administrative centers in stone, large amounts of coins, jewelry, gold, etc.	Landlocked; altered trade routes; decline in navigability of rivers
West Africa / Songhay Empire	Trade routes of the Sahara, linking Mediterranean and Niger valley; astute leadership (Muhammad Askia) and alliance with Muslim clerics, scholars	Canals, dikes, reservoirs; extension of cultivable land; rich trade with Niger valley goldfields	Limited long-range communication; adverse Atlantic winds/currents
Central Africa / Kongo	Domination of Congo River; alliance with Portuguese; abundant natural resources	Use of Western firearms, Christian religion and symbols to legitimate and maintain control; trading of slaves from conquered territories to Portuguese	Ultimate loss of control over slave trade to Portuguese leads to decline and fall
South America / Inca	Diversity of environments, resources; tribute system allows exchange of products between zones	Quick expansion and use of extreme methods of control; extensive road system; large shrines for dead leaders	Mass executions and other methods of subjugation alienate subject peoples and allies
Mesoamerica / Aztecs	Environmental diversity; hundreds of tributary communities; efficient recordkeeping; large array of natural resources	Intensive transformation of environment in/around capital (Tenochtitlán); abundance of commodities, both necessities (food, tools) and luxuries; widespread human sacrifice; monumental architecture	Loose administrative control; fragile alliances; alienation of tributary peoples; excessively rapid expansion

open, flat expanses of land and widely scattered populations contributed to an environment in which states could form with ease but only survive with difficulty. Most came and went quickly, vulnerable to external attack and internal rebellion.

In the fifteenth century, however, the rulers of Moscow established a state of imperial dimensions. Muscovy—as the early Russian Empire was called—has always been volatile at the edges, but it has been exceptionally enduring. One of the features that made Muscovy different was the shape of its heartland. It was based on control of the Volga River, a north–south axis of trade. Earlier empires, including the Mongols', were based on the east–west axis of the steppes, which served as highways for horse-borne armies.

The new empire's beginnings in the fourteenth century were almost imperceptible to those who experienced them or witnessed their effects. As we have seen, Russian princes could sometimes use Mongol dominance to their own advantage. Rulers of Moscow were the most adept in exploiting the Mongols to secure independence of and—increasingly—power over other Russians. Ivan I, known as Kalita or "Moneybags" (r. 1325–1340), got his nickname from his success as a tax collector for the Mongols. In 1378–1382, shortly after the collapse of Mongol rule in China, Muscovy attempted to drive the Mongols out of Russia. The challenge was premature, but Moscow's privileged relationship with the overlords survived. Mongol supremacy faded gradually.

The Russian world was expanding northward in the late fourteenth and early fifteenth centuries, as missionaries opened roads to convert people in the forests and tundra. An astonishing example of expansion by sea occurred in the 1430s. The evidence comes from a monastery on an island—bare, poor, and ice bound for much of the year—in the White Sea, on the edge of the Arctic. The monks painted their home not as it was but as they envisioned it, with a golden sanctuary and domes like candle flames. They showed the founders of their monastery rowing to the island, while whip-wielding angels expelled the original inhabitants. The paintings show merchants arriving, and monks rescuing shipwreck victims, with help from the ghosts of the monastery's saintly founders, who drive back the pack ice. Angels supply bread, cooking oil, and salt. All the ingredients of a typical story of European colonialism appear: the religious inspiration, the heroic voyage into a perilous environment, the ruthless treatment of the natives, the struggle to adapt and establish a viable economy, the quick arrival of commercial interests, and, finally, success through perseverance.

Muscovy's sudden take-off in the second half of the century, when conquests of neighboring peoples turned it into an imperial state, overshadowed early efforts at expansion. Indeed, when Constantinople fell to the Turks in 1453, Muscovites could see their city as, potentially, the "Third Rome," replacing Constantinople as Constantinople had replaced Rome, the former imperial capital (see Chapter 9). By the 1470s, Ivan the Great (r. 1462–1505) had absorbed most of Russia's other surviving principalities and was ready to throw off Mongol overlordship. He married a Byzantine princess, incorporated an imperial eagle into his coat of arms, forged a genealogy that traced his family back to the Roman Caesars, imported Italian technicians to fortify his palace complex, the Kremlin, and contemptuously dismissed an offer from the German emperor to invest him as king. "We have been sovereign in our land from our earliest forefathers," he replied, "and we hold our sovereignty from God."

"It was the borderlands that straddle Europe and Asia that nurtured the really big, really enduring new or resumed empires of the age, those of the Turks and Russians."

Russian expansion. The monastery these Russian Orthodox monks—Zosima and Savatti—founded in the White Sea off the Arctic coast of Siberia was really a modest and precarious little community, housed in wooden buildings in an icy desert. But the monks painted it as they would like it to be—big, grand, prosperous, and frequented by commerce.

During his reign, Ivan the Great more than trebled the territory he ruled—to over 240,000 square miles (see Map 15.4). His realm also took a new shape around most of the vast length of the Volga, stretching across the breadth of Eurasia, uniting the fur-rich north and the cash-rich fringes of Asia, and reaching for the Baltic and Caspian Seas. The city of Novgorod, which Muscovy absorbed in the 1470s, formed the northern pole of the state. Fur was the "black gold" of the north, inducing Russians to conquest and colonization, just as gold and spices lured other European peoples to Africa and the East.

War parties gathered pelts as tribute along a northern route that missionaries pioneered in the late fourteenth century, by way of the rivers Vym and Pechora. Repeatedly from 1465, Ivan sent expeditions to the rivers Perm and Ob to levy tribute. The expedition of 1499 numbered 4,000 men, equipped with sleds drawn by reindeer and dogs. They crossed the Ob in winter, returning with 1,000 captives from the forest-dwelling peoples who hunted for the furs. Ivan's ambassador to the rich Italian duchy of Milan boasted that his master received 1,000 gold ducats' worth of tribute annually in furs—five or six times an Italian nobleman's income. In the south, Russian dominance extended over Muslim-ruled Kazan (kah-ZAHN), near the Black Sea, Russia's great rival for control of Siberia's fur trade. While in the north missionaries, seeking to convert pagans, formed the vanguard for Russian conquests. Russian expansion therefore became a conscious crusade. Rulers justified it on religious grounds.

MAP 15.4

The Russian Empire, ca. 1505

Russian Empire

routes used by fur traders

fur

Timurids and the Ottoman Empire

In the early fifteenth century, Turkish—and therefore Muslim—expansion resumed in southern Europe and Asia, still under the leadership of the Ottoman dynasty. The Mongol supremacy had been a traumatic challenge to the Islamic world, shattering the reputation of Muslim armies, breaking the monopoly of Sharia or Islamic law, exposing the limitations of the clergy, and inspiring the religious minded to withdraw from the world in a spirit of resignation. The Black Death had also battered the Islamic world. In some ways, indeed, it never fully recovered. Muslims' numerical preponderance over Christians never got back to earlier levels. But, for global history, the Islamic recovery is a much bigger story than the temporary setback.

To understand recovery, we turn to one of its most brilliant Muslim observers after the Black Death, the historian Ibn Khaldun (ihb-ihn hahl-DOON). In 1377,

"*Everywhere in Ibn Khaldun's day, Islamic survival and success depended on Muslims' ability to tame the invaders challenging them from the deserts and the steppes, and turn their power to the service of Islam.*"

he sat down in a village in what is now Algeria "with ideas pouring into my head like cream into a churn." His efforts produced one of the most justly admired works of all time on history and political philosophy, the *Muqaddimah*. Its theme was the counterpoint of herder and tiller, which Ibn Khaldun saw as the motivating force of historical change. He had plenty of opportunity to observe the often violent interplay of nomads and sedentarists, their periodic collaboration, the incorporation of herder communities into Islamic states, and the way they launched new empires of their own. The consequences were clear. Everywhere in Ibn Khaldun's day, Islamic survival and success depended on Muslims' ability to tame the invaders challenging them from the deserts and the steppes, and turn their power to the service of Islam. Despite the disasters of the Black Death, new manpower stoked the Islamic world's potential for expansion. The pastoral peoples of Central Asia continued to provide converts. Islam's unique appeal to steppelanders was one of the great formative influences in the late medieval world. Most Turkic peoples and many Mongols were converted into warriors for Islam. Consequently, Central Asia stayed Muslim, and the Indian Ocean linked mainly Muslim shores. In other words, the Silk Roads and maritime routes of Eurasia had to pass through Muslim-ruled territory. Equally important, human fuel renewed the Islamic world's capacity to wage war and expand its frontiers.

The most conspicuous mobilizer of steppeland manpower in Muslim service in the late fourteenth and early fifteenth centuries, was the self-proclaimed "world conqueror," Timur (tee-MOOR) the Lame. Western writers, who traditionally call him Tamerlane, have tended to see him, romantically, as an embodiment of the superior virtues and simple lives of pastoral peoples. In reality, Timur was a nobly born townsman from Central Asia. Unlike most steppeland upstarts, he could justly claim to be descended from Genghis Khan (see Chapter 13). His court historian represented him as "the being nearest to perfection" and a pious devotee of holy war, but his role models were the pagans, Alexander the Great (see Chapter 5) and Genghis Khan.

When Turkic nobles rebelled against their Mongol masters in his homeland, Timur emerged as their leader. Deftly eliminating his rivals, he emerged as ruler of the region by 1370. By the time he died in 1406, he had conquered Iran, halted the growth of the Ottoman Empire, captured and caged its sultan, invaded Syria and India, and planned the conquest of China (see Map 15.5). Wherever he went, he heaped up the skulls of citizens unwise enough to resist his sieges. But this destruction was for efficiency, not for its own sake. It made most conquests submit cheaply. His success was by no means uniform, but it was impressive enough and consistent enough, to seem decreed by God. He addressed enemies in terms reminiscent of Mongol tradition: "Almighty God has subjugated the world to my domination, and the will of the Creator has entrusted the countries of the Earth to my power."

The day after his death, as his heirs turned on one another, his achievements seemed transitory. Even today, Timur's impact on the Islamic world is usually seen as negative. His success against the Ottomans gave Christendom a reprieve. By humbling the Mongols, he encouraged Christians in Russia. By weakening the Muslim sultans of Delhi, he liberated millions of Hindus. These reflections, however, overlook his psychological legacy. He was a champion of Islamic orthodoxy and exerted great influence as a patron of Muslim education. He is also important as an example of the process that converted pastoralists. Having been the scourge of the Islamic world, they became its sword.

Timurid horoscope. Despite their fearsome reputation, Timurid princes—the descendants of the Muslim Turkic conqueror whom Westerners called "Tamerlane"—were great patrons of both astronomers and astrologers. This horoscope was drawn up in Shiraz, Iran, in 1411 for one of Timur's grandsons, Iskandar Sultan. The date of his birth, 1384, is given in Persian, Uighur, and Chinese.

Timur was like a hurricane—his force soon spent. The Ottomans were more like a monsoon: Their armies returned and receded as each season came and went, but they constantly made new conquests. The fate of the Mongols—expelled from China, retreating from Russia—shows how hard it was for a great Eurasian empire to survive in the aftermath of the Black Death, which jarred economies and felled manpower. Yet, falteringly in the early fifteenth century but with renewed strength thereafter, the Ottoman Empire managed to do so.

The Ottomans' great advantage was location. The heartlands of the empire were at the crossroads of some of the world's great trade routes, where the Silk Roads, the Indian Ocean routes, the Volga, the Danube, and the Mediterranean almost converged (see Map 15.5). The history of the Byzantine Empire showed the importance of holding on to this location. Byzantium flourished while it occupied these lands, faltered when its control there slackened and ceased (see Chapter 12). From their own past, the Ottomans inherited the traditions of steppeland imperialism. They were content, at first, to levy tribute and allow their tributaries to govern themselves or to exist as puppet states to be manipulated according to Ottoman needs.

Gradually, the Ottomans adapted to the conditions of the environments they conquered, which were predominantly agrarian, urban, and maritime. As their conquests grew, their methods of governing became, necessarily, more bureaucratic and centralized. As their frontiers touched formidable foes, they modified their military traditions. Other empires of nomadic origins failed when required to adapt to new military technologies, but the Ottomans' readily became a gunpowder empire. Their forces could blow away cavalry or batter down city walls.

The Ottomans even took to the sea. In the 1390s, the sultans began to build permanent fleets of their own. It was a long process and hard to catch up with

MAP 15.5

Timur and the Ottomans, ca. 1370–1500

Empire of Timur, 1405

Ottoman Empire, 1500

Mamluk Sultanate

ROMANIA modern country

Campaigns of Timur: 1379–1405

against Persia 1379–1388

against Golden Horde 1388–1391 and 1395

against sultanate of Delhi 1398–1399

against Mamluk Sultanate and Baghdad 1399–1401

against Ottomans 1402

city sacked by Timur, with date

Scale varies with perspective
15,138 km
(9,346 miles)

7,720 km
(4,490 miles)

INDIAN OCEAN

Red S

Gulf of Aden

*Arabian
Peninsula*

*Arabian
Sea*

Persian Gulf

Bag

Gulf of Oman

Hormuz

Shiraz

Isfahan
1387

PERSIA

**EMPIRE
OF TIMUR**

KHURASAN

Nishapur

Herat

Ca

Indus

Kandahar

Oxus (Amu Darya)

Urgench

1381

1383

Kabul   Balkh

Bukhara   **1379**

**SULTANATE
OF DELHI**
1398 Timur invades
India and sacks Delhi

Multan

Samarkand
Timur's capital

Otrar
1405

Tashkent

INDIA

TRANSOXIANA
1370 Timur becomes master
of Transoxiana, part of the
Chagatai khanate

Delhi

*Bay
of
Bengal*

Ganges

CHAGATAI KHANATE

Lake
Balkhash

Equator

long-established naval powers. As late as 1466, a Venetian merchant in Constantinople claimed that to win a battle Turkish fleets needed to outnumber those of Venice by four or five to one. By the end of the century, however, the Ottomans had overturned the 400-year-old Christian maritime supremacy in the Mediterranean. Never since Rome defeated Carthage (see Chapter 7) had such an unlikely candidate become a naval power.

Like other imperialists of steppeland origin, the Ottomans mastered the art of keeping subjects of diverse religions loyal to them. At the same time, Ottoman leaders, as self-appointed warriors of Islam, took whatever steps were necessary to strengthen the Islamic state. They tolerated Jews, Christians, and Shiites, but had no qualms about levying punitive taxes on these minorities. On Christians, they imposed a levy of male child slaves, who were brought up as Muslims to form the **Janissaries**, an elite corps of the armed forces, and staff the ranks of the administration. The system provided servants for the state, and converts for Islam, while keeping Christian communities in submission. From the 1420s, consistently with the character of the empire as a Muslim state with people of many religions and customs, the sultan functioned as head of two linked systems of law and justice. The first consisted of secular laws and

A Turkish fleet at anchor off Toulon, in southern France, in 1543, from a chronicle written to celebrate the wide-ranging campaigns of Sultan Suleiman the Magnificent (r. 1520–1566). The Ottomans were able to wage naval war in the western Mediterranean, thanks to the many harbors along the North African coast controlled by Muslim chiefs who were subjects of the sultans.

customs that the sultan's appointees administered. The second was enshrined in the Quran and the traditions of Islamic law, with a body of experts to run it, who met in the sultan's palace.

In 1451, Mehmet (MEH-meht) II became sultan at the age of 19, uninhibited by caution, committed to reform. This was a decisive step in the shift from indirect rule to centralized government. Mehmet's predecessors had prudently allowed self-rule to continue in the city of Constantinople and its few surviving dependencies—the last fragments of the Byzantine Empire that still proclaimed itself the heir of Rome. The Ottomans controlled what happened in Constantinople by threatening and bribing political factions there. But some factions in the city were determined to challenge the Turks and formed an alliance with Western Christendom. Mehmet laid siege to Constantinople. He built huge forts to command the sea approaches to the city and fired the heaviest artillery ever made at its walls. He transported ships overland in pieces to get round the great chain the defenders stretched across the entrance to the harbor. In the end, the sheer weight of numbers was decisive. The attackers climbed the walls over the bodies of dead comrades. The last Byzantine emperor, Constantine XI, fell fighting—only the eagles on his purple boots identified his corpse.

With the fall of Constantinople in 1453, Mehmet II could see his empire as a continuation of Rome. He looked westward for fashions to incorporate into his court culture and chose Italians to paint his portrait, sculpt his medals, and write some of his propaganda. The direction of Ottoman conquests tilted toward Europe as Mehmet attempted to recreate the Byzantine Empire. He extended his territory into most of what are now Greece, Romania, and Bosnia, seeking to control the shores of the Adriatic and Black seas.

THE LIMITATIONS OF CHINESE IMPERIALISM

Ottoman imperialism in the fifteenth century resumed its former course after setbacks caused by the Black Death and the rise of Timur. An observer at the time might have predicted that China, too, would resume expansion and even anticipate the Ottomans in bidding for a maritime empire. The best way to understand why such developments seemed likely—and why they were frustrated—is to look back at China's recovery from the mid-fourteenth-century plagues. Like so many decisive episodes of Chinese history, the story begins among the people on whose labor the empire depended: peasants.

The rhythms of peasant life sometimes seem slow and changeless, peasants' expectations low: deferring hope, shrugging off promises of improvement. Their response, in a surprisingly wide variety of cultural contexts, is to wait and pray for the millennium—a fabled future, when divine intervention will either perfect the world or end it. Often, however, in times of extreme disaster, peasant movements arise to try to trigger the millennium. One of the most explosive of all such movements began among Chinese canal workers in 1350.

Mid-fourteenth-century China was particularly wretched. Peasants were the victims of the slow-grinding effects of economic misery and the survivors of terrible environmental disasters. The plagues that began in the 1320s kept returning. Not until well into the 1350s did the plagues begin to lose their virulence or to encounter naturally immunized populations. In 1344, the Yellow River flooded. Persistent droughts followed. Decayed communications that prevented timely help made local famines worse. The population of the empire had fallen, by some calculations, to half what it had been at its height. In this setting, peasants were forced to repair the Grand Canal, which carried essential food supplies from southern and central China to Beijing.

The peasants' millenarianism—their hope of deliverance in a transfigured world—was based on a Buddhist myth. The lord Maitreya, the last of the earthly Buddhas, would come to prepare the world for extinction. Now, however, given the peasants' miserable lives, the myth acquired a political edge. Maitreya would put a triumphant end to the struggle of good against evildoers and give his followers power over their oppressors. A similar movement was current at the same time in Western Europe, where the Fraticelli, a group of Franciscan friars, identified with the needs and interests of the wretched of the Earth. The Franciscans predicted that a cosmic hero would come to wrest treasures from the soil and enrich the poor. Fulfilling the biblical prophecy uttered by the mother of Jesus that the prayers of the church repeated every day, he would put down the mighty from their seat and exalt the humble and meek.

In China, the mood was particularly dangerous. Along with their desire for deliverance, peasants harbored a folk memory of the Song dynasty (see Chapter 12) and a hankering for the good times supposed to have preceded the Mongol invasions of a century before. Peasant revolts are often revolutionary in the most literal sense of the word, wanting to turn the world back, "revolve" it full circle, to an imagined or misremembered golden age. Therefore, when the Mongol rulers executed a pretender to the throne who claimed to be the heir of the Song in 1351, a revolt broke out among his followers. They easily recruited thousands of peasants

Sultan Mehmet II (r. 1451–1481) extended the Ottoman Empire westward into Europe, taking great interest in the culture of lands that had once belonged to the Roman Empire—especially after he captured the old Roman capital of Constantinople in 1453. Gentile Bellini, who worked at Mehmet's court and was one of the best Venetian painters of the day, painted this portrait of the sultan in the realistic style that was popular in Italy at the time. Bellini framed the sultan's image with columns decorated in the European style.

to their cause. Some members of the elite even joined in, out of resentment at the ruling dynasty's partiality for foreign advisers.

The leader who emerged from the chaos of rebellion was Zhu Yuanzhang (joo yoo-ehn-jhang), the recruiting officer of a rebel band. By the end of the 1350s, the empire in the Yangtze region had dissolved into a chaos of small states run by similar upstarts. Between 1360 and 1363, in river warfare of reckless daring, Zhu conquered his rivals. At this stage, he was careful to represent himself as a mere servant of the rebel cause. By 1368, however, he was so powerful that he proclaimed the start of a new dynasty.

Zhu cleverly managed the coalition that had brought him to power. He juggled all the rebels' conflicting ideologies while reconciling former enemies. To please the Confucian establishment, he restored ancient court ceremonies and the examinations for public service. He kept the military command structure and even dressed in some of the same ways as the previous Mongol dynasty had. He renounced the cult of Maitreya, but only after making it clear that he had fulfilled it in his own person by adopting the name "Ming" for his dynasty. The word, which means bright, was traditionally used to describe the lord Maitreya.

Giraffe. "The ministers and all the people gathered to gaze at it and their joy knows no end," commented Zhen-tu, the Chinese court painter who recorded the arrival of one of several giraffes at China's imperial zoo in the early fifteenth century. Imperial propaganda identified giraffes with mythical beasts of good omen.
1977–42–1. Tu, Shen. "The Tribute Giraffe with Attendant". Philadelphia Museum of Art: Gift of John T. Dorrance, 1977.

Zhu had the self-educated man's typical contempt for the academic establishment. "Chewing on phrases and biting on words," he said, "they have never had any practical experience. When you examine what they do, it is nothing." But he recognized that the Confucian bureaucrats had expertise he could use. His empire—vast and literate, as it was—needed a civil service that would heed a traditional code of ethics. He also needed to keep the Confucian elite under his control. He therefore kept the traditional power centers of his court in balance: the military top brass, the eunuchs who ran the imperial household, the foreign and Muslim advisers and technicians, the Buddhist and Daoist clergies, and the merchant lobby. Together, they limited the power of the Confucian elite.

The result was a brief period when expansionist policies prevailed over Confucian caution. Zhu's son, the Yongle (yuhng-leh) emperor (r. 1402–1424) aggressively sought contact with the world beyond the empire. He meddled in the politics of Vietnam and enticed the Japanese to trade.

The most spectacular manifestation of the new outward-looking policy was the career of the Muslim eunuch-admiral, Zheng He (jehng heh). In 1405, he led the first of a series of naval expeditions. Their purpose has been the subject of long and unresolved scholarly debate, but in part, at least, it was to show China's flag all over the Indian Ocean (see Map 15.6). He replaced unacceptable rulers in Java, Sumatra, and Sri Lanka, founded a puppet state on the commercially important Strait of Malacca, and gathered tribute from Bengal in India. He displayed Chinese power as far away as Jiddah, on the Red Sea coast of Arabia and in major ports in East Africa as far south as the island of Zanzibar. "The countries beyond the horizon," he announced with some exaggeration, "and from the ends of the Earth, have become subjects." He restocked the imperial zoo with giraffes, ostriches, zebra, and rhinoceroses—all hailed as beasts bringing good luck—and brought Chinese geographical knowledge up to date.

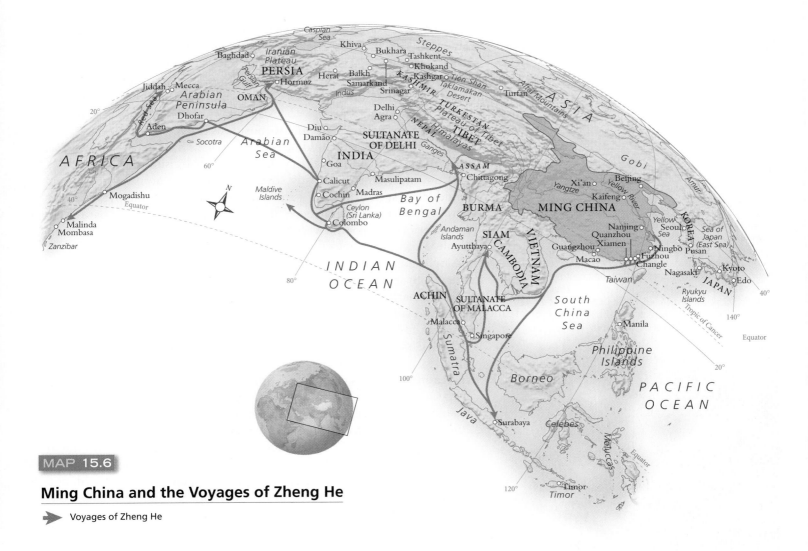

MAP 15.6

Ming China and the Voyages of Zheng He

➤ Voyages of Zheng He

Can Zheng He's voyages be called an imperial venture? Their official purpose was to pursue a fugitive pretender to the Chinese throne—but that would not have required such vast expeditions to such distant places. The Chinese called the vessels treasure ships and emphasized what they called tribute gathering (in the more distant spots Zheng He's ships visited, what happened was more like an exchange.) Commercial objectives may have been involved. Almost all the places Zheng He visited had long been important in Chinese trade. In part, the voyages were scientific missions: Ma Huan, Zheng He's interpreter, called his own book on the subject, *The Overall Survey of the Ocean's Shores,* and improved maps and data on the plants, animals, and peoples of the regions visited were among the expeditions' fruits. But flag showing is always, to some extent, about power or, at least, prestige. And the aggressive intervention Zheng He made in some places, together with the tone of his commemorative inscriptions, demonstrates that the extension or reinforcement of China's image and influence was part of the project.

Indeed, it is hard to see how else the huge investment the state made in his enterprise could have been justified. Zheng He's expeditions were on a crushing scale. His ships were much bigger than anything European navies could float at the time. His first fleet was said to comprise 66 junks of the largest ever built, 225 support vessels, and 27,870 men. The seventh voyage—probably the longest in reach—sailed 12,618 miles. The voyages lasted on average over two years each. Some silly claims have been made for Zheng He's voyages. Ships of his fleet did not sail beyond the limits of the Indian Ocean—much less discover America or Antarctica. His achievements, however, clearly demonstrated China's potential to become the center of a maritime empire of enormous reach.

But the Chinese naval effort could not last. Historians have debated why it was abandoned. In many ways, it was to the credit of Chinese decision makers that they pulled back from involvement in costly adventures far from home. Most powers that have undertaken such expeditions and attempted to impose their rule on distant countries have had cause to regret it. Confucian values, as we have seen, included giving priority to good government at home. "Barbarians" would submit to Chinese rule if and when they saw the benefits. Attempting to beat or coax them into submission was a waste of resources. By consolidating their landward empire, and refraining from seaborne imperialism, China's rulers ensured the longevity of their state. All the maritime empires founded in the world in the last 500 years have crumbled. China is still there.

Part, at least, of the context of the decision to abort Zheng He's missions is clear. The examination system and the gradual discontinuation of other forms of recruitment for public service had serious implications. Increasingly scholars, with their indifference to expansion, and gentlemen, with their contempt for trade, governed China. In the 1420s and 1430s, the balance of power at court shifted in the bureaucrats' favor, away from the Buddhists, eunuchs, Muslims, and merchants who had supported Zheng He. When the Hongxi (huhng-jher) emperor succeeded to the throne in 1425, one of his first acts was to cancel Zheng He's next voyage. He restored Confucian office holders, whom the Yongle emperor had dismissed, and curtailed the power of other factions. In 1429, the shipbuilding budget was cut almost to extinction. The scholar-elite hated overseas adventures, and the factions that favored them so much that they destroyed all Zheng He's records in an attempt to obliterate his memory. Moreover, China's land frontiers became insecure as Mongol power revived. China needed to turn away from the sea and toward the new threat.

By the late fifteenth century, the scholars' position seemed unshakable, and the supremacy of Confucian values could not be challenged. The Hongxi emperor aspired to Confucian perfection. He ordered the slaughter or expulsion of court magicians and exiled 1,000 Buddhist and Daoist monks. He resumed a Confucian priority: study of the penal code, which previous Ming emperors had neglected. He reintroduced the palace lectures, during which Confucian professors instructed the emperor. He endowed a library alongside the Confucian temple at the sage's birthplace in Qufu (choo-foo). He patronized artists whose work radiated Confucian serenity. Wu Wei (woo way), the emperor's favorite painter, had Daoist patrons, too, but his representations of ascetics meditating in sketchy landscapes demonstrate the triumph of thought over nature and, therefore, by implication, of Confucianism over Daoism.

By the end of the fifteenth century, there was little chance the Chinese would resume a strategy of expanding the empire and no chance

Wu Wei was one of the most original and influential artists of late-fifteenth-century China. But his values were those of his patrons, the conventional scholar-elite of the imperial court. This painting is typical. The scholar staring thoughtfully into the distance is drawn in delicate and flattering contrast to the heavy, blotchy ink used to depict the tree. *Wu Wei, "Scholar Seated Under a Tree," China. Ink & traces of colour on silk. 14.7 × 8.25. Chinese and Japanese Special Fund. Photograph © 2007 Courtesy Museum of Fine Arts, Boston*

that they would expand by sea. For the rest of the Ming period (1368–1644), China did not cease to be a great imperial power, but frontier stability became far more important to the ruling elite than frontier expansion. The transfer of the imperial capital from the southern citty of Nanjing to the northern city of Beijing under the Yongle emperor symbolized this concern. The state never resumed the active patronage of overseas expansion. The growth of trade and of Chinese colonization in Southeast Asia was left to the private initiative of merchants and migrants. China, the empire best equipped for maritime imperialism, opted out. Consequently, lesser powers, including those of Europe, were able to exploit opportunities in seas that Chinese power vacated.

Chronology: The Early Ming Dynasty	
1350s	Yangtze region dissolves into small warring states
1360–1363	Zhu Yuanzhang conquers his rivals
1368	Zhu Yuanzhang founds Ming dynasty
1405	Zheng He leads first naval expedition
1425	Hongxi emperor succeeds to throne; Zheng He's voyages cancelled; Confucian values ascendant

THE BEGINNINGS OF OCEANIC IMPERIALISM

Even under the Yongle emperor, China confined its seaward reach to the monsoonal seas of maritime Asia and the Indian Ocean—seas of terrible hazards and fabulous rewards. As we have seen, the Indian Ocean was relatively easy to cross but relatively hard to enter or exit. For most of history, therefore, it was the preserve of peoples whose homes bordered it or who traveled overland—like some European and Armenian traders—to become part of its world. Moreover, all the trade was internal. Merchants took no interest in venturing far beyond the monsoon system to reach other markets or supplies.

From Europe, however, access to the Indian Ocean was well worth seeking. Merchants craved a share of the richest trades and most prosperous markets in the world, especially the spices, drugs, and aromatics that were the specialities of producers in Sri Lanka, and parts of India and what is now Indonesia. These products, sold to rich buyers in China and Southwest Asia, and, to a lesser extent, in Europe, were the most profitable in the world, in terms of price per unit of weight. Many Europeans sought to find out where they came from and to take part in the trades. But the journey was too long, laborious, and hazardous to generate much profit. From the Mediterranean, merchants had either to travel up the Nile and proceed by camel caravan to a Red Sea port, or to negotiate a dangerous passage through the Ottoman Empire to the Persian Gulf. In either case, they obviously could not take ships with them. This was a potentially fatal limitation because Europeans had little to offer to people in the Indian Ocean basin except shipping services. For most of the fifteenth century, until the 1490s, Europeans were not sure if it was possible to approach the Indian Ocean by sea at all.

To understand why, until the late fifteenth century, Europeans were so backward in navigation compared with Indian Ocean peoples and unable to gain direct access to Asian markets and supplies, we must look at the wind map (see Map 15.7). For most of history, winds and currents have played a huge part in conditioning, and even determining, who and what went where in the world.

Europe's only effective access by sea to the rest of the world is along its western seaboard, into the Atlantic, which has a fixed-wind system. That is, instead of changing direction seasonally, as in monsoonal systems, the prevailing winds in the Atlantic are always the same. It took a long time to develop navigation with fixed-wind systems because, until navigators explored and decoded those winds' path-

"China, the empire best equipped for maritime imperialism, opted out. Consequently, lesser powers, including those of Europe, were able to exploit opportunities in seas that Chinese power vacated."

MAP 15.7

Winds and Ocean Currents Worldwide

Ocean Currents

	warm
	cold

Prevailing Winds

	warm
	cold

Local Winds

	warm
	cold

ways, adventurers could not get home. Navigators either sailed into the wind—which usually resulted in their being blown back without discovering any useful new lands or routes—or they sailed with the wind, never to be heard of again.

The Norse explorers of the North Atlantic in the tenth and eleventh centuries (see Chapter 11) overcame these limitations by sailing west with the currents that cross the Atlantic below the Arctic, and then picking up the westerlies, which took them home. But this route led only to relatively poor and underpopulated regions. For the Atlantic to become Europe's highway to the rest of the world, explorers had to develop ways to exploit the rest of the fixed-wind system. They had to discover the winds that led to commercially important destinations. There were, first, the northeast trade winds, which led to the resource-rich, densely populated regions of the New World, far south of the lands the Norse reached. There was also the South Atlantic wind system, which led, by way of the southeast trade winds and the westerlies of the far south, to the Indian Ocean.

The technology needed to exploit the Atlantic's wind systems only gradually became available during a period of long, slow development in the thirteenth, fourteenth, and fifteenth centuries. Like most technology, for most of history, it developed by trial and error. We know little about the process, because the work went undocumented. Humble craftsman labored to improve hull design and rigging—and therefore the maneuverability of ships—and to make water casks secure for the long voyages explorers had to undertake. Historians have traditionally emphasized the contribution of formal science in developing maritime charts and instruments

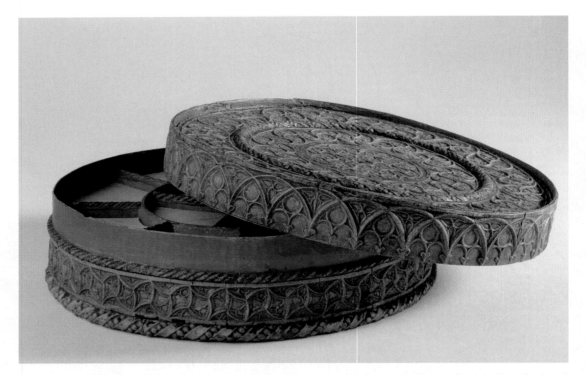

Spice box. This sixteenth-century leather box was used to house specimens of spices from Southeast Asia. Around the outer rim would have been different kinds of pepper, which accounted for as much as 70 per cent of the global trade in spices in the early modern period; cloves (the most valuable spice per unit of bulk, production of which was overwhelmingly concentrated in the islands of Ternate and Tidore); and ginger. The inner compartment would have contained nutmeg and mace (which are both products of the nutmeg tree, the former being the inner kernel of the seed, the latter its outer coating, grown in the Banda Islands in what is today Indonesia); and cinnamon (most of which came from what is now Sri Lanka, though production was widely diffused across the region as far as the Philippines).

for navigating by the stars. Now it seems that these innovations were irrelevant. No practical navigator of this period in Europe seems to have used them.

In addition to gradually developing technology, gradually improving knowledge of winds and currents prepared Europeans to explore maritime routes to the rest of the world. The European discovery of the Atlantic was launched from deep in the Mediterranean, chiefly by navigators from Genoa and the island of Majorca. They forced their way through the Strait of Gibraltar, where the strength of the adverse current seemed to stopper their sea, in the thirteenth century. From there, some turned north to the familiar European Atlantic. Others turned south into waters unsailed, as far as we know, for centuries, toward the Madeira and Canary Islands and the African Atlantic. Early efforts were long and laborious because explorers' vision was limited to the small patches of the ocean before them, with their apparently unremitting winds. Navigators were like code breakers deprived of information to work with. Moreover, the Black Death and the economic downturn of the mid–fourteenth century interrupted the effort, or at least slowed it down.

Only the long accumulation of information and experience could make a breakthrough possible. Navigators had no means to keep track of their longitude as they beat their way home against the wind. They made increasingly huge deep-sea detours to find westerlies that would take them home. Those detours led to the discovery of the Azores, a mid-ocean string of islands more than 700 miles west of Portugal. Marine charts made not later than the 1380s show all but two islands of the group. Much longer open-sea voyages now became common. From the 1430s, the Portuguese established way stations, sown with wheat or stocked with wild sheep, on the Azores, so that passing crews could find provisions.

Several attempts were made during the fifteenth century to explore Atlantic space, but most doomed themselves to failure by setting out in the belt of westerly winds. Presumably explorers chose this route because they wanted to be sure that they would be able to get home. We can still follow the tiny gains in the slowly unfolding record on rare maps and stray documents. In 1427, a Portuguese pilot called Diogo de Silves established for the first time the approximate relationship of the islands of the Azores to one another. Shortly after 1450, the westernmost islands of the Azores were reached. Over the next three decades, the Portuguese crown often commissioned voyages of exploration farther into the Atlantic, but none is known to have made any further progress. Perhaps they failed because they departed from the Azores, where the westerlies beat them back to base.

Not only was exploitation of the Atlantic slow, but at first it yielded few returns. One exception was Madeira, which paid enormous taxes to the Portuguese crown thanks to sugar planting in the mid–fifteenth century. The explorers' hope of establishing direct contact with the sources of West African gold proved false, though they were able to get gold at relatively low prices through trade with West African kingdoms. This trade also produced something that could be sold in European markets. From 1440, Portuguese desperadoes obtained increasing numbers of slaves through trading and raiding. But markets for slaves were limited because great slave-staffed plantations, of the sort later familiar in the southern United States, hardly existed in Europe, where most slaves were still domestic servants. The Canary Islands attracted investment because they produced natural dyestuffs and seemed exploitable for sugar. But their inhabitants fiercely resisted Europeans, and the conquest was long and costly.

In the 1480s, however, the situation changed, and Atlantic exploration began to pay off. In the North Atlantic, customs records of the English port of Bristol indicate that quantities of whaling products, salt fish, and walrus ivory from the ocean increased dramatically. In West Africa, the Portuguese post at São Jorge da Mina, near the mouth of the Benya River, was close to gold fields in the Volta River valley, and large amounts of gold now began to reach European hands. In 1484, sugar production at last began in the Canary Islands. In the same decade, Portuguese made contact with the kingdom of Kongo. Although voyages toward and around the southernmost tip of Africa encountered unremittingly adverse currents, they also showed that the far south of the Atlantic had westerly winds that might at last lead to the Indian Ocean. By the end of the 1480s, it was apparent that Atlantic investment could yield dividends.

Imperial marker. Portuguese explorers erected carved stone pillars to mark their route and to record their claim to have annexed territory for Portugal. Diogo Cão raised this example, the Padrão de Santo Agostinho, at Santa Maria, south of Benguela in Angola in 1482 (see Map 15.8).

The 1490s were a breakthrough-decade in Europe's efforts to reach out across the ocean to the rest of the world (see Map 15.8). In 1492–1493, Christopher Columbus, in voyages financed by Italian bankers and with backing from the Spanish 'monarchs, discovered fast, reliable routes across the Atlantic that linked the Mediterranean and the Caribbean. In 1496, John Cabot, another Italian adventurer, backed by merchants in Bristol and the English crown, discovered a direct route across the North Atlantic, using variable springtime winds to get across and the westerlies to get back. His route, however, was not reliable and, for over 100 years, was mainly used to reach the cod fisheries of Newfoundland.

MAP 15.8

European Oceanic Exploration up to 1500

→	European explorers with names and dates
→	Norse voyages of the 10th and 11th centuries
▬	extent of Portuguese exploration of West African coast up to 1487
✚	Portuguese markers erected in token of their claim to sovereignty
Thule Inuit	people

**Economic activity associated with early
European exploitation of the Atlantic**

⬇	sugar plantation
➤	fisheries
⬇	slaves

Meanwhile, the Portuguese sought to determine whether the Indian Ocean was genuinely landlocked. In 1497–1498, a Portuguese trading venture, commissioned by the crown and probably financed by Italian bankers, attempted to use the westerlies of the South Atlantic to reach the Indian Ocean. Its leader, Vasco da Gama, turned east too early and had to struggle around the Cape of Good Hope at the tip of Africa. But he managed to get across the Indian Ocean anyway and reach the pepper-rich port of Calicut at the tip of India. The next voyage, in 1500, reached India without a serious hitch.

The breakthroughs of the 1490s opened direct, long-range routes of maritime trade across the world between Europe, Asia, and Africa. Success may seem sudden, but not if we view it against the background of slow developments in European chronology and knowledge and the accelerating benefits of Atlantic exploration in the previous decade. Was there more to it than that?

Making Connections | THE BEGINNINGS OF OCEANIC IMPERIALISM IN EUROPE

DESIRE	OBSTACLES	BREAKTHROUGHS, 1200–1500
European merchants crave access to Indian Ocean trade	Long, laborious journey across hostile territories Europeans have little to offer in exchange for the spices, drugs, and aromatics of the East Fixed-wind system of Atlantic makes oceanic voyages impractical Black Death and consequent economic downturn slow down efforts to explore Atlantic	Technology to exploit Atlantic wind system slowly develops Knowledge of winds and currents gradually improves Thirteenth century: Navigators from Genoa and Majorca force their way through the Strait of Gibraltar Portuguese discover the Azores in the late fourteenth century *1450–1480*: Portuguese commission Atlantic voyages of exploration *after 1480*: Exploration of Atlantic begins to pay returns *after 1490*: Europe begins to reach out across the ocean to the rest of the world.

Was there something special about European culture that would explain why Europeans rather than explorers from other cultures discovered the world-girdling routes, linking the Old World to the New and the Indian Ocean to the Atlantic? Some European historians have argued just that—that Europeans had something others lacked.

Such a suggestion, however, seems ill conceived. Compared to the peoples of maritime Asia, Europeans were special mainly in being slow to launch long-range voyages. The Atlantic, the ocean they bordered, really was special, however, because its wind system inhibited exploration for centuries but rewarded it spectacularly once it was launched. Moreover, the breakthrough explorations were not the work of "Europe" but of people from a few communities on the Atlantic seaboard and in the Mediterranean. What distinguishes them is not that they set off with the right kind of culture, but that they set off from the right place.

THE EUROPEAN OUTLOOK: PROBLEMS AND PROMISE

In some ways, indeed, Western Europe in the fifteenth century was beset with problems. Recovery from the disasters of the fourteenth century was slow. Though plagues were less severe, they remained frequent. And though used to the severe climate of their little ice age, Western Europeans did not reoccupy the high ground and distant colonies that they had abandoned in the fourteenth century. In most places, population increase was modest and probably did not reach levels attained before the Black Death. Food supplies were unreliable, and harvests frequently failed.

Human foes joined impersonal enemies—plague, war, and famine. In 1396, a crusade to drive the Turks from the Balkans failed. It marked the beginning of a long period of Turkish advance on the Balkan and eastern Mediterranean frontiers of Christendom. Meanwhile, in the northeast, Lithuanians, most of whom remained pagan until the late fourteenth or early fifteenth century, eroded the conquests of German knightly orders along the Baltic Sea (see Chapter 12). In the early fifteenth century, Thule Inuit raiders finally obliterated the Norse colony on Greenland (see Chapter 14).

Meanwhile, hard times created opportunities for those with the skill or luck to exploit them. High mortality opened gaps in elites, which bureaucrats could fill, thanks, in part, to a revolution in government. The use of paper made it cheap and easy to transmit rulers' commands to the farthest corners of their realms. To help legitimize the newcomers' power, Western moralists redefined nobility as the product of virtue or education rather than ancestry. "Virtue is the sole and unique nobility," declared a Venetian coat of arms. A doctrine of late fifteenth-century Italian social thought invoked Greek mythology to make its point: "Neither the wealth of Croesus [reputedly the richest man in the world] nor the antiquity of the blood of Priam [the king of Troy in Homer's epics] could rival reason as an ingredient of nobility."

New economic divisions appeared. The line of the Elbe and northern Danube Rivers and the lands between became a cultural fault line. To the west of this line, underpopulation boosted the value of labor. The effects were to liberate peasants and urban communities from landowners' control, split up landholdings, encourage tenancies, and convert cropland to pasture. In the east the opposite occurred. Landholders responded to the loss of manpower and revenue by clamping down on peasants' rights and forcing formerly free towns into submission. New definitions of nobility were rejected. East of the Bohemian forest, nobility was ancient blood or acquired "by martial discipline," and that was that.

Scored by heresies, trenched by conflicting social values, and riven by economic cracks, Western Europe nevertheless showed signs of self-confidence and optimism. Scholars and artists pursued, with renewed vigor, the project of recovering the legacy of classical antiquity—the cultural achievements of ancient Greece and Rome. The movement is commonly called "**the Renaissance**" on the grounds that the civilization of classical antiquity was reborn—but "the" is a much-abused word. Scholarship has now identified renaissances in almost every century for the previous 1,000 years. No radically new departure occurred in the fifteenth century from what had gone before—merely an accentuation of long-accumulating tendencies.

An event traditionally said to be representative of the Renaissance occurred in 1400, when the Cloth Importers' Guild of Florence launched a competition for a new set of bronze doors for the greatest monument in their care: the Baptistery that faced the city's cathedral. The Baptistery had been built in the eighth century as the place where infants and converts could receive the sacrament of baptism. Urban myth, however, claimed it was orginally a Roman temple of the god Mars. Two great geniuses were the finalists in the competition: Filippo Brunelleschi and Lorenzo Ghiberti both used classical models for their startlingly realistic and dramatic trial plaques depicting the Sacrifice of Isaac. Both works represent the moment in the biblical story when God stays Abraham's hand from sacrificing his son Isaac. Ghiberti won the commission, perhaps because he was technically more ingenious, using less bronze and therefore cutting the cost. In 1425, his second set of Baptistery doors genuinely marked a breakthrough in the power of the art of bronze reliefs: "gates of paradise," as Florentines called them, which acquired the realism of an extra dimension through the use of perspective. In 1440, Donato Donatello, the most devoted student of classical art in Florence, produced his free-standing bronze statue of David, which, under the form of a sacred subject,

"Scholarship has now identified renaissances in almost every century for the previous 1,000 years. No radically new departure occurred in the fifteenth century from what had gone before—merely an accentuation of long-accumulating tendencies."

(a)

(b)

Renaissance competition. In 1400, when the Cloth Workers' Guild of Florence sponsored a competition for new designs for the doors of the baptistry in the city's cathedral, Florence's leading designers competed for the job. The subject to be portrayed was the story from the Book of Genesis when God intervened to prevent Abraham from sacrificing his son Isaac. The model entered by Filippo Brunelleschi, the cathedral's architect, was more dramatic, with an angel literally staying Abraham's hand to save Isaac from being slain (a). But Lorenzo Ghiberti's winning design was more classical. The angel's foreshortening, the musculature of Isaac's body, which was copied from ancient Greek and Roman sculpture, and the technically dazzling way in which Abraham's elbow jabs from the plaque help explain Ghiberti's success (b).

again from the Bible, seemed to bring a vanished pagan world back to life: secular, sensual, homoerotic.

For there was no notion of "art for art's sake" in fifteenth- and sixteenth-century Italy. Artists were practical. The technology of bronze casting developed along with experience in casting cannon. Many masters of the Renaissance had sidelines in gunnery. Ironically, increased demand for bronze guns starved art of a vital raw material and even led to the melting down of antique bronzes, just when artists and collectors most valued them. Similarly, painters had to be good at every kind of design, including urban planning, architectural drawing, interior decoration, jewelwork, stagecraft, party-planning, and engineering. When Leonardo da Vinci—universally hailed as one of the greatest painters of the early sixteenth century—sought new patrons, he advertised himself as skilled in every kind of handiwork, including the making of weapons and the constructions of siege engines. When he worked for the dynasty that ruled Milan, one of his jobs was to paint their coat of arms on the ceilings of their apartments.

Admirers of classical learning adopted a predominantly secular curriculum: grammar, rhetoric, poetry, history, and moral philosophy, imbibed mainly from classical texts. The classics as well as—even, instead of—Christianity came to inform common ideas of morality, politics, and taste. Spreading, at first, from a few French and north Italian schools, **humanism** gradually became Europe's most prestigious form of learning. Political thinkers turned back to Greek and Roman history for instruction. Religious innovators modeled their ideas on evidence from early Christianity. Artists adopted realism and perspective from what they thought were Greek and Roman models.

Florence demonstrates humanism's power and limitations. In the fifteenth century, classical taste transformed its art and architecture. Comparisons with the Roman republic inspired its citizens to think of themselves as free and self-governing.

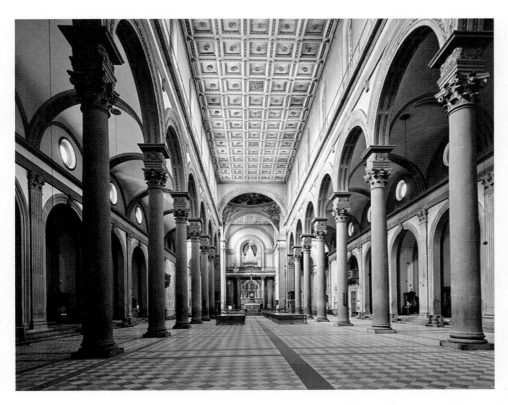

The Church of San Lorenzo. Filippo Brunelleschi, the trend-setting architect of Florence, got the commission to design the parish church of the ruling Medici family in 1418. He based his concept on laws of mathematical proportion that, he believed, ancient Greek and Roman architects had followed. He copied the ground plans of the most ancient churches he knew, and, to support the clergy's growing desire to make congregations participate actively in worship, he opened domes above the sacred spaces to fill them with light.

Yet power gradually fell into the hands of a single family, the Medici, who patronized art in the classical tradition but who actually spent more on jewels and on gaudy, gem-like artworks that could display their wealth. When they were temporarily overthrown in 1494, after their banking business collapsed, the state that replaced them was no Roman-style republic. Rather, it was the rule of a "godly" clique, inspired by a hell-fire preacher, who preferred piety to humanism. Botticelli (1444–1510), the great artist who had painted pagan erotica for a Medici villa, turned to biblical subjects.

Still, across Europe, the rise of humanism had lasting consequences for Christian culture. Humanists painstakingly scrutinized the language of the Bible and the historical traditions of the church, exposing incorrect translations and departures from the practices of early Christianity. New styles in church architecture reflected classical taste and, more deeply, arose from the desire to create a setting for the kind of devotion that humanism inspired. Open sanctuaries, brilliantly lit and approached through wide naves and aisles allowed worshippers to see and take part in events at the altar.

Humanism also helped arouse European interest in the wider world. Some important and provocative geographical writings of classical antiquity became widely known in the West. In the early fifteenth century, the work of the ancient Greek scholar Ptolemy, originally written in Alexandria in the second century, invited intense speculation about geography, mapping the world, and the limits of exploration. The first-century B.C.E. work of Strabo, a Greek geographer who sought to reconstruct Homer's mental map of the world, prompted questions

Chivalrous hero. When Albrecht Dürer painted an altarpiece for the family of wealthy merchants Stephan and Lucas Paumgartner in Nuremberg Germany, probably in 1498, both brothers wanted to appear as figures of chivalry. Stephan was shown as St. George, the knightly dragon-slayer, and Lucas, depicted here, took on the role of St. Eustace, displaying a banner with the image of Christ between a stag's antlers to recall the moment when Eustace, according to legend, was converted during a hunt.

about finding previously unknown continents in the ocean. Humanists' fascination with the history of language reinforced the search for "primitive" peoples who might cast light on the question of how language originated.

Magic was at least as much a part of the learned culture of the Renaissance as humanism. Florence, like everywhere else in the world at the time, as far as we know, was full of popular spells and superstitions. Three nights before the death of the Medici banker and art patron, Lorenzo the Magnificent in 1492, lightning struck the cathedral, sending stones from the famous dome crashing to the street. Florentines said Lorenzo had a demon trapped in his ring and had released it as he sensed his impending death. In 1478, when Jacopo Pazzi was hanged for his part in a conspiracy against Medici rule, heavy rains threatened the survival of the grain crop. Popular wisdom was that it was Jacopo's fault: His burial in consecrated ground had offended God; so he was dug up and dragged stinking through the streets, while the mob battered his remains before flinging them into the Arno River.

Belief in magic was not just a vulgar error. There was learned magic, too. The notion that human agency could control nature was a perfectly rational one. Promising approaches included techniques we now classify as scientific, such as observation, experiment, and the exercise of reason. Astrology, alchemy, conjuration, and sorcery had not yet proved to be false leads. For what is the difference between magic and science? Both are attempts to explain and therefore to control nature. Western science of the sixteenth and seventeenth centuries grew, in part, out of magic. The vocations of scientists overlapped with those of magicians—wielders of magical techniques for mastering nature.

In any case, chivalry was more characteristic than humanism in the values and education of most members of the elite. **Chivalry** could not, perhaps, make men good, as it was supposed to do. It could, however, win wars. In 1492, for instance, the monarchs of the Spanish kingdom of Castile extended the frontier of Christendom by conquering Granada, the last Muslim kingdom in Spain, in what the Venetian ambassador called "a beautiful war." "There was not a lord present who was not enamored of some lady," who "often handed warriors their weapons…with a request that they show their love by their deeds." Queen Isabella II of Castile (r. 1474–1504) died uttering prayers to the Archangel Michael as "prince of the chivalry of angels."

The typical chivalrous hero of the time took to the sea, conquered an island, married a princess, and became a ruler. Explorers—often men of humble social origins—tried to embody these fictions in real life. Adventurers in the service of the Portuguese Prince Henry (1394–1460), included former pirates and violent criminals. They indulged in chivalric rituals and gave themselves storybook names, like Lancelot and Tristram of the Island. They also colonized the Madeira Islands and parts of the Azores, and explored the coast of West Africa as far as Sierra Leone. The commercial sector that helped to back overseas adventures was looking for new opportunities—especially the Genoese, whose role in the eastern Mediterranean at this period was largely confined to high-bulk, low-profit shipping and trading. Marginal noblemen, shut out from advancement at home and imbued with chivalric ideas, were willing to take amazing risks. That, together with the availability of high-risk investment, helps to explain many early forays in Atlantic exploration.

Prince Henry himself—traditionally misrepresented as a navigator motivated by scientific curiosity—imagined himself a romantic hero, destined to perform great deeds and win a kingdom of his own. The truth is that he never went exploring, and his desperate efforts to make enough money to pay his retainers included slave raiding and a soap monopoly. His followers included the father-in-law of Christopher Columbus, a weaver by training who reinvented himself as a "captain of cavaliers and conquests," and who took to exploration to escape the restricted social opportunities of home.

Alongside chivalry, millenarian fantasies may have influenced overseas expansion. The first king of Portugal's ruling dynasty was actually called "Messiah of Portugal." Columbus claimed that the profits of his discoveries could be used to conquer Jerusalem and help complete God's plans for a new age. Franciscan friars who supported Columbus believed that an "Age of the Holy Spirit," which would precede the end of the world, was coming soon, and some of them came to see the New World as the place where such an age might begin.

Europe's outreach into the Atlantic was probably not the result of science or strength, so much as of delusion and desperation. This was a space race where it helped to come from behind. The prosperous cultures with access to the Indian Ocean felt no need to explore remote lands and seas for new resources. For cash-strapped Europe, however, the attempt to exploit the Atlantic for new products was like the efforts of underdeveloped countries today, anxiously drilling for offshore wealth from oil or natural gas. In some ways, it paid off.

> *"Europe's outreach into the Atlantic was probably not the result of science or strength, so much as of delusion and desperation. This was a space race where it helped to come from behind."*

In Perspective
Beyond Empires

The imperial habit was spreading, and new empires were forming in environments that had never experienced imperialism before. Russia, for example, extended empire to the Eurasian far north. Mwene Mutapa introduced it in sub-Saharan East Africa. The Aztecs and Incas practiced it in the Americas on an unprecedented scale. Nonetheless, most of Africa and the Americas, as well as the whole of Australia and most of the Pacific island world, as far as we know, had still not experienced anything like empire. While some empires revived, most of the world remained in the hands of communities with modest political ambitions. These were still organized as kinship networks, chiefdoms, or small states. More remarkably, perhaps, some regions with an imperial past, or under imperialist threat, shied away. Instead, they developed systems in which independent states coexisted with varying degrees of mutual hostility. The world of the late fourteenth and fifteenth centuries had four such areas.

In North Africa, Mamluk Egypt was an immensely rich and productive state but remained confined to the Nile valley, unable to expand beyond the deserts that fringed it. A second area lay westward, along Africa's Mediterranean coast. Here numerous small states, founded on the profits of trade or piracy, flourished where Mediterranean and Saharan trade routes met. At the western end of North Africa, Morocco emerged as a kingdom on the edge of the Islamic world, holding Christendom at bay.

South and southeast Asia was a third empire-free region. In India, the sultanate of Delhi never fully recovered from the setbacks of the mid–fourteenth century. Hindu states proliferated, some warlike, specifically, toward Islam. The most militaristic, perhaps, was Vijayanagar—the name means "City of Victories"—with its 60 miles of sevenfold walls (see Map 15.9). This was the state, for

MAP 15.9

Vijayanagar

extent of Vijayanagar Empire, circa 1500

Absolute sovereignty. The artist of the Wilton Diptych is unknown, but it is regarded as one of the most exquisite paintings of the fourteenth century. It is a propaganda work, emphasizing the claims of King Richard II of England (r. 1377–1399), to sacred responsibilities. His heavenly patrons, St. John the Baptist, and two earlier, sainted English kings, present him to the Blessed Virgin Mary, whose angel-attendants wear Richard's badge—the emblem of the white stag—and carry the English flag. Most interpreters suppose that the message of the painting is that the Virgin is entrusting Richard with the realm of England, symbolized by the flag, but his hands seem open to receive the Christ Child himself—symbolism suitable to a traveling altarpiece, probably designed to be set up whenever the king wished to hear mass during a journey.

which Abd-ar-Razzak, the Persian ambassador mentioned at the start of the chapter, was bound in 1417. It impressed another Muslim visitor in 1443 as "such that the eye has seen nothing like it." Chinese expansion nibbled at the edges of southeast Asia, but China's renunciation of imperialism left the native states of the region free to try one another's strength. The Thai—founders of what is now called Thailand—certainly had expansionist ambitions. In the early fifteenth century, they created the region's largest state at the expense of their neighbors, the Burmese, Khmer, Mons, and Malays (see Map 15.8). Nonetheless, the region lacked a dominant empire and remained home to a state system in which a number of regional states contended with each other.

Finally, most of Europe continued to enclose a state system. East of the Vistula River, where geography favored the formation of large, unstable states by conquest, Russia, as we have seen, undertook a massive imperial enterprise. A brief union of the Polish and Lithuanian states in 1386 created what, on the map, at least, also looked like an empire of daunting dimensions, stretching from the Baltic to the Black Sea. Farther west, however, small states got stronger, and the dream of reuniting them and recreating the old Roman Empire faded—or began to look unrealistic.

Something like what we now call **nationalism** emerged. That is, group feeling developed where people's mutually intelligible speech and a common sense of identity defined by birth caused them to merge into a single community. In the fifteenth century, for instance, the kings of England began to use English, alongside

French and Latin, in official documents and correspondence. National communities adopted patron saints. At international gatherings, such as universities and church councils, people defined themselves according the nation to which they belonged and engaged in ferocious disputes over precedence. At a Council of the Church in 1415, the Castilian delegation settled such a dispute with the English by overturning the bench on which their rivals were sitting, so that the Castilians could occupy a higher place in the hall.

States increasingly asserted their absolute sovereignty, rejecting any obligation to defer to such traditionally supranational authorities as the church or the Holy Roman Emperor. When, for instance, the Emperor Sigismund visited England in 1415, a knight rode into the sea to challenge him to renounce all claim to authority in England before he was allowed to disembark. Kings of France called themselves "emperors in their own realm" and those of Castile in Spain asserted "my sovereign absolute power."

Some rulers developed ideological grounds for their claims to absolute sovereignty. French kings were supposedly endowed with divine powers to heal and able to perform "miracles in your own lifetime." Richard II of England (r. 1377–1399) had himself painted in a sumptuous image, attended by angels, opening his hands to receive the body of Christ from the hands of the Virgin Mary herself.

At the same time, the power of the state really did increase. One reason was improved communications. As paper replaced parchment, increasing the output of documents, royal bureaucracies reached more people in more parts of the realm. Changes in the concept of law also strengthened the state. Traditionally, the law was seen as a body of wisdom handed down from the past. Now it came to be seen as a code that kings and parliaments could endlessly change and recreate. The state's power also expanded over vast new areas of public life and common welfare: labor relations, wages, prices, forms of land tenure, markets, the food supply, livestock breeding, and even, in some cases, what personal adornments people could wear.

Finally, while the state was growing more powerful, the power of the church declined. Between 1378 and 1415, rulers in Latin Christendom could not agree whom to recognize as pope. The power vacuum eroded what little unity Christendom still had. Secular states became stronger as heresies arose. Under the influence of reformers who demanded—among other changes—lay control of appointments in the church and worship in everyday language instead of Latin, Bohemia for a time refused to recognize papal authority. Reformers known as conciliarists argued that the church should become a kind of republic, with power transferred from Rome to a council of bishops who would meet periodically in a kind of parliament.

Chronology

ca. 1325	Aztecs found city of Tenochtitlán
1368	Beginning of Ming dynasty
1370–1406	Reign of Timur
Late fourteenth century	Ethiopia expands into surrounding regions
1401	Lorenzo Ghiberti wins competition for the bronze doors of the Bapistery in Florence
1405	First voyage of Zheng He
1417	Voyage of Abd-ar-Razzak to Vijayanagar (India)
1430s	Portuguese establish way stations in Azores
1440s	Portuguese begin to obtain slaves from West Africa
ca. 1450	Inca begin period of expansion and conquest
1453	Ottomans capture Constantinople
1462–1505	Reign of Ivan the Great
ca. 1475	Center of power in southern Africa shifts from Zimbabwe to Mwene Mutapa
1480s	Portuguese make contact with kingdom of Kongo
1482	Portuguese establish trading post of São Jorge da Mina on West African coast
1484	Sugar production begins in Canary Islands
1490s	First Portuguese diplomatic missions arrive in Ethiopia
1492–1493	First voyage of Christopher Columbus; Spanish kingdom of Castile captures Granada, last Muslim kingdom in Spain
1496	John Cabot discovers direct route across North Atlantic
1497	Pilgrimage of Muhammed Touray Askia, ruler of Songhay, to Mecca; first voyage of Vasco da Gama
1500	Vasco da Gama reaches India; Aztec Empire at its peak

"The expanding empires of the age were reaching toward each other. Where they made contact, they became arenas of unprecedented scale for trade and for transmitting technology, ideas, sentiments, and ways of life."

How much difference did the state system make to Europe's prospects? Historians have engaged in a pointless debate over this question. On the one hand, the state system deprived Europeans of unified command, of the sort found, for instance, in the Chinese or Ottoman Empires. On the other hand, it stimulated competition among rulers, multiplying the possible sources of patronage available to innovators. For European maritime expansion, the state system was not decisive in launching most initiatives. The explorers and would-be empire builders relied on private enterprise, with little or no state backing. Columbus, for instance, got no direct financial support from the Spanish crown—the myth that Queen Isabella of Castile pawned her jewels for him is nonsense. Prince Henry's Atlantic enterprise was a private venture. Furthermore, as the example of Southeast Asia shows, a state system was not in itself sufficient to produce overseas imperialism; for that, the stimulus of coming from behind was necessary. Asian states were at the nodes of the world's richest trades. They had no need to explore new markets or conquer new centers of production, because everything came to them anyway. Europeans, on the other hand, had to expand if they were to gain access to anything worth exploiting.

For all its hesitations and limitations, fifteenth-century expansion was new and potentially world changing. The new routes pioneered in the 1490s linked the populous central belt of Eurasia to the Americas and Africa, and Europe to Asia by sea. We can see the beginnings of an interconnected globe—a **world system** able to encompass the planet. The expanding empires of the age were reaching toward each other. Where they made contact, they became arenas of unprecedented scale for trade and for transmitting technology, ideas, sentiments, and ways of life. The consequences would transform the world of the next three centuries: Worldwide encounters, commerce, conflict, contagion, and cultural and ecological exchange would follow.

PROBLEMS AND PARALLELS

1. Why was the last half of the fifteenth century an age of expansion? How did the beginnings of a world system emerge around 1500?

2. Why were African states fragile in this period? How did Muhammad Touray Askia use Islam to make Songhay the dominant power in West Africa?

3. What does the term *ecological imperialism* mean? How did the Inca exploit the many different ecosystems of their empire? What was role of tributary networks in the Aztec Empire?

4. How did the Russian and Turkish worlds expand in the fourteenth and fifteenth centuries? What was the impact of Timur's conquests on the Islamic world?

5. Why did the Chinese turn away from maritime expansionism after the voyages of Zheng He? Why was frontier stability more important than overseas expansion for China? Why did the Hongxi emperor reinstate Confucian values at the Chinese court?

6. Why were wind systems so important in world history? Why did the beginnings of European oceanic imperialism have as much to do with geography as with culture?

7. How did the rise of nationalism and the state system drive European expansion? Why were there no major empires in North Africa or in South Asia during this period?

READ ON ▶ ▶ ▶

The material on Abd-ar-Razzak comes from R. H. Major, ed., *India in the Fifteenth Century* (1964). D. Ringrose, *Expansion and Global Interaction, 1200–1700* (2001) gives the background.

On Ethiopia, S. C. Munro-Hay, *Ethiopia: the Unknown Land* (2002) and R. Pankhurst, *The Ethiopians: A History* (2001) are valuable general histories. W. G. Randles, *The Empire of Monomotapa* (1975) is excellent on Mwene Mutapa. On West Africa in this period, E. W. R. Bovill, *The Golden Trade of the Moors* (1995) is a readable classic. Songhay is not well served by books in English but a useful collection of sources is J. O. Hunwick, ed., *Timbuktu and the Songhay Empire: Al-Sa'di's Ta'rîkh al-Sudan down to 1613, and Other Contemporary Documents* (1999). Anne Hilton, *The Kingdom of Kongo* (1985) is outstanding.

Of histories of the Inca and Aztecs, J. V. Murra, *The Economic Organization of the Inca State* (1980), T.N. D'Altroy, *The Incas* (2003), and M. Smith, *The Aztecs* (2002) are particularly strong on ecological aspects.

My material on the White Sea comes from R. Cormack and D. Gaze, eds, *Art of Holy Russia* (1998). J. Martin, *Treasures of the Land of Darkness* (2004) is enthralling on the economic background to Russian expansion. I. Gray, *Ivan III and the Unification of Russia* (1972) is a businesslike introduction. Ibn Khaldun's great work is *The Muqaddimah: An Introduction to History*, tr. Franz Rosenthal (1969). B. F. Manz, *The Rise and Rule of Tamerlane* (1999) is the outstanding work on its subject.

For the Ottomans, see H. Inalcik, *The Ottoman Empire: the Classical Age* (2001). E.L. Dreyer, *Early Ming China* (1982) and *Zheng He: China and the Oceans in the Early Ming Dynasty* (2006) cover the Chinese topics of this chapter admirably. L. Levathes, *When China Ruled the Seas* (1997) is readable and reliable.

On Europe C. Allmand, ed, *The New Cambridge Medieval History, VII* (2005) is comprehensive, while M. Aston, *The Prospect of Europe* (1968) offers a short introduction. On Portuguese expansion, P.E. Russell, *Henry the Navigator* (2001) is admirable and F. Bethencourt and D. Curto, eds, *Portuguese Oceanic Expansion* (1998) provides a broad survey. P.O. Kristeller, *The Cambridge Companion to Renaissance Humanism* (1996) is an unsurpassed classic on its topic and M.H. Keen, *Chivalry* (1986) is on the way to attaining the same status.

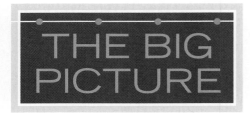

THE BIG PICTURE

The World in 1491

In the thirteenth century, as we pointed out in Chapter 13, the Mongol peace proved a greater stimulus to the migration of ideas and technologies across Eurasia than all previous empires had achieved. In part, the Mongols' outreach was a response to climate change, as cooling shriveled their grasslands. In the fourteenth century, observers began to notice unsteadily increasing cold. Glacial evidence shows that global cold lasted—with varying intensity—until the eighteenth century. In most of Eurasia and North Africa, climate change nourished the diseases contemporaries called plague. As long as the cold period lasted, so did frequent plagues.

The Mongol peace exceeded previous empires as a stimulus to the migration of ideas and technologies, while merchants, missionaries, and pilgrims pioneered ever more intensive communications that bound together Eurasia and parts of North, East, and West Africa. Gradually, with gathering pace in the fifteenth century and dramatic acceleration from the sixteenth century onward, convergence began to replace divergence as the dominant theme in the history of human cultures. After millennia of divergence, it seems amazing that the process should have been halted and reversed.

Explorers found routes across the Atlantic, which for the first time linked Europe and Africa to the Americas. They sailed around Africa to connect Europe by sea with the lands around the Indian Ocean, the world's richest zone of commerce. Cultural exchange stimulated Western arts and learning, though from the perspective of Islam, India, or China—Westerners remained relatively backward and poor. Over a longer period, empires and trade overleaped oceans, taking people, animals, plants, deadly microbes, and forms of culture with them. Parts of the globe that had grown unalike now began, slowly and selectively at first, to resemble each other once again as they had before the continents had drifted apart millions of years ago.

▶ QUESTIONS

1. Based on the globes shown here, which cultures were experiencing the most convergence in 1491? Which cultures were mostly divergent from other cultures?

2. In 1491, which ocean was the biggest and richest zone of long range commerce? Is there any evidence in the globes shown here that the Atlantic would emerge in the sixteenth century as a major zone of cultural and ecological exchange?

To view an interactive version of this map, as well as a video of the author describing key themes related to this Part, go to www.myhistorylab.com

Chinese Exploration by c. 1491

- ■ Known and mapped in detail
- □ Known by observation or report but not mapped in detail

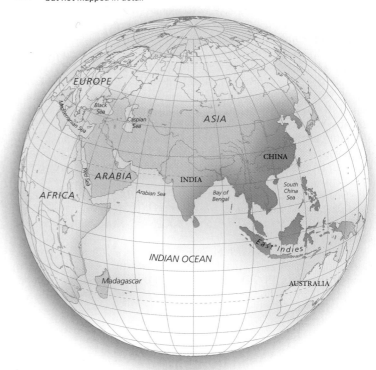

Japanese Knowledge of the World, c. 1491

- ■ Known in detail
- □ Known by report

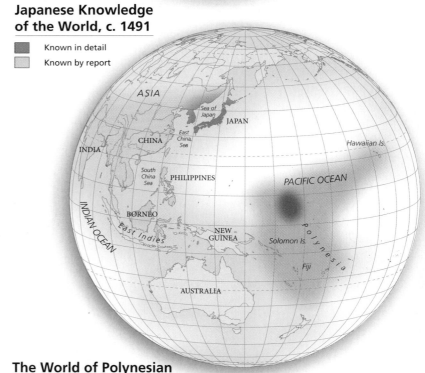

The World of Polynesian Navigators by c. 1491

- ■ Known and mapped in detail
- □ Known but not mapped

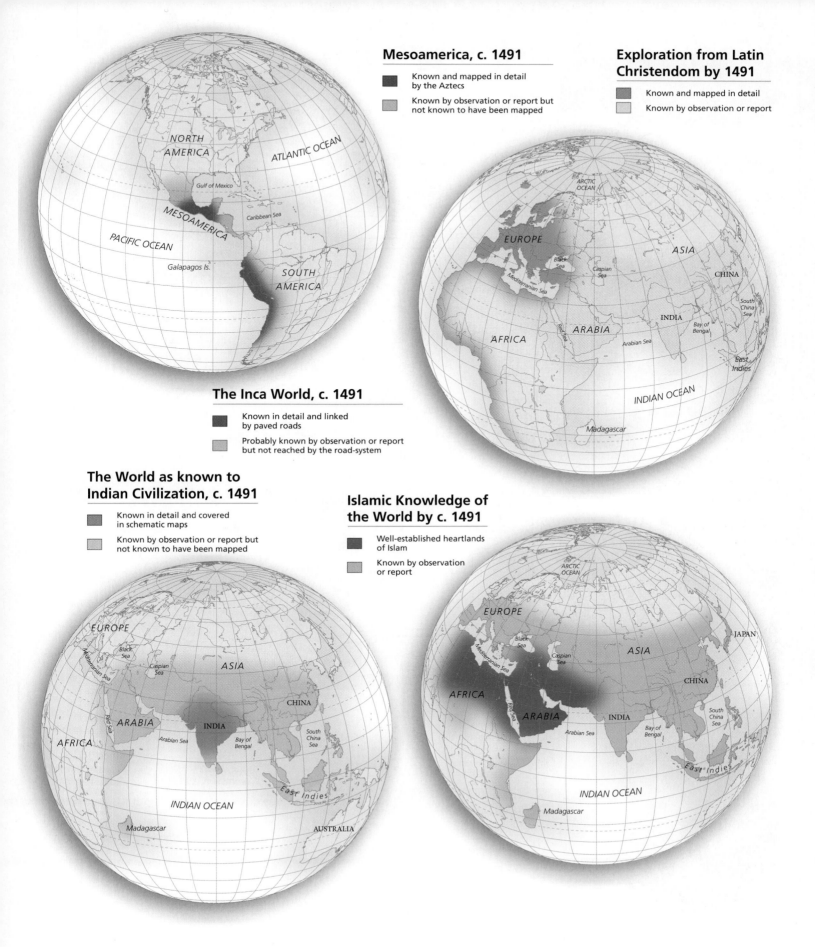

Mesoamerica, c. 1491

- Known and mapped in detail by the Aztecs
- Known by observation or report but not known to have been mapped

Exploration from Latin Christendom by 1491

- Known and mapped in detail
- Known by observation or report

The Inca World, c. 1491

- Known in detail and linked by paved roads
- Probably known by observation or report but not reached by the road-system

The World as known to Indian Civilization, c. 1491

- Known in detail and covered in schematic maps
- Known by observation or report but not known to have been mapped

Islamic Knowledge of the World by c. 1491

- Well-established heartlands of Islam
- Known by observation or report

PART 7

ENVIRONMENT

since 1492
Columbian exchange

since 1513
Atlantic navigation—
Gulf Stream mastered

CULTURE

ca. 1500–1600
Portuguese maritime
empire at its height

Convergence and Divergence to ca. 1700

◀ **A Mixtec world-view,** ca. 1500, painted on deer hide. At the center of the world the god Xiutecutli or Yahui spills the life forces of fire and blood. Trees grow toward each of four directions. At the top, a sun disc, rising over temple steps, signifies east. In the west, where the sun sets, the tree is uncolored.

National Museums and Galleries on Merseyside, Liverpool, England, U.K.

since 1565
Pacific navigation—Japan
current mastered

since early 1600s
Dutch navigation of
"roaring 40s"

since ca. 1640
Decline of steppelands

mid–16th century
Atlantic slave trade takes off

ca. 1550–1650
Expansion of Asian
empires

1640
Closing of Japan

1600–1700
Western Scientific Revolution

CHAPTER 16

Imperial Arenas: New Empires in the Sixteenth and Seventeenth Centuries

▲ **Imperial conflict.** Portuguese, armed mainly with bows, resist the attack on Hormuz, which restored the island fortress to Persian rule, in 1622. This was the first of a long series of campaigns in which indigenous powers ejected the Portuguese from their trading outposts on the coasts of Asia and East Africa.

PERSIAN GULF

The letter was only one page long. But Jeronimo de Quadros put his heart into it, as he poured out his troubles to his king. In 1572, after a career spent fighting up and down the east coast of Africa and Arabia and in the Persian Gulf, he had succeeded his father as commander of a Portuguese fort on the Persian mainland, at a spot the Portuguese called Comorão, modern Kumora. Sixteen years later, he was concerned about the rewards for service he hoped to receive back home. By the end of the 1580s, those concerns were becoming urgent. Native enemies had captured all the other Portuguese strongholds in the region. Jeronimo de Quadros's own fort was becoming indefensible. He had, he wrote, only 7 Portuguese and 45 native mercenaries under his command. With these, he had to man the fort, control local marauders, and escort traders who might want to do business with Portugal. He had difficulty keeping his men supplied with arrows. Gunpowder and shot were so far beyond his reach that they were not even worth mentioning. Every year, he explained, he had to rebuild his fort after the rains "because it is made of mud." His most revealing problem was the want of sufficient opium to meet the needs of his men. Their task was so hopeless, in this remote and abandoned corner of an overextended empire, that they could only face it with the help of narcotics. Though the fate of Jeronimo de Quadros is unknown, his fort finally fell into enemy hands shortly afterward. Now, like all the Portuguese forts that once dotted the region, it lies in ruins. Quadros's predicament was typical of the sixteenth, seventeenth, and eighteenth centuries, when empires seemed to overreach the limits of the possible and to exceed the scope of the technology at their command.

Nowadays, *empire* has become one of the dirty words of politics. Politicians, exchanging abuse across the world, commonly call each other "imperialists." We recoil from the idea that any political community should be subject to another. It seems to go against our respect for principles we call freedom or self-determination. But from the sixteenth century to the eighteenth, when the unprecedented growth of empires was one of the most dramatic features of the history of the world, empires spread as much by collaboration as by conquest. They were not usually held together by force, because no state had enough resources for such a task. The moral effects of empires on their subjects were mixed. Some communities were victimized, subjugated, exterminated, or enslaved, while enhanced economic opportunities enriched others, as markets grew and trade routes lengthened. Above all, empires were arenas of exchange—and not solely or primarily of exchange of trade. They stimulated—and sometimes enforced—human migrations on a scale never previously undertaken, over unprecedented distances, and in unprecedented

FOCUS questions

How were empires the agents of change in the sixteenth and seventeenth centuries?

Why did the Dutch replace the Portuguese as the main European imperial power in Asia?

How were maritime empires different from land empires in Asia during the sixteenth and seventeenth centuries?

What roles did war and conquest play in the Mughal and Ottoman empires?

Why were Native Americans so important in the Spanish conquests of the Aztec and Inca empires?

Why did the global balance of trade begin to shift during the seventeenth century?

directions. Technologies, religions, political ideas, and artistic tastes became interchangeable across vast distances as never before.

Finally—and perhaps most importantly—**imperialism** helped to introduce a new era in evolution. Formerly, for hundreds of millions of years, ever since the continents of the world began to drift apart, the life forms of landmasses divided by uncrossable oceans developed independently of one another. Each continent had its own peculiar plant and animal life. Everything tended to be different—from human types to microbes. About 500 years ago, this long history of divergence ended. As empires crossed oceans, the continents came into mutual contact. They swapped life forms. The world we inhabit today began to take shape—in which you can find specimens of the same creatures, wherever climate permits, all over the world (see Chapter 17).

So empires offer a framework for understanding all the major long-range, long-run changes of the period. Western historians used to see the empires founded from Western Europe as the sources of the most important initiatives, and even to call the period as a whole the "Age of European Expansion." But imperialism was not a peculiarly Western vice. Asian, African, and Native American peoples created and led some of the most impressive empires of the period. And the "European" empires usually depended on non-European collaborators who saw an advantage in cooperating with the Europeans. Indeed, the numbers of Europeans involved in creating the empires and making them work were normally small compared with the numbers of native peoples or of non-European migrants from elsewhere. The influences that shaped the empires and made them different from one another generally owed more to environmental or economic circumstances than to their home countries and the traditional allegiances of their ruling elites.

MARITIME EMPIRES: PORTUGAL, JAPAN, AND THE DUTCH

Until about 500 years ago, most empires were concerned with controlling large amounts of two resources: people and land. They may have had ideological or religious reasons for wanting to extend their territorial control; or they may have engaged in conquests out of hatred or insecurity. The economic purpose underlying empire, however, was usually to gain control of, or power over, the places and people that produced valuable goods.

Less commonly, imperial communities could enrich themselves by controlling trade as well as, or even instead of, production. By land, imperialism of this kind is hard to achieve without occupying vast amounts of territory, because traders tend to find ways to outflank imperialists. At sea, however, the opportunities are better. By seizing what is often a limited number of suitable ports, or by patrolling what are often limited routes of access that winds, currents, and straits shape, imperial-minded people can obtain a stranglehold on trade in some commodities, within some climatic or geographical zones. Or they can colonize limited amounts of coastal territory that seaborne communications link, to produce and ship commercial commodities for their own profit. As we have seen, empires of these kinds flourished—briefly and at intervals—in the ancient and medieval Mediterranean and in parts of maritime Asia.

From the sixteenth to the eighteenth centuries, opportunities multiplied to found and extend such empires. Technological improvements accompanied the new opportunities. European or European-designed ships began to rival, and even excel, those of traditional Asian construction, partly thanks to borrowings from Asian technology, such as rudders, bulkheads between the ship's interior compartments, more streamlined designs for long-range commercial vessels, and technical aids that enabled navigators to determine their position by the sun and stars. Improvements in artillery and fortifications made it ever easier to defend coastal forts and trading posts. Naval powers that mustered enough shipping and shipboard firepower could use convoys to control sea lanes or even exclude rival ships by aggressive policing. Meanwhile, sea charts—which professional seamen traditionally despised because it was a matter of professional pride for them to navigate by memory and experience—gradually became an accepted and necessary part of nautical equipment. The expanding reach of exploration helped to improve these nautical maps. Gradually, too, longitude-finding techniques improved. In 1584, King Philip II of Spain decreed a prize for anyone who could solve the problem of determining longitude at sea. Other states initiated similar schemes. A long and fitful series of improvements followed, although no really reliable method was devised until the late eighteenth century.

Improved technology, however, was of little use without new routes where it could be deployed. As we saw in detail in Chapter 15, until the sixteenth century, the world's only really effective long-range, ocean-crossing routes were confined to monsoonal seas. This was chiefly because **monsoons** are seasonal. They blow toward land in summer—sucked landward by warming air, rising over large landmasses. In winter, the direction of the wind is reversed. Navigators therefore know that if they venture out to sea with a following wind, they will be able eventually to return home. By contrast, in the **fixed wind systems** of the Atlantic and Pacific oceans, the direction of the prevailing winds never shifts for long. The ambitious navigator's choice is bleak: to risk a voyage with a following wind, taking you ever farther from home, with the prospect of never being able to return; or to sail against a headwind and probably never get far. In consequence, shipping crossed and re-crossed the monsoonal seas of the Indian Ocean and maritime Asia for

Navigator. The Florentine adventurer, Amerigo Vespucci (1451–1512), presides triumphantly over this world map of 1507. The map's maker, Martin Waldseemüller, considered Vespucci as the equal of the greatest cosmographers of antiquity, and shows him here wielding a huge pair of mapmakers's dividers, alongside a map of the lands Waldseemüller called "America" in Amerigo's honor. Yet Vespucci's reputation as a navigator and explorer rested entirely on his own say-so. He campaigned for "scientific" navigation—using instruments to sail his ships, rather than relying on tradition and practical knowledge—but used instruments incompetently. He often promised to make maps of the lands he encountered in his voyages but never seems to have done so.

> "As explorers cracked the wind codes of the world's oceans, previously inconceivable interconnections became possible: directly between Europe and the Indian Ocean; between America and Asia; or among Europe, Africa, and the Americas."

centuries, creating dynamic economies and generating enormous wealth, before the Atlantic or Pacific was developed as a major trading space. In the sixteenth century, however, the monopoly of the Indian Ocean ended. With the discovery of the Gulf Stream in 1513, the last major element of the wind and current system of the Atlantic became known to navigators. Thereafter, the principal routes of trade from Europe to Africa and the Americas and back were established in the form that has remained normal for seaborne commerce to the present day: outward bound with easterly trade winds, toward the Caribbean and the central zones of the Americas, then northward with the Gulf Stream to the region of westerlies that bring ships back to Europe. In the Pacific in the 1520s and 1530s, Spanish navigators explored the easterly wind corridors that link the New World to Asia, but the route back long eluded explorers. After many unsuccessful attempts to find it, an expedition of 1564–1565 solved the problem by exploiting the way the winds circulate in the northern Pacific, using the Japan Current to get back to the west coast of America from the Philippines. Finally, in the early seventeenth century, Dutch sailors began to exploit fierce westerly winds that enable sailing ships to circle the globe around 40 degrees latitude south. This made it possible to link the commerce of the Atlantic, Pacific, and Indian oceans with new speed and reliability. In particular, the Dutch opened a fast new route between Europe and the East Indies, sailing nonstop, if necessary—or with a stop or two at the island of St. Helena in the middle of the South Atlantic and at the Cape of Good Hope on the southern tip of Africa—all the way from Holland to Java in what is today Indonesia. The speediest method was to bypass the Indian Ocean to the south with the westerlies, then turn north with the Great Australia Current, skirting the coast of western Australia, and heading directly for the Sunda Strait toward the East Indies (see Map 16.1).

As explorers cracked the wind codes of the world's oceans, previously inconceivable interconnections became possible: directly between Europe and the Indian Ocean; between America and Asia; or among Europe, Africa, and the Americas.

Making Connections | LAND EMPIRES AND MARITIME EMPIRES COMPARED

TYPE OF EMPIRE	CHARACTERISTICS
Maritime	Control of international trade via strategic seizure of suitable ports, control of sea-lanes
	Colonization of limited coastal territory
	Production and shipment of high-value commodities
	Limited military confrontation and investment in imperial colonies
	Exploitation of improved maritime technology
	Expanded use of sea charts for exploration, control of far-flung regions
	Dependence on native collaborators
Land	Emphasis on control of large amounts of people and land
	Large military investment required to staff outposts and fund armies
	Land and sea access routes vulnerable unless controlled
	Massive capital investment to support imperial colonies and build infrastructure
	Superior technology needed to overcome resistance from natives
	Expanded social and cultural contacts with imperial subjects
	Dependence on native collaborators

The Portuguese Example

On an unprecedented scale, Europeans could now gain access to the commerce of the Indian Ocean and maritime Asia. The main motive was simple. The economies of the region were hugely richer and more productive than those of Europe. Anyone who could get ships into the region and carry some of its trade could make money here. Moreover, the region produced luxury manufactures of a quality Europeans could not produce for themselves: textiles, especially, from India and China, and increasingly, as time went on and trade developed, porcelain from China and Japan. Even more important were the foodstuffs, drugs, and spices that only grew in environments that could not be reproduced in Europe, and that were expensive because they were as much in demand in China as in Europe. Pepper dominated the spice trade because cuisine at the time in both Europe and China privileged it as a flavor and because—with other spices—it was much used in pickling processes that, along with drying and salting, were for a long time the only

MAP 16.1

Maritime Imperialism in the Indian and Pacific Oceans, 1500–1700

- ◆ Portuguese trading post with date
- ◇ Dutch trading post with date
- ◆ Spanish trading post with date
- ◆ English trading post with date
- ○ major Chinese port
- → Japanese campaigns in Korea, 1592–1598
- → Japanese expansion
- → trade routes
- → Manila galleon from Mexico
- → Dutch route to the East Indies
- → Great Australian Current

ways to preserve food. Finally, eastern seas attracted European traders because their markets were highly exploitable. Gold was relatively cheap, in exchange for silver, in China, but relatively expensive in India. Canny traders could make fortunes out of the difference.

Portugal was well placed to take advantage, partly thanks to a position on the Atlantic edge, close to the place from which the trade winds spring. After dividing up zones of navigation by agreement with their Spanish neighbors, the Portuguese began to penetrate the Indian Ocean. Portuguese venturers opened direct trade with the pepper-growing region of southern India in 1500 and founded a coastal trading post nearby at Goa in 1510. They established direct access to the trading world of the islands off Southeast Asia within a few years more. They began direct contact with Thailand and China in the second decade of the sixteenth century and with Japan in the 1540s.

In some ways, the Portuguese enterprise in Asia was a classic case of maritime imperialism. Portuguese took over Malacca in modern Malaysia to try to gain an advantage in directing trade through the Strait of Malacca. They used force to compel unwilling partners to trade with them, especially in the "Spice Islands" of what is now eastern Indonesia, where low-bulk, high-value goods, such as cloves and the products of nutmeg and sandalwood and other aromatic woods were obtainable. They attacked rival shipping to damage other people's trade. They established expensive bases at the mouth of the Red Sea, on the coast of East Africa, and in the Persian Gulf—and, eventually, even on the Persian coast—in unsuccessful efforts to divert trade into their own hands and to strangle alternative routes. In 1529,

Chronology: Maritime Imperialism: Technology and Sea Routes

1513	Gulf Stream discovered
1520s–1530s	Spanish navigators explore easterly wind corridors that link the New World to Asia
1564–1565	Northern Pacific route between Asia and New World discovered
1584	Philip II of Spain offers prize for solving problem of longitude at sea
Early seventeenth century	Dutch use westerlies to circumnavigate globe

The Portuguese in India. "Unmarried Christian ladies" of contrasting complexions, with their chaperone watching from her palanquin, exchange courtesies with a gentleman in sixteenth-century Portuguese India.

they agreed with Spain to extend to the Pacific the system they had already agreed to observe in the Atlantic, in which each guaranteed the other's monopoly over selected routes, while denying access to the shipping of other powers. In effect, they divided between them seaborne routes to the non-European world. In the early seventeenth century, Portugal tried to control by force the trade of Sri Lanka—the world's main source of cinnamon (see Map 16.1).

Still, Portuguese imperialism was, by the standards of native Asian empires of the day, a feeble and shallow affair—a minor irritant, causing only local or temporary disruption. Portugal was a small country, with only 1.5 million inhabitants and few natural resources, except large salt pans and privileged access to the sea. It was poorer and less populous even than the Netherlands.

The main business of the Portuguese was to participate as shippers and traders in the existing commerce of Asia, along traditional routes. Direct trade with Europe was not significant for Asia, but was important for Europe; and it grew throughout the period. Three or four Portuguese ships a year carried the whole of the Indian pepper trade to Europe in the 1590s. In the 1680s and 1690s, when other European trading communities had joined in the business, 800 ships left Europe for Asia, most of them destined to return with Asian goods. But direct dealing with Europe was only a secondary element in the lives of most Portuguese in Asia. Most of Asia's Portuguese, indeed, lived beyond areas of Portuguese rule, as servants, mercenaries, technicians, missionaries, or commercial agents in Asian states. They were welcome, because their trading activities and their work as shippers in established trades contributed to the further enrichment of existing economies.

Francisco Vieira da Figueiredo was a representative figure. Like many poor Portuguese soldiers in the east, he resorted to trade to make a living. He was a chameleon who moved with ease through the various colorful islands between the Indian Ocean and the South China Sea. He served in 1642 as the envoy to

The *Estado da India*. The empire that the Portuguese called the *Estado da India* was actually a string of trading posts around the edges of the Indian Ocean and East Asia. The outposts depicted here were in India in 1630, shortly before Portugal began to withdraw from most of the region in the face of native hostility and Dutch competition. Note how lightly fortified most of these places are and how several of them include mosques—sometimes within, sometimes outside the walls. Like other European overseas expansion, that of Portugal depended on native people's willingness to collaborate with it and tolerate it.

Cambodia of a Spanish governor of Manila. He dealt with the Dutch East India Company, even when they were at war with Portugal. He became the intimate adviser of the sultan of Makassar in what is today Indonesia, the envoy of the ruler of Golconda in India, and a commercial agent for both of them. His object, according to English competitors, was "gain of wealth." Though he often talked of returning to Portugal, he was in his element in the east, where he could affect gentlemanly rank and presume on princely friends. His life was adapted for mobility. In Makassar, like other foreigners, he was forbidden to build a permanent residence. So he lived in a bamboo shack. But his real palace was his magnificently appointed yacht. As a trader, his first interest was in textiles from Coromandel in southeast India. He then specialized in aromatic woods from Indonesian islands, gold and silver from Sumatra and the Philippines, and cloves from the Molucca Islands, which were the chief item of Makassar's trade. In 1664, when the Dutch forced him out of Makassar, he went to the island of Timor and dealt in sandalwood until his death three years later.

Typically, the Portuguese blended into local society as well as local politics and regional trade by marrying or living with local women, who supported their husbands' business. Schemes to promote the supply of "eligible maidens" from Europe for Europeans living in the east were frequently launched and usually failed, or they supplied women of dubious background and morals. African or Indian wives administered their Portuguese husbands' estates while the latter were away on trading voyages. According to an English male visitor, wives acquired in the Portuguese East African possession of Mozambique excelled European women for "fidelity, behaviour to their husband, good-natured dispositions and agreeable conversation, so far as their little knowledge extends." Moralists accused some Portuguese in Goa and Bassein in Burma (today called Myanmar) of large-scale pimping, training dancing girls in their personal harems, and selling them as Hindu-temple prostitutes. The usual pattern, however, more resembled a scene engraved on a famous ivory casket from seventeenth-century Sri Lanka in which a Portuguese merchant or soldier and his Sri Lankan wife share a luxurious table of local dishes. Such marriages could be mutually beneficial. The merchant got access to valuable commercial contacts, whereas his bride acquired substantial rights to share the profits of his business under Portuguese law. Her family was often rewarded with offices in Portuguese firms or trading posts.

Until well into the second half of the seventeenth century, most European involvement in Asia was of the same sort—what some historians have called "trading-post empires." Aspiring monopolists conducted direct trades with

Europe, chiefly in spices, principally pepper. These monopolists were the Portuguese crown, and, from about the turn of the seventeenth century, English and Dutch companies. A similar trade with the New World, chiefly in Chinese silks and porcelain, traveled annually in a single Spanish galleon via Spain's colonial outpost in Manila in the Philippines. But European participation in commerce between Asian countries and in shipping ventures within Asian waters eclipsed these trades in value and extent.

Asian Examples

To understand the increased opportunities for Europeans, we need to look at the context of the enormously increased activity—as merchants, colonists, and even, occasionally, maritime imperialists—of native Asian states and communities. At either end of maritime Asia—in Japan in the east and in Oman on the coast of Arabia and the Ottoman Empire in the west—were rulers and adventurers interested in maritime imperialism (see Map 16.1).

Toyotomi Hideyoshi, the warlord who took over Japan at the end of a long era of civil war in 1585, is a case in point. He sent demands for submission to the kingdoms of Southeast Asia and to the Spanish governor in the Philippines. He vowed to ravish China "like a maiden" and "crush it like an egg." He proclaimed himself the gods' choice for mastery of the world. It sounds insane. But it was a rational strategy in the circumstances. The civil wars had militarized Japanese society. Professional warriors needed employment. Arms industries needed markets. Warlords' energies had to be redeployed. Japanese pirates had shown how vulnerable China was, sucking wealth into Japan, raiding Chinese cities far inland, and holding them to ransom.

Hideyoshi imagined his future conquests vividly. The Koreans and Chinese would "learn Japanese customs." Kidnapped children were taught Japanese. The land of China would be split among Japanese notables, and the Japanese emperor would be invested with the mandate of heaven. At first when the Japanese invaded in 1592, Korea, enfeebled by two centuries of peace, seemed easily conquerable. But the Korean navy had long experience of conflict against pirates and was equipped with startling new technology: "turtle ships" with reinforced hulls and ship-killing cannon. In combination with the typhoon-lashed seas and in collaboration with the Chinese fleet, the Korean sailors made it impossible for the Japanese to supply and reinforce their armies in Korea. Shortly after Hideyoshi's death in September 1598, the Japanese aborted their campaigns on the mainland of Asia.

It was not, however, the end of Japanese expansion. Okinawa and the Ryukyu Islands south of Japan became, in effect, a Japanese dependency by conquest in 1609. The northern land frontier of Japan gradually expanded to fill the whole of what we now think of as the Japanese home islands, at the expense of the native Ainu people, during the rest of the seventeenth century (see Chapter 19). And in the eighteenth century, Japanese expansion met that of Russia in the northern Pacific, where the two powers disputed control of the huge but barren and fog-bound island of Sakhalin. Meanwhile, although the Japanese state formally renounced southward expansion and, from the 1630s, practically forbade its subjects to travel overseas, illegal migrants and "pirates" continued to pour out of the country to take part in the new economic opportunities trade and colonization opened up in Southeast Asia. Some were Christians, fleeing from persecution after the definitive abolition of religious

"At either end of maritime Asia—in Japan in the east and in Oman on the coast of Arabia and the Ottoman Empire in the west—were rulers and adventurers interested in maritime imperialism."

"Red Seal" ship. From 1592, the shogun Hideyoshi licensed foreign trading ventures by Japanese ships under the "Red Seal." Until the abolition of the trade in the 1630s, about ten voyages a year took handicrafts, copper, silver, and foodstuffs from Japan mainly to the Portuguese settlement of Macao on the coast of China, Vietnam, Thailand, and the Philippines in exchange for silk. This silk scroll of about 1630 shows Vietnamese galleys towing one of these "Red Seal ships" into a river mouth. The umbrellas indicate the market in front of the Japanese quarter. The three long houses across the river represent the Chinese quarter.

tolerance in Japan in 1639, like the community whom a Portuguese missionary met in mid-seventeenth century Burma—close-knit, hungry for the sacraments, longing to build a church. Most Japanese migration, however, was, like that of the Chinese, economically motivated. Many letters home survive, showing that the Japanese authorities were only half-hearted in suppressing the migrants' movements and content to allow them to send money home to enrich the domestic economy.

Frontiers affected cultures by changing individual lives. In the Rijksmuseum in Amsterdam, a painting of 1644 depicts the family of the rich Dutch merchant, Pieter Cnoll. His wife, Cornelia, is a beauty in an unmistakably Japanese style— daughter and fabulously wealthy heiress of one of the first officials of the Dutch East India Company and of his Japanese concubine. She called Holland "the fatherland" and corresponded with relatives in Japan. Later, she was to be a formidable businesswoman in her own right, administering her fortune after her husband's death. Then she became the tragic heroine of one of the most protracted and expensive legal cases of the seventeenth century, in her efforts to get a divorce from her grasping, tyrannical, abusive, and exploitative second husband, and to defend her fortune against him. In the background of the portrait, stealing an apple, stands her handsome Malay slave, Untung. His future would include leading a guerrilla band of runaway slaves in the backlands of Batavia, capital of the Dutch East Indies (at what is now Jakarta in Indonesia). He became king of a realm he carved out for himself in the interior of Java. Cornelia's is hardly a typical story of the overseas Japanese, but it demonstrates the fantastic range of unprecedented experiences that the empires of the time made possible.

Even greater was the outpouring of colonists from China. In many colonial outposts, in the Spanish colony of Manila, for example, though the nominal authority, the garrisons, and the guns were European—or, at least, under European officers—the real colonists, who settled the towns in large numbers and exploited the economy on a grand scale, were Chinese. Without a metropolitan government of their own committed to overseas imperialism, the migrants used Western empire builders to protect and promote their own activities.

Batavia, for example, bore the old Roman name for Holland. Its founder in 1619 was a Dutch soldier, Jan Pieterszoon Coen. Its sovereign proprietors were the

The Dutch merchant Pieter Cnoll painted in 1644 by Jacob Coeman. At one level, this seems an ordinary scene: a rich colonial trader with his elegant family and the trappings of his wealth. But the slave stealing an apple went on to become a famous bandit chief, while Cornelia, Cnoll's half-Japanese wife, became, after Cnoll's death, the richest businesswoman in the Dutch East Indies and the notorious protagonist of an agonizingly long and expensive divorce case against her second husband.

directors of the Dutch East India Company, which had a government-granted monopoly on trade between Holland and Asia. But the entrepreneurs who created its economy and attracted settlers to it in its great days were Coen's two principal Chinese collaborators: Souw Beng Kong, known as Bencon—the godfather figure of the Chinese community—and the energetic labor broker whom the Dutch called Jan Con. Lanterns inscribed, "The Original Founder of the Region" flanked the entrance to Bencon's country house. In Chinese eyes, the Dutch role was subordinate. Jan Con, who arrived from China in 1619 or 1620, rose to prominence by farming coconuts and collecting the town's taxes on gambling and cattle raising. His main business was importing labor from China, hiring Chinese laborers from Fujian (foo-jee-ehn) in southern China on annual contracts to work on canals and fortifications. He diversified into the hinterland, starting a sugar plantation and harvesting lumber. He opened salt pans and minted lead coins—giving Batavia a brief and rickety boom in the 1630s. But poor sugar yields and high salt-production costs ruined him—combined with English competitors' devastating policy of dumping lead coins in Batavia. He died, broke, in 1639. The Dutch never fully trusted Chinese businessmen again. But the Chinese character of the colony became even more marked after 1684, when the Chinese government relaxed controls on emigration. Thousands of Chinese residents enriched China by sending money home—like Jan Con himself, who never ceased to feel guilty for deserting his parents' home. Chinese shipping in Batavia's harbor normally outnumbered that of any other country by at least two and a half to one.

Overwhelmingly, the migrants were what we would now call economic refugees—escapees from poverty and contempt at home. In 1603, when the first of a long series of hate riots provoked a massacre of the local Chinese by native Filipinos in Manila, the emperor of China refused to intervene on the grounds that his murdered subjects were "scum, ungrateful to China, their land, their parents and ancestors for they had failed to return to China for so many years that such people were deemed to be of little worth." Yet the Chinese colony in the Philippines kept growing. By 1621, it had regained its premassacre level of 15,000, and it had more than doubled by the time of the next massacre in 1639.

Chinese and Japanese participated in empires—chiefly in the seventeenth century and increasingly as it went on as colonists, because their home governments, in attempts to control trade, restricted their commercial opportunities. Most merchants who operated in maritime Asia and the Indian Ocean therefore tended to come from other parts of Asia—especially from India and Armenia—and, to a limited but growing extent, from Europe. The most important single source of long-range commercial enterprise was Gujarat, in northern India. Gujaratis linked maritime trade with that of the Armenian and Indian traders dispersed throughout Central Asia and Persia. They were the biggest operators in banking as well as in commerce in the Arabian Sea. Sometimes the same individuals engaged in both types of business. Virji Vora, reputedly the richest man in the world in the early seventeenth century, was the biggest creditor of European merchants in India. He was a capitalist in the truest sense of the word, ever reinvesting his profits in commercial enterprise, so that looters who attacked his house were disappointed not to find great riches there. At times, European merchants felt oppressed by Gujarati power in key markets. In 1692, for instance, the Dutch East India Company had to sell a large cargo of nutmeg, cloves, and mace at half price to a Gujarati broker, because the company's representatives feared the power of another Gujarati—Muhammad Sahid, who was trying to control the market and was willing to undercut any competitor.

Capitalism—contrary to the traditional assumptions of Western historians—was not a European specialty. Nor—contrary to assertions still regularly made in old-fashioned history books—was it peculiar to any religious tradition. In 1904, Max Weber, one of the most influential sociologists ever, first proposed the idea that religion predisposes some communities to particular kinds of economic behavior. But in most cases, the theory does not seem to work. Jains, Christians, and Muslims were all prominent in Gujarat's trading community. In some places, despite the common belief that Hinduism generally regards commerce as a polluting and demeaning activity, even Hindus could engage in capi-

Gujerati merchant. Though most merchants in sixteenth-century Gujarat were Jains or Muslims, the Portuguese annotator of this sketch from the port city of Cambay (now officially called Khambat) calls the subject a banian—a term Europeans adopted from various languages of Sanskritic origins, usually to mean a Hindu merchant, moneychanger, or loan agent. Hindus could engage in commercial occupations at the time with little danger of loss of caste, and some of them were among the richest operators in the Indian Ocean. The woman's provocative attire, make-up, jewelry, and gesture—offering the merchant an apparently symbolic flower—and the fact that the man reciprocates with a bulging purse of money leave no doubt that the scene is of prostitution. Western writers on India in the late middle ages and early modern period rarely omit references to the glamour, luxury, and abundance of brothels, and the charms of the prostitutes.

talism without losing caste. Hindus dominated the trade of Goa, although nominally this was a Portuguese-controlled city. In an auction in 1630, for instance, the local Hindu merchants numbered nearly half of the bidders and outbid their Portuguese counterparts and the government itself for about half of what was on offer. In seventeenth-century Kerala, south of Goa, most bankers were Brahmins—Hindus of the highest caste—who, according to Dutch complaints "by and large control the pepper trade."

The Dutch Connection

For over 100 years, from their arrival in the Indian Ocean in 1498, the Portuguese fitted into this Asian-dominated world without provoking seriously disruptive conflicts. At first, Spaniards were their only European rivals, and the Portuguese came to a series of advantageous arrangements with them. Gradually, however, from roughly the 1620s, the situation changed. Asian hosts lost patience with the presence of sovereign ports and offshore trading establishments, where Portuguese religious intolerance damaged trade by discriminating against Muslim and Hindu merchants. As Asian empires expanded or grew in power, or became more assertive, they eliminated key Portuguese outposts. Even after the capture of the mainland forts of which Jeronimo de Quadros was a commander, Portuguese occupation of the offshore trading post of Hormuz was tolerated until 1622, when the Portuguese were expelled from the Persian Gulf. A series of similar expulsions followed: from Hooghly—their fort in Bengal—in 1632, from Ethiopia in 1634, and from Japan in 1639. From 1640, their own attitude to their Asian interests changed. Portugal became involved in a long and destructive war against Spain that deflected Portuguese resources from the east. Atlantic priorities took over, as Portugal's Brazilian sugar plantations became increasingly profitable and the transatlantic slave trade boomed (see Chapter 20).

One reason Asian communities could become more selective about their partnerships with the Portuguese was that far more European buyers and shippers were now operating in maritime Asia. English, French, and Scandinavians all played increasing roles in the seventeenth century, but the contribution of the Dutch eclipsed them all.

The provinces of Holland and Zeeland, in what is today the Netherlands, were, like Portugal, poor communities, with relatively unproductive hinterlands, on Western Europe's ocean edge. Their people had a longstanding maritime vocation as fishermen, whalers, and shippers in northern seas, particularly in the lucrative trade in timber and dried fish with the Baltic.

In the late sixteenth century, merchants from the Netherlands broke into the trading world of the Mediterranean. In part they were driven by necessities arising from their rebellion against their ruler—who, by a series of dynastic accidents, happened also to be king of Spain. In part, too, a civil war drove them in which they were pitted against the neighboring provinces to their south in what is today Belgium. Netherlanders' contact with long-distance trade began because the Portuguese used Antwerp in the southern Netherlands as the clearing house for distributing Asian spices into northern Europe. During the war, many merchants from Antwerp migrated north to escape Spanish control. The commercial center of gravity in the Low Countries shifted with them to Holland. Meanwhile, in 1580, the king of Spain also succeeded by hereditary right to the throne of Portugal. This made Portuguese ships and possessions, potentially, fair game in the eyes of Dutch rebels.

"One reason Asian communities could become more selective about their partnerships with the Portuguese was that far more European buyers and shippers were now operating in maritime Asia."

The Netherlands. Although the Netherlands were divided into 17 provinces, all determined to preserve their own separate institutions and ways of life, the inhabitants long had a sense of common identity. This map of 1550 expresses that unity by depicting the provinces as "the Belgian lion"— which was already a traditional image—strong and warlike, clawing and snapping at Germany across the Rhine, lashing the North Sea with its tail. But it also hints at the cultural differences that divided the provinces from each other by showing how the traditional dress of Holland and Belgium, shown on the right, was different from that of the province of Frisia, shown on the left. From the 1560s to 1648, religious and political conflicts heightened the differences between the northern and southern provinces of the Netherlands and shattered their sense of unity. In consequence, two separate states emerged: a Protestant-ruled republic took shape in the seven northern provinces, while the rest of the Netherlands, which eventually became modern Belgium, remained loyal to the Catholic Habsburg dynasty.

In the 1590s, Jan van Linschoten, a Dutch servant of the Portuguese archbishop of Goa, explored the prospects of extending Dutch business into the Indian Ocean. The publication of his findings ignited a craze. In 1602, after three years of hectically free competition, leading merchants of the port of Amsterdam, who largely controlled government in the province of Holland, formed a **joint-stock company** to exploit, as a monopoly, the opportunities of trade with Asia.

Historians have generally supposed that such private limited companies were more efficient than the state monopolies by which Portugal and Spain attempted to regulate long-range trade. But the English, whose system was similar to that of the Dutch, were by comparison seriously undercapitalized and could make only a modest success of it. More important for outstripping other European trading ventures was the new outward route to the East Indies, which the Dutch began to explore in the second decade of the seventeenth century.

Even at its height, Holland's would-be monopoly of the rarer spices—cloves, nutmeg, cinnamon, and mace—was a leaky vessel. Dutch shipping never accounted for more than a seventh of the total involved in carrying the trade in these products. The Dutch never got control of pepper, which, in the seventeenth century, accounted for about 70 percent of the spice trade by value and even more by volume. Pepper demand and production grew constantly throughout the century, steadily increasing the sum of global commerce and supplying many traditional routes and handlers.

Nevertheless, the Dutch did establish a clearly dominant position as carriers of Europe's Asian trade in the seventeenth century, effectively replacing the Portuguese while keeping well ahead of other European rivals in all theaters and—in combination with political instability in Central Asia—helping to deflect trade from the Silk Roads. Four reasons underpinned Dutch success: the speed and efficiency of their route; the problems that harassed so much of the Portuguese seaborne empire in the east as some indigenous states transferred their favor to the Dutch; the selectively aggressive policies that, as we shall see, gradually brought the Dutch control of more—and more valuable—production of Asian communities than any European rivals; and above all, the privileged position they established in trade with Japan.

Overwhelmingly, the most valuable of the trading enterprises of maritime Asia led to Japan, because Japan was the world's leading producer of silver. Silver was relatively cheap in Japan. Merchants who took goods there, or performed services for Japanese businesses or rulers, could exchange it on favorable terms for profitable trade goods elsewhere. They used Japanese silver to buy pepper and cotton textiles in India and aromatic woods and spices from Indonesia. In China they acquired silks, porcelain, and rhubarb, which was prized as a laxative in Western medicine at this time. Increasingly they bought tea, which grew in importance as time went on and tastes spread, along with other aspects of culture, along new trade routes. Injections of Japanese silver supplied more cash for the world's markets, stimulating economic activity.

However, Japan's willingness to participate in the spreading web of economic interconnections came close to collapse in the 1630s. The main reason for this was the phenomenal success of Catholic missionaries, who had accompanied Portuguese and Spanish merchants in the country and made hundreds of thousands of converts. Fears that this alien religion would undermine traditional loyalties to the state provoked an official ban on Christianity in 1597 and led to the bloody martyrdom of Catholic clergy and converts until Christianity was driven underground in 1638–1639. From 1640, Dutch merchants were the only Europeans allowed in Japan—tolerated because they were willing to let their servants take part in an annual rite called "Trampling the Crucifix." Most of the Dutch merchants were Calvinists, Protestants who repudiated "graven images" such as crucifixes anyway as contrary to the Ten Commandments (see Chapter 18). The Japanese government channeled Dutch trade through an island off the port of Nagasaki and strictly monitored the merchants' contact with Japanese subjects for more than 200 years.

Yet, to be able to continue to trade in Japan at all was an enormous bonus. For the rest of the century—until other Europeans began to build up their trade in other parts of Asia to levels at which they could generate comparable earnings—the Dutch dominated the handling of all the most valuable products of China and Southeast Asia for European markets. The Netherlands—formerly a poor, cramped, beleaguered, divided, and marginal part of Europe—experienced a "Golden Age" of wealth, art, empire-building, and military and naval power. Dutch imperialists challenged the Spanish monarchy in parts of the New World. Taking advantage of changed Portuguese priorities, and of help from some expanding Asian powers, they drove the Portuguese out of Malacca in 1641, Sri Lanka in the 1650s, and from many places in India thereafter. They resisted Spanish and French attempts at conquest in the seventeenth century. Meanwhile, they drove the English out of the Spice Islands and defeated them in the seas around England itself. Eventually, in 1688–1699 the Dutch ruler, taking advantage of internal conflicts in Britain, invaded England and became its king by deposing his English father-in-law.

A further consequence of the growing wealth and power of the Dutch was growing ambition in empire-building in Asia. Increasingly, from the 1660s, they aimed to control not only trade in valuable commodities, but also their actual

Chinese view of the Dutch. Jingdezhen, on the south bank of the Yangtze River, eclipsed other centers of porcelain production in China, for quality and quantity, from the eleventh century until the eighteenth. Under the Qianlong emperor (r. 1735–1796), some 60 million pieces of porcelain a year were produced there. To a Jesuit visitor in 1712, Jingdezhen had so many furnaces that at night "one thinks the whole city is on fire." Some of the output was for export, especially to Holland, but these satirical figurines of Dutch merchants—now in a French museum—seem more likely to have appealed to Chinese collectors.
Reunion des Musees Nationaux/Art Resource

The Fall of Makassar, June 12, 1660, painted by Frederik Woldemar. The capture of Makassar in what is today Indonesia was part of the Dutch campaign to build an empire in the East Indies. Makassar was an independent sultanate whose ruler was supported by the Portuguese, and the painting shows a Portuguese ship that the Dutch had already taken. While the guns in the sultan's palace exchange fire with the Dutch ships, native troops march to the sultan's aid. The neutral English trading post flies the flag of St. George. The decisive moment of the encounter came when a Dutch landing party seized the stronghold.

production. Refugees from Dutch aggression elsewhere poured into Makassar. Malays swelled its ships' crews. Moluccans brought their know-how in growing spices. Portuguese from Malacca introduced their long-range trading contacts. Makassar became their "second and better Malacca." According to a Dominican friar who visited in 1658, it was "one of the greatest emporia of Asia" with a ruler who collected European books and scientific instruments.

In the 1650s, the Dutch began a relentless war, first of coercion, then of conquest, in the East Indies. "Do you believe," sneered the sultan of Makassar, "that God has reserved for your trade alone islands which lie so far from your homeland?" The conquest took nearly 20 years. That of Bantam, on Java, with its big pepper output, followed in the early 1680s. Southeast Asia's age of trade was ending as native Asian cultivators abandoned cash crops, which had once enriched their cultivators but now seemed only to attract foreign predators.

The Dutch policy set a fateful example, as other European trading communities also undertook more aggressive policies. Europeans began to turn from maritime imperialism, based on control of trade, to territorial imperialism, which aimed to control production. At first their efforts were modest and unsuccessful. The Portuguese expanded outward from Goa and in the 1680s conquered the passes leading toward the Deccan, acquiring a subject population of about 30,000 people. The French crown, which had opened a permanent trading establishment at Pondicherry in southeast India in 1674, contemplated taking over Thailand but had to withdraw in humiliation. The English East India Company, founded in 1600, challenged the Mughal Empire in India to war, in an attempt to increase its share of trade, but was defeated in 1685–1688.

Chronology: European Maritime Imperialism in the Indian and Pacific Oceans, 1500–1700

1500	Portuguese begin direct trade with southern India
1510	Portuguese trading post at Goa established
1571	Spanish trading post of Manila founded
1600	English East India Company established
1602	Dutch East India Company founded
1619	Dutch found trading post of Batavia (Indonesia)
1620–1640	Portuguese expelled from trading posts in Persian Gulf and Indian Ocean
1640	Dutch merchants only Europeans allowed in Japan
1674	French establish trading post at Pondicherry (India)

Gradually, however, in the eighteenth century, Europeans would take more and more production under their own direct control, building up land empires in Asia that genuinely transformed the global economy. The profits Europeans made in Asian trade in the sixteenth and seventeenth centuries had modified Europe's age-old trading deficit with Asia in Europe's favor. Now it could be reversed, as Europeans not only influenced markets, but also manipulated production.

LAND EMPIRES: RUSSIA, CHINA, MUGHAL INDIA, AND THE OTTOMANS

The European land empires in Asia were, however, all modest affairs until well into the eighteenth century—with one exception. Russian imperialism gleams from the heavily gilded surface of a remarkable painting: the "Icon of the Hosts of the Heavenly King," made in the third quarter of the sixteenth century. Led by the biblical kings Solomon and David, Russians march across a fantastic landscape of mountains and rivers, from a city of infidels, ringed by fire, toward a shrine of the Virgin Mary. Heavenly hosts, ghostly cavalry, and the Christian founder-emperors of the Russian Orthodox tradition, Vladimir and Constantine (see Chapter 9), flank the earthly army. "Although the martyrs were born on earth," reads the commentary, "they succeeded in attaining the rank of angels." Two real leaps of Russian imperialism inspired this art. First, the conquest of Kazan in 1552 gave the **czars**—as the Russian ruler was styled in allusion to "Caesar"—command of the entire length of the Volga River, which was the great corridor of commerce at the western edge of Asia, and eliminated Russia's great rival for control of Siberia's fur trade. Furs summoned Russians to conquest and colonization, as gold lured Spaniards and spices captivated the Portuguese. The czars' next task was to conquer Siberia itself and control the production of furs as well as the trade in them (see Map 16.2). In 1555, Czar Ivan IV began to call himself Lord of Siberia. Three years later, he cut a deal with a big dynasty of fur dealers, the Stroganoffs, who were prepared to pay to turn that title into reality. The language of a chroniclers' account reflects the typical mind-set of European conquerors in new worlds: the assertion that pagans have no rights; that their lands are "empty"; that they are subhuman—bestial or monstrous; that financial privileges can promote colonization; and that the work is holy.

The Icon of the Hosts of the Heavenly King is one of the most spectacular works of Russian imperial propaganda of the sixteenth century. Mounted on a warhorse, the Archangel Michael leads a Russian army from the conquest of Kazan, shown in flames on the extreme right, into the presence of the Mother of God and her son. Constantine, the first Christian emperor, and Vladimir, Russia's first Christian ruler, carry banners.

MAP 16.2

Eurasian Land Empires of the Sixteenth and Seventeenth Centuries

- Ottoman Empire
- China (Ming/Qing Empires)
- Russian Empire
- Mughal Empire
- Safavid Empire
- — Silk Roads

From the 1570s, the "protection" of Russian armies "against the fighting men of Siberia" was proclaimed for native peoples who submitted and paid tribute in furs. Like other European military operations on remote frontiers, the Russians ascribed their success to technology: firearms mounted on river barges, from which the waterborne conquerors exchanged bullets for bowshots with defenders on the banks. The Siberian khan was said to be dismayed to hear that "when they shoot from their bows, then there is a flash of fire and a great smoke issues and there is a loud report like thunder in the sky. . . . and it is impossible to shield oneself from them by any trappings of war."

Native peoples were subjected to tribute and controlled by oaths of traditional, pagan kinds. One Siberian people, the Ostyaks, were made to swear on a bearskin on which a knife, an axe, and a loaf were spread. The oath breaker would choke to death or be cut to pieces in battle with men or bears. The Yakuts had to swear by passing between the quarters of a dismembered dog. The first object of the conquest, however, was not to vanquish these "savages" who ranged the pine forests and tundra but to eliminate the only state able to challenge Russia in the region: the Mongol khanate of Sibir, which dominated the eastern tributaries of the Irtysh River. Thus the conquest was sold as a Crusade and depicted symbolically by representations of gospel rays spread from the eyes of Christ between colonists' cities. Russians credited Khan Kuchum with a prophetic vision in October 1581: "The skies burst

Chronology: Russian Expansion Eastward	
1552–1556	Russian conquest of Kazan
1555	Czar Ivan IV claims title of Lord of Siberia
ca. Late seventeenth century	Russian and Chinese expansion meet
1689	Treaty of Nerchinsk with China checks Russia's eastward expansion

open and terrifying warriors with shining wings appeared. . . . They encircled Kuchum's army and cried to him, 'Depart from this land, you infidel son of the dark demon, Muhammad, because now it belongs to the Almighty.'"

China

By the late seventeenth century, Russian expansion in eastern Siberia met China's, which was preempting or pursuing Russian rivals in a war zone along the Amur River. The road that led here was kept smoother, according to a Jesuit visitor, "than Catholics in Europe keep the road on which the Sacrament is to be conveyed." The Treaty of Nerchinsk of 1689 formalized Chinese claims to vast unexplored lands of doubtful extent in northeast Asia, where some mapmakers imagined a huge landmass pointing to or even joining America.

Much of this territory was effectively beyond any practical frontier of settlement. Generally, however, Chinese imperialism was of an intensive kind, compared with Russia's: dedicated not merely to economic exploitation and trade, but also to colonization and to spreading Chinese ways among native peoples. Before the end of the seventeenth century, Outer Mongolia had been crudely incorporated into the Chinese Empire, and more than 1.5 million settlers had been lured into Sichuan (seh-chwhan) in southern China by the promise of immunities from taxation. The Xinjiang (sheen-jeeahng) frontier in western China was peopled next, more thinly, by a mixture of enforced deportation and inducements to voluntary settlers. By the end of the century, 200,000 Chinese migrants had settled there. Manchuria, homeland of the ruling dynasty, the Manchus or Qing (see Chapter 21), was normally closed to settlers, but its rich soils drew them unofficially in the hundreds of thousands, until the Chinese government was obliged to accept their presence. Meanwhile, the people of Manchuria were progressively converted to Chinese ways. On all fronts, the pressure of intensive new settlement provoked a cycle of conflicts and solutions ominously familiar to students of European colonialism: tribal peoples reshuffled or penned in reservations; militarized agricultural colonies growing wheat, barley, peas, and maize (which had been introduced to Asia from the Americas; see Chapter 17), while keeping the natives in check. Schools were erected to spread Chinese language and values.

The Mughal Example in India

The Russian and Chinese empires practiced large-scale colonization, with attempts at new kinds of exploitation of conquered or resettled soil. That was to be the pattern of most new imperialism from this period onward. But there were still empires of what one might call an old-fashioned kind: conquest states that tended to leave the political, social, demographic, and economic structures of their conquests largely intact and to exploit them indirectly by levying tribute. The Mughal (the name means Mongol and refers to the ruling dynasty's supposed origins) Empire in India was the newest and fastest-growing empire of this type in the late sixteenth and seventeenth centuries. If we can trust its founder's memoirs, it began in a mood of distraction. Babur (1483–1530) was an adventurer from Central Asia, in the mold of his ancestor, Timur (see Chapter 15). In the volatile world west of the Hindu Kush, the rugged mountains that separate India from Afghanistan, he raised war bands and exchanged kingdoms with a rapidity of turnover unattainable elsewhere. His dream was to rebuild Timur's empire from the city of Samarkand in Central Asia, but after he had won and lost that city twice

"Generally, however, Chinese imperialism was of an intensive kind, compared with Russia's: dedicated not merely to economic exploitation and trade, but also to colonization and to spreading Chinese ways among native peoples."

The assault on Chittorgarh. The Mughal Emperor Akbar (r. 1556–1605) commissioned artists to record his campaigns. This painting shows a notable moment in his siege of the supposedly impregnable fortress of Chittorgarh. A tunnel mined by Akbar's engineers exploded, killing hundreds of his own men. When the fort fell, most of the defenders were massacred.

over, he turned to India. From 1519, conquering it became his obsession. India seduced him. He rebuked Afghan followers who claimed to prefer the Afghan capital of Kabul, where he had been "the sport of harsh poverty." After 1526, when he conquered Delhi in north India and made it his capital, he never left India, though he missed the "flavor of melons and grapes" of his Afghan home (see Map 16.2).

The state Babur founded remained small and unstable until the long rule of his grandson, Akbar (r. 1556–1605). The priorities of Akbar's empire emerge vividly from the account compiled by his friend and minister, Abul Fazl Allami, who begins by describing the emperor's jewel chest, then turns to the treasury, the coinage, the mints for gold and silver, the stupendous court cuisine with its gold-laced dishes, the emperor's writing room, his arsenal, his elephants, horses, cows, and camels. When he turns to what he considers the lesser aspects of government, he deals first with protocol, before insisting on a ruler's responsibilities for spiritual welfare; then come accounts of building projects, the army, revenue raising and rites (including hunting and games), lists of great nobles and court personalities.

In short, the Mughal Empire was like a business, run for profit—an investment in power and majesty, with rich returns in the form of tribute and taxes. The heartlands it ruled directly never extended much beyond the limits of Babur's conquests, in the Punjab and the Ganges valley in north India. Beyond this area, existing power structures and local rulers remained in place, supplying money and manpower for future conquests, and linked to the imperial court by every device of networking. The 800 wives Akbar assembled from the rulers who paid him tribute were, in effect, hostages and mediators of sometimes uneasy alliances. Religious tolerance was an essential ingredient of internal peace in an empire that straddled the Hindu and Muslim worlds.

The Mughal war machine was so big and costly that it was impossible to operate at a profit without the constant stream of victories that Akbar had his court artists commemorate in still ravishing, still terrifying miniature paintings. The most dramatic battle of his reign was the assault on Chittorgarh, the clifftop stronghold of a Hindu prince, in 1567–1568—recalled by a depiction of the deaths of hundreds on both sides in the accidental explosion of the mines that Akbar's engineers bored and burrowed into the cliff. Of the defending garrison of 8,000 and their 40,000 servants, 30,000 reputedly died in the last onslaught.

In some ways the Mughal Empire seems ramshackle, stumbling between victories, with no central institutions except the imperial court and army, no agreed rules of succession to the throne, and an elite divided by ethnic and religious differences and economic jealousies. The death or old age of every emperor triggered rebellion and civil war. Yet the frontier kept growing, reaching deep into south India by the time of Akbar's death in 1605, slowing during the half century that followed, and again advancing rapidly under the Emperor Aurangzeb (r. 1656–1707) to cover almost the entire subcontinent.

The Ottomans

West of India were states superficially similar to the Mughals, where Muslim rulers—the Safavid dynasty in Persia and the Ottomans, based in Turkey—dominated huge territories and diverse populations by mobilizing large armies equipped with up-to-date firepower. Historians call both of them empires, but the Safavids ruled a compact state, more or less corresponding to modern Iran and—not for want of trying—never managed permanently to annex much territory farther afield. Their story belongs in Chapter 19.

The Ottomans, by contrast, were among the most effective empire builders the world had ever known. What we have already seen of them (see Chapter 15) demonstrates that; what happened in the sixteenth and seventeenth centuries would confirm it. And although the areas they conquered had all been part of big empires before, the empire the Ottomans built up had no exact precedents. The diversity literally echoed around Lady Mary Wortley Montagu, an English ambassador's wife, in 1718, who heard her servants chatter in ten different languages. "I live," she went on, "in the perpetual hearing of this medley of sounds, which produces a very extraordinary effect upon the people that are born here. They learn all these languages at the same time and without knowing any of them well enough to write or read in it."

In the Ottoman world, boundless ambitions seemed possible. The Ottomans inherited three universalist traditions: one from their steppelander ancestors, whose aim was to make the limits of their empire match those of the sky; another from Islam, whose caliphs' legacy and title the Ottoman sultans claimed; and a third from ancient Rome, whose legacy they wrenched into their own grasp by conquering much former Roman imperial territory.

The Ottomans could afford to invest in strategies of conquest, because the sixteenth and seventeenth centuries were an era of prosperity in Turkey unprecedented at the time and unparalleled since. Their heartlands were in the Anatolian plateau. Beyond it, the Ottoman lands were grouped around three great waterways: the eastern Mediterranean, the Black Sea, and the twin rivers of Mesopotamia. Beyond what they called Rumelia, the westernmost of the provinces they ruled directly, lay a broad frontier zone that they controlled and that reached beyond Budapest in Hungary in Central Europe. In North Africa, beyond Egypt, the sultans enjoyed nominal allegiance, at least, from the principalities of the Barbary coast, as far west as what is now Algeria. They got control of most continental transit points between Asia and Europe: the western reaches of the Silk Roads, the Persian Gulf, the Red Sea, and the main ports of Egypt and the eastern Mediterranean seaboard. New trade routes from Europe to south and southeast Asia did not deflect existing trade from Ottoman territories. On the contrary, with improved communications and expanding demand, the total volume of the spice trade continued to grow, and more of this trade passed through Ottoman hands in the sixteenth century than ever before.

"The Ottomans could afford to invest in strategies of conquest, because the sixteenth and seventeenth centuries were an era of prosperity in Turkey unprecedented at the time and unparalleled since."

On the other hand, the Ottomans were, in some respects, disadvantageously placed. They had no outlets to the Atlantic or the Indian Ocean—or even to the western Mediterranean, except through narrow straits that enemies easily controlled. Wars frequently broke out on frontiers with permanently hostile neighbors—Persians in the east, Christians in the north and west. Armies shuttled back and forth across the empire in successive seasons to keep Europeans inhibited and Safavid Persians at bay. Beset, as the Ottomans were, by enemies on every side, their state needed extraordinary strength to survive. Only a state of extraordinary efficiency could expand.

Yet expand they did. They overran Egypt in 1517 and exploited it for huge annual tax surpluses that sustained campaigns elsewhere. The armies of Suleiman the Magnificent (r. 1520–1566) reached Belgrade in Serbia in the northwest Balkans in 1521 and the island of Rhodes in the Aegean in 1522. What

Ankara. The artist Jean-Baptiste Vanmour, who lived in Istanbul in the early eighteenth century, and helped to make Westerners familiar with images of the city and its people, also depicted other Turkish cities of the time, including this view of Ankara in Anatolia. Vanmour emphasized the aspects of commercial, domestic, and civic life that made the Ottoman Empire seem exotic to Western eyes.

began as a punitive expedition against Hungary in 1525 ended as the conquest of most of that country. Until Suleiman's death, the pace of conquest was enormous. He conquered Iraq from Persia and most of the shores of the Red Sea, while exerting more informal lordship over much of the rest of Arabia. Suleiman extended his rule over almost the whole southern shore of the Mediterranean, where his naval commanders, the Barbarossa brothers of Algiers, organized a seaborne empire of war galleys and pirate havens (see Map 16.2). In 1529, Suleiman was called from besieging Vienna in Austria to fight the Persians in Iraq, while a Turkish fleet raided the city of Valencia in Spain. During a single campaigning season in 1538, Ottoman forces conquered Moldavia in the northeast Balkans, besieged the Portuguese stronghold of Diu in India, and wrecked a Christian fleet off the shores of Greece. His court poet Baki hailed Suleiman as "the monarch with the crown of Alexander . . . the earth before his gate served as prayer mat for the world."

The pace of expansion was slower under Suleiman's successors, but not because the empire was running out of energy. Rather, it was because remoter conquests brought diminishing returns. The Ottoman naval effort—it is true—faltered: outgunned in the Indian Ocean by Portugal and in the central Mediterranean by Spain. But every generation brought a net gain of territory until the last years of the seventeenth century.

The degree of imperial authority could hardly be uniform in the outlying parts of so extensive an empire, but it was felt everywhere. The younger Barbarossa, who ruled the remotest outposts on the North African coast, was loosely called a king, even in Turkish accounts. He recruited ships and men with his own resources, won his victories by his own strength—so many of them that he sold Christian captives "at an onion a head." In Islamic North Africa, the sword carved the right to rule. Yet when Suleiman summoned him to Constantinople, Barbarossa did not hesitate to obey. The khans of Crimea in what is today Ukraine negotiated terms of pay—often in the form of captive slaves—for joining the sultans' campaigns and sometimes simply disobeyed the sultan. Turks garrisoned but did not directly rule Wallachia and Moldavia (in modern Romania). Transylvania, on the western edge of the empire, was a vassal state, with low taxes and a Christian prince whom its medieval parliament elected. In Arab lands, the sultans used religion as a source of legitimacy, but—with only sporadic displays of force to back it up—they found it hard to turn that legitimacy into effective allegiance. As we shall see in Chapter 19, even the parts of their empire that the sultans ruled directly were a patchwork of different methods and conventions of rule that were often hard to keep under close control.

Chronology: Mughals and Ottomans	
1517	Ottomans conquer Egypt
1519	Babur founds Mughal Empire
1520–1566	Reign of Ottoman sultan Suleiman the Magnificent
1526	Babur makes Delhi his capital
1529	Ottomans besiege Vienna
1656–1707	Aurangzeb extends Mughal Empire over most of Indian subcontinent

NEW LAND EMPIRES IN THE AMERICAS

Across the Atlantic, meanwhile, European imperialism led landward. Columbus (see Chapter 15) envisaged no more than a trading setup when he first saw what he thought was Japan, the Caribbean island of Hispaniola (modern Haiti and the Dominican Republic) in 1492, imagining a European merchant-colony under Spanish control, trading in cotton, mastic (a resin used to make varnish), and slaves. However, none of these products was available in large quantities in the Caribbean. Columbus based his initial hopes on the illusion that the riches of Asia lay only a short way farther west. But he had grossly underestimated the size of the world. Instead, therefore, the Spaniards had to focus on exploiting the gold mines of the island. Columbus's war of conquest in Hispaniola of 1495–1496 was—albeit on a small scale—the first step toward creating a Spanish territorial empire.

The settlement of more Caribbean islands and, between 1518 and 1546, the conquests of Mexico and Peru, confirmed this trend. As a result, Spaniards found themselves obeyed over huge tracts of the most densely populated territory in the Americas. Indeed, Spain—which was a relatively poor and underpopulated country—had acquired, within a few years, and in their entirety, two of the fastest-growing and most environmentally diverse empires of the age—those of the Aztecs and the Incas (see Chapter 15). This achievement was effected thousands of miles from home, with relatively primitive technology, few resources, and privately recruited bands of only a few hundred men (see Map 16.3).

How was it possible? In early colonial times, four explanations occurred to those who tried to make sense of the way the conquest had turned out. The clergy favored the view that the conquest was miraculous and providential—procured by God for his own purposes. The warriors who took part in successful expeditions, their heirs, and cronies explained it as the result of their own godlike prowess. But this was incredible and self-interested—an account designed to maximize rewards from a grateful crown. The Spaniards' Native American allies saw the overthrow of the Aztecs and Incas as their own work, with a little help from their Spanish friends. Illustrations in documents of the Tlaxcalteca (tlash-kahl-TEK-ah)—the most numerous and formidable of the Indian communities who joined the alliance against the Aztecs—show Native Americans in the vanguard of every attack and Spaniards, typically, bringing up the rear. Along with the Tlaxcalteca, the Huexotzinca (weh-hot-SEEN-kah), another people hostile to the Aztecs, claimed exemption from taxation in postconquest times on the grounds that the conquest had been mainly their own work.

Finally, according to early colonial analysts, the Native American empires were victims of their own shaky morale. Hernán Cortés (1485–1547), the adventurer who led the band that conquered Mexico, spread the claim that the Aztec Emperor

"Indeed, Spain—which was a relatively poor and underpopulated country—had acquired, within a few years, and in their entirety, two of the fastest-growing and most environmentally diverse empires of the age—those of the Aztecs and the Incas."

MAP 16.3

Land Empires in the Americas, ca. 1700

- Spanish possessions
- Portuguese possessions
- English possessions
- French possessions
- Dutch possessions

Tlaxcalteca native peoples described on pages 553–561

→ Portuguese slaving raids

→ Manila galleon

→ Treasure Fleet to Seville

→ Humboldt Current

Native conquistadores. The conquest of Michoacán was—apart from the capture of the Aztec capital of Tenochtitlán—the toughest and bloodiest episode of the Spanish conquest of Mexico. This account by the Spaniards' native allies, the Tlaxcalteca, made in the mid-sixteenth century, emphasizes the leading role played by Native American conquistadores. The Spaniards bring up the rear, though one of their dogs takes an enthusiastic role in the vanguard.

Moctezuma II (mok-teh-ZOO-ma) (r. 1502–1520) had surrendered power into his hands in the belief that Spanish supremacy was the fulfillment of a prophecy. This claim was almost certainly false, made up to head off awkward questions churchmen and lawyers in Spain raised about whether the Spaniards had any right to rule in Mexico. In early colonial times, rumors spread that omens and signs from their gods had predisposed the Aztecs to surrender, or that they regarded the Spaniards as gods or the representatives of a departed god, destined to return as ruler. But these rumors were made up after the event, and the reported omens were borrowed from European books. The aggressive, confident, dynamic, and expanding Aztec state showed no signs of weak morale and resisted ferociously.

Yet similar stories were invoked to explain Spanish success elsewhere, too. To refer to Spaniards, the people of the Inca Empire used a term that was also the name of a god or legendary hero. So the notion that they mistook Spaniards for gods attracted people in that region, too. When the last independent Maya kingdom submitted to the Spanish monarchy in 1697, the priest who negotiated the surrender convinced himself that the Maya had yielded in supposed obedience to an ancient prophecy.

Historians have added other explanations. The technology gap is often assumed to have been instrumental in the conquests. And in some respects, Spanish war technology was important. In 1521, in the final siege of the Aztec capital Tenochtitlán, Spanish-designed, gun-carrying ships patrolled the lake that surrounded the city. Spanish steel-edged weapons were probably more effective in disabling and killing enemy warriors than the blades made from volcanic glass native armorers used. Crossbows, as long as new bolts were available, could outperform Native American slings and bows. The importance of guns and horses, however, was probably slight. Horses are of limited value in mountain warfare and street fighting—conditions in which some of the most critical episodes of the conquests occurred. It is hard to credit claims that the defenders were awestruck by these devices or inhibited by the belief that they were magical. Such claims were always linked with efforts to mock the natives' intellectual and rational powers. In practice, Native Americans quickly adapted to European styles of warfare and used horses and firearms, where these were effective, themselves.

As we shall see in the next chapter, disease was, in the long run, of enormous importance in weakening Native American resistance to European conquerors. It is more doubtful, however, whether it was decisive in the early stages of conquest. Maladies hard to identify, made worse by malnutrition, weakened and killed many of the defenders of the Aztec capital. By the time of the conquest of Peru in the 1530s, smallpox was devastating unimmunized populations. Spanish carriers unwittingly spread it wherever they went. Yet its effects cut both ways, harming the Spaniards' allies as least as much as their enemies, while still leaving formidable numbers of foes in the field. Spaniards themselves, after all, were also operating in unfamiliar and debilitating environments.

It is worth bearing in mind that many—perhaps most—European successes were by-products of war among Native Americans themselves. Some Maya communities identified more closely with the Spaniards than with their hated neighbors, exploiting Spanish help to settle feuds sometimes centuries old. The French in Canada in the next century were drawn into wars between different Iroquoian peoples. The Aztec and Inca worlds were full of conflict. Civil war wracked the Inca Empire when the Spaniards arrived. Most of its subject peoples resented Inca rule. The Huari (WAH-ree) nursed hateful memories of the Inca conquest. Only a few years before the Spaniards' arrival, the Inca had massacred thousands of recently conquered Cañari in an apparent attempt to terrorize them into obedience. Even some of the Incas' former allies had grown disenchanted. The Incas' demands for forced labor, which drove many workers hundreds of miles from their homes, were acutely resented. When the empire fell, tens of thousands of conscripted workers left their posts to return to their original communities.

The Aztecs' demands similarly alienated tributary peoples. The tribute system was both the strength and weakness of their state: strength, because it embodied their power to command resources from a vast area; weakness, because Tenochtitlán became dependent on tribute for basic necessities—the food and cotton the city could not produce for itself—and the luxuries from distant climates, needed to sustain the way of life of the elite: the ritual cacao and incense, the rubber for the ball game, the gold, the jade, the amber, the seashells, the exotic featherwork and ceremonial clothing. When the Spaniards' allies denied Tenochtitlán its tribute, they effectively starved the Aztec capital into submission.

The Spaniards' triumph was therefore less a battlefield victory than a diplomatic maneuver. In forming an alliance able to defy the Aztecs, the Spaniards enjoyed crucial advantages. The Aztecs at first treated the Spaniards' arrival as a diplomatic mission, rather than a hostile force, which gave the Spaniards time to make useful contacts in disaffected Native American communities. The Spaniards acquitted themselves so impressively in tests of battle that the Tlaxcalteca adopted them enthusiastically as allies and remained in alliance even after the Spaniards suffered a severe defeat at Aztec hands in 1520. The single most important ingredient in Spanish diplomatic success was probably their interpreter, whom they called Doña Marina. She was a native speaker of the main language of central Mexico and quickly learned Spanish. She was, at a crucial phase, the only person with the linguistic qualifications to mastermind negotiations. Tlaxcalan pictures

> *"It is worth bearing in mind that many—perhaps most—European successes were by-products of war among Native Americans themselves."*

of the conquest invariably show her center stage, mediating between Spaniards and Native Americans in peaceful scenes, and actually supervising military operations in depictions of war.

None of these explanations, however, really matches what happened in the Americas when Europeans arrived. For, usually, the transition to new kinds of European-led imperialism happened with little or no violence. Traditionally, historians have concentrated on conflicts between Europeans and their native "victims." Indeed, Spanish conquests in the New World have had a bloody reputation. Terror was a common tactic, not because the conquistadores were morally different from other warriors, but because they were subject to peculiarly intense strains of operating in hostile environments, often with little help of relief, surrounded by enemies whose cultures seemed savage and unintelligible. Yet considered from another aspect, the Spanish "conquest" seems remarkably peaceful. Most communities, especially within the regions previously subject to the Aztecs and Incas, offered the Spaniards little resistance or actively welcomed them, so eager were they to escape from their Native American overlords.

The Native American Doña Marina rather than the Spaniard Cortés directs the battle of Tenochtitlán in the Lienzo de Tlaxcala, a mid-sixteenth-century Native American portrayal of scenes from the conquest of Mexico. The same source also always shows Doña Marina center-stage negotiating alliances. Here she commands along the central causeway, where native warriors lead the attack against the Aztecs, and in the Spanish gunboat that native paddlers help propel across Lake Texcoco.

Even where no oppressive native empires existed, Native Americans were often surprisingly hospitable to European intruders, who usually seemed at first too few, vulnerable, and unused to local conditions to be much of a threat. Most European communities relied on native collaboration for food or allies, or both. Sexual alliances with native women of elite rank, especially in areas of Spanish and Portuguese operations, helped the newcomers to get established and, according to native custom in many areas, conferred on the host communities a duty to help with labor and food. Spanish friars were amazingly successful in making themselves useful as holy men, healers, arbiters of disputes, and protectors against secular exploiters. In short, the reception of Europeans owed much to a remarkably widespread feature of Native American cultures: what we might call the **stranger effect**—the tendency some peoples have to esteem and defer to strangers, whose usefulness as arbitrators of disputes, dispensers of justice, and preservers of peace, arises from the objectivity that their foreign origins confer.

Making the New Empires Work

By the end of the sixteenth century—before the French or English had established a single enduring colony anywhere in the Western Hemisphere—the Spanish monarchy in the New World effectively included all the biggest and most productive islands of the Caribbean and a continuous swathe of territory from the edge of the Colorado plateau in the north to the River Bío-Bío in southern Chile. It extended from sea to shining sea over the narrow reaches of the hemisphere, and along the Atlantic coast of what is now Venezuela, with a southerly corridor to the Atlantic, across what is now Bolivia, and along the Paraguay River and River Plate. In most areas that the Atlantic wind system made easily accessible from Europe, Spain had preempted potential rivals, except on the Brazilian coast, where, by agreement with Spain, Portugal had a series of sugar- and timber-producing colonies. The relatively late start other colonizers and would-be colonizers, in particular, the English and French monarchies, made was not the result of any inherent inferiority on their part. The best portions of the hemisphere were in other hands and only the dregs were left. It took a long time to find the will and ways to exploit them.

Unsurprisingly, therefore, in the Americas, the colonial societies of the north lived in awe of those of the south: envying their gold and silver, imitating their plantations and ranches, trying to rival their cities, coveting their territory but fearing their further expansion. English conquerors, for instance, aped those of Spain. In 1609, the first instructions to the colonists of Virginia—the first enduring English colony in North America—ordered them to maintain a pretense of divinity in dealing with the natives; and to conceal any white men's deaths to project an image of immortality. This was naive. Captain John Smith (1580–1631), the most dynamic leader of early Virginia, was a voracious reader with a storybook self-image. He claimed—in imitation of a story Columbus told about himself in Jamaica—to hold natives spellbound by his knowledge of the stars. Smith also applied methods apparently modeled on Cortés: using terror and massacre to keep natives cowed, and trying to exploit a special relationship with the natives' dominant chieftain to rule through him.

The Spanish Empire preempted European rivals in regions selected precisely because they were densely populated, with productive, established economies. In consequence, Spanish policy—rarely successful in practice—was always to preserve the Native American population. This was not the case in most other parts of the Americas, where the Indians were too few, too warlike, or too unaccustomed to large-scale production to meet the colonists' labor needs. In most colonies, once reliance on native charity was no longer necessary, Native Americans seemed at best a nuisance, unless they were needed to keep trade going (as in the parts of mainland America France nominally ruled).

Throughout British America, for instance, the native peoples were a source of conflict between frontiersmen and the representatives of the crown, who wanted the protection of Indian buffer states and the benefit of a relatively dense pool of white labor, which frontier conquests would disperse. For most colonial subjects, however, the Native Americans merely got in the way of land grabbing. Genocide was the best means to deal with them. In 1637, an explicit attempt to exterminate an entire Native American people—the New England Pequots—was half finished in a massacre on Mystic River in Connecticut, where, the governor reported, the victims could be seen "frying in the fire and the streams of blood quenching the same." The tribe's very name was banned. In defiance of official policy, a settler malcontent, Nathaniel Bacon, launched war in Virginia in 1675 with the explicit aim of destroying all Native Americans, friendly and hostile alike. This was a characteristic outrage in the late seventeenth century: a period of increasing tension—which also provoked violent clashes in areas of Spanish settlement in Florida and New Mexico—between growing colonies and threatened Native Americans. In terms of the sacrifice of life on both sides, the worst such episode was King Philip's War in New England in 1676. Launched by a Native American chief, who managed to put together an uncharacteristically big Indian coalition to stem white expansion, this resistance movement threatened to reverse the direction of extermination. The white presence was, for a few months, genuinely at risk, until Native American peoples from the interior who were willing to fight for the colonists restored the balance in the white man's favor. In areas of predominantly British

> *"The relatively late start other colonizers and would-be colonizers, in particular, the English and French monarchies, made was not the result of any inherent inferiority on their part. The best portions of the hemisphere were in other hands and only the dregs were left. It took a long time to find the will and ways to exploit them."*

A CLOSER LOOK

The Meeting of Cortés and Moctezuma

Part of a series of canvases painted in Spain about 150 years after the fall of Mexico, The Meeting of Cortés and Moctezuma is a remarkable record of how the Spanish memorialized the conquest.

By the late seventeenth century, Spaniards in New Spain were so used to Chinese and Filipino textiles and imitations that they treated the patterns as indigenous.

For "creole" apologists, who defended the New World against jibes that America was inferior to Europe, the might and majesty of Popocatapetl were symbolic. (see p. 681)

In earlier, indigenous depictions, Doña Marina, Cortés's mistress and interpreter, occupies pride of place, receiving more honor than Cortés, who appears more or less as her assistant.

The lake-bound environment of pre-colonial Tenochtitlan is recalled, reflecting Spaniard's pride in "civilizing" the environment by smothering it with a great new city.

Spaniards who possessed armor probably did wear it to suit the sense of occasion associated with the encounter with Moctezuma. Usually, however, they preferred the native cotton armor, suited to the climate and altitude.

What does this painting say about the way the Spanish mythologized the conquest of Mexico?

The Pequot War. The capture of Fort Mystic in eastern Connecticut in May 1637 was the decisive event of the war of extermination waged by New England colonists in search of security against the Pequot people. Surprised by the ferocity of Native American resistance, the settlers burned the houses in which hundreds of Indian women and children were sheltering. This illustration, made just after the war, shows the settlers' opening volleys and the routes of their two-pronged attack.

colonization or "Anglo" rule, preconquest population levels for Native Americans have never really revived, outside the formerly Spanish-ruled Southwest of the United States.

In some places, Native Americans were useful as slaves. On the fringes of the Amazon jungles, slaving became a major industry for Portuguese based in the port of São Paulo in southern Brazil. The early economy of the Carolinas depended on the slave trade with Native Americans, who raided neighbors as far inland as the Mississippi River valley. In this part of the North American South, there were more Native American slaves than black slaves until the destructive nature of the trade led to its abandonment in the early eighteenth century.

Generally, however, the English colonies relied on imported labor—whether enslaved or not—and so could afford to massacre their Native Americans or drive them west. They had a ready-made ideology of extermination. They were the new Israel. The Native Americans were the "uncircumcized," to be dealt with as the biblical Israel dealt with its pagan enemies: smitten hip and thigh. The English, indifferent to clerical discipline, rarely endured Spanish-style agonies of conscience about the justice of their presence in America or the morality of their wars. People who left their land underexploited or unfenced deserved to lose it. Only the line of the fence or the marks of the plow proved true tenure. Native Americans in British areas of expansion were too poor to exploit for tribute. It was more economical to dispossess them and replace them with white farmers or black slaves. The only colony where this reasoning was modified was early Pennsylvania. Here moral and material considerations combined to favor a policy of friendly collaboration with the Native Americans. Thanks to the founder's Quaker high morality, supposedly just prices were paid for land purchases from the Indians, who were encouraged to stay on the frontier as buffers against hostile tribes or rival European empires.

Whether expelled, exterminated, diminished by disease, or absorbed into colonial society by marrying Europeans or adopting European ways, the Native Americans retreated to the margins of colonial life wherever European colonies were founded. European involvement in the affairs of the Western Hemisphere had begun—like European penetration of Asia—as a collaborative venture in which Native American communities and states were the newcomers' essential hosts and helpers. By the late seventeenth century, however, those relationships, almost everywhere in the Americas where European and Indian cultures confronted each other, had broken down in violence or simply been transformed as the Native American population fell. Unlike Asia, the New World was not an arena in which native and European states could coexist side by side—although, as we shall see, in the eighteenth and nineteenth centuries, short-lived attempts to found native states and empires revived beyond the frontiers of European settlement.

Chronology: Spanish and English Land Empires in the New World	
1492	Columbus arrives in Caribbean
1495–1496	Columbus begins war of conquest in Hispaniola
1518–1546	Spanish conquests of Mexico and Peru
1609	English found colony of Virginia
1675	Bacon's rebellion (Virginia)
1676	King Philip's War (New England)

In Perspective
The Global Balance of Trade

It is not generally realized that in the colonial New World precolonial patterns of exchange often remained intact. European merchants joined existing Native American trading communities, extending the reach or increasing the volume of traffic, enhancing what Indian Ocean venturers called **country trades**, which involved local or regional exchanges that never touched Europe. In North America, trade in deerskins and beaver pelts in colonial times extended precolonial practice. The French backwoodsmen and buckskin-clad frontiersmen slotted into an existing Native American framework that linked hunting grounds and routes of trade and tribute. The Huron, Native American farmers and traders who did not need to hunt, except for exercise and to supplement their diet, were the middlemen of the early seventeenth-century fur trade, supplying French buyers in Quebec in Canada. Spanish entrepreneurs took part in a profitable canoe-borne trade in local textiles, healing plants, and dyestuffs along the coast of Venezuela in the 1590s. Similarly, the economy that sustained the Spanish conquerors of Yucatán was no transoceanic affair of precious goods, but an extension of the age-old Maya trade with central Mexico, based largely on cacao for consumption in Mexico City.

Of course, Spanish activity was not confined to modest ventures of these kinds, along traditional grooves. The Spanish monarchy was a great inaugurator of new intra-American trade routes. New cities, founded in places never settled on a large scale before, especially on the Pacific and Atlantic coasts, became magnets to suppliers of foodstuffs, cotton textiles, and building materials. The conquest of Peru demanded a new transcontinental route from the Caribbean to the Pacific across the Isthmus of Panama in Central America, which became, like the alternative later opened from Bolivia to the Atlantic via the River Plate, a major silver-bearing artery of the Spanish Empire. Mule-train routes that the Native American civilizations, which had no horses or mules before the arrival of the Europeans, had never required, served the new mining ventures in remote hinterlands. The conquest of much of Chile in the mid-sixteenth century stimulated the creation of a heroic new seaborne route, far into the Pacific, to overcome the Humboldt Current. Sailing ships took longer to get from Lima in Peru to Concepción in Chile than from Seville in Spain to Santo Domingo in the Caribbean.

The slow but steady spread of Spanish frontiers brought regions formerly unknown to each other into touch. The link between Mexico and Peru is the most startling case, since it seems incredible—yet true—that the Native American civilizations of those areas never had significant mutual contact until the Spaniards arrived. Although the places Spaniards occupied in New Mexico, Arizona, and Texas showed some signs of having received cultural influences from Mexico in the past (see Chapter 10), California was a genuinely new discovery, where Spanish missions in the eighteenth century first created ventures in settlement and agriculture that made the region a potential trading partner for other parts of the Spanish monarchy (see Chapter 21). Native American merchants could have navigated the Amazon and the Orinoco rivers before the Spaniards arrived, but, as far as we know, they never did so. No one fully exploited those

"The slow but steady spread of Spanish frontiers brought regions formerly unknown to each other into touch. The link between Mexico and Peru is the most startling case, since it seems incredible—yet true—that the Native American civilizations of those areas never had significant mutual contact until the Spaniards arrived."

> *"The Americas were a huge bonanza—of land, of food and mineral resources, of opportunities for the productive deployment of labor, of new markets and manufactures. Western Europeans' privileged access to those resources made a new era in world history possible."*

mighty and mysterious waterways as arteries of commerce until well into the seventeenth century.

Meanwhile, new commerce opened with the wider world. A system of convoys linked Spain to America and injected Europe's cash-starved economies with veins of gold and silver. The need for slaves led other European merchants to Spanish colonies and linked the Americas to Africa. The route of the Manila Galleon, a Spanish ship that made an annual crossing of the Pacific from the Philippines to Acapulco on the Pacific coast of Mexico, facilitated the direct exchange of Mexican silver for Chinese silk and porcelain. For the first time, trade girdled the world, tying the Americas, Africa, and Eurasia into a single, interconnected system.

Suppose Columbus had been right. Suppose the globe was small, and no Americas lay in the way of Europeans' westward approach to Asia. Europeans would still, of course, have taken part—presumably a bigger part—in Asia's carrying trades. They would have made money out of it and closed the wealth gap that separated them from the richer economies of maritime Asia. They would have contributed to recycling Japanese silver and helped to make the world's economy more liquid. They would probably have gone on to found the land empires that began to take shape in Asia in the late seventeenth century. The total volume of resources at their command would, however, have remained modest. The Americas were a huge bonanza—of land, of food and mineral resources, of opportunities for the productive deployment of labor, of new markets and manufactures. Western Europeans' privileged access to those resources made a new era in world history possible. The traditional poor relations of Eurasia—the formerly impoverished West—could now challenge previously towering economies,

Gathering Brazil Wood. "Because this wood is dense and hard to cut," as a French observer of Brazil's logwood trade noted, "if the foreigners who voyage over there were not helped by the savages, they could not load even a medium-sized ship in a year." The quality of this carving from Rouen, France in the 1530s, made to decorate a timber merchant's house, suggests that fortunes could be made from the trade in tropical woods. The carver glamorizes the Native Americans as innocently naked and classically posed.

Yohann Deslandes, cg76-Agence photographique des sites et musees departementaux

such as those of India and China, that had been dominant in Eurasia for thousands of years.

The dazzle of American silver, however, should not blind us to the continuing importance of the Indian Ocean as the world's major arena of large-scale, long-range trade, where the world's biggest fortunes were still made and lost, and where Europeans were interlopers, striving for toeholds. Traditionally, historians concentrated on the spice trade as an index of world-shaping changes, and especially on pepper, which accounted for as much as 70 percent of the total trade by value in the seventeenth century. It is true that by value per unit of weight, spices—especially cloves, mace, nutmeg, and cinnamon—were the world's most valuable products at the time. And it is also fair to say that by the end of the seventeenth century the major share of the trade had passed into the hands of European shipping agents, to the detriment of ancient land routes and indigenous shipping. It is important, however, to bear some qualifications in mind. China still dwarfed the rest of the world as a market for spices, and only a few ships a year carried part of the trade from the Indian Ocean to Europe. European shipping probably expended far more time and labor on moving spices around maritime Asia than on exporting them elsewhere. In this respect, the role of Europeans in the spice trade was part of a bigger picture, in which Europeans, with little to sell in Asian markets except space aboard their ships, began to accumulate wealth as suppliers of services to their richer Asian hosts. By taking advantage of the price differentials between various Asian markets—and especially, as we have seen, of the differential values of silver in Japan, China, and India—they were able gradually to take more and more of the initiative as independent traffickers in the goods, such as Indian textiles, aromatic woods of the

Chronology

1492–1493	Columbus discovers routes to and from the New World
1500	Portuguese begin direct trade with southern India
1510	Portuguese trading post at Goa established
1513	Discovery of the Gulf Stream
1518–1546	Spanish conquest of Mexico and Peru
1519	Babur founds Mughal Empire
1519–1521	Spanish navigators complete first global navigation
1520–1566	Reign of Suleiman the Magnificent (Ottoman Empire)
1521	Spanish capture Tenochtitlán; end of Aztec Empire
1529	Spain and Portugal divide Pacific seaborne routes between themselves
1530s	Spanish conquest of Peru
1552–1556	Russian conquest of Kazan
1556–1605	Mughal expansion and centralization under Akbar
1564–1565	Northern Pacific sea route between New World and Asia discovered
1585–1598	Reign of Toyotomi Hideyoshi (Japan)
1600	East India Company founded (England)
1602	Dutch East India Company founded
Early 1600s	Dutch use westerlies to circumnavigate globe
1609	English found Virginia colony
1619	Dutch found Batavia (Indonesia)
1620–1640	Portuguese expelled from trading posts in Persian Gulf and Indian Ocean
1640	Dutch merchants only Europeans allowed in Japan
1656–1707	Mughal Empire covers most of Indian subcontinent under Aurangzeb
1674	French establish trading post at Pondicherry (India)
1676	King Philip's War (New England)
1689	Treaty of Nerchinsk with China checks Russian expansion eastward

South Seas, sugar, rice, and the pharmaceuticals and porcelain of continental East Asia, which were in high demand around the Indian Ocean. As time went on, they gained more advantages by introducing products from elsewhere that were inaccessible to native Asian traders, such as African slaves, American silver, and, later, as we shall see (Chapter 25) opium. Though their activities sometimes resembled piracy, and they sometimes jeopardized their role by resorting to force in an attempt to concentrate trade in their own hands, they were, on the whole, tolerated or welcomed as a useful and exploitable addition to the shipping stocks of a region so overflowing with trade that it could absorb almost any amount of strangers, as long as they had ships. The beginning of the "rise of the West" to parity with the wealth of the East happened in the Indian Ocean as much as or rather more than in the Atlantic. It started modestly, with Westerners in a subordinate role. And its foundation was the volume and strength of intra-Asian trade: Europe generally was still economically underproductive compared with the powerhouse economies of the East.

PROBLEMS AND PARALLELS

1. How were empires agents of change in the sixteenth and seventeenth centuries?
2. What are the differences between land and maritime empires? Why were Mughal emperors such as Akbar and Ottoman sultans such as Suleiman the Magnificent so warlike?
3. How did the maritime imperialism of Japan compare with Portuguese and Dutch imperial ventures? Why did the shogun Hideyoshi try to conquer an empire on the mainland of Asia?
4. What roles did native collaborators, interpreters, merchants, and middlemen play in the empires of the sixteenth and seventeenth centuries? What does the term *stranger effect* mean?
5. What are the differences and similarities among the Russian, Chinese, Ottoman, and Mughal Empires of this period?
6. How was Spain able to achieve such a vast empire in so short a time? Why were Spain's Native American allies and collaborators such as the interpreter Doña Marina so crucial in the conquest of the Aztec and Inca empires?
7. How did a global trade network emerge in the sixteenth century? How did the Indian Ocean continue to be the major arena of large-scale, long-range trade in the sixteenth and seventeenth centuries?

READ ON▶ ▶ ▶

The best introductions to the Portuguese maritime empire are A. J. Russell-Wood, *The Portuguese Empire, 1415–1808* (1992) and F. Bethencourt and D. Curto, eds., *Portuguese Overseas Expansion* (2007). P. Pérez-Mallaína, *Spain's Men of the Sea: Daily Life on the Indies Fleets in the Sixteenth Century* (trans. Carla Rahn Phillips, 1998) is a superb social history of shipboard life in the age of maritime expansion. C. R. Boxer, *The Dutch Seaborne Empire: 1600–1800* (reprint, 1991) is a slightly dated but still valuable and very readable account of the rise of Dutch colonial power. Its perspective on Southeast Asia should be balanced by W. Cummings, *Making Blood White: Historical Transformations in Early Modern Makasar* (2002), a sophisticated recent study of the transition from oral to literate culture in an area of increasing Dutch influence. K. So, *Japanese Piracy in Ming China during 16th Century* (1975) explores the impact of *wako* raids around the South China Sea in the sixteenth century. M. Berry, *Hideyoshi* (2001) is a superb study of that ruler. B. Walker, *The Conquest of Ainu Lands: Ecology and Culture in Japanese Expansion, 1590–1800* (2001) is important on continuing Japanese expansion.

R. L. Edmunds, *The Northern Frontier in Qing China and Tokugawa Japan: A Comparative Study of Frontier Policy* (1985) is valuable. On Qing expansion, J. Waley-Cohen, *Exile in Mid-Qing China* (1991) is important. On Batavia, L. Blusse, *Strange Company* (1986) is outstanding. J. F. Richards, *The Mughal Empire* (1996) is a fine introduction to Mughal history, while P. M. Brand and G. D. Lowry, *Akbar's India: Art from the Mughal City of Victory* (1985) explores the cultural expressions of Mughal might and ruling style. R. Murphey, *Ottoman Warfare, 1500–1700* (1999) analyzes Ottoman military power in its social, economic, and geographic contexts. K. Chase, *Firearms. A Global History to 1700* (2003) offers an overview of the dynamics of power in Eurasia whose central thesis is simplistic but whose details on the spread of gunpowder weaponry are valuable.

My material on Russian icons comes from the Royal Academy exhibition catalog *The Art of Holy Russia: Icons from Moscow, 1440–1660* (1998). On Siberia, T. Armstrong, ed., *Yermak's Campaigns in Siberia* (1975) unites the main chronicles. J. Forsyth, *A History of the Peoples of Siberia* (1994) is the best overall study.

M. Restall, *Seven Myths of the Spanish Conquest* (2003) is essential on New World imperialism. J. H. Elliott, *Empires of the Atlantic World* (2006) compares English, later British, and Spanish experience. B. E. Mundy, *The Mapping of New Spain: Indigenous Cartography and the Maps of the Relaciones Geograficas* (2000) offers an excellent scholarly analysis of the local maps and surveys collected by the Spanish government in the late sixteenth century as part of its effort to govern its new empire more effectively. A fine edition of W. Bradford, *Of Plymouth Plantation* (1999) gives a first-hand account of the creation of the Plymouth colony. E. H. Spicer, *The American Indians* (1982) is an authoritative summary of Native American history, including relations with the expanding European presence in North America.

On global trade balances in the sixteenth and seventeenth centuries, see A. Gunder Frank, *ReOrient: Global Economy in the Asian Age* (1998), a provocative study that argues forcefully for Asia, especially China, as the center of gravity of global trade right through to 1800. E. van Veen, *Decay or Defeat? An Enquiry into the Portuguese Decline in Asia* (2000) makes some important corrections, and R. Barendse, *The Arabian Seas* (2002) is extremely helpful. J. Goody, *The Theft of History* (2008) investigates the myth of the Western origins of capitalism, and much else of relevance.

CHAPTER 17

The Ecological Revolution of the Sixteenth and Seventeenth Centuries

▲ **Ledger's legacy:** the quinine plantations established in Java, thanks to the seeds Charles Ledger transplanted to the Dutch East Indies from Bolivia in the late 1850s, are now the world's major source of this antimalarial drug.

BOLIVIA

PERU

Charles Ledger's captors were taking him to the regional capital, where the Bolivian police would lock him up indefinitely if he fell into their hands. But Ledger could not afford that sacrifice of time. It was already mid-April 1855. The deadly winter of the Southern Hemisphere in the high mountains was drawing on. Ledger's men and flocks needed him. Luckily, he had a strong narcotic in his saddlebags, left over from a bout of toothache. He slipped a heavy dose into his guards' brandy, drove off their mules, and escaped into the night. Shots echoed around him as he fled, but the policemen were too dazed with the drug to aim straight.

The crime for which he was under arrest was attempting to export alpacas, small, llama-like creatures famous for their fine wool. The authorities in Peru, where Ledger began his odyssey, did not want breeding animals to fall into potentially rival hands. The law forbade anyone to drive alpacas toward the coast. Therefore, having bought hundreds of specimens and gathered them high in the Andes, near the Peruvian-Bolivian border, Ledger conceived a plan the local Indians condemned as insane. He would turn inland, drive his herd over the mountains and across deserts, via Bolivia and Argentina, to Chile. There he would board them on ships and sail them to Australia, where the government promised him a handsome reward if he could get adequate breeding stock into the country. On the way, he would cross-breed alpacas with llamas, which are much larger but have coarser coats, to improve the yield of good-quality wool.

If ever there was a nightmare journey, this was it. The authorities hunted him—alleging not unreasonably that he was breaking the spirit of the law. Rustlers mounted attacks. Indians shadowed and harried him, like hidden raptors, striving to steal animals. Ledger tried to elude his pursuers by following secretive, dangerous routes amid precipices and high passes, up to 17,000 feet above sea level. Yet he also had to organize vast amounts of fodder and water to cross high badlands where neither was available. Men he sent to gather wood for campfires froze to death in snowdrifts. More died in gunfights with pursuers. The animals perished in their hundreds from starvation or thirst or heat or cold. Ledger kept up their numbers by breeding them and replenishing them with purchases in Bolivia along his way.

Ledger spent his fortune and beggared his family. He never saw again the wife he left behind in Peru, because she died before his journey ended. So did the baby daughter with whom she was pregnant at Ledger's departure, and whom he never saw at all. It took him six years to get to the

FOCUS questions

Why was the Columbian Exchange so important, and how did it affect nutrition in Europe and Asia?

How did the introduction of new diseases by Europeans affect population levels in the Americas?

Why did the Europeans import slaves to the Americas?

Why did the balance of power change between nomads and settled peoples?

In what new ways did people around the world exploit the natural environment in the seventeenth century?

How did the European settlement in the Americas and increased contact across Eurasia redirect the course of evolution?

Chilean frontier, and even then he still had to cross the Atacama Desert—one of the most arid environments in the world. The French consul offered him a fortune for his flock, intending to send the animals to Algeria and start an alpaca textiles industry there, but Ledger persevered in what he conceived as a patriotic mission for the British Empire. When he got to Australia, the authorities reneged on their promises, dispersed the flock, and left Ledger penniless.

Ledger would have starved to death or been dependent on charity, but for the fact that the alpacas were just a sideline. Ledger's other—and even greater—contribution to world history was to discover, while he was in Bolivia, a stock of the highest-quality fever-tree seeds the world had ever seen. The tree's bark yields quinine, the universally acclaimed "miracle drug" that Jesuits had produced in Peru in the seventeenth century and had administered, with startling effects, to sufferers across the world. It supresses fevers and shivers and has regularly saved the lives of patients afflicted with malaria. Until the discovery of quinine, the only remedies known in Europe were magical mumbo jumbo—putting a peach stone in an orange and eating the fruit, for instance, or having a young virgin tie magic paper around a sufferer's neck with a long string.

In Ledger's day, efforts to propagate the miracle-seeds outside the Andean region had largely failed. But Ledger's seeds thrived in Java, where quinine kept Dutch soldiers and the Dutch Empire alive. A pension from the Dutch government sustained Ledger until his death in a suburb of Sydney, Australia, senseless with senile dementia, at the age of 87, in 1906.

Ledger's life was a small episode in the story of what was, by most standards, the greatest revolution ever to have occurred in the history of the world by means of human agency. The sheer, staggering audacity of taking Andean life forms to Australia, Algeria, or Java only became possible as a result of what historians now generally call the **Columbian Exchange**—the global redistribution of life forms, beginning in 1492 and accelerating thereafter, that accompanied the era of world-wide travel by intercontinental routes.

A divergent pattern of evolution had made the life forms of the various continents ever more different from one another from the moment, perhaps about 150 million years ago or more, when Pangaea—the unified world landmass—split and the continents began to drift apart. Relatively suddenly, by the scale of the long preceding period, the Columbian Exchange reversed that pattern. About 500 years ago, Earth-girdling travel and a mixture of deliberate and unconscious transplantation of plants, animals, and bacteria substituted a new pattern in which the life forms of different continents began to be swapped. It became possible to grow and breed plants and animals in environments that had never seen their like before. Products migrated between hemispheres, across previously impassable barriers of climate and expanses of ocean. So did people. So did pests.

Three huge transformations in humans' relationship with the environment were among the consequences or coincidences. First, the human relationship with fatal pathogens underwent puzzling lurches. At one level, as we have seen, the period from the mid-fourteenth century to the eighteenth was an age of plagues, when lethal diseases spread over the world and ravaged populations. On the other hand, the micro-organisms that were chiefly responsible seem, late in the period, to have retreated, with surprising and still unexplained suddenness, from their accustomed eco-niches. Partly as a result, a worldwide "population explosion" began toward the mid-eighteenth century.

Second, human settlement changed both its range and its nature, invading new ecological frontiers on an unprecedented scale: farming grasslands, felling forests, climbing slopes, reclaiming bogs, penetrating game preserves and deep-sea fisheries, expanding and founding cities, turning deserts into gardens and gardens into deserts. This was part of a drive for resources and energy sources in an increasingly populous and competitive world. Hunters ransacked previously unmolested wild zones for animal furs, fats, and proteins. Much of this hunting took place at sea, in pursuit of migrating fish and wandering whales. The exploration and exploitation of new frontiers created an illusion of abundance that inspired ecological overkill; yet imperialism also had positive environmental effects, as colonialists came, in some cases, to see themselves as custodians of "tropical Edens," preparing the way for a revived respect and even reverence for nature in the eighteenth-century West.

Finally, climate underwent global fluctuations: The "Little Ice Age" was in progress for most of the period and revived briefly at its end, though temperatures generally took an upward turn in the eighteenth century. The effects of the temperature changes, however, are hard to calibrate and, on the basis of present knowledge, seem surprisingly slight. We have to set them aside as an unknown quantity and look in turn at each of the other aspects of an ecological revolution, which, though its effects were global, is primarily part of the story of Western civilization, because it began as a result of world-ranging European initiatives and, in particular, changed Europe and the Americas.

THE ECOLOGICAL EXCHANGE: PLANTS AND ANIMALS

It is tempting to pick out the well-documented introductions of life forms as the highlights of the story, or focus on the legends of heroes who bore life-changing new foodstuffs across the oceans. Christopher Columbus is fairly credited with a lot of "firsts." From his first ocean crossing in 1492, he brought back descriptions and samples of New World plants, including pineapple and cassava or manioc. On his second transatlantic voyage in 1493, he took sugarcane to the island of Hispaniola—but let it grow wild. Pigs, sheep, cattle, chickens, and wheat made their first appearance in the New World on the same occasion. Other heroic firsts are the subjects of legends or fables. Juan Garrido, a black companion of Cortés, supposedly first planted wheat in Mexico. The story of Sir Walter Raleigh, the sixteenth-century poet, courtier, historian, and pirate, introducing potatoes to England is false but has an honored place in myth.

The real, though unwitting, heroes, however, are surely the plants and animals themselves, which survived deadly journeys and successfully adapted to new climates, sometimes—in the case of seeds—by accident, with little human help. They traveled in the cuffs or pleats of the clothing of carriers who didn't know they were there, or were caught in the fabric of cloth bales and sacks. In terms of volume and contribution to global nutrition, a few instances stand out. Out of Eurasia to new worlds in the Western and Southern Hemispheres went wheat, sugar, rice, bananas, coconuts, apples, pears, apricots, peaches, plums, cherries, olives, citrus fruits, and major meat-yielding and dairy livestock. The European grape variety *vitis vinifera* (the only grapes native to the Americas are Concord grapes) should perhaps be included, because of the importance that American wines made from varieties of it have attained in the world market. Yams, okra, and collard greens were among vegetables that made the crossing from Africa (see Map 17.1).

"The real, though unwitting, heroes, however, are surely the plants and animals themselves, which survived deadly journeys and successfully adapted to new climates, sometimes—in the case of seeds—by accident, with little human help."

Ecological and Microbial Exchange, Americas to Africa and Eurasia

maize	cacao
potatoes	chillies
sweet potatoes	cassava
tomatoes	peanuts
beans	squash
quinine	vanilla
pineapples	turkeys
tobacco	syphilis?

1492: Columbus brings back to Europe descriptions of pineapples and cassava

1510: First importation of slaves to Spanish colonies

ca. 1519: Supposed first planting of wheat in Mexico; introduction of smallpox to the New World

1535: Influenza introduced by French explorers wipes out Indians in St. Lawrence River valley

1560s: First record of sweet potatoes in China

1490 1500 1510 1520 1530 1540 1550 1560 1570

1493: Columbus takes sugarcane to island of Hispaniola

1513: First sugarcane plantation in the Americas opens in Hispaniola

1530s: First Brazilian sugar plantations

1555: First record of maize in China

1563: Plague strikes Bahia (Brazil)

1580s: Brazil becomes world's major producer of refined sugar

1605: Portuguese introduce potatoes to Asia

1644: Coffee arrives in France

1570 1580 1590 1600 1610 1620 1630 1640 1650

1590s: Potatoes planted in Ireland, northern Spain, and southwestern France

1633–1635: Epidemic of measles and smallpox strikes Chesapeake Indians

1648: Chocolate introduced to England

1666: first rhubarb planted in Amsterdam

1680s: potatoes arrive in Belgium

1700s: approximately 24,000 African slaves a year taken to the Americas

1650 1660 1670 1680 1690 1700 1710 1720 1730

1679: Plague strikes Venice

1690s: Dutch transplant coffee in Java

1720: Last recorded outbreak of plague in Europe

Ecological and Microbial Exchange, Eurasia to the Americas

wheat	onions
rice	coffee
sugar	sheep
bananas	chickens
coconuts	pigs
apples	horses
pears	cattle
peaches	whooping cough
plums	diptheria
cherries	chicken pox
oranges	typhoid
lemons	influenza
dandelions	smallpox
almonds	measles
grapes (*vitis vinifera*)	

Ecological and Microbial Exchange, Africa to the Americas

yams
okra
collard greens

MAP 17.1

Ecological, Microbial Exchanges, 1500–1700

→ ecological and microbial exchange, Eurasia to the Americas

→ ecological and microbial exchange, Americas to Africa and Eurasia

→ ecological and microbial exchange, Africa to the Americas

➤ European immigration to the Americas, 1500–1700

➤ forced migration of Africans to the Americas

⚑ sugar plantation

⚒ major importer of slaves

⊘ coffee plantation

Huron peoples

Genetic Sameness

The distribution of the O-blood type among native peoples of the world

Percentage:

■ 90
■ 80
■ 70
■ 60
□ 50?

Before 1500, the distribution of the blood group O gene was far higher among the native peoples of the Americas than anywhere else in the world. This confirms their protracted isolation from the people of the Old World that left them exposed to disease.

Tobacco was thought to be good for the digestive system. In this seventeenth-century Dutch illustration, Cupid carries the smoker's pipe and pouch because tobacco, like lovemaking, is a fleeting pleasure that quickly goes up in smoke.

Along with the fancy foodstuffs and flavors already mentioned, the Americas supplied medicinal plants for Africa and Eurasia. Quinine, which Spanish physicians borrowed from among the medicinal plants of the peoples of Peru, had enormous long-term significance, because, as we have seen, it can control the effects of malaria and was therefore vital for Europeans struggling to survive in the mosquito-ridden, swampy tropics. Tobacco—"with which," said a Spanish reporter in the 1540s, Native Americans "perfume their mouths"—was thought to aid digestion. But the staple products—and therefore the most important gifts of the New World to the rest, because they could feed vast populations—were maize, potatoes, and sweet potatoes.

Maize, Sweet Potatoes, and Potatoes

Maize at first revolted Old-World taste buds but fascinated plant specialists. As the Spanish botanist Juan de Cárdenas reported in one of the first scientific studies of maize in 1591, it thrives "in cold, hot, dry, or wet climates, in mountainous regions or grasslands, as a winter or summer crop, irrigated or dry-farmed," with a high yield and short land-use cycle that made wheat seem difficult to cultivate by comparison. Maize appeared in China so quickly after it emerged from America that some scholars insist that it must somehow have arrived there earlier. Two independent routes seem to have brought maize to Asia: overland from the west, maize was borne to China as a tribute plant by Turkic frontiersmen and first recorded in 1555. Meanwhile, it came by sea to Fujian in southern China, where a visiting Spanish friar saw it cultivated in 1577. At first, Chinese welcomed it as a curiosity, not a serious source of food. It rated only a footnote in a standard Chinese agricultural work of the early seventeenth century. But its advantages over millet and rice—it required less labor per unit of production and could grow in eco-niches where those crops were unsuitable—gradually made it popular, especially in areas of new settlement. Europeans were initially even less enthusiastic than the Chinese about eating maize themselves, rather than feeding it to livestock, but it slowly established a place as human food in the eighteenth century in parts of the eastern and central Mediterranean, the Balkans, Ukraine, and southern Russia.

Like maize, the sweet potato had a transforming effect in parts of China. First reported in southern China near the Burmese border in the 1560s, it probably came overland from the south. Its flavor had a bad reputation with ethnic Chinese, but it found favor in hill country among immigrants and settlers who were obliged to occupy land previously thought marginal. Used, at first, only for horse fodder, sweet potatoes were rapidly adopted as human food. In 1594, a governor of Fujian supposedly recommended sweet potatoes when the conventional crops failed. The enthusiasm with which different cultures received the crop varied unpredictably. In Japan sweet potatoes never caught on, after following a south-to-north route perhaps indicated by variations in their name: they are called "Chinese potatoes" in the Ryukyu Islands, "Ryukyu potatoes" farther north in Satsuma in the southern Japanese home islands, and "Satsuma potatoes" in the rest of Japan.

Potatoes, which the Portuguese introduced to Asia in 1605, similarly failed to win popular favor in Japan, Korea, or China. They had remained a regionally restricted food in the Americas—cultivated at high altitudes in the Andes. Yet when Portuguese migrants took them to Bengal in India, they became an inescapable ingredient of Bengali meals. Potatoes conquered northern Europe,

Harvesting potatoes in India. Although Westerners tend to think of rice as the staple food of India, the country is now the third largest potato producer in the world, after China and Russia. Bengal—where potatoes have been an essential ingredient of the regional cuisine since the Portuguese introduced them from the New World in the 1600s—is no longer the major producer. Other provinces, especially in the highlands of northwest India have overtaken Bengal, and Andra Pradesh, shown here, is catching up.

where they gradually replaced rye as the food base of a vast swathe of humankind from Ireland across Scandinavia and Germany to Poland and Russia. War spread them, for peasants favored a crop that grew concealed in the ground and so eluded seizure by plundering troops. Tried out with success in the Basque country of northern Spain and southwest France and in Ireland before the end of the sixteenth century, the potato began its war-linked career in Belgium in the 1680s under the impact of French invasion, and spread eastward with every subsequent war. Scholars and bureaucrats promoted it because of its impressive nutritional qualities. If eaten in sufficient quantities, it is the only major staple that provides all the nutrients essential to human health.

Weeds, Grasses, and Livestock

Transplantations in the opposite direction—into the New World from the Old—turned much of the Americas into farmland for food for European palates and digestions, and ranch land for European livestock. The first stage was colonization by European weeds and grasses that made parts of the New World able to support sheep, cattle, and horses instead of just bison and llamas. European plants, such as purslane and Englishman's Foot, created what Alfred Crosby, the great historian of the ecological exchange, called "empires of the dandelion." Weeds made the revolution work. They "healed raw wounds" invaders tore in the earth, bound soil together, saved it from drying out, refilled "vacated eco-niches," and fed imported livestock.

Conscious transpositions followed. Horses and cattle came first—the New World had no similar big domesticated animals. The Spanish army that invaded New Mexico in 1598 was accompanied by thousands of head of cattle, which their masters drove over mountains and deserts—including the terrible 60-mile waterless stretch known as the March of Death. To Spanish cattlemen, the South American pampa and the North American prairie were the last frontiers of an enterprise that began in the Middle Ages, when they had adopted ranching as a way to exploit the empty, conquered lands in Spain after the Muslim population had fled or been expelled.

"To Spanish cattlemen, the South American pampa and the North American prairie were the last frontiers of an enterprise that began in the Middle Ages, when they had adopted ranching as a way to exploit the empty, conquered lands in Spain after the Muslim population had fled or been expelled."

Transporting horses. This eighteenth-century illustration from a Spanish manual of horsemanship makes it look easy. But transporting horses by sea was a delicate, hazardous, and technically demanding business. Once across the ocean, a few runaway steeds could transform the Americas. In 1536, Spaniards released 12 horses on the plains of Argentina. Within a few years, the herds "looked as dense as forests."

Embarcadero de los Cavallos.

Meanwhile, wheat arrived. The lower levels of the central valleys proved highly suitable for wheat, and although most of the Indian population continued to rely on maize, wheat bread became a badge of urban sophistication. Within a few years of the Spanish conquest, the city council of Mexico City demanded a supply of "white, clean, well-cooked and seasoned bread." The valleys of Mexico supplied Spanish garrisons all over Central America and the Caribbean with wheat flour.

Not all efforts to introduce wheat in other parts of the Americas were successful, at least at first. The Spanish colonists of Florida in 1565 brought wheat seed, together with grapevine cuttings, 200 calves, 400 pigs, 400 sheep, and unspecified numbers of goats and chickens. But the crops did not "take," and the animals went wild or died for lack of fodder or were slaughtered in desperation. By 1573, "herbs, fish, and other scum and vermin" sustained the colonists when rations were short. Corn bread and fish, foodstuffs copied from the Native American diet, were their mainstays. Similarly, the first English colonists in Virginia were unable to grow food for themselves and relied on handouts from the natives to see them through their "starving time." Investors and imperialists back home blamed colonists' moral deficiencies for these failures. But the problems of the mutual adaptation of Old World farming and New World environments were formidable, especially for settlers of exposed seaboards in an era of imperial competition. Colonies sited for defense, behind marshes or swamps, in difficult climates, needed generations of investment and long periods of heartbreakingly high rates of mortality before they could be made viable. At every stage of European colonization of new worlds, the remarkable thing is not the high rate of failure but the perseverance that led to ultimate success.

Cane Sugar

Of all the Old World arrivals in America, cane sugar was the first transplanted product to have a major impact on world markets. It is, perhaps, the first food to have conquered unaccustomed markets by the power of supply. Instead of following the usual laws of economics, according to which demand comes first and supply responds, sugar was the first of a series of tropical products that were recommended by their availability. European taste buds became enslaved to it.

Sugar rapidly became the most important item of transoceanic trade. The first sugar refinery in the Americas opened in Hispaniola in 1513. Portuguese enterprise launched the Brazilian sugar industry. For the first 30 years of their presence in Brazil, the Portuguese exploited its coasts for nothing but logwood bought in vast quantities—perhaps 19,000 tons a year—from the natives. From the 1530s, however, they began to plant sugar around Salvador and in Pernambuco in northern Brazil. It was a difficult crop to plant, harvest, and refine, greedy of capital and demanding lots of specialized labor. And it yielded surprisingly low profits for the planters—typically only 3 percent a year.

Trading in sugar, however, was highly profitable. So it was important for planters to retain an interest in the trade after the sugar left their hands. The value of the crop doubled or even quadrupled as it crossed the Atlantic. The sugar-growing area was never extensive—parts of Brazil, some Caribbean islands, patches of coasts around the Spanish Main, and French Louisiana around New Orleans—but it was highly productive. By the 1580s, four effects were evident. First, Brazil had become the world's major producer, and the economies of the older sugar islands of the eastern Atlantic—Madeira, the Azores, the Cape Verdes—(see Chapter 15) went into eclipse. Second, the need for labor in the sugar plantations and mills

A water-driven sugar mill in Pernambuco during the Dutch occupation of northern Brazil, depicted here in a Dutch atlas of 1662. Slaves carry the mill owner, slung in a hammock under a rich awning in the foreground. The sugar cane arrives by ox cart, to be ground by the power of the mill.

caused an explosion in the transatlantic slave trade. Third, the growing volume of sugar production created new American industries: refining sugar and distilling rum. In the seventeenth century, Brazilian sugar was refined locally, before export.

Finally, the competition for sugar-producing lands was becoming a major cause of imperial rivalry among European states. Dutch invaders took over the Portuguese sugar plantations in Pernambuco in 1630, then, on their expulsion nearly a quarter of a century later, concentrated on creating plantations of their own in the Caribbean and on the Guiana coast of South America, where they proclaimed a "second Brazil" in Surinam in 1667. English, French, Spaniards, Scandinavians, and even Courlanders from a duchy on the Baltic coast all set up sugar industries on Caribbean islands in the second half of the seventeenth century. Where sugar could be grown successfully, unprecedented prosperity was possible. In the 1680s, the British island of Barbados sustained a population of more than 300 people per square mile—the average figure for Western Europe at the time was 92 people per square mile. By then, the sugar trade was undergoing a further revolution that would transform it into one of the world's most popular products: the popularization of the taste for hot sugar-sweetened beverages in Europe.

Coffee, Tea, and Chocolate

For, where sugar led, coffee—and, ultimately, tea and chocolate—followed. By 1640, the coffee of Yemen rivaled or exceeded pepper as the main trading commodity of the Arabian Sea. It continued to boom, supplying markets in Persia, where coffee consumption quadrupled to nearly a million pounds a year by 1700. Even larger amounts—about 17 million pounds—went to the Ottoman Empire via the Red Sea and Egypt. Coffee arrived in France in 1644 with a returning ambassador from Turkey, along with old porcelain cups of great beauty and small napkins of fine cotton muslin, embroidered in gold, silver, and silk. The coffee-drinking habit soon found patrons. In 1657, Jean de Thévenot noticed that Parisian aristocrats hired Moorish and Italian coffeemakers. Armenian importers and street brewers popularized coffee drinking in France. Within half a century, coffee became the West's favorite addictive stimulant. In his satirical domestic comedy, the "Coffee Cantata," Johann Sebastian Bach (1685–1750) credited

Turkish coffeehouse. In the late eighteenth and early nineteenth centuries, coffee was still a luxury item in much of the world, and coffee drinking was a social ritual for the rich, as in this coffeehouse scene in Istanbul. Mass production in Java and later in Brazil, however, was already turning coffee into a cheap drink for the West's industrial workers.

Chocolate. In this canvas of about 1640—presumably intended to adorn a dining room—the Spanish painter Juan de Zurbarán (1620–1649) exalts chocolate, raising it on a silver pedestal and placing it center stage as if he were painting its portrait. In the seventeenth century, rich Europeans consumed chocolate the way the Aztec elite had—as a luxury beverage. Zurbarán here depicts a truly global experience in conspicuous consumption: expensive chocolate imported to Spain from Mexico is to be drunk in even more costly porcelain cups imported from China.

it with breaking up marriages because so many husbands stayed away from home to drink coffee in cafes, while wives sang love-songs to coffee.

Once the popularity of the new beverage was established, the next stage was to transplant it to new lands where Europeans could control the supply. The great coffee boom of the eighteenth and nineteenth centuries took it to Brazil, to the French islands of the Indian Ocean, and to the French colony of Saint-Domingue on Hispaniola, which for a while—until the black slaves there rebelled and proclaimed the Republic of Haiti in 1804—was the most productive island in the world for coffee and sugar alike. One of the most enduringly successful of the new coffee lands was Java, where the Dutch introduced the plant in the 1690s, gradually expanded production during the eighteenth century, and, in the nineteenth, fought wars to boost production on ever more marginal soils.

While coffee spread across the world from the Middle East, chocolate followed a similar path from a starting place in Mesoamerica. It took longer than coffee to penetrate European markets. In a work of 1648, credited with introducing chocolate to the English-speaking world, Thomas Gage described how colonial Mexico liked it—mixed with Old-World flavors, such as cinnamon, cloves, and almonds, as well as in the stews of bitter chocolate and chilles that were traditional Mesoamerican recipes. As the new drink became fashionable in Europe, the cacao (cah-COW) from which chocolate was made was transplanted to West Africa, where Danish plantations helped supply the growing trade in the eighteenth century. Tea also contributed to the growth of global trade, but not to the ecological exchange. China was able to supply almost the whole of world demand until the nineteenth century when the British established tea plantations in India and Sri Lanka.

Patterns of Ecological Exchange

It would be a mistake to think of the ecological exchange as merely bouncing back and forth across the oceans between the Old World and the New. Some ecological exchanges happened within the Americas. Domesticated turkeys formed no part of the first Thanksgiving meal. They were introduced to New England from Mexico later in the seventeenth century. The real maker of English economic success in Virginia was John Rolfe. He was the husband of the Indian princess Pocahontas—the forger of a kind of understanding with the natives, based on collaboration, mutual benefit, and sexual alliance that was normal in Spanish, Portuguese, and French colonies but remained rare in English colonial practice. Rolfe's vital economic contribution was to introduce "Spanish tobacco" (from the West Indies), which became Virginia's monoculture: the large-scale export crop that turned the colony from an unprofitable swamp into a field for settlers. It had to be transplanted because Europeans could not stand the taste of Virginia's native tobacco. Sweet potatoes were first recorded in Virginia in 1648, probably introduced not directly from South America, but via Europe or Africa with the slave trade.

Along the routes of transmission, gardens where plants could be adapted and bred for new climates were way stations of ecological exchange. Dutch horticulture led the way. Gardening was already a Dutch national obsession in the seventeenth century, when tulips from Turkey and chrysanthemums from Sri Lanka inspired costly "manias"—competition to grow the rarest and most spectacular varieties.

Dutch plant collectors crisscrossed the world. The Dutch Prince John Maurice of Nassau grew African and Indonesian plants in his garden in Brazil and sent Chilean monkey-puzzle trees to Germany. Nicolaas Witsen, a director of the Dutch East India Company, planted the first rhubarb in Europe in the town garden of Amsterdam in 1666—no mean achievement, as powdered rhubarb was by then one of the main products traded on the old Silk Roads. A fellow director made it his life's work, or folly, to try to grow oranges and lemons in cold, damp Holland. By the end of the seventeenth century, the company's gardens at the Cape of Good Hope on the southern tip of Africa had become the meeting place of hundreds of ornamental or potentially useful European, African, American, and Asian plants.

The result of the ecological exchange was a better-nourished world in the eighteenth century, better equipped than before with medicinal drugs derived from plants. This presumably contributed to the population explosion that then began, and has continued, with increasing pace, more or less ever since.

Human population, however, depends not only on what people do but also on how disease-bearing microorganisms behave. In the sixteenth and seventeenth centuries, a long and hazardous period of relatively low and uncertain growth preceded the upward surge of world population. Why population patterns change is still poorly understood. Clearly, social structures—and marriage disciplines above all—play a big part in explaining why people seem to breed at different rates at different moments of history. (We will discuss the global social history of the sixteenth and seventeenth centuries in Chapter 19.) Nutrition is important, because it affects fertility, and, when it improves, it keeps more people alive for more of their fertile years. But we cannot even begin to understand changing world patterns of population in the sixteenth and seventeenth centuries without looking at history under the microscope and examining the microbial world.

Dutch garden. An idealized view of the garden that Johann Maurits of Nassau created in Holland, to complement the gardens he planted in Brazil, when he was governor of the Dutch colony there from 1637 to 1644. The printed verses compare Johann Maurits with ancient Persian emperors, who were thought to have invented gardening.

THE MICROBIAL EXCHANGE

Instead of increasing population, in accordance with known precedents, colonization in the New World in these centuries provoked the worst recorded demographic disaster in history. Smallpox, in a virulent form, fatal to the immune systems of populations that had never encountered the disease, was probably the most effective killer. But some pestilence was doubtless unclassifiable in terms of current diseases, because the organisms responsible have evolved unrecognizably since that time. Symptoms often baffled their beholders. When a plague struck in Bahía, in 1563, José de Anchieta, the Jesuit "apostle of Brazil," could make no sense of symptoms that rotted the liver and produced a noxious pox, but he treated Indians by bleeding and peeling "parts of the legs and almost all their feet, cutting off the corrupt skin with scissors." Even if we assume that Native American societies were like those in the rest of the world and had suffered undocumented pestilence before the Europeans arrived, it seems incontestable that the diseases colonization brought were new and the effects unprecedented. "The breath of a Spaniard" was said to be enough to make a Native American die. The first Spanish navigators of the Amazon, in 1542, beheld cities built on stilts on the river banks, fed by aquaculture and the intensive cultivation of bitter manioc. The Spaniards did no more than pass through, yet by the time of the next European visitors a generation later, that populous world had vanished.

"But we cannot even begin to understand changing world patterns of population in the sixteenth and seventeenth centuries without looking at history under the microscope and examining the microbial world."

Smallpox victims. A native artist drew these victims of smallpox in sixteenth-century Mexico to illustrate a history that a Spanish friar wrote in Nahuatl—the language of the Aztecs. At top left, an Aztec physician is talking to his patient, who was almost certainly doomed. Hardly any Europeans died of smallpox at the time, but the disease killed millions of Native Americans, who had had no opportunity to develop immunity to it.

Demographic Collapse in the New World

Demographers have been unable to produce convincing figures for the extent or duration of the collapse, but even at the most optimistic estimates, the Indian population of Hispaniola, where New World colonization began, was virtually wiped out. In the densely settled and highly exposed regions of Mesoamerica and the Andes, Indian populations typically fell by 90 percent before they began to recover—which they did only patchily and intermittently until well into the seventeenth century and in many places not until the eighteenth.

Benevolent attitudes by colonial authorities made no difference. No empire has ever legislated so persistently, or so ineffectually, for the benefit of its victims as Spain's in the New World. It is impossible to imagine a system more benevolent—in paternalist fashion—than that of the Jesuits in the vast areas of Brazil and Paraguay that the crown separated from Spain's secular dominions for an experiment in building a self-sustaining Christian community. A picture in a work of propaganda in praise of this enterprise, published in 1700, displays its idealistic inspiration. A jaguar lies down with a tapir, and a little child leads them. Somehow, however, this paradise had got mislaid. Baptismal records show that by 1650, of the 150,000 people the Jesuits had baptized in their missions in the four most forward frontier provinces, only 40,000 survived the raids of Portuguese slavers and the visitations of plague.

The more spacious environments of North America bred equally devastating diseases. The influenza French explorers unwittingly introduced in the St. Lawrence River valley in Canada in 1535, and the nameless plague a Spanish expedition spread in what is now the American Deep South in 1538, inaugurated a history in which every attempted European settlement infected the Native Americans. The first English settlement in Virginia spread a quick-killing disease among the Indians, "so strange that they did not know anything about it or how to cure it." The next major epidemic, of 1633–1635, was recognizably of measles followed by smallpox. The Chesapeake Indians disappeared by the end of the seventeenth century. The numbers of the Huron in Canada collapsed so dramatically after contact with Europeans that one Jesuit argued desperately that it was a sign of divine favor. God was gathering his chosen to him. By the end of the seventeenth century, the Native American population in regions Europeans penetrated had fallen—according to rival estimates—by between 60 and 90 percent.

Plague and New Diseases in Eurasia

Some regions outside the Americas suffered comparable devastation. In the remoter parts of Siberia, visitors from the wider world were almost as much of a novelty as in the New World, and the unimmunized natives were equally vulnerable to unaccustomed diseases. Eighty percent of the tribespeople Russian imperialism touched east of the Yenisey River perished in the 1650s. Later, European penetration of Australia and parts of the Pacific had similar effects.

So, in a sense, the "age of plague" that started in the Old World in the late Middle Ages increased in virulence as disease-bearing microorganisms spread across the world. Microbial evolution, meanwhile, altered the patterns of disease in Eurasia. Leprosy diminished in range, but new diseases arose or old ones mutated. Tuberculosis does not seem to have been around in Europe on a significant scale—and certainly was not a major killer—until the sixteenth century when a more virulent form of the disease may have been brought back from the Americas. New strains of venereal disease developed in Europe—also perhaps as a result of transference from the New World.

Visitations of lethal sicknesses that Europeans continued vaguely to call plague remained a constant problem, holding down population growth in the seventeenth century in parts of southern Europe. The plague of Venice of 1679 left thousands of dead lying in a ditch, smothered in quicklime "like pickled game in a barrel" to dissolve the bodies. Plague in Spain in 1657 inspired terrifying paintings of lives stalked by death or focused on putrefaction. In a hospital in Seville, a carved altarpiece of the descent from the cross inspired a brotherhood of aristocrats who sought to atone for their sins by burying the plague dead and tending the plague sores of the poor with their own hands. China in the 1580s and 1640s endured more epidemics of greater virulence than in the more notorious plagues of the fourteenth century. A survivor of the plague in Hunan in 1657 claimed that nine of ten inhabitants were smitten, with a third of them breaking out in fever at midday to "become delirious in the evening and be partly eaten by rats when found dead at sunrise."

Yet for reasons that remain ill understood, the age of plagues gradually exhausted its virulence. The last recorded outbreak of plague in Europe was in the port of Marseilles on the Mediterranean coast of France in 1720. The deaths of unimmunized populations left well-adapted survivors. As a result of the ecological exchange, improved nutrition fortified increasing numbers of people. Microbes shifted their targets, perhaps, or mutated for evolutionary reasons to become less deadly. After all, it is not necessarily efficient for microorganisms to kill off their hosts. Whatever the reasons for it, deadly disease receded in the late seventeenth and early eighteenth centuries from all the areas in which it had previously been most destructive.

Of course, other diseases occupied the eco-niches retreating microbes vacated, or leaped into new ones that social, economic, or environmental change opened up. Cholera and yellow fever, for instance, broke out of their tropical heartlands to attack people in some of the fast-growing, densely populated, heavily polluted cities and ports in the industrializing West (see Chapter 29). Dysentery and typhus thrived in the undersanitized environments of rapidly growing towns. Dense concentrations of people helped tuberculosis to spread. Bubonic plague, in its modern form, may be another new disease of this period—or, at least, a recurrence of an old disease with new characteristics. As we have seen (see Chapter 14), historians' longstanding assumption that bubonic plague was the sole or main affliction of the "age of plague" in Europe is probably false. In China, there is no decisive evidence that any epidemic before the nineteenth century was of bubonic plague in its modern form. In Yunnan province, however, on China's southwest border, a new kind of environment, in which new kinds of disease had an opportunity to emerge, was taking shape in the late eighteenth century. In the last quarter of the century, mining towns mushroomed as 300,000 immigrants moved in from other parts of China. At the same time, strong similarities with modern bubonic plague characterized a particularly intense series of epidemics from the 1770s to the 1790s, followed by slightly less intense

Burial of the dead—plague-stricken or impoverished—was one of the obligations of the brethren of the religious brotherhood, or confraternity, that ran the Hospital de la Caridad in Seville, Spain. The sculptures on the high altar therefore depict the entombment of Christ. This altarpiece represents a characteristically emotional baroque theme: the paradox of inhabitants of a glorious heaven sharing the miseries and suffering of earthly life.

outbreaks until the 1820s. The most significant similarity was the presence of rats as agents of disease. Modern bubonic plague is endemic in particular kinds of rodents. It spreads to humans when rat fleas bite people and inject the bacillus into human bloodstreams. The Yunnan plague was incontestably associated with rats, according to observations made at the time, not only by physicians but also by a young poet who wrote,

> Dead rats in the East!
> Dead rats in the West!
> . . .
> A few days following the death of the rats,
> Men pass away like falling walls!

Still, the impact of modern bubonic plague was not as severe as that of the Black Death or the other scourges of the age of plague. When plague receded from Yunnan in the 1830s, it became dormant or sporadic. The next—or, by strict standards of interpretation, the first—unquestioned major outbreak in China did not occur until 1894. In any case, the new or spreading diseases of the eighteenth and nineteenth centuries generally could no longer keep pace with growing world population or, it seems, seriously restrain its growth.

Meanwhile, however, for as long as the age of plague lasted, problems of severe regional labor shortages had to be faced. The gravest of these were in the last region to suffer devastating losses of population to disease: the New World. The solution lay in transplanting human labor. This was, in a sense, yet another kind of ecological exchange. Along with plants, animals, and germs, another life form, another ingredient of ecosystems—human beings—was swapped and shifted across the ocean and—for the most part—ended up in the Americas.

"Along with plants, animals, and germs, another life form, another ingredient of ecosystems—human beings—was swapped and shifted across the ocean and—for the most part—ended up in the Americas."

LABOR: HUMAN TRANSPLANTATIONS

Even before native numbers thinned, the colonial Americas suffered from shortages of useful labor. The new economic activities Spaniards wished to promote were impossible without new sources of labor even in the most densely populated areas of Spanish rule. Native Americans were, with few exceptions, ill suited to the kind of work Europeans wanted done, such as plantation labor, domestic service, and specialist skills in mining and sugar refining. Most of them were—as a companion of Columbus commented when dismissing the idea that the native peoples of the Caribbean could usefully be enslaved—"not suited to hard work" as Europeans understood the term.

Europe, however, was unsatisfactory as an alternative labor source. Spanish schemes to introduce colonies of Spanish laborers failed in the sixteenth century. The Dutch encountered similar failure in the seventeenth. North America proved particularly hard to populate. Sixteenth-century attempts to found North American colonies almost all failed. Those founded in the seventeenth century took a long time to become viable—renewing their populations, that is, by sustainable birth rates. They could not rely, as most of Spain's early American conquests could, on native population levels to keep them viable. There are no reliable estimates of the size of the native population of North America when the Europeans arrived—well-informed guesses range from two to seven million—but there is no doubt that the region was sparsely populated. And such people as it did have were not well suited to be a labor force for colonial empires, such as the big, densely packed native populations of Mesoamerica and the Andes provided for Spain.

Immigration could not, at first, make up the deficit. Virginia was farmed mainly with a form of forced labor imported from England—"indentured" poor, escapees from social exclusion at home, who contracted with masters to serve for years at a time, on subsistence wages or payments in kind, with no hope of release. But there were never enough of them, and as the market for black slaves gradually opened up to the English, Africans replaced them. Again, the model of exploitation was found in the Spanish, Portuguese, and (by now) Dutch colonies to the south.

Until the second half of the seventeenth century, life expectancy in Virginia remained low. Few colonists survived into their 50s. The Virginia swampland, where the first permanent settlements were founded from 1607 onward, was so unhealthy that of the first 100 or so settlers, only 38 were still alive nine months after landing. Of the first 3,000, only a couple of hundred were still alive, after a bloody war with the Indians in 1622. The population did not begin to increase naturally until some 50 years after the first settlement. The breakthrough was accompanied by increased rates of immigration, which tripled from about 1650 to 1670.

New England's environment was less hostile: "endowed with grace and furnished with means," as a Puritan settler declared. From early in the 1630s (Plymouth, the first New England colony, was founded in 1620), the colonists could grow enough to feed themselves, and natural increase kept the population growing. Without valuable cash products, however, the region had little appeal for immigrants. Only 21,000 came in the whole seventeenth century, and the numbers of immigrants diminished over time—only a third of that total arrived after 1640. These were problems general to northern colonies. There were only 5,000 settlers in New Netherland when the English conquered the colony, which became New York, in 1664. New France, founded in Canada in 1608, received fewer than 4,000 immigrants in the second half of the seventeenth century. France, though densely populated by European standards in early times, never persuaded many colonists to go to America.

In the Spanish colonies, as early as 1510, the importation of slave labor began from the only source near enough and demographically buoyant enough to provide it: Africa. By the 1570s, Spanish America was importing, on average, about 2,500 African slaves a year. The average figure over the next century and a half, during which the trade to Spanish America was fairly stable, was 3,500 a year. Brazil became a major importer of slaves from the 1570s. Brazil probably had fewer than 15,000 black slaves in 1600, but numbers soared thereafter with the growth of sugar plantations, and the colony was soon absorbing more slaves than the whole Spanish Empire.

For the first 150 years or so of the colonial era, Spanish naval supremacy and Portuguese control of many of the sources of slaves denied adequate supplies of this resource to the British, Dutch, and French colonies. But as demand for slaves grew, routes of supply diversified—through piracy and illicit trading at first, then increasingly by agreement of the Spanish and Portuguese authorities with slavers of other nationalities. In the 1640s, Dutch slavers turned the island of Curaçao, off the coast of Venezuela, into a huge slaving station, supplying Spanish colonies at first and, increasingly, their own. Scandinavian traders entered the market in the 1650s. From the late 1660s, French and English companies tried to break into the slave trade. In the third quarter of the seventeenth century, nearly 15,000 slaves a year left Africa on average. In the final quarter, the number increased to 24,000 a year.

After experiments with other kinds of enforced labor, slavery became the universal method to develop the plantation crops, including the rice and cotton that, in preference to tobacco and sugar, suited some of the land the English seized in North America. The system was imitated from Spanish and Portuguese precedents

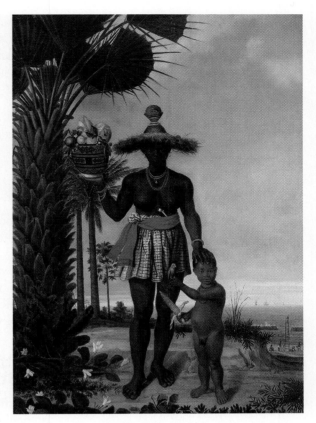

African woman and child. This painting of 1641 by the Dutch painter Albert Eckhout illustrates the range of racial types in Brazil. The woman's calm stance, her rich clothing and jewels, the lavish foodstuffs, the exotic birds, the pipe at her breast, and her son's markedly different complexion all signify an image of order, stability, variety, and abundance. In the background scaffolding rises to signal trading opportunities to passing ships.

Chronology: The Columbian Exchange: Plants, Animals, Microbes, and People

1492	Columbus arrives in the New World, beginning process of biological exchange
1500s	Horses and cattle introduced to New World
1510	Importation of slave labor in the Spanish colonies begins
1555	First record of maize cultivation in China
1570s	Brazil becomes a major importer of slaves
1580s	Brazil becomes the world's major sugar producer
1700s	Coffee becomes popular in Europe and Middle East
	Coffee production begins in Brazil and Indonesia

in areas where Native Americans were reduced by disease or refused to do plantation work. Climate drove it, as is apparent from the failure of early antislavery laws in Georgia, which was founded in 1733 as a refuge for the British poor. Subtropical America could not be made to pay without labor from Africa. No other area could supply enough workers adaptable to the climate.

WILD FRONTIERS: ENCROACHING SETTLEMENT

The slave trade was part of a bigger phenomenon: the development of new ways to exploit the soil, which, in combination with the widening of trade, hugely increased the wealth of the world. This could be called the economic dividend of imperialism: the extension of land exploited for ranching, farming, and mining, and the conversion of some land from relatively less productive to relatively more productive methods of exploitation.

Northern and Central Asia: The Waning of Steppeland Imperialism

In northern and Central Asia, the political background was of a shift of power, as steppeland imperialism waned and the growing strength and reach of settled empires in China, Persia, and Russia squeezed the pastoralists' domains. New attempts to galvanize the power of the steppelanders, by a succession of leaders who claimed descent from Genghis Khan or his heroic lieutenants (see Chapter 13), brought little success. Most new imperial initiatives remained penned inside the steppes. At the beginning of the sixteenth century, for instance, two new enemies locked horns in Southwest Asia. The pastoralist Uzbek Empire, under the Shaybanid dynasty, with its heartlands in the steppes between the Aral Sea and Lake Balkhash, celebrated the identity of "men of the steppe: all our wealth consists of horses; their flesh is our favorite food. . . . Houses have we none." The Safavid Empire of Persia, which was largely based on settled agriculture, was their neighbor to the south (see Chapter 19). To judge from the record of the previous 500 years, anyone tempted to bet on the outcome of a clash between these two states would back the steppelanders to win. But, during nearly a century of warfare, the Safavids repeatedly got the upper hand, until a final Persian victory in 1597 provoked the breakup of the Uzbek state into small khanates.

Meanwhile, at the eastern end of the steppes, the Mongols found it impossible to reunite their power for long enough, or in sufficient strength, to renew a lasting threat to China. The Mongols could not even, for much of the time, securely dominate Tibet, which in the seventeenth century became the objective of the most ambitious Mongol chiefs.

There was, however, one uncharacteristic and perhaps deceptive instance of steppeland dynamism in the period. In the 1640s, a Manchu army, which the Chinese Empire had created to help police the Mongol frontier, intervened decisively in a Chinese civil war, conquered China (see Chapter 19), and dethroned the last Ming emperor in 1644. In some ways—in practice, more or less token ways—the Manchus imposed their own values on China. One of the first commands of the new regime, which survived until 1912, was that Chinese should signify their submission by shaving their hair in Manchu fashion. According to Confucian notions of filial piety, hair was part of the sacred legacy children inherited from their parents and therefore should not be cut off. But the Manchu commander replied to objectors, "I spared your heads and now you want to keep your hair?" In most respects, however, the new dynasty rapidly adopted Chinese ways. Indeed, the great achievement of the Qing (cheeng)—the name the Manchu dynasty adopted in China—was to reverse the direction of empire. The Qing conquered much of the steppeland and spread Chinese culture deep into Central Asia.

Disputes over Tibet eventually provoked China into sustained war against the Mongols. In the 1690s, the Kangxi (kong-shee) emperor, himself a Manchu, campaigning in person on the Mongol front, described in letters home his days of early rising, "braving the sand and the dust" with "hands all blistered from holding the reins." By 1697, he was able to announce, with only a little exaggeration, "There is no Mongol principality that has not submitted to my rule." The historic pattern of imperialism in Central Asia was undergoing a kind of inversion. The Chinese Empire was reaching into the Mongol steppe, instead of lying at the periodic mercy of steppeland conquerors.

Why did the balance of power between settled life and pastoralism shift in favor of the former? The usual answer appeals to the so-called **military revolution** that accompanied the rise of firepower technology. Large forces of well-drilled, fire-armed infantry, with heavy artillery behind scientifically designed fortifications, made "gunpowder empires" invulnerable to steppeland cavalry. Demographic change also favored the settled peoples, whose populations grew faster than those of pastoralists. The progress of Islam and Buddhism in Central Asia supposedly eroded the ideologies of conquest that had animated earlier steppeland empires. Changes in the pattern of trade in the seventeenth century, when the role of the Silk Roads declined in relation to oceanic trade routes, cut off some of the liquid wealth that mobilized nomad war bands.

None of these explanations seems adequate. Steppelanders had adapted to new warfare technologies in the past. The Mongols, for instance, would never have been able to conquer China without incorporating infantry and siege engines into their armies (see Chapter 13). Settled neighbors had always outnumbered pastoral peoples, whose economic system, by its very nature, demands a lot of grazing land to feed relatively fewer mouths. Although many new trade routes carried more commerce than those of Central Asia, steppelanders still had plenty of wealth-creating opportunities to exploit. Chinese tribute lists and trading licenses show steppeland communities getting gradually richer, especially in horses, furs, and silks. Without definitive evidence, the best we can say is that all these changes, in combination, weakened the steppelanders relative to the empires that surrounded them. Whatever the reasons for it, the decline in the relative power of Eurasia's steppelanders was irreversible, as farmers from the Russian and Chinese empires colonized areas of steppeland and left the pastoralists with less territory. The retreat of the steppelanders was a conspicuous element in the making of the modern world. It formed part of a broader change: an ecological revolution that extended the range and productivity of settled farming around the world.

Steppeland defeat. The Uzbek Empire of the sixteenth century never had the power or potential to fulfill its declared aim to conquer the world. At times, the Uzbeks were even hard-pressed to defend their steppes against invaders from Persia. The late seventeenth-century Persian painter of a palace mural remembered the Uzbek Khan Shibani as the victim of defeat by Shah Ismail I (r. 1501–1524). Persia's defeat of the Uzbeks showed that the age-old pattern—in which agrarian states felt menaced by the steppelanders—had been reversed.

"The retreat of the steppelanders was a conspicuous element in the making of the modern world. It formed part of a broader change: an ecological revolution that extended the range and productivity of settled farming around the world."

MAP 17.2

The Moroccan invasion of Songhay, 1591

- Morocco
- Moroccan occupied territory
- → Moroccan invasion route
- gold mine
- salt mine
- alluvial gold

Pastoral Imperialism in Africa and the Americas

In some parts of the world, meanwhile, pastoralism remained or became a predominant way of life, and pastoral imperialism remained or became robust. In the African Sahel, for instance, the native tradition recovered after a challenge in the late sixteenth century from Morocco. In the 1580s, Morocco's long-cherished dreams of crossing the desert and conquering a gold-rich empire in black Africa began to look practical. The Moroccan sultan al-Mansur collected an army equipped with formidable firepower—2,500 marksmen and a train of camel-mounted artillery. The desert was not impassable, he argued. What merchant caravans could do, so could a well-organized army. From a Moroccan perspective, the Sahara was a sea of sand with an inviting shore. Like Spain's Atlantic, Morocco's Sahara was an obstacle course that could be crossed to a land of gold.

In 1588, al-Mansur declared war on Songhay. Nine thousand camels accompanied his task force on a march of 135 days across 1,500 miles, mostly of desert. Half the force may have died on the way, but the survivors dispersed the mounted hosts of Songhay as efficiently as Spanish conquerors had shattered the Aztecs and Incas (see Map 17.2). Morocco turned the western Sahel into a colony settled with 20,000 men. But the settler communities, often marrying locally, gradually slipped out of Moroccan control. After an initial bonanza, the gold shipments dwindled, and by the 1630s, Morocco's gold reserves were running out. No outside power again attempted to conquer the Sahel until the French arrived in the nineteenth century. The supremacy of the Sahel pastoralists remained secure.

The centuries-old process of expansion of arable farming from the Ethiopian highlands went into reverse in the sixteenth century, as pastoralist invaders from the east and south—pagan Oromo, Muslim Adil—seized lands and destroyed the monasteries that were the engines of Ethiopian frontier settlement. At the extreme southern tip of Africa, herding grew in economic importance. The region of the Cape of Good Hope had long been heavily grazed by thousands of head of long-horned cattle, herded by pastoralists who called themselves Khoi and who had probably themselves been driven into the region by the expansion of Bantu farmers from the north. The numbers of livestock doubled in the second half of the seventeenth century, when Dutch settlers introduced sheep following the establishment of a colony of the Dutch East India Company on the Cape in 1652. The Dutch followed Khoi strategies for selecting seasonal grazing and corralling their herds against predators. Although the Dutch also practiced arable farming, the extent of their ranching activities was incomparably greater.

In the Americas, of course, there had never been much pastoralism because there had never been large domesticable livestock herds, except for the llamas and their cousins in the Andes. In the sixteenth and seventeenth centuries, however, the introduction of horses, cattle, and sheep made new ways of life possible, raising the prospect of empires whose economy was based on herding livestock. In some ways, it is tempting to see Spanish and Portuguese imperialism in some parts of what are now Mexico and Brazil as a form of pastoral imperialism imposed on sedentary Indian peoples. Sheep and cattle, unknown before the Europeans arrived, numbered millions by the early seventeenth century and grazed hundreds of thousands of square miles of land—some of it previously unexploited, but much of it vacated by native farmers and hunters. As we shall see, in the late eighteenth and early nineteenth centuries (see Chapter 21), horse-borne Native American empire builders threatened to dominate the prairie and the pampa.

MAP 17.3

Imperialism and Settlement in Eurasia, 1600–1725

- Russian Empire, ca. 1600
- Russian Empire, ca. 1600–1725
- • Russian cities founded 1587–1718
- Qing Empire in ca. 1644
- Qing Empire in ca. 1660
- Qing Empire by ca. 1770
- → internal migration in China in the 18th century
- Mughal Empire, ca. 1700
- Mughal Empire, ca. 1605
- → Japanese expansion northward
- *Ainu* people

So in some parts of the world, arable farming lost acreage or yield. In other areas, methods of exploiting the soil remained limited to hunting and gathering. Although California and parts of Australia, for instance, were highly suited to arable farming, their native inhabitants were uninterested in changing methods of feeding themselves that had worked satisfactorily for thousands of years. Not until European intrusions in the eighteenth century did ranching and tillage begin fundamentally to alter their landscapes. But the main trend of the period was the extension of new forms of exploitation—especially arable farming—onto lands where it had never before been practiced. The new empires, which encouraged colonists and drove and mined for new resources, forced the pace of this change (see Map 17.3).

IMPERIALISM AND SETTLEMENT IN EUROPE AND ASIA

The Russian conquest of Kazan in the 1550s made possible the colonization of the fertile "black earth" regions of the lower Volga River and southwest steppeland, pressing back and penning Mongol and Turkic herdsmen. By 1600, a million settlers had turned a quarter of the region to grain cultivation, turning over the heavy sod with ox-drawn plows. Although the conquest of Siberia was launched for the fur trade, the ambition to see the land colonized gradually eclipsed the original vision. The foundation of frontier cities marked the progress of colonization:

A CLOSER LOOK

The Remezov Chronicle

Several narrative accounts document the Russian conquest of Siberia. In the Remezov Chronicle, written in a monastery about 1700, and illustrated with 154 pen and ink drawings, Russian territorial expansion is depicted as an evangelizing and civilizing mission. Shown here is the title page from the Chronicle.

"From the beginning of time, our Christian God, the All-Seer ... decreed for the Gospels to be preached throughout Siberia to the ends of the universe and the limit of the mountains to the famous city of Tobolsk."

"And he will dwell in righteousness, and towns will arise to the Lord."

The hen is a motif taken from the Gospels of Luke, where it symbolizes Jerusalem's resistance to God's will. The words above it, (only partly legible), read, "Just as the hen gathers its chicks under its wing, so shall I. . . . my name."

Set beneath the eye of God, the words in the open book, from the Gospels of John and Matthew, read "If any man serve me, let him follow me; and where I am there shall also my servant be. . . . where two or three are gathered together in my name, there am I in the midst of them."

Tobolsk is flatteringly depicted, while rays from the Gospel spread to 21 other towns.

How does this illustration connect territorial expansion with the Russian state's self-proclaimed mission to spread Christianity?

Tobolsk on the Irtysh River in 1587, Tomsk in 1604, Barguzinsk on Lake Baikal in 1648, Nerchinsk on the Amur River in 1654. In the mind of an eighteenth-century chronicler, Siberia had become a land of cities—22 of them, dispersed throughout the territory, depicted in an illustrative engraving as joined by rays of light to the eye of God. By then, over 300,000 peasants inhabited these settlements—outnumbering the surviving native Siberians.

Meanwhile, on a smaller scale, similar appropriations of territory by encroaching farmers displaced traditional peoples at the extremities of Eurasia, in the British Isles and Japan. The English and lowland Scots waged wars to seize land, from Ireland to the Highlands and islands of Scotland. These were, from one point of view, culture wars that self-styled civilization waged against so-called savagery, by Protestants against Catholics, by speakers of Germanic tongues against those who spoke Celtic, by feudalism against tribalism. They were also economically inspired wars fought to convert pastoral land to arable. In Japan, after the Ainu War of 1669–1672, about half of Hokkaido was set aside for Japanese peasants to settle, at the expense of the displaced Ainu natives, whom the Japanese classed as primitive and savage, using language similar to that of English and Scots propaganda about the highlanders, islanders, and Gaelic Irish.

"These were, from one point of view, culture wars that self-styled civilization waged against so-called savagery, by Protestants against Catholics, by speakers of Germanic tongues against those who spoke Celtic, by feudalism against tribalism."

China

Imperial China sponsored the biggest movements of agricultural settlers in frontier regions and new conquests. Uncultivated land was wasted land. That was what late-sixteenth-century Chinese officials thought, denouncing the "laziness" of gatherers of wild reeds on land that could be adapted to grow food. Manchu conquest of Sichuan in southern China was exceptionally savage, eliminating—so it was said—three-quarters of the people. Yet between 1667 and 1707, tax exemptions lured more than 1.5 million settlers to Sichuan. Here and on the southeast frontier, the pressure of intensive new settlement provoked a cycle of conflicts. Rebellious native tribes were penned in reservations. Militarized agricultural colonies grew wheat, barley, peas, and maize while keeping the natives obedient. Schools brought Chinese language and values to the tribes.

The civil wars of the third quarter of the seventeenth century, which pitched the last Ming loyalists against the Manchu conquerors, drove Chinese peasants out of the densely populated provinces of Fujian and Guangdong (gwahng-dohng) into Guangzxi (gwahng–jshee) and the Yangtze highlands to the tea and timber industries or to cultivate sweet potatoes or maize. Celebrating his conquests against the "half-human" natives of Guizhou (gway-joh) in the mid–seventeenth century, a Manchu general described "chiseling" through the "forests that extend beyond the horizon. . . . Every day, for our imperial court, we've developed new arable lands. . . . So these far-off wastelands and tribal domains yield us menials and serving girls."

Large-scale immigration preceded the Chinese conquest of Taiwan in the 1660s. During some four decades of Dutch rule, which preceded the Chinese conquest, Dutch colonialists rewarded Chinese migrants with land concessions, cheap seed, draft animals, and tax breaks. By the time Chinese took over the government, over 35,000 settlers had brought nearly 25,000 acres under the plow, growing mainly rice and cane sugar. When the Manchu government assumed control of the island in 1684, the "raw aboriginals" enjoyed a period of official favor. The Manchus used the native deerstalkers to repress the suspect immigrant Chinese population in an offshore province where resistance to Manchu conquest had been

Building a dike in seventeenth-century China.
Peasant conscripts rig screws to drive piles into the mud to form the walls of the dike. Others use heavy wooden hammers to level the dike, or dig earth, which fellow-workers shift in baskets yoked by poles.

strong. But that did not prevent the depletion of the deer herds, as Chinese peasants continued to encroach on land officially reserved for the native Taiwanese.

To the north of traditional China, in the borderlands of Mongolia and Manchuria, colonization proceeded on a different basis. The Kangxi emperor (r. 1661–1722) tried to stop the colonization of Manchuria on the grounds that he "wished to maintain the original equestrian and hunting ways and martial virtues of the Manchus and Mongols in their home territory, which should remain a recruiting ground for soldiers." In practice, however, the frontier of settlement could not be controlled. The cultivated zone of Manchuria grew by nearly 30,000 acres in the decade following Kangxi's decree. (See Map 17.3.)

The exploitability of illegal immigrants made them welcome. The earliest colonization had a camp-life quality of roving communities of wild ginseng diggers. (Ginseng is prized in Chinese medicine.) Farmer pioneers came not far behind. In the frontier town of Ninguta (neen-goo-tah) (today known as Ning'an) on the River Hurka, in the generation after its foundation in 1660, only 400 households lived inside the ruined wall of mud. There was "no person of leisure," and the exiles' womenfolk—"descendants of the rich and honorable families of China"—slid barefoot down the icy hillside under the burden of water from the only well.

Yet even in this environment, some metropolitan values triumphed, while the winds of change overturned others or blew them away. Anyone with scholarly pretensions—let alone degrees—was prized in Ninguta. The deference the natives accorded to the Chinese and the prosperity of the settlers impressed a visitor in 1690. The older merchants even "greeted the military governor as a younger brother": in other words, they affected superiority over him. The hierarchies of home persisted alongside new rankings the emerging society of the frontier had evolved.

India

We can detect the same trends—imperial expansion, fostering new settlement, increasing the range of farming, and exploiting new resources—in the same period in India. Forest clearance was a policy the Mughal emperors (see Chapter 16) embraced determinedly, in their heartlands and new conquests alike. In Bengal, deforestation was part of a longstanding struggle to advance the frontier of settlement and of Islam by granting forested areas to Muslim holy men and communities, who planted wet rice in the cleared zones. On the edges of the Mughal heartland, deforestation was an instrument of enhanced control, uprooting the jungles where bandits and rebels sheltered, and encouraging settlement and, therefore, increasing revenues for the state. The emperor received a third of every harvest. Indian peasants were extremely efficient, producing two crops a year almost everywhere they planted—whether of millet, rice, or wheat. Lumberjacks accompanied seventeenth-century Mughal armies. Colonists who followed them to new lands received tax concessions and cheap plows. When the Mughals conquered areas from Burma in 1665, they evicted the existing population as ruthlessly as any European imperialists and introduced hundreds of Muslim religious foundations to clear the forest and plant rice.

NEW EXPLOITATION IN THE AMERICAS

The decline of the Native American population may have led to the abandonment of vast zones that the Indians had farmed before the Europeans arrived. But colonial regimes found alternative methods to exploit the land that, in total, probably made the colonial economy as productive as the Indian system had been: mining, ranching, and plantations (see Map 17.4). The arrival of plows, which had been unknown in the Americas before the Europeans brought them, meant that heavy soils could be exploited for the first time. Horses, mules, and oxen took on burdens Native American porters formerly bore on their backs.

The Spanish Empire

The Spanish Empire in the Americas had every avenue to wealth at its disposal. Suitable environments for all the new kinds of activity were available in abundance, while traditional native economies continued to produce their time-honored crops—such as maize, beans, squash, cotton, and cacao in Mesoamerica or coca, potatoes, and sweet potatoes in the Andes—and generate tribute. The most vivid mark and measure of success were the cities of Spanish America. As soon as Columbus returned from his first voyage, and news of America began to circulate in Europe, engravers imagined what they called the Indies filled with magnificent cities. In areas of Spanish rule, the vision was quickly realized, for Spanish imperialism was uncompromisingly urban minded. It is said that when two Englishmen meet on a savage frontier they found a club. Two Spaniards in the same circumstances found a city.

Spanish colonization slotted into the existing framework of Native American civilizations. In an extraordinarily productive period of expansion in the 1520s and 1530s, while the Spanish monarchy absorbed the existing great urban centers of Mesoamerica and the Andean region through conquest or diplomacy, the biggest cities of the Americas acquired new characteristics: Spanish-speaking elites, a new Native American middle class that served Spaniards' economic needs, an African American slave class for domestic service, Spanish courts and town councils, Christian religious foundations, cathedrals, and even, in Mexico City, a university and printing press. Similar developments followed Spanish colonization in other parts of the Americas in succeeding decades. Spanish colonists founded cities wherever they went. The new cities

Cuzco, home city of the Incas, never really looked like this. Built amid mountains, its monumental palaces, temples, and fortifications, constructed of huge blocks of stone, enclosed irregular spaces. But when Georg Braun and Franz Hogenberg published their views of the world's great cities in the late sixteenth century, they imagined Cuzco as a flat grid—the supposedly ideal form of Renaissance urban planning that inspired many colonial American cities.

Chronology: Founding Dates for Spanish Cities in the Americas

Caribbean and North America		South America	
Santo Domingo	1496	Cajamarca	1532
San Juan (Puerto Rico)	1509	Cartagena	1532
San Cristóbal (Havana)	1515	Cuzco	1533
Panama City	1519	Quito	1534
Mexico City	1521	Lima	1535
Guadalajara	1531	Buenos Aires	1536
Santa Fe de Bogotà	1538	Santiago	1541
Mérida	1542	La Paz	1548
Zacatecas	1546	Mendoza	1561
San Juan Bautista	1564	Caracas	1567
San Augustín (Florida)	1565		
Santa Fé (New Mexico)	1610		

rooted easily in areas where native cities and a strong urban tradition already existed. In other areas of mainland Spanish America—California, the frontier grasslands of North and South America—urbanization was harder, growing slowly from seeds that missions, military garrisons, and naval stations planted.

European styles in buildings smothered or supplemented the old angular look of Native American architectures with arches and domes. Some old Indian cities were flattened and rebuilt. Others were lightly adapted and recrafted. Some were abandoned, as a terrible demographic crisis unfolded with the collapse of the Native American population. New cities on new sites, like Lima, Peru, still perhaps the most Spanish of Spanish American cities in looks and atmosphere, replaced some Native American capitals. Parts of Old San Juan in Puerto Rico look exactly like a Spanish city of the seventeenth and eighteenth centuries, complete with walls, sea gates, courtyard gardens, and cathedral square. The civic model of life, the city-centered model of administration, was extended into new areas. From the 1570s, the Spanish crown issued exact regulations to construct new cities, with their grid plan and classically inspired buildings and monumental scale, the exact placing of cathedrals, government buildings, hospitals, and schools. The archives are full of the plans of projected cities, and many of them were actually built. But in North America in the seventeenth and early eighteenth centuries, beyond the Spanish frontier, cities of English and French construction generally remained, in a sense, in the Iroquois tradition. They were largely built of wood and, though intended for permanent occupancy, had a gimcrack air of instant shabbiness.

Brazil

Other European empires in the Americas lacked the advantage of local labor sources that they could exploit on the scale of the Spanish lands. As a result, they tended at first to expand to landward on only a modest scale, so that they could increase the areas of cultivation of the crops they introduced, such as sugar in the Caribbean, West Indian tobacco in Virginia, rice in the Carolinas, and wheat almost everywhere. In Brazil, sugar was suitable only to coastal enclaves where it could be successfully grown and easily shipped to Europe. It would never, on its own, have induced planters to create a large territorial domain in Brazil's hinterland. Rivalry with Spain to control the Amazon, however, turned Portuguese thoughts toward the Brazilian interior, especially after rival Spanish and Portuguese expeditions tested the navigability of the great Amazon River system in the 1630s. Gold and diamonds, discovered in the Brazilian province of Minas Gerais (meaning "general mines") in the 1680s, proved the incentive required for Portugal to drive its Brazilian frontier inland.

British North America

Elsewhere, though explorers scoured the Americas for natural resources in the late sixteenth and seventeenth centuries, major sources of gold, silver, pearls, and precious gems remained a Spanish monopoly. The areas left for the English and French to exploit contained only fool's gold, such as the iron pyrites Martin Frobisher found in Canada in 1576, which deceived investors into ruin and lured adventurers to their deaths. Furs were the "black gold" of the north, but, like the timber and fish that also abounded in and around North America, resources of these kinds could not alone sustain permanent or populous colonies: only the French fur trappers who lived among the Indians, migrant merchants and hunters, and seasonal visitors.

Except in the Caribbean, where sugar and, later, coffee would grow on islands seized from or ignored by Spain, it was hard to find crops suitable to sustain colonial life. Tobacco was the first such crop, introduced into Virginia in 1614. Later in the century, rice made fairly large-scale settlement practical in the coastal areas of South Carolina. Independent farmers could always cultivate small holdings for their own subsistence, as they did with remarkable success even in the inhospitably rocky soils of New England from the 1620s. But this form of exploitation could never be the foundation of prosperity. New England only really began to reveal its potential as a great world center of wealth and civilized life in the eighteenth century, not because of its own resources but because so many of the inhabitants took to the sea. Like classical Greece and ancient Phoenicia (Chapter 5), New England became a maritime civilization, making up for the poverty of its home soils by trade and the exploitation of marine resources. Three trades in particular contributed to transforming New England's economy into one of the richest, per capita, in the world by the late eighteenth century: first, the slave trade, in which New England merchants worked both as shippers and dealers; second, the export of locally produced rum and manufactured goods to the slave-producing and slave-consuming markets with which the slave trade connected the New Englanders; and finally the so-called **East India trade**—mainly with China, by way of Cape Horn on the southern tip of South America—for tea and porcelain to sell at home.

From Virginia southward, English North American colonies naturally—literally, naturally—resembled those that Spanish, Dutch, and Portuguese investors were already exploiting in Mesoamerica and South America. They were hot and wet, with torrid lowlands that could be adapted to plant cash crops with the labor of imported slaves. The first English-run sugar industry in Barbados was directly copied from the Dutch enterprise in Pernambuco, with Dutch capital and know-how. The effects on settler society were predictable. Economic reliance on large-scale, capital-intensive enterprises created huge disparities of wealth. Large-scale English planters in parts of North America and the Caribbean became, in effect, the lords of huge estates, more reminiscent of the Mediterranean or Brazil, than of England or New England. In 1700, the top 5 percent of settlers by wealth owned half of one county in Virginia.

HOME FRONTS IN EUROPE AND ASIA

New wealth-creating activities were not confined to imperial frontiers. Equal efforts were under way to exploit the homelands of the empires. Governments all over the world undertook land surveys to determine the extent of production and

A Chinese porcelain punch-bowl acquired in the East Indies trade late in the eighteenth century by the Rhode Island merchant John Brown. The decoration shows the American *hong* (or warehouse and place of business) in Guangzhou, as well as *hongs* for traders from other Western countries, overlooking the Pearl River.

Chronology: Imperialism and Coloniziation in Europe, Asia, and the Americas	
1520s–1530s	Absorption of Mesoamerican and Andean cities into Spanish Empire
1550s	Russian conquest of Kazan
ca. 1560–1650	Russian colonization of lower Volga and Siberia
1600s	Expansion, colonization, and intensive farming in Mughal India
	Outflow of Chinese and Japanese settlers to Southeast Asia
	Export of African slaves, especially to the Americas
	British colonization of North America
ca. 1620s–1660s	Large-scale Chinese immigration to Taiwan
1667–1707	1.5 million settlers arrive in Sichuan
1680s	Discovery of gold and diamonds prompts further Portuguese expansion in Brazil
Late seventeenth century	Japanese peasants displace native inhabitants of Hokkaido
1700s	New England becomes a world center of trade

Great Slave Lake

Carrier
Chipewyan

Beaver

Lake Athabasca

Fort Churchill

Churchill

York Factory **1682**

Nelson

Hudson Bay

Severn Factory

RUPERT'S LAND

East Cree

James Bay

Fort Albany **1670**

Eastmain

Cree

Moose Factory **1671**

Rupert House **1668**

Labrador

Naskapi

Montagnais

Beothuk

Newfoundland

Gulf of St. Lawrence

Cape Breton Island

Micmac

Halifax **1749**

NOVA SCOTIA

Saskatchewan

Cree

Lake Winnipeg

Assiniboine

Fort Kaministikwia

Ojibwa

Ottawa

Nipissing

Algonquin

St. Lawrence River

Quebec **1608**

Montreal **1642**

NEW FRANCE

NEW ENGLAND

Kutenai

Nez Perce

Flathead

Blackfoot

Gros Ventres

Crow

Great Plains

Lake Superior

Huron

Lake Huron

Pentun

Michilimackinac

Menomini **1697**

Lake Michigan

Sauk Fox

Lake Champlain

Fort Orange **1624**

Albany **1664**

Mohican

Boston **1630**

Narraganset

ROCKY MOUNTAINS

Northern Shoshoni

Teton Dakota

Santee

Arikara

Yanktonai

Cheyenne

Yankton

Winnebago

Iowa

Oto

Mascouten

Kickapoo

Miami

Niagara

L. Ontario

Detroit **1701**

L. Erie

Iroquois

Susquehanna

Delaware

Newport

East India Trade

Bannock

Western Shoshoni

Shoshoni

NORTH AMERICA

Pawnee

Missouri

Missouri

Illinois

Ohio

Shawnee

Powhatan

New Amsterdam **1625** (New York **1664**)

Philadelphia **1682**

Ute

Southern Paiute

Hopi Queres

Navajo

Zuni Acoma

Taos **1680**

Santa Fe **1609**

Pecos

Apache

Arapaho

Arkansas

Kiowa

Kansa

Osage

Kaskaskia

The Illinois Post **1700**

Quapaw

Mississippi

Chickasaw

Yuchi

Cherokee

Catawba

Monacan

Tutelo

Tuscarora

Pamlico

Richmond **1733**

Jamestown **1607**

Appalachian Mountains

ATLANTIC OCEAN

Mojave

Western Apache

Colorado

Cocopa

Imuris

Jocome

Jano

Mescalero Apache

Lipan

Comanche

Wichita

Caddo

Tunica

Tonkawa

Coosa

Alabama

Hitichi

Creek Confederacy

Yamasee

Charleston **1672**

Savannah **1733**

INDIAN TERRITORY

Waicuri

Cochimi

Papago Lower Pima

Opata

Suma

Concho

Jumano

Atakapa

Karankawa

Choctaw

Houma

Chitimacha

Acolapissa

New Orleans **1718**

Apalachee

Potano

Timucua

St. Augustine **1565** **1565**

Ais **1566**

Seminole

Calusa **1567**

Tekesta **1567**

1567

Bahamas **1629**

Tropic of Cancer

Nevome

Tarahumara

Tubar

Toboso

Coahuilteco

Mayo

Guasave

Tepehuan

Zacatecas

Guachichil

Gulf of Mexico

Havana **1511**

Arawak

Cuba

Hispaniola

San Juan **1509**

Danish Virgin Islands

Antigua **1632**

Cuyute

Loco

Mazatec

Jonaz

Pame

Tampico

Mérida **1542**

Yucatan Peninsula

ROYALTY OF NEW SPAIN

SAINT-DOMINGUE

Santo Domingo **1497**

Puerto Rico **1509**

Ciboney

Guadeloupe **1635**

Coca

Tlazcatan

Mexico City **1521**

Veracruz **1519**

Yucatan

Maya

West Indies

1509-1655

1655

Jamaica

Martinique **1635**

St Lucia **1605**

Barbados **1605**

Aztec

Zoque

Gulf of Honduras

BELIZE

Mixe

Chorti

Trujillo **1525**

Cholulec

Paya

Mosquito

Grenada **1650**

Xinca

Pipil

MOSQUITO COAST

Matagalpa

Caribbean Sea

Aruba

Bonaire

Curaçao

Trinidad **1577**

PACIFIC OCEAN

Talamanca

Güymi

Panama **1519**

Nicarao

Cartagena **1532**

Caracas **1567**

VICEROYALTY OF NEW GRANADA

500 km

500 miles

N

Caribbean Sea

Santa Marta 1525
Panama 1519
Gulf of Darien
Maracaibo 1529
Cartagena 1532
Caracas 1567
Cumaná 1521
Gulf of Panama
AUDIENCIA OF SANTA FÉ 1548
Lake Maracaibo
Santa Fé de Bogotá 1538
Orinoco
VICEROYALTY OF NEW GRANADA 1739
Guiana Highlands
New Amsterdam 1627
SURINAM
Paramaribo 1613
ATLANTIC OCEAN

Equator
Quito 1534
PRESIDENCIA OF QUITO 1563
Rio Negro
Branco
Putumayo
Equator
Belém do Pará 1616
PARÁ 1616
São Luís (Maranhão)
Ceará
Tumbes 1526
Cuenca 1557
Marañón
Amazon
Rio Negro
Amazon
Amazon
Manaus 1674
Tapajós
MARANHÃO 1615
PIAUÍ 1532
CEARÁ 1613
Natal 1597
DUTCH BRAZIL 1630–1654
Paita 1532
MAYNAS 1638–1767
Juruá
Purus
Madeira
PARAÍBA 1532
Paraíba 1585
Olinda
Cajamarca 1532
VICEROYALTY OF BRAZIL
PERNAMBUCO 1532
Recife ca.1535
Trujillo 1525
AUDIENCIA OF LIMA 1543
SOUTH AMERICA
SERGIPE 1532
Fort Maurits 1637
Sergipe del Rey
Callao 1537
Lima 1535
Huancavelica
Madre de Dios
MATO GROSSO 1748
BAHIA 1532
Bahia (Salvador) capital 1549–1763
Cuzco 1533
MOJOS 1659–1767
Vila Bela (Mato Grosso) 1752
Planalto de Mato Grosso
GOIÁS 1744
Goiás 1744
Minas Novas 1727
PORTO SEGURO 1532
Ilhéus 1534
Arequipa 1540
Lake Titicaca
La Paz 1548
CHIQUITOS 1691
Paraguay
Corumbá 1788
Diamantina 1730
MINAS GERAIS 1720
ESPIRITO SANTO 1532
Arica 1537
Lago Poopó
La Plata 1538
PRESIDENCIA OF CHARCAS 1559
ITATÍN 1609–1660
Paraná
SÃO PAULO 1709
RIO DE JANEIRO 1532
Vitória
Potosí 1545
VICEROYALTY OF PERU 1543
Pilcomayo
Gran Chaco
GUAIRÁ ca.1630–1632
São Paulo 1532
Santos 1545
Rio de Janeiro 1565 capital from 1763
Tropic of Capricorn
Asunción 1537
Ciudad Real 1630
São Vicente 1532
Coquimbo 1537
CHACO 1732–1767
Paraná
SANTA CATARINA 1532
Desterro 1640
Córdoba 1573
Uruguay
GUARANÍ 1630–1660
RIO GRANDE DO SUL 1777
Laguna 1654
CAPTAINCY-GENERAL AND PRESIDENCIA OF CHILE 1606
Mendoza 1561
Porto Alegre
Rio Grande 1737
Valparaíso 1541
Santiago 1541
Salado
Buenos Aires 1536
Colônia do Sacramento Portuguese 1680–1750
Concepción 1550
Pampas
Montevideo 1726
Valdivia 1552
Araucanians
Rio Negro
Colorado
Carmen de Patagones 1779
MAP 17.4
San Carlos de Ancud 1763
Patagonia
Deseado
Golfo de San Jorge
Golfo de Penas
Bahía Grande
Strait of Magellan
Islas Malvinas
Cape Horn

Land Exploitation in the Americas up to ca. 1725

	British ca. 1725	
	Spanish before 1650	
	Spanish after 1650	
	Portuguese by 1600	
	Portuguese by 1750	
	French ca.1725	
	French influence	
	approximate western limit of French claim	
	Dutch	

- - - - - fur trade routes
1682 date of foundation
Houma native people
✝ Jesuit missions
✝ major Franciscan missions
Spanish fort

Economic Activity

hides and deerskins
copper
gold
silver mine
drugs
cocoa
diamonds
dyes
rice-growing region
sugar-growing region
major fisheries
tobacco cultivation

***Shinsen Dainibon Zukan* (Revised Map of Japan) of 1687.** The maps of Japan that the shogun Hideyoshi commissioned have not survived, but this is one of a series based on them. Each province is marked with the name of its feudal lord or *daimyo* and the amount of his salary. The placard at the top lists each province's topographical information, including place names, temples, and shrines. The blank land to the left of it, labeled Chosenkoku, is Korea.

the possibilities to increase it. In the 1570s, King Philip II of Spain ordered the most comprehensive survey of his realms that any European state had ever undertaken. It was soon extended to the New World and illustrated with maps that Native Americans made. In Japan in 1580, the shogun Hideyoshi (see Chapter 16) commanded a survey of Japan that would penetrate "the deepest caves of the mountains and the reach of oars at sea." It was to include the dimensions and soil quality of every rice field and the location of every irrigation channel. Villagers who withheld information would be crucified. Landowners who failed to cooperate would be put to the sword. Begun in 1583, driven by unpitying force, the job was finished by 1598. The Mughal regime in India was not given to such bureaucratic exertions but achieved something similar in the late sixteenth century, including a tally of average yields and market prices, field by field. In 1663, frustrated by his inability to locate undeveloped resources in France, Jean-Baptiste Colbert, the chief minister of King Louis XIV, ordered the first scrupulously accurate map of the country to be made by the latest surveying techniques. It was not fully complete until 1789 on the eve of the French Revolution.

New Energy Sources

Efforts to explore the environment led to the discovery and release of new energy sources. Timber from deforestation made an enormous contribution, together with oil from aggressive whaling by European and Japanese seamen in previously unfrequented seas. Cottonseed oil and rapeseed oil in Japan came into use as oil-lamp fuel in the early 1600s. Extracting peat to be burned as fuel from the bogs of Holland became a major industry. In some places, people shifted to coal, mined in increasing quantities in Great Britain, Germany, and the southern Netherlands (modern Belgium; it was a territory of the Spanish monarchy at the time). Londoners in the mid–sixteenth century burned more than 20,000 tons of coal annually—a little less than a quarter of a ton per inhabitant. By 1700, coal imports to London totaled almost 400,000 tons for a population of about 600,000. In the late seventeenth century, miners in Kyushu, Japan, began to make a success of marketing coal: to peasants for fuel, to refiners of salt and sugar. The Japanese government, meanwhile, adopted policies to conserve and replant forests, reserving valuable timber for official purposes, excluding intruders from endangered forest zones, and rewarding tree planting. "Cherishing the mountains," for the local ruler of Tugaru in the 1660s, was essential to nurture life and reverse forest shrinkage so severe that loggers were invading the northernmost Japanese island of Hokkaido for timber. Coal was abundant in China, but the market for it remained static. Wood and charcoal were still adequate to meet China's energy needs.

Land Reclamation

Land reclamation complemented the struggle to expand and settle new frontiers. In Holland, after terrible losses of lands to the encroaching sea in the sixteenth century, reclamation became a matter of survival. New windmill-pumping technology drained 57,000 acres of land in North Holland between 1610 and 1640. In all, the Dutch added nearly 370,000 acres to the land available for farming during the century. A minor social revolution accompanied the transformation of the landscape, as smallholders lost access to the sea and were forced to sell out to big landowners. In England, the drainage of the fenlands, which lay just across the sea from Holland in the eastern counties, began in 1600. Enforced by military occupation, against the protests of the local inhabitants, who were dispossessed, the project brought about 480,000 acres under the plow by the early 1650s. In Japan, government-sponsored schemes drained the Yodfo River delta. The Nobi plain in northern Honshu was transformed from "a marshy plain of water birds" to an area with hundreds of villages. The Aka River, which once flowed through marshes, fed 12,000 acres of wet rice lands by 1650. The cultivated land area of Japan grew by 82 percent between 1600 and 1720.

FRONTIERS OF THE HUNT

Imperialism promoted more efficient—sometimes more ruthless—exploitation of the Earth. Beyond the edges of empires, we do not know enough to be sure, but improvements in the range and effectiveness of hunting, and the extension of cultivation, were happening in other parts of the world, too. When the English arrived in Virginia, they found thousand of acres under cultivation and maize stocks "of sufficient quantity to fill the holds of several ships."

The Iroquois country of northeast North America is a case in point. Toward the end of what we think of as the Middle Ages, Indians developed a form of maize suitable for latitudes as north as the Great Lakes. This zone, which extends just north of Lakes Ontario and Erie and along the southern shores of Lakes Huron and Michigan, had about 140 frost-free days a year. Increasingly in the sixteenth and seventeenth centuries, Indians planted the new crop in forest clearings between the upper Hudson River and Lake Erie, on the frontier between deciduous and evergreen trees, where ecological diversity made ambitious ways of life possible.

The very diversity of their food sources imposed a mobile way of life on the Native Americans of the region. Periodically, soil erosion and forest depletion forced them to shift the sites of their

Huron women. Published in 1664, the *History of Canada* by the Jesuit priest François du Creux summarized the vast output of the author's fellow missionaries on the subject and helped to spread a favorable image of the Huron among learned readers in Europe. Here the engraver shows industrious Huron women peacefully engaged in a civilized, agrarian activity—maize production, in an idealized setting, while an infant's cradle alludes to sentiments and social conventions that European readers would have found comforting and familiar.

towns. Maize exhausts soil more quickly than other grains. The biggest settlement in the Great Lakes region was the Illinois town of Kaskaskia, with over 7,000 people in 1680, but villages of about 1,000 people were not unusual. To make glades for planting without hard-metal tools, Native Americans cut a ring in the trunk of a tree and set it on fire until the stump burned through. The method yielded ash for fertilizer, but left a landscape strewn with stumps. Farming under these disadvantages could never entirely replace a traditional way of life based on hunting, fishing, gathering wild berries, and tapping maple trees for syrup. But, like other forest peoples of the Americas who came into contact with colonial and overseas markets, the inhabitants improved their techniques and turnover as hunters too. They adopted firearms for the kill and steel knives to skin and butcher game. Beavers, once hunted for their meat, were now more valuable for the pelts European fur traders demanded. Beavers were almost gone from southern Ontario by the mid-1630s and had virtually disappeared from New England by 1700. In southern parts of North America, below the beaver's natural range, deerskins for the European leather trade became an equally valuable product. They made suede breeches and book bindings and smooth yellow gloves. In the 1690s and early 1700s, Charleston, South Carolina, exported up to 85,000 deerskins a year, and the numbers increased until the deer herds were depleted in the 1770s.

"In some parts of the world, the effects of the ecological revolutions were delayed until the eighteenth or nineteenth centuries. But the decisive transformations had already occurred by the end of the seventeenth century. Across the densely populated belt of the world, from China to Mesoamerica and the Andes, a single network of communications transmitted the same varieties of plants and animals."

In Perspective
Evolution Redirected

In some parts of the world, the effects of the ecological revolutions were delayed until the eighteenth or nineteenth centuries. But the decisive transformations had already occurred by the end of the seventeenth century. Across the densely populated belt of the world, from China to Mesoamerica and the Andes, a single network of communications transmitted the same varieties of plants and animals. The empires that dominated the zone responded in similar ways to the problems and opportunities of the time. New crops and animals helped the great colonizing movements of the era. They enabled farmers to penetrate new environments and exploit old ones more efficiently. The results included a huge increase in the amount of food people in affected regions could coax from the fields or cull from the wild. Not only did total food production go up, but a revolution in nutrition also occurred, as a wider variety of foodstuffs became available worldwide. Sometimes, when traditional crops failed, the products of the ecological exchange could fill the gap. In some places, on the other hand, newly introduced crops displaced traditional ones without increasing people's choices. In parts of northern Europe, for instance, by the nineteenth century, people became dependent on potatoes. In parts of the Americas, wheat displaced maize, which is, in many ways, a more efficient crop.

The indirect consequences of the ecological exchanges were equally impressive. People could farm new areas with new crops, creating new communities and the kernels of new states. In southeast Europe, for instance, maize cultivators could move upcountry to higher altitudes, where the Ottoman Empire's tax gatherers and enforcers never penetrated. A global revolution in the organization and distribution of labor was among the effects, as slavers shifted manpower from Africa across the Atlantic and Indian oceans to grow transplanted crops such as sugar and coffee on a huge scale.

Making Connections | NEW WAYS OF EXPLOITING THE NATURAL ENVIRONMENT

REGION/ECOLOGICAL ZONE	NEW FORMS OF EXPLOITATION	RESULTS
Western Hemisphere (North and South America, Caribbean)	Mass importation of slaves from Africa after depopulation of Native Americans due to disease	Large areas of North, Central, and South America transformed into plantations for cultivation of sugar, cotton, rice, tobacco, and indigo; creation of large African and mixed-race populations throughout Western Hemisphere
Steppeland; mountainous regions of Asia, including Mongolia and Xianjang	Chinese takeover of traditional adversaries, exploitation of natural resources	Well-trained infantry, advanced artillery, well-designed fortifications end the nomadic threat; highland and steppe regions become source for raw materials
Cape of Good Hope, South Africa, Australia	Introduction of sheep and new breeds of cattle, extensive farming by European settlers	Displacement of natives
North and South America/lowlands, high plains	Farming pampas/prairies; felling forests	Creation of large-scale agricultural complexes focusing on wheat, maize, and other commodities for human and livestock consumption for domestic use and export
Mexico, South America	Development of silver and gold mines	Boost global supply of cash
Mexico, South America, and North America	Development of extensive livestock herding	Millions of square miles of lightly populated areas claimed for cattle and sheep herding
North America	Large-scale fur trade in American Midwest, West, and Canada	Beaver, deerskins, and other furs/skins become basis for gradual penetration, settlement of western and northern North America
Eurasia	Land reclamation projects; expansion of timber harvesting, mining	National leaders attempt to solidify control, expand state revenues through systematic exploitation of resources, beginning with thorough mapping and surveying projects

Chronology

1492	Columbus arrives in the New World, beginning process of biological exchange
1500s	Horses and cattle introduced to New World
1510	Importation of slave labor in the Spanish colonies begins
1520s and 1530s	Absorption of Mesoamerican and Andean cities into Spanish Empire
1550s	Russian conquest of Kazan
1555	First records of maize cultivation in China
ca. 1560–1650	Russian colonization of lower Volga and Siberia
1570s	Philip II of Spain orders survey of his realms
	Brazil becomes a major importer of slaves
1580s	Brazil becomes the world's major sugar producer
1580	Shogun Hideyoshi orders a survey of Japan
1600s	British colonization of North America
	Expansion, colonization, and intensive farming in Mughal India
ca. 1620s–1660s	Large-scale Chinese immigration to Taiwan
1667–1707	1.5 million settlers arrive in Sichuan
1680s	Discovery of gold and diamonds prompts further Portuguese expansion in Brazil
1690s	Charleston, South Carolina, exports up to 85,000 deerskins a year
Late seventeenth century	Japanese peasants displace native inhabitants of Hokkaido
ca. 1700	Native American population in regions penetrated by Europeans declines 60 to 90 percent
1700	Popularity of coffee booms in Europe and Middle East, and coffee production begins in Brazil and Indonesia
	New England becomes a world center of trade

Evolution, meanwhile, was launched on a new course. In one respect, at least, the ecological exchanges constituted the biggest revolution humankind had wrought in the natural history of the planet. Ever since the continents began to split apart from one another, perhaps about 130 million years ago, they had begun to nurture different life forms. Species peculiar to each continent developed in different ways, divided from each other by uncrossable seas. This divergent history now gave way to a convergent trend that has produced the world we inhabit today, when the same germs, plants, and animals occur all over the world, wherever climate permits. In a sense, human intervention began to reverse the effects of tens of millions of years of evolution.

The ecological revolution was the essential precondition for some of the global changes of the next few centuries, fueling some of the major themes of the next two parts of this book: population growth, radical breakthroughs in exploiting the globe's resources, and the globalization of empires and trade. But such effects depended on more than the physical environment. People's mental attitudes to the world changed, too, and, like the ingredients of ecological exchange, voyagers carried these new attitudes with them across the globe through long-range travel, trade, and empire-building. These mental revolutions are the subjects of the next chapter.

PROBLEMS AND PARALLELS

1. Why should the Columbian Exchange be regarded as one of the biggest revolutions in history?

2. What are some of the explanations for the "age of plagues"? Why did it suddenly end in the eighteenth century?

3. How did human settlement expand its range in the sixteenth and seventeenth centuries? What were the motives behind this expansion? What effect did it have on ecological frontiers? On the way colonialists viewed the natural world? Why did rulers like Hideyoshi in Japan initiate detailed land surveys of their domains?

4. Why was there a massive transplantation of human labor during the sixteenth and seventeenth centuries? Why did colonial America suffer from severe labor shortages?

5. Why did the balance of power between settled life and pastoralism shift in favor of the settlers? In which parts of the world did pastoralism remain a predominant way of life? Why did the Moroccan conquest of Songhay under al-Mansur ultimately fail to control the pastoralists of the Sahel?

6. What factors made Spanish colonialism in the Americas more advantageous than the ventures of the English or French?

READ ON▶ ▶ ▶

Ledger's story can be found in G. Gramiccia, *The Life of Charles Ledger* (1988) and F. Rocco, *The Miraculous Fever-tree* (2003). The major works on the ecological exchange are A. W. Crosby, *The Columbian Exchange* (1972) and *Ecological Imperialism* (1986). J. F. Richards, *The Unending Frontier* (2003) is a superb, if necessarily selective, environmental history of the period. Classics on particular crops include N. Deerr, *The History of Sugar* (1949); S. Mintz, *Sweetness and Power* (1986); N. Salaman, *History and Social Influence of the Potato* (1985); and A. Warman, *Corn and Capitalism* (2003). M. Elvin, *The Retreat of the Elephants* (2004) is an inspiring general history of the Chinese environment. My book, *Near a Thousand Tables* (2002), puts the exchanges in the context of the history of food. R. Grove, *Green Imperialism* (1996) is an amazingly rich work that argues that European colonialism nurtured environmentalism.

On plague in general, see the works recommended in Chapter 14. The demographic disasters of the New World are the subject of intense controversy: see D. Henige, *Numbers from Nowhere*, (1998) and contrast W. M. Denevan, *The Native Population of the Americas in 1492* (1992). The most balanced general treatment is in D. N. Cook, *Born to Die*, (1998) though the author's argument that demographics explain the course of "conquest" should be considered critically. On plague in China, C. Benedict, *Bubonic Plague in Nineteenth-Century China* (1996) is important. O.J. Benedictow, *The Black Death, 1346–53* (2004) is a valuable recent contribution to plague epidemiology.

On the Atlantic slave trade, H. Thomas, *The Slave Trade* (1999) is a lively history. R. Blackburn, *The Making of New World Slavery* (1998) is an engaging introduction. J. Thornton, *Africa and Africans in the Making of the Atlantic World* (1998) is a model of scholarship and presentation. P. D. Curtin, *The Rise and Fall of the Plantation Complex* (1998); S. W. Mintz and R. Price, *The Birth of African-American Culture* (1992), B. Solow, ed., *Slavery and the Rise of the Atlantic System* (1993); D. Eltis, *The Rise of African Slavery in the Americas* (1999) are all valuable studies of the economies and societies of slave plantations.

M. Sobel, *The World They Made Together* (1989) is important on the slave world of Virginia, and L. Ferguson, *Uncommon Ground* (1995) is full of interesting material on plantation life in the North American South generally.

C. D. Totman, *Early Modern Japan* (1995) is an account particularly strong on environmental awareness. B. Walker, *The Conquest of Ainu Lands* (2001) is admirable. R. L. Edmonds, *Northern Frontiers of Qing China and Tokugawa Japan* (1985) makes an admirable comparative introduction. On Chinese expansion, R. H. G. Lee, *The Manchurian Frontier in Ch'ing History* (1970), and J. Waley-Cohen, *Exile in mid-Qing China* (1991) are indispensable. Ping-ti Ho, *Studies on the Population of China* (1959) is a valuable broad survey of its subject.

D. Twitchett and J. K. Fairbank, eds., *The Cambridge History of China*, vol. 7 (1988), is an invaluable guide to China in the period. On the Manchu conquest of China, L. Struve, *Voices from the Ming-Qing Cataclysm* (1998) is a well-selected and structured collection of sources.

There is, as far as I know, no dedicated study in English, but there are some useful pages on al-Mansur's conquest of the Sahara in A. C. Hess, *The Forgotten Frontier* (1978), and J. O. Hunwick, *Timbuktu and the Songhay Empire* (2003) contains some useful documents.

On Russian Siberia, J. Forsyth, *A History of the Peoples of Siberia* (1994) is an impressive and masterful introduction. B. Dmitrishyn et al., eds., *Russia's Conquest of Siberia* (1986) is an enormous compendium of sources. The best edition of the chronicles is T. Armstrong, ed., *Yermak's Campaigns in Siberia* (1975). J. Martin, *Treasure of the Land of Darkness* (2004) is superb on the background of the fur trade. M. Rywkin, ed., *Russian Colonial Expansion* (1988) contains some important papers.

C. Wilson, *England's Apprenticeship* (1965) is an excellent introduction to the economic history of England in the seventeenth century. For the inland see K. Lindley, *Fenland Riots and the English Revolution* (1982). J. de Vries and A. M. van der Woude, *The First Modern Economy* (1997) is the standard work on the early modern Dutch economy.

On the Mughal frontier in Bengal, R. Eaton, *The Rise of Islam and the Bengal Frontier* (1996) is of great value and importance.

On Spanish American cities V. Fraser, *The Architecture of Conquest* (1990) is a monograph (on Peru) crafted well enough to serve as an introduction.

For Brazil, J. Hemming, *Red Gold* (1978) and *Amazon Frontier* (1987) are superb and chilling accounts of the fate of the natives at the time of European conquest and colonization. S. Schwartz, ed., *Tropical Babylons* (2004) is the most up-to-date collection on the sugar colonies. G. Freyre, *The Masters and the Slaves* is a classic of such significance in Brazilian historiography that it should still be read by anyone interested in the subject. C. R. Boxer, *The Golden Age of Brazil* (1995) is almost in the same category.

B. Trigger's magnificent *A History of the Huron People*, 2 vols. (1976), is unequaled in its field.

CHAPTER 18

Mental Revolutions: Religion and Science in the Sixteenth and Seventeenth Centuries

▲ **Astronomy lesson:** from the sacred seclusion of a private chamber, King Narai of Siam listens in while Jesuits teach astronomy to his courtiers during an eclipse. Owing to the king's presence, the courtiers must attend to the lesson while lying face down on the floor. Celestial events triggered traditional royal rituals in the kingdoms of East Asia, so Jesuits' expertise in astronomy made them useful to many rulers there.

FRANCE

SIAM

The beds were strange—"raised like thrones, girded with hangings and curtains, and with thick mattresses and covers to protect sleepers from the cold.'" That was the first thing Kosa Pan saw when he spent his first night ashore in France in 1686, as ambassador of the king of Thailand (the country Westerners used to call Siam until the twentieth century). "I am told," he went on, "that entire families sleep in one large bed, all enclosed in wooden shutters; we were spared such an indignity.'" The account that follows—which narrates the embassy's journey from the coast to Paris—is so mixed up with satirical comment intruded by a European editor that it is often hard to tell Kosa Pan's voice. Still, many comments on French customs ring true. French dancing, Kosa Pan the writer found, resembled "a military parade performed by both sexes." He literally turned his nose up at the unperfumed common people he met, for they "found our habit of bathing curious. . . . Truly I think our buffaloes smell sweeter than most French people, for we wash them more often."

When Kosa Pan at last arrived at the French king's palace, Louis XIV (r. 1643–1715) spared no effort or expense to impress the ambassador. He received him, seated on a silver throne and dressed in cloth of gold, studded with huge diamonds in imitation of Siamese royal robes. The layout and the lavish floral decorations of the audience chamber were designed to match what travelers had reported of the appearance of Siam's royal apartments. When Kosa Pan presented his credentials, Louis rose, bowed, and doffed his hat—gestures of condescension he would never have made to honor a European diplomat.

But why had Kosa Pan traveled so far? What was this Buddhist gentleman from an agrarian state in a corner of Southeast Asia doing halfway across the world, struggling across two oceans, to a continent his countrymen had only just discovered, dragging 132 crates—as he recalled—filled with gifts from his king to the king of France?

It was not the first time that King Narai of Siam had tried to forge an alliance with France. The first embassy was shipwrecked off the coast of Madagascar and never even reached the Atlantic. The second made it to Paris, initiated contacts, and caused a sensation in Europe, prompting the French court to respond with a mission to Siam. The idea for an alliance seems to have originated with a Greek adventurer whom Narai employed as a trusted confidant. Narai's objectives seem to have been twofold. First, he wanted France to supply him with soldiers, to deter other European powers from attacking Siam and keep potential rebels in awe. This alone shows that European military technology and techniques were already respected in Southeast Asia. But Narai admired another, more peaceful Western attainment, too.

FOCUS questions

Why did European elites attempt to change Christian practice and teachings during the sixteenth century?

How did Native Americans and Africans influence Christian beliefs and worship?

Where were Muslim and Buddhist missionaries most active in the sixteenth and seventeenth centuries?

How did the Mughal emperors deal with religious diversity?

Why was the spread of scientific thought important for the West?

Why were the Chinese so interested in astronomy?

A contemporary engraving shows him listening to an astronomy lesson from a visiting Jesuit missionary. Court dignitaries struggle to follow the lesson, while abasing themselves in the ritual fashion Siamese court etiquette demanded. Astronomy in parts of East Asia was more than a learned curiosity: it was a means to power. Like many other rulers who modeled their practices on those of Chinese emperors, Narai had to perform official rites at prescribed moments during the cycle of the sun, moon, and stars, to preserve—supposedly—harmony between his kingdom and the heavens. Westerners, despite their barbaric manners and offensive smell, had the advantage of mastery of two technologies— the telescope and clockwork timekeeping—that could help to guarantee the accuracy of the calendar. Kosa Pan traveled in search of knowledge as well as power—indeed, he and his king regarded the two quests as inseparable. His journey illustrates an ever more common and characteristic feature of the world of his day: the way human encounters brought cultures into contact and initiated cultural exchanges that crossed the planet.

In one respect, Kosa Pan's journey was unusual. More commonly, it was Westerners who crossed the world and initiated the contacts that brought cultural exchange, but Christianity, Islam, and Buddhism all contributed. The sixteenth and seventeenth centuries were an unprecedented era for the revitalization and spread of all three religions. They were also centuries of unprecedented development for Western science and secular values. Western science reached parts of the world where previously, like Thailand, it had been unknown. At the same time, the ways people thought, felt, and, in some respects, behaved in the West changed as a result of encounters with non-Western cultures.

CHRISTIANITY IN CHRISTENDOM

Western Christendom and, to a slightly lesser extent, the Eastern Orthodox world had developed a new sense of mission in the late Middle Ages. Fervor to renew the dynamism of the early history of the church combined with a new conviction of the obligations of the godly. Those obligations included a growing sense of the need to compel "right thinking" alongside outward conformity, and to combat heresy, unbelief, and supposedly satanic forces. People with vocations or responsibilities in the church, or with a strong personal sense of their relationship with God, increasingly took it upon themselves to spread active, committed, Christian awareness, informed by a knowledge of dogma. Among the consequences were new religious orders, new techniques of prayer, new fashions in devotion, and increased coercion and social control (see Chapter 19). But there were still parts of society and places in the world where, so far, Christianity had hardly reached or only superficially penetrated. In the sixteenth and seventeenth centuries, the mission-minded felt the need of a new conversion strategy, addressed to people low on the social scale: the poor; the rootless masses of growing cities; the neglected country folk; the peoples of forest, bog, and mountain, who had barely entered the candle-glow of the church; and the vast world that exploration and improved geographical learning revealed or suggested. Self-consciously, godly elites set themselves the task of re-Christianizing Europe, reviving the fervor of lukewarm Christians, and trying to root out pagan survivals and demonic intrusions or delusions from popular customs. Like peasants and pagans, children were part of the previously submerged world to which clerical zeal now penetrated. By the last quarter of the sixteenth century, thousands of Christian catechisms for the education of children were in print.

The countryside was Europe's pagan backyard, full of potential converts to a more intense, aware, and devout Christian life. Rural communities still lived in worlds full of spirits and demons, where natural forces were personified and placated. A miller in northern Italy in the early sixteenth century could describe a remarkably coherent universe made "of cheese and worms," from which Christian traditions about creation were entirely absent. A Jesuit priest in the city of Bordeaux in France in 1553 was appalled to find people in the nearby countryside "who have never heard of mass nor of a single word of the faith." Another Jesuit in Spain in 1615 expressed disbelief that so many of his colleagues wanted to be missionaries in Asia or America "when we have so many people here who do not know whether they believe in God." In 1628, a member of the English parliament complained of regions of the country "where God was little better known than among the Indians." In 1693, the Swedish governor general of Livonia (in the modern Baltic States) ordered the smashing of the rocks and groves people worshipped "so that not the least memorial may be left which could be used for superstition."

Campaigns like these were part of a more general attempt by ministers of religion to enforce their claim to a monopoly over ritual. For instance, in Spain, the church hierarchy had normally been happy, in the fifteenth century, to validate laypeople's claims to have experienced saintly visions. But from the early sixteenth century, the church endorsed no more such claims. The same unease was directed against the deities of local religion: the local saints and virgins, whose cults the churches swept away or replaced with the universal veneration of Christ and his mother, the Virgin Mary.

All kinds of lay competition in the clergy's proper fields became subject to attempts at control or eradication, especially such practices as fortune telling, folk healing, magic, and even fairs and festivals. The Council of Trent—a series of meetings held from 1545 to 1563 by bishops who acknowledged the pope's authority—ordered that "all superstition shall be removed" and the cults of saints and relics purged of "perversion by the people into boisterous festivities." Dancing was banned from church—and in some places forbidden altogether. Bull fighting and contests between bears and dogs were prohibited or restricted, or at least banned on holy days, not because they were torture to animals but because they were temptations for people to behave in ways of which the church disapproved—gambling, getting drunk, or having sex.

The war on popular religion was an attempt, under the constant menace of natural disasters, to wean people away from a religion of survival in this world toward one of salvation in the next. Trials of rats and exorcisms of swarms of locusts, appeals to folk healers and wisewomen, vows to saints for worldly purposes, charms to master nature, and spells to conjure the supernatural—these were the common enemies the clergy of all Christian traditions strove to control or abolish. A German law of 1669, typical of hundreds of others, condemned such magical practices as "putting pigs' hairs in fires, binding trees on New Year's Eve, and putting St. John's wort on walls to drive out spirits, and Easter bonfires

Catechism class. Balls of wool as rewards for good students, blows for the bad from the rods the schoolmaster keeps under his desk: a catechism class in progress in 1593. Thanks to printing, every student could follow the text of a lesson in a relatively cheap copy of his or her own. The illustration comes from the first catechism of the Church of England, by Alexander Nowell (ca. 1507–1602).

Witchcraft. The south German draftsman of these scenes of witchcraft turned the subject into a pretext for dark humor and social satire. Artists traditionally contrasted scenes of worldly pleasures with depictions of the pangs of hell. Here women cavort with demons in a forest clearing, where dancing hints coyly at sex, while a devil roasts meat. But the witches' executioners, stoking fires and armed with pitchforks, are almost equally demonic.

accompanied by all sorts of songs that take the name of our Lord in vain while a good deal of devilry goes on." In the seventeenth century, Catholic clergymen were prominent in reclassifying witchcraft as a psychotic delusion, but all kinds of Christians, with diminishing frequency, were inclined to persecute it.

Public rituals affect private lives. Formal religion now intruded as never before in Europe into the most private sphere of activity: sex. In the sixteenth and seventeenth centuries in most of Europe, successful campaigns brought under the supervision of the clergy all contracts in which men and women agreed to live with each other as man and wife. Ostensibly, for instance, the Spanish Inquisition, founded in 1478, was a tribunal of faith, originally designed to monitor the sincerity of former Muslims and Jews who had converted to Christianity under pressure from the Spanish authorities. In practice, most of its efforts in the second half of the sixteenth century were devoted to getting laypeople's sex lives under clerical control. Bigamy and fornication were among the most common crimes the Inquisition investigated. Church leaders had never completely approved of sex, but they were united in thinking it did least harm when they themselves licensed it. Charity, as well as power lust, motivated them. It seemed vital, as a saintly campaigner claimed in 1551, "to invalidate all marriages where there is no witness," because "an infinite number of maidens have been deceived and undone . . . trusting in the promise of marriage made to them; and some have left their parents' house and gone to their perdition."

The newly self-conscious godly elites did not, however, consist entirely of clergy. On the contrary, clerical demand for more responsive congregations and a more committed flock met lay demand for more access to the mysteries of religion. Indeed, the more the clergy weaned people from pre-Christian or non-Christian superstitions, the more they aroused lay appetites for a share in the experience of Christian devotion: prayer, the sacraments, scripture, preaching—all the means by which the Church claimed to deliver experience or knowledge of God. Different parts of Christendom met this lay demand in different ways, but always by finding forms of devotion that could connect laypeople with God: through increased access to the sacraments of the church, in some places; through preaching and translations of the Bible and liturgy in others; and everywhere by encouraging private prayer.

One of the most effective communicators of the Christian message to a wider public was the German theologian Martin Luther (1483–1546). He began with himself—a conviction of his own sinfulness and of his redemption by the grace that God freely offered to all humankind. In a personal mission that he began toward the end of the second decade of the sixteenth century, he looked first to his fellow priests, with patchy success. He was more successful in reaching secular rulers, whom he encouraged to take power over the church and to confiscate its wealth to purify it and restore it to the simplicity Jesus and his apostles had practiced. Luther's greatest effect, however, was on the lay public. For he appealed to laypeople over the heads of the church hierarchy, whose authority he gradually came to reject in favor—in practice—of his own reading of scripture. The printing press—a medium unavailable to earlier religious reformers—spread his message and illustrated it with pictures that even illiterate people could appreciate. He devised a style of writing vivid beyond crudity in images, for example, of the papacy as the whore of Rome copulating with the Antichrist foretold in the Bible, or the pope defecating lies. (Some of Luther's opponents gave as good as they got. Catholic cartoonists, for example, depicted Luther as Satan, complete with horns and tail.) What was more, Luther crafted his language out of various northern German dialects. Many communities in the German-speaking world could understand it, and it spread relatively easily around the trading zone of the North Sea and Baltic. Here, in Scandinavia and parts of Germany—assisted by rulers grateful for an excuse to take power over the churches of their realms and seize their property—Luther's version of Christianity became the majority religion. Patchily, it also spread, or was carried in even more radical forms by Luther's unruly disciples, into parts of Europe that major trade routes connected, along the corridors of the Rhine, Rhone, and Danube rivers.

Within these corners and patches of Europe, Luther not only reached places and classes where Christianity had previously been superficial, but changed the lives of individuals whose Christian awareness he touched. Rumors of his death drove the great German painter, Albrecht Dürer, to despair: "who," he asked, "will expound the gospel to us with such clearness?" Hans Sachs, the poet of Nuremberg in southwest Germany, said simply, "Luther spoke—and all was light." In some provinces, the church had anticipated his project. Cardinal Cisneros, for instance, who was head of the Spanish Inquisition from 1507 until his death in 1517, had cheap editions of devotional books published in Spanish to wean readers from the pulp fiction of the day. But Luther went further, advocating reading the Bible and conducting the liturgy of the church in languages people actually spoke instead of in Latin.

Luther, however, was politically and socially conservative. He feared social revolutionaries who claimed religious inspiration to justify rebellion against established authority. In 1525, for instance, he condemned "thieving, murderous hordes" of German peasants who claimed that his works had inspired them to rebel. The revolution of 1525 in the city of Münster alarmed him even more. Radical Christians, who claimed that God absolved them from following rules or obeying laws, seized control of the town and imposed a reign of terror, massacring their enemies and indulging—so their orthodox critics said—in orgies of looting and sex. Luther urged responsible nobles and rulers to save the town and punish the heretics. He wanted the reformed church to remain hierarchical under the rule of bishops and to adhere to the orthodoxy he preached. Some talented Protestant theologians could not accept this discipline and broke with him to found churches of their own.

The most influential in the long run were Ulrich Zwingli (1484–1531) and Jean Calvin (1509–1564). With Zwingli, Luther's main dispute was about doctrine—specifically, about what happens at communion when Christians consecrate gifts of bread and wine. Luther insisted, with modifications, on the truth of the tradition of the church: communicants really ingested the essence of Christ's flesh and blood along with bread and wine. When they met to discuss it, and Zwingli argued that flesh and blood could only be present in a metaphorical or symbolic sense, Luther chalked or carved Christ's words from the Bible—'THIS IS MY BODY'—in capital letters on the table.

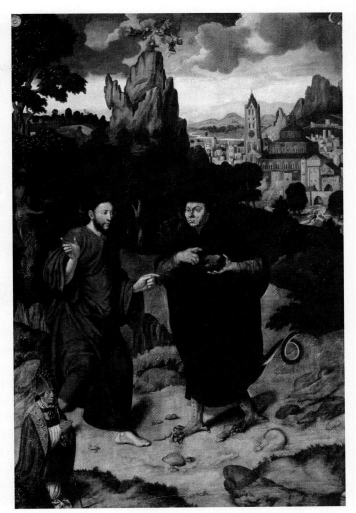

Martin Luther as Satan tempting Jesus (1547). Protestant propaganda during the Reformation often depicted the pope as Satan. Here Catholic propaganda turns the tables by portraying Martin Luther as the devil (note his cloven hooves and tail.) Like Satan in the Bible, Luther asks Jesus to make bread out of stones. Implicitly, the artist is accusing Luther of warping the Church's teaching that the bread of the eucharistic becomes 'the body of Christ,' though Luther was emphatic that the bread of the sacrament was 'not bread alone' but also real flesh.
Versuchung Christi (1547), Gemalde, Bonn, Landschaftsverband Rheinland/Rheinisches Landesmuseum Bonn. Inv. Nr. 58.3.

Inextinguishable light: Pope, friar, and devil cannot blow out the candle of the Reformation lit by Martin Luther, who sits behind it surrounded by other Protestant theologians of the sixteenth century. The Frenchman Jean Calvin is next to Luther, aptly turning away from him. The standing figure touching Luther's arm is the Scots reformer John Knox. Immediately behind Luther is the Swiss Ulrich Zwingli. Luther's disciple Philip Melancthon is seated to his left. The scene is imaginary. All these reformers never gathered together, and Luther and his followers were bitterly opposed to the theological ideas of Calvin, Zwingli, and Knox. The border of the engraving alludes to Jesus' claim to be "the true Vine."

"Having broken the principle that the church was indivisible and that authority within the church was unique and binding on all Christians, the new Christian movements tended to split among themselves in often bitter and bloody disputes over Christian dogma and how to organize the church."

Calvin differed from Luther on a further point of dogma. He insisted that logically if, as Luther believed, God had chosen some people for salvation from before time began, he must have excluded others. So some people would spend eternity in hell, no matter how virtuous they were in this life. More important than this doctrine, called "predestination," in making Calvinism appealing to Christians were Calvin's gifts as a writer and administrator. His theology seems austere and chilling. Yet when he wrote about it he made it moving and humanly compelling. Strictly speaking, if everyone was saved or damned from before time began, Jesus' life and sacrifice seem pointless. Yet Calvin's writings are full of a sense of Jesus' reality and effectiveness as the focus where human and divine love meet. Calvin established a power base in the Swiss city of Geneva, where revolutionaries renounced allegiance to their ruler, the duke of Savoy, and organized missionaries who radiated from there across Europe. No state church in Europe, except those of Scotland, some German principalities, and the United Provinces of the Netherlands, adopted his teachings; but many of his followers came to occupy influential positions in the church hierarchy in England, and communities of his adherents took root in many parts of France and Switzerland, and were scattered in patches around Germany and parts of northern Italy, Hungary, and Transylvania. Having broken the principle that the church was indivisible and that authority within the church was unique and binding on all Christians, the new Christian movements tended to split among themselves in often bitter and bloody disputes over Christian dogma and how to organize the church.

The schism within Christianity endures to this day (see Map 18.1). Some national or local churches in the affected areas—northern and eastern Germany; parts of France, Switzerland, Hungary, and Holland; Scandinavia; Scotland , England, and Wales—seceded from obedience to the Church of Rome, calling themselves "Evangelical" or "Protestant," or "Reformed" (hence the term *Reformation* for the movements they formed.) A Catholic movement that historians commonly call the Counter-Reformation or the Catholic Reformation reconverted some churches to Roman obedience. Partly in reaction against Protestantism, but at a more profound level to pursue the common, underlying project to re-Christianize Europe that all Christian elites shared, new religious orders sprang up within the Catholic Church. The most significant of these for the future of world history was the Society of Jesus or Jesuits, which Ignatius Loyola (1491–1556)

1529: At Diet of Speyer, Charles V attempts to reach compromise with Lutheran princes

1535: John Calvin formulates doctrine of predestination in Geneva

1545: Start of Council of Trent, which defines modern Catholicism

| 1510 | 1520 | 1530 | 1540 | 1550 | 1560 |

1517: Martin Luther posts 95 Theses condemning abuses of Catholic church at Wittenberg

1532: Henry VIII of England declares himself head of Church of England

1555: At Peace of Augsburg; Lutheran princes win right to choose their religion

MAP 18.1

Spread of the Reformation by c. 1580

Protestant majorities

Large Protestant minorities

Areas regained by Catholic efforts from c. 1535

• Centers of Protestant evangelization

founded in 1540. Loyola was an ex-soldier under the Spanish crown who brought martial virtues to the movement he founded: tight discipline, comradeship, self-sacrifice, and a sense of chivalry. He was also a gifted mystic, who taught his friends and followers self-transforming techniques of prayer, and a natural intellectual, who insisted on the highest standards of learning for those who joined his order. The Jesuits became the Roman Catholic Church's most effective missionaries and educators, both in Europe and in the wider world, and the schools they established were nurseries of science and scholarship.

Having broken the principle that the church was indivisible and authority within the church was unique and binding on all Christians, the Protestant movements tended

Jesuit missionaries. The Jesuits' pride in the success of their overseas missions radiates from this eighteenth-century painting in which three of the order's sixteenth-century saints are prominently depicted. Flanked by personifications of the four continents in the foreground, the mythical giant Atlas presents the world to the Jesuits' founder, St. Ignatius Loyola. St. Francis Borja on the left-hand pedestal represents the order's preaching vocation; St. Francis Xavier, on the right, represents the ministry of the sacraments. Xavier also wears a Chinese-style vestment, a reminder of the Jesuits' long efforts to convert China. One of the leading Jesuit missionaries in China, Matteo Ricci, is in the background, among other Jesuit saints and heroes. Representatives of peoples the Jesuits converted kneel in prayer.

to split among themselves in often bitter and bloody disputes over Christian dogma and how to organize the church. A sense of hostility among the different forms of Christianity grew up in the aftermath of the schism—leading to wars justified, if not caused, by religious cant. As a result of this climate of hostility, traditional history has exaggerated the differences between Protestant and Catholic Christianity. Few people understood or cared about the subtleties of doctrine and worship that divided theologians. The doctrine most commonly said to define the Protestant reformers is that of "salvation by faith alone," according to which God imparts grace freely to anyone who professes belief in him without the sinner needing to perform pious works or obey church rules. Yet many Catholics stayed in the church while sharing Protestant views on this point, while Luther himself repeatedly insisted, in his own catechism for young Christians, "We should fear God because of his threat to those who transgress his law and love him for his promise of grace to those who keep it."

The missionary impulse within Europe produced no great revolution in spirituality. Most people remained as indifferent and shallow-minded as ever. But the language and imagery—the total communication—of the Christian faith were genuinely transformed. For Protestant clergy, services in the vernacular and the promotion of the Bible in translation were ways to help the laity become more actively involved in their faith. For Catholics, frequent communion and—to involve women in particular—the extension of the cults of the Virgin Mary and the founding of new orders of nuns who taught the young and nursed the sick served the same purpose.

Both traditions made God more intelligible, more accessible. "You seem to think that Christ was drunk," thundered Luther against radically subversive readings of the story of the Last Supper by rival Protestants like Zwingli, "and wearied his disciples with meaningless words!" This daring joke had the great virtue of treating Christ's humanity as literal and picturing him in the flesh of human weakness. In 1573, the Inquisition in Venice forced the Italian painter Veronese to re-label his painting of the Last Supper as *Dinner at the House of Levi*, because it contained scenes of feasting and mirth, but by the century's end, another Italian painter, Caravaggio, could depict the *Last Supper*, without irreverence, as an episode of tavern low life. The German artist Mathias Grünewald in the 1520s had to hide his drawing of Jesus as a low-browed, warty-faced loser, but a century and a half later, the Spanish painter Murillo could revive the ancient tradition of depicting the Christ child as a naughty boy. As a result of the church's mission to bring Christianity to the people, relevance to the lives of ordinary folk sanctified sacred subjects.

In eastern Christendom, too, reform movements led to conflicts between the Christianity of the clergy and the religion of ordinary people, and ultimately to splits in the Orthodox Church as they did in the West. A reformation parallel to that of the West began in 1621, when the Patriarch of Constantinople, Cyril Lukaris (1572–1638), renounced what he called the "bewitchment" of tradition "and took for my guide," he said, "Scripture . . . and Faith alone." The Russian priest Avvakum, "though a miserable sinner," tackled popular excesses violently. He drove mummers from his village, breaking their masks and drums, clubbing one of their dancing bears senseless, and releasing the other into the wild. In 1648, the Russian Orthodox clerical brotherhood known as the Zealots of Piety captured the czar's attention. At their insistence, the czar banished the vulgarities of popular piety from the Russian court and banned popular music as a presumed survival of paganism. Yet within 20 years, the clergy who had triumphed together in championing these changes fell out among themselves over a further proposed elimination of impurities: the standardization of texts and the harmonization of rituals. The leader of one party was exiled in 1666, the other burned at the stake in 1681.

Exaltation of the ordinary. The Italian painter Caravaggio's "Supper at Emmaus" (1599) is famous among art historians for its innovative, dramatic use of light and shade, but it is equally extraordinary for its treatment of a sacred subject: a meeting at which Jesus revealed himself to his disciples after his Resurrection. Caravaggio depicted the disciples, not as glorious saints, but as shabby, commonplace peasants.

CHRISTIANITY BEYOND CHRISTENDOM: THE LIMITS OF SUCCESS

Beyond Europe, the world that exploration and imperialism disclosed was a magnet for missionaries. "Come over and help us," said the Indian on the official seal of the trading company responsible, under the English crown, for colonizing Massachusetts in the early seventeenth century. On the whole, however, overseas missionizing was a rare vocation in Protestant Europe. There were a few exceptions. The conviction that the Algonquin Indians were a lost tribe of ancient Israel inspired John Eliot (1604–1690), who created "praying towns" in New England where Native American pastors preached and led congregations in prayers and readings from the Bible. Normally, however, only Roman Catholic religious orders had enough manpower and zeal to undertake the missions on a large scale, and outside areas of Spanish rule, their efforts were patchy.

In Asia, the contrast between the Philippines, where Spanish rule built up what is by far the biggest Christian community in Asia, and the many mission fields that proved barren or only briefly productive illustrates this patchiness. Even in the Philippines, Christian success in direct competition with Islam was limited. In the Sulu Islands, where Muslim missionaries were active within reach of protection from a strong Islamic state in Brunei, the Muslim threat could be met by force of arms, but Christian preaching could not eradicate it. In the Philippine island of Mindanao, Muslim intruders arrived from the small but spice-rich sultanate of Ternate in the 1580s. The Christian mission on Mindanao had barely begun and could not be sustained. In the late sixteenth and early seventeenth centuries, it was all Spanish garrisons could do to keep at bay Muslim hotheads who launched holy wars against the Spaniards' main base in Luzon. Yet, responding to his advisers' view that the mission was not worth the cost and effort, King Philip II of Spain (r. 1556–1598) insisted that he would rather spend all the gold in his treasury than sacrifice one church where the name of Christ was praised.

SOCIETAS ASIATICA.

P. Sebastianus Vieira Lusitanus, cum quinq, Socijs Iaponibus Soc:IESV, triduano Scrobis tormento, et Subiecto igne pro Fide Christi necatus, in Iaponia Iendi. 6 Iunij A. 1634.
C. Screta d.   Melch: Küsell.

Christian missionaries. In late sixteenth- and early seventeenth-century Japan became victims of their own success. Not only did they attract hundreds of thousands of followers, but they also established close ties to many of the daimyos, regional lords whom the central authorities distrusted. The missionaries' Spanish and Portuguese allegiance also made them suspect as potential foreign agents. A series of persecutions, beginning in the 1590s, included many martyrdoms, like that of the Jesuit Sebastião Vieira, tortured to death with some of his converts in 1634 in an episode depicted here. After 1639, the only Christians allowed in Japan were a small group of Dutch Calvinist merchants, whose servants had to trample on a crucifix in an annual ceremony, in order to prove their rejection of Christianity.

For a while, Franciscans and Jesuits in Japan encountered amazing success by targeting lords whose conversions were catalysts for the conversions of their followers. Once the missionaries had a place to say mass and a conspicuous aristocratic patron to make Christianity respectable, they could attract potential converts by displays of devotion, such as the magnificent requiem mass sung for the local ruler's wife, Lady Gracia, at Kokura that attracted thousands of mourners in 1600. By the 1630s, more than 100,000 Japanese had been baptized. Successive central governments in Japan had been suspicious of the new religion, as a source of subversive political ideas, foreign influence, and encouragement to local lords to usurp central authority. Sporadic persecution from the 1590s, however, had failed to halt the progress of Christianity. So from 1639, it was banned outright, and Christians who refused to renounce their faith were forced into exile or put to death.

China could not be converted by means similar to those the Jesuits followed in Japan. It was a relatively centralized state with no intermediate lords to serve as local flashpoints of Christian illumination. The Jesuits made most of their converts at modest social levels but focussed disproportionate efforts on the scholar officials, or mandarins, who enjoyed huge social influence. Some of their converts were impressively committed: using Christian baptismal names, passing Christianity on to their friends and families, and proclaiming their faith in public. Yang Tingyun (yahng teeng-yuhn) recalled a vivid conversion experience in the presence of one of the Jesuits' pictures of Jesus, which inspired him "with feelings of the presence of a great lord." Debates with Jesuits followed. Why could reverence for the Buddha not be accommodated alongside acknowledgment of Jesus? How could the Lord of Heaven be subject to disgrace and suffering by being crucified? How could bread and wine be turned into the body and blood of Jesus? (Answer: "My Lord's love for the world is boundless.") After much agonizing, Yang repudiated his mistress—a more impressive test, perhaps, of Christian commitment than baptism—and went on to build a church, finance the printing of Christian works, and write books explaining Christianity. His fellow Christian, Xu Guangqi (shew gwang-Kee), explained as an act of God his failure to pass the exam to enter the civil service that first brought him into contact with the missionaries and attributed to divine revelation, by way of a dream, his insight into the doctrine of the Trinity.

Despite such promising instances, the Jesuits failed to convert China for three reasons. First, as we shall see, most Chinese were more interested in the Jesuits' scientific learning and technical skills as mapmakers, astronomers, artists, clock makers, and designers than in their religious teaching. Second, the strategy the Jesuits adopted to convert China was a long-term one, and the revolutions of Chinese politics tended to interrupt it. No sooner had the Jesuits converted an empress than the Manchus overthrew the Ming dynasty in 1644 (see Chapter 17). Finally, the church lost confidence in the Jesuits' methods. This was the outcome of a conflict that began with the founder of the mission, Matteo Ricci (1552–1610). He developed a healthy respect for Chinese wisdom. Indeed, the Jesuits became mediators not only of Western culture to China but also of Chinese learning in the West. Ricci decided that the best way to proceed with Chinese converts was to permit them to continue rites of reverence for their ancestors, on the ground that it was similar to Western veneration for saints. As we have seen, this was just the sort of practice that, in the West, the clerical elite was attacking. The missionaries split over the issue, and the effectiveness of the mission suffered when Pope Clement XI ruled against the veneration of ancestors early in the eighteenth century.

In parts of South and Southeast Asia, missionary strategists targeted potential converts at various social levels. In the seventeenth century in the Molucca Islands and Sulawesi (formerly Celebes) in what is today Indonesia, Protestant and Catholic missions alike approached sultans, local notables, and village headmen, with results that usually came to embrace many ordinary people but that never seem to have lasted for long. In Manado in northern Sulawesi, Franciscans launched an intensive mission in 1619. They began by obtaining permission from an assembly of village headmen at the ruler's court. But these notables disclaimed power over their fellow villagers' religious allegiance. The friars preached from village to village, encountering universal hostility. The audience would shriek to drown out the preaching, urge their unwelcome guests to leave, and profess fidelity to their gods. They withheld food and shelter. The friars therefore withdrew in 1622. Their Jesuit successors made some progress by concentrating on the ruler and his family. When Franciscans returned to the villages in the 1640s, they enjoyed a much more positive reception. By the 1680s, under Dutch sponsorship, a Protestant mission in Manado made further headway by employing converted native schoolmasters to work among the children of the elite, wherever a local ruler would permit it. In Sri Lanka, Portuguese missionaries were more successful, but the Dutch who took over the island in 1656 were as keen to undermine Catholics as to convert Buddhists to Protestantism, and the long-term impact of Christianity proved slight.

In the New World, the bottom-up strategy of conversion was more usual. After initial contact, which, of course, often brought missionaries into touch with local leaders, ambitious programs of mass baptism and mass preaching rapidly followed. In the 1520s and 1530s, Franciscans baptized literally millions of Native Americans in Mexico, in an experiment typical of the time. It was an effort to re-create the actions and atmosphere of the early church, when a single example of holiness could bring thousands to baptism and altar as if by a miracle. Clearly, most conversions in these circumstances cannot have been profound, life-changing experiences of the kind specified in traditional definitions of conversion. The doctrinal awareness the friars succeeded in communicating was limited. The first catechism the Franciscans used in Mexico does not even refer to the divinity of Jesus, which is the central doctrine of Christian belief. Dominican friars denounced the superficiality of Franciscan

Chinese Madonna and child. When Jesuit missionaries first brought images of the Madonna and Child to China in the late sixteenth century, they were alarmed to find that the Chinese misidentified the Virgin Mary with Guanyin, goddess of mercy, who, in fertility charms, was often depicted with a child in her arms. But in a new mission field, unencumbered with local versions of Christianity, the Jesuits could not resist promoting the great universal cults of the Church: those of the Savior and his mother. Native Chinese artists began producing images of Mary with her son in her arms in the early seventeenth century, blending Western and Chinese treatment and technique.
The State Hermitage Museum, St. Petersburg. Photograph © The State Hermitage Museum

Chronology: The Revitalization and Spread of Christianity

1478	Spanish Inquisition founded
1500s	Spanish Christians compete with Muslims for dominance in the Philippines
Early sixteenth century	Martin Luther initiates Protestant Reformation in Europe
1520s and 1530s	Franciscans baptize millions of Native Americans
1540	Ignatius Loyola founds Jesuits
1545–1563	Council of Trent meets
Seventeenth century	Jesuits lead Christian missionary effort in China
1621	Reformation in Eastern Orthodox Church begins
1630s	Over 100,000 Japanese baptized
1639	Christianity banned in Japan

First book printed in the New World. "In a plain style for common understanding": the first book printed in the New World was a catechism issued by Juan de Zumárraga in Mexico City in 1543. The tasseled hat signifies that the book was published under the patronage of the archbishop of Mexico. The ornamented borders were fashionable decoration for books at the time in Europe. Zumárraga was a Franciscan friar who was committed to spreading Catholic doctrine to poor and uneducated people who knew little or nothing about the faith. The church in New Spain was not just a missionary effort directed at Native Americans, but also part of a movement active throughout the Christian world, in which the clergy and the godly tried to re-express Christian doctrine in simple terms that a wide audience could understand.

teaching, but the same problems of deficient manpower, daunting terrain, and linguistic and cultural differences hampered their own efforts.

The fear of backsliding and apostasy by new converts haunted the missions. As early as 1539, clergy in Mexico worried about the multiplication of small chapels "just like those the Indians once had for their particular gods." In central Mexico, in the mid-sixteenth century, fears that new cults disguised pagan practices convulsed the church. Doubts arose even concerning the purity of the veneration of Our Lady of Guadalupe herself—the apparition of the Virgin Mary, supposedly to an Indian shepherd boy on the site of a pre-Christian shrine, which had demonstrated the sanctity and grace of Mexican soil in the 1530s. In 1562, one of the worst recorded cases of missionary violence erupted in Yucatán, when the head of the Franciscan mission became convinced that some of his flock were harboring pagan idols. The reports that alerted him came from native informants, motivated, probably, by traditional hatred and rivalry among Indian communities, rather than by any zeal for the facts. In the subsequent persecution, 4,500 Indians were tortured, and 150 died.

In a similar case in central Peru in 1609, a parish priest was condemned for using excessive violence toward backsliders. The papers he collected include the story of a revealing trauma. Don Cristóbal Choque Casa, the son of a local Indian notable and community leader, reported that, some 30 or 40 years after a vigorous Jesuit mission had nominally converted his people, he was on his way to meet his mistress at the abandoned shrine of a tribal god, when the devil in the form of a bat attacked him. He drove out the demon by reciting the Lord's Prayer in Latin, and the following morning he summoned his fellow natives to warn them not to frequent the shrine on pain of being reported to the parish priest. But that same night, he dreamed that he was irresistibly drawn to the accursed spot himself and compelled to make a silver offering to the god. The story evokes a vivid picture of the consequences of "spiritual conquest": old shrines, so neglected that they are fit only for bats and fornicators; abiding powers, so menacing that they can still haunt the dreams, even of a sinner sufficiently indoctrinated to be able to pray in Latin.

For the rest of the colonial period, the eradication of pre-Christian devotions in Peru became the work of professional "extirpators." In most of the rest of the Spanish American world, every new generation of clergy repeated the frustrations and disillusionment of their predecessors. The Indians seemed unable to forget their old rites for appeasing nature. In the early eighteenth century, in Guatemala and Peru, priests were still making the same complaints as their predecessors a century and a half before. Indians were attached to "idols" and to their own healers and seers. They turned the saints into pagan deities. They accused each other of superstition and of working with demons. Only with extreme caution could they be trusted to revere sacred images of Jesus and the saints without idolatry.

Still, ordinary people's accessibility to the ministry of missionaries made the New World an extraordinarily rich and rewarding mission field. Aided by the tendency—exceptionally common in the Americas—of some cultures to welcome and defer to strangers, missionaries could penetrate areas otherwise untouched by any European presence, establish an honored place in their host societies, learn the languages, and guide congregations, by intimate, personal contact, into redefining themselves as Christians.

THE MISSIONARY WORLDS OF BUDDHISM AND ISLAM

Other religions paralleled Europe's mission to the infidel within.

China and Japan

In China, Zhu Hong (jew-hung) (1535–1615) and Han Shan (hahn-shahn) (1546–1623) presented Buddhism afresh as a religion people could practice "at home," eliminating the priestly character that had formerly made it seem inaccessible and unintelligible to lay followers. Lay devotees could perform the same rituals at home as monks did in a monastery. Laymen could worship the Buddha, fast, adopt vegetarianism, and even don the saffron robe that signified a religious vocation. In the eighteenth century, Peng Shaosheng (pahng show-shuhng) took the same line of reform further by explaining techniques of mental prayer, unprompted by images of gods. This emphasis on direct religious experience, unmediated through a priestly class, strikingly resembled what was going on in Europe.

In seventeenth-century Japan, comparable movements, embracing both Buddhism and native religion, began with the reexamination of ancient texts, just as Christian reformers began by going back to the Bible. The monk Keichu (1640–1701) was a pioneer in recovering authentic texts of the *Manyoshu*, poetic native scriptures of the eighth century. These scriptures, along with other old myths known as the *Kojiki*, became the basis of a born-again local religion, stripped of the additions of intervening centuries and of influences from outside Japan. Among Keichu's successors in the following century, Motoori Morinaga (1730–1801) used the *Manyoshu* as Protestants used the Gospels—to reconstruct a model of purity and to denounce the degeneracy of the latter days. Meanwhile, the suppression of Christianity in Japan created an opportunity for Buddhism. Wealthy lords, merchants, and peasants endowed many new Buddhist foundations.

The Mongols

The decisive initiative in reenergizing missionary Buddhism came from within Mongolia in the 1570s. Altan Khan (1530–1583) ruled a swathe of territory along the northern loop of the Yellow River to the border of Tibet. He founded Koke Khota—the "Blue City"—to be a permanent Mongol capital near the present border of Inner and Outer Mongolia. The Chinese called it Guihua—"Return to Civilization." He was a determined pagan, who treated his gout by sacrificing a human victim and paddling inside the victim's split open body. Realizing that Buddhist help would be vital to his schemes to extend his realm by conquest, he founded monasteries, sent for scriptures to Beijing, and had them translated on tablets of polished apple wood. Shrines and monasteries filled the slopes above his capital. Cultivation of Buddhism gave his khanate a distinctive profile among the client-states on China's northwest border.

At Altan Khan's invitation, the ruler of Tibet, known as the **Dalai Lama,** visited Mongolia in 1576 and 1586. Tibet was a priestly Buddhist state, and the Dalai Lama was, by unalterable convention, the head of the Buddhist establishment. He guided reform of Mongol customs. Human sacrifices were forbidden, and blood sacrifices of all sorts stopped. The ongons—the felt images in which spirits resided, except

The Ongons, or Ongghot, small figures of cloth or wood kept in a box or—like these, which once dangled from a tent pole in a pouch—are the most conspicuous feature of Mongolian shamanism. In traditional Mongol belief, the souls of the dead "become ongghot" with the power both to help and harm living people. Using the little images, the shaman, in his ecstasy, can transmit the presence and power of these spirits into himself. In the late sixteenth and seventeenth centuries, Buddhist missionaries tried with varying success to stamp out shamanism and belief in the Ongons.

Chronology: The Spread of Buddhism and Islam

Fifteenth and sixteenth centuries	Merchants and missionaries spread Islam
1570s	Mongol ruler Altan Khan stimulates the revival of missionary Buddhism in Mongolia
Late sixteenth century	Zhu Hong and Han Shan stress direct experience of Buddhism in China
Seventeenth century	"Jihad of the sword" takes on greater importance in spread of Islam
1630s	Missions initiated by Prince Neyici Toyin bring Buddhism to Manchuria
1690s	Torokawa scholars incite revival and jihad in Hausaland in modern Nigeria

when the rites of shamans liberated them (see Chapter 13)—were to be burned and replaced by Buddhist statues. The new religion was at first limited to the aristocracy. But over the next century, Buddhism spread through society and outward across the Mongol dominions. The next Dalai Lama was the son of a Mongol prince. His training for his role in the 1590s took place in Mongolia, amid scholars engaged in the systematic translation of the vast body of Buddhist scriptures into Mongolian. Young noblemen joined the priesthood. Altan Khan had 100 of them ordained as priests to celebrate the Dalai Lama's first visit. Increasingly in the late sixteenth and early seventeenth centuries, the documents Mongol chiefs issued during diplomatic exchanges contain allusions to Buddhism, and when they made alliances with pagan peoples, Buddhist and pagan language and ceremonies marked the occasions.

From the 1630s, a mission that Prince Neyici Toyin (1557–1653) organized took the Buddhism of Tibet beyond Mongolia into Manchuria, building the great Yellow Temple in Shenyang (shehn-yahng) to house an antique statue of the Buddha. Toyin worked by "miracles" of healing that may have owed something to the superiority of Tibetan and Chinese medicine over the unscientific therapies of the shamans. Manchu political power, after they conquered China in 1644, reinforced the mission. The Manchu emperors perceived Buddhist missionaries as pacifiers and potential agents of imperial policy. They appointed Tibetan lamas to instruct the Mongols, presumably in part to reconcile the Mongols to Chinese rule.

Like Catholic missions in the New World, political conquests and violence shadowed and disfigured Buddhist missions in northern Asia. Neyici Toyin burned before his tent a bonfire of ongons ten tent-frames high. The following advice was given to Buddhist missionaries in the extreme west of Mongolia in the mid-seventeenth century: "Whoever has worshipped ongons, burn their ongons and confiscate their cattle and sheep. From those who let the shamans and shamanesses perform fumigations, take their horses, fumigate the shamans in their turn with dog dung." In practice, the old gods reemerged as Buddhist deities, just as in Christian America the Native American gods survived as saints and representations of the Virgin Mary. In both Mongolia and the Americas, the old gods continued to mediate between humans and nature.

Islam

The trend to what might be called low-level strategy—missionary efforts targeting ordinary people—also seems to have affected Islamic missions (see Map 18.2). In Southeast Asia (in what were to become Malaysia and Indonesia) and Africa, which were the two great arenas of Islamic expansion at the time, the means of conversion were fourfold: commerce, deliberate missionary effort, holy war, and dynastic links. As in Southeast Asia, on the Islamic world's African front, the arrival of Christian Europeans hardly affected the retreat of paganism. Except in the coastal toeholds of Christendom, the same combination of merchants, missionaries, and warmongers ensured the dominance of Islam.

Merchants and missionaries spread Islam together. Trade shunted pious Muslims from city to city and installed them as port supervisors, customs officials, and agents to local rulers. Missionaries followed: scholars in search of patronage, discharging along the way the Muslim's obligation to convert unbelievers; spiritual

Jesuit missions to Japan from 1549; persecuted from 1620; banned in 1639

Philippines colonized by Spanish from 1530s

from Europe

from Europe

MAP 18.2

The Spread of Christianity, Islam, and Buddhism in Asia and Africa by 1750

→ major Christian missions after 1500

→ Buddhist missionaries, 1650–1750

— trade route

Regions predominantly Buddhist or with strong Buddhist traditions

under Muslim rule by 750

under Muslim rule by 1500

under Muslim rule by 1750

athletes in search of exercise, anxious to challenge native shamans in contests of conspicuous austerity and supernatural power. In some areas, **Sufis**—mystics, with a feel for popular worship of natural forces, for whom, as one of them said, God was "closer than the veins of my neck"—made crucial contributions. In Southeast Asia, Sufis congregated in Melaka, and after the city fell to the Portuguese in 1511,

The Chronicles of Java. Islam in Southeast Asia has often been mixed with elements from other religions. This illustrated manuscript tells the history of the island of Java in what today is Indonesia and the spread of Islam there by Sufi saints and rulers up to 1647. Written in Javanese, it seeks to give the Muslim rulers of the state of Mataram legitimacy by telling of how one of their ancestors had ties to three different religious traditions: He was blessed by a Muslim saint, practiced Hindu asceticism, and married the goddess of the southern ocean.

they fanned out from there through Java and Sumatra. In the late sixteenth and seventeenth centuries, the sultanate of Aceh in northwest Sumatra in modern Indonesia was a nursery of Sufi missionaries of sometimes dubious Islamic orthodoxy, such as Shams al-Din, who saw himself as a prophet of the end of the world and whose books were burned after his death in 1630. Even peaceful Muslim missionaries tended to see themselves as warriors of a sort, waging a "jihad of words." During the seventeenth century, perhaps under the goad of competition from Christianity, the "jihad of the sword" grew in importance, and the extension of the frontier of the Islamic world depended increasingly on the aggression of sultans, especially from central Java.

In West Africa, merchant clans or classes, like the Saharan Arabs known as Kunta, who made a habit of marrying the daughters of holy men, were the advanced guard of Islam. The black wandering scholars known as the Torokawa incited revivalism and jihad in Hausaland in modern Nigeria from the 1690s. Schools with a wide curriculum played a vital part in diffusing Islam among the Hausa, scattering pupils who in turn attracted students of their own. A sheikh who died in 1655 was able, at school in Katsina, near the present border of Niger and Nigeria, to "taste to the full the Law, the interpretation of the Quran, prophetic tradition, grammar, syntax, philology, logic, study of grammatical particles, and of the name of God, Quranic recitation, and the science of meter and rhyme." Paid by donations according to pupils' wealth, the master of such a school sat on a pile of rugs and sheepskins before his niche of books, equipped with his tray of sand for tracing letters with his finger. He might have his brazier filled with burning charcoal to warm him in winter and his spittoon for the husks of kola nuts that were eaten for their caffeine content. Students' manuscripts survive, smothered in annotations from the teacher's commentary, which was often in a native language instead of Arabic, the language of the Quran. At the end of this course, the student

Making Connections | REVITALIZATION OF WORLD RELIGIONS

RELIGION	REASONS FOR REVITALIZATION	CONSEQUENCES	NEW ADHERENTS
Christianity	To renew dynamism of early church To combat heresies, paganism, witchcraft To engage unevangelized and underevangelized people	New religious orders; new techniques of prayer; new types of devotion; increased coercion and social control by church–state alliances; sharp restrictions on localized beliefs and rituals; emphasis on missionary efforts	Lower-class Europeans, urban and country; colonized peoples in America, Africa, Asia
Buddhism	To popularize Buddhism in China and Japan To adapt to native religious beliefs (China and Japan) As a vehicle for strengthening political control (Mongolia, Manchuria)	Eliminating the need for priestly leadership; simplified rituals; emphasis on direct religious experience via meditation, ritual; creation of new systems of monasteries throughout Asia; Tibetan lamas restructured Mongol spiritual practices	Laymen, peasants, and other social classes throughout Japan, China, Central Asia
Islam	To spread belief to Southeast Asia, Africa To adapt to native religious beliefs To enhance Muslim spirituality	Use of merchants, Sufi missionaries, holy war (jihad), and dynastic alliances to expand Islamic influence; intermarriage as a method of advancing Islam; spread of Islamic schools increases literacy	Ordinary people, especially in Southeast Asia, Africa

acquired a certificate, emblazoned with a long pedigree of named teachers going back to Malik ibn Anas, the eighth-century codifier of Islamic law.

THE RESULTING MIX: GLOBAL RELIGIOUS DIVERSITY—AMERICAN AND INDIAN EXAMPLES

The forms of Catholic Christianity that became characteristic of Spanish America were, in their way, every bit as different from the Catholic mainstream as was the Protestantism of most of the English colonies. In part, this was because of the imperfections of the "Spiritual Conquest" of Spanish America by Catholic missionaries. Missionaries were few. Cultural and linguistic obstacles impeded communication. Pre-Christian religion was probably too deeply rooted to be destroyed. In partial consequence, Native American features ripple Latin American Catholicism to this day.

Secular scholars, and Protestant critics of Catholic missionaries, sometimes call these Native American influences **syncretic** features or pagan survivals because Christianity and paganism seemed to fuse in a new religion that was not quite either but was a blend of both. Yet the proper comparison for colonial religion is not—or not solely—with the religion of the Native American past but with that of Europe of the same era, where clerical bafflement at the stubborn survival of popular religion was just as great. The Christianity of the American countryside was deficient in similar ways to that of the European countryside. Anxiety about how to survive in this world interfered with people's concern about their salvation in the next. Rites to induce rain, suppress pests, elude plague, and fend off famine drove Scripture and sacraments into neglected corners of ordinary lives. As the programs of reform unfolded in Europe, clergy and educated laity acquired ever-higher standards of doctrinal awareness, ever-deeper experiences of Christian self-consciousness. Their expectations of their flocks increased accordingly—which accounts for the continual renewal of their dissatisfaction. The more Christianized the elite became, the more Christian the clergy expected ordinary people to behave. Meanwhile, the Christianity of Indians in Spanish America had as much variety as that of Europeans in Anglo-America.

Black America

The religion of black people in the Americas—though it varied a lot from place to place, molded into conflicting traditions by the influence of Protestantism and Catholicism, respectively—always had one thing in common: it was always black—different, that is, from the religion of white people. Brazil is the best-documented area and has a characteristic profile. Here, in colonial times, black artistic vocations and religious devotion were centered on cult images that charitable associations of black Catholic laypeople often supported financially. These **confraternities,** as they are called, were vital institutions for colonial society generally, melding the culturally uprooted into a coherent community, renewing their sense of identity and belonging. They were even more important for black people, who were compulsory colonists, traumatically transferred as slaves from Africa to an alienating environment on another continent. Confraternities cushioned and comforted them in a white world. The confraternities were unstable organizations, "created and dissolved with extraordinary rapidity," as one of their most distinguished historians has said. Encouraged by the church, and especially by the Jesuits and Franciscans, the black brotherhoods were hotbeds of disorder.

For the guardians of the colonial power structure, the confraternities' choice of patron saints, whose statues they paraded through the streets and elevated in shrines, was often self-assertive, sometimes defiant. St. Elesbaan, for instance, was a warrior-avenger, a black crusading emperor of Ethiopia, who led an expedition to avenge the massacre of Christians by a Jewish ruler in Yemen in 525. He was easily reinterpreted as a symbol of resistance to the many plantation owners of Portuguese-Jewish ancestry. St. Benedict of Palermo, perhaps the favorite patron of black confraternities, was born the son of Nubian slaves in Sicily in 1526. He became a hermit in his youth, to escape taunts about his blackness. Then, as a Franciscan lay brother, he rose to become guardian of his friary and worked miracles after his death in 1583. The cult of St. Iphigenia, a legendary black virgin, who resisted the spells of her suitor's magicians with the help of 200 fellow virgins, embodied the triumph of faith over magic. But it had its subversive aspect,

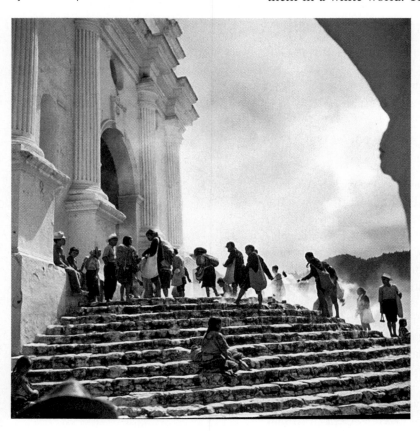

Shamans still burn incense on the steps of the church of Saint Thomas at Chichicastenango in the Guatemala highlands, where worshippers leave offerings of flowers and rum. The steps—a mound similar to pre-Hispanic Maya temples—seem to rival the church interior as a place of devotion. Is this paganism, Christianity, or a mixture of the two? Most local shamans now serve as officials of societies dedicated to Christian saints, and the religion of Chichicastenango may be best understood as one of the many local forms of Christianity that developed in the colonial New World.

too, sanctifying virginity in a slave society where women wished sterility on themselves in order not to produce children who would become slaves. Veneration of the Mother of God was closer in spirit to the fertility religions supposedly traditional among migrants from Africa and more consistent with the interests of slaveowners, who wanted their human livestock to breed. Black Catholicism was an excitant, not an opiate. Rather than playing the role commonly assigned to religion—keeping believers in their place—it inspired hopes of betterment in this world. A commonly depicted scene in black religious art was that of black tormentors torturing white Judas in hell.

Colonial black Catholicism really was different from that of white people. Masters excluded slaves from mass, ostensibly "on account of the [slaves] smell," but really to keep them away from dangerously radical clergy. White confraternities reviled black people "with their guitars and drums, with their *mestizo* prostitutes," and with their revolutionary pretensions, "just as though they were no different from honest white people." Fugitive black slaves who set up their own backwoods communities and independent kingdoms were formally excommunicated. The church hierarchy usually refused their requests for chaplains.

Missionary activity in Brazil began in the early sixteenth century before the Counter-Reformation, when the clergy were still content with superficial levels of Christian teaching. It continued in an era of growing Catholic sensitivity to the native heritage of potential converts, who were not always called on to renounce all their culture to become Christians. The mulatto priest António da Vieira (1608–1697), who became a royal chaplain in 1641, imported "masks and rattles to show the heathen that the Christian religion was not sad." In partial consequence, Brazilian Catholicism is an umbrella term for a bewildering range of styles of devotion. Outside the Spanish and Portuguese colonies—and especially in those of the British and Dutch, where plantations were inaccessible to Catholic religious orders—the lack of missionary activity was even more marked. As a result, African religions persisted, and syncretism happened because the slaves on these plantations often learned Christianity by themselves and blended it with African religious beliefs.

"As a result, African religions persisted, and syncretism happened because the slaves on these plantations often learned Christianity by themselves and blended it with African religious beliefs."

White America

As for the religion of white Americans in colonial times, its great common—albeit not constant—feature was enthusiasm. Refugees from religious persecution in Europe, who took religion seriously, formed or infiltrated many colonies: Catholics and radical Protestants in British North America, Jews or so-called New Christians—descendants of Jews, whose Christianity Judaism deeply influenced—in Spanish and Portuguese colonies. Even hard-headed laymen could prove open to religious enthusiasm in the heady atmosphere of a New World where everything seemed possible and a new church might be constructed from scratch, without the corruption and distortions that had warped Jesus' teaching in the Old World. Columbus and Cortés—neither of whom showed much interest in religion in their early lives—both had visions of a restored apostolic age in the lands they explored and conquered.

The most extreme form of enthusiasm is **millenarianism**. Millenarianism is, in some ways, the characteristic form of religious fervor of the Americas. It can be detected in pre-Christian Native American religions. In central Mexico, most peoples celebrated rites of renewal of the Earth in fire every 52 years and nourished

The Cult Image of St. Elesbaan

Devotion to St. Elesbaan, shown here in an early eighteenth-century statue from the Confraternity of Our Lady of the Rosary, was one of a number of politically charged, socially subversive cults that attracted black worshippers in colonial Brazil.

Black saints were inspiring models for the black confraternities, lay Christian brotherhoods that flourished in Brazil.

Elesbaan is dressed as priest and emperor, ruler of the Christian kingdom of Ethiopia in East Africa.

Elesbaan supposedly led an Ethiopian invasion across the Red Sea to Yemen in southern Arabia in 525 to dethrone a Jewish ruler who was persecuting Christians. The many black slaves in Brazil felt persecuted by their masters, many of whom were of Jewish or allegedly Jewish ancestry.

How does this statue show the uniqueness of black Christianity in colonial Brazil?

myths of the destruction of the world in a divine furnace. But for these and other Native American cultures we know about, time was cyclical. Each destruction was the start of a new cycle. For Native Americans, the end of time—which for Christians would be the climax of history—was unimaginable.

Franciscans introduced Christian millenarianism to the New World in the sixteenth century. Most of the early missionaries came from a few Franciscan communities in southern Spain, where friars nurtured obsessions with the coming end of the world, which would be preceded by a cosmic war between good and evil leading to the Age of the Holy Spirit.

Fantasies of this kind unhinged unorthodox minds at frequent intervals. The Spanish adventurer Lope de Aguirre, during a harrowing navigation of the Amazon in the 1560s, imagined himself as the embodiment of God's wrath. His Franciscan contemporary, Francisco de la Cruz, was the self-proclaimed universal pope and emperor of the last days. The fervor of the spiritual Franciscans mingled with whatever forms of millenarianism were inherited from Native American tradition. In Mexico in 1541, an Indian chief called Don Martín Ocelotl (oss-ehl-OT-el) proclaimed the second coming of Christ, embodied in himself. In 1579, in Paraguay, another Indian chief, Oberá the Resplendent, launched a rebellion against Spanish rule with a similar message. In Peru, so-called *Inkarrí* (een-kah-REE) movements kept legendary memories of the Inca Empire alive into modern times and fused them with expectations of the coming of a "Last World Emperor."

North America merged similar traditions with the original forms of millenarianism that grew up in Protestantism. Because millenarianism was generally considered heretical, or was associated with heresies, it became common in America, driven there by persecution, nourished there by toleration. Anabaptism (the belief that only adults should be baptized), world's-end biblical fundamentalism, and sects invented by prophets who preached that the last days of the world were at hand have all contributed to the formation of the United States. The founders of Massachusetts saw the colony as a refuge for those God intended "to save out of general destruction." The Puritan minister John Cotton predicted the end would come in 1655. Another Puritan minister, Increase Mather, felt he could hear God's "murdering pieces go off" as he watched the comet of 1680. The Shakers, another Protestant sect, called themselves "The United Society of Believers in Christ's Second Coming."

"Because millenarianism was generally considered heretical, or was associated with heresies, it became common in America, driven there by persecution, nourished there by toleration."

India

Religious frontiers, where rival creeds and communions meet, are often places of conflict. But they can also stimulate creative thinking, as contrasting religious groups strive to understand and live with each other. Sixteenth-century India produced an enduring new religion: **Sikhism,** which blended elements of Hindu and Muslim tradition—or, as Sikhs would say, went beyond both. Neither Hindu nor Muslim paths to God suffice, said Guru Nanak (1469–1539), the Sikh founder, "so whose path should I follow? I shall follow the path of God."

Nanak was a widely traveled pilgrim of enormous learning. The Mughal Emperor Akbar (r. 1556–1605), who was illiterate and traveled mainly on military campaigns, sought to outdo him by founding a religion of his own. Like Nanak he recognized that in a religiously plural world, it made better sense—and better served the peace of his realm—to look at what religions had in common rather than at what divided them. "God should be adored with every form of adoration,"

Religious debate. The Mughal Emperor Akbar (r. 1556–1605) devised his own religion in an attempt to defuse conflicts among his subjects, who were mostly Muslims and Hindus. He also presided over debates—like the one shown here from his album of paintings of the life of his court—in which Muslims, Hindus, Buddhists, Sikhs, and Christians (represented by black-robed Jesuits, whom Akbar greatly admired) were supposed to reconcile their differences. But the debates ended in bitterness and mutual antagonism.

he said, according to a Jesuit who lived at his court. And indeed, he exhibited broad-mindedness unparalleled in Christendom in his day. Awestruck by the realism of a European painting of the Virgin Mary in the chapel he gave to the Jesuits in his palace, Akbar and his courtiers "could not contain their joy at seeing the infant Jesus in his mother's arms and it seemed as if they would like to play with him and talk to him." The emperor acquired European prints for his own painters to copy. Catholic religious imagery became part of the decor of his court.

Akbar promoted debates between teachers of rival religions in an attempt to establish a synthesis, which he called the "Faith of God"—the Din-i-ilahi. In what sounds like a standard story of saintly conversion, enlightenment came to him while he was hunting, in the late 1570s. Unsurprisingly, the new religion seemed like an attempt to make the Mughal state itself sacred. Akbar came to see himself as a manifestation, even an embodiment of God. Most Muslims were repelled and resolved never to try to accommodate other religions again. Later Mughal emperors felt torn between strategies of tolerance and of hostility toward non-Muslim faiths. The need to appease Hindus caused a mid-seventeenth century revival of Akbar's efforts by Dara Shukoh, a pretender to the Mughal throne, who proposed "the mingling of the two oceans" of Muslim and Hindu teaching. But his fanatically Muslim brother, Aurangzeb (r. 1658–1707), beat him to the throne and promoted Islam aggressively. He executed the Sikh leader, Guru Hari Rai, for blasphemy and discriminated against Hindus in distributing offices and rewards. The result was a backlash. When a Sikh prince seized the city of Jodhpur, for example, in 1707, he banned Islam and burned the mosques.

THE RENAISSANCE "DISCOVERY OF THE WORLD"

In the long run—according to traditional readings of world history—religious diversity, which arose from the splitting and mingling of religions in the sixteenth century, made the world more secular. People became less committed to their religions because they had to live at peace with neighbors of different faiths. The mutual challenges of rival religions weakened all of them by comparison with other godless or materialistic ways of looking at the world.

But these changes, if they happened at all, took a long time to take effect. In Europe, for instance, in the sixteenth and seventeenth centuries, most of the ideas contemporaries denounced as atheism turn out, on close examination, to have been challenges to traditional Christian descriptions of God. Secular subjects did become more common in art, and religious subjects less so. But this may have had less to do with changing ideologies than with the economics of art. As wealth spread, so did art patronage. The church's dominance of the art market weakened. Religions did become more mutually tolerant, in some places where they mingled, and forfeited their claims to exclusive truth. In other cases, however, the opposite occurred and, overall, on a global scale, religious warfare and persecution probably became more bitter and more widespread.

In the first half of the sixteenth century, fashions in learning, art, and letters informed by the inspiration of classical Greece and Rome, leaped from Italy, where they had originated, across Europe, in a movement traditionally called the Renaissance (see Chapter 15). During his invasion of Italy in 1515, King Francis I of France saw "all the best [art] works"; he began to collect casts of ancient sculptures and acquire the services of Italian artists, including Leonardo da Vinci (1459–1519). The sixteenth-century courts of Henry VIII of England, the Habsburg Archduchess Mary of Hungary (who ruled the Low Countries for her nephew, the Emperor Charles V), Sigmund I and II in Poland and Lithuania, and Ferdinand I and Maximilian II in Austria and Bohemia became similar centers for spreading the Renaissance. In the 1520s, returning poets took Italian verse forms to Spain, Portugal, and England. In Spain, the great new buildings of the period—the cathedral and royal palace of Granada, the town hall of Seville, the hospital in Toledo—introduced a new look, based on classically inspired shape, harmony, proportions, space, and light. Beyond royal courts, the trade in engravings, the migrations of artists and scholars, and the taste of civic patrons, took the same classicizing tradition to the great cities of Germany and Switzerland.

Poets who scoured the era of the Roman Emperor Augustus (r. 27 B.C.E.–14 C.E.) for models and churchmen who looked back to the time of Christ shared the same perspective. Virgil (70–19 B.C.E.), Augustus's favorite poet, was generally, if mistakenly, credited with having prophesied the birth of Jesus. Fusions of Christianity with classical philosophy became popular as never before since the fourth century, when Christianity conquered the thinking classes of the Roman Empire. Christian Platonism and Christian stoicism (see Chapter 6) were characteristic fashions of the era, and the most influential thinker of the first half of the sixteenth century, Erasmus of Rotterdam (1466–1536), made "the philosophy of Christ" a current term. Benvenuto Cellini the Florentine (1500–1571) sculpted a *Crucifixion* that expresses serene stoicism, rather than the searing passion earlier sculptors had represented. In a series of sculptures by Michelangelo (1475–1564), "captives" in human shape emerge from the coarse particularity of rocks. Michelangelo seems to have been trying to embody the notion that matter hides reality—which is spiritual—from our senses and that we need genius or grace to see it.

Meanwhile, the discoveries of explorers transformed the way Europeans pictured the world. They confirmed the vastness of the globe and disclosed the existence of a New World in the Western Hemisphere. In particular, the discoveries challenged European notions of what it means to be human, as encounters unfolded with a previously unsuspected range of cultures and civilizations.

The most exciting moment of all occurred when Christopher Columbus first glimpsed what he called "naked people," on Friday, October 12, 1492, on an island he called San Salvador, which most scholars identify with Watling Island in the Bahamas. The natives were therefore probably Lucayos—a people of whom little is known, though archaeological evidence endorses Columbus's account of their material culture. His description deploys many of the categories, comparisons, and images available in his day to help Westerners understand other cultures. Many of his observations cut two ways. The natives' ignorance of warfare established their innocent credentials but also meant they would be easy to conquer. Their nakedness evoked a primitive Eden or an ideal of dependence on God, but also suggested savagery and similarity to beasts. Their lack of commercial skills showed that they were both morally uncorrupted and easily fooled. Their rational faculties made them identifiable as human and exploitable as slaves. Columbus seemed genuinely torn between conflicting ideas about the Native Americans. After all, he and his men were undergoing an experience no European had ever had before.

Michelangelo's "captives" are often described as unfinished. But they illustrate an idea of the ancient Greek philosopher Plato: Like captives from their bonds, or reality from the shadows, true forms emerge struggling from the rocks that enclose them.

Columbus's Encounter with Indians. One of the engravings that illustrated an early edition of the first printed report of Columbus's first transatlantic voyage illustrates a scene that never happened but that Columbus himself imagined and described. Asian traders do business with the naked, timid people Columbus met on Hispaniola. The image was designed to bolster his claim that he had reached a point close to and in touch with the riches of Asia.

Throughout his journeys to the New World, Columbus remained undecided between rival perceptions of the people—as potential Christians, as types of pagan virtue, as exploitable slaves, as savage, as civilized, as figures of fun. A long quest began to understand the diversity of humankind. Discoveries in the natural world complicated it. In the seventeenth century, as Europeans increasingly got to know the great apes of Africa and other primates, the problem of where to draw the limits of humankind grew increasingly puzzling. Discoveries about the human body kept pace with those of human cultures. Traditional ideas of human nature reeled under the impact of discoveries on every side.

Eyes adjusted slowly to the newly revealed realities. Influenced by missionaries eager to save souls among newly encountered peoples, the church took a positive view of their natural qualities to protect them from secular exploitation and extermination. The question of whether the native peoples of the New World were fully human, endowed with rational souls, was settled—at least for Catholics—affirmatively by Pope Paul III in the 1530s, but their status needed frequent shoring up against slippage. Missionary scholars in the Americas built up files to demonstrate the social and political sophistication of native societies. A case like that of the Aztecs posed typical problems. Cannibalism and human sacrifice tarnished the record of a people who otherwise appeared highly "civil." In evidence—vividly painted by native artists at the court of the Spanish Viceroy of Mexico—compiled under missionary guidance in the 1540s, one can still see the range of qualities the clergy held up for admiration. The training of an Aztec candidate for the priesthood of the pre-Christian gods is shown in gory detail, as his teachers beat his body to bleeding. But this was evidence not of barbarism but of the similarity of Aztec values to those of their Franciscan evangelists, who also practiced devotional whipping and tortured their own flesh. The Aztec state was depicted as a well-regulated pyramid, symmetrically disposed to administer justice, with an emperor at the top, counselors below him, and common pleaders at the lowest level: a mirror image of the society the missionaries had left in Spain. The Aztecs' sense of justice was shown to conform to the standards Europeans deemed natural. An adulterous couple, stoned to death, suggested a comparison with the ancient Jews and, therefore, openness to the milder Christian message. Justice was tempered with mercy. Though drunkenness among the Aztecs was punishable by death, the aged were depicted as enjoying exemption. Mild restraint took the place of execution. When the Aztecs went to war, provocations on their enemies' part were shown to precede hostilities, which followed only after diplomatic efforts had been rebuffed. The natives, it seemed, practiced "just" war by traditional Christian standards—something that the Spanish monarchy strove to do with imperfect success. Missionaries could cite examples like these for every native community where they worked.

In the mid-sixteenth century, a Spanish bishop, Bartolomé de Las Casas (1474–1566), was the loudest spokesman for broadening the definition of humankind to include Native Americans. He was a convert to conscience—an exploiter of Indian labor on Hispaniola, who reformed when he heard a Dominican preacher's challenge: "are the Indians not human beings, endowed with rational souls, like yourselves?" He joined the Dominicans and became the official Protector of the Indians. In effect, despite unsuccessful spells as a missionary and a frontier bishop, he was a professional lobbyist who managed, albeit briefly, to get the Spanish crown to legislate for Indian rights. Human sacrifice, according to Las Casas, should be seen rather as evidence of the misplaced piety of its practitioners, or of their pitiable state as victims of the devil, than as an infringement of natural law. His conclusion—"All the peoples of mankind are human"—sounds self-evident, but it was a message important enough to bear repetition. It was applied patchily at first. Black people hardly felt the benefits for centuries. It made possible a new view of history, according to which all peoples were created equal, but passed through various universal stages of historic development. Broadly speaking, this model prevailed in educated European minds in the seventeenth and eighteenth centuries.

THE RISE OF WESTERN SCIENCE

Partly because of privileged access to the recycled learning of classical antiquity and partly owing to the new data accumulated during the exploration of the world, Western science registered leaps in the seventeenth century that science in other parts of the world could not match.

Renaissance view of Africans. The world map of Italian navigator Sebastian Cabot of the 1540s includes positive images of black Africans. The manicongo—the ruler of Kongo—appears with crown, scepter, and elegant European clothes. Pygmies, though small and poorly clad, carry sticks to prove their rational ability to use tools and "understand each other"—as the inscription on the map puts it—in civilized conversation.

If secularism did not displace religion to any great extent in the West, science did, in some degree, probably displace magic. Just by offering this opinion, we raise a problem: What is the difference between magic and science? Both are attempts to explain and therefore to control nature. The Western science of the sixteenth and seventeenth centuries grew, in part, out of magic. Starting with Marsiglio Ficino (1433–1499), an Italian priest and physician who worked for the Medici, Renaissance writers argued that magic was good if it was used to heal or to accumulate knowledge of nature, and that some ancient magical texts were lawful reading for Christians.

The most influential text was the work supposedly written by an ancient Egyptian known as "Hermes Trismegistos" (Hermes Thrice-Blessed), but which was actually composed by an unidentified Byzantine forger. It arrived in Florence in 1460 among a consignment of books bought from the Balkans after the fall of Constantinople to the Turks in 1453 for the Medici library, and it caused a sensation. Renaissance scholars felt inspired to pursue "Egyptian" wisdom in search of an alternative to the austere rationalism of classical learning—a fount of older and supposedly purer knowledge than could be had from the Greeks or Romans. The distinction between magic and science as means of attempting to control nature almost vanished in the sixteenth century.

Doctor Faustus, who sold his soul to the devil in exchange for magical access to knowledge, was a fictional character, but he symbolized a real yearning. In his world, wisdom was supernatural knowledge. The Habsburg Emperor Rudolf II (r. 1576–1612), who patronized mysterious arts in his castle in Prague in what is now the Czech Republic, was hailed as the new Hermes. Here magicians gathered to probe the secrets of nature and to practice astrology, alchemy, cabbalism (the ancient mystical and magical wisdom of the Jews), and *pansophy*—the attempt to classify all knowledge and so unlock access to mastery of the universe.

None of this magic worked, but the effort to manipulate it was not wasted. Alchemy fed into chemistry, astrology into astronomy, cabbalism into mathematics, and pansophy into the classification of nature. Would-be wizards constructed what they called "theaters of the world" in which all knowledge could be divided into compartments and displayed and "wonder chambers" where specimens of everything in nature could be gathered. The eventual outcome of this work included the methods for classifying plants, animals, and languages that we still use today. Wonder chambers developed into museums. Many of the great figures of the scientific revolution in the Western world of the sixteenth and seventeenth centuries either started with magic or maintained an interest in it. Johannes Kepler (1571–1630), who worked out the path of the planets around the sun, was one of Emperor Rudolf's favorites. Sir Isaac Newton (1642–1727) was a part-time alchemist. The philosopher and mathematician Gottfried Wilhelm Leibniz (1646–1716) studied ancient Egyptian hieroglyphs (though he could not read them) and cabbalistic notation.

If Western science of the time owed a lot to magic, it gradually developed a direction of its own: toward empirical methods, rational explanations, and verifiable facts. One of the most conspicuous examples is the abandonment of the image of the universe centered on the Earth that appeared in the Bible and was generally accepted in the ancient world. In 1543, the Polish astronomer and churchman Nicolaus Copernicus (1473–1543) proposed reclassifying the Earth as one of several planets revolving around the sun. His theory was formulated tentatively, advocated discreetly, and spread slowly. He received the first printing of his great book on the heavens when he was on his deathbed. It took nearly a century after his death to remold people's vision of the universe. In combination with Kepler's work on the mapping of orbits around the sun published early in the seventeenth century, the Copernican revolution expanded the limits of the observable heavens, substituted a dynamic for a static system, and wrenched the universe into a new shape around the paths of the planets, accurately represented. This shift of focus

Wonder chamber. In Europe in the late sixteenth and seventeenth centuries, art collection expanded to include the "curiosities" of nature and science. This seventeenth-century painting records the splendors of a Dutch gentleman's collection. Portraits of the owner and his wife preside over an array of objects that is modestly representative of the world: scenes from nature, the Bible, classical myth, and antique ruins—all the traditional sources of wisdom—are on the walls. A personification of the Tiber River—representing ancient Rome—is over the door. Wonders of nature—coral and shells—mingle with classical statues. On the tables, learned visitors contemplate the sphere of Earth and the heavens, and the new wonders revealed by exploration. In the center, the artist warns against religiously inspired vandals who destroyed art and learning.

Adriaen Stalbent (1589–1662) "The Sciences and the Arts." Wood, 93 x 114 cm. Inv. 1405. Museo del Prado, Madrid, Spain. Photograph © Erich Lessing, Art Resource, NY

The Copernican Universe. Personifications of Justice and Learning flank a vision of the cosmos, as late seventeenth-century European scientists imagined it. A rim of stars, signified by the signs of the Zodiac, surrounds the six planets that were known at the time. The planets move around the sun in the elliptical orbits discovered by Johannes Kepler (1571–1630). The Earth, with moon attached, is no longer at the center of the universe. But as the most important planet, it is shown in detail, with emphasis on how day, night, and the seasons change as the Earth moves.

from the Earth to the sun was a strain on eyes adjusted to an outlook that made the Earth the center of the universe. Every subsequent revelation of astronomy has reduced the relative dimensions of our dwelling place and ground its apparent significance into tinier fragments.

Scientific reasoning grew more systematic. Two particularly influential styles of thinking are illustrated—and were first fully formulated—in the work, respectively, of the English experimenter, Francis Bacon (1561–1626), and the French philosopher and logician, René Descartes (1596–1650). Bacon took from the Dutch scientist, J. B. van Helmont (1577–1644) the motto, "Logic is useless for making scientific discoveries." Bacon prized observation above tradition and was said to have died a martyr to science when he caught a chill while testing the effects of low temperatures on a chicken. He devised the method by which scientists turn observations into general laws: the so-called **inductive method** by which a general inference is made from a series of uniform observations and is then tested. The result, if it works, is a scientific "law." Scientists can then use this law to predict how natural phenomena will behave under similar circumstances.

Descartes, who affected laziness and detested the restless lives of men such as Bacon (who also pursued an ambitious career in politics), made doubt the key to the only possible certainty. Striving to escape from the suspicion that all appearances are false, Descartes reasoned that the reality of his mind was proved by its own self-doubts. His starting point was the age-old problem of **epistemology**: How do we know that we know? How do we distinguish truth from falsehood? Suppose, he said, "some evil genius has deployed all his energies in deceiving me." Then nothing in the world might be certain except that "without doubt I exist

"This shift of focus from the Earth to the sun was a strain on eyes adjusted to an outlook that made the Earth the center of the universe. Every subsequent revelation of astronomy has reduced the relative dimensions of our dwelling place and ground its apparent significance into tinier fragments."

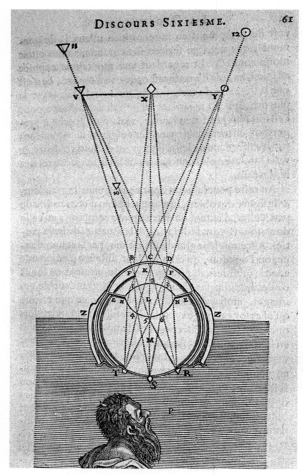

DISCOURS SIXIESME.

A vision of vision. The French philosopher René Descartes (1596–1650) described how we see things in his *Optics,* which was published in 1637. Light travels—in waves, Descartes guessed—between object and eye. The eye itself works like a lens, bending the light to form an impression. Science, like magic, had the power to make humans "masters and possessors of nature."

[even] . . . if he deceives me, and let him deceive me as much as he will, he will never cause me to be nothing so long as I think that I am something." This left a further problem: "What then am I? A thing which thinks. What is a thing which thinks? It is a thing which doubts, understands, conceives, affirms, denies, wills, refuses, which also imagines and feels."

The work of Isaac Newton (1643–1727) typified the achievements of seventeenth-century Western science. In a bout of furious thinking and experimenting, beginning in the 1660s, Newton seemed to discover the underlying "secret of the universe" that had eluded the Renaissance wise men. He imagined the universe as a mechanical contrivance—like the wind-up models of the heavens in brass and gleaming wood that became popular toys for gentlemen's libraries. It was tuned by a celestial engineer and turned and stabilized by a universal force—gravity—observable in the swing of a pendulum or the fall of an apple, as well as in the motions of moons and planets.

Newton was a traditional figure: an old-fashioned humanist and an encyclopedist, obsessed by trying to determine the chronology of the Bible. He was even, in his wilder fantasies, a dabbler in magic, hunting down the secret of a systematic universe, an alchemist seeking the Philosophers' Stone, which legend said could turn base metals into gold. He was also a representative figure of a trend in the thought of his time: **empiricism,** the doctrine beloved in England and Scotland in his day, that reality is observable and verifiable through our senses. The universe consisted of events "cemented" by causation, of which Newton found a scientific description and exposed the laws. "Nature's Laws," according to the epitaph the eighteenth-century poet Alexander Pope wrote for Newton, "lay hid in Night" until "God said, 'Let Newton be!' and there was Light."

If so, it turned out to be an act of divine self-withdrawal. Newton thought gravity was God's way of holding the universe together. Many of his followers disagreed. Belief in a supreme being (though not necessarily in God as Christianity describes him) thrived in eighteenth-century Europe, partly because the mechanical universe could dispense with the divine "Watchmaker" after he had given it its initial winding. By the end of the eighteenth century, the French astronomer and mathematician Pierre-Simon de Laplace (1749–1827), who interpreted almost every known physical phenomenon in terms of the attraction and repulsion of atomic particles, could boast that he had reduced God to "an unnecessary hypothesis."

WESTERN SCIENCE IN THE EAST

It would be wrong, however, to speak of the rise of science at the expense of religion. There is no necessary conflict between the two, and no one in the sixteenth or seventeenth centuries, as far as we know, even suspected that there could be. Science did prove, however, in one respect, to be more powerful than any single religion. It showed more cultural flexibility, appealing more widely across the world. The spread of Christianity, Buddhism, and Islam was among the great movements of the age—but they all ran up against cultural limits. Buddhism grew mainly in Central Asia. Islam registered little appeal in Europe outside of the Turkish-controlled Balkans. Christianity was rejected in most of China and India and all but wiped out in Japan. The new Western science, however, had the power to penetrate everywhere. The cultural exchange that took Christianity to Asia also took Western science across Eurasia. Indeed, the same Jesuit scholars were the agents of both transfers.

In some respects, the intellectual climate in Eastern Asia was unwelcoming to Western ideas. In the seventeenth century, a Confucian revival in China, Japan, and Korea impeded Western thought because it spread ancient Confucian prejudice against Western "barbarians." The Dutch, on whom, from 1639, Japan depended exclusively for information about the West, were generally regarded—said one of their few Japanese admirers—as "scarcely men, a sort of beast." According to the Korean Confucian scholar Yi T'oegye (1501–1570), "It is no exaggeration to liken [Westerners] to birds and beasts." In some ways, Japanese scholars welcomed the Western view of the world as undermining Chinese claims to cultural superiority and to China being the center of the world, but they hesitated to adopt Western ideas as uniquely true. When the Zen monk Ishin Suden (1569–1633) explained the nature of Japan as a "divine land," he used all the traditional language. In Confucian terms, Japan was "born of Earth and Heaven"; by Daoist thought, it was "grounded in the opposing principles of Yin and Yang"; and it was a "Buddhaland" for good measure.

In China, the change of dynasty in 1644 from the Ming to the Qing stimulated the Confucian revival. Because he did not want to serve rulers whom he considered to be usurpers, Wang Fuzhi (wahng foo-jih) (1619–1692) withdrew to the hills of Hunan in the distant south. There he celebrated the values of eleventh-century Confucians and dreamed of "the order of heaven" restored on Earth. Gu Yanwu (goo yehn-woo) (1613–1682), similarly alienated from the new dynasty, returned to Confucian guidelines for life: "study all learning" and "have a sense of shame." Like any determined Renaissance scholar in Europe, he dedicated himself to "the search for antiquities." "Anything legible I copied by hand, and when I saw an inscription unseen by my predecessors I was so overjoyed that I could not sleep." He and his fellow scholars consciously guarded the spoils of time against erosion, damage, and oblivion.

This Chinese renaissance was comparable in kind with that of Europe, but did not achieve the same effects. For the first time in recorded history, China slipped behind Europe, in some fields, in the rate of scientific achievement. On the whole, the global history of technology up to this time reflected consistent Chinese superiority. World-shaping innovations typically happened first in China. Take a few key examples. Printing and paper, the bases of modern communications until the late twentieth century, were Chinese inventions. So was paper money—without which modern capitalism would be unthinkable. So was gunpowder, the key to modern warfare. So were the rudder and the method of shipbuilding that protected the vessel against sinking by dividing the hull into separate compartments—these were vital innovations in the development of global shipping. The blast furnace, essential for modern industrialization, also came from China. In what we think of as the late Middle Ages, however, Western technology edged ahead in two areas: clockwork and lens-making (see Chapter 13). These came together in the science of astronomy.

The impact of Western astronomy in China is immediately visible in one of the world's most extraordinary books, the *Tianwen Lue* (tee-ehn-wen lehw) *(A Treatise on Astronomy)* that Manuel Dias, a young Jesuit missionary, wrote in Latin and, with native help, in Chinese in 1610—the year after the great Italian astronomer Galileo Galilei (1564–1642) first used a telescope to study the heavens. "Lately," Dias told Chinese readers, "a famous Western sage has constructed a marvelous instrument." Through the telescope, he said, "the moon appears a thousand times

"This Chinese renaissance was comparable in kind with that of Europe, but did not achieve the same effects. For the first time in recorded history, China slipped behind Europe, in some fields, in the rate of scientific achievement."

The Observatory at Beijing. In 1674, the Chinese government handed over the observatory at Beijing to the Jesuits for reorganization. Among the results was a new observatory, shown in this eighteenth-century engraving, that the Jesuits set up on the roof of the imperial palace using instruments built to European specifications. Some of these instruments have survived and have only recently been removed to a museum.

larger"; Saturn's rings become visible; "Jupiter appears always surrounded by moons. . . . The day this instrument arrives in China we shall give more details of its admirable use."

For a simple reason, Jesuit mastery of astronomy was the most important of the many technical skills with which they impressed the Chinese. The Chinese Board of Astronomy, an official department of the Chinese imperial court, existed not for the disinterested study of the heavens but to devise a ritual calendar. The ceremonies of the imperial court, like those of King Narai of Thailand, were attuned to the rhythms of the stars, so that earthly order should reflect heavenly harmony. To perform the rites for movable feasts and unique occasions, the stars had to be favorable. The Chinese believed that the success of imperial enterprises, the survival of the dynasty, and the life of the empire depended on it. The environment of a star-struck court stimulated scientific knowledge. Though the Board of Astronomy was young—created in the early seventeenth century—the Chinese tradition in astronomy was ancient, and it had been practiced at court for centuries. The imperial observatory had a continuous history of some 400 years behind it, and the number and quality of recorded observations available to Chinese astronomers had been unequaled anywhere in the West until well into the sixteenth century.

Yet when the Jesuits arrived, their superiority over the Muslim personnel who then ran the observatory seemed so marked that the imperial court abandoned the entire native Chinese tradition and turned the practice of astronomy over to the newcomers. After a couple of false starts, the Jesuit Ferdinand Verbiest took over the Board of Astronomy in 1669 and systematically reformed the calendar. In 1674, at the emperor's request, the observatory was re-equipped with instruments of Jesuit design. The rooftop observatory, with the instruments erected like shrines on little platforms, provided European engravers with one of their most popular Chinese pictures. The astronomy lesson of King Narai had parallels in many parts of Asia.

Influences from the East reflected back at the West. Gottfried Wilhelm Leibniz, was one of the greatest admirers of China in his day, devouring everything he could learn about the country from Jesuit writings. In 1679, he published his own book on Chinese learning. He believed that Chinese wisdom was superior to Europe's in civilized values, ethics, and politics: "I almost think," he wrote, "that Chinese missionaries should be sent to us to teach us the aims and practices of natural theology, as we send missionaries to them to instruct them in revealed religion." But he thought Europe was ahead in mathematics and what we would now call physics. The reversal in the balance of technical skill in Eurasia had begun. In succeeding centuries, similar reversals in historic patterns of power and wealth would elevate the West in other respects.

In Perspective
The Scales of Thought

Despite the shortcomings of the missionaries or of their congregations, the enormous extension of the frontiers of Islam, Buddhism, and Christianity remains one of the most conspicuous features of the world of the sixteenth and seventeenth centuries. Buddhism and Islam expanded into territories that bordered their existing heartlands. By overleaping the Atlantic and Pacific oceans, Christianity registered a spectacular difference. Islam, however, had the advantage of expanding in the demographically vigorous worlds of Africa, Malaysia, and Indonesia, whereas the territories Buddhism won in northern Asia were vast but sparsely populated. As we saw in the last chapter, the millions Christianity won in the Americas quickly withered with the rapid decline of the Native American population.

In the long run, however, the sheer size of the New World counted for most. Because of the exclusion of Islam from the Western Hemisphere, Muslim predominance among world religions slipped in the eighteenth and nineteenth centuries, when the Americas made up and exceeded their lost population. In the balance of resources, Christendom acquired potentially vast extra weight. For reasons no one has ever been able fully to explain, Christianity proved more flexible—more adaptable to more cultures—than Islam or Buddhism did. Islam continued to spread, but only within a relatively narrow band of the world, bounded on the north by the Mediterranean basin and the Eurasian steppelands and in the south by the tropics and the Indian Ocean. The expansion of Buddhism into Central Asia was a conspicuous triumph by earlier Buddhist standards: the religion had not spread far and had even retreated from some of its former heartlands, in the previous 500 years or so. But by the standards of Christian and Muslim expansion in the sixteenth and seventeenth centuries, the Buddhist achievement was modest. It is worth reflecting on how much the conditions governing the spread of these religions seem to have changed today. Christianity still exhibits remarkable adaptability, with dramatic levels of conversions and rates of growth in parts of Asia and sub-Saharan Africa. Islam has begun to overleap its traditional boundaries, thanks mainly to the wide-ranging migrations of Muslims, especially from parts of North Africa and South and Southeast Asia. Buddhism has developed a new appeal, attracting adherents for the first time in cultural environments it never penetrated before, especially in Europe and North America.

Equally remarkable, in the period this chapter has covered, and equally significant for the history of the world over the following few centuries, was the spurt of Western science and the recognition it achieved, in some respects, in China. Although China, the Islamic world, and, to some extent, India, had rich scientific

"Despite the shortcomings of the missionaries or of their congregations, the enormous extension of the frontiers of Islam, Buddhism, and Christianity remains one of the most conspicuous features of the world of the sixteenth and seventeenth centuries."

Chronology

Fifteenth century	Study of classical Greece and Rome provides foundation for the rise of Italian humanism
Fifteenth and sixteenth centuries	Merchants and missionaries spread Islam
Early sixteenth century	Martin Luther initiates Protestant Reformation in Europe
1500s	Spanish Christians compete with Muslims in the Philippines
Sixteenth and seventeenth centuries	Royal courts in northern Europe spread humanism; Contact with Native Americans challenges European notions of what it means to be human; elites take on task of "re-Christianizing" Europe
1520s and 1530s	Franciscans baptize millions of Native Americans
1540	Ignatius Loyola founds Jesuit order
1543	Nicholas Copernicus proposes heliocentric theory
Mid-sixteenth century	Catholic Church begins Counter-Reformation
1545–1563	Council of Trent meets
1596–1650	René Descartes, French philosopher and proponent of deductive reasoning
1570s	Mongol ruler Altan Khan stimulates the revival of missionary Buddhism in Mongolia
Late sixteenth century	Mughal emperor Akbar attempts to establish the "Faith of God"
Seventeenth century	Jesuits lead Christian missionary effort in China
1621	Reformation in Eastern Orthodox Church begins
1630s	Missions initiated by Prince Neyici Toyin bring Buddhism to Manchuria
1639	Christianity banned in Japan
1669	Jesuit Ferdinand Verbiest takes over the Chinese Board of Astronomy
1687	Sir Isaac Newton publishes *Principia Mathematica*

traditions of their own, and although the Islamic world, like the West, had privileged access to the scientific legacy of the ancient Greeks and Romans, Westerners now caught up and pushed ahead in some fields. Of these fields, astronomy was of key importance in the seventeenth century because it won acceptance for Westerners in other cultures. The only two major fields of innovation in which Western technicians exceeded those of China in the Middle Ages were glasswork, especially lens-making, and clockwork. In astronomy, these fields came together, giving Western sages an advantage in competition with indigenous rivals in China, India, and Southeast Asia. Meanwhile, Westerners absorbed and developed technologies of Chinese origin that would ultimately multiply Westerners' advantage in competition with Asian states and economies, including those of China. Printing and paper-making (the insuperable ingredients of modern communications until the twentieth century) were Chinese inventions. So were paper money and the blast furnace (without which capitalism and industrialization would have been impossible). So were gunpowder and vital direction-finding and shipbuilding techniques, without which the West might never have caught up with China in nautical or military endeavors. In the eighteenth century, as we shall see, Western superiority in some military, naval, and industrial technologies would begin to have an impact. The resulting shift in the world balance of power and resources is the subject we have to tackle next.

PROBLEMS AND PARALLELS

1. Why were the sixteenth and seventeenth centuries an unprecedented era in the revitalization of Buddhism, Christianity, and Islam? How did the missionary strategies of these different faiths compare? What strategies did the Jesuits use to try to convert China and Japan? Why did Altan Khan patronize Buddhist missionaries in Mongolia?

2. Why did pre-Christian religious practices persist among Native Americans? Why has millenarianism been so important in American Christianity? How did Guru Nanak and the Emperor Akbar seek to bridge the rivalry between Hinduism and Islam in India?

3. How did the Renaissance "discovery of the world" influence European thinking and spirituality? How did their encounters with non-Western cultures transform the way Westerners saw the world? Why were Christopher Columbus's attitudes toward Native Americans so conflicted?

4. Why were the sixteenth and seventeenth centuries significant in the development of Western science and secular values and in the transmission of Western science to other parts of the world? How did the relationship of Western science to magic evolve over time?

5. What Western ideas were most welcome in the East and which were not? Why was King Narai of Siam so interested in astronomy?

READ ON ▶ ▶ ▶

The Diary of Kosa Pan (2002) is available, edited by M. Smithies and D. van der Cruysse. J. D. Tracy, *Europe's Reformations* (1999) is a reliable account, but J. Bossy, *Christianity in the West* (1985) and J. Delumeau, *The Catholic Church from Luther to Voltaire* (1977) are radical and searching. My account follows F. Fernández-Armesto and D. Wilson, *Reformations* (1997). On China and Indonesia, respectively, I am indebted to W. J. Peterson, *Why Did They Become Christians?* Y. T'ing-yün, L. Chih-tsao, and H. Kuang-ch'i' in J. W. O'Malley et al., eds., *The Jesuits: Cultures, Sciences and the Arts, 1540–1773,* which is an important collection generally, and A. Meersman, *The Franciscans in the Indonesian Archipelago, 1300–1775* (1967). L. M. Brockey, *Journey to the East* (2007) reveals the extent of the Jesuits' work in China. M. C. Ricklefs, *A History of Modern Indonesia: c. 1300 to the Present,* (1981) is an excellent general history that traces Islamic missionary efforts in Indonesia in the seventeenth century. On Buddhist missions, W. Heissig, *The Religions of Mongolia* (2000) is fundamental, as is M. Hodgson, *The Venture of Islam* (1977) on Islam.

R. Ricard, *The Spiritual Conquest of Mexico* (1966) is an enduring classic. P. U. Bonomi, *Under the Cope of Heaven: Religion, Society, and Politics in Colonial America* (1986) and S. Schwartz, *"A Mixed Multitude": The Struggle for Toleration in Colonial Pennsylvania* (1987) explicate the emergence of religious diversity in North America's Middle Atlantic colonies in the seventeenth century. M. Deren, *Divine Horsemen: The Living Gods of Haiti* (1985) is the best introduction to the Afro-Caribbean religion A. Métraux, *Black Peasants and Their Religion* (1960) is an enduring classic.

J. Rubiés, *Travel and Ethnology in the Renaissance. South India through European Eyes, 1250–1625* (2000) is a brilliant analysis of European perceptions of religious diversity in India during the Renaissance. L. Jardine, *Worldly Goods: A New History of the Renaissance* (1998) reexamines the cultural achievements of the Renaissance in the context of the material and commercial world that produced them. L. Jardine and J. Brotton, *Global Interests: Renaissance Art between East and West* (2000) sets the global context.

S. Shapin, *The Scientific Revolution* (1998) examines how the world of seventeenth-century scientists shaped their understanding of nature. A. Grayling, *Descartes* (2006) is up-to-date, readable, and provocative; L. Jardine and A. Stewart, *Hostage to Fortune: The Troubled Life of Francis Bacon* (1999) is masterly. J. Waley-Cohen, "China and Western Technology in the Late Eighteenth Century." *American Historical Review* (1993) traces the reception of various Western technologies, including gunpowder, in China. M. Jacob, *Scientific Culture and the Making of the Industrial West* (1997) offers a detailed analysis of how the cultural dissemination of Newtonian mechanics affected the emergence of industrial technology, especially in Britain.

CHAPTER 19

States and Societies: Political and Social Change in the Sixteenth and Seventeenth Centuries

▲ **Queen Nzinga.** In 1622, before she came to the throne of Ndongo, Nzinga made a treaty with the Portuguese. This contemporary engraving shows her conducting negotiations, seated on a slave's back to avoid standing in the presence of a white man of lower rank than herself.

NDONGO

At an uncertain date, sometime in the 1640s, Queen Nzinga of Ndongo, in southwestern Africa, announced that she would "become a man." Her husbands, of whom she had several, were labeled as concubines, dressed in women's clothes, and made to sleep among her maids (under pain of instant beheading, should any illicit sex ensue). Her ladies-in-waiting were re-equipped as bodyguards. Henceforth she led her troops into battle. She could still handle weapons skillfully as late as 1662, at the age of 80, when an Italian visitor to her court witnessed a military parade. Like many other female pretenders to thrones that men normally occupied, she had overcome challenges to her right to rule by reclassifying herself as masculine.

The decision to switch gender was not the first challenging transformation in Nzinga's life. She came to power as regent for her nephew, the rightful king according to the normal rules of succession, in 1615, but, fearful of having to surrender power, she killed him and declared herself queen. In 1622, she adopted Christianity, less—it seems—out of conviction than to secure Portuguese help against the enemies who sought to dethrone her. She used the ferocious mercenaries known as Imbalanga—private war bands that grew by kidnapping boys—to fight her battles. When they cheated her, she vowed to "become an Imbalanga" herself and lead her own war band. As this involved bloody rituals of sacrifice, cannibalism, and child killing, she had to renounce Christianity. But she returned to the faith in the 1640s to obtain more reliable help again from the Portuguese.

Hers was a surprising and bizarre career. In one respect, however, it was a representative episode of early modern politics. All Nzinga's self-transformations were strategic moves in her struggle for power in Ndongo—a hard-fought series of wars, in which she repeatedly clawed her way back from defeat and repeatedly returned victorious after being driven from her realm. That struggle was part of a longer, broader, deeper story of political change that many parts of the world echoed: the rise of strong, central monarchies, the subduing of unruly aristocracies, the shift of power from the hands of nobles into those of royal dependants. In the 1560s, when Portuguese explorers, slavers, and missionaries first described Ndongo, it was a loosely defined kingdom, where big landowners wielded the most power and claimed the right to elect the monarch. Over the next few decades, kings asserted their hereditary right to the throne, without the need to consult the nobility. They also used slaves as administrators, wrenching authority away from aristocrats and confiding it to their own creatures. Nzinga was the slaves' candidate for kingship. Her first rivals in the wars she fought to secure the throne were nobles. Her attachment to the hereditary principle was passionate. Twice she lost control of the burial grounds of her ancestors. Twice she defied military priorities to win them back and defend them at heavy cost. Her effort to assert the legitimacy of female rule was successful. Her nominee, her sister, Barbara, succeeded her as queen. Women occupied the throne of Ndongo for 75 of the 100 years that followed Nzinga's death.

FOCUS questions

How did European rulers strengthen their power in the sixteenth and seventeenth centuries?

Why were the Ottomans able to build such a successful and long-lasting empire?

What role did Shiite Islam play in Safavid Persia?

How did Chinese society change under the Qing dynasty?

How did the Tokugawa shoguns govern Japan?

How did the "creole mentality" affect Spanish America?

What roles did African states play in the Atlantic slave trade?

What common features affected the development of states all over the world during this period?

Nzinga's realm was small but fiercely contested. As we look around the world of political and social change in the sixteenth and seventeenth centuries in this chapter, first at Europe, then at parts of Asia and the Americas before returning to Africa, we see similar conflicts unfold, albeit with many differences from region to region and state to state, as monarchs searched and struggled to redistribute power to their own advantage, and new or newly empowered classes contended for a share in the growing might and resources of states. Though many of the problems rulers and elites faced were similar world-wide, the variety of responses cannot be crushed to fit an easy formula: we have to acknowledge the diversity and make the best sense of it we can. Global history is difficult and delightful because, although, as I hope this book shows, there is a single story that encompasses the world, there are also contrasting and sometimes conflicting stories within it, which fit into the framework in different ways.

POLITICAL CHANGE IN EUROPE

Europe already had a state system (see Chapter 11). Events of the sixteenth and seventeenth centuries enshrined that system and made the political reunification of Western Europe—which had been a dream or mirage since the fall of Rome—unthinkable for centuries. There were three principal reasons for this.

First, the ideal of Western political unity faded as the various European states solidified their political independence and exerted more control over their inhabitants. In the Middle Ages, hopes of such unity had focused on the prospect of reviving the unity of the ancient Roman Empire. The term *Roman Empire* survived in the formal name of the group of mainly German states—the Holy Roman Empire of the German Nation—that an elected emperor ruled. When King Charles of Spain was elected to be Emperor Charles V in 1519, the outlook for uniting Europe seemed favorable. Through inheritance from his Habsburg father, Charles was already ruler of the Netherlands (modern Belgium, Holland, and Luxembourg), Austria, and much of Central Europe (see Map 19.1). His propagandists speculated that Charles V or his son would be the "Last World Emperor" foretold by prophecy whose reign would inaugurate the final age of the world before the Second Coming of Christ. Naturally, however, most other states resisted this idea, or tried to claim the role for their own rulers. Charles V's attempt to impose religious uniformity in the form of Roman Catholicism on his empire failed, demonstrating the limits of his real power. After his abdication in 1556, no one ever again convincingly reasserted the prospect of a durable universal state in the tradition of Rome.

Second, the power of individual European states increased rulers' power against rivals to their authority and the states' power over their own citizens. In 1648, almost all European states signed the **Treaty of Westphalia**, which ended a long war that had devastated much of Central Europe in the name of religion. The treaty gave rulers the right to impose their religions on their subjects. Though most European states experienced civil wars in the sixteenth and seventeenth centuries, monarchs usually won them. Cities and churches surrendered most of their

The Dominions of Charles V

Habsburg lands of Charles V

boundaries of the Holy Roman Empire

privileges of self-government. Aristocracies—their personnel transformed as old families died out and rulers elevated new families to noble status—became close collaborators in royal power, rather than rivals to it, as aristocrats had been so often in the past. Offices under the crown became increasingly profitable additions to the income that aristocrats earned from their inherited estates. Countries that had been difficult or impossible to rule before their civil wars became easy to govern when their violent and restless elements had been exhausted or became dependent on royal rewards and appointments. England and Scotland had been particularly hard for their monarchs to tax in the sixteenth and early seventeenth centuries. The so-called Glorious Revolution of 1688–1689, which its aristocratic leaders represented as a blow against royal tyranny, actually turned Britain into Europe's most fiscally efficient state. In place of a dynasty committed to peace, the revolution installed rulers who fought expensive wars. Taxation trebled during the reign of the monarchs the British revolutionaries crowned.

Finally, Spain, the only power capable of imposing unity on Europe, failed. Spain seems, in retrospect, an unlikely superpower. It was a weakly united monarchy, consisting of several distinct states, each with its own languages and laws, linked only by imperfect allegiance to a single dynasty. The biggest of these states—Castile and Aragon—permanently shared the same monarchs only from 1516.

Castile acquired two other realms—Granada in the south and Navarre in the north—in conquests as late as 1492 and 1511, respectively. Spain's internal resources were small compared with those of France, which probably had, at the start of the sixteenth century, a population twice as big, substantially more territory, a more favorable climate, and enormously more productive farmland. About a third of the surface of Spain is mountainous or virtually desert.

Yet Spain was unrivaled for military and naval effectiveness in Europe throughout the sixteenth century and well into the seventeenth, while also maintaining, man for man and woman for woman, Europe's best-educated population—rivaled or excelled only in parts of the Netherlands and Italy—and generating some of the continent's most vibrant art and literature. Knowledge of Spanish became, like English today, a mark of education among Europe's elites.

How was Spain's strength possible? It was the result, in part, of the feebleness of its potential competitors. France spent much of the period racked by civil wars between aristocratic factions and did not fulfill its potential until the late seventeenth century, after the last of the wars was over. England, crippled by a low tax yield and split by religious dissent, failed to exploit the maritime advantages of its strategic position between the Atlantic and the North Sea. Germany was only a geographical expression, a loose collection of semi-independent states, incapable of working together. Poland, though vast in area, had insecure frontiers and a powerful nobility that defied or crippled royal power. Italy was a muddle of small states that no one could unify and only Spain could dominate. As a result, smaller, less naturally favored states had moments as major powers: Sweden for much of the seventeenth century, Holland in the second half of it.

Spain had the advantage of privileged access to the silver mines of Mexico and Peru. But the importance of the silver sent back to Spain was not so much in its total value as in its predictability. While these shipments remained regular, until the second or third decade of the seventeenth century, they gave Spanish kings much better credit ratings than other rulers of the time. The total contribution silver imports made to the cost of sustaining Spanish power was small compared with the yield from taxation in the realm of Castile. Moreover, in contrast to most of the rest of Europe, where rivalry for power among monarchs, church, nobles, and city authorities caused frequent breakdowns and occasional wars, Castile was exceptionally united in loyalty to its monarchs. The close collaboration of crown and aristocracy began in war against Muslim Granada, from 1480 to 1492, solidified in the early 1520s, when crown and aristocracy combined to suppress rebellion in some cities, and lasted until the 1640s, when the aristocratic spirit of service to the crown collapsed—and tax revenues collapsed along with it. While religious conflicts divided other parts of Western Europe, Spain became increasingly united in religion. Almost all minority religious communities—Jews, Muslims, the few Protestants—were subjected to forcible conversion, or persecuted out of existence. Finally, Spain's opportunity resulted in part from a factor ever present in monarchical state systems: dynastic accident. Throughout the period, the ruler of Spain also ruled southern Italy and Sicily. From 1519 to 1556, Castile's king happened also to be ruler of the Holy Roman Empire. From

Potosí in Bolivia—the world's most productive silver mine in the late sixteenth and seventeenth centuries. The "Silver Mountain" really does have an abrupt, conical outline, but all early modern representations exaggerate that shape and emphasize its dominance over the puny dwellings and almost ant-like workers.

1504 until 1648, Spanish monarchs were nominally rulers of the Netherlands—though substantial parts of those countries were permanently in revolt from the 1570s. Between 1580 and 1640, kings of Spain were also undisputed kings of Portugal and of its vast overseas possessions in Africa, Asia, and Brazil.

There was a moment in the 1580s and 1590s when Spain seemed able to bid for the role of arbiter of Europe, or even—in the minds of some Spaniards, who fantasized about conquering Cambodia, China, and Japan—of the world (see Map 19.2). In 1588, Spain sent the first of a series of invasion fleets, the Spanish Armadas, against England, and although all of them were turned back or wrecked by bad weather, they demonstrated England's vulnerability to invasion. In the early 1590s, the uniform success of Spanish armies in mainland Europe made the conquest of France and the suppression of Netherlandish rebels seem likely. And all this happened while the frontiers of the Spanish monarchy continued to advance in the Americas and Asia.

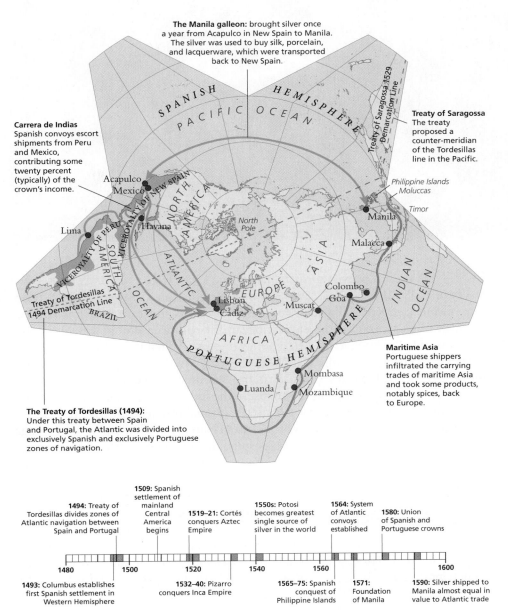

The Manila galleon: brought silver once a year from Acapulco in New Spain to Manila. The silver was used to buy silk, porcelain, and lacquerware, which were transported back to New Spain.

Carrera de Indias
Spanish convoys escort shipments from Peru and Mexico, contributing some twenty percent (typically) of the crown's income.

Treaty of Saragossa
The treaty proposed a counter-meridian of the Tordesillas line in the Pacific.

Maritime Asia
Portuguese shippers infiltrated the carrying trades of maritime Asia and took some products, notably spices, back to Europe.

The Treaty of Tordesillas (1494):
Under this treaty between Spain and Portugal, the Atlantic was divided into exclusively Spanish and exclusively Portuguese zones of navigation.

MAP **19.2**

The Spanish Monarchy in 1600

■ Dominions of the king of Spain

→ Carrera de Indias

→ Portuguese trade with maritime Asia

1494: Treaty of Tordesillas divides zones of Atlantic navigation between Spain and Portugal

1509: Spanish settlement of mainland Central America begins

1519–21: Cortés conquers Aztec Empire

1550s: Potosi becomes greatest single source of silver in the world

1564: System of Atlantic convoys established

1580: Union of Spanish and Portuguese crowns

1493: Columbus establishes first Spanish settlement in Western Hemisphere

1532–40: Pizarro conquers Inca Empire

1565–75: Spanish conquest of Philippine Islands

1571: Foundation of Manila

1590: Silver shipped to Manila almost equal in value to Atlantic trade

The Surrender at Breda. Diego Velázquez (1599–1660), the greatest painter of the Spanish Baroque, leaves us in no doubt who won the struggle in 1624–1625 for the fortress city of Breda in the Netherlands. The Spaniards' lances are proudly erect. Those of the defeated Dutch are in disarray. The pain of war, however, is shared. No one is triumphant. The symmetry of the canvas gives almost equal space to both sides. The Spanish commander, Ambrosio Spinola, shown on the left foreground, seems to be consoling a colleague rather than humbling a defeated enemy.

Still, the success proved unsustainable. The 1590s were a turning point, as the loyalty of Philip II's (r. 1556–1598) subordinate kingdoms showed signs of strain, state revenues ebbed, and a catastrophic decline of population, which would last for most of the seventeenth century, began. By the time Philip II died, he had already decided to leave to his heir a policy of peace. When that peace broke down in a general renewal of conflicts in Western Europe in the 1620s, the strain proved unbearable. Spanish naval supremacy in the Atlantic wavered in the late 1620s and faltered in northern Europe in the 1630s. In the following decade, Spanish armies' long unbroken record of victory collapsed with major defeats by the French.

Meanwhile, serious rebellions broke out in Naples and Catalonia, and Portugal recovered its independence in 1640. Despite an impressive recovery in the eighteenth century from this critical low point, Spain never again attempted to outclass all Europe's other powers.

WESTERN POLITICAL THOUGHT

Along with the growth of the power of the state, the way people thought about politics changed. They came to take the sovereignty of the state for granted. A French political philosopher, Jean Bodin, formulated the doctrine of sovereignty in 1576. Sovereignty defined the state, which had the sole right to make laws and distribute justice to its subjects. Sovereignty could not be shared. There was no portion of it for the church, or any sectional interest, or any outside power.

More radically, in 1513, the Florentine historian and office seeker, Niccolò Machiavelli, challenged traditional thinking about the purpose of the state. Political theorists of antiquity and the Middle Ages recommended various kinds of state, but they all agreed that the state must have a moral purpose: to increase virtue or happiness or both. Even the Legalist school in ancient China (see Chapter 6) advocated oppression in the wider interest of the oppressed. When Machiavelli wrote *The Prince*, his rules for rulers, the book shocked readers not just because the author recommended lying, cheating, ruthlessness, and injustice, but because he did so with no apparent concession to morality.

Machiavelli cut all references to God out of his descriptions of politics and made only mocking references to religion. The only basis for decision making was the ruler's own interest, and his only responsibility was to retain his power. He should keep faith only when it suits him. He should pretend virtue. He should also pretend to be religious. Machiavelli's other books are strongly republican in sentiment, and he may have intended *The Prince* to be ironical. Irony, however, can be the hardest form of rhetoric to detect. Later thinking borrowed two influences from *The Prince*: first, the doctrine of **realpolitik**, which says that the state is not subject to moral laws and serves only itself; second, the claim that the end justifies the means and that any excesses are permissible to ensure the survival of the state, or public safety, or national security, as some later formulations put it. Meanwhile, among moralists, *Machiavel* became a term of abuse, and the devil became known as "old Nick."

In the absence of any overriding authority or mechanism for sharing sovereignty, the European state system needed international laws. When Thomas Aquinas (see Chapter 12) summarized the previous state of thinking in the Western world in the thirteenth century, he distinguished the laws of individual states from what he called the **law of nations**, which all states must obey and which governs the relationships between them. Yet he never said what this law was or where or how it could be codified. Many jurists assumed it was just natural law or the basic, universal principles of justice—but this is also hard to identify in complex cases. The Spanish Jesuit theologian Francisco Suárez (1548–1617) solved the problem in a radical way. The law of nations "differs in an absolute sense," he said, "from natural law" and "is simply a kind of positive human law." It says whatever people agree it should say.

This made it possible to construct an international order along lines first proposed earlier in the sixteenth century by one of Suárez's predecessors at the University of Salamanca in Spain, the Dominican Francisco de Vitoria, who advocated laws "created by the authority of the whole world"—not just pacts or agreements between states. In 1625, the Dutch jurist Hugo Grotius worked out the system that prevailed until the late twentieth century. Natural law obliged states to respect each other's sovereignty. The commercial and maritime laws that they formally ratified or traditionally embraced, and the treaties they made between themselves regulated relations among them with the strength of contracts, enforceable by war. This system did not need the support of any particular ideology or religion to back it. It could embrace the world beyond Christendom. It would remain valid, Grotius said, even if God did not exist.

"When Machiavelli wrote The Prince, his rules for rulers, the book shocked readers not just because the author recommended lying, cheating, ruthlessness, and injustice, but because he did so with no apparent concession to morality."

WESTERN SOCIETY

Modern societies are divided into horizontally stacked classes that are defined according to their income or wealth—upper class, middle class, working class. But in the sixteenth and seventeenth centuries, classes intersected with other structures, in which most people were more likely to situate themselves: vertical structures—interest groups, professions, trades, the entourages and clients of powerful noblemen and officials, social orders, such as the nobility or the peasantry, religious sects, clans—whose members' sense of mutual belonging depended on the differences they felt between themselves and outsiders rather than on shared values, wealth, priorities, or education (see Figure 19.1). The elite estates or social groups, the nobility and clergy, were not classes in any sense that a modern market researcher or opinion pollster would recognize. They were communities of privilege uniting people of hugely different degrees of wealth whose tax privileges and legal advantages marked them out from the rest of society. A prince-bishop ruling a semi-independent state like Cologne in Germany or Liège in Belgium belonged to the same clerical estate as a penniless priest who wandered from parish to parish saying mass for a fee. Nobility embraced a duke with an income exceeding a king's and a rural nobleman whose only possession was a lance for hire.

Cities formed communities of a similar kind, jealous of their jurisdiction, walled against the world, and fortified in their civic identities by the enjoyment of economic "liberties"—such as the right to hold markets or fairs, or levy tolls on travelers or merchandise. In most countries, Jews formed similar communities, also distinguished by economic and legal privileges as well as disabilities. So did the Protestant minorities in France and Poland. The kinsmen and retinues of noble families had some of the same characteristics, often embracing poor and remote relations as well as retainers at every level of wealth and rank, tenants, servants, and other dependants, who gathered for festivals or accounting days and sometimes lived together in considerable numbers under a single vast roof, eating their meals in common. On a smaller scale, the "families," as they were usually called, or extended households of urban artisans, with generations of apprentices sharing their roofs, had the same characteristics.

A vast, slow process of erosion changed this way of organizing society. In most of Europe, the family was redefined as an ever-smaller knot of close kin. Between the sixteenth and eighteenth centuries, in aristocratic households, family dining rooms came to provide a privileged retreat from the communal life of the great hall of the medieval castle. This was true even for kings. Court portraits of Philip IV (r. 1621–1665) of Spain and Charles I (r. 1625–1649) of England reveal a world of nuclear families, in which the royal children and parents cluster together. In Protestantism, the family grew in importance because so many other structures of life—religious brotherhoods, guilds, and monasteries—were abolished. The glittering courts of monarchs sucked provincial aristocracies away from their estates and hereditary followings, breaking the bonds of vertical structures. "Take but degree away," as a character says in a play of William Shake-

FIGURE 19.1 ORGANIZATION OF WESTERN SOCIETY IN THE SIXTEENTH AND SEVENTEENTH CENTURIES COMPARED TO MODERN SOCIETIES

(a) Modern societies

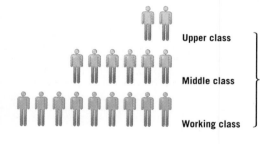

Upper class

Middle class

Working class

Classes of people differentiated by income, wealth, shared values, or education

(b) Societies in sixteenth and seventeenth centuries

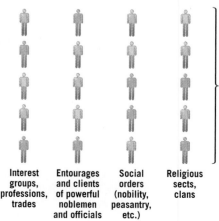

Widely varying groups whose sense of mutual belonging depends on differences between themselves and outsiders

Interest groups, professions, trades

Entourages and clients of powerful noblemen and officials

Social orders (nobility, peasantry, etc.)

Religious sects, clans

speare's, written around 1602, "untune that string and hark! What discord follows!" Everywhere that string was retuned to the clink of moneybags, as monarchs put titles up for sale. "Ducats make dukes," quipped an early seventeenth-century Spanish satirist. Women's status was transformed. In Padua in northern Italy in the 1550s, the anatomist Gabriele Falloppio sliced open women's cadavers and found that they worked in unsuspected ways. Women were not just nature's bungled attempts to make males, as earlier medical theory claimed. In the late Middle Ages, there had been isolated and discouraging examples of women in power as regents or sovereign queens. Now women rulers appeared in unprecedented numbers in Europe. Some—like the flighty Mary, Queen of Scots (r. 1512–1567), or Catherine de' Medici (1519–1589), Regent of France—reenacted in their lives cautionary tales of the biblical Eve: submitting to lovers or favorites, manipulating men. To the Scots Protestant preacher John Knox (ca. 1513–1572)—expressing a common opinion strongly—women in power were a "monstrous" aberration. But most women rulers earned praise for what Elizabeth I of England (r. 1558–1603) called her "heart and stomach of a king." In other words, men praised them for ruling like men even though they were women.

In ordinary homes, struggles between different forms of Christianity gave new importance to women's traditional domain—as the guardians of household routine. Mothers were the hearthside evangelists who transmitted simple religious faith and devotional practice from one generation to the next. Their choices ensured, in some places, the survival of Catholicism, in others the rapid progress of Protestantism. Women who married according to the clergies' new rules (see Chapter 18) could be better protected against male predators and more secure in keeping their property when their husbands died. In late seventeenth-century Massachusetts, the Puritan preacher Cotton Mather believed women were morally superior beings, because of their constant fear of death in childbirth.

There could, however, be no corresponding increase in what feminists today call women's "options." New economic opportunities on a sufficient scale were unavailable until industrialization that began in the late eighteenth century. Widowhood remained the best option for women who wanted freedom and influence. The most remarkable feature of this situation, which might have tempted wives to murder, is that so many husbands survived it. In most of sixteenth- and seventeenth-century Europe, husbands committed more detected domestic murders than wives. And women, despite their improved status, were still often victims: beaten by husbands, scolded by confessors, repressed by social rules, and cheated by the courts. "Long Meg of Westminster"—hero of an English story of 1582—proves her superiority over men in a series of fair fights, but "never let it be said," she announced when she married, "that Long Meg shall be her husband's master."

Conflicts along class lines were rare. The so-called Wars of Religion between Catholics and Protestants in sixteenth-century France resembled old-fashioned civil wars, in which aristocrats recruited private armies from their retainers, relatives, and tenants to battle each other. Other sixteenth-century rebellions were of the same character, or else were the protests of threatened minorities, such as Catholics in England, or descendants of Moors in Spain. Or else they were assertions of provincial identity, like those Aragonese who rioted against Spanish royal power in defense of their provincial liberties in 1590, or Netherlanders who rose up

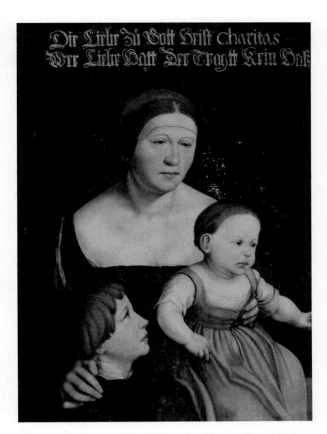

Married Charity. As an allegory of the love of God, "which is called Charity," according to the inscription, Hans Holbein painted his wife, Elsbeth, with their children, Philip and Catarina, during a rare moment at home in the Swiss city of Basle in 1529, after a trip to England, where commissions from the king and the court bought the painter a spell of prosperity. But he spent most of his life grubbing for commissions far afield, and Elsbeth was left to bring up the family on her own for years at a time. She eventually sold this painting to make ends meet.

Chronology: Early Modern Europe: Politics, Ideas, and Society

Sixteenth through eighteenth centuries	Nuclear family grows in importance
1513	Machiavelli writes *The Prince*
1519	Charles V becomes Holy Roman Emperor
Mid- to late sixteenth century	French Wars of Religion
1576	Jean Bodin formulates doctrine of sovereignty
1588	Defeat of the Spanish Armada
1618–1648	Thirty Years' War
1640s	Strain of empire precipitates decline of Spanish power
r. 1682—1725	Peter the Great attempts Westernization of Russia

in 1568 against the foreign methods and officials of an absentee monarch, Philip II of Spain. The English Civil Wars of 1640–1653 used to be held up as a classic case of class revolution—the birth pangs of bourgeois society, struggling to emerge bloody from the womb of feudalism. But the war seems better understood as a mixture of a traditional aristocratic rebellion, a provincial revolt against intrusive central government, a struggle of "ins" and "outs," and a genuine war of religion.

Patterns of social change were not uniform across Europe. From the fifteenth century, an economic divide opened in Central Europe. The fault line ran roughly along the Elbe and upper Danube rivers. In the west, peasants could take advantage of intense demand for labor and a relative glut of exploitable land. Forms of land tenure grew more diverse. Traditional limitations on peasants' freedom to move and acquire property weakened. Similar conditions prevailed selectively in Eastern Europe. In parts of Brandenburg in Germany, for instance, the countryside had so few people in the fifteenth century that noble landlords took to the plow themselves. Generally, however, as Eastern Europe gradually took over the Mediterranean Basin's former role as grain supplier to the continent, landlords increasingly restricted peasants' freedom to sell their labor.

This was a remarkable reversal of the course of history as conventionally understood. In the Middle Ages, such restrictions on peasants had not been a characteristic institution of the regions where it now began to take root. Indeed, at modest social levels, colonization beyond the Elbe had been the work of peasant escapees from a society of restricted opportunities and lordly oppression in the west. Now even the free towns, in what are now Poland, eastern Germany, the Czech Republic, Slovakia, and Hungary, lost their rights of jurisdiction on a massive scale to aristocrats and rulers. In Poland, Hungary, and Bohemia, the nobility reclaimed or enforced their right to elect the king. A world of aristocratic dominance was emerging.

Traditional notions about nobility became entrenched. According to István Werbоćky, Hungary's key theorist on this issue in the early sixteenth century, only the nobles were the nation. Their privileges were rights of conquest, inherited from presumed Hunnic and Scythian ancestors. Other classes descended from natural slaves or criminals. Werbоćky did acknowledge that new men could join the aristocracy "by the exercise of martial discipline and other virtues and gifts of mind or body." But to him these were means to strengthen a hereditary caste—not, as most Westerners maintained, methods to open up a social group to outsiders.

Despite these growing differences between east and west, Peter the Great of Russia (r. 1682–1725) tugged and wrenched the frontier of Europe eastward by striving to make Russia more like Western Europe. It was an information revolution—a transfer of technology as well as fashion and taste from west to east. Peter's reforms redesigned his empire. He moved the capital from Moscow to the new city of St. Petersburg that he built on the Baltic, redrafted the Russian alphabet, and remodeled the aristocracy's facial hair. A popular print showed a demon barber executing Peter's command that the Russian nobility shave off their beards to make them look like "modern" European aristocrats. Preachers called Peter the sculptor and architect of Russia, remolding the country, carving the palace furni-

Making Connections | FACTORS CONTRIBUTING TO EUROPEAN STATE-BUILDING

HISTORICAL DEVELOPMENTS	INFLUENTIAL CONTRIBUTING FACTORS	SOCIAL AND POLITICAL CONSEQUENCES
Renaissance: development of Western political thought	Sovereignty becomes dominant way to identify the state Retaining power becomes dominant political motivation Need for international cooperation leads to commercial, maritime laws	Machiavelli's *The Prince* becomes handbook for gaining and maintaining power Law of nations becomes important factor in states honoring each other's sovereignty The "ends justify the means" to ensure states' survival
Spanish dominance 1500–1600	Access to silver mines of Mexico, Peru Relatively unified monarchy; aristocracy ennobled by service; religious hierarchy Developed superior military and naval forces Dynastic connections	First wealthy colonial superpower controls Portugal, much of Africa, Asia, Central and South America; challenges England, France; controls much of Italy, Netherlands, Germany Economic, military decline in seventeenth century leaves opening for other European states
Social transformation of Europe	Smaller family units become primary social unit Intermarriage between aristocratic, royal families Expansion of the role of women as moral exemplars	Religious conflicts supercede class conflict Increasing economic freedom, opportunity for urban dwellers Traditional notions of nobility become entrenched Western "progress" becomes a model for Peter the Great of Russia and others

ture with his own hands. He allowed women out of the home where traditional Russian practice had tried to confine them. He made two great journeys through Europe in semidisguise to learn Western ways. His role models were foreign: Dutch, German, Swedish. He aimed to be for his country both Romulus and Numa—the founder, that is, of ancient Rome and the king who supposedly crafted its laws. He appeared in engravings in Roman tradition, baton-wielding on a rearing horse, with the title "Imperator" engraved in Roman letters. He seriously considered making Dutch the official language of his court. He became an honorary Danish admiral and a member of the French Academy of Sciences. But rebels regarded him as Antichrist or, at best, the, satanic imposter of a true czar. Western admirers saw him as Russia's modernizer, but the report of a visit to St. Petersburg illustrates the uneasy, short-term impact of his reforms. High society there, said the report, was just like those of Paris or London, except that Russian ladies still put cosmetic blacking on their teeth. Henceforth, Russia was permanently part, by wars or alliances, of European politics. Peter the Great's daughter, Elizabeth (r. 1741–1762) was the last ruler of her dynasty, the Romanovs, in the male line. Thereafter, all the czars were products of the European dynastic marriage market.

Peter's policy, and, in particular, his decision to relocate the capital of Russia on the Baltic, should be considered in a further context: the northward shift of

Demon barber: Czar Peter the Great (r. 1682–1725) enforces conformity to the religion of the state in Russia. The Old Believers, religious dissidents who split from the Russian Orthodox Church in the 1660s, believed that beards were part of the image of God, and that therefore it was a sacrilege to shave. Peter saw beards as signs of Russia's backwardness and of resistance to his rule, and he imposed a tax on facial hair.

Europe's center of gravity. The newly rising powers of the seventeenth century—the Netherlands, Sweden, England, France—were all in the north. So were some of the most spectacularly growing cities—Amsterdam, Paris, London. The Mediterranean seemed stagnant by comparison. It was in the north that the great global trading companies and banks arose. There were undeniable advantages to being in business in northern rather than southern Europe in the sixteenth and seventeenth centuries. Inflation flowed from south to north—stimulated by new sources of gold and silver, by new forms and expanded levels of credit, and by the demand an increase of population created. This meant goods were cheaper in the north. Northerners used that price advantage to break into the Mediterranean in the late sixteenth century. Demand for their shipping helped—to bring in grain to meet food shortages and to counter losses to Turkish and North African piracy. From shipping, northerners diversified into slaving and banking, handling—and creaming off—the wealth of the cash-rich empires of Spain and Portugal, diverting the trade of Venice and the eastern Mediterranean.

THE OTTOMANS

Europe's shifting axis of wealth affected the Ottoman Empire, a partly Mediterranean power. Yet this was a state that straddled Europe and Asia and, as we saw in Chapter 16, combined diverse traditions of political thought. The nerve center of the empire was the sultan's palace in Constantinople, the Topkapi Saray. Its layout embodies much of the way the sultans thought about their role and is a guide to how politics worked. The throne room is a pavilion, and many apartments are scattered through the grounds, like the tents of a nomad camp. The imperial stool is big enough for a sultan of the most morbid obesity. This was an empire that sustained memories of its ancient nomadic origins through centuries of settled life.

The harem could accommodate 2,000 women, the stables 4,000 horses. The scale of everything in the Topkapi Palace attests to the size of the empire and the effectiveness of Ottoman authority. The grounds of 7,500,000 square feet enclosed 10 mosques, 14 bathhouses, and 2 hospitals. The kitchens were equipped to serve 5,000 diners daily and 10,000 on holidays.

The Topkapi was a fortress, a sanctuary, and a shrine. The bustle of the outer courts, where the kitchen noise competed with the clatter of the guards, contrasted with the inner silence of the sacred spaces where the sultan was cocooned, close to his vast collection of relics of the Prophet Muhammad. Here, according to a visitor in 1700, "even the horses seem to know where they are."

Inside the sultan's private quarters, with its lavish alleys and secret hideaways, we can sense the hidden methods of government. Here talk was of politics: pillow talk and conversation in the baths, as well as the diplomatic encounters and the sultan's meetings with his ministers. In the absence of rules of succession to the throne, women and eunuchs conspired to manipulate the transfer of power from one sultan to the next. Sultans commonly exercised their privilege to put their brothers to death as security against rebellion, or confined them in the luxurious prison quarters known as the cages. A knock on the door might be a summons to become sultan or the rap of an executioner: Sultan Ibrahim I (EE-brah-heem) (r. 1640–1648) heard both and mistook each for the other. Access to a sultan's mother or favorite concubine was an avenue of politi-

The sultan's birthday party. Members of the imperial family, officials, and dignitaries line up, one by one, in strict order of protocol, to congratulate Ottoman Sultan Selim III (r. 1789–1807) in the Topkapi Palace in Istanbul. Konstantin Kapidagli, the painter, was highly favored at the sultan's court and imitated by painters in the West.
Dagli Orti/Picture Desk, Inc./Kobal Collection

cal influence. For much of the seventeenth century, the effective chief executives of the state were queen mothers who knew little of the world beyond the harem walls, but who learned much from spies and servants, and who can be seen in paintings of court life, listening, from behind elaborate screens, to audiences with ambassadors and political council meetings. "Although Western visitors all went away heady with the exotic scents of palace life, the efficiency of the Ottoman state from the fifteenth to the seventeenth centuries could rival any Western competitors, many of whose traditions it shared." Other empires of nomadic origins failed to keep up with advances in the technology of war, but the Ottomans could float a vast navy, batter the walls of Byzantium with cannons in 1453, or blow away the Safavid cavalry of Persia with gunpowder. The modernization of the army influenced social change. The traditional aristocracy, the mounted "protectors"—cavalrymen who served in war and were maintained by tribute—lost roles and revenues.

The direction and balance of the conquests, which, in the fifteenth and sixteenth centuries, tilted toward Europe, gave the sultans access to huge numbers of Christian subjects, who paid discriminatory taxes and supplied a quota, the **devsirme** (dehv-SHEER-meh), of their male children to serve as Muslims in the elite slave army, the **Janissaries**, or in the sultan's administration. In the seventeenth century (see Chapter 15), the Janissaries became a hereditary corps, probably at the cost of their military efficiency, and conquests on the Christian front ceased.

To Western observers, the sultan seemed a model of despotism. He made and unmade laws, both religious and secular, at will. His subjects had no rights against his anger. And unlike Christian rulers, sultans had no need of a Reformation to curb the power of clergy. Though they had to be wary of the moral vigilance of the Islamic clerical establishment, as caliphs as well as sultans, they controlled the power structure of Sunni Islam themselves. Westerners regarded Ottoman government as disturbingly alien, but in the 1570s, the Ottoman jurist Ebu us-Suud

"Although Western visitors all went away heady with the exotic scents of palace life, the efficiency of the Ottoman state from the fifteenth to the seventeenth centuries could rival any Western competitors, many of whose traditions it shared."

Ottoman law book. Written in Arabic in Istanbul in 1517 by Ibrahim al Halabi, the Islamic legal textbook known as *Multaqa al-Abhur (Confluence of the Currents)* remained an authoritative guide to the laws of the Ottoman Empire for 300 years. It contains rules for almost every human activity: spiritual rites, domestic relations, inheritance, commercial transactions, and crimes. The section shown here refers to buying and selling done by third parties. Various commentators made notes on this copy of the text.

produced a justification of the ruler's power that revealed a thorough command of Roman law and was not unlike Jean Bodin's near-contemporary theory of sovereignty in France. Still, the Ottoman system was unquestionably more autocratic than anything European "absolute" monarchs could manage. Even allowing for the inefficiencies that arise when preindustrial technology transmits commands over vast distances, the dominions of Sultan Murad IV (r. 1623–1640) were more tightly reined to the center than those of his counterparts in most of Europe. His Spanish contemporary, Philip IV, for instance, was generally regarded as the most powerful Christian king of his day. He ruled multiple kingdoms with the aid of an up-to-date bureaucracy, but without an overarching source of authority. In different places, his rule was known by different titles, legitimized by different theories, embodied in different institutions, and constrained by different laws. Not so Murad's.

In most of the Ottoman Empire, for instance, the sultan's representatives were chosen in a remarkably uniform way. It is not true, as Europeans used to say, that these men were all in a formal sense the sultan's slaves. The head of the civil service, the Grand Vizir was indeed a slave, but lesser officials and provincial governors were drawn from every class and every part of the empire. Typically, in the sixteenth century, they trained as pages in the sultan's household before taking provincial commands, where they were maintained by revenues from designated areas. They rose through the administrative ranks of the provinces to which they were assigned.

Military and administrative life was incomparably the best route to wealth in the empire. Provincial governors made more out of their offices than even the richest merchants made from trade. The emphasis was not quite on plunder to the same extent as in Mughal India. Suleiman the Magnificent (r. 1520–1566; see Chapter 16) regulated the fees courts charged to litigants and practiced restraint in taxation and exploitation as part of the ideology of the state. Still, rational exploitation of subjects' wealth was the aim of the rulers of the empire. *Dirlik* (DEER-leek)—the term applied to provincial government—literally meant "wealth."

Increasingly, in the seventeenth century, the need to make the state efficient in war, in the face of the mounting costs of modern weaponry, drove changes in administrative practices. The lower ranks of the provincial administration became a career dead end, as governors came more and more from the army. The result was the rise of enormously powerful provincial governors. When some of them rebelled in 1658, the state barely mustered the resources to beat them.

Despite the central training of the ruling elite, and its close dependency on the sultan, it is easy to overrate the degree of control the empire exercised in the provinces. The system could perhaps best be characterized as centralization tempered by chaos. Rival governors, for instance, sometimes got simultaneous letters of appointment to the same place and were left to fight it out. Banditry usurped authority—fed with manpower by deserters from the army and peasants whom immoderate tax gatherers forced into outlawry. In a typical incident in 1606, Canboladolu Ali Pasha (jahn-boh-LAHD-oh-loo AH-lee PAH-shah), a notorious bandit chief, proposed to police the eastern front on the Persian border with 16,000 men in exchange for lucrative governorships for himself and his kin. The sultan granted his request.

The following year, the army overthrew him, but his success shows at once a weakness of the state and a form of internal diplomacy sultans had to practice. Many states of the time faced problems with bandits, but most tried to deal summarily with them. The Ottomans negotiated with them and tried to manipulate them. This was typical of the Ottoman approach, which was always flexible and adaptable. There was one law, but it could always be modified to take into account local custom. The sultan derived his authority from religious principles, but these could be emphasized in different ways to suit different communities. Uniform rules, in theory, governed taxation, but in practice it was arbitrary and changeable. Historians always tend to date "decline" too early, because they know what follows. To speak of Ottoman decline in the seventeenth century seems premature. It might be fairer to say that the Ottomans ceased to expand. In 1683, an attempt to capture the Habsburg capital Vienna failed, and in subsequent treaties, the Ottomans gave up further ambitions in Europe. If they faltered, it was not so much because of imperfections in their system of government—which, after all, had proved itself in the past—as because of an unexplained stagnancy in the population of their empire. Its growth did not match that of the populations of Europe, India, China, or Japan. And in the eighteenth century, Ottoman population growth slowed, relatively speaking, even more.

MUGHAL INDIA AND SAFAVID PERSIA

Like the empire of the Ottomans, that of the Mughals in India thrived on the economic success of the people they ruled. Or perhaps it would be fairer to say that the Mughals and their subjects enriched each other. The Mughals' fantastic demand for revenues stimulated economic inventiveness and forced peasants to produce for urban markets. Spectacular spending on war, buildings, and luxuries recycled wealth and stimulated an economy that high taxation might otherwise have stifled.

The Mughals' understanding of the nature of sovereignty was rooted in their conviction that they descended from Timur and ultimately from Genghis Khan (see Chapters 13 and 15). The names they gave their children and their dynasty reflect their Mongol and Islamic heritage. They ran their empire as a conquest—which, of course, it was, but it is more usual for conquerors to come to identify with the realms they rule. As we have seen (see Chapters 16 and 17), outside the relatively small, centrally administered core of the empire, Mughal methods of control relied on dividing tribute among a network of their relations, followers, clients, and allies. Like the Mongols and the Ottomans, they never established clear rules of succession to the throne. Every reign saw dynastic rebellions and wars of succession. Rivalries and alliances shifted unstably. The Mughals had always to balance the conflicting claims of rival aristocracies—the descendants of Timur, the Afghans and Persians who helped establish the dynasty in the 1520s, and the native Indian warrior chiefs on whom they relied increasingly to keep their empire together and extend it. A painting for the Emperor Akbar (r. 1556–1605) captures a familiar scene. A chain gang of captured rebels—some of them clad as beasts, others stripped naked—appears at his palace, shaking their chains defiantly, while their captors exult.

The Emperor Aurangzeb (r. 1658–1707) found the formula to keep the system going for a time: constant war to keep the aristocracies occupied, and continual conquests to multiply their rewards. A new generation of leaders arose, "born in the camp," as one of his ministers observed. New nobles, recruited from the frontier regions of the Deccan in south India as Aurangzeb's conquests grew, were

Captive rebels arrive at the palace of the Mughal Emperor Akbar (r. 1556–1605) in 1573, wearing animal skins to symbolize the unnatural perversity and bestiality of the act of rebellion. The emperor is offstage to the right, because it would diminish his dignity to depict him in the company of rebels. The painting is one of a series Akbar commissioned to commemorate the great events of his reign.

promoted above old ones, getting the choicest shares of tribute. Newcomers composed nearly half the upper ranks of the aristocracy by the end of the reign. Restlessness and rebellion in the heartlands and older conquests were among the results as ambitious or disaffected nobles clashed with each other and fought with the imperial administration. Rural disruption and loss of revenues followed. In part, the Mughal Empire was a victim of its success. It expanded too fast to sustain the system of keeping nobles dependent by assigning them revenues. Still, when he died in 1707, Aurangzeb left a treasury stuffed with reserves greater than Akbar's.

Squeezed between the Ottomans and the Mughals, the Safavids of Persia (1501–1773) ran, in some respects, a similar state to both of them, with universalist rhetoric, a nominally all-powerful ruler, and flexible relationships between the ruler and subordinate sources of authority. Like the Ottomans, the Safavids benefited from the growth in trade across Eurasia: especially, in the Safavid case, in the silk trade of the lands they ruled. Like the Ottomans, they drew on ancient traditions of kingship, as well as Muslim political thought, to legitimize their rule. The first ruler of the dynasty commissioned a lavishly illustrated history of the ancient Persian kings. Their rules of succession were, like the chaotic systems that prevailed among the Ottomans and Mughals, divisive and bloodily enforced. Shah Abbas I (ah-BAS), the Great (r. 1588–1629) imprisoned his sons and exterminated his remoter relations. Isfahan, his capital, resembled a great Indian or Ottoman city, full of unmistakable evidence of power, wealth, confidence, and energy. Its central plaza was seven times the size of St. Mark's Place in Venice. The goalposts installed there for games of polo were of marble. At one end, the great mosque was offset at an angle to guarantee a good view of the domes and minarets, displayed behind a gate 90 feet high. There were 273 public baths and 1,802 inns for commercial caravans.

Nevertheless, Safavid rule never relied on the kind of uniform bureaucracy the Ottomans used. Practices resembling those of the Mughals kept them in power. Except in some frontier regions, where they relied on accommodations with local rulers, the Safavids deployed a hereditary class of warrior horsemen of Turkic origin, known as the Qizilbash (KIH-zihl-bahsh), to enforce taxation and repress rebellion. As time went on, however, the Qizilbash tended to put down roots in the regions they ruled and frequently became rebels themselves. To tie elite loyalties firmly into the center, the Safavids used marriage, distributing the womenfolk of the ruling house around the provinces. Where possible, rulers exterminated

Isfahan, a vital center of trade, provides unmistakable evidence of the power, wealth, and dynamism of Safavid Persia. In this illustration, from the 1725 edition of *Voyages to Moscow, Persia, and the East Indies* by the Dutch traveler Cornelis de Brun (1652–1726), a camel caravan approaches the city.

PONT ALLA-WERDIE-CHAN

troublesome Qizilbash clans or replaced them with their own personal representatives. But the dynasty rarely had the power to put these devices into practice.

The Safavids, however, practiced politics that were unique in two respects. First, they were fiercely Shiite. They contemplated neither the religious pluralism of the Mughals nor the toleration of the Ottomans. They wanted to rule an exclusively Shiite Muslim people. Shiism was the basis of their claim to legitimacy. Religious minorities were forced to convert or were persecuted toward extinction. Second, the Safavids had no nostalgia for a mythic steppelander past. On the contrary, they claimed to be enemies of the nomads, and as we saw in Chapter 17, defeated the Uzbek steppelanders (see Map 19.3).

The Safavids' religious policies are hard to understand, since—at the start of the period—most of the people they ruled were not Shiites. A desire to have a distinctive ideology, in opposition to that of the Ottomans, seems to have impelled them. Or perhaps, like Akbar in India, they wanted a religion of their own. Like so many dynasties—like Islam itself—the Safavid line started with warrior holy men, who turned tribesmen from deserts and mountains into formidable armies. The first Safavid shah, Ismail I (ihs-mah-EEL) (r. 1501–1524), was a visionary who conversed with a vision of Muhammad's nephew Ali (see Chapter 8) and who appears, from his powerful, egocentric poetry, to have considered himself to be an incarnation of God. To a Venetian traveler, it seemed that throughout Iran "the

MAP 19.3

The Safavid Empire, 1501–1736

- Safavid Empire, 1722
- territory under Ottoman rule, 1722
- Mughal Empire, 1722
- easternmost limit of area contested by Ottomans to 1736
- ➤ Uzbek invasion, 1587

Uzbeks steppe people

Flagellants. Iranians shout religious slogans and beat themselves with iron chains in Tehran during the Shiite religious festival of Ashura in March 2004. Ashura marks the day when Imam al Hussein, the "leader of the martyrs" and grandson of the prophet Muhammad, was killed in Karbala in 680 C.E. in what is today Iraq.

name of God is forgotten and only that of Ismail remembered." Ismail imposed Shiism by force. But force is never enough to change emotional allegiances. In subsequent reigns, dazzling, frightening ceremonials impressed Shiism on the people's minds. In 1641, a visiting Western observer described a typical ritual, designed to commemorate the death of one of the great martyrs of Shiism: a terrifying mock conflict, a melee of horses, camels—some painted black to appear more fearsome—and "naked persons who struggled and screamed as if in despair, gashed with wounds, which they beat to make them spurt blood." An accompanying parade featured mourning women, and children, dressed in hides that were pierced with arrows and smeared with blood. Throughout such ceremonies, messages of hatred were directed against the supposed heirs of the martyr's murderers—the Safavids' Sunni Ottoman neighbors.

Paradoxically, perhaps, Safavid rulers never seemed very pious—tending to exempt themselves from Islamic rules about drink and sex—until one of the last shahs of the dynasty, Husain (r. 1694–1722), who engraved Islamic law in stone, smashed the 6,000 wine bottles in the imperial cellars, forbade song, dance, coffee, games, and prostitution, and banished even respectable women from appearing in the streets. In retrospect, these commands seem like a desperate attempt to capture the allegiance of an alienated clergy.

It is remarkable not so much that the Safavids ultimately failed as that they succeeded for so long. Whereas the Ottomans and Mughals were able to renew their strength by making new conquests, the Safavids' opportunities to match that means of success were limited. Ismail I thought himself invincible. When Ottoman artillery stopped his cavalry at the Battle of Chaldiran in Iraq in 1514, he flew black banners inscribed with the word *revenge.* But he never achieved it and withdrew into a world of drinking and womanizing. The Safavids did make some gains against the Turks later in the sixteenth century, and Safavid armies won impressive successes well into the seventeenth century. They raided Ottoman Baghdad twice. Scores of thousands of Georgian, Armenian, and Circassian prisoners were drafted into the slave corps that served the shahs as administrators. Portuguese intruders were turned out of the Persian Gulf. But the strength of the Ottomans to the west and of the Mughals to the east left the Safavids nowhere to expand.

CHINA

While Europe became ever more divided among competing states, and the Ottoman, Mughal, and Safavid empires consolidated, the unity of China survived potentially devastating threats.

Under the Ming dynasty (1368–1644), sixteenth-century China enriched its subjects. Fernão Mendes Pinto, a

Chronology: Islamic Empires: The Ottomans, Safavid Persia, and Mughal India	
Fifteenth and sixteenth centuries	Ottomans create an elite slave army, the Janissaries
1501–1722	Safavid dynasty in Persia
r. 1501–1524	First Safavid ruler, Shah Ismail I, imposes Shiism by force
1520s	Afghans and Persians help establish Mughal power in India
1570s	Ottoman jurist Ebu us-Suud justifies the Sultan's power
1658	Rebellion of provincial governors against Ottoman authority
1683	Ottomans fail to capture Vienna and cease conquests on the Christian front
r. 1658–1707	Emperor Aurangzeb engages in almost constant warfare in India
r. 1694–1722	Last Safavid ruler, Husain, imposes strict Islamic law
ca. Eighteenth century	Mughal power begins irreversible decline
1857	End of Mughal Empire

A CLOSER LOOK

A Safavid Battle Tunic

Throughout the Muslim world from the fifteenth century onward, soldiers wore talismanic shirts, designed to protect them in battle and ensure victory over enemies. This Safavid battle tunic, most likely from the late sixteenth century, was worn next to the warrior's skin and is embroidered with verses from the Quran.

"Help is from God and speedy victory. So give the good news to the believers." (61:13)

"Truly we have given you a glorious victory." (48:1)

"And may God give you his mighty help." (48:3)

"This is the Glorious Quran, preserved in writing." (85:21–22)

Why was there a close connection between Islam and war in Safavid Persia?

Portuguese window shopper in Beijing, walked around markets "as if in a daze" at the "silk, lace, canvas, clothes of cotton and linen, furs of marten, musk ox, and ermine, delicate porcelain, gold- and silver plate, seed pearls and pearls, gold dust and gold bullion." And as for the base metals, gems, ivory, spices, condiments and foods—"well, all these things were to be had in such abundance that I feel there are not enough words in the dictionary to name them all." The wealth gap between China and most of the rest of the world probably went on increasing over the next two centuries, as demand soared for newly popular goods in which China dominated world markets: porcelain, fine lacquerware, tea, ginseng, and rhubarb. By the mid-seventeenth century—before prolonged civil wars limited its growth—China probably contained about a third of the population of the world.

Chinese Politics

The emperors' authority, unlimited in theory, was restricted in practice by the power of the 20,000 or so scholar **mandarins** who ran the administration. They qualified for their jobs by passing competitive examinations in knowledge of classical Confucian texts. In consequence, most of them never questioned Confucian ideas. They wanted emperors to stick to the performance of sacred rites and the administration of justice. The empire, they felt, was best left in a state of peaceful balance, without undertaking the risks of aggression against its neighbors. Traditionally, emperors had escaped the control of bureaucrats by appealing to other factions, such as the Buddhist clergy, the court eunuchs, and the army. In the sixteenth century, however, the supremacy of the mandarins appeared unshakable. The emperor was not allowed to leave the capital—ostensibly, to prevent the delegation of power into profane hands while he was away. For example, the Zhengde (jehng-duh) emperor (r. 1505–1521) moved out of the palace and surrounded himself with eunuchs and monks. In a series of incidents beginning in 1517, he insisted on going on campaign on the Mongol frontier, in defiance of the mandarins, to escape the suffocating presence of his ministers. But he was obliged to abandon the expeditions when the scholars, in effect, went on strike, crippling the administration.

Chinese porcelain. Ming dynasty porcelain bowls from China, with their distinctive blue and white glazes, make superb ceiling ornaments. Two hundred sixty of them decorate a room in the Santos Palace in Lisbon, Portugal. The ceiling dates from the 1660s, but some of the bowls are more than a century and a half older.

The gravest crisis arose in 1587, when the Wanli (wahn-lee) emperor (r. 1572–1620) resolved to defy the mandarins. Evidence of widespread corruption in the civil service had undermined his confidence in the moral order traditional Confucianism recommended. He proposed to assert his power by altering the rules of succession, passing over his eldest son in favor of a son by his favorite concubine. Factions supporting the rivals traded accusations of witchcraft and distributed pamphlets among the people. After 10 years of stalemate, in which government effectively came to a halt, the emperor backed down. Intellectual trends reflected the shift in the location of power. The philosopher Li Zhi (lee jeh) wrote a new version of Chinese history, in which emperors counted for nothing, and the heroes were mandarins. Ming government was never fully effective after this crisis.

The Ming Empire seemed unable to cope with ecological disasters—floods and famines—in the 1630s. Peasant rebellions became civil wars as independent army commanders fought each other to control or even capture the throne. Meanwhile, from about 1590, the Ming delegated defense on the Mongol frontier to the north-west to Nurhaci, a chief of a pastoral war band in Manchuria (see Chapter 17). Chinese support enabled him to unite the Manchus. He began to call himself emperor and to represent himself as the spiritual heir of Manchu ancestors who had conquered northern China in the twelfth century. In 1636, Nurhaci's successor, Abahai, decreed a new ideology, which he called "Qing." The name was an allusion to "pure" water, which would quench the "bright" flame of "Ming." After intervening decisively in China's civil wars, the Manchus methodically and bloodily took over the country, proclaiming the Qing (chihng) dynasty. It was a long drawn-out business. The last Ming claimant to the throne was executed in 1662. The last Ming loyalists were not rooted out from their nests on the island of Taiwan until the 1680s. Yet the partisans of the defeated dynasty dictated ideology to the newcomers.

The shock of conquest by the Manchus made Chinese intellectuals rethink the whole basis of political legitimacy. The most startling and innovative result was the development of a doctrine of the sovereignty of the people, similar to that of Western Europe. Huang Zongxi (hwang dzohng-shee) (1610–1695) thought that a state of nature had once existed when "each man looked to himself" until benevolent individuals created the empire. Corruption set in, and "the ruler's self-interest took the place of the common good. . . . The ruler takes the very marrow from people's bones and takes daughters and sons to serve his debauchery." Lü Liuliang (loo lee-o-lee-ahng) (1629–1683) went further: "The common man and the emperor are rooted in the same nature." "It might seem as though social order was projected downwards to the common man," but, from the perspective of heaven, "the principle originates with the people and reaches up to the ruler. . . . Heaven's order and Heaven's justice are not things rulers and ministers can take and make their own."

"Unlike the West with the memory of ancient Greece and Rome, China had no examples of republicanism or democracy to look to in its history or idealize in myth."

Yet, whereas in the West, this sort of thinking helped to justify republics and generate revolutions, nothing comparable happened in China until the early twentieth century, when a great deal of Western influence had done its work. There were plenty of peasant rebellions under the Qing whose rule lasted until 1912, but, as throughout the Chinese past, these revolts aimed to renew the empire and replace the dynasty, not end the imperial system and transfer the **mandate of heaven** from a monarch to the people. Unlike the West with the memory of ancient Greece and Rome, China had no examples of republicanism or democracy to look to in its history or idealize in myth. Still, the work of Huang, Lü, and similar theorists passed into Confucian tradition. It helped to keep radical criticism of the imperial system alive and prepare Chinese minds for the later reception of Western revolutionary ideas.

Chinese Society

China experienced a sometimes violent revolution in the ownership of land. Peasant revolts in the 1640s challenged landowners' privileges. An incident from 1645 shows what was going on. A powerful clan's poor relation called Huang Tong (hwang tohng) roused tenants "for the pleasure of working off their petty grievances"—as a hostile court official put it—into attacking his rich kinsmen. He broke into the county capital and, after looting and bloodletting, tore down the

Erotic Deformity. There is a market in body shapes, as in everything else. In Qing China, the feet of women deformed by binding in childhood—typically at about five or six years old—became increasingly popular among families who could afford to remove their womenfolk from the workplace. Erotic literature enhanced the appeal of the practice, which also served patriarchy by making women less mobile and more dependent on men.

walls. Over the next few decades, the government gradually abolished limitations on peasants' freedom to sell their labor. In 1681, peasants could no longer be sold along with the land they farmed but were free to "do as they please." The last restrictions on peasant freedom were swept away in the early eighteenth century. As a result, the landlord life became less attractive. Land was still valued as a source of prestige or security, but agriculture was despised as "the labor of fools," while peasant fierceness made rent collection "a task to be feared." Individuals determined to reacquire ancestral lands no longer sought to restore estates that had been broken up by dividing the property among all the heirs. China became increasingly a land of peasant smallholders. Rural investment took the form of pawnbrokering by urban loan sharks who lent money to peasants to buy seed grain. A history of hatred between city and country began that still endures.

So in China, as in Europe, economic change broke down some of the traditional structures of society. Migrations probably contributed to the effect. The clan, or extended family that persisted from one generation to another, however, was a social structure that could not be destroyed. Ancestor worship made the clan into a religion. The administrative system perpetuated its role because Chinese clans, thousands strong, combined to select the best candidates from among their members to take the exams to enter the civil service and become mandarins. The rich members of the clan would pay for the education of the children of their poorest relations, if there was a chance that some bright young boy (girls could not take the exams) would rise to an office of influence in the state and favor his kin. Men normally married women from outside their own clan, and these wives then came to support the interests of their husbands' clan. There are signs that the restriction and even oppression of women got worse in seventeenth-century China. Female foot binding literally hobbled its victims and restricted their mobility (see Chapter 12). Widow suicide, though it never attained the degree of compulsion that it did in Hindu India, was increasingly encouraged. Widows who stayed alive often prospered in business, but remarried much less often than in Europe, where the remarriage of widows and widowers was a standard way to cope with the effects of high mortality.

Elements in China's seventeenth-century experience combined to strengthen and spread the sense of Chinese identity. This may seem surprising. We might expect the disruptions caused by civil war and the Manchu conquest, the dislocations of mass migrations over vast distances, the spillage of population by immigration overseas to Taiwan and Southeast Asia, or migration to the plains of Mongolia on an unprecedented scale to have weakened allegiance to the state. The vastness of the empire meant that China's new rulers had to exhibit great skill in adapting their legitimacy: as Manchus in Manchuria, as khans in Mongolia, as protectors of the Buddhist establishment in Tibet. Only on their extreme western frontier, where their subjects were Muslims, did the Qing emperors show hostility to the local culture. In the rest of the empire, however, their policy was to favor the adoption of Chinese culture. By the end of the eighteenth century, China's ethnic minorities had largely come to think of themselves as Chinese. Internal migra-

Chronology: Ming and Qing China: Politics and Society

1368–1644	Ming dynasty
1500s	Commercial economy booms
1587	The Wanli emperor precipitates a crisis by challenging the mandarins
1630s	Ecological disasters undermine Ming power
1640s	Peasant revolts challenge landowners' privileges
1644–1912	Qing dynasty
Seventeenth and eighteenth centuries	Mandarins reconciled to Qing power
Early eighteenth century	Last restrictions on peasant freedom eliminated

tions helped. They induced minorities to leave their traditional homelands and encouraged a sense that everyone within the empire was Chinese. Meanwhile, the overseas Chinese found themselves thrust into communities composed of migrants from many parts of China. As a result, they increasingly felt—paradoxically, perhaps—a common sense of belonging to the same community, which they projected home in their letters.

Qing strategy was to reconcile the different Chinese elites, especially the scholar-gentry, from among whom the mandarins were mostly recruited, to Manchu rule with generous rewards and with complete deference to the Confucian point of view that was deeply rooted among the Chinese elites. The Kangxi emperor (r. 1661–1722), who was the second Manchu to rule China, took lessons in the Confucian classics daily before dawn. The Qing avoided the impasse with the mandarins, in which late Ming rule had been mired, for three reasons. First, the scholars clung to the Qing as guarantors against disorder. Second, the dynasty and the bureaucracy had a common enemy in the warlords whose armies survived the civil wars that had brought down the Ming and who ruled vast areas with little input from the central government. The Kangxi emperor overthrew them in 1673. Finally, the Qing had their own power base in the Manchu warrior-elite. A twofold problem arose: how to perpetuate the martial readiness of Manchus, softened by adopting Chinese ways, and how to preserve a balance in the dynasty between Chinese and Manchu identities. Though the Qing emperors spoke and wrote Chinese, they kept up their knowledge of the Manchu language, privileged Manchus who remained loyal to their traditional culture, and founded schools of martial virtue for Manchu sons.

TOKUGAWA JAPAN

Compared with the multiethnic, religiously and socially diverse societies that the Qing, Ottomans, or Mughals ruled, the Japanese already had a remarkably uniform set of notions about themselves. The only ethnic minority in the Japanese islands was the Ainu people of the far north, and most of them lived outside the boundary of the Japanese Empire in 1600. The Japanese treated those Ainu whom they did conquer with deep suspicion and forbade them to mix with Japanese people. In any case there were relatively few Ainu.

Nevertheless, in other respects, the dynamic features of the period affected Japan as sweepingly as any of the other newly or lately interconnected regions in Eurasia that we have been discussing. Historians have always regarded the seventeenth century as a period of deepening Japanese isolationism. And Japanese governments did try increasingly to exclude foreign culture—but only that of "barbarian" Westerners. Chinese and Korean arts and ideas remained welcome, and, indeed, Confucianism revived spectacularly in the Japanese elite's scale of values (see Chapter 18). Imperial expansion went on. Although the government severely controlled merchants and shipping, this was not to prevent trade. On the contrary, Japan's overseas commerce grew throughout the seventeenth and eighteenth centuries, partly through the Dutch and Chinese agents who were allowed restricted trading privileges in Japan, and partly through illegal trade that the Japanese authorities condemned as piracy but never wholly suppressed. In any case, Japan was big and booming enough to generate its own internal commercial revolution. The area under cultivation doubled in 100 years from the mid sixteenth century. Population rose from something like 12 million in about 1550 to 30 million, according to a census of 1721.

Manchu warrior. "The bandits' heads were strung together. . . . Without even combing his horse's mane, he returned to make his report." The poem about this portrait of Zhanyinbao, of the Chinese Imperial Guard, in 1760, praises his prowess in law enforcement, but the artist shows him in hunting dress, armed with the bow that the Qianlong emperor, in the Manchu tradition, favored for the hunt. The realism and animation with which the subject's face is portrayed suggest that one of the Jesuit court artists painted this picture. *The Metropolitan Museum of Art, Purchase, The Dillon Fund Gift, 1986 (1986.206) Photograph © The Metropolitan Museum of Art*

Racing to Edo. The harbor of Osaka, in about 1670, where ships laden with the new cotton crop are about to sail for the imperial courtly city of Edo (modern Tokyo). Merchant's warehouses line the way. It was an annual race: whoever got to the capital first would sell at the highest price.

Peasants and merchants were the big gainers from the new prosperity, as peasants switched to surplus production to feed the growing cities, and merchants exploited the expanding markets. Edo (EH-doh), the old name for Tokyo, was one of the biggest cities in the world, with at least 600,000 people in 1700. A service-industry bourgeoisie of merchants, clerks, and craftsmen thrived in booming cities. Peasant prosperity eased the former cycle of famine and rebellion. In an atmosphere of social peace, governments encouraged people to concentrate on getting rich. The writer of novellas, Saikaku, was the spokesman of the age. "Heaven says nothing," announces his most famous book, *The Japanese Family Storehouse* (1688), "and the whole earth grows rich beneath its silent rule." He collected stories about money making and "placed them in a storehouse to serve each family's prosperity." Most of his stories tell of self-enrichment by hard work or intelligence. A street scavenger who picks up sticks becomes a chopstick-manufacturing millionaire. A desperate widow makes a fortune by raffling off her own house. "Now, if ever, trade is an exciting venture. So let none of you risk slipshod methods in earning your livings." The new economic climate had losers, too. Peace was bleak for the traditional warrior class, the samurai, who suffered from effects of the commercial boom: relatively low land values, high interest rates, and stagnation in the amount of rice the peasants had to provide to pay samurai pensions. Many samurai were reduced to the role of ronin—underemployed freelance soldiers, drifting between service to different lords. Lords (called **daimyo**) rarely paid samurai proper salaries. Exploitative pay was sometimes masked as "emergency reductions," sometimes as loans from the samurai that the daimyo never repaid.

Korea experienced similar problems with impoverished members of its noble class, or *yangbans*, as they were called. Traditionally, they discharged responsibilities in war and administration and, in official positions, could obtain land and wealth. But those excluded from office led lives of impoverished idleness, amid prostitutes and low-life hangers-on, satirized in popular literature and art.

Clearly, however, for those who shared it, Japanese prosperity was founded on what Japanese call the Great Peace: the era of internal peace that followed the reunification of Japan early in the seventeenth century under a dynasty of chief ministers, the Tokugawa, who ruled as *shoguns* in Edo, while the emperors remained secluded figureheads, performing sacred rites in a provincial court at

Making Connections | CHINA AND JAPAN: STABILITY AND CHANGE, 1500–1700

STATE AND SOURCES OF STABILITY	CHALLENGES	SOCIAL, CULTURAL, AND POLITICAL ADAPTATIONS
China / Confucianism; scholar mandarins run the state regardless of emperor, dynasty	Ecological disaster—floods and famines in the 1630s	Development of the docrine of sovereignty of the people
	Peasant rebellions, civil wars resulting from natural disasters	Elimination of right to sell peasants along with land
	Conquest by Manchus	Breakup of large estates
	Pressure for land reform, challenges to landowners	Continuation of clan loyalty, ancestor worship amid social, economic change
Japan / ethnic homogeneity; imperial system of rule; stable population and economic prosperity	Christian missionaries convert many people	Enforced isolationism from West balanced by continuing trade with Asia
	Disenfranchisement of traditional warrior class (samurai)	New emphasis on Confucian, Buddhist beliefs
	Need to maintain peace between shoguns and provincial rulers (daimyo)	Encouragement of commercial revolution, urbanism

the old capital in Kyoto. The key to stability was management of relations between the shoguns and the 260 or so daimyo who ruled Japan's provinces. The daimyo had to be drawn from a limited number of noble families, but the shogun appointed and frequently transferred them from one domain to another. Some daimyo, however, effectively managed to secure hereditary succession in their chosen regions. The Shimazu lords of the huge domain of Satsuma in southern Japan, for instance, built up enough regional power to exercise effective autonomy (and, eventually, in the nineteenth century to challenge the shoguns.) Normally, the Tokugawa obliged daimyo to maintain houses—and, in effect, leave hostages—at the shogun's court in Edo and reside there for part of each year. The shoguns also arranged marriages between daimyo families. In these respects, the system resembled the way many European monarchs dealt with their most powerful nobles.

THE NEW WORLD OF THE AMERICAS

Historians' favorite question about European overseas colonization is whether it created frontier societies—removed from models of society in the European homelands by generation gaps and pioneer radicalism—or exact duplications of home: transplanted Old Worlds. The answer of course is that the colonies were both. Molded and changed by new challenges and opportunities, settler communities usually tugged at nostalgic images of a home they aped or mirrored. An early apologist for the Spanish Empire conceived it as the colonists' obligation to rebuild New Spain in the image of the old Spain. Hence Spaniards built European-style arches in earthquake zones in the Americas, even though earth tremors could—and did—easily reduce such structures to ruin. Even Puritans, who did consciously want to make something new of New England, went about it by fencing and planting to create English-style fields.

Yet the results nearly always did mark the beginning of something that was different from Europe. Colonies had to adapt to new environments and, in many cases, to the presence of new neighbors. Sectarian religious communities, democratic commonwealths, and plantation economies were all new, for instance, to the English experience. A bureaucratic state, with little delegation of authority to nobles and towns, was unknown in Spain. While slaves had existed in Europe in the Middle Ages, slavery on the American scale was unprecedented. Huge mixed-race populations, of the kind that filled Spanish and Portuguese America, had never before had a chance to emerge outside the Muslim world. The new colonies were products of their environments, which changed the people who lived in them.

The New World really was new. The Spanish experience there was one of the biggest surprises of history: the creation of the first great world empire of land and sea, and the only one, on a comparable scale, erected without the aid of industrial technology. A new political environment took shape. Historians have scoured sixteenth-century Europe for the origins of the "modern state," in which the authority of the aristocracy shrank to insignificance, the crown enforced an effective monopoly of government jurisdiction, the independence of towns withered, the church submitted to royal control, and sovereignty—formerly definable in terms of the right to pronounce justice—became increasingly identified with supreme legislative power, as laws multiplied.

States in Europe developed along those lines, but only the Spanish Empire in the New World fully matched all the criteria. Great nobles were generally absent from the Spanish colonial administration, which was staffed by professional, university-trained bureaucrats whom the crown appointed and paid. Town councils were largely composed of royal nominees. Church patronage was exclusively at the disposal of the crown. With a few exceptions, feudal tenure—combining the right to try cases at law along with land ownership—was banned. Though Spaniards with rights to Native American labor or tribute pretended to enjoy a sort of fantasy feudalism, speaking loosely of their "vassals," they were usually denied formal legal rights to govern or administer justice and the vassals in question were subject only to the king. Meanwhile, a stream of legislation regulated—or, with varying effectiveness, was supposed to regulate—the new society in the Americas. The Spanish Empire was never efficient, because of the vast distances royal authority had to cover. Remote administrators could and did ignore royal commands. But this was a modern state because it was a bureaucratic state and a state governed by laws.

It also threw up new kinds of social effects, new microsocieties: the shipboard world of to-ing and fro-ing across the Atlantic and Pacific; the missions; the slave plantations; the little kingdoms runaway slaves called **maroons** set up; the households Spanish conquerors founded with pretensions to nobility and native wives or concubines. In Spanish colonies, **creole** consciousness arose at an early stage among persons of at least partly European descent who were born in the colonies. In some ways it was evident in the first generation of the conquerors. Pride in mixed ancestry—or false claims to it, especially claims to be descended from Indian nobility—was one sure sign of creole self-assertion. So was the use of Native American languages alongside or instead of Spanish. In the late sixteenth and early seventeenth centuries, Fernando de Alva Ixtlilxochitl's was a typically self-conscious creole voice: a historian of his community in Texcoco in Mexico, an interpreter of Native American language in the law courts, a government representative on municipal councils, a promoter and collector of Aztec literature. In the same period in Peru, the royal Inca blood of Garcilaso de la Vega made him highly

"The New World really was new. The Spanish experience there was one of the biggest surprises of history: the creation of the first great world empire of land and sea, and the only one, on a comparable scale, erected without the aid of industrial technology."

sought after as a godparent by young families in the Spanish town where he lived.

Historians have often supposed that the trauma of conquest and the catastrophic effects of the unaccustomed diseases Europeans introduced shocked Native Americans into docility. In many ways, however, it is remarkable how much—and how long—their society survived. Sometimes it simply evaded the Europeans. The Inca state, for instance, withdrew in the 1530s to a new, lowland environment centered on the fortress city of Vilcabamba (veel-kah-BAM-bah) in Peru, until a further Spanish conquest uprooted it in 1572. Independent Native American states survived for generations and sometimes for centuries beyond the reach of Spanish power in the rain forests of Guatemala, the Mexican desert, the Florida swamps. In other cases, Native American communities survived by forming partnerships with Spanish religious orders as their protectors, or— especially in the former Aztec and Inca subject areas— by collaborating with the Spanish monarchy and simply continuing to pay to the new elite the tribute they had formerly paid to Native American imperialists.

Mixing of the races. One of the most popular subjects for painters in eighteenth-century Spanish America was the vast range of skin complexions that intermarriage among Europeans, Native Americans, and black Africans produced. Hundreds of sets like this one survive, each consisting of many portraits of couples and their children, with every imaginable gradation of skin color. No one knows exactly what these paintings were for, but Spaniards who returned to Europe brought them home as souvenirs.

In some places, the substitution of new elites, not conquest, transformed politics and society. The new elites were not just composed of Europeans but also of newly elevated Native American individuals and communities. In the Aztec world, for instance, where war and disease wiped out much of the former generation of leaders, Spaniards—especially missionaries—formed new relationships with surviving youngsters, who became committed to Christianity and new values under the influence of mission schools. In urban environments a new class of opportunistic Native American *ladinos* arose—who learned Spanish and earned Spanish trust. In Panama the Spaniards elevated new local big men, mistrustful of the ritual functions of the leaders they displaced and whom they identified as "demonic." Everywhere, the children of marriages between Spaniards and Indians assumed a potentially advantageous place in colonial society. Because people at the time were more sensitive to differences of class than of race, these *mestizos*, as the descendants of Europeans and Native Americans were called, had access to positions of power and opportunities of wealth.

Of all the new kinds of society the global interconnections of the period created, the most novel were surely those of "the world the slaves made" in the Americas. From Virginia to Bahía in Brazil, much of Atlantic-side America became, in early colonial times, a world that was more African than European. In 1553—when black people in Mexico were doing little more than domestic labor—the viceroy, the representative of the king of Spain, was afraid that they would swamp white settlers. Black people rarely came to form a majority in the Spanish colonies— Cuba and Santo Domingo were two exceptions. Elsewhere, however, Africans were often the largest part of the population. By the end of the seventeenth century, England's Caribbean colonies had over 120,000 black slaves and only about 15,000 white inhabitants. The slaves practiced their own religions (see Chapter 18), maintained their own household patterns, and ate their own food. They created languages of their own to bridge the communication gaps among people from so many different parts of Europe and Africa. One of the earliest documented of these

Sranan, Dutch, and English Compared

Sranan	Dutch	English
brada	broder	brother
buku	boek	book
datra	doctor	doctor
faya	vuur	fire
gado	god	god
ingi	Indiaan	Indian
kerki	kerk	church
masra	meneer	mister
noso	neus	nose
omeni	hoeveel	how much
skribi	schrijven	write
srudati	soldaat	soldier
trow	trouwen	marry

new languages is Sranan, still the main language of Surinam, the former Dutch colony in South America. Slaves invented it in an amazingly short time, under a brief period of British rule, in the 1650s and early 1660s. Despite high mortality and rapid turnover in the slave population, they stuck to it through the subsequent 300 years of Dutch rule—adopting some Dutch words, but maintaining Sranan essential structures and vocabulary.

Even in tightly controlled plantations, slave communities often created autonomous institutions. In Jamaica, the British could never eliminate the secret power of the *obeah-men*, whom they denounced as sorcerers, or curb the "benches" of elders, who were the self-regulating judges of the slaves. Though specialists debate the issue, the evidence from British North America suggests that slaves themselves seem to have evolved the social order of plantation life—the family structures, the regulation of relationships, the norms of behavior. Their African culture was only slowly transformed, because most owners resisted Christianizing their slaves. The Bible might give them subversive ideas about the equality of men. Clergy might interfere with owners' rights of abuse.

As well as African ways of life, there were African political structures in America: independent states established by runaways, sometimes in collaboration with Native Americans. Colonial authorities were forced to recognize the most successful maroon kingdoms. It was easier to establish a working relationship than run the risks of war and of inflaming slaves' grievances. The best-known case is that of a maroon kingdom in Esmeraldas in the hinterland of what is today Colombia, which signed a treaty with the Spanish crown in 1599. The Spanish viceroy commissioned a commemorative painting of the event from Alonso Sánchez Galque, the best painter in the colony at the time. It shows a maroon leader and his sons, richly attired as Spanish gentlemen, but bejeweled with ear and nose ornaments of gold in Native American fashion.

Beyond the reach of British colonies, too, in the seventeenth and eighteenth centuries, maroon states in South Carolina and Jamaica enjoyed arrangements with the colonial authorities that guaranteed their peaceful toleration in exchange for joint regulation of the fate of new fugitives from the plantations (see Map 19.4). In the backcountry of Surinam, a maroon state was established in 1663 (the year the maroons of Jamaica received the first treaty acknowledging their autonomy), with the connivance of planters who sent their slaves there to evade the head tax on them

Don Francisco Arove and his sons, leaders of a maroon kingdom in Esmeraldas, who submitted to the Spanish crown by treaty in 1599. A government official commissioned the painting for presentation to King Philip III. The mixed culture of this community of runaway slaves is reflected in the appearance of its leaders: their black faces, their rich clothing in the style of Spanish noblemen, the costly ear and nose ornaments borrowed from Native American tradition.

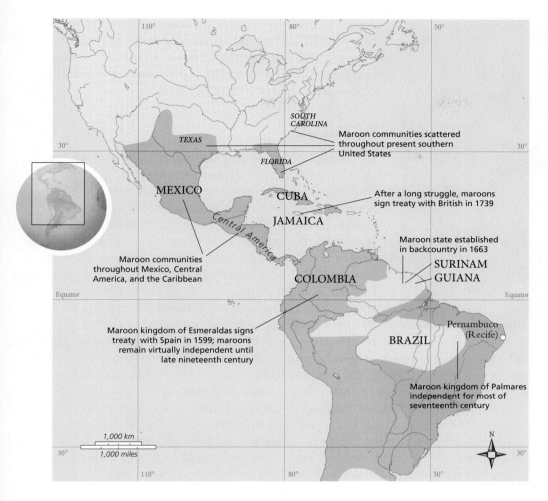

MAP 19.4

Maroon Communities in the Americas, 1500–1800

- Spanish territory after 1650
- Portuguese territory by 1750

that they were required to pay to the colonial government. The best documented and longest lasting of the runaways' states was upcountry from Pernambuco (pehr-nam-BOO-koh) in Brazil, where the kingdom of Palmares (pal-MAHR-eshs) defended its independence from Portugal for almost the entire seventeenth century. At its height, under King Zumbi, in the late seventeenth century, it had a royal guard 5,000 strong, an elaborate court life that impressed visiting Portuguese, and a black elite rich enough to have many slaves of their own.

Europeans dealing in the slave trade convinced themselves that slavery represented a civilizing process: the recovery of one of the virtues of the ancient Greek and Roman worlds, which slave energy had fueled, and the removal of slaves from the supposedly "barbarous darkness" of Africa to the "light" of Christian European civilization. In practice, it is hard to imagine anything more destructively barbarizing. Slavery nourished its own forms of lies and cant: racism, which depicted blacks as inherently inferior to whites, or claimed that they were better off enslaved than at home. It corrupted owners, by giving them power over the lives and bodies of their slaves and encouraging them to abuse it. It corrupted shippers, who overcrowded their cargoes to maximize their profits and, in verifiable incidents, tossed slaves overboard for the insurance ship owners could earn for dead "cargo." It kept black and white people in mutual fear and loathing, driving black rebels to horrific and despairing acts to find refuge or gain revenge, and trapping colonial governments in policies of inhuman rage and repression. It let loose predatory gangs of

"Europeans dealing in the slave trade convinced themselves that slavery represented a civilizing process: the recovery of one of the virtues of the ancient Greek and Roman worlds, which slave energy had fueled, and the removal of slaves from the supposedly 'barbarous darkness' of Africa to the 'light' of Christian European civilization. In practice, it is hard to imagine anything more destructively barbarizing."

Archibald Dalzel's *History of Dahomey* of 1793 was a slaver's defense of the slave trade, and the engravings in it reflect the author's prejudice against black Africans. The royal court of Dahomey in West Africa is presented as a contemptible blend of despotism, silliness, and immorality.

FIGURE 19.2 THE ATLANTIC SLAVE TRADE, FIFTEENTH TO EIGHTEENTH CENTURIES

From Cañizares-Esguerra, Jorge; Seeman, Eric, The Atlantic in Global History: 1500–2000, © 2007. Electronically reproduced by permission of Pearson Education, Inc., Upper Saddle River, New Jersey.

slavers and bounty hunters. It encouraged war in Africa between predator states that profited from the trade and their victims. The moral effects are important because every memory of inhumanity is precious in a world still riddled with vices of cruelty and greed.

AFRICA

The social, political, and demographic effects of the slave trade in Africa are hard to measure. The slaves who crossed the Atlantic came especially from the West African bulge, the Congo Basin, and Angola. The New World needed substantial numbers of them. Outside British North America, most slave communities in the Americas did not reproduce naturally, for reasons that historians still do not fully understand. Constant new imports were therefore required just to maintain labor levels. Over 1.5 million black slaves reached the New World by 1600, and nearly six million more in the eighteenth century (see Figure 19.2). The numbers shipped out of Africa were even larger, because many slaves died during the passage across the Atlantic. From the best available figures, almost 400,000 of those exported from Africa before 1800 never reached the Americas.

Overwhelmingly, black African sellers procured them by war and raiding that reached hundreds of miles into the interior. Despite the size of the catchment area, it is hard to believe that the export of manpower on the scale demanded did not seriously affect the victim societies. For a time the Angola region of West Africa seems to have developed a marked excess of females over males because many more men than women were shipped across the Atlantic. On the fringes of African slave-trading societies, some areas may have been depopulated.

Dahomey—one of many slave-trading states that sprang up or grew in West Africa during the slaving era (see Map 19.5)—illustrates the political effects. The kingdom arose in the interior of the present state of Benin in the early seventeenth century. Europeans already called the region the Slave Coast. Dahomey lived by war, and subordinated all other values to a ferocious warrior cult. Guests at the king's table dined with silver-handled forks on food European-trained cooks prepared, but they had to approach the king's palace over a path paved with skulls and were obliged to witness the human sacrifices with which Dahomeyans celebrated royal funerals and annual commemorations of former kings. Around the midseventeenth century, Dahomey began to accumulate muskets in exchange for slaves it obtained by raiding farther north. The 18 trading communities subject to Dahomey in the 1680s grew to over 200 within 20 years. Dahomey acquired a strip of coast—so King Agaja told European traders—to control outlets for slaves.

Yet with a productive territory in an area of varied commerce, Dahomey did not depend on slaving, which, by the best available calculations, accounted for perhaps 2.5 percent of its economy. Slaving apologists frequently pointed out that a war ethic motivated Dahomeyan aggression and that Dahomey prized captives more as potential human sacrifices than as slaves. White slave traders claimed that they performed a work of mercy by redeeming their victims from certain death. Dahomey's wars were not

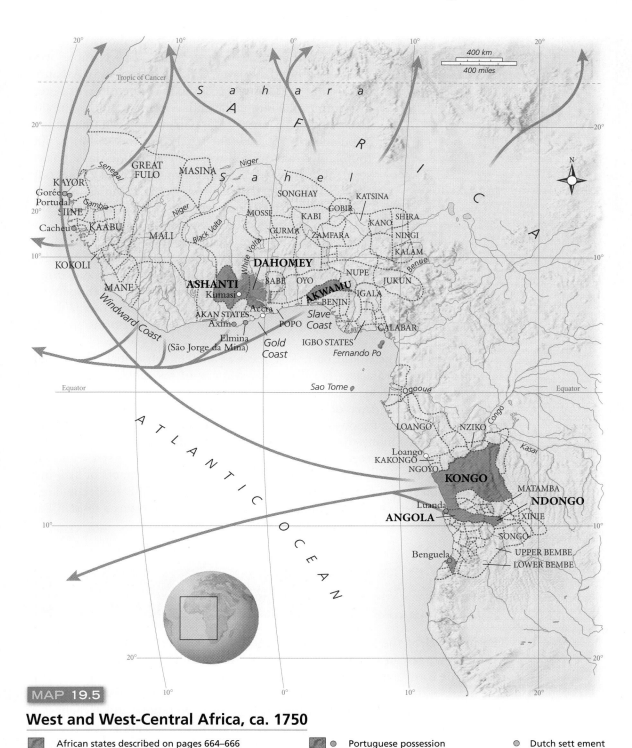

West and West-Central Africa, ca. 1750

- African states described on pages 664–666
- Portuguese possession
- Dutch sett ement
- s a e trade

fought primarily for slaves. Indeed, only a third of the campaigns acquired enough victims to cover the costs. Still, some facts are clear. Dahomey rose and fell with the rhythms of the slave trade, and its cult of ferocity coincided with the market for captives of war. The economics of the slave trade obliged African suppliers to be warriors or bandits, because the prices Europeans paid made it worth raiding for slaves, but not worth raising them.

Chronology: Africa, the Americas, and the Slave Trade

Late sixteenth century	Maroon kingdom of Esmeraldas
Seventeenth and eighteenth centuries	Slave states proliferate in West Africa; Maroon states in South Carolina and Jamaica
Late seventeenth century	Black slave population of British Caribbean reaches 120,000
	Maroon kingdom of Palmares reaches its height
ca. 1700	Number of slaves shipped to New World reaches 1.5 million
ca. 1800	Number of slaves shipped to New World reaches 7.5 million

Farther west, the history of Ashanti shows that state-building on an even greater scale was possible with resources other than slaves. Gold was the basis of Ashanti's spectacular rise from the 1680s to the dimensions of a great kingdom by the mid-eighteenth century, occupying 10,000 square miles of present-day Ghana and commanding a population of 750,000. The royal chest was said to be able to hold 400,000 ounces of gold. The throne was a golden stool said to have been called down from the sky. The court sheltered under ceremonial umbrellas as big as trees. For the annual yam ceremony, when the king's tributaries gathered with their followers, the capital at Kumasi housed 100,000 people. More adaptable than Dahomey, Ashanti used firepower to defeat mounted armies from the Sahel, while coping with a variety of environments and fronts. Part of its armies' success was owed to outstanding intelligence and logistics, with fast runners operating along cleared roads. Even Ashanti, however, increasingly relied on slaving to supplement its gold during the eighteenth century.

To the east of the Gold Coast, Akwamu was another substantial slave-stealing state of a distinct character. Its ruler enslaved many of his subjects by arranging phoney denunciations for adultery—a crime many African states punished by servitude—and mobilizing gangs of "smart boys" to kidnap victims. Similarly, in the other main slave-producing region—the Congo Basin and Angola—the profits of slaving enabled ambitious monarchs to consolidate and centralize states. Kongo became a hereditary kingdom, whose rulers appointed the chiefs of subordinate states, and who succeeded, on the whole, in preventing, or at least limiting, enslavement of their own subjects. Ndongo, in the interior of what is now Angola, grew similarly rich and centralized and, as we saw, under the formidable warrior queen, Nzinga, resisted Portuguese attempts at conquest for most of the seventeenth century.

In Perspective
Centuries of Upheaval

The upheaval of the sixteenth and seventeenth centuries affected much of the world. As we saw in Chapter 18, ecological exchanges had reversed, in a crucial respect, the course of evolution. Empires had overflowed like tidal waves and covered much of the globe. The balance of power between pastoral and settled peoples in Eurasia had shifted definitively toward the latter. Migrations and exchanges of culture crossed oceans and continents, sometimes with profoundly transforming effects. For the first time, a single—if small-scale—system of trade encircled the Earth. Some regions were still outside this system: Australia and most of the South Pacific, parts of inland Africa, the far interiors of the Americas. But they were unlikely to be left outside it for long.

Increasing demand was the result of gradually rising population and of huge increases of cash, which the silver mines of Japan and the Americas unlocked. New economic opportunities enriched new countries and new classes. A military revolution, as scholars now call it, introduced new technology to war: firearms that a peasant could handle with little training; fortifications that were proof against traditional horse-borne warriors; armies disciplined in the routines of battle rather than being trained, like knights of old, in individual combat. These changes started in Europe, but they transformed warfare in all the "gunpowder-empires" of the Old World. The military revolution loosened aristocracies' hold on one of the most basic forms of power, creating easily drilled armies of massed infantry, equipped with guns. Stronger states emerged in Europe and Africa; stronger empires in Asia; unprecedented empires in the Americas.

Although empires still seemed to dominate the map of the world, and although small chieftaincies and tribal states continued to occupy much of it, there was some evidence, in some regions, of a trend toward the kind of state familiar today: the relatively small and self-contained state, with internal sovereignty. In Europe, the Habsburg dynasty failed to turn Spanish preponderance into imperial control. Even in Germany, Habsburg power waned and, though Habsburg emperors continued to speak of their empire, it was transformed into a mass of loosely linked, small, effectively sovereign entities. In Southeast Asia, many rulers dreamed of creating an empire that would stretch from the Indian Ocean to the Pacific, and from India to China, but the traditional state system survived largely intact. In western Africa, while slaving states grew in strength, none reconstructed the extensive sway Mali had enjoyed in the fourteenth century or Soghay, for a while, in the sixteenth (see Chapters 14 and 15). Safavid Persia, though historians usually refer to it as an empire, more closely resembled a compact and—by the standards of its neighbors—a relatively homogeneous state. Although the Tokugawa imposed peace on Japan, there were limits to the political unification they imposed: in many ways, the daimiyos functioned like the rulers of loosely confederated states.

It is tempting to seek a connection between political instability, especially in the spell of civil wars and revolts that afflicted many states in the mid- to late seventeenth century, and the environmental changes described in Chapter 17. Although the ecological revolution and the spread and intensification of agriculture were sweepingly global phenomena, their effects took a long time to register. The seventeenth century was generally, as far as we can tell, a period of demographic stagnation in most of Eurasia and Africa, and even of decline in some places, posing a challenge for states that had to raise money and men for war. The concentrated aggravation of Eurasia's age of plague in the seventeenth century (see Chapter 17) made the problem worse. Like visitations of plagues in Eurasia in the fourteenth century (see Chapter 14), it accompanied protracted freak weather and abruptly falling temperatures, as a spell of unusually dense sunspots coincided with many volcanic eruptions, spraying the atmosphere with dust and shrouding the planet from solar energy. The period from the end of the 1640s to the 1680s was particularly hard. In the same decades, some of the most spectacular political revolutions of Eurasia occurred, including the collapse of the Ming Empire, the fragmentation of the Spanish monarchy, the temporary dissolution of the Polish Commonwealth, the splitting of the Netherlands, a major re-casting of the Holy Roman Empire, and, in England and the Ottoman Empire, revolutions in which rulers were killed. At the least, it seems likely that environmental changes added to the strains of war that disrupted these states.

Remarkably, however, they all emerged strengthened. The Qing, who dethroned the Ming in 1644, renewed the Chinese Empire and made it more effective militarily. The northern Netherlands became the launch-pad of a great global empire and the nursery of a "Golden Age" of wealth and art. Germany more or less split into many small states—but individually they were stronger than ever. The Poles recovered sufficiently to challenge the Ottomans, whose empire was barely affected by the palace revolution. Although Spain lost control of Portugal and the Netherlands, rebellions elsewhere failed, and the Spanish crown emerged with a tighter hold on

"For the first time, a single—if small-scale—system of trade encircled the Earth. Some regions were still outside this system: Australia and most of the South Pacific, parts of inland Africa, the far interiors of the Americas. But they were unlikely to be left outside it for long."

Chronology

1368–1644	Ming dynasty
Fifteenth and sixteenth centuries	Ottomans create an elite slave army, the Janissaries
Sixteenth through eighteenth centuries	Nuclear family moves to the center of European society
1500s	Chinese commercial economy booms
1501–1722	Safavid dynasty in Persia
r. 1501–1524	First Safavid ruler, Shah Ismail I, imposes Shiism by force
1513	Machiavelli writes *The Prince*
1519	Charles V becomes Holy Roman Emperor
1520s	Afghans and Persians help establish Mughal power in India
1570s	Ottoman jurist Ebu us-Suud justifies the Ottoman Sultan's power
1576	Jean Bodin formulates doctrine of sovereignty
1603–1868	Tokugawa shogunate
1618–1648	Thirty Years' War
1630s	Ecological disasters undermine Ming power
1640s	Strain of empire precipitates decline of Spanish power
1644–1911	Qing dynasty
Seventeenth and eighteenth centuries	Mandarins reconciled to Qing power
1658	Rebellion of provincial governors against Ottoman authority
1658—1707	Emperor Aurangzeb engages in almost constant warfare
r. 1682–1725	Peter the Great attempts Westernization of Russia
1683	Ottomans fail to capture Vienna and cease conquests on the Christian front
Late seventeenth century	Maroon kingdom of Palmares reaches its height
Seventeenth and eighteenth centuries	Slave states proliferate in West Africa; Japan undergoes a "commercial revolution"
Eighteenth century	Last restrictions on freedom of Chinese peasants eliminated; Mughal power begins irreversible decline
1721	Population of Japan reaches 30 million
ca. 1800	Number of slaves shipped to New World reaches 7.5 million

what was still a vast and—overall—growing empire. England's convulsions were traumatic, but in the course of them, the English crushed the independence of the Irish and Scots. France's time of troubles ended with the reign of Louis XIV (r. 1643–1715), whose image ever since has stood for royal power and the pursuit of gain and glory by war.

Growing state power went hand in hand with social changes. Rulers in Christendom and Islam challenged clergies for control of their subjects' private lives, especially their marriages. Where aristocratic government had formerly prevailed, bureaucrats and courtiers tended to replace local and provincial aristocrats as the main props of monarchical power. Remarkably, this trend was especially marked in Spain's American empire, where royal commands waned in effectiveness with the distance they traveled and the time it took. Although it would be going too far to speak of "the rise of the bourgeoisie," it is true that over much of the world—encompassing most of Europe, much of Asia, and significant parts of Africa and the Americas—new social configurations took shape, as the old vertical structures of society grew weaker, in which people identified with each other on the basis of kinship or local or provincial allegiance, or caste, or membership of an order or estate, or adhesion to a religious tradition. Instead, or alongside them, new sources of common interest grew in strength, with people identifying with others of similar wealth—or lack of it—and way of life. The trend was particularly strong in Europe, where family life grew ever more intimate and ever more narrowly focused on the home. Longstanding traditions dissolved or weakened, while new contexts for creating wealth and wielding power emerged, making possible the developments to which we must turn in the next part of the book: startling innovations in the global distribution of wealth and power, and revolutionary ways of thinking and behaving that became conspicuous in the eighteenth-century West and—as we shall see—then spread over the world.

PROBLEMS AND PARALLELS

1. How did the power of the state grow in the sixteenth and seventeenth centuries? How did monarchs such as Queen Nzinga seek to redistribute power to their own advantage? Which newly empowered classes contended for a share in the growing might and resources of states?

2. What were the sources of Spanish power in the sixteenth and seventeenth centuries? Why did Charles V fail to establish a dominant state in Europe? Why did Spain eventually lose its preeminent position in Europe?

3. How did the way Westerners think about sovereignty and international law change in this period? Why was Machiavelli's advice to rulers so shocking? How did European society change during this period?

4. What are the similarities and differences among the Ottoman, Mughal, and Safavid empires during this period? Why did Shah Ismail I impose Shiism on Persia?

5. What economic and social changes occurred in China during the early Qing dynasty? How did these changes affect Chinese politics? How did Japanese society change under the Tokugawa shoguns?

6. In what ways were European colonies in the Americas products of their environments? In what ways was the Spanish Empire a modern state? How did the creole mentality affect colonial societies?

7. How did slave communities in the Americas create autonomous institutions? What effect did the slave trade have on African states during this period?

READ ON ▶ ▶ ▶

The account of Queen Nzinga is indebted to work by J. K. Thornton, whose *Africa and Africans in the Making of the Atlantic World* (1995) is fundamental. A very readable introduction to the social transformation of early modern Europe is G. Huppert, *After the Black Death: A Social History of Early Modern Europe* (2nd ed., 1998). G. Parker, *The Military Revolution: Military Innovation and the Rise of the West, 1500–1800* (1988) is a vastly influential, though technologically oriented, statement of the connection between military and political change in Europe and globally. B. Downing, *The Military Revolution and Political Change* (1992) takes a closer, regionally differentiated look at political transformation. R. Carr, ed., *Spain: A History* (2000) is the best introduction to its subject. R. Harrison, *Hobbes, Locke, and Confusion's Masterpiece: An Examination of Seventeenth-Century Political Philosophy* (2002) is a masterful explication of seventeenth-century political philosophy. O. Hufton, *The Prospect Before Her* (1996) and I. Maclean, *The Renaissance Notion of Woman* (1983) are important for understanding the role of women in the West.

I. M. Kunt, *The Sultan's Servants: The Transformation of Ottoman Provincial Government* (1983) looks at the local and bottom-up forces affecting Ottoman governance, while H. Inalcik, *The Middle East and the Balkans under the Ottoman Empire: Essays on Economy and Society* (1993) explores the mutual impact of rulers and ruled in the most ethnically and religiously diverse area of Ottoman control. K. Barkey, *Bandits and Bureaucrats: The Ottoman Route to State Centralization* (1994) studies Ottoman state formation from the perspective of the central government.

I. Gallup-Diaz, *The Door to the Seas and the Key to the Universe. Indian Politics and Imperial Rival in Darien, 1640–1750* (2002) takes an ethnohistorical perspective on Indian responses and resistance to European encroachment in this period. Peter Jackson and Lawrence Lockhart, eds., *The Cambridge History of Iran: Volume 6, The Timurid and Safavid Periods* (1986) is the standard history of Persia during this period.

R. Huang, *1587: A Year of No Significance* (1982) tells the story of the crisis of that year in China. My account of the rise of the Qing is indebted to L. Struve, *Voices from the Ming-Qing Cataclysm* (1998). F. Wakeman, Jr., *The Great Enterprise* (1985) looks at the social bases of early Qing political and military power. Pak Chi-won, *Tale of a Yangban* (1994) offers a story of Chinese influence in Korea. C. Totman, *Politics in the Tokugawa Bakufu* (1967) is the classic study of the political transformations of Japan after unification. S. Morillo, "Guns and Government: A Comparative Study of Europe and Japan," *Journal of World History* (1995) uses Japan as a case study in the primacy of social over military change, challenging Parker's "military revolution" thesis.

P. P. Boucher, *Cannibal Encounters. Europeans and Island Caribs, 1492–1763* (1999), traces cultural interactions in the Caribbean and demonstrates the effectiveness of Carib resistance to Europeans.

The intense instability of the mid-seventeenth century is studied in G. Parker and L. Smith, eds., *The General Crisis of the Seventeenth Century*. G. Parker, *The World Crisis: Climate, Collapse and Recovery in the Seventeenth Century* (forthcoming) brilliantly sets the phenomenon in a global context.

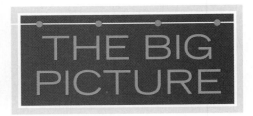

THE BIG PICTURE

The World in 1700

The way life-forms began to cross the world in the sixteenth century halted one of the longest-standing trends on the planet. Scores of millions of years of divergent evolution, continent by continent, were reversed. But the big effects on the diversification of food and the increase of global population had not yet been felt. The lurches of climate sped transformations of states—leading to retreating aristocracies, encroaching bureaucracies, and the multiplication of laws—but the transformations were patchy and incomplete. The worldwide reach of explorers, traders, missionaries, and conquerors from Atlantic-side Europe demonstrated the imperial potential of Europe, but the empires were still feeble, outclassed by those of indigenous Asian powers. Prowess in astronomy and cartography won Europeans new respect in parts of Asia where they had formerly longed in vain for access. The global balance of wealth and power, however, remained undisturbed: indeed, China benefited most from the growing range and scale of global trade. Christianity was reaching previously unevangelized populations in Europe and around the world—but the spread of Islam and Buddhism echoed and, in some regions matched or exceeded, that of Christianity.

From inside a European *Wunderkammer* or Memory-Theater, such as the one shown on this map, the world did look different. Riches were pouring into Europe as never before, thanks above all to previously unexploited resources in the Americas. Maps, reports, curiosities, and exotica garnered from all over the globe were beginning to give European science a privileged view of the world and to stimulate imperial imaginations. Glimmeringly, the prospects of "the rise of the West" to global hegemony were beginning to be discernible.

▶ QUESTIONS

1. If the ecological revolution was the essential precondition for the major global changes of the sixteenth and seventeenth centuries, why was Europe better able to take advantage of these new resources?

2. How did mental attitudes to the world change as the result of ecological exchange?

To view an interactive version of this map, as well as a video of the author describing key themes related to this Part, go to www.myhistorylab.com

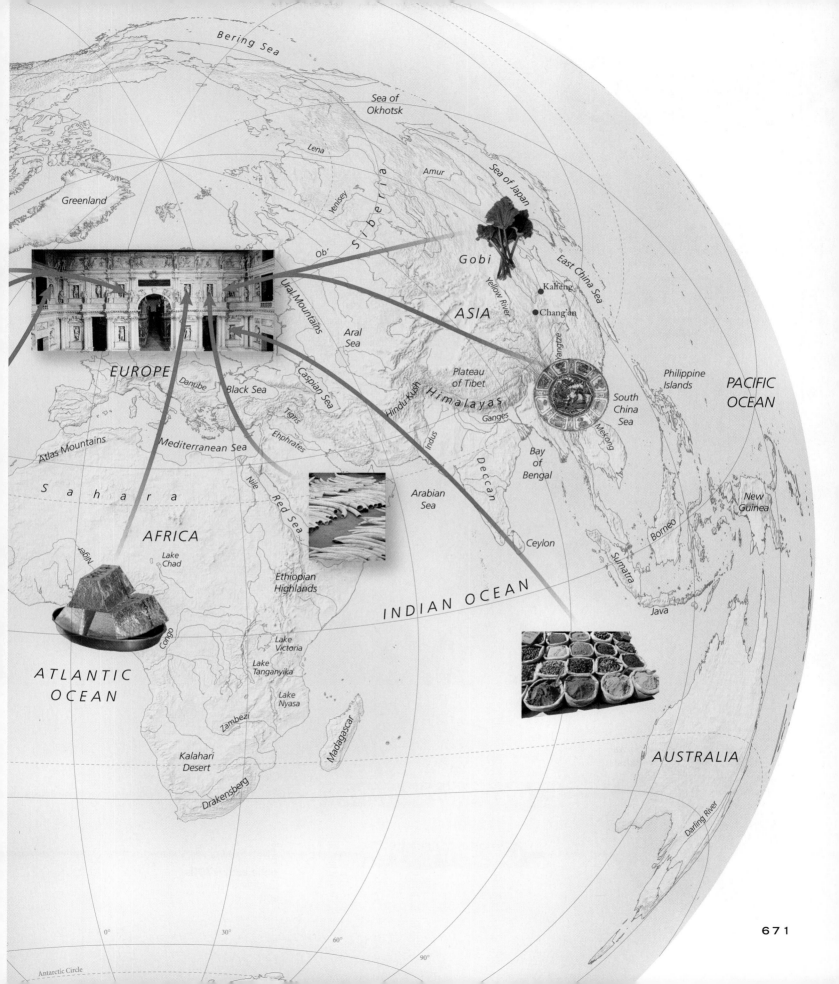

Bering Sea

Sea of
Okhotsk

Greenland

Lena

Amur

Sea of Japan

Siberia

Yenisey

Ob'

Gobi

East China Sea

ASIA

Kaifeng

Yellow River

Chang'an

Ural Mountains

EUROPE

Aral
Sea

Danube

Black Sea

Caspian Sea

Plateau
of Tibet

Hindu Kush

Himalayas

Yangtze

South
China
Sea

PACIFIC
OCEAN

Philippine
Islands

Atlas Mountains

Mediterranean Sea

Tigris

Ephrates

Ganges

Indus

Deccan

Mekong

Sahara

Nile

Red Sea

Arabian
Sea

Bay
of
Bengal

Borneo

New
Guinea

AFRICA

Lake
Chad

Ethiopian
Highlands

Ceylon

Sumatra

Niger

Congo

INDIAN OCEAN

Java

ATLANTIC
OCEAN

Lake
Victoria

Lake
Tanganyika

Zambezi

Madagascar

Lake
Nyasa

AUSTRALIA

Kalahari
Desert

Drakensberg

Darling River

0°   30°   60°   90°

671

Antarctic Circle

PART 8

After that, plague never returned to Europe. Changes in the distribution of carrier species of rats, fleas, and lice may have played a part (see Chapter 14). But the demise of plague could be like most other forms of species extinction: a product of evolution. The microorganisms that bear disease are more volatile, more apt to evolve, than other, bigger organisms, because they are individually short lived. They go through many generations in a relatively short span of time. Viruses are especially mutable. So species come and go much faster in the microbial world than among the great, lumbering plants and animals whose evolution we normally observe. We think of evolution as a slow-working process. Microbes experience it fast. Those that kill off their hosts are obviously not adaptively successful. They need to find new eco-niches to ensure their own survival, or they are self-condemned to disappear. For reasons we do not know—but which must be connected with their own evolutionary advantage— hostile microorganisms may sometimes switch their attention away from one set of victims to another. Historically, our improving health may owe less than we suppose to our own cleverness and more to the changing habits and nature of microbes.

> *"Historically, our improving health may owe less than we suppose to our own cleverness and more to the changing habits and nature of microbes."*

ECONOMIC TRENDS: CHINA, INDIA, AND THE OTTOMAN EMPIRE

More population means more economic activity. That is not surprising. But eighteenth-century economic activity did mark a new departure from long-prevailing global patterns, as the gap in production, and therefore in wealth, began to narrow. The West began to catch up with China and India. The new rich among the world's economies began to emerge in Europe and America. By the end of the eighteenth century, India went into sharp relative decline. China maintained its supremacy, but signs suggested that its days as the world's richest society were numbered.

China

The distribution of the world's most productive and profitable industries indicates what was going on. The most intensive concentrations of industrial activity were still in East and South Asia. Take the case of the Beneficial and Beautiful wholesaling firm, founded in the seventeenth century in the city of Hangzhou (hahng-joh) on the coast of central China. According to records collected in the early nineteenth century, the firm built up its cloth sales to a million lengths a year by making bold rebates to tailors. In the early eighteenth century, the firm employed 4,000 weavers and several times that number of spinners. The dyeing and finishing were concentrated in a specialized suburb of the city, where in 1730 10,900 workers were gathered under 340 contractors and, claimed the firm's publicity, "for two hundred years now there has been no place, either north or south, that has failed to consider Beneficial and Beautiful cloth to be lovely."

The tale of the Beneficial and Beautiful Company was an exceptional but not an uncharacteristic story. A porcelain center in eighteenth-century Jiangxi (jee-ahng-shee) province in southern China "made the ground shake with the noise of tens of thousands of pestles. The heavens are alight with the glare from the furnaces, so that one cannot sleep at night." Farther south were ironworks that employed 2,000 to 3,000 men, and water-driven hammers pounded incense "without any expenditure of muscular effort." In the southwest provinces, similar machines for husking rice were lined up by the hundred, while water-driven paper-makers hummed "like the whirr of wings." The great city of Nanjing had three imperial textile factories at the start of the eighteenth century, employing 2,500 artisans and 664 looms. Near what is today Shanghai, in 1723, there were about 20,000 textile workers and dyers. The imperial government appointed the entrepreneurs in state factories, and they could make fabulous private fortunes without cheating the throne. A typical example, Zaoyin, whose career was largely spent managing imperial factories, was a shy, modest man who pretended to read as he was carried in his litter to screen his eyes from the sight of the common people rising in respect as he passed. But he made a famous collection of rare art works and curiosities, "without speaking of silver, treated like mud," as his own nurse reported. "No matter what thing there is on earth, there it was piled up like mountains or the waters of the sea."

The sheer size of China's internal market guaranteed a dynamic economy (see Map 20.2). In about 1800, over 10 percent of grain production was for sale rather than eaten by the farmers who grew it, together with more than a quarter of the raw cotton produced throughout the empire, and over half the cotton cloth—amounting to 3 billion bolts of cloth a year. Nearly all the silk, tea, and salt in the empire likewise were sold on the market.

Foreign trade, against this background, was of relatively small importance to China. It was vital, however, for the economies of much of the rest of the world. In the foreign trading posts (called **factories**), of Guangzhou, the world clamored for admittance at China's barely open door. All the trade of Europeans and Americans in search of Chinese tea, silk, rhubarb, and porcelain was funneled through this narrow opening. A privileged group of Chinese merchants controlled the trade. China's favorable trade balance, moreover, continued to expand, thanks to the growth of the European tea market. Dutch tea purchases in Guangzhou rose from about 1.5 million guilders (in Dutch currency) in 1729–1733 to nearly 16.5 million in 1785–1791. By that time, the British had taken over as the main customers, transporting nearly 300 million pounds of tea in the 20 years after Britain reduced the tea tax in 1784.

The "barbarians," as the Chinese called the Europeans, still paid almost entirely in silver. Eventually, Western merchants found a commodity they could market in China. Opium was the only foreign product Western suppliers con-

Guangzhou. In 1800, Guangzhou harbor still carried more international trade than any other port in the world. European traders were not allowed anywhere else in the Chinese Empire. Their residential quarters and warehouses are the white buildings in the center foreground. A European merchant probably commissioned the painting as a souvenir of his stay in China.
Photograph courtesy Peabody Essex Museum.

MAP 20.2

China in the Late Eighteenth Century

Qing Empire, 1770

Great Wall

trolled that Chinese consumers wanted, or came to want, in large quantities. The poppies from which opium was derived were grown in northern India under British rule. As with the milder drug China exported in exchange—the tea that banished sleep or, at least, promoted wakefulness—supply seems to have led demand. When China first banned the opium trade, in 1729, imports were reckoned at 200 of what the Chinese called "chests" a year. Each "chest" contained about 170 pounds of opium. One thousand chests were recorded in 1767. In 1773, the British East India Company imposed a monopoly on the opium trade in India. By the early nineteenth century, 10,000 chests of opium were entering

China annually. This was a significant new element in global trade. Foreigners now had, for the first time in recorded history, a chance to narrow their habitual trade gap with China (see Chapter 25).

China's economic supremacy had lasted a long time, but it was vulnerable to erosion in three ways. First, foreign suppliers could exploit the opium market. Second, they could find substitutions for their imports from China—making their own porcelain and silk, growing their own rhubarb, finding alternative places, such as India and Sri Lanka, where they could plant tea. Finally, they could outstrip Chinese production by mechanizing their industries. All these changes would occur in the nineteenth century. In the long run, the last of these changes made the greatest difference. For China could not mechanize production. The empire was caught in what the historian Mark Elvin has called a "**high-level equilibrium trap.**" Industries that were meeting huge demands with traditional technologies had no scope to increase output. An economy with a vast pool of labor had no means or incentive to replace human muscle with machines.

Comparison with Britain illustrates the point. Starting from a low threshold, Britain could triple cotton-cloth production between the 1740s and 1770s. A similar rise in Chinese output would have glutted the world. The entire world supply of raw cotton would have been insufficient to meet it. In about the 1770s or 1780s, a single Chinese province imported yearly, on average, six times as much raw cotton as the whole of Britain. Cheap labor is good for industrialization, but cheap capital is better. In the teeming worlds of India and China, the cost of labor relative to that of capital may have been too low for industry's good. The trap was typified by the experience of a Chinese official in 1742 who proposed to save peasants in his charge four-fifths of their labor by installing expensive copper pumps at a wellhead. Aghast at the immobilization of so much hard wealth, the peasants continued to prefer to draw water by hand. China's unwillingness to mechanize is not surprising. The frustration some of us feel today at our continued dependence on the internal combustion engine and fossil fuels shows how the inertia of inferior technologies can arrest progress.

India

The Indian economy was even more vulnerable than China's to manipulation by foreign imperialism and competition from mechanizing systems. Yet Indian industries in the eighteenth century were scarcely less impressive than those of China. In Bengal, where it seemed to a British observer that "every man, woman, or child in every village was employed in making cloth," each major type of textile was the specialist product of a particular subcaste. A Dutch silk factory in Bengal, with 700 or 800 workers, was modeled less on European precedents than on the official textile factories the Mughals sponsored to supply the imperial wardrobe with fine cloth. Other kinds of economic specialization concentrated vast amounts of manpower and produced goods of outstanding quality and high value. Kurnool, a town of only 100,000 people on the Krishna River, is said to have had 30,000 to 60,000 iron ore workers. Until Benjamin Huntsman perfected the manu-

Dutch trading post. With its huge fluttering flag, formal grounds, spacious quarters, and splendid gates in the Mughal style, the Dutch trading post at Hoogly in northeast India looks like an outpost of empire. In fact, however, it represents how dependent European merchants of the seventeenth century were on the wealth of the East. The post opened for trade in 1635, so that the Dutch East India Company could acquire relatively cheap silk in India and exchange it at a handsome profit for silver in Japan.

India in the Eighteenth Century

● important city or trading center

facture of cast steel in the 1760s, "the finest steel" in Britain "was made by the Hindoos" in India and imported at £1,000 per ton (which was more than 40 times the annual wages of a skilled British worker). By the conventional economic standards of Europe, the Mughals' tax demands—exacting perhaps 50 percent of the gross product of the empire—might seem depressing to any developing industrial spirit. But high taxation created a huge administrative class with surplus spending power (see Chapter 21). Their demand may have stimulated the concentration of production. Mughal India was almost certainly the world's most productive state in terms of manufacture for export, despite the modest technical equipment with which its industries were generally supplied (see Map 20.3).

Against this background, India's industrial collapse is astonishing. The ancient drain of Westerners' silver into India, which had been going on since pre-Roman times (see Chapter 7), was reversed in Bengal by the 1770s, In 1807, John Crawfurd reported that "kite makers, falconers, astrologers, and snake-charmers" had replaced useful trades in Bengal. A French missionary claimed, "Europe is no longer dependent on India for anything, having learned to beat the Hindus on their own ground,

Chronology: Global Population and Economic Trends

ca. 1500	Population of Europe reaches 80 million
Eighteenth century	Urbanization increases in Europe and the Americas; most intense concentrations of industry found in East and South Asia
ca. 1750–1800	Indian industry goes into decline
	Population of China doubles; population of the Americas increases sixfold
1784–1814	British import 300 million pounds of tea from China
Late eighteenth century	Ottoman Empire loses control of its shipping industry
1794	Condorcet's *The Progress of the Human Mind* published
1796	Edward Jenner improves smallpox vaccine
1798	Malthus's *Essay on Population* published
ca. 1800	Population of Europe reaches 180 million

even in their most characteristic manufactures and industries, for which from time immemorial *we* were dependent on *them*. In fact the roles have been reversed and this revolution threatens to ruin India completely."

How did this collapse happen? Indian industry may have been caught, like China's, in an equilibrium trap. But it was more fragile in any case: less high powered, less technically advanced. The decline of Indian industry probably started with the decline of the Mughal Empire in the eighteenth century—skewered at its heart by Persian and Afghan invaders who sacked the capital, and shredded at its edges by usurping officials and rebellions. The impoverishment of the Mughal court deprived native industry of its best market. After Persian invaders looted the imperial treasury at Delhi in 1739, the nobles could no longer buy the products of Bengal. Then, with an exactness rare in history, India's industrial debacle coincided with one of the dramatic new developments of the next chapter of this book: the establishment of British rule or influence over most of India and, in particular, over its former industrial heartlands. Between the 1760s and the 1780s, in the early years of British rule in Bengal, silver imports into India virtually ceased. Instead, the British used tax revenues they extracted from the country to pay for the goods they exported to it. The British East India Company and its servants shamelessly exploited their monopoly by cutting prices to suppliers and acquiring allegedly low-quality Indian goods at confiscatory prices before reselling them to Indians and Europeans at enormous profits. Nor did the British neglect the opportunity to impose high prices for primary materials on Indian manufacturers. In 1767, for instance, the company's representative sold silk yarn to weavers at double the price he paid for it.

The rapidity of the transformation of India from an economic powerhouse to a declining economy surprised contemporaries. For the Irish statesman, Edmund Burke (1729–1797), it was one of the "stupendous revolutions that have happened in our age of wonders." The dual nature of India's predicament, political and commercial, decorates the ceiling of the East India Company's headquarters in London, where Britannia, enthroned, receives the riches of the East from an abject procession led by India.

The Ottoman Empire and Its Environs

As in India, some of the same inducements and problems affected the industrial development of the Ottoman Empire. Here, too, raw materials were abundant. The vitality of the luxury market impressed every European visitor. But the selectivity of Turkish talent for industry and the lack of technical inventiveness in important trades made the empire as vulnerable as India to European competition. According to a voyager in the Persian Gulf in the mid-eighteenth century, the expensive spending habits of local notables mainly benefited French importers. In the second half of the eighteenth century, the carrying trade of the Ottoman Empire passed entirely into foreign hands—mainly French, English, and Venetian. In 1775,

Making Connections | ECONOMIC TRENDS: CHINA, INDIA, AND THE OTTOMAN EMPIRE

REGION	TRANSFORMATIONS IN ECONOMIC ACTIVITY	POLITICAL/SOCIAL EFFECTS
China	increased scale of traditional crafts/industry; employment of thousands of urban workers; Westerners clamor for entry into dynamic market seeking tea, silk, porcelain via trading posts in South China; development of opium as viable commodity	increased supply = increased demand for opium, greater dependence of Chinese population; gradual decline of Chinese power after Westerners mechanize traditional industries (textiles, porcelain, etc.)
India	increased scale of textile industries spread throughout subcontinent; other economic specialization also booms (iron-ore mining, steel making, etc.); high taxation and large administrative class with surplus spending power	Britain's colonization of India, taxation, and confiscation of goods leads to decline of Indian power
Ottoman Empire	abundance of raw materials, limited industry leads to competitive disadvantage with Europe by late 18th century; lavish lifestyles of Ottoman elites benefit European importers of luxury goods; decline of Persian silk, Egyptian linen as trade goods	gradual encroachment of European powers; decline of sultan's power, and prestige

Tunisian shippers (Tunis in North Africa was nominally part of the Ottoman Empire) abandoned a heroic effort to compete with French shippers, whose home government supported them with tax breaks and naval protection. Persian silk, previously transmitted through Ottoman territory, and Egyptian linen disappeared from the export lists of the empire, as British, French, and Italian manufacturers produced cheaper alternatives. A critical observer of the Turks in 1807 admitted that "Europe certainly cannot surpass them in several of their manufactures"—essentially fine textiles—and that "in many of the inferior trades," Turkish workmen were equal to those of France. But he added that from laziness or lack of enterprise they "have not introduced or encouraged several useful arts of later invention."

THE WEST'S PRODUCTIVITY LEAP

The overall picture is clear. In the eighteenth-century world, economies in Western Europe were becoming more developed, catching up with, and, in some respects, surpassing the parts of Asia that had previously been enormously more productive. At first sight, **industrialization** in Europe looks like one of those great transformations of history that just happen beyond human control because of economic, demographic, and environmental forces—necessities that mother invention. No one in Europe thought about it until the process had already begun to unfold. Yet a conspicuously active and fruitful period in the history of Western science preceded and accompanied—though it did not cause—industrialization (see Chapter 18). Science and technical innovation were parallel results from growing curiosity about the real world and growing interest in tinkering with things to see how they work. It makes sense to look into the realm of ideas to try to find the origins of Europe's leap in production.

"Science and technical innovation were parallel results from growing curiosity about the real world and growing interest in tinkering with things to see how they work."

The moon. By the time Galileo published the results of his astronomical observations through a telescope in 1610, the instrument was famous throughout Europe, and a Jesuit missionary had even written a book about it in Chinese. The telescope revealed that the moon, formerly perceived as being a perfect sphere, was in fact ridged and pitted.

Demonstrations of the power of invisible forces in nature were domestic entertainments for rich people in eighteenth-century Europe. Intently, and with indifference to suffering, the scientist who dominates this painting of such a scene by Joseph Wright of Derby, in 1768, proves the vital necessity of air by depriving a bird of it. As the bird dies, a girl is revolted. Lovers carry on regardless. A father tries to explain science; a young man is enraptured by it.
Joseph Wright of Derby (1734–1797). "An Experiment on a Bird in the Air Pump." Oil on canvas. National Gallery, London, UK/The Bridgeman Art Library.

The Scientific Background

The scientific revolution that occurred in the West during the seventeenth and eighteenth centuries extended the reach of human knowledge to subjects that had formerly been too remote or too difficult to understand. Galileo Galilei (1564–1642) could see the moons of Jupiter through his telescope. Anton van Leeuwenhoek (1632–1723) saw microbes through his microscope. Marin Mersenne (1588–1648) measured the speed of sound. Robert Hooke (1635–1703) could sniff what he called "nitre-air" in the acrid smell of vapor from a lighted wick, before Antoine Lavoisier (1743–1794) proved the existence of oxygen by isolating it and setting it on fire. Isaac Newton (1642–1727) could wrest the rainbow from a shaft of light or feel the force that bound the cosmos in the weight of an apple (see Chapter 17). Luigi Galvani (1737–1798) could feel the thrill of electricity in his fingertips. Friedrich Mesmer (1734–1815) thought hypnotism was a kind of detectable animal magnetism. Through life-threatening demonstrations with kite and keys, Benjamin Franklin (1706–1790) claimed to show that lightning is a kind of electricity. Their triumphs made believable the cry of philosophers: "Nothing that we do not sense can be present to the mind!"

These discoveries accustomed Europeans to the idea that barely detectable forces can have enormous power, just as the strength of the body reposes in threadlike muscles. Nature was full of invisible powers that could replace human effort. The idea of harnessing natural energy arose unsurprisingly in the context of scientific thought. Steam, the first such power source in nature to be harnessed to replace muscles, was a fairly obvious case. You can see it and feel its heat, even though it takes imagination to believe that it can work machinery and make things move. But engineers in late eighteenth-century Britain used a discovery of "pure" science—atmospheric pressure, which is invisible and only an experiment can detect—to make steam power exploitable. Still, it is not enough to have a good idea. Conditions have to be right before good ideas get applied. The principles of the steam engine had been known in ancient Rome, and the science of the West had largely been anticipated in China. But, just as conditions in China restrained industrial output in the eighteenth century, conditions in parts of Europe promoted it. Population was rising fast enough to boost demand, without activating a high-level equilibrium trap. The global context favored economies that had privileged access to the Atlantic sea lanes of global commerce. And, within Europe, new energy sources were being explored and released. The most conspicuous case is Britain's, where, in the second half of the eighteenth century, industrial output exhibited the most dynamic increases of any economy in the world (see Map 20.4).

The British Example

Britain, in population terms, was puny compared with the industrial giants of Asia. Britain still had fewer than 9 million people in 1800. But this was a dramatic increase from the 5.3 million recorded in 1731. To make up for the lack of manpower, Britain had unrivaled resources of untapped energy just below the surface of its soil. Coal production throughout Western Europe rose dramatically in the

MAP 20.4

Industrial Britain, ca. 1800

⚒	iron works
⚓	shipbuilding
●	major urban growth
♉	pottery
X	cutlery
📖	woolens/cloth/cotton
📕	silk
▬	coalfields
═══	turnpike road network, 1750

Manchester 33   journey time from London, in hours

eighteenth century, but the biggest supplies, of the best quality, were in Britain. In the late seventeenth century, the annual output of British coal miners was less than 3 million tons. By 1800, it had reached almost 14 million tons. Part of the increase was due to steam pumps, which enabled miners to dig deeper, below the water table, into shafts that could be drained. In turn, the pumps got people thinking about wider applications of steam-driven technology.

Britain, moreover, was an outstanding example of success in exploiting a position on the Atlantic. Britain tightly controlled the economies of its colonies in and across the Atlantic, so that their trade enriched British shippers and suppliers. British-ruled Ireland's agricultural surplus helped feed England and Scotland. Some of the profits of the slave economy of the West Indies went into agricultural improvement in Britain or investment in the infrastructure of roads, canals, and docks. The same shippers handled slave transfers and raw cotton imports, and exported the produce of the first major industrialized sector of the economy: cotton textile manufacture. By the 1770s, the Atlantic world of Africa and the Americas absorbed more of Britain's exports than Europe or Asia did and almost the entire export output of the British cotton and iron industries. The merchant marine tripled to nearly 700,000 tons by 1776. Investment in infrastructure transformed the road network and stagecoach services. During the century, the time it took to get to London from Scotland was cut from 256 to 60 hours, and the journey from London to the city of Manchester fell by about 75 percent to 33 hours (see Map 20.4).

The cumulative effect of all these changes was a sharp increase in Britain's national product in the 1780s. For the rest of the century, annual output grew at 1.8 percent compared with 1 percent previously. Pig-iron production doubled and then doubled again. Exports, which had more than doubled in the first three-quarters of the century to over £14 million in value, reached £22 million by the century's end.

It would be an exaggeration, however, to speak—as historians used to do—of an eighteenth-century Industrial Revolution. In most industries, development was piecemeal, and methods remained traditional. Huge gains in productivity resulted simply by supplying traditional methods with more manpower and more capital investment to meet rising demand. In England, between 1785 and 1800, beer production rose by about a third, as did that of tallow candles. Soap manufacture rose by over 40 percent in the same period. Overwhelmingly, these industries grew without significant mechanization, and the spectacular growth of London provided their market. In the same period, sales of imported commodities, which required little processing, grew comparably or even more impressively. Tobacco sales increased by over half. Tea sales more than doubled.

The great exceptions—where transformed methods did boost production—were the textile and iron industries. Improved smelting techniques using coke, made from coal, drove changes in how the iron and steel trades were organized. By eliminating charcoal smelting and producing iron goods to replace wooden ones, these techniques doubly relieved pressure on failing timber resources. Output of iron rose from 17,350 tons in 1740 to over 125,000 tons in 1796. The first iron bridge spanned the River Severn in 1779. The first iron ship sailed in 1787. In 1767, Richard Arkwright patented a machine that enabled a single operative to spin 16 threads of yarn at once. In 1769, he adapted it to be powered by a water mill, turning—with improvements achieved over the next few years—100 spindles at a time. In 1779, Edmund Crompton found a way to use water or steam to power a machine to weave the yarn into cloth. In consequence, the cost of processing 100 pounds of raw cotton into cloth was cut by more than half in 20 years. The first steam-powered textile mill opened in 1785. Raw cotton imports, which amounted to under 3 million pounds weight in 1750, reached nearly 60 million pounds in 1800. A new way of working evolved in mechanized factories, with huge concentrations of workers, a pattern that would revolutionize the societies it affected in the next century.

Historians have always wondered and often asked whether there was anything special about British values or mind-sets or "spirit" that might help to explain why Britons took up the opportunities of the age with so much enthusiasm and effectiveness. Commercial values may have occupied a relatively high priority in British culture. Certainly, people thought so at the time. Napoleon—who developed intense hatred for Britain after he became ruler of France in 1799—sneered at "a nation of shopkeepers," but Britons accepted the sneer with pride. Early in the eighteenth century, the English novelist Daniel Defoe exulted in the incalculably huge number of British tradesmen. You may as well, he said, "count the stars in the sky." The agricultural writer Arthur Young (1741–1820) jokingly advised his sons to "get children" because "they are worth more than ever they were."

There was a serious theory behind Young's joke. The British economist David Ricardo (1772–1823) recognized a principle of economics—that labor adds value to a product. He went further. Value, he argued, is

The first iron bridge. The Iron Bridge spanning the River Severn at Coalbrookdale in England was the world's first cast-iron bridge. Completed in 1770, it has come to be regarded as a symbol of the beginning of the Industrial Revolution. The Iron Bridge is also one of the last of its type to have survived intact. It was erected in just three months using sections made in a local foundry.

proportional to the labor invested in it, "labor . . . being the foundation of all value, and the relative quantity of labor . . . almost exclusively determining the relative value of commodities." In its crude form, the theory is wrong. Goods are not always exchanged at values proportionate to the labor invested in them. Capital plays a part (and is not always just stored-up labor, since raw natural assets can be sold for cash). So does the way the goods are perceived. Rarity value—which Ricardo did recognize, citing objects of art and "wines of a peculiar quality"—is the most obvious example. Advertising and recommendation can also add value. Still, the principle is right. Ricardo drew from it a counterintuitive conclusion. If labor makes the biggest contribution to profits, one would expect high wages to reflect this (as generally, in modern industrial societies, they do). Ricardo, however, thought that to maximize profits, capitalists would always keep wages low. "There can be no rise in the value of labor without a fall in profits." In fact, wages were static in England and rose a little in Scotland. Industrialization did not drive wages down, because the growth of population and of trade continually drove demand upward.

In broad context, however, Britain's eighteenth-century experience seems more characteristic than extraordinary—just a more pronounced case of an effort to maximize the use of resources that was happening all over Western and northern Europe. By the time the French Revolution began in 1789, for instance, similar, if smaller, industrial complexes were emerging in France, Belgium, eastern Germany, and northern Spain. This effort was most widely generalized in the case of land—universally recognized, along with labor, as the most basic resource of all. In Britain, landholdings were considerably consolidated during the eighteenth century, with important consequences for efficiency. By 1790, over a quarter of the land in England was concentrated in estates of over 3,000 acres. In much of the highland zone of Scotland, landlords expelled or exterminated smallholders to make way for large sheep-grazing estates. Over most of the country, landowners adopted a common program: reducing labor costs, replacing inefficient grain farming with grazing, improving soils by draining and fertilizing, enhancing livestock by scientific stockbreeding, diversifying crops to maximize use of the earth, and, perhaps most importantly, by "enclosing" land—fencing off underexploited land that had been open to anyone in the community for their own use. French agriculturalists who called themselves "physiocrats" recommended ways to improve agriculture to enrich France. Agricultural improvement societies promoted English-style changes in Spain and Spanish America. Similar approaches spread over much of Europe, as far east as Poland and as far south as northern Italy.

These European changes had parallels in East Asia beyond the reach of the equilibrium trap. In Korea and Japan, many works of popular agricultural advice were published to satisfy a passionate market for agricultural improvement. In Korea, farmers began to sow barley after the rice harvest to boost grain production. As in England, small landholdings were consolidated into huge farms for cash crops: ginseng, tobacco, and cotton. A measure of the Korean economic boom was the 1,000 new markets that sprang up in the first half of the eighteenth century. In Japan, too, agriculture

Agricultural improver. Thomas Coke of Norfolk (1752–1842), shown on the left, was an exemplary British agricultural improver, whose work with sheep was particularly influential. He boosted his flock from 800 to 2,500 without increasing the amount of grazing land the sheep needed, thanks in part to the scientific improvement he made in the South Down breed, depicted here, which produced highly prized mutton.

became commercialized, as peasant subsistence agriculture virtually disappeared. Cotton cultivation spread from Osaka almost throughout the country. Osaka also lost its monopoly of oil lamp and soy sauce production, and Kyoto its dominance over silk output. The new crops that ecological exchange made available also played their part. In 1732, for instance, a locust plague in Kyushu destroyed the grain, but people had sweet potatoes to fall back on. Famines still occurred, but now local communities could afford social-welfare schemes to mitigate their effects. Landowners paid a wealth tax to supply emergency rice stocks, make loans to new businesses, and support the elderly. The leveling off of Japanese population trends looks like a classic case of prosperity having a restraining effect on birthrates. In Okayama, over the century as a whole, the average size of a household declined from seven persons to five.

THE EXPANSION OF RESOURCES

The effort to coax more food from the soil was only one aspect of a worldwide search for new food resources—a search in which Western Europeans occupied a privileged place.

Global Gardening

In the late eighteenth century, the botanical garden of Madrid in Spain was the nursery of a uniquely widespread empire. In the half-century after its foundation in 1756, it was one of the grand ornaments of European science, forming the last link in a chain of such gardens in Manila in the Philippines, in Lima in Peru, in Mexico City, and in the Canary Islands off the coast of Africa. At least in theory, samples of the plant life of every climate the Spanish monarchy occupied could be centralized in a single place of research. From Peru, for instance, in 1783, came 1,000 colored drawings and 1,500 written descriptions of plants. Perhaps the most important collections were those of Hipólito Pavón, whose expedition to Chile and Peru in 1777–1788 allowed him to indulge his personal passion—the study of the healing properties of plants—and to produce the most complete study of quinine yet attempted. Another prolific contributor was José Celestino Mutis, who presided over scientific life in one of the heroic outposts of the Spanish Empire at Bogotá, in what is today Colombia, from 1760 until his death in 1808.

The Botanical Garden of Madrid. By establishing a series of botanical gardens on both sides of the Atlantic, the Spanish monarchs in the eighteenth century promoted the transplantation of scientifically interesting or useful plants—including species good for health or nutrition—between continents. Today, the Botanical Garden of Madrid is little more than a park, but it retains reminders of its original functions, including the eighteenth-century plant house in the background of this photograph and the bust of the great Swedish botanist, Carolus Linnaeus (1707–1778), in the foreground.

At their best, empires could gather useful specimens from an astonishing diversity of climes and make their flowers bloom together in scientific proximity. The Botanical Garden in Paris performed a comparable role. The French Jesuit missionary, Pierre Nicolas le Chéron d'Incarville, sent rare Chinese and Japanese plants there with Russian caravans across Asia. In England, the Royal Botanical Gardens at Kew, London, and the garden of the University of Oxford had similar functions, as, in the Netherlands, did the town gardens of Amsterdam and Utrecht and the University Garden of Leiden.

The plants of the world could gather in Europe and be redistributed around European empires, because only these empires were scattered widely enough around the globe, and had the environmental range, to exploit the opportunities to the full. European empires became laboratories of ecological exchange. Pierre Poivre, for instance, launched one of the most breathtaking experiments in France's Indian Ocean island colonies in 1747. Until he transformed them, the islands were economically unsuccessful—diminishing assets, wasted by deforestation and repeated attempts to introduce plantation monocultures. Poivre trained to be a Jesuit but, too young for ordination, filled in his time by traveling widely in Asia to study natural history. He smuggled 3,000 valuable spice plants out of Southeast Asia and planted them in the island of Mauritius off the east coast of Africa, where they eventually became the basis of a commercially successful operation in cloves, cinnamon, and pepper. When he became governor of France's Indian Ocean colonies 20 years after his first introductions, he combined the policy of diversifying crops with a strategy to restore the islands' forests to maintain rainfall levels.

Similar transplantations occurred to and fro, as the ecological exchange became more systematic and planned. Coffee is a case in point. Southern Arabia had long enjoyed a world monopoly of coffee. But in 1707, the Dutch introduced it into Java, the main island of what is today Indonesia, as part of a system of political control in which local rulers guaranteed to deliver it at prices that exploited producers, who had to be forced to grow it. Coffee was one of the most commercially successful products of the eighteenth century. The French planted it in the island of Bourbon (modern Réunion) in the Indian Ocean and in Saint-Domingue (modern Haiti) in the Caribbean, and the Portuguese in Brazil (see Chapter 17). By mid-century, the Arabian coffee trade had ceased to grow, and the British East India Company no longer sent regular ships there (see Map 20.5). Since almost all coffee drinkers of the era took their cups heavily sweetened, the sugar and coffee trades grew together, and sugar, of course, had wider applications. The expansion of sugar lands in the seventeenth-century Atlantic was followed, in the eighteenth century, by a similar expansion around the Indian Ocean. By 1800, sugar had probably replaced pepper as Southeast Asia's major export.

Even places too isolated for the global ecological exchange to affect could achieve high levels of productivity. Hawaii is a case in point, since it remained outside the range of European navigation until 1778. The earliest European accounts of Hawaii were full of praise for the native farmers. Expeditions from the late 1770s to the 1790s recorded fields outlined with irrigation ditches and stone walls, "made with a neatness approaching to elegance," planted with taro, breadfruit, sweet potato, sugarcane, and coconut, and laid out in a pattern calculated to impress readers at home as civilized. The roads "would have done credit to any European engineer." An engraving made on the basis of reports from the expedition of the British navigator, George Vancouver, early in the 1790s shows a field system of a regularity that arouses one's suspicions that it was made up to present a picture attuned to European ideals. Yet the same array of farmers' geometry is visible today, under the surface of fields no longer tilled, in the noon sunlight on the slopes of Hualalai and the Kohala Mountains on the Big Island of Hawaii. Only in Hawaii, moreover, among Polynesian settlements, was fish farming fully developed. Into the grid of fields and pools, other constructions were slotted. Massive platforms of stone supported temples of exact symmetry, and the wall-building techniques were adaptable to the demands of fortifications two or three times the height of a man. Early European visitors could recognize not only institutions of statehood but also an islandwide empire in the making—a process completed in 1795, when the first king, Kamehameha I, defeated the last of his enemies and extended his rule over all the Hawaiian islands.

Mauritius in 1835. In the eighteenth century, French administrators introduced forest conservation to the Indian Ocean island and banned colonists there from growing what were thought to be ecologically unsuitable crops, such as cotton and wheat. The map shows the surviving forests in the center and the lower left.

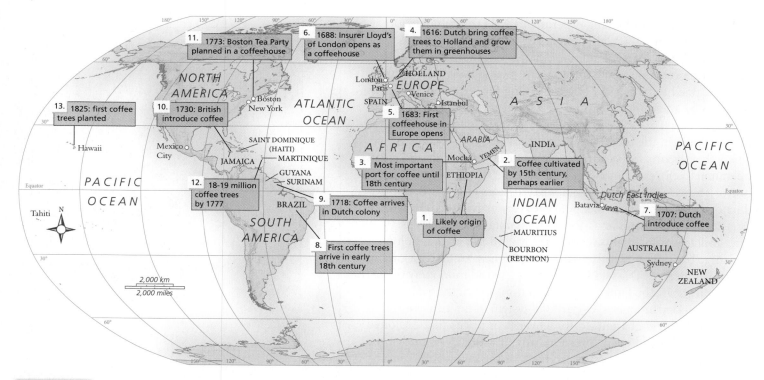

MAP 20.5

The Spread of Coffee Worldwide

The Pacific generally was a latecomer to the great ocean-borne exchange of foodstuffs. In 1774, a Spanish expedition tried to annex Tahiti. It failed, but left Spanish hogs behind, which first improved, then replaced, the native breed of pigs. By 1788, the small, long-legged, long-snouted native pigs had disappeared. In consequence, Tahiti had an advantage in the pork trade that soon transformed the Pacific as a result of two developments. First, Captain James Cook (1728–1779) perfected a method to keep salt pork edible after a long sea voyage. Second, Australia became a British colony. In 1792, George Vancouver shipped 80 live pigs from Tahiti to Sydney in Australia to create a food source for the colonists. But it proved more economical for Australia to import pork ready salted from Tahiti than to breed its own pigs. In the first year of the trade, 1802–1803, merchants in Sydney—Australia's first middle class—handled 300,000 pounds of the meat. By the time the trade waned in the late 1820s, ten times that amount had changed hands. The muskets that paid for the pork stimulated civil war and turned Tahiti into a monarchy.

The breadfruit was an eye-catching part of the abundance that made the South Sea islands wonderful to eighteenth-century European sailors: places of restoration that supplied the long-felt wants of seaboard life. Along with the sexual license of Tahitian life, on an island where "the only god is love," ample fresh food helped to make the South Seas seem "certainly the paradise of the world," according to a British visitor in 1787. In the lingo of modern economists, this was a world of "subsistence affluence," where there was little specialization in food production and limited trade in food products, but where, in normal times, abundance was spectacular.

In most islands, yams, taro, and plantains contributed most to the basic diet, but when in season, breadfruit was the making of every feast, the starchy complement to the festive meats: pigs, turtles, dogs, chicken, fish, and some prestigious larvae, such as the grubs of the longhorn beetle, which infests coconuts. The most widely favored way to prepare breadfruit was to bake it whole in hot embers or in pits with hot stones. It was also eaten in fish stews, cooked in coconut milk. Because it is a seasonal product, and—unlike taro—rots if not harvested when it is ripe, it was also dried, fermented, and smoked. It helped to communicate an illusion of nutritional richness and became a fixture in Europeans' mental picture of the South Sea–island Eden in the eighteenth century.

The "inestimable benefit" of this "new fruit" was among the prizes that lured the French explorer, the Count de La Pérouse, to his death in the South Pacific in 1788. The same search inspired the voyage that ended with events Hollywood turned into the most famous episode of eighteenth-century naval history: the mutiny on the *Bounty*. Captain William Bligh's mission as commander of the British warship *Bounty* in 1787 was to pluck a bit of the paradise of the South Pacific in the form of breadfruit tree seedlings and transfer it to the slave hell of the Caribbean. On Jamaica, Bryan Edwards, a planter who was always on the lookout for ways to improve the slave economy, believed that breadfruit could energize slaves and turn his island into a hive of industry. So the British government sent Bligh to Tahiti.

William Hodges' vision of Tahiti, remembered from his experiences as resident artist with Captain Cook's expedition of 1772: "a voluptuaries' paradise . . . a habitat for nymphs."

Bligh brought his single-minded, demonic energy to the task. In the South Pacific, most of his men mutinied. The captain and the loyal survivors were cast adrift in midocean and saved, after terrible deprivations, only by Bligh's startling ability as a navigator. Meanwhile, some of the mutineers lived in self-condemned exile with their Tahitian women on Pitcairn, an uncharted island where predictable quarrels led to feuding in which most of them were killed. The Royal Navy hunted down and executed others. After six years' bloodshed and hardship and with a new ship, Bligh completed his mission. But there was an ironic twist—the breadfruit experiment proved disastrous. Breadfruit is not a particularly useful food. It has few nutrients. It does not keep well. The slaves would not eat it.

Other food transfers were more successful. Captain James Cook, the explorer who was responsible for so many more famous initiatives in Pacific history, was also the prophet of pigs and potatoes in New Zealand. The Dutch had discovered New Zealand in 1642, but it was then forgotten. Cook rediscovered the islands in 1769. The native inhabitants of New Zealand, the Maori, who preferred their own food, resisted his first efforts to introduce new foodstuffs (see Chapter 14). "All our endeavours for stocking this country with useful animals are likely to be frustrated by the very people we mean to serve." But Maori in the north of New Zealand were trading potatoes by 1801, and pigs became a trading item by about 1815. Other attempted introductions, such as goats, garlic, cattle, and cabbage, failed because they did not fit into traditional Maori ways of farming. Cook's shipboard scientist, Johann Reinhold Forster, suffered for his efforts to introduce sheep and goats to the islands, especially from the smell their manure produced when they were stabled in the cabin next to his to protect them from the weather. Potatoes, however, proved popular in New Zealand because they were sufficiently like the kumara or sweet potatoes that had long been familiar to the Maori, who also welcomed Europe's pigs, which could be grazed and eaten.

The same expedition succeeded in a series of other introductions. Forster reported:

> We have imported goats into Tahiti and laid the foundations of a numerous breed of animals most excellently calculated for the hills occupying the inland parts of this isle . . . and in all the isles we made presents of garden seeds and planted potatoes in Queen Charlotte's Sound with a good quantity of garlic: so that future navigators may be refreshed in these seas more than they would expect.

"The breadfruit was an eye-catching part of the abundance that made the South Sea islands wonderful to eighteenth-century European sailors: places of restoration that supplied the long-felt wants of seaboard life."

Sydney. Crowned by brushland, with natives in canoes in the foreground, this is what the harbor of Sydney, Australia looked like soon after the colony of New South Wales was founded in 1788. The governor's house is high on the hillside to the left, and fields are taking shape around the cove.

New Zealand was an outstanding example of what Alfred Crosby called **Neo-Europes** (New Europes): lands in other hemispheres where the environment sufficiently resembled Europe's for European migrants to thrive, European plants to take root, and a European way of life to be transplanted. Even with help from the climate, however, it was not easy to catch reflections of home in such distant mirrors. The strenuous efforts the British had to apply to adapt in the Australian colony of New South Wales are vividly documented. Take, for instance, the case of James Ruse. He was a pardoned convict who had been a farmer in England. In 1789, he received a grant of 30 acres at Parramatta in Australia. The "middling soil," it seemed to him, was bound to fail for want of manure. He burned timber, dug in ash, hoed, clod molded the earth, dug in grass and weeds, and left the soil exposed to sun for sowing. He planted turnip seed "which will mellow and prepare it for next year" and mulched it with his own compost, made from straw rotted in pits. He and his wife did all the work themselves.

Success with such untried soils depended on experimentation with varied planting strategies. Early Australia was a strange sort of New Europe at first—made with yams, pumpkins, and maize. On the warm coastal lowlands where the first settlers set up, maize did better than the rye, barley, and wheat that the founding fleet shipped from England in 1788. Firs and oaks were planted, but the food trees were more exotic: oranges, lemons, and limes grew alongside indigo, coffee, ginger, and castor nut. On the outward voyage, the fleet acquired tropical specimens, including bananas, cocoa, guava, sugarcane, and tamarind. In 1802, visitors could admire "the bamboo of Asia" in the governor's garden in Melbourne, the capital of New South Wales. The most successful early livestock were introduced from Calcutta in India and the Cape of Good Hope in South Africa, which also supplied fruit trees.

In the long run, a European model did prevail, but it was primarily a Mediterranean one. Sir Joseph Banks, the British botanist who equipped the founding expedition, believed that over most of its extent the Southern Hemisphere was about 10 degrees cooler at any given latitude than the Northern. He therefore expected Botany Bay in southern Australia to resemble southwest France and sent over citrus fruits, pomegranates, apricots, nectarines, and peaches. "All the vegetables of Europe" fed the colonists in the 1790s, but Mediterranean colors predominated in visitors' descriptions. The first governor had oranges in his garden, "as many fine figs as ever I tasted in Spain or Portugal," and "a thousand vines yielding three hundredweight of grapes." Watkin Tench, whose study of the soils was vital to the colony's success—his samples can still be seen, dried to powder, in a Sydney museum—commended the performance of grape "vines of every sort. . . . That their juice will probably hereafter furnish an indispensable article of luxury at European tables has already been predicted in the vehemence of speculation." He also spotted the potential of oranges, lemons, and figs. By the time of a French visit in 1802, peaches were so plentiful that they were used to fatten the hogs. The French commander saw, in the governor's garden, "the Portugal orange and the Canary fig ripening beneath the shade of the French apple tree." The Mediterranean world also provided Australia with an exportable staple—wool. The first consignment of merino sheep, a Spanish breed, left for New South Wales in 1804. Only five rams and one old ewe survived the journey, but these were enough to begin the stocking of the country, which today has more sheep than people.

This Australian experience set the pattern for the colonial New Europes of the nineteenth century, where "the roots are European but the tree grows to a different pattern and design." The North American West, New Zealand, and to a lesser extent, the "cone" of South America—Uruguay, Argentina, and Chile—were all settled, displacing the native cultures with dynamic, outward-going, and relatively populous economies. All defied their original planners and developed their own distinctive characters—tricks that the alchemy of settlement worked in the crucible of new environments.

Transplanting breadfruit. Thomas Gosse, the official artist of the British expedition that took breadfruit from Tahiti to Jamaica in the 1790s, gave pride of place to the Tahitians in the pictures he painted of the voyage. He depicted the British in a marginal, subordinate, and passive role. The breadfruit was supposed to provide cheap food for Jamaica's slaves, but the slaves rejected it.

Making Connections | EXPANDING RESOURCES IN THE EIGHTEENTH CENTURY

TYPE OF FOOD RESOURCE	METHODS OF SPREADING	RESULTS
Botanical Garden of Spain, Madrid and similar gardens throughout Spanish empire (Peru, Mexico, Canary Islands, Manila); Botanical gardens in Paris, London, Netherlands	via naval expeditions of exploration, trading expeditions	cultivation of exotic plants previously confined to specific areas (spices in Indonesia, for example) now able to be dispersed to colonized regions for economic gain
Coffee	Dutch introduction to Java; French introduction to Indian ocean and Caribbean colonies; Portuguese to Brazil	growth of worldwide coffee industry via systematic planning, growth of supply
Pork	new forms of salting, preserving pork leads to introduction of pigs on Pacific islands to provision European ships	Pacific islands become increasingly important as strategic stops for provisions
Potatoes	spread to New Zealand, other Pacific islands by James Cook and other explorers	successful introduction because of similarity to native sweet potato (kumara)
Maize, yams, wheat, oranges, lemons, limes	spread to New Zealand, Australia by James Cook and early settlers	creation of "new Europes" with crops, climate similar to Europe, but also able to grow citrus, coffee, indigo near coasts and in sub-tropical areas

In Perspective
New Europes, New Departures

"There was never," observed Samuel Johnson (1709–1784), the English man of letters, contemplating his own era, "from the earliest ages a time in which trade so engaged the attention of mankind, or commercial gain was sought with such general emulation." The world was encircled by a cycle that was speeding up: growing population, growing demand, growing output, growing commerce, all stimulated by each other. The big gainers were economies that bordered the Atlantic, where traders and shippers could participate in the increasing opportunities worldwide. For the Atlantic led to the wind systems of the world and, by relatively easy access, to exploitable empires.

Overseas colonies were an unmixed blessing for the states that founded them. Colonies demanded heavy investment and paid modest returns. They drained manpower from home countries without always adding much to long-term demand. On the contrary, colonies tended to develop regional economies, "creole mentalities," and—as we shall see in the next chapter—independence movements. The biggest, most precocious, and, in terms of cash yield, richest of the empires—that of Spain—never stimulated much of a commercial or industrial revolution in Spain itself. Yet gradually, in less obvious ways, overseas imperialism did contribute to European world dominance.

The New Europes made the West big. A culture crammed, for most of its history, into a small, remote, and beleaguered corner of Eurasia, now had much of the Western Hemisphere and important parts of the Pacific and Africa at its disposal. Even without the technical and scientific advantages the West was beginning to build up, the growing resources available to Western economies were enough to change the world.

Silver was of special importance among the products for which Europeans exploited the New World, because the critical shortage from which Westerners had suffered, in their efforts to penetrate Asian markets, had always been a shortage of cash. But the new plants of American origin that crossed the world and enhanced the productivity of other regions grew in importance. So did the sheer extent of exploitable terrain the Americas added to the resources of European empires, once they solved their labor problems by enslaving millions of Africans. The plantations and ranchlands of the Americas helped the West to even up the traditional imbalance of global resources that had formerly favored Asian economies.

Chronology

ca. 1500	Population of Europe reaches 80 million
Seventeenth and eighteenth centuries	Scientific revolution in the West
ca. 1700	Population of Europe reaches 120 million
Eighteenth century	Urbanization increases in Europe and the Americas; concentration of landholdings in Britain; most intense concentrations of industry found in East and South Asia; economic boom in Korea and Japan
1721–1804	Population of Japan stabilizes
ca. 1750–1800	Indian industry goes into decline
1750–1850	Population of China doubles; population of the Americas increases sixfold
1756	Botanical Garden of Madrid founded
1769	Captain James Cook rediscovers New Zealand
1760–1808	José Celestino Mutis leads scientific study in Colombia
1770s	The Atlantic world absorbs more British exports than Europe or Asia
1777–1788	Hipólito Pavón's expedition to Chile and Peru
1780s	Sharp increase in Britain's national product
1784–1814	British import 300 million pounds of tea from China
1787	*Bounty* begins journey to South Pacific
Late eighteenth century	Ottoman Empire loses control of its shipping industry
1794	Condorcet's *The Progress of the Human Mind* published
1796	Edward Jenner improves smallpox vaccine
1798	Malthus's *Essay on Population* published
ca. 1800	British coal production reaches 14 million tons; population of Europe reaches 180 million; 10,000 "chests" of opium imported into China annually
1805	Merino sheep introduced to Australia

China and Japan were also big gainers from the economic and demographic changes of the eighteenth century. But a future in which the West would be increasingly dominant was already visible. In the late eighteenth and early nineteenth centuries, the industrialization of Britain would keep rough pace with the deindustrialization of India at British bayonet point. Domination of India acquired even greater significance in the nineteenth century when the British turned Indian land over to the production of tea and opium, which destroyed China's trade balance, and ultimately to the farming of quinine in industrial quantities, which enabled European armies to treat malaria, one of the most deadly hazards of tropical environments. Meanwhile, other eighteenth-century developments, which are the subjects of the next two chapters, contributed to reshaping world history: the growth, strain, instability, and—in some cases—collapse of land empires, and the increasing exchange of ideas between parts of Asia and the West.

"The world was encircled by a cycle that was speeding up: growing population, growing demand, growing output, growing commerce, all stimulated by each other."

PROBLEMS AND PARALLELS

1. Why is the population increase of the eighteenth century central to understanding the history of this period? What are the various explanations for the demographic growth of the eighteenth century? How did increased urbanization affect the demographic trends of this period?
2. How did global economic patterns change during the eighteenth century? Why did the disparity in productivity and wealth between China and India and the West begin to narrow? Why did Ottoman economic activity decline?
3. How did the demographic changes and the speeding up of economic activity affect the global balance of power? Why did Europe's productivity leap in the eighteenth century? How did science contribute to European technical innovation in this period?
4. How did "global gardeners" like Pierre Poivre and Captain James Cook affect the economies and societies of islands in the Indian Ocean and the Pacific? What does the term *New Europes* mean? How did European plants and animals transform Australia?
5. What are the social, economic, and political reasons for the rise of Britain as a world power in the eighteenth century? What factors led to its military and economic strength?

READ ON ▶ ▶ ▶

On the great eighteenth-century thinkers about population, see J. Avery, *Progress, Poverty and Population: Re-Reading Condorcet, Godwin and Malthus* (1997). Robert Duplessis, *Transitions to Capitalism in Early Modern Europe* (1997) contains much nuanced information on European demographics and is a good overview of the run-up to industrialization, distinguishing Britain from the Continent. Margaret Jacob, *Scientific Culture and the Making of the Industrial West* (1997) shows the cultural conduits through which Newtonian mechanics influenced technological progress. See also Joel Mokyr, *The Lever of Riches: Technological Creativity and Economic Progress* (1990), which is perhaps overly optimistic.

On China during the eighteenth century, Pamela Crossley, *The Manchus* (1997) is useful, as is Joanna Waley-Cohen, "China and Western Technology in the Late Eighteenth Century," *American Historical Review* (1993). But now fundamental are Kenneth Pomeranz, *The Great Divergence: China, Europe, and the Making of the Modern World Economy* (2001) and Andre Gunder-Frank, *ReORIENT: Global Economy in the Asian Age*. For a contrasting view, see David Landes, *The Wealth and Poverty of Nations* (1998). Huri Islamoglu-Inan, *The Ottoman Empire and the World Economy* (1987), puts the Ottoman economy in perspective. Seema Alavi, ed., *The Eighteenth Century in India* (2002) collects the most significant work on the Indian economy and the impact of British commercial and political interventions.

Richard Grove, *Green Imperialism: Colonial Expansion, Tropical Island Edens and the Origins of Environmentalism, 1600–1860* (1996) is excellent for the development of resources. *The Journals of Hipólito Ruiz: Spanish Botanist in Peru and Chile, 1777–1788*, trans. Richard Schulte et al. (1998) provides a fascinating first-hand account. Ernest Dodge, *Islands and Empires: Western Impact on the Pacific and East Asia* (1976) is useful, while Alfred Crosby, *Ecological Imperialism: The Biological Expansion of Europe, 900–1900* (1993) is a classic.

CHAPTER 21

The Age of Global Interaction: Expansion and Intersection of Eighteenth-Century Empires

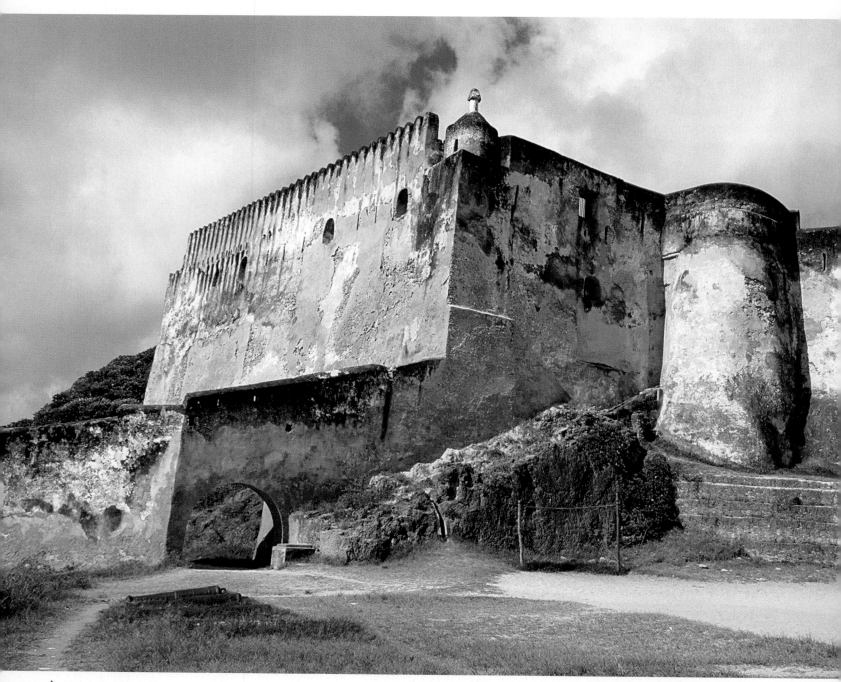

▲ **Fort Jesus, Mombasa,** in what is today Kenya, was one of a string of forts the Portuguese founded around the rim of the Indian Ocean. It fell to Omani attackers in 1698—one episode in Portugal's long retreat from most of its eastern outposts in the face of hostility or competition from non-European empires.

In September 1697, after 18 months of siege, all the 2,500 defenders were dead, except a few Swahili mercenaries under a local sheikh known as Bwana Daud. Fort Jesus, at Mombasa, on the east coast of Africa, in what is now Kenya, was the principal Portuguese station at the western end of the monsoon wind system of the Indian Ocean. It looked as if it was bound to fall to new rivals for the creation of a seaborne empire: the Sayid (SEYE-yihd) dynasty of Oman, in southeast Arabia.

MOMBASA

"Loyalty counted more with me than ambition or maternal love," wrote Daud later to the king of Portugal. By heroic efforts, he held out until a relief force of 200 men arrived. But the Omanis did not give up, and by December 1698, the situation was again desperate. Only 10 defenders survived. They retreated into the innermost bastion of the fort and resolved to die fighting. A few hours after the last of them was cut down, a relief force from the Portuguese colony of Goa in India appeared offshore. They saw the red flag of Oman fluttering over the ramparts, turned around, and headed for home. Over the next three decades, despite periodic reversals, Sayid imperialism mopped up all the Portuguese stations on the Swahili coast of East Africa.

It was part of a deliberate Omani strategy to control westward trade along the old monsoonal routes. Oman was an unusual kind of state. It created an unusual kind of empire. The Omani brand of Islam was neither Sunni nor Shi'a, but maintained that the true heir of the Prophet Muhammad was whoever was the best qualified to lead the people: the **imam**, as the Omanis called him. In practice, the Sayids had established a hereditary monarchy, but they remained formally committed to the idea of the imamate. This religious principle ensured that their people rejected the ideologies of neighboring empires: the Sunni Ottomans, Shiite Persia, and the Christian Portuguese.

On the coast of East Africa, peaceful colonization by Omani merchant families had preceded armed intervention. Independent city-states had dotted the region and the islands offshore since at least the twelfth century when local rulers began to mint the earliest coins so far discovered in this region. These states had a common economic culture—commercial and maritime—a common religion in Islam, and a common language, Swahili. In grammar, Swahili was like the Bantu languages that neighboring inland peoples spoke, but influences from the sea, especially Arabic, increasingly saturated its vocabulary. Portuguese incursions in the sixteenth century had disrupted the trade of all but a handful of East African ports—Mombasa was one of the exceptions—but merchants from Arabia and, to a lesser extent, India never stopped trading in the area.

Omanis established garrisons at Mombasa, Kilwa, Zanzibar, and Pemba. At first, the imam directly appointed governors from Oman. For the native East Africans, the Omanis were as foreign as the Portuguese. Resentment and rebellions among the Swahili followed. At home in Oman, splits in the political elite were common, as some of the Sayids' subjects felt that the

FOCUS questions

Why did China rely more on colonization than on conquest to expand its empire in the eighteenth century?

What internal problems and foreign foes did the Ottoman Empire face in the eighteenth century?

How did Britain become the dominant power in India?

Why was the slave trade so important for the economies of West Africa, Europe, and the Americas?

Why did new Native American and African empires begin to arise during the eighteenth century?

Why did the British and Spanish colonies in the New World come to resent imperial control from Europe?

dominance of one dynasty betrayed the spirit of the imamate. Oman could not fully exploit commercial opportunities, because it never had enough shipping to handle all the African ivory and Indian cloth that crossed the ocean, though Omanis did dominate the large East African slave trade. Political control was weak. The Omani Empire became a loose network of autonomous small states, tied by a sense of kinship among Sayid clan members, like the regional branches or offshoots of a family business.

Beyond the reach of Omani naval power, even more informal networks spread, as Omani migrants crossed the Indian Ocean. They were welcome, wherever Islam was practiced, as descendants of the Prophet and speakers of perfect Arabic. They became judges, royal advisers, and the husbands of rich women. They founded dynasties in the Southeast Asian islands of Borneo and Sumatra. "They have spread everywhere throughout the Malay countries," complained a Dutch governor in Melaka in 1750, "and have revealed too much to the natives": too much, that is, about the vulnerability of European outposts.

In one respect, the emergence of Omani power is a typical story of the time—intelligible in a context of multiplying opportunities to accumulate wealth and multiplying temptations to invest it in empire. Yet in other ways, the Omani network seemed an old-fashioned empire in its day—concerned to control trade, not production, clinging to maritime outposts, and stringing them together into the loosest kind of web—whereas the trend was for maritime empires to turn landward, build up territorial conquests, and centralize power. On the whole, in the eighteenth century, Europeans were becoming relatively more successful in encounters with enemies in other parts of the world. Though they still did not dare to tackle China or Japan, European arms gradually established their superiority against Indian and Southeast Asian foes. At the least, it could be said that European operations in Asia were no longer at the mercy of native empires, as they had been, in most areas, in the seventeenth century. These are related problems: the growth of land empires and the rise of Western power, wealth, and inventiveness.

ASIAN IMPERIALISM IN ARREST OR DECLINE: CHINA, PERSIA, AND THE OTTOMANS

Empires grew not only or even mainly by conquest, but by colonization. In the eighteenth century, an era of colonization worldwide or, at least, world widespread, peopled the border lands of the expanding empires and lined political frontiers with settlers. Painstakingly recruited, thinly spread, colonists began to extend the limits of the inhabited world. At the edges of the empires to which they belonged, where they reached out to touch the outposts of other expanding peoples, they helped to mesh the world together.

China

The Qing ruled by most standards, the world's fastest-growing empire in the eighteenth century. It engulfed Tibet in 1720, thrust deep into Central Asia, and made territorial gains along the borders with Mongolia, Russia, Burma, and Vietnam. Chinese continued to colonize recently absorbed lands in Manchuria and Taiwan (see Chapter 19). The conquest of China's "wild west" in Xinjiang was complete by 1759. When the scholar Ji Yun (chuh-ywuhn) made his journey of exile there 10 years later, he felt the awe of entering "another world"—the usual sentiment of a Chinese traveler on leaving China. Yet he soon settled down on a formerly wild frontier that was being tamed with remarkable speed. The hick town of Urumqi (oo-room-chee), where he made his new home, had bookshops selling classical Chinese texts. His neighbors grew Chinese peonies and peaches. Settlers kept coming from the east. By 1788, an emancipated convict was able to make a fortune by opening a shop selling Chinese delicacies.

By the end of the century, at least 200,000 Chinese immigrants had settled in Xinjiang. Plenty of them were criminals and political undesirables, but many others were volunteers. For merchants the opportunities in Xinjiang were so profitable that they were punished for wrongdoing by being sent back home. A government that reimbursed travel costs and offered loans for seeds, livestock, and housing, with a grant of four-and-a-half acres of land per family and temporary exemption from taxes sweetened the paths of legitimate migrants. Settlement was concentrated beyond the mountains on arable land where market towns mushroomed. The lead and iron mines of Urumqi produced nothing for export. The frontier's own boom absorbed everything the mines produced.

For the ruling Manchu Qing dynasty, colonization of the frontier was too important to be left to the Chinese. In a reshuffling of tribal peoples, reminiscent of the frontier defense strategies of the late Roman Empire (see Chapter 8), the Qing moved Mongol bands about like knights on a chessboard, shifting some between weak points in the borderlands, inducing others into the empire from outside. In an affecting ceremony in Beijing in 1771, the Qianlong (chee-ehn-luhng) emperor (r. 1735–1796) welcomed back into the imperial fold the Khan Uphasha of the Torghut people. China had wooed this tribe for nearly 60 years. The Torghut now abandoned Russian overlordship in the Volga valley, where they had found refuge for over a century, to return to their long-lost homeland in western Mongolia. It sounds like a happy story—but the vacancy had arisen only because the Chinese had fought the local inhabitants to extinction to clear the way for the Torghut.

Tribute. The Qianlong emperor of China loved horses, as a good Manchu should. Here, in a painting probably produced by Chinese and Jesuit painters at the emperor's court, he receives some of the famed horses of Central Asia from Mongol envoys. The background to this scene was the expansion of the Chinese Empire and the emperor's efforts to bring nomadic peoples under imperial discipline.
The Tartar envoys presenting their horses to Emperor Qianlong. 1757. 45 × 257 cm. Musee du Louvre/RMN Reunion des Musees Nationaux, France. SCALA/Art Resource, New York

Meanwhile, Chinese continued to overspill the borders of China by sea. They became miners in Malaya and farm laborers in the Spanish-ruled Philippines. Some of them made fortunes as businessmen and brokers. In Manila, the capital of the Philippines, in 1729, the archbishop and other leading citizens complained that a Spaniard had tried to obtain the contract to supply the city with bread, but was unable to wrest the concession from the Chinese. Immigrants went on repeopling Chinese quarters in Manila and Batavia, the capital of the Dutch East Indies, despite the periodic massacres inflicted by native Filipinos and Javanese who feared the Chinese would "swamp" them. The migrants flowed in, in defiance of the efforts of the Chinese government to stop them—or, at least, to persecute those who returned home. A famous case was that of Zhen Yilao, who made a fortune in the Dutch East Indies and acted as "introducer" of new Chinese colonists for the Dutch after a massacre in 1740. He returned to his home province of Fujian in southern China in 1749, he said, to "fulfill his filial duty of looking after his ageing mother." But as punishment for having left China in the first place, the government seized his fortune and condemned him to exile—this time, to be spent inside the borders of the empire. Chinese traders benefited increasingly, as trade in Southeast Asia slipped out of the control of states and large companies. Armenians, independent Europeans, and Bugis from Sulawesi (formerly Celebes) in Indonesia also stepped into the breach, but the Chinese predominated. In 1732, Chinese controlled 62 percent of the shipping into Batavia from other parts of Southeast Asia.

Content with profit, they rarely made bids for power. A rebellion broke out in the Chinese quarter of Batavia in 1740, not so much to seize power as for self-defense. In Batavia, according to the rebels, "so few Dutchmen and so many Chinese live, and . . . nevertheless the Dutch dare to treat the Chinese so harshly and oppress them so unjustly that it cannot be tolerated. The Chinese nation is forced to unite and declare war against the Dutch." In Manila, the sense of common identity among the Chinese became so strong that it overcame the usual Chinese emphasis on clan or family lineage, especially as the Chinese became entangled in new kinship structures as a result of locally contracted marriages. A Chinese had to woo his intended bride's family and placate them with gifts. Traditionally, Filipino women remained part of their parents' families, which their husbands joined. But the Chinese were ghetto dwellers; that is, they lived in exclusively Chinese neighborhoods. So mixed marriages, unlike those between two Filipinos, took a bride away from her parents' home. The structure was neither wholly Filipino nor particularly Chinese, but something new.

Multicultural city. Batavia, the capital of the Dutch East Indies, was, according to Captain Cook, the unhealthiest port in the world. It was also one of the busiest. This engraving from 1764 showed the teeming shipping in the harbor and revealing scenes in the foreground of life in what was effectively a Dutch-Chinese city. From under her umbrella, a Chinese lady in grand Western dress, scowls at tipsy Dutchmen. Crocodiles share the canal with a Chinese pleasure boat and commercial barges.

At some times and in some places, overseas Chinese took power for the sake of trade. For instance, after trouble with European advisers and French envoys in the late seventeenth century, the Thai kingdom of Siam underwent a revulsion against European influence. But the Thai court had a long tradition of installing foreign favorites. So from 1700, Chinese were dominant, occupying the position of royal favorite and purchasing most of the other principal offices in the kingdom. Chinese concubines, selected by Chinese favorites, surrounded King Thaisa (r. 1709–1733). But the Chinese community was too successful for its own good. The Thai became jealous of its growing profits and afraid of its growing numbers. When a new Thai king, Borommakot, suspended the pro-Chinese policy in 1733–1734, the Chinese, who by now numbered 20,000, fell under suspicion of plotting to oust him. Expected vengeance from China did not materialize. Overseas adventures remained private initiatives, in which the Chinese state was uninterested.

Back in mainland China, the economic dynamism of the empire was evident from the tax returns. Revenues rose by about two-thirds in the eighteenth century, despite substantial tax reductions, especially the abolition of the poll tax in 1712. The increase in the revenue was the result of rising population, rising production, and rising trade. The Qianlong emperor enjoyed an annual surplus of 8 to 9 million silver dollars and left 400 million silver dollars in his treasury at his abdication in 1796—probably more than twice as much as the Mughal Empire in India amassed at its height. By the emperor's last years, however, Chinese expansion was slackening or stagnating. Territorial expansion stopped. The emperor grew old and inert. His last portraits show him wasted, wrinkled, shrunk into old age—a sad contrast with his youthful portraits as huntsman, warrior, or pilgrim to sacred shrines. The influence of the corrupt favorite, Hensho, was blamed for the state's lack of vigor. But China had reached the limits of expansion with the technology at its disposal and had little wish or will to make new conquests, adopt new technologies, or undertake new initiatives. The giant, as Napoleon noticed, had "fallen asleep."

The Qianlong emperor. When the Qianlong emperor attained an advanced age, Chinese portraits generally showed him splendidly enthroned and enveloped in gorgeous robes, embroidered with images of power and virility. But the artist, William Alexander, who visited China with an ill-fated British embassy in 1793, was free to capture this informal, intimate likeness of the emperor.

The Asian Context

It is tempting to see this as part of an Asian general crisis of the late eighteenth century. Most of the other great Asian empires—Ottoman, Mughal, Persian, Japanese, Thai—lost impetus during the eighteenth century. The large states that had taken shape in Southeast Asia stopped expanding or broke up, as kings complained that "officials and monasteries" usurped their power. Burma, which today calls itself Myanmar, first shrank, then split, and finally collapsed in 1752, after long civil wars between ever more-powerful provincial rulers. Partial recovery directed Burmese energies against the neighboring Thai Empire in what the Burmese represented as holy wars on behalf of Buddhism. This was a crisis for which an era of internal peace from 1709 to 1758 had left the Thai ill prepared. Burmese invaders effectively wiped out the Thai capital at Ayutthaya in 1767. The Thai Empire shattered among five small states. Vietnam also fell apart in the chaos of peasant rebellions between 1771 and 1778.

Persia and the Ottoman Empire

In Southwest Asia, static population levels held back the Persian and Ottoman worlds. The Safavid Empire in Persia fell in 1722. Like Humpty Dumpty, no one seemed able to put it back together. Although Safavid shahs regained the throne at intervals until the 1770s, the dynasty had lost the allegiance of its subjects (see Chapter 19). Ironically, the Safavid emperors, who had forced their Shiite Islam on their people, found themselves condemned for their own lack of piety. Between

1719 and 1730, Persia was the playground of invading Afghan warlords. The former bandit chief, Nadir (NAH-deer) Shah, who drove them out, tried to end internal strife by turning Persian ambitions outward and to discipline the Shiite clergy by privileging Sunni Islam. He sought to bring the Afghan chiefs into line by reviving the old Afghan practice of raiding India. He even sacked the Mughal court in Delhi and stole its treasure in 1739. He bought English warships to regain control of trade in the Caspian Sea and the Persian Gulf. But he could never escape from rebellions—not even when, in an attempt to secure his throne, he killed the heirs of the Safavids and had his own son blinded. After his assassination in 1747, rulers survived only by leaving the power of regional warlords intact, or playing them off against each other. State institutions were neglected. Nadir Shah's navy rotted away.

The Ottoman Empire—the Safavids' neighbor and longtime enemy—was more robust, but encountered difficulties that seemed crippling. The check to Ottoman expansion toward the end of the seventeenth century (see Chapter 19) shocked the ruling Ottoman elite, who embarked on long and inconclusive self-examination to try to understand why the empire was beginning to stagnate. The efficiency of the state declined, as hereditary officeholders gradually took over the administration. This surrender of power to men whom sultans could not easily remove or replace was precisely what the traditional Ottoman system of government was designed to avoid. The numbers of slave-bureaucrats, who tended to strengthen central control because they depended on the sultan's patronage, declined as the empire lost control of the various Christian subject-peoples in Europe and the Caucasus, from whom the administration traditionally recruited fresh intakes of slaves. Sultans had to rely increasingly on the Muslim clergy to keep the administration going. But clerics were hard to manage because, unlike the Sultan's slave-bureaucrats, they were not reliant on his patronage. As early as 1717, the wife of an English ambassador noted how the clergy "engrossed all the learning and almost all the wealth of the Empire. 'Tis they that are the real authors, tho' the soldiers are the actors, of revolutions."

As a result of the economic changes described in Chapter 20, trade revenues fell. Trade with France, for instance—formerly the Turks' best overseas customer—accounted for only 5 percent of France's imports by the late eighteenth century, compared with about 16 percent when the century began. Imports from Turkey had accounted for 10 percent of Britain's trade in the mid-seventeenth century. The total fell to less than 1 percent by the end of the eighteenth. The end of the coffee monopoly of southern Arabia, as coffee production grew in the East Indies and West Indies, was a serious blow to the Ottoman economy.

The balance of power between the empire and its neighbors, which, for so many centuries, had favored the Ottomans, was clearly shifting. A long series of border wars with Russia led in 1774 to the Treaty of Küçük Kaynarca (koo-CHOOK kye-NAHR-jah), in which the Ottomans ceded control of the north shore of the Black Sea. Compared with the former glory of the empire (see Chapter 19), this was a serious setback, for not only did the Ottomans lose control of important trade routes, but they also conceded sovereignty over a Muslim population to a Christian power. This undermined the sultans' traditional status as protectors of Islam. Russia consolidated its gains in further campaigns that diminished the area under Ottoman rule in the Caucasus. In 1798, France invaded Egypt and Syria. The French soon withdrew to fight more urgent wars in Europe, but henceforth, Ottoman overlordship in the empire's North African provinces,

Rainy parade. In 1720. the Ottoman Sultan Ahmad III held fifteen days of celebrations to mark the circumcision of his sons. On the eleventh day the French and Russian ambassadors (shown at the top right of this account by the court painter, Abdulcelil Levni, "the colorist") were among the guests, watching a procession of trade guilds, each bearing its own characteristic gift. Levni does not record that rain kept most of the guilds away that day. Alongside the saddle-makers guild is their advertisement—a giant statue of a black woman wearing the same leopard skin as the saddlecloth exhibited in the float.

which, in addition to Egypt, included Algeria, Tunisia, and Libya, existed in name only. These areas became virtually autonomous.

Meanwhile, the empire's control of other outlying areas also weakened. In the Balkans, many Christian communities dodged Ottoman control by withdrawing into hill regions, where they planted maize on the upper slopes, beyond reach of the Turkish tax collectors. On the empire's Balkan frontier with Russia in what is today Romania, the empire conceded autonomy to the local inhabitants. The Arabian provinces—never a secure part of the Ottoman dominions—seceded in a religiously inspired rebellion. Muhammad ibn Abd al-Wahhab (1703–1787) launched a religious reform movement named **Wahhabism** after him, calling for a return to Quranic purity and rejecting the legitimacy of the Ottomans' claims to the caliphate. The Wahhabites conquered Arabia and pressed on the borders of Ottoman-controlled Iraq (see Map 21.1).

The Ottomans' difficulties can be measured in their loss of prestige. Long feared and admired in Europe, they had been loathed but never before disdained. From 1739, Austrians first, then Europeans generally, began conventionally to call the empire the "sick man of Europe" and to eye the sultans' possessions like greedy creditors around a rich man's deathbed. In reality, the empire's sickness was by no means terminal, but its relative decline by the standards of its European neighbors was obvious. In 1807, a Spanish spy, who, like so many double agents, found it impossible to resist all sympathy with the culture of his enemy, wrote an account of the empire in his pretended character as a friendly critic. "Although I am a Muslim," he wrote,

> when I see a nation without the slightest idea of public law, or of the rights of man; a nation in which scarcely one in a thousand knows how to read and write; a nation where no one enjoys security of property, and where human blood is made to flow for trivial reasons and without any just process; a nation—in short—determined to close its eyes to enlightenment and to reject the torch of civilization that shines quite clearly before it, will, for me, always seem a nation of barbarians.

MAP 21.1

Wahhabi Expansion

- Ottoman Empire ca.1800
- Wahhabi territory ca.1800
- → Wahhabi expansion in the early nineteenth century
- **1805** date captured by the Wahhabis

IMPERIAL REVERSAL IN INDIA: MUGHAL ECLIPSE AND BRITISH RISE TO POWER

The most dramatic reversal of fortune—and the one with the most profound implications for the future—happened in India. The Emperor Aurangzeb (r. 1658–1707) had driven the frontiers of the Mughal state southward with relentless energy (see Chapter 19). But after his death, expansion halted, and gradually, the empire exhibited signs of the strains that arise from success. Widened borders enclosed ever more-diverse cultures, religions, political systems, and ethnic identities. Sikhs and Hindus were hard to accommodate in the fiercely Muslim ideology that Aurangzeb had imposed. The Emperor Muhammad Shah (r. 1719–1748) exploited the opportunity to take control of the Muslim clergy by claiming the privilege of judging between rival schools of Islamic law. He appealed to the Shiite minority by calling himself "heir of Ali," the Prophet Muhammad's son-in-law who had been murdered in the seventh century, and revived imperial pretensions to religious leadership by giving

Chronology: Trends in Asian Imperialism	
Eighteenth century	China is world's fastest-growing empire; Persia and Ottoman populations static; Ottoman government goes into prolonged decline
1720	China conquers Tibet
1722	Safavid Empire collapses
1759	Chinese conquest of Xinjiang complete
1767	Burmese invasion leads to disintegration of Thailand
1771–1778	Vietnam collapses under strain of peasant rebellions
1774	Ottomans cede land to Russia in the Treaty of Küçük Kaynarca

himself the title of "Shadow of God on Earth." But these measures only alienated the emperor further from most religious communities in the realm.

Victories could be profitable. In the past the Mughals had always made money out of war. But empire was a capital-intensive business, subject to diminishing returns. The tax burden necessary to sustain Aurangzeb's policy provoked increasingly frequent peasant rebellions. Accommodations with conquered elites became increasingly generous—triggering the anger of the Mughal's old comrades and supporters, who resented the privileges granted to the elites in recently conquered lands. The growing importance of merchants to whom the government farmed out the collection of taxes and from whom the government borrowed large sums deepened this resentment. In the remoter parts of the empire, the Mughals, in effect, delegated power to local elites.

The danger of this policy became obvious in a dramatic sequence of events, beginning in 1719–1720. The emperor made spectacular concessions to petty Hindu princes, called the **Marathas**, who ruled in Maharashtra, and whom their Muslim neighbors despised as little better than bandits. The Nizam al-Mulk, who governed for the Mughals on the frontier with Maharashtra, responded by defying Mughal authority. In 1725, he conquered Hyderabad in central India and established it as an effectively independent Muslim state. He paid no tribute to the Mughal emperor in Delhi. He handed out offices and parcels of tribute without reference to the emperor. He took three-quarters of the tribute due to the Mughals and left the remaining quarter to buy peace with his Hindu neighbors. The Mughal Empire still claimed "lordship of the universe" and monopolized reverence and religious rituals. Prayers for the emperor were still offered in mosques throughout India right through the eighteenth century. It was becoming clear, however, that the Mughal state was in permanent decay and that India was up for grabs (see Map 21.2).

Native princes contemplated replacing the empire or seizing control of what remained of it. Or else they simply ceased to obey the emperor. After 1761, for instance, the Marathas expressed obedience to the Mughals only in treaties. Otherwise, they largely ignored the emperor, though some continued to send formal petitions to court and issue coinage with the imperial stamp. But tradition still counted. Regional or local rulers could not challenge the empire without calling into question their own legitimacy, which emperors conferred. Traditionally, conquerors or reunifiers of India had always come from outside, as had the Mughals themselves, who originated in Afghanistan. It was easier for Indians to accept a foreign conqueror than one from inside the empire. Huns, Afghans, Mongols, Turks, and Persians had all played this role in the past. Now, because of the huge shifts of power that had overtaken the world, potential imperialists were unlikely to come from within Asia. By an unforeseeable sequence of events, the successors of the Mughals would be British.

As late as 1750, the British East India Company, which had been founded in 1600, insisted that its officials think of themselves as the "agents of merchants" rather than as a military colony. The circumstances of violent competition with French rivals in India, however, were already forcing the company's men to rethink their roles. Young Robert Clive (1725–1774), for instance, was a clerk in the southwest Indian port of Madras. His family thought him useless for any job more demanding. But he spent his leisure reading military history, and when fighting broke out, he found soldiering to be his true vocation.

MAP 21.2

The Marathas

- ▨ Core territories
- ▨ Maratha's expansion, 1708–1800
- ▨ Maratha's subject states
- ▨ areas of irregular tribute
- 1739   date of acquisition by Marathas
- (–75)   date of subsequent loss by Marathas to ca. 1800
- →   Maratha campaigns into neighboring territory, with date

In 1756, Clive turned what was to have been a punitive expedition into a campaign of conquest. The province of Bengal in northeast India was by far the most important trading area in India for European commerce. In the 1730s, for instance, nearly half Holland's imports from Asia, and as much as two-thirds of all Asian exports to England, originated in Bengal. The *Nawab*, the local ruler, alienated the British by allying with France, seizing the British port of Calcutta, and allegedly allowing the mistreatment and murder of British women and children. In dealing with him, passion replaced the usual prudence of British policy, and Clive enjoyed greater freedom of action to pursue vengeance than frontier colonels were usually allowed. The French were unreliable allies for Indian rulers. During wars in Europe, the British could rely on continental allies to distract them. Bengal was full of internal dissent: Hindu resentment of Muslim rule, warlord rivalry with the Nawab, popular resentment of heavy taxation, military unrest at overdue pay.

Clive blundered into this tense arena. His barely professional army of a little over 1,000 Europeans and 2,000 Indian trainees was outnumbered in the field by over 12 to 1 and had hardly any technical advantages. The Nawab had French guns and gunners. But, like so many conquerors, Clive aimed to destroy the enemy by dividing them. He succeeded by putting together a coalition that ousted the Nawab at Plassey in 1757 by what was in effect a battlefield coup. Traditionally, historians have represented the battle as the result of British superiority, whereas it showed only the superiority of some Bengali factions over others. A delightful illustration made at the time to celebrate Clive's heroism displays the propaganda image: Clive's army is drawn up in neatly ordered lines of fire. The Nawab's force is a straggly tangle, and appears to flee before a relentless British advance. What really happened is that, confronted by a conspiracy among his supposed followers, the Nawab fled after little more than exchanges of cannon and skirmisher fire.

Bengal was easily the richest of the fragments into which the Mughal Empire dissolved. Clive looted it—"astonished," he said, "at my own moderation." Booty never dulls the appetite it feeds. Clive's men almost mutinied in dissatisfaction with their share of the plunder even though it had made them all rich. Yet, well managed, Bengal was the biggest prize of any pirate since Pizarro seized Peru for Spain in the 1520s (see Chapter 16). The East India Company raised £2 million in 1761–1764 and almost £7.5 million in 1766–1767. The riches of Bengal paid for the conquest of other Indian principalities. By 1782, the Company, whose motto had once been "trade, not war," was keeping an army of 115,000 men in India (see Map 21.3).

The parallel with the Spanish conquerors in the Americas is striking. The British first installed a puppet ruler in Bengal and then used the profits of confiscatory policies to conquer the Ganges River valley and the shore of the Bay of Bengal, just as the Spaniards had used the wealth and manpower of the formerly Aztec-dominated highlands of Mexico to conquer the surrounding regions. As in Mexico and Peru, the speed of the conquerors' triumph gave it the illusion of inevitability. Once the growth of a land empire had begun, it had to continue. Security always demanded control of the next frontier. The existing setup in India, in which native princes bargained with rival Western buyers and shippers, became intolerable to the British once they

Conspirators exchange congratulations. The Battle of Plassey in 1757, usually celebrated as a great British victory over the Nawab of Bengal, was really the outcome of the dissolution of the Bengali army, as various of its units deserted or went over to the British. Here the British commander, Robert Clive, receives a sum of money from the Nawab as compensation for officers and soldiers injured in battle.
Erich Lessing ©The Trustees of the British Museum/Art Resource, NY

"The parallel with the Spanish conquerors in the Americas is striking . . . As in Mexico and Peru, the speed of the conquerors' triumph gave it the illusion of inevitability."

MAP 21.3

European Expansion in South and Southeast Asia, ca. 1800

- area under British rule, ca. 1800
- area under Dutch control and possessions, 1765
- Spanish possessions
- French possessions
- area under Portuguese control and possessions, 1765
- petty tribal polities
- China
- —— frontiers, ca. 1765

realized they could enforce a monopoly. With Bengal in their power, the British extended their control over the spice-rich south.

Under cover of the next European war in the 1790s, which again neutralized the French threat, Britain put together a coalition of Indian clients and mercenaries to defeat piecemeal the only regional powers capable of reversing the trend. Tipu Sultan, ruler of Mysore in south India, posed the biggest threat. His ambitions were obvious. He spurned the Mughals, took imperial trappings for himself, and looked to the distant Ottomans to legitimate his claims. In the 1780s, while the Mughal emperor swallowed his pride and sought the protection of a Maratha leader, Mahadji Scindia, Tipu confronted the British for supremacy in India. He wrote accounts of his dreams in a revealing book. Amid scenes of emeralds, tiger shoots, and white elephants, it includes visions of French troops and of the expulsion of the

British. Yet Tipu was more than a dreamer. Political realism, idealized as holy war, underpinned his anti-British policy. He realized that Indians could no longer deal with the British in the traditional frameworks of commerce and politics. They had to be expelled or obeyed.

Their own revolution, which began in 1789 (see Chapter 22), and then the need to defend France against invaders in the 1790s distracted Tipu's French allies. His neighbors preferred to back the British rather than to support him. If they had to submit to rulers, they preferred to have them far away in London rather than dangerously close in Mysore. Hopelessly besieged in his capital at Seringapatam in 1799, Tipu died in the fighting. The Maratha states in south India accepted British overlordship after a defeat in 1806.

British supremacy was only the latest variant on an old theme of Indian history: the establishment of dominance over India by foreign military elites. But in a crucial sense, the phenomenon was new. Britain's India was the first big European empire on the mainland of Asia. The British could now seize or clear much of India to grow products that suited them. They could smother the potential competition of Indian industries, shifting the balance of the world's resources in favor of the West (see Chapter 20). Britain's Indian Empire was at once the last of the old adventurer conquests, achieved with native collaboration and without conspicuous technical advantages, and the forerunner of the new industrial conquests, by which Europeans would extend their empires in the next century. There were, as yet, no machine guns or ironclad ships or quinine pills to give Westerners technical advantages. Steam power and rifles were in their infancy. But British industry affected—if it did not effect—the conquest of India. By the 1790s, standard British artillery was so superior to the Indian product that the finely decorated cannon of Tipu Sultan were good to the British only for their value as scrap metal.

Tiger mauling a British soldier. A British officer's death in a tiger's jaws in 1792 became a symbol at the court of Tipu Sultan of Mysore of the fate he wished to inflict on the British. Tipu's very name meant "tiger," and he adopted the beast as his badge.

THE DUTCH EAST INDIES

Events in India vividly illustrated the way European imperialism elsewhere in Asia was also turning to territorial conquest. The Spanish, painfully slowly, continued to build up their empire in the Philippines, crushing a rebellion after the British briefly seized Manila in 1762. The Portuguese, despite being expelled from their East African outposts by the Omanis, hesitantly expanded their frontiers around Goa on the southwest Indian coast into what they called the New Conquests, pushing to control trade routes into south India, and acquiring 30,000 new Indian subjects. The Dutch, meanwhile, built up a land empire on Java in Indonesia. In 1740, they intervened to support the ruling dynasty and exacted coastal territory as the price of their help. In 1749, they took the whole of Mataram, and in the second half of the century, they effectively controlled most of the rest of the island, dividing the kingship between rival Javanese clients. In 1774, the heir to one of the resulting kingdoms, Yogyakarta, composed a poem in which the Dutch were converted to Islam, while sheikhs in Mecca in Arabia accused the Muslim puppet rulers of being "the devil's kings," taunting, "Shall the Europeans be more powerful than Allah?" Dutch rule was usually indirect, through Dutch-appointed regents on whose collaboration the Dutch relied.

Chronology: Mughal Decline	
1600	East India Company (EIC) founded
Eighteenth century	Spanish, Dutch, and Portuguese expand holdings in Southeast Asia
1707	Death of Aurangzeb and the end of Mughal expansion
1725	Nazim al-Mulk conquers Hyderabad
1756–1757	Robert Clive leads EIC conquest of Bengal
Late eighteenth century	Marathas offer only nominal obedience to the Mughals
1761–1764	EIC revenues: £2 million
1766–1767	EIC revenues: £7.5 million
1806	Maratha states accept British overlordship

These were always leading members of traditional elites, but their right to rule was often—from a Javanese point of view—doubtful. So they depended on the Dutch just as the Dutch depended on them, and the relationship benefited both sides.

In the end, the landward turn did the Dutch little good. Their strength was in their shipping, and a seaborne, piratical empire suited their talents and technology. Their weakness was a shortage of manpower. Territorial acquisitions gradually overstretched and exhausted them. The Dutch could only pay for war by enforcing high prices. As they devastated rivals' lands, uprooted surplus crops, and destroyed competitors' ships, they ran the risk of ruining the entire region and being left profitless, as one of their leaders warned, "in depopulated lands and empty seas."

Yet what choice did the Dutch have? Unlike the Spaniards and Portuguese, they had little access to marketable assets, such as gold and silver mines or sources of slaves. They could finance their inroads into eastern markets in only two ways: by the profits of intra-Asian trade and shipping, or by diversifying into production by growing their own cash crops. By opting for the latter strategy, they committed themselves to seizing the spices and, in the end, the land the spices grew on, by force. They ended up with an empire, the Dutch East Indies (modern Indonesia), whose costs exceeded its profits. Only the conversion of much of Java to the cultivation of coffee closed the gap between expenses and returns.

THE BLACK ATLANTIC: AFRICA, THE AMERICAS, AND THE SLAVE TRADE

Equaling or exceeding the vast movements of internal colonization in Asia was the shift of people across the Atlantic. Most of them were black Africans, forced into slavery and transported to the New World. In the eighteenth century, nearly 400,000 were imported into English North America, nearly 1 million into Spanish colonies, over 1 million into the Caribbean, and some 3 million into Brazil. The structures of the trade were the same as in the previous century (see Chapter 19), but its scale grew (see Map 21.4).

Our traditional image of the horrors of the Atlantic crossing comes from slave memoirs and the writings of abolitionists who sought to do away with the slave trade. Skeptics have wondered whether shippers can really have been so careless of their cargo as to tolerate—and even invite—heavy losses of life en route. Yet such evidence as the often-reproduced deck plan of the British slave-ship *Brooks* in 1783 is decisive. Slaves were stacked "like books on a shelf," in spaces little more than 5 feet high by 4 feet wide. The ship's surgeon explained that the slaves were not supposed to be able to turn round: "the slaves that are out of irons are . . . closely locked to one another, and those which do not get quickly into their places are compelled" by the lash. He watched their "laborious and anxious efforts for life," which resembled those "we observe on expiring animals subjected by experiment to bad air of various kinds." In an autobiography published in 1789, Olaudah Equiano, a West African who claimed to have been enslaved there as a boy, described the conditions of his own experience as an item of cargo. "The closeness of the place, and the heat of the climate, added to the number in the ship, which was so crowded that each had scarcely room to turn himself in, almost suffocated us. This produced constant perspirations, so that the air soon became unfit . . . and brought on a sickness among the slaves, of which many died, thus falling victim to the improvident avarice, as I may call it, of their purchasers." The *Brooks* lost 60 slaves out of 600 on the crossing.

The slave ship *Brooks*. Over 600 slaves were crammed into a space on the *Brooks* designed to carry no more than 450 persons. The extent of the inhumanity in the slave trade is shocking. The inefficiency is more surprising. By herding too much cargo into too little space, the slavers doomed much of their valuable cargo to death before delivery.

Yet, strictly from the point of view of profits, the slavers knew what they were doing. Tight packing had no noticeable effect on rates of mortality, compared with such figures as are available for comparison with the more humane conditions specified—though not always observed—for Portuguese ships. In a telltale case, a captain from the British port of Liverpool in 1781 had 130 slaves thrown overboard to claim the insurance for lost cargo. It was a peculiarly horrifying instance, but it was normal to dispose of sick or mutinous slaves in the same way.

The economics of slavery are hard to understand. Forced labor, according to economic theory, is never efficient, and the difficulty of managing slaves to maximize production is one of the few conclusions on which all observers of slave plantations in the eighteenth century agreed. Yet slavery was just one form of forced labor, on which, in various forms, most eighteenth-century economies relied. Indentured workers, peasants tied to the land, unpaid apprenticeships, and convict workers all made compulsion seem normal. Traditional forms of employment generally gave employers—masters, as they were commonly called—enormous power over their workers' lives: where the workers lived, how they spent their leisure, whom and when they married. So until economic thought began to challenge such practices in the late eighteenth century (see Chapter 22), it is not surprising that people tolerated the savageries and inefficiencies of the slave plantations. And demand for slave-grown commodities was such that plantations managed to make profits. Sometimes planters could enjoy spectacular results in a small space. France's colony of Saint-Domingue (modern Haiti) in the eighteenth century occupied only one-third of the island of Hispaniola. It was hardly much of a land empire in terms of size, but Saint-Domingue was what we would now call an economic miracle. It became, for a while a source of enormous wealth, the world's major producer of coffee and sugar, with important sidelines in indigo and cacao.

Depictions of the life of black societies in the Americas range from the idealized through the colorful and the satirical to the horrific. But the crack of the lash can be heard between the lines even of idealized accounts—like the Englishman William Beckford's acount of Jamaica, where he was a slave owner in 1788. He claimed that "the situation of a good negro under a kind owner . . . is very superior (the idea of indiscriminate punishment excepted) to those of the generality of labouring poor in England." His arguments against excessive whippings included that "They should not be chastised in such a manner as to lay them up, for the end of punishment is defeated by a loss of labour," and "When a negro becomes familiarized to the whip, he no longer holds it in terror." More typical was his contemporary Edward Long, who justified slavery in 1774 on the grounds that black Africans were so unlike other peoples—among other reasons, because of a "narrow intellect" and "bestial smell"—that they were almost a different species.

In contexts where such crude racism was commonplace, the defense of slavery on the grounds that slaves might be well treated rang hollow. In South America, no area had a rosier reputation than eighteenth-century Minas Gerais, a mining district in Brazil, for the "liberty" that slaves there could enjoy. Yet even here, slaves were "free" chiefly to obtain their gold quotas by extortion or prostitution. White Portuguese preserved order by techniques of selective terror, exploitation of dislike between rival black nations, and large rations of rum and tobacco.

Punishment for disobedient slaves—as for mutinous soldiers and seamen—was brutal not because the offenses merited it, but to terrorize and cow the victims. This early nineteenth-century depiction of the whipping of a slave in Brazil is based on the tradition of representing the scourging of Christ in paintings. The planter, turning casually aside to his rum and tobacco, seems contemptible. The slave woman tied to the tree looks more innocent in her nakedness than the onlookers.
Dagli Orti (A)/Picture Desk, Inc./Kobal Collection

"The economics of slavery are hard to understand. Forced labor, according to economic theory, is never efficient, and the difficulty of managing slaves to maximize production is one of the few conclusions on which all observers of slave plantations in the eighteenth century agreed."

MAP 21.4

The World Slave Trade, ca. 1800

�-	main source areas of African slaves
➤	main slave trade routes
▰	main slave settlement area in the Americas
⚓ 1,250,000	estimated total of African slaves imported

Trade Goods

🌰	cocoa beans
☕	coffee
◇	cotton
⚓	sugar
⚲	tobacco

GREENLAND

Hudson Bay

C A N A D A

Rocky Mountains

NORTH AMERICA

Quebec
Montreal
Newfoundland

UNITED STATES OF AMERICA

Boston
New York
Richmond

Mississippi

⚓ 400,000

New Orleans
Mobile
Charleston

Gulf of Mexico
San Augustín

Greater Antilles

A T L A N T I C   O C E A N

Mexico City
Veracruz
Acapulco

⚓ 1,000,000

🌰

Havana
Cuba

Puerto Rico
Virgin Is.

Jamaica
HAITI ⚓ +1,000,000

Hispaniola

CENTRAL AMERICA

VICEROYALTY OF NEW SPAIN

Caribbean Sea

Cartagena
Lesser Antilles

Portobelo

VICEROYALTY OF NEW GRANADA

P A C I F I C   O C E A N

Cape Verde Islands

Saint Gor...

🌰

SURINAM

GUIANA

Amazon

VICEROYALTY OF PERU

Callao
Lima

SOUTH AMERICA

B R A Z I L

Recife
Salvador (Bahia)

Potosí

⚓ 3,000,000

MINAS GERAIS
Rio de Janeiro
São Paulo

VICEROYALTY OF RÍO DE LA PLATA

Buenos Aires

Tropic of Cancer
Equator
Tropic of Capricorn

Andes

1502: Introduction of African slaves to the Caribbean

1739: Stono rebellion in South Carolina

1739: Slave revolt in Haiti

1804: Foundation of independent Haitian state

1867: Last known arrival of a slave ship in Cuba

| 1450 | 1500 | 1550 | 1600 | 1650 | 1700 | 1750 | 1800 | 1850 | 1900 |

1522: First American slave revolt in Hispaniola

1685: French *Code Noir* restricts slavery in French Caribbean colonies

1807: Slave trade outlawed in Britain

1850: Effective end of slave trade in Brazil

1888: Slavery abolished in Brazil

1863: Emancipation proclamation frees slaves in United States around the Caribbean, slaves rebelled frequently, ran away when they could, and—above all—refused to reproduce. Colonial authorities could usually suppress rebellions. In 1739, the British authorities in Jamaica solved the problem of runaways inventively, by negotiating a treaty with Captain Cudjoe, the ruler of the maroon state of runaway slaves in the interior of the island (see Chapter 19). In return for British recognition of his autonomy, he agreed to return future fugitive slaves to their plantations. But the slaves' most effective form of resistance was to refuse to give birth. Hard labor, harsh punishment, poor food, meager clothing, and unsanitary housing all worked against the natural increase of population. Even more significant were low birthrate and high infant mortality. It seems likely that slave women chose not to bring children into the wretched world they were forced to inhabit. The British West Indies had only 350,000 slaves in 1780, although planters had imported 1.2 million by that time.

In the second half of the eighteenth century, slaves exported from West Africa in British ships were worth ten times the value of all other African exports put together. This disparity protected African states from European imperialism, as Europeans were not particularly interested in controlling the products of the land, or—yet—of developing plantations of their own in Africa. Disease, mainly malaria and yellow fever, was another factor. Europeans had a hard time surviving in West Africa in the eighteenth century. On the underside of the West African bulge, the slaving states established in the seventeenth century enjoyed a certain stability or at least a power of survival in the eighteenth. Oyo, Dahomey, Allada, Whydah, and Ashanti were secure against all enemies except each other. European slave stations multiplied along the coast, changing hands with the rhythms of European wars. Danish enterprise in the 1780s was still adding to the numbers of slave forts begun 100 years previously along the Gold Coast. St. Louis, the chief French station on the Senegal River in the same period, had 600 French officials and soldiers. The biggest station was at Gorée, south of Cape Verde, where the chaplain in the 1780s secured the prettiest slave girls for himself on the pretext of founding a sisterhood of the Sacred Heart. At that time, Miles Barber of London had 12 establishments on the west coast of Africa, handling about 6,000 slaves a year. Near one of his stations off Conakry in modern Ghana, a remarkable independent trader dominated business at the mouth of the River Bereira: Betsy Heard was the English-educated daughter of a British trader and an African slave. The slave-trading compound on Bence Island in West Africa in midcentury was owned by a syndicate of Scots eccentrics, who built a golf course, served by black caddies in kilts woven in Glasgow—a canny example of how even small-scale imperialism stimulated home industry.

White colonialism exerted little pressure in other parts of Africa. In Kongo, the long struggle against Portuguese domination wore down the state, which crumbled in the late seventeenth century. King Pedro IV (Kongolese kings had Portuguese names—see Chapter 15) effected a brief revival. In 1706, he captured and burnt at the stake Beatriz Kimpa Vita, a visionary rebel who claimed to be a virgin and mother and who decreed the use of the "Salve Regina," a hymn to the queenship of the Virgin Mary, in her own honor. During her rebellion she claimed to have replaced Christianity. She expelled white people, and installed a puppet king. The wars wasted Kongo and ruined its former agricultural prosperity. The fruitful collaboration with Portuguese missionaries and officials could not be fully restored.

Slave states as rapacious and militaristic as anything known earlier (see Chapter 19) grew up in the savanna toward the south of the Congo drainage area, from the Kwango River to Lake Tanganyika. Luanda was the greatest of these states. A bracelet of elephant sinews confirmed its kings' sacred nature. But a network of women, who strengthened the dynasty by marriage, exercised the real power. A

Cudjoe making peace. The British commander, Colonel John Guthrie, extends a hand in peace to the maroon leader, Captain Cudjoe, in Jamaica in 1739. After eight years of indecisive war, the British conceded autonomy to a maroon state in the interior of the island. The maroons in turn agreed to harbor no more runaway slaves.

Elmina. The Portuguese founded the fort of Elmina, on the underside of the West African bulge, near the rivers Pra and Benya, in 1482 to trade mainly for gold from the Volta valley. But, as with most European trading posts in the region, slaving rapidly became the main activity. The Dutch captured the fort and took over the trade in slaves there in 1637.

Fulani cavalrymen. The strength of the Fulani Empire was its cavalry, deployed to good effect in the grasslands of the African Sahel. European firepower checked Fulani expansion in the nineteenth century and overthrew the empire in the early 1900s, but horsemanship and the use of traditional weapons remain practices of high prestige in parts of West Africa.

female elder, known as the *Lukon-kashia*, played a major role in selecting the king. In Luanda, court "cities," as Europeans called them, attracted praise for their cleanliness, rational grid plans of streets, and public squares. Slavery was the basis of Luanda's domestic economy as well as of its commerce. Slaves were needed to work soil adapted for cassava and maize, New World crops that revolutionized productivity in Africa.

Meanwhile, the northern Zambezi valley experienced renewed Portuguese interest with a gold rush in the 1740s. Most of the lower valley ended up in the hands of adventurers called *prazeros*—Portuguese colonists who established personal dominance over the native populations. The once-mighty empire of Mwene Mutapa, which had defeated Portuguese attempts at conquest in the sixteenth century, had broken up. In coastal East Africa, as we saw at the beginning of this chapter, the Omanis replaced the Portuguese definitively from 1729, when the Portuguese failed to recapture Mombasa. In the long run, Omani rule benefited trade. The biggest European menace appeared in the southern tip of the continent, where the Xhosa (KOH–sah) felt increasing pressure from the Dutch expansion from the Cape. But here the black and white antagonists were evenly matched. The Dutch farmers (or "Boers") halted at the edge of the Zuurveld in wars that ended in 1795. By that time the Boers had fallen out among themselves, and the British had seized the Cape Colony from the Dutch East India Company.

The greatest threats to African states came not from European imperialism but from within Africa. Ethiopia continually tried and continually failed to contain Oromo migrations. Early in the eighteenth century, the Oromo began to organize in what were recognizably states of their own and to become Muslims. Oromo became high officials and commanders inside what was left of Ethiopia and rulers of effectively independent provinces. A siege mentality took over the Ethiopian elite, with rival factions and sects squabbling over a diminishing power base. In the 1760s, the most powerful provincial governor, Mika'el Suhul, who built up a well-trained army, equipped with firearms, dispensed with the normal conventions of loyalty and took government into his own hands. Ethiopia's "Era of Princes" began, in which the emperor was a pawn or puppet of warlords. "How is it," wailed a chronicler of the 1780s, "that the kingdom has become contemptible to striplings and slaves? How is it that the kingdom is a laughing-stock of the uncircumcised?"

In parts of West Africa, meanwhile, the continuing expansion of the Islamic world put relentless pressure on local African states. Senegambia fell to Muslim-led revolutions that displaced native dynasties. Bundu fell in 1690 (though its kings remained pagans for over 100 years thereafter), and Futa Jallon fell in 1725. Samba Gelaajo Jeego, ruler of Futa Toro, who is still a subject of popular songs in the region, enlisted French help, but to little long-term result. Muslims conquered Futa Toro in 1776. Muslim Tuareg warriors and Kunta holy men proved, in combination, an irresistible force along the middle Niger River. The process gathered pace. In 1794, a holy man in the Sahel, Usuman da Fodio, had a vision in which he was "girded with the Sword of Truth, to unsheathe it against the enemies of God." The strict Islamic Wahhabite movement from Arabia inspired him. He saw himself as the "Renewer of Faith" promised by prophesies, and the forerunner of the **Mahdi**, a Muslim messiah, whose

Making Connections | THE ATLANTIC SLAVE TRADE, 1700–1800

REGION		ECONOMIC ROLE OF SLAVERY		SOCIAL EFFECTS
Africa		main source of slaves for the Americas, large scale slave export trade mostly depend on African slavers for supply; slave states sustain the trade in the interior, slave-forts operated by Europeans multiply along Atlantic coast; expanded presence of Europeans leads to discovery of goldfields, and settlement in South Africas		expansion and strengthening of slave states, local traders contrast with occasional rebellions; use of slaves spreads to domestic economy to sustain agriculture, commerce; displacement of tribes in South Africa with increased Dutch settlement of temperate region
Europe		initially slavery in the Americas sponsored by Spanish and Portuguese enriches Europeans through profits derived from slave trading and plantations developed with slave labor		increased racism; profits sent to Europe lead to domestic prosperity, increased military and political/power/status; by 1800 a strong anti-slavery movement established in England
Americas		establishment of vast plantations as well as smaller-scale slave enterprises decreases cost of labor, allows for expanded profit when combined with inexhaustible supply of inexpensive land		growth of racial divisions enforced by codes, laws; social divisions widen separating races, classes; increased incidence of slave rebellions; expansion of public infrastructure, private commerce primarily fueled by slave labor

coming would inaugurate a cosmic struggle, preceding the end of the world. A poet among his followers announced "a time to set the world in order."

Usuman attracted a fervent following among the Fulani, traditional herdsmen of the Sahel, who called themselves "a cloud that has settled upon God's earth, so dense that escape from it is impossible." Their empire was a combination of three traditions: another pastoralist attempt to exploit the Sahel's potential for long-range grazing of flocks; another frustrated step to unify the area politically; and another holy war inspired by Islamic militancy. By 1820, Usuman's followers had conquered an empire that stretched from Bornu to beyond the Niger, with a capital of sunbaked clay buildings at Sokoto (see Map 21.4). This really was the world's last great pastoralist empire. It lasted until British conquest in 1906.

LAND EMPIRES OF THE NEW WORLD

The case of the Fulani had parallels in the Americas. By the eighteenth century, horse-borne hunting made the South American pampa and North American prairie desirable places to live in. Intrusions of farmers and city dwellers on the edges enhanced the new economic opportunities that horses, cattle, and sheep offered.

The Araucanos and the Sioux

Pastoralism and mining enabled native peoples of the pampa in what is today Argentina to open new trade with Chile and to absorb lessons in large-scale chieftaincy from the Araucanos—the impressive warriors of the South American Southwest, who maintained effective independence beyond the frontiers of the Spanish Empire. By the mid-eighteenth century, chieftains on the rivers Negro and Colorado, such as Cacapol and his son Cangapol "the Wild," could turn the elective position of

MAP 21.5

The Spread of the Horse in the North American Prairie, 1600–1800

→ Horses

⊞ Spanish Missions in California, late eighteenth century

war chief into hereditary rule. They could organize lucrative trade in furs, assemble harems of a size to mark their status, impress a Jesuit visitor as "monarchs over all the rest," raise thousands of warriors, and threaten the city of Buenos Aires.

A similar transformation began to affect the North American prairie. Huge kills of buffalo for their hides generated a trading surplus, which in turn introduced maize to Native American hunters' diets, whiskey to their religious rites, and guns to their armories. As the horses multiplied, the plains became a source of supply for the white colonies on the edges of the region. Even before white men disputed control of them, the prairies became an arena of competition between ever-growing numbers of immigrant Native American peoples—many driven, as much as drawn, from east of the Missouri River by the pressure of white empire building (see Map 21.5). Those with agricultural traditions edged toward or into nomadism. All tended to become herders of horses as well as hunters of buffalo—which forced them into unstable contact with each other on shared trails and pastures. The Sioux were converts to nomadism. Numbering 25,000 by 1790, increasing rapidly thereafter, they were a potentially imperial or at least domineering people who became the terror of a settled Native American world still intact on the upper Missouri River.

Even when they had adopted a horse-borne way of life and an economy based on the slaughter of bison, the Sioux kept an interest in their traditional forest economy. Even when their conquests covered the plains, they extended them into new forests farther west, where deer hunting still conferred special prestige. The Black Hills in South Dakota were their "meat store," which they seized from Kiowa,

Cheyenne (who ran a smaller but equally dynamic empire of their own), and Crow. Meanwhile, trade exposed the region to killer diseases of European origin. Smallpox epidemics eased the Sioux's conquest of the Arikara and Omaha peoples just as diseases had paved the way for white imperialism among unimmunized Native Americans. The Sioux adopted the values of imperial society, rewarding skill in battle above other qualities and tying social status to the possession and distribution of booty. White people did not introduce imperialism to the plains. They arrived as competitors with a Sioux Empire that was already taking shape there.

Portugal in Brazil

East of this region, France's attempt to create an American land empire failed. The French, despite the density of their home population, were reluctant emigrants in the eighteenth century. Before France ceded it to Spain in 1763, Louisiana—a vast territory that took in most of the Mississippi valley—was little more than an outline on the map. In 1746, it had only 3,300 settlers, mostly concentrated around New Orleans at the mouth of the Mississippi River, while South Carolina alone, in a poorer region with a less congenial environment, had 20,000.

The black Brazilian sculptor Aleijadinho (ca. 1730–1804) carved this statue of the prophet Ezekiel for the church of Nosso Senhor do Bom Jesus de Matosinho, in the province of Minas Gerais. Because Aleijadinho's hands were crippled, he would not have been able to depict the animation, emotion, and decorative detail displayed here if he had not been carving in soapstone, which is soft when freshly quarried but hardens on exposure to air.

Other European empires, however, made substantial inroads in other parts of the hemisphere. The Portuguese got a second wind after their seventeenth-century troubles with the Dutch (see Chapter 17) and the Omanis, developing a vast, rich domain to landward in their previously neglected outpost of Brazil. As Portugal withdrew from or lost most of its sovereign outposts in Asia and East Africa, Brazil became, for want of anything better, the jewel in the crown of a now compact empire. Most of the Brazilian coast was less than two months' sail from Lisbon or the African slave ports on the other side of the Atlantic.

Exploitation of the Brazilian hinterland remained largely an affair of private slavers and ranchers, operating out of the southern city of São Paulo, until the 1680s, when reports of gold and diamond finds deep in the interior began to accumulate. In the "golden century" from the 1690s, gold and diamonds replaced sugar as Brazil's cash crops. We can see the effects in the depth of gilding that coats countless eighteenth-century Portuguese church walls. An era of ambitious demand for high art began in a land awash with wealth. Some cash went on British service industries and manufactured goods, stimulating industrialization in Britain. Some of it ended up in India and China, funding the West's persistent balance of payments deficit with the east. Much of it funded the creativity of sculptors and painters, like Aleijadinho, the crippled, black genius whose sculptures are among the wonders of the churches in Minas Gerais. Other black slaves produced impressive church music for wealthy Portuguese-Brazilians. Gold and silverwork were banned in Brazil in 1766 to protect Portuguese craftsmen. By then, the Portuguese had pushed Spanish outposts back roughly to the line of the present linguistic boundary between Spanish and Portuguese in South America. Although Spain's New World land empire was much bigger, Portugal's was in some ways more impressive: carved out of hostile jungle environments. Brazil had little useful Native American manpower, and most of what there was—when the Portuguese could catch them—had to be enslaved and forcibly redistributed to work the mines and plantations.

Spanish America

Eighteenth-century Spanish expansion happened more modestly, through a collaborative approach, winning over native communities that could not be conquered. The experience of the late seventeenth and early eighteenth centuries showed that

This idealized view of the main square of San Juan Bautista, Texas, in 1754 illustrates the way the Spanish monarchy eventually won over native communities it could not conquer. It shows the consecration of the main square by the erection of crosses at its corners. The mission is at the top, with its garden and magnificent church, and the town hall is to the right. Nuns, with the children from their school, emerge from the mission buildings to attend the ceremony. Parties of Indians are arriving at all the main entrances to the square, while Spanish troops and Native Americans parade and fire salutes.

the Spanish Empire could triumph by force only on exceptionally well-settled frontiers, like New Mexico, which the Spanish bloodily reconquered from Native American rebels in the 1690s. The policy of scattering frontier garrisons over a wide area often left their defenders surrounded by enemies and isolated. Instead, in the eighteenth century, Spanish strategy switched to a method that proved surprisingly successful: attracting peoples into the monarchy through prolonged negotiations, on equal terms. Communities that accepted Spanish rule moved into the supposed security and prosperity of rationally planned settlements.

In the second half of the century, the Spanish persuaded Indians to settle in 80 new towns on the Argentine and Chilean frontiers, and in many more settlements on and beyond the northern edge of effective Spanish power, in what is now the southwestern United States. The triumph of the process is represented by scenes like that of the foundation of San Juan Bautista in Texas in 1754, sketched by a native artist in a report sent home to Spain. Through the neat files of the colonnaded streets, processions of Indians and Spaniards thread, with their traditional arms and dress and music, to meet the mission folk in the main square and erect celebratory crosses in each of its corners: an idealized scene, no doubt, but one that represents, at least, the way Spanish administrators wanted their empire to be. Similar means drew runaway slaves back into the empire. At San Antonio in Texas, black settlers had the right to exclude white colonists, except for a priest. By 1779, San Antonio had nearly 1,500 citizens.

In California, 21 new missions extended Spain's reach beyond its remotest garrisons in the late eighteenth century (see Map 21.5). From 1769 to his death in 1784, the Franciscan missionary Brother Junípero Serra founded a string of mission stations along the coast of upper California, where the arrival of an annual ship was the only contact with the rest of the Spanish monarchy. Here he converted the environment as well as its inhabitants, wrenching the natives out of nomadism, producing new crops—wheat, grapes, citrus, almonds, olives, figs—from the soil. His foundations stretched from San Diego to San Francisco, to keep the wilderness, paganism, and rival empires—British and Russian—at bay. In these respects, the missions were successful. They worked economically, too. They had 427 head of cattle in 1775 and at least 95,000 by 1805. But prosperity did not help the Native Americans survive the unfamiliar diseases that contact with Europeans brought. The Indians, as a missionary observed, "fattened and sickened."

At the other end of the empire, where the Jesuits tended the southeastern frontier in Paraguay until the Spanish government expelled them in 1768, dozens of mission churches, now ruined or restored, mark the boundaries. Even on Spain's most troublesome frontier, in what is now southern Chile, progress was made in the 1770s and 1780s, when the Spaniards adopted the policy of treating with native peoples on equal terms, conceding their claim to possess sovereignty. Previously hostile Indian peoples joined the Spanish monarchy, and even the Mapuche, whom the Spanish could not conquer, allowed Spaniards to build a road and a string of missions to promote trade.

Creole Mentalities

Colonies laboriously created, carefully built in the image of Europe, gradually grew away from home. Creole sentiments and values began to emerge almost as soon as colonies were established. Some settlers came to the Americas to escape their mother countries. Others, determined to remold the frontier in the image of home, were nonetheless seduced by the novelties of the New World, turning their backs on the ocean, striking inland, and seeking a new identity. In some ways the New World tended to drift away from the old almost as soon as the two shores were linked, slipping as if from newly tied moorings. Internal economic systems developed, followed by new loyalties, and finally by political independence.

By the eighteenth century, creolism—it might fairly be said— was a strong Spanish-American ideology. In 1747, the enlightened French naturalist, Georges-Louis, Count de Buffon, lost patience with overly idealistic depictions of the New World, which, it must be admitted, owed a lot to empires' desires to make themselves look good. He sketched out an alternative America, a grim world of harsh climates, dwarfish beasts, stunted plants, and ugly and degenerate people. His views sparked fiercely patriotic reactions in the New World. Creole science responded to European scholars' contempt for America by arguing that American nature was superior to that of the Old World—according to some claims, even the sky in the Western Hemisphere was more benign, and the influences of the stars were more favorable there. The creole elite of Peru affected Inca dress and collected Inca artifacts. In Mexico, discoveries in the late eighteenth century, including in 1773 the ruins of Palenque, the "Maya Pompeii" (Pompeii, a Roman city in southern Italy buried by a volcanic eruption in 79 C.E., had been rediscovered in the 1730s), and the uncovering of the Aztec "calendar stone" under the paving of the main square of Mexico City in 1790, boosted interest in Native American antiquities. Scholars began to describe the ruins of Xochicalco—the most complete surviving city from Aztec times—at about the same time.

These movements in Hispanic America had parallels in British colonies. Until independence in 1776, most of the leaders of the colonies that became the United States still thought of themselves as Englishmen, but the sense of being American was beginning to take shape. Gradually, elites in British North America identified with fellow colonists. In Thomas Jefferson's (1742–1826) mind, the rights of true-born Englishmen came to include the right to renounce English identity. Americans were founding a new society, independent of Britain, just as their Saxon ancestors had founded a new society when they went to Britain in the fifth century, independent of their native Germany. This was the reason behind Jefferson's frustrated efforts to have Hengist and Horsa, the supposed founders of Anglo-Saxon England, adorn the seal of the United States. At Monticello, Jefferson's estate in Virginia, his domestic museum was rich in American specimens and Native American artifacts. Painted buffalo hides hung in his hall. "Savage" carvings from Tennessee lined the atrium, rather as a Renaissance Italian palace might exhibit Roman inscriptions and statues (see Chapter 15). The portraits Jefferson collected included supposed makers of America—the explorers Christopher Columbus and Amerigo Vespucci hung alongside heroes of the American Revolution, such as George Washington and the Marquis de Lafayette. After the Revolutionary War, in the 1780s, the French traveler Michel-Guillaume Jean de Crèvecoeur, who had once believed that American freedom was an overseas version of England's "national genius," revised his opinion. Americans, he thought, were "neither Europeans nor the descendants of Europeans" but "a new race of men." Joel Barlow (1754–1812), the first epic poet of independent America, hailed, "call'd from slavish chains, a bolder race."

Aztec calendar stone. Just after European scholars had proclaimed the natural inferiority of the New World, spectacular archaeological finds in Mexico seemed to vindicate pre-Columbian America's claim to house great civilizations. This "Aztec calendar," unearthed in 1790, appeared to demonstrate mathematical proficiency, elevating the knowledge its makers had from "superstition" to "science." The glyphs on the carving surround an image of the god Tonatiuh who is crowned with a sunbeam and arrayed with images of a jaguar's head and claws, a sky serpent, a feathered shield with an emblem of the sun, and a basketful of the remains of human sacrifice.

Toward Independence

The America that broke away from Britain in the war of 1775–1783 was in many ways a brand new society, though its origins had been laid more than 150 years before. Until the mid-eighteenth century, British settlements were sparse and scattered, clinging to the eastern rim of the continent. As a destination for migrants in the seventeenth century, the attractions of the West Indies outclassed mainland North America. After 100 years of colonization, the total white population of the mainland colonies was around 250,000. Many of the successful colonies had been conscious experiments by idealists and religious pilgrims. Economic self-betterment had been the explicit aim only of those desperate enough to sign away their liberty and labor for the term of an indenture, to buy a passage from home and a few tools and clothes with which to start an independent life when their bond was paid. In the eighteenth century, as colonial horizons broadened and the prospects of a good life in America became better defined, the mood of migrants changed. Their numbers exploded. In the 1770s, on the eve of the Revolution, the total population was probably over 2.5 million (see Figure 21.1).

This astonishing increase—by a factor of 10 within three generations—had no precedent or parallel elsewhere in the New World. It was an accelerating process, most of which was crammed into the last third of the entire short period. Between the mid-eighteenth century and the outbreak of the Revolution in 1775, the number of towns founded in New England tripled each year, as—roughly—did the populations of Georgia and South Carolina. In the 1760s, the population of New York rose by nearly 40 percent and that of Virginia more than doubled.

From about 1760, a rush of settlers scaled the previously impassable wall of the Appalachian Mountains to found a new biblical "land of Canaan" between the Susquehanna and the Ohio rivers. Crèvecoeur, whose book *Letters from an American Farmer* was to make him a founding father of American identity, imagined himself joining a mass of immigrants, heading out from Connecticut to the wilds of western Pennsylvania. There he found "a prodigious number of houses rearing up, fields cultivating, that great extent of industry opened up to a bold and indefatigable people." In 1769, on the day the land office opened at Fort Pitt on the site of what is today Pittsburgh, 2,790 claims were staked. By 1771, 10,000 families were living on this frontier. The most adventurous imaginations were overstimulated by what they saw. George Washington dreamed in the 1760s of laying "with very little money the foundation of a noble estate" on the Ohio River. He was disappointed and eventually had to make do with being president of a new republic instead.

The migrants who stimulated and swelled this growth came with alienated loyalties. Those from within England itself were almost all young. Those from within Britain were mostly from Scotland and, within Scotland, mostly from the Highlands and Islands—regions that the English and Lowland Scots establishment had only recently conquered and that were subject to vicious political and religious persecution. Many of the hearts and minds in which the Revolution was conceived were those of newcomers, gripped in a ferment of exciting possibilities. British America was a colonial region in flux, exploding with instability. Independent America was, to a great extent, a nation of latecomers.

New Englanders could never fully participate in the landward turn. Except in the Connecticut River valley and as domestic servants, slaves were largely unsuited to the climate. Nor could the New England economy pay for them. Farmer-settlers worked wonders with rocky soils—which were duly abandoned, to

> *"British America was a colonial region in flux, exploding with instability. Independent America was, to a great extent, a nation of latecomers."*

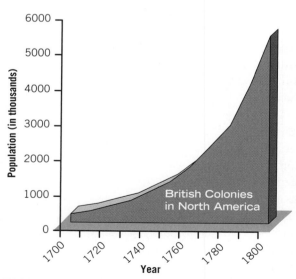

FIGURE 21.1 POPULATION GROWTH IN BRITISH NORTH AMERICA, 1700–1800
Historical Statistics of the United States (Washington, DC: U.S. Government Printing Office, 1976), 1168.

be replaced by mills or returned to forest, as newer, better farmland opened up farther west. Mountains and the boundaries of rival states cut the maritime colonies off from the interior. They were best equipped for a seaborne trading economy. The impoverished hinterland of New England drove work and wealth creation seaward, to the cod and whale fisheries and long-range trade.

In a sense, these were the wages of success. Early in the eighteenth century, New England's population outgrew its capacity to grow food. A trading vocation replaced the farming vocation with which the founding fathers had arrived. Yet New Englanders in their own way, by sea, drifted apart from the mother country, just as the landward-driving settlers and investors in the Ohio valley edged away by land. For the ocean led to the world. Ever-improving maritime technology was always—slowly, by small step-by-step advances, or by sudden leaps, such as the introduction of a method to determine longitude in the late eighteenth century—opening more of the globe to commerce. Gradually, during the century, it became a marked disadvantage for a trading people to be limited by the regulations of empire. New England's quarrels with Britain focused increasingly on issues of barriers to trade and the freedom of the seas, and disputes over the definition of contraband—what goods were legal to trade in and what taxes merchants and consumers had to pay on those goods. The great symbolic acts of resistance that preceded the Revolutionary War happened offshore and made these issues explicit in acts of civil disobedience: the Boston Tea Party in 1773 and the seizure of the small British warship *Gaspée* in Narragansett Bay, Rhode Island, in 1772—"God damn your blood!" screamed the respectable merchants who boarded and burned this piracy-control vessel.

Long Wharf, Boston. In 1770, when Paul Revere engraved and published this view, Long Wharf still extended out further than any other wharf in colonial Boston. The view shows the arrival in September 1768 of British troops sent to quell disorders that rocked the city almost continuously from the late 1760s.

Meanwhile, under the stress of war with France in the 1750s and 1760s and in the flush of victory that followed the end of France's American empire in 1763, Britain's attitude to America had become more centralizing and interventionist. The British colonies had their own institutions and liberties that got in the way of some of the most crucial functions of government, especially the housing of troops and the levying of taxes. Increasingly vigorous government from Britain was designed to make the colonial administration more uniform, to exploit the colonies' growing wealth and security by taxing them, and to organize defense on modern, efficient, and, therefore, more centralized and expensive lines. These measures aroused the resentment of colonists anxious to retain the privileges and liberties that they had secured during the long period in which the home government had taken little interest in their affairs. The new demands of the pre-Revolutionary years came not so much from the colonists as from a Britain anxious to exact efficiency from its empire. The threat to the colonies' comfortable habits of effective self-rule and cheap government provoked confrontation.

It became increasingly obvious, moreover, in the early 1770s that British rule threatened two vital colonial interests. In 1772, a British judge declared slavery illegal on English soil, in a judgment that aroused premature anticipation among black people in America. Vermont rapidly adopted the ruling into its own laws, but it was unwelcome in the slave-dependent economies of much of British America. It seemed only a matter of time before colonial slave owners clashed with an elite in

Britain that increasingly favored abolishing both the slave trade and slavery itself. Moreover, the British government was determined to keep the peace on the "Indian" frontier, and to preserve Native American buffer states between the British and Spanish empires in the interior of North America. This was precisely where American colonists were looking to expand.

A period of increasing interventionism from Europe and increasing friction with colonial elites was broadly paralleled in the Spanish monarchy, where reformist governments in the same period took increasingly burdensome measures in a similar spirit: reasserting bureaucratic controls, reorganizing imperial defense, eliminating traditional colonial customs, maximizing the power and fiscal reach of the crown. Spanish administrators were as intrusive and troublesome in Spanish colonies as royal governors were in those of Britain. In both empires, the home governments tried to ease local bigwigs out of influential offices and replace them with creatures of the home government. In both empires, the results included growing, and potentially revolutionary, resentments. For both empires, the Americas housed some of the most remote, most difficult to govern provinces, with local populations that stubbornly sought to protect their own interests. In both empires, home governments encouraged militarization—mobilization and training for defense. These measures were a rational response to the problems of security in vast territories with ill-defined frontiers, but the effect was to create potential reservoirs of armed revolutionaries.

The Seven Years' War, which began in 1756 and ended in 1763, removed the French threat to the colonists' security with the British conquest of Canada and the French cession of Louisiana to Spain. The colonies were now free to challenge their rulers in England. By imposing high costs on imperial defense, the war encouraged Britain to seek new ways to tax America, with all the familiar consequences. It trained American fighters in the skills they would need if they were ever to challenge British forces. The experience of military collaboration between American militias and British regulars initiated or exposed cultural differences. The floggings and other brutalities of discipline that troops in the British army were subject to repelled the volunteers in the colonial militias, while the British attacked colonial resistance to stationing troops in private houses, which was the usual practice elsewhere in the British Empire, as "neglect of humanity" and "depravity of nature." The colonists saw themselves as true-born Englishmen but were shocked to find that their fellow countrymen from across the Atlantic did not share their self-perception. Mutual alienation led to violence.

Historians used to depict the uprising in 13 of the English mainland colonies in the 1770s as a peculiarly English affair—the inevitable outcome of long-standing traditions of freedom that colonists took with them as a heritage from deep in the English past. On the contrary, current scholarship tells us, it was an improvised solution to short-term problems, a typical convulsion of a colonial world that was full of rebellions in the late eighteenth century: against the British government in the north of Ireland, against Spain in Colombia and Peru.

The war was in one sense an English civil war, pitting self-styled free-born Englishmen against an intrusive government, recycling the rhetoric of sev-

British defeat. John Trumbull (1756–1843) painted the surrender of British to American forces at Yorktown in Virginia in 1781 in symbolic fashion. American General Benjamin Lincoln accepts the surrender on a horse with a raised forepaw—a traditional symbol of triumph, under a darkening sky that suggests the shadowing power of divine providence. Only the Americans are shown victorious in the painting, whereas the war against the British was brought to this conclusion thanks to French and Spanish help. A large French army participated in the siege of Yorktown, and the French fleet forced the surrender by preventing the British from escaping by sea.

MAP 21.6

The Americas in 1828

- ▨ area gaining independence from imperial control or claims, ca. 1783–1828
- ▨ British possession
- ▨ Russian possession
- → Sioux expansion
- ➔ Scientific expedition of Alessandro Malaspina, 1790–1793

enteenth-century conflicts in England, where the "commonwealth" had fought the crown. American revolutionaries' favorite philosopher was John Locke (1632–1704), who in an attempt to justify revolution in England, advocated what he called natural rights of freedom (but not for black people), religious toleration (but not for Catholics), and property (but not for Native Americans).

But if the revolt of the colonies was, in part, a war between rival visions of the rights of "true-born Englishmen," it was also an American civil war, in which at least 20 percent of the white population, and most of the black people and Native Americans, sided with the British. Increasingly, it also became an international conflict. After the first three years' campaigns, when the raw American forces proved surprisingly effective, France in 1778 joined by Spain in 1779 saw the opportunity to inflict a defeat on the British. Usually, the British won eighteenth-century wars by buying the alliance of other powers on the continent of Europe.

Alejandro Malaspina's Spanish expedition to the Americas and the Pacific was the last and most elaborate of the great voyages of scientific research inspired by the Enlightenment and funded by European governments. The expedition's first ethnographic fieldwork took place in Patagonia, recorded by the official artist, José del Pozo, who captured features the Spaniards' reports stressed: the inhabitants' legendary stature, their monogamous habits, their affection for children, their adoption of horses, and the authority of their chief, Juncar, who dominates the center foreground. As with all the peoples the expedition studied, the specialist scholars on board created a vocabulary of the language. Malaspina thought the Patagonians "worthy of the attention of philosophers" and proposed further research into their origins, but doubted whether other, more isolated groups could be as "civilized" as those he met.

This time, no such allies were available. French and Spanish intervention proved decisive, and the colonies that now began to call themselves the United States of America were the main beneficiaries (see Map 21.6).

The Spanish colonies, with their longer, stronger tradition of creole consciousness, were likely to follow the example of the northern revolutionaries. Indeed, rebellions and conspiracies multiplied in Spanish America during the 1770s and 1780s. Soon after the emergence of the independent United States, Alessandro Malaspina—one of the new breed of scientifically trained Spanish naval officers—prepared an official fact-finding voyage across the Hispanic world. In part, it was to be Spain's answer to the great Pacific voyages of the Briton Captain James Cook and the Frenchmen Bougainville and La Pérouse (see Chapter 20): the most ambitious survey of the Americas and the Pacific ever undertaken. The results were dazzling—the product of the efforts of an enlightened government, which, as the German naturalist Baron von Humboldt (1767–1835) acknowledged, spent more on scientific research than any other monarchy of the day. Malaspina and the scholars who accompanied him gathered hundreds of thousands of samples, drawings, maps, and reports about plants, animals, native peoples, geology, climate, and the oceans.

Yet Malaspina was also responsible for reporting on the political state of the empire and the best measures of reform. Much of the background of rebellion in the English colonies was also visible in those of Spain: the emergence of distinctive political identities, the political unrest, the resentment over taxes. The eighteenth-century Mexican revolutionary, Servando de Mier, announced the political program of creolism: "America is ours, because we were born in it." He asserted the "natural right of peoples in their respective regions. God has separated us from Europe by an immense sea and our interests are distinct."

Spanish America was poised, for a moment, between two possible futures. On the one hand, as Malaspina envisioned, Spain could delegate authority into provincial hands, slash defense costs, and open trade to universal competition. On the other, the monarchy could continue to attempt to enforce an eighteenth-century model of ever more rigorous centralization, regulate trade for the benefit of Spain, not the colonies, spend heavily for defense, and risk provoking the kind of revolution that had already shattered Britain's American empire. Unfortunately, Malaspina's voyage was a long affair, which outlasted the moment when the Spanish government might have embraced reform. By the time he returned to Spain in the 1794, the French Revolution was sending shudders of horror down establishment spines. The Spanish government was in no mood to embrace reform. Malaspina was disgraced, and almost all the vast feedback of information from his scientific team was locked up, unpublished, in state archives. In America, two decades later, when war against French invaders immobilized the Spanish state, local elements, in both Spain and America, fell back on the old Spanish tradition of setting up local councils, or juntas, to handle affairs in an emergency. Once in place, most of the American juntas saw little reason to accept a return to Spanish rule, even after the French were driven from Spain in 1814, except under terms that left them in effective control.

The independence revolutions had similar causes across the Americas but, in important respects, differing outcomes. The Caribbean saw only one successful revolution: that of Haiti from 1791 to 1802 (see Chapter 19). On few other islands were there more than feeble and brief efforts to join or mimic the revolutions on the North and South American continents. Canada remained aloofly loyal to the British crown. Britain's recently acquired French Catholic subjects in Quebec evidently thought it better to be ruled from distant London than from Boston or Philadelphia. Peru and Brazil embraced independence with some reluctance. Peru's revolutionaries included elements for whom the royal government in Spain was too liberal. Independent Brazil remained a monarchy until 1889, ruled by emperors descended from the royal house of Portugal, the former colonial power. This was understandable, since, for Brazil, the Napoleonic Wars (1799–1815) had brought the colonies closer to the mother country after the Portuguese royal family chose exile in Brazil when France overran Portugal in 1807. For the Spanish Empire, the Napoleonic invasion of Spain in 1808 was an alienating experience that exposed new quarrels between the colonial and metropolitan elites. Despite the republican rhetoric that had been prominent in the rebellions, Mexico and Peru also flirted with ideas for monarchical government at intervals during their rebellions and after they won independence in 1821 (see Map 21.6).

As for the ways in which they unfolded, there were huge differences between North and South America—or, at least, what would become the United States, on the one hand, and the Spanish-speaking republics, on the other. Anglo-America and Latin America began to take divergent courses, much to the advantage of the former. The Spanish wars started later and lasted longer. Fighting in North America, though traumatic and divisive, lasted barely 8 years, from 1775 to 1783. Unlike the Anglo-American revolutionaries, whose success depended on French and Spanish help, the Latin American rebels fought on their own, against tenacious royalist resistance. Because the Latin American wars started later, the cultural context was different. The principles of the Enlightenment (see Chapter 22) no longer commanded the respect with which the founding fathers of the United States revered them. Armies, which in the eighteenth century were small, highly professional organizations, were now composed of mass levies. Militias were no longer constrained by the strict laws of war that had formerly helped to mitigate the horrors of warfare. Although there were massacres and atrocities in the American Revolutionary War, they were mainly directed against Native Americans—whom the revolutionaries regarded as outside the constraints of civilized behavior—or occurred at a late and desperate phase of the conflict, mainly in the Carolina backcountry, where the mutual hatred of rebels and crown loyalists was peculiarly intense. In Latin America, however, terror and massacre became routine features of the revolutions. The loyalists mobilized slave armies—something the British barely attempted in North America—to wreak vengeance on the former masters.

The exchange of atrocities intensified in 1813 when Simón Bolívar, the Venezuelan revolutionary who has, perhaps, the best claim to be the overall mastermind of Spanish American independence, proclaimed what he called "war to the death. . . . Let the monsters who have infested our land and covered it in blood vanish forever. . . . Every Spaniard who does not join us against tyranny in our just cause, wholeheartedly and effectively, will be classed as a foe and punished as a

Chronology: Slavery and Empire in the New World

1690s	Gold and diamonds replace sugar as Brazil's main revenue source
Eighteenth century	Nearly 3.5 million African slaves brought to the Americas. European expansion into South American pampa and North American prairie
1756–1763	Seven Years' War
1775–1783	American colonies gain independence from Britain
1791–1802	Haiti gains independence from France
1821	Mexico and Peru gain independence
1822	Brazil proclaims independence from Portugal

A CLOSER LOOK

Imagining Brazilian Independence

"The Founder of the Fatherland." José Bonifacio de Andrade e Silva was one of the outstanding figures in scientific circles in late colonial Brazil. His prestige helped to legitimize the establishment of the independent Brazilian Empire in 1822. Expelled during later political troubles, he died in exile in 1838. This late nineteenth-century engraving depicts him as a disillusioned hero of Brazil's struggle to create a state in which white people, black people, and Native Americans could live in harmony.

The figure representing Brazil's Native Americans is romantically depicted, as Native Americans were in most nineteenth-century Brazilian art, but he has an unmistakable air of detachment, implying that Native Americans were fascinating and exotic but on the fringe of Brazilian society.

A fundação da Patria Brazileira
(7 de Setembro de 1822)

The imperial crown and regalia represent Andrade's hopes of preserving Brazil in peace as an independent monarchy ruled by an "emperor" from the Portuguese royal family.

An adoring woman represents Brazil's large black population. Her deferential attitude implies that black Brazilians "looked up" to their white compatriots.

How does this depiction of independent Brazil idealize its society?

traitor to the fatherland and, therefore, will be unremittingly harried to death." This was not mere rhetoric. Massacre and the destruction of property were systematic strategies, applied on both sides. Bolívar himself summed up the consequences: "Blood flows in torrents. Three hundred years of culture, enlightenment, and industry have disappeared. The ruins of nature or of war appear on every side. It is as if every kind of evil had descended on our miserable peoples."

Brazilian independence came rapidly and almost bloodlessly in 1822 when a Portuguese prince was proclaimed Emperor Pedro I of Brazil. Though some destructive internal conflicts followed, they were resolved relatively quickly, and loyalty to the new monarchy preserved the unity of Brazil. The Spanish colonies, meanwhile, were condemned to nearly two decades of destruction in merciless violence against Spanish armies that demonstrated surprising strength. The wars of independence, which had caused long and total interruptions of foreign trade, also ruined the economies of the Spanish colonies, whereas the United States, enjoying the protection of the French and Spanish navies, actually gained new trading partners and multiplied its shipping during its struggle against the British.

In Perspective
The Rims of Empires

Within the Americas, a new gap opened between what became the United States—increasingly prosperous, advantageously connected to a growing global economy—and Latin America, stagnant or arrested in development, unable to lick clean the wounds of its wars. After independence, U.S. society showed few signs of having been militarized by the experience of war. George Washington, the first president, rose to supreme civil command by virtue of his role as supreme commander of the revolutionary armies. But, like a dictator of the ancient Roman republic, he withdrew to civilian life when his term of power was over, and he nurtured the civil institutions of the republic he hoped to found. The Latin American republics, by contrast, emerged thoroughly militarized, with their armies identified as the makers and guardians of the political settlement, and their generals destined for power in society. To some extent, the process had begun in the colonial period, when the Spanish monarchy encouraged all white males to take part-time responsibility for imperial defense. But the long, vicious wars, in which unprecedented numbers of soldiers were mobilized, were decisive in molding society in the likeness of an army. The sheer destruction and bloodshed of the era of the wars of independence crippled the economies of the former colonies, which were, in any case, poorly positioned to take part in the expansion of global trade, in which their neighbors in the United States enjoyed a head start. For much of the nineteenth and twentieth centuries, people in the United States would behold Latin America with mingled pity, greed, and contempt.

It was not only in the Americas that the rights of empires were questioned. When the French navigator Louis de Bougainville left the island of Tahiti in the South Pacific in 1768, he set up an engraved plaque with the words, "This land is ours." The French satirist, Denis Diderot, who was also one of the most influential intellectuals of the era (see Chapter 22), put a rejoinder into the mouth of a fictional Tahitian: "If a Tahitian landed one day on your shores, and scratched on one of your rocks or the bark of your trees, 'This country belongs to the people of Tahiti,' what would you think?" Diderot went further: "Every colony, whose authority rests in one country and whose obedience is in another, is in principle a vicious establishment." Much of

"For much of the nineteenth and twentieth centuries, people in the United States would behold Latin America with mingled pity, greed, and contempt."

Chronology

1690s	Gold and diamonds replace sugar as Brazil's main revenue source crop
1707	Death of Aurangzeb and the end of Mughal expansion
1720	China conquers Tibet
1722	Safavid Empire collapses
1756–1757	Robert Clive leads East India Company (EIC) conquest of Bengal
1756–1763	Seven Years' War
1759	Chinese conquest of Xinjiang complete
1761–1764	EIC revenues: £2 million
1766	Gold and silverwork banned in Brazil to protect Portuguese craftsmen
1766–1767	EIC revenues: £7.5 million
1767	Burmese invasion leads to disintegration of Thailand
1771–1778	Vietnam collapses under strain of peasant rebellions
1774	Ottomans cede land to Russia in the Treaty of Küçük Kaynarca
1775–1783	American colonies gain independence from Britain
Late eighteenth century	Marathas offer only nominal obedience to the Mughals; slaves become West Africa's most valuable export
1780s	Spanish and French laws protect the rights of slaves
1789	French Revolution begins
1791–1802	Haiti gains independence from France
1799	British conquer Mysore
ca. 1800	200,000 Chinese immigrants settled in Xinjiang
1806	Maratha states accept British overlordship
1821	Mexico and Peru gain independence
1822	Brazil proclaims independence from Portugal

the European elite was happy to applaud the independence of the former colonies in the Americas.

There was little revulsion of feeling between the mother countries and their rebellious children. The independence of most of the Americas might have opened a new chasm in the Atlantic, splitting the Atlantic world that had grown up in the previous three centuries. On the contrary, Atlantic trade continued to grow after the wars of independence, as did migration from Europe. Nor did conflict interrupt the exchange of ideas. Independence did, however, make a difference. The independent colonies had the prospect of becoming empires in their own right by expanding in their own hinterlands. For the United States, the outlook was particularly encouraging. The circumstances in which it achieved independence left the new country strong and wealthy, by comparison with other parts of the hemisphere, and the states had enormous, underexploited resources in nearby lands.

The exploitation of colonial frontiers had hardly begun. No recorded crossing of North America from the Atlantic to the Pacific was made until 1793. Knowledge of the interior of the hemisphere was so ill recorded that patriots in Washington, D.C., in the early 1800s were unsure where the Rocky Mountains were. Scholars in Europe did not know that the Amazon and the Orinoco Rivers in South America were connected until Baron von Humboldt—one of the world's most adventurous scientists—made the journey between them in 1800. Only a beginning had been made. Yet what had been achieved did matter.

Empire-building initiatives had become—for a while—almost a European monopoly. Native Asian empires had crumbled, or their expansion had largely halted. The nineteenth century saw few if any reversals comparable to those the Omanis had inflicted on the Portuguese, for instance. From now on, successful empire builders would need continually to update their war-making technology with industrially produced guns and ships. For most of the nineteenth century, only a few powers—European, for the most part, and the United States—had effective access to such technology.

Although most of the world remained outside the rule of the empires of the age, imperialism had bridged some of the world's great chasms of communication. There were touch points of empire, at which the colonialism of rival powers met, in some of the most impenetrable places of the globe. In the late eighteenth century, Chinese and Japanese agents vied to collect tribute from native chiefs in Sakhalin Island, north of Japan, where Russia was also beginning to cast covetous looks. In the depths of Brazil, Portuguese soldiers wiped out the Jesuit missions in 1755, with Spanish permission, in a murderous rationalization of a previously vague frontier.

In 1759, tiny British and French armies of 2,000 or 3,000 men settled the fate of Canada in a battle the British won under the modest church spires of Quebec City. In 1762–1763, the British occupied Spanish Manila in the Philippines, on the edge of the South China Sea, where the purely commercial maritime expansion of China had met the rival, armed imperialisms of Portugal, Holland, England, and Spain. In 1788, a French expedition anchored off Botany Bay in Australia only to find that a British colonizing venture—using convict exiles—had just beaten them to it.

In 1790, Britain and Spain almost went to war when Spanish forces seized British ships, dispatched from Sydney in Australia, at Nootka Sound, on the northwest coast of America, where British, Spanish, and Russian expansion converged. In 1796, the Spanish crown's glib Welsh agent, John Evans, persuaded the Mandan Indians of the upper Missouri to hoist the Spanish flag, defining a new frontier with the British Empire, represented by the formerly French fort of La Souris, two-weeks' march away. The hand of empire may have lain lightly on some lands, but it stretched long fingertips over the world.

PROBLEMS AND PARALLELS

1. How did China use colonization and settlement to expand its territory? What impact did Chinese immigration have on Southeast Asia? Why did the Chinese government not support overseas immigration?
2. Why did native Asian empires lose impetus in this period? Why did the Mughal Empire go into permanent decline?
3. Why did the British gain ascendancy in India? What are the parallels between British imperialism in India and the Spanish conquest of the Americas? Why did Tipu Sultan resist the British so tenaciously?
4. Which land empires expanded in this period in Asia and Africa? How was Usuman da Fodio able to build an empire in the Sahel?
5. Why did the slave trade last so long in the Americas? What was the economic rationale for slavery?
6. How did black people in the Americas craft their own social customs and norms of behavior? Why did laws designed to protect slaves mostly fail?
7. How did ecological change and the presence of Europeans strengthen some Native American peoples in the eighteenth century? Why did the Sioux become an imperial people?
8. How did the growth of national identity affect relations between European mother countries and their colonies? Why did Spanish America suffer more than Anglo-America or Brazil from the struggles to gain independence? Why did Latin American leaders like Simón Bolívar fight so much more bitterly for independence than the North American rebels against Britain did?

READ ON ▶ ▶ ▶

On Mughal decline and the rise of British influence, Jos Gommans, *Mughal Warfare: Indian Frontiers and Highroads to Empire 1500–1700* (2003) provides important background, and Marshall Hodgson, *The Venture of Islam, Volume 3: The Gunpower Empires and Modern Times* (1977) is a classic that also covers the Ottoman and Persian experiences in this age. A. Newmann, *Safavid Iran* (2006) is valuable. Dirk Kolff, *Naukar, Rajput, and Sepoy: The Ethnohistory of the Military Labour Market of Hindustan, 1450–1850* (2002) shows the complexity of the political and military interaction between Indian and European powers. Evelyn Rawski, *The Last Emperors* (1999) covers China and the slowing of Qing imperialism.

Jorge Cañizares-Esguerra and Erik Seeman, eds., *The Atlantic in Global History: 1500–2000* (2006) is a broad-ranging introduction to the contours of Atlantic history, including the slave trade. Hugh Thomas, *The Slave Trade: The Story of the Atlantic Slave Trade, 1440–1870* (1999) is massively detailed and comprehensive.

The classic first-hand account of Oludah Equiano is readily available in *The Interesting Narrative and Other Writings* (2003).

Fascinating work is being done on the dynamics of American land empires in the late colonial period. See Jorge Canizares-Esguerra, *How to Write the History of the New World: Histories, Epistemologies, and Identities in the Eighteenth-Century Atlantic World* (2001), which is brilliant on creolism, while T. Burnard, *Creole Gentlemen: The Maryland Elite, 1691–1776* (2002) is excellent on the same phenomenon in North America. R. Price, ed., *Maroon Societies: Rebel Slave Communities in the Americas* (1996) collects important work on Atlantic slave rebellions. *The Malaspina Expedition 1789 to 1794: Journal of the Voyage by Alejandro Malaspina: Cadiz to Panama*, ed. Andrew David, Felipe Fernández-Armesto, et al. (2002) provides a first-hand account of the Spanish crown's attempt to improve its knowledge of its American colonies, fix frontiers, improve scientific and geographical knowledge, and generate maps.

CHAPTER 22

The Exchange of Enlightenments:
Eighteenth-Century Thought

▲ **Raja Rammohan Roy.** As a portrait painter, the British artist Henry Perronet Briggs made a specialty of theatrical subjects. His study of Raja Rammohun Roy (1774–1833) seems romantic and dramatic, giving the Indian sage a visionary stare and a strange, vaguely oriental outfit, in a setting that seems to recall the Mughal Empire.

In the spring of 1829, an exciting rumor reached the English bishop of Calcutta. India's most respected thinker, Raja Rammohan Roy, had turned to Christianity. Roy, who was born in 1774, had spent most of his life in Bengal under British rule, except for a period of study in London. He had become an admirer of Western ways, a master of Western languages, a scholar of Western science. He was only 16 when he wrote a rejection of his ancestral religion, *A Reasoned Renunciation of the Idolatrous Religion of the Hindus*. As a teacher, he introduced his pupils to the writings of Western philosophers. He translated Western literature into Indian languages. He promoted printing and popular education as ways to spread critical new readings of ancient Hindu scriptures, and he challenged rituals that he thought contrary to right reason. He led movements to abolish female infanticide and the custom that required widows to burn themselves to death on their husband's funeral pyres. He argued for freedom for women.

In short, many observers saw Roy as representative of a new phase of global history: the slow but unstoppable triumph, from the late eighteenth century onward, of Western ideas, as growing Western power and the example of Western economic and military strength spread them around the world. Indeed, there is much truth in that image. But it does not do justice to the complexity of Roy's thought or to the diversity of the traditions he inherited. He was a scholar of the Veda and of classical Persian literature long before he became a student of Western learning, and his liberal, radical, humane, and skeptical notions were confirmed, not created, by Western influence. He seems to have known about Aristotle from Arabic editions before encountering the original Greek texts. He sought not to turn India into an eastern version of the West, but to use Western help to restore India to what he saw as a golden age of reason, from deep in its own past. He rejected popular superstition and social abuses, whether they were Indian or Western.

Roy was selective, moreover, in the Western culture he admired. The authors he loved and taught were, above all, those connected with the great, innovative movement of eighteenth-century European thought that we call the **Enlightenment**—writers who elevated reason, science, and practical utility, challenged conventional religion, and sought ruthlessly to expose every kind of cant. When the bishop of Calcutta congratulated him on his supposed conversion to Christianity, Roy quickly denied it with the kind of irreverent wit he had picked up from European writers he

FOCUS questions

What was the Enlightenment, and how did it influence Western social, political, and economic thinking?

How did China and Japan view Europe in the eighteenth century?

Why were the ideas of Rousseau so influential?

Why was there a reaction against the cult of reason, and what forms did it take?

How did Enlightenment ideas influence the course of the French Revolution and Napoleon's policies?

What intellectual trends did Europe, the Americas, Islam, and East Asia have in common in the eighteenth century?

"Like all topics in the history of thought, the Enlightenment is complex and elusive. We had better begin by admitting that and relishing the challenge it presents."

admired: "My Lord, I assure you, I did not abandon one superstition merely in order to take up another." The Enlightenment, indeed, was the source of the most powerful influences that spread from Europe over the world of the nineteenth and twentieth centuries. Even before the eighteenth century was over, the Enlightenment made a home in the Americas, with some modifications, and gripped finger holds in Asia.

The Enlightenment was global in its inspiration, as well as its effects. Much debate among historians has focused on the problem of where the Enlightenment started. England, Scotland, France, and the Netherlands all have their partisans. In some ways, we can trace its origins all over Western Europe. This debate misses the more fundamental contribution made by the interaction of Western European thought with ideas from overseas, and, in particular, from China. Like all topics in the history of thought, the Enlightenment is complex and elusive. We had better begin by admitting that and relishing the challenge it presents.

The best way to approach the Enlightenment may be by first telling a story that expresses its character better than any attempt at a dictionary-style definition. We can then look at the global exchange of influences that surrounded enlightened ideas, the key texts that encoded them in Europe, and the changes that overtook and—ultimately—transformed the Enlightenment during the eighteenth century.

THE CHARACTER OF THE ENLIGHTENMENT

To understand what the Enlightenment was like, a good place to start is Kittis in northern Finland, near the Arctic Circle, where a French scientist, Pierre Louis Moreau de Maupertuis, pitched camp in August 1736. The light reflected and refracted among the rocks and ice made it seem, he said, "a place for fairies and spirits."

Maupertuis was engaged in the most elaborate and expensive scientific experiment ever conducted up to that time. Traditionally, Western scientists had assumed that the Earth was perfectly spherical. Seventeenth-century theorists, however, led by Isaac Newton in England, argued that it must be distended at the equator and flattened at the poles, owing to centrifugal force (the thrust or sense of thrust you get on the edge of a circle in motion, which tends, for instance, to fling you off a merry-go-round). Meanwhile, mapmakers working on the survey of France for King Louis XIV (see Chapter 18) made a series of observations that suggested the contrary. The world seemed to be football-shaped: elongated toward the poles. The French Royal Academy of Sciences decided to end the debate by sending expeditions—of which Maupertuis's was one—to measure the length of one degree along the surface of the circumference of the Earth. If measurements at the Arctic Circle matched those at the equator, the globe would be spherical. Any difference between them either way would indicate where the world bulged.

In December 1736, Maupertuis began to measure his baseline, some 12 miles long—"the longest baseline that ever was used"—on the ice of the river. The measuring rods were made of fir wood because of all available materials it was least likely to shrink from the intense cold. "Judge what it must be like," he wrote, "to walk in snow two feet deep, with heavy poles in our hands, . . . in cold so extreme that whenever we would take a little brandy, the only thing that could be kept liquid, our tongues and lips froze to the cup and came away bloody, in a cold that congealed the extremities of the body, while the rest, through excessive toil, was bathed in sweat."

It should have been all but impossible to achieve total accuracy under such conditions, but Maupertuis's readings were overestimated by less than a third of 1 percent. They helped to convince the world that the planet was indeed shaped as Newton had predicted—squashed at the poles and bulging at the equator. On the front page of his collected works, Maupertuis appears in a fur cap and collar over a eulogy that reads, "It was his destiny to determine the shape of the world."

Like many scientific explorers seared by experience, Maupertuis eventually became disillusioned by science but inspired by nature. He set off believing that every truth was quantifiable and that every fact could be sensed. By the time of his death in 1759, he had become something of a mystic. "You cannot chase God in the immensity of the heavens," he concluded, "or the depths of the oceans or the chasms of the Earth. Maybe it is not yet time to understand the world systematically—time only to behold it and be amazed." In the *Letters on the Progress of the Sciences*, which he published in 1752, the next experiments for science to tackle, he felt, would be on dreams and the effects of hallucinatory drugs—"certain potions of the Indies"—as the only way to learn what lay beyond the universe. Perhaps, he speculated, the perceived world is illusory. Maybe only God exists, and perceptions are only properties of a mind "alone in the universe."

Maupertuis's mental pilgrimage between certainty and doubt, science and speculation, rationalism and religious revelation reproduced in miniature the history of European thought in the eighteenth century. First, in a great surge of optimism, the perfectibility of man, the infallibility of reason, the reality of the observed world, and the sufficiency of science became common assumptions. In the second half of the century, the Enlightenment flickered as intellectuals rediscovered the power of feelings over reason and sensations over thoughts. Then revolutionary bloodshed and warfare, in which the century ended, seemed for a while to put out the torch completely. But embers remained: enduring faith that freedom can energize human goodness, that happiness is worth pursuing in this life, and that science and reason—despite their limitations—can unlock progress and enhance lives.

Pierre Louis de Maupertuis (1698–1759), on his return from the Arctic in 1737, seems to flatten the globe in this portrait by the French artist Robert Lervac-Tournières. The hero points the way forward. A map of the area he surveyed in Finland is on the table, with the Laplanders' fur-lined cap he wore on his expedition.

THE ENLIGHTENMENT IN GLOBAL CONTEXT

During the eighteenth century, despite the long reach of some European empires, China's was, as we have seen (see Chapter 21), by almost every standard, still the fastest-growing empire in the world. China was also the homeland of a more modern society—in key respects—than any you could find in the West. It was a better-educated society, with over a million graduates from a highly demanding educational system, and a more entrepreneurial society, with bigger businesses and bigger clusters of mercantile and industrial capital than you could find anywhere else. It was a more industrialized society, with higher levels of production in more specialized concentrations, and a more urbanized society, with denser distributions of population in most areas. China's was even—for adult males—a more egalitarian society, in which the hereditary landed gentry had social privileges similar to those of their Western counterparts, but had to defer to scholar-bureaucrats who were drawn from every level of rank and wealth in society.

The Chinese Example

Described with frank admiration by the Jesuits on whom Europeans relied for information, China was bound to excite positive interest among European thinkers who were looking to improve the societies they inhabited. One of China's greatest fans was also one of Europe's most influential thinkers. The French philosopher François-Marie Arouet (1694–1778), who wrote under the name Voltaire, was the best-connected man of the eighteenth century. He corresponded with Catherine the Great of Russia (r. 1762–1794), corrected Frederick the Great of Prussia's (r. 1740–1786) French poetry, was friends with the official mistresses of Louis XV of France (r. 1715–1774), and influenced statesmen all over Europe. His works were read in Sicily and the Balkans, plagiarized in Vienna, and translated into Swedish. He saw China, in part, as a source of inspiration for his own art. In 1733, he adapted a Chinese play for the Parisian stage under the title, *The Orphan Boy of China*. More generally, Confucianism attracted him as a philosophical alternative to organized religion, which he detested. And he sympathized with the Chinese conviction that the universe is orderly, rational, and intelligible through observation. In the Chinese habit of political deference to scholars, he saw an endorsement of the power of the class of professional intellectuals to which he belonged. In the absolute power of the Chinese state, he saw a force for good.

Not everyone in Europe's intellectual elite, not even in his native France, shared Voltaire's admiration for China. His colleague and collaborator, Denis Diderot (1713–1784), ridiculed him for believing Jesuit propaganda. In 1748, in *The Spirit of Laws*, a work that inspired constitutional reformers all over Europe, the baron de Montesquieu (1689–1755) claimed that "the cudgel governs China"—a claim Jesuit accounts of Chinese habits of harsh justice and judicial torture endorsed. He condemned China as "a despotic state, whose principle is fear." Indeed, a fundamental difference of opinion divided Montesquieu and Voltaire. Montesquieu advocated the rule of law and recommended that constitutional safeguards should limit governments. Voltaire never really trusted the people and felt that strong, well-advised governments could best judge the people's interests. Montesquieu, moreover, developed an influential theory, according to which Western political traditions were benign, and tended toward liberty, whereas the governments of Asian states were hopelessly despotic and concentrated power in the hands of tyrants. "This," he wrote, "is the great reason for the weakness of Asia and the strength of Europe; for the liberty of Europe and the slavery of Asia." *Oriental despotism* became a standard term of abuse in Western political writing.

François Quesnay (1694–1774), Voltaire's colleague, who echoed the idealization of China, countered that "enlightened despotism" would favor the people rather than elites. Confucianism, he argued, restrained despotism. In their day, Quesnay's ideas were more influential than Montesquieu's. He even persuaded the heir to the French throne to imitate a Chinese imperial rite by plowing land in person as an example to agrarian improvers. **Enlightened despotism** also entered the political vocabulary, and many European rulers in the second half of the eighteenth century sought to embody it. One way or another, whether you favored China or rejected its examples, Chinese models seemed to be shaping European political thought. By the 1760s, a satirist in England could complain that busts of Confucius were replacing those of Plato and Aristotle in fashionable houses, and that instead of relying on the classics, "we take our learning from the wise Chinese." In the same decade, the leading minister of the French crown conceived a plan to develop a policy of intellectual exchange with China and arranged for

Voltaire. When Voltaire died in 1778, the sculptor Jean-Antoine Houdon (1741–1828) used the great writer's death mask (a plaster cast of the face made just after a person died) to represent him realistically. But this sculpture remains highly charged with symbolic meaning. Voltaire is robed like an ancient philosopher-sage; his hands are wrinkled with useful toil; a sardonic smile represents his use of irony and humor to challenge the institutions of church and state.

two Chinese scholars to study in the Academy of Sciences. The plan failed, however, because the two Chinese decided to work as Christian missionaries instead. The English dramatist Oliver Goldsmith (1728–1774) composed fictional *Letters of a Chinese Philosopher* to express disapproval of his own society.

Meanwhile, Chinese influence was changing elite taste in Europe. Until the eighteenth century, China exercised its artistic influence on the West almost entirely through porcelain, lacquers, and textiles. Now the delights of Chinese wallpaper became accessible to a rich elite, and European furniture and dishes were decorated with genuinely Chinese themes. The French painter, Jean-Antoine Watteau (1684–1721) inaugurated a taste for Chinese-style schemes with his designs for an apartment for Louis XIV. It spread through all the palaces of the royal dynasty of Bourbon, which ruled France, Spain, and Naples, and was connected by marriage with many of Europe's other leading dynasties. From Bourbon courts, the Chinese look radiated throughout Europe. In England, King George II's son, the Duke of Cumberland, sailed on a fake Chinese pleasure boat. William Halfpenny's *Chinese and Gothic Architecture* (1752) was the first of many books to treat Chinese art as equivalent to Europe's. Sir William Chambers, the most fashionable British architect of the day, designed a pagoda for Kew Gardens in London and Chinese furniture for aristocratic homes, while "Chinese" Thomas Chippendale, England's leading cabinetmaker, popularized Chinese themes for furniture. By mid-century, engravings of Chinese scenes hung even in middle-class French and Dutch homes.

The Duke of Cumberland's "Mandarin Yacht"—a fake Chinese junk, built to sail on his large artificial lake near London. Cumberland was a son of King George II (r. 1727–1760), and the Mandarin Yacht helped to influence a fashion for things Chinese—gardens, porcelain, furniture, interior design—among European elite in the eighteenth century.

Japan

Enthusiasm embraced Japan as well as China. Jesuits, of course, did not praise Japan, whose rulers had expelled them in the 1630s. Since then, Japanese governments had relentlessly persecuted Christianity. The Japanese policy of excluding foreigners kept Europe in ignorance of Japanese life. But the activities of the Dutch East India Company in Japan opened a window. Engelbert Kaempfer, a company envoy, published the most influential account of Japan in 1729. He presented Japan in an ambiguous light, as a land of heavy punishments and light taxation. His portrait of a rampant Lord High Executioner and of a people in "slavery and submission" fed into European ideas of Japan for centuries to come, but he was also frank about the peace, order, and prosperity he observed. Opinion about Japan in Europe split as it did over China. Montesquieu saw Japan as another oriental despotism. Voltaire saw it as the embodiment of "the laws of nature in the laws of a state."

India

Voltaire found an even better model in India. In 1756, he published *Dialogue Between a Brahman and a Jesuit*. The Brahman speaks with Voltaire's voice. He wants, above all, "a state in which the laws are obeyed." Voltaire's work on India was more profound than his assertions about China and Japan, because he recognized how much Western thought owed to ideas that had originated in Indian civilization. "It is probable," he averred, "that the Brahmins were the first legislators of the earth, the first philosophers, the first theologians." The study of Asian languages in the West strengthened this contention as the century went on. The elite Collège Royal in France introduced Chinese studies in the 1730s, but it was Jesuit work on Indian languages, especially Sanskrit, that facilitated the most remarkable disclosure. In 1786, the English scholar Sir William Jones realized that Sanskrit—the language of the Indian classics—was related to Latin and Greek and probably shared with them a common root. Although Western observers found little to praise or imitate in Indian science, they could not help but note the effectiveness of traditional methods of inoculation against smallpox, which were similar to the practices Europeans were copying from Turkey (see Chapter 20).

Edward Wortley Montagu in Turkish dress. Turkish dress was more than an affectation for the English traveler, Edward Wortley Montagu, painted here in 1776, the year of his death. His father had been British ambassador in Constantinople. His mother, Lady Mary, had written appreciatively about Turkey, where she learned the technique of inoculation against smallpox and had it tried out on her son.

The Islamic World

Muslim Turkey and Persia, too, influenced Western minds in the eighteenth century, mainly as sources of exotic imagery, and also, in Turkey's case, as a model of good and bad practice in government. Montesquieu added objectivity and credibility to his critiques of Western society in his *Persian Letters* (1721) by pretending that they were the work of a Persian sage. Playwrights favored Turkish settings and characters for social satire. In 1782, Mozart's *The Abduction from the Seraglio*, one of the great comic operas of the age, showed Turks outfoxing Europeans in cunning and exceeding them in generosity. In its plot, a lovelorn European youth fails comically to rescue his girlfriend from the harem of an Ottoman official, who, however, generously allows the lovers to go free, together. Turkey was often cited as a model for Europe to follow in hygiene, education, charitable institutions, and generally in what a late seventeenth-century traveler praised as their "order, . . . economy and the regulation of provisions." In 1774, Simon-Nicolas-Henri Linguet pointed out that in Turkey and Persia the Quran protected political liberty by restraining the power of rulers. Well-informed observers of Turkey commended the Ottomans for religious toleration, respect for laws, customs, and property rights, and for benevolence toward minorities—the very virtues that some political philosophers of the Enlightenment thought that Europe lacked.

Nonetheless, over the century as a whole, European critics of Ottoman life and customs became increasingly strident. Features of government formerly praised as evidence of strength and wisdom—the lack of a governing aristocracy, for instance, the docility of the sultan's subjects, the vulnerability of high officeholders to the sultan's mood—came to be seen, through the lens of the Enlightenment, as arbitrary and despotic. Turkey, even more than China, became a reference point for denunciations of oriental despotism. "In such distressful regions," wrote a follower of Montesquieu, "man is seen to kiss his chains, without any certainty as to fortune and property; he adores his tyrant; and without any knowledge of humanity or reason, is reduced to have no other virtue but fear."

Making Connections | GLOBAL INFLUENCES ON THE ENLIGHTENMENT

COUNTRY	INFLUENTIAL IDEAS/PRACTICES	IMPACT ON EUROPE
China	Confucianism; absolute power of the state; art forms	Chinese models shape European political thought; many European rulers seek to embody enlightened despotism Chinese influence changes elite tastes in Europe
Japan	Publication of Engelbert Kaempfer's account of Japan in 1729	Its portrait of a country both despotic and peaceful divides European opinion and shapes impressions of the country
India	Antiquity of Indian civilization: Western thought indebted to ideas that originated in ancient India	Voltaire publishes Dialogue Between a Brahman and a Jesuit (1756) William Jones shows that Sanskrit is related to Latin and Greek and shares a common root with them (1786)
Islamic World	Inoculation against smallpox Hygiene, education, charitable institutions Oriental despotism	Turkish practice of inoculation introduced in Europe in early/mid-1700s Turkey often cited as model to follow Turkey becomes leading reference in the West for negative features associated with absolute power.

THE ENLIGHTENMENT'S EFFECTS IN ASIA

European interest in Asia transformed Europe but changed Asia only a little.

The Enlightenment and China

Historians have generally regarded the Chinese attitude to European ideas at the time as arrogant, unrealistic, and restricted by outmoded traditions. But it reflected the historic world balance of power. Westerners had always had more to learn from China than the other way round. Even in the eighteenth century, the inferiority of the West was only beginning to be reversed. So it is not surprising that the Chinese were still highly selective in their receptivity to Western ideas. At the beginning of the century, when Jesuits were already installed as the emperors' favorite astronomers, mapmakers, and technicians (see Chapter 18), one of them, Father Chavagnac, complained that the Chinese still "cannot be persuaded that anything which is not of China deserves to be regarded." Chavagnac found it particularly distressing that some Chinese scholars still expressed skepticism when he showed them his map of the world. "They all cried out, 'So where is China?' 'It is this small spot of land,' said I. 'It seems very little,'" was their reply.

Nevertheless, the Jesuits did extend their activities at court in eighteenth-century China. "Every day," they claimed in letters home during the reign of the Kangxi emperor (r. 1661–1722), "from two hours before noon to two hours

Concubine. In the eighteenth century, Chinese emperors inaugurated a fashion at the imperial court for having one's portrait painted in Western dress. Here the favorite concubine of the Qianlong emperor (r. 1735–1796) wears a Western suit of armor. The artist, Giuseppe Castiglione, was a member of the Jesuit mission in China from 1730 until 1768. He also helped design the gardens of the imperial summer palace, with their complicated series of fountains that constituted a feat of hydraulic engineering.

after noon, we were at the emperor's side, lecturing on Euclid's geometry, or on physics, astronomy, etc." The emperor wrote a famous poem in praise of one of his Jesuit-made clocks and commissioned Jesuits to map inner Asia. He commanded and—according to his flatterers—supervised the translation of a collection of Western mathematical works, including Euclid's *Elements of Geometry* and all the texts Jesuits recommended on the calendar. The Yongzheng (yung-jheng) emperor (r. 1722–1735) restricted missionaries' freedom to make converts but had himself painted in a Western curled wig and coat. For the Qianlong emperor (r. 1735–1796), European artists painted his favorite concubine dressed in Western armor and the horses of his stable in Western style. Other Jesuits designed his gardens and engineered its fountains and mechanical statues.

A story often told to demonstrate the Chinese attitude is that of a British embassy that arrived in China in June 1793. The mission lacked nothing that might embellish its dignity and emphasize its prestige. King George III (r. 1760–1820) had made its leader, Lord Macartney, an earl and equipped him with a staff of 84 attendants. The king's gifts for the Chinese court, worth over £15,000—a huge sum in the eighteenth century—included a letter to the emperor in a box made of gold and all the most new-fangled hardware of early British industrialization: a planetarium, globes, mathematical instruments, chronometers of apparently magical accuracy, a telescope, instruments for chemical and electrical experiments, plate glass, Wedgwood ware (the best pottery British factories could provide), silver-plated knives and forks, and samples of textiles woven on power looms.

The Chinese were not wholly contemptuous of these efforts. Esteem for Western technical ingenuity was high, and the Qianlong emperor had a formidable collection of Western mechanical devices. Indeed, restrainedly pleased at the arrival of this "first tributary mission" from Britain, the emperor ordered that because of the envoys' long journey they should be given a better welcome than equivalent missions from Burma and Vietnam. He did not, however, endorse the high value the British put on themselves. He indulged, as a bit of barbarian bad manners, the ambassador's refusal to follow Chinese custom by knocking his head on the ground in deference to the throne. The British, the emperor said, were incapable of "acquiring the rudiments of our civilization." They possessed nothing China wanted. Their representatives could not be allowed to reside permanently at the imperial court. "It is your bounden duty," the emperor concluded in his reply to George III, "reverently to appreciate my feelings and to obey these instructions henceforth for all time."

Western technology made its biggest impact, perhaps, on war. In 1673, the emperor threatened to expel all Christians from China unless the Jesuits consented to design and manufacture artillery for him. The priests' designs continued in use until the mid-nineteenth century. They supervised gunnery practice, under compulsion, insisting that they were men of peace. In the mid-1780s, when news of the development of hot-air balloons in the West reached the Chinese court, the Chinese immediately inquired about its possible military applications. "Only in war," an imperial prince explained, "do we have no regard for expense, difficulty or danger. We are ready to try anything." Nonetheless, Chinese interest in adopting new technology waned for a while thereafter. Westerners still seemed just clever barbarians to the Chinese, useful in their place, dangerous when they aimed higher.

Western Science in Japan

Admiration for the West penetrated deeper—though still not very deep—in Japan. The shogun Yoshimune (r. 1716–1745) took an interest in science and technology comparable to Kangxi's. From 1720, he allowed Chinese translations of Western books to circulate in Japan. The Japanese scholar Miura Baien (1723–1789) recognized that Western astronomy had revolutionized knowledge of the universe. Like many Western philosophers of the time, he advocated practical utility and technical efficiency above traditional values. "A tiny lantern that lights humble homes," he wrote, "is worth more than gems." Iron and copper, from which goods were made that people could use, should be valued above silver and gold. Yet despite Japanese sympathy for aspects of Western thought, it was hard to find ways to promote Western knowledge. Japan's seventeenth-century experience (see Chapter 19) still made its government determined to exclude Christianity and limit foreign access to the country. Since the representatives of the Dutch East India Company were the only Europeans allowed in Japan—and even then only under tight restrictions—access to sources of scientific information was haphazard. Japanese scholars had no way to judge what information was accurate or up to date. The interpreters who negotiated with the Dutch worked exclusively in Portuguese, the traditional language of Western commerce in East Asia. Japanese scholars who wanted to read the Western books that reached Japan had to teach themselves Dutch from scratch.

The case of Rembert Dodens's *Cryidetboeck*, a Dutch study of plants published in 1554, is instructive. In 1659, a Dutch embassy presented a 1618 edition of the book to the shogun. Hidden away in the palace library, it was extracted at Yoshimune's command in 1717, in the belief that it might contain useful medical knowledge. It was handed over to a translator, who eventually produced his translation in 1750. The work was by then nearly 200 years out of date. The same translator worked on another supposed guide to plants for 24 years before realizing that it was a zoological work that had no medical information.

Something like a breakthrough came only in 1771, when the dissection of a corpse demonstrated the accuracy of European books of anatomy. A group of enthusiastic beginners in **Dutch studies** started meeting six or seven times a month to puzzle over the meaning of Western books. "After about a year," wrote one of them, "we became capable of reading as much as ten or more lines of text per day if the particular passage was not too difficult."

So China remained the dominant intellectual influence in Japan, and Confucianism remained the foundation of Japanese thought. Most new developments came not from the West but from Japanese reactions against Confucianism. Independently, Japanese thinkers discovered principles similar to those philosophical radicals in Europe and America advocated: the virtues, especially, of universal reason—*ri*, the Japanese called it—approached scientifically, through observation. Ogyu Sorai (1666–1728) advocated experience in place of speculation as the key to truth. "History," he declared, "is ultimate knowledge." Tominaga Nakamoto (1715–1746) went further, doubting the possibility of any universally valid statements because experience seemed too diverse. In 1713, Kaibara Ekken argued that nature was in a constant state of flux and so could only be understood by observation, not by the grand generalizations of Confucian theory. Some radicals embraced an egalitarian theory of human nature. Ishida Baigan (1685–1744), a strong advocate of reason as the unique means to truth, was one of many teachers who opened their classes to people of modest social backgrounds, in the belief that commoners had the same mental powers as the gentry.

Chinese clock. Although the history of clock making in China dates back to the eleventh century, clockwork was not used for timekeeping until the Jesuit missionary Matteo Ricci arrived in the late 1500s (see Chapter 18). Western technology thereafter played a key part in diplomatic relations between the West and China. In the reign of the Kangxi emperor (1661–1722), an imperial clock and watch factory was established within the imperial palace at Beijing. The emperor himself studied mathematics and applied science, and one of his surviving poems reads, "The skill originated in the West / But, by learning, we can achieve the artifice / Wheels move and time turns round / Hands show the minutes as they change." The clock above, made in Guangzhou in about 1790, is an automated musical table clock sounded by 12 bells and 22 hammers. The exquisite design displays both Chinese and European artistic styles.

Dutch studies. "When I first observed that book of anatomy and ascertained its accuracy by actual observation, I was struck with admiration by the great difference between the knowledge of the West and that of the East. And I was inspired to come to the determination that I must learn and clarify the new revelation for applying it to actual healing and also for making it the seed of further discoveries among the general physicians of Japan." After heroic labor, the Japanese scholar Sugita Genpaku published his translation of *A New Book of Anatomy* (Katai-Shin-Sho), in the late 1770s—the culmination of years of "Dutch studies."

Korea and Southeast Asia

In Korea and Vietnam, too, national revulsions from Confucianism and Chinese cultural dominance stimulated new thinking. In Korea, the movement called "practical learning" started as a reaction against Confucianism but acquired some knowledge of Western technology by way of China. A design for a Western crane, copied from a Chinese book, helped to build a castle. Koreans began to model world maps on Western examples. In the mid-eighteenth century, Yi Ik began a systematic study of Western learning in Chinese books. In the 1780s, a group of Korean intellectuals spontaneously founded a society to introduce Catholicism into the country. In Vietnam, meanwhile, the most remarkable case of independent thinking echoing new ideas from the West appeared in the work of the poet, Ho Xuang Huong. "Down with husband-sharing!" she exclaimed when her husband took a second wife. "One [wife] rolls in warm blankets, the other freezes. . . . I've turned into a half-servant, an unpaid maid! Had I known, I would have stayed single."

Other Asian cultures were even less hospitable to Western thought. In Thailand, an exchange of embassies with France in the 1680s (see Chapter 18) stimulated, at first, enormous interest in both countries. For the French, Thailand, or Siam as the French called it, offered a model of the exotic. For the Thai, the French presented an insight into the Western technical proficiency already admired in China. Kosa Pan, the Thai envoy to France, took home a large collection of European maps, and the French mission to Thailand established an observatory in the royal palace. The king—suitably screened from the profanity of contact with ordinary people—attended lectures that Jesuit astronomers gave. But this period of receptiveness did not last long. Western influence in Thailand receded after a palace revolution there in 1688.

A Meeting of China, Japan, and the West

Eastern and Western Enlightenments meet in this late eighteenth-century Japanese painting on silk.

The Japanese man, who seems the dominant presence in this discussion group, is perhaps a self-portrait of the artist, Shiba Kokan, who played a big part in promoting "Dutch learning" in Japan. His position near the European suggests his admiration for Western science.

In the background, firefighting teams from Japan, China, and the Netherlands tackle the same blaze with their respective techniques. The Dutch seem to be most effective.

The unidentified Dutchman displays a book of anatomy—one of the sciences in which the Japanese acknowledged Western superiority. The closeness of the Dutch and Japanese figures is emphasized, while the Chinese participant sits somewhat apart, listening critically.

How does this painting illustrate the global exchange of ideas in the eighteenth century?

Making Connections | ENLIGHTENMENT INFLUENCES IN ASIA

COUNTRY	INFLUENTIAL IDEAS	SOURCES	SOCIAL/POLITICAL/ECONOMIC CONSEQUENCES
China	Western astronomy, mathematics, scientific methods, technology	Jesuit missionaries; European diplomats	Imperial leaders collect Western mechanical devices; use Western-designed artillery
Japan	Western astronomy, mathematics, scientific methods, technology; Japanese concepts of universal reason, scientific observation	Dutch diplomats, merchants; Japanese thinkers (Sorai, Nakamoto, Ekken)	Restrictions on trade and contact with foreigners limit exposure to Western ideas, technology; reaction against Confucianism
Korea	"Practical learning"	Reaction against Confucianism and interest in Western technology, religious inspiration	Development of new technology aids in construction, mapmaking; Catholicism introduced by intellectuals
Vietnam	Interest in women's rights	Ho Xuan Huong (writer)	Critique of traditional marriage practices

The Ottomans

Inhibited by Muslim religious scruples, the Turks and Persians, too, were relatively slow to open up to the worldwide exchange of ideas. The first printing press in Turkey was only set up in 1729. When the authorities closed it down in 1742, it had produced only 17 titles. In 1798, French armies invaded Egypt and Syria, leaving—after their early withdrawal—seeds of Western-style thinking. Here, as in India, aspects of Western thought were enthusiastically embraced but only in the nineteenth century, and only after unmistakable demonstrations of Western military strength (see Chapter 25).

THE ENLIGHTENMENT IN EUROPE

Even in Europe, in some quarters, new thinking met distrust, censorship, and persecution. To understand why—and to identify the defining themes of the thought of the time—the best source is the French *Encyclopedia*, subtitled *Reasoned Dictionary of the Sciences, Arts and Trades*, which appeared in 17 volumes of texts and 11 volumes of illustrations between 1751 and 1772. By 1779, about 25,000 sets had been sold throughout Europe, in the teeth of condemnation by reactionary governments and established churches (See Map 22.1). This may not seem a large number, but the ideas the *Encyclopedia* contained reached the entire European elite, one way or another, and circulated in countless spinoff works. Denis Diderot, who masterminded the entire project, wanted a comprehensive work that would "start from and return to Man," while covering every intellectual discipline along the way. The aim of the *Encyclopedia*, he announced, was "to assemble the knowledge scattered over the face of the Earth . . . that we may not die without having deserved well of mankind."

Of course, the book was not merely a disinterested panorama of knowledge. It had a slant. First, its values were practical. There was enormous emphasis on utility, engineering, mechanics, and technology. There was, according to Diderot, "more intelligence, wisdom, and consequence in a machine for making stockings" than "in a system of metaphysics." Second, the writers of the *Encyclopedia* advocated reason and science as means to truth, drawing heavily on the work of Scottish and English philosophers of the early 1700s. The first page depicted Reason pulling a veil from the eyes of Truth. Third, although the contributors by no means agreed among themselves on questions of political philosophy, the tone of the *Encyclopedia* was generally highly critical of the existing record of Europe's monarchies and aristocracies. Drawing on the English apologist of revolution, John Locke (see Chapter 21), most contributors on political questions seemed to favor constitutional guarantees of the liberty of the citizen against the state. Many contributors to the *Encyclopedia* insisted on the "natural equality" of all men. Finally, the work was uniformly hostile to organized religion.

The Belief in Progress

Underlying the whole project was a heady kind of optimism: belief in progress. Indeed, only optimists could have undertaken such an ambitious project. To make progress credible, someone had to think up a way to understand evil, and explain away all the disasters and woes of the world. This was a long-unfulfilled task of theologians, who never satisfactorily answered the atheists' challenge, "If God is good, why is there evil?" In the seventeenth century, the growth of atheism made the task seem urgent. "To justify the ways of God to man" was the objective the English poet John Milton (1608–1674) set himself in his great verse epic, *Paradise Lost*. But it is one thing to be poetically convincing, quite another to produce a reasoned argument. In 1710, the German philosopher Gottfried Wilhelm Leibniz (1646–1716) did so. He was the most wide-ranging thinker of his day, combining outstanding contributions to philosophy, theology, mathematics, linguistics, physics, and law with his role as a courtier to the ruler of the German state of Hanover. He started from a truth traditionally expressed and witnessed in everyday experience: good and evil are inseparable, because each is meaningless without the other. Freedom, for example, is good, but must include freedom to do evil. Altruism is good only if selfishness is an option. But of all logically conceivable worlds, ours has, by divine decree, the greatest possible surplus of good over evil. So—in the phrase Voltaire used to mock this theory—"All is for the best in the best of all possible worlds." "Whatever is, is right," echoed Alexander Pope (1688–1744), the most elegant English poet of the age, in his verse *Essay on Man*. Leibniz formulated his argument in an attempt to show that God's love was compatible with human suffering. It was not Leibniz's purpose to endorse progress, and his "best world" could have been interpreted as one in which nothing ever changed, in which the ideal amount of evil was inherent in human beings. But, in alliance with the conviction of human goodness, which most thinkers of the Enlightenment shared, it made the goal of a secular golden age possible, toward which people could work by using their freedom to adjust the balance, bit by bit, in favor of goodness.

Camera obscura. Denis Diderot's *Encyclopedia* promoted technology and "useful" knowledge—in this case, the construction of a camera obscura, which was the forerunner of modern photography. The camera obscura captured an image by projecting rays of light from an object through a pinprick opening onto the inner wall of a chamber. Painters used this technique to ensure realism in their art.

Even then, the suspicion that it was merely a historical phase, enjoyed by their own times, but exceptional by the standards of history in general, inhibited believers in progress. The Marquis de Condorcet (see Chapter 21), for instance, thought he could see "the human race . . . advancing with a sure step along the path of truth, virtue, and happiness" only because political and intellectual revolutions had subverted the crippling effects of religion and tyranny. The human spirit was now at last "emancipated from its shackles" and "released from the empire of fate."

New Economic Thought

If you believe in human goodness, you believe in freedom. Thinkers pessimistic about human nature, like the Chinese Legalists (see Chapter 6), tend to favor strong, even repressive governments to keep destructive instincts in check. Optimists hope to liberate people to do good. Montesquieu and the authors of the *Encyclopedia* were particularly concerned to recommend political freedom, but economic freedom was an equally important theme in the thought of the time.

Free trade was a new doctrine. The long experience of an unfavorable trade balance with Asia had induced two obsessions in Western economic thought: bullion—gold and silver—is the basis of wealth; and to grow rich, an economy must behave like a business and sell more than it buys. According to the Spanish moralist, Tomás de Mercado (ca. 1523–1575), what "destroys this abundance and causes poverty is the export of money." All European governments came to believe this. In consequence, they tried to evade impoverishment by hoarding bullion, trapping cash inside the realm, limiting imports and exports, regulating prices, defying the laws of supply and demand, and founding empires to create markets for their goods that they could control.

The consequences were woeful. Overseas investment was restricted, except in imperial ventures. The protection of trade nourished inefficiency and squandered resources on policing. Competition for protected markets caused wars and, consequently, waste. Money drained out of circulation. These conditions, which clearly inhibited economic growth, were much criticized from the late seventeenth century onward. The eighteenth-century French school of economic thinkers known as the physiocrats devised the slogan **laissez-faire** to mean "leave the market to itself." The British economist David Ricardo (see Chapter 21) agreed. "Wages," he recommended, "should be left to the fair and free competition of the market, and should never be controlled by the interference of the legislature." The decisive moment in the shift toward economic freedom came in 1776, when the Scots professor of moral philosophy, Adam Smith, published *The Wealth of Nations*.

Smith had a lofty view of the importance of the law of supply and demand, believing that it affected more than the market. "The natural effort of every individual to better his own condition" was the foundation of all political, economic, and moral systems. Taxation, Smith felt, was more or less an evil. First, it was an infringement of liberty. Second, it was a distortion in the market. "There is no art which one government learns sooner than another than that of draining money from the pockets of the people." Self-interest could be left to serve the common good. "It is not from the benevolence of the butcher, the brewer or the baker that we expect our dinner, but from their regard to their own interest." "In spite of their natural selfishness and rapacity," Smith declared, the rich "are led by an invisible hand to make nearly the same distribution of the necessaries of life which would have been made, had the earth been divided into equal portions among all its inhabitants."

The Wealth of Nations appeared in the same year as the Declaration of Independence and should be counted among the United States' founding documents. It

"The decisive moment in the shift toward economic freedom came in 1776, when the Scots professor of moral philosophy, Adam Smith, published The Wealth of Nations.*"*

1790: King of Prussia proclaims absolute authority over the clergy in his realm

1762: Catherine the Great secularizes property belonging to Orthodox Church

1762: Jesuits expelled from France
1794: Cult of the Supreme Being briefly replaces Catholicism as the official religion

1773: Pope Clement XIV dissolves the Jesuit Order

1767: Jesuits expelled from Spain and the Kingdom of Naples

1759: Portugal expels the Jesuits and confiscates their property

200 km
200 miles

MAP 22.1

The Enlightenment in Europe

Subscriptions to the *Encyclopedia* by 1779

- • 1–10
- ● 11–50
- ● 51–100
- ● more than 100
- ▬▬ anticlerical act, 1759–1794

encouraged the American Revolution, for Smith said that government regulations limiting the freedom of colonies to engage in manufacture or trade were "a manifest violation of the most sacred rights of mankind." The United States has remained the homeland of economic liberalism ever since.

Social Equality

Smith's arguments for freedom included the claim that freedom would deliver equality. This is not necessarily true, but it was characteristic of the time. Reason suggested that all men are naturally equal. So what about women? Montesquieu saw no reason to exclude them. The ideas we now call **feminism**—that women collectively constituted a class of society, historically oppressed and deserving of emancipation—appeared in two works of 1792, the *Declaration of the Rights of Woman and of the Female Citizen* (*Déclaration des droits de la femme et de la citoyenne*) by Marie-Olympe de Gouges, and *A Vindication of the Rights of Woman* by Mary Wollstonecraft. Both authors had to struggle to earn their living. Both led irregular sex lives. Both died tragically. Wollstonecraft died in childbirth in 1797 at the age of 38. De Gouges was guillotined in 1793 during the French Revolution for defending the king and queen of France. "Women may mount the scaffold," she said, "they should also be able to ascend the bench," that is, to become judges. Both writers rejected the entire previous tradition of female championship, which praised women for their domestic and maternal virtues. Instead, they admitted women's vices and blamed male oppression.

Anticlericalism

For most of the philosophers who worked on the *Encyclopedia*, the great obstacle to progress was the Church. They catalogued the crimes of the church—inquisitions, persecutions, clerical abuses of power. They ridiculed the doctrine that one person could be both God and man. The reader of the article on cannibalism was referred to articles on the Eucharist, Communion, altar, and such. "We must show that we are better than Christians," wrote Diderot in a letter to a contributor, "and that science makes more good men than grace." In his *Persian Letters*, Montesquieu had carried the attack further, blaming Christianity and Islam alike for inhibiting sex and discouraging procreation. Voltaire erected his own temple to "the architect of the universe, the great geometrician" but regarded Christianity as an "infamous superstition to be eradicated—I do not say among the rabble, who are not worthy of being enlightened and who are apt for every yoke, but among the civilized and those who wish to think." Many people in France ceased to mention God and the saints in their last wills. Donations to religious foundations dwindled. King Louis XV abandoned the rites, traditional for French kings, of touching subjects with scrofula, a disfiguring skin disease, in the hope of a miracle cure, because he found belief in miracles embarrassing.

We can measure the progress of the Enlightenment across Europe in anticlerical acts (see Map 22.1). In 1759, Portugal expelled the Jesuits and confiscated their property. In 1762, Catherine the Great of Russia secularized a great portfolio of property belonging to the Orthodox Church. Between 1764 and 1773, the Jesuit Order was abolished in most of the rest of the West. In the 1780s, European governments confiscated church lands and forced 38,000 monks and nuns into lay life. A Spanish official proposed seizing most of the church's land. In 1790, the king of Prussia, one of the largest German states, proclaimed absolute authority over the clergy in his realm, both Protestant and Catholic. Meanwhile, among the European elite, the cult of reason was taking on the characteristics of an alternative religion. In the secret ceremonies of freemasonry, a profane hierarchy celebrated the purity of its own wisdom, brilliantly portrayed in Mozart's opera *The Magic Flute*, first performed in 1791. In 1793, revolutionary committees banned Christian worship in parts of France and erected signs proclaiming, "Death is an Eternal Sleep" over cemetery gates. In the summer of 1794, the government in Paris tried to replace Christianity with a new religion, the cult of the Supreme Being.

To some extent, the success of science encouraged mistrust of religion. From John Locke, eighteenth-century radicals inherited the conviction that it was "fiddling" to waste time thinking about what, if anything, lay beyond the scientifically observed world. The evidence of our senses was all true and—with certain exceptions about sound and color that experiments could confirm—it was all caused by the real objects our senses seemed to disclose to us. Thus, the jangling is proof of the bell, the heat of the fire, the stink of the gas. "Freethinking" atheism got a boost from the microbial world, with its apparent evidence of spontaneous generation. The very existence of God—or at least, the validity of claims about God's unique power to create life—was at stake.

THE CRISIS OF THE ENLIGHTENMENT: RELIGION AND ROMANTICISM

This attitude, which we would now call **scientism**, did not satisfy all its practitioners. The Scottish philosopher David Hume (1711–1776) pointed out that sensations are not really evidence of anything except themselves—that objects cause them is just an unverifiable assumption. Many scientists, like Maupertuis, drifted back from atheism toward religion, or became more interested in speculation about truths beyond the reach of science. In 1799, with the aid of a powerful microscope, Lorenzo Spallanzani observed fission—cells reproducing by splitting. He demonstrated that if heating killed bacteria—or *animalculi*, to use the term favored at the time, or germs, as he called them—they could not reappear in a sealed environment. He concluded that living organisms did not appear from nowhere. They could only germinate in an environment where they were already present. No known case of spontaneous generation of life was left in the world.

"Despite the hostility of the Enlightenment, the eighteenth century was actually a time of tremendous religious revival in the West."

Religious Revival

The churches, moreover, knew how to defeat unbelievers. Censorship did not work. But appeals, over the intellectuals' heads, to ordinary people did. Despite the hostility of the Enlightenment, the eighteenth century was actually a time of tremendous religious revival in the West. Christianity reached a new public. In 1722, Nicolas Ludwig, Count Zinzendorff, experienced an unusual sense of vocation.

George Whitfield. Long after his death, George Whitfield (1714–1770) was remembered for the emotional effects of his preaching. In the 1770s, the artist John Wollaston recalled Whitfield's charisma. The congregation concentrate on him, yet he seems spiritually absent, as if transported by rapture, unengaged with his audience. His hands stretch out to lay people, including women, in the gesture his church—the Church of England—reserved for the rite in which bishops ordain priests. Whitfield's message was indeed that gifts of the Holy Spirit were universal, given to laypeople as well as to ordained clergy.
John Wollaston, George Whitefield, ca. 1770. National Portrait Gallery, London.

He built the village of Herrnhut (meaning "the Lord's keeping") on his estate in eastern Germany to be a place of refuge, where persecuted Christians could share a sense of the love of God. It became a center from which evangelical fervor—or "enthusiasm," as they called it at the time—radiated over the world. Zinzendorff's was only one of innumerable movements of religious revival in the eighteenth century to offer ordinary people an affective, unintellectual solution to the problems of life: proof that, in their way, feelings are stronger than reason and that religion—for most people—is more satisfying than science. As one of the great inspirers of Christian revivalism, Jonathan Edwards (1703–1758) of Massachusetts, said, "Our people do not so much need to have their heads stored, as to have their hearts touched." His meetings, characteristically, were occasions for congregations to purge their emotions in ways intellectuals found repellent. "There was a great moaning and crying through the whole house," observed a witness to one of Edwards's sermons, "What shall I do to be saved—Oh, I am going to Hell—oh, what shall I do for Christ, etc., etc., so that the minister was obliged to desist—the shrieks and cries were piercing and amazing."

Preaching was the information technology of all these movements. Between 1740 and his death in 1758, George Whitfield (or Whitefield—he spelled it both ways) was always on the move, all over Britain and across the American colonies. Addressing a congregation composed of almost the entire population of Boston, he made the town seem "the gate of heaven. Many wept enthusiastically and cried out under the Word, like persons that were hungering and thirsting after righteousness. The Spirit of the Lord was upon them all." In 1738, with a "heart strangely warmed," John Wesley (1703–1791) began a mission to the workers of town and country in England and Wales, traveling 8,000 miles a year and preaching to congregations of thousands at a time, at open-air meetings. He communicated a mood rather than a message—a sense of how Jesus can change lives by imparting feelings of love. Catholic evangelism was equally stirring and targeted the same enemies—materialism, rationalism, apathy, and formalized religion. One observer compared Alfonso Maria Liguori's (1696–1787) mission among the poor in Naples in Italy to the preaching of a biblical prophet. In 1765, the pope authorized devotion to the Sacred Heart of Jesus—a bleeding symbol of divine love.

Music contributed to the mood. The eighteenth century was a time when God seemed to have all the best tunes—from the moving hymns that John Wesley's brother, Charles wrote, to the stirring settings of Christ's passion by the German composer Johann Sebastian Bach (1685–1750). In 1741, George Friedrich Handel wrote *Messiah*, telling the life of Jesus in music so sublime that when the first London performance approached its climax, King George II rose to his feet and heard the "Hallelujah Chorus" standing, a custom the audience at modern performances still repeats. The scriptures Handel set to music made an effective reply to skeptics: Jesus was "despised and rejected," but "I know that my Redeemer liveth, and though worms destroy this body, yet in my flesh shall I see God." Mozart's music, too, ultimately served the church better than the Masonic movement. He died in 1791 while at work on his great *Requiem Mass*—his own triumph over death.

Cynically, the so-called enlightened despotism of some European monarchs collaborated with religious revival as a means to distract people from politics and strengthen churches as institutions of social control. King Frederick the Great of Prussia was a freethinker who liked the company of philosophers at dinner. He employed, for a while, both Maupertuis and Voltaire. But he favored religion for his people and his troops, founding hundreds of military chaplaincies and requiring religious teaching in schools. He was applying a principle his sometime friend, Voltaire, uttered: "If God did not exist, it would be necessary to invent him."

The Cult of Nature and Romanticism

The cult of nature was something Christians and their enemies could agree on. Nature seemed both more beautiful and more terrible than any construction of the human intellect. In 1755, an earthquake centered at Lisbon, Portugal, shook even Voltaire's faith in progress. One of Europe's greatest cities, home to nearly 200,000 people, was reduced to ruins. It was the single most destructive natural disaster on record in European history. As an alternative to the return to God, radical philosophers responded to the call, "Return to Nature," which one contributor to the *Encyclopedia*, Baron d'Holbach, uttered in his *System of Nature* in 1770: "She will console you, drive out from your heart the fears that hobble you . . . the hatreds that separate you from Man, whom you ought to love." "Sensibility" became a buzz word for responsiveness to the power of feelings, which were valued even more than reason.

It is worth remembering that exploration in the eighteenth century was constantly revealing new marvels of nature. New World landscapes strongly inflamed the minds of the kind eighteenth-century people called romantic. Modern scholars seem unable to agree about what this term really meant. But it signified a mindset that became increasingly characteristic of Europeans in the second half of the eighteenth century, and increasingly dominant in the world thereafter. Romantic values included imagination, intuition, emotion, inspiration, and even passion, alongside—or in extreme cases, ahead of—reason and scientific knowledge as guides to truth and conduct. Romantics professed to prefer nature to works human beings created, or, at least, wanted art to demonstrate sympathy with nature. The influence of American landscapes on romantic minds began with the beautiful and exciting drawings that two young Spanish scientists, Jorge Juan and Antonio de Ulloa, made during a scientific expedition to the equator. In work published in 1752, they combined scientific diagrams with images of awestruck reverence for untamed nature. Their drawing, for instance, of the volcanic Mount Cotopaxi erupting in Ecuador, with the phenomenon, depicted in the background, of arcs of light seen in the sky on the mountain slopes, combines precision with rugged romance. The Andean settings they recorded remained the source of the most powerful romantic images of America. Cotopaxi became a favorite subject of American landscape painters.

The merging of science and romance is apparent in the work of one of the greatest scientists of the age, Baron Alexander von Humboldt (1769–1859). In the 1790s, he began a series of journeys of scientific exploration in America. His aim, he declared, was "to see Nature in all her variety of grandeur and splendor." The high point of his endeavors came in 1802, when he tried to climb Mount Chimborazo—Cotopaxi's twin peak. Chimborazo was thought to be the highest mountain in the world—the untouched summit of creation. Sickened by altitude, racked by cold, bleeding copiously from nose and lips, Humboldt had almost reached the top when he was forced to turn back. His story of suffering and frustration was just the sort of subject romantic writers were beginning to celebrate in Europe. The English poet John Keats (1795–1821) hymned the lover who "canst never have thy bliss." The German novelist Friedrich von Hardenberg (1772–1801) praised the "blue bloom" that

> *"The cult of nature was something Christians and their enemies could agree on. Nature seemed both more beautiful and more terrible than any construction of the human intellect."*

Cult of the unattainable. Alexander von Humboldt stoops to pluck a botanical specimen near the foot of Mount Chimborazo. His account of his climb to the top of Chimborazo is a poignant litany of the cult of the unattainable so characteristic of romanticism.

can never be plucked. The cult of the unattainable—an unfulfillable yearning—lay at the heart of romanticism. Humboldt's engravings of the scenery he encountered inspired romantic painters in the new century.

This new **Romantic Movement** was not just a reaction in favor of nature against the cult of reason. It was also an attempt by intellectuals to adopt the feelings and attitudes of the uneducated populace. Its poetry, said the leading English figure in the movement, William Wordsworth (1770–1850), was "the language of ordinary men." Its grandeur was that of solitude rather than cities, mountains rather than mansions. Its religion was "enthusiasm," which was a dirty word among the intellectuals of the old regime but which drew thousands to listen to popular preachers. The music of romanticism ransacked traditional songs for melodies. Its theater and opera borrowed from the entertaining antics of street performers. Its prophet was Johann Gottfried Herder (1744–1803), who praised the moral power of the "true poetry" of "those whom we call savages." Its philosopher was Jean-Jacques Rousseau (1712–1778), who taught the superiority of natural passions over cultivated refinement. Its portrait paintings showed society ladies in peasant dress in gardens landscaped to look natural, reinvaded by romance. The German collector of folk tales, Jakob Grimm (1785–1863), devised its slogan: the people make poetry. "The people" had arrived in European history as a creative force and as a remolder of the educated elite in the people's own image.

Rousseau and the General Will

Of the thinkers who broke with the outlook of the *Encyclopedia*, Rousseau was the most influential. He was a restless super tramp with a taste for low life and gutter pleasures. He changed his formal religious allegiance twice without once appearing sincere. He betrayed all his mistresses, quarreled with all his friends, and abandoned all his children. Addiction to his own sensibilities became the guideline of his life. In 1750, in the prize-winning essay that made his name, he repudiated one of the most sacred principles of the Enlightenment—"that the Arts and Sciences have benefited Mankind." That the topic could be proposed at all shows how far disillusionment with enlightened optimism had gone. Rousseau's denunciations of property and the state offered nothing in their place except an assertion of the natural goodness of humankind in its primitive state. Voltaire loathed these ideas. "One wants to walk on all fours," like an animal, he said, after reading Rousseau.

Nonetheless, Rousseau's political thinking helped shape the politics of his day and has remained influential ever since. Rousseau regarded the state as a corporation, or even a sort of organism, in which the individual identities of the citizens are submerged. At a previous, unknown stage of history, the act occurred "by which people become a people, . . . the real foundation of society." "The people becomes one single being . . . . Each of us puts his person and all his power in common under the supreme direction of the general will." Citizenship is fraternity—an organic bond, equivalent to the blood bond between brothers. The commands of the general will are perfect freedom—social or civil freedom, Rousseau called it—and anyone constrained to obey them is simply being "forced to be free." "Whoever refuses to obey the general will shall be compelled to do so by the whole body."

"Rousseau regarded the state as a corporation, or even a sort of organism, in which the individual identities of the citizens are submerged."

Rousseau was vague about the moral justification for this obviously dangerous doctrine. The German philosopher Immanuel Kant (1724–1804), however, provided one. By setting aside one's individual will or interests and exercising reason instead, one can identify objective goals of a kind whose merit everyone can see. Submission to the general will limits one's own freedom in deference to the freedom of others. In theory, the "general will" is different from unanimity or sectional interests or individual preferences. In practice, however, it just means the tyranny of the majority. Rousseau admitted that "The votes of the greatest number always bind the rest." In Rousseau's version of the way his system works, political parties are outlawed because "There should be no partial society within the state." The same logic would forbid trade unions, religious communions, and reformist movements. Yet the passion with which Rousseau invoked freedom made it hard for many of his readers to see how illiberal his thought really was. Revolutionaries adopted the opening words of his essay of 1762: "Man is born free and everywhere he is in chains!"

Pacific Discoveries

Underlying the elevation of the common man and woman to be fit for participation in government were influences from surprising directions: the Pacific and the Americas. The Pacific in the eighteenth century stretched between myths: an unknown continent called *Terra Australis*, supposedly awaiting discovery in the south, and the rumored sea passage around America in the northwest. Investigation of those myths became the objective of the English navigator Captain James Cook (see Chapter 19). After sailing on coal carriers in Britain, he had joined the Royal Navy as an able seaman. War service in the North Atlantic drew attention to his uncanny gifts as a coastal surveyor and chart maker. In 1769, he was ordered to Tahiti in the South Pacific to observe the transit of the planet Venus and returned with a burning vocation to sail "not only farther than man has been before but as far as I think it possible for man to go."

In three voyages of Pacific exploration, Cook ranged the ocean with a freedom never before attained. He crossed the 70th parallel north and the 71st south. By charting New Zealand, the west coast of Alaska, and the east coast of Australia, he defined the limits of the Pacific Ocean (see Map 22.2). He also filled in most of its remaining gaps on the map. He brought a new precision to mapmaking, using the latest technology for finding longitude—the exquisitely accurate chronometer the English inventor John Harrison (1693–1776) had developed. Cook exploded the myth of Terra Australis, or at least pushed its possible location into latitudes "doomed to lie forever buried under everlasting snow and ice." His achievements overflowed the map of the Pacific. By rigorous standards, for instance, of hygiene and nutrition aboard ship, he contributed to the conquest of scurvy (see Chapter 19). He suggested the colonization of Australia and New Zealand. His ships brought back sketches and specimens of plants and beasts unknown in Europe.

Cook was the spearhead of an enormous scientific invasion of the Pacific by late eighteenth- and early nineteenth-century expeditions from Britain, Spain, France, Russia, and the newly independent United States. They acquainted the European public as never before with the dimensions and diversity of the world. As with the case of the Americas in previous centuries, another "new world" became available for Western imperialism to exploit, and another treasury of natural resources was open to enrich Western economies. From the point of view of intellectual history, the most important discoveries Western explorers made in the Pacific were of its peoples.

Chronometer. Outwardly, it looks like other timepieces of its era, but John Harrison's marine chronometer revolutionized navigation in the eighteenth century. Three problems made clocks inaccurate at sea: moisture got into the cases, pendulums changed length with changes in temperature, and friction disturbed the moving parts. Harrison's solutions to these problems were so perfect that when the famous explorer Captain Cook tested the chronometer at sea in 1774, he found it accurate to within a few seconds over any distance in any conditions. Because differences in longitude match differences in time, navigators could now always be sure of their position and could safely judge their distance from charted dangers.

MAP 22.2

The South Pacific Voyages of Captain James Cook, 1768–1779

→ Cook, 1768–1771   → Cook, 1772–1775   → Cook, 1778–1779

Observers dismissed some of the inhabitants as intellectually insignificant. William Dampier, author of the first description of aborigines of Australia, published in 1697, found their material culture "nasty" and their appearance repellent, with "no one graceful feature in their faces." The aborigines attracted little scientific study in the eighteenth and early nineteenth centuries, but the inferior status to which Westerners assigned them seemed to require no endorsement from science. It struck those Westerners who met them as obvious. Despite the British government's pious orders to its subjects "to live in amity and kindness" with the natives, ruthless persecution and exploitation followed. In contrast to the practices Europeans adopted toward Native Americans or the Maoris of New Zealand, British imperialists never bothered to make treaties with Australian aborigines. Colonists hunted such people without qualms, like kangaroos. Early painters of the "black fellows" were divided in their perceptions. There are some noble-looking "savages" among their subjects. More commonly, however, the aborigines are like monkeys, crawling on the earth or scampering in the trees.

From other parts of the Pacific, however, explorers brought home fine specimens of Pacific manhood, whom admirers instantly classed as **noble savages**—exemplars, that is, of the fact that to be morally admirable you did not need to be white, or Western, or Christian, or educated in social customs or intellectual traditions that Europeans recognized as "civilized." In 1774, English society lionized Omai, who had been a restless misfit in his native Polynesia. Duchesses praised his natural graces, and Sir Joshua Reynolds, Britain's most fashionable painter, painted him as an example of calm, uncorrupted dignity. Lee Boo, from Palau in Micronesia, was equally convincing as a "prince of nature." Visitors to the Pacific found a sensual paradise. The French explorer, Louis Antoine de Bougainville (1729–1811), called Tahiti the island of Venus after the Roman goddess of love. The ease with which visitors could obtain sexual favors from Tahitian women was one of the most persistent themes of literature about the place. Romantic primitivism became inseparable from sexual opportunity. Images of Tahiti as the ravishing home of inviting nymphs filled Westerners' minds and paintings. Diderot focused on sex to highlight the mutual incomprehension of a Tahitian girl and a French chaplain: "Honest stranger, do not refuse me. Make me a mother."

Omai—the restless young Tahitian who sailed to England with Captain Cook in the 1770s—became the darling of London society. He is shown here painted by Sir Joshua Reynolds, the most fashionable portrait painter of the day, in heroic fashion, in misplaced oriental attire, and bare feet, against a majestic backdrop. In Western eyes, Omai embodied the idea that the untutored, "natural" man could be effortlessly noble.

Wild Children

The disappointments of previous centuries had not ended the quest for "natural" humans. On the contrary, interest in such problems as the origins of language and of political and social life, and the moral effects of civilization was never so acute, and scholars' anxiety to examine specimens of primitive humanity untouched by rules of civilized society was greater than ever. "Wolf children" seemed, for a while, to be likely to supply the required raw material for analysis. Carolus Linnaeus (1707–1778)—the Swedish botanist who devised the modern method of classifying species—thought that wild children were a separate species of human beings. Plucked from whatever woods they were found in, wrenched from the wolves and foxes that suckled them, they became experiments in civilization, subjected to efforts to teach them language and manners.

The number of recorded cases of wild children increased in the seventeenth and eighteenth centuries. Was this because of renewed interest, stimulated by comparisons with the "savages" discovered by overseas expansion? Or was it simply a function of the explosion of population in the Europe of the day, expanding the limits of towns and cultivation, squeezing the remaining tracts of unpopulated "wilderness"? All the experiments to "civilize" these children failed. Boys whom bears supposedly raised in seventeenth-century Poland continued to prefer the company of bears. "Peter the Wild Boy," whom rival members of the English royal family struggled to possess as a pet in the 1720s, hated clothes and beds and never learned to talk. The "savage girl" kidnapped from the woods in France in 1731 preferred raw frogs to

Wild child. "Peter the wild boy" was found, naked and silent, in the woods of Hanover in 1725 as a young teenager. Under learned tuition in London, he learned to mime polite greetings. The writer Daniel Defoe defended him from the charge of mere idiocy as an example of how "mere nature" needs society to civilize it. He spent much of his life tethered to prevent escape, popularly reported in the *Gentleman's Magazine* as "more of the Ouran Outang species than of the human."

food cooked in the kitchen, and for a long time, she imitated birdsong better than she spoke French. The most famous case of all was that of another French child, the "Wild Boy of Aveyron." Abandoned in infancy in the high forest of southwest France, he survived by his own wits for years until he was kidnapped for civilization in 1798. He learned to wear clothes and to dine elegantly, but never to speak or to like what had happened to him. His tutor described him drinking fastidiously after dinner in the window of the room, "as if in this moment of happiness this child of nature tries to unite the only two good things which have survived the loss of his liberty—a drink of limpid water and the sight of sun and country."

The Huron as Noble Savage

The most prolific and influential source of ideas about the nobility of savagery were the Native American Huron of the Great Lakes region of North America (see Chapter 19). Although missionaries who worked among the Huron were candid about the defects of their savage way of life, the secular philosophers who read the missionaries' accounts tended to accentuate the positive and eliminate the negative. Cautionary tales were filtered out of the missionary texts, and only an idealized Huron remained. This transformation of tradition into legend became easier as real Hurons literally disappeared—first decimated, then virtually destroyed by the diseases to which European contagion exposed them.

The great secularizer of legends about the Huron was Louis-Armand de Lom de l'Arce, who called himself by the title his family had sold for cash, Sieur de Lahontan. Like many refugees from a hostile world at home, he left France for Canada in the 1680s and set himself up as an expert on its curiosities. The mouthpiece for his free-thinking anticlericalism was an invented Huron called Adario, with whom Lahontan walked in the woods, discussing the imperfections of translations of the Bible, the virtues of republicanism, and the merits of free love. Lahontan's devastating satire on the church, the French monarchy, and the pretensions and pettiness of the French elite fed directly into Voltaire's tale of the 1760s of a "natural" Huron sage in Paris.

The socially intoxicating potential of the Huron myth was distilled in a comedy performed in Paris in 1768, inspired by or plagiarized from Voltaire's portrait. The Huron in this comedy excels in all the virtues of noble savagery as huntsman, lover, and warrior against the English. He travels around the world with an intellectual's ambition: "to see a little of how it is made." When urged to adopt French dress, he denounces imitation as fashion "among monkeys but not among men." "If he lacks enlightenment by great minds," comments an observer, "he has abundant sentiments, which I esteem more highly. And I fear that in becoming civilized he will be the poorer." Unhappy in love, the Huron urges the mob to breach the prison fortress of Paris, the Bastille, to rescue his imprisoned love. He is therefore arrested for sedition. "His crime is manifest. It is an uprising."

THE FRENCH REVOLUTION AND NAPOLEON

Believers in the nobility of the savage found it relatively easy to believe in the wisdom of the common man. The Bastille was a symbol of oppression. Copies of the *Encyclopedia* that the government had seized were kept there, and Voltaire had been briefly and comfortably imprisoned there. Urban myth insisted that hundreds of prisoners of conscience suffered in the Bastille. Yet, like most organs of the

French state, it was rickety, and like the government's treasury, virtually empty. Rebels who broke into it in search of arms and gunpowder on July 14, 1789, found only a handful of inmates, none of whom were political prisoners.

Background to the Revolution

To those who endured it, or experienced its consequences, the Revolution that— according to the conventional narrative—broke out in France on that day seemed so momentous that they searched the past for its causes. Historians have looked deep into the history of the pre-Revolutionary old regime in France for explanations. Like most political upheavals, however, the French Revolution arose suddenly in the particular circumstances of the time and unrolled rapidly in ways previously unforeseeable. The costs of wars—especially French participation in the American Revolutionary War, which ended in 1783 and added substantially to the French state's debts—left the monarchy desperate to increase tax yields. France was a rich country with a poor government. In 1788, to resolve the fiscal crisis, royal ministers, in desperation, took a big risk: they summoned, for the first time since 1614, the Estates General, the medieval assembly of the realm. Deputies to the estates expected to be able to demand changes that would go far beyond finance. Many arrived resentful, having sat on consultative bodies whose advice the government had dismissed. Most belonged to the literate minority the Enlightenment had affected. They had strong inclinations toward constitutionalism in politics and anticlericalism in religion. All of them had read the gutter press of the day: scandal sheets about alleged sexual and financial shenanigans at court.

> *"Historians have looked deep into the history of the pre-Revolutionary old regime in France for explanations. Like most political upheavals, however, the French Revolution arose suddenly in the particular circumstances of the time and unrolled rapidly in ways previously unforeseeable."*

Local assemblies elected the deputies. "Public opinion," King Louis XVI (r. 1774–1792) once wrote in one of his schoolbooks, "is never wrong." The regulations for electing the Estates General emphasized that "His Majesty wishes that everyone, from the extremities of his realm and from the most remote dwelling places, may be assured that his desires and claims will reach him." As a result, the deputies arrived charged with "books of grievances," many of them full of the complaints of peasants hungry after bad harvests, venting their rage on big landowners. Most of them demanded lower taxes and relief from traditional obligations of peasants and the traditional privileges of lords—the lords' exclusive rights to keep pigeons, hunt game, and grind grain into flour, to evade taxes, to charge fees to hold markets and fairs, to mobilize forced labor. In June, 1789, the Estates General gave itself the title of National Assembly with the right to "interpret the General Will of the nation." In August, it enacted the Declaration of the Rights of Man and the Citizen. "Men are born free and remain equal in rights," this document proclaimed. Sovereignty, said the Declaration, no longer rested with the king but with the whole people. As in all revolutions, radicals exploited the mood in favor of change to organize and agitate for even more change than most people wanted.

Tennis Court Oath. On June 20, 1789, the members of the French National Assembly responded to the king's attempt to force them to disband by swearing "never to separate… until the constitution of the realm is drawn up and fixed upon solid foundations." The painter Jacques-Louis David, who supported the Revolution, dramatized the moment by exaggerating the wind and light, and romanticized it by giving the members heroic poses, based on ancient Roman rituals. He crowded the canvas with more individuals than were actually present when the oath was taken. The foreground scene, in which a Catholic priest, a Protestant pastor, and a lay deputy embrace, never took place. In the right foreground, Martin-D'Auch, the only member to refuse to take the oath, resists pleas to join with the others.

Revolutionary Radicalism

In 1790–1791, the revolutionaries concentrated on the church, enacting a "Civil Constitution of the Clergy" that turned priests and bishops into public servants and nationalized church property. The pope rejected it. So did Louis XVI, who had never been wholehearted in his support of radical reform. Once his opposition became known, the king became a virtual prisoner of the assembly. Opponents of the Revolution began to leave the country. Foreign powers feared the Revolution might be exported abroad. In March 1792, war broke out, and Austria and Prussia invaded France.

In the atmosphere of war, anything can happen, and only harsh measures can give governments control over events. In August 1792, when it was obvious that Louis XVI was in contact with the invaders, a mob ransacked the royal palace in Paris and massacred the king's servants and Swiss Guards. In 1793, the royal family was executed. Aristocrats, priests, and government officials were slaughtered in urban riots and peasant rebellions. The most ruthless revolutionary factions seized power over what remained of the state, while local committees of militants and self-appointed "people's tribunals" imposed revolutionary unity by terror. In the bloodiest spell, during June and July 1794, 1,584 heads were chopped off in Paris, and thousands of peasants and workers were killed in the provinces. "It was not," admitted a member of the government, "a question of principles. It was about killing."

It was also about politics. The ruling faction used terror to perpetuate its power. But like so much fanaticism, the Reign of Terror was genuinely principled in the eyes of its perpetrators. The effective leader of the revolutionary government at the time was a true idealist. Maximillien Robespierre (1758–1794) joined the Estates General in 1789 as a popular representative. He embraced the role of legislator with enthusiasm for the chance to do good. He was passionate for the early gains the Revolution made: the curtailment of aristocratic power; the transfer of wealth to the peasantry; the installation, as he saw it, of religious liberty by the humbling of the church; the establishment, as he put it, of the world's first real democracy. When counterrevolutionaries and invaders threatened these achievements, he responded with violence. In February, 1793, he explained the rationale of terror. "Our aim is the peaceful enjoyment of liberty and equality, and the reign of that eternal justice whose laws are engraved not in stone or marble but in the hearts of all people." So far, so good. But Robespierre had learned from Rousseau that people "must be forced to be free." He never fully trusted ordinary people to know what was good for them without help from their intellectual superiors. He believed in perfection by purgation, healing by cauterization. To Robespierre, the blade of the guillotine was like a surgeon's knife, chopping off whatever was dangerous and corrupt. He continued, "If the basis of popular government in time of peace is virtue, its basis in time of revolution is both virtue and terror—virtue without which terror is disastrous and terror without which virtue has no power." People had to be killed so that the Revolution and the virtuousness it claimed to represent could triumph. It was a claim that would find even bloodier expression in the twentieth century (see Chapters 28 and 29).

The idealism that had launched the Revolution became hard to sustain in the face of so many crimes committed in the name of liberty. Take the example of a leading revolutionary propagandist, the Marquis de Sade (1740–1814), who called himself Citizen Sade after the revolutionaries liberated him from what amounted to a luxury suite in the Bastille to which his family had begged the government to confine him in the 1780s. His private correspondence exposes his revolutionary enthusiasm as a sham and his enlightened idealism as hypocrisy. His offenses included torturing, imprisoning, and poisoning prostitutes, and—so he claimed—"proving that God does not exist" by inserting consecrated communion wafers in their posteriors. His sexual antics were a

Revolutionary France began executing people by guillotine in 1792. The guillotine was supposed to be an efficient and humane death-machine because it killed quickly with a single blow, without torture. But during the Revolution, it made a horrible spectacle of mass executions and became a symbol not of the Enlightenment but of barbarity. France continued to guillotine condemned criminals until 1977. Today the laws of France, like those of almost every Western country, acknowledge that even criminals have basic human rights, of which the most fundamental is the right to live.

distortion of liberty, his egotism a warped version of individualism, his violence and cruelty a caricature of the vicious fervor of revolutionary injustice. Morbid forms of sexual cruelty are still called "sadism" after him. As if in parody of Rousseau, de Sade thought no instincts could be immoral because all are natural. And as if in parody of Pierre Laplace's elimination of God from science (see Chapter 20), he thought no passions should be condemned because chemical forces in the body govern them. In his brief political career as a revolutionary spokesman—he ended his days in an insane asylum— he was unable to find a way to combine the extreme individualism to which he was inclined with the social responsibility the Revolution demanded.

Napoleon

When revolutions unleash chaos, people often turn to a "strong man." In 1799, a military coup brought France's best general to power as dictator. Napoleon Bonaparte (1769–1821) called himself First Consul of the Republic, and then, from 1804, after more victories had increased his popularity, Emperor of the French. His military genius and the skill and strength of his armies turned Europe into a playground for his political experiments. French power extended at its height over Spain, Portugal, Italy, Belgium, the Netherlands, Switzerland, most of Germany, Poland, and parts of Austria and Croatia. French influence overshadowed Scandinavia. French armies carried revolutionary ideas into Ireland, Russia, Egypt, and Syria (see Map 22.3). The wars were the nearest thing to world war that the world had yet seen, igniting contests for trade and dominion in India, where the British seized the opportunity to extend their conquests, and in the Americas, where British armies attacked Buenos Aires in Argentina and burned the White House in Washington, D.C. Colonies changed hands in the Caribbean, North America, the Indian Ocean, the East Indies, and South Africa, and even, in Haiti's case, achieved independence (see Chapter 21). But the major global effects arose from the new political forms and ideas generated in Europe and the way an increasingly interconnected and well-informed world took them up.

In an age of political innovations, Napoleon was one of the most inventive rationalizers of states. He imposed a uniform law code on his conquests. The **Code Napoleon** is still his most impressive legacy and forms the basis of the civil and criminal laws of much of Europe, Latin America, and sub-Saharan Africa. He subordinated the church to the state. He decreed the abolition of ancient monarchies and republics. He summoned new states into being, changed the boundaries of old ones, and imposed constitutional government where it had never existed before. He substituted aristocracies at will, demoting ancient families and raising up new ones. He cultivated a romantic image of himself as "a fragment of rock hurled into space"—a meteor that changed the fate of a continent. To the poor, he was the man who fulfilled the French Revolution, and to the rich, the man who tamed it. The heirs of the Enlightenment admired him for making reason, rather than ideology, the guide of his politics. But critics charged that for Napoleon reason was a substitute for morality. In some ways, he ruled a barbarian empire, descended as much from that of Charlemagne (r. 768–814) as from Rome. Sometimes he had himself painted as a Roman emperor. Sometimes he preferred to be depicted among ancient German gods. Historians have detected opportunism and lack of any general principles in his behavior. A cruel police state operated wherever he ruled.

Napoleon's power was unsustainable because it was based on victory, procured, from 1805 onward, in campaigns at escalating cost against enemies who never accepted his hegemony for long. By 1810, he had defeated Austria and

Napoleon. The French painter Jean Ingres's (1780–1867) portrait of Napoleon enthroned as Emperor of the French amazes the onlooker. How could so much majesty, magnificence, and power come within the reach of an outsider? Napoleon came from Corsica, a poor Mediterranean island that had only become part of France in 1768; his army service began in the artillery—a corps other soldiers despised at the time; his father though claiming aristocratic blood, had been a lawyer—a bourgeois occupation. Yet Napoleon turned France from a republic into a monarchy and crowned himself emperor in 1804. Though regal and romantic, Ingres's image also seems showy and vulgar. Napoleon's brother, Lucien, told the emperor that it was more distinguished to be head of a republic than to be an emperor.
Jean Auguste Dominique Ingres (1780–1867), Napoleon on His Imperial Throne, 1806. Oil on canvas, 259 × 162 cm. Musee des Beaux-Arts, Rennes. Photograph © Erich Lessing/Art Resource, New York

MAP 22.3

Napoleon's Empire, ca. 1799–1815

- territories under direct French control
- other states ruled by Napoleon or members of his family
- other dependent states
- ⚔ selected battles
- ⚔ selected naval battles

Prussia with crushing effect and occupied Spain. Of the other major powers that opposed him, Britain was unassailable because of British command of the sea, and Napoleon's attempt to choke the British into submission by strangling their continental trade proved unenforceable. That left Russia—a power Napoleon cowed into an uneasy alliance that could not last. In 1812, he attempted an invasion to bring the Russians to heel. As a great general once said, "There are few rules in war: one of them is, Never Invade Russia." The Russians withdrew, fighting only delaying battles, and relying on winter to destroy Napoleon's army—which it did with stunning effect. He never fully recovered from the defeat, and he became increasingly desperate for loss of allies and lack of manpower back home in France. The old coalition of Britain, Russia, Prussia, and Austria re-formed in 1813 and dethroned him in 1814. He returned from exile in 1815 for a final throw but could not match the resources his enemies brought to the battle-field. Waterloo—the scene of his final defeat in Belgium that June—has become a proverbial term for an irrecoverable disaster.

In Perspective
The Afterglow of Enlightenment

To the disappointment of the idealists who advocated "liberty, equality, and frater-nity," the French Revolution had failed to change the world. The wars the Rev-olution started were the real anvil of change, and Napoleon was their smith and hammer. After the shake-up of the Napoleonic Wars, no form of political legitimacy would be beyond challenge in Europe. Constitutional struggles domi-nated European politics and influenced those of the world, along with the conflict of new or newly effective political ideas, which we shall look at in the next part of this book: nationalism, militarism, secularism, democracy, and socialism.

The French Revolution was part of the dark side of the Enlightenment—both its creation and its destroyer. It opened with noble cries—for liberty, equality, and fraternity, the rights of man and of the citizen, the sovereignty of the people. It ended with the sickening scream that forms the last line of the "Marseillaise," the French revolutionaries' anthem, calling for troughs full of the "impure" blood of aristocrats, traitors, and foreigners.

In Britain, the statesman and philosopher Edmund Burke (1729–1797) was so appalled by the Revolution's excesses that he reached for the comforts of conservatism. In Spain, in the black paintings of Francisco Goya (1746–1828) and in Germany, in the private darkness of Beethoven's (1770–1827) late music, we can sense another response: retreat into hag-ridden disillusionment. In the *Critique of Pure Reason* of 1781, Immanuel Kant proposed a rickety, human-scale world of "crooked timber" in place of the grand ruined structures of the Age of Reason. The Enlightenment was streaked with shadows. In Paris in 1798, Étienne Robert Gaspard displayed a freak light show in which he made monstrous shapes loom at the audience from a screen or appear to flicker eerily, projected onto clouds of smoke. In other demonstrations of the wonders of electricity, the real-life forerunners of Frankenstein made corpses twitch to thrill an audience. It was not the sleep of reason that produced these monsters. They were creations of its most watchful hours—the hideous issue of scientific experimentation, the brutal images of minds tortured by revulsion at revolutionary crimes.

The Enlightenment survived in America. The United States' Constitution of 1787 embodied some of the dearest political principles of Montesquieu and the authors of the *Encyclopedia*, substituting the sovereign people for a sovereign gov-ernment, switching many powers from the executive to the legislature, creating a long list of constitutional guarantees of freedom, outlawing any "establishment of religion," and expressing confidence in the people's fitness to decide their own fate. Assumptions about equality—though they did not yet extend to black people, Native Americans, or women—typified American society. No formal aristocracy was acknowledged. Servants treated employers with a familiarity that shocked European visitors. Money became a more powerful indicator of social distinction than birth.

An image of war. Francisco Goya's art began to desert the conventional subjects demanded by his early patrons in the 1790s. Under the dark and bloody impact of the French Revolution, he pro-duced scenes of witchcraft and torture. It was the Spanish War of Independence against Napoleon in 1808–1814, however, that released from his imagination colossal monsters like this: an image of war wading through the land and overshadow-ing the wreckage of lives.

"Napoleon's power was unsustainable because it was based on victory, procured, from 1805 onward, in campaigns at escalating cost against enemies who never accepted his hegemony for long."

Chronology

r. 1661–1722	Kangxi, Chinese emperor, tutored by Jesuit scholars
1680s	Louis-Armand de Lom de l'Arce leaves France for Canada
1685–1750	Johann Sebastian Bach, composer
1694–1778	François Marie Arouet (Voltaire), leading philosopher and admirer of China
1703–1758	Jonathan Edwards, New England preacher
1703–1791	John Wesley, founder of Methodism
1712–1778	Jean-Jacques Rousseau, author of the *Social Contract*
1713–1784	Denis Diderot, publisher of the *Encyclopedia*
1720	Chinese translations of Western books allowed to circulate in Japan
1728–1779	Captain James Cook, Britsh explorer
1736	Maupertuis's expedition to the Arctic Circle
1740–1758	George Whitfield, emotional preacher
1752	Publication of Maupertuis's *Letters on the Progress of Science*
1759–1773	Jesuits expelled from most West European countries
1769–1859	Baron Alexander von Humboldt, scientist and explorer
1771	Japanese "Dutch studies" group begins study of Western books
1776	Publication of Adam Smith's *The Wealth of Nations*; United States Declaration of Independence
1783	End of the American Revolutionary War
1789	Convening of the Estates General; Estates General becomes the National Assembly
Late 1700s and early 1800s	Romantic movement
July 14, 1789	Storming of the Bastille
1790–1791	Creation of Civil Constitution of the Clergy (France)
1792	Austria and Prussia invade France; publication of Mary Wollstonecraft's *A Vindication of the Rights of Women*
1793–1794	Reign of Terror; Louis XVI executed
	Lord Macartney's mission to China
1799	Napoleon seizes power
1804	Napoleon crowns himself Emperor of the French
June 18, 1815	Napoleon suffers final defeat at Battle of Waterloo

To the surprise of much of the world—and even of some Americans—the United States managed to avoid becoming a military dictatorship, the fate of so many other supposedly republican and egalitarian revolutions.

Even in Europe, the idea of progress survived. In the nineteenth century, it strengthened and fed on the "march of improvement"—the history of industrialization, the multiplication of wealth and muscle power, the insecure but encouraging victories of constitutionalism against tyranny. It became possible to believe that despite human failings progress was irreversible. Evolution programmed it into nature. It took the horrors of the late nineteenth and twentieth centuries—a catalogue of famines, failures, inhumanities, and genocidal conflicts—to make most people question whether progress was inevitable or even real.

The effects of the Enlightenment rippled over the world. Europeans and the inhabitants of European colonies in the Americas felt growing confidence as a result of their sense that their societies were making scientific and technical progress. Rivals in Asia seemed stagnant by comparison. Western visitors to Turkey in the last decade of the century felt certain that the Ottomans had not only lost their lead in power and wealth—they had slipped into inferiority through neglect of science, "too stupid to comprehend," an English observer averred, "or too proud to learn." Even China seemed to have sacrificed former advantages. A Dutch envoy in 1794 declared

that the scientific knowledge possessed by the Chinese is of very ancient date, and they obtained it long before the sciences were known in Europe. But everything has remained in its primitive state, without their even seeking, like the Europeans, to make further progress, or to bring their discoveries to perfection . . . . We have consequently so far surpassed them.

The former greatness of Asia—it was commonly alleged by the end of the century—had shifted to Europe.

During the following century, Asians increasingly shared this Western point of view. Rammohun Roy was not alone in his day in trying to appropriate the scientific learning of the Enlightenment for Indians' use. Indians joined the scientific societies that the British founded in India and founded others of their own. Bal Shastri Jambedkar, a professor of mathematics who collaborated closely with English colleagues in the scientific community in Calcutta (now called Kolkota) in the 1830s, published his work in Indian languages and translated useful texts. In the same period, the work of surveying India began increasingly to rely on Indian, not British, experts. Where Western scientific impact led, the influence of Western thinking on political, economic, and philosophical subjects soon followed.

India had privileged access to Western ideas because of the vast number of Westerners, especially Britons, whom British imperialism introduced to that country. Other European empires had similar effects in areas they colonized. And, increasingly in the nineteenth century, the effects of Western intellectual movements spread beyond the reach of imperialism. French invaders spread them in Egypt and Syria. Missionaries spread them—selecting those ideas that were not anti-Christian or anticlerical—almost wherever they went. So did the many Westerners who were employed as technicians throughout the world in the nineteenth century. Jesuits were instrumental in China. Dutch merchants and ambassadors penetrated Japan. Books helped to make Western ideas accessible worldwide and communicated them to parts of the world Westerners in person could hardly hope to remold. The consequences are apparent in most of the rest of this book. Up to this point in our story, the exchanges of culture we have chronicled have been mutually influential or have tended to be dominated by influences exerted on Europe from outside. From this point onward, global history becomes increasingly a story of Western influence.

> *"Up to this point in our story, the exchanges of culture we have chronicled have been mutually influential or have tended to be dominated by influences exerted on Europe from outside. From this point onward, global history becomes increasingly a story of Western influence."*

PROBLEMS AND PARALLELS

1. How was the Enlightenment global in its inspiration, as well as in its effects? Why were Asian influences more influential in the West during the Enlightenment than Western influences were in Asia? Which Western ideas and products appealed to elites in China, Japan, Korea, India, and Thailand?

2. Why did Enlightenment writers like Voltaire, Diderot, and Montesquieu disagree about whether Asian cultures were models for Europe or negative examples to be avoided? Why did the Western view of the Ottoman Empire become more negative during the eighteenth century?

3. Why were so many Enlightenment thinkers opposed to religion? Why was there a religious revival in the eighteenth century? How did George Whitfield and Charles Wesley use emotional fervor to win converts?

4. How did the *Encyclopedia* promote Enlightenment thinking? Why have Adam Smith's economic ideas been so influential? In what sense were Marie-Olympe de Gouges and Mary Wollstonecraft feminist writers?

5. Why was Romanticism often seen as antithetical to the Enlightenment? What was Rousseau's concept of the state? Why did he argue that obedience to the general will was more important than individual rights?

6. How did influences from the Pacific and the Americas shape the elevation of the "common man"? What does the term *noble savage* mean?

7. Why did reform lead to revolution in France in 1789? How did Robespierre justify the use of terror? Was Napoleon a ruler who symbolized the Enlightenment or who undermined its ideals?

READ ON ▶ ▶ ▶

S. C. Crawford, *Raja Rammohun Roy and Progressive Movements in India: A Selection from Records, 1775–1845* (1983) is useful. Maupertuis is best approached through his own writings, but there are useful studies by D. Beeson, *Maupertuis* (1992), and M. Terrall, *The Man Who Flattened the Earth* (2002).

On the Enlightenment in general, P. Gay, *The Enlightenment* (1995), is a classic that is still stimulating. J. Israel, *Radical Enlightenment: Philosophy and the Making of Modernity* (2001) is a superb study that emphasizes the Dutch contribution. G. Gunn, *First Globalization* (2003) is a useful introduction to the global context.

A. Çirakman, *From the "Terror of the World" to the "Sick Man of Europe"* (2002) traces changes in the image of the Ottomans in the West. Li Yan and Du Shiran, *Chinese Mathematics: A Concise History* (1987) is fundamental. J. Waley-Cohen, *The Sextants of Beijing* (1999) is a broad survey of Chinese science, with special attention to interchange with the West. Her 1993 article in the *American Historical Review*, "China and Western Technology in the Late Eighteenth Century," puts the Macartney mission in context. F. Wakeman, *The Great Enterprise* (1986) is a good introduction to China in the period.

For the context of Dutch studies, L. Blussé et al., *Bridging the Divide* (2001) is enthralling. J. B. Bury, *The Idea of Progress* (1982) is an unsurpassed classic.

T. Ellingson, *The Myth of the Noble Savage* (2001) is an important revisionist work. M. Newton, *Savage Girls and Wild Boys: A History of Feral Children* (2003) is a fascinating overview of its subject. A. Pagden, *European Encounters with the New World from Renaissance to Romanticism* (1994) is indispensable.

C. L. Johnson, ed., *The Cambridge Companion to Mary Wollstonecraft* (2002) is a mine of information and a valuable guide to work on early feminism.

J. C. Beaglehole's classic *The Life of Captain James Cook* (1992) is still the best biography.

S. Schama, *Citizens* (1991) tells the story of the French Revolution with vision and verve. C. Jones, *The Great Nation* (2003) is excellent on the background of eighteenth-century France. There are so many books about Napoleon: P. Geyl, *Napoleon: For and Against* (1967) is a magisterial survey of the literature.

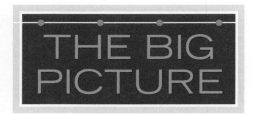
The World in 1800

Creole languages are scattered around the world, like jetsam left by the receding tides of early modern empires. Slaves created many of the new languages, while other languages took shape in the communities of traders or settlers. Mapping them is a way of demonstrating the length and breadth of the reach of empires. The distribution of creole speech recalls the way the world shrank in the eighteenth century, as migrants criss-crossed the world in the service of empires or in an attempt to exploit them.

The existence of these languages and the literatures many of them generated are reminders that colonialism, which was destructive of so much of the culture it touched, could also be amazingly creative, calling into being not only new languages but also new religions, new cuisines, and new ways of thought and life.

The effects of the global exchange of culture were visible and audible not just in the far-flung outposts of empires, where creole languages emerged, but also in the homelands of the imperial powers. News and views from the Americas deeply influenced European imaginations and helped to form romantic aesthetics. The political thought of the European Enlightenment would have been radically different without input from the worlds of Islam, India, China, and Japan. Without reports about the Huron and the Polynesian islanders, Europeans would not have formulated the notion of the noble savage—and so ideas about common wisdom and popular sovereignty might have been arrested. Cultures traditionally hostile to foreign influences began to respond positively to global exchanges, as Dutch studies introduced Japanese thinkers to revised models of how the world worked and as the Jesuits influenced Chinese arts and engineering.

▶ QUESTIONS

1. How did the world shrink in the eighteenth century? How were empires the touch points that helped mesh the world together?

2. How did China's continued economic dynamism in the eighteenth century contribute to the global exchange of ideas?

To view an interactive version of this map, as well as a video of the author describing key themes related to this Part, go to www.myhistorylab.com

770

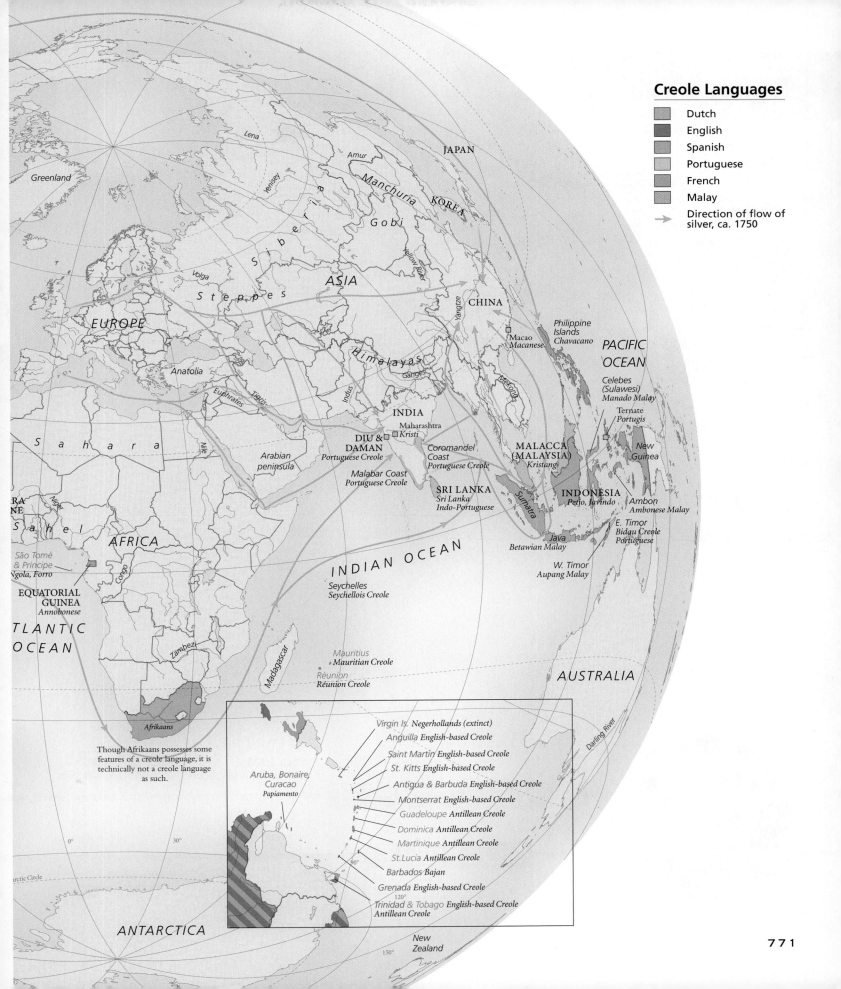

Creole Languages

	Dutch
	English
	Spanish
	Portuguese
	French
	Malay
→	Direction of flow of silver, ca. 1750

Greenland

Lena

Amur

Manchuria

JAPAN

KOREA

Siberia

Gobi

Yenisey

Volga

ASIA

Steppes

Yellow River

CHINA

Macao
Macanese

Philippine
Islands
Chavacano

PACIFIC
OCEAN

EUROPE

Yangtze

Anatolia

Himalayas

Ganges

Euphrates

Tigris

Indus

Mekong

Celebes
(Sulawesi)
Manado Malay

INDIA

Maharashtra
Kristi

Ternate
Portugis

New
Guinea

Sahara

Nile

Arabian
peninsula

DIU &
DAMAN
Portuguese Creole

Coromandel
Coast
Portuguese Creole

MALACCA
(MALAYSIA)
Kristang

INDONESIA
Petjo, Javindo

Ambon
Ambonese Malay

São Tomé
& Principe
Ngola, Forro

Sahel

AFRICA

Malabar Coast
Portuguese Creole

SRI LANKA
*Sri Lanka
Indo-Portuguese*

Sumatra

E. Timor
*Bidau Creole
Portuguese*

EQUATORIAL
GUINEA
Annobonese

Congo

INDIAN OCEAN

Java
Betawian Malay

W. Timor
Aupang Malay

ATLANTIC
OCEAN

Seychelles
Seychellois Creole

Zambezi

Madagascar

Mauritius
Mauritian Creole

Réunion
Réunion Creole

AUSTRALIA

Though Afrikaans possesses some
features of a creole language, it is
technically not a creole language
as such.

Afrikaans

Darling River

Aruba, Bonaire,
Curaçao
Papiamento

Virgin Is. *Negerhollands (extinct)*

Anguilla *English-based Creole*

Saint Martin *English-based Creole*

St. Kitts *English-based Creole*

Antigua & Barbuda *English-based Creole*

Montserrat *English-based Creole*

Guadeloupe *Antillean Creole*

Dominica *Antillean Creole*

Martinique *Antillean Creole*

St. Lucia *Antillean Creole*

Barbados *Bajan*

Grenada *English-based Creole*

Trinidad & Tobago *English-based Creole*
Antillean Creole

ANTARCTICA

New
Zealand

since 1800
Global population boom

since ca. 1800
Coal and steam power

ENVIRONMENT

CULTURE

1800–1880
Decline of slavery

The Frustrations of Progress
to ca. 1900

◀ **Ottoman world map.** In 1803, the Turkish Military Engineering School published this world map—the first Ottoman map based on Mercator's projection—in an atlas using European geographical knowledge and mapmaking techniques.

since 1850
Industrialization of food production

ca. 1850
Electricity

1870–1900
Famine and drought worldwide

1840s–1860s
Opium Wars, China

1860s–1910
Mass migrations

1870–1871
Franco-Prussian
War

1885
Berlin Conference–
Partition of Africa

CHAPTER 23

Replacing Muscle: The Energy Revolutions

▲ **Encounter between man and beast.** Ambroise-Louis Garneray (1783–1857) was among the artists whose heroic whaling scenes helped to inspire Herman Melville's novel *Moby Dick*. Garneray's depiction of whalers at work in the North Atlantic in 1836 emphasizes the solitary combat between the heroic harpooner and the great, black sea beast, and shows other dangers—the fragile boat, its frantic crew, the spurt of blood from the wounded whale, the foaming sea. In the background, the ship is calm—with fires ready to render the whale's blubber.
Photograph courtesy of the Peabody Essex Museum

In this Chapter

THE WORLD

It is a tale of monsters, but not a horror story. *Moby Dick* is one of the most gripping, moving sea sagas ever written: the tale of a seaman's hunt for revenge against a huge white whale that snapped off his leg: a monstrous man, a monstrous beast, a monstrous obsession. When Herman Melville wrote it in 1851, whaling was still a close encounter between man and beast in the wild, in an open boat that the lash of a whale's tail could easily crush or smash to splinters. The harpoonists had to weary, worry, and bleed the whale to death. Then they would haul the carcass alongside their ship, dismember it, and the whole crew would kneel between decks in blood and blubber to chop and melt down the fat before it turned putrid. The fat was precious. Before the development of the fossil-oil extraction industry, whaling was the world's main source of oil. Blubber supplied lipids—fat for human food—and lubricants to grease machinery and to light lamps.

The world was facing a fat crisis—a worsening shortage of both lipids and lubricants. Within a few years, however, a series of developments and innovations solved the problem. In 1856, a French experimenter won an official competition to find a cheap kind of edible fat for the French navy. He called his mixture of beef fat and milk "margarine" because its pallid gleam was supposed to resemble the little pearls known in France as marguerites. This did not increase the world's stock of fat, but it did make what was available go further. Soon after, in 1858, fossil oil emerged in the New World, skimmed out of the ground in Ontario, Canada, then pumped from the earth in Pennsylvania in 1859. People had been using fossil oil for thousands of years in small ways where it was available through natural seepage. Tunnels under rivers in Mesopotamia in the second millennium B.C.E., for example, used bitumen mortar derived from petroleum in their bricks. Now, for the first time, extraction on a massive scale began, as a way to replace other increasingly scarce and expensive sources of fat. In 1865, the first fully industrial whaling ship was launched in Norway, with explosive harpoons and a fast steam engine that could tow dead whales into port for quick processing. Even the gigantic blue whale—which previous hunting techniques could not touch—now became whalers' prey.

Meanwhile, the search was on for other sources of fat. Increasingly intensive methods to produce feed supported more livestock and therefore boosted supplies of animal fat. New grazing areas opened up in Argentina, Australia, and the American West. Demand for edible oil drove European powers into colonial ventures to produce palm, peanut, and coconut oil.

FOCUS questions

Why did the world's population begin to rise rapidly during the nineteenth century?

Why did industrialization increase the world's food supply?

How was industrialization related to the growth of military power?

Why did the economies of the United States and Latin America develop in different ways?

Why did Japan and China pursue different policies toward industrialization?

How did British imperialism affect the economic development of India and Egypt?

Fat—oil from animals, plants, and minerals—made the world of the nineteenth century work. It supplied raw energy for growing numbers of human consumers. It was used in products from soap to shoe polish. It greased the machines of industrialization. It induced new adventures in long-range empire-building. But fat was just one of many sources of energy that nineteenth-century people exploited on a scale previously never experienced in the history of the world. Oils and fats, along with muscle power, traditional fuels (wood, peat, and coal), and relatively limited exploitation of wind-power and water-power were the only means humans had to supplement the power of the Earth and the sun and devise ways to deliver energy that particularly suited human activities. The fat crisis was part of a bigger picture: a revolution in the sources of energy that kept human society working. The way people responded to the crisis brought together major themes of the nineteenth century: new ways to exploit the planet's resources; new ventures to release energy and redirect it to new uses.

The main reason why people needed to multiply the sources of energy in the mid-nineteenth century is the first subject of this chapter: population explosion, which strained supplies of exploitable energy. We then turn to the response: industrialization, which, in the parts of the world where it happened, replaced muscle-power with machines. The following three chapters will cover the major consequences of industrialization: new forms of imperialism, and the effects of industrialization on society and politics.

GLOBAL DEMOGRAPHICS: THE WORLD'S POPULATION RISES

Population growth, with consequent rising demand, lay at the heart of the drive for new sources of energy. In 1800, by the best available calculations, there were about 950 million people in the world. By 1900, there were about 1.6 billion (see Map 23.1). After centuries when 0.5 percent per year growth was hard to sustain for more than a few decades, to have more than 1 percent growth yearly for over a century was revolutionary. Around 1800, only four large areas in the world could reasonably be called densely settled—with, say, more than four people per square mile: in East Asia (China, Japan, and Korea), Southeast Asia (Indochina, Malaysia, and Indonesia), the Indian subcontinent, and Western Europe. By 1900, parts of Africa and the Americas, especially along the coasts, had become regions of comparable density.

In part, population increase was the result of the continuing favorable pattern of global disease (see Chapter 17). In some ways, it is surprising that the world stayed relatively healthy. There were good reasons to expect— as many students of population trends supposed at the time—that global health would get worse. As people got more crowded together, new eco-niches opened for disease. The improvements in long-range communications, with consequent huge increases in the range and rate of travel and migration, made it easier for disease to spread. The danger, which threatened throughout the century, finally struck in 1917–1919, when an influenza pandemic killed at least 30 million people worldwide. But by then, the rate of population increase was so quick that the disaster hardly made a dent in the world's population.

Yet epidemics multiplied. The growing cities of the period were ill planned and poorly equipped with drainage and sanitation. Urban plagues—especially cholera and dysentery, which are contracted through contaminated water, and typhus, which is spread by body lice—arose in areas that had never experienced them before. Cholera arrived in China from India in 1820 and soon became a common problem in Europe. Populations uprooted and transferred from countryside to town often suffered nutritionally, especially in the early stages of urbanization, before the food supply was properly organized and regulated. Polluted and nutritionally inadequate food was a major problem in nineteenth-century cities. Infected milk helped to spread one of the century's killer diseases in urban environments: tuberculosis. Heating milk to make it safe only began in the last couple of decades of the century. Manufacturers and grocers who could successfully promote their wares as healthy made fortunes. Nevertheless, the "age of plague" did not return, and new killer-diseases were never generalized enough or lethal enough to check demographic growth.

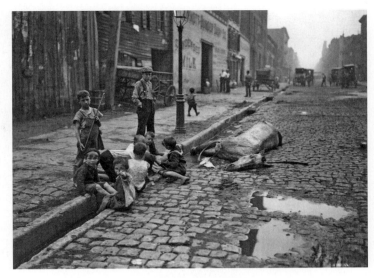

Slum life. Social reformers of the late nineteenth century listed sanitation, children's welfare, and animal abuse as some of the most pressing problems associated with urban conditions. This snapshot, taken around 1900 in New York City, captures all three issues: The ragged children play in a filthy gutter while a dead horse, presumably used to pull a cart or a trolley car, rots a few yards away.

Nor were rural populations exempt from ecological disasters. Although food production soared in global terms, its effects were unevenly distributed, and the ravages of famine were worse—in terms of the numbers of people killed—in the nineteenth century than at any other period in recorded history. Political neglect made the effects even worse, especially in the territories of large empires under distant or indifferent rulers. In some ways, the most successful crops of the period—the most prolific, the most nutritious—were traps, because people became overreliant on them. When fungal disease ruined the potato crop, horrific famines followed in 1845–1849 in Ireland, where a million people died and a million more were driven overseas, and in Belgium and Finland in 1867–1868. People who usually ate the potatoes to survive had no other crop to fall back on.

Famine killed at least 4.3 million people in India in 1876–1878, or probably more like 7 million if one allows for the caution of official British estimates. The famine that afflicted China at the same time was officially "the most terrible disaster in twenty-one dynasties." In the 1890s, droughts associated with an unusual concentration of El Niño events caused 12 million deaths in India and 20 million in China. Famines triggered plagues. In India, for instance, smallpox had killed a third of the population of the densely populated province of Bengal—almost wiping out a generation of children—after a famine in 1770. A cholera epidemic killed half the population of Guntur in eastern India, after the crops failed in 1833. Smallpox and cholera also followed the great Indian famine of 1896.

The Irish Potato Famine of 1845–1846 challenged English assumptions about the benefits of their rule in Ireland. George Frederick Watts (1817–1904), one of the most fashionable British painters of the day, depicted the human tragedy of the famine in this work of 1850. The grieving father stares at the onlooker with inescapable reproach.

Nonetheless, population growth proved irrepressibly robust, recovering from every catastrophe. In the Western world, the ascent of population was uninterrupted. The United States had 76 million people by the end of the nineteenth century—making it the most populous state in the Western world. Spectacular population increases also occurred in Europe. Most European countries roughly doubled their populations during the nineteenth century. The continent, which had about a fifth of the world's population at the start of the century, had about a quarter by its end. The population of the Russian Empire, including the peoples it conquered in Asia, increased fourfold to over 130 million. Taken together, the demo-

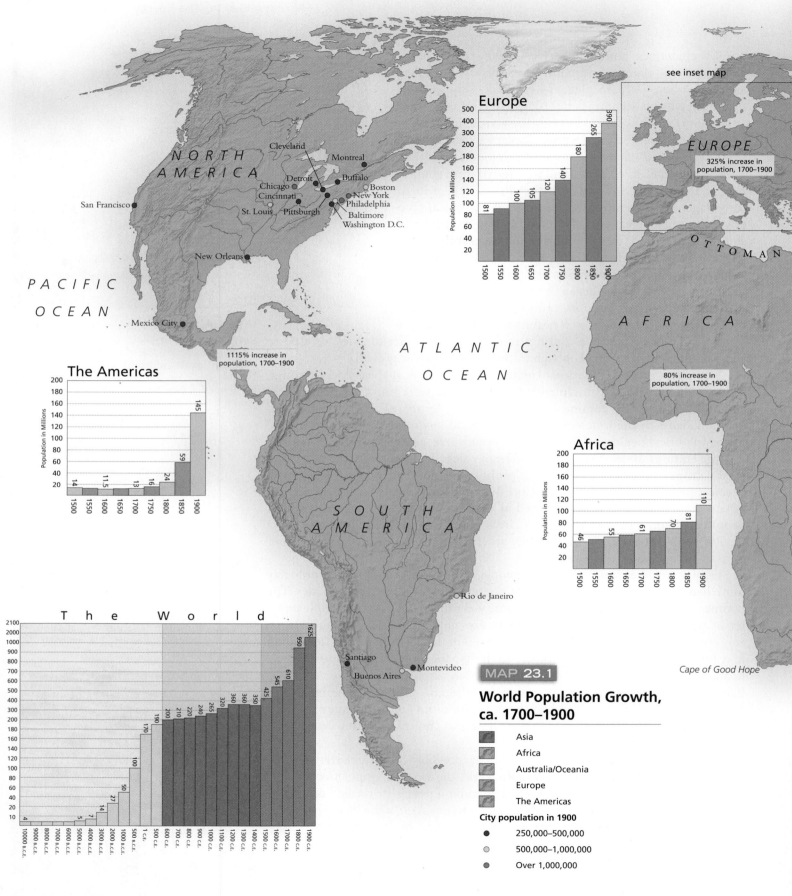

MAP 23.1

World Population Growth, ca. 1700–1900

Asia

Africa

Australia/Oceania

Europe

The Americas

City population in 1900

● 250,000–500,000

○ 500,000–1,000,000

● Over 1,000,000

RUSSIAN EMPIRE

ASIA

QING
EMPIRE

234% increase in
population, 1700–1900

Beijing
Tianjin
Nagoya
Kyoto   Tokyo
Kobe   Yokohama
Osaka

Alexandria
Cairo

Wuhan
Chongqing   Shanghai

Lucknow

Calcutta   Guangzhou

Bombay
Hyderabad

Madras   Bangkok

INDIAN

OCEAN

Dutch East Indies

AUSTRALIA
OCEANIA

281.3% increase in
population, 1700–1900

Sydney
Melbourne

Asia

Population in Millions

1500	1550	1600	1650	1700	1750	1800	1850	1900
280		375	370	415	495	625	795	970

Australia/Oceania

Population in Millions

1500	1550	1600	1650	1700	1750	1800	1850	1900
2					2.5	2.25		6.75

EUROPE

Manchester
and
Liverpool
Stockholm
St Petersburg
Glasgow
Copenhagen   Riga
Belfast   Leeds and   Amsterdam   Moscow
Bradford   Rotterdam
Dublin   Sheffield   Hamburg   Lódz
Birmingham   London   Cologne   Berlin   Warsaw
Leipzig
Bristol   Antwerp   Dresden
Brussels   Nuremburg
Paris   Frankfurt
Munich   Vienna   Odessa
Lyons   Budapest
Milan   Bucharest
Bordeaux   Turin
Marseilles
Barcelona
Madrid
Lisbon   Istanbul

graphic trends of the nineteenth century represented a real shift in the global balance of resources in favor of the West. The traditional pattern of global history, in which the hugely populous and productive societies of East and South Asia predominated, was ending or over. In some ways, the population figures mask an even greater shift: the extra people that Europe and the United States acquired produced hugely disproportionate increases in wealth, thanks to giant strides in the output of food and manufactures.

FOOD: TRANSITION TO ABUNDANCE

In view of the way famine and disease accompanied population growth, it is tempting to see Malthusian logic (see Chapter 20) linking demographic increase to ecological disaster. According to Malthus, population "naturally" increased faster than food resources. People could be expected to breed with little restraint unless and until disasters—plague, war, and, above all, famine—checked them. In reality, things never worked out the way Malthus predicted, for two reasons.

First, population increase did not conform to Malthus's prophecies. In all parts of the world for which we have data, people practiced forms of population control. In Europe, for instance, they postponed marriage. In France, uniquely as far as we know, married couples routinely practiced contraception. In India, relatively large numbers of people took up celibate ways of life, and the remarriage of widows was severely restricted. In Japan, traditionally, men postponed marriage until their late 20s or early 30s, whereas women were usually about 21 years old when they adopted one of the distinctive hair-styles that advertised their availability for marriage. As the century progressed, however, there was a clear drift toward marrying later. Moreover, for unknown reasons, Japanese women ceased to have children relatively early—in their mid-30s, some five years earlier than was normal in Europe at the time. Marriage in Japan became a privilege for the head of the household, so that most households had only one childbearing couple. The average size of a household fell from nearly 5 persons in 1800 to 4.25 in 1870, a demographically significant drop.

Second, new ways to produce food outstripped population growth. In this respect, Malthus's critics, who expected "progress" to prevent disaster, were right. It is hard to distinguish cause and effect, but population increase and the growth of the food supply were inseparably connected. Food production soared, partly because more land was devoted to it and partly because of new, more efficient methods of exploitation. In the Philippines and in Java, for instance, where population growth had long been static, rates of increase rose to 1 percent a year, largely because women started marrying at under 20 years of age. But this was an adjustment to new conditions that boosted food stocks and generated wealth. Large-scale deforestation released land for food production. Wetlands were adapted for rice farming. Previously marginal soil was exploited to grow coconuts, not necessarily for food but for the fiber, which was much in demand for matting, and for coconut oil, which was used in everything from cooking to making soap.

Sometimes food production rose simply because farmers applied traditional methods more systematically. This seems to have been the case in Japan, where agrarian output rose throughout the second half of the century, and well into the next, without any significant increase in the amount of land devoted to farming. In Egypt, wheat and barley production nearly doubled in the last two decades of the nineteenth century,

Rice cultivation in Japan. Hiroshige (1797–1858) specialized in painting comforting images of traditional Japan. Here bent-backed peasants labor virtuously under enriching rain in regularly patterned rice fields, surrounded by benign landscape. In the 100 years after the artist's death, enhanced efficiency enabled the Japanese to harvest more rice without extending the area under cultivation.

while the acreage under cultivation increased by less than half. But in most regions for which evidence survives, numerous small increases of the grazed or cultivated area amounted to a huge total increase. More spectacularly, a few major initiatives or accidents incorporated vast, previously unexploited frontiers. Occasionally, this happened through natural growth with little or no human effort. Natural means added almost 600 square miles, for instance, to the fertile Yellow River delta in China in the second half of the century. But natural losses—to encroaching seas and deserts—always tend to offset natural increases. So human hands have to intervene to stop losses and reclaim land. In the Netherlands, for instance, 11,000 acres were reclaimed from sea and wasteland during the nineteenth century. Partly in consequence, in the second half of the century, the number of cattle doubled, and pigs increased fourfold.

Beyond question, the greatest extension of the frontier of food production happened in the vast open lands of Argentina, Brazil, Uruguay, Australia, and North America. The incorporation of the North American prairie to raise cattle and grow grain was the most conspicuous large-scale adaptation of the environment for human purposes ever recorded (see Map 23.2). It may therefore be regarded as one of the most important events in history. In 1827, when James Fenimore Cooper wrote his novel *The Prairie*, the region seemed a place without a future: "a vast country incapable of sustaining a dense population." People called it "the Great American Desert." Almost nothing grew naturally that human stomachs could digest. Except in a few patches, the soil was too tough to plow without industrial technology. Yet by the end of the nineteenth century, the same plains had become the world's granary, with some of the most productive farming the world has ever seen—to say nothing of the great cities that were scattered across it.

The extension of grazing was the first stage in the region's transformation. This was the common experience of previously underexploited grasslands in the period. Much of southeast Australia and New Zealand became sheep-rearing country, though at first more for wool than for meat. The South American grasslands of the pampa, the sertão in Brazil, and much of Patagonia in southern Argentina bred cattle and sheep. Refrigeration on steam ships enabled Argentina to become a major exporter of beef and mutton. But the scale of production possible on the North American prairie exceeded that of other areas because so many markets were close at hand there. Partly, this was a result of railway construction, which concentrated large, though temporary, labor forces in parts of the region. Driving cattle herds from grazing lands to railway construction centers was a lucrative new business of the mid-nineteenth century. When the railways were built, the big concentrations of population in the Mississippi River valley and along the seaboards of North America became easily accessible to the products of the prairie.

Grains soon became more important than meat products. Planted by human hands, new kinds of humanly edible grass—wheat and maize above all—began to replace the native prairie grasses. But the change could not have happened without help from new industrial technologies. Steel plows turned the sod of the prairie. Railways transported the grain across what would otherwise be uneconomic distances. Houses built from precision-milled lumber and cheap nails made in Chicago spread cities in a region where most construction materials were simply unavailable. Repeating rifles destroyed the vital links in the earlier ecosystem: the buffalo herds and their human hunters, the Native Americans.

"The incorporation of the North American prairie to raise cattle and grow grain was the most conspicuous large-scale adaptation of the environment for human purposes ever recorded."

Grain elevator, 1879. Farmers packed their harvested grain into burlap sacks and brought the wagonloads to country elevators like this one in Moorhead, Minnesota. Note the pile of wood on the left to power the elevator's steam engine.

MAP 23.2

The Incorporation of the American Prairie

- ⌁⌁ railroads
- — cattle drives
- ▬ gold
- ▬ silver

Major industries, ca. 1890

- 🗌 cotton goods
- 👓 copper refining
- 🌲 lumber products
- 🏔 meat packing
- ⚒ iron and steel
- 🏭 flour mill products
- ↧ sugar refining
- ⛩ products for railroads
- ● rubber products
- ⚑ petroleum refining
- ▯ lead smelting

Grain elevators, introduced in 1850, made it possible to store grains without vast amounts of labor. Harvesting machinery enabled a few hands to reap large harvests. Wire enclosed farmland against buffalo and cattle. Giant mills—which still stand in many midwestern towns, where nowadays, they tend to get converted into apartments and shopping malls—processed the grain into marketable foodstuffs.

In 1861, the British novelist and postal official Anthony Trollope saw the results while touring the United States on official business: concentrations of food resources that had no precedent or parallel. Trollope was "grieved by the loose manner in which wheat was treated" in Minneapolis—"bags of it upset and left upon the ground. The labour of collecting it was more than it was worth." In Buffalo, New York, he saw some of the 60 million bushels of grain that passed through the city every year. But the transformation of the prairie was only beginning. The year after Trollope's visit, the Homestead Act made land in the West available to anyone—in practice, almost exclusively to white people—who wanted it at nominal prices. Five hundred million acres were added to the United States' farmland by 1900. In more modest degree, similar changes occurred in other parts of the American grasslands. Argentina had been a net importer of grain in the 1860s. By 1900, it exported 100 million bushels of wheat and maize a year. Canada also became a major grain exporter.

Not only did the amount of land for food production increase, but fertilizers increased productivity, too. To some extent, the increase was due to the spread of age-old techniques using natural fertilizer to enhance soils. In Europe, farmers kept their fields constantly productive, alternating beets or turnips with clover or alfalfa, which are good crops for renewing the soil because they recycle significant amounts of nitrogen. Root crops, such as turnips, rutabagas, and potatoes, could keep cattle alive throughout the winter, generating more manure. In 1860, British farms still got 60 percent of their fertilizers from recycling their own animal waste. But the system increasingly needed supplements because the market demanded increasing quantities of meat. Turnips, moreover, demand a lot of fertilizing on most soils. The first consequence was the mid-century guano boom. The guano of Peru was rich in nitrogen: mountains of excrement on islands off the Pacific coast, where huge concentrations of birds fed off the abundant fish. The normally rainless climate preserved the nitrogen from being washed away. In the 1850s, the main handler of Peruvian guano exported over 200,000 tons a year to Britain alone. Meanwhile, in 1843, new sources of guano began to be mined in southwest Africa, and the first chemical fertilizers came into production. There was "a manfactory of fertilizer in almost every town" in Britain by 1863, according to the *Farmer's Magazine*. British output of "superphosphates," as the new chemical fertilizers were called, rose from 30,000 tons in 1854 to 250,000 tons in 1866. At first, manufacturers mainly enhanced the fertilizing properties of bone meal and ash, but as time went on, mineral phosphates became increasingly important.

In a context of growing population—and therefore of increasing demand—farming became ever more of a business, in which producers looked to boost production and make farms bigger to cut relative costs. In consequence, more and more capital was reinvested in research in scientific agronomy. The self-taught American agronomist Luther Burbank (1849–1926) was the most extraordinary figure in the field. He started a market-gardening business in California in 1875 and became the world's most inventive practitioner of hybridization, grafting, and breeding for selection. He experimented obsessively and seemed to value sensationalism above science. He produced 1,000 new species, including white blackberries and the plumcot, a fruit that was half-apricot, half-plum. He was a self-taught scientist, and his methods were notoriously wasteful—he would destroy hundreds of plants before he found one that suited his purposes. But his enormous commercial success encouraged the spread of scientific techniques to improve strains and develop new plants for newly exploited environments.

Alongside the growing output of farming, industrialization revolutionized the availability of food by transforming techniques of preserving, processing, and supply. Lazaro Spallanzani's late eighteenth-century observations of bacteria (see Chapter 22) revealed new possibilities. Simultaneous heating and sealing could keep food edible indefinitely. Stimulated by the demands of the large armies Europe mobilized in the early nineteenth century, huge bottling and canning operations began. When the wars were over, canned foods became widely available to civilians. By 1836, a French firm was selling 100,000 cans of sardines a year. By 1880, factories on the west coast of France were producing 50 million tins of sardines annually. Canning soon became adapted to virtually every kind of food. The results were hugely significant. Canning kept more food in the supply chain for longer. It also made it possible to transport unprecedented quantities of easily perishable food in bulk over long distances. This in turn promoted more regional specialization in the production of particular foods and more economies of scale.

Luther Burbank started with "ten dollars and ten potatoes," but went on to develop thousands of new species of fruits, vegetables, and flowers like the poppies he is holding here. Burbank spoke almost constantly of "working with Nature," but he was an obsessive experimenter whose guiding principle was "quantity speeded up." He tried so many hybrids his critics claimed that some of them were bound to work. But his influence was in some ways benign: He encouraged plant breeders to think ecologically and inspired imitators to develop new species.

"Alongside the growing output of farming, industrialization revolutionized the availability of food by transforming techniques of preserving, processing, and supply."

Chicago meat packinghouse, 1892. Once cattle had been slaughtered and turned into dressed beef, the carcasses sat in immense cooling rooms before being shipped by rail across North America.

"Part of the vast increase of population that the food boom fed was free to engage in other kinds of economic activity. Trade, industry, agriculture, and urbanization were linked in a mutually sustaining cycle of expansion."

In the 1870s, Australian engineers made an even more dramatic breakthrough in preservation techniques: the compressed-gas cooler. Meat from Australia or South America or New Zealand could now be refrigerated and shipped to Europe, say, at relatively modest cost. The resulting economies of scale actually made meat processed in this way cheaper in some markets than locally produced meat. In combination with new means to ship large quantities of grain over long distances by railroad and steamship, new production and processing techniques changed the world pattern of food production (see Map 23.3). Food no longer had to be produced near where it was eaten. In industrializing areas, agriculture declined. British agriculture virtually collapsed in the last generation of the nineteenth century. All over Western Europe, farmers abandoned wheat for other crops, such as dairy products, smoked meats, fruits, and vegetables, in the face of long-range imports.

Food itself became an industrial product, as manufacturers took on more and more processing, until they were delivering some foods, mass produced on a vast scale, in forms in which consumers could eat them without further preparation. Cookies and crackers, once artisanal products or foods baked a few dozen at a time at home, became factory-made items. In 1859, the world's three major producers, all in Britain, made six million pounds of cookies. By the late 1870s, the same firms were producing 37 million pounds. Other industries created new foodstuffs. In the 1840s, chocolate, formerly a luxury beverage, became a cheap food, manufactured as "candy bars" especially in Britain, Switzerland, and Holland. In 1865, the German chemist Baron Justus von Liebig perfected cubes of beef extract that could be made into broth by adding water. Moral crusaders sought a low-protein food that would reduce "passion" and promote chastity. They found it when the American Reverend Sylvester Graham, inventor of the "graham cracker," also invented breakfast cereals in the 1830s. These products were suitable for industrial production methods and, by the 1890s, absorbed much of the world's increased output of grain.

For all its inefficiencies—the scars of famine, the failures of distribution—the huge increase in available food had an unprecedented impact on the world. Because so much of it was the result of new kinds of science and technology, it was achieved with a relatively small input of additional labor. Part of the vast increase of population that the food boom fed was free to engage in other kinds of economic activity. Trade, industry, agriculture, and urbanization were linked in a mutually sustaining cycle of expansion.

ENERGY FOR POWER: MILITARIZATION AND INDUSTRIALIZATION

Even food, however, was a modest source of extra energy compared with those mobilized for militarization and industrialization. Again, these developments were linked to the mid-century fat crisis, for armies and industries put relatively intense pressure on sources of fat compared with other resources.

Militarization

Nineteenth-century armies were big. The trend to make them bigger than they ever had been started in Europe in the 1790s when fear of the French Revolution induced a coalition of conservative countries to invade France with apparently invincible force. The French responded by drafting a "citizen army" or

By 1870s Refrigerated container ships transport lamb and mutton to world markets

Railroads transport beef cattle from Western grasslands to the populated east coast

Refrigerated container ships transport bananas to world markets

Panama Canal opens in 1914. Journey times reduced by up to 40%

Refrigerated container ships transport South American beef to world markets

Suez Canal opens in 1869. Journey times reduced by up to 60%

Invention of canning opens up world fruit markets

NEW ZEALAND

AUSTRALIA

Melbourne
Sydney
Adelaide
Perth

PACIFIC OCEAN

Manila
Singapore
Hong Kong
Shanghai
Tokyo
Beijing
BURMA
CHINA
INDIA
Delhi
Bombay

INDIAN OCEAN

RUSSIAN EMPIRE

San Francisco
CANADA
U.S.A.
Chicago
MEXICO
Mexico City
New Orleans
Montreal
New York
CUBA
PANAMA

Moscow
Constantinople
Aden
Arabian Peninsula
MADAGASCAR

Berlin
EUROPE
London
Paris
Rome
OTTOMAN EMPIRE
EGYPT
AFRICA
Johannesburg
NIGERIA
Cape Town
LIBERIA

ATLANTIC OCEAN

BRAZIL
Valparaíso
CHILE
Santiago
ARGENTINA
Buenos Aires
Montevideo
URUGUAY
Rio de Janeiro

Equator

MAP 23.3

Industrialization, Technology, and Food Manufacturing in the Nineteenth Century

- highly industrialized region
- industrializing region
- less industrialized region

Improvements in communication

- major rail networks, ca. 1914
- North Atlantic shipping route
- other shipping route
- underwater telegraph cable route

Manufacturing industry outside of Europe

- heavy machinery
- iron and steel

- textile production

Export markets opened up by technology

- beef cattle
- lamb and mutton
- fruit

Major cash crops

- coffee
- cotton
- rubber
- sugar cane
- tea

"nation in arms"—imposing military service on the entire active adult male population. This was not, in principle, intended to militarize society. On the contrary, it was an old-fashioned ideal, supposedly inspired by ancient Greek and Roman models, and much advocated by classical scholars, such as Machiavelli, in the Renaissance (see Chapter 18), on the grounds that citizens would fight more effectively than professional warriors who were fighting for monetary rewards. The same idea lay behind American revolutionaries' insistence on the moral superiority of voluntary citizen "militia" armies over the professional and mercenary troops the British employed.

The effect, however, was to create mass armies. The "Grand Army" with which the French Emperor Napoleon invaded Russia in 1812 numbered over 600,000 men, and the Russian forces opposing him were even larger. In the second half of the century, many European powers could mobilize armies numbering millions. The effects on warfare were enormous. The German theorist, Karl von Clausewitz (1780–1831), formulated the doctrine of "total war"—waged not just against the enemy's armed forces, but against the entire population of a hostile country (see Chapter 26). The results made war worse—multiplying the victims, spreading the destruction, and encouraging preemptive attacks. Similarly, the era of mass armies transformed society by taking young men from their homes, gathering them in barracks, drilling them in military discipline, and teaching them loyalty to the state. "Peasants," it was said, "became Frenchmen" through their service in the army in the late nineteenth century. Armies became forges of national identities.

The economic consequences of militarization were, perhaps, even more significant. Armies concentrated huge numbers of men, straining food supplies and transport resources. Navies consumed unprecedented amounts of iron and steel for shipbuilding and of coal to keep the ships going. Every serviceman had to be nourished with efficient energy-sources. We have already seen plenty of examples of how war stimulated energy-delivering industries. Margarine was invented expressly for the French navy. Canning was a response to war in early nineteenth-century Europe. Milk canning developed in the American Civil War (1861–1865). Massive armed forces demanded unprecedented quantities of mass-produced munitions, guns with ever more rapid rates of fire, and ever-bigger and more complex artillery and engineering services. Every gun and cartridge had to be greased to function. In 1857, the issue of cartridges supposedly greased with pig and beef fat that soldiers had to break open with their teeth sparked a major rebellion among the native troops of Britain's Indian army. To the Muslims, pigs were unclean. To the Hindus, cows were sacred. (In fact the cartridges were greased with vegetable oil.) Wartime logistics provided models and, sometimes, generated innovations in production, supply, and communications. Huge production lines, for instance, first appeared in state bakeries that produced dry bread for navies. These bakeries inspired the factory system of production that was necessary for large-scale industrialization.

Industrialization

New energy-resources—what we now call **fossil fuels**—fueled industrialization Peat and coal were the first to be exploited; traditional fuel-sources, they were now extracted from the ground on an unprecedented scale. Oil followed (and, eventually, in the twentieth century, natural gas.) In effect, mining and drilling for coal and oil released buried sunlight, accumulated millions of years ago

---

"Massive armed forces demanded unprecedented quantities of mass-produced munitions, guns with ever more rapid rates of fire, and ever-bigger and more complex artillery and engineering services."

when plants and creatures—which store energy from the sun in the carbons that form their bodies—were buried and crushed. Fossil fuels are therefore a form of concentrated energy. A few pounds of coal can produce as much heat as an acre of timber. So the first effect of the release of coal from the ground was to liberate land for farming that had formerly been used to produce wood for fuel, boosting the massive growth of food production. The second was to provide energy for new forms of power.

Coal-generated energy and steam power were inextricably linked. Steam powered the pumps that drained the coal mines. Coal fueled the furnaces that produced the steam. Iron and steel were inescapably part of the picture. They were the materials from which the machinery was made to convert coal to energy and steam to power—the rods and the pistons, the cogs and casings of the engines. Coal produced the heat that fused the ores and forged the metals. The metals in their turn enclosed the spaces in which the coal burned.

An early Union ironclad on the Mississippi River during the Civil War. Although the British and French navies already had ships built entirely of iron by 1860, U.S. naval experts were reluctant to believe that these vessels could be effective. But the Union navy put iron plates on wooden ships and began building iron-hulled vessels in 1862, in response to Confederate plans to launch similar ships and buy others from Britain.

Fuel consumption and production leaped. Coal purchases accounted for over a quarter of the expenses of the world's biggest steamship company in the 1860s. Japanese coal production had always been modest, but it rose from 390,000 tons in 1860 to 5 million tons in 1900. Increases of a similar order of magnitude occurred in Belgian and Spanish coalmines over the same period. The most productive coalfield in the world was already that of South Wales in Britain. Here, in the same period, output soared from 11.4 million to 35.1 million tons a year. German coal was of problematic quality, but nineteenth-century developments made its exploitation worthwhile. Over 100 million tons were being mined annually by the end of the century.

But what was all this extra energy for? Statistics seem to dominate the story of industrialization—whenever historians tell it. Understandably, economic historians, looking to quantify the subject and make it seem scientific, like to measure industrial change in terms of productivity figures. These figures are sometimes suggestive, sometimes spectacularly revealing. Machinery in use in Britain by the 1830s, for instance, could produce in 135 hours the same amount of cotton that took 50,000 hours to spin by hand. This certainly helps to explain the appeal of industrialization. But a paradox remains to be explained. In an age of increasing population, more muscle power was becoming available worldwide. So why bother to mechanize?

In part, the explanation lies in the geography of industrialization. On the whole, it happened earliest and fastest in regions where labor was relatively expensive: in areas such as Europe and Japan, where the size of the workforce was relatively modest compared with, say, China and India; or in the United States, which, despite the huge increase in its population, was still seriously underpopulated in the nineteenth century. Second, and perhaps more significant, industrialization was a function of demand. Population increase accounted in part for increasing demand, but so did the multiplication of sources of wealth—the new resources unlocked from the soil, the enormous expansion of financial institutions, the growth in the money supply as governments took on increasing responsibilities and minted cash to pay for them, using the output of new mines, which were particularly productive in this period in North America, southern Africa, and Russia. Figures are not available, but it seems likely that the growth in the money supply worldwide would have been hugely inflationary if production and trade had not increased proportionately and absorbed its effects. Although mechanization stripped workers of employment in traditional industries and in

Power to rival Nature's: Philippe-Jacques de Loutherbourg, born in France in 1740, made his career as a painter in England, where his work as a stage designer helped to add a showy, theatrical quality to his art. His painting of the great ironworks of Coalbrookdale in the English Midlands shows the rural setting typical of early industrial sites, and displays the "sublime," "picturesque," and "romantic" qualities for which he became famous. The smoke and flames from the forge are more on the scale of a volcano than of a factory.

"Industrial technology represented, for its early witnesses, the triumph of imagination over nature. Admirers of mechanization saw it as romantic—a perspective we have lost today."

unindustrialized parts of the world, it generated new wealth and, therefore, new employment opportunities in other activities and other areas. Trade and capital were essential extra spokes in the cycle that linked food, population, and industry. They provided incentives to mechanize and money to invest in mechanization.

Economic circumstances alone, however, cannot explain industrialization. Indeed, it was more than an economic phenomenon. For the contemporaries who took part in it, the appeal of industry was a form of enchantment. Like magic, or like today's information technology, which seems to affect many people in the same way, it multiplied power and effected dazzling transformations. A passenger aboard the first commercially viable locomotive train—George Stevenson's Rocket in Britain, which achieved a speed of 35 miles per hour in 1829—called it a "magical machine with its flying white breath and rhythmical unvarying pace. When I closed my eyes the sensation of flying was delightful." A witness of the unveiling of one of the century's most impressive technologies—Sir Henry Bessemer's process for turning iron into steel in 1856—described the event with the slack-jawed awe of a sorcerer's apprentice: "Out came a volcanic eruption of such dazzling coruscations as had never been seen before. When combustion had expended all its fury, most wonderful of all, the result was steel!"

Industrial technology represented, for its early witnesses, the triumph of imagination over nature. Admirers of mechanization saw it as romantic—a perspective we have lost today. The English artist Joseph Turner (1775–1851) painted the speed of the locomotive. The German composer Felix Mendelssohn (1809–1847) turned the noises of steam navigation into music. The British author Samuel Smiles (1812–1904), whose writings convinced the English-speaking world of the virtues of industrialization, declared, "We may justly look upon the steam engine as the noblest machine ever invented by man." Engineers became heroes. Smiles wrote their lives in the style of romances of chivalry, or even of fairy tales. A band played "Hail! The Conquering Hero Comes" when the most inventive engineer of the age, I. K. Brunel (1806–1859), appeared at the opening of a bridge he designed across the River Severn in England.

Industrialization had martyrs as well as heroes. One hundred workers died digging two miles of a railway tunnel Brunel designed. And, of course, industrialization had its enemies. It threatened the livelihoods of workers in traditional crafts. Moralists condemned production techniques that forced workers into soulless rhythms of work in the backbreaking, disease-breeding environments of factories and mines, and as we shall see in Chapter 25, their laments were justified. Not everyone appreciated the romance of steam. For some, railways desecrated the countryside or damaged and stole the land. Nostalgia for the fate of the land inspired artists, novelists, and reactionary social movements (see Chapter 26) wherever industrialization occurred.

Even industrialists often seemed uncommitted to what we should now call the "entrepreneurial spirit." In England, "captains of industry" typically devoted their wealth to creating a rural idyll for themselves—buying country estates and building country houses, in imitation of traditional landed aristocrats. Their managers, who could not afford country estates, imitated the longed-for way of life in so-called garden suburbs, leafy oases of large houses and private parks that were built outside the big industrial cities. In France, industrialists commonly affected scorn for entrepreneurship. In 1836, a member of a great textiles dynasty of northern France went on a pilgrimage "to obtain illumination from the Holy Ghost, so that we should never undertake anything in business above our strength, lest we should be troubled by hazardous speculations." Another French industrialist, François Wendel, died in 1825, leaving a fortune of 4 million francs (about $80 million in today's money) from his iron works, having become, he said, an iron master and owner of profitable businesses "against my will." His fellow-countryman, the industrial magnate Jules Siegfried, engraved "to work is to act" on his cufflinks, but defied the prevailing work ethic to retire from manufacturing textiles at the age of 44. In Japan (as we shall see), entrepreneurs insisted on motives for their work that were connected with "honor" or patriotism rather than profit. Again, they sought to imitate the warrior aristocracy. Even in the United States, which, as a "young" country, was less subject to old-fashioned inhibitions, industrialists practiced similar evasions. Cornelius Vanderbilt (1794–1877), the steam-power multimillionaire owner of ships and railroads, liked to see himself as a "knight of industry" and had himself depicted in a church window dressed in a medieval suit of armor. In the southern states, manufacturers aped planters' lifestyles. Industrialization, in short, succeeded only where people could reconcile it with traditional values.

The romance of steam. Joseph Mallord Turner (1775–1851)—the most defiantly original English artist of his day—made the railway seem part of nature, blurring the steam into the clouds, the rails into the landscape.

Of course, industrialization impacted on the rest of the world—by creating global inequalities of wealth and power that are the subjects of later chapters of this book and by linking unindustrialized regions in a grid of high-speed communications. Even parts of the world that had few or no factories or mechanized production-methods, such as China, India, and South America, got railways, steam shipping, and electric telegraphs. The first successful experiment in steam locomotion was carried out in 1804, when Richard Trevithick carried 10 tons of iron along 9 miles of tracks in Britain. The local paper predicted "a thousand instances" of uses "not yet thought of." Trevithick's designs were too slow and cumbersome to be commercially useful, but viable railways were being built in Britain by 1830, and they spread around the world with amazing speed. Although the web of railways was densest in industrial regions, the rails also stretched across vast distances of the unindustrialized world, delivering to ports and factories ingredients for the machines to turn into saleable goods, and food and drugs to keep the workers at their tasks. By the 1840s, the United States had more rails than Britain. The first line across the American continent opened in 1869. By 1900, the United States had nearly 170,000 miles of track. Most of the network linked regions of primary products to centers of industrial processing and consumption.

Knight of industry. Far from keeping upstarts in their place, the code of chivalry has for centuries encouraged and equipped enterprising men who have risen in Western society. The swashbuckling, self-made American tycoon Cornelius Vanderbilt (1794–1877) is depicted in this stained glass window in the most socially respectable church in Newport, Rhode Island, with the armor and Christian symbols of a medieval knight.

Among the most intensive scenes of railway building in the mid-nineteenth century were India and Cuba—colonial lands where the ruling powers discouraged manufactures and exploited their basic products to serve industries in Britain and Spain, the "home countries." India's case is especially spectacular. Railway construction began in 1852. Fifty years later, India had nearly 42,000 miles of track—more than all the rest of Asia put together. £150 million of British capital made the enterprise possible. In terms of labor, however, this was a genuinely Indian enterprise, with over 370,000 Indians a year working on the lines by the 1890s. Indian contractors, who supplied workers and, in most cases, supervised the work, made the biggest fortunes in railway construction. Jamsetji Dorabji Naegamwalla (1804–1882) was the most successful of all. He was an illiterate carpenter in a

Indian railway. When it began to operate in 1881, the Darjeeling Railway in northwest India ran 55 miles from the port of Calcutta, mounting steep slopes to reach the tea-growing regions. This loop, photographed in the late nineteenth or early twentieth century, shows one of the devices the British engineers who built the railway used to conquer the sharp ascent. The tea the trains carried eventually went to England, supplying a cheap stimulant for the workforce of British industry.

The steamship *Brittania*. In this painting of the 1840s, the sailing vessel seems doomed to shipwreck, while the steamship braves the gale. Owners commissioned ship portraits of this sort to encourage business and build confidence in the sailing qualities of their vessels.
Photograph courtesy of the Peabody Essex Museum

British-run dockyard when, in 1850, he realized the potential of the railways. He employed thousands of Indians and a handful of European engineers, ensuring the smooth running of the operations the government assigned to him by getting to know his men and boosting their morale by his constant presence on the job. When a viaduct he built collapsed in 1855, he bullied the authorities to let him rebuild it at extra cost and waive their usual demand for cash securities in advance. Unlike most British contractors who worked on railway construction, he made money and retired in 1870 to enjoy his wealth.

The development of steam-powered shipping kept pace with that of the railways. In 1807, the first commercial steamboat, built by Robert Fulton, navigated the Hudson River, traveling 150 miles upriver from New York City to Albany in 32 hours. Twelve years later, the steamship *Savannah* crossed the Atlantic in 27 days. The voyage, however, was a failure. The *Savannah* spent only 80 hours of the crossing under steam, relying on sails for the other 568 hours. The engine was gutted, and the ship was sold as a sailing vessel. To be successful, steamships needed technical improvements in propulsion and fuel consumption. The first regular transatlantic steam service began in 1838. Ten or 12 days instead of 6 weeks became the normal length of an Atlantic crossing between Western Europe and North America.

Paintings collected in the Peabody Essex Museum in Salem, Massachusetts, show the advantages of the early steamers. Owners chose to have their vessels depicted in stormy seas because the regularity of all-weather sailing was an important selling point. When the English novelist Charles Dickens crossed the Atlantic in 1842, he endured the "staggering, heaving, wrestling, leaping, diving, jumping, pitching, throbbing, rolling and rocking," as the ship braved headwinds "with every pulse and artery of her huge body swollen and bursting." It was in adverse weather that the steamers demonstrated their superiority over sail. British steam tonnage at sea exceeded that under sail by 1883.

Intersecting rail and shipping lines were the scaffolding of the world, along which trade and travelers could clamber to every part of it. James Hill, the American railway millionaire and philanthropist who built the cathedral of St. Paul, Minnesota, founded a steamship line that connected the fastest rail route across the Rockies with the Russian Trans-Siberian Railway, which opened in 1900 and linked Moscow and St. Petersburg with Russia's Pacific port of Vladivostok. Steam transport linked the great food-producing and consuming belt of the world, from Vladivostok to Vancouver on Canada's Pacific coast. The railways made a startling difference. They wrenched trade in new directions. They made it possible for land-based systems of communications to carry freight on a scale previously possible only by sea. The world's great hinterlands, far from seas and ports and even navigable rivers, in the innermost parts of the continents, could be integrated into an increasingly global economy.

It was hard to think of a power-source better than steam, but electricity—normally, like steam, generated by burning coal but also by hydroelectric power—began to rival steam power in some applications. The English physicist Michael

Making Connections | INDUSTRIALIZATION AND MILITARIZATION

INDUSTRIAL DEVELOPMENT	MILITARY ADAPTATION	EFFECTS
Food technology: preservation, production, innovation	To supply massive armies of nation-states: canning of food, beverages; automated production lines for baked goods; new products like margarine to supply naval personnel	Extension of ability to provision large-scale armies/navies across continents and ocean; projecting military power; ability to manage colonies more effectively
New energy sources: fossil fuels	Coal-generated energy and steam power fuel industrialized production of weapons, ammunition	Largest industrial nations (Europe, United States) develop massive armies, navies equipped with weapons and ammunition that are more deadly
Transportation technology	Railroads, steamships used to transport troops and supplies rapidly across oceans, continents	Tighter control of homelands, colonies through technologically advanced military forces
Electrical technology	First practical application focuses on communication—telegraphy, used by military forces to coordinate troop movements	Ability to maintain control of large-scale armies on battlefields, or across continents and oceans via telegraph messages

Faraday, a self-educated amateur, conducted remarkable experiments in the 1830s and 1840s that demonstrated the possibilities of various applications, including electric lighting. The biggest contribution arose from one of his first gadgets: an electromagnetic induction machine, made in 1831. The following year, the American Samuel Morse used Faraday's discovery to transmit messages. The first long-range telegraph line linked Washington, D.C., to Baltimore, Maryland in 1844. Submarine cables to transmit telegraph messages crossed the Atlantic in 1869, shrinking the ocean to the dimensions of a pond. An electric age was about to succeed the age of steam. The gasoline-fueled internal combustion engine, invented in the 1890s, also pointed the way to a further stage of locomotion, without rail tracks. It would have as transforming an impact on the twentieth century as the steam-powered engine had on the nineteenth.

Transatlantic telegraph line. An 1866 lithograph depicts the third and finally successful attempt to lay an underwater telegraph line between Europe and North America. This cable reduced the time it took messages to cross the Atlantic from the length of a sea voyage to a few minutes.

INDUSTRIALIZING EUROPE

One way to measure the spread of industrialization is to map the distribution of steam-powered businesses. By these standards, Europe developed early and mightily. In the first half of the nineteenth century, Britain, Spain, Italy, and Belgium all doubled their steam-driven industrial capacity. France and Russia tripled theirs. In what is now the Czech Republic (but what was then part of the Austrian Empire), capacity grew fivefold, and Germany's capacity multiplied by 6. So industrialization was a genuinely widespread phenomenon. It transcended traditional national boundaries. In 1830, the Englishman John Cockerill's core business was manufacturing textiles in Belgium. He set up a heavy machinery factory in the city of Liege to manufacture his own equipment. He diversified into

Chronology: Population, Food, and Energy

1780–1831	Karl von Clausewitz, developer of theory of "total war"
ca. 1800	Global population: 950 million; areas with regions in excess of 4 people per square mile: East Asia, Southeast Asia, India, Western Europe
1804	First successful railroad locomotion
1807	First commercial steamboat
1850s	British imports of guano reach 200,000 tons per year
1850–1900	500 million acres added to U.S. farmland
1860–1900	Japanese coal production rises from 390,000 to 5 million tons; British coal production rises from 11.4 million to 35.1 million
1866	British output of chemical fertilizers reaches 250,000 tons
1869	First transcontinental railroad in United States; first telegraph messages cross the Atlantic
1870s	Australian engineers develop compressed-gas cooler
ca. 1900	German coal production reaches 100 million tons annually
	Argentina exports 100 million bushels of wheat per year; global population: 1.6 billion; new areas with regions in excess of 4 people per square mile: Americas, Africa

weaving in Germany and Russian-ruled Poland and into producing cotton yarn in Spain. He went into mining in various European countries to obtain raw materials for his engineering factories and into international banking to finance his operations. He even dabbled in unrelated businesses—he had a sugar plantation in the Dutch colony of Surinam on the northeast coast of South America. His empire collapsed in 1837. He then went on to build railways in Russia.

From 1815 to 1914, city growth matched and even came to exceed army growth as the motor of change in Europe. Industrialization helped shape what remains, on the map, a conspicuous feature of the modern world: a zone of densely clustered industrial cities from Belfast in northern Ireland and Bilbao in northwest Spain to Rostov and St. Petersburg in Russia (see Map 23.4). By 1900, 9 European cities had more than a million people. Most of the population of Britain and Belgium had forsaken agriculture for industry and rural life for the cities. In the rest of industrializing Europe, the same drift to the towns was evident. The Russian Empire remained an overwhelmingly peasant country, but two-thirds of the inhabitants of St. Petersburg, Russia's capital, were former peasants. The biggest factories in Europe were state undertakings in Russia. Twenty percent of Austrians were factory workers. In 1896, factories in Hungary made the machines and equipment for the world's first electric underground railway in London.

Still, if industrialization was becoming a European phenomenon, capacity tended to be concentrated in particular areas. Only Belgium, which is small, was a fully industrialized country in the sense of having industry evenly scattered throughout its territory. Southern Britain actually lost industrial capacity, which became concentrated in northern and central England and along the River Clyde in Scotland. In France, the northeast had most of the country's industry. In Switzerland, it was in the north. In Germany, most industry was located in two regions: the Ruhr in the west and in Silesia and Saxony in the east. Italy's industries were concentrated in the north in Piedmont and Lombardy and focused on the cities of Turin and Milan. In Russia, the two favored areas were in St. Petersburg and in the Donets Basin to the north of the Black Sea. In Spain, only the Basque Country and Catalonia were industrialized.

What made the difference between zones of industrialization and the unindustrialized regions that remained alongside them? Most of the key regions were favored by the availability of coal and iron deposits and access to major markets, but some places bucked this trend. Catalonia in Spain, for instance, had major metallurgical industries despite lacking iron or coal and being ill placed to communicate with other urban areas. Except by appealing to some sort of "commercial 'spirit'" that remains hard to describe or define, no one has ever really been able to explain this anomaly.

To try to understand why neighboring areas responded differently to the opportunity to industrialize, the Low Countries are a good place to look. If Britain was, as is commonly said, "the first industrial nation," Belgium was the second. Yet Belgium's neighbor, the kingdom of the Netherlands, hardly participated in industrialization until late in the nineteenth century. Belgium had the highest density of population in Europe—698 persons per square mile—but the Netherlands was also relatively

MAP 23.4

The Industrialization of Europe by 1914

Land use 1914

- mountainous area/wasteland
- agriculture and stock rearing
- forest
- industrial area

Resources

- coalfield
- oil
- potash

Manufacturing industry

- textiles
- iron smelting
- machinery
- shipbuilding

Population growth

- city with population over 500,000 in 1850
- city with population over 500,000 in 1914
- city with population under 500,000 in 1914
- principal railways 1914

Dutch agriculture. The firm of W. Hoogstraaten & Co., founded in Leiden in the Netherlands in 1856, illustrates the dependence of early Dutch industrialization on agriculture. In 1862, the firm's pickling and bottling factory had 12 workers, 4 of whom were women. Half their production was for export. By 1900, when the firm's advertising had made its products well known, it had become a major enterprise with several factories, hundreds of workers, and a large line in prepared foods.

thickly settled, with 487 people per square mile. Indeed, in no other region of comparable size in Europe, outside England, was population so concentrated.

As the century wore on, Belgian entrepreneurs increasingly concentrated on iron and steel production, for which their country was well supplied with raw materials. Belgium had the most efficient iron- and steel-making equipment in the world by 1870, each furnace producing on average a third more iron than those of Britain, over half as much again as those of Germany, and more than double those of France. Zinc and glass were other Belgian specialities. Belgium was also well served by railways. Its 1,800 miles of track in 1870 constituted a substantial network for such a small country.

The Netherlands, meanwhile, remained overwhelmingly agricultural. Its industrial sector was dedicated to food processing, especially to making candy, using the cane sugar from Dutch colonies in the Caribbean and the East Indies and, increasingly, the beet sugar Dutch farmers produced. (French scientists had discovered how to extract sugar from beets in the early 1800s.) Dutch milk-processing firms supplied 80 percent of the British market for condensed and powdered milk by 1900, and the Netherlands was Europe's biggest manufacturer of margarine. Despite the traditional importance of shipbuilding, Dutch iron and steel production only began to catch up with European averages in the 1890s.

So what explains the difference between the two countries, which had similar histories and cultural profiles? If anything, the Netherlands had historic advantages: a large colonial empire in what is now Indonesia, and a tradition of long-range trade—both of which, according to some economic theorists in the nineteenth century, should have stimulated industrial development. Dutch coal was mainly anthracite and hard to mine, but similar limitations did nothing to restrain industry in Germany. If there is such a thing as an industrial or a capitalist spirit, it is unlikely that it should have been prevalent in one country and not in its neighbor. Indeed, when global conditions changed in the late nineteenth and twentieth centuries, the Netherlands did industrialize.

In the nineteenth century, however, the two countries' economies were complementary: Belgium specialized in heavy industries, whereas the Netherlands specialized in producing and processing food for industrializing markets, including those of Belgium. The patchiness of industrialization, in short, was essential to industrialization's success. It was part of a pattern of specialization in which some regions supplied food and raw materials while others concentrated on manufacturing. If some places had comparative advantage in resources, others had comparative advantage in finance and access to markets, or a relatively disciplined or suitably educated labor force. The system was reproduced at the global level, as large areas of the world became suppliers of primary produce to industrializing economies.

INDUSTRY IN THE AMERICAS

The United States was a surprising industrializer. It was a country with a long history of supplying raw materials—pelts and skins, whaling products—for other people's industries. The southern states produced raw cotton for mills in Britain, as well as tobacco and sugar, which contributed to the world economy mainly as mild drugs to make workers' dreary lives more bearable. The Midwest had, by the mid-nineteenth century, an obvious future as a source of food for the world. The rest of the American interior had vast stocks of lumber, agricultural land, and mineral deposits. The states' main manufactures in the eighteenth century had specialized in part-processing raw products.

Still, in other ways, the United States was a suitable arena for industry. High per capita incomes meant there was money for investment. A large, active merchant marine enabled the country to participate in global markets. A relatively small population meant there was a labor shortage that mechanization could make up. The fact that slavery was lawful in almost half the country until 1865 meant that a lot of labor was unproductively tied down, raising labor costs elsewhere. Nor did the abolition of slavery do much for this problem, because most former slaves remained in the South as sharecroppers or owners of small, relatively unproductive farms. On the other hand, high immigration rates from Europe meant that enough manpower became available to make factory systems viable and ensured growing domestic demand for the products of industry. There was plenty of coal and iron, especially after huge iron ore deposits were discovered in the region of the Great Lakes in 1844. The United States also had high tariffs for most of the nineteenth century, which were designed to shut out European products and foster native industry.

Andrew Carnegie (1835–1918)—a self-made millionaire and immigrant from Scotland who had risen from a child laborer in a textile factory by sacrificial saving and shrewd investing in the steel industry—called in professional chemists to make the most of technological innovations. By 1900, the United States was producing 10 million tons of steel a year. Productivity in Carnegie's plants was spectacular. His workers produced more than 10 times as much per man as their German counterparts—the best steel at the lowest prices. "The Republic," wrote Carnegie in 1885, "thunders past with the rush of an express." By the 1890s, factories in the United States produced twice as much as those of Britain and half as much again as the whole of Europe. Railroad expansion became faster and fuller than in Europe. As we shall see in Chapter 25, European, especially British, investors were alert to the opportunities the United States offered.

The magic of industry. An engraving of Andrew Carnegie's Pittsburgh steelworks in 1886 captures the magic-like brilliance—glittering sparks, thunderous noise, mysterious haze, dynamism, and light—of the Bessemer converter. The result is gleaming white steel. The human agents are dwarfed.

Canada

Nothing like this industrialization happened in the rest of the Americas. Canada became an agricultural country, thanks to the domestication of its own prairie, but not an industrial one. Fewer than 500,000 Canadians, out of a total of some 7 million, worked in manufacturing at the beginning of the twentieth century, and a third of them processed timber and food.

Latin America

Most of Latin America was even less industrialized. The Latin American wars of independence were unlike that of the United States. Theirs were mostly long struggles, unaided by outside powers, leaving many of them exhausted and divided (see Chapter 22). The newly independent nations, after spending heavily

Ankle-deep in coffee on a plantation in Brazil in the early twentieth century. The freshly harvested beans are tipped into troughs to be washed. Business imperialism continued to promote long-range ecological exchange as global trade increased, making South American coffee a major product alongside coffee from Southeast Asia, and sending Brazilian rubber trees to Southeast Asia.

to fight Spain, had to maintain big armies in wariness of each other and to suppress domestic discontent. They lacked the north's incentive to mechanize. Latin America had plenty of ex-slaves, Indians, and illiterate laborers. In a sense, the region never fully emerged from colonial-style exploitation. Its own elites became the exploiters of their own peasants, whereas at first, until the emancipation of the slaves, the United States hardly had any dependent peasants, and none lived in the areas that industrialized. In North America, small farmers were their own bosses. Big ranchers used the mobile labor of "cowboys."

Free trade, which most of the independent Latin American states practiced, favored industrializing economies that could produce cheap goods, and condemned Latin American economies to underdevelopment. Having fought Spanish monopolists under the banner of free trade, the new countries were unable to protect their native industries, such as they were, against European imports. They became locked into a role as producers of primary products: the ore, timber, and rubber that supplied the factories of Europe and the United States; the foods and fertilizers that fed the workforces; the tobacco and coffee that provided the stimulants that fought workers' need for sleep; the sweets that kept their blood sugar up (see Map 23.5). The grasslands of South America never followed the grain-rich, city-sprinkled model of the North American prairie: not even in Argentina, which had plenty of prairie-like land—the pampa—that remained ranching country throughout the century. The pampa was too far from most centers of population. "The promises of the pampa, so generous, so spontaneous, many times go unfulfilled," wrote the Spanish philosopher and diplomat José Ortega y Gasset (1883–1955). "Defeats in America must surely be worse than elsewhere. A man is suddenly mutilated, . . . with no treatment for his wounds." The success of the United States became a standing reproach to the economically frustrated countries to its south.

Much of Latin America became a continent of disillusioned hopes. In 1857, Carlos Barroilhet, who did more than anyone else to explain the merits of guano to the world, prophesied that Peru was destined to be "at once the richest and happiest nation on Earth," but by the 1880s," guano, much depleted by overexploitation, was considered a "curse." Competition from African guano and chemical super phosphates undermined a monopoly on which governments had staked all their economic plans. Similarly, Brazil lost its rubber monopoly when British businessmen smuggled out some plants and replanted them in Malaya. Late nineteenth-century Brazil relied more on coffee—another asset subject to increasing global competition—than rubber. Mexico lost its potentially most valuable territories—unmined gold and silver, untapped oil—in war with the United States in 1846–1848. At the century's end, Argentina seemed in some ways more than ever a land of promise. Frozen meat exports and a meat-extract processing industry made the dominance of ranching in the pampa seem like a wise strategy. According to an "oath to the flag" that educational reformers introduced in 1909, Argentina was simply "the best land in the world," which would know "no history without a triumph." But its economy remained at the mercy of foreign investment and precarious global markets, and its promise was never fulfilled.

JAPAN INDUSTRIALIZES

Commodore Perry sailed into Tokyo Bay on July 8, 1853. His mission was to persuade or force the Japanese to open their ports to trade with the United States. He meant business in every sense of the word. He had four heavily armed steamships

MAP 23.5

South American Economies, ca. 1900

Major export products

- 🍌 bananas
- 🐄 beef
- cacoa
- ☕ coffee
- copper
- cotton
- ▲ guano
- hides
- ▽ nitrates
- rubber
- ↓ sugar
- silver
- tin
- 🌱 tobacco
- wheat
- wool
- railways by 1910
- 1853 date slavery abolished
- ✳ major port

with him. "The universal Yankee nation," wrote the expedition's interpreter, Samuel Williams, had arrived to end Japan's "apathy and long ignorance" with the example of "a higher civilization," elevated by "the success of science and enterprise." Nevertheless, what Williams actually saw in Japan conformed only in part to the stereotype of a country consigned to backwardness by isolation. Williams noted a mixture of "railroads," which dock areas already had, "and telegraph, . . . shaven pates and nightgowns, soldiers with muskets and drilling in close array, soldiers with petticoats, sandals, two swords, all in disorder." Japan's "modernization" had already begun in selective respects, and the country was well poised to invest in innovative technologies: rich, urban, with a long history of commercial growth and a large middle class see (see Chapter 20).

At first, Japanese industrializing policies focused on the army and navy. The urgent task in the mid-nineteenth century was to close the technology gap that had opened up between Japan and the Western powers. But the slogan "Increase Production, Promote Industry" soon replaced "Prosperous Nation, Strong Military" as Japan's guiding principle. The project for the elites of late nineteenth-century Japan was to create an industrial economy like those taking shape in Europe and the United States. Japan would become the "floating wharf of the Pacific." "We need industry to attain the goal of becoming a rich nation," declared the government in 1868.

At first, unfair terms of trade held Japan back. Western powers, exploiting their temporary military advantage, imposed "unequal treaties" that allowed them to sell products in Japan cheaply and exempted their nationals from having to obey Japanese laws or be judged in Japanese courts. The trade balance remained adverse—Japan imported more than it sold abroad—until the 1880s: "a source of lamentation," according to a government report of 1880. In 1884, only 176 non-government factories employed more than 50 people, and only 72 were steam-powered. By 1899, however, Japan was able to break out of the unequal relationship and revise the terms of trade with the West, while imposing terms on China after defeating that country in a war over Korea in 1895. Japan's total foreign trade increased tenfold from 1877 to 1900. The Meiji emperor presided at the opening of the first long-distance railway in 1872, but there were still only 100 miles of track in 1880. Nearly 5,000 miles were added in the next two decades. At the century's end, 50 cities had telephone exchanges, handling 45 million calls a year.

There were surprising successes. Buttons, previously unknown in Japan, became a major export by 1896. The textile-producing area of Lancashire in Britain inspired Japanese entrepreneurs to reorganize their country's cotton production. The value of the weaving output quadrupled in the 1890s. Cotton yarn production swelled more than sixfold to 250 million pounds—25 percent of Japan's total industrial output—by 1900. This was a remarkable achievement because cotton textiles were one of the world's most competitive sectors. But to some extent, women's labor financed the enterprise by keeping costs down.

Two strategies were essential: first, expanding traditional economic activities and reinvesting the profits in new industries; and second, heavy investment by the state to kick-start industrial enterprises. Exports of traditional Japanese products, especially raw silk and tea, paid for industrialization, taking up what would otherwise have been China's expanding markets. Raw silk was by far the main export, still accounting for over a third of Japan's export trade in the 1890s. By 1900, Japan exported practically as much silk as China.

Meanwhile the strategy of involving state finance in the establishment of industry began to pay off, at the cost of huge losses for the treasury. In the 1880s, state enterprises sold off mining interests and textile centers to private companies.

"The project for the elites of late nineteenth-century Japan was to create an industrial economy like those taking shape in Europe and the United States. Japan would become the 'floating wharf of the Pacific'."

A CLOSER LOOK

Japanese Views of American Naval Technology

Commodore Matthew C. Perry's expedition to Tokyo in 1853 aroused great interest among the Japanese, who closely observed the American "black ships" anchored offshore. In his diary, Perry wrote that "at early sunrise . . . a corps of artists . . . came close to the ship's side, but made no attempt to come on board, busying themselves in taking sketches of the strange vessels." One of the purposes of the sketches was to give the shogun and his officials accurate information about the barbarians and their technology.

The paddle wheel from one of the expedition's steamers. Intended to be a technical drawing, it shows the passion with which the Japanese studied every detail of the American expedition, even though they were unfamiliar with the workings of a steamship.

The steamship *Susquehanna*, which served as Perry's command ship. The Japanese inscription indicates that the flag at the stern of the warship had "about 30 white stars on navy blue background, said to be the number of states."

The care with which the artist depicts the black smoke billowing out of the ship's funnel shows that he had never seen anything like this before.

How do these sketches illustrate Japan's attitudes toward "modernization" and the adoption of Western technology in the nineteenth century?

The Tokyo terminus of the new Tokyo-Yokohama railway line, built in 1872 with the aid of foreign engineers. From a series of prints called "Famous Places on the Tokaido: A Record of the Process of Reform," it was published only seven years after the Meiji Restoration opened Japan to foreign trade and ideas in 1868.

Shipyards, established to build warships in the 1850s and 1860s, diversified into civil engineering and the production of iron and steel for industry. The foundations of wealth were available at cut price. The Hiroshima Spinning Mill cost the state 49,000 yen to set up. It was sold to private investors for 12,000 yen. Great corporations, of the kind that still dominate Japanese economic life, such as Mitsui and Mitsubishi, were able to take advantage, thanks to connections with the government and to the wealth they had accumulated during the era of the Tokugawa shoguns (1603–1868; see Chapter 19). Powerful, dictatorial company chairmen dominated them—but this was not a conservative style of leadership. On the contrary, it ensured that innovation for long-term success remained more important than short-term profiteering. Myths multiplied of heroic entrepreneurs, just like the heroic engineers in England whose lives Samuel Smiles romanticized. The head of Mitsui supposedly began his career as a newspaper boy, while the employee who rose to head Mitsubishi started in life by selling flowers. The theme of rags to riches was old and prominent in Japanese literature (see Chapter 19) and was probably an incentive or inspiration for capitalism. The Japanese government primed the pump with huge issues of coinage. Between 1816 and 1841, it increased the amount of money in circulation by 80 percent, and increased it by 50 percent more before it started cutting back in the 1880s.

Japan's industrialization was Japanese-style, not a copy of that of the West. Japanese responded to the West by trying to adapt rather than ape, equal rather than imitate. Symbolically, the artist who drew one of Japan's first steam-powered factories in 1872 made the smoke from the factory chimneys curl in a pattern that matched the steam from the summit of Mount Fuji, the sacred volcanic mountain near Tokyo. Western theorists of the merits of private enterprise and "enlightened self-interest" were well known in Japan, and, indeed, some Japanese thinkers advocated them. "The government should never attempt to compete with the people in pursuing industry or commerce," wrote Matsukata Masayoshi in 1878. He claimed that self-interest made private enterprise efficient. But the Japanese preferred to see business as a form of service to the community and the state. They knew the laws of supply and demand, but preferred to regulate consumption for moral reasons. Industrialists claimed to have patriotic motives. Fukuzawa Yukichi (1835–1901) convinced samurai of the merit of trade "for profit and for Japan." His books and pamphlets sold 10 million copies in his lifetime. Eiichi Shibusawa, who spent a long time as the government minister responsible for industrial development, confessed that he began by thinking that only the military and political classes were honorable. "Then I realized that the real force of progress lay in business."

These mental habits and convictions made collaboration between the state and the private sector easy. Government and business worked together. The Western division between the state and private enterprise did not apply. Industrialists collaborated with government to restrain domestic demand and prioritize strength for war. Governments responded with contracts and concessions. In part this was because some influential Japanese misunderstood Western models. Okuba Toshimichi, who visited the manufacturing cities of Birmingham and Glasgow in Britain in the 1870s, reported that there was "no instance" in Europe where "a country's productive power was increased without the patronage and encouragement of its officials." This was not a false observation, but the inference he drew

MAP 23.6

The Industrialization of Japan to 1918

Modernization under the Meiji

■ main industrial areas by 1918

- - - railways built 1868–1918

Traditional industries

♦ ceramics

▢ textiles

▢ silk

Industries developed after 1868

▦ manufacturing

✳ machine building

⚓ shipbuilding

♦ chemicals

● city of over 500,000 in 1918

○ other major city

was misleading. The engine of Western capitalism—unless you count Russia as Western—did not need the state to stoke it, only to keep hands off the damper.

More mattered than just profit. Japanese firms had strong corporate identities, whereas in the West, class divisions tended to prevent bosses and workers from developing close partnerships. Occasionally, Japanese investors behaved like those in other countries. The Kyoto Pottery Company collapsed in 1892 because shareholders grew impatient after five years without dividends. But investors generally seem to have preferred capital growth to quick rewards. As in the West, "modern" enterprises such as railways were disproportionately popular with investors. Cement manufacturers made low profits and rarely issued dividends, but they rejoiced in producing from "dirt at home" instead of spending "gold abroad." Similar attitudes prevailed in brick making, shipyards, and the gas industry.

The price was paid in more than cash. In the 1890s, the Ashio copper mines became a scandalous symbol of the costs of industrialization: rabid expansion, deforestation, flooded villages, and the poisoning of downstream waters. Nonetheless, the overall achievement of industrialization in Japan was remarkable. Compared with the beginning of the nineteenth century, Japan's national output of manufactured goods, raw materials, and agricultural products had quadrupled, and the proportion contributed by industry had at least doubled (see Map 23.6).

CHINA AND INDUSTRIALIZATION

As so often in Chinese history, peasant rebellion, rather than foreign example, was the spur to change. Western industrialization should have alarmed Chinese officials and intellectuals in the first half of the nineteenth century. It eroded Chinese domination of the global economy and reversed the military balance of power—with effects that

China painfully felt, as we shall see in the next chapter. But influential Chinese did not develop their response until 1861. They called it "self-strengthening."

In 1860, two events brought on a sense of crisis. First, huge areas fell into the hands of peasant revolutionaries, notably the Taipings, who mounted a serious threat to the ruling Manchu Qing dynasty from 1852 to 1864 (see Chapter 25). Second, an Anglo-French army occupied Beijing. The immediate pretext for this invasion was an apparently trivial matter of diplomatic procedure: Chinese failure to comply with a promise to receive British and French ambassadors at the emperor's court in Beijing rather than in the southern city of Guangzhou. But the background included a series of incidents that convinced the Westerners that they had to humble China to secure freedom of action for Western merchants and missionaries.

While smarting under their humiliations, China's elites took comfort from the outcome. The Western barbarians clearly had no intention of trying to wrest the mandate of heaven from the Qing like earlier invaders. Their aims were commercial, and the Chinese could buy their goodwill with trade. The result was a new openness toward the "barbarians" whose armies the imperial government could hire to suppress the peasant rebels. Barbarian skills could perhaps be employed to strengthen China. As an official memorandum of early 1861 put it, China had the chance "to snatch good fortune out of disaster, to transform weak to strong, this should provide China with cause of great rejoicing." Civil servants reporting to the emperor during this period insisted that the technology that gave the barbarians a present advantage was all of Chinese origin, anyway. They were largely right.

In November 1861, Wei Muting used these facts to sugar a bitter pill. China would have to relearn its old skills from the foreigners. Shipbuilding and munitions manufacture were technologies China could adopt from Europe. "Now that we know what they depend on for victory," agreed Prince Gong, the emperor's chief minister, "we should try to master it."

Because European soldiers of fortune and merchants helped the Chinese government suppress the Taiping rebellion, General Li Hongzhang could inspect Western munitions closely. "If China were to pay attention to these matters," he concluded, "she would be able to stand on her own a hundred years from now." He called for a revolution in values that would elevate technicians and engineers above scholars and writers.

> Seek machines that make machines and men who make machines. Western machinery can produce farming, weaving, printing, and pottery-making equipment for the daily use of the people. It is not solely for the purpose of making weapons. What is wondrous is that it utilizes the power of water and fire to save labor and material resources.... Several decades hence, among the rich peasants and prosperous merchants of China, there will inevitably be men who follow the example of Western machine-manufacturing in their pursuit of profit.

As in Japan, the early impact of mechanization was confined to munitions. The Kiangnan arsenal opened in 1865 to manufacture guns and ships. It also had a translation department charged with keeping up to date with Western knowledge in armaments. It was an important initiative but never managed to produce rifles as good or as cheap as imported models. Its ships cost twice as much as those available from competitors abroad. A naval yard inaugurated in 1866 built 40 ships, none of which performed well.

Zeng Guofan (dzung-gwoh-fan), the model administrator responsible for modernizing China, insisted that imperial rule and rites were perfect. "Propriety and righteousness" came above "expediency and ingenuity." After his death in

"China and the West were mutually blinded by perceptions of each other's "barbarism." From 1840, the Opium Wars exposed China's weakness and dispelled the Western respect for the empire and its people that had featured so prominently during the Enlightenment."

1872, the focus of self-strengthening switched to civilian industries, the infrastructure, and the economic basis of a strong state: civilian steamships, mechanization of coal mining and textile manufacture, and the telegraph system. A railway-building boom, paid for with foreign capital, followed in the 1880s, linking coal mines and agricultural hinterlands to the ports. Yet China remained a preindustrial power. Private investment was channeled through state-run monopolies in all these fields.

In war against Japan over who would dominate Korea in 1894–1895, the difference between the belligerents showed. On paper the Chinese navy, which had cost more than Japan's, looked more formidable—bigger and more heavily armed with two ironclads of 7,000 tons each—than the Japanese navy, which had no ship bigger than 4,000 tons. But before the conflict, a Japanese officer noted with disgust that piles of garbage littered the Chinese decks and washing hung from the guns. The Chinese war machine was like "an over-fired sword, no sharper than a rusty kitchen knife." The imperial household had diverted money for munitions to rebuild a palace outside Beijing that the British and French had burned in 1861. When battle began, the Chinese guns had only three rounds of ammunition each. Most of their ships avoided action. The Japanese captured or sank those that did fight.

Self strengthening. Chinese interest in Western technology sometimes wavered, but was always strongest in military contexts. Here, Qing officials examine a machine gun and a rocket launcher at the Nanjing Arsenal.

China and the West were mutually blinded by perceptions of each other's "barbarism." From 1840, the Opium Wars (see Chapter 25) exposed China's weakness and dispelled the Western respect for the empire and its people that had featured so prominently during the Enlightenment (see Chapter 22). In China, it was heresy to acknowledge the West as civilized. For Westerners, the Chinese were "Asiatic barbarians" to be treated with contempt. For most of the Chinese elite, the big problems were those of longest standing: the peasant uprisings, of which the Taiping was the most threatening; the unrest of Muslim minorities, whose rebellions the Qing repressed with difficulty; and the erosion of state power to provincial strongmen. Carefully measured deference to selective Western superiority seemed the best course. "Chinese essence, Western practice" became the government's slogan after the defeat by Japan.

In the 1880s, the tea trade shrank in the face of Indian competition. Although Chinese silk exports remained significant despite Japanese competition, new exports from China were geared to an industrializing world: primary foodstuffs intended for processing abroad, skins and straw, hog bristles and timber, coal and iron ore. Much of the trade supplied Japanese industries that were outstripping those of China. The era of dominance for China through its luxury products was largely over.

INDIA AND EGYPT

In the nineteenth century, India deindustrialized. Was this the inevitable result of the unbeatable competitiveness of mechanized textile production in Britain? Or was it a deliberate effect of empire, as the British wrecked India's industries to boost their own? It was probably a bit of both. India's traditional industries, particularly cotton textile weaving, began to collapse in the 1820s, before Britain had a systematic policy with regard to India. The disappearance of the great courts and armies of the Mughal era (see Chapter 21) left India without the motors of demand that once drove its economy. Indians had to turn back to the land.

1879 Abolition of all tariff duties on British textiles
1895 Britain imposes excise of 5% on Indian cotton goods
1924 Cotton excise suspended

1815–1860 British cotton textile production expands at a rate of 6–7% per annum and by the midcentury British cotton constitutes 50% of world production of commercially produced cloth

Late 18th century Cotton production in Lancashire is great growth industry of Industrial Revolution

1793 Invention of cotton gin leads to a massive increase in the production of short staple cotton

1861–1865 'Cotton famine' caused by Civil War restrictions in U.S. leads British textile manufacturers to look to India for raw materials

1800–1860 U.S. annual raw cotton production increases from 100,000 bales to 4 million bales

1861 During Civil War, Confederate states restrict cotton exports to try and force European intervention in war

1861 onwards Boom in raw cotton production in India

1820–1850 India loses in world market for textiles as it is forced by excises to import cotton cloth from Lancashire.

MAP 23.7

The Politics of Cotton

→ raw cotton from U.S. to Britain
→ cotton textiles to India
→ raw cotton from India to Britain
⬦ cotton-producing region
▨ textile town
▬ major cotton-producing states

The British made matters worse. They bureaucratized tax collection, cutting out native Indian capitalists. From an industrial giant, India became a producer of raw materials for the British Empire: tea, coffee, quinine, opium, jute, cotton. Early in the century, while Britain's balance of trade with China was still unfavorable, Britain's trade drained cash from India's economy. Industrialization elsewhere lowered prices for Indian products. The export of labor began. Millions of Indian laborers emigrated in the second half of the century, most to work on construction projects or plantations elsewhere in the British Empire, in East Africa, the Pacific, or the Caribbean. India still had a favorable trading balance with its Asian trading partners but not with Britain. The machinery of British cotton mills pulverized Indian manufactures. By 1900, British-made textiles accounted for over a third of India's total imports. India bought two-fifths of Britain's cotton exports. The British set the tariffs to favor their own exports. British firms effectively monopolized India's shipping, insurance, and international banking (see Map 23.7).

The British built a new economic infrastructure in India: dams, bridges, tunnels, roads, harbor installations, and, above all, as we have seen, railways. But the railways moved troops, administrators, travelers, and the primary goods the empire demanded. They did not contribute, as they did in Europe or North America, to internal industrialization.

In most of the rest of the world, industrial models of development had little appeal. Rulers wanted to get their hands on modern munitions—generally by buying them from the West—and to hire Western technicians to train their armies to use those armaments. In some places these minimal strategies achieved remarkable success. Elsewhere, rulers or elites welcomed Western investment to build railways and bridges, but rarely tried to start factories to compete with Western manufactures.

The big exception was Egypt. Its population had grown rapidly, even by nineteenth-century standards, from 2.5 million inhabitants in 1800 to 6.8 million in 1882. The passage of French Revolutionary armies through the country in

1798–1799 was an experience Egypt shared with much of Europe. While they were in Egypt, French officials saw opportunities for industrialization. They opened factories for guns, gunpowder, food, and beer. After they departed, the far-sighted Mehmet Ali (1769–1849)—who, from 1805, was nominally the viceroy or khedive for the Ottoman Empire but was, in effect, an independent monarch and the founder of a dynasty that ruled Egypt until 1953—bought in the services of Western, mostly French, experts to reproduce the activities already characteristic of industrializing Britain: cotton mills, munitions factories, steel-works, shipyards, a printing press. One of his French hired hands, Louis-Alexis Jumel, introduced a new strain of cotton that proved amazingly successful as the basis of fine textiles. In 1826, Mehmet Ali imported 500 steam-powered looms from Britain. About 10 years later, Egypt was producing 1.2 million bolts of cotton cloth a year. The industry was a state monopoly. Mehmet Ali suppressed private competitors. He found, however, that British industrialists were equally hostile to competition from him. In 1839, Britain forced Egypt to abandon protective tariffs when they blocked Mehmet Ali's attempt to overthrow the Ottoman Empire with French support. As a result, the Egyptian cotton industry dwindled, and Egypt, like the American South, became a major exporter of cash crops—sugar cane and raw cotton. Continuous irrigation was required to force the extra output, which was needed to support the military and government facade of a modern state, from the land. The peasants were impoverished and overburdened, and the opportunity to modernize on the Western European model slipped out of Egypt's grasp.

Egyptian intellectuals remained faithful to Western models of development. Rifaa Tahtawi (1801–1871) introduced the notion of a secular state and advocated universal education. Ali Pasha Mubarak (1824–1893) produced Western-inspired

The Suez Canal. The French artist Edouard Rion (1833–1900) went to Suez to record Egyptian life for the French illustrated press just before the opening of the canal. Engravings of many of his paintings—including this bustling interpretation of the inaugural procession of ships through the canal in November 1869—appeared as illustrations to the account of the canal's construction written by Ferdinand de Lesseps, the canal's promoter and chief engineer.

"In 1800, Britain and Germany combined contributed less than 5 percent of global industrial production. By 1900, those two countries alone accounted for nearly a third of the output of the world's industries."

writings and public works for the government on engineering, fortifications, irrigation, and mechanized agriculture. Khedive Ismail (r. 1863–1879), Mehmet Ali's grandson, tried to revive his grandfather's program. Ismail proclaimed Egypt to be "part of Europe." Borrowing money at outrageous interest from European bankers, he built docks, sugar mills, an opera house in Cairo, and a school for girls. He had the Suez Canal driven across Egyptian land using French engineers and French capital. The canal opened in 1869 and, by connecting the Mediterranean to the Red Sea, reduced the sailing time from Europe to India and the Far East from months to weeks. But his extravagances bankrupted the state. In 1875, Britain purchased Ismail's shares in the canal. In 1879, his European creditors forced him to abdicate. Much of Egypt's revenue was assigned to repay foreign debts, and 1,300 foreign bureaucrats arrived to manage the country's finances and armed forces. In September 1881, the handful of native Egyptian officers still left in high ranks rebelled under the slogan "Egypt for the Egyptians."

Britain responded by occupying key parts of the country "to save," as a British official claimed, "Egypt from anarchy, and all European nations interested in Egypt from incalculable losses in blood and treasure." The intervention was more self-interested than the rhetoric implied. Egypt became, in effect, a British dependency with a puppet government and a large British garrison until after World War II.

In Perspective
Industrialization, Causes and Consequences

In 1800, China was probably about eight times as productive as Britain. By 1900, Britain produced about three times as much as China. In 1800, Britain and Germany combined contributed less than 5 percent of global industrial production. By 1900, those two countries alone accounted for nearly a third of the output of the world's industries. China's share in the same period fell from over a third to barely 6 percent (see Figure 23.1). Industrialization had dwarfed a giant and hoisted jacks-of-all-trades to the top of the beanstalk. Why did the West beat the rest—or most of the rest, if we include Japan—to the benefits of industrialization?

The West had few of the advantages commonly alleged. Traditional Western values, which were those of the landed aristocracy and the church, were industrialization's antibodies, training elites to have contempt for trade. Factories went up in a world where, according to the English essayist William Hazlitt (1778–1830), "people were always talking of the Greeks and Romans." Nor did Europe's supposedly "scientific" culture breed industry. The late eighteenth-century inventors of industrial processes—coke smelting, mechanized spinning, steam pumping, and the steam-driven loom—were all heroes of what Samuel Smiles called "self-help." They were self-taught artisans or entrepreneurs with little or no formal scientific training. Science had no inbuilt practical vocation until the late nineteenth century. It would be fairer to say that industry hijacked European science—bought it for "useful research," diverted it to social responsibility.

FIGURE 23.1 SHARE OF WORLD MANUFACTURING OUTPUT, 1750–1900 *Derived from B. R. Tomlinson, "Economics: The Periphery." in Andrew Porter (ed.). The Oxford History of the British Empire: The Nineteenth Century, Oxford 1990, p. 69 (Table 3.8).*

Share of World Manufacturing Output, 1750–1900

	1750	1800	1830	1860	1880	1900
Europe	23.1	28.0	34.1	53.6	62.0	63.0
China	32.8	33.3	29.8	19.7	12.5	6.2
India	24.5	19.7	17.6	8.6	2.8	1.7

Nor is it enough—though it is important—to say that the distribution of coal and iron privileged some economies for industrialization. In some places outside the West and beyond Western control, coal and iron reserves were left unexploited. In others, such as New England and parts of northern Spain and Italy, industrializers, carried ahead by their own determination, found ways to compensate for the lack of them.

The West's real advantage was commercial. Commerce makes specialization possible. Without extensive systems of long-range trade, large concentrations of labor dedicated to manufacturing particular items or producing particular primary products are impossible. In the eighteenth and nineteenth centuries, Western Europe and North America were excellent environments for banking and what would now be called financial services industries, thanks to the climate of economic liberalism (see Chapter 22) and the commitment of states to foster commerce. Europe was not unique in this respect. "Capitalism" and commercial entrepreneurship were also ingrained in many communities and ruling elites in Asia. In China, however, commerce did not enjoy the same level of support from the state. Moreover, China was slow to change this attitude in the nineteenth century.

The pace of commerce is a function of the size of the market, and it is worth noting that European populations experienced exceptionally high growth rates in the nineteenth century. The population of Europe more than doubled to over 400 million in 1900, even though during the same century over 40 million Europeans migrated to other continents. Was this increase a cause or an effect of industrialization? At least we can say that population growth was particularly strong in the most industrialized zones. The populations of Belgium, Britain, and Germany all rose faster than the average.

Westerners, finally, came from behind. That is where innovation usually comes from, because leaders in any field have little interest in promoting change. Economies like those of India and China, which had productive traditional industries and enormous reserves of labor, felt no call to mechanize.

Industrialization was disastrous for many of the people who took it up. Like the ancient adoption of farming, it had adverse consequences for nutrition, health, and what we would now call quality of life. It nourished oppression and tyranny. So why did people accept it? Why,

Chronology

1780–1831	Karl von Clausewitz, developer of theory of "total war"
1798–1799	French armies occupy Egypt
Nineteenth century	India deindustrializes
ca. 1800	Global population: 950 million; areas with regions in excess of four people per square mile: East Asia, Southeast Asia, India, Western Europe
1800–1850	Increase in steam-driven industrial capacity: Britain, Spain, Italy, Belgium doubled; France, Russia tripled; Czech Republic increased fivefold; Germany increased sixfold
1804	First successful railroad locomotion
1805–1849	Reign of Mehmet Ali in Egypt, proponent of industrialization
1807	First commercial steamboat
1835–1918	Andrew Carnegie, American industrialist
1839	Britain forces Egypt to end protection of cotton industry
1846–1848	Mexican-American War
Mid-nineteenth century	Japanese industrialization focuses on military technology
1850–1900	500 million acres added to United States farmland
1850s	British imports of guano reach 200,000 tons per year
July 8, 1853	Commodore Perry sails into Tokyo Bay
1857	Sepoy Mutiny in India
1860	Peasant revolutionaries take control of large parts of China; Anglo-French army occupies Beijing
1860–1900	Japanese coal production rises from 390,000 to 5 million tons; British coal production in South Wales rises from 11.4 million to 35.1 million
1861–1865	American Civil War
1861	China begins "self-strengthening" program
1866	British output of chemical fertilizers reaches 250,000 tons
1869	First transcontinental railroad in United States
1870s	Australian engineers develop compressed-gas cooler; Belgium leads world in iron- and steel-making equipment
1877–1900	Japan's foreign trade increases tenfold
1890s	United States produces twice as much steel as Britain
1895	Japan defeats China in war over Korea
Late nineteenth century	Belgium and Netherlands develop increasingly complementary economies
1900	German coal production reaches 100 million tons annually; Argentina exports 100 million bushels of wheat per year; global population: 1.6 billion; 9 European cities have populations of more than a million

indeed, did they relish it so much that almost every community that has had the chance to industrialize over the last 200 years has opted to do so?

Industrialization had one immediately obvious benefit: it released land for food production. It was no longer necessary, for instance, to maintain forests to provide wood for fuel. Forests in England halved between 1800 and 1900. The conservation policies of eighteenth-century Japan (Chapter 20) were abandoned. In the nineteenth century, the carefully husbanded woodlands that formerly covered much of the islands of Honshu, Kyushu, and Shikoku largely vanished as coal replaced wood as a source of fuel, and Japan devoted more land to agriculture. The opposite happened in much of New England, where the rock-ribbed soil, which had largely been under the plow in 1800, began to revert to forest as food production shifted westward in the 1820s and 1830s.

Further, as we shall see in Chapter 26, the long-term consequences of industrialization tended to spread the benefits surprisingly widely. In its early stages, mechanization hugely increased the burden of labor for the workers who operated the machines. But it was labor saving for others. And technical improvements gradually liberated even the machine workers to enjoy increased leisure.

Finally, it is worth dwelling for a moment on the example of agrarianization. As readers of earlier parts of this book know, early farming communities adopted new production methods despite adverse short-term effects (see Chapter 2). In part, this was because most people—especially those most likely to suffer, because they were poor and powerless—had no say in decision making. Industrialization, like farming, was an elite option. It appealed to people whose power it increased. It enabled the controllers of industrial wealth to join or replace existing elites, and it empowered industrialized and industrializing communities to dominate the rest of the world and extort or exploit its resources.

PROBLEMS AND PARALLELS

1. How did fat—oil from animals, plants, and minerals—make the world of the nineteenth century work? What other sources of energy were exploited in the nineteenth century?

2. How did the population rise of the nineteenth century lead to new ways to exploit the Earth's resources?

3. Why did population increase not conform to the predictions of Thomas Malthus?

4. Why was the agricultural exploitation of the North American prairie and the South American pampa so important?

5. How did industrialization affect the world's food supply? What was the relationship between industrialization and militarization?

6. Why did some parts of the world industrialize and not others? Who benefited most from industrialization?

7. Why did Japan industrialize more rapidly than China? How did British imperialism affect India's economy in the nineteenth century? Why were Mehmet Ali and his successors unable to make Egypt an industrial power?

READ ON ▶ ▶ ▶

C. A. Bayly, *The Birth of the Modern World* (2004) is an insuperable survey of global history in the nineteenth century. E. A. Wrigley, *Peoples, Cities and Wealth: The Transition of Traditional Society* (1989) provides an overview of some of the most conspicuous issues. P. N. Stearns, *The Industrial Revolution in World History* (1998) is an introductory essay.

On food, F. Fernández-Armesto, *Near a Thousand Tables* (2003) is a short, general history. J. Burnett, *Plenty and Want* (1988) surveys the topic for Britain. J. Goody, *Cooking, Cuisine and Class* (1982) is an ingenious, anthropologically informed work that opens up comparative perspectives. P. N. Stearns, *Fat History* (2002) studies attitudes to fat in France and the United States. On famine, M. Davis, *Late Victorian Holocausts* (2002) is important and challenging.

On the domestication of the prairie, W. Cronon, *Nature's Metropolis* (1991) is essential reading. R W. Paul, *The Far West and the Great Plains in Transition* (1998) is an excellent study. W. Cronon et al., eds., *Under an Open Sky* (1993) includes some important essays. On fertilizers W. M. Mathew, *The House of Gibbs and the Peruvian Guano Monopoly* (1981) is a most helpful monograph. On Burbank, F. W. Clampett, *Luther Burbank* (1926) provides a rather uncritical outline.

On the militarization of society, E. Weber, *Peasants into Frenchmen* (1979) is a classic study. P. Paret, *Clausewitz and the State* (1985) is a useful study of Clausewitz's work in social and political perspective.

G. R. Taylor, *The Transportation Revolution* (1951) is an old but still authoritative study of the infrastructure of industrialization. On the industrialization of Europe, T. Kemp, *Industrialization in Nineteenth-century Europe* (1969) provides an overview. D. Landes *The Unbound Prometheus* (1969) is a classic survey. P. N. Stearns, *Lives of Labor* (1975) takes a comparative approach focused on workers' experience.

On Britain and France, P. O'Brien and R. Quainault, eds., *The Industrial Revolution and British Society* (1993), and P. O'Brien and C. Keyder, *Economic Growth in Britain and France* (1978) are in some respects correctives of the still important classic study, P. Mathias, *The First Industrial Nation* (1969). T. Zeldin, *France 1848–1945*, 2 vols, (1973) is a wonderful book: sensitive and stimulating with an impressively original method. For Germany, T. Pierenkemper and R. Tilly, *The German Economy during the Nineteenth Century* (2005) is a good brief introduction. J. Mokyr, *Industrialization in the Low Countries* (1976) is basic. E. H. Koss-

mann, *The Low Countries 1798–1914* (1978), and J. C. H. Blom and E. Lamberts, eds., *History of the Low Countries* (1998) provide useful overviews. J. L. Van Zanden, *The Economic Development of the Netherlands since 1870* (1996) includes a brief history of Dutch industrialization. J. de Vries and A. van de Woude, *The First Modern Economy* (1997) is an influential survey of pre-nineteenth-century Dutch economic history. Spain is superbly covered by D. Ringrose, *Madrid and the Spanish Economy* (1983), and N. Sánchez-Albornoz, ed., *The Economic Modernization of Spain* (1987). For Italy, J. Cohen and G. Federico, *The Growth of the Italian Economy* (2001) is an efficient introduction. D. C. North, *The Economic Growth of the United States* (1966) is a venerable and reliable work. G. J. Kornblith, ed., *The Industrial Revolution in America* (1998) contains some stimulating essays. M. Girouard, *The Return to Camelot* (1981), and D. C. Lieven, *The Aristocracy in Europe 1815–1914* (1993), are helpful on the survival of an aristocratic ethos in the industrializing West.

J. Batou, ed., *Between Development and Underdevelopment* (1991) is an important collection on attempts at industrialization in the extra-Western world in the nineteenth century.

R. Bin Wong, *China Transformed: Historical Change and the Limits of European Experience* (2002) is of fundamental importance; L. Aiguo, *China and the Global Economy since 1840* (1999) is a helpful introductory work. India is covered in D. Kumar, ed., *The Cambridge Economic History of India, II* (2005), and I. J. Ker, *Building the Railways of the Raj* (1998). M. B. Jansen, ed., *The Cambridge History of Japan* V (1995), and S. Sugiyama, *Japan's Industrialization in the World Economy* (1988) deal with Japan; S. Hanley and K. Yamamura, *Economic and Demographic Change in Pre-industrial Japan* (1967) is valuable on the background and takes a critically acute approach to controversial issues in historical demography. On the Middle East, R. Owen, see *Cotton and the Egyptian Economy* (1969), and *The Middle East and the World Economy* (1993). C. Issawi, ed., *The Fertile Crescent, 1800–1914* (1988) is a useful economic overview of the Middle East, with many documents. P. J. Vatikiotis, *The History of Modern Egypt* (1991) is an outstanding survey.

Debate on the reasons for the West's great leap forward is mainly conducted in K. Pomeranz, *The Great Divergence* (2001); A. Gunder Frank, *ReOrient* (1988); D. Landes, *The Wealth and Poverty of Nations* (1999), J. Goody, *The East in the West* (1996), and J. Hobson, *The Eastern origins of Western Civilization* (2004).

CHAPTER 24

The Social Mold: Work and Society in the Nineteenth Century

▲ **Samurai.**   Akira Kurosawa's epic movie of 1954, *The Seven Samurai*, was set in the Japan of the sixteenth century, but it depicted the predicament of the samurai in modern times. By the nineteenth century, the samurai had become an obsolete class, whose prestige and wealth had been diminished by social, economic, and political changes. But in their own eyes, and in those of most Japanese, they still embodied timeless values of honor and courage. In the movie, the seven find work as mercenaries, defending villagers from bandits. In the process, they teach the peasants the art of war, thus rendering themselves—and by extension, all samurai—useless.

JAPAN

As the police closed in, four fugitives struggled in bitter March cold through the mountains south of Osaka, Japan. When the first one faltered, his companions accepted his offer to commit ritual suicide. Indeed, they helped by slicing off his head. Another of the party soon dropped from exhaustion and then hanged himself from a tree.

Now only Oshio Heihachiro—a former police magistrate who had led an unsuccessful rebellion—and his son were left. They doubled back to their home city, disguised as priests, and forced a former client to take them in. When the police caught up with them, Oshio's son wanted to flee, but, screaming, "Coward! Coward!" Oshio stabbed him to death, set fire to the house, stood defiantly on the threshold, slashed his own throat, and perished amid the flames on May 1, 1837. When his charred remains were carried off, the heat had so bloated and twisted his head that he looked, said onlookers, like a great toad.

In Japan, Oshio has always been regarded as a hero, despite, or perhaps because of, his horrific suicide. He was a member of the hereditary warrior caste—a samurai and proud of it—who had grown up believing that nobles' obligations to the poor were more important than their privileges over them. Early in his career, he acquired a reputation as an infallible and incorruptible detective, rooting out secret practitioners of Christianity—which still had faithful followers 200 years after Japan banned the religion—and exposing scandals in the administration. He then retired, after a mystical vision, to meditate and found a small school.

The circumstances that drove him to rebellion were not new. But it was a new kind of revolt in Japanese history. For the first time, noble samurai made common cause with the poor and the peasants against the middle class. As had happened so often before in Japan, and as happened sooner or later in every society dependent on one staple crop, the 1830s were a decade of rice failures and famine. In 1837, as the price of rice reached unprecedented levels, Oshio saw poor people dying of starvation in the streets of Osaka. Yet the state granaries were well stocked, and the officials who ran them and got rich by driving up prices were shipping rice to the capital. Oshio petitioned local officials to open the warehouses, but they threatened him with prosecution for meddling where he had no official status.

Oshio sold his library, bought a cannon and muskets, and hired an artillery expert to train his men in the use of firearms. He then issued a summons to revolt, promising to "visit Heaven's vengeance" on the officials and merchants, and calling on peasants to join the revolt and burn the tax records on which the authorities relied. He stressed, sincerely, that he did not aim to seize power, only to right injustice.

FOCUS questions

How did industrialization change society and the economy?

Why was Marx wrong in predicting that industrialization would lead to violent revolution?

Why were the slave trade and slavery abolished in the nineteenth century?

How did the roles of women and children change in the nineteenth century?

Why were some aristocracies able to adapt to the changes industrialization brought?

The modernization and industrialization of Japan (see Chapter 23) would soon destroy Oshio's world. But his type of revolt, and the kind of alliance of aristocrats and peasants he led, was repeated over and over. Not just in Japan but wherever they arose, the new kinds of wealth that commerce and, in some places, industry generated threatened to subvert traditional society by diminishing the old role of aristocracies, elevating the middle class, reducing and ruining peasants, creating an industrial working class, and eliminating traditional forms of labor such as slavery and serfdom.

In the nineteenth century, Oshio's call was echoed in surprising places around the world. In Bengal in India, for instance, a landlords' agent, Titu Mir, led a peasant revolt against moneylenders, tax collectors, and rent gougers in 1831. In England, at about the same time, conservative aristocrats saw workers and landowners as natural allies in a struggle to save the old economy of the land against the new economy of capital. In North America, some slave owners appealed to their slaves to fight alongside them against would-be liberators who wanted to subordinate the states to the federal government. In Latin America aristocratic rebels recruited peasant guerrillas to fight in civil wars. In France middle-class intellectuals—typified by the apologist of terrorism, Auguste Blanqui (1805–1881)—dreamed of leading the masses to progress. In the Ottoman Empire Butrus Bustani, a Western-influenced aristocrat, spoke up for rebellious peasants in Lebanon. In Russia the great novelist, Count Leo Tolstoy (1828–1910), renounced his wealth and adopted a peasant's way of life.

Traditional resentments—of merchants by aristocrats, of profiteers by peasants—grew with the growing wealth gaps of the age. Increasing trade generated new wealth, but little of it reached the workers who grew and mined raw materials in the unindustrialized world. And it took a long time even for industrial workers in the West to obtain a substantial share in the new prosperity. As the pace of commerce speeded up, and its reach broadened, so did the range of economic opportunities and rewards, and so did the numbers of people worldwide who were left behind or left out. Industrialization accelerated these effects. And it affected more than just the regions in which it happened, because it made global wealth gaps gape, turning some regions and peoples into suppliers of staple products for consumers in industrial economies that were located hundreds or even thousands of miles away.

Even in unindustrialized societies, economic status rivaled age-old ways of determining people's place in society—parentage, ancestry, birthplace, learning, strength, sanctity. Where industry flourished, social change was even more convulsive. Instead of identifying with communities that embraced people at all levels of rank and prosperity—neighborhoods, cities, provinces, sects, families, clans, big households, ethnic groups—people, uprooted and regrouped in industrial centers, came to define themselves in terms of wealth or what they increasingly called class. It was a common assumption of nineteenth-century observers in the West that the world was being redrawn along class lines. Some governments even adopted class as a way to categorize their populations. Everyone had a place in the world as a noble, a bourgeois, a peasant, or a worker. In Europe, the German revolutionary philosopher Karl Marx (1818–1883) championed a new theory of history: that all change was part and product of inevitable **class struggles** that pitted the rich against those whom they exploited.

Marx's view was exaggerated, but it helps to show how people at the time perceived the often traumatic social changes that accompanied the economic changes of the nineteenth century.

This chapter is about how people could fit into this changing world: the spaces they occupied, the way their work patterns altered, the shifts in the nature and location of labor, the new relationships people developed, the shaken kaleidoscope of class and rank. In the first half of the chapter, we concentrate on industrializing societies, because they exerted a disproportionate influence on everyone else. After looking at the differences that industrialization made to people's lives and experiences of work in industrializing areas, we shall turn to changes in the way labor was recruited and distributed beyond—and in the shadow of—the industrializing world, and finally to the way industrialization affected the elites, who employed or commanded that labor.

THE INDUSTRIALIZED ENVIRONMENT

Machines created unprecedented differences of power and wealth: between regions and countries, of course, but also, within industrializing regions, between classes, sexes, and generations.

Palaces of Work: The Rise of Factories

Industrialization transformed the way people worked and the places they worked in. It is easy to say that—especially now, when the age of the vast factories is over in much of the West. But at the time, industrialization was a strange experience for those caught up in changes that seemed disruptive, disturbing, and often hard to endure. Work moved from country to city, from outdoors to indoors, from homes and small workshops into factories and mines, from relatively healthy to relatively unhealthy environments: deafening, psychologically straining, mentally exhausting, personally alienating, in ways that the traditional rural economy had never been. One kind of traditional workplace practically disappeared in industrializing societies. In the past, small groups of workers had shared intimate surroundings: workshops in which a few equals or near equals collaborated, or households in which a master craftsman marshaled apprentices who lived together like a large family. Now seismic social upheavals raised factories, like "smoking volcanoes" (as contemporaries said), burying the world of artisans and flattening the traditional social hierarchies.

Factories were new settings that reorganized work and reordered life. They are the best markers of the changes industrialization brought. They made startlingly different impressions on different people, but the passions they inspired—for and against—were always profound. For their admirers, factories represented a truly noble achievement: proof of progress, a seemingly magical extension of human power over the rest of nature, a romantic adventure in making a new future for humankind. In 1802–1803, for instance, the German artist, C. A. G. Goede, traveling between the industrial cities of Birmingham and Shrewsbury in England, marveled at "mountain and valley in flames" for miles around, where "fire-spitting volcanoes" turn the horizon purple, "beautifully lit by the gleaming glow of coal. One might believe oneself in Vulcan's workshop"—the forge of the ancient Roman god who supposedly stoked the world's volcanoes. Indeed, there were no precedents, except in myth, for what machines could do. The power of mechanization

". . . at the time, industrialization was a strange experience for those caught up in changes that seemed disruptive, disturbing, and often hard to endure."

Unthreatening industry. William Ibbitt's engraving of industrial Sheffield, in northern England, in the mid-nineteenth century, depicts the towering factories, which rival the city's churches, the outpouring smoke, and the huge sprawl of the growing city. But, nestling in nature, industry seems at ease with the environment, and traditional rural life is undisturbed in the foreground.

did make people feel godlike. The ways early nineteenth-century artists painted factories are full of echoes of volcanic imagery.

Early depictions, moreover, show factories in remarkable harmony with nature, sited in the countryside for convenient access to raw materials. The French artist Philippe-Jacques de Loutherbourg painted Coalbrookdale in England in 1801, with furnaces ablaze in a cozy pastoral setting (see page 788). In 1830, Karl Schurz painted the new Lendersdorf steel works, near Cologne in Germany, in the style of a farmyard scene against a background of rolling hills. Only the smoke from the chimneys hints at the revolutionary nature of the activity under the rather rickety roof. William Ibbitt painted mid-nineteenth-century Sheffield, another English industrial center, as an ideal city, merging into the surrounding light, clean despite the smoke of the 50 factory chimneys that rose parallel with the spires of churches. On a hill in the foreground, workers relax, children play, a middle-class family surveys the city with pride.

Even as they got bigger and multiplied, factories were still remarkable creations of the imagination: spaces of a type never before conceived and, therefore, never before designed. Architects sought models from the ancient world and fiction, raising fantasy buildings, bristling with turrets, battlements, spires, and domes, to be what contemporaries called cathedrals of work or castles of industry. In a newspaper's praise of the factories of Sabadell, outside Barcelona in Spain, in 1855, we can detect all the emotions factory builders invested in their efforts. "These factories, grand and elegant . . . are sumptuous palaces that ought to inspire their owners and all the people with pride. . . . These palaces house no pharaohs, no orgies, but are a means of life for hundreds of families. These palaces are not there to inspire insanity or arrogance, but love of work and respect for effort and for merit." The words express genuine belief in the nobility of work. The language also reveals the power hunger of industrialists who based their claims to influence on merit rather than wealth. The moral tone of bosses' **paternalism** leaps from the page. More than just money inspired industrialization at its best.

Paternalism also made economic and political sense. One of the big problems for historians of industrialization is to explain why people left the land for factories and abandoned the country for the towns. Most of those who did probably had no choice. The mechanization of agriculture reduced the amount of rural work available. Landowners' own economies of scale concentrated more land in fewer hands. Global specialization shifted production of food and industrial raw materials out of the industrializing world, leaving some rural workforces unemployed. Yet the very success of industrialization meant that factory owners had to compete with one another for labor, as industries multiplied and businesses crowded the marketplace. Farsighted factory owners, moreover, realized that contented workers were the most productive.

Some entrepreneurs were genuinely motivated by vision or vocation, by religion and charitable sentiments. The British writer Samuel Smiles spoke of the spirit of industry as "the gospel of work." Henry J. Heinz (1844–1919) of Pittsburgh epitomized that spirit. His example can stand for hundreds. His pious Lutheran family had migrated to Pennsylvania from Germany, and his early ambition was to be a minister. Biblical quotations filled the notebooks in which, in his teens, he began to collect recipes for pickles and catsup. When he made a fortune from his canned and bottled food business, Heinz chose a famous slogan: "57 Varieties," not because there were really 57 of them—there were soon many more—but because the number came to him during a vision while he was riding an elevated railway in New York City. The vast factory he built in Pittsburgh resembled a church, with huge arches and stained-glass windows. In its workers' refectory, organ music entertained the diners. Heinz treated his employees as members of a religious congregation. They were expected to work hard. In 1888, entry-level employees got five cents an hour for a 10.5-hour day—lower wages than many other local employers paid.

Fantasy castle. Barcelona's factories made perhaps the most extravagant ensemble anywhere of "palaces of progress." The Casarramona factory was designed in 1910 by Josep Puig i Cadafalch, a figure of heroic stature in antiquarian scholarship, art patronage, and Catalan politics, as well as an architect of high repute and enormous influence. He experimented with a variety of medieval sources of inspiration and made this textile factory into a Moorish fantasy castle, with minaret-like towers.

But Heinz provided generous benefits, calculated to promote the common good of everyone in the firm. His workers, for instance, got free uniforms, medical and dental treatment, and, if they handled food, a daily manicure. There were dressing rooms with hot showers, a gymnasium, a roof garden, and a reading room. The firm organized employees' recreation. Heinz had carriages to take workers for rides in the park and hired trains for outings to local beauty spots. He provided lectures, concerts, and free courses in dressmaking, hatmaking, cooking, drawing, singing, and citizenship. There were four dances a year, at which, a worker recalled, "Mr. Heinz stayed on the balcony, waving down at us," and a Christmas party, where Heinz welcomed Santa Claus. Critics branded this style of management as paternalist and self-serving, but Heinz's methods had a strong and, in their own way, a genuinely benevolent message: capital and labor were not inevitable enemies but natural allies. Management—not exploitation and profiteering—was the key to success. Heinz's good works went beyond the factory walls and the employees' lives. His philosophy stressed the purity of his products. In a period when state controls on hygiene were in their infancy, and mass-produced food was often watered down or even polluted, Heinz delivered nutritious, safe food, and he made it pay.

Critics of Industrialization: Gold from the Sewers

Philanthropic industrialization was important because it showed that industry did not only benefit people who were already rich. It could spread the benefits of prosperity widely and increase leisure for workers as well as bosses. Its reach, however, was limited. Most bosses did not share Heinz's devotion to good works. And with the rush to industrialize came unplanned evils. Outside the relatively few exemplary factories and model industrial towns, in the streets and slums that the concentration of labor created, the effort to erect a romantic environment for the industrial society was a horrible failure.

Industrialization plunged workers into misery: uprooting lives, disrupting families, imposing bleak new working conditions, throwing up hideous cities rife with filth and disease. Visiting the British city of Manchester in 1835, the French aristocrat Alexis de Tocqueville, who was widely admired as the greatest analyst of the societies of his time, recoiled from the atmosphere of the "palaces" of industry. "These vast structures," he wrote, "keep air and light out of the human habitations which they dominate; they envelop them in perpetual fog; here is the slave, there is the master; there is the wealth of some, here the poverty of most. . . . Here humanity attains its most complete development and its most brutish; here civilization effects its miracles, and civilized man is turned back almost into a savage." He

Cholera epidemic. On the night of March 29, 1832, when a cholera epidemic broke out in Paris, the visiting German poet, Heinrich Heine, reported that "the balls were more crowded than ever…when suddenly the merriest of the harlequins felt a chill in his legs, took off his mask, and…revealed a violet-blue face." Wagon loads of sufferers "were driven directly from the ball" to the main hospital, where the heir to the French throne showed solidarity by visiting the sick and dying.

found "men, women and children yoked together to the machine, which knows no weariness." Yet "from this filthy sewer, pure gold flows." A popular hymn called on Englishmen to build Jerusalem among "England's dark satanic mills." The will to do so was certainly present, but the task was evidently overambitious.

Karl Marx foretold that industrialization would aggravate class warfare. At first, as he contemplated the industrializing world in the 1830s and 1840s, it looked as if he must be right. Industrialization increased the opportunities for people at all levels of society to indulge sociable habits—including, of course, those of riot and rebellion. Employers—despite many glowing examples of good works and kind bosses—commonly set out to exploit their workers to the limit. Workers, Marx thought, must soon discover their power, realize that their labor was the source of society's wealth, and demand their fair share of prosperity. The result would be a bloody revolution, in which the working class would overthrow the bourgeoisie and impose its own dictatorship. "Workers of the world arise," he proclaimed in 1848, "you have nothing to lose but your chains!" Riots, if not rebellions, were commonplace in industrializing cities. Socialists, who demanded that workers should get the full economic benefits of their labor, threatened—and sometimes shattered—civil peace.

Yet, in the world's most industrialized societies, Marx's warnings that impoverishment would drive the workers to revolution went unfulfilled. In part, this was because those warnings were heeded in time. Workers soon had more than chains to lose. Increasingly, they had a genuine stake in the societies of which they formed part. In the second half of the nineteenth century, reformers responded with a new concept: "public health"—sewers and clean water provided by municipal authorities. The rise of town planning was in part the triumph of a romantic sense of the beauty of light and air, but it also showed the power of industrial capitalism to "improve." Light and air contributed to public health. The uniformity of the grid plan for city streets spoke to the depths of an ideal of social equality. Governments stepped up their services to their citizens, especially by regulating health, education, and the food supply.

Meanwhile, moral restraint, Christian good works, and "enlightened self-interest" blunted the fangs of industrial capitalism and helped to ensure, in the long run, that workers benefited from the wealth that industries created. Warned, perhaps, by prophets like Marx and the social movements he helped to inspire, or driven by the energy of the market, employers raised wages and improved working conditions. Cheap food, better pay, and declining disease smothered or at least diminished revolutionary inclinations. Prosperity bought out proletarian rage. As William Cobbett (1763–1835), one of the leading English reformers of the early nineteenth century, observed, "You can't agitate a man on a full stomach."

Businesses and governments were not inspired by pure benevolence. States wanted to be able to recruit large and effective armies. Employers realized that good wages and healthy workforces enhanced production and increased demand for their manufactures. In many countries, churches championed the workers, forestalling revolutionaries' appeal and making revolution unnecessary.

A CLOSER LOOK

Pullman, Illinois

Pullman, Illinois was a town of 12,000 inhabitants at its height in the early 1890s. George Pullman built the town to house workers to produce luxury railway carriages in his enormous factory. His aim was to extract more productivity by providing a morally elevating environment for workers to live in. In practice, however, they resented living in dreary paternalism "under Mr. Pullman's thumb."

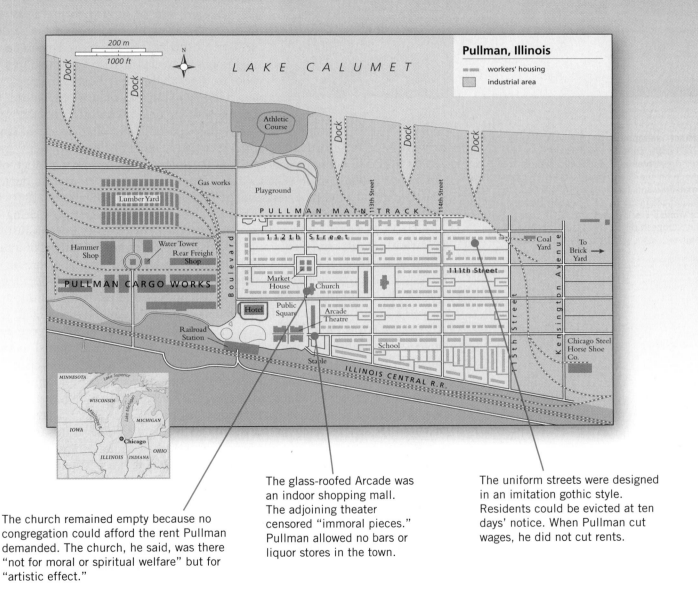

The church remained empty because no congregation could afford the rent Pullman demanded. The church, he said, was there "not for moral or spiritual welfare" but for "artistic effect."

The glass-roofed Arcade was an indoor shopping mall. The adjoining theater censored "immoral pieces." Pullman allowed no bars or liquor stores in the town.

The uniform streets were designed in an imitation gothic style. Residents could be evicted at ten days' notice. When Pullman cut wages, he did not cut rents.

How does the layout of Pullman embody nineteenth-century paternalism?

THE CITY OF CHICAGO.

Instant metropolis. In the second half of the nineteenth century, exploitation of the North American prairie and the development of commerce on the Great Lakes turned Chicago from a small fort and trading post into a vast city. This image was made in 1892, when the city shaped its World's Fair to mark the 400th anniversary of the European discovery of the New World.
Dagli Orti (A)/Picture Desk, Inc./Kobal Collection

The case of the United States is the most remarkable, because Marx expected revolution to start there. Instead, socialists in America were the first to sell out to capitalism. Rather than leading the world into socialism, America led the world in revulsion from it. Industry developed so fast that it soaked up all the new labor that immigration and procreation created, so that the United States rapidly became a high-wage economy. The frontier (see Chapter 23) sucked restless and rebellious individuals westward, out of industrializing areas. Cheap land in the West enabled even poor settlers to achieve prosperity. The American Dream became a nightmare for socialists, diverting the hopes of the poor from revolution to self-enrichment.

Socialists yearned for a better future. Other critics and enemies of industrialization yearned for a lost past. Traditional workers smashed machinery to defend their jobs. In 1811–1813, the British government assigned 12,000 troops to repress machine-wrecking rioters—more soldiers, though of inferior quality, than Britain sent to fight Napoleon in 1808. Romantics deplored a world that the English priest and poet, Gerard Manley Hopkins (1844–1889), described as "seared with trade, bleared, smeared with toil, . . . wearing man's smudge." Some of them tried to escape. Ironically, the escapees from industrialization were often also its beneficiaries. G. Poldi-Pezzoli, one of the fathers of industrial Milan in northern Italy, had a medieval-style room in his house, where he would retreat among his collection of medieval art. In Barcelona, in the last decades of the century, the sublime architect Antoni Gaudí professed to hate the machine age and created fantasy buildings in which captains of industry could feel secluded.

Cragside was the most extravagantly escapist mansion of nineteenth-century England. It was built in remote, rural Northumbria and was designed to embody the doctrines of the artists of the **Arts and Crafts** movement, who championed craftsmanship and opposed industrial uniformity. The owner and builder of the house, however, was William Armstrong (1810–1900), Britain's biggest arms manufacturer. Cragside was also the first house in England to be lit by electric light. The machine age enabled the rich to live out their romantic fantasies in comfort.

When factory workers got home, however, they would often find the misery that Philip Kay, a doctor who treated cotton workers, described in Manchester in 1832: "loathsome wretchedness" in houses "dilapidated, badly drained, damp." Or the worker might be confined to one of the cellar dwellings swilling with filth from the street and sopping with wetness from underground. Disease got trapped in the bad ventilation.

Reformers stressed the effects of an industrial environment on workers' morale. Jaume Balmes, the great ethical critic of Barcelona's industrialization, thought the workers were worse off than ancient slaves, who had at least some protection from the economic ups and downs that could turn poverty into destitution overnight. Moral criticism, of course, tended to reflect the values of the critics, and workers did not necessarily share it. Philip Kay watched the tenants of vile housing "denying themselves the comforts of life in order that they might wallow in the unrestrained license of animal appetite." For workers, the vices he had in mind were rational survival strategies. Gambling was a form of investment for people with too little spare cash to save. Alcohol was a lubricant for lives stuck in drudgery.

One of the most effective criticisms of urban over-crowding was—in the words of a London physician in 1858—that "it almost necessarily involves such negation of all delicacy, such unclean confusion of bodies and bodily functions, such mutual exposure of animal and sexual nakedness, as is rather bestial than human." Karl Marx, the middle-class theorist of communism, who slept with his maid, claimed that ruthless bosses sexually abused their workers. Popular songs—the genuine utterances of the working classes—tended to mock middle-class prudery and praise pleasures that moralists attacked, including drink, gambling, idleness, and promiscuous sex.

Bosses—according to critics of industrialization—were in moral danger, too. A Barcelona newspaper urged workers to see their masters as divine instruments for the workers' own welfare. It warned owners that "the mechanics in your factories are made of the same clay of which you are formed . . . and must not be confused with the machines you have in your workshops." This mixture of conscience tempered by common sense was typical of the Catholic response to industrialization in countries where the church molded the moral consensus. Archbishop Affré of Paris died at the barricades that workers erected in the revolution of 1848. Pope Leo XIII (r. 1878–1903) acknowledged the need to bring Catholic social teaching up to date if only to save workers from seduction by socialism. He would not undermine a social hierarchy in which the church had a strong vested interest, but he did authorize trades unions and encouraged Catholics to found their own. He could not denounce property—the church had too much of it for that—but he could remind socialists that Christians, too, were called to social responsibility. He could not endorse socialism, but he did condemn naked individualism.

Cragside. The study is the most modest room at Cragside, the gigantic baronial-style mansion built in the romantic countryside in northern England for William Armstrong (1810–1900). Armstrong made a fortune by inventing and manufacturing, among many other things, the Armstrong gun, one of the first modern forms of artillery. The house is full of gadgets—including the earliest electric lighting in any private house in Britain—although the architect, C. Norman Shaw, belonged to the Arts and Crafts movement, which favored old-fashioned artisanship.

URBANIZATION

Nineteenth-century urbanization was on a scale the world had never known. There had been gigantic concentrations of people before, especially in China, but never had so much population, in so many places, been gathered together in big cities.

In the industrializing world, this was hardly surprising. Some factories remained relatively isolated or attached to small towns. Overwhelmingly, however, economic considerations drove industry into cities, and people settled where the factories were. Owners needed to concentrate labor and communications and realized that they could make "economies of scale," saving on costs by making big investments and getting disproportionately big returns. As steam power and improved transport came on line, production could move nearer to convenient markets, making cities even bigger. As the scale and number of factories grew in any one place, so did the size of local markets, leading yet more businesses, especially those supplying food, to gather in the same places. The result was a new way to organize life around specialized production processes. The dynamics of locating production in factories turned former villages, such as Manchester and Birmingham in Britain and Essen in the German Rhineland, into great cities.

In most of the places it affected, industrialization created, at first, flimsy, ill-built cities: fearsome breeders of disease and disorder. Manchester in the 1830s and 1840s and Barcelona in the 1850s and 1860s are the best-known examples, because

Most Populous Cities in 1900	
Name	Population
1 London, United Kingdom	6,480,000
2 New York, United States	3,437,000
3 Paris, France	3,330,000
4 Berlin, Germany	2,707,000
5 Chicago, United States	1,717,000
6 Vienna, Austria	1,698,000
7 Tokyo, Japan	1,497,000
8 St. Petersburg, Russia	1,439,000
9 Manchester, United Kingdom	1,435,000
10 Philadelphia, United States	1,418,000

United Nations; United States Census Bureau

Shantytown. Construction workers in a shanty-town outside Berlin, depicted by Kurt Ekwall in 1872. Begging children implore a prosperous couple, who have come to "do good" among the poor and hungry.

Izmir on the Mediterranean coast of Anatolia was one of the busiest ports in the Ottoman Empire in the eighteenth and nineteenth centuries. By 1829, when this view was painted, it was handling more than half the empire's exports. Izmir was also the port of entry for most of the foreign textiles, brought principally by French shippers, that the empire imported.
Photograph courtesy of the Peabody Essex Museum

of the many philanthropic reformers, inquiries, and reports that exposed the horrors of the conditions in which workers lived. In the 1840s, works such as Edwin Chadwick's *Sanitary Conditions of the Labouring Population* in Manchester, or Jaume Salarich's survey of working-class health in Barcelona in the 1850s, clinically described the effects of breathing in the atmosphere of the textile mills: profuse sweat, exhaustion, gastric trouble, difficult breathing, poor circulation, mental weariness, nervous prostration, corrosion of the lungs, poisoning from machine oils and dyes. Slums clung to city centers. Shanties spread around city edges. Kurt Ekwall painted Berlin's shantytown in 1872, complete with a visiting middle-class family doling out pennies to ragged children.

Food is an even more basic index of the standard of living than hygiene and housing. Even in this connection, it took a long time for urbanization to deliver benefits, because growing towns make fresh foods relatively expensive and hard to obtain. As late as 1899, R. Seebohm Rowntree conducted pioneering investigations into the working class of the city of York in northern England. He found most families were inadequately fed for the work they had to do, and many were actually sick for want of food. The normal diet of working families was monotonous, with only occasional treats of meat and fish. Unlike their rural counterparts, they could not normally grow vegetables or keep a pig. Workers saved by living almost entirely on oatmeal and water.

It was not only the industrialized world that experienced the madcap growth of cities. It also happened in parts of the world that played only a minor or marginal role in industrialization. Mining, for instance, was a way to produce raw materials that could create mushroom-growth towns, such as San Francisco in California and Kimberley and Johannesburg in South Africa. In 1871, diamonds were found on a farm at Kimberley. By the end of the century, 100,000 miners worked there. Gold turned Melbourne, on Australia's farthest Pacific edge, from a rudimentary settler village in 1837, the year Queen Victoria came to the throne, into the third largest city in the British Empire, with over 800,000 people, by the time she died in 1901. Growth during Melbourne's mining boom years from the 1850s surpassed "all human experience" in the opinion of a citizen astonished by the crowded wharves, the "scream of the engines, the hubbub of the streets" and the "swarming masses."

Global trade, meanwhile, stimulated port cities all over the world. The most conspicuous examples were in regions where industrialization was taking off. New York, for instance, experienced enormous growth—from 60,000 inhabitants at the beginning of the nineteenth century to nearly 3.5 million by 1900. But outside the industrializing world, ports from which primary produce was shipped overseas could experience, in proportion, much the same growth. Alexandria on Egypt's Mediterranean coast had only a few thousand people at the start of the nineteenth century, but it had grown to about 250,000 by the century's end because it was a transitional port for Egyptian cotton. Lagos on the Nigerian coast boomed in the late nineteenth century because of palm oil and cocoa. Buenos Aires in Argentina grew rapidly thanks to the refrigerated meat trade. Calcutta (known today as Kolkata) in India, which was a small settlement when the nineteenth century began, started the twentieth century with more than 750,000 people, because of its role in exporting the dyes and coarse fibers of Bengal. In the 1850s, Shanghai became the port of choice for European merchants operating in China. It soon replaced Guangzhou as the great trading metropolis of China. Thanks in great part to its role in exporting opium, the population of Izmir on the Mediterranean coast of Turkey grew at a rate of 2 percent a year from the 1840s, to house more than 200,000 people by the 1880s.

Izmir dramatically illustrates another feature of the new cities of the nineteenth century. It had French-built boulevards and British gas lighting. There were 5 newspapers, 17 printing houses, a public library that filled 10 houses, and one of the first theaters in the Ottoman Empire. This demonstrates how a new kind of cultural life became possible. Cities now were different from those of earlier times—fearsome, heavily policed, filled with rootless populations, and stalked by new diseases. But they gradually acquired new benefits: the facilities for recreation, education, and welfare that are only possible where many people congregate and large resources concentrate.

Towns were remodeled or enlarged on new principles of urban planning. Paris and Vienna acquired the boulevards familiar today. Vast grids of rationally planned streets were added to Madrid and Manhattan. In Cairo and Alexandria, spectacular new quarters enveloped the chaotic old cities in networks of straight streets (see Map 24.1). Opera houses arose in places as surprisingly remote as Cairo and Manaus, the center of the rubber-producing region in the Amazon jungles of Brazil. City walls fell because modern artillery had made them obsolete. New roads, sewerage, water-supply systems, public baths, large stores, street lighting, cafes and clubs, sporting facilities, and such urban means of transport as trolleys and buses multiplied. New kinds of public spaces arose on cast-iron arches: snaking bridges and so-called crystal palaces—glass-covered markets, railway stations, greenhouses, shopping arcades. London's Crystal Palace, scene of the first great Universal Exposition of 1851—set the trend and housed, appropriately, a display of the industrial arts of the world. Madrid's main market was the most innovative example, built in 1870 and designed by an amateur (for it was beyond the imagination of most professional architects) to enclose more than 100 acres in a pyramid of glass.

New urban spaces permitted new kinds of social activity. Mass education was a remarkable development. In some places investment by the state spurred education, partly because states wanted boys to be trained for soldiering. In 1890, 70 percent of boys—and 35 percent of girls—went to school in Japan. Compulsory universal education, introduced in many European countries and the United States during the nineteenth century, was in one respect the most remarkable development of all, for it defied two cherished beliefs of the time: the doctrines of parental responsibility for children and individual freedom.

BEYOND INDUSTRY: AGRICULTURE AND MINING

The new trends rightly capture our attention, but even the spread of industry and the growth of towns left most individual lives in the nineteenth century unaffected. Urbanization seemed to skip huge areas of the globe, which remained largely a world of peasants even in the West. In those parts of Asia and Africa that fell under colonial rule, many of which like British India and French Indochina had long and ample

MAP 24.1

Cairo, ca. 1900

☐ old city
☐ expansion, 1869–1900
═ new streets and neighborhoods after 1869
╌╌ railways

Opera in the jungle. The nineteenth-century rubber boom turned Manaus, in the Brazilian rain forest, into a grand, rich city, with this enormous opera house that attracted famous singers and musicians from Europe. But Manaus was ruined toward the end of the century, when rubber production shifted to the British colonies in Malaya.

Making Connections | INDUSTRIAL TRANSFORMATIONS IN THE NINETEENTH CENTURY

ECONOMIC/POLITICAL TRANFORMATIONS	SOCIAL CHANGES	CHANGES IN DAILY LIFE
Development of industrial/factory-based employment	Urbanization, increased population density; increased labor specialization, formal division of work and leisure time	Work moves from country to city, outdoors to indoors; from homes and small workshops to factories and mines; large, impersonal work environments, bleak working conditions
Salary-based labor system	Shift from proprietorship to large-scale enterprises where power is concentrated in small number of factory, mine owners	Plentiful workers relatively powerless to negotiate unless organized; strict organization of daily routines
Urbanization and mixture of factory–residential districts	Proximity of work offset by increase in air and water pollution; grimy surroundings, lack of public sanitation in high-density cities	Increased exposure to epidemics of cholera, dysentery, and chronic diseases such as tuberculosis
Increased power of municipal, national governments to regulate economic and social conditions	Development of idea of "public health" to fight disease, child mortality rates, epidemics	Increased town planning, public sanitation lead to longer life spans, better urban conditions
Growth of global trade	Increased movement of goods and traders in ports all over the world; creation of wealth	Foreign goods, luxury items, and technological innovations spread rapidly in industrialized countries

Industry joins agriculture: The McCormick Company of Chicago helped transform the prairie in the late nineteenth century by supplying a mechanical reaper to make up for the shortage of farm labor. The spider's web shown here on a hand-held sickle symbolizes the demise of old methods.

urban traditions, the proportion of town dwellers in the population hardly grew. The rise of urban workplaces was just one of many contexts in which the role and nature of labor changed. Even in Europe, most people still lived and worked on the land in the nineteenth century.

Nonetheless, unindustrialized and deindustrialized regions lived in the shadow of industrialization and were affected by its demands and subjected to similar pressures for social change. Even in the country, the context of work in ever larger fields, employing ever less labor, bred different feelings and ways of life from traditional agriculture, with its communal habits, companionship, and shared rituals that marked the passage of the seasons or the festivals of local saints and gods.

The big areas of growth in agriculture were of two kinds. On one hand, prosperous, independent farmers and ranchers in the American Midwest, Australia, and Argentina could produce meat and grain with methods that involved relatively little labor. Advertisements for the harvesting machines that the McCormick Company of Chicago made in the midcentury illustrated the point vividly. Two horses and one man were all that were needed—the poster seemed to say—for vast fields that stretched toward distant mountains. The company produced 1,500 reapers a year in the 1850s—and nearly 15,000 in the 1870s. Ranching remained unmechanized but required only a small and specialized workforce—cowboys or, in Argentina and Uruguay, *gauchos*, who tended to be freelancers, cultivating and celebrating their personal independence.

On the other hand, farmed products, such as palm oil and cocoa from West Africa, cotton from Egypt and India, and opium from India and Turkey were labor intensive. To satisfy the market, peasants had to be mobilized—induced or compelled—into growing these crops, along with other lesser but still important items of growing demand, such as rubber, coffee, and easily transportable foodstuffs like bananas and citrus.

The pressures or promise of the market made peasants switch from subsistence agriculture or farming only to supply local outlets to export crops. *Max Havelaar* is the best-known Dutch novel—indeed, it is virtually the only Dutch novel widely known outside the Netherlands. It is a fearless condemnation of colonialism and, in particular, of the system by which the Dutch, in collaboration with native elites, forced peasants in the Dutch East Indies to grow coffee, because it was a cash crop, whether their land was suitable for it or not. In the late nineteenth century, the Dutch forced about half the population of Java to take part in this system. Elsewhere in the Dutch East Indies in the 1870s, people seem to have had more children to meet the colonial government's demands for forced labor. In Egypt, too, world demand for primary materials forced peasants to grow a product—cotton—they could not eat and could sell only at prices they could not influence. Peasant landholdings tended to split under the strain. By 1900, Egypt had some 2 million landless peasants, who were subject to forced labor in the irrigation works and conscription into the army.

So agriculture, like industry, became increasingly a specialized activity, with particular crops concentrated in favored regions and large domains. Revolutions in tenure arose as the brokers or middlemen who sold peasants' crops to merchants began to invest in land themselves, using their control of credit to obtain holdings cheaply.

The Ottoman Empire, for instance, became a net exporter of crops for the first time in history, thanks to the grapes and opium of western Anatolia, where exports increased by more than 500 percent between 1845 and 1876. Private owners took over state landholdings, while much land passed from the hands of peasants into those of tribal or local chiefs, city merchants, moneylenders, and officials. Sixty percent of the soil of Ottoman Syria—once a peasant land—was officially reclassified as large estates in the early twentieth century. The estate owners included some local families, but many were outsiders—especially Armenians, Greeks, and Jews.

In West Africa, palm-oil production, formerly the work of gatherers of wild plants, became, from the 1840s, a focus of increasingly systematic farming. Harvesting palm fruits, pounding the nuts to extract the oil, and getting the product to market demanded plenty of labor. Typically, a group of independent farmers would combine under an elected leader. In some areas, especially in what is now Nigeria, families could operate small, independent palm-oil farms. Alternatively—and more insistently as time went on—merchants would grab land and start slave-operated plantations. Much of the profit went into private armies, maintained to fight for power or to seize more slaves. Labor was wrenched out of food production to keep the oil flowing. Transporting and marketing the oil enriched a growing commercial class.

In southern Bengal, indigo planting was the big new opportunity. But it required capital investment, which forced peasants to borrow. Getting a loan— said a magistrate in 1830—was a "misfortune" that reduced the borrower to "little better than a bond slave to the factory." In the second half of the century, jute—a cheap fiber good for making rope and bags—became dominant. Small cultivators could grow jute economically with little capital on plots of an acre or two. Peasants abandoned rice to grow it. But reliance on a single exportable crop left producers at the mercy of the market and led to high levels of debt, incurred

Coffee plantation in Java. The coffee plantation owned by the Dutch conglomerate, Insinger, on the island of Java in the Dutch East Indies, c. 1920. The Dutch introduced coffee to Java early in the eighteenth century. Huge growth in global demand induced the Dutch to encourage and, increasingly, to enforce production, even in areas where coffee was hard to grow, turning Java into the world's leading coffee producer by the mid-nineteenth century. Most coffee grown on Java came from inferior *coffea robusta* plants, like those in the photograph.

The face of Africa, scarred and pitted by colonial exploitation: open-cast diamond mining in the "blue earth" at Kimberley, South Africa in 1872. At that early stage—not much more than a year after the first diamond was discovered on the De Beers's farm—the diggings were checkered with the square plots of individual prospectors. The inability to dig deep enough to find diamonds on small plots led to the consolidation of these shallow digs into bigger holdings and to the formation of the De Beers Mining Company in 1874. By 1914, the Kimberley pit had become the largest man-made crater ever dug.

Chronology: Industrialization, Mechanization, and Urbanization

Nineteenth century	Factories in the United States and Western Europe reorganize work and reorder workers' lives
1811–1813	British use 12,000 troops to repress machine-wrecking rioters
1842	Poor living conditions in Manchester detailed in Edwin Chadwick's *The Sanitary Condition of the Labouring Population*
1844–1919	Henry J. Heinz, industrialist and proponent of paternalist management
1845–1876	Ottoman agricultural exports increase fivefold
1848	Publication of Marx's and Engels's *The Communist Manifesto*
1851	London's Universal Exposition held at Crystal Palace
1867	Publication of Marx's *Capital*
1870	New central market built in Madrid
ca. 1875	McCormick Company of Chicago produces 15,000 reapers per year
r. 1878–1903	Pope Leo XIII, advocate of social reform
Late nineteenth century	Arts and Crafts movement
ca. 1900	Cotton cultivation in Egypt contributes to the creation of 2 million landless peasants
	Urban populations: Izmir, 200,000; Alexandria, 250,000; Calcutta, more than 750,000; Melbourne, 800,000; New York, 3.4 million, London, 6.5 million

to tide them over hard times or meet high rents. The peasant class survived, but the rising standards of commercial and industrial activity elsewhere in the world left them impoverished. A poet of the early twentieth century summed up the effects:

> The Westerners came and took control.
> Now look how much money they have made.
> They can now be disdainful of the Bengalis . . .
> Look, the Bengali race is ruined.

The **caste system** gripped India more tightly than ever, as the British imposed burdens and forms of discrimination that were supposedly traditional because they were enshrined in ancient texts, but that people had not formerly practiced much. In southern India, especially, British policy favored the concentration of the best agricultural land in the hands of a few dominant families, reducing many peasants to abject poverty and to social and economic dependency.

In some places, where Western immigrants themselves took to the land, they could also end up joining the ranks of the losers in the global marketplace. In the mid-nineteenth century, the Portuguese government began settling poor white farmers in Angola, in southwest Africa, as a way to extend and perpetuate Portuguese control of the native Africans. Most of these settlers never made a success of their ventures, renouncing the opportunities to grow export crops, turning instead to subsistence farming to feed their own families, living in hovels, and dressing in rags. The plight of black peasants in Angola was even worse. Before the 1870s, having their land seized and being enslaved were their usual fate. Late in that decade, when Portugal officially abolished slavery, their status hardly improved in practice. Not until the early twentieth century did the authorities make serious or sustained efforts to stop the illegal export of slaves.

The erosion of independence and of local prosperity was a common—but not universal—consequence of the specializations the global market encouraged. In the second half of the century, Thailand, formerly a self-sufficient country, began to specialize in a few exportable commodities: rice—which accounted, on average, for 60 to 70 percent of total exports—tin, and teak. The emphasis on rice ensured that some traditional ways of life continued. The Thai stayed on the land, increasing output almost entirely by extending the amount of land under cultivation. They resisted the lure of high wages or returns from activities outside agriculture and left commerce to Chinese immigrants. The amount of capital investment required for growing rice was modest, and, among foreigners, Chinese supplied most of it. Thailand therefore never succumbed to foreign "business imperialism" (see Chapter 25). Relative to

MAP 24.2

Major Mineral Finds of the Late Nineteenth Century

	cobalt
	copper
	diamonds
▼	iron ore
	gold
	manganese
	silver
	tin

other staple foods, rice earned good profits for the people who grew it. Only about 50 percent of the export price went to the middleman, miller, and shipper.

As well as the fruits of increasingly specialized agriculture, the unindustrialized world also supplied the industrializing world with raw minerals in ever larger quantities (see Map 24.2). Where mines were located, the impact was often intense. The Kimberley diamond mines in South Africa were a good example. "Every foot of the blue ground," said Cecil Rhodes (1853–1902), one of the big early investors in the enterprise and a champion of the British Empire in Africa, "means so much power." Mines meant power to their owners. To workers, they signified the destruction of traditional life. As soon as diamonds were discovered, black African workers wrenched from agrarian and pastoral communities poured in, struggling to re-create the layouts and routines of their characteristic home villages in the squalid, lawless vicinity of the mines. Black mine workers were forbidden to acquire licenses to establish their own diggings. Though nominally not slaves, they could be fined or flogged for desertion of employment, and their wages were never more than a fifth of what white miners earned for similar work.

Although miners in Europe and North America were better treated, it was not necessary to go far beyond the frontiers of the industrializing world to see mines wreak comparable havoc. The Río Tinto copper mines in Spain recruited thousands of workers from all over Iberia in the 1870s and 1880s. The company aimed to practice the sort of productive benevolence associated with the best factories at the time. But decent housing and modest health care and schooling did little to ease the feelings of alienation understandable in uprooted communities, or the impatience workers felt at the company's paternalism. Living conditions were always overcrowded, because the building program could not keep up with the demand for labor. The environment was literally poisonous, as sulfurous fumes hung over the area whenever the wind fell. Most of the British staff—the management and most of the top technicians were Britons—were housed apart in what would now be called a gated community, where ordinary workers and local people were forbidden to enter.

CHANGING LABOR REGIMES

The virtual disappearance of slavery—and the total disappearance of plantation slavery in the Americas—was perhaps the most surprising episode of the nineteenth century. Almost every preindustrial society we know about has considered slavery a normal and legitimate relationship—a suitable status for supposedly inferior people, for captives, or for those unable to survive except as a master's chattel. Nineteenth-century Western science produced new justifications for slavery, stronger than any previously advanced: certain races were inescapably inferior to others. Black people were, according to schemes of classification that some anthropologists proposed, more like apes than Europeans.

Slavery and the Slave Trade

On the other hand, slavery repelled believers in three doctrines of growing appeal in the world, and especially in parts of the West: evangelical Christianity, egalitarianism, and economic liberalism. According to evangelical Christians, Jesus' message of universal love outlawed slavery. According to egalitarians, all people were equal, and it was nonsense for anyone to be born into slavery. For economic liberals, and especially for those who believed in free trade, slavery was irrational, because people worked better when they did so freely and for wages.

Impeccable in theory, the free-trade doctrine did not seem to be borne out in reality. On the contrary, the world economy relied, as it had relied for centuries, on compulsion to work. In much of Africa, according to early nineteenth-century observers, slaves were both a vital labor force and a major export product. In the tropical and subtropical latitudes of the Atlantic-side New World, slavery was the only labor force available. It was not only the plantation economies of the Americas that depended on slavery. The trade in slaves sustained shipping in Europe and America and many states in Africa. In Liverpool, Britain's leading port, a quarter of the ships were engaged in the slave trade in 1800. Without slavery, cotton textile manufacture in Europe, the rum industry of New England, and the arms trade to Africa would all be jeopardized. In the long run, mechanization might make slavery out of date. But no one could foresee this in the early nineteenth century. On the contrary, the kind of plantation environment in which slavery was entrenched seemed unsuitable for mechanization. In any case, in slave-owning societies, slavery was part of culture and tradition. People practiced it not because it was profitable but because it was part of the fabric of life. So it was not just economics that eliminated slavery. The rise of a new morality changed cultural assumptions. Reformers dismantled the system despite the dictates of tradition, ideology, economics, and what passed for science.

Reformers started with the slave trade. This was an easier target than slavery, because it did not involve problems of how to compensate slave owners or dispose of liberated slaves. In the 1790s, in Europe and America, a tremendous wave of sentiment against the trade broke against the fears and obstacles that vested interests raised. But in 1803, Denmark outlawed the trade. Britain and the United States followed within less than a decade. The abolition of the slave trade became a sort of British national crusade, in which the navies of other European

Anti-slavery Society. Thomas Clarkson, veteran campaigner against slavery, was 80 years old, "grey and bent . . . feeble and tottering" and weak-voiced when he addressed the international Anti-slavery Society Convention in London in 1840. But here the painter, Benjamin Haydon, presents a rejuvenated and vigorous Clarkson. Though several women were allowed to attend the meeting, they were not permitted to speak on the grounds that such exhibitionism would be unseemly for ladies.

and American countries joined. The crusade transferred to the African mainland. Indeed, it became a way to justify British imperialism and inspired destructive wars in which thousands of native slave traders and their families, who thought they were simply engaged in a traditional and lawful activity, died. Meanwhile, Britain paid rulers in parts of Africa and the Indian Ocean to stop dealing in slaves.

Reformers expected the abolition of the slave trade to lead to the disappearance of slavery. Demographic trends suggested this possibility. As we have seen, plantation slave populations in the eighteenth century normally had high death rates and low birth rates (see Chapter 20). But abolition had two unforeseen effects that combined to frustrate the abolitionists' predictions.

First, abolition made slaves more expensive and therefore gave new life to the slave trade. The total number of slaves shipped across the Atlantic from Africa to the Americas in the nineteenth century was about 3.3 million. Slavers made great fortunes, charging premiums for the risks they faced in running the gauntlet of the British navy's patrols. By the 1830s, Pedro Blanco of Cadiz in Spain became known as the "Rothschild of slavery"—an allusion to the world's richest banking family at the time. Blanco reckoned that if he could save one vessel in three from capture he could make a profit. At his slaveholding camp on a group of islands in the mouth of the Gallinas River in West Africa, he could keep 5,000 slaves at a time, guarded by lookout posts 100 feet high equipped with telescopes to warn of approaching British patrols. He permanently employed a lawyer, 5 accountants, 2 cashiers, 10 copyists, and a harem of 50 beautiful African slave girls.

Second, abolition of the slave trade made slave owners more careful of their slaves. As a result, in some areas formerly destructive of the fertility of slave women, such as the Caribbean islands, the number of slaves began to grow, or at least to stay steady, through natural reproduction. When Spain joined the movement to end the slave trade in 1818, its government allowed owners a period of grace during which they could import slave women of fertile years, so that "by propagating the species, the abolition of the commerce in slaves should be less noticeable in future." Meanwhile, in the southern United States, the number of slaves multiplied from under 1 million at the start of the century to almost 4 million by 1860. The upward trend was unstoppable. Even when federal law banned the trade in 1809, world demand for cotton continued to drive the rise of slavery in the South.

Slaves played surprisingly little part in their own liberation. Though rebellions were frequent—and frequently bloody—most plantation societies learned to live with them, absorbing the costs of suppression or confining the runaways to roles that were troublesome rather than fatal to planter control. The big exception was Haiti, the French colony called Saint-Domingue where rebellious slaves seized power in the 1790s. The French Revolution, igniting expectations about "the rights of man" (see Chapter 22), provided Haitian slaves with a basic ideology of liberation. Yet controversy in Haiti early in the Revolution focused not on whether slavery was right or wrong but on whether free black and mixed-race people should have the right to vote. The slave revolt that began in 1791 seems to have started outside enlightened and revolutionary circles—with rumors that the king of France had freed the slaves, with voodoo ceremonies, and with a slave leadership barely connected with free black people, some of whom rebelled against white rule at the same time (see Map 24.3).

In late 1792, a new phase began when Léger-Félicité Southonax arrived as the representative of the French Republic with orders to pacify the colony. The following year, impelled in part by revolutionary fervor and in part by concern at the

> *"So it was not just economics that eliminated slavery. The rise of a new morality changed cultural assumptions. Reformers dismantled the system despite the dictates of tradition, ideology, economics, and what passed for science."*

MAP 24.3

The Haitian Revolution

······ 1790: border

······ 1820: border between Haiti and Santo Domingo

worsening security situation, with the British poised to invade, he freed the slaves of the northern province—creating at a stroke, he said, "200,000 new soldiers for the republic." He befriended and promoted the most talented officer among the freed slaves, Toussaint L'Ouverture (1746–1803), who, in effect, seized power in 1797. A visiting Englishman admired the "perfect system of equality" he observed under the new regime, with black and white people of different social ranks eating together.

After the French captured L'Ouverture in 1802, Haitian resistance became desperate, and the rule of former slaves much harsher. In 1804, L'Ouverture's successor as leader of the revolt, Jean-Jacques Dessalines, proclaimed "Independence or Death." In a remarkable reversal of the white man's usual rhetoric, he denounced the French as barbarians:

> What have we in common with that bloody-minded people? Their cruelties compared to our moderation—their color to ours—the extension of seas that separate us—our avenging climate—all plainly tell us they are not our brethren.... Let them shudder... at the terrible resolution we are going to make—to do to death any native of France who shall defile, with his sacrilegious footstep, this land of liberty.

The Haitians officially won their liberty in 1825 at the cost of agreeing to pay a crippling indemnity to compensate French property owners. But by excluding white colonists, the Haitians deprived their country of much-needed capital investment and technical expertise. They also sent tremors of fear through the planter societies of other parts of the Americas. In 1823, Thomas Clarkson, who was the British representative of the Haitian state, came close to threatening planters elsewhere with the same fate those in Haiti had suffered.

Even without the Haitian example, emancipation of slaves was likely to follow the abolition of the slave trade. Otherwise, the work of the abolitionists would have been largely fruitless. In the 1820s and 1830s, some Spanish American republics led the way, not because they were peculiarly virtuous, but because slavery played a relatively small part in their economies. Paraguay, where most of the slaves were Native Americans, was exceptional in delaying emancipation until 1869. Although slavery had been unlawful in England itself since the 1770s, the British Empire as a whole did not ban it until 1834. It took the Civil War (1861–1865) to free the slaves of the Southern United States—and even then the federal government's Emancipation Proclamation in 1863 was more a practical response to war conditions than an act of morality. After various false starts, Spain freed its slaves—but not those of its colonies—in 1823. France decreed emancipation in 1848, and the Netherlands in 1863. The Spanish colony of Cuba held out until 1886 and the Empire of Brazil until 1888.

Slavery survived longer in Africa and what we think of as the Middle East, but thanks in part to British insistence, its scope gradually diminished, as did the numbers of slaves. Persia signed an antislave trade treaty with Britain in 1882 but never enforced its terms. Egypt made slavery illegal in 1885. Formal laws against the slave trade were proclaimed in the Ottoman Empire in 1889 and in Zanzibar in 1897—which, as part of an Omani trading empire that had ousted the Portuguese from much of East Africa (see Chapter 21), thrived as a slave-trading center. In practice, state bans were hard to enforce in Islamic society, where religious law licensed slavery and where many Islamic authorities regarded antislavery legislation as contrary to Islam (just as many Christian planters cited the Bible to justify their support for slavery). There were still, by the most widely accepted estimate, 100,000 black slaves in the Sahel in sub-Saharan Africa at the end of the nineteenth century.

Slavery was not the only form of forced labor to dwindle in the nineteenth century. There was also serfdom in which peasants were tied to the land they worked and could be sold along with, but not apart from, it. When the century began, the

Tippu Tip, "the biggest slaver of them all," whose activities on behalf of Sultan Barghash of Zanzibar (see Chapter 25) almost succeeded in preempting European imperialism, before he became a collaborator in the empire-building efforts of King Leopold II of the Belgians. In the opinion of Jerome Becker, one of Leopold's agents in the Congo in the 1880s, "From his [Tippu's] immense plantations, cultivated by thousands of slaves, all blindly devoted to their master, and from his ivory trade, of which he has the monopoly, he has in his duplex character of conqueror and trader, succeeded in creating for himself in the heart of Africa a veritable empire."

hereditary rule of lords limited the freedom of the peasant serfs of Eastern Europe to move, trade, and marry. The wars that arose early in the century in the aftermath of the French Revolution shifted the frontiers of serfdom eastward, forcing the emancipation of the peasants of Prussia in central and eastern Germany. In the Habsburg Empire, serfdom vanished bit by bit—often at the insistence of lords who thought free peasants would be more economically efficient. After peasant revolts, the Habsburg monarchy finally granted all former serfs freedom and land in 1853–1854. The Habsburg government made this concession to win peasant loyalty and free up labor for railway construction. In Thailand, almost the entire male population was bound by forced labor laws, which the Thai government abolished bit by bit throughout the century.

Even Russia, where most people were still serfs, joined the trend. In 1847, an influential German travel writer, Baron von Haxthausen, claimed that Russian society would never come to resemble that of the rest of Europe. Some Russians were proud of their country's distinctive reputation and wanted to keep it as different as possible. The ruling elite, however, found it embarrassing that Western Europe considered Russia backward. They postponed the liberation of the peasants only because of prudent fear of unforeseen consequences. However, increasing peasant violence in the 1840s, and, in 1855, the shock of defeat in the Crimean War by Turkey, France, and Britain helped to concentrate minds in favor of reform. The Czar proclaimed emancipation of the serfs in 1861. In the background, Russia felt the irresistible pressure of a European model of economic change: recognition that Russia had to enter the railway age and that the empire had to reorganize its manpower for industrialization.

In Japan, meanwhile, peasants became participants in an enlarged marketplace as communications improved, and cities grew and multiplied. Individual farms tended to replace the traditional village collectives in which all the village families had worked the land in common and shared the harvests. There were crosscurrents. New regulations favored landowners, especially by limiting traditional tenants' rights in common land. But the peasants' lot generally improved. In 1868, the government promised, "the common people, no less than the civil and military officials, shall be allowed to pursue their own individual callings so that there may be no discontent." In the 1870s, government decree freed the dependent peasants and workers of Japan. In 1877, when disaffected samurai attempted a rebellion of the type Oshio Heicharo had tried to launch in 1837, the peasants were on the other side, drafted into the government's army, armed with guns, and drilled in obedience.

In some parts of the world, convicts became a substitute for slave labor. "Hard labor" became a way to exploit criminals' potential for work and to exact retribution from them on behalf of society. In Japan, criminals worked in the notorious Ashio copper mine (see Chapter 23). Governments in Europe deported convicts in the hundreds of thousands—often for minor crimes—to remote, previously uncultivated lands. Australia alone, for instance, absorbed over 150,000 convicts from Britain between 1788 and 1868. Some Pacific Islands, Siberia, former slaveholding states in the United States after the Civil War, and French Guiana in northeast South America relied on convict labor to sustain their economies.

Chronology: Slavery in the Nineteenth Century	
1790s	Abolitionist sentiment on the rise in Britain and the United States
1791–1803	Haitian Revolution
1800	1 million slaves in the United States
1800–1900	3.3 million slaves shipped from Africa to the Americas
1803	Denmark outlaws slave trade
1807	Britain outlaws slave trade
1809	Importation of slaves outlawed in United States
1823	Spain outlaws slavery
1825	Haiti wins official independence
1834	Slavery abolished in the British Empire
1848	France outlaws slavery
1860	4 million slaves in the United States
1863	Emancipation Proclamation (United States)
1869	Paraguay outlaws slavery
1885	Egypt outlaws slavery
1886	Cuba outlaws slavery
1888	Brazil outlaws slavery

Coolies. Picks and shovels, wheelbarrows, one-horse dump carts, black gunpowder, and hand drills were the meager tools and materials with which coolies hired by the Central Pacific Railroad dug and hacked their way over the towering Sierra Nevada Mountains of California. Because white workers were scarce in the American West in the late nineteenth century, the railroad brought in thousands of Chinese to do the most backbreaking labor.

The slaves' main successors worldwide, however, were millions of **coolies**: laborers, mainly from poor communities in India and China, conned or coerced at miserable wages as contracted or indentured workers for some of the era's most demanding work on sugar plantations, tropical mines, and colonial railway-building projects (see Map 24.4). Technically, the Chinese government required that every recruit from Chinese jurisdictions should enter "freely and voluntarily" into his agreement with his employers and shippers. In practice, officials connived in what were effectively deportations or abductions. In the 1860s and 1870s, French recruiters shipped some 50,000 laborers from India to the Caribbean, where, Indian government officials complained, the French "tried everything they could to keep Indians in perpetual servitude." A British report of 1871 characterized the condition of Chinese and Indian laborers in British Guiana in South America as the new slavery. A Chinese government inquiry in 1873 found that "the lawless method by which the Chinese were—in most cases—introduced into Cuba, the contempt there shown for them, the disregard of contracts, the indifference about working conditions, and the unrestrained infliction of wrong, constitute a treatment which is that of a slave, not of a man who has consented to be bound by a contract." After Spain abolished slavery in Cuba in 1886, slave catchers stayed in business—now hunting down runaway Chinese workers. There were perhaps 25,000 Chinese in California

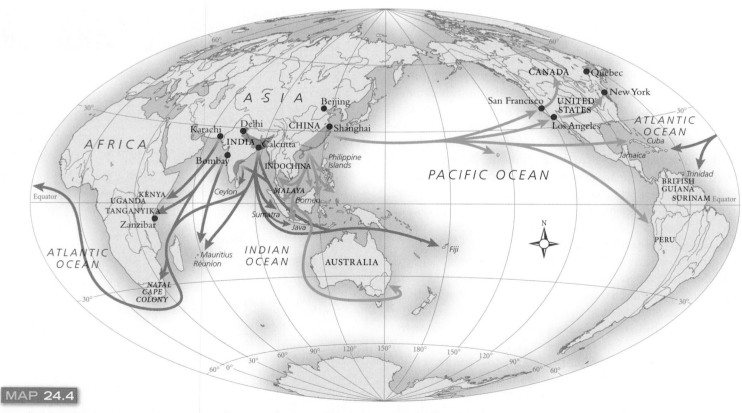

MAP 24.4

The Movement of Indentured Labor in the Late Nineteenth Century

- ▨ core area of Indian migration
- ▨ core area of Chinese migration
- ➡ Indian migrants
- ➡ Chinese migrants

in the 1850s. The Central Pacific Railroad employed 10,000 of them. From 1868, by agreement with China, 16,000 arrived annually. Many went to factories in San Francisco, where "Little China" had nearly 50,000 residents by 1875. Violence and immigration controls followed. When the British writer Rudyard Kipling visited California in 1889, he could see "how deep down in the earth the pigtail [which all Chinese men had to wear under the Qing dynasty] has taken root."

From 1834, when the British Empire abolished slavery, until the eve of World War I in 1914, 4 million workers, mainly from India and China, kept the empire supplied with cheap labor. France conquered Indochina from the 1850s to the 1880s in part to solve the problems of a labor shortage elsewhere in the French Empire.

Female and Child Labor

So although slavery was abolished in most places and legal serfdom disappeared from Europe, other forms of forced and dependent labor survived and spread. In industrializing economies, it is doubtful how far wage labor was morally superior to slavery. Unlike the masters of slaves, factory owners did not have the legal right to sell their workers or, at least in theory, sexually abuse them. But work in the factories and mines of the West and its colonies was highly disciplined, unless and until governments allowed workers to organize in trade unions and bargain collectively for their wages. Women and children joined the workforce. Child labor was, of course, entirely forced labor, as was much of the work that women did. Both categories made a substantial contribution to the success of industrialization. In Germany in 1895, nearly 700,000 workers were under 16 years of age. In France in the 1890s, 32 percent of the manufacturing workforce was women. Well over half the industrial workforce in late nineteenth-century Japan were women, mostly from rural backgrounds, living in supervised dormitories and sending most of their meager pay back home to their village relatives. The biggest source of employment for women was the result of other social and economic changes. Urbanization increased demand for domestic servants and for retail staff in shops and markets.

Trends similar to those of the West were visible in patches wherever industrialization—on however small a scale—occurred. In Ottoman-ruled Syria and Lebanon, for instance, 85 percent of the workforce in silk reeling, which was the only steam-powered industry in the area, was female on the eve of World War I. Women were dragged into new forms of work in the unindustrialized or deindustrialized worlds, too. Indian tea plantations relied on female labor to pick the tea leaves, partly because women were supposedly nimble fingered, partly because they were cheap to hire and easier to exploit. In northern Bengal, stripping jute and plucking tea leaves joined the dehusking of rice as women's work. Most families came to depend on women's wages. In West Africa, men took over much of the work of pounding the palm nuts to extract their oil, which was traditionally women's work. But women were diverted into selling oil and food. Their menfolk benefited. As in the industrializing world, the new economic opportunities of the era led men to assert claims to women's labor and to the proceeds that labor earned.

Although some women turned to jobs outside the home to escape the domination of parents or husbands, it is hard to resist the impression that women were—as usual—employed where men could best exploit their labor. In a German factory, a survey in 1900 revealed that half the women employed claimed that they worked because their husbands could not earn enough to support their families. The problems of balancing factory work and family life were formidable—especially since

Tea picker. Tea was an imperial beverage in the nineteenth century. First, Britain encouraged mass production of tea in India to undermine Chinese exports. Then the British introduced the crop to Sri Lanka, where this harvester is shown at work in a photograph from the 1890s. This "Ceylon tea" is now prized, but it was originally a cheap, inferior beverage to help keep British industrial workers alert.

Decorative and unproductive womanhood. This nineteenth-century advertisement for soap was aimed at lower-middle-class women whose incomes—or those of their husbands—enabled them to purchase goods like soap that had once been considered luxuries. The industrialization of the West would have been impossible without the exploitation of the labor of women and children, but industrialization also emancipated them and brought them a measure of prosperity. As a gender women were oppressed, but even at the relatively low social and economic level at which this ad was aimed, a new idea of womanhood—decorative and unproductive—can be detected. A similar change affected children, who became during the period of industrialization at once an exploited underclass, a source of cheap, unskilled labor, and the image of angelic perfection.

factory workers in the late nineteenth century married relatively young, typically in their early twenties in highly industrialized countries, such as Britain and Germany. Even women who stayed at home worked harder, as factories and mines sucked in their menfolk and deprived wives of their husbands' help at home. In the growing cities, prostitution boomed, often employing, in effect, enslaved women.

In the long run, industrialization led Westerners to reevaluate womanhood and childhood. By comparison with men, women and children were, somewhat contradictorily, perceived as ideal for certain industrial tasks but were also treated as marginally efficient workers. Gradually, mechanization took them out of the labor market. Society rationalized the process by representing it as a form of liberation and even of elevating the status of women and children. Womanhood mounted a pedestal. Children were treated as a distinct rank of society—almost a subspecies of humankind—whereas formerly they had often been seen as little adults, or as "enemies" who needed discipline, or simply as negligible, even expendable, given the high rates of child mortality.

These were uniquely Western cults, barely intelligible in cultures where women and children were still men's partners in production. The status looked enviable in artists' and advertisers' images of delicate femininity or angelic childhood. But there were disadvantages. Societies that freed children from the workplace tried to pen them inside schools. For many children, and for parents who needed their children's wages, compulsory education was a form of tyranny. In 1863, the English novelist Charles Kingsley wrote a popular and sentimental story about boy chimney sweeps—a dirty and dangerous form of child labor—who changed magically into spirits or "water babies." This sort of transformation, however, did not occur naturally. The romantic ideal of childhood was more often forced than coaxed into being. Schools were repressive and designed to mold pupils according to adult agendas.

Women liberated from work were assigned a role and rights that resembled, in some respects, those of children. In the early nineteenth century, Montréal in Canada was the only place in the world where, owing to a constitutional quirk, women could assert the right to vote. But the suffrage for women was withdrawn in 1834 after a single election, "to protect their modesty." Stiflingly male-dominated, middle-class homes confined women. The Norwegian dramatist Henrik Ibsen (1828–1906) brilliantly captured the atmosphere in 1879 in his most famous play, *A Doll's House*, which depicts the married household as an oppressive pen from which a woman must struggle to escape. For middle-class women, the fall from the pedestal could be bruising. In 1858, the British artist Augustus Egg painted an adulteress in three terrible stages of decline and destitution. Great composers devoted operas to sexually promiscuous heroines who invariably came to a bad or a sad end—Giuseppe Verdi's *La Traviata* (1851), Georges Bizet's *Carmen* (1875), Giacomo Puccini's *Manon Lascaut* (1891) and *La Bohème* (1896). The fallen woman became the favorite villain or victim of the age.

Still, women did exert new influence in traditional male arenas without succumbing to new forms of exploitation. Education was the principal lever of their ascent. Feminists realized this. Elizabeth Cady Stanton (1815–1903) was one of the most prominent feminists of the late nineteenth and early twentieth centuries. She devoted a lifetime to campaigning for women in the United States to have the same access to education and political participation as men. "The responsibilities of life," she argued before a Senate committee in 1894, "rest equally on man and woman." Therefore, "they need the same preparation for time and eternity. The talk of sheltering woman from the fierce storms of life is the sheerest mockery, for they beat on her from every point of the compass, just as they do on man, and with more fatal results, for he has been trained to protect himself, to resist, to conquer." But for Stanton, "the strongest reason for giving woman all the opportunities for higher education, for the full development of her faculties, for . . . the most enlarged freedom of thought and action" was a distinctly American value: the integrity and independence of every individual.

Such reasoning did not play equally well in all cultures. As Malaka Hifni Nasif, an Egyptian advocate of education for her fellow-women put it in 1909, "I am the first to admire the activities of the Western woman, and her courage, and I am the first to respect those among them who deserve respect, but respect for others should not make us overlook the good of the nation." She was a professional, independent woman, but she contracted a polygamous marriage with a Bedouin chief and lived with him in the desert. Her role in public life was strictly as an advocate for education, health, and charities—not for women's social emancipation or political rights. She opposed female suffrage. At times her writings seemed to extol education mainly as a way of making Egyptian women more attractive to men. Egyptians who sought brides abroad were the most consistent targets of her criticism.

In Egypt—and, perhaps, generally outside the West—the most effective spokesmen for women were men. Qasim Amin (1863–1908), for instance, was a more radical advocate than Malaka Hifni Nasif, championing women's right to education and participation in public life in equality with men. In *The Liberation of Women* (1899), he argued that women's rights were consistent with Muslim teachings—especially in connection with the cases against polygamy, arbitrary divorce, arranged marriages, veiling, and seclusion.

Even for peoples formerly enslaved, only a modified form of freedom emerged. Even in Haiti, the army kept slaves at work. In areas of previously slave-staffed plantations, a labor crisis followed emancipation. It was met, in different degrees in different places, by enforcing new sources of labor, but also, in general, by going back to an older pattern of tenure with peasants, renting the land and sharecropping, forced to give landlords a percentage of their harvests. Liberated slaves were too numerous to command much power in a free labor market. In the British West Indies, they made up 80 percent of the population. In the French and Dutch Caribbean, the proportions were 60 and 70 percent, respectively. Poor European immigrants supplied the labor that industry needed in the United States, while Indian and Chinese coolies kept labor in the Caribbean relatively cheap. For most black people in the United States, part of the results of emancipation was economic misery and subjection to "color bars:" In many states, white people excluded them not just from the right to vote and equal opportunities in employment, but from supposedly public spaces and services. Black Americans were subjected to the petty humiliations, enforced by violence if necessary, of exclusion from white churches, schools, libraries, restaurants, hotels, athletic and recreational facilities, hospitals, and even streetcars, railroad cars, drinking fountains, cemeteries, and park benches.

Free Migrants

Massive migration of free labor was the final feature that helped to reshape the world's labor force. Population increase—so great as to overspill from some areas—combined with improved, cheap, long-range communications to make unprecedented migration rates possible.

Russian and Chinese migration into northern Asia—Siberia and Manchuria—illustrates this well. Russia's population exceeded 167 million in 1900—an increase

Reactionary Feminist: "If we pursue everything Western we shall destroy our own civilization." Though Malaka Hifni Nasif (1886–1918), pictured here, advocated women's education and rights in marriage, her purpose was conservative and nationalist—equipping Egypt with wives and mothers to prepare a new generation of men for greatness.

Italian immigrants. The photographs Lewis Hine (1874–1940) took of immigrants arriving at Ellis Island in New York City in 1904–1905 launched his career as one of the most socially influential photographers in U.S. history. This shot of an Italian mother and her children, which Hine hand colored, typifies his talent for capturing the dignity and promise of the poor and oppressed.

of nearly 20 million in the last two decades of the nineteenth century. Siberia relied on convict labor until the 1870s, but by the end of the century, almost all the migrants there were free. Nearly 1 million settlers entered Siberia during the 1890s while the Trans-Siberian Railway was under construction (see Chapter 23). About 5 million followed in the first decade or so of the twentieth century, when the railway was complete. Chinese colonization of Manchuria increased after 1860 when the Qing relaxed the rules restricting it. China, indeed, was still the world's most prolific source of long-range colonists. The age-old Chinese diaspora in Southeast Asia gathered pace, rising to a total of almost 14 million in the 1890s and leaping further in the years before World War I.

Meanwhile, the steamship trade, which also facilitated coolie migration, helped to populate underexploited frontiers in the Southern Hemisphere and the North American West, and to provide labor for North American industrialization. Europe, because of its exceptional rise in population, was the main source of free migrants. "New Europes," areas with similar climates and environments to those the migrants left behind, were the most attractive destinations. There were areas of this kind in North America, the southern cone of the Americas—Brazil, Argentina, Chile, and Uruguay—Australia, New Zealand, Algeria, and South Africa. Transatlantic routes were the most popular and carried the most traffic, chiefly because of the economic opportunities that North American expansion created.

Most transatlantic migrants headed for the United States, which gained more than 128,000 migrants in the 1820s and over 500,000 in the 1830s. Numbers trebled in the next decade. Until then, most migrants came from Germany, Britain, and Ireland. A further leap in the 1880s brought the total to over 5.25 million, from all over Europe and especially from Scandinavia, Italy, Central Europe, and the Russian Empire. This was the manpower that fueled continental expansion and industrialization. In 1884, the Statue of Liberty arrived in New York City from France in 214 crates to welcome the wretched of the Earth into America. The cost of erecting it ($100,000, around $5 million in today's money) almost prevented it from being unpacked.

From 1890 to 1920, migration brought a net gain of 18.2 million people to the United States—more than in the entire previous history of the country (see Map 24.5). In combination with industrialization, this turned the United States into a major world power. After 1892, the United States enforced new rules. Immigrants were subject to strict quotas and questioned for suitability. Political undesirables and the morally suspect, including prostitutes and polygamists, were excluded, as were those suffering from infectious diseases, such as syphilis and tuberculosis. Canada and the South American countries of the River Plate region, especially Argentina, also made huge gains. By 1914, when 13 percent of the population of the United States was foreign born, the corresponding figure in Argentina was 30 percent. Nearly half of Argentina's immigrants came from Italy and nearly a third from Spain. Most of the rest were Eastern Europeans.

HUNTERS AND PASTORALISTS

When the pattern of world population settled after the shake-up, some former parts of it had vanished or shrunk. After slaves, the numbers of pastoral and foraging peoples diminished the most. In some places, the advance of mechanized agriculture simply wiped them out or penned them in reservations where they were doomed to decline. In others, they were converted to settled ways of life.

Alternatively, the unfamiliar diseases that contact with outsiders introduced diminished or destroyed them. They survived only in environments that were too unappealing for better-armed peoples to contest, such as the harsh Kalahari in southern Africa, where San hunters fled to elude their black and white persecutors, or in the vast but merciless Australian interior, where aboriginals retreated from white settlers, or in the North American and Eurasian Arctic. Occasionally, the hesitations of potential enemies saved them: inhibitions that were sometimes romantic, sometimes practical, sometimes a bit of both. In 1884, for instance, when the Swedish government was considering the fate of the Sami—the reindeer herders of the far north—some theorists argued that the pastoralists were relics of an inferior race, whom the laws of nature doomed to extinction. Opponents countered that Sami culture was "the only one suited to expansive regions of the country." The "small peoples of the north," as Russians called them, benefited from the perceptions of romantics who saw them as embodiments of the ideal of the noble savage (see Chapter 22), and of Russian and Finnish sympathizers, who saw them as survivors from an earlier phase of their own peoples' past.

An Auracano chief in native dress with the Andes behind him, painted in 1853. The native peoples of the extreme southern cone of the Americas fought off Spanish conquistadores and resisted the Chilean and Argentine republics, until industrially produced machine guns defeated them in the late nineteenth century.

Most pastoralists and foragers, however, lacked such protectors. Railways carved up the lands of the surviving hunter peoples of the North American West. Reservations broke up their communities. Phoney treaties shifted them onto marginal lands where survival was hard. Exemplary massacres harassed them into submission. Thanks to rifles and machine guns, frontier generals could plan to exterminate native peoples "like maniacs or wild beasts." Free rations of cattle bought off the survivors of wars. In 1872, an American army officer reported of the Shoshone of the Great Plains: "Their hunting grounds have been spoiled, their favorite valleys are occupied by settlers and they are compelled to scatter in small bands to obtain subsistence." He described the same depths of demoralization and beggary to which other Native American peoples of the Midwest and the far West had plunged.

Similar ruthlessness solved the problem of what to do with foragers in the grasslands of South America. In the 1840s, an Argentine president decided that white competition doomed his country's Indians "to disappear from the face of the Earth." In the 1880s, machine guns fulfilled his prophecy. In that decade, the discovery of gold in the far south of Argentina in Tierra del Fuego turned the remotest limits of the American hemisphere into contested territory. Professional man hunters arrived to wipe out the native foragers, charging around five dollars for every Indian they killed. At the opposite end of the hemisphere, in the Aleutian Islands off the coast of Alaska, missionaries and bureaucrats saved the native fishing communities from extermination by Russian conquerors, but could not mitigate the effects of diseases to which the inhabitants had no resistance. An epidemic in 1838–1839 wiped out half the population, by official estimates. When Russia sold Alaska to the United States in 1867, another wave of casual looters arrived, with another alien culture, imposed by force.

Less dramatically, but equally effectively, governments in the Old World induced nomads to change their way of life. Mehmet Ali (r. 1805–1848), the khedive of Egypt (see Chapter 23), turned nomadic Arab tribal leaders into landowners, mobilized the desert warriors, and seized their horses. The former nomads shifted to the towns or became "lost among the peasants." Russian governments in the 1890s forced Muslim Khazaks and Kirgiz nomads in Central Asia into agriculture by confining them to land grants too small for them to sustain themselves by grazing their flocks.

Ethnic Neighborhoods in Manhattan, ca. 1920

Legend:
- African-American
- Chinese
- Czech, Hungarian
- French
- German
- Irish
- Italian
- Jewish
- Scandinavian, Finnish
- Syrian, Turkish, Armenian, Greek

New Jersey

Hudson River

Tenth Avenue
120th Street
100th Street
110th Street
Central Park
Eighth Avenue
Broadway
90th Street
80th Street
70th Street
Fourth Avenue
Third Avenue
Second Avenue
First Avenue
60th Street
Eleventh Avenue
Ninth Avenue
Sixth Avenue
Fifth Avenue
50th Street
40th Street
Broadway
30th Street
Madison Square
20th Street
Seventh Avenue
Union Square
10th Street
Houston Street
Canal Street
Broadway

East River

Queens

Brooklyn

2 km
2 miles

INDIA

30°
90°
120°

Batavia
Singapore
MALAYA
SIAM
Mekong

DUTCH EAST INDIES

Hong Kong
Manila
Shanghai

AUSTRALIA

JAPAN
Yokohama

Melbourne
Sydney

0°

Equator

PACIFIC OCEAN

180°
30°

1 million

NEW ZEALAND

Timeline:

1818: 20,000 Irish emigrate to U.S. as a result of famine

1845–54: Irish Potato Famine leads 1.6 million to emigrate

1849: California Gold Rush draws large numbers of migrants from Europe, Australia, Chile, and China

1882: Beginning of major Jewish emigration from Russian Empire; 80,000 Scandinavians emigrate to U.S.

1900: Start of major Italian emigration to U.S. and Argentina; by 1910, more than two million have arrived

1800   1820   1840   1860   1880

1816–1817: Emigration from southwest Germany following Napoleonic wars

1831–41: 200,000 people leave Ireland for Canada, many traveling on to the U.S.

1848–49: Revolutions lead to political crackdown and exodus of democrats from Central Europe

1850s: Height of emigration from England and Scotland; more than 50,000 per year

1881–90: Peak years of German emigration to U.S. (1,300,000)

1888: Abolition of slavery in Brazil; next decade sees over a million immigrants

MAP 24.5

World Migration, ca. 1860–1920

Transatlantic migration
- to North America
- to South America and the Caribbean
- to Europe from the Americas

Other European migration
- to Australia and New Zealand
- to North Africa

Asian migration
- to the Americas and Australia
- Russian migration into Siberia
- Indian migration within British Empire
- transcontinental railroad
- major exporters of people
- major importers of people

INDIAN OCEAN

MADAGASCAR

SOUTH AFRICA
Cape Town

Lake Nyasa
Mombasa
Lake Victoria
Mogadishu
Lake Tanganyika

CEYLON (Sri Lanka)
Bombay
INDIA
AFRICA
Congo
Nile
Suez Canal 1869
Lagos

CALCUTTA
BURMA
SIAM
Mekong
Tashkent
Baku
OTTOMAN EMPIRE
Tigris
Euphrates
Niger
Dakar

CHINA
ASIA
Yangtze
Novosibirsk
Moscow
Constantinople
Odesa
Naples
AUSTRIA-HUNGARY
ITALY
Genoa
Marseille

Yellow River
Beijing
Trans-Siberian Railway
EUROPE
St. Petersburg
GERMANY
Hamburg
Amsterdam
Antwerp SPAIN
Southampton
PORTUGAL
Liverpool
BRITAIN IRELAND

4 million
3 million

6 million
Ob
RUSSIAN EMPIRE
Yenisei

Vladivostok

ATLANTIC OCEAN

3 million (2.5 million British)

ARCTIC OCEAN

7 million returnees

8 million

24.1 million

60°

30°

Halifax
Quebec
Boston
New York

see inset map

Belém
BRAZIL
Rio de Janeiro

PUERTO RICO
Amazon

CANADA
Canadian Pacific
NORTH AMERICA
Northern Pacific
Central Pacific
Vancouver

San Francisco
UNITED STATES
New Orleans
CUBA
JAMAICA
Panama Canal 1914

SOUTH AMERICA

URUGUAY
Montevideo
Buenos Aires

Los Angeles
MEXICO
Mexico City

PERU
Lima

ARGENTINA
CHILE
Valparaíso

Equator

60°

837

ELITES TRANSFORMED

Industrialization created proletariats. The dwindling of slavery, serfdom, and foraging transformed rural lives and work patterns. Migration and new forms of social control shook up the role and distribution of the world's labor. At the top end of society, the changes of the period were almost as traumatic for those they touched. While peasantries and working classes suffered, the era of industrialization transformed aristocracies or, at least, severely tested them. They survived by diversifying from an emphasis on landed estates into new economic activities. When they failed to adapt, they perished.

In Japan, the government abolished samurai privileges in the 1870s. A military draft for all able-bodied men in 1873 effectively eliminated the main legal distinction—the right to bear arms—between samurai and commoners. Japan now had no warrior caste. Many samurai benefited from the abolition of distinctions within their own class. Lower samurai were now free to accumulate wealth and honor. Professions that had formerly been considered socially beneath them, such as those of merchants and civil servants, opened up to the gentry, and many of them became dependents of the government. They also served as officials and as officers in the new European-trained army and navy, or invested in new industries. Others declined into poverty and merged into the ranks of the commoners.

Traditionally, in China, merit had been the means to attain high social rank. But families with inherited wealth had an advantage because they could afford good schooling for their sons and tended increasingly to monopolize access to the scholar elite in the nineteenth century. "The gentry are at the head of the common people," said imperial instructions to magistrates, "and to them the villagers look up." The impoverished landowners of China shook off the ties of extended kin and the traditional social obligations of their status. Thanks to their efforts to find new sources of wealth, by engaging in trade, or by exploiting the labor of poor neighbors and tenants on their land, they found themselves demonized as "evil gentry."

The British aristocracy survived the collapse of land prices by diversifying into commerce, by marrying American heiresses, and by absorbing into its ranks the "beerage"—the new class of wealthy entrepreneurs, such as those who owned the massive, mechanized breweries that supplied the workers' beer. Reversals of traditional class relationships were the favorite theme of comic writers. W. S. Gilbert and Sir Arthur Sullivan, whose works dominated musical theater in late nineteenth-century Britain, devoted much of their satire to merciless jokes about egalitarianism and most of their plots to reversals of rank in topsy-turvy worlds, in which noblemen become working-class apprentices, common seamen, and gondoliers, while an attorney's clerk rises to be Lord High Admiral and an ex-convict becomes Lord High Executioner.

The **new rich** were among the most satirized villains and clowns of the age. In Charles Dickens's novel *Our Mutual Friend* (1864–1865), the middle-class Mr. Veneering suddenly emerges with a mansion, an aristocrat's coat of arms, and the ambition to win a seat in parliament. The type was familiar in real life. Sir William Cunliffe Brooks (1819–1900) was a British banker, but so "common"—in the opinion of an aristocratic friend—that even his housekeeper made fun of his lower-class accent. He bought a castle in 1888 and turned the old kitchen of his hunting lodge into a chapel, decorated with hunting trophies. "The effect," said a visitor, "was that you were in a baronial hall, or the comfortable private chapel of an old baron."

The sons of the new rich acquired the habits, friends, and tastes of gentlemen at the numerous new and expensive schools—called "public" in Britain only because they sought to be of public importance—and the growing universities. Old blood

> *"While peasantries and working classes suffered, the era of industrialization transformed aristocracies or, at least, severely tested them. They survived by diversifying from an emphasis on landed estates into new economic activities. When they failed to adapt, they perished."*

allied with new money. Industrialization shifted the balance of power and wealth away from landed estates and into cities. But landowners could also benefit, by mining coal and iron ore on their estates or by leasing or selling the land on which to build towns and docks. The third Marquess of Bute (1847–1901) did all these things and left an estate equivalent to several hundred million dollars today. As early as the 1840s, about a sixth of England's landed gentry earned a significant part of their wealth in business, mainly through manufacturing, banking, and railways. Aristocracies were becoming middle class while the middle class was adopting aristocratic tastes.

Every industrializing economy had its new rich and its declining aristocracies. In Spain, the vulgar tycoon, the Marquis de Salamanca, who made a fortune out of Madrid real estate, typified new money, with his shady deals and showy ways. The novelist Pérez Galdós satirized the decline of old money in one of his best novels, *Mercy* (1897), about hard times for an aristocratic family, who were maintained by their maid's talents as a beggar. In Russia, Anton Chekhov's play *The Cherry Orchard* (1904) features an old landed family compelled to sell its estate, and the upwardly mobile local entrepreneur who buys them out, after enduring years of their exploitation and contempt.

In the United States, "old" money, which was in truth not very old, was more vulnerable to intrusion by the new rich because the country had no landed aristocracy and no titled nobility. Nonetheless, in a book entitled *Our Benevolent Feudalism* in 1902, W. J. Ghent argued that American millionaires were developing into an hereditary nobility. In 1899, Thorstein Veblen proposed in *The Theory of the Leisure Class* that America had acquired an elite whom inherited wealth exempted from having to worry about money. In the 1870s and 1880s, Samuel Ward McAllister attempted to create high society, based on the admission of supposedly suitable people to entertainments given by socially exclusive hostesses in New York City—exclusive, that is, according to McAllister himself. "We want the money power," he explained in 1872, "but not to be controlled by it." In effect he was admitting that the American aristocracy was open to new money, and indeed, merchants

Elite uniforms. The Freemason's Lodge of Freetown, in Sierra Leone in West Africa, presents an address to the Duke of Connaught, a son of Queen Victoria, on December 15, 1910. The white ladies, in their tea dresses under the canopy, and the top brass with ceremonial swords and pith helmets, look positively informal by the standards of the black dignitaries, who wear what appears to be full court dress in the heat of the tropical day. It would be hard to find a more telling image of determination to defy the environment.

Cultural exchange. The fashion for Japanese art and taste in the late nineteenth-century West extended to women's clothing. Paintings of Westerners in Japanese kimonos—like these American women painted in San Francisco around 1880—demonstrate the fashionable appeal of Japan. Note the view of Mount Fuji in the background on the left-hand panel.
Photograph courtesy of the Peabody Essex Museum

and railroad men's sons and daughters got into McAllister's list of America's "First Four Hundred." Old money did occasionally resist. At Newport on the Rhode Island coast, Southern planters and New York tycoons built palatial summer "cottages" of marble and gilt. But the coal merchant's wife who built the breathtaking mansion called Rosecliff there found herself alone at her house's inaugural ball. Her neighbors boycotted her party. Snobbery was indissoluble, even in champagne.

Outside the West, too, the rise of the new rich was probably the biggest change in the composition of the elite. As we have seen, most purchasers of land came from outside the peasantry or aristocracy. Westernization made the rise of a new class easier, by spreading values and tastes distinct from those of traditional aristocracies. In the 1870s, one Angolan chief looted his own people to build a medieval-looking castle and collect violins. In the 1890s, another hired an ex-slave who had worked for the Portuguese as a maid to teach him European etiquette. Almost everywhere, Western dress became the uniform of the world's elite—at least for men. Formal suits with top hats, ties, stiff collars, and striped pants were the uniform of male power, whether affected by the well-to-do of Freetown in Sierra Leone in West Africa or the Maori chiefs of New Zealand. The self-reinvented samurai who staffed the Japanese government chopped off the top-knots from their hair and clamped shiny top hats to their heads. Among the relics of José Rizal, the leader of Filipino nationalism in the last years of the nineteenth century, are his yellowing stiff collars, lovingly preserved at the fort of Santiago in Manila (see Chapter 26).

In Perspective
Cultural Exchange—Enhanced Pace, New Directions

Despite differences of pace, texture, and density in the spread of railways and mechanized production, and despite the complexity and perplexities of social change, the common experience of industrialization restored a kind of uniformity to Western society. A gap opened between the developed and underdeveloped worlds. The technology gap became a wealth gap between the regions that supplied commodities and those that turned them into manufactured goods. These worldwide inequalities were hugely bigger, and would prove more enduring for the future, than the internal class differences that divided industrializing societies.

Meanwhile, exchanges of culture crossed the world with greater intensity and speed than ever before. No example is more eye catching or more obviously attuned to the pace of industrialization than the standardization of time. Until the nineteenth century, every place determined its own time of day according to the sun and set its clocks accordingly. But the railway made it impossible to maintain this "natural" time. People could move too fast. The railway schedules became too complex. In 1852, an electric telegraph system was set up to transmit the time at the Royal Observatory in Greenwich across Britain. In 1880, Greenwich time became by law the official standard time for the whole country.

"No example is more eye catching or more obviously attuned to the pace of industrialization than the standardization of time."

MAP 24.6

Time Zones of the World

At the International Meridian Conference, held in Washington, D.C. in 1884, the same standard became the basis for a sequence of time zones covering the entire globe (see Map 24.6).

Cultural exchange got faster and more complicated than ever. In part, this was because people—who in every age have been the most effective agents of cultural change—could travel farther and more frequently than formerly. The world's first travel agent, Thomas Cook and Company, founded in Britain in 1841, began by organizing a local trip for a temperance society in England. By 1900, Cook's was selling 3 million travel packages a year. Most of the trips the firm organized were still within Britain and were sold to working- and middle-class tourists. But Cook's also took luxury travelers, big-game hunters, business-people, and high officials of the British Empire across the world.

Cultural exchange, however, was not one-way Westernization. What Europeans considered exotic became fashionable in the West. The Japanese-inspired style that Western designers called "Japonisme" was the most striking case. The French painter Claude Monet (1860–1926) portrayed his wife in a kimono. Camille Pissarro (1830–1903) copied Japanese prints—notably in his famous painting of umbrellas in Paris. Giacomo Puccini, the leading operatic composer at the turn of the century, borrowed from what little he knew of Japanese, Chinese, and even Native American music and put it in his operas. These exchanges took in wider influences, too. In the 1890s, the Czech Anton Dvořák was among the first European composers to draw on African American music. European painters and

Chronology

1791–1803	Haitian Revolution
1800	1 million slaves in the United States
1800–1900	3.3 million slaves shipped from Africa to the Americas
1807	Britain outlaws slave trade
1809	United States outlaws importation of slaves
1825	Haiti wins official independence
1834	Slavery abolished in the British Empire
1838–1839	Epidemic wipes out half of the native population of the Aleutian Islands
1842	Edwin Chadwick's *The Sanitary Condition of the Labouring Population*
1845–1876	Ottoman agricultural exports increase fivefold
1848	France outlaws slavery; publication of Marx's and Engels's *The Communist Manifesto*
1850s	25,000 Chinese live and work in California
1853–1854	Serfs in Habsburg Empire emancipated
1860s and 1870s	French ship 50,000 Indian laborers to their Caribbean colonies
1861	Serfs in Russia emancipated
1863	Emancipation Proclamation (United States)
1867	Publication of Marx's *Capital*
1870s	Japanese workers and peasants freed by official decree; samurai privileges abolished
ca. 1875	McCormick Company of Chicago produces 15,000 reapers per year
1880s	5.25 million immigrants arrive in the United States; bounty offered for killing Indians in Argentina
1885	Egypt outlaws slavery
1886	Cuba outlaws slavery
1888	Brazil outlaws slavery
1890s	32 percent of French work force is female; 14 million people migrate from China
1890–1920	Immigration adds 18.2 million people to U.S. population
Late nineteenth century	Arts and Crafts movement
1899	Publication of *The Liberation of Women* by Qasim Amin
ca. 1900	Cotton cultivation in Egypt contributes to the creation of 2 million landless peasants
	Urban populations: Izmir, 200,000; Alexandria, 250,000; Calcutta, more than 750,00; Melbourne, 800,000; New York, 3.4 million; London, 6.5 million
1914	30 percent of the population of Argentina is foreign born

sculptors began to discover the wonders of what they called primitive art from Africa and the South Seas. Some exchanges bypassed the West altogether. In the 1890s, Chief Mataka of the Yao—deep in the East African interior—made his people don Arab dress, launched Arab-style ships on Lake Nyasa, planted coconut groves and mangoes, and rebuilt his palace in the mixed Arab-African Swahili style that had long dominated the East African coast (see Chapter 21). "Ah!" he exclaimed, "now I have changed Yao to be like the coast!"

Although cultural transmissions increasingly crisscrossed the world, one route was new and would become dominant. The big new influences came from the United States, heralding trends that would dominate the twentieth century. This was surprising at the time. North America had previously followed European and, to some extent, Latin American cultural leadership. In politics, as we shall see, the United States launched, nurtured, or revised some ideas of enormous and growing influence in the world—including, notably, democracy and socialism—but it is hard to find a movement of any significance in the arts, literature, science, or philosophy that started in the United States before the 1890s. Then, however, the flood began, as European composers discovered the wonders of American ragtime. It was a small beginning, but it was the herald of the dawn of an "American century" in which the United States was increasingly to be the source of worldwide trends in popular culture, entertainment, the arts, taste, food, and, ultimately, the major source of new technology and ideas.

PROBLEMS AND PARALLELS

1. What were the advantages and disadvantages of industrialization in Japan and Europe in the nineteenth century? Who were the winners and losers from this process?
2. How did industrialization change daily life for the average urban dweller? In what ways did these changes improve life or make it more difficult?
3. How was Henry Heinz's treatment of his workers an example of paternalism? Why did Karl Marx's prediction of a workers' revolution not come to pass?
4. How did cities cope with highly concentrated populations? Why did so many people abandon the land for cities? Why did the populations of many port cities expand rapidly during the nineteenth century?
5. Why was slavery abolished in the nineteenth century? What forms of labor replaced slavery?
6. How did industrialization change women's and children's lives? Why did Western governments enforce compulsory education for children? Why did some non-Western women like Malaka Hifni Nasif reject social emancipation for women?
7. How did massive migration of free labor reshape the world's labor force? Where did most immigrants go before World War I? Why did pastoralism decline as a way of life in the nineteenth century?

READ ON ▶ ▶ ▶

My version of the story of Oshio Heicharo is based on I. Morris, *The Nobility of Failure* (1988). The best general survey of the nineteenth-century world is C. A. Bayly, *The Birth of the Modern World* (2003).

T. Hunt, *Building Jerusalem*, (2004) and A. Briggs, *Victorian Cities* (1993) deal with urbanization in the British state and empire. J. Merriman, ed., *French Cities in the Nineteenth Century* (1981) is a good survey of France; C. Chant, D. Goodman et al., eds., *European Cities and Technology: Industrial to Post-industrial City* (1999) is a valuable six-volume collection of essays and documents. Peter Hall, *Cities in Civilisation* (1998) is particularly good on urban culture. On the effects on health, D. Brunton, *Health, Disease, and Society in Europe* (2004) is a highly useful collection of documents. R. J. Evans, *Death in Hamburg* (1987) is an impressive case study.

On working conditions in the industrializing world, P. Stearns, *Lives of Labor* (1975) is particularly good. J. Burnett, ed., *Useful Toil* (1994) is a valuable collection of English working-class autobiographical materials. A. Kelly, *The German Worker* (1987) does a similar job for Germany. R. C. Alberts, *The Good Provider* (1973) is a lively biography of Heinz. G. Marks and S. M. Lipset, *It Didn't Happen Here* (2000) is a useful attempt to explain the failure of socialism in the United States.

M. Lynch, *Mining in World History* (2004) is a magisterial survey, with emphasis on technological aspects. S. Kanfer, *The Last Empire* (1995) is an enjoyable history of De Beers. D. Avery, *Not on Queen Victoria's Birthday* (1974) studies the Río Tinto case.

On rural conditions in the unindustrializing world, S. Bose, *Peasant Labour and Colonial Capital* (1993) is an outstanding study of Bengal; for Thailand, J. C. Ingram, *Economic Change in Thailand* (1971) is excellent. On Africa, M. Lynn, *Commerce and Economic Change in West Africa* (2002), and W. G. Clarence-Smith, *Slaves, Peasants, and Capitalists in Southern Angola* (1979) are important. J. McCann, *Green Land, Brown Land, Black Land* (1999) surveys sub-Saharan Africa with emphasis on the ecological effects of economic development. C. Issawi has published a series of invaluable works, rich in documents, on the Middle East, notably *The Economic History of the Middle East* (1966) and *An Economic History of Turkey* (1980), which can be supplemented with R. Kasaba, *The Ottoman Empire and the World Economy*; P. Richardson, *Economic Change in China* (1999) is a good introductory survey on that country.

For changes in labor regimes, H. Thomas, *The Slave Trade*, (1999) and D. Northrup, *Indentured Labor in the Age of Imperialism* (1995) are fundamental. The eight volumes of P. J. Kitson and D. Lee et al., eds., *Slavery, Abolition, and Emancipation* (1999) make an invaluable collection of mainly literary and theoretical source materials. S. Miers and R. Roberts, eds., *The End of Slavery in Africa* (1988) and P. C. Emmer and M. Morner, eds., *European Expansion and Migration* (1992) are useful collections. P. Kolchin, *Unfree Labor* (1990) compares America and Russia.

CHAPTER 25

Western Dominance in the Nineteenth Century: The Westward Shift of Power and the Rise of Global Empires

▲ **Unequal combat in the Opium Wars.** The British ironclad, *Nemesis*, blows Chinese war junks to smithereens with impunity, on January 17, 1841, off Guangzhou. The print was circulated at the British shipbuilders' and arms-makers' expense, partly to advertise their wares.

On February 10, 1842—Chinese New Year's Day—General Yijing (yee-jing) consulted the oracles in the Temple of the War God. China was at war with Britain. Yijing was the commander of a force sent to root the invaders from Ningbo (nihng-boh), a key port for controlling the Yangtze River system. He could succeed, the oracle warned, only if "you are hailed by humans with the heads of tigers." A few days later, a band of aboriginal recruits arrived dressed in tiger-skin caps. The general was delighted and distributed similar caps throughout the army. Following ancient Chinese war magic, he ordered his forces to attack at the hour designated as that of the tiger on the day of the tiger in the month of the tiger.

CHINA

Yijing also tried other ways to secure victory, some magical, some original, but all with a touch of desperation about them. He flung a tiger's skull into the Dragon's Pool to arouse the dragon to attack the foreigners. He contemplated attacking the British ships with monkeys strapped with firecrackers to their backs. But the plan proved impracticable, and the monkeys died of starvation.

The campaign was chaotic. Chinese troops mistook and fought their own men. The supply department failed, inflicting unendurable hunger on the army. Thousands of porters who carried the army's baggage died or deserted. Commanders received rewards for writing reports on nonexistent victories. Embezzlers raided the war chest. Only a fraction of the army arrived in time for the battle. Misunderstanding their orders, troops attacked the main city gate armed only with knives.

They faced, moreover, a new kind of "barbarian." The British forces had state-of-the-art munitions—products of the early phases of industrialization—and steam-powered gunboats. They could recruit large numbers of men—"black devils," as the Chinese called them—from India, where Britain was building up an empire of its own. The Chinese proved powerless to stop the invasion. The aggressors could go where they liked and do what they liked.

At first glance, the outcome of the campaign looks like a triumph for modernity. Ancient methods and magic failed in the face of professional, disciplined forces equipped with industrially produced guns and ships. The dynamic out-thrust of a go-ahead Western nation shattered an inward-looking, self-satisfied empire.

Such conclusions would be unfair or at least exaggerated. Chinese respect for ancient rituals, such as omen taking and the invocation of dragons, did not usually cloud rational judgment or get in the way of military efficiency. The deficiencies of organization and generalship in Yijing's command were not unique to, or typical of, Chinese warfare. The Chinese government was actually negotiating with France at the time to buy the latest military and naval technology from the West, but the war broke out before the Chinese could acquire the much-needed equipment.

Nevertheless, the conflict revealed how much the balance of power in the world had shifted during the early stages of industrialization. For most of recorded history—for most of this book—China had been the source of most world-shaping technological innovations. In partial consequence, China had also been the world's greatest power, secure in its unique status as the "central country," with the strength to influence and sometimes dictate politics far from its own borders and shores. Britain, by contrast, had spent most of history on the edge of Eurasia—literally, a marginal part of the world—absorbing influences from outside rather than radiating its own influence to the rest of the world. Now the positions were reversed. Thanks in part to the substitution of machine power for manpower, a small country like Britain could easily defeat a giant, such as China. Thanks to the exploration of the wind systems of the world and the development of technologies of long-range communications, a position on the edge of the West had turned from a disadvantage into an advantage. From the shores of the Atlantic, powers in Western Europe and North America could reach out across the world, using seaborne communications to mesh together increasingly ambitious, increasingly vast territorial domains. The broader context of General Yijing's failures reveals a further vast shift in global history: an economic shift—upheaval in the traditional balance of wealth and reversal in the traditional structures of trade.

THE OPIUM WARS

A trade dispute had provoked the war of which Yijing's campaign formed part. At the center of the dispute was opium. The British wanted to sell opium in China. The Chinese authorities wanted to stop them. As we have seen (see Chapter 21), British merchants in the eighteenth century found that there was growing demand in China for opium, a product they could ship from India at large profit. The opium trade represented an important breakthrough into a market in which, previously, most foreigners had virtually nothing to sell. To buy the products of China, and to meet booming demand, above all, for tea in Europe and North America, Westerners had to pay cash. To earn that cash, they had to work hard, trading and shipping products between Asian markets or exploiting resources in other parts of the world. In the early nineteenth century, the trade in opium expanded sharply. The annual value of the opium that reached China rose fivefold in the 20 years preceding the mid-1830s. As the trade increased, so did the alarm it caused in China, much as today's global traffic in heroin and cocaine alarms the West. Because narcotics are addictive, they create their own captive markets and command high prices. This makes them ideal commodities for relatively poor producer economies seeking markets in rich economies.

Chinese statesmen and intellectuals were united in blaming opium addiction for demoralizing, enfeebling, and impoverishing increasing numbers of Chinese. They were also aware that the drain of revenues threatened one of China's great historic sources of strength: its favorable balance of trade with the rest of the world. The situation became acute in the 1830s, because Britain abolished trading monopolies among its own subjects and opened free trade with China. In 1839, therefore, the Chinese emperor appointed Commissioner Lin to end the opium trade.

That February, Lin drafted a letter for the British monarch, Queen Victoria. The letter was never sent, but it is an admirable summary of Chinese thinking. The draft begins by declaring that human nature is the same in all peoples and climes and that all peoples have the same capacity to distinguish evil from good. The document stresses the benevolence of the Chinese Empire in allowing commerce with foreigners: "Rhubarb, tea, and silk are all valuable products of ours, without which foreigners could not live."

"But there is a class of evil foreigner," the draft went on, "that makes opium and brings it for sale, tempting fools to destroy themselves, merely in order to reap profit. Formerly the number of opium smokers was small; but now the vice has spread far and wide. . . . Our great, unified Manchu Empire regards itself as responsible for the habits and morals of its people and cannot rest content to see any of them become victims to a deadly poison. For this reason we have decided to inflict very severe penalties on opium dealers and opium smokers. . . . What it is here forbidden to consume, your dependencies must be forbidden to manufacture, and what has already been manufactured Your Majesty must immediately search out and throw into the sea, and never again allow such a poison to exist in Heaven or on Earth. When that is done, not only will the Chinese be rid of this evil, but your people too will be safe. For so long as your subjects make opium, who knows but they will not sooner or later take to smoking it?" The draft added an appeal to something the British understood: commercial considerations. "The laws against the consumption of opium are now so strict in China that if you continue to make it, you will find that no one buys it and no more fortunes will be made. Rather than waste your efforts on a hopeless endeavour, would it not be better to devise some other form of trade?"

The British—those of them in charge of trade and government, at least—were unresponsive to appeals grounded in morality. Nor were they disposed to suspend opium production while the trade remained profitable. Commissioner Lin was wrong to think that the threat of suspending commerce in rhubarb or tea would force Britain to accede to Chinese wishes. Rhubarb sold in relatively small quantities, and the British had huge stockpiles of tea. It was no good hoping for British cooperation. If China wanted to stop the opium from reaching its people, China had to act on its own.

In the spring and summer of 1839, Lin confiscated all the opium he could find and flushed it into the sea—writing a poem of apology to the Spirit of the Sea for this act of pollution. He was unable, however, to secure promises from the British merchants that they would withdraw from the trade, and in January 1840, the imperial court suspended dealings with Britain. The British acknowledged that China could punish its own subjects for smoking opium. But to ban the trade itself was unlawful interference in the freedom of commerce, and to confiscate the chests of opium from British merchants was an outrage against private property.

Britain responded to Chinese provocations with obviously disproportionate counter demands: for compensation and indemnities for the confiscated opium, for territorial concessions, and for the liberalization of trade. In the summer of 1840, a British expeditionary force blockaded China's ports, occupying the Guangzhou waterfront and reopening trade by force. The following year, after the Chinese refused Britain's terms, British warships, with opium vessels in their wake, sacked China's coastal and river towns. The British hardly noticed General Yijing's counterattack of 1842.

In the Treaty of Nanjing, which ended the war, China ceded Hong Kong to Britain, opened five other ports to British trade, and paid a colossal indemnity of 21 million silver dollars (equivalent in purchasing power today to around $2 billion). Henceforth, British officials, not Chinese, would have the right to settle disputes between British and Chinese subjects. Britain would have what we now call

Destroying opium. Commissioner Lin destroyed the opium he confiscated from Western—chiefly British—merchants at Guangzhou in 1839 by mixing it with lime and flushing it into the sea or, in the example here, setting it on fire.

"most favored nation" rights in China. British subjects would automatically enjoy any privileges and immunities that China conceded in future to other foreigners. The United States, France, and Sweden soon persuaded or forced the Chinese to grant them similar treaties.

To the Westerners' surprise, the subsequent growth of trade still favored the Chinese, at least until the late 1850s. Tea was a more valuable drug in the West than opium was in China, and the market for it was bigger and faster growing. Britain's official deficit with China rose from under $20 million in the year of the Treaty of Nanjing to nearly $55 million in 1857. It took a further series of British incursions and invasions from 1856 onward to wrest from China terms of trade weighted in Westerners' favor. In 1860, the Taiping rebellion virtually paralyzed the Chinese state. A French and British task force found it easy to march to Beijing, burn the imperial summer palace, and exact the terms the Westerners wanted from the Chinese government (see Chapter 23).

Henceforth, foreigners dominated China's trade and bought up the best real estate in the major trading centers (see Map 25.1). In 1880, for instance, two British steamship companies handled between them 80 percent of China's shipping business. The effects of the wars partly account for this relatively sudden leap to Western ascendancy. In the background, other influences piled up. First, industrialization in the West compensated for China's size and enabled Western economies to overtake China's in wealth. Meanwhile, Western imperialism in other parts of the world increased the resources available to Western powers.

The rise of the West to economic superiority over China—and, indeed, of some Western powers to economic dominance within China—was one of the major reversals of history. Since then, the world has experienced an abnormal situation, in which—until the last few years, at least—China has been stagnant and, by the technical standards of Western powers, backward or underdeveloped, while historical initiative—the capacity for some groups in the world to influence others—has been concentrated in the West. Whereas for centuries China had been the only country to occupy the position of a *superpower*—a state exceeding in strength that of all rivals combined—Western states became the main contenders for that role. Britain exercised it briefly in the nineteenth century, and the United States has enjoyed it—briefly again, so far—in the late twentieth and early twenty-first centuries.

> "The rise of the West to economic superiority over China—and, indeed, of some Western powers to economic dominance within China—was one of the major reversals of history."

THE WHITE EMPIRES: RISE AND RESISTANCE

The change occurred in the context of a new feature of global history in the nineteenth century: the rise—beginning, like industrialization, in Western Europe and rapidly coming to include Russia, the United States, and Japan—of enormous empires that spread across the globe and virtually carved up the world among them. Previously, most of the really big empire-building initiatives in the world had originated in Asia, and the empires expanded by land into territories that bordered on those of the conquerors. Such was the nature of the empires of the Persians, Arabs, Chinese, Indians, and steppelanders such as the Mongols—the empires whose stories have dominated much of this book. Even at the height of their predominance, Chinese rulers had never sent fleets beyond the Indian Ocean, or armies beyond Central Asia (see Chapter 15).

Alongside the great empires, smaller imperial ventures had also set out to control trade rather than production, to dominate sea lanes and harbors rather than large stretches of land. Most European imperialism had been of this character. Until the eighteenth century, as we have seen (see Chapter 21), no empire except Spain's had been able to combine these roles on a large scale. Europeans overseas

MAP 25.1

Foreign Imperialism in East and Southeast Asia, 1840–1910

Area of control or influence

	Russian
	Japanese
	French
	British
	Dutch
	American
	Portuguese
	German

1898   date of acquisition by foreign power

Leased territory   **Treaty ports**

Leased territory	Treaty ports
Japanese	Japanese
French	French
British	British
Portuguese	American
German	open port

Qing Empire at its greatest extent ca. 1850

Foreign attacks on China

→ British (Opium War 1840–1842)

→ Anglo-French campaigns 1858–1860

→ French 1883–1885

had generally depended on the goodwill of local collaborators in existing economic systems. Now their relationship with the world they had entered changed, as they exploited the advantages of industrially equipped armies and navies to control the production of the key commodities of global trade. The combination of land and sea empires became commonplace.

As in industrialization, Britain established an early lead in imperialism. The first world war—different, of course, from the First World War of 1914–1918—began during the French Revolution in the 1790s and ended with the final defeat of Napoleon in 1815 (see Chapter 22). The British government had already begun to think globally, locating colonies in strategic positions along the world's trade routes. While continental European powers fought and distracted each other, British governments pushed global thinking to new extremes. In 1807, they launched an unsuccessful invasion of the River Plate region of South America. In 1812–1814, Britain fought to check the ambitions of the United States. Britain took advantage of wars in Europe to wrest colonies from France, Spain, and Holland and to seize useful stations to control global communications by sea, including Malta and other Mediterranean islands, South Africa, parts of the Dutch East Indies, French islands in the Indian Ocean, and islands and coastal positions in and around the Caribbean.

An allegory of the British Empire, by the Scottish painter William Dyce, decorated the favorite residence of Queen Victoria (r. 1837–1901). Britannia's lion signifies empire, and her trident stands for Britain's rule of the sea. The gods of wisdom, science, and industry attend her with personifications of liberty, work, and war. Other figures representing beauty and commerce humbly reach for the hem of her garment, hoping to be saved from storms and sea monsters.

Other governments had, as yet, no such vision. China was still self-absorbed, confident of its role as the central country and barely aware of events in the wider world. Japan was still proudly ignorant of global events—content to rely on Dutch informants, who managed to conceal the fall of Holland to French revolutionary armies in 1794 from the Japanese government for years. Even the French closed windows to the world in the early nineteenth century, although they had invaded Egypt and Syria in the late 1790s, with the aim of establishing an empire in the east, where, as Napoleon said, "great reputations are made." First, France withdrew from Egypt, then abandoned the effort to reconquer Haiti from rebellious slaves, then, in 1803, sold to the United States its claims to the vast territory in North America known as Louisiana. The British could consolidate the conquests they had already made, thanks to a long period of peace with other European countries that lasted for almost 40 years after 1815.

For other powers, the empire-building process really took off in the second half of the century, when the world experienced a tremendous increase in imperialism (see Map 25.2). For European powers, Africa was the biggest arena. African resistance and tropical disease had deterred or defeated earlier would-be conquerors from Europe, who seized patches of coast but never got far inland. Now, however, in a notorious scramble for territory, in the last two decades of the nineteenth century, seven European powers seized 10 million square miles of Africa. The Pacific was sliced up in similar fashion. In Southeast Asia, in the same period, only Thailand eluded European, Japanese, or American imperialism. Even in parts of the world largely exempt from the rule of these empires, in most of continental Latin America, and East and Southwest Asia, local governments had to accept economic domination—a form of exploitation that has come to be known as **business imperialism**—and political interference in both their internal and foreign affairs.

Existing empires enlarged. The extent of land under French rule doubled between 1878 and 1913. The total territory of all European empires more than doubled to more than 20 million square miles over the same period, while the total population of their empires increased from a little over 300 million to over 550 million people (see Figure 25.1). New empires emerged: those of Germany, Italy, and Belgium (or rather, strictly speaking, of King Leopold II of the Belgians, for his empire in the Congo was, at first, a so-called free state under the king's personal rule). These were new countries, outcomes of European rebellions and wars: Belgium only came into being in 1830, while Italy and Germany were forged by the unification of many smaller states in the 1860s. Italy's was a particularly significant empire, because it was built up by a state with no direct access to the Atlantic. Italy used the Mediterranean as a route to expand into North Africa and the Levant, and the new Suez Canal, which opened in 1869, as a means of access to imperial conquests in East Africa. Portugal acquired a "third" African empire in Angola and Mozambique to replace those it had lost in the Indian Ocean and Brazil. The Netherlands withdrew from West Africa to concentrate on building up a huge empire in Indonesia. Other European countries took little part: the Scandinavian powers and Spain engaged in the outreach of this period only to a modest extent, while the Habsburg Empire, centered in Austria and Hungary, with limited access to the sea, showed no interest in overseas expansion. Russia's vast land empire left it little scope and energy for maritime adventures (see Chapter 21). With these exceptions, however, it is fair to speak generally of "European" global imperialism.

In part, we need to understand European expansion against the background of demographic change. Europe's population was soaring. At the beginning of the nineteenth century, most of Malthus's fellow intellectuals (see Chapter 20) believed that what they called "progress" could sustain population growth and, in particular, that agricultural improvement could enhance nutrition in Europe and generate enough surplus food to feed many mouths. Broadly speaking, they were right. During the nineteenth century, most European countries roughly doubled their populations. Russia's increased 400 percent. At the same time, Europe generated enough surplus population to populate "New Europes" in the temperate parts of the Americas, Australia, New Zealand, Algeria, and South Africa. Over the eighteenth and nineteenth centuries as a whole, despite big rises in population in some parts of Asia, Europe's share of world population rose from around a fifth to over a quarter.

In places that European outreach targeted, native populations declined as a proportion of the global whole. In some places they declined in absolute terms. Africa illustrates the role of demography. The figures are glaring. From rough parity with Europe's population in the seventeenth century, Africa's share of world population dropped to little more than 8 percent by 1850. The reasons for this decline are unknown. It seems, however, that while plague (see Chapter 14) receded from Europe, sub-Saharan Africa's killer diseases—malaria, sleeping sickness, yellow fever—remained rampant, and in North Africa plague lingered. Although we lack the data to make comparisons with earlier periods, the incidence of recorded plagues in North Africa grew in the eighteenth century—in the very period when plague disappeared from Europe. The last outbreaks in the Maghrib, as far as we know, were in 1818–1820 and in Egypt in 1835. The decrease of population in Africa altered the continent's role in the world. For European intruders, it came to make more sense to take over African soil and exploit its products and potential directly, instead of milking the continent for slave labor.

Even so, demographic changes alone cannot account for the ascent of Europe to global hegemony. Europe still did not have enough manpower to dominate the world. Industrial technology, however, made up much of the shortfall. Europe's advantage became visible in the late eighteenth century. In the 1770s, the chronometer solved the problem of how to find longitude at sea. This invention hugely increased the security of long-range navigation because it enabled sailors to know when they were approaching dangerous coasts. New steel-making technology (see Chapter 23) enhanced guns of European manufacture. Rifled guns and breach-loading artillery improved in the same period, as did techniques for making tropical-weight clothing. Gradually, medicines good enough to keep European armies alive in the tropics came into use, especially, in the second half of the century—quinine pills and powders from plantations in India and Java. Quinine could stave off the effects of malaria, the biggest tropical killer disease. Steam power, meanwhile, made European workers more productive and improved the precision, adaptability, and reliability of European armies in hostile environments. Victim-peoples of Western imperialism found it hard to resist invaders borne on steamboats, fortified by quinine, and armed with steel guns.

"Victim-peoples of Western imperialism found it hard to resist invaders borne on steamboats, fortified by quinine, and armed with steel guns."

FIGURE 25.1 EUROPEAN EMPIRES: AREA AND POPULATION, CA. 1939
Niall Ferguson, Empire: The Rise and Demise of the British World Order and the Lessons for Global Power, *New York: Basic Books, 2003, p. 242.*

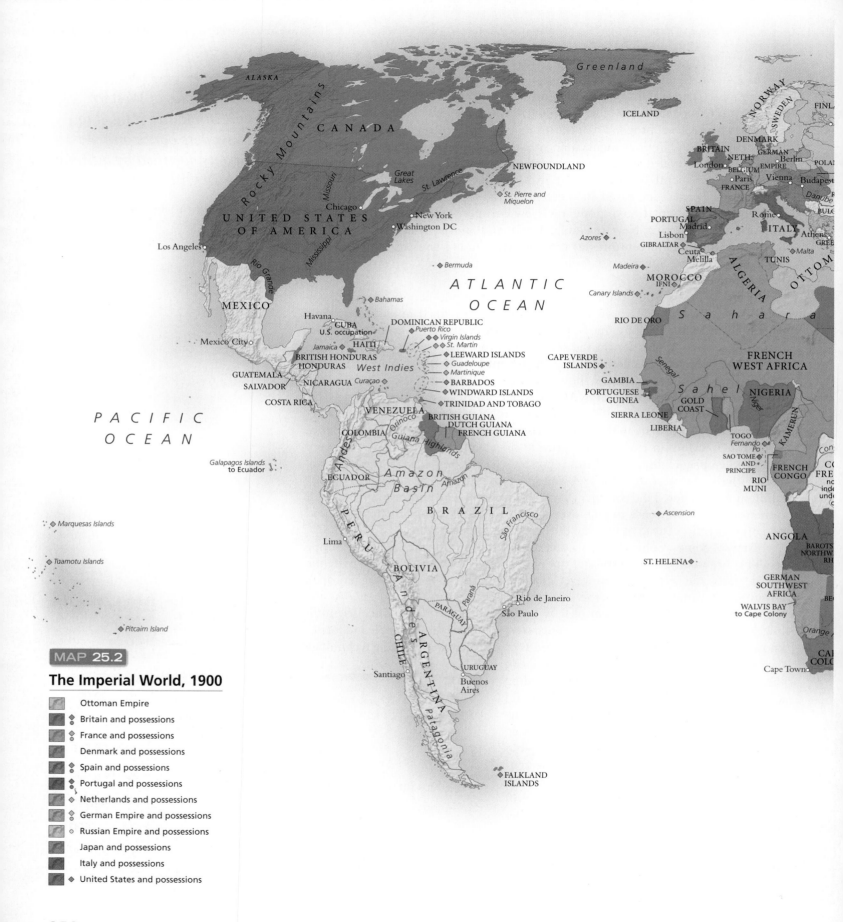

ALASKA

Greenland

CANADA

NEWFOUNDLAND

ICELAND

NORWAY

SWEDEN

FINLA...

DENMARK

BRITAIN

NETH.

GERMAN

London

BELGIUM

EMPIRE

Berlin

POLA...

Paris

Vienna

Budapest

FRANCE

Danube

Rome

ITALY

BULG...

Athens

GREE...

ATLANTIC
OCEAN

SPAIN

PORTUGAL

Madrid

Lisbon

Azores

GIBRALTAR

Ceuta

Malta

Melilla

Madeira

MOROCCO

IFNI

Canary Islands

ALGERIA

TUNIS

OTTO...

UNITED STATES
OF AMERICA

Rocky Mountains

*Great
Lakes*

Missouri

St. Lawrence

Chicago

New York

Washington DC

*St. Pierre and
Miquelon*

Los Angeles

Mississippi

Rio Grande

Bermuda

RIO DE ORO

Sahara

MEXICO

Bahamas

Havana

CUBA

U.S. occupation

Mexico City

Jamaica

HAITI

DOMINICAN REPUBLIC

Puerto Rico

Virgin Islands

St. Martin

CAPE VERDE
ISLANDS

FRENCH
WEST AFRICA

Sahel

BRITISH HONDURAS

West Indies

LEEWARD ISLANDS

GAMBIA

NIGERIA

HONDURAS

Guadeloupe

PORTUGUESE
GUINEA

GOLD
COAST

GUATEMALA

NICARAGUA

Martinique

SIERRA LEONE

SALVADOR

Curaçao

BARBADOS

LIBERIA

COSTA RICA

WINDWARD ISLANDS

TOGO

TRINIDAD AND TOBAGO

*Fernando
Po*

KAMERUN

VENEZUELA

Orinoco

BRITISH GUIANA

SAO TOME
AND
PRINCIPE

Con...

PACIFIC

COLOMBIA

DUTCH GUIANA

FRE...

OCEAN

Guiana Highlands

FRENCH GUIANA

RIO
MUNI

FRENCH
CONGO

*no...
ind...
und...
C...*

*Galapagos Islands
to Ecuador*

ECUADOR

*Amazon
Basin*

Amazon

Ascension

ANGOLA

Marquesas Islands

B R A Z I L

São Francisco

ST. HELENA

BAROTS...
NORTHW...
RH...

Tuamotu Islands

Lima

PERU

Andes

BOLIVIA

Rio de Janeiro

São Paulo

GERMAN
SOUTHWEST
AFRICA

BE...

WALVIS BAY
to Cape Colony

Pitcairn Island

Paraná

Paraguay

Orange ...

CHILE

Andes

ARGENTINA

URUGUAY

CAP...
COLO...

Santiago

Buenos
Aires

Cape Town

Patagonia

MAP **25.2**

The Imperial World, 1900

- Ottoman Empire
- Britain and possessions
- France and possessions
- Denmark and possessions
- Spain and possessions
- Portugal and possessions
- Netherlands and possessions
- German Empire and possessions
- Russian Empire and possessions
- Japan and possessions
- Italy and possessions
- United States and possessions

*FALKLAND
ISLANDS*

FINLAND

St. Petersburg

Moscow

Volga

POLAND

AUSTRO-HUNGARIAN
EMPIRE

pest

ROMANIA

Danube

BULGARIA *Crimea*

GREECE *Black Sea*

Istanbul

ns

OTTOMAN EMPIRE

EGYPT

Cairo *Suez Canal*

Red Sea

Nile

ANGLO-
EGYPTIAN
SUDAN

ERITREA

Addis
Ababa

ETHIOPIA

BRITISH
EAST
AFRICA

Congo

CONGO
FREE STATE
nominally
independent
under Belgian
control

GERMAN
EAST
AFRICA

NORTHEASTERN
RHODESIA

BAROTSELAND-
NORTHWESTERN
RHODESIA

Zambezi

BRITISH
CENTRAL
AFRICA

PORTUGUESE
EAST
AFRICA

SOUTHERN
RHODESIA

BECHUANA-
LAND

SOUTH AFRICAN
REPUBLIC

Orange River

ORANGE FREE STATE

NATAL

CAPE
COLONY

BASUTOLAND

Yenisey

Ob'

RUSSIAN EMPIRE

Lena

S i b e r i a

Amur

Caspian Sea

BUKHARA

PERSIA

Tehran

Tigris

Euphrates

KUWAIT

BAHRAIN

*Arabian
Peninsula*

OMAN

HADHRAMAUT

Aden

FRENCH SOMALILAND

BRITISH
SOMALILAND

ITALIAN
SOMALILAND

Socotra

Seychelles

Zanzibar

Amirante Islands

Comoro Islands

MADAGASCAR

Mauritius

Réunion

AFGHANISTAN

Himalayas

Indus

Delhi

Ganges

NEPAL

BHUTAN

Diu
Damão
Bombay

Chandernagore

Goa

INDIA

Yanaon

Madras
Pondicherry
Karikal

Mahé

CEYLON

Gobi

QING
EMPIRE

Yellow River

Beijing

KOREA

Port Arthur

Jiaozhou

Nanjing

Yangtze

Shanghai

Macao

Hong Kong

Guangzhouwan

Taiwan

JAPAN

Tokyo

Burma

SIAM
(Thailand)

Bangkok

Mekong

FRENCH
INDOCHINA

Saigon

BRITISH
NORTH BORNEO

BRUNEI

MALAYA SARAWAK

Singapore *Borneo*

Sumatra

DUTCH EAST INDIES

Batavia

Java

MALDIVE
ISLANDS

Chagos Islands

Cocos Islands

INDIAN
OCEAN

PHILIPPINE
ISLANDS

Manila

*Christmas
Island*

PORTUGUESE
TIMOR

*Mariana
Islands*

Guam

*Marshall
Islands*

*Caroline
Islands*

PACIFIC OCEAN

KAISER WILHELM'S
LAND

*New
Guinea*

PAPUA

BISMARCK
ARCHIPELAGO

*Gilbert
Islands*

*Solomon
Islands*

*Ellice
Islands*

*Santa Cruz
Islands*

Fiji

*New
Caledonia*

AUSTRALIAN
COLONIES

Darling

Sydney

*Lord Howe
Island*

NEW
ZEALAND

N

**Percentage of Earth's Land Surface
Controlled by Colonial Empires in 1914**

Independent: 29.8%

Chinese: 6%

Ottoman: 1.5%

Russian: 15%

Portuguese: 1%

Spanish: 1%

French: 7.7%

Belgian: 1.6%

Italian: 1.8%

German: 1.6%

Japanese: 0.4%

United States: 7.6%

Dutch: 1.4%

Danish: 1.5%

British: 21.5%

The Battle of Omdurman. "Whatever happens, we have got the Maxim gun and they have not," wrote a British cynic about combat between modern Western armies, armed with machine guns, repeating rifles, and heavy artillery, and their non-Western foes who still fought with spears, swords, and shields. This contemporary commemorative panorama of the British victory over the Sudanese at the Battle of Omdurman revels in the slaughter wrought by irresistible technical superiority. Almost 11,000 Sudanese were killed, and at least 16,000 wounded in this battle, at a cost of 48 British lives—half of which were lost when a British colonel insisted on fighting one anachronism with another by launching a cavalry charge.

In the last quarter of the century, machine guns, especially the Maxim gun, patented in 1884, made a huge difference because unlike heavy artillery, they could be easily transported to almost any destination. In 1880, General Roca machine-gunned his way through the Native American defenders of the pampa in central and southern Argentina. The following year, a similar campaign of extermination began against the Yaqui Indians in northwest Mexico. The government expropriated their lands, giving 1 million acres to a frontier rancher and over 1.2 million acres to a United States construction company. In 1884, French guns silenced opposition to their takeover of Indochina. British gunships blasted the Southeast Asian kingdom of Burma out of existence in 1885. In 1893, white settlers in what is now Zimbabwe in southern Africa shot the spear-armed Ndebele warriors to pieces. In a typical gesture of despair in 1895, Ngoni priests in Mozambique in East Africa threw away their bone oracles after defeat by invincibly well-armed Portuguese. In 1898, the classic case occurred: the Battle of Omdurman, where the British mowed down the previously invincible forces of a Sudanese leader. The Sudanese losses were 11,000 dead and 16,000 wounded. British losses are usually put at 48 killed, 382 wounded. "Whatever happens, we have got/The Maxim gun and they have not," wrote a cynical British versifier. Like all technological advantages, the West's military superiority could not be permanent, but it was vital while it lasted.

Still, it would be a mistake to attribute the empires' dominance to technology alone, any more than to demographics alone. Despite medical advances, disease could still defeat white armies in tropical climes throughout the century. In South Africa in 1879, it killed twice as many British soldiers as were lost in combat to the Zulus. In Cuba in 1898, during the Spanish-American War, three times as many Americans fell to yellow fever as to enemy action. Partly because of the ravages of disease, it took France 13 years of brutal warfare, from 1882, to conquer Vietnam (known to the French as Tonkin China), even with an army of 35,000 men. "Tonkin cholera, Tonkin misery, Tonkin famine, Tonkin cemetery" became a grim joke in Paris. Nor did Western armies always have things all their own way on the battlefield. Their supremacy was patchy at first, for technological advantages were slow to mature. During wars against the Sikhs of northwest India in the 1840s, the British found that the defenders could almost match their firepower. In 1876, an alliance of Sioux and Cheyenne almost annihilated a force of United States' cavalry at the Battle of the Little Bighorn. In 1879, a Zulu army surprised a British force at Isandlhwana in South Africa. Of 1,800 British troops, only about 350 escaped alive.

After all these defeats, the white man took effective revenge, but as well as waging and winning conventional battles in wars of resistance, underequipped native defenders on colonial frontiers could prolong the wars with guerrilla tactics. Such tactics kept the British out of Afghanistan in the 1840s and 1870s and harassed the French in the interior of Algeria, where native fighters never ceased to resist the colonizers after the French occupied the city of Algiers in 1830. In the 1870s, the French logged 2,380 guerrilla incursions in Algeria. In the East Indies, the Dutch lost 15,000 men subduing resistance in Java in the 1820s. It later took them 30 years, from 1873, to bring the sultanate of Aceh in northern Sumatra under control, thanks to the deadly combination of fierce native guerrillas and killer diseases.

Two cases illustrate the possibilities of successful native resistance in conventional warfare. The Maori wars in New Zealand lasted a long time: from 1845 to

1872, on and off. British forces only reported victories against Maoris, but British propaganda masks a remarkable fact. Maoris repeatedly got the better of the British by devising effective tactical and technical responses to the invaders' superior firepower. The Maori quickly became masters of musket warfare, copying the volley-firing discipline of European troops. Indeed, the Maori were among the most effective users of muskets. In the 1830s, in a frightening imitation of European methods, musket-armed Maori conquered the Chatham Islands, southeast of New Zealand, dispossessing and slaughtering the native fisher folk. In 1862, a British missionary thought that the Maori were "apparently equal to an English regiment as regards order and discipline."

Dutch attempts to conquer Aceh began in 1873 and raged on and off for 30 years. Aceh had been an independent sultanate for centuries, and it was still imperfectly subdued when the Dutch conceded Indonesian independence in 1949. The photograph shows one of the small units the Dutch organized in response to the guerrilla methods of the Acehenese, with three Dutch officers for only 16 native riflemen.

Moreover, the Maori developed an ingenious method of defense, digging underground bunkers of the kind Western armies later adopted in fighting each other, while posting snipers to break up British attacks. In consequence, they sometimes won offensive battles—at least in the early phases of the wars, before the British had the advantages of newer rifles—while in defensive engagements, the Maori were virtually unbeatable, despite being habitually outnumbered. They also made cunning use of strategic withdrawals. Frequently, British artillery expended a fortune's worth of shells against Maori defenses, only to find they were unoccupied. When the Maori finally ceased to resist, it was partly because their own ranks were divided—the British had seduced some to their side. Partly, too, the inequality of numbers between settlers and Maori had become too great. The Maori were outnumbered by more than three to one in a land that by the end of the century had nearly 750,000 white settlers. Even after the conclusion of the wars in 1870, an independent Maori zone remained unconquered, gradually integrating, by peaceful accommodation, into the emerging New Zealand state (see Chapter 26). The Maori also proved adept at European business and technology, developing their own sawmills and European-style shipping.

Ethiopia proved to be even more robust. Emperor Menelik II (r. 1889–1913) beat the European imperialists at their own game. He came to the throne as a passionate modernizer with a love of gadgets—the sort of man, said one of his European aides, who "would build an escalator to the moon." He used revenues from expanding trade to buy Western military technology. By the mid-1890s, he had 100,000 modern rifles. He also reformed the army's supply services, while upholding the traditional methods of recruiting soldiers, via the warrior aristocracy and local chiefs, and the traditional ideology of crusade. He proved that an African state could compete with European empires on equal terms in the scramble for Africa.

While respecting areas of European control, Menelik conquered an empire of his own as far as Lake Turkana in the south and the swamplands of the upper Nile to the west. Campaigns began with traditional chants of self-praise from the troops and ended in "terrible butchery," as a European observer reported, "by soldiers drunk with blood." Menelik scattered garrisons in conquered territory, imposed Christianity on pagan communities, and introduced the customs and dress of his native province of Shoa. In 1896, Italy attempted to take over his empire. At the Battle of Adowa, the Italian army crumbled in the face of Ethiopian firepower. The Italians lost a third of their 18,000 men killed, plus a further 1,500 wounded and 1,800 captured. Ethiopia emerged from the scramble for Africa as the only enlarged native African state.

Ethiopia is a reminder that even in the nineteenth century imperial expansion was not a white privilege. Other native African states tried it, but all succumbed, sooner or later, to conquest by Europeans. Khedive Ismail of Egypt (r. 1863–1879),

"Ethiopia is a reminder that even in the nineteenth century imperial expansion was not a white privilege."

A European view of the Battle of Adowa. In contrast to the Ethiopian version of the battle depicted on the Closer Look on page 857, the European press managed to invest the Italian defeat with the heroic quality of a last stand against overwhelming odds. In this typical example from a British newspaper, *The Graphic*, the light is falling on the Italians' gleaming uniforms, which convey an impression of civilization and almost of sanctity, in contrast to the demonic savagery of their Ethiopian attackers. The Italian troops are surrounded by spent cartridge cases. The kneeling soldier on the right, with his transfixed look and prayerful posture, is trying to reload despite a mortal wound. Outlined against the gunsmoke, on a rearing horse, General Baratieri, the Italian commander, raises his helmet in a last salute to rally his doomed troops.

for instance, was, for a time, one of Africa's most successful native imperialists. He proclaimed his ambitions openly. The opera he commissioned for the opening of the Cairo Opera House in 1871 was Giuseppe Verdi's *Aida*, a celebration, in Ismail's eyes if not in those of Verdi, who was an empire-hating liberal, of ancient Egyptian wars of conquest southward. In 1878, Ismail announced that he would present, at the Universal Exposition of that year in Paris, a map showing Egypt's borders resting on Lake Chad in Central Africa, with a project to open a route to the Atlantic.

Ismail realized that steam power could open up the potential of the African interior. He believed that he could exploit Western sympathies to help him create an empire for Egypt among the remotest reaches of the Blue and White Niles. Posing as the policeman of slave-trading routes, he would raise finance for empire-building among anti-slavery philanthropists in Britain and France. He employed Europeans to lead armies and administrators into what he called the "province of Equatoria," on the Nile in Central Africa, in a world of great lakes and waterfalls that were only beginning to find their way onto maps in Europe. But the difficult environment and vast distances defeated him. His armies were overwhelmed or isolated. Along the Red Sea and Blue Nile, he encountered invincible resistance from the native states. Meanwhile, his ambitions bankrupted Egypt, and his westernizing ways helped provoke a nationalist rebellion. In 1882, Britain took control of the Egyptian government (see Chapter 23). What remained of Ismail's conquests eventually became the Anglo-Egyptian Sudan—in effect, an unruly part of the British Empire.

In northwest Africa, meanwhile, the sultan of Morocco, Mulay Hassan (r. 1873–1894), tried to preempt European imperialism by claiming dominion over the Sahara, as ruler of "all the tribes not subject to another sovereign" and of "the land of all the tribes who mention the sultan in their prayers." These were unrealistic pretensions. The desert peoples acknowledged "no other chief than Allah and Muhammad." Religious leaders commanded respect and sometimes organized resistance to imperialism from whatever quarter it came. In the 1890s, the holy man Ma el Ainin (ma ehl-eyein-NEEN), whose breath supposedly made sand miraculously medicinal, fought off French and Spanish invaders in the western Sahara, without even paying lip service to the sultan. His stronghold at Smara still stands in the desert. After Mulay Hassan's death, rebellious sheikhs and jealous European powers weakened his empire until, in 1904, France and Spain partitioned Morocco between them.

The sort of empire Mulay Hassan imagined in North Africa, Said Barghash (r. 1870–1888), sultan of the island of Zanzibar in East Africa, dreamed of in the heart of the continent. "Chosen," he claimed, "by Providence to found a great African kingdom which will extend from the coast to the great lakes and beyond to the west," he realized that he needed to conciliate European powers. He therefore posed as a foe of the slave trade—but, along with ivory, slaves were the wealth of the region he claimed. Instead of relying, like Khedive Ismail, on European officers, Barghash employed African and Arab agents to represent him in the African interior. They were often deeply implicated in slaving, which was a provocation to the Europeans. In the early 1880s, Barghash's governor in Ugogo, Mwinyi Mtwana, gave Germany an excuse to intervene by charging outrageous tolls on caravan traffic. The Germans put him to death and took over his territory. Barghash's system was doomed. By the time of his death, Britain and Germany had dismembered and shared out his territories. Zanzibar became a British protectorate in 1890.

A CLOSER LOOK

An Ethiopian View of The Battle of Adowa

Menelik calmly directs his troops. He is dressed in imperial regalia and accompanied by officials and holy men who survey the action from underneath umbrellas that signify their rank. The umbrellas are dark as a sign of mourning that both sides were shedding Christian blood.

In the Battle of Adowa in 1896, the Ethiopians under the command of Emperor Menelik II (r. 1889–1913) annihilated an invading Italian army. An Ethiopian painting from early in the twentieth century shows the victors in a more positive light than in the European version of the same battle on page 856.

Astride a white horse, and protected by a halo painted in the national colors of Ethiopia, St. George leads Menelik's army.

Ethiopian firepower includes cannon, machine guns, and repeating rifles.

Legendary Ethiopian heroes, clad in traditional dress, slash the Italian infantry with swords.

With his horse facing backward, the Italian commander, General Baratieri, appears ready to order a retreat.

How does this painting provide a different perspective on imperialism from the version that most Westerners believed in the nineteenth century?

Making Connections | TECHNOLOGY AND IMPERIALISM

TOOLS AND TECHNOLOGY	REGION OF DEVELOPMENT/DATE OF INVENTION	EFFECTS
Invention of chronometer	Britain/1770s	Allowed for precise location of longitude at sea, increasing security of long-range navigation; effective planning of voyages
Steelmaking technology	Britain and Western Europe/1730s–1800s	Increased productivity of steel products; more effective small arms and artillery
Rifles and breach-loading artillery	Britain and Western Europe/1840s–1900	Combined with better materials (see above) to improve weaponry
Tropical-weight clothing	Britain and Western Europe/1850s–1900	Allowed more mobility, comfort in tropical zones for colonial military and officials
Quinine pills, powders, and other medicines	Europe (1750); wide use by 1850	Used to stave off effects of malaria; increased survival rates and mobility of European colonial officials and soldiers in tropics
Steam power	England/1769–1900 (continuously improved)	Vastly increased speed over wind-propelled ships or horsepower on land
Machine guns	Europe/1860s–1900 (continuously improved)	Helped annihilate native foes of colonialism in the Americas, Asia, and Africa; in turn, they abetted native resistance to European imperialists

METHODS OF IMPERIAL RULE

If white imperialism was not imposed by weight of numbers, or solely by force of superior technology, it must have relied—indeed, it did rely almost everywhere—on native collaborators. Thanks to historians' work in the last 50 years or so, we know much more about how people in territories that received European imperialism reacted to it. Far from being passive playthings of white superiority, we can now see that native Asian, African, and Pacific states were participants in the process and that native peoples were its exploiters and manipulators, as well as its victims. Without the consent of native communities, empire was expensive. Even at its best, empire was probably only marginally profitable in most places. Without native help in policing and administration, the Western colonial empires could never have functioned.

India, for instance, had fewer than 1,000 British administrators in the 1890s in a country of 300 million people. European observers considered Java, with 300 Dutch administrators for 30 million people "overgoverned." British troops in India never numbered more than 90,000 men—0.03 percent of the population. The rest of the Indian army, more than 200,000 men, was made up of Indian troops under British officers. Though empires sometimes shipped large armies to their colonies for conquests or to repress rebellions, they could never afford to keep such forces in place for long.

The most common device for harnessing native cooperation was what the British called **indirect rule** (or *dual role* as the Dutch called it, or *association* to use the term the French applied in Indochina.) "The keynote of British colonial method," said Frederick Lugard (1858–1945), the official largely responsible for developing the system of indirect rule in Africa, was "to rule through and by the natives." As a British parliamentary committee recommended in 1898, "Adopt the native government already existing; be content with controlling their excesses and maintaining peace between them."

Lugard exaggerated when he claimed that this was a uniquely British method, which "has made us welcomed by tribes and peoples in Africa." On the contrary, it was how most successful empires succeed and have succeeded throughout history. Europeans were welcome in many places that became regions of indirect rule because of the *stranger effect* (see Chapter 16). Some cultures are disposed to grant what to us seem surprising degrees of power to outsiders—sometimes because of the high esteem accorded to the exotic and strange, such as we show for rarities and curiosities from distant shores, and sometimes because of a shrewd calculation. The foreigner is a useful arbitrator in disputes, because outsiders can be—or appear to be—objective. So, as long as they retained local power, many native elites in colonial lands were willing to grant the topmost level of authority to European intruders and pay them to exercise it.

Indirect rule worked particularly well in British colonies because British administrators, even though they were usually middle class, had an aristocratic outlook and education and came from an old monarchy. They could sympathize with traditional elites and aristocracies and could even sense that they had more in common with them than with many of their fellow Britons. In 1897, the aristocratic wife of a British governor in Fiji in the Pacific made the point in her diary: "How can I make it clear to Nanny," she wrote, that the "native ladies," as she called the wives of local chiefs, "are my equals?" whereas "Nanny," who was a working-class English woman, was emphatically not. Especially after 1877, when Queen Victoria of Britain officially took the title of Empress of India, British administrators sought to link the traditional Indian elite to the crown with aristocratic trinkets: coats of arms, lavish ceremonies, knighthoods, and other titles.

Indirect rule was more than a charade, however. Local, regional, and subordinate native rulers retained real power. More than one-third of India was divided among states ruled by Indian princes, and native sultans ruled virtually the whole of Malaya. Friendly native chiefs administered parts of German East Africa (modern Namibia). Regents, as the Dutch called traditional local rulers, and autonomous sultanates survived in the Dutch East Indies. Even the French, whose republican principles should have made them hostile to the idea of working with the traditional hereditary elites of their colonies, accepted the necessity of indirect rule. Morocco and Tunisia were French *protectorates* under the formal rule of figurehead Arab monarchs, for instance, whereas the parts of Algeria that bordered the Mediterranean were considered part of France, run by the same system of provincial administration as was France itself. In their tropical African possessions, the French delegated awkward jobs, such as tax collecting, to native chiefs. They also ruled through native monarchs in Cambodia, Laos, and Vietnam. In practice, European powers could exercise jurisdiction at their discretion, even in territories classed as protectorates or nominally shared, like the Anglo-Egyptian Sudan, with native co-rulers. When they thought it necessary, they could change the personnel

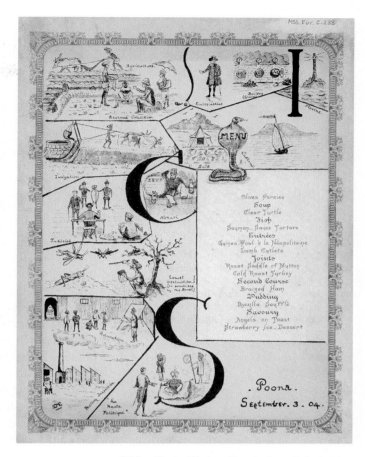

White Man's Burden. The Indian Civil Service (ICS) was the highly paid, professional bureaucracy that governed Britain's Indian Empire. Until the 1920s, its members were overwhelmingly British. This dinner menu for members of the ICS in 1904 looks lavish and self-indulgent at first but reveals much about the difficulties of governing distant empires: the range of activities for which the civil servants felt responsible; the differences in development in the largely rural India of the day; nostalgia for the tastes of home; and the self-mocking humor that helped English administrators cope with their jobs.
© *The Trustees of the British Museum*

Indirect rule. Snapped in late 1920, the French ambassador to Cambodia takes center-stage, in a posture of rigid authority, as the effective ruler of the country, King Sisowath Monivong (r. 1904–1927), stands to his right, in French uniform and a subordinate role. Like other imperial powers elsewhere, the French in Indochina preferred to mask the reality of their power behind the facade that native monarchs and elites retained control of their own countries.

or nature of local and regional government in their colonies. But the trouble and expense of direct rule were always best avoided if possible. Everywhere, local collaborators kept the European empires going. A local chief named Ngailema settled the boundary between French and Belgian spheres on the lower Congo River, extorting rich gifts from both sides.

Still, even in areas of indirect rule, European imperialism could have transforming effects on methods of government and ways of life. Changes in legal systems are a good way to measure the impact of empire. In Malaya, in the second half of the century, the court of the Sultan of Kedah closely imitated European practices, while the Sultan of Johor, Abu Bakr, who ruled for most of the second half of the nineteenth century, struck English visitors as "a perfect English gentleman." The sultans' subjects still regarded the ruler's power as supernatural and revered the symbols of royalty as sacred, but trial by jury replaced magical ordeals and appeals to oracles. The state enforced its exclusive right to violence. Cases traditionally settled by private vengeance became matters of public law. Male adulterers—formerly fair game for injured husbands—now paid steep fines. Such transformations, however, remained dependent on local sympathies. In 1892, a French administrator in Senegal in West Africa proposed that the ordeal of the hot blade (which supposedly would not burn the mouth of an innocent man) be discontinued, together with the practice of punishing not just the offender, but his entire family. The suggestions struck local chiefs as so radical that they had to be shelved.

The British far preferred to rely on traditional aristocracies rather than on the "educated natives" whom the French favored. But educated natives were indispensable. Interpreters were vital. "The commanders come and go," ran a French saying in West Africa, "but the interpreters are always there." Even though most colonial regimes privileged some particular set of laws—usually those of their own mother country—in practice many competing systems of traditional and customary law inevitably applied in vast territories inhabited by many different historic communities. Locals, who knew their way around the native cultures, were vital guides. Four thousand of them served in the administration of the British-ruled parts of India in the late 1860s. Twenty years later, Indians occupied nearly two-thirds of the jobs. Bankimcandra Chattopadhyaya, whom Bengalis regard as one of their greatest writers, showed the contradictions of this class of *babus*, as the British called their Indian helpers. Bankim accepted office under the British as a deputy magistrate. He earned British admiration and won British rewards, including a medal, which, in one of his own short stories, features as a payoff for a corrupt magistrate. The hero of his novel, *Anandamath*, of 1882, warns his fellow countrymen, "There is no hope of the revival of true faith if the English do not become rulers. . . . Our knowledge of ourselves cannot grow without knowledge of the world. The English are well versed in knowledge of the world and they are great teachers too. Therefore we shall make them kings." On the other hand, his work has terrifying passages of revolutionary bloodshed directed against the British. His attitude toward Indian independence in the late nineteenth century was like St. Augustine's toward chastity in the late fourth century. He wanted it but not yet.

An alternative strategy to indirect rule or reliance on native administrators was to ship collaborators in from far away. When Frederick Lugard marched into Uganda in East Africa in 1890, his forces included many African Muslims: a Somali chief porter, Sudanese soldiers, and sharpshooters from Zanzibar. When Henry Morton Stanley claimed the lower Congo in Central Africa for King Leopold II of the Belgians in 1880, he found a French outpost commanded by a black Senegalese sergeant, dressed "in dirty African rags," who declared "in all seriousness that, being the only White man there, he was glad to see others arrive to keep him company." In Sierra Leone in West Africa, Britain established a black colony of freed slaves from the Caribbean, who created an imitation of England in their capital at Freetown, with garden parties, lecture circuits, concerts, and a temperance union to combat alcoholism. Sawyer's bookshop in Freetown sold such English middle-class manuals of behavior as *The Ballroom Guide* and *Etiquette and the Perfect Lady*.

In other places, local allies enabled the Europeans to rule. The British fought the Zulus with the help of other peoples of South Africa and recruited Hausa gunners from what is today Nigeria to keep order in West Africa. The French conquerors of Tukolor on the Niger River in West Africa in 1889 incorporated thousands of other Africans into their army. Then, when their native soldiers rebelled, the French enlisted the conquered Tukoloros against them. In the 1890s, the British Empire nurtured the kingdom of Lozi in southern Africa while pulverizing the neighboring Ndebele people into submission. The Lozi king acquired a portrait of Queen Victoria, visited London to great acclaim, and became a satisfied client of white imperialism.

In getting and keeping the empires going, women were among the most important native collaborators. "White" women were in short supply in the European colonial territories in the first half of the nineteenth century, but relations between European men and native women could be advantageous to both parties, opening useful local links for the colonizers and, for local groups, exploitable channels of communication with the incoming elite. The future British field marshall Sir Garnet Wolseley (1833–1913) wrote as a young officer to his mother from India that with a native concubine he could supply "all the purposes of a wife without any of the bother." Concubinage, however, virtually ceased in India after a rebellion among native soldiers against British rule in 1857, which panicked the British into distancing themselves further from native society. Female emigration from Europe stepped up in the late nineteenth century. In the Dutch East Indies, less than a quarter of the European settler population was female in 1860. The proportion had risen to well over a third by the end of the century. India saw a similar rise in the numbers of British women. In former times, the children of sexual alliances between natives and newcomers had often played important roles in cementing the alliances on which empires relied. In the nineteenth century, that became ever harder, because racism classed "half breeds" as inferior and kept them on the margins of the communities from which they sprang.

Female bravery. Legend has it that a young Scots woman was first to hear the bagpipes of the relief force that on March 5, 1858 raised the siege of Lucknow. Some 3,000 British and Indian troops and civilians had been besieged at Lucknow since July 1, 1857 during the rebellion against British rule in 1857–1858 that the British called the Indian Mutiny. Balladeers celebrated the incident, and the fashionable English artist, Frederick Goodall (1822–1904), painted it.

"In getting and keeping the empires going, women were among the most important native collaborators."

BUSINESS IMPERIALISM

The most indirect form of imperial rule was economic control—business imperialism, which left government in local hands but bought up resources, skimmed off wealth, introduced foreign business elites, reduced economies to dependency, and diverted wealth and political influence abroad. Again, industrialization made business imperialism possible. The world was increasingly divided between primary producers and industrial manufacturers. This division made interregional trade vital as never before. It opened a wealth gap between the primary and secondary producers and gave the rich of the industrialized countries surplus capital with which to buy up the productive capacity of much of the rest of the world. Though

Business imperialism. Even countries that "business imperialism" condemned to produce primary products for the industrialized world could experience industrialization of their own. Some cotton-growing countries, for example, sought to become textile manufacturers. This early twentieth-century photograph of a factory in Ecuador shows automated spinning under way on the right, and cylinders full of carded cotton on the left.

the evidence is insufficient, scholars debate whether large-scale foreign enterprises blocked development of smaller and more local initiatives, frustrating economic growth and industrialization in regions where business imperialism was rife.

Latin America registered the most obvious effects. In a sense, colonialism never really ended there. Native communities, or "indios," as they were called, constituted most of the population in most of the region, but they never exercised a fair share of power or acquired a fair share of wealth. Instead, they became the quasicolonial victims, the exploited human "resources" of their countries' own elites. These elites, though they drove out the representatives of the Portuguese and Spanish crowns, continued themselves to represent European culture—to speak the languages and maintain the customs and privileges of the European conquerors.

Moreover, in the second half of the nineteenth century, foreign investors became a powerful extra elite tier in much of Latin America. A new form of colonial-type dependency arose, this time on international big business. Overwhelmingly, the investors were Europeans, from the major imperial powers of the day—Britain, Germany, and France—and from the United States. In the **Monroe Doctrine** of 1823, the United States had unilaterally decreed a ban on European colonialism in the New World. Thanks in large part to European agreement, the ban worked, and European powers stayed out of most of mainland Latin America for most of the time. Now European capital found a way around the ban. Indeed, business imperialism almost became the forerunner of reimposed European rule. In 1864, the French government installed a puppet ruler in Mexico, on the pretext of securing Mexican debts owed to European creditors. The adventure proved a fiasco. Popular rebellion, the need for troops in Europe, and United States' diplomacy drove the French away in 1867, but the involvement of foreign business in the Latin American economy kept growing.

British investments in Latin America rose from $425 million in 1870 to $3.785 billion by 1913. This added up to two-thirds of the total foreign investment in the region. British companies controlled over half the shipping in Argentina and Brazil and most of South America's railways. By 1884, Europeans owned two-thirds of Chile's nitrates—the valuable new fertilizers of the period (see Chapter 23). Argentina's foreign trade almost trebled between 1870 and 1900. Foreign capital led the boom. Similar developments occurred in other parts of Latin America. Like other forms of imperialism, business imperialism was a collaborative project between locals and strangers: local elites and foreign capitalists. In 1870, a British firm opened for business in Rosario, Argentina's second city, to provide water and drainage. The local authorities demanded high levels of investment and a high share of the yield for themselves. In Brazil, British power in the coffee market aroused many complaints, but Brazilians owned or acquired most plantations, and the government accepted underdevelopment and economic inferiority to foreigners as inevitable.

Hostility to foreigners was more normal, though rarely effective. In 1860, the president of Peru, Ramón Castilla, restive under foreign control of the trade in natural fertilizers, voiced what became the standard complaint: "On many occasions we have been treated with grave lack of respect, as if for the great international potentates there did not exist a common law of nations." The Argentine epic poem of 1872, *Martín Fierro*, by José Hernández, celebrated a gaucho of expansive tastes, for whom the land could never be big enough. It recalled a golden age before bosses, "gringos," and Englishmen, demonic and effeminate, who were "good only to give work." In the last years of the century, nationalists who resented business imperialism adopted the text as a call to independence.

A pattern emerged: local interests attracted foreign investment. This led to foreign control of key technologies for the production and transportation of primary commodities. The consequence was dependence on foreign markets and financiers and, often, political control by foreign businessmen. In 1870, for instance, the government of Costa Rica contracted out its railway-building program to an engineer from the United States. A few years later, his nephew began using the railway to ship bananas to North America. His firm eventually grew into the United Fruit Company—a conglomerate so rich and monopolistic that it became more powerful in the early twentieth century than any government in Central America.

The United States itself, meanwhile, was an important arena for European businessmen, who plowed massive investments into industrial outlets and construction projects. The British novelists Anthony Trollope and Charles Dickens made fun of European investors who sank their money in towns that were never built and railways that went nowhere in the Americas. But there were plenty of genuine and profitable opportunities.

The scale and success of business imperialism raise a further question: Was all imperialism really economic? Imperialism was the result of capitalism and industry: a drive for markets. Between 1850 and 1859, the value of world trade increased by 80 percent. During the last quarter of the century, world trade roughly doubled in volume and increased in value by a third. Between 1870 and 1900, world industrial production roughly quadrupled. World shipping nearly doubled to about 30 millions tons.

In some cases imperialism was clearly profitable. Between 1831 and 1877, revenues from the Dutch East Indies covered a quarter of Dutch state expenditure. Phosphates in Morocco, diamonds in South Africa, and gems, ivory, and rubber in the Congo enriched, respectively, France, Britain, and the king of the Belgians. It used to be thought that the Portuguese Empire in Africa was a silly extravagance for such a poor, small country, but it seems to have been acquired as an act of economic calculation. Russia's expansion into Central Asia was—in part at least—directed toward lands that could grow cotton for Russia's fledgling textile industries. France, as we have seen (see Chapter 24), embarked on the conquest of Indochina in the 1880s partly to solve its labor problems. Indochina also yielded coal, zinc, rubber, and tin for French industry.

Few parts of Africa with exploitable resources were left out of the global economy. Traditional traders were exterminated or became extinct. Some suffered because they were slavers, others because they got in the way of armed greed. King Leopold II proclaimed war on slave traders in the Congo. But his real aim was to cloak his ruthless ivory and rubber grabbing in moral rhetoric. The native palm-oil traders of the Niger delta in West Africa were innocent of slaving, but British merchants cheated and impoverished them. Driven into rebellion in 1895, the natives apologized for their attack on the representatives of the British Niger Company, "particularly in the killing and eating of parts of its employees. . . . We now throw ourselves entirely at the mercy of the good old Queen [Victoria], knowing her to be a most kind, tender-hearted and sympathetic old mother." The face of Africa was scarred and pitted with roads, railways, and mines, or scratched and scrubbed for plantations and new crops.

The **Scramble for Africa** was, in part, a scramble for resources. Even as late as 1880, European imperialists had only appropriated about 10 percent of Africa—most of it on or near the coasts. But improved technology—especially antimalarial treatments, steamboats, and highly efficient

Exploitation. Carefully posed in the self-conscious style favored by photographers at the time, this scene of ivory-bearers in French Congo in 1890 served as a postcard. Part of the message that the person who sent it wrote is on the largest tusk and in the margin at the right. Europeans' exploitation of the Congo was so ruthless that the population fell by 8-10 million under the brutal rule of King Leopold II of the Belgians from 1885 to 1908.

killing machines—encouraged them to try to dominate the interior. As Germany and Italy—recently unified—began to consolidate, new imperial ambitions were added to the longstanding rivalries of Britain and France. Between 1880 and 1884, all four powers bid to annex parts of the continent. So did King Leopold II of the Belgians, acting as an independent entrepreneur. Portuguese empire-builders responded by trying to extend their hold inland from their old colonies on the coasts of Angola and Mozambique. To forestall the danger that competing bids would spark a European war, representatives of the powers gathered in Berlin in 1884 and agreed, in effect, to partition the continent between them (see Map 25.3).

MAP 25.3 **The Scramble for Africa**

Territory controlled by European nations by 1914

- Belgium
- Britain
- France
- Germany
- Italy
- Portugal
- Spain

1883 date of taking control

—— borders in 1914

European routes of expansion

- → Belgian
- → British
- → French
- → German
- → Italian
- → Portuguese
- → Spanish

1888 foundation date of colonial settlement

Colonial settlements

- ● Belgian
- ○ Boer
- ● British
- ● French
- ● German
- ● Italian
- ● Portuguese
- ○ other settlement

Important mineral deposits

- ◆ coal
- ▣ copper
- ◻ diamonds
- ▣ gold

Over the next 25 years or so, no part of Africa—except, as we have seen, the Ethiopian empire, which grew at its neighbors' expense, and the quasi-American colony of Liberia—was exempt from some form of European control.

In view of the strength of economic imperialism, it is tempting to see greed as the spur to empire-building. But there was more to it than that. Purely political competition among the powers drove imperialism, too, and patriotic pride and the pursuit of glory inspired imperialists who were indifferent to economics. Like other external wars, imperial adventures were ways to export unrest. In Britain, the empire rewarded otherwise potentially rebellious groups. The Scots and Irish, who tended to resent English rule, were disproportionately represented in the ranks of British colonial officials and merchants. The empire gratified the working class, and popular culture celebrated it. Nationalist rhetoric encouraged imperialism and spread pride in empire throughout society. "C is for colonies," trumpeted *An ABC for Baby Patriots*, "Rightly we boast/That of all great countries/Great Britain has the most." The "Great Game"—Anglo-Russian rivalry for power and prestige in Central Asia—drew Russia deeper into Asia to forestall the expansion of British India. It is true, too, that the Scramble for Africa was prompted by rivalries among European powers—initially, over control of access to the natural riches of the Congo Basin.

In some ways, however, competition among the great powers did more to frustrate empires than promote them. Iran (Persia) and Afghanistan stayed independent, partly by playing off the British against the Russians. Thailand staved off colonialism by balancing French and British power. China was so weakened by 1900 that it seemed ripe for partition among European powers and Japan, but they could not agree on how to divide the spoils.

Chronology: European Imperialism in Africa and Asia	
Nineteenth century	European population explosion fuels economy and creates surplus population for global migration; Africa's population declines
ca. 1815–1835	Value of opium exported to China increases fivefold
1820s	Dutch lose 15,000 men in conquest of Java
Summer 1840	British blockade Chinese ports in response to Chinese suspension of trade
1842	Treaty of Nanjing ends Opium War
1850–1859	Value of world trade increases by 80 percent
1857	Formal end of Mughal rule in India
1860–1861	Anglo-French force occupies Beijing
1863–1879	Khedive Ismail attempts to build an Egyptian Empire
1869	Suez Canal opens
1870–1900	World industrial production quadruples; world shipping doubles; world trade doubles in volume
1870s	French fight guerrilla warfare in Algeria
1877	Queen Victoria takes title of Empress of India
1880–1914	Most of Africa brought under European control
1884	Maxim machine gun patented
r. 1889–1913	Emperor Menelik II modernizes Ethiopian army and expands empire in Africa
1896	Battle of Adowa
1898	Battle of Omdurman

IMPERIALISM IN THE "NEW EUROPES"

Some lands were subjected to empire not primarily because of their potential contribution to global trade but because they were "New Europes"—regions similar in climate to much of Europe and therefore exploitable for European colonization. By a combination of accidents, most of these regions—in South Africa, New Zealand, and Australia—belonged to the British Empire, or, like Chile and Argentina, were deeply influenced by British business imperialism.

South Africa had already become a New Europe. In some ways, it was less oppressive than those elsewhere in the world, for here, at least, the European settlers allowed the native peoples to survive, so that they could exploit their labor. In most other regions of similar climate—in the South American cone of Argentina, Chile, and Uruguay, the North American West, Australia, and, with less success, in New Zealand—white settlers waged wars of extermination against the native inhabitants. Australia and New Zealand were exploited at first mainly for sheep raising. This was a marginal activity from the perspective of the global economy, though Australian wool, in particular, was an exportable commodity. But toward

Vancouver, British Columbia, on the Pacific coast of Canada. The crammed houses, bravely flying their flapping laundry, trapped amid telegraph wires, and dwarfed by warehouses seem to imply that space was at a premium. In fact, Canada was thinly populated, and a vast expanse of wilderness and small, isolated prairie settlements separated Vancouver in the early twentieth century from eastern Canada.

the end of the century, refrigeration enabled both countries to export meat and dairy products to Britain. Gold rushes, meanwhile, attracted huge investment and coaxed large cities into being in Australia, California, and South Africa.

Canada was exemplary among the New Europes. In some ways, Canada's nineteenth century seems unspectacular. During the century that followed the end of the War of 1812, in which the Canadian colonies repelled attacks from the United States, the population grew—modestly by the standards of other parts of the Americas—tenfold to about 8 million people. The vast territorial expansion across the continent to the Pacific—which mirrored and matched that of the United States—included much unproductive territory. The Canadian prairies did produce grain, but never as much as those of the United States. A railway crossed the continent on Canadian territory, but it carried less freight and fewer passengers than the parallel railways in the United States. Yet merely to survive, alongside a United States that frequently seemed to be threatening to annex it, was an achievement for Canada. Even though the Atlantic-side Canadian provinces, with their English-speaking inhabitants, had little in common, commercially or culturally, with the mainly French settlements in Quebec, all of them managed to combine in 1867 in a confederation that the British largely put together. Thanks in part to the dynamic vision of the man the British chose to be the first Canadian prime minister, Sir John A. Macdonald (1815–1891), the confederation took responsibility for the whole of British North America except Newfoundland (which did not join the confederation until 1949), incorporated British Columbia on the Pacific coast in 1871, drove rails across the continent, and created a state with the potential Canada subsequently came to exhibit, as a country remarkable for social welfare, cultural pluralism, constitutional flexibility, prosperity, and peace. The main casualties of the process of creating a Canadian nation in the nineteenth century were the native peoples—ignored in the making of the constitution, brushed aside in the westward drive. By the early twentieth century, they had declined at a rate similar to that of most Native Americans of the United States, to a total of around 100,000 people.

The system Britain had established in Canada was really a variant of indirect rule, with elected colonial leaders exercising direct power instead of native chiefs and traditional aristocracies. Demographics, combined with improved communications, made this possible. Toward the end of the nineteenth century, Britain's other colonies of white settlers in Australia and New Zealand were approaching population thresholds—about 4 million and about 750,000, respectively—that enabled them to have the same status as Canada in the British Empire. South Africa, the last of Britain's New Europes, was more of a problem. Unlike the other colonies, it still had its native population. Indeed, black people made up a majority in South Africa. It had even more mineral wealth than Australia—by the end of the century, South Africa was the world's main supplier of gold and diamonds. It also had a sizable community called *Boers*, white citizens, mainly of Dutch ancestry, who spoke not English but *Afrikaans*, their distinctive derivative of Dutch, whose attitude to the British Empire was, at best, wary, and who had to be forced into collaboration in a series of wars, ending only in 1902. Effectively, Britain bought the Afrikaaners' loyalty by giving them power over black South Africans. As one of the Afrikaaner leaders wrote, rejecting British desire to grant civil liberties to "every civilized man" regardless of color, "I sympathize profoundly with the Native races of South Africa, whose land it was long before we came here to force a policy of dispossession on them. . . . But I don't believe in politics for them. . . . When I consider the political future of the Natives in South Africa I must say that I look into shadows and darkness; and . . . feel inclined to shift the intolerable burden of solving the . . . problem to the ampler shoulders and stronger brains of the future."

French imperial planners imagined Algeria in North Africa as a New Europe, too, or a sort of Old World America, where France could encourage American levels of input and achievement among the colonists, while penning the native races—Arabs and Berbers— in doomed desert reservations. Algeria was a "promised land," to be farmed "with gun in hand," as Alexis de Tocqueville put it. The Algerian city of Philippeville looked American to him; distorted into Wild West ugliness by an economic boom. The city of Algiers would become like a town in the American Midwest—"Cincinnati in Africa." Tocqueville believed that Algeria, with its narrow but rich coastlands along the Mediterranean, its vast inland plains, its great open spaces, and its untapped resources would play a crucial role in the future of France. Thomas Bugeaud, the French general charged with the conquest of the Algerian interior in 1837 thought that "conquest will be fruitless without colonization. . . . Agriculture and colonization are the same thing." Tocqueville was convinced that native races, whether in Africa or America, were incapable of civilization. The best the natives could hope for was to be joined with their conquerors and absorbed by them. In 1850, 130,000 Europeans lived in Algeria. There were more than 500,000 by 1900. The more extravagant schemes to make colonization prosper included flooding the Sahara to make a navigable inland lake.

Sydney. New Europes rapidly came to look like old Europe. George Street, Sydney, Australia, photographed in 1899, when the population was some 450,000, looks like a commercial street in a prosperous English provincial city of the same era.

Where they worked, New Europes really did reproduce much of the look and feel of old Europe. In 1850, Jorge Mármol, one of the first of Argentina's long line of great novelists, described the lives of the elite of the capital Buenos Aires, surrounded by embossed wallpapers, Italian carpets, Spanish paintings, and French perfume. To this day, New Zealand has the English-style municipal gardens colonists planted in the spent craters of volcanoes to remind them of home. The University of Dunedin, founded in 1869, near New Zealand's most remote, southernmost point, is modeled on that of Glasgow in Scotland. In 1885, an English historian visiting Australia found "English life all over again."

EMPIRES ELSEWHERE: JAPAN, RUSSIA, AND THE UNITED STATES

Japan, Russia, and the United States lagged only slightly behind Western Europe, in imperialism, as in industrialization.

Japan

Japanese intellectuals began to envy Europeans their empires in the late eighteenth century, when Honda Toshiaki, one of the leading Japanese scholars of Western literature, argued that Japan needed long-range shipping, munitions, and an empire of its own. Colonies could be stripped of resources and their populations exploited for labor, while "the ruler father" could "direct and educate the natives in such a manner that there will not be a single one of them who spends even one unproductive day." Japanese rule extended into the islands that lay north of Japan. Overseas empires were like unified nationhood, parliamentary constitutions, codified laws, industrial economies, trousers, and bow ties: signs of modernization, qualifications for admission to the circle of the great powers.

MAP 25.4

Russian and Japanese Expansion, 1868–1918

Russian Empire, ca. 1855		**1868**	date of foundation or acquisition	→	Japanese attacks in Sino-Japanese War, 1894–1895
acquisitions 1856–1876			Trans-Siberian Railway, built 1891–1917	→	Japanese attacks in Russo-Japanese War, 1904–1905
acquisitions 1877–1914			Japanese Empire, 1870	—	borders 1914
temporary acquisition, with dates			Japanese, 1874–1895	*Chechens*	people
southern limit of Russian sphere of influence, 1914			Japanese, 1905–1910		

The era of Japanese adventures overseas coincided almost exactly with the great age of Western imperialism. A sense of urgency drove Japan to compete for the diminishing living-space that rival empires claimed. Japan's long period of demographic stability ended in the late nineteenth century when its population began to grow. Soldiers and businessmen allied to advocate empire. For samurai who had lost their social privileges (see Chapter 24), external wars were a means of discipline, a purifying ritual for a society polluted by change at home. Victory in the war of 1894–1895 against China (see Chapter 24) equipped Japan with the foundations of an empire: possession of Taiwan and the Pescadores Islands, semicontrol of Korea, and a springboard for further expansion at Russian and Chinese expense (see Map 25.4).

Russia

In Siberia, Russians, of course, already had an empire in territory that bordered their own. They continued to build up their land empire in Europe itself on their western and southern frontiers. Russian imperialism took a huge leap in the Napoleonic Wars (1799–1815), with the annexation of Finland from Sweden in 1809 and the consolidation of Russia's hold on Poland and the Baltic states. The colonization of "New Russia"—southern Ukraine—followed. The port of Odessa on the Black Sea had 30,000 people in 1823 and 630,000 in 1914. In 1853–1856, in the Crimean War, Britain and France intervened to halt the Russian advance into the Balkans at Ottoman expense. So Russian efforts turned to Central Asia. A huge domain there was converted to cotton cultivation to supply industries in Russia's heartlands. A struggle to overcome the Chechens in the Caucasus Mountains extended from the 1830s to the 1860s. Meanwhile, the fantasy of a seaborne empire on the Pacific, reaching to the Antarctic, haunted Russian naval planners' imaginations. Not much came of it. In 1867, Russia sold Alaska to the United States and withdrew from the North American mainland. But the Aleutian Islands off the coast of Alaska remained a maritime frontier, divided between Russia and the United States (see Map 25.4).

Retreat from Alaska made Russia focus even more on Central Asia. In 1868, the Russian Empire declared the native aristocracy of Transoxania dispossessed. Sparing only a few places, which were left to particularly powerful or particularly obedient native dynasties, Russian armies enforced a new system of direct rule and direct taxation. In 1891, a new law limited landholding in the steppes of what is now Kazakhstan to 40 acres per person—far less than a nomad needed to survive. Russia, meanwhile, ruled Chechnya by terror, on the grounds, as a Russian viceroy in the Caucasus put it, that "One execution saved hundreds of Russians from destruction and thousands of Muslims from treason." As the Russian novelist Fyodor Dostoevsky (1821–1881) said, "In Europe we were hangers-on and slaves, whereas in Asia we shall go as masters." Finally, in the 1890s, Russian imperialism concentrated on the Far East, where it met Japanese empire-building, with grave consequences for the future.

The Russian bear. The first satirical Muslim journal in the Russian Empire was published from 1905 to 1917 in Tbilisi, Georgia, the administrative capital of Russian Transcaucasia. Although the Russian Empire had many Muslim subjects, they were divided into competing and often mutually hostile national groups. This journal targeted educated Azerbaijani readers, many of whom had more in common with Shiite Iran than with the Sunni Islam practiced by other Muslims in the Caucasus. The cover page of the November 22, 1909, issue shows the Russian bear growling menacingly while the symbol of Turkish wisdom, the legendary popular philosopher Mullah Nasreddin, sleeps unaware.

The United States

The United States was also an empire. Most nineteenth-century Americans were perfectly frank about it and proud of expanding their territory at other people's expense. They called this America's "manifest destiny." The United States absorbed Mexicans, Canadians, and Native Americans by force or the threat of it. Canada was driven back on the borders of Minnesota in 1818, Maine in 1842, and what are now the states of Oregon and Washington in 1846. The United States' great leap across the continent began in earnest in the 1830s, with attempts to sweep all the native peoples of the Midwest and Southeast into a small, resource-poor Indian territory in what is today the state of Oklahoma. It was a genocidal act that the Cherokees called the Trail of Tears, in which thousands died from disease, exposure, and starvation. Many United States planners hoped that it would kill off most Native Americans. Indeed, by 1900, the total Native American population of the United States was recorded as 237,196—a decline of probably 50 percent during the nineteenth century. Only in the Southwest did Indians escape eclipse. In the last quarter of the nineteenth century, the United States launched a war of extermi-

Manifest Destiny: The spirit of "American Progress," depicted by John Gast in 1872, hovers over the westward march of white settlers. She trails a telegraph wire, as the land behind her is turned into fertile fields. Symbols of technological advance race across the plains. Rather than leading the march, the Native Americans on the left flee, casting frightened glances at their pursuers. By the 1890s, Native Americans had either been wiped out or confined to reservations by the U.S. army.

nation against the remaining Native American peoples in its territory. Meanwhile, in the 1840s, conquests gobbled up Mexican territory north of the Rio Grande, adding most of what are now the states of Arizona, New Mexico, Utah, Nevada, Colorado, and California to the growing empire.

In 1890, the United States census bureau officially declared the land frontier closed. The country was now settled from coast to coast. Almost immediately, American imperialism spilled into the oceans. In the Pacific, the Hawaiian kings had fended off European predators for years and sustained a clever diplomatic balance to keep potential conquerors at bay. But the numbers of foreign immigrants to Hawaii increased, and the economic power of traders from the United States became dominant. The game Hawaii's native rulers played therefore got harder, until white settlers overthrew the Hawaiian monarchy in 1893 with American military and diplomatic support. Annexation to the United States followed in 1898. Meanwhile, the United States also annexed American Samoa in the South Pacific and seized the Philippines, Guam, and Puerto Rico, after defeating Spain in 1898. Spain's former colony Cuba, which was nominally independent after 1901, became a virtual United States protectorate, and the United States took permanent possession of a naval base there at Guantánamo Bay. It also acquired the Canal Zone from Panama in 1904 after enabling Panama to secede from Colombia. The whole American hemisphere became a United States sphere of influence and "Uncle Sam's backyard."

RATIONALES OF EMPIRE

How did imperialists justify their activities? Two rationales were overwhelmingly popular: what imperialists called their **civilizing mission**, and the doctrine that they were inherently, naturally superior. These two justifications overlapped and shaded into each other.

Doctrines of Superiority

Chronology: The Imperial Ambitions of Japan, Russia, and the United States	
1803	Louisiana Purchase transfers vast territory from France to the United States
1809	Russia annexes Finland
1823	United States issues the Monroe Doctrine
1830–1860	Russians struggle to conquer Chechens
1867	United States purchases Alaska from Russia
1890	Land frontier of the United States declared closed
1890s	Russian imperialism focuses on the Far East
1894–1895	Japan defeats China, takes Taiwan
1898	United States annexes Hawaii, seizes Philippines, Guam, and Puerto Rico after defeating Spain
1904	United States acquires Panama Canal Zone

The most influential doctrine originated in a different context: in the search for a scientific way to explain the tremendous diversity of nature, and in the development of a theory of change that, originally conceived to apply to biology, got wrenched out of its original background and applied to society.

In 1800, the "Creation Oratorio" of the Austrian composer Joseph Haydn proclaimed in ravishing music the traditional, biblical account of how the planet got filled with so many different plants and creatures. God had created the world and everything in it in six days. It was a metaphor—a poetic myth, designed to reveal more than literal truth. Most people who thought about it already knew that the planet was immensely old—fossils discovered in the eighteenth century had proved that—and that life developed slowly, growing in complexity, from simple, primitive forms. What remained unknown—the "mystery of mysteries," as the young English scientist, Charles Darwin, remarked in the 1830s—was how those life forms changed, or how God changed them, into the amazing variety visible in the natural world.

Darwin's earliest scientific interests were in sponges and beetles—indications of his interest in life forms regarded as primitive. In 1839, he got a chance to extend his observations, when he accepted a post as the resident scientist on a small round-the-world mission by the British navy. Two stops on the expedition's route inspired new thinking. First, in Tierra del Fuego at the southern tip of South America, he was shocked to see how little the natives had, at least in European eyes, of material culture or intellectual or spiritual lives. "Man in his natural state," Darwin reported, was "so beastly, so vile, a foul, naked, snuffling thing." He was particularly surprised that the local Indians could endure the ferocious, freezing climate in a state of virtual nakedness and guessed that their bodies must have adapted to the environment in which they lived. He began to see humans for what they are—well-adapted animals.

Later in the voyage, further revelations occurred to him off the northwest coast of South America, in the Galápagos Islands, where the diversity of species, and the differences among species from island to island, seemed so great as to be almost inexplicable. "I never dreamed," he wrote, "that islands would be so differently tenanted. Temples filled with the varied productions of God and Nature … filled me with wonder." Clearly, by some means, the different conditions from island to island must have encouraged life forms to develop in different ways. When Darwin got home, two circumstances made his thinking crystallize.

First, Darwin devoted himself to the study of how species change under the influence of domestication: how farmers, stockbreeders, and pigeon fanciers, for instance, select for breeding or hybridization to ensure that the offspring of their animals will inherit favored characteristics. Maybe nature functioned in the same way, favoring characteristics most suitable to particular environments. Ill-adapted specimens of plants or animals would be unlikely to pass on their characteristics to subsequent generations. They would tend to die earlier and have a shorter fertile life span than more successful specimens. Or, in the case of breeding species, they might find it harder to attract mates. Conversely, the fittest would survive longest and breed most.

Second, Darwin's personal circumstances affected his theories. He had married his cousin, and, to their distress, the couple had produced sick children who struggled to survive. When his favorite daughter died, it became "impossible," he said, "for me ever to feel joy again." He found himself secretly beginning to hate God. Indeed, in his later years, he ceased to go to church, subscribed anonymously to an atheist society, and, to his wife's disappointment, treated the local Anglican clergyman with contempt, while avoiding former friends whose religious faith was undisturbed. More important for the world, however, than Darwin's personal agonies and religious doubts was his growing conviction that his own family demonstrated the truth of the theory that was forming in his mind. Nature was "clumsy, wasteful, blundering, low, and horribly cruel," or rather, indifferent to sentiment. Nature would allow only strong, well-adapted specimens to survive and pass on their characteristics to their offspring. He held the struggle for life in awe, partly because his own children were victims of it. "From the war of nature, from famine and death," he wrote, "the production of higher animals directly follows."

Darwin published that opinion in *The Origin of Species by Means of Natural Selection* in 1859. As his theory became accepted, other thinkers proposed terrible refinements that came to be known as **Social Darwinism**. Nature decreed "the survival of the fittest" and the extinction of the weak. Conflict is natural, therefore

A Fuegian on the frontispiece of Robert Fitzroy's *Narrative of the Surveying Voyage of HMS Adventure and Beagle* (1839). "Nothing," wrote Darwin in his *Beagle* journal, "is more likely to create astonishment than the first sight in his native state of a barbarian—of man in his lowest and most savage state. One's mind hurries back over past centuries, and asks, could our progenitors have been men like these, men who do not appear to boast of human reason. I do not believe it is possible to describe or paint the difference between savage and civilized man. . . . It is greater than between a wild and domesticated animal." The remarkable environmental adaptation that made the Native American inhabitants of Tierra del Fuego, at the tip of South America, able to withstand the cold was one of the observations that influenced Darwin's thinking about a theory of evolution.

"Scientific" racism. The British anatomist Charles White (1728–1813) believed that "various species of men were originally created and separated by marks sufficiently discriminative" to enable a scientist to rank them in a hierarchy of nature. The skeletons of white people showed that they were "most removed from brute creation," while the bodies and, especially, the skulls of black people "differed from the European and approached to the ape."

"Unsurprisingly, many saw Darwin's theories as justifying the inequalities of their day: a world sliced by the sword and stacked in order of race."

good. The elimination of weak specimens serves society. Inferior races are justly exterminated in favor of master races. The feeble or stupid should not be allowed to breed. Nature decrees the rule of more evolved races and individuals over those less evolved. "Degenerate" people—what we would now call the underclass—represented throwbacks to some more primitive stage of evolution. It would be unfair to blame Darwin for these consequences. He advocated the unity of creation and so, implicitly, defended the unity of humankind. He was the enemy of self-styled anthropologists of the day, who claimed that different races belonged to different species. Darwin was an unfailing opponent of slavery.

Nevertheless, no clear line divided Social Darwinism from scientific Darwinism. Darwin was the father of both. As early as 1839, he claimed that "When two races of men meet, they act precisely like two species of animals. They fight, eat each other. . . . But then comes the more deadly struggle, namely: which have the best fitted organization or instincts (i.e., intellect in man) to gain the day?" Black people, Darwin speculated, would have evolved into a distinct species had European imperialism not ended their isolation. He even admitted that a scientist of nature confronted with examples of black and white humans "without any further information" would undoubtedly classify them as separate species. As it was, he thought, black people were doomed to extinction in competition with white people. Unsurprisingly, many saw Darwin's theories as justifying the inequalities of their day: a world sliced by the sword and stacked in order of race.

A French anthropologist, Joseph-Arthur de Gobineau, who died in 1882, the same year as Darwin, arrayed humankind in order of excellence, with white people at the top, black people at the bottom, and others in between. Craniologists measured skulls and proved to their own satisfaction that the skulls of black people resembled those of apes. The French and Belgians said that black Africans who adopted European culture had "evolved" into a higher state of being human. "No full-blooded Negro," stated the *Encyclopedia Britannica* in 1884, "has ever been distinguished as a man of science, a poet, or an artist, and the fundamental equality claimed for him by ignorant philanthropists is belied by the whole history of the race." The governor of the Dutch East Indies in 1850 thought "the right of rule" was "a characteristic of the pure white race" to which "the black man bows down humbly." Some black people and Eskimos in Europe were actually displayed in zoos and World Fairs alongside exotic animals.

The Civilizing Mission

Alternatively, imperialists appealed to what they called their moral superiority. "The basic legitimization of conquest over native peoples," a French administrator insisted, "is the conviction of our superiority, not merely our mechanical, economic, and military superiority, but our moral superiority." Sir Francis Younghusband, who led a British military expedition to Tibet in 1902, claimed to have witnessed evidence of European superiority over Asian and African peoples—"not due to mere sharpness of intellect, but to that higher moral nature to which we have attained."

Moral may seem an odd word for the kind of superiority that enabled some people to kill, dispossess, and exploit others. A British administrator in South Africa was surely right when he observed "how thin is the crust that keeps our Christian civilization from the old-fashioned savagery—machine guns and modern rifles against knob sticks and assegais are heavy odds and do not add much to the glory of the superior races." But in part moral superiority signified what we should now call superior morale. Europeans, white North Americans, and Japanese certainly seemed more determined in the late nineteenth century than their counterparts in other parts of the world to seize other people's lands and wealth. To some extent, this seems to have been a reaction to historic positions of inferiority—Europe's with respect to Asia, Japan's with respect to China and Korea, that of the United States to most of the rest of the Americas and, indeed, to most of the rest of the world. In part, too, it is worth remembering that in the nineteenth century, ancient ideas of virtue were still current in classically educated minds. For nineteenth-century Europeans and white North Americans, virtue still included personal strength—physical and, therefore, military strength—as it had for the ancient Greeks and Romans.

The civilizing mission, New Guinea, 1919. The British missionary stands in a position of authority, on the right. The white women are relaxed and wear hats. The New Guineans are presumably receiving instruction, but it might as well be orders. Almost everything in the scene is mysterious. Is a class or a religious service taking place? Why do only females, not males, hold books? Why is the lady in the black hat seated facing the back of her chair?

The civilizing mission seemed inapplicable to much of the colonial world, and especially to India, whose civilization was older and, arguably, richer than that of Europe. But the British managed to think themselves into what they saw as a civilizing role even in India. In 1835, the British historian and legislator Thomas Babington Macaulay dismissed Indian civilization as "absurd history, absurd metaphysics, absurd physics, absurd theology." A single shelf of a good European library, he claimed, "is worth the whole native literature of India and Arabia." The English, he predicted, would be to the Indians as the Romans, in their day, had been to the ancient Britons. English would be the new Latin. "Indians in blood and color" would become "English in tastes, in opinions, in morals and in intellect."

Civilization was also undeniably a property of Chinese and Japanese societies. Western admiration for China never died out entirely, though the Opium Wars did much to subvert it. Thereafter, China's backwardness was widely acknowledged in the West, but most commentators realized that it was a temporary trick of history and would soon be reversed. Japan's potential to catch up was obvious from the 1870s onward (see Chapter 24). For Westerners, therefore, China and Japan were potential rivals, who could be recruited or resisted. Many Europeans adopted a defensive attitude to what they called "the Yellow Peril." The German emperor, Wilhelm II (r. 1888–1918), was among the loudest such voices, as was his contemporary, the United States president Theodore Roosevelt. In 1900, Wilhelm exhorted German members of an international task force sent to Beijing to rescue European residents from Chinese rebels, the so-called Boxers, who had killed the German ambassador and murdered European missionaries and their Chinese Christian converts: "You should give the name of German such a cause to be remembered in China that for a thousand years no Chinaman shall dare look a German in the face."

On the whole, it is hard to assess imperialists' claims to have governed for the benefit of their victims. Under the grasping rule of King Leopold II of the Belgians, 8-10 million people in the Congo died in massacres or from stunningly callous neglect. Native peoples who perished to make room for white empires in the Americas and Australia had no opportunity to count blessings. The British Empire can claim to its credit to have spent much blood and treasure in suppressing the slave trade (see Chapter 24). But even this was not an exclusively benign business.

MAP 25.5

The Global Drought of 1876–1878

dry regions

Empire of Hunger: The failure of the monsoon in 1900 triggered one of the many famines, that afflicted India under British rule. A cholera epidemic followed. The Viceroy, who observed the effects "from his carriage window," banned "indiscriminate alms-giving," which might have "weakened the fibre and demoralized the self-reliance of the population." Famine relief was late and inadequate.

Photograph courtesy of the Peabody Essex Museum.

In 1879, in southern Sudan, General Charles Gordon, who was in charge of anti-slaving operations, was sickened by the skulls and skeletons his men's work left: slavers' womenfolk slaughtered to stop them breeding, thousands of slaves abandoned to starve when slavers' caravans were disrupted or destroyed.

For those who suffered from it, imperialism was often a path to hell, paved with the good intentions of white people who stumbled under the burdens of their self-imposed and self-proclaimed imperial responsibilities. Outside Europe, North America, and a few other lucky locations, the last three decades of the nineteenth century were an age of famine, exceeding all others up to that time for mortality and perhaps for every other kind of measurable severity (see Map 25.5). Equally adverse conditions, including a worldwide drought, associated with a series of El Niño events, returned toward the end of the 1880s and in the second half of the 1890s. Lake Chad in Central Africa shrank by half. Nile flood levels fell by 35 percent. Thirty million people may have died in India and an equal number in China. In some respects, imperialism helped people find food for survival. Cheap iron from Europe increased food production enormously in West Africa when it was turned into plows. Before the arrival of European imports there, a hoe blade cost a cow. It is hard, however, to exempt European imperialism from some of the blame for the consequences of famine. "Europeans," a missionary in India heard, "track famine like a sky full of vultures." Cteshwayo, the Zulu king who tried to defeat the British Empire in South Africa in 1879, thought "the English chiefs have stopped the rain." If they did not engineer famine, white imperialists at least mismanaged it. Humanitarian sentiment, like food, was plentiful in their countries, but they found no way to turn their surplus of either to practical use.

Earlier, native states had handled famine relatively well. China coped with protracted crop failure in 1743–1744. In India in 1661, to the admiration of European observers, the Mughal emperor Aurangzeb (see Chapter 21) "opened his treasury" and saved millions of lives. Western countries—with the exception of the Russian Empire, where crop failures killed millions around the middle Volga and in Ukraine in 1878–1881—seemed able to save people from famine in the late nineteenth century if they so wished. The American Midwest suffered as badly as almost any other part of the world from the drought of 1889–1890, but relief was well organized and deaths were few.

In Perspective
The Reach of Empires

At the start of the nineteenth century, the English poet and artist William Blake could still draw Europe as one of the Graces among equals in the dance of the continents. But over the century as a whole, unprecedented demographic, industrial, and technological strides transformed Europe's place in the world. The result was a period of European world dominance. By 1900, European powers directly ruled much of the world, and European political influence and business imperialism combined to guide or control much of the rest.

It was, by the standards of world history, a brief phenomenon. By the end of the nineteenth century, Japan and the United States had overtaken many European countries in industrial strength and in their capacity for war. In the twentieth century, European empires would collapse as spectacularly and as quickly as they had arisen (see Chapter 28). Meanwhile, even under imperialism, people continued to make their own history, thanks to systems of indirect rule and the empires' reliance on collaborators. Still, the nineteenth remains a century of a "European miracle": the sudden, startling climax of long, faltering commercial outthrust, imperial initiatives, and scientific progress.

Despite their defects, the empires were of immense importance in global history as arenas of cultural exchange. As we saw in Chapter 23, imperial commerce followed the lines laid down by the effects of industrialization, dividing the world into specialized areas of primary production and manufacturing, encircling the Earth with steamship routes and railroads. As Chapter 24 made clear, these arteries carried culture as well as commerce. Empires intensified the process of exchange. Like distorting mirrors, the colonies reflected imperfect images of Europe around the world.

Cultural exchange happened despite climate and distance. Indian thinkers and writers gave a discriminating welcome to Western influence. The first great Indian advocate of Western ideas, Raja Rammohan Roy (1772–1833), was a child of the Enlightenment (see Chapter 22). Yet the roots of his rationalism and liberalism predated his introduction to Western literature. They came from Islamic and Persian traditions. The next great figure in Roy's tradition, Isvarcandra Vidyasagar (1820–1891), did not learn English until he was on the verge of middle age. When he argued for the remarriage of widows or against polygamy, or when he advocated relaxing caste discrimination in the schools, he found ancient Indian texts to support his arguments. But he dismissed the claims of pious Brahmans who insisted that every Western idea had an Indian origin. He resigned as secretary of the Sanskrit College of Calcutta in 1846 because of opposition to his program to include "the science and civilization of the West" in its curriculum. "If the students be made familiar with English literature," he claimed, "they will prove the best and ablest contributors to an enlightened Bengali renaissance." And, indeed, vernacular Indian writers did inject Western influences into their work, with revitalizing effect. The British in India were like many foreign, "barbarian" conquerors before

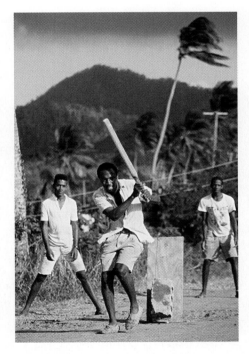

Imperial game. Soccer and cricket originated in expensive English boarding schools but spread around the world and to all classes. Soccer rapidly became popular almost everywhere in the world, outside the United States and Canada. Cricket, however, caught on only—with few exceptions—in lands subject to the British Empire. Here boys improvise a game with makeshift equipment, against the tropical background of St. Kitt's in the British West Indies.

Chronology

Nineteenth century	European population explosion fuels economy and creates surplus population for global migration; Africa's population declines
1803	Louisiana Purchase transfers vast territory from France to the United States
1807	British launch unsuccessful invasion of River Plate region of South America
1809	Russia annexes Finland
1812–1814	War of 1812
1823	United States issues the Monroe Doctrine
1830s–1860s	Russians struggle to conquer Chechens
1839	Charles Darwin begins around-the-world expedition
1842	Treaty of Nanjing ends Opium War
1845–1872	Maori Wars in New Zealand
1850	130,000 Europeans live in Algeria
1850–1859	Value of world trade increases by 80 percent
1857	Formal end of Mughal rule in India
1863–1879	Khedive Ismail attempts to build an Egyptian Empire
1867	United States purchases Alaska from Russia; Canadian Confederation is formed
1869	Suez Canal opens
1870–1900	World industrial production quadruples; world shipping doubles; world trade doubles in volume
1870s	French battle guerrilla warfare in Algeria
1877	Queen Victoria takes title of Empress of India
1878–1913	Total territory of European empires doubles to 20 million square miles; population of European empires expands from 300 million to 550 million
1884–1914	Scramble for Africa: most of Africa brought under European control
1884	Maxim machine gun patented
1889–1913	Emperor Menelik II modernizes Ethiopian army and expands empire in Africa
1890s	Russian imperialism focuses on the Far East
1894–1895	Japan defeats China, annexes Taiwan
1896	Land frontier of the United States declared closed
1898	Battle of Omdurman; United States annexes Hawaii and seizes Philippines, Guam, and Puerto Rico from Spain
1899–1902	Boer War
1900	500,000 Europeans live in Algeria, 4 million live in Australia, 1 million live in New Zealand
1904	United States acquires Panama Canal Zone

them, adding a layer of culture to the long-accumulated sediments of the subcontinent's past.

Today, what were once British colonies still have legislatures and law courts modeled on those of England, universities copied from Scotland, and sports that colonists from England's public schools brought with them (see Chapter 24). The French Empire spread French culture, Parisian cuisine, and the Code Napoléon (see Chapter 22) to Africa, the Caribbean, and the Pacific. Africa became the great growth land of Christianity, thanks to the missionaries who followed or, in some cases, carried the flags of European empires. Europeans spread their languages everywhere. In much of the ex-colonial world, English, Spanish, Portuguese, French, and Russian remain the language of first choice. The colonial worlds reciprocated the exchange. Mughal style adorned nineteenth-century British buildings. The industrialists of Paisley in Scotland copied Indian patterns for their textiles. Curry from India has become virtually an English national dish, as has Indonesian rijstafel in Holland and North African couscous in France. From the end of the nineteenth century, images and works of art looted from empires affected European imaginations and gave artists new models to follow. Despite the barriers to understanding that pseudoscientific racism erected, far frontiers kept increasing the white world's stock of examples of noble savagery (see Chapter 22). In the twentieth century, as we shall see in Chapter 27, social scientists found, among the subject peoples of empire, disturbing new perceptions: new ways to see not only the "primitives" and "savages," but also themselves and the nature of human societies.

PROBLEMS AND PARALLELS

1. Why did foreign powers gain significant control of the Chinese economy by the late nineteenth century? Why did China's relative decline prove temporary?

2. How do the Opium Wars illustrate a shift in global history? Why were the British unresponsive to Commissioner Lin's argument against the trade in opium?

3. Why were Western powers able to control so much of the world in the nineteenth century? Where did Britain and France try to create "New Europes"?

4. Why was Emperor Menelik II of Ethiopia able to resist European imperialism? What was the Scramble for Africa? Why were the rulers of Egypt, Morocco, and Zanzibar unable to build lasting African empires?

5. What methods did Europeans use to govern native peoples in their colonial possessions? What does the term *business imperialism* mean? Why was business imperialism so dominant in Latin America?

6. How did Europeans and white North Americans justify imperialism? What was the "civilizing mission"? How were Charles Darwin's biological theories used to justify imperialism?

7. Where did Japan, Russia, and the United States build empires in the nineteenth century? Why did the Native American population decline in the nineteenth century?

READ ON ▶ ▶ ▶

On the Opium War, A. Waley, *The Opium War Through Chinese Eyes* (1979) is a lively collection of sources. J. Y. Wong, *Deadly Dreams: Opium, Imperialism, and the Arrow War (1856–1860) in China* (1998) is excellent on the consequences and on the second Opium War.

H. L. Wesseling, ed., *Expansion and Reaction* (1978) contains ground-breaking papers on imperialism. H. L. Wesseling, *The European Colonial Empires* (2004) is the best overall survey. The same author's *Divide and Rule: The Partition of Africa* (1996) and T. Pakenham, *The Scramble for Africa* (1991) are outstanding in different ways—the first for impeccable judgment, the second for thrilling vividness. On Britain, W. R. Louis, ed., *The Oxford History of the British Empire*, vol. 3 (2001), ed. by A. Porter, is sweeping in its coverage. D. R. Headrick, *Tools of Empire* (1981) is important on the technology of imperialism. A. Knight, *The Mexican Revolution*, vol. 1 (1990) is a model work, from which I drew the details on the Yaqui. J. Belich, *The New Zealand War* (1998) is a brilliant work that reset the agenda of the study of colonial warfare. On indigenous imperialism see ch. 21 above and P. Hämäläinen, *The Comanche Empire* (2008). On Congo, A. Hochschild, *King Leopold's Ghost* (1998) is frighteningly revealing.

On Africa, *The UNESCO History of Africa*, vol. 7 (1990) and *The Cambridge History of Africa*, vol. 6 (1985) offers expert general surveys. G. Prins, *The Hidden Hippopotamus* (1980) is a sensitive, anthropologically informed study of Lozi history. N. R. Bennett, *Arab Versus European: Diplomacy and War in Nineteenth-Century Central Africa* (1986) is useful, especially on Zanzibar. The details on Ma el-Ainin come from J. Mercer, *Spanish Sahara* (1976).

On Johor, J. Gullick, *Malay Society in the Late Nineteenth Century* (1987) is invaluable. Many novels of Bankimcandra Chattopadhyaya are available in English, as are those of Jorge Mármol. On business imperialism, D. C. M. Platt, *Business Imperialism* (1977) is the indispensable introduction. A. de Tocqueville, *Writings on Slavery* is the source of the material on that writer. On the Russian Empire, D. Lieven, *Empire*, is the best survey.

On Darwin, the best books are the provocative A. Desmond and J. Moore, *Darwin* (1994), and E. J. Brown, *Charles Darwin* (1996) of which two volumes have appeared so far. M. Bates and P. S. Humphrey, eds., *The Darwin Reader* (1956) is a good introduction to Darwin's writings.

CHAPTER 26

The Changing State:
Political Developments in the Nineteenth Century

▲ **Maori warrior.** Nene, leader of Maori in Hokianga in northern New Zealand, took the name Tamati Waka after Thomas Walker, his British godfather, when he was baptized a Christian in 1839. Nene sought to befriend and, if possible, exploit the British. He sided with them in the Maori wars of the 1840s, achieving fame as the Maori "who did more than any other to establish the queen's (meaning Queen Victoria of England) authority."

NEW ZEALAND

In 1882, a British visitor wandered into an ill-mapped area in New Zealand's North Island. James Kerry-Nicholls called himself an explorer, but he was really engaged in what we might now call adventure tourism. He thought he was still in the British Empire. Instead, he found an "extensive region ruled over by the Maori king" that was, to all intents and purposes, a sovereign state, "inhabited exclusively by a race of warlike savages, ruled over by an absolute monarch, who defied our laws, ignored our institutions, and in whose territory the rebel, the murderer, and the outcast took refuge with impunity."

Kerry-Nicholls was in an independent Maori state in what is still known as the King Country. In the early 1880s, it occupied over a fifth of the territory of the North Island and had a population, by contemporary estimates, of some 7,000. The truth about it hardly justified Kerry-Nicholls's indignation. The Maoris reserved the right to imprison or kill outsiders who entered their territory without a visa, but they were not warlike savages. In the King Country, they had given up war and practiced peaceful resistance to the British—simply ignoring British orders. Invited to parley with the British in the year of Kerry-Nicholls's visit, King Tawhiao, "habited in European attire," bejeweled with a polished greenstone in one ear and a shark's tooth in the other, listened patiently to their proposal to give up his independence in exchange for land. "I approve," said the King, referring to the boundary of his kingdom,

> of you administering affairs on that side—the European side. . . . My only reason for going on that side is to hear—to listen. . . . I will remain in the place where my ancestors and my fathers trod. . . . What I have said to you is good: it has been said in the daylight, while the sun is shining. . . . You can remain on your side, and administer affairs, and I will remain on my side.

The King Country was the last stronghold of a movement that had originated in the 1850s to unify the Maori into a single state to confront British aggression and stop individual chiefs from ceding Maori land. In 1858, 26 Maori tribal groups had come together, numbering in all perhaps 25,000 or 30,000 souls, to elect a king by agreement among the chiefs. The groups had no ties of kinship or traditional alliances with each other. "Do not be concerned for your own village," said one native prophet to his people. "No, be concerned for the whole land." "I and my people," said a chief, "will march to show sympathy for the island." In 1861–1863, the British tried to destroy this new state, sending in armies up to 14,000 strong, with mortars, cannon, and a gun that fired 110-pound shells. But after defeats and inconclusive engagements (see Chapter 25), they simply gave up. The King Country gradually settled into uneasy coexistence with the British Empire.

FOCUS questions

Why was Westernization often equated with modernization in the nineteenth century?

Why was nationalism so potentially disruptive for empires and states?

Why did some African and Asian states succeed in resisting Western imperialism?

How did the growth of armies and bureaucracies increase the power of states?

What roles did nineteenth-century socialists want government to play?

Why did organized religion and the state come into conflict in the nineteenth century?

Presumably, the Maori got the idea of a unitary state, ruled by a "king," by imitation from the British. Their purpose, as one Maori leader explained, was "that they should become united, to assemble together and become one, like the Pakehas," as they called the white men. Presumably, too, had the Maori not faced a common enemy, they would have continued their long-standing methods of political organization in mutually warring chiefdoms. The idea of switching from armed to peaceful resistance was attributed to native prophets, but perhaps it owes something to the influence of Christian missionaries and the model of Jesus' kingdom (which was, as the Bible says, "not of this world"), or maybe even to the secular notion of civil disobedience that some Western intellectuals at the time advocated to effect peaceful change.

The political inventiveness of the Maori happened on a small scale, but it illustrates general features of the way nineteenth-century states grew and changed. New states emerged out of disunited traditional groupings, such as chiefdoms and tribes. Old states made themselves more systematic by eliminating political anomalies, devising constitutions, codifying laws, rationalizing institutions, breaking the power of rival sources of authority (such as clergies, aristocracies, city councils, or heads of tribes or clans), and imposing centralization or, at least, increasingly consistent methods of administration, on their subjects. *Modernization* is, strictly speaking, a meaningless word, since every era produces its own modernity, but we can follow tradition in using it as a label for these processes, because they produced states similar to those that prevail today.

Some models of state development or refashioning began in Europe and North America and spread through the world in the course of the "white man's" outreach—by example, or by the power of imperialism. The process certainly did not end where white rule ended, and some instances, at least, probably happened independently of any white initiative. Examples we have already met illustrate this: the reforging of Japan and Egypt in response to European industrialization and imperialism, Ethiopia's success in the scramble for Africa, or the Sioux's efforts to create an empire in the North American prairie. As we shall see in this chapter, some states modernized far from the frontiers of European empires or the reach of European influence.

Nevertheless, the story of state modernization, and the study of the problem of how and why it happened, must begin in the West, partly because some features of modern states emerged there first. For much of the world, modernization really was *Westernization*, the conscious imitation of the world's most powerful and prosperous states: Britain, France, Germany, and the United States. While the scope and power of states grew in many parts of the world, the strongest and most enduring influences of the period came from the West. Here models of state development unfolded and were imitated around the world. Here theories about politics and society were formulated that achieved global importance and, often, global impact. From this point in the story of the world, Westernization is one of the most conspicuous global themes.

We will look at its clearest manifestations—nationalism, constitutionalism, militarization, centralization, and bureaucratization—before turning at the end of the chapter to some of the other influential but, for the time being, frustrated political movements of the period: religiously inspired utopianisms, democracy, and other new or developing forms of political radicalism that radiated from the West.

NATIONALISM

Nationalists claimed that a people who shared the same language, historic experience, and sense of identity made up a nation, an indissoluble unit, linked (to quote a Finnish nationalist) by "ties of mind and soul mightier and firmer than every external bond." Nationalists believed that everyone must belong to a nation of this kind, and that every nation had to assert its identity, pursue its destiny, and defend its rights. "The voice of God" told Giuseppe Mazzini (1805–1872), the republican fighter for Italian unification, that the nation was the essential framework in which individuals could achieve moral perfection.

Strange as this notion seems, many people believed it. In the nineteenth century, most people in Europe came to believe it. Nationalism triumphed in the West, stimulated by the American and French Revolutions and the Napoleonic Wars, and encouraged by belligerents who wanted to inspire their people to fight. It spread from the West to touch or transform much of the world by the end of the century.

Nationalism in Europe

Almost all European states contained more than one nation (see Map 26.1). Many European nations straddled the borders of states. **Nationalism** was therefore a potentially disruptive doctrine. German nationalists yearned to unite all German-speaking people in a single state. French nationalists wanted to meld France's historic communities into a unified force and secure what they claimed to be France's natural frontiers—by incorporating all the land west of the Rhine River and north of the Alps. Spain remained, as a British visitor observed, a "bundle" of nations—including, notably, Castilians, Catalans, Basques, and Galicians—unsure whether they wished to become a single Spanish nation. British statesmen kept talking about England, forgetting that the English, Irish, Scots, and Welsh were all supposed to have combined in a new British nation. Italian nationalists wanted to convert their peninsula from a "geographical expression" into a state. In Central Europe the Habsburg monarchy juggled minorities that often quarreled with each other, privileging Germans, Hungarians, and, to some extent, Poles in areas where they predominated, acknowledging in various ways other groups that had more or less distinct homelands, such as the Slovenes, Croats, and Czechs. Even more than that of the Habsburgs, the Ottoman Empire in southeast Europe had uncontainably conflicting nations within its borders. "Judge what would happen," wrote the Ottoman foreign minister in 1862, "if free scope were given to all the different national aspirations. . . . It would need a century and torrents of blood to establish even a fairly stable state of affairs." The Greeks achieved independence from the Ottomans in 1830. Romania and Serbia did so by 1878. Bulgaria, though still technically subject to Turkey until 1908, functioned effectively as a sovereign state hostile to the Ottoman Empire from the 1880s.

Some large states that enclosed many nations tried to stir themselves into consistency, usually by oppressing minorities. Government campaigns of "Russification" in the Russian Empire or "Magyarization" in Hungary meant, in practice, suppressing historic languages and sometimes persecuting

The year 1848 was one of largely failed constitutionalist revolutions in Europe. One of several women among the leaders of the Romanians who rebelled against Russian and Turkish domination was Ana Ipatescu, who had scandalized society by leaving her first husband and mobilizing revolutionary sentiment. Here, having proclaimed a provisional government, she leads a rather inauspicious band of followers. Onlookers seem to anticipate the inevitable defeat.

MAP 26.1

The Peoples of Europe

—— frontiers 1815

Nationalities Within the Habsburg Empire

- Croats
- Czechs
- Italians
- Poles
- Serbs
- Slovaks
- Germans
- Hungarians (Magyars)
- Romanians
- Slovenes
- Ukrainians

minority religions. In Britain, Scotland's Highlanders, who formed a nation with its own language, religious traditions, and ways of life, were expelled from their land and sent into exile in a vicious campaign that was euphemistically called "clearances." Governments in London proposed to deal with the problem of the cultural and religious distinctiveness of the Irish by implanting an "agent of civilization"—an English Protestant clergyman—in every Irish parish. In effect, this was a failed attempt to eradicate or weaken native Catholicism.

Without bringing fulfillment to big communities, nationalism threatened minorities with destruction or repression. Some of them, like Finns and Poles in the Russian Empire or Slavs and Romanians in the Habsburg Empire, could respond with counternationalisms of their own. The Jews were not so lucky.

The Case of the Jews

The Jews had no national homeland. Their rising population—with a rate of increase remarkable even by European standards—seemed to provoke or aggravate **anti-Semitism.** So did changes in Jewish society and its relationship to the world around it. The triumph of enlightened principles in the French Revolution and their spread in the Napoleonic Wars extended the "rights of man" to the Jews, for whom governments relaxed legal and financial disabilities, except in Spain and Portugal and in the Russian Empire. Many European Jews discarded the traditional exclusiveness of the ghetto in favor of assimilation into secular society. Heinrich Heine (1797–1856), a German Jew, filled his poetry with Jewish self-awareness but regarded Christian baptism as "a ticket into European culture." Part of Jewish self-emancipation was to adopt the dress and manners of host societies and conform to their way of life. From 1810, a reform movement that started in Germany brought these new ways into synagogues, introducing organ music, singing in melodic unison, and sermons. The very success of Jews in blending into gentile society seemed to excite anti-Semitism. This growing and increasingly conspicuous community, anti-Semites claimed, might take over the wealth and power of the world.

When the world's biggest synagogue opened in Berlin in 1866, the Chief Rabbi preached in German about his hopes of a "common Messiah" to unite all nations in brotherhood. This seemed an overoptimistic program. There were two other options. The first was for Jews to espouse Jewish nationalism—which some did with increasing desperation as anti-Semitism grew. They turned to the search for a homeland, perhaps somewhere in Africa, or perhaps in Palestine (an idea first suggested by a Balkan rabbi in the 1840s). The second possibility, which most Jews embraced, was to join in the nationalism of the country in which they lived. Joseph Moses Levy (1812–1888), owner of England's biggest newspaper, sought, in a rival journalist's sneer, "to be numbered among the Anglo-Saxon race." The young Walter Rathenau (1867–1922), whose family owned the largest electricity-producing firm in Germany, believed that German Jews could help Germany achieve world supremacy.

Assimilation, however, was always risky for unconverted Jews, unless they were immensely rich. The prayer book of French Jews in the 1890s praised France as the country "preferred by God," and the French, according to the country's chief rabbi in 1891, were "the chosen race of modern times." None of this prevented French anti-Semitism, as became all too clear in the case of a Jewish officer in the French army accused of spying for the Germans in 1893. Captain Alfred Dreyfus was obviously innocent, but the French gutter press bayed for his blood, in effect because he was Jewish. He was led into exile and imprisonment crying, "Long live France!" and later, after his innocence was proved, he won medals fighting in the French army in World War I.

Assimilation and alienation. Funded by congregants' subscriptions, the Synagogue of Berlin, which opened in 1866, was the largest in Europe. Its patrons hoped it would symbolize Jews' attainment of an honorable place in Germany. Anti-Semites, however, interpreted the ostentatious gold decoration of the dome and the oriental-style design as evidence of Jews' unassimilably alien nature.

In Romania, in 1875, the press threatened a prominent British Jew, Sir Moses Montefiore (1784–1885), with lynching when he went there to plead for the rights of Jews. Yet a Jew wrote the period's most heartfelt celebration of Romanian nationhood in Yiddish, a language only Jews spoke.

Nationalism beyond Europe

Beyond Europe, nineteenth-century nationalism is hard to distinguish from patriotic resistance against European imperialism. It seems clear, however, that by the end of the century, many independence movements in European empires overseas had adopted nationalism as their own ideology. Rebels proclaimed as "nations" countries, such as "the Philippines," "Indonesia," "Algeria," and "India," that had never existed before and that housed many different historic nations.

This phenomenon started in the Americas. Propagandists in the United States popularized the idea of an "American nation" during their Revolutionary War. Before the war, residents of the 13 North American colonies that rebelled against Britain had all considered themselves "true-born Englishmen." In Latin America, similar sentiments developed during the wars of independence fought against Spanish rule between 1810 and the 1820s. The success of the idea of nationalism was even more surprising in Latin America than in the United States. Though the Creole elites shared a common identity as "Americans," their desire to exercise power in states of their own creation exceeded their willingness to remain united. Spanish American unity was a Humpty Dumpty, smashed by its fall. Paraguay and Uruguay fought to stay apart from Argentina and Brazil. Bolivia and Ecuador rejected union with Peru. In the 1830s, large states that had emerged from the independence wars dissolved into small ones. Gran Colombia split into Colombia

MAP 26.2

The Americas in 1828

■ area gaining independence from imperial control by 1828

The Americas in 1905

■ European colonies

and Venezuela. Venezuela, like Uruguay, was a country seemingly invented on the spur of the moment. It had no identity as a distinct administrative or social unit in colonial times. The United Provinces of Central America crumbled into Guatemala, Honduras, Nicaragua, Costa Rica, and El Salvador. The fissures continued to spread, detaching Texas and California from Mexico, and almost detaching Yucatán as well in the 1840s (see Map 26.2). Texas and California became independent republics, before joining the United States. Nationalist sentiments existed, especially among people who called themselves Californios, but since the late colonial period the balance of wealth and power in those states had gradually shifted to the large numbers of immigrants from the United States, who identified more readily with their folks back home than with the natives of their adopted lands.

Brazil, meanwhile, like the United States, emerged formally united but, unlike the United States, was highly fragile in the short term (see Chapter 21). Offshore currents in the South Atlantic divided coastal Brazil into two zones, between which it was hard to communicate. The ranch-rich São Paulo region in the south had always been a law unto itself. In the interior, there was a Wild West of mining, slaving, and logging with its own boss class. Northern Brazil was the domain of rich coffee and sugar planters. Unity survived destructive civil wars in the 1830s only because the regions were incapable of collaborating in revolt and because the emperor supplied a powerful symbol of legitimacy for the new country. Ethnic diversity added to the complexity of regional divisions. Brazil had more black people than other Latin American states—an inheritance of the importance of slavery in the sugar plantations in the colonial economy. As slave labor became ever harder to obtain, the country needed more and more free immigrants of diverse origins.

Yet the new states of the nineteenth-century Americas rapidly bred a sense of nationhood in at least some of their citizens. When the United States seized California from Mexico in 1846, one youngster there was appalled "because I am a *Californio* who loves his country and a Mexican on all four sides." In 1843, a Bolivian intellectual found his country's constitution excessively nationalistic, because it "declares from the start . . . that the Bolivian nation comprises all Bolivians. Beyond Bolivians, no other elements of the nation exist." In consequence, Bolivia had become a narrow-minded country, dedicated to "independence and isolation, without limit, without quarter."

In the second half of the century, nationalist sentiment in the individual Latin American states increased, partly in detestation of interference from the United States, and the countries fought each other. In Argentina, nationalism tended to get distracted by romantic identification with the *gauchos*—the rugged cattle drovers of the pampa. In Brazil and Paraguay, the romantic sympathy took the form of yearning for an idealized "Indian" world, though poetry written in praise of the Indians excited little political activity on their behalf. The first fully independent Mexican state in 1822 based the official symbol of the nationhood it claimed—an eagle devouring a snake atop a prickly pear cactus—on an Aztec carving. In Colombia, Ecuador, and Venezuela, it was the landscape that inspired nationalist poetry and art.

In sub-Saharan Africa, too, the nationalist idea was implanted, at least in part, from the United States. It started in Liberia, a colony of ex-slaves founded in 1821 as a private venture by philanthropists, with help from racists who wanted to rid the United States of black people. Liberia proclaimed its independence in 1847, with a constitution based on that of the United States, but more radical in its insistence on "national rights and the blessings of life." In 1856, one of the earliest Liberian presidents, Stephen A. Benson, perceived "the makings of a great nation" in the colony. In 1872, Edward Blyden, an outstanding black intellectual who had settled in Liberia, where he taught Latin and Greek, proclaimed "Africa for the African."

An Argentine gaucho. The painter Eduardo Morales specialized in romantic landscapes of his native Cuba. Here he portrays an Argentine cowboy, a gaucho, and the landscape of Argentina itself in a similar romantic style. The man's horse, however, seems groomed for a formal riding contest, with forepaw raised in a tradition more appropriate for depicting rulers and warriors than cowboys.

West African missionaries helped to spread nationalism, imagining national churches similar to those that Protestants maintained in Europe. Black intellectuals saw the political potential of this model. James Africanus Horton, for instance, a black doctor from the colony of ex-slaves that the British established alongside Liberia in Sierra Leone, pointed out in 1868 that "We have seen European nations who in long years past were themselves as barbarous and unenlightened as the negro Africans are at present, and who have exhibited wonderful improvement within the last century. This should urge the Africans to increased exertions, so that their race may, in course of time, take its proper stand in the world's history." Talk of nationalism began to have real political effects in West Africa. In 1871, Fanti chiefs in what is now Ghana met to found a confederation "to advance the interest of the whole Fanti nation."

North of the Sahara, meanwhile, nationalism emerged among communities forced into self-definition as the Ottoman Empire retreated and European imperialism threatened. In the second half of the nineteenth century, Egyptian intellectuals began to give the Arabic word *watan*—which originally just meant something like "birthplace"—the sense of the European term *nation*, with the same romantic associations. One of the most influential of them was Ali Mubarak Pasha (see Chapter 23), who published a nationalist novel in 1882, the very year when opponents of British and French influence rose up with the cry, "Egypt for the Egyptians!" Mubarak wrote in the preface to his book:

> One of the strongest things, we feel indebted to, and on which we, being steeped in its sacred rites, make demands, is the nation. . . . For at every moment it enlarges us, . . . enriches us, just as it has done to our . . . ancestors and will do to our sons and grandsons who follow us. We are thus obliged to give it our boundless duty, as it deserves.

To some extent, Western empires deliberately encouraged nationalism around the world, regarding its spread as evidence of successful Westernization and of the fulfillment of Westerners' supposedly civilizing mission. In the early 1850s, a British statesman, Lord Grey, believed that by bringing the chiefs of the Gold Coast (modern Ghana) together, Britain had turned "barbarous tribes . . . into a nation." British administrators in Canada assumed that nation making was an obligation of empire. Even without official collaboration, Western empires tended to have this effect. In colonial settings, budding nationalists could read and learn about what was going on in Europe. Many of them went to Europe to study or at least attended European-style schools at home. To them, nationalism seemed an alternative form of political legitimacy with which to confront traditional elites allied with or controlled by outsiders.

José Rizal (1861–1896), for instance, the great spokesman of Filipino nationalism in the late nineteenth century, was the best student in Greek at Madrid University in Spain in his day. He was also competent or excellent in Latin, French, English, German, Italian, Dutch, Swedish, and Portuguese, as well as his native Malay and Chinese. He dressed and conversed like a typical upper-class Spaniard. La Solidaridad—one of the cells from which the nationalist movement in the Philippines was formed—was founded in Spain among Filipino students in 1888. Rizal crammed his writings with allusions to classical, Spanish, English, and German literature, but he also searched for inspiration in the poetic traditions of his homeland. He was a hybrid of Europe and Asia—a misfit wherever he went, known in Hong Kong as "the Spanish doctor" and labeled in the Philippines as a "Chinese half-breed." Spanish observers noticed Rizal's patriotic poetry as early as 1879 and identified him as "a man who bears watching, a rare and new kind of man . . . for

"To some extent, Western empires deliberately encouraged nationalism around the world, regarding its spread as evidence of successful Westernization and of the fulfillment of Westerners' supposedly civilizing mission."

whom the mother country is the Philippines, not Spain." He spent his last years in exile, charged with conspiring with other nationalists to make the Philippines independent. The experience only deepened his sense of rootedness in his own country. When he returned to Manila and was shot by the Spaniards as a rebel, he struck out the words "Chinese half-breed" on his death warrant and wrote "pure native" instead.

Rizal's subversive novels—especially *El Filibusterismo*, which, he said, is about "patriots waiting to be hanged"—showed how literature could help forge nationalism in colonial environments. Equally powerful in India were the novels of another culturally ambiguous figure whom we met in the last chapter, Bankimcandra Chattopadhyaya. Bankim wrote Western-style fiction, but often chose politically inflammatory themes. His most overtly nationalist novel, *Anandamath* (1882), is about a guerrilla leader inspired by visions of shedding British blood. *Anandamath* and *El Filibusterismo* both became handbooks of their respective countries' nationalist movements.

In a further level of ambiguity, Bankim himself served the British as a deputy magistrate. This was typical of the nationalists who formed the first enduring all-Indian political organization, the Indian National Congress, in 1885. Most of the founder members and early recruits belonged to the civil service or the legal profession. Most of the leading figures were graduates of the British-style universities founded in 1857 in Calcutta (now called Kolkata), Bombay (now Mumbai), and Madras (now Chennai).

While Western models promoted the growth of nationalism worldwide (see Map 26.3), other influences were also at work. Toward the end of the century, Japan became a model for Asian nationalists because its success demonstrated that Asian nations could rival or even surpass Western powers. Vietnamese nationalism, meanwhile, fed on memories of age-old resistance to the Chinese as well as on opposition to the French in the nineteenth century. To some extent, nationalism happened independently wherever big empires provoked subject-peoples to react or rebel. The Russian, Habsburg, Chinese, and Ottoman empires all faced similar problems. Chinese nationalism was itself an expression against the ruling Qing dynasty, even though the emperors' Manchu origins were now a long way in the past (see Chapter 21). Opponents of the regime appealed to Chinese "purity." The first rebellion of the movement that called itself "nationalist," in Guangzhou in 1895, was an attempt to found a Chinese state free of Manchu domination.

José Rizal. In 1887, José Rizal published, in the form of a novel, what he called "the first impartial and bold account" of the Filipino independence movement and the injustice that inspired it. "Felicity," Rizal wrote, "is proportional to liberty." He compared Spanish rule to a wooden bridge—vulnerable to wind and rot.

CONSTITUTIONALISM

The rise of nationalism becomes intelligible against the background of rapid shifts of power: revolutions, conquests and counterconquests, and the rise of imperialism dethroned old regimes, reshaped states, and challenged long-established forms of political legitimacy. Nationalism was one way to justify the new structures of power or challenge old ones. **Constitutionalism**—the doctrine that the state is founded on rules that rulers and citizens make together and are bound to respect—was another.

Constitutionalism was not confined to Europe, but Europe was its great battleground. After the French Revolutionary Wars, most European states tried to prevent another such explosion by sanctifying existing frontiers and outlawing or restricting constitutional reforms. By mutual agreement, they intervened to repress

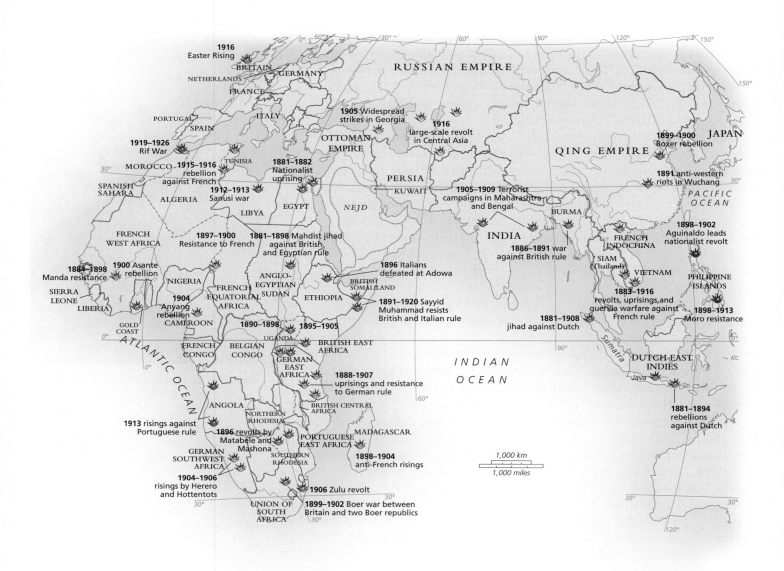

MAP 26.3

Examples of Resistance to European and United States Imperialism, 1880–1920

Anti-colonial uprisings and incidents

⚜	anti-British
⚜	anti-Dutch
⚜	anti-French
⚜	anti-German
⚜	anti-Italian
⚜	anti-Portuguese
⚜	anti-Russian
⚜	anti-Spanish
⚜	anti-American
—	boundary at 1914

each other's revolutions. The system worked well, and revolutionaries achieved freedom to act only in the relatively short periods when the major European powers fell out among themselves. The nineteenth century was therefore a great age for monarchies. All the new European states of the period—Belgium, Greece, Romania, Serbia, Bulgaria, newly united Italy and Germany—were monarchies. Republics that fell during the Napoleonic Wars—in Venice, Genoa, and the Netherlands—were not restored. Even in Latin America, some states toyed with plans for monarchical systems. Mexico and Haiti had monarchs for a time. Brazil's monarchy survived until a military coup in 1889.

Most European monarchies, however, eventually felt compelled to compromise their authority by granting or accepting constitutions, or passing laws to enlarge the numbers and nature of those of their subjects admitted to the political process. Constitutionalism not only redistributed power; it also changed the way people thought about the state—no longer the domain of the ruler, but of the rule of law, to which the monarch and government were themselves subject. Constitutionalism did not necessarily embody the idea that the people were sovereign, but it at least implied that more than one person and more than one class shared sovereignty. In Britain, for instance, though no written constitution was ever granted, or even formally sought, a series of Reform Acts turned Parliament from an enclave of the aristocracy and gentry into an assembly that was still heavily aristocratic but also representative of the middle class and even, from 1867, of the more prosperous workers.

On the fringes of Europe, the Ottoman and Russian empires staved off constitutionalism with difficulty. In 1864, the Russian monarchy permitted district assemblies with representatives from all classes to meet, while judges became at least nominally independent of the government. The Ottoman court convened an assembly of provincial representatives in 1845, explicitly limited to "those who are respected and trusted." The sultan quickly abandoned this experiment in constitutionalism, but in 1876, a constitutional revolt proclaimed "respect for the national will" and made the executive responsible to the legislature. "All Ottoman subjects," the new constitution decreed, "regardless of whether they possess property or fortune, shall have the right to vote." Religious liberty and equality before the law were enshrined. The constitution lasted only a few months before the sultan reimposed his authority, but resentment festered among the educated classes of the empire.

Constitutionalism spread, along with other Western ways, to Japan, where experiments with various kinds of legislatures began in 1868. In 1882, the decision to draw up a constitution was based on the results of a fact-finding mission to Berlin, Vienna, Paris, and London. Because Japan was now an industrializing economy, thought the framers of the constitution, the middle class would be sure to rise to power. The constitution, introduced by decree of the emperor in 1889, had to provide a framework in which this change could occur peacefully, without jeopardizing the powers of the throne or the interests of other classes, such as the landlords, peasants, and industrial workers. Sovereignty remained the prerogative of the "sacred and inviolable" emperor, The ruler would govern "with the consent" of a representative assembly, elected by a franchise restricted to those rich enough to pay property taxes, and an upper house, modeled on Britain's House of Lords, composed of hereditary nobles and distinguished men whom the emperor appointed for life. The assembly could initiate new laws and veto the budget. The constitution also enshrined what we now call civil and human rights—including rights to hold and transfer property, to speak and associate freely, to practice religion without hindrance, and to be tried under the law, as well as the right of all men to compete for office under the state without discrimination as to birth or creed. The emperor, however, could suspend these rights in emergencies. Political parties were recognized as playing a role in running the assembly, but not the country. Because it was considered vital for the emperor to remain "above politics," he appointed ministers, on the advice of senior statesmen, without reference to party. Prussia, one of the more authoritarian states in Germany, provided the closest Western model to Japan's constitution.

In other parts of the world, constitutionalism was rarely more than a series of movements that never achieved power, or a dream of intellectuals who were largely without influence until the twentieth century. As we have seen, copycat constitutions accompanied the independence of all the new Latin American states of the nineteenth century, but they were usually mere formalities that disguised the rule of military strongmen, dictators, and oligarchies. The same can be said of Liberia's constitution. Nonetheless, there were impressive attempts to create effective constitutions. In the North American Southeast, under the influence of German missionaries who began work in 1817, and the inspiration of their charismatic chief, Sequoia

Constitutionalism in Japan. On April 6, 1868, the Meiji Emperor (r. 1867–1912) proclaimed the Charter Oath—the first principles of what became Japan's constitution. Henceforth, the emperor ordered, public discussion would be open to all social classes and would precede policy-making. All Japanese subjects would enjoy the right to pursue the means of life. All laws and customs contrary to natural justice would be abolished, and knowledge would be "sought throughout the world so as to strengthen the foundations of imperial rule." The emperor remained partially hidden from his audience behind a screen when he proclaimed the Oath, and a scribe read his speech for him, but no emperor had intervened so publicly in politics for centuries. Paradoxically, his listeners submitted to constitutionalism because, as one of them said, "we had no choice but to follow the imperial will."

(1770–1843), the Cherokee people established their own republic alongside the United States, with representative institutions and laws codified in a written version of their own language. The Cherokee state flourished until the United States crushed it, seized its land, and expelled its peoples in the 1830s. The Fanti confederacy in West Africa, as James Africanus Horton described it, was "the pivot of national unity, headed by intelligent men, to whom a great deal of the powers of the kings and chiefs are delegated. . . . Through it the whole of the Fantee race, numbering some 400,000 souls, can . . . boast of a national assembly." The chiefs between them elected a king-president. Education and road maintenance were among the responsibilities of the government.

Although constitutionalism was Western inspired, traditional societies often had similar systems or conceptions of government of their own that limited rulers' power or subjected them to control or scrutiny by aristocratic or (less often) popular assemblies. When, for instance, the war leader Atiba reconstructed the collapsed kingdom of Oyo in what is now central Nigeria in the 1850s, he looked back to his people's traditions, restoring the rites of ancient gods, founding temples for guardian deities, instituting worship of royal ancestors, even though he and most of his people were nominally Muslims. He enjoyed such grandiose titles as Owner of the World and of Life, Owner of the Land, and Companion of the Gods. In practice, however, the king could not act without the support of the council composed of representatives of noble families, who nominated officials and had the right, rarely exercised, to demand his self-sacrifice by ritual suicide. In what is now Ghana, the king of the Asante was known as "He Who Speaks Last" because, although he made policy decisions, he listened first to the views of the rest of the chiefs.

CENTRALIZATION, MILITARIZATION, AND BUREAUCRATIZATION

"Because armies consumed large amounts of taxes and conscripts, their growth was an important—though not a necessary—condition for centralization and bureaucratization."

Whether monarchical or republican, constitutional or absolutist, nineteenth-century states tended to become more centralized. Industrialization and militarization boosted the power of governments. It became possible, as never before, to enforce unity and exact obedience from areas remote from a country's capital. We have already seen what a powerful source of industrial and social change militarization was (see Chapter 23). It is not surprising, therefore, that it should also have had enormous political consequences. Because armies consumed large amounts of taxes and conscripts, their growth was an important—though not a necessary—condition for centralization and bureaucratization.

In and Around the Industrializing World

In the Ottoman Empire, for instance, Sultan Mahmud II (r. 1808–1839) reorganized the army on European lines in 1826 and used his new troops to wipe out the Janissaries, the old, politically unreliable, hereditary military corps. He introduced European officers, training methods, and manuals. The army became the spearhead of movements of political reform and the self-appointed guardian of what increasingly—as the multinational empire shrank—felt like a Turkish nation-state. Under the next sultan, a new bureaucracy took over tax collecting, which the state had formerly farmed out to local agents. To some extent, these Ottoman reforms were inspired not directly by European examples, but by those of Muhammad Ali in Egypt (see Chapter 23). He had launched a similar program as early as 1820, conscripting peasants into an army he called the New Order. To recruit and pay for this army, he radically overhauled the administration, dividing Egypt into 24 provinces and creating layers of bureaucracy that reached from the capital into every village. To a lesser extent, rulers in Libya, Tunisia, and Morocco imitated the Ottoman reforms and created bureaucracies that, however, remained largely confined to the cities and functioned elsewhere, if at all, alongside traditional local and tribal authorities.

In the industrializing world, the most spectacular cases of restructured state power were those of Germany, Italy, the United States, and Japan. In the 1860s, all these countries experienced wars that were broadly similar in four respects. First, the wars unified countries that were either fragmented or in danger of fragmentation. Germany and Italy had long been disunited—"geographical expressions" divided among many different and often hostile states. Japan had a long history as a unitary state, but power over remote provinces had slipped out of the central government's control. The United States was still a new state, but its constitution had never really settled a crucial issue: whether the separate states had permanently and irrevocably renounced their sovereignty in favor of the federal government. When some of the slave-holding states exercised what they claimed was their right to secede from the Union, the federal government contested it by force.

Second, the civil wars in all four places pitted relatively industrializing or industrialized regions against one another. In Japan, the regions of Choshu and Satsuma in the south supplied most of the manpower and equipment on the victorious side. These were areas where the local rulers had invested most in modernizing their armed forces and producing munitions on a massive scale. In Italy, the armies that conquered the rest of the peninsula came mainly from the kingdom of Piedmont in the northwest, where most Italian industry was concentrated. In Germany and the United States, the stories of the wars were similar: broadly speaking, industrializing regions overcame unindustrialized ones, though in Germany the divisions were less clear-cut than in the American case.

Third, the effects of consolidation were similar in all four cases. Germany emerged instantly as a major power. In 1870–1871—only four years after the creation of a superstate in which most German states joined—the new Germany crushed France in a test of strength that lasted only a few months. Little more than a decade later, the German Empire—as it was now called—was contending for overseas colonies in Africa and Asia. Political unity also had a stimulating economic effect, and Germany's economy began to rival Britain's as the most industrialized and productive of the time. Italy, Japan, and the United States were slower to emerge as potential superpowers after their wars of unification, but by the end of the century, they were all beginning, at least, to display the same characteristics: rapid industrialization, military efficiency, and colonial expansion.

Finally, in all four countries, the leaders appealed, with varying degrees of sincerity, to conservative values to justify the revolutions that had imposed centralization and unity on sometimes reluctant communities. In Japan the term *Meiji Restoration* was coined to describe the revolution, on the spurious grounds that by abolishing the shogunate in 1868 the new regime "restored" the Meiji emperor (r. 1867–1912) to his

ARMÉE OTTOMANE

SADIK-BEY
Colonel d'infanterie, aide de camp de
S. M. I. le Sultan.

RIZA-BEY
Commandant de cavalerie, aide de camp
de S. M. I. le Sultan.

CHEFKET-BEY
Lieutenant-colonel d'artillerie.

Ottoman military officers of the late nineteenth century. Westernization and modernization in the Ottoman Empire in the nineteenth century often focused on the armed forces. Foreign officers, especially from Germany and Britain, helped to train and reorganize Ottoman forces, and many Ottoman officers studied at military academies in Western Europe. A Parisian illustrated paper from 1895 showed officers of the sultan's household in uniforms modeled—except for the fezzes—on those worn in Western armies.

Making Connections | NINETEENTH-CENTURY CIVIL WARS IN GERMANY, ITALY, THE UNITED STATES, AND JAPAN

FACTOR	OUTCOME
Unification	Civil wars unify countries that were either fragmented (Italy, Germany) or in danger of fragmentation (Japan, the United States)
Industrialized regions versus less industrialized regions	Industrialized regions overcome less industrialized ones
Political power	Consolidation leads to military efficiency, economic growth, and colonial expansion
Justification for wars of unity	Leaders appeal to conservative values: "restoration" in Japan, medieval past in Italy and Germany, Founding Fathers and "Reconstruction" in the United States

rightful place at the head of the empire. In Italy, the victors quoted medieval poets in praise of political unity and claimed to have contained radical elements in the nationalist movement. In part, this claim was valid, since the supporters of monarchy triumphed over republicans, and the more radical elements in the nationalist movement were excluded from government. Yet the radicals—under their romantic, red-shirted leader, Giuseppe Garibaldi (1807–1882)—dominated the image of the movement abroad and enforced the incorporation, as part of the new kingdom, of Sicily and Naples, regions their conservative comrades would have preferred to leave outside it. In Germany, the victors called their new state an "empire"—evoking memories of medieval German empires—while adopting truly radical measures, including an aggressively secularist campaign against the social influence of the Catholic Church, and the introduction of the world's first state-run social insurance scheme. In the United States, the victorious North invoked the country's Founding Fathers and claimed to defend the Constitution, while undertaking profoundly radical policies, including the emancipation of all slaves and "Reconstruction," which was really an attempt to enforce policies of racial equality on the defeated South that many of the Northern states themselves did not practice.

China also underwent a "restoration" after troubles in the 1860s, but they were troubles of a different order from those experienced in Germany, Italy, Japan, and the United States. China endured old-fashioned rebellions—Muslim risings on the edges of the empire, peasant revolutions at its heart—and the invasions by Britain and France recounted in the last chapter (see Map 26.4). The restoration, moreover, did not involve the radical recrafting that circumstances really required. In some ways decentralization continued, in defiance of the trend in the industrializing world. The Chinese government sold offices—effectively wrecking the virtues of the ancient examination system as a method for filling high positions under the state by merit. The number of magistrates who bought their jobs doubled in the second half of the nineteenth century. Partly to maximize sales, the government appointed magistrates for unhelpfully short terms, so the local administration of justice tended to fall into the hands of petty officials who, once appointed as magistrates' underlings, remained in their jobs indefinitely.

MAP 26.4

Revolts in the Qing Empire, 1850–1901

Qing Empire

tribal risings

Muslim revolts

area of Northwestern Muslim rising 1863–1873

area controlled by Taiping rebels 1853–1863

Taiping rebellion

area of Boxer uprising 1900–1901

Guizhou Muslim uprising 1854–1872

opium trade

Centralization did not always, or even primarily, mean extending the power of central institutions. It was also a matter of sentiment—overcoming traditional provincial, regional, and communal loyalties with a common sense of allegiance to the state. Governments increasingly used universal military service (see Chapter 24) to create a statewide sense of political community, usually in combination with efforts to cultivate nationalism and spread nationalist feelings. Japan's army, typically, became a nursery for reeducating young men in a new version of samurai values, focused on the notions of obedience to the emperor and self-sacrifice for the state. "I wish the army," declared the emperor in 1875, "to be the entire nation." "We are your supreme commander in chief," stated the emperor's instructions to soldiers in 1882, "Our relations with you will be most intimate when we rely on you as our limbs and you look up to us as your head."

The Japanese army, in consequence, felt no loyalty to the civil government and remained, in effect, outside and above the constitution. A similar pattern can be

"But neither the new doctrines of militarism nor the new awareness of its effects eliminated the old way of looking at war as a chivalrous, romantic, and glorious adventure full of dashing heroes, waving flags, and colorful uniforms."

discerned in Spain and in the Latin American states, where the wars of the early nineteenth century armed and militarized huge proportions of the populations. Armies became the agents of independence and in some cases of modernization, the guardians of the state, and, therefore, the arbiters of constitutional conflicts. To some extent, all countries that used their armed forces to mobilize the entire society ran the same risk of suffering or actually did suffer similar consequences: militarized societies produced politicized armies. The United States was fortunate that by the time of its Civil War (1861–1865) the country had developed civil institutions and traditions strong enough to survive the trauma. Civil conflict in the United States never led, as it has done in most countries, to military dictatorship. Britain, too, escaped the danger by keeping its army small and avoiding conscription until 1916 during World War I.

As well as bringing armies into politics, militarization made wars worse. The Prussian military theorist Carl von Clausewitz (1780–1831) assumed that wars were inevitable and that they were bound to involve the entire populations of the warring powers. Everyone was an enemy. The only rational way to wage war, he thought, was "to the utmost. . . . He who uses force unsparingly, without reference to the bloodshed involved, must obtain a superiority." He advocated attrition and general destruction to "wear down" the enemy. The ultimate objective was to leave the enemy permanently disarmed. This encouraged belligerents to fight for unconditional surrender when they were winning, to resist it obstinately when they were losing, and to impose harsh terms in victory. Clausewitz's ideas eventually influenced the entire military and political establishment of Europe and America.

In combination, the improved technology of war, the doctrines of militarism, and the transformation of society into a battleground all made the horrors of war worse. The disasters of the Crimean War in the 1850s and the carnage of the American Civil War also set the stage for what followed. Many of the most gruesome aspects of World War I in Europe were foreshadowed by trench and scorched-earth warfare in the United States. Photographers and chroniclers of the American Civil War and the Franco-Prussian War of 1870–1871 introduced a chilling new awareness of war's consequences. The photographs of Matthew Brady (1823–1896) showed fields full of dead and dying Confederate and Union soldiers. The novels of the French writer Emile Zola (1840–1902) depicted foul hospital scenes, decaying dead, gangrenous wounded, and frenzied amputations. His most vivid material, supplied by a field surgeon, brought a new kind of brutal realism to fiction. But neither the new doctrines of militarism nor the new awareness of its effects eliminated the old way of looking at war as a chivalrous, romantic, and glorious adventure full of dashing heroes, waving flags, and colorful uniforms. So wars went on. Peace Congresses were for cranks. Alfred Nobel (1831–1896), the guilt-racked, lonely Swedish weapons magnate who invented dynamite, took refuge in extravagant projects for world peace. War would "stop short instantly," he promised in 1890, if it were made "as death-dealing to the civilian population at home as to the troops at the front." The best hope Nobel could see for peace was the invention of a method of germ warfare or a weapon of mass destruction.

"Honored dead." The reality of the field of Gettysburg was litter-strewn and squalid, with gaping, crumpled corpses. Photography helped to take romance out of depictions of war.

Beyond the Industrializing World

It is tempting to suppose that similar effects on the state could not happen outside the industrializing world. But major new military technologies always affect political and social organization, and, as we have seen many times before in this book, relatively simple innovations in war could have big consequences in preindustrial societies. This remained true in the nineteenth century. In southeast Africa, for instance, King Shaka reorganized the Zulus into a unified kingdom capable of putting an army of 50,000 men into the field. He invented or adapted a heavy-bladed thrusting spear and developed intensive drills to accustom infantry to use it. The parallel with the effects of firearms drill on Western armies is irresistible. When Shaka claimed his kingdom in 1816, his clan had perhaps 350 warriors. By the time family conspirators murdered him in 1828—a common hazard of kingship in his part of the world—he was ruler of perhaps 250,000 subjects.

In any case, as the arms trade spread industrially produced weaponry around the world, militarization accompanied it. The Zulus began to rearm with firearms after encountering them in the hands of Boer enemies in 1838. Baskore of Maradi (r. 1854–1875) in what is now northern Nigeria, developed the existing bureaucratic traditions of the region of Katsina, where his realm was centered, to keep an effective army mobilized to gather booty and tribute.

In the first half of the century, the most remarkable case in sub-Saharan Africa was that of the kings of Asante in West Africa. Before the kingdom's conquest by the British in the late nineteenth century, the Asante kings imposed the rule of their own dependents in the provinces, burdened rich rivals with punitive taxes, and employed what historians have not hesitated to call a bureaucracy to systemize the tax system. Held together even after the British abolished the slave trade, the Asante kingdom at its height covered 150,000 square miles and had 3 million to 5 million inhabitants. Beyond a core area around the capital, Kumasi, where the ruler's war companions ruled their own followers without much interference from the court, a central treasury that also ran the kings' own commercial transactions—mining, slave trading, and hunting for ivory—regulated tribute, poll taxes, inheritance taxes, and tolls. Early in the century, the kings adopted Arabic as a language of record keeping, which thereafter was done on paper instead of in the old form of piles of shells and coins, used as tokens and counters. The Asante usually did not displace traditional rulers of conquered peoples but redesignated them as captains of the Asante king and placed resident agents alongside them to keep them in order. Bureaucrats were at the disposal of the king. "We are willing to prove to your majesty," ran the declaration of office of the highest treasury official, "our devotion to your person by receiving your foot on our necks, and taking the sacred oath that we will perform all your commands. Our gold, our slaves and our lives are yours, and are ready to be delivered up to your command."

Remarkable as the Asante case was, it never made the kingdom invulnerable to European conquest. By that standard, Ethiopia was the most successful case of political modernization in sub-Saharan Africa. In the third quarter of the century, Ethiopia emerged from a long period of internal war and weak leadership. The emperors never enjoyed uncontested legitimacy or universal obedience, but at least they had credible programs of reunification. The system of government had to be loosely federal, with regional rulers exercising authority without reference to the center, except for paying tribute and defending the country from external enemies. Even the most powerful of the warlords, Menelik of Showa, who subsequently rebelled and captured the throne for himself, paid dazzling tributes. In 1880, for instance, he sent the emperor 600 horses and mules with saddles and bridles

King Shaka. Struggling to make a living, the black South African painter Gerard Bengu (1910–1990) worked as an illustrator for children's textbooks on Zulu history. His historical works have all the vices of these kinds of books in any country, as this overidealized and romanticized vision of King Shaka (ca. 1787–1828) shows. Yet in his private work, Bengu painted the lives of his people with moving realism.

Asante King. Reminiscences of the greatness of the Asante kings persisted after defeat by the British in the late nineteenth century. In this photograph of the 1890s, King Agyeman Prempeh I, borne by slaves, sits on his litter under the royal umbrella, surrounded by drummers and praise singers. Shortly after the photograph was taken, the British arrested and exiled him and provoked a further—and, for the Asante, disastrous—war by demanding custody of the Asante's sacred golden stool.

trimmed in gold and silver, $80,000 worth of cotton goods, and $50,000 in cash. Provincial rulers could assemble treasure on this scale only by conquering more territory. So expansion and the enrichment of the emperor's treasury went on simultaneously, and as resources built up at the center, Ethiopia began to show potential for transformation into a centralized state.

In the 1870s, as a result of victories against Egyptian invaders, Emperor Yohannes IV (r. 1872–1889) began to build up a huge supply of captured modern weapons and to reorganize the army, so that it had a professional core. When Menelik II became emperor in 1889, he concentrated on creating a militarily efficient state, armed with the best guns he could buy from Europe. He established garrisons in remote parts of the empire, dominating the country, stimulating markets, and spreading Christianity. Local farmers had to keep the soldiers supplied. Intermarriage between soldiers and provincials generally eased the potential conflicts the system risked and turned the garrisons into effective agents of the central authority. Huge provinces remained effectively autonomous under their traditional chiefs, but Ethiopia looked increasingly like a modern state, acquiring, by the time Menelik died in 1913, extensive postal, telegraph, and telephone services, and a rail link to the outside world through the French colony of Djibouti on the Red Sea. The emperors were architects of Ethiopia's modernization, but they imported technical know-how from Europe. Alred Ilg, a young Swiss engineer, was Menelik's chief aide, attending to everything from the palace plumbing to foreign policy. Menelik also made much use of Italian technical advice and arms shipments before the outbreak of conflict with Italy in 1896. As a result of all these changes, Ethiopia played a unique role among native African states in the late nineteenth century. As we saw in Chapter 24, Ethiopia not only repulsed European invasion but participated in imperial expansion on its own account alongside European powers.

The case of Ethiopia calls to mind that of Thailand (then still known in the West as Siam), a Southeast Asian state that modernized even more thoroughly than Ethiopia and also achieved the distinction, unique in its region, of avoiding Euro-

Making Connections | STATE MODERNIZATION IN THE NINETEENTH CENTURY

TYPE OF DEVELOPMENT/ IDEOLOGY	CORE IDEA/PURPOSE	SCOPE AND RESULTS
Nationalism	Uniting people who shared same language, historic experience, and sense of identity into a cohesive state	Worldwide; positive effects include increased self-government, popular sovereignty; negative effects include repression of minorities (ethnic, religious, racial) within larger states; promotion of assimilation
Constitutionalism	Belief that state is founded on rules that rulers and citizens create and are bound to obey within a legal framework	Worldwide; beginning in Britain, United States, and Europe; vigorously opposed because of the implication that sovereignty was shared by more than one person/one class; threatened divine right of monarchy and aristocracy; eventual spread to Middle East and Asia
Centralization	Overcoming traditional provincial, regional, communal loyalties by fostering allegiance to the state; often extending power of central institutions	Worldwide, especially in quickly developing regions; often propelled by civil wars (United States, Japan, Germany, Italy) and in areas threatened with fragmentation
Militarization	Use of armed forces to mobilize populations; boosts power of governments to tax and spend on a large scale	Worldwide, especially in industrializing regions and colonial territories; use of larger armies, advanced technology expands warfare to civilian population, increases military and civilian casualties; arms race for improved technologies
Bureaucratization	Systemizing tax collecting, census taking, and regulation; growth of professional civil service with loyalty to the state	Worldwide, in old empires (Ottoman), new industrial states (United States, Germany, Britain), and regions with ambitious rulers (Ethiopia, Thailand, Egypt, Asante kingdom); improved ability to harness economy to government goals

pean conquest. In the 1830s, Prince Mongkut, who already had a reputation as an outstanding Buddhist scholar and reformer, came into contact with French Catholics and American Protestant missionaries and immediately appreciated that Thailand had a lot of catching up to do if it were to survive in a Western-dominated future. He studied Latin, Greek, and Western science and mathematics, and he read British newspapers from Hong Kong and Singapore to keep in touch with Western news. When he became king in 1851, he began cautious reforms, inaugurating a government newspaper, printing laws, and—in a break with a tradition formerly thought sacred—allowing his face to be seen in public. He permitted his subjects to petition him, gave women rights to choose marriage partners, and educated his successor, Chulalongkorn, in a Western as well as a traditional curriculum.

Chulalongkorn (r. 1868–1910) inherited an enormous empire—bigger than any that Southeast Asia had ever seen. But it was highly decentralized and variegated: a tributary empire at its edges, with hundreds of traditional communities in every kind of dependence, all with their own peculiar relationships to the throne. When

Modernization personified. The clothes suggest an upper-class Englishman of the era and an expensively educated English schoolboy. But the faces are those of Chulalongkorn, the king of Thailand, and his son, photographed in about 1890. Westerners' image of Thailand at the time has been distorted, thanks to the much-loved Hollywood and Broadway musical *The King and I*, which depicts an exotic court, presided over by an unbending patriarch king, whereas King Chulalongkorn (r. 1868–1910), was Westernized in his sentiments as well as in his outlook and policies.

Chulalongkorn came of age in 1873, he immediately created a Privy Council and a Council of State with advisory and legislative powers. He abolished the slave trade. He established a palace school and placed royal princes in charge of departments of government, bypassing the old custom by which ministers succeeded by hereditary right or by choice of hereditary patrons. In the 1870s and 1880s, royal commissioners brought outlying autonomous regions of the Thai Empire under control of the central administration. From 1888 onward, after a royal prince had visited England to report on British methods of government, a British-style cabinet system of decision making was gradually introduced. In 1897, the king went to Europe and professed himself "convinced that there exists no incompatibility" between the acquisition of Western know-how "and the maintenance of our individuality as an independent Asiatic nation." Although Western examples obviously inspired his reforms, he presented them as triumphs of Buddhist morality.

Examples of bureaucratic centralization could be multiplied in every continent. Until the British invasions of the 1840s, the Sikh state in northern India was developing by creating a bureaucracy, taking a census, surveying the territory it occupied, and introducing a consistent scheme of taxation, with the help of foreign—including British—experts. In the Central African highlands, King Mutesa (r. 1857–1884) of Buganda in what is now Uganda imported European weapons to equip his own servants and clients and Christian missionaries to strengthen his bureaucracy. He was able to dismiss local chiefs at will and concentrate unprecedented power in his own hands. In West Africa, the empire of Sokoto survived throughout the nineteenth century, in part because it created a bureaucracy to replace the local power of chiefs. The kingdoms of Fouta Toro and Fouta Jalon became elective monarchies, relying on Muslim clergy as servants of the state in the localities (see Map 26.4). Tawhiao, the proud Maori who impressed and alarmed James Kerry-Nicholls in New Zealand, had counterparts in state creation all over the world.

RELIGION AND POLITICS

State power mopped up traditional rivals. Nationalism, militarization, and centralization eclipsed other traditional allegiances. Aristocracies, as we saw in Chapter 24, were on the wane anyway in most places. Religion, however, was more problematic. Religions often had their own powerful institutional structures and rich clergies. They also had the moral authority to challenge governments. States often needed religion for support or to uphold claims to political legitimacy. In the nineteenth century, morality, family life, and the spaces in which social relationships were forged—the household, educational institutions, and the workplace—became arenas fiercely contested between religious institutions and states. In the West, civil marriage was perhaps the state's most important intrusion on what in the previous four centuries had become a precinct of religion. Most countries with codified law made at least some provision for it. Education was another battleground, usually resolved by compromise, because clerical teachers were too cheap and too valuable to eliminate from schools. States that had not already done so, in some cases, even took over existing religions, funding them and appointing clerics. Japan's ancient popular religion, Shintoism, which had always been a chaotic mix of local nature and ancestor cults, became a national organization with the emperor as chief priest, largely because nineteenth-century intellectuals in Japan perceived state control of religion to be one of the strengths of Western powers.

Europe and the Americas became arenas of state-church competition—what in Germany after 1873 came to be called a **Kulturkampf,** "a conflict of cultures" between the state and the Roman Catholic Church. Church-affiliated and secularist political parties engaged in constitutional struggles over the degree to which constitutions should embody religious traditions and reflect religious values. Secularists used the word "liberal" to denote a program of religion-free politics. In this respect, as in so many others, the United States provided a model. Its Constitution had insisted from the first that the federal government shall "make no establishment of religion." This was not, however, because Americans were irreligious or because the state was jealous of religion. Rather, it was to protect religious freedom. Secularism in Europe, by contrast, was a program to increase state power, and it therefore aroused much opposition. In Latin America, too, the conflict was fierce. A story about Simón Bolívar (1783–1830) (see Chapter 21), the principal leader and spokesman of the successful independence movements of the early nineteenth century in Spanish America, illustrates this. In 1812, he was in Caracas, the main city of Venezuela, when an earthquake struck. Monks took to the streets to bless the dying and denounce the rebels against Spain. Bolívar dragged a monk from the pulpit of a church, threatened him with the sword, and said, "If nature opposes us, we will fight against it and make it obey us." But politicians could not change nature, and religious sentiment was too deeply rooted in human nature and communities to be defied. Churches continued to be able to mobilize people for political action.

In Europe, the Catholic Church fought back with surprising success. Pope Pius IX (r. 1846–1878) responded to challenges to church authority and Christian belief with defiance. He refused to submit to force or defer to change. He condemned almost every social and political innovation of his day. When Italy occupied Rome in 1870 and put an end to papal rule, he retreated into virtual seclusion in the Vatican. Earlier that same year, his fellow bishops had rewarded him for a godly vocation undiluted by compromise by proclaiming papal infallibility in religious doctrine and morals. His successor, Leo XIII (r. 1878–1903), turned the church into a reforming institution, a privileged critic of abuses of secular power. But after Leo's death, the political fashion changed in Rome, and the church became much more conservative. There were always clergy in every faith who were prepared to collaborate with repression and authoritarianism on the political right.

Meanwhile, religion resisted a deeper challenge from an atheism that science claimed to validate. Charles Darwin's theory of evolution (see Chapter 25) suggested, to some of its advocates, a new God-free explanation for life. Impersonal evolution threatened to replace divine Providence as the motor of change. If science could explain a problem as "mysterious"—to use Darwin's word—as the diversity of species, it might yet be able to explain everything else. Religious doubts multiplied among European and American elites. From the 1870s, groups

Chronology: Nationalism, Constitutionalism, Militarization, Centralization, and Bureaucratization in the Nineteenth Century	
1783–1830	Simón Bolívar, leader in the fight for Latin American independence
ca. 1800–1850	Asante kings centralize and bureaucratize their West African kingdom
1805–1872	Giuseppe Mazzini, Italian nationalist
1810	Beginning of Jewish reform movement
ca. 1810–1830	Wars of independence from Spain fought in Latin America
1820	King Shaka of the Zulus controls much of southeast Africa
1821	Founding of Liberia
1822	First fully independent Mexican state
1827	Constitution of Cherokee Republic
1829	Greece gains independence from Ottoman Empire
1830s	Large Latin American states dissolve into smaller ones
1832	Reform Act increases middle-class representation in British Parliament
1845	Ottoman sultan convenes and dissolves an assembly of provincial representatives
1873–1901	British conquest of kingdom of Asante
1861–1896	José Rizal, Filipino nationalist
1864	Creation of district assemblies in Russia
1868	Meiji Restoration in Japan abolishes shogunate and restores the emperor as the head of the administration
r. 1868–1910	King Chulalongkorn modernizes Thailand
1878	Romania and Serbia gain independence from Ottoman Empire
1889	Japanese constitution created by imperial decree
1893	French Captain Alfred Dreyfus accused of spying for the Germans
Late nineteenth century	Ethiopia modernizes army, administration, and infrastructure

Zwischen Berlin und Rom.

Church-State Conflict. The struggle between the Imperial German government and the Catholic Church was one of the most intense cultural conflicts of the late nineteenth century. In this cartoon from the 1870s, Pope Pius IX and Otto von Bismarck, the German chancellor, play a game of political chess. Pieces captured represent German church leaders whom Bismarck sought to remove from public life. A standard-bearer demanding the closure of monasteries leads Bismarck's attack. The pope's remaining pieces represent spiritual sanctions and intellectual arguments. Bismarck is clearly winning the game, while the Pope considers his next move.

calling themselves "humane" or "ethical" societies aimed to base moral conduct on humane values rather than on the fear of God or the dogmas of religious institutions. Christianity was stirred in response, rather than shaken. Evangelizing movements spread Christian awareness in the new industrialized, urban workforces of the period. In 1867, the English poet, Matthew Arnold, stood on Dover Beach and heard in his mind the "melancholy, long, withdrawing roar" of the "the Sea of Faith." But in 1896, the Austrian composer Anton Bruckner died while writing his great "Ninth Symphony"—a dark document of religious doubts smothered in a glorious finale of resurgent faith.

Among many instances of the continuing vitality of Islam as a source of political inspiration in the nineteenth century, none was more spectacular than the movement the self-taught prophet, Muhammad Ahmad, proclaimed in the Sudan in 1881. Calling on his followers to "put aside everything that resembles the customs of Turks and infidels," he came to see himself as the *Mahdi*—the successor of the Prophet Muhammad, the restorer of the faith, whose coming would herald the end of time. His support grew. He organized his followers into a war machine on Quranic principles—the Quran was the only text he knew. He claimed to speak with the Prophet. He condemned as infidels all who opposed him. His domain on the upper Nile was impregnable—"a desolation of desolations, an infernal region, a howling waste of weed, mosquitoes, flies and fever, backed by a groaning waste of thorns and stones—waterless and waterlogged," as a European described it. The Mahdi's typical follower was, as the British admitted (in lines by the great poet of the British Empire, Rudyard Kipling [1865–1936]) "a pore benighted 'eathen, but a first-class fightin' man." The Mahdi himself had a different explanation for his success: "Every intelligent person must know that Allah rules, and his authority cannot be shared by muskets, cannons, or bombs. . . . He who surrenders shall be saved, but if . . . you persist in denying my divine calling, . . . you are to be killed." The Egyptian and British governments sent armies that failed to suppress the movement until 1898, when a crushingly well-armed British force slaughtered the Mahdists at the Battle of Omdurman (see Chapter 25).

The Mahdi was only one of many founders of Islamic states or disturbers of secular ones (see Map 26.5). In 1852, al-Hajj Umar, leader of an austere Muslim sect known as the Tijjaniya, launched religious war in the western Sudan, creating a revolutionary state. Ma Ba did the same, probably in imitation, in Senegambia in West Africa about a decade later. Before attacking a city, he would pray in public amid a crowd of chanting holy men and distribute written charms to his warriors. "You are my equals and my brothers before Muhammad. . . . I am a man of little value, but one who calls you to God and his prophet." In 1860, also in West Africa, the king of Sine told the French that they wanted to do with subject-peoples "as we have always done. These people are my slaves . . . I will take their property, their children and their millet." But Muslim holy men summoned them to revolt, which the French only repressed with difficulty.

In other regions, too, religion remained a revolutionary force in the world, generating movements of popular rebellion that always failed but that kept cropping up. A few examples illustrate this fact. In 1847, a conflict known as the Caste War broke out in Yucatán in southeast Mexico. Maya rebels threatened to kill all white

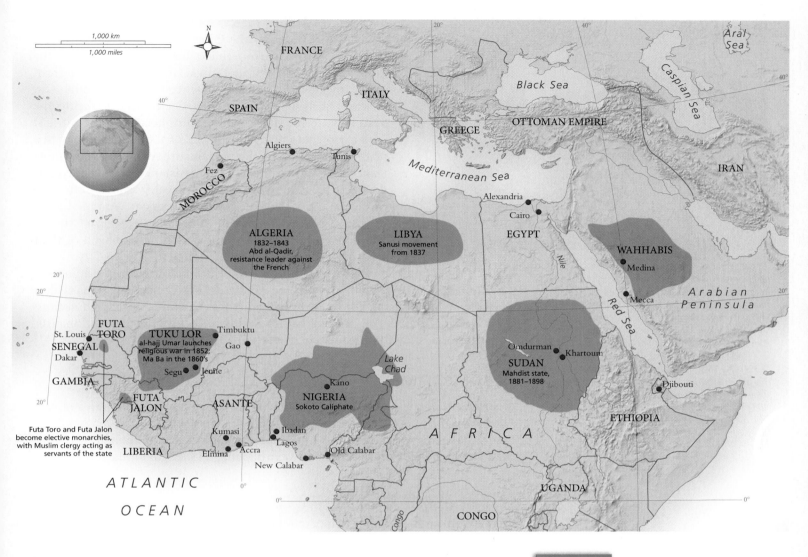

Muslim Reform Movements in Africa and Arabia in the Nineteenth Century

 Islamic reform movement

people. Government supporters retorted with threats to exterminate the Maya. The rebels' rallying point was the so-called Talking Cross of the shrine of Chan Santa Cruz—an oracle proclaiming divine sanction and success for the rebel cause. In the 1850s, in the South African Transkei, the Xhosa people were powerless to rebel against the British, because their cattle were dying from a new kind of lung sickness. A woman prophet urged them to a gesture of despair as an alternative to rebellion: sacrificing their surviving livestock to persuade the gods to get rid of the British.

In Ethiopia, when a new emperor seized the throne in 1855, he called himself Tewodros II to appeal to peasants who expected the resurrection of a fifteenth-century emperor of the same name who had befriended the peasantry. This movement transcended religious boundaries. Tewodros II (r. 1855–1868) was a Messiah for Christians and a Mahdi for Muslims. He behaved in this respect, as in so many others, like a modernizer in the Western mold, secularizing much church property.

In Japan in the 1860s, samurai reactionaries were the most menacing opponents of Westernization, but a woman who claimed to be a divine incarnation inspired thousands of peasant followers to rebel. She preached equality and peasant solidarity. In China at around the same time, a failed examination candidate and school teacher, who came to see himself as a "brother of Jesus," led

Ghost dance. The American artist Frederick Remington (1861–1909) was the most famous and popular illustrator of the life of the "Wild West." He painted this version of the Sioux Ghost dancers for *Harper's Weekly*, allegedly from sketches made by members of the South Dakota Home Guard, who suppressed the movement, massacring and scalping 75 Sioux, in December 1890. As the painting suggests, Remington had no personal sympathy for Native Americans.
Ogallala Sioux performing the Ghost Dance at the Pine Ridge Indian Agency, South Dakota. Illustration by Frederic Remington, 1890. The Granger Collection.

the Taiping rebellion that, as we have seen, paralyzed China and almost overthrew the Qing Empire (see Chapter 25). In 1866, a woman who called herself the Virgin of the Rosary led a rebellion in Bolivia. In the North American plains, meanwhile, the Ghost Dance was a traditional—or, at least, fairly old—Native American ritual to bring the dead back to life. In the 1880s, prophets associated it first with a project to bring on the end of the world, then with a plan to invoke divine help against the whites. Most Ghost Dancers never intended violent resistance, but alarmed settlers called in the United States' cavalry. Shortly after the cavalry massacred Sioux Ghost Dancers at Wounded Knee in 1890, Native American rebels in northern Mexico adopted a local woman prophet as the figurehead of their revolt against a modernizing regime in Mexico City.

On the whole, despite the continuing vigor of religiously inspired politics, religion lost out in its conflicts with secular states. The charms religious zealots such as the Mahdi issued did not work against the machine gun. Sacred notions of political authority succumbed to new kinds of legitimacy that nationalists, constitutionalists, and bureaucrats advocated.

NEW FORMS OF POLITICAL RADICALISM

In principle, popular revolutionary movements of religious inspiration were not new. We have met them many times before in this book. In the nineteenth century, however, even more radical challenges—even more subversive ways of thinking about the state and forms of political behavior—were building up strength for the future.

Steps toward Democracy

In the West, enthusiasm for democracy began to mobilize popular movements and became a major force for change independent of any sect. Increasingly, in the nineteenth-century West, citizens sought to take the constitutional changes of the era further and create states in which the political process was open to all. But where did the idea of democracy come from? The two usual—but not necessarily mutually exclusive—answers are from ancient Greece and primitive Christianity. Greek examples provided models of states in which all citizens shared decision making, even though Greek citizenship was restricted to free adult males who usually also had to own property to participate in political life. The Christianity of the apostolic age enshrined the notion of the equality of all members of the group.

However that may be, the United States—perhaps because men steeped in reverence for both the classics and Christianity founded the country—was the laboratory of democracy for the nineteenth-century world. Democracy as we usually understand it today—with a representative legislature, elected on a wide suffrage, and political parties—was, in effect, an American invention. Although the American executive is not formally subordinate to Congress, all major officeholders under the president have to submit to confirmation by the Senate, and all, including the president, report to Congress, which has—and sometimes indulges in—a right to impeach them. Despite major imperfections (slaves, Native Americans, Asian immigrants, and women were excluded from political rights), democracy developed early in the history of the new republic. Some of the states were more generous than others in enlarging the franchise, but by the early 1840s, almost all adult, white, and free males could vote in all the states of the United States.

From the perspective of Europe, however, democracy seemed at first to be one of America's "peculiar institutions," like slavery, that it would be best to avoid. It appeared to be foolish for elites to share power with poorly educated masses who tended to vote for populists, demagogues, and charlatans. The bloodshed of the French Revolution seemed to show that the "common man" was an untrustworthy political partner. In consequence, the first half of the nineteenth century was a time of democratic retreat in most of Europe, as rulers withdrew or diluted constitutions that they had conceded to enlarge political nations in the crises of the Napoleonic Wars. The new constitutions that did emerge in Europe at this time were designed to create alliances among monarchs, aristocrats, churches, and the upper middle classes and thus to defend traditional privileges by enlarging support for them. Whenever possible, the birth of working-class organizations was aborted, radical presses censored, demonstrators shot. In Britain, the Reform Act of 1832, often hailed as a first step toward democratic progress because it increased middle-class representation in Parliament, actually disenfranchised working-class voters.

Nevertheless, the model of the United States became increasingly attractive as the young country proved itself. European radicals who visited America returned enthused. The first influential apologist for American democracy was a German, Karl Postl, who in 1828 recommended a "system which unites the population for the common good." In 1831, Alexis de Tocqueville, one of the most influential voices of the nineteenth century (see Chapters 24 and 25), followed Postl. Tocqueville was a French aristocrat, not previously noted for liberalism, keen to see equality in action—much as one might decide to visit a fairground freak. Between 1835 and 1840, he published *Democracy in America*. His aristocratic self-confidence in the face of popular sovereignty helped reconcile Europeans to democratic change. Tocqueville was not an uncritical admirer of the United States. On the contrary, he noted grave faults: the costliness and inefficiency of government; the corruption and ignorance among public officials; the political bombast; the conformism that offset individualism; the intellectually feeble popular religion; the tension between crass materialism and religious enthusiasm; the "tyranny of the majority"; the threat of rule by and for the rich. But he predicted an American-style future for the world. While most Europeans of his class felt the terror and menace of the revolutionary mob, Tocqueville saw "the same democracy . . . advancing rapidly toward power in Europe." Properly managed, the result would be "a society which all men, regarding the law as their work, would acknowledge without demur." Where rights were guaranteed, he wrote, democracy would "shelter the state" from tyranny, on the one hand, and lawlessness, on the other.

With all its shortcomings, the America Tocqueville described seemed exemplary. Its bottom line was expressed in dollars and cents—the prosperity America delivered for Americans—and in military clout—the success in war the United States demonstrated against Mexico in the 1840s. "Democracy," announced a Hungarian revolutionary after a visit to America, "is the spirit of our age." Democracy became the first American cultural product to conquer Europe—even before jazz, rock music, casual manners, fast food, and tight jeans. The decisive moment came in the 1880s, when James Bryce, a future British ambassador to the United States, revisited the subject of democracy in *The American Commonwealth*. The

Stump Speaking. George Caleb Bingham (1811–1879) chronicled the life of the Missouri valley in the mid-nineteenth century in his accomplished, well-observed paintings. He was also active in politics on behalf of Andrew Jackson, which gives his political scenes an edge of personal commitment. Typically, as here in *Stump Speaking* (1853–1854), a politician's passion contrasts with the attitudes of his audiences—variously cool, critical, idly curious, sneering, bored, or depraved.
George Caleb Bingham (American, 1811–1879), "Stump Speaking," 1853–54. Oil on canvas, 42 1/2 × 58 in. The Saint Louis Art Museum, Gift of Bank of America.

Women's suffrage. In 1905, Norway's legislative assembly called a referendum to dissolve the union with Sweden that had been imposed 90 years before, after the Napoleonic Wars. Women were soon to have equal voting rights with men in independent Norway, but the referendum was held under the old Swedish election rules, which restricted the vote to men. So women organized their own say-so by signing a petition in favor of independence. More than 250,000 women signed the document, an impressive number, given that Norway's population at the time was less than 2.5 million.

book provided a blueprint for constitutional change around the world. Bryce recommended a wide suffrage, but with some property qualifications, since for the poor, he thought, "a vote is a means to mischief." He advised against salaried politicians, who were likely to accept bribes and be overly influenced by money. He felt the American system was too prone to be dominated by the rich. (This was perhaps unfair. In Bryce's Britain, members of Parliament were unpaid, and only the rich or their protégés could normally afford to run for office.) But on the whole, Bryce approved of America. Democracy was like a "lamp, whose light helps those who come after it."

The efforts of Tocqueville, Bryce, and their like changed the way European elites perceived democracy. In the last two decades or so of the nineteenth century, most European countries modified their constitutions in a democratic direction and, in particular, enlarged the franchise. New states of the early years of the new century—Norway, Australia, New Zealand, and Iceland (which was under the Danish crown but autonomous)—had even more determinedly democratic constitutions than the United States. Norway and New Zealand even allowed the vote to women and to formerly despised ethnic minorities, the Sami in Norway and the Maori in New Zealand. It is rarely appreciated that in Europe, though France, Switzerland, and—with less consistency—Spain were beacons of universal male suffrage, the most conspicuous concentration of states with democratic franchises was in the former Ottoman dominions in the Balkans. In Greece, Bulgaria, Serbia, and Romania, the right to vote was more widely shared than in Britain or Scandinavia. In this respect, the dawn of European democracy, it is fair to say, came up in the east. This was understandable. The newest states, repudiating the empires that preceded them, had the least historic baggage to discard in adopting democracy.

There was, however, no uniform march of progress toward practical democracy in most of Europe. On the contrary, democracy remained marginal throughout the century. For effective democracy is not just a matter of how many people can vote. Everywhere, small groups tried to manipulate mass electorates. In Romania, the constitution was often suspended or ignored. In Britain, the biggest single extension of the franchise—in 1884–1885—which added 2 million voters to the rolls, was accompanied by a redistribution of parliamentary seats to preserve the existing parties' shares of power. Constitutional reform in Europe never completely pried open the half-closed world of the dominant political caste and its adopted recruits. The aristocracy retained formal power. Parliamentary dictatorship in Greece subverted the democratic constitution by patronage and intimidation. Greek governments regularly hired thugs to frighten voters at election times. When Germany introduced universal male suffrage in 1871, it was limited to elections for one chamber of the national legislature, the Reichstag, whose power was limited.

The Expansion of the Public Sphere

Even where there was little or no democracy, more people got involved in what historians and sociologists now like to call the **public sphere**: in clubs, institutions, and associations outside the home, in arenas of debate in cafes and bars, and in places of worship. Newspapers brought affairs of state home to everyone who was literate. To some extent, public readings of newspapers made even illiterate people politically informed. In Cuba, this was the normal entertainment for workers in factories while they rolled cigars. In Spain in 1852, a young friar visited a factory in Barcelona at lunchtime to find the workers all listening to young children reading aloud from "highly colored political journals which generally spread subversive doctrines, mocked holy things . . . spoke ill of the proprietors and government, and preached socialism and communism." Catholic clergy provided reading material for factories to deflect workers from hearing too much inflammatory or revolutionary propaganda.

The public sphere was widest and most developed in North America and parts of Europe. That is why democracy got a foothold in those regions. But there were outposts and echoes in other parts of the world. Although relatively few people took part in political life in Latin America, compared with the United States, they contested power with great commitment and sustained ferocious debates in the press. In Brazil, the proliferation of political clubs, newspapers, and rallies preceded the abolition of slavery in 1888 and the proclamation of the republic in 1889. In Cuban cigar factories, lectors employed to read to the workers spread radical political messages. In the last two decades of the nineteenth century, most Argentine intellectuals generally and genuinely regarded their country as a democracy: that was the message of the leading newspaper, *La Nación*, and its founder, the former president, Bartolomé Mitre.

In Japan the spread of education (see Chapter 24) was bound to enlarge the public sphere. The state replaced samurai privileges with examinations as a means of recruiting officials. Even in China, the political class expanded, thanks in part to the creation of hundreds of provincial academies to train officials. On the whole, the Qing rulers responded to crisis by resisting social or political change and clinging to the notion that the inherited order of society was sacred. The terms of public debate, however, were enlarged. The work of Feng Guifen (fung gway-fun) (1809–1874), director of one of the largest provincial academies, included radical proposals, based on study of Western politics. At the height of the crisis caused by rebellion and Anglo-French invasion in the 1860s, he advocated the professionalization of the civil service and popular election of village headmen to provide the lowest level of the judiciary. The government, however, shelved his proposals.

WESTERN SOCIAL THOUGHT

The clash of political visions in the nineteenth-century West was the echo of a mightier clash of rival philosophies: part of a worldwide tension between secularism and religiosity in everyday conceptions of life and the world. Were men apes or angels? Were they images of God or heirs of Adam? Would the goodness inside them emerge in freedom, or was it corroded with evil that had to be controlled? In 1816, just after the Napoleonic Wars, the English writer Thomas Love Peacock, gathered fictional philosophers in the setting of his comic novel, *Headlong Hall*. "Mr. Forster, the perfectibilian," expected "gradual advancement towards a state of unlimited perfection," while "Mr. Escot, the deteriorationist," foresaw, with gloomy satisfaction, "that the whole species must at length be exterminated by its own imbecility and violence." These extremes of optimism and pessimism echoed real debates. In France, for instance, Louis Blanc (1811–1882) believed that the state could eliminate all human wickedness, while his contemporary, Alphonse Karr, looked for no improvement in society and thought that attempted reforms only made things worse. The politics of fear and hope collided in conflicts that pitted rival kinds of radicalism—reformist philosophies that claimed to get to the root of the world's problems—against each other.

Socialism was an extreme form of optimism. Socialists believed in the ideals of equality and fraternity that those thinkers in the Enlightenment who believed in the perfect ability of human nature had proclaimed (see Chapter 22). Early socialist communities in Europe and America practiced sharing and cooperating. Charles Fourier (1772–1837) planned a settlement called New Harmony, where even sexual orgies would be organized on egalitarian principles. In Texas in 1849,

"The clash of political visions in the nineteenth-century West was the echo of a mightier clash of rival philosophies: part of a worldwide tension between secularism and religiosity in everyday conceptions of life and the world."

Socialist utopia. A bird's-eye view of design for Robert Owen's socialist utopia of New Harmony, Indiana. Owen's socialism had Christian origins, though the minaret-like towers and central pavilion make this view of New Harmony resemble Mecca. The symmetry recalls classical models of an ordered life. The grandeur and fantasy are typical of the "progress-palace" tradition of nineteenth-century factory architecture.

Étienne Cabet (1788–1856) founded a town he called Icaria, where abolishing property and forbidding rivalry would prevent envy, crime, anger, and lust. Clothes, according to Cabet, ought to be made of elastic to make the principle of equality "suit people of different sizes."

These experiments, and others like them, failed, but the idea of reforming society as a whole on socialist lines appealed enormously to people unrewarded or outraged by the unequal distribution of wealth in the industrializing world. Economic theorists maintained that since workers' labor added the greater part of the value of most commodities (see Chapter 24), the workers should get the lions' share of the profits—or so some socialists inferred. This was a capitalist's kind of socialism, in which ideals carried a price tag. Louis Blanc convinced most socialists that the state could impose their ideals on society. John Ruskin (1819–1900) echoed these arguments in England. For him "the first duty of a state is to see that every child born therein shall be well housed, clothed, fed and educated," and he relished the prospect of increased state power to accomplish it.

Meanwhile, Karl Marx (1818–1883) predicted the inevitability of socialism's triumph through a cycle of class conflicts. As economic power passed from capital to labor, so workers—degraded and inflamed by exploitative employers—would seize power in the state. "Not only," he announced, "has the bourgeoisie forged the weapons that bring death to itself. It has also called into existence the men who are to wield those weapons—the modern working class, the proletarians." The transition, he believed, would inevitably be violent. The ruling class would try to hold on to power, while the rising class struggled to gain it. So he tended to agree with the thinkers of his day who saw violence as good and conducive to progress. In part, the effect was to help inspire revolutionary violence, which sometimes succeeded in changing society, but never seemed to bring the communist utopia into being or even into sight. All Marx's predictions, so far, have proved false. Yet the brilliance of his analysis of history ensured that he would have millions of readers and millions of followers.

While mainstream socialists put their faith in a strong, regulatory state to realize revolutionary ambitions, or sought to capture the state by mobilizing the masses, visions of revolutionary violence sidetracked others. Some of these "anarchists," as they called themselves, turned increasingly to the bloodstained ravings of Johann Most (1846–1896), the first great ideologue of terror. The entire elite—including their families, servants, and all who did business with them—was, for Most, a legitimate target of armed struggle, to be killed at every opportunity. Anyone caught in the crossfire was a sacrifice in a good cause. Most devised the phrase "propaganda of the deed" as a euphemism for murder. In 1884, he published a handbook on how to explode bombs in churches, ballrooms, and public places, where the "reptile brood" of aristocrats, priests, and capitalists might gather. He also advocated exterminating policemen on the grounds that these "pigs" were not fully human. The bombs of terrorism exploded in elite ears. The propaganda of the deed captured the world's press. Social outcasts and the chronically disaffected formed solemn pacts to assassinate rulers, provoke revolutions, fight wars of resistance against the state, and defy the repressive realities of politics and economics.

In most European countries in the late nineteenth century, socialists built up mass organizations for political and industrial action. They believed their triumph was determined by history. The questions that divided them were whether that triumph should be triggered violently, pursued democratically, or engineered

A CLOSER LOOK
Educating Native Americans

Education in the nineteenth century generally sought to promote the interests of the state by imposing national identity and social conformity. The effort to turn Native American children into submissive U. S. inhabitants was an extreme case. "I believe in immersing the Indians in our civilization and when we get them under holding them there until they are thoroughly soaked," said Richard Henry Pratt, who founded the Carlisle Indian Industrial School in 1879. He was a humane man, but his program of integration was as destructive of Native American culture as the extermination policies he opposed.

The Chiricahua Apache fiercely resisted conquest by the U. S. In 1886, Pratt began to recruit the children of mistreated Chiricahua prisoners for his school.

On arrival, the photographer simply lined them up in their first experience of regimentation.

The students' dress shows signs of assimilation to standard U. S. models, but their hair styles are highly individualistic.

Pratt's background and method were military. He put the students in uniform, cut their hair, and made them do daily drill. Students spent their vacations as servants in white households.

"You are here to learn the ways of white men. Do it well," said Geronimo, the famous Apache war chief, to the students when he visited the school in 1905. Most graduates returned to their reservations, making their "education" seem pointless.

How do these photographs show education as a tool to further interests of the state in the nineteenth century?

by industrial action. In Milan in northern Italy, in 1899, Giuseppe Pelizza, a convert to socialism from a guilt-ridden middle-class background, began a vast symbolic painting. He depicted a crowd of workers, advancing, "like a torrent, overthrowing every obstacle in its path, thirsty for justice." Except for a Madonna-like woman in the foreground—who seems bent on a personal project, appealing to one of the rugged leaders at the head of the march—the workers are individually characterless, moving like parts of a giant machine, with a mechanical rhythm, slow and pounding. No work of art could better express the grandeur and grind at the heart of socialism: noble humanity, mobilized by dreary determinism.

Opponents of socialism included philosophical pessimists, who believed that humans could not be reformed and that only law and order could redeem their wickedness. Between extreme optimism and extreme pessimism, centrist political thinking developed. In the nineteenth century, the English philosopher Jeremy Bentham (1748–1832) devised the most influential form of centrist thinking, called **utilitarianism.** Bentham proposed a new way to evaluate social institutions without reference or deference to their antiquity or authority or past record of success. He thought good could be defined as a surplus of happiness over unhappiness and that the aim of the state was "the greatest happiness of the greatest number." For Bentham, social utility was more important than individual liberty. His doctrine was thoroughly secular. Bentham's standard of happiness was pleasure, and his index of evil was pain. His views therefore appealed to the irreligious. Today, he is treated like a secular saint. His body is exhibited at University College, London, to encourage students. Bentham and his friends also attempted austerely rational and scientific thinking about how to run society. But the greatest happiness of the greatest number means sacrifices for some. It is strictly incompatible with human rights because the interest of the "greatest number" will always tend to leave some individuals without benefits.

Modifying, then rejecting utilitarianism, Bentham's disciple, John Stuart Mill (1806–1873), came to adopt a scale of values with freedom at the top. Liberty, he thought, is absolute, except where it interferes with others. "The only purpose," he wrote, "for which power can be rightfully exercised over any member of a civilised community, against his will, is to prevent harm to others"—not to make him happier. For Bentham's "greatest number," Mill substituted the individual. "Over himself, over his own body and mind, the individual is sovereign." Mill's individualism, however, never excluded social priorities. "For the protection of society," the citizen "owes a return for the benefit." He can be made to respect others' rights and to contribute a reasonable share of taxes and services to the state. Freedom and social priorities, however, did not commend themselves to everybody. Philosophical opponents of liberalism—the most eloquent of whom was the German Friedrich Nietzsche (1844–1900)—favored "heroes" and "supermen" to solve social problems. Dictators in the next century would adopt these ideas.

Meanwhile, Benthamism was amazingly influential. The British state was reorganized along lines Bentham rec-

Chronology: Religion, Utopianism, Democracy, and Political Radicalism in the Nineteenth Century

1748–1832	Jeremy Bentham, proponent of utilitarianism
1772–1837	Charles Fourier, created planned community of New Harmony based on egalitarian ideals
1788–1856	Étienne Cabet, founded utopian community of Icaria
1806–1873	John Stuart Mill, combined individualism with social reform
1811–1882	Louis Blanc, argued that the state could eliminate human wickedness
1818–1883	Karl Marx, predicted socialism's inevitable triumph through violent revolution
1835–1840	Publication of Alexis de Tocqueville's *Democracy in America*
ca. 1840	Almost all adult white males can vote in the United States
1844–1900	Friedrich Nietzsche, rejected liberalism and religion
r. 1846–1878	Pope Pius IX, opponent of social and political innovation
1847	Caste War begins in southeast Mexico
1873	*Kulturkampf* launched by Bismarck
r. 1878–1903	Pope Leo XIII urges social reform
1881	Muhammad Ahmad calls on Muslims in the Sudan to join his reform movement

ommended. The penal code was reformed to minimize unhelpful pain. The government bureaucracy was restaffed with administrators who had passed competitive exams. Capitalist and libertarian prejudices could never quite exclude public interest from legislators' priorities, even under nominally right-wing governments. Benthamism made social welfare seem like the job of the state. In promoting social welfare, Germany led the way, introducing pensions, health services, and education for all in the 1880s. The German policy is often seen as an attempt to preempt the appeal of socialism—as indeed it was. But it was also the out-

Noble workers. Giuseppe Pelizza's painting *Il Quarto Stato*, completed between 1899 and 1901. Pelizza was convinced that artists were workers who had a social responsibility to educate, elevate, and inspire other workers. Although he himself was born into a well-off, middle-class Italian family, he believed that only a person who was born, bred, and lived among the working class could undertake this duty.
G. Pellizza da Volpedo "The Fourth Estate." Milano, Galleria Civica D'Arte Moderna. © Canali Photobank.

come of a trend, begun during the Enlightenment, of philosophical respect for the common man. Australia and New Zealand copied German initiatives in an attempt to create a common identity for settlers—an identity, moreover, distinct from those of the snobbish and class-ridden society that migrants from Britain had left behind. A worldwide consensus in favor of a socially responsible state gradually emerged. The main disagreements, which would be bloodily fought out in the following century, were over how far that responsibility extended.

In Perspective
Global State-Building

All the transformations of nineteenth-century states need to be understood against a common background: the declining credibility of traditional forms of authority, as conflicts overthrew old supremacies and economic change enriched new aspirants to power. During the changes that followed, the sphere of the state unquestionably expanded. States still had not penetrated vast areas of the globe, but these regions were now clearly the exception—underpopulated and relatively inaccessible environments. In most of the rest of the world, the state had arrived: imposed from outside by imperialist invasions, or created from within by monarchs or elites, usually in imitation of Western powers. In parts of the world with long experience of states, such as Japan, Egypt, and Thailand, governments had extended their reach. States took on new responsibilities as their power increased. Education, as we have seen, received a boost from militarization. States interfered more and more in religion and family life. It even became increasingly accepted that the state was responsible for the total well-being of its citizens. Public health schemes became the norm in Europe and America. The first systems of social insurance and universal education were among other consequences.

In addition to imposing their will on their subjects or citizens with unprecedented force, states confronted each other with wariness or hostility. Indeed, competition, defensiveness, and fear were among the motive forces that made states cohere. Alliances normally sought the self-interest of states and the containment or humiliation of enemies rather than collaboration and deep friendship. The notion that the interests of the state came above those of the individual or of religion or of morality was widely upheld. People called it by the German term, *Staatspolitik*.

After all the wars, reforms, constitutional conflicts, radical thinking, and administrative tinkering, how strong were the states and empires that covered most of the world by 1900? Had they reformed for survival? Or were they, as socialists thought,

"All the transformations of nineteenth-century states need to be understood against a common background: the declining credibility of traditional forms of authority, as conflicts overthrew old supremacies and economic change enriched new aspirants to power."

Chronology

1748–1832	Jeremy Bentham, proponent of utilitarianism
1772–1837	Charles Fourier, created planned community of New Harmony based on egalitarian ideals
ca. 1800–1850	Asante kings centralize and bureaucratize their West African kingdom
1805–1872	Giuseppe Mazzini, Italian nationalist
1806–1873	John Stuart Mill, combined individualism with social reform
ca. 1810–1830	Wars of Independence from Spain fought in Latin America
1811–1882	Louis Blanc, argued that the state could eliminate human wickedness
1818–1883	Karl Marx, predicted socialism's inevitable triumph through violent revolution
1820	King Shaka of the Zulus gains control of much of southeast Africa
1821	Founding of Liberia
1822	First fully independent Mexican state
1829	Greece gains independence from Ottoman Empire
1830s	Large Latin American states dissolve into smaller ones
1832	Reform Act increases middle-class representation in British Parliament
1835–1840	Publication of Alexis de Tocqueville's *Democracy in America*
1844–1900	Friedrich Nietzsche, rejected liberalism and religion
1845	Ottoman sultan convenes and dissolves an assembly of provincial representatives
1846–1848	Mexican-American War
r. 1846–1878	Pope Pius IX, opponent of social and political innovation
1847	Caste War begins in southeast Mexico
1861–1896	José Rizal, Filipino nationalist
1868	Meiji Restoration in Japan abolishes shogunate and restores the emperor as head of the administration
r. 1868–1910	King Chulalongkorn modernizes Thailand
1871	German unification
1873–1901	British conquest of kingdom of Asante
1873	*Kulturkampf* launched
r. 1878–1903	Pope Leo XIII urges social reform
1878	Romania and Serbia gain independence from Ottoman Empire
1881	Muhammad Ahmad calls on Muslims in Sudan to join his reform movement
1889	Japanese constitution created by imperial decree
1893	French Captain Alfred Dreyfus accused of spying for the Germans
Late nineteenth century	Ethiopia modernizes army, administration, and infrastructure

doomed to disappear? Age-old rivals of the state—religious institutions and allegiances—had proved remarkably strong. And although local, regional, and tribal loyalties were in retreat, they had only been checked, not destroyed. As we shall see, they would often reemerge in the twentieth and twenty-first centuries. At the end of the nineteenth century, some states, such as Japan, the United States, and the British Empire, looked as it they had met the challenges of the century successfully and recast themselves in lasting form. Others, such as the Ottoman Empire and China, seemed inadequately reformed and vulnerable. In between were superficially strong states, such as the German and Russian empires, and that of the Habsburgs, which were to prove surprisingly fragile when tested in the twentieth century. While white empires continued to grow, there were signs that the days of their supremacy were numbered. Their power was founded on technological superiority, which was a wasting asset. Nonwhite powers in Asia and Africa had already demonstrated that they could copy the trick, either by buying European technology with which to fight back against the empires, as Ethiopia had or, like Japan, launching their own industrialization programs.

To maintain its power in the world, Europe needed peace at home. Only brief wars broke that peace in the nineteenth century. For almost 40 years after the defeat of Napoleon in 1815, no major war flared on Europe's home ground. The wars of the midcentury to 1870 were short and did not overstrain the belligerents. After 1870, short-term military service became the universal fashion in the West—with the major exceptions of Britain and the United States but including almost all of Latin America—and Japan, as states sought to give more male citizens experience of military service. Armies therefore had to make up in technology what they lacked in professional ability, because most recruits did not serve long enough to become skilled soldiers. Ever more efficient means of mobilizing armies were called on, as railways linked front lines to barracks and bases all over Europe. Ever more accurate and long-range weapons were required to compensate for soldiers' lack of expertise in firing them. The result was an arms race that made peace precarious, and an atmosphere of anxiety among the powers to mobilize rapidly should a new war threaten: a recipe, in short, for rupturing peace. Still, until the end of the nineteenth century, enough powers were sufficiently evenly matched to keep the peace for most of the time.

By then, however, the fear of revolution had so diminished, and the habit of short wars had become so familiar, that neither the fragility of peace nor the fear of war excited much alarm in Europe. The balance of power, on which peace depended, was beginning to tilt toward war because of the uneven distribution of heavy industry. By 1900, Germany produced vastly more coal, iron, and steel than all the other European powers combined. The Russian Empire, with its huge population, was beginning to show signs of being able to catch up. This fact—little noticed outside Germany—made a trial of strength seem urgent. In the arena of Europe, the sand that the changes of the nineteenth-century kicked up was raked into new patterns of alliance, made with war in mind rather than to contain change or maintain the balance of power. The arena was ready for the gladiators.

PROBLEMS AND PARALLELS

1. What roles did nationalism, constitutionalism, militarization, and bureaucratization play in state development in the nineteenth century? How did King Shaka of the Zulus and Emperors Yohannes IV and Menelik II of Ethiopia use modernized armies to strengthen their states?
2. What were the differences between European nationalism and nationalist movements outside Europe? What was the relationship between constitutionalism and modernization in the nineteenth century? Why did King Chulalongkorn reform Thailand's government along Western lines?
3. Why did many nineteenth-century states emphasize centralization? Who benefited from centralization? Which groups lost power?
4. Why did religion and politics clash in the nineteenth century? Why did religious leaders like Pope Pius IX oppose political and social innovation?
5. Why was religion a "revolutionary force in the world" during the nineteenth century? How did Muhammad Ahmad use Islam to inspire his political movement in Sudan?
6. Why did democracy become more widespread in the nineteenth century? Why did Alexis de Tocqueville think that Europe should adopt American-style democracy? Why did new forms of political radicalism emerge in the nineteenth century? Why did most European Jews seek to identify with the nations in which they lived in the nineteenth century?

READ ON ▶ ▶ ▶

The opening story comes from J. H. Kerry-Nicholls, *The King Country* (1974), J. Belich, *The New Zealand Wars* (1988), and *Making Peoples* (1996) are gripping revisionist studies of New Zealand. B. Anderson, *Imagined Communities: Reflections on the Origin and Spread of Nationalism* (1991) is the fundamental starting point for contemporary thinking about nationalism. G. Wawro, *Warfare and Society in Europe, 1792–1914* (2000) is a solid introduction to the impact of militarization on European states and society. Lord Durham's *Report on the Affairs of British North America*, ed. by C. Lucas (1970), shows the thinking that went into the emerging political structure of the British Empire.

Nationalist state-building beyond Europe is beginning to receive more attention in the literature. Among the many books by B. Lewis, *The Middle East* (1997) is a good introduction to the politics of the Arab world. F. R. Hunter, *Egypt under the Khedives, 1805–1879: From Household Government to Modern Bureaucracy* (1984) is the foundational work on the emergence of the modern Egyptian state. H. S. Wilson, *Origins of West African Nationalism* (1969) analyzes the impact of colonial rule on the emergence of African nationalisms, while *West African Kingdoms in the Nineteenth Century*, ed. by D. Forde and P. M. Karberry (1967), studies the range of successes in indigenous African state-building. B. Farwell, *Prisoners of the Mahdi* (1967), recounts the story of three Western prisoners of the Mahdi in the Sudan who lived to tell the story, and explores this religiously inspired revolt against colonial encroachment. M. A. Klein, *Islam and Imperialism in Senegal, 1847–1914* (1968) provides a more analytical account of the interaction of religion and imperial pressure. M. Rajaretnam, ed., *José Rizal and the Asian Renaissance* (1996), sets a very broad context. His novels and many of Bankim's are available in English translations.

C. A. Bayly, *The Birth of the Modern World, 1780–1914* (2004) is indispensable for understanding the nineteenth-century state in global dimension. D. Ralston, *Importing the European Army: The Introduction of European Military Techniques and Institutions in the Extra-European World, 1600–1914* (1996) studies several key examples of non-European states attempting to the new world of militarized centralization. D. Wyatt, *A Short History of Thailand* (1984) explores one of the few cases of successful Asian resistance to imperial pressures. R. Scheina, *Latin American Wars: Volume I, The Age of Caudillos, 1791–1899* (2003) gives a detailed military narrative that reveals the reasons behind the failures of Latin American state-building. K. Pomeranz, *The Great Divergence: China, Europe, and the Making of the Modern World Economy* (2001) is excellent on the different paths taken by Britain and China after 1800, linking political regimes to economic development in unexpected ways.

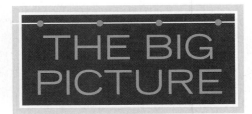
The World in 1914

Industrialization, the biggest story in the nineteenth-century world, was a response to a global energy crisis. It happened when and where global population was exploding—which might have made mechanization seem unnecessary. But up to a critical threshold, population increase generated demand for new scales and new kinds of production. Beyond that threshold, as in China, the amount of surplus manpower available inhibited mechanization. A startling result was the shift in the global balance of wealth and power away from China and South Asia to Europe and—by the end of the century—the United States.

Industry opened a vast energy gap between industrializing and unindustrializing zones. The industrializing areas imposed their power on the unindustrializing, enforcing political unification, for instance, in Germany, Italy, Japan, and the United States. The world split between industrializing regions and those that, by choice or coercion, produced primary goods for the industrializers. Peoples untouched by industrialization became the victims of the disparities it empowered. In Africa and much of Southeast Asia, indigenous states could not resist European imperialism unless they "modernized" along European lines. In the Americas, industrially equipped armies and colonists displaced native peoples.

Industrialization transformed the world's labor force. States got stronger. Intellectual trends became mass movements and attracted worldwide followings. Finally, by demanding huge amounts of coal and, increasingly, oil, industrialization transformed the scale on which people valued resources and edged the world toward conflicts over increasingly precious fossil fuels.

▶ QUESTIONS

1. In 1800, China contributed over 30 percent of global industrial production. By 1914, it accounted for just 3.5 percent, whereas the United States and Western Europe accounted for two thirds of the output of the world's industries. What accounted for this stunning reversal?

2. How did the energy gap between industrialized and unindustrialized regions underpin the motives behind imperialism, nationalism, socialism, and racism?

PEARSON
myhistorylab

To view an interactive version of this map, as well as a video of the author describing key themes related to this Part, go to www.myhistorylab.com

Industrialization and Urbanization, ca 1914

Major oil fields in the early twentieth century

46% percentage of population living in urban areas in 1914

Industrial potential as a percentage of global total, 1914

Greenland

Lena

2.7%

JAPAN

40%

Amur

Manchuria

KOREA

Gobi

8.3%

Yenisey

RUSSIA

Siberia

14%

United Kingdom 13.6%

Germany 14.8%

Volga

Steppes

ASIA

Yellow River

5%

Europe

CHINA 3.5%

5%

PLOESTI

France 6.1%

Italy 2.5%

Anatolia

BAKU

Himalayas

Yangtze

Philippine Islands

PACIFIC OCEAN

Euphrates

Tigris

MIDDLE EAST

Indus

Ganges

INDIA 1.4%

Mekong

Sahara

Nile

Arabian peninsula

8%

Sahel

Niger

5%

AFRICA

Congo

Borneo

New Guinea

SUMATRA

ATLANTIC OCEAN

INDIAN OCEAN

Zambezi

Madagascar

Orange River

AUSTRALIA

Darling River

ANTARCTICA

New Zealand

Arctic Circle

0°   30°   60°   90°   120°   150°

PART 10

ENVIRONMENT

since 1905,
1918, 1930
Relativity—
Quantum
Mechanics

CULTURE

1914–1918
World War I

1929–1939
Great Depression

Chaos and Complexity: The World in the Twentieth Century

◀ **An upside-down world.** How you see the world depends on how you look at it. By making Australia central and dominant, the "Australia map of the world" makes the Northern Hemisphere seem insignificant. The intention is satirical, but many countries have sponsored self-enhancing map projections and perspectives to promote nationalism and belittle rivals.

since 1950s
Global warming

since 1960s
Intensive deforestation

since mid-1980s
AIDS epidemic

since 1990s
Genetically modified crops

1939–1945
World War II

1945–1989
Cold War

since early 1950s
Television

since mid-1990s
Internet

CHAPTER 27

The Twentieth-Century Mind: Western Science and the World

▲ **Western medicine in China.** Dr. Edward H. Hume taking a patient's pulse at the Yale-Hunan Clinic. Dr. Hume founded the clinic in the city of Changsha, in Hunan, China in 1914 and was its dean until 1927. The presence of guards shows that this photograph was taken after the clinic began to attract socially elevated patients.

CHINA

Edward H. Hume's heart sank when he saw the gateway to the city where he was to begin his new life. After researching bubonic plague in India, he arrived in China in 1905 as part of a team from Yale University. His aim was to start a clinic, and his ambition, if possible, was to found a medical school. His destination was Changsha, in remote Hunan province, where the Chinese government allowed foreigners to settle as part of its policy to develop the interior. The city gate stared back at him, blindly and defiantly—symbolically bricked up against him at the orders of the local gentry, who resented having foreign barbarians stationed in their midst. The local officials did their best to obstruct him. The notables of the town shunned him. For the poor, however, Hume's services were attractive. With the backing of Yale alumni, he could afford to treat them for nominal sums. So they frequented his clinic, as well as visiting the shops of his Chinese rivals—an astrologer, a fortune-teller, a physiognomist who diagnosed illnesses by scrutinizing the faces of the sick, and an old soldier who had retrained as a folk pediatrician. Some members of the merchant class favored Hume, too, because he carefully kept corpses off his premises, shipping hopeless cases away before they died. Observers therefore judged his methods to be superior to those of traditional Chinese medicine. A notorious bandit, who had a bullet in his leg, was one of the first patients at Changsha's Yale Clinic.

For nearly three years, Hume had no patients from among the mandarins, the scholar-elite who monopolized positions of authority in China. Then one morning he heard harsh voices outside his clinic. "Carefully! Set the chair down! . . . Stand aside, you brats! This is a mandarin's chair!" The newly arrived visitor expected to jump the waiting line of patients, but Hume's doorman insisted on the rules. "Yes, Great One," the doorman explained, "I know you are an official; but this foreign doctor would dismiss me in an instant if I admitted you out of turn. . . . I am not worthy, Great One, to stand opposite you."

A few minutes later, Hume welcomed into his surgery his first mandarin patient. The newcomer seemed apprehensive, but appeared reassured when the foreign doctor began to check his pulse. The mandarin even complimented the physician on his mastery of a technique long practiced in China. But when Hume dropped his patient's wrist and shoved a thermometer into his mouth, the mandarin exploded with rage. "Why," he said to the attendant who accompanied him, "did you let this foreigner put this strange, hard thing inside my mouth? Can't you see that he knows nothing of medicine?" Only subsequently did Hume learn how he had offended his patient. He had read his pulse by taking his left wrist; but Chinese tradition dictated that a doctor must also check a series of pulse points on the right arm. By proceeding straight to taking the patient's temperature, Hume had exposed himself, in his patient's eyes, as an ignoramus.

It was a disappointing episode for the young physician. He realized that the authorities had sent the mandarin to report on the foreigner's practices. He hoped to make a favorable

FOCUS questions

Why was Western science so dominant during the first half of the twentieth century and how did science spread to the non-Western world?

What former certainties about the cosmos and human nature did science undermine during the twentieth century?

Why did many people turn away from science in the late twentieth century?

How did styles in the arts mirror developments in science?

Why have many people in the West come to rely on non-Western forms of medical treatment?

impression since he knew that official approval would expand and enrich his practice. His failure was an episode in a long, slow, and sometimes fitful story of the assimilation of Western medicine in China—which was itself a strand in a larger fabric of history: the spread of Western science—led by Western medicine and military technology, but extending to every kind of science and to scientific habits of thought—across the world. In no area was the rise of the West to world dominance more apparent than in the worldwide appeal of Western science. Hume played his own modest part in the story with increasing success. Gradually, painstakingly, he won Chinese confidence, building up support not only by successfully treating many difficult cases, but also by using the accumulated goodwill of the school for boys and girls that the Yale mission maintained alongside the clinic. Hume's experience, in micro-cosm, echoed that of Western influence generally.

In the twentieth century, science came to set the agenda for the world. Whereas previously scientists had tended to respond to the demands of society, now science drove other kinds of change. The pace of scientific discovery—with the dazzling revelations scientists disclosed about the cosmos, nature, and humankind—commanded admiration and radiated prestige. In Europe and the Americas, the period was convulsively innovative. A scientific counterrevolution exploded certainties inherited from seventeenth- and eighteenth-century science. Revolutions in psychology and social anthropology made people rethink cultural values and social relationships. A new philosophical climate eroded confidence in traditional ideas about language, reality, and the links between them. Ever larger and costlier scientific establishments in universities and research institutes served their paymasters—governments and big business—or gained enough wealth and independence to set their own objectives and pursue their own programs. New theories shocked people into revising their image of the world and their place in it.

The lessons of Western science proved equivocal. New technologies raised as many problems as they solved: moral questions, as science expanded human power over life and death; practical questions, as technologies multiplied for exploiting the Earth's resources of energy. Increasingly in the twentieth century, ordinary people and nonscientific intellectuals lost confidence in science. Uncertainty corroded the hard facts with which science was formerly associated. Faith that science could solve the world's problems and reveal the secrets of the cosmos evaporated.

In part, this was the result of practical failures. Although science achieved wonders for the world, especially in medicine and communications, consumers never seemed satisfied. There was no progress without problems. Every advance unleashed side effects. Technological advances seemed to privilege machines that fought wars and destroyed or degraded environments. Science seemed best at devising engines of destruction, but could only make people happy in modest ways, and it did nothing at all to make them good. Even medical improvements brought equivocal effects. The costs of treatment sometimes exceeded the benefits. Health became a purchasable commodity. In prosperous countries, medical provision buckled under the weight of public expectations and the intensity of public demand.

As the power of science grew, more and more people came to fear and resent it and react against it. Despite its stunning successes, science proved strangely self-undermining. It stoked disillusionment, even as it spread. It disclosed a chaotic cosmos, in which effects were hard to predict, and interventions regularly went wrong. A century dominated by Western science ended with the recovery of alternative traditions that Western influence had displaced or eclipsed.

The stories of these changes fill this chapter—starting with the global diffusion of Western science, then turning back to the West to see how science changed from within and how art mirrored the changes. In the remaining chapters, we can look at the effects of the changes on politics, culture generally, and the environment.

"Paradoxically, the only way for the rest of the world to beat the West, or catch up with it, was to 'modernize'—code for imitating the West in science and technology."

WESTERN SCIENCE ASCENDANT

The early twentieth-century world seethed with discontent at Western hegemony and sparkled with visions of a brighter future that political leaders, religious enthusiasts, and secular intellectuals promised or called for. Yet the allure of Western science proved irresistible (see Map 27.1). Its global appeal was twofold. First, it worked. Western military technology won wars. Western industrial technology multiplied food and wealth. Information systems devised in the West revolutionized communications, business, leisure, education, and methods of social and political control. Western medical science saved lives. Paradoxically, the only way for the rest of the world to beat the West, or catch up with it, was to "modernize"—code for imitating the West in science and technology. Second, Western science offered the promise of infallibility: of knowledge that was certain because it matched observation, fulfilled predictions, and withstood tests. Chinese revolutionaries actually called science a faith and represented "scientism" as an alternative to Confucianism.

China

The Chinese reception of Western science began in a continuous and systematic fashion in the 1860s, at the start of the "self-strengthening" movement (see Chapter 23). In 1866, Beijing's Foreign Language Institute opened a "mathematics" department. More accurately it was a Department of Science and Technology, with the aim of emulating the West or, as its first director said, "for the use of logical reasoning, methods of manufacturing and being practical," as well as mathematics strictly understood. "If we can concentrate on being practical," the director added, "and learn all the essentials, then this is the path to strengthening China." It was a promising beginning, but, as we have already seen, Chinese self-strengthening was patchy in the nineteenth century, and the absorption of Western ideas was always slow and subject to the restraining effects of mistrust of foreigners, whom Chinese continued to see, all too often, as barbaric or demonic.

Nor was the pace of change uniform in all the sciences. At first, medicine lagged behind mathematics and military and industrial technology. In 1876, for instance, a comparative study of Chinese and Western medicine by Chinese physicians upheld the superiority of ancient Chinese methods. In 1883, however, the Beijing School of Medicine launched a Western-style curriculum. Chinese students began to go abroad to study medicine. In 1900, the United States government received an indemnity from China for the losses caused to American business interests by the chaos and bloodshed of a rebellion in China that Western forces helped to suppress. The government used the money to finance scholarships for Chinese students in America. By 1906, 15,000 Chinese students were studying science abroad—13,000 of them in Japan, where

Jesuit university in Shanghai. Founded in 1903, Aurora University became a model of Western education in China, pre-eminent in medicine, botany, and biology, with students drawn both from the native Chinese and the foreigners who thronged the foreign trading concessions in the city. Aurora's founder, the Chinese Jesuit, Joseph Ma Xiangbo, did not want to impose a Catholic curriculum on the school, and left in 1905 to found Fudan University, with which Aurora merged in 1952 after the communist revolution.

1900 First Ottoman University designed on Western model opens

EUROPE

Istanbul

TURKEY

1961 Al-Azhar University reorganized along Western lines

Cairo

EGYPT

AFRICA

1922 Makerere University founded, though few contributions are made to education of locals

UGANDA

GABON

CONGO

Albert Schweizer spearheads Western medicine in French West Africa in the early- to mid-twentieth century

SOUTH AFRICA

ASIA

1866 Foreign Language Institute opens a "mathematics" department with aim of emulating the West

1883 Beijing School of Medicine launches Western-style curriculum

1914 University of Beijing acquires a medical department; Science Society of China founded by Chinese students at Cornell University, USA

Beijing

CHINA

Changsha

Japan Western science prevalent by 1900

1905 Edward H. Hume of Yale University opens medical clinic

INDIA

1897 Jagadis Chandra Bose awarded research grant

By 1906 research institutes devoted to veterinary science, agriculture, and forestry

By 1914 scientific research teams in various fields

1930 Chandrasekhara Venkata Raman awarded Nobel Prize for physics

MALAYA

1920 Sultan Idris Training College for Medicine opens

DUTCH EAST INDIES

Bandung

INDONESIA

1920 local investors finance opening of Royal Institute for Higher Technical Education at Bandung

1922 construction begins of astronomical observatory at Lembang, near Bandung

1930 A third of the students at Bandung are Indonesians

AUSTRALIA

2,000 km
2,000 miles

MAP 27.1

Spread of Western Scientific Learning, 1866–1961

the Western scientific curriculum was already triumphant. European and American doctors, meanwhile, acquired Chinese assistants and, in some cases, took advantage of growing Chinese interest in Western methods to move to China to practice. Dr. Hume was one of about 100 Western physicians in China in his day. In 1903, the University of Beijing acquired a medical department. Meanwhile, in essays published from 1895 onward, the scientific translator Yan Fu (yen foo) introduced Darwin's theory of evolution to China (see Chapter 25), and 20 or 30 Western scientific books were being translated into Chinese each year, with dozens more reaching China via Japan.

The revolution of 1911 that overthrew the Qing dynasty and made China a republic stimulated the pace of change, bringing to positions of power and authority intellectuals indebted to the West for many of their political ideas. They proclaimed what they called New Culture, in which science would play a prominent part, to modernize and "save" the country from Western and Japanese competition. After the revolution, syllabus reforms replaced ancient Chinese mathematics—apart from the use of the abacus—with a Western-style mathematical curriculum. Translations of Western science textbooks helped in a vital part of the process: developing a modern scientific vocabulary in Chinese. Until the term *kexue* (keh-shweh-jahng) became current from 1915, no Chinese word expressed everything the word *science* meant in English. New journals applied scientific methods and principles to social and personal problems.

Chinese who studied abroad continued to infuse China with Western intellectual influences. In 1914, Chinese students at American universities met at Cornell University in New York State to found the Science Society of China. When they returned home, it became one of the most influential organizations in the country, dedicated to popularizing Western-style science and promoting scientific education. The society succeeded. Science as Westerners understood it became part of the general curriculum, as well as the core of professional training. By 1947, for instance, China had 34,600 medical practitioners trained according to Western methods. The numbers more than doubled over the next 10 years. By the end of the twentieth century, all Chinese physicians had at least some Western-style training.

In China, Western science had to rely chiefly on its inherent appeal to make headway. While the Qing had ceded a few, relatively small urban areas to foreign custody or control, in most of the country Western power was exercised only indirectly. Westerners had to buy or bribe their way into positions of influence. Yet Western science still exercised an irresistible fascination, even where it could not be forced on people. It is not surprising, therefore, that in parts of the world under the direct rule of Western empires, the uptake was even greater, for European empires acted as agents for the spread of Western science. India is the best example to concentrate on. It had a colonial government committed to promoting science and a native intelligentsia anxious to learn.

India

In 1899, the British viceroy of India, Lord Curzon, declared that the British had come to India to bring the benefits of their law, religion, literature, and science. The value of the first three for India might be debatable, but the benefits of "pure, irrefutable science" and, in particular, of medical science were indisputable. Science also served, incidentally, the aims of British policy, breaking through traditional barriers of caste and community, serving "rich and poor, Hindu and Mohammedan, woman and man." Curzon made the colonial government invest heavily in scientific education and the employment of Western scientists, and he induced the native princes who still ruled much of India to do the same. By 1906, India had research institutes devoted to veterinary science, agriculture, and forestry. The central government employed its own scientific research teams. By 1914, these teams existed for medicine, meteorology, veterinary science, botany, agriculture, forestry, and geology. In 1913, the Indian *Journal of Medical Research* was launched. These efforts were paralleled in neighboring parts of the British Empire. In Malaya, for instance, where the native elite had begun to accept Western schooling in the 1890s, the Sultan Idris Training College for Medicine opened its doors to students in 1920.

In the first couple of decades of the century, European personnel, of course, hugely predominated in the new scientific institutions. To achieve Indianization—training Indians in scientific work—the government had to overcome ingrained racial prejudice, typified in 1880 by the British superintendent of the Geological Survey of India, who declared Indians "utterly incapable of any original work in natural science." Outstanding Indian scientists, trained in Britain, had to struggle for recognition, accept lower pay than their British counterparts, or take

Sir Jagadis C. Bose, Indian physicist and botanist, in 1896. Bose was a professor at Calcutta and studied the polarization and reflection of electric waves. He also worked on experiments that demonstrated the sensitivity and growth rates of plants.

"Outstanding Indian scientists, trained in Britain, had to struggle for recognition, accept lower pay than their British counterparts, or take service with native princes. But their achievements gradually began to speak for themselves."

service with native princes. But their achievements gradually began to speak for themselves. In 1897, the viceroy—not without opposition from prejudiced individuals—awarded a research grant to Jagadis Chandra Bose, as "the first explorer and inventor in the electrical sciences that India has yet produced." The numbers of native scientists multiplied, thanks in part to Western-inspired educational institutions—especially the Jesuits' schools and the Indian universities the British had founded—and, in part, to the networks of education and exchange of ideas that Indian intellectuals established for themselves.

Prafulla Chandra Ray was at the heart of these networks, establishing an international reputation in chemical research and founding his own successful pharmaceutical business in Bengal. By 1920, he and his students and colleagues had published over 100 research papers, many in British and American journals. "Our age," he announced at the Indian Science Congress that year, "is preeminently an age of science. The fate of a nation will depend henceforth more upon the achievements of its students of science than upon the skill of its generals or the adroitness of its diplomatists and statesmen." In the 1920s, when the government proposed to add a chemistry department to the teams of scientists it maintained, Indian scientists opposed the idea because the teams were led by British bureaucrats, while Indian experts were better qualified for the work. In 1930, Chandrasekhara Venkata Raman, a pupil of Jagadis Chandra Bose, won the Nobel Prize in physics for work on the diffusion of light in liquids—the first non-Westerner to be so honored.

The Wider World

Although the achievements of Indian science were exceptional, the Indian model—imperial promotion of science, the multiplication of educational opportunities for natives of the country, the emergence of an indigenous scientific establishment—were reproduced in other areas of European dominion or influence in South and Southeast Asia, in the Middle East, and, to some extent, in the Philippines, which was ruled by the United States.

The Indian model, however, was not followed slavishly wherever European empires ruled. In Dutch Indonesia, for instance, the reception of Western science owed little or nothing to government initiatives. Wealthy plantation owners financed an astronomical observatory at Lembang, where stargazers could escape Holland's cloudy skies in an effort to construct a reputation. The University of Leiden in the Netherlands maintained field centers in South Africa and Java. These institutions served largely as laboratories for Dutch scientists. Some scientific initiation, however, was available to Dutch colonial subjects. From 1913, Indonesians could study Western medicine without leaving their homeland. The following year, secondary schools dropped admissions policies that discriminated against native Indonesians. In 1920, local investors financed the opening of the Royal Institute for Higher Technical Education in Bandung. Its reputation as a center of scientific education quickly came to rival schools in Europe. By 1930, a third of the students at Bandung were Indonesians.

Resistance to Western science was strongest in other parts of the Islamic world, where Western dominance was absent or shaky. In the nineteenth century, the Ottoman Empire had produced many intellectuals interested in the benefits of Western science, but their work was slow to take effect. In 1900, the first Ottoman university designed on Western lines opened, but its library subscribed to no scientific research periodicals. After 1908, however, when self-styled modernizers seized control of the Ottoman government, the pace of change quickened. Learned societies in dentistry, agriculture, veterinary medicine, engineering, and geography took shape.

When a European adventurer demonstrated an early airplane in Istanbul in 1909, popular revulsion forced him out of the country. But, especially after 1911, when Italian planes bombed Turkish troops in Libya during a brief war, the government took a keen interest in promoting aviation. Kemal Ataturk (1881–1938), the leader who overthrew the Ottomans after World War I and made Turkey a secular republic, proclaimed "science and reason" to be his legacy (see Chapter 28). Said Nursi, the enemy of Ataturk's revolution, opposed the new leader's secularism but agreed with him about the need to embrace science. He devoted his exile in the 1920s in part to demonstrating that science was compatible with Islam.

On the fringes of the Ottoman Empire, and outside areas of Ottoman control, Muslim modernizers of the nineteenth century had praised science as a proper occupation for a Muslim—but without winning the argument against religious critics. One of the most influential modernizers, Jamal al-Din al-Afghani, had exposed the historic hostility of religious establishments—Christian and Muslim alike—to scientific projects. The Lebanese Shiite scholar, Husayn al-Jisr, who died in 1909, was the first great apologist for Darwin in the Islamic world. The Egyptian Ismail Mazhir (1891–1962) continued his work in a series of translations of Darwin, beginning in the 1920s but incomplete until 1961. His great project to demonstrate that Darwin's theories were consistent with Quranic accounts of creation was still in progress at the end of the twentieth century, when the Pakistani intellectual, Ziauddin Sardar, championed it. Scientific interpretation of the Quran was, at that time, one of the most popular types of literature in the Muslim world.

Meanwhile, other forms of Western science also seeped into and soaked the educational systems of much of the Muslim Middle East. Science was a foreign implant there. A survey of scientific research in the Middle East, conducted during World War II (1939–1945), found only a handful of Muslim scientists to consult. In 1952, a survey in Egypt counted 1,392 individual practitioners of science. At that stage, more than 70 percent of them had at least one degree from a university abroad—most from British and American institutions. By 1957, the total number of Egyptian scientists had risen to 3,600. By 1973, there were 10,655. In 1961, the great Muslim educational center of Cairo, known as al-Azhar, was reorganized along the lines of a Western university. Similar changes were under way throughout the Arab world. Over the following two decades, at least 6 million Arabs studied Western-style science at universities.

In sub-Saharan Africa, meanwhile, Western science spread more slowly and selectively. While European empires lasted, racist assumptions inhibited the colonial authorities from training native African scientific elites. Britain founded some research institutes in its East African colonies, notably Makerere University in Uganda, but their scientific staffs were recruited in Britain, and they educated few Africans. French research institutes had many African field centers, but these, too, were unconnected to indigenous communities. Belgian scientific work in the Congo was locally financed but otherwise uninvolved with native Congolese. For most of the first half of the century, therefore, black Africans were the passive recipients of Western science, especially of medicine. Albert Schweizer (1875–1965), a Swiss theologian who retrained as a doctor and devoted himself to the care of the sick in Gabon in French West Africa for nearly 30 years, typified the spirit of the medical missionary, transforming the life expectancy of his patients not so much by his medical skill, which was never advanced,

Muslim nursing students. Cairo University in Egypt, where female Muslim students wear *hijab* (headscarves). Some women students cover their faces completely. Many aspects of Western culture, including science, spread in part because they adapt easily to a variety of cultural environments. Western science has eastern roots—Islamic and Chinese influences—that many non-Westerners who study it can recognize.

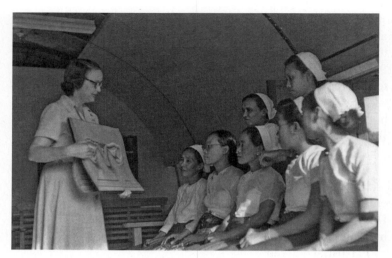

Colonial science. A British midwife instructs Burmese nurses in midwifery in the 1950s. The picture is posed to suggest Western superiority. The students—some older and presumably wiser than their teacher—are in Western-style uniforms, submissively listening to a lesson reinforced by simple diagrams.

Chronology: Major Inventions—1850–1914

Year	Invention
1852	Gyroscope
1853	Passenger elevator
1856	Celluloid
	Bessemer converter
	Bunsen burner
1858	Refrigerator
	Washing machine
1859	Internal combustion engine
1862	Rapid-fire gun
1866	Dynamite
1876	Telephone
1877	Phonograph
1879	Incandescent lamp
1885	Motorcycle
	Electric transformer
	Vacuum flask
1887	Motorcar engine
1888	Pneumatic tire
	Kodak camera
1895	Wireless radio
	X-rays
1897	Diesel engine
1902	Radio-telephone
1903	Airplane
1911	Combine harvester

as by his efficient hospital buildings, his emphasis on hygiene, and his ability to dispense Western medicine. Thousands of idealistic young Western volunteers followed similar vocations. From the 1930s until the 1980s, as Western medicine increasingly relied on medication with new pharmaceuticals, which were invented at a dizzying pace, the power of Westerners to save African lives slashed death rates and helped bring a population explosion to Africa.

Medicine everywhere was the banner bearer of Western science, partly because that of the West probably was more effective than any other tradition, and partly because it attracted official support around the world. Missionaries valued and practiced it as an antidote to what they called superstition and magic. Western administrators saw it as a means to gain favor from indigenous elites and power over native populations who became dependent on Western medicines.

THE TRANSFORMATION OF WESTERN SCIENCE

Even while it achieved enormous influence and registered enormous effects across the world, Western science was changing from within. The very qualities that made it attractive—its benign inventions, its power to increase knowledge, its promise to disclose truths you could trust—crumbled. The inventions proved equivocal, the knowledge elusive, the certainties unattainable.

With hindsight, we can also detect the origins of the conflicts that beset science in the early twentieth century. On the one hand, they were years of impressive progress. Conventionally, historians represent the first decade or so of the new century as a spell of inertia, a golden afterglow of the romantic age that the real agent of change, World War I, would turn blood red. But even before the war broke out in 1914, the worlds of thought and feeling were already alive with new colors. Technology hurtled into a new phase. The twentieth century would be an electric age, much as the nineteenth had been an age of steam. In 1901, Guglielmo Marconi broadcast by wireless radio across the Atlantic. In 1903, the Wright brothers took flight in North Carolina. Plastic was invented in 1907. The curiosities of late nineteenth-century inventiveness, such as the telephone, the car, and the typewriter, all became commonplace. Other essentials of technologically fulfilled twentieth-century lives—the atom smasher, the steel–concrete skyscraper frame, even the hamburger and Coca Cola™—were all in place before World War I.

On the other hand, when the century opened, the scientific world was in a state of self-questioning, confused by rogue results. In the 1890s, X-rays and electrons were discovered or posited, while puzzling anomalies became observable in the behavior of light. In 1902, a young French mathematician, Henri Poincaré, questioned what had previously been the basic assumption of scientific method: the link between hypothesis and evidence. Any number of hypotheses, he said, could fit the results of experiments. Scientists chose among them by convention—or even according to "the idiosyncrasies of the individual." Among examples he cited were Newton's laws (see Chapter 19) and the traditional notions of space and time. He provided reasons to doubt everything formerly regarded as demonstrable. He compared the physicist to "an embarrassed theologian, . . . chained" to contradictory propositions. His books sold in the thousands. He became an international celebrity, whose views were widely sought and reported.

Science usually affects society less by what it does or says, than by how it is misunderstood. This was particularly so for most of the twentieth century, when all academic disciplines became highly professionalized and specialized, with their own jargon and long training programs designed to exclude outsiders and amateurs. Practitioners of other kinds of learning tended to treat science as a benchmark discipline, whose objectivity they wish to emulate, but whose language and findings they could barely comprehend. Readers misinterpreted Poincaré to mean that "Scientific fact was created by the scientist," and that "Science consists only of conventions. . . . Science therefore can teach us nothing of the truth; it can only serve us as a rule of action."

Physics

Poincaré claimed that he had never intended to say or imply such things. But he set the tone for at least 100 years of struggle between science and skepticism—skepticism about our ability to know anything for certain. "The nature of our epoch is multiplicity and indeterminacy," announced the Austrian poet, Hugo von Hofmannsthal (1874–1929). "Foundations that other generations believed to be firm are really only sliding." Science seemed a laboratory transformed by the magic of a sorcerer's apprentice.

The result of this skepticism was that science, for all its achievements, could never replace ideology. It could not command ordinary people's allegiance the way that religious or political systems could. Science strode ahead, proposing solutions to theoretical problems about the nature of the universe and practical problems in every field. Its admirers and many of its practitioners came to believe in its unique virtue and even in its potential power to supplant other guides to life, such as religion, reason, instinct, and common sense. But there were always people who sneered at it, or snubbed it, or doubted its claims, or feared its consequences.

Thanks to the way Poincaré shook up perceptions of the nature of science, people became more willing to listen to radical theories from unlikely people, such as Albert Einstein (1879–1955), a minor official in the Swiss Patent Office, whose academic vocation had become frustrated because his teachers undervalued the originality of his mind. In 1905, he emerged from obscurity, like a burrower from a mine, to detonate an intellectual explosion. His theory of relativity exploded traditional physics and reshaped most educated people's image of the cosmos. The impact registered only gradually, as, up to 1915, Einstein worked out the implications of his thinking and knowledge of it spread.

According to traditional physics, and to commonplace observation and intuition, the speed of a body ought to affect the speed of the light it reflects or projects, rather as a ball gains speed from the vigor with which it is thrown. Yet experimental data, which accumulated in the 1890s, seemed to show that the speed of light never varied. Most people assumed an error in the measurements. Einstein proposed, instead, that the invariability of the speed of light was a scientific law. He resolved the contradiction by proposing that the apparent effects of motion on speed were illusions. Rather, time and space change with motion. Mass increases with velocity, whereas time slows down.

Einstein's work broke on the world with the shock of genius: the jarring sensation of seeing something obvious that no one had ever noticed before. The implications of

The vitascope was an early device for projecting cinematic images, displayed here showing the ballet *Giselle* in an advertisement of 1896. The gilt frame, prominent orchestra, and choice of theme all evoke the marketing context: a tasteful art-form for the middle class.

Theoretical physicist Albert Einstein writes an equation on a blackboard while turning to his audience at the California Institute of Technology, ca. 1931. Einstein's distinctive looks—the ever-alert eyes, the deliberately disordered hair—became the universal image of a "typical," perhaps ideal, scientist.

a cosmos in which time was unfixed took a lot of getting used to. In Einstein's universe, every appearance deceived. Mass and energy could be changed into each other. Twins aged at different rates. Parallel lines met. The curvature of the trajectory of light literally warped the universe. Intuitive notions vanished as if down a rabbit hole to Alice's Wonderland. Scientists hungered for an explanation that would resolve the apparent contradictions. Nonscientists were confused. Beyond doubt, however, experiment confirmed that, broadly speaking, Einstein was right. "The spirit of unrest," the *New York Times* said in 1919, "invaded science."

While Einstein proposed a restructured universe, other scientists repictured the tiniest particles, or *quanta* of which the universe is composed. Ernest Rutherford's work in Britain in 1911 proved a conjecture first discussed in the 1890s: that atoms consist of masses and electric charges, including a *nucleus* surrounded by *electrons*. The basic structure of matter, it seemed, was being laid bare. But it kept dodging and slipping out of the experimenters' grasp. For the rest of the century, ever smaller particles, ever more elusive charges continued to come to light. Between 1911 and 1913, work on atomic structures revealed that electrons appear to slide erratically between orbits around a nucleus. Findings that followed from the attempt to track the untrappable particles of subatomic matter were expressed in a new field of study called **quantum mechanics**.

The terms of this new science were paradoxical—like those employed by the Danish Nobel Prizewinner, Niels Bohr (1885–1962), who described light as consisting, simultaneously, of both waves and particles. By the mid-1920s, more contradictions piled up. When the motion of subatomic particles was plotted, their positions seemed irreconcilable with their momentum. They seemed to move at rates different from their measurable speed and to end up where it was impossible for them to be. Working in collaborative tension, Bohr and his German colleague, Werner Heisenberg (1901–1976), proposed a principle they called uncertainty or indeterminacy. Their debate provoked a revolution in thought. Interpreters made a reasonable inference—observers are part of every observation, and there is no level of inspection at which their findings are objective.

This was of enormous importance because practitioners of other disciplines at the time—historians, anthropologists, sociologists, linguists, and even students of literature—were seeking to class their own work as scientific, precisely because they wanted to escape from subjectivity. It turned out that what they had in common with scientists, strictly so-called, was the opposite of what they had hoped—they were all implicated in their own findings.

Maybe it was still possible to pick a way back to certainty by following mathematics and logic. These systems, at least, seemed infallible, and they guaranteed each other. Mathematics was reliable because it was logical and logic was reliable because it was mathematical—or so people thought, until 1931, when the Czech logician, Kurt Gödel, severed mathematics from logic and showed that both systems, ultimately, must yield contradictory results.

Gödel inspired an unintended effect. Like many earlier philosophers, he thought that we can reliably grasp numbers, but he helped make others doubt it. He believed that numbers really exist, objectively, independently of thought, but he provided encouragement to skeptics who dismissed them as merely conventional. The effect of Gödel's demonstrations on the way the world thinks was comparable to that of termites in a wooden ship that the passengers had thought was watertight. If mathematics and logic leaked, science would sink. "Logics die" was the comment of the Irish poet, Brendan Behan (1923–1964).

Of course, the implications of the discoveries of Bohr, Heisenberg, and Gödel took a long time to change minds. Only gradually, through percolation within the scientific community and vulgarization in the press and popular science books, could they modify how ordinary people thought about the world. In the light of the theoretical contributions of quantum science and revolutionary logic and mathematics, however, the world was beginning to look increasingly disorderly. Meanwhile, practical discoveries and empirical observations jarred, even more uncomfortably, the equilibrium of the old picture of the cosmos.

In 1929, thanks to a powerful new telescope operated at Mount Wilson, near Los Angeles, by Edwin Hubble, the universe was found to be expanding. It seemed so strange a finding that some physicists sought to explain away the evidence for 50 years. By the 1970s, however, most cosmologists took the view that expansion started with a **big bang**, an explosion of almost infinitesimally compressed matter, which is still going on. For some interpreters, notably Pope John XXIII (r. 1958–1963), this was evidence of divine creation, or, at least, a description of how God did it. For others, it was a naturalistic explanation of change in the universe that made divine intervention an unnecessary hypothesis.

Contributions later in the century only seemed to put more space between science and certainty. In 1960, in one of the most challenging works a philosopher ever wrote about science, Thomas Kuhn argued that scientific revolutions were the result not of new discoveries about reality but of what he called paradigm shifts, changing ways of looking at the world, and new ways of expressing them. Most people drew an inference Kuhn repudiated—that the findings of science depended not on the objective facts but on the mindset of the inquirer.

In the 1980s, **chaos theory** cast doubt on one of the blessings science still promised for the world. Science specialized in inferring laws from experience and in using those laws to make predictions about the future. Chaos theory made the world seem unpredictable. The idea emerged in meteorology, as a result of the dawning awareness that weather systems are so complex that, ultimately, causes and effects are untraceable. A butterfly flapping its wings, according to an image that became the most popular way to sum up the theory, can work up a storm. There is still, according to this way of thinking, some deep order in nature, some chain of cause and effect in which the whole of experience is linked—but we cannot see it whole.

Throughout these shake-ups, workers in theoretical physics never abandoned the search for a comprehensive way to explain the cosmos—a "theory of everything" that would resolve the contradictions of relativity theory and quantum mechanics. The way matter behaves—at least, the way it behaves when we observe it—is riddled with paradoxes that subtle thinking has to reconcile. By the end of the century, cosmologists were proposing terms for understanding the universe that described nothing anyone had ever experienced or could easily imagine: infinite dimensions, superstrings, supersymmetry, supergravity. No experiment validated any of these models of how the universe is structured.

Superstrings. The superstring theory is a "Theory of Everything" (or "Grand Unification Theory") that seeks to unite gravity as a force along with the other fundamental forces (electromagnetism and nuclear forces). The theory states that fundamental particles such as quarks and electrons are not points of energy or matter, but result instead from the vibrations of "string-like" entities that are much smaller.

Human Sciences

In some respects science did deliver measurable progress. Two fields of study transformed human biology. Beginning in 1908, T. H. Morgan at Columbia University in New York initiated experiments in animal breeding that ultimately demonstrated how some characteristics are inherited by means of the transmission of genes. This led, in the second half of the century, to a new form of medicine in which doctors could manipulate people's genes to treat disease. Meanwhile, neuroscience made enormous progress in mapping the brain, demonstrating the distribution of mental functions, and recording how electrical impulses and releases of proteins occur, as different kinds of thinking, feeling, memorizing, and imagining take place.

Evolution on trial. People gather at an open-air bookstall during the Scopes "Monkey Trial" in Dayton, Tennessee in 1925 to examine the antievolution offerings. Books by William Jennings Bryan, the former presidential candidate who led the struggle to ban evolution from the public school curriculum, are prominently advertised.

Partly as a result of progress in human biology, practical medicine registered spectacular advances. Doctors could control diseases ever more effectively by imitating the body's natural hormones and adjusting their balance. That story began in 1922 with the isolation of insulin, which controls diabetes. In 1931, penicillin was discovered. It was the first *antibiotic*—a killer of microorganisms that cause disease inside the body. Preventive medicine made even bigger strides, as inoculation programs and health education became—gradually, during the century—available almost everywhere.

Many of the fiercest battles concerned biology, where advances challenged people to rethink human nature. In 1925, in a notorious case in Tennessee, an American court upheld the right of school boards to ban Darwin from the curriculum, on the supposed grounds that the theory of evolution was incompatible with the Bible. Belief in creation and belief in evolution are not necessarily contradictory. Evolution, which is the most convincing description we have of how and why species change, could, to a religious mind, be part of God's creation and Providence's plan. But simplistic-minded people on both sides of the debate kept picking fights with one another. Cases over whether schools could or should be compelled to teach evolution are still cropping up in courts in Europe and America, affecting Muslim as well as Christian schools. In some ways, evolution became more controversial as its proponents' claims became more strident. Some late twentieth-century Darwinians claimed to have found an evolutionary explanation for morality, for instance, and even to be able to explain cultural change in evolutionary terms. These claims got headlines but left most people unconvinced.

While disputes about evolution rumbled, the new science of genetics posed even more searching problems. In 1944, the Austrian physicist, Erwin Schrödinger, predicted that a gene would resemble a chain of basic units, connected like the elements of a code. His speculations invigorated the search for "the basic building-blocks" of life. A few years later, scientists in England built up the picture of what DNA (deoxyribonucleic acid) was really like. Genes in individual genetic codes—it soon emerged—were responsible for some diseases and perhaps for many kinds of behavior that changing the code could regulate. The codes of other species could be modified to obtain results that suit humans: producing bigger plant foods, for instance, or animals designed to be more beneficial, more palatable, or easier to transform into human food.

This discovery shed painfully strong new light on an old controversy—the **nature versus nurture** debate. On one side of the conflict were those who believed that character and capability were largely inherited and therefore could not be changed by "social engineering." Ranged against them were those who believed that experience—nurture—produced these qualities, and that social change can therefore improve our moral qualities and collective achievements. Genetic research seemed to confirm that we inherit more of our makeup than we have traditionally supposed. Meanwhile, sociobiology, a new synthesis devised by the ingenious Harvard entomologist, Edward O. Wilson, rapidly created a scientific constituency for the theory that evolutionary necessities determine differences between societies and that we can rank societies accordingly. Two fundamental convictions survived in most people's minds: that individuals make themselves, and that society is worth improving. Nevertheless, genes seemed to limit our freedom to equalize the differences between individuals and societies. Genetic and sociobiological claims inhibited reform and encouraged a mood we shall examine in the next two chapters: the prevailing conservatism of the late twentieth and early twenty-first centuries.

By the 1990s, genetically modified plants promised to solve the world's food-supply problems. The potentially adverse economic and ecological consequences, as we shall see in Chapter 30, evoked a chorus of protest. Modification of human genes presented more profound problems and provoked more profound unease. On the one hand, it promised a brighter future—eliminating genetically transmitted disease and enabling infertile couples to have children. On the other, it posed terrifying moral questions, best illustrated by the controversy over therapeutic cloning of human embryos, which was developed in the 1990s. This meant breeding or "farming," as people said, human embryos to extract useful cells from them. A woman could produce as many embryos as she might wish and pick the healthiest or most perfect specimens, or those she most preferred. The rest could be stored but, at some stage, would have to be discarded. In effect, this meant destroying human beings, since embryos, whatever their status in other respects, are unquestionably human. In the early twenty-first century, "designer babies" were already being produced where the process could prevent genetically transmitted diseases.

Subtle nightmare: the fear that human cloning could suppress individuality and eliminate diversity, is cleverly aroused in this seemingly charming and innocent scene. But these are not real babies: On close examination the computer-generated images look disturbingly identical.

Research into less morally troubling methods of treatment would soon replace therapeutic cloning for infertile couples and to treat inherited disease. But the prospect of designer babies selected for particular features of character or appearance was even more troubling. It might lead to people capriciously cloning and discarding embryos to engineer children for themselves with fashionable looks or exploitable talents. The prospect arose that some societies would want to engineer human beings along the lines once prescribed by eugenics—improving the human species through controlled breeding. Governments could legislate supposedly undesirable personality genes out of existence. States could enforce normality at the expense, for instance, of genes supposed to dispose people to be criminal, or homosexual, or just plain uncooperative. Morally dubious visionaries foresaw societies without disease or deviancy. In a world recrafted, as if by Frankenstein, humans now had the power to make their biggest intervention in evolution yet: selecting unnaturally not according to what is best adapted to the environment, but according to what best matches what humans happen to want at a particular moment. In 1995, a coalition of self-styled religious leaders in the United States signed a declaration opposing the patenting of genes on the grounds that they were the property of their real creator: God. The World Health Organization, UNESCO, and the European Parliament all condemned human cloning as unethical. Many countries banned it.

Meanwhile, the genetic revolution profoundly affected human self-perceptions, nudging people toward a materialist understanding of human nature. It became increasingly hard to find room in human nature for nonmaterial ingredients, such as mind and soul. "The soul has vanished," announced Francis Crick, a leading pioneer of genetic research. Cognitive scientists subjected the human brain to ever more searching analysis. Neurological research showed that thought is an electrochemical process in which synapses fire and proteins are released. These results made it possible, at least, to claim that everything traditionally classed as a function of mind might take place within the brain.

Artificial intelligence (AI) research reinforced this claim—or tried to—with a new version of an old hope or fear: that minds may not even be organic but merely mechanical. Pablo Picasso (1881–1973) painted a machine in love in 1917. Robots became the antiheroes of science fiction—the imaginary next stage of evolution, who would inherit the Earth from humankind. In the second half of the century, computers proved so dextrous, first in making calculations, then in responding to their environments, that they seemed capable of settling the debate over whether mind was

> *"In a world recrafted, as if by Frankenstein, humans now had the power to make their biggest intervention in evolution yet: selecting unnaturally not according to what is best adapted to the environment, but according to what best matches what humans happen to want at a particular moment."*

The Electronic Numerical Integrator and Computer —one of the first electronic digital computers in the United States—was commissioned by the U.S. Army and first installed at the University of Pennsylvania in Philadelphia. The choice of female programmers was presumably dictated by the public relations objectives of this photograph.

different from brain. The debate was unsatisfactory because people on either side were really talking about different things. Proponents of artificial intelligence were not particularly concerned with building machines with creative, artistic imaginations, or with intuitive properties, or with the ability to feel love or hatred—qualities that opponents of AI valued as indicators of a truly human mind. These kinds of questions could be resolved only by working on ever more sophisticated robotics and seeing whether robots with highly complex circuitry developed the cognitive properties of humans.

Meanwhile, two areas of scientific research previously thought to be of purely academic interest posed a further challenge to human self-perception: primatology (the study of apes, monkeys, and their ancestor-species) and paleoanthropology (the study of prehistoric humans and their ancestors). Paleoanthropologists discovered, among remains of humans' nonhuman ancestors and related primates, features formerly thought unique to our own species, *Homo sapiens*. The most challenging discoveries came from Neanderthal burials, which demonstrated that Neanderthals, who belonged to a species different from ours, had ritual lives and moral practices, including care of the elderly and reverence for the dead. Skeptics displayed apelike agility in challenging these facts, explaining them away as the result of accident or fraud. But there was too much evidence to discount altogether. It proved, in combination, that nonhuman species, morally indistinguishable from human beings, have existed. The question was important because, as we shall see in Chapter 29, it emerged at a time when the notion of **human rights** became current—a notion based in part on the assumption that being human constitutes a meaningful moral category that excludes nonhuman creatures.

Animal rights movements challenged that assumption. Improved knowledge of surviving species of nonhuman primates tended to support them. First, scientists working with macaque monkeys in Japan realized that these creatures, though modestly endowed with brains, have culture. They can learn and transmit what they learn across generations. The breakthrough discovery came in 1952, when a monkey called Ima was observed teaching her community how to wash the dirt off sweet potatoes. The tribe took up the technique. The monkeys continued to practice it, even when supplied with ready-washed potatoes, showing that washing had become a cultural rite, not a practical measure (see Chapter 1, p. 5).

In subsequent decades, led by a brilliant field-worker, Jane Goodall, primatologists came to realize that chimpanzees have, albeit to a much smaller extent than

Chimp painting. It's painting, but is it art? Works by Congo, the most famous chimpanzee painter, and others of his kind, sell for thousands of dollars. Chimps often label their work in sign language, but their paintings never represent images in ways that are recognizable to humans. Their minds are both like and unlike ours. They seem to see the world differently from the way we do.

human beings, all the features of culture that were formerly thought to be peculiarly human, including tool-making, language, war, rules for distributing food, and political habits. Further studies of other social animals—beginning with other great apes, such as gorillas and orangutans, and, by early in the twenty-first century, including whales, dolphins, elephants, and even rats—seemed to show disturbingly similar results, suggesting that culture is uniquely human only as a matter of degree. Meanwhile, many observations and experiments cast doubt on the belief that humans have unique cognitive properties. Nonhuman apes, for example, proved to be self-aware and showed sensibilities hard to distinguish in practice from the senses of morality and transcendence formerly thought to be human peculiarities. By the end of the twentieth century, some ethicists were campaigning for animal rights or for the redefinition of the moral community to embrace great apes.

The discoveries of primatologists and comparative zoologists belonged in a broader context of scientific change: the rise of ecology, the study of the interconnectedness of all life and its interdependence with aspects of the physical environment. The development of ecology—ecologists' exposure of a vast range of new practical problems arising from human overexploitation of the environment—became a major source of influence on changes in the late twentieth-century world. Chapter 30 is devoted to discussing these problems.

Anthropology and Psychology

In anthropology, as in science, the opening decade of the twentieth century was decisive. Among the supposedly scientific certainties the late nineteenth-century West treasured was that some peoples and societies were evolutionarily superior to others: an image of the world sliced and stacked in order of race. This picture suited Western imperialists, who treated it as justification of their rule over other peoples (see Chapter 25). But it was upset in the first decade of this century, largely thanks to an undersung hero: Franz Boas (1858–1942). Boas showed that no race was superior to any other in brainpower. He made untenable the notion that societies could be ranked in terms of a developmental model of thought. People, he concluded, think differently in different cultures not because some have superior mental equipment but because all thought reflects the traditions to which it is heir, the society that surrounds it, and the environment in which it exists.

At the end of the first decade of the century, Boas summarized his findings: "The mental attitude of individuals who . . . develop the beliefs of a tribe is exactly that of the civilized philosopher."

> There may be other civilizations, based perhaps on different traditions and on a different equilibrium of emotion and reason, which are of no less value than ours, although it may be impossible for us to appreciate their values without having grown up under their influence. The general theory of valuation of human activities, as developed by anthropological research, teaches us a higher tolerance than the one we now profess.

In addition to being a teacher who dominated anthropology in the United States, Boas was a field-worker in his youth and a museum keeper in maturity; he was in touch with both the people and the artifacts he sought to understand. His pupils had Native American peoples to study who lived little more than a railway ride away. The habit of fieldwork piled up enormous quantities of data that were used to bury the crude hierarchical schemes of the nineteenth century. The new anthropology took a long time to spread beyond Boas's students, but it was already influencing British methods in the first decade of the twentieth century, and the other major centers of anthropological research in France and Germany gradually accepted it.

The result was **cultural relativism**: the doctrine that we cannot rank cultures in order of merit but must judge each on its own terms. As we shall see in Chapter 30, this doctrine proved problematic. Should cannibals be judged on their own terms? Or cultures that licensed slavery or the subjection of women? Or those that practiced infanticide or head-hunting or other abominations? Or even those that condoned relatively milder offenses against values the West cherished—offenses such as the mutilation or torture of criminals or female circumcision? Cultural relativism had to have limits, but anthropology compelled educated people everywhere to examine their prejudices, to see merit in cultures they formerly despised, and to question their own convictions of superiority.

". . . anthropology compelled educated people everywhere to examine their prejudices, to see merit in cultures they formerly despised, and to question their own convictions of superiority."

Margaret Mead. "I lived like a visiting young village princess. I could summon informants to teach me everything I wanted to know: as a return courtesy, I danced every night." The photograph shows the celebrated anthropologist Margaret Mead (1901–1978) in Samoan dress with her collaborator Fa'amotu. Fieldwork seems to have been a liberating experience for Mead.

Sigmund Freud on holiday in 1913 with his daughter Anna, who herself became a distinguished psychoanalyst. It was a momentous year for Freud. His most brilliant disciple, Carl Jung, broke with the master, and Freud published *Totem and Taboo*, which he later privately repudiated as "a scientific myth," full of inaccuracies. Feeling defensive about the reputation of his work Freud wrote *The Claims of Psychoanalysis to Scientific Interest* in the same year.

The noble savage (see Chapter 22) reemerged from the eighteenth-century Enlightenment. Perhaps the most influential anthropological book of all time was Margaret Mead's *Coming of Age in Samoa*, published in 1928. Mead worked with pubescent girls in a sexually permissive society. She claimed to find a world liberated from the inhibitions, hang-ups, anxieties, and neuroses that psychology was busily uncovering in Western cities and suburbs. In the long run, as she rose to the top of her profession, to academic eminence and social influence, her work helped to feed fashionable educational ideas: uncompetitive schooling, rod-sparing discipline, cheap contraception.

Western educators could learn from Samoan adolescents in a world without barbarians and savages, where the language of comparison between societies had to be value free. What had once been called "primitive cultures" and "advanced civilizations" came to be labeled "elementary structures" and "complex structures." The longstanding justification for Western imperialism—the civilizing mission—lapsed, because no group of conquerors could any longer feel enough self-confidence to impose their own standards of civilization on their victims.

Psychology was even more subversive than anthropology, because its discoveries or claims reached beyond the relationships between societies to challenge the notions individuals had about themselves. In particular, the claim, first advanced by an Austrian psychiatrist, Sigmund Freud (1856–1939), that much human motivation is subconscious, challenged traditional notions about responsibility, identity, personality, conscience, and mentality. In an experiment Freud conducted on himself in 1896, he exposed his own *Oedipus Complex*, as he called it: a supposed, suppressed desire, which he believed to be subconsciously present in all male children, to supplant his father. In succeeding years he developed a technique he called **psychoanalysis**, designed to make patients aware of their subconscious desires. Hypnosis or, as Freud preferred, free association, could retrieve repressed feelings and ease nervous symptoms. Many patients who rose from his couch walked more freely than before.

Freud seemed able, from the evidence of a few of his patients, to illuminate the human condition. Every child, he claimed to show, experienced before puberty the same phases of sexual development. Every adult repressed similar fantasies or experiences. Women who only a few years previously would have been dismissed as hysterical malingerers became, in Freud's work, case studies from whose example almost everyone could learn. This made an important indirect contribution to the reevaluation of the role of women in society (see Chapter 29). Freud's science, however, failed to pass the most rigorous tests. When the philosopher Karl Popper asked how to distinguish someone who did not have an Oedipus complex from someone who did, the psychoanalytic fraternity had no answer. Nevertheless, for some patients, psychoanalysis worked.

Returnees from the horrors of twentieth-century wars became patients of psychiatry. The nightmares of trench survivors in World War I (see Chapter 28) were too hideous to share with loved ones, their experiences unimaginable to people back home. The guilt of those who missed the war echoed the shellshock of those who fought it. Introspection, formerly regarded as self-indulgence, became routine in the modern West. Repression became the modern demon and the analyst an exorcist. The "feel-good society," which bans guilt, shame, self-doubt, and self-reproach, was among the results. So was the twentieth- and twenty-first century habit of sexual candor. So was the fashion—prevalent for much of the twentieth century—to treat metabolic or chemical imbalances in the brain as if they were deep-rooted mental disorders. The good and evil that flowed from Freud's theory are nicely balanced and objectively incalculable. Psychoanalysis and other, sub-Freudian schools of therapy helped millions and tortured millions—releasing some people from repressions and condemning others to illusions or futile treatments.

The most profound influence psychology exercised, however, was not on the treatment of mental disorder but on the way children were raised. In 1909, the Swedish feminist Ellen Key proclaimed the rediscovery of childhood. Children were different from adults. This was, in effect, a summary of the state of the idea of childhood as it had developed in the nineteenth-century West (see Chapter 24). It was, perhaps, a valid observation. But it had questionable consequences for the way children were brought up. Children who were not treated as adults in childhood "never grew up"; they were like the tragic hero of J. M. Barrie's classic novel of 1911, *Peter Pan*, who withdrew into Neverland and whose childhood sweetheart outgrew him. Generations raised on the assumption that they could not face adult realities found themselves deprived of truths about their own lives and became fodder for the new therapies of psychiatry. Generational "hang-ups" became a new curse for Western children. People outside the West, where the new image of childhood arrived patchily and late, had fewer such troubles.

In the West, better treatment for childhood disease enabled more children to lead longer lives. So children became more suitable objects in whom to invest time and emotion and, of course, study. Working on Freud's insights, educational psychologists in the West built up a picture of mental development in predictable, universal stages, as people grow up. School curricula changed in the 1950s and 1960s to match the supposed patterns of childhood development. Generations of schoolchildren were deprived of challenging tasks because child psychology said they were incapable of them. While formal education got longer and longer, most children emerged from it with no experience of traditional elements of the curriculum that were now thought unsuitably difficult, such as calculus, foreign and classical languages, sophisticated vocabulary, ancient authors, even grammar. Other developments, which belong in Chapter 29, stimulated this trend, including, notably, the economic changes that made vocational qualifications seem disproportionately important in education and the social pressures that made for "dumbing down."

Idealized childhood. The first story of Peter Pan—"the boy who never grew up"— appeared in 1902, hit the London stage in 1904, and became the subject of illustration by Arthur Rackham (1867–1939), the most famous children's illustrator of his day, in 1906. Infant deaths were still common, and writers found romantic euphemisms with which to mask the horror. Peter flies from his crib when seven days old, over the smoke-shrouded roofscape of London—Rackman includes recognisable though distorted vignettes of such landmarks as St. Paul's Cathedral and the tower that houses Big Ben—and makes his home with fairies. In the next book, in 1911, Peter became an equivocal character, trapped in immaturity.

Philosophy and Linguistics

To scientific uncertainty and cultural relativism, the opening decade of the century added potentially devastating philosophical unease. In combination with Einstein's disquieting revelations about the nature of time, the theories of the French philosopher Henri Bergson (1859–1941) proved both unsettling and inspiring. He formulated a concept he called "duration"—the new sense of time we get when we realize that there is no clear "separation between present states and preceding states." This seemingly difficult idea helped to fortify educated people's faith in free will. Time is not a constraint that nature imposes on us, but a concept that we impose on nature. Bergson coined the term *élan vital* to express the freedom we retain to make a future different from the one that science predicts—a spiritual force with the power to reorder matter. Time, the way Bergson saw it, became not a sequence of atomized events, but a product of memory, which is different from perception and therefore "a power independent of matter."

Bergson's thinking infuriated scientists and inspired artists, especially novelists, who began to write stories that involved the reader in coils of tumbling, jumbled thoughts and events. He argued that the theory of evolution needed rethinking. Evolution, he said, was not a scientific law but an expression of the creative will of living entities, which change because they want to change. Critics accused Bergson of irrationalism on the grounds that he was attacking science and representing objective realities as purely mental concepts. Indeed, consistent with his principles, he never tried to demonstrate the validity of his ideas by logical exposition or scientific evidence. This did not make them less attractive, or less effective in liberating people who felt limited or inhibited by all the supposedly scientific determinism of the late nineteenth century. Bergson reassured those who doubted whether, for example, history really led inevitably to the revolutions Marx predicted, or to the white supremacy "scientific" racism preached, or to the destruction the laws of thermodynamics predicted. Nature was unorganized. The chaos that made scientific minds despair offered hope to Bergson's readers.

Bergson's followers hailed him as the philosopher for the twentieth century. His first great rival for that status was an American, William James (1842–1910). The start of James's tragedy was his family's prosperity—he felt guilty when he was not earning his own living. Inside the philosopher, a capitalist was always striving to get out. James wanted a distinctively American philosophy, reflecting the values of business and hustle. He joined patriotic organizations, resisted attempts to Europeanize him, and always scampered back thankfully to America from trips abroad.

Seeking reasons to make other people share his belief in God, James argued that "if the hypothesis of God works satisfactorily in the widest sense of the word, it is true." He called this doctrine **pragmatism**. The work in which he popularized it in 1907, *The Will to Believe,* was hailed as the philosophy of the future. But what one individual or group finds useful, another may find useless. James's claim that truth is not what is real, but is whatever serves a particular purpose, was one of the most subversive claims a philosopher ever made. James had set out as an apologist for Christianity, but by relativizing truth, he undermined it.

Linguistics produced similarly subversive developments—doubts about the reality of truth and whether language could express it. Ferdinand de Saussure, a teacher at the University of Geneva in Switzerland, is usually credited with decisive influence in this respect. But, like Einstein's, his influence was slow to affect the wider intellectual community. Saussure began his lectures in 1907, but they were not published until after his death in 1913, in a form his pupils perfected or distorted. Mostly, they seemed revolutionary only to other students of language. But they contained a revolutionary idea: the distinction between social speech, the *parole* addressed to others, and subjective language, the *langue* known only to thought. As most students and readers interpreted it, Saussure seemed to say of language what Poincaré seemed to say of science—any language we use refers only to itself and cannot disclose remoter realities.

Mainstream philosophers were at first reluctant to pursue the implications of this idea. The dominant philosophy of the 1920s and 1930s, the years between the First and Second World Wars, was *positivism,* which asserted that what the human senses perceived was real and that reason could prove that what our senses perceive is true. As we have seen, however, developments in science and logic were making it impossible to feel such confidence. The most significant boost to the tradition Saussure inaugurated came in 1953 with the publication of *Philosophical Investigations,* by the English-trained Austrian philosopher, Ludwig Wittgenstein. The printed pages retained the flavor of lecture notes, full of anticipated questions from the audience. Wittgenstein's argument was that we understand language not because it corresponds to reality but because it obeys rules of usage. Therefore, we do not necessarily know what language refers to, except its own terms. Wittgenstein imagined a student

"James's claim that truth is not what is real, but is whatever serves a particular purpose, was one of the most subversive claims a philosopher ever made. James had set out as an apologist for Christianity, but by relativizing truth, he undermined it."

asking, "So you are saying that human agreement decides what is true and what is false?" And again, "Aren't you at bottom really saying that everything except human behavior is a fiction?" Wittgenstein tried to distance himself from such devastating skepticism. The impact of a writer's work, however, often exceeds his intentions.

Equally disturbing, because of what it implied about human nature, was the work a linguist at the Massachusetts Institute of Technology, Noam Chomsky, published in 1957. Chomsky was impressed at how quickly and easily children learn speech. They can, in particular, combine words in ways they have never actually heard. He also found it remarkable that the differences between languages appear superficial compared with the "deep structures"— the parts of speech, the relationships between terms that we

Language in action. Does this picture show conversation? Debate? Performance? Oratory? Are the protagonists talking to each other or using each other to express themselves or to appeal to the onlookers? How much of the language they exchange is gesture and how much words? Taken during the 1948 election that restored democracy to post-war Italy, this photograph raises profound questions about how we should understand language.

call *grammar* and *syntax*—that are common to all of them. Chomsky suggested a link between the structures of language and the brain. We learn languages fast because their structure is already part of the way we think. This was a revolutionary suggestion. Experience and heredity, nurture and nature, it implied, do not make us the whole of what we are. Part of our nature is hardwired and unchangeable. As Chomsky saw it, at least at first, this "language instinct" or "language faculty" was untouchable—and therefore perhaps not produced—by evolution. Chomsky's views remained theoretical and were, perhaps, beyond proof. But they resonated in minds worried about the problems of using language and science to access reality. He rapidly became the most-quoted figure in academic literature.

Even more fundamentally, Chomsky argued that our language prowess, on which we tend to congratulate ourselves as a species—and which some people even claim is a uniquely human achievement—is like the special skills of other species: that of cheetahs in speed, for instance, or cows in ruminating. "It is the richness and specificity of instinct of animals," Chomsky said in a work of the mid-1980s, "that accounts for their remarkable achievements in some domains and lack of ability in others, so the argument runs, whereas humans, lacking such . . . instinctual structure, are free to think, speak and discover . . . . Both the logic of the problem and what we are now coming to understand suggest that this is not the correct way to identify the position of humans in the world." This observation coincided with the disarming discoveries of primatology and paleoanthropology.

By the time Chomsky entered the academic arena, unease and pessimism were rampant, especially in Europe and parts of Asia, where the material destruction and moral horror of World War II had been most keenly felt. The most widely accepted response to the war had emerged from a group of philosophers in Germany known as the Frankfurt School. Their great project was to find alternatives to Marxism and capitalism. They defined what they called alienation as the central problem of modern society. Economic rivalries and short-sighted materialism divided individuals and wrecked common pursuits. People felt dissatisfied and rootless. Martin Heidegger proposed a strategy to cope with this feeling. Specifically, he said, we should accept our existence between conception and death as the only unchangeable thing about us and tackle life as a project of self-realization, of "becoming"—who we are changes as the project unfolds. This **existentialism** represented the retreat of intellectuals into the security of self-contemplation, in revulsion from an ugly world.

Heidegger was discredited because he collaborated with the Nazis, a vicious German regime that provoked world war and massacred millions of people. In France in 1945, however, Jean-Paul Sartre (1905–1980) relaunched existentialism

Existentialists. Jean-Paul Sartre (1905–1980) and Simone de Beauvoir (1908–1986) became icons of radicalism—she for her feminist classic, *The Second Sex,* he for the influence of his philosophy on postwar Western youth. At home in Paris, however, they seem like a model middle-class couple, stiffly sharing a newspaper in their under-decorated apartment.

Making Connections | TRANSFORMATIONS OF WESTERN SCIENCE AND THOUGHT

DISCIPLINE	NEW THEORIES	EFFECTS ON SOCIETY
Physics/ Mathematics	Henri Poincaré: notes elastic connection between hypothesis and evidence and how multiple hypotheses can fit results of experiments Albert Einstein: proves speed of light is a constant and that time and space change with motion (theory of relativity) Ernest Rutherford: establishes basis of sub-atomic world Niels Bohr: describes light as consisting simultaneously of both waves and particles; links to Werner Heisenberg's indeterminacy principle (uncertainty principle); questions objectivity of scientific observations	Helped unleash the power of charged subatomic particles in technology, including weapons (atomic bombs), communications (transistors, microprocessors, integrated circuits) The "new physics" revolutionizes astronomy, chemistry, other physical sciences
Astronomy	Edwin Hubble: discovers that universe is expanding	Combined with the "new physics" and jet propulsion, astronomical findings set the stage for exploration of solar system, challenge or confirm religious beliefs; "big bang" theory of the origins of the universe
Biology	T. H. Morgan: demonstrates that genetic transmission influences physical characteristics Neuroscience demonstrates how mental functions operate within the brain	Discoveries in human biology lead to advances in medicine: curing infections with antibiotics and other drugs; controlling diabetes; developing preventive public health programs (inoculations, health education); controversy over theory of human evolution; development of artificial intelligence (AI)
Genetics	DNA discovered in the 1950s; belief that manipulation of genetic codes could solve medical and behavioral problems	Ability to modify genes of plants and animals for human use; debate over cloning and genetic engineering of human beings
Primatology and paleo-anthropology	Primatology: discovery that, like humans, animals also have culture, language, tool-making skills Paleoanthropology: discovery of features originally thought uniquely human (rituals, morality) among nonhuman ancestors	Reinforced connection between humans and other animals; deeper understanding of ecology and the interconnectedness of all life forms; animal rights movement
Anthropology	Franz Boas: comparative study of societies shows that no race is superior to any other in brainpower, mental development Margaret Meade: claimed so-called primitive cultures are free of neuroses and anxieties that plague West	Cultural relativism studies communities in context of their own traditions; widened appreciation for non-Western cultures (Native American, Samoan, etc.)
Psychology	Sigmund Freud: argued that subconscious motivates human behavior; developed psychoanalysis to uncover subconscious feelings, thoughts New theories on child raising and education by Freud, Ellen Key and others emphasize childhood as a separate phase of life	Therapeutic treatment for mental and emotional problems; transformation of school curriculums, child raising to conform with stages of child development; widespread interest in popular psychology, including psychoanalysis and dream analysis
Philosophy and Linguistics	Henri Bergson and others reconceptualize time and causation as part of human-determined memory and experience F. de Saussure and others deconstruct language as a human-constructed medium that cannot convey objective reality	Noam Chomsky argues that language, speech, grammar, and syntax are linked to the brain and are part of the way humans think

as a new creed for the postwar era. "Man," he said, "is . . . nothing else but what he makes of himself." For Sartre, self-modeling was more than an individual responsibility. Every individual action is an exemplary act, a statement about humankind, about the sort of species you want to belong to. Yet there is no objective way to put meaning into such a statement. God does not exist. Everything is permissible, and "as a result man is forlorn, without anything to cling to." "There is," he wrote, "no explaining things away by reference to a fixed . . . human nature. In other words, there is no determinism, man is free, man is freedom."

Sartre's version of existentialism fed the common assumptions about the life of educated young Westerners in the 1950s and 1960s. Critics who denounced it as a philosophy of decadence were not far wrong in practice because it was used to justify every form of self-indulgence. Sexual promiscuity, revolutionary violence, indifference to manners, consideration for others, defiance of the law, and drug abuse could all be part of becoming oneself. The social changes of the 1960s, to which we shall return in Chapter 29, would have been unthinkable without existentialism: beat culture, and permissiveness—ways of life millions adopted or imitated—as well, perhaps, as the late twentieth-century's libertarian reaction against social planning. Existentialism was, briefly, the philosophical consensus of the West. But it never caught on in the rest of the world; and even in the West, people who saw more urgent problems than shaping one's personal future detested it. By the 1970s, a reaction was in the making: conservative in politics, mistrustful of materialism, inclined to religion, anxious to recover tradition and rebuild social solidarity—especially through the family. This was a global reaction. It was particularly strong in the Americas, while in Asia and Africa revulsion from Western-dominated thinking strengthened the trend.

THE MIRROR OF SCIENCE: ART

The twentieth century was a graveyard and a cradle: a graveyard of certainties, the cradle of a civilization of crumbling confidence in which it would be hard to be sure of anything. We can see the effect of this unsettling period—literally, see it—in the work of painters. Never more than in the twentieth century, painters tended to paint not the world as they saw it directly, but as science and philosophy displayed it for their inspection. The revolutions of twentieth-century art, the chronologies of artists' changing perceptions, exactly match the jolts and shocks science and philosophy administered.

In 1909, the Italian Emilio Filippo Marinetti (1876–1944) published a manifesto for fellow artists, proclaiming what he called **futurism**. At the time, most artists professed modernism: the doctrine that the new was superior to the old.

Chronology: The Diffusion and Transformation of Western Science

1842–1910	William James, American philosopher, developed the doctrine of pragmatism
1856–1939	Sigmund Freud, developer of psychoanalysis
1860s	China's "self-strengthening" program begins
1875–1965	Albert Schweizer, medical missionary to Africa
1879–1955	Albert Einstein, developer of the theory of relativity
1881–1938	Kemal Ataturk, founder of modern Turkey and proponent of secularism and Western science
1883	Beijing School of Medicine adopts Western curriculum
1885–1962	Niels Bohr, won Nobel Prize in 1922 for work on the structure of the atom
1891–1962	Ismail Mazhir, translator of Charles Darwin's work into Arabic
1897	Jagadis Chandra Bose awarded scientific research grant by the British viceroy
1901–1976	Werner Heisenberg, developed uncertainty principle
1902	Henri Poincaré, questions the link between hypothesis and evidence
1903	Powered flight
1905–1980	Jean-Paul Sartre, French philosopher associated with existentialism
1907	Plastic invented
1912	Overthrow of the Qing dynasty increases pace of Westernization in China
1913	Indian *Journal of Medical Research* launched
1914	Science Society of China founded by Chinese students at Cornell University
1920	Royal Institute for Higher Technical Education founded in Indonesia
1928	Margaret Mead's *Coming of Age in Samoa* published
1930	Chandrasekhara Venkata Raman of India, first non-Westerner to win Nobel Prize in physics
1931	Penicillin discovered
1944	Erwin Schrödinger predicts structure of the gene
1953	Ludwig Wittgenstein's *Philosophical Investigations* and Simone de Beauvoir's *The Second Sex* published

Man as machine, speeding and striding into the future. The Italian artist Umberto Boccioni (1882–1916) captured the spirit of futurism in this sculpture of 1913. "Our straight line will be alive and palpitating", he wrote, aiming to "embed" the math and geometry of machines "in the muscular lines of a body".

Umberto Boccioni, "Unique Form of Continuity in Space." 1913 (cast 1931). Bronze, 43 7/8" x 34 7/8" x 15 3/4" (111.4 x 88.6 x 40 cm). Acquired through the Lillie P. Bliss Bequest. The Museum of Modern Art/Licensed by Scala-Art Resource, New York.

"The power Marinetti praised—the power of science, the power of states—could not bring the world to order or order to the world."

Marinetti wanted to go further. He believed that what was traditional had not only to be surpassed but repudiated and wrecked. He rejected coherence, harmony, freedom, conventional morals, and conventional language—even conventional grammar—because they were familiar. Comfort was artistically sterile. Instead, futurism glorified war, power, chaos, and destruction, which would shove humankind into novelty. Marinetti, with the followers he soon acquired, celebrated the beauty of machines, the morals of might, and the syntax of babble. Sensitivity, kindness, and fragility he dismissed as the mawkish values of old-fashioned art, created by the followers of the styles called romantic and aesthetic. Futurists preferred ruthlessness, candor, strength.

Marinetti's machine-age imagery appealed to a wide public and found echoes in the work of many artists, not all of whom accepted his brutal, radical program. Painters inspired by Marinetti's lectures painted "lines of force"—symbols of coercion. The excitement of speed—attained by the new-fangled internal combustion engine—represented for Marinetti the spirit of the age, speeding away from the past. The movement he founded united adherents of the most radical politics of the twentieth century: fascists, for whom the state should serve the strong, and communists, who hoped to incinerate tradition in revolution. The fascists and communists hated each other and relished the battles they fought with each other, first in the streets and later, when they took over states, in wars bigger and more terrible than any the world had ever seen. But they agreed that the function of progress was to destroy the past.

In retrospect, Marinetti seems uncannily prophetic. The deepening destructiveness of wars and the quickening speed and power of machines did indeed dominate the future. The speeding machines turned the world into a global village where every place was within, at most, a few hours' travel of every other place and where information was accessible everywhere, instantly. The machines also achieved dazzling power to destroy. Toward midcentury, people devised massive gas chambers and incinerators that put millions to death and disposed of their bodies economically and efficiently. Bombs obliterated tens of thousands at a time, and spread deadly, corrosive radiation capable of killing millions more. Marinetti claimed, "The future has begun." It sounds like nonsense or, if not nonsense, a platitude, but, in a way, he was right. He had devised a telling metaphor for the pace of the changes that he and his contemporaries experienced. It was an exhilarating time, but it was also full of terror and foreboding.

Ultimately, Marinetti's future also failed because tradition could never quite be outstripped; it always clung to the coattails of the speeding world. But the world had to pass through the flames of war and the furnace of tyranny before settling for mere instability and insecurity. By the end of the century, power seemed to have passed outside the realm of conventional politics. The programs of scientists and technologists mattered more than those of politicians. Big business wielded more influence over people's lives than voters exercised. Institutions of security, defense, and justice tended to slip not just out of democratic control, but even out of the control of governments. The power Marinetti praised—the power of science, the power of states—could not bring the world to order or order to the world.

Other artists, meanwhile, turned in disgust from the ideal of a machinelike universe and an engineered society, preferring a vision that atomic theory suggested—of an elusive, ill-ordered, uncontrollable world. In 1907, an artistic style called **cubism** began to hold up to the world images of itself reflected as if in a distorting mirror, shivered into fragments. Pablo Picasso and Georges Braque (1882–1963), the originators of the movement, denied they had ever heard of Einstein. But scientific vulgarizations, especially, of course, of the work of Poincaré, reached them through the press. As painters of an elusive reality from many different perspectives, they were reflecting the science and philosophy of their decade (see Map 27.2). Even Piet Mondrian (1872–1944)—the Dutch artist whose work so perfectly captured the sharp angles of modern taste that he represented the rhythms of boogie-woogie music as a rectilinear grid and Broadway in Manhattan as a straight line—had a shivered-mirror phase in the early years of the second decade of the century. Formerly, he loved to paint the trees along the River Geyn in his native Holland with romantic fidelity. Now he splayed and atomized them.

The French artist Marcel Duchamp (1887–1968) denounced his own expertise in science as mere smattering. But he, too, tried to represent Einstein's world. He called his painting, *Nude Descending a Staircase* of 1912, an expression of "time and space through the abstract presentation of motion." His notes on his baffling masterpiece of sculpture, *Large Glass*, revealed how closely he had studied relativity. Meanwhile, in 1911, the Russian artist Vasily Kandinsky had read Rutherford's description of the atom. "The discovery hit me with frightful force, as if the end of the world had come. All things become transparent, without strength or certainty." After that, he painted the world as he now saw it, suppressing every reminder of real objects. The tradition he launched, of entirely "abstract" art, which depicted

MAP 27.2

Centers of European Art Movements, 1900–1940

- ■ centers associated with Cubism
- ■ centers associated with Futurism
- ■ centers associated with Expressionism
- ■ centers associated with Dada
- □ centers associated with Surrealism
- — state borders as of 2000

Marcel Duchamp's painting, _Nude Descending a Staircase_ (1912) was shockingly avant garde when first exhibited, but in retrospect, it seems representative of the most prominent trends in its day: dehumanizing, mechanistic, informed by science and technology, and subversive of tradition. _Marcel Duchamp (American, born France, 1887–1968) "Nude Descending a Staircase, No. 2," 1912, oil on canvas, 58 x 35 in. Philadelphia Museum of Art: The Louise and Walter Arensberg Collection. Color transparency by Graydon Wood, 1994. © 1998 Artists Rights Society (ARS), New York/ADAGP, Paris/Estate of Marcel Duchamp._

objects unrecognizably or not at all, became dominant for the rest of the century. The new rhythmic beat of jazz and the noises of atonal music—developed in Vienna by Arnold Schoenberg from 1908 onward—subverted the harmonies of the past as surely as quantum mechanics began to challenge its ideas of order.

In art, the effects of the new anthropology were even clearer than those of the new physics. Picasso, Braque, and members of Kandinsky's circle (known as the Blue Rider School) copied "primitive" sculptures from museums of natural history, with the indigenous arts of the Pacific and Africa dominant at first. The range of influences broadened, as Western artists in the Americas and Australia rediscovered the art of native peoples. As in science and philosophy, Asian traditions made a big impact in the West in the last four decades of the century, especially in music, architecture, and stage design. The vogue for primitivism ensured that craftsmen outside Europe had a market for their traditional arts. Yet whenever innovations occurred in art, as in science, Western initiatives predominated globally throughout the century.

As in so many areas of modernization, Japanese artists led the way in assimilating Western influences. Outstanding painters, such as Kuroda Seiki and Wada Eisaku, were already studying in Europe in the 1890s and the early 1900s. In China, influence radiated chiefly from Russia, especially from the late 1940s, as Russian-inspired communists became first prominent, then all-powerful. Their characteristic subjects were stocky, heroic peasants and workers in poster-art style. This still dominated the art of Wang Guangyi (wahng gwang-yee) in the last years of the twentieth century. Meanwhile, China had opened up to every kind of Western influence. The outstanding young artist of the 1990s, Zhou Chunya (joe chwun-yah), was reported as saying, "Even though Western art dominates my painting style, I would say I am a Chinese painter . . . because I maintain a Chinese lifestyle within myself." For painters working in the shadow of Western influence, his was a typical sentiment.

Among artists who resisted or selectively filtered Western influences, those from India were most conspicuous. To a great extent, this was thanks to Abindranath Tagore, who, at the end of the nineteenth century, rejected his Western-style training as a painter to find inspiration in Mughal art (Chapter 19). His followers and successors—notably Nandalal Bose (1882–1966)—made anticolonialism part of the message of their work. At the end of the century, many artists around the world turned to folk art to supply new styles. But even painters who were most vocal in their rejection of the West were unable to escape altogether the magnetism of Western techniques, materials, and models.

The novel, modeled on the Western tradition rather than the independently developed Japanese form, became a universal genre. Cinema, a new medium of Western origin, rapidly became the most popular art form in the world, and, although different cultures evolved their own schools of cinema, the American style, known as "Hollywood" from the Los Angeles suburb where most of the film studios had their headquarters, dominated the global market. New initiatives in sculpture and architecture, and some interesting new genres, such as video art and computer-generated art, depended on technologies that the West invented.

Paradoxically, it was in the West that the influence of Western art declined as the century wore on, but it took a long time for this to become apparent. Although governments patronized conventional artists, the characteristic art of World War I and its aftermath was **dada**—externalized disillusionment, deliberately brutal, ugly, and meaningless. The "Dada Manifesto" of 1918 celebrated World War I as the "great work of destruction." In Germany, Kurt Schwitters (1887–1948) scraped collages together from bits of smashed machines and ruined buildings. Max Ernst (1891–1976) exposed postwar nightmares, often using hostile materials—barbed wire and rough planks of wood. The artists who called themselves surrealists continued this trend in the 1920s and 1930s, reflecting psychology by creating paintings and films in which they aimed to externalize subconscious neuroses and desires. To some extent, their project overlapped with a school that established a more enduring tradition: expressionists, most of whom were more concerned with color and sometimes texture than with form, reached inside themselves and their subjects to represent emotion and mood.

After that, art seemed to lose some of its power to make people see the world afresh. **Surrealism** and **expressionism** were the last great global movements to start in the art world and overspill into ordinary people's perceptions. Plenty of great artists challenged onlookers' world picture, but none succeeded in changing it. Why was this? In part, it was because propaganda seduced art, especially the most powerful new art of the twentieth century, cinema. Most of the great movie directors and music composers of the 1930s and 1940s in Europe, America, and Russia got caught up in the ideological conflicts of the time. The Russian dictator, Josef Stalin (1879–1953), wrote music criticism anonymously, dictated style for the Soviet Union, and insisted on "socialist realism" in all the arts as the only school worthy of state patronage and the only style in which it was safe for artists to paint, compose, or write. The German dictator, Adolf Hitler (1889–1945), fancied himself a painter and an architect and banned artists, writers, and composers whom he regarded as Jewish or "decadent." Even after World War II and into the 1950s, American movie makers had to answer questions from Congress about how much "anticommunist" cinema they produced, and actors, directors, and screenwriters were banned if they were seen as being or even having once been procommunist.

More treacherously, art, like so much else in the twentieth-century West, became fodder for consumerism, commercialism, celebrity, and fashion. Artists escaped from political control by appealing to the mass market and to rich collectors. Salvador Dalí (1904–1989) was probably the most accomplished painter of the age in a technical sense. No one excelled him in mastery of his materials. His paintings, film–set designs, and the marketing of his images in poster form communicated the spirit of surrealism to a worldwide public. But many of his fellow artists hated him for his dedication to self-promotion and vulgar exhibitionism to boost the prices of his works. The great theorist of surrealism, André Breton (1896–1966), expelled Dalí from the movement and coined an anagram of his name: Avida Dollars. Picasso, the most prolific artist of the century, also became the richest by exhibiting uncanny business sense and by becoming a celebrity, famous for being famous almost as much as for his art.

Art lost influence, too, because taste splintered. The pace of change quickened in art as in everything else. From the 1930s onward, the market lurched rapidly among fashions. Every school of artists had to repudiate every other school to attract buyers. Technology multiplied media exponentially from the 1960s onward, and the market responded by huddling in niches. Fans of one kind of music might

Art both Indian and modern. Under the Raj, British taste in Indian art was mainly antiquarian and favored styles that had been dominant in India's past. Nandalal Bose (1883-1966) responded to Western modernism by drawing on native Indian, Japanese, and Western traditions to create art that was both Indian and "modern." He was a nationalist and used his work to advance the claim that the whole of India shared a distinctive cultural identity. In this painting of 1943, and many similar pieces, he glorified the custom—banned by the British—of suttee: widows burning themselves to death on the funeral pyres of their dead husbands.

Evidence suggests that in Nigeria an enormous and thriving industry exists of inexpensive domestic productions, perhaps as many as twenty per week, that go directly to DVD in a country where there are few movie theatres.

MAP 27.3

World Film Production, 2007

- over 100 films
- 50–100 films
- 4–49 films

Chronology: "Modern" Art	
1866–1944	Vasily Kandinsky, Russian artist, launched tradition of entirely abstract art
1872–1944	Piet Mondrian, Dutch abstract artist
1876–1944	Emilio Filippo Marinetti, proponent of futurism
1881–1973	Pablo Picasso, cofounder of cubism
1882–1966	Nandalal Bose, Indian artist, incorporated anticolonialism in his work
1887–1968	Marcel Duchamp, French artist influenced by Einstein's theory of relativity
Early twentieth century	Karoda Seiki and Wada Eisaku, Japanese painters, create works that assimilated Western influences
1918	Proclamation of the "Dada Manifesto"
1920s and 1930s	Emergence of surrealist and expressionist movements

know nothing of any other kind. Theatergoers might avoid films and film buffs never go to plays. The two groups might never communicate with each other, despite the obvious opportunities for cross-fertilization between their arts. To a large extent, intellectual and economic differences determined the niches of taste, as some artists, seduced by theory or lured into a price-range accessible only to the super rich, lost interest in communicating with people of modest means or ordinary education. This became especially the case from the 1960s, when artists influenced by the new theories in philosophy and linguistics lost belief in the power of symbols generally. Images, like words, some of them came to feel, have no direct relationship to reality.

Painting and sculpture yielded popularity to film and to mass entertainment industries (see Map 27.3). Arts suited to the new media—cinema, radio, photography, and the gramophone at first, television in the second half of the twentieth century, computers and video toward the century's end—spread secondhand experiences, received wisdom, and hand-me-down values. The artists who really touched people were cartoonists. Walt Disney (1901–1966)—a film studio chief who specialized in anthropomorphic characters and adaptations of famous fairy tales for the screen—became, perhaps, the world's most influential artist ever because his cartoon movies depicted the most commonplace emotions, morals, and character types in ways that people of all ages in all cultures could immediately grasp. Musical theater, sacrificing sophistication for memorable melody, displaced opera. Pop music was to art what factory products were to crafts: cheap to make and capable of generating huge profits. In the second half of the century, when—for reasons we shall discuss in the next chapter—vast masses of young people in the West acquired unprecedented spending power, the record industry became the home of the most socially revolutionary and subversive arts, a role writers had once filled. Now it was rock bands that issued messages of political protest and sexual liberation to the masses. These messages proved less saleable, in the long run, than escapism.

By the end of the twentieth century, the most commercially successful genre was fantasy—the depiction of worlds that magic regulated or transformed, which suited computer-generated imagery. It seemed an ironic end to a century dominated by science, but it was symptomatic of the impatience with or revulsion from science that came to characterize popular responses. Meanwhile, the art form that attracted the most investment, and therefore attained the highest technical standards, was television advertising. Advertising jingles and images became the common artistic culture of the time—the only things you could rely on just about everyone to recognize. Sport, especially soccer, was the only rival, largely because it was telegenic and broadcast brilliantly all over the world.

Architecture ought to be the most popular art of all because people who never enter an art gallery live in some form of architecture and see buildings around them every day. Indeed, after World War II, architecture replaced painting and rivaled cinema as the most socially powerful of the arts. The world had to be rebuilt, after the destruction of the war and the neglect of colonialism. However, doctrines that proved hostile to most people: **functionalism** and **rationalism**, which favored machinelike buildings, fashioned by necessity, stripped to their most elementary forms, angular in appearance, and unrelated to human scale, dominated the architecture of the period. So much had to be built so quickly that officialdom decided what and how to build, without giving much time or thought to the needs and feelings of the people who had to live in the huge apartment blocks, work in the offices, factories, and schools of the era, and recover or die in the hospitals. Only in the 1970s did architects and urban planners begin to turn back to popular demands, tear down some of the worst excesses of functionalism, and start again on a smaller scale and along more traditional lines.

The Hobbit. The stories of the British writer J.R.R. Tolkien (1892–1973) launched a new type of literature: the fantasy novel, in which authors combined myths from different cultures to create imaginary worlds—located sometimes in the past, sometimes in space, sometimes in a "parallel universe"—where events could unfold without the limitations imposed by reason or reality. Science could not displace magic from people's minds and tastes. In some cases, the fantasy novel even became the basis of new kinds of religion.

THE TURN OF THE WORLD

In the second half of the twentieth century, a reaction set in. The West rediscovered "Eastern wisdom," alternative medicine, and the traditional science of non-Western peoples. Other cultures renewed their confidence in their own traditions. One of the first signs of this reaction was Niels Bohr's decision in 1947 to adopt a Daoist symbol on his coat of arms when the Danish government ennobled him. He saw the wavelike double curve, interpenetrated by dots, as a description of the universe that prefigured that of the quantum physics of which he was the leading practitioner. "Opposites," according to the motto on his coat of arms, "are complementary." In the same period, J. Robert Oppenheimer, the American physicist who led the research team that developed the A-bomb, was one of many Western scientists who turned to the ancient Indian texts, the Upanishads (oo-PAH-nee-shahdz), for consolation and insights, in a West disillusioned by the horrors of war (see Chapter 28).

Then in 1956, Joseph Needham, who had served as director of scientific cooperation between the British and their Chinese allies during World War II, began to publish, in the first of many volumes, one of the momentous books of the twentieth century, *Science and Civilisation in China*, in which he showed that, despite the poor reputation of Chinese science in modern times, China had a scientific tradition of its own from which the West had learned the basis of most of its progress in technology until the seventeenth century. Indian scientists, meanwhile, had made similar claims for the antiquity—if not the global influence—of scientific thinking in their own country. In the 1960s, India became a favored destination for young Western tourists and pilgrims in search of values different from those of their own cultures (Chapter 29). By the 1980s, some Western scientists, dissatisfied with the terms at their disposal for describing the complexities of the cosmos that their work revealed, turned to Asian philosophies. Zen Buddhism (Chapter 14) and Daoist descriptions of nature provided some Westerners with models to interpret the universe that seemed to match scientific discoveries.

Even in medicine, the showpiece science of Western supremacy in the early twentieth century, non-Western traditions gained ground. Westerners with experience of the world often came to respect and learn from the healers they met far afield. Edward Hume himself commented favorably on the work of traditional Chinese herbalists, from whom he had learned much during his years at the Yale Clinic in Changsha. But it took a long time for such respect to become general in the West. In the 1980s, the World Health Organization began to realize the value of traditional healers in delivering health care to disadvantaged people in Africa. In 1985, for instance, Nigeria introduced alternative medicine to hospitals and health-care centers. South Africa and other African countries set up similar programs.

Meanwhile, in the West, traditional healing arts of non-Western peoples attracted big followings. Ethnobotany became fashionable, as medical practitioners discovered the healing plants of Amazonian forest dwellers, Chinese peasants, and Himalayan shamans. Scientists—led by anthropologists impressed by the knowledge of medicinal plants that the peoples they encountered in their work had—began to appreciate that so-called primitive peoples had a cornucopia of useful

The Beatles in India. Maharishi Maheshi Yogi, who claimed to be able to levitate and to procure world peace through meditation, was the most commercially successful of the Indian gurus who became fashionable in the West in the 1960s. Here members of the star rock band, the Beatles, sit at his feet. They incorporated some Indian influences into their music, and George Harrison (center, right) remained a devotee of the Maharishi's techniques.

A CLOSER LOOK

A "Vertical Village" from the 1950s

Today, the architecture of Charles-Édouard Jeanneret Gris ("Le Corbusier," 1887-1965) looks brutal, sterile, mechanical, and over-planned - symbolic of the failures of utopianism. But work like this, a fragment of a projected "vertical village" in Marseille in southern France, of the late 1940s and 1950s, was important not only for its influence, but also for the nobility of the architect's vision and ambition.

High-rise buildings have a bad reputation nowadays, because of the alienating effect people experience in large blocks of apartments, but Le Corbusier realised that in theory his thin, high building could give everyone a pleasant outlook and proximity to nature.

This was the world's first building clad in raw concrete, but for Le Corbusier concrete was a material that could capture the essence of nature, grained with the texture of the wooden planks between which the slabs were pressed.

"Violent, clamorous, triumphant polychromy" was Le Corbusier's aim for the façade, designed "to make people think."

Le Corbusier liked to elevate buildings on stilts as a virtuoso gesture. He believed the technique created a feeling of freedom, even of fantasy; but the result was dark, sinister, useless spaces detested by residents.

Interiors reporduce the outward aesthetics of the building.

How does this building embody many of the artistic doctrines of the postwar period?

African healing cult. In Cape Town, South Africa, a ritual of initiation into Ngoma—a shamanistic cult widespread in Africa. Practitioners use music and dance to attain a trance-like state in which they communicate with spirits, usually to access powers of healing.

drugs unknown to Western medicine. Traditional medicine had never died out in India and China. In a remarkable reversal of the direction of influence in the late twentieth century, Western patients seeking alternative medicines turned to Indian herbalism and Chinese acupuncture, along with other forms of traditional medicine in both countries. Westerners began to travel to China and India to study herbal treatments, just as at the beginning of the century, Asian students had headed to the West for the medical learning fashionable in their day. Western demand for alternative medicine became an economic opportunity for Chinese and Indian physicians in the West. The world had come full circle since Edward Hume's day.

In Perspective
Science, Challenging and Challenged

In the first half of the twentieth century, the intellectual hegemony of science was linked, unchallengeably, with the global dominance of the West. All the major new scientific initiatives came from Europe and America. The rest of the world could only endure this supremacy or attempt to imitate it. In the 1960s, however, the pattern began to shift significantly. Western scientists began to turn to non-Western, and especially to Asian, traditions of thought to help interpret some of the conflicting data their observations accumulated. These contradictions seemed, especially to nonscientists, to expose the imperfections of science as a system of knowledge that could explain the universe. Non-Western countries, especially in East and South Asia, imitated Western technologies so well that they began to build up enough wealth to invest in their own scientific institutions.

Meanwhile, revulsion from science increased prestige for what came to be known as alternative methods. Some people, especially professional scientists, remained convinced of the all-sufficiency of science and scorned these trends. Their critics called them scientistic. Toward the end of the century, divisions—sometimes called culture wars—opened between apologists of science and advocates of alternatives.

The search for the underlying or overarching order of the cosmos seemed only to lead to chaos. "Life is scientific," says Piggy, the doomed hero of William Golding's novel of 1959, *Lord of the Flies*. The rest of the characters prove him wrong by killing him and reverting to instinct and savagery. Golding died in 1993, hailed as one of the great storytellers of the century, largely because of the impact of this one novel, which seemed to be an allegory of its times. Science, in most people's judgment, soared and failed. It sought to penetrate the heavens, and it ended by contaminating the Earth. Among its most influential inventions, the effects of which are among the subjects of our remaining chapters, were bombs and pollutants. The expansion of knowledge added nothing to wisdom. Science did not make people better. Rather it increased their ability to behave worse than ever before. Instead of a universal benefit to humanity, science was a symptom or cause of disproportionate Western power. Under the influence of these feelings, and in response to the undermining of science by skepticism, an antiscientific reaction set in during the late twentieth century. It generated conflict between those who stuck to Piggy's opinion and the vast global majority who, as we shall see in Chapter 29, turned back to religion or even magic to help them cope with the bewildering world of rapid change and elusive understanding.

William Golding's *Lord of the Flies* in the movie version directed by Peter Brook (1963). The story of the British choirboy-castaways who turn to tyranny and savagery when cut off from the disciplines of adult control is not just an antidote to the idealization of childhood but also a reminder of the fragility of civilization. In this scene the gang turns on their companion, Piggy, who maintains a touching faith that "Life is scientific."

The revival of unscientific ways to picture reality surprised most observers. But by making the cosmos rationally unintelligible to most people, science actually stimulated a religious revival. Quantum science encouraged a revival of mysticism—a "reenchantment" of science, according to a phrase the British theologian David Griffin coined. Quantum experiments accustomed people to reliable observations that no one has been able to check objectively and to valid experiments that no one can repeat. Motions we cannot measure, events we cannot track, causes we cannot trace, and effects we cannot predict all became familiar and seemed to license metaphysical and even supernatural explanations. Modern Japan is a land of high-tech Shinto, where spirits infest computers and where an office tower of steel and plate glass can be topped off with a shrine to Inari, the fox-god. Some medical practitioners collaborate with faith healers. Even religious fundamentalism—one of the most powerful movements in the late twentieth-century world—owed something to science.

The last wave of revulsion from science—or, at least, from scientism—in the twentieth century was a form of humanism: a reaction in favor of humane values. Science seemed to blur the boundaries between humans and other animals, or even between humans and machines. It seemed to take the soul out of people and substitute genes for it. It seemed to make freedom impossible and reduce moral choices to evolutionary accidents or genetically determined options. It turned human beings into subjects of experimentation. Ruthless regimes abused biology to justify racism and employed psychiatry to imprison dissidents. Extreme scientism denied all nonscientific values and became, in its own way, as dogmatic as any religion. The "new humanism" was much more, however, than an antiscientistic reaction. It tended to blame religion—or, at least, religious conflicts—as much as science for the failures of history, and its thinkers and practitioners sought a morality based on universal or potentially universal values. More than either science or religion, the barbarities of the violent, conflictive political history of the twentieth century stimulated the new humanism.

"Science, in most people's judgment, soared and failed. It sought to penetrate the heavens, and it ended by contaminating the Earth."

Chronology

1856–1939	Sigmund Freud, developer of psychoanalysis
1858–1942	Franz Boas, anthropologist, proved that races are of equal intelligence
1860s	China's "self-strengthening" program begins
1866–1944	Vasily Kandinsky, Russian artist, launched tradition of entirely abstract art
1883	Western-style curriculum at Beijing School of Medicine
1871–1937	Ernest Rutherford, postulated concept of the atomic nucleus
1875–1965	Albert Schweizer, medical missionary to Africa
1876–1944	Emilio Filippo Marinetti, proponent of futurism
1879–1955	Albert Einstein, developer of the theory of relativity
1881–1938	Kemal Ataturk, founder of modern Turkey and proponent of secularism and Western science
1881–1973	Pablo Picasso, cofounder of cubism
1882–1966	Nandalal Bose, Indian artist, incorporated anticolonialism in his work
1885–1962	Niels Bohr, won Nobel Prize in 1922 for work on the structure of the atom
1891–1962	Ismail Mazhir, translator of Charles Darwin's work into Arabic
1897	Jagadis Chandra Bose awarded scientific research grant by the British viceroy
1901–1976	Werner Heisenberg, developed uncertainty principle
1902	Henri Poincaré questions the link between hypothesis and evidence
1903	Powered flight
1905–1980	Jean-Paul Sartre, French philosopher associated with existentialism
1906	15,000 Chinese study science abroad
1907	Plastic invented
1913	Indian *Journal of Medical Research* launched
1914	Science Society of China founded by Chinese students at Cornell University
1920s and 1930s	Emergence of surrealist and expressionist movements
1920	Royal Institute for Higher Technical Education founded in Indonesia
1925	Scopes "Monkey" Trial
1928	Margaret Mead's *Coming of Age in Samoa* published
1930	Chandrasekhara Venkata Raman, first non-Westerner to win Noble Prize in physics
1931	Penicillin discovered
1944	Erwin Schödinger predicts structure of the gene
1953	Ludwig Wittgenstein's *Philosophical Investigations* published
1956	Publication of Joseph Needham's *Science and Civilisation in China*

For the story of politics in the twentieth century matched that of science. In politics, too, the new century opened with new departures. The world's first full democracies—full in the sense that women had equal political rights with men—took shape in Norway and New Zealand. In 1904–1905, Japanese victories in a war with Russia foreshadowed the end of white supremacy. Encouraged by Japan's example, independence movements sprang into action in Europe's overseas empires. In 1911, the first great "rebellions of the masses" began. Contrary to the expectations of Karl Marx, these rebellions were not launched by urban workers, but by peasant revolutionaries in Mexico and by a combination of underemployed intellectuals and disaffected soldiers in China. In Mexico, the effect was to end the power of the two elements of society that had been dominant since colonial times: the church and the big landowners (see Chapter 29). In China, the Qing dynasty, which had reigned since 1644, was overthrown, the mandate of heaven abolished, and a republic proclaimed. This was an extraordinary reversal for a system that had survived so many convulsions for more than 2,200 years, and a sign that no form of political stability, however longstanding, could now be taken for granted. Both revolutions soured, turning into civil wars, breeding dictators. This too was an omen of the future. Most of the many violent regime changes of the twentieth century had similar consequences.

The future that the radicals of the nineteenth century imagined never happened. Ordinary people never really got power over their own lives or over the societies they formed—even in states founded in revolutions or regulated by democratic institutions. The progress people hoped for in the early years of the twentieth century dissolved in the bloodiest wars ever experienced. And just as Western science receded in the second half of the century, so did Western empires. To those stories we must now turn.

PROBLEMS AND PARALLELS

1. How did science come to set the agenda for the world in the twentieth century? How did Western empires spread Western science? How was Western science received in China and India? Why was Western science slow to be accepted in the Islamic world? Why did Kemal Ataturk consider science and reason to be the foundations of the Turkish republic?

2. How was Western science transformed in the twentieth century? What effects did uncertainty have on human self-perception and religious values? Why were the philosophies of Henri Bergson and William James so influential in the twentieth century?

3. Why is twentieth-century Western art a mirror of twentieth-century science? How did the revolutions in twentieth-century art match the jolts and shocks of science and philosophy? Why were communists and fascists attracted to the artistic ideas of Emilio Filippo Marinetti?

4. Why did a reaction against Western science take hold in the second half of the twentieth century? Why did scientists like Niels Bohr and J. Robert Oppenheimer turn to Daoism and ancient Indian texts for inspiration and consolation?

5. Why were existentialism and the ideas of Jean Paul Sartre so influential in the West in the 1960s? Why did existentialism fail to take hold in the non-Western world?

6. What is cultural relativism? How did anthropologists such as Franz Boas and Margaret Mead undermine Westerners' conviction of Western civilization and culture?

READ ON ▶ ▶ ▶

T. Dantzig, *Henri Poincaré, Critic of Crisis: Reflections on His Universe of Discourse* (1954) is still the fundamental study of the thought of one of the founders of modern science, whose own philosophy of science is available in Henri Poincaré, *The Foundations of Science* (1946). Also valuable for the emergence of modern physics, and more recent, is G. J. Holton, *Einstein and the Cultural Roots of Modern Science* (1997).

On the history of psychology, see the very readable book by C. P. Bankart, *Talking Cures: A History of Western and Eastern Psychotherapies* (1996), which sets the different traditions in their cultural contexts. A good study of one of the founders of modern psychology is R. B. Perry, *Thought and Character of William James* (1935). The key work by a founder of modern anthropology is F. Boas, *Mind of Primitive Man* (1911), while a foundational work of modern linguistics is available as *Saussure's First Course of Lectures on General Linguistics (1907): From the Notebooks of Albert Riedlinger*, ed. E. Komatsu and G. Wolf (1996). For those willing to tackle one of the hardest of twentieth-century philosophers, L. Wittgenstein, *Philosophical Investigations*, translated by G. E. M. Anscombe (1953) is accessible.

On the influence of Western science beyond the West, a number of fine works are available. E. H. Hume, *Doctors East, Doctors West: An American Physician's Life in China* (1949) is a first-hand account of the meeting of medical cultures, from which the story that opens the chapter comes. Li Yan and Du Shiran, *Chinese Mathematics: A Concise History* (1987), trans. by J. N. Crossley and A. W. C. Lun, and L. A. Orleans, ed., *Science in Contemporary China* (1980) both illuminate the influence of Western science in China, while J. Reardon-Anderson, *The Study of Change: Chemistry in China 1840–1949* (1991) examines the crucial transitional period of Chinese contact with Western learning. D. Arnold, *Science, Technology, and Medicine in Colonial India* (2000) does the same for the subcontinent, as does L. Pyenson, *Empire of Reason: Exact Science in Indonesia, 1840–1940* (1997) for Southeast Asia. E. Ihsanoglu, *Science, Technology and Learning in the Ottoman Empire: Western Influence, Local Institutions, and the Transfer of Knowledge* (2004) traces in detail the routes and methods of the transmission of Western science into the Ottoman world. A. B. Zahlan, *Science and Science Policy in the Arab World* (1980) brings elements of that story into recent times. *The Political Economy of Health in Africa* (1991) ed. by T. Falola and D. Ityavyar, brings us into sub-Saharan Africa and back to medicine as a crucial vector of the spread of Western science globally.

P. Conrad, *Modern Times Modern Places* (1999) is a sophisticated analysis of modern art globally as a reflection of changing social and cultural trends. The iconoclastic J. Waller, *Fabulous Science* (2002) debunks many scientific myths. W. Hung, ed, *Chinese Art at the Crossroads* (1991), examines the challenges posed by modernity to historical artistic traditions with specific attention to China.

D. Edgerton, *The Shock of the Old* (2006) is brilliantly revisionist on technology. T. Judt, *Postwar* (2006) helps explain the context of the new humanism.

CHAPTER 28

World Order and Disorder: Global Politics in the Twentieth Century

▲ **1931: News of the Manchurian Incident** flashes around the globe, as imagined by the brilliant Belgian cartoonist, Hergé. The Japanese propaganda version of the incident was false. Rogue Japanese agents, not Chinese "bandits," had blown up the railway track, and there were no casualties. The cartoon strip's boy hero, Tintin, discovers the truth and becomes entangled in the Japanese invasion of China for which the incident was a pretext.
© Hergé/Moulinsart 2006.

In the Manchuria of the 1920s and 1930s, the brothels in the city of Harbin were not merely, or even primarily, places of vice, but they resembled clubs, where the regular clients became friends and met each other. The Russian journalist Aleksandr Pernikoff frequented a brothel called Tayama's, which was Japanese owned and flew the Japanese flag. At the time, Manchuria was part of the sovereign territory of China, but Tayama's displayed signs of the gradually increasing level of Japanese infiltration. The Chinese government—run by the nationalist, republican party known as the Guomindang (gwoh-meen-dohng)—rightly suspected Japan of plotting to seize Manchuria, detach it from China, and turn it into part of the Japanese Empire.

On September 19, 1931, Pernikoff arrived at Tayama's as usual, crossing the seven-foot high fence of rough boards that screened the windows of the brothel from the street. The door was opened not by the regular attendant but by a clean-shaven, scholarly looking Japanese man with gold-rimmed glasses. As he shook hands with his friends, Pernikoff became aware of the tension in the atmosphere:

> "What's all this about?" Pernikoff whispered.
> "Didn't you hear?" replied one of the men. During the night, he explained, the Japanese had seized the Manchurian capital of Shenyang and "exterminated the Guomindang vermin," on the alleged grounds that the Chinese "tried to blow up a Japanese train near Shenyang."
> "Did they blow it up?" asked Pernikoff.
> "No," answered the man, with a crooked half-smile. "The mine went off after the train had passed. But the Japanese troops were ready and waiting—they occupied the town within thirty minutes after the explosion."
> "How did they know it was going to happen?"
> "You're a fool! The mine was set wrong. . . . The Japanese expected it to wreck the train and create a proper turmoil. That's why there wasn't a single Jap on the train. Clean work," he added with admiration. A Japanese member of the brothel's clientele, who—Pernikoff now realized—was really a secret agent, gathering intelligence on his fellow clients, rose to read out the official Japanese report of the incident. "Chinese bandits" had tried to blow up the train. Fortunately, a Japanese officer, who happened to be nearby, "being a samurai, knelt in the direction of Japan and humbly invoked the help of Amaterasu, the Sun Goddess, the divine ancestress of all Japanese." Miraculously, "by divine intervention," although thrust "up into the air" by the force of the explosion, the train descended back onto the rails, resumed its journey, and reached its destination without loss. "All of us in the room," wrote Pernikoff, "felt uneasy at hearing this childish account."
> "What will happen now?" he asked.
> "War."

MANCHURIA

FOCUS questions

How did the world wars weaken Europe's global dominance?

Why were totalitarian and authoritarian regimes so numerous and widespread during the twentieth century?

How did the United States become the world's only superpower?

Why did the Soviet Union collapse?

How did decolonization affect Asia and Africa?

Why did democracy spread around the world in the late twentieth century?

Are the European Union and China likely to become superpowers in the twenty-first century?

This episode, known to historians as the **Manchurian Incident**, was the first in a series of crises that Japanese militants manufactured over the next six years—not always with the knowledge or approval of their own government. Usually, rogue elements in the army, who conspired to force militaristic and expansionist policies on the rulers in Tokyo, contrived the incidents and began the violence that always followed them. The first results were to sever Manchuria from China and convert it into Manchukuo, a Japanese puppet monarchy. Then, in 1937, full-scale war broke out, and Japan began a long and tenacious attempt to conquer China and rule it as a subject territory (see Map 28.1).

It was a titanic conflict between states that history seemed to have earmarked to be contenders for global power. China was still by far the world's most populous country, needing only good government and a modernized economy to resume its traditional role as a superpower. Japan at the time had Asia's only industrial economy and was the only Asian state that European and American diplomats classed as a great power. Japanese motivation was simple. War was a preemptive strike, before China became too strong and outclassed all rivals.

The war in China dragged on until 1945. The Japanese occupied much of the country and set up a puppet regime in Beijing but could never eradicate resistance. The conflict escalated, merged with other struggles, and became part of a world war in which all the world's potential superpowers—Japan, China, the United States, Russia, and Germany—were locked, together with the British, French, and Dutch Empires and most of the other sovereign states that then existed.

The war was part of a long series of global conflicts. Catastrophically violent and destructive warfare punctuated the first half of the century. A **Cold War** between ideologically opposed antagonists dominated most of the second half, waged in local or regional conflicts and in economic, diplomatic, and ideological competition.

We can follow the story of politics in the twentieth century along a path picked between these struggles. To make space for the enduringly important cultural and environmental history of the century, we need to try to tell the political story briefly, rather than dwelling, as textbooks usually do, on the many twists and turns, and the forgettable statesmen and generals whose effects on their times were slight, and whose legacy—mercifully, in most cases—has not lasted. In the pages that follow, we divide the century roughly into three periods: first, that of the world wars, which ended in 1945; then, the so-called Cold War era of superpower confrontation that began as world war ended, continued for most of the rest of the century, and entered a new phase, dominated by the global breakup of European empires, in the 1960s. Finally, toward the end of the century, a "new world order" arose, as the United States outstripped, outgunned, or outlasted rivals.

The story foreshadows, but does not include, the end of Western world hegemony. Western initiatives—influences that originated in Europe and the United States—continued to dominate global history throughout the conflicts of the century. When the Sino-Japanese War began, China seemed, to people in Europe, a minor theater of conflict. In 1939, the British writers W. H. Auden and Christopher Isherwood abandoned their journalistic assignments to cover the war in China as soon as they received news of the deteriorating situation in Europe. They emigrated to the United States, shifting their focus amid an impending conflict that seemed more relevant to them and more vital to the world.

THE WORLD WAR ERA, 1914–1945

One way to understand Japan's conflict with China in the twentieth century is as a sort of civil war within a single civilization, between peoples who shared many values and had overlapping legacies of thought, religion, and art. That, indeed, was how Japanese usually represented the conflict to themselves—as a decisive struggle to determine which country would be the "big brother" and which the "little brother" in a future common empire, or, as Japanese propagandists said, the Great East Asia Co-Prosperity Sphere.

The European conflicts that merged with this intra-Asian war, and that spread beyond Europe itself to become a global war, had similar characteristics. At first, in the episode known as World War I, from 1914 to 1918, national and imperial rivalries triggered hostilities. The European powers disagreed about little except how to distribute power and territory among themselves. Ideological differences only took over after the war had begun. To the great question of which country would dominate Europe, the war raised another, greater question: which ideology would dominate Europe? Would the common culture of European peoples in the future be religious or secular, liberal or authoritarian, capitalist or socialist, individual or collective? And which particular forms of those choices would prevail as fascist, communist, and democratic states fought one another?

MAP 28.1

Japanese expansion, 1875–1936

- Japanese territory, 1910
- Spheres of influence by 1918
- Japanese treaty ports
- occupied by 1936

World War I

When the struggles began in 1914, all the belligerent states had more or less the same ideology. Except for France, they were all monarchies. They were all nationalistic and imperialistic. Although most were not democratic, they all had constitutions and parliaments, and they all aspired to mobilize the allegiance of their peoples. They also all used the same rhetoric of chivalry, idealism, and crusade.

Yet for each of the countries involved in World War I, the conflict embodied Clausewitz's statement that war was a "continuation of politics by other means" (see Chapter 26). For Germany, it was an attempt to resolve two obsessions: first, to strike a preemptive blow against Russia, before industrialization and rearmament turned that country into a superpower; second, to break out of maritime containment by Britain, for Germany's only access to the ocean highways lay through narrow seas easily policed by British naval power. For France, the war was an attempt to wreak revenge on Germany for the humiliation it had suffered and the territory it had lost in their last war in 1870–1871. For Britain, it was an exercise in traditional British grand strategy: pinning down a world-imperial rival—Germany—in a continental war.

For the old, multinational, Habsburg Empire of Austria-Hungary, striving to contain restless and violent national minorities, war was a desperate act of impatience with Serbian subversion, which threatened to detach the empire's southern, Slavic provinces. "Better an end with terror than terror without end" became a common saying in Vienna, the Habsburg capital, in the last years before the war. For Italy, the objective was frontier snatching at Austria's expense. For the Ottoman

A trench with wounded and dead, June 1915, on the Western Front in northern France during World War I. The apparently unposed photograph is shocking because of the standing soldiers' apathetic acceptance of the plight of their wounded comrade in the foul, brutalizing environment of the trenches.

Empire, fearing Russian expansion, it was a miscalculated gamble to risk survival on an alliance with Germany. For the Russian czar, war in defense of fellow Slavs in the Balkans was an obligation of honor. "For Serbia," he said, "we shall do anything." His ministers also feared that Germany had "a gigantic plan of world domination" that it was vital to preempt. War broke out in August 1914 when Serbia refused to accept responsibility for the actions of a Serbian terrorist band that had assassinated the heir to the Austrian throne, with Germany supporting Austria and Russia hastening to Serbia´s defense.

For all the major belligerents, the war went wrong. On the western front in northern France and Belgium, the rival armies—French, British, and Belgians on one side, Germans on the other—got stuck in the mud in long trenches that stretched from the English Channel to the Swiss border and that could be neither outflanked nor penetrated. In the east, Germans, Austrians, and Turks collided blunderingly with Russians in the vastness of the terrain. In the Alps, Italians hurled themselves futilely against Austrians who occupied the higher ground. In the Balkans, Germany, Austria, and Bulgaria overran Serbia and Romania, but those conquests and Greece's intervention on the Allied side had little effect on the outcome of the war. The elites who had started the war could not control its course or its costs.

Russia dropped out in revolution and disorder toward the end of 1917—the first of the major belligerents to collapse under the strain. Germany could therefore switch its main effort to the western front. The balance of forces, however, was already shifting decisively against the Germans, for in April 1917, the United States joined the fray.

This was a surprising development. If the war was essentially a European dispute, it was—many, perhaps most, Americans felt—no business of America's. It made sense for Americans to stick to peace and take the profits it offered. This policy, known as **isolationism**, was, however, gradually becoming impractical in the years leading up to World War I. By the end of the nineteenth century, Western Europe and North America were growing increasingly like each other. Britain, Spain, France, Austria, and Norway were all roughly as democratic, at least in terms of their franchise, as the United States, or more so, considering the racist laws that prevented black people and other minorities from voting in large parts of the United States. Meanwhile, the United States and, to a lesser extent, Canada, while remaining big producers of raw materials, had copied the manufacturing and industrial economies of Western Europe. With the official closing of the American frontier in the 1890s, America lost the appearance of a pioneer country. "Uncle Sam," in the language of the British press, had become "Brother Jonathan, a power among the powers."

America might have favored the Germans. There was a big German lobby as well as millions of German immigrants inside the United States. The British Empire was a rival that Americans viewed with traditional distaste—and many Irish Americans detested—and had no particular reason to help. But Britain was America's biggest creditor and trading partner. Germany, meanwhile, offended against two of America's pet values: peaceful problem solving and freedom of the seas. Faced with British superiority in warships, Germany had forced the pace of the arms race in the years leading up to the war by building an enormous navy. Squeezed between France and Russia, the Germans practiced militarism partly as a survival technique. In consequence, rightly or wrongly, Americans tended to see Germany as the greater threat and the more alien society. Once war in Europe broke out, Britain continued to command the Atlantic and to place huge orders for war material with American industry, while Germany had to resort to submarine warfare—which, being sneaky and secretive, offended American sensibilities—to unblock access to its own ports and damage British commerce. Since 1915, German submarines had occasionally sunk American merchant ships that traded with Britain. The Germans had always backed down in the face of American protests but in 1917 announced that their submarines would engage in unrestricted sinking of ships sailing in British waters. By then, the United States was already looking for a pretext to join the war against Germany. Intervention was decisive, because no other belligerent could match America's power. By 1914, American industrial output was nearly equal to that of the whole of Europe combined.

The United States did not enter the war to serve its allies. Indeed, it refused to become a formal ally and instead called itself an "associated power." It went to war to meet an American agenda: to crush militarism, free the seas, weaken European empires, lift American debts, consolidate America's growing superiority in wealth, liberate the Eastern European homelands of million of American citizens, and make the world safe for democracy. But the war was a unifying process for the powers that joined each other across the Atlantic. Three million Americans had the transforming experience of serving in Europe. "How ya gonna keep 'em down on the farm," a popular song inquired, "now that they've seen Par-ee?" Three of the world's most powerful, resourceful, and predatory states—the United States, Britain, and France—were now in partnership. The rest of the world faced a source of cultural influence of peculiar force.

America had a chance to reshape the politics of the world. World War I was a crucible in which the world seemed to dissolve, awaiting an alchemist to reforge it in a better form. The war destroyed states, elites, empires, and traditional ways of life. Almost 10 million men died in action. There were 25 million casualties in all (see Figure 28.1). Nine million tons of shipping sank. The statistics concealed the real depths of the destruction. The war wiped out a generation of the natural leaders of Europe. That in itself ensured disruption and discontinuity in European history. The war ended by provoking political revolution or transformation wherever its armies marched. Twelve new sovereign, or virtually sovereign, states emerged in Europe or on its borders (see Map 28.2). Superstates were demolished, frontiers reshuffled, overseas colonies swiveled and swapped. The Russian, German, Austro-Hungarian, and Ottoman empires were felled at a stroke. Even the United Kingdom lost a limb, when revolution and civil war broke out in Ireland in 1916 and ended with, in effect, independence for most of the island in 1922. Huge migrations redistributed peoples. After the war, more than one million Turks and Greeks shunted to safety across the newly drawn borders of their mutually hostile states.

President Woodrow Wilson (1856–1924) appreciated the opportunity and rose to the challenge. He rejected imperialism (except in the Western Hemisphere where the United States continued to intervene whenever and wherever it felt its interests were threatened). His country made its last permanent acquisition of territory

FIGURE 28.1 TOTAL CASUALTIES IN THE FIRST WORLD WAR.

Country	Dead	Wounded	Total Killed as a Percentage of Population
France	1,398,000	2,000,000	3.4
Belgium	38,000	44,700	0.5
Italy	578,000	947,000	1.6
British Empire	921,000	2,090,000	1.7
Romania	250,000	120,000	3.3
Serbia	278,000	133,000	5.7
Greece	26,000	21,000	0.5
Russia	1,811,000	1,450,000	1.1
Bulgaria	88,000	152,000	1.9
Germany	2,037,000	4,207,000	3.0
Austria-Hungary	1,100,000	3,620,000	1.9
Turkey	804,000	400,000	3.7
United States	114,000	206,000	0.1

Niall Ferguson, The Pity of War *(New York: Basic Books, 1998).*

MAP 28.2

Europe, the Middle East, and North Africa in 1914 and 1923

Europe, the Middle East, and North Africa, 1914

Europe, the Middle East, and North Africa, 1923

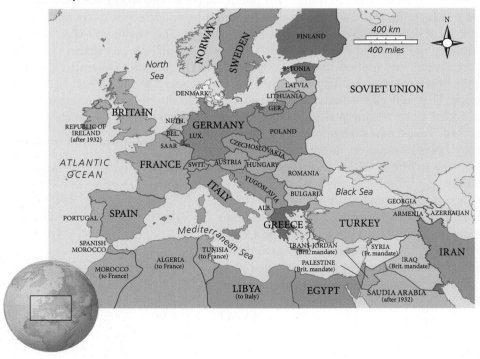

(three of the Virgin Islands in the Caribbean) shortly before entering the war by buying them from Denmark. Wilson also did his best to discourage the imperialism of his allies, though France, Britain, and Italy took little notice, carving up captured German, Turkish, and Austrian territories among themselves. Wilson further insisted, within Europe, on "self-determination" for the peoples of the collapsed empires of Russia, Germany, Austria-Hungary, and Turkey. New nations sprang into being or reemerged at the rhythm of a State Department typewriter: first, what Wilson called

"Czecho-slovakia," then "Jugo-slavia," Poland, Finland, Estonia, Latvia, and Lithuania.

On the other hand, the claims of Ukraine, Georgia, Armenia, Belarus, the Kurds, and the Muslim peoples of the Russian Empire were ignored. In Africa, the belligerents swapped colonies, with no thought for self-determination. The aspirations of the Arab subjects of the Ottoman Empire were patchily treated. A leader of anti-Ottoman resistance in Arabia, Sharif Husayn (1856–1931), proclaimed himself king of the Arabs in 1917, with popular support, but the British and French divided much of his territory between them. They left only what are now Jordan and Iraq to his heirs, and allowed a disaffected Islamist chieftain, Ibn Saud (1880–1953), to conquer what is now Saudi Arabia in 1924–1925. Meanwhile, in what is now Libya, rebels against the Italians who had seized the country from the Ottomans in 1911–1912 proclaimed an Arab republic in 1918, but Italy suppressed them shortly afterward. From 1917, moreover, the British outraged Arabs by following—albeit half-heartedly—the policy of setting aside formerly Arab land in Palestine as what they called a "national homeland" for the persecuted Jews of Europe.

For Turkey itself, the loss of empire seemed a relief. The new, secular Turkish republic, founded by the war-hero Mustafa Kemal in 1923 (he later took the surname Atatürk, meaning "Father of the Turks"), had universal male suffrage in 1924 and women there had the right to vote from 1934. Atatürk uprooted the capital from Istanbul to new ground at Ankara in the middle of Anatolia. He made Friday, the Muslim Sabbath, a workday, imposed the Roman alphabet on a language formerly written in Arabic characters, and founded an opera, a university, and a symphony orchestra. That Turkey remained overwhelmingly Muslim still made it seem exotic to Western outsiders, but Atatürk's success inspired secular nationalists in other parts of the Muslim world. In neighboring Iran, for instance, an army strongman, Riza Khan (REH-zah hahn), seized power in 1925, proclaimed himself shah, and imitated, on a more modest scale, Atatürk's secularizing policies, abolishing the veil for women and banning Islamic religious schools.

Finally, as a result of World War I, the balance of power, which had failed to guarantee peace, would give way to a new order of international cooperation that a global institution, the **League of Nations**, would regulate. President Wilson proposed the League as a forum to resolve international disputes peacefully. Taken together, these initiatives promised a reformed world, which, had it worked, would have been better—more peaceful, more stable, more just—than the world the First World War destroyed. But the United States Senate rejected Wilson's vision and refused to ratify the treaty that would have permitted America to join the League. Americans had no taste for world leadership. The costs of the Great War, in blood and treasure, had been enough for them (even though, compared to the losses European armies suffered, relatively few Americans had been killed in the war, and the United States emerged from it the richest nation in the world.) When America retreated into isolation, the new world order was doomed.

Or perhaps it was doomed anyway. The treaties the Allies imposed left too many dissatisfied states. German resentment was massive and unyielding. Germany had been barely defeated, but, after it sued for peace in November 1918, the victors treated it with contempt: subject to huge reparations, loss of territory, and partial occupation by French armies, with humiliating restrictions on the right to rearm. It was also forced to

Arab delegates. When the Ottoman Empire entered World War I on the side of Germany, the Allies determined to carve it up. As part of that effort, they promoted Arab efforts to secure independence. Delegates to the Paris Peace Conference of 1919–1920, which ratified the dismemberment of the Ottoman Empire, included British Colonel T. E. Lawrence ("Lawrence of Arabia"), who helped lead the Arab rebellion, and representatives from the Mideast. Prince Faisal, whom the British were to make king of Iraq in 1921, stands in the foreground. Lawrence is second from the right in the middle row, demonstrating his Arab credentials by wearing traditional Bedouin headgear.

Chronology: World War I, 1914–1920	
1914	United States industrial production equal to whole of Europe combined
August 1914	World War I begins
1915	Mohandas K. Gandhi, leader of Indian independence movement, returns to India from South Africa
1917	Russian Revolution begins; United States enters World War I
November 1918	World War I ends
1919	First meeting of Pan-African Congress
1919–1920	Paris peace conference

Gassed. Poison gas was ineffective on the battlefield during World War I, but it symbolized the nature of technologically "advanced" weaponry: inhuman and undiscriminating. Except in the U.S. cinema, wartime artists almost entirely abandoned heroic images in favor of scenes of horror. Blindness and blundering—as here in John Singer Sargent's painting *Gassed*—became metaphors for the misconduct and incompetence of political and military leaders.

John Singer Sargent (1856–1925), "Gassed, an Oil Study". 1918–19 Oil on Canvas. Private Collection. Imperial War Museum, Negative Number Q1460

"In the long run, perhaps, the big effects of the postwar settlement were on morale and changed expectations for the future. For those who took part in it, the war was an experience of unmatched horror."

accept sole guilt for causing the war. Italy remained discontented that its heavy casualties had been rewarded with only modest territorial gains. Japan, meanwhile, which had joined the Allies in 1914 expecting a free hand in East Asia, felt let down by them. Russia, stripped of its traditional influence over Eastern Europe, was excluded from any real say in the postwar settlement and looked for ways to unpick it. Most of the newly erected nation-states were raggedly hemmed with irrational borders that included large, resentful national minorities that caused conflict among neighbors. For example, besides Czechs and Slovaks, Czechoslovakia included Germans, Hungarians, Ukrainians, and Poles, none of whom were happy to be in the new state. The new kingdom of Yugoslavia was dominated by Serbs, to the simmering discontent of its Croat, Slovene, Albanian, Macedonian, and Muslim Bosnian subjects. Even with American participation, it is doubtful whether the League of Nations could have sorted out this mass of mutual resentments. As it was, the League was useless, its representatives—in the words of an English comedian—turning up for meetings "in taxis that were empty."

In the long run, perhaps, the big effects of the postwar settlement were on morale and changed expectations for the future. For those who took part in it, the war was an experience of unmatched horror. The men who marched away expected another war like those of nineteenth-century Europe: short, with opportunities for heroism. What they got was more than four years of suffering of an intensity never known before. Soldiers on the western front spent weeks or months on end in filthy trenches, contending with rats, lice, mud, and poison gas. While they cowered underground, artillery more powerful than any the world had ever seen pounded their dugouts. When they went over the top of the trenches to attack, they faced machine guns and died, or watched their comrades die, in the millions. Experiences too terrible to confide to loved ones back home became secret neuroses. Shell shock was the characteristic mental disease among the demobilized soldiery of the postwar years. The battlefield became soulless, desolate, a blasted, blackened, barbed-wired Golgotha. Tanks displaced cavalry. Machines crushed life out of the landscape and chivalry out of war. The soldiers' feelings of alienation were foreseen and captured in the awesomely strident music of the British composer, Gustav Holst (1874–1934). The war destroyed "even the survivors" of battle, said the German writer Erich-Maria Remarque (1898–1970) in *All Quiet on the Western Front*, the most influential of all the war-born novels and memoirs.

Postwar Disillusionment

Optimism, however, survived in other places—especially where people resented the power of European empires. The war was a collective humiliation for Europe in the eyes of the world, for only American intervention had seemed to be able to end the bloody stalemate. The United States was revealed as unquestionably the world's leading power. Japan emerged more dominant than ever in East Asia and the western Pacific, where it mopped up formerly German-owned islands and naval bases in China. Almost before the gun smoke had cleared, nationalist movements, directed against European imperialists, got under way in India, Indonesia, Egypt, Indochina, and parts of sub-Saharan Africa. In Dutch-controlled Indonesia in 1916, the group known as Sarekat Islam mobilized a mass movement for self-government. At its 1919 congress, it claimed to have 2 million members. The Pan-African Congress, which claimed to represent all black Africans under European colonial rule, met for the first time in 1919 to demand that Africans play a part in governing their own countries "as soon as their development permits." In the same year, the Egyptian Wafd or Nationalist Party was founded to pressure the British into leaving.

In India in the same year, amid riots against the continuation of strict wartime police measures, the British authorities effectively suspended civil liberties. Mohandas K. Gandhi (1869–1948), who had made a reputation before the war in South Africa as a spokesman for the rights of oppressed black Africans and Indian migrants there, emerged as leader of the protests. He launched a movement he called **satyagraha**—literally, "the force of truth"—relying not on violence but on "passive disobedience": strikes, fasts, boycotts, and demonstrations against British rule. Other protesters derailed trains, clashed with police, and cut telegraph wires. The British responded nervously. In Amritsar in northern India, troops fired on demonstrators "to teach," their commander said, "a moral lesson": 379 unarmed people were killed and 1,200 wounded. Britain's hold on popular sentiment in India, such as it was, deteriorated rapidly after that. Gandhi's optimism was only briefly dented. "Just wait for the next European war," cried a character in the 1924 novel, *A Passage to India*, by the scholarly English liberal, E. M. Forster, who had been to India and knew the mood there. Much of the Indian intelligentsia was indeed looking forward to dismantling Western hegemony and dismembering Western empires.

In the euphoria of peace, even some Western politicians were free with optimistic rhetoric. The war would "end all wars." Its survivors would return to "homes fit for heroes." The year after the war ended, the architect Walther Gropius (1883–1969) founded an art school in Weimar, where Germany's new republican constitution had been written in 1919, to create built environments that would be both works of art and "would arise toward heaven from the hands of a million workers." The West would climb back out of its dugout. Progress would resume. The British writer H. G. Wells published his *Outline of History* in praise of progress in 1920. The destruction pleased, at least, those formerly excluded from the prewar order: the poor, the previously suppressed nations, men—and women—who had been denied the right to vote, the political radicals and extremists. As we have seen (see Chapter 27), some artists reveled in the wreckage of the battlefield. President Wilson also spoke with the voice of optimism. Almost as soon as the war ended, he went to Manchester in Britain to foretell an age "not perhaps golden, but brightening."

In America, where no fighting took place, this story was believable, at first. But war-scarred Europe found it hard to match this mood. Europeans were already becoming convinced of the imminent "decline of the West"—the title of the postwar blockbuster by the German historian Oswald Spengler. For those who could

Gandhi as he wished to be seen. He squats in a traditional position for Indian mystics, working calmly in a scholarly, reflective manner. His gaunt body, modest loincloth, and simply furnished home proclaim his selflessness and asceticism. He adopted a spinning wheel as the symbol of his movement for Indian independence to signify tradition, patience, constructiveness, self-sufficiency, and peace.

afford it, the 1920s in Europe were an age of desperate pleasure seeking—what England's wittiest songwriter, Noel Coward, called "twentieth-century blues." For the rest, it was a time to try to salvage something from disillusionment. The results included labor unrest, extremist politics, welfare efforts crippled by economic failures, and impoverishing inflation.

Disillusionment hit America later. The war made the United States economy boom. After short-term dislocations of the peace, Americans enjoyed "seven fat years" from 1922 to 1929. Millionaire "titans" of business and industry bestrode corporate "pyramids" of millions of share owners. A spiraling stock market seemed to promise literally universal riches. In 1924, a total of 282 million shares of stock changed hands on Wall Street. In 1929, that figure rose to 1.824 billion. That same year, the crash came. In three weeks, beginning on October 24, American stocks fell in value by $30 billion (almost $400 billion in today's money)—equivalent almost to the entire cost of America's war effort. The effects ricocheted off the rich, bounced the economy into recession, bounded across the Atlantic, and set off a string of bank failures. Meanwhile, ecological disaster—part of the subject of Chapter 30—struck farms in the American West. "Brother, can you spare a dime?" sang crooners in the character of a war hero down on his luck. Economic depression was hard to take in communities that had become used to the accumulating prosperity of economic growth. Hollywood did wonders for Americans' morale, spinning celluloid stories of riches to rags, rags to riches.

Disillusionment afflicted parts of Latin America particularly deeply, because expectations there were so enormous. Argentina, Chile, Uruguay, Mexico, and Brazil were all self-styled lands of promise. For a while in the early twentieth century, Argentina was the world's most desired destination for migrants. In 1914, nearly a third of its population was of foreign birth—Italians, Spaniards, Germans, Britons, Slavs. The oath of allegiance schoolchildren recited proclaimed Argentina "the finest country on Earth." But after booming during World War I, Latin America's economies went into dramatic reverse after the war when European and United States demand plummeted for the raw materials the region produced. Violent changes of government ensued. In 1930, army officers ousted elected politicians and seized power or installed "emergency" governments with dictatorial powers in Argentina, Peru, and Bolivia. Guatemala, the Dominican Republic, and El Salvador followed suit over the next couple of years.

In the 1920s, Mexico experienced the end of more than a decade of conflict and chaos—"a whirlwind in which," people said, "the dirt came up," as young, violent, macho leaders seized the country, or parts of it (see Chapter 29). Now, as the people recoiled from violence, well-educated professionals took over and decreed that revolution was "institutionalized"—a discreet way of saying it was over. Their political heirs would rule the country until 2000.

The economic disasters of Europe and the Americas in the 1920s and 1930s seemed to show that the West was wormwood. The rot went deeper than the corrosive international politics that caused wars and blighted peace. It was an age of fault-finding with Western civilization. Some of the things people blamed were so fantastic as to be rationally incredible—yet impoverished and miserable millions were ready to believe the rabble-rousers' claims and were susceptible to the appeal of "noisy little men" proposing easy and even "final" solutions. Anti-Semites, for instance, blamed Jews, who, they claimed to believe, controlled the world's economies and exploited gentiles for their own enrichment. Advocates of eugenics claimed that unscientific breeding weakened society by encouraging "inferior" classes and races and "feeble" or "mentally defective" individuals to have children who would be as weak and useless as their parents.

"The Pillars of Society," according to the German artist Georg Grosz (1893-1959), were force, fear, and folly, represented in this cartoon by evil-looking soldiers, a noxious inquisitor (whose welcoming gesture ushers us toward a grid of fire), and bourgeois politicians, journalists, and industrialists, who are shown as shallow and empty-headed, or capped with a pot of human feces.
George Grosz (1893–1959), "Stuetzen der Gesellschaft (Pillars of Society)". 1926. Oil on canvas, 200,0 x 108,0 cm. Inv.: NG 4/58. Photo: Joerg P. Anders. Nationalgalerie, Staatliche Museen zu Berlin, Berlin, Germany. Art © Estate George Grosz/Licensed by VAGA, New York, New York.

According to the most widespread analysis, the fault lay with what people called "the system." Capitalism did not work. Marx's predictions seemed to be coming true. The poor were getting poorer. The failures of capitalism would drive them to revolution. Democracy was a disaster. Only authoritarian governments could force people to collaborate for the common good. Perhaps only totalitarian governments, extending their responsibility over every department of life, including the production and distribution of goods, could deliver justice.

Broadly speaking, there were three ways to approach the problems. First, people who still believed in democracy and capitalism thought the system could be reformed from within. The English economist, J. M. Keynes (1883–1946), advocated the most persuasive program. Governments could tweak the distribution of wealth through taxation and public spending, without seriously weakening enterprise or infringing freedom. Well-judged interventions of this sort would stimulate the economy without overstoking inflation (see Chapter 29). Britain, France, and Scandinavia successfully adopted this kind of solution to economic depression. So did President Franklin D. Roosevelt (1887–1945) in the United States. Federal debt nearly doubled to over $40 billion in the 6 years of his peacetime administration (1933–1939).

"The economic disasters of Europe and the Americas in the 1920s and 1930s seemed to show that the West was wormwood. The rot went deeper than the corrosive international politics that caused wars and blighted peace. It was an age of fault-finding with Western civilization."

The Shift to Ideological Conflicts

The two other approaches were authoritarian or totalitarian. The right-wing or *corporatist* solution was to allow private enterprise to continue to contribute to the economy, but only on the understanding that individual rights, freedoms, and property were not to be allowed to exist for their own sake, but were at the service and disposal of the state. The state would force all citizens to collaborate in the collective effort and coerce or, in extreme versions of the doctrine, exterminate any groups thought to resist the common pursuit. Left-wing versions proposed to collectivize virtually all economic activity, seizing most private property and, if necessary, eliminating "class enemies." This would end exploitation and have a morally, as well as economically, improving effect. The other main difference between right and left was that the right was unashamedly nationalist, whereas the left proclaimed internationalism, at least in its rhetoric. The left was divided between those—usually called *anarchists*—who wanted collectives of workers to run economic activities, and *communists*, who wanted the state to own and control all production, distribution, and exchange.

Long-accumulating class hatreds underlay ideological differences. In the years before the war, European elites talked themselves into expecting a showdown with the working class. Workers' demonstrations kindled fear and provoked massacres, painted in the early twentieth century in Barcelona in Spain by Ramon Casas and in Russia by Ilya Repin. The elation of middle-class onlookers, in feather-trimmed hats, fur muffs, and stiff collars, echoed the screams of peaceful petitioners shot by Russian troops. On the eve of war in August 1914, the British Foreign Secretary Sir Edward Grey predicted, "There will be socialist governments everywhere after this."

Such predictions were exaggerated. The first and, for a long time, the only successful revolution was hardly a workers' triumph. The Bolshevik uprising in Russia of October (or November, by the Western calendar) 1917 was a well-planned coup, which elevated a party—the Communist Party—to the role of an aristocracy, and charismatic dictators—first Vladimir Ilyich Lenin (1870–1924), then Josef Stalin

Workers' demonstration. The Spanish painter Ramon Casas (1866–1932) specialized in meticulously painted scenes of bourgeois life of his native Barcelona, but he could also play the role of a social commentator. In 1902 he exhibited this scene of police dispersing a crowd of striking workers against a backdrop of gaunt factories. In the sky, there is gold beyond the industrial smog and perhaps a patch of hope.

Indonesian communists. In 1925, when this photograph was taken in Batavia (now Jakarta), the Indonesian Communist Party had just launched a new policy of armed insurrection, after a series of unsuccessful strikes and a growing sense of desperation, as the Dutch authorities expelled its leaders. The three languages of the placard tell a story. Chinese immigrants were prominent in the movement. Malay—written here in Arabic script rather than the Roman alphabet currently preferred—was the language of the masses. The elite who ran the party, however, used Dutch. The rebellion launched the following year was another failure.

(1879–1953)—to the power of atheist czars, indeed to greater power than the czars had ever enjoyed. The country formerly known as the Russian Empire became the Union of Soviet Socialist Republics, after the Russian term for a workers' collective, although in practice the party and the state exercised control or tyranny in workplaces. Over the next few years, attempts to launch copycat revolutions were defeated in Finland, Germany, Hungary, Bulgaria, and Italy. Socialists made compromises with bourgeois rulers, often submitting to domestication and political collaboration as the price of a share of power. But left-wing militancy kept up the struggle. Moscow encouraged and eventually financed international communism. Communists often attached more importance to suppressing anarchists and other left-wing splinter groups than to overthrowing capitalist regimes. "Aren't we all socialists?" asked the bewildered English writer and freedom fighter, George Orwell (1903–1950), during a firefight between communists and anarchists in Barcelona in 1938. It was like asking, "Aren't we all Christians?" at the Massacre of St. Bartholomew's Day in 1572 when French Catholics had killed French Protestants in Paris. It may seem odd that leftists fought each other under the guns of their common enemies, but it is worth remembering that most of them accepted the Marxist dogma that revolution was inevitable. For the communists it was more important to ensure their own leadership of the revolution than to provoke it prematurely (see Map 28.3).

Even in some places beyond Europe, in the 1920s and 1930s, conflicts over power were increasingly seen as clashes of classes or ideological showdowns. In China, for instance, the main contending parties called themselves Nationalist and Communist. Their conflict escalated in the 1930s, despite the menace Japanese invasion posed to both of them. In Peru in the same period, rival would-be dictators adopted the language of socialism and fascism, respectively. But the "socialist," Raúl Haya de la Torre, was really an old-fashioned rouser of peasant millenarians, while his opponents were equally old-fashioned Catholic oligarchs. In parts of the British, French, and Dutch empires, rebels and malcontents identified with socialism. They saw a similarity between the plight of their own peoples, oppressed by imperialism, and the worker-victims of capitalism, many of whom they got to know when they worked or studied in the metropolitan centers of the empires to which they, unwillingly, belonged. Ho Chih Minh (1890–1969), for instance, who later led a communist revolution in Vietnam, worked as a waiter in Paris after World War I. Tan Malaka, leader of Indonesian communists, learned communism in the Netherlands after the Dutch colonial authorities expelled him from his homeland as an agitator for independence in 1922. Leopold Senghor (1906–2001), later founder of the Senegalese Socialist Party and first president of his West African country, felt drawn to socialism as a schoolteacher in France in the mid-1930s. Thus the West exported the semblance, if not the substance, of its ideological conflicts, along with so many other aspects of its culture, around the world.

Whether **fascism**—an extreme and extremely violent corporatist movement—was

Chronology: The Interwar Years, 1922–1939	
1922	Benito Mussolini's Fascist Party seizes power in Italy
1923	Turkish Republic founded
1924	Vladimir Lenin, leader of Russian Revolution dies; Josef Stalin emerges as new Soviet leader
1929	U.S. stock market crash
1930–1931	Military seizes power in Argentina, Peru, Brazil, Guatemala, El Salvador, and the Dominican Republic
1931	Japan invades Manchuria
1933	Nazis take power in Germany
1936–1939	Spanish Civil War

MAP 28.3

The Great Depression and Political Extremism in Europe, 1922–1939

Nazi or fascist regime by 1933

other right-wing regime

communist regime

more than 20% unemployment by 1932

strikes and riots during the 1930s

decrease in industrial output since 1929 (1932 figures as a percentage of 1929)

another splinter ideology of socialism has been passionately debated. Fascism could as well be classified as an independently evolved doctrine or as a state of mind in search of a doctrine. Or it could be merely a slick name for unprincipled opportunism: an agile insect, never still for long enough to swat. Stubbornly undefinable, its symbols best expressed its nature. In ancient Rome, the *fascis* was a bundle of rods with an axe through the middle of it, carried before magistrates as an emblem of their power to scourge or behead wrongdoers. Italian fascists adopted these bloodstained images of law enforcement as what we would now call their logo. They proclaimed the welts of the rod and the gash of the axe. They appealed

Argentine President Juan Perón salutes in military garb as wife Eva waves in a fur coat from the back of a convertible on a street in Buenos Aires, Argentina in June 1952, with the Ritz Hotel in the background. Despite their showiness and wealth, and the policies they championed that were candidly designed to protect capitalism from revolution, the Peróns managed to convince Argentina's "shirtless masses" that they were on their side.

to a system of values that put the group before the individual, cohesion before diversity, revenge before reconciliation, retribution before compassion, the supremacy of the strong before the defense of the weak. They justified the enforcement of order by violence and by the obstruction or obliteration of misfits, subversives, deviants, and dissenters.

When they took power, communists tended to be as ruthless as fascists. Communists persecuted and massacred class enemies. Fascists victimized or exterminated "inferior" communities and races. The German Nazis, in a conscious program of genocide, put more than 6 million people to death simply because they were Jews or Gypsies. In the Soviet Union, Stalin's campaign of extermination of small rural landowners and troublesome ethnic minorities claimed even more lives. Fascists and communists alike empowered the state at the expense of individuals and sacrificed liberty to social cohesion. Both sets of extremists shared belief in the omnipotence of the state, and built similar monuments—crushingly heavy, jarringly angular. Fascism had, perhaps, wider appeal. Advocating policies that could be summarized as socialism without the abolition of private property, fascists could mobilize small property owners from among the inflation-impoverished bourgeoisie. The cults of violence were equally characteristic of the militants of both left and right. Both extremes recruited their street armies from the same cohorts of unemployed, demobilized victims of economic slump and recession and social dislocation. The same ideals of fraternal community kept parties at both extremes together.

The politics of the twentieth century were horseshoe shaped, and the fanatics at each end seemed, in key respects, close enough to touch each other. Individuals moved between fascism and militant socialism as if through connecting doors. Benito Mussolini (1883–1945), who, as leader of the first successful Fascist Party—indeed, he coined the word *fascist*—seized power in Italy in 1922, began his political life as a socialist. The Nazi Party—whose program was essentially fascist, with a particularly virulent anti-Semitic driving force—was officially called the National Socialist German Workers' Party and campaigned for "Work and Bread." Britain's failed "man of destiny," Sir Oswald Mosley (1896–1980), was a socialist cabinet minister before he took to the streets as the leader of what he called the British Union of Fascists. Colonel Juan Perón (1895–1974), who took over Argentina in 1946 and founded a movement that remains influential there, seemed closer to fascism than socialism. He promised employers that with "workers organized by the state, revolutionary currents endangering capitalist society can be neutralized." But he was free with socialist demagoguery, a hero to trade unionists. His wife Eva (1919–1952), a former radio diva, became, in government propaganda, a proletarian goddess, "the faithful voice of the shirtless masses."

By 1933, when the Nazis took power in Germany, it was clear that in European politics, ideological defiance now transcended national hatreds. But the conflicts that followed were not straightforward struggles of left and right. Old hatreds crisscrossed the killing grounds. In some cases, liberals hunted clericalists; in others, local and regional majorities stalked racial or ethnic victims. Nationalists and imperialists gunned for liberals and separatists. Neighboring peoples indulged traditional feuds. Between 1936 and 1939, for instance, civil war in Spain seemed to project to the rest of the world images of a dress rehearsal for a global struggle of left against right. In reality, however, the fighting was between broad coalitions pursuing domestic Spanish agendas. The right-wing coalition partnered virtual fascists with awkward allies: traditional Catholics, who were defending the church against the seizure of its property; old-fashioned liberal centralists, who were equally numerous on the other side; romantic reactionaries who yearned to reinstate a long-excluded branch of the royal house; constitutional monarchists, who wanted to return to the cozy, corrupt, profitable parliamentary system of the previous generation; worshippers of "the sacred unity of Spain," who thought they were fighting to hold the country together. On the other side, along with all the mutually warring sects of the left, were conservative republicans, liberal anticlericals, admirers of French and British democratic standards, and right-wing regionalists, who, recognizing the Nationalists as the greater threat, supported the Republicans as the lesser evil.

Ideology, in any case, could still be sacrificed to national interest. The Nazi dictator, Adolf Hitler (1889–1945), regarded Jews and communists as his main enemies, but one of his chief aims, which he made no attempt to conceal, was to crush Russia and conquer an empire of "living-space" and slave labor for Germany in Eastern Europe. He never compromised with Jews, but in August 1939, he made a nonaggression pact with his communist counterpart in Russia, Josef Stalin. For both dictators, the pact was a temporary expedient. Hitler wanted to clear the ground for a knock-out war against France and Britain to free himself to deal with Russia in the future. Stalin wanted to get his hands on the resources of Finland, Romania, the Baltic states, and eastern Poland to fortify his country against enemies farther west and re-create as much of the czarist empire as he could.

The pact was a disaster for the peace of the world. By neutralizing Germany's main foe, it wrecked the Western democracies' strategy for containing Hitler. Britain and France had attempted to buy time for their own rearmament by conceding a series of demands Hitler made and ignoring a series of his provocations. Beginning in 1934, Hitler disregarded agreed restrictions on the size of German armed forces, built up a massive military regime, and reoccupied demilitarized parts of Germany. Then he forced German-Austrian unification, and seized most of Czechoslovakia after dispute over that country's German minority. The French and British hoped that fear of Russia would keep him in check, or, perhaps, that a war between Germany and Russia would exhaust both dictatorships. Many people in France and Britain also preferred to make almost any concession rather than risk the slaughter of another European war. The pact between Hitler and Stalin crushed those hopes and made war inevitable. The French and British had gambled that they could restrain Hitler by guaranteeing the integrity of his next target, Poland, even though geography made it impossible for them to offer Poland any effective assistance. The German invasion of Poland, launched in September 1939, plunged them into a war that they had never wanted to fight and for which, as events were to prove, their armed forces were not ready.

Hitler and Stalin. "Kem" Marengo (1907–1988), who became a major contributor to British propaganda campaigns in World War II, drew this cartoon while he was a student at the University of Oxford. He depicts the Nazi-Soviet Nonaggression Pact that was signed in August 1939 as an unworkable tie-in between partners pointing in opposite directions, compelled to share a jackboot because of their threadbare, shabby, unshod poverty, strung together like participants in a "three-legged race"—an entertainment in which the runners are tied to each other with comical results.

World War II

In Europe, World War II (1939–1945) reran aspects of World War I. This time, however, France, not Russia, crumbled, and it was on their eastern front, rather than in the west, that the Germans became stuck. Hitler overplayed his hand, turning against Russia prematurely in June 1941, without first knocking Britain out of the war. Aided by those traditional allies, "Generals January and February," and by Hitler's strategic blunders, Russia proved unconquerable. The decisive element again was American intervention—again procured against the grain of American isolationism and public unwillingness to get involved in policing the world. President Roosevelt wanted to save Europe from Hitler. Hollywood chimed in with wonderful propaganda films on behalf of the war. *Mrs. Miniver* showed plucky little Britain resisting Nazi aggression. *Casablanca*—still one of the world's favorite films—showed a wisecracking but glamorous Humphrey Bogart as an American exile in French Morocco sacrificing love for the Allied cause. In the end, Hitler made America's decision himself, declaring war in December 1941 in support of his own ally, Japan.

Japanese society, already highly militarized, had become consecrated to war in the struggle to conquer China. The conflict escalated, as Japan realized that it would have to procure the energy resources it needed to subdue China by conquering Dutch and British colonies in Southeast Asia. Such a vast extension of the Japanese Empire at other powers' expense was bound to become a global conflict. If Japan were to succeed, the United States would have to be neutralized or intimidated into standing aside. In December 1941, Japan launched a preemptive strike against the American Pacific Fleet at Pearl Harbor in Hawaii, gambling on being able to fix a deal with the Americans later when Japan was in a position of strength after having overrun Southeast Asia. The attack was a startling success, but the strategy was miscalculated. The Americans were knocked out long enough for Japanese forces to occupy French Indochina, overrun Dutch Indonesia and British Hong Kong, Malaya, and Burma, drive the United States from the Philippines and Guam, and fan out over the western Pacific. But America was enraged, Japanese forces were overstretched, and a terrible war of attrition began, in which the Americans, with help from Britain, Australia, New Zealand, and the Chinese refusal to give up, gradually thrust the Japanese back (see Map 28.4).

MAP 28.4

The Second World War, Sept 1939–Dec 1941

——	political boundaries in 1939
▨	Axis and its allies, March 1940
▨	Allies, May 1940
▨	Allies, Dec 1941
——	Axis territorial expansion, June 1940
----	Axis territorial expansion, Dec 1941
◆	Axis satellites following the German invasion of France, May 1940
▢	neutral or non-belligerent state

The war to December 1941

Sept 1939: Invasion of Poland by Germany and Soviet Union

June 1940: Italy declares war on Britain and France

June 1941: Germany invades the Soviet Union (operation Barbarossa)

Dec 1941: Japan attacks Pearl Harbor, US enters the war

Sept 1939: Britain and France declare war on Germany

June 1940: German troops enter Paris, fall of France

Jul–Oct 1940: Battle of Britain waged in air over southern England

Jul 1941: Soviet Union and Britain sign pact of mutual assistance

Dec 1941: Germany declares war on US

Jan 1940   Jan 1941   Jan 1942

America and Britain constructed a vast coalition—known informally as the Allies and officially as the United Nations—to fight or, at least, to legitimate the war. But most members of this global alliance could contribute little—in many cases because Germany or Japan occupied their national territories. In 1940, Italy joined Germany in what became known as the Axis. Mussolini gambled recklessly on a quick German victory, but his help proved more of a drag on German resources than an asset. Italians felt little solidarity with Mussolini's regime and even less enthusiasm for war. German troops became overcommitted pursuing Italian adventures in North Africa, where the British forces triumphed in 1943, and the Balkans, where fierce guerilla resistance in Yugoslavia and Greece tied the Germans down. Meanwhile, the campaign in Russia—Hitler's enemy of choice for ideological reasons—relentlessly ground down the German armies. Once American troops became available for the European front in large numbers in the Italian campaign in 1943 and, above all, with the invasion and liberation of France that began in June 1944, Allied victory in Europe became irreversible. But Hitler fought on—partly out of a fanatical refusal to surrender, partly out of hope that secret weapons would emerge from his research laboratories or that the Western Allies would fall out with the Soviet Union, and partly out of the sheer lust for destruction that was fundamental to Nazi ideology. Indeed, the Germans were able to launch terrifying new rocket bombs, the V-1s and V-2s, against Britain in 1944, but

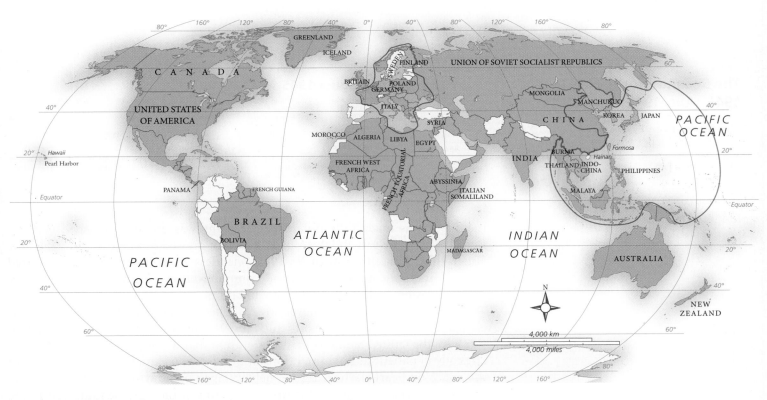

The Second World War, December 1941–July 1943

— extent of Axis powers Dec 1942

▨ Axis powers, July 1943

▨ Allies, July 1943

☐ neutral state

The war to July 1943

Feb 1942: Surrender of British forces to Japan in Singapore

Aug 1942: US bombing raids over Europe begin

Oct–Nov 1942: British defeat Germans at El Alamein

Feb 1942 | Jan 1943 | Jul 1943

Mar 1942: Dutch surrender East Indies to Japan

Sept 1942: Start of German seige of Stalingrad (ends Jan 1943)

Jan 1943: Roosevelt and Churchill meet at Casablanca

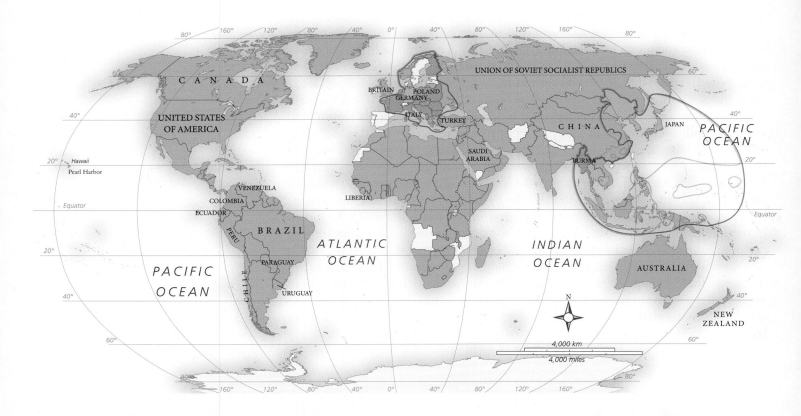

The Second World War, July 1943–Aug 1945

____ area controlled by Axis powers, July 1943

▨ countries liberated by Allied forces by Feb 1945

___ extent of Axis powers, Jan 1945

▨ Axis powers, May 1945

▨ Allies, May 1945

☐ neutral state

The war to August 1945

July 1943: Allied forces land in Sicily

Sept 1943: Italy surrenders to Allies; German forces occupy Milan and Rome

Aug 1944: Allied forces liberate Paris

Oct 1944: Battle of Leyte Gulf against Japan

May 1945: Germany surrenders

Aug 1945: Atomic bombs exploded over Hiroshima and Nagasaki

July 1943

Oct 1943: Italy declares war on Germany

Jan 1944

Nov 1943: Roosevelt, Stalin, and Churchill meet in Tehran

June 1944: D Day: Allied landings in Normandy

Jan 1945

Nov 1944: US begins direct aerial bombing of Japan

May 1945: Berlin surrenders to the red army

Oct 1945

Sept 1945: Formal Japanese surrender

these weapons made little difference. Germany was gradually crushed between Russians from the east and the Allied forces that pressed from the west. By the time Hitler killed himself on April 30, 1945, relentless aerial bombing had pulverized German industry, infrastructure, and communications; Germany's armed forces were collapsing, and the Russians were in Berlin.

In the Pacific, there was never any real likelihood of Japanese victory. Japanese leaders were aware of the difficulty. In 1941, their naval command compared war with the United States to a risky operation that would either save the life of a critically ill patient or kill him. Even Admiral Isoroku Yamamoto, the architect of the attack on Pearl Harbor, did not believe Japan could win the long war that he foresaw. "I shall run wild for the first six months of the war," he said, "but I have utterly no confidence for the second and third years." The need for oil and gasoline for the machines of war obliged the Japanese to drive ahead rapidly to gain control of the oilfields of Southeast Asia. They ended up with too many enemies and overextended lines. Once Germany surrendered and the Allies were able to turn their full strength against Japan, the outcome was inevitable. Even so, Japan fought on, improvising weapons and refusing to surrender, which, in Japanese culture, was labeled as shame. The end came only because the war stimulated

U.S. research into the devastating new technology of the atom bomb, which forced the Japanese, who had no such bombs, to surrender to the Americans, who had them and used them. In August 1945, American planes dropped atom bombs on two Japanese cities, Hiroshima and Nagasaki, virtually obliterating them, killing over 220,000 people, and poisoning the survivors with radiation.

THE COLD WAR ERA, 1945–1991

Foreign involvement is a smooth-sided pit, and America found it impossible to get out. The peace was harder to win than the war. Roosevelt's, like Wilson before him, had a vision of a new world order. In Roosevelt's, the United States, Britain, Russia, and China would, in effect, divide the world among them and collaborate to police peace. But protracted conflict threatened from three sources: civil wars in "liberated" countries, the ambitions of international communism, and Russia's desire for security or power along its borders. Stalin seized or garrisoned much of Eastern Europe. In March 1946, Winston Churchill (1874–1965), who had led the British government for most of the war years, announced the descent of an "Iron Curtain" from the Baltic to the Adriatic seas dividing Soviet-dominated Eastern Europe from the West.

Hiroshima, Japan after the explosion of the atomic bomb. In August 1945, Japan's defeat was already manifest, but rather than negotiate a conditional surrender or sacrifice thousands of American lives by invading the Japanese islands, President Truman (1884–1972) decided on a terrible alternative: the incineration of the Japanese cities of Hiroshima and Nagasaki with atom bombs.

Making Connections | THE WORLD WAR ERA, 1914–1945

BELLIGERENTS	CONFLICT	CAUSES	OUTCOMES
Germany, Austria-Hungary, Ottoman Empire, versus Great Britain, France, Russia, Italy, other European powers	World War I, 1914–1918	Imperial and national rivalries	Defeat of Germany: dismantling of Austro-Hungarian and Ottoman Empires; Bolshevik Revolution in Russia; Britain and France victorious but empires weakened and discredited; United States emerges as richest nation in the world; League of Nations formed; postwar disillusionment pervades Europe
Japan versus China	Second Sino-Japanese War, 1937–1945	Various incidents instigated by Japan lead to full-scale war in 1937 in an attempt by Japan to turn China into a subject territory	Japanese invade China and turn Manchuria into a puppet state (Manchukuo); Sino-Japanese conflict merges with World War II
Allies (Great Britain, United States, Soviet Union, other powers) versus Axis (Germany, Italy, Japan, other powers)	World War II, 1939–1945	Clash between different ideologies and forms of government (fascism, communism, democracy), and national/imperial interests	Germany, Italy, and Japan defeated; Eastern Europe falls under Soviet domination; Germany divided; Holocaust and forced migrations transform European society; Japanese Empire dismantled; European powers begin to decolonize; formation of United Nations; United States and Soviet Union emerge as nuclear superpowers

Superpower Confrontation

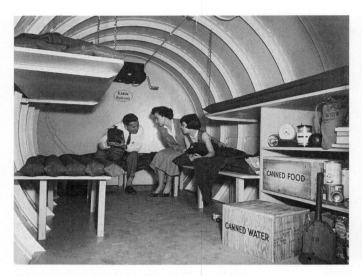

Bomb shelter. A U.S. public information campaign photograph of the 1950s makes the "shadow of the bomb" seem almost comfortable with a family posed earnestly together around a radio in their well-stocked bomb shelter. But this reassuring propaganda was a sham. Only the elite had shelters, and if their shelters had survived an atomic bomb, these people would have emerged into a deadly, poisoned environment.

In 1947, America tried one of the most generous foreign aid programs ever, the **Marshall Plan** (named after Secretary of State George C. Marshall (1880–1959)), to try to seduce former enemies into dependence on the United States and "create the social and political conditions in which free institutions can exist." American taxpayers cheerfully surrendered the money for European reconstruction, and Western Europe rapidly began to recover. But it was too late for the east. Reparations debts tied most of Eastern Europe to the Soviet market. By choice, Russian occupation, or communist seizure of power, almost all the states east of the Iron Curtain—Poland, Czechoslovakia, Romania, Hungary, Bulgaria, Albania, the Soviet-occupied part of Germany—became Soviet satellites. At Stalin's orders, they turned down Marshall aid. Europe's civil wars had resulted in partition between armed camps. A ring of American client states, of varying degrees of obedience to Washington, faced a heavily fenced-in Soviet Empire.

So another opportunity had arisen to reconstruct world order—and again, the opportunity had been lost. In one respect, however, the American vision worked. Democracy took root in countries American forces occupied. Japan was the most conspicuous success, thoroughly transformed into a demilitarized, democratic state, and a staunch American ally. Italy also democratized without difficulty, though it had too large a Communist Party for American taste and was prone to chronic changes of government. Germany had to be partitioned into two zones. The Soviet zone in the east became a rigid communist dictatorship, but the American-, British-, and French-occupied zones in the west were combined to form another model democracy, the Federal Republic of Germany.

The world shivered uneasily under a nuclear cloud. British experimenters had noted the explosive properties of nuclear fission as early as 1911. H. G. Wells popularized the prospect with a novel about the emergence of a utopian world from the ashes of civilization, incinerated by an atomic war. In 1935, the French researcher, Frédéric Joliot, in his speech receiving the Nobel Prize for work on nuclear energy, warned that an atomic chain reaction could destroy the world. By 1939, European scientists had nearly overcome the technical obstacles to the manufacture of the imagined bomb, but war, which ought logically to have speeded research in Europe, actually stymied it. The more immediate demands of the war effort distracted British researchers. Nazi conquest dispersed Joliot's team in France. In Germany, Werner Heisenberg (see Chapter 27) led a team equipped with essential ingredients: German uranium and Norwegian-made deuterium oxide, or heavy water, which helps control the flow of neutrons in a nuclear reaction. But Heisenberg was unwilling or unable to put a bomb in Hitler's hands.

So the first bombs were made in America. J. Robert Oppenheimer (1904–1967), a left-wing mystic with a genius for scientific administration, led the team. Had the United States kept its monopoly of the weapon, the country would have been permanently secure in the role of world arbiter for which its size and wealth equipped it. But the government felt obliged to share the secret with Britain, whose collaboration had been vital in making the bomb. Partly as a result of treason by Soviet sympathizers in the British foreign service, Russia's research team produced its own "A-bomb" in 1949.

Nevertheless, since Russia's main strength was in manpower, the new technology did not favor it. Outside the Soviet sphere of influence, Western Europe, under the nuclear shadow, could enjoy a security unthinkable without such protection, because the bomb canceled Soviet superiority in nonnuclear military prowess. On the other hand, nuclear equivalency with the United States guaranteed Russia's free hand in territories it had already conquered or coerced. Yugoslavia broke free of Russian hegemony in 1947–1948 before the completion of the Soviet bomb. Afterward, other East European satellite states tried to do the same and failed. Within a few years, technical improvements in the nuclear arsenal brought Russian and American firepower to the level of "mutually assured destruction." The balance of terror kept the peace between them.

Soviet and Western blocs confronted one another in a cold war that never quite reached the boiling point. In ideological terms, the story of the Cold War was of resistance to international communism by liberals and democracies, or of resistance to capitalism and imperialism by self-designated representatives of inevitable progress. In international terms, it was a confrontation between the United States and the Soviet Union for world domination or, at least, for global influence. Each side looked threatening to the other. The Western allies ringed the Soviet world with treaty organizations: alliances of anticommunist states in Europe, the Middle East, and Asia. The Soviet Union turned the flank of the West by nurturing revolutionary allies among the poor and developing countries of the world (see Map 28.5).

Depending on one's point of view, the conquests of international communism were battering rams pointing at Western Europe and the rest of the world, or giant buffers projecting the natural caution of a Russia that had barely escaped destruction in World War II. Russian leaders' own rhetoric wavered between defensive anxiety and aggressive bravado, reflecting struggles for supremacy within the Soviet elite. Contenders for power drew attention to themselves by loud language. Stalin's eventual successor, Nikita Khrushchev (1894–1971), hammered loudly on the table at international conferences to distract attention from his weakness, and practiced "brinkmanship"—periodically scaring the world with the threat of nuclear war—to deter the West from aggression. One of these crises—in 1962, over the housing of Soviet missiles in Cuba—nearly did lead to nuclear conflict. But both sides backed down. The Russians removed their missiles from Cuba, the Americans theirs from Turkey. This showed that both powers recognized the need for what they called coexistence, at least between themselves.

In retrospect, the Soviet phenomenon was bound to fail. Russia's postwar power reflected its natural endowments for hegemony: a larger population than most of its neighbors, vast natural resources, and a heartland that was too big for enemies to conquer. Yet the Soviet Empire was ramshackle, no more capable than that of the czars had been in containing the ancient national and religious identities of its subject-peoples. Empires of the eastern European plains have always been short lived. State-run economies tend to fall behind those managed by private enterprise, which guarantees rewards for those who create wealth. The Soviet elite compounded the problem by bad policies: collectivization of agriculture, which deprived individual peasant farmers of any stake in the land; repression

"Each day of labor—a step toward communism!" Russian communists adopted the hammer and sickle emblem to symbolize the alliance of peasants and workers. In practice, however, landowning peasants remained hard to convince. Josef Stalin had millions of them massacred and exiled in the 1920s and 1930s for refusing to join collective farms. As late as 1968, however, propaganda still featured images of steel and grain—the privileged products of Soviet economic planning.

КАЖДЫЙ ДЕНЬ ТРУДА-

ШАГ К КОММУНИЗМУ!

MAP 28.5

The Alliances of the Cold War

U.S., allies, and satellite states

- U.S. and original NATO 1949
- later NATO
- NATO dependencies 1960
- other nations allied to the Western bloc by treaty

U.S.S.R. and allies

- U.S.S.R.
- Warsaw Pact 1955
- Communist satellite states
- China

Non-aligned movement

- members as of 1961

of the free market for goods and services, which led to nightmares of central planning and a chronic shortage of even basic consumer goods; suppression of traditional ethnic and national cultures, which created festering resentment in the non-Russian areas of the Soviet Union; and a horrific disregard for the environment, which wasted natural resources and polluted the landscape. The survival of the Soviet system from 1917 to 1991 is more surprising than its eventual collapse.

For a long time, however, it seemed that communism would win the ideological struggle and that the Soviets would get most of the world on their side. In 1949, for instance, China appeared to have joined the Soviet camp when the Chinese communists defeated the nationalists in a civil war. Since the overthrow of the Qing dynasty in 1911 (see Chapter 29), no Chinese government had been able to replace the lost legitimacy of the old imperial order or hold the country together for long. Japanese conquest brought order, or at least a suspension of chaos, to much of the country but at a terrible price in violence, exploitation, and humiliation. The Chinese communists succeeded where others had failed: mobilizing popular enthusiasm, unifying the country, creating a new, uniform political elite—the Party—to replace the old mandarinate. Mao Zedong (mao dzeh-dohng) (1893–1976) was the most effective leader the Chinese Communist Party had, organizing its weak forces into an army that could never be defeated because it could never be pinned down. His most famous maxim was: "When the enemy advances, we withdraw. When he rests, we harass. When he tires, we attack. When he withdraws, we pursue." His triumph in 1949 seemed to have altered the world balance of power.

At first, China's revolution seemed a decisive triumph for international communism and a great addition to Soviet power. The United States struggled to hold the line—or what was perceived as a line—against communist encroachments in Korea. The country had been divided at the end of World War II because Soviet troops had occupied its northern half while American forces had garrisoned the south. Supposedly, North and South Korea would be reunited after elections, but the rulers Russia installed in the north and those the United States backed in the south never allowed the elections to take place. In June 1950, the north invaded the south. America stepped in, with the authorization of the United Nations and strong military support from Britain and Australia. Despite Chinese intervention on the other side, the Americans and their allies were just about able to drive the invaders back to the north. Thereafter, Korea remained, and still remains, divided.

In Vietnam, however, a similar situation led to a disaster for the United States. In the 1950s, after French imperialism in Indochina collapsed, a partition of Vietnam between communist and anticommunist regimes led to civil war. American troops poured into South Vietnam in increasing numbers from 1961. The war of containment the Americans tried to fight proved impracticable against guerrilla incursions from communist North Vietnam. The United States got trapped in what was called *escalation*: rising costs, mounting casualties, plunging morale. Public opinion at home would neither approve perseverance nor admit defeat. America entered a 12-year agony that dominated the world's media. No war had ever before been so ruthlessly exposed on television and in the newspapers. Nightly images of dead and wounded young soldiers, atrocities, and ineptitude disturbed domestic audiences. In the morning, photojournalism splattered the previous day's bloodshed over America's breakfast tables.

> *"The survival of the Soviet system from 1917 to 1991 is more surprising than its eventual collapse."*

Atrocity. This 1973 Pulitzer Prize-winning photo shows South Vietnamese forces casually walking behind terrified children, including Kim Phuc, center, as they head down a highway after a plane dropped napalm on suspected communist guerrilla hiding places. The terrified girl had ripped off her burning clothes while fleeing.

"But the effects of Vietnam seemed cataclysmic for one side in the Cold War. Defeat when it came, with the complete collapse of South Vietnam in 1975, diminished American prestige."

Peace movements arose in response and spread beyond America across the Westernworld. Cults of "flower power" celebrated "love, not war." Increasing numbers of young men sought to evade serving in the military. Western youths now had a cause for their generational habits of rebellion or indifference. Protesters recoiled from the establishment decision makers. In 1968, massive street demonstrations across Europe and America toppled some governments and disturbed others. The would-be revolutionaries mostly talked themselves into inertia or grew out of rebelliousness. Protest ebbed with the war. But the effects of Vietnam seemed cataclysmic for one side in the Cold War. Defeat when it came, with the complete collapse of South Vietnam in 1975, diminished American prestige. The horrors of the war undermined America's moral authority. The insurgents' success encouraged America's enemies on other fronts. The American people recoiled from the exercise of responsibility for other people's liberty. The newly independent countries of the era were disinclined to take America's side. A communist takeover in Cambodia and Laos in the 1970s made the American rout seem worse. Cambodia's regime was one of the most brutal in a savage century, but its communism proved unique and demented. Its leader, Pol Pot (1926–1998), conceived a return to a purely agrarian state, such as had supposedly prevailed in Cambodia's medieval golden age. He proposed to restore it by massacring the bourgeoisie and the educated, wrecking industry and commerce, and depopulating the cities.

As if these political setbacks were not enough, the West also seemed to be losing in the economic and scientific stakes against the Soviet system. In 1957, Russia launched the first successful spacecraft, *Sputnik I*, and in 1961 put the first man in space. Space exploration was expensive and brought virtually no useful economic or scientific returns. But America, in danger of forfeiting world prestige, was forced to play catch-up, which it did, putting the first man on the moon in 1969. Meanwhile, the world had the impression that Russia was ahead in the struggle to forge what a British prime minister in the early 1960s called the "white heat" of technology. Russian technical prowess seemed to do credit to Russia's economic system. Its surplus production, especially of oil and natural gas, subsidized its satellite states without impoverishing its own economy.

MAP 28.6

The Collapse of Communism in Eastern Europe

- Soviet Union to 1991
- Soviet-dominated Eastern Europe and the Caucasus to 1989
- Yugoslavia to 1991
- other communist state before 1991
- 1993   date of first multi-party election

Gradually, however, evidence mounted that the Soviet economy was not as strong as it appeared, or as propaganda painted it. "Socialism is management," Lenin once said. But no Russian government managed the economy well. In 1954, for instance, Khrushchev launched a disastrous economic initiative known as the Virgin Lands scheme. He intended to turn vast areas of steppe into farmland—the way the great ecological revolution of the nineteenth century had transformed the North American prairie (see Chapter 23). In this case, however, the result was large-scale desertification and a food crisis in Russia. By the 1960s, intensive farming had exhausted the soil of the grasslands the Russians plowed up. In all, an area greater than that of the entire farmland of Canada was lost.

In most respects, however, the era of Soviet economic success lasted until the world oil crisis of 1973, when oil-exporting countries, combining to hike the price of fuel, triggered massive global inflation. The economies of Russia's satellite regimes in Eastern Europe slipped out of economic dependence on Moscow, which could not afford to go on subsidizing them as lavishly as before, and into heavy indebtedness to Western bankers who loaned them vast sums. Then, in the 1980s, after sending troops into Afghanistan to replace a strongman ruler who was showing signs of becoming too independent with a more pro-Moscow puppet government, Russia found itself embroiled in a hopeless war against fanatical Islamic guerrillas who were financed by conservative Arab regimes and armed by the United States. The costs in blood and cash were greater than Russians were willing to bear. The American president, Ronald Reagan (1911–2004), saw the opportunity and stepped up the arms race, outstripping Russia's ability to pay for new weapons. The Chicago economists (see Chapter 29) on whom Reagan relied for advice helped to convince the world that private enterprise made for prosperity and that economics was too important to be left to the state. The thinker who inspired them, the Austrian social scientist, F. A. von Hayek (1899–1992), became the source of the era's fashionable idea: order in the service of freedom.

The pope also played a part in dissolving Soviet power. In 1978, a Polish cardinal, Karel Wojtyla, became Pope John Paul II (1920–2005), the first non-Italian pontiff in over 450 years. He had witnessed persecution of the church by Nazis and communists alike. He used his wide range of acquaintances among Catholics in Eastern Europe to build up movements of resistance to Soviet domination. The first and most effective of these was the Polish trade union, Solidarność (Solidarity), which launched a series of strikes and demonstrations from 1980 onward, first against economic mismanagement by Poland's communist regime and then against the regime itself.

From 1985, the Soviet Union floated off the shoals and into the wake of the West, under a leadership that had ceased to believe in traditional socialist rhetoric. Mikhail Gorbachev (b. 1931) dismantled the command economy, freed the market, introduced accountable government, and, in the end, submitted to demands for democracy and for self-determination by the Soviet Union's ethnic minorities. Moscow manipulated or permitted similar revolutions in the satellite states—the last act of a dying supremacy. Dissidents were on hand to take over revolutions they had not started but long wished for. Satellite states zoomed out of the Soviet orbit. The two European communist supranational states—the Soviet Union and the Yugoslav federation—cracked and splintered. Europe seemed to go straight from the world of Karl Marx to the world of the Marx Brothers, a popular Hollywood slapstick comedy act, with bewildering new states—Macedonia, Bosnia, Azerbaijan, Belarus, Moldava, Slovenia, Croatia, Montenegro, Kososvo—bubbling over the map like *Duck Soup* in the brothers' chaotic 1933 movie of that name (see Map 28.6).

Solidarity. Going to confession and receiving communion in public became rituals of public protest in Poland under communist rule, because the Catholic Church was too popular for the Party ever to suppress or control it. By 1980, when this photograph was taken, the shipyard workers' union leader, Lech Waleśka (the mustached figure in the left foreground) had organized what was in effect a Church-sponsored political resistance movement called Solidarity to restore democracy.

MAP 28.7

Chinese Expansion and Influence Since 1949

🌿 Territorial/border dispute

➡️ Chinese invasion

★ Chinese support for
  communist insurgents

China, meanwhile, had become an enemy to both sides in the Cold War. Mao Zedong disappointed Moscow almost from the moment he took power. He was better read in Chinese pulp fiction than in Marxist theory. He admired the bandit heroes of Chinese romance more than he did Lenin or Stalin. He was a peasant by birth and developed his own theory of peasant revolution. "He doesn't understand the most elementary Marxist truths," said Stalin, who disliked and feared Mao. In any case, Mao was determined to go his own way. Under his rule, China remained as resolutely aloof from the Soviet Union as from the West and joined in the global game to offset American and Russian power. Mao denounced America for imperialism and the Russians for what he called "bourgeois deviationism"—turning the Communist Party into a new kind of privileged middle class. He competed with both for the friendship of the successor states of dismantled colonial empires in Asia and Africa, while pursuing aggressive policies toward neighboring states. China overran Tibet, intervened in the Korean War, provoked confrontations on the Indian, Vietnamese, and Russian borders, and encouraged insurgents in Nepal (see Map 28.7).

Mao's domestic policies arrested China's development. He thrived on crises and created his own when circumstances failed to provide them. He caused famine by communalizing agriculture and environmental disaster by absurdly impracticable schemes of industrialization. He launched campaigns of mass destruction from time to time against a sequence of irrationally selected enemies: dogs, sparrows, rightists, leftists—even, at one point, grass and flowers. He outlawed romantic love as bourgeois and, proclaiming that vice was hereditary, reduced the descendants of ancient elites—scholars, landowners, officials—to the ranks of an underclass. In 1966, his regime proclaimed a **Cultural Revolution**. In practice, this meant victimizing professionals—including teachers, scientists, doctors, and technicians, on whom the country relied—and forcing them into manual labor or degrading them with humiliating punishments. For more than three years, intellectuals were brutalized, antiquities smashed, books burned, beauty was despised, study subverted, work stopped. China's economy reverted to chaos.

The long-term outcome of Mao's moral and economic failures was the reconversion of China to capitalist economics. Between 1969 and 1972, United States President Richard Nixon (1913–1994) reversed America's traditional policy of hostility, accepting Communist China into the United Nations and opening American trade with it. It was an attempt to wedge Russia and China further apart, while mopping up some of the spoilage from America's failure in the Vietnam War. Still, Nixon's strategy worked, especially after Mao's death in 1976.

Mao's successor, Deng Xiaoping (1904–1997), recommended the Chinese "to get rich"—not an objective either Mao or Confucius would ever have approved. After making remarkably liberal trade agreements with America and Japan, Deng freed up the Chinese economy, gradually returning more and more production

A CLOSER LOOK

Reporting our Harvest to Chairman Mao

Mao Zedong's "Great Cultural Revolution" was meant to remake society by forcing the privileged to share the lives of peasants and workers. But by victimizing the educated and the enterprising, Mao wrecked the economy and impoverished China. Propaganda strove to conceal the truth—not least from Mao himself.

The bystanders and the little girl nestled protectively in Mao's arm represent peasants and youth—the groups Mao tried to mobilize against professionals and intellectuals, whom he saw as enemies.

Mao, godlike in stature and simple in dress, recites his "Thoughts" to implausibly smiling adorers.

The girl wears the badge of the Communist Party on her peasant's wide straw hat. Under Mao, the party became the country's only permitted elite.

Peasants bring agricultural abundance to Mao—like tribute-bearers to a traditional emperor or worshippers to a god. In reality, China had no abundance of food or anything else. Mao's policies undermined productivity in agriculture as well as industry.

How does this painting differ from what we know about China under Mao?

and finance to the private sector. In 1986, Vietnam, too, adopted a policy of market liberalization. By the 1990s, China's was the fastest-growing economy in the world, averaging nearly 10 percent a year in output. In the first decade of the twenty-first century, China's economy grew even faster, and Chinese demand for oil, food, raw materials, and, increasingly, consumer goods is now helping to drive up the prices of energy and commodities worldwide. North Korea is the only state in the region—in the world, really—that remains inward looking, isolated, and hostile to even limited economic freedom.

DECOLONIZATION

Before the Cold War could end, the world had to endure the agonies of decolonization—the breakup of the old European empires in Asia and Africa (see Map 28.8). The moral bankruptcy of imperialism was apparent in agonizing resistance struggles and wars of attempted reconquest. Between 1941 and 1945, self-

MAP 28.8

Decolonization in Africa and Asia Since World War II

- before 1950
- 1950–1956
- 1956–1970
- since 1970

interested Japanese aggression drove white rulers out of Southeast Asia. The United States responded, after the war, by granting independence to the Philippines. In other parts of the region, the colonialists returned, only to be forced into surrendering power by fierce nationalist resistance.

The Dutch "police operation" in the Netherlands East Indies (1945–1949) was really a brutal war that ended in Dutch retreat and the foundation of the independent Republic of Indonesia in a spirit of mutual resentment. The French suffered ignominious defeat in Indochina in 1954. By pouring in 40,000 troops, the British managed to defeat communist insurgents in Malaya, but colonial rule ended there in 1957 when a British-selected Malay government took over.

Meanwhile, in 1947, the British pulled out of India in haste, escaping horrific problems of famine control and ethnic and religious conflict. Partition of Britain's Indian Empire between Hindu and Muslim states—India and Pakistan, respectively—claimed at least half a million lives before borders were stabilized. The British bullied or blackmailed the rulers of the native states into joining either India or Pakistan. In both countries, the old patchwork of princely states was resewn into a uniform pattern. Eventually, the maharajahs were stripped of their powers.

This scenario was typical of European decolonization, which dismantled more than empire. In many places, colonial powers abandoned or sidelined the old elites—both European settlers and traditional native aristocracies—in favor of the newly anointed: upstart leaders, who came from the rising native middle classes. Usually, the newcomers had been educated in Europe, or sometimes in isolated mission schools at home. Generally, the retreating colonialists felt forced to favor them. Once the colonial armies left, the new men, who commanded popular support, or revolutionary armies, or help from abroad, stepped into leading roles from backgrounds of violent resistance, cutting out traditional elites or reducing the old aristocracies and monarchies to purely ceremonial functions. This policy usually ensured instability and tyranny in decolonized regions. In India, which became the world's most populous democracy, it worked exceptionally well. Pakistan was a less successful case. After about a generation of independence, the country was defeated in two wars against India, partitioned to accommodate secessionists in what became known as East Bengal or Bangladesh, and subjected to long periods of military rule.

Most Westerners assumed that Africa would take much longer to decolonize than Asia, but the winds of change quickly blew up a storm in that continent, too. Because sub-Saharan Africa largely escaped World War II, some forms of production—especially of rubber and food—were relocated there. As a result, an ambitious African middle class developed. Meanwhile, the benefits of modern medicine produced a population boom. Uncontrollable growth in the numbers of needy people made empires obviously unprofitable. Rather than shoulder unmanageably escalating costs, it became cheaper for European powers to grant independence and foreign aid.

The role the Japanese played in Asia—uncovering the weakness of European empires and hastening their downfall—had an African counterpart. In Africa, Egypt led the way. Britain and France, the two main colonial powers, were humiliated in a showdown with Gamal Abdel Nasser (1918–1970), an Egyptian nationalist whom an officers' coup elevated to power in 1952. When he seized the Suez Canal Company in 1956, Britain and France, joined opportunistically by Israel,

Guerrillas, not rebels. In line with U.S. policy, which favored Indonesian independence and the end of Dutch colonialism in Southeast Asia, the caption for this Associated Press photograph, in July 1947, identified these fighters not as rebels against Dutch colonialism, but as "non-uniformed combat guerrillas" of "supporting units to the regular military forces" of the "Republic of Indonesia." After bitter fighting, the Dutch finally ceded Indonesian independence in 1949.

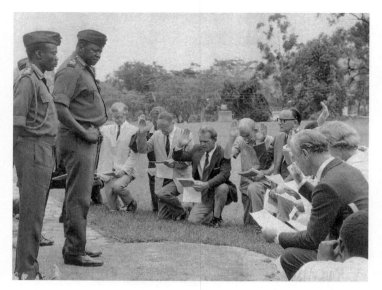

Leader cult. When colonial powers rushed ill prepared to disengage from Africa in the 1960s, they left dysfunctional states behind, prey to ruthless dictators, sprung from the new elites that Europeans promoted to offset the power of traditional leaders. Idi Amin, for instance, of Uganda, who seized power there in 1971, had been a sergeant under the British. This photograph from 1975 captures an incident of his increasingly unbalanced behavior as ruler of his country, when he forced white subjects and employees into taking bizarre and humiliating oaths of allegiance to him, drafting them into the armed services, so that they would be under military discipline, and exacting vows to fight against the white-dominated South African regime.

sent in troops hoping to topple his regime. Liberal British opinion thought "Nasser was right"—in the words of a character in Evelyn Waugh's great antiwar novel, *Unconditional Surrender*. For reasons of its own, the United States repudiated the Franco-British operation and, in effect, forced its allies to accept Egypt's case. A flight of colonial powers from Africa followed.

The cracks spread outward from Egypt. In the year of Suez, Britain evacuated Sudan, and France left Tunisia and Morocco—"protected" territories under European control but not formal European sovereignty. Algeria was a more problematic case. Although the vast interior of the country was a French colony, the parts of Algeria on the Mediterranean had been one of the "New Europes" (see Chapter 25). They were considered an integral part of France itself, and their inhabitants elected members to the parliament in Paris. By the 1950s, these areas had over one million settlers of European descent, many of whom were prepared to fight France, if necessary, to remain French and secure what they considered a European way of life. A savage war that broke out in 1954 between the French army and Muslim rebels settled the question in favor of independence by 1962, but not before mutinous generals and enraged settlers threatened to topple the government of France itself.

Meanwhile, in 1957, Ghana in West Africa became the first sub-Saharan African state to gain its independence. After that, the skirts of empire were lifted with indecent haste. In 1960, 14 new states came into being in Africa, including a vast tract of continuous territory from the southern Sahara to the River Congo or Zaire. Ultimately, even Ethiopia, the one native African empire to survive and grow in the nineteenth century (see Chapter 25) lost territory. Emperor Haile Selassie (r. 1930–1974), having survived another Italian attempt to take over his empire in the 1930s, withdrew as he aged into complacency and inertia. A military coup launched in the name of socialism dethroned—and ultimately murdered—him in 1974 and substituted a Marxist-inspired "totalitarian autocracy" for the ancient Ethiopian monarchy. Before they were overthrown in 1991, the new military rulers imprisoned or killed thousands from the old elite. The economy collapsed, famine broke out, and rebels in outlying regions of the old empire launched independence movements, one of which succeeded in detaching the former Italian colony of Eritrea on the Red Sea as an independent republic in 1991.

Newcomers to the power game, schooled in resistance, usually replaced old elites. In Ghana, for instance, the independence leader Kwame Nkrumah (1909–1972) had "PG" for prison graduate embroidered on his cap. In Kenya, the first president, Jomo Kenyatta (1889–1978), was generally—and probably correctly—assumed to be the secret leader of the terrorists who had developed a fearsome reputation for the slaughter of white settlers and African loyalists under British colonial rule in the 1950s. Colonel Haile Mariam Mengistu in Ethiopia was a classic case of a leader who "rose without trace," though his grandfather was commonly said to have been a slave. He justified his massacres of opponents as revenge for historic oppression by the Ethiopian elite.

Most postcolonial rulers in Africa adopted or affected secular programs, usually heavily influenced by socialism, and flirted with Moscow or Beijing, either out of ideological conviction, or in an attempt to play off rivals to maximize their freedom of maneuver and opportunities for graft or aid. The ease with which many of them slid into despotic habits, and reduced their countries to dictatorships and destitution, dismayed Western liberals who had hoped that decolonization would bring freedom and prosperity.

Leader cults filled the gaps that the extinction or subversion of traditional loyalties left open. Some cases were truly shocking, especially in Africa. Nkrumah, who called himself the Redeemer, became prey to messianic delusions, as his troops sang, "Nkrumah never dies." Jean-Bedel Bokassa (1921–1996) declared the Central African Republic an "empire" and crowned himself its emperor in imitation of Napoleon in 1977. He later massacred school children and was accused, not without evidence, of cannibalism. Idi Amin (1925–2003) in Uganda in East Africa, who, like Bokassa and Mengistu, rose by another of the new routes, through the ranks of the army, used terror as a method of government and plunged his country into chaos by torturing and murdering thousands of opponents and victimizing minorities. In Sierra Leone in West Africa, Siaka Stevens (1905–1988) became preoccupied with a mission to justify polygamy. In Congo, Joseph Mobutu (1930–1997) milked the economy of billions of dollars and gave himself a nickname that meant "the rooster that leaves no hen unmated." Even Félix Houphouet-Boigny (1905–1993) of Ivory Coast, long admired as a model for Africa because of his friendliness toward the former French colonists, gave way to self-indulgence, building himself a grandiose mausoleum, guarded by golden rams and sacred crocodiles, inflicting the world's biggest Roman Catholic cathedral on his home village, and banking billions in tax-proof Swiss bank accounts. Francisco Macías Nguema in Equatorial Guinea—executed by his own nephew after a coup in 1979—and Robert Mugabe (b. 1924) in Zimbabwe impoverished their countries and deployed armed gangs to tyrannize and murder opponents and intimidate electors.

In fairness, it must be said that decolonization left decolonized lands staggering under terrible burdens. Their populations were normally growing at an unprecedented pace, for which the colonial regimes had not prepared them. They were usually encumbered with irrational, indefensible, and unsustainable borders that the departing colonialists had hastily outlined. The principle of national self-determination, which had guided, however imperfectly, the dismantling of imperialism inside Europe after World War I, was ignored in the wider world. Colonial regimes adopted three exit strategies: they crammed historically hostile communities into single states; they forced reluctant partner communities and nations into unstable "federal" superstates; or they imposed borders between newly independent states that neither side found acceptable. International law treated postcolonial borders as inviolable, even where they were oppressive or unworkable.

As a result, civil wars commonly accompanied or followed decolonization, and disputes over the divisions of territory often remained unresolved into the twenty-first century: between new states, such as India and Pakistan; or between Catholics and Protestants in Ireland; Jews and Arabs in Israel and Palestine; Turks and Greeks in Cyprus; Christians and Muslims in Nigeria, Sudan, Ivory Coast, and the Philippines; Tamils and Singhalese in Sri Lanka; centralists and secessionists in Congo, western Sahara, and Uganda; rivals for resources in Angola and Mozambique; and traditional elites and historically underprivileged groups in Liberia, Sierra Leone, Rwanda, Burundi, and many other new countries in Africa and Asia.

All the ensuing wars multiplied the sufferings of the people who endured them, but the Palestinian conflict had the worst long-term effects on global history. In 1948, the British, who had occupied Palestine since the collapse of the Ottoman Empire in 1918, packed up and left in the face of murderous conflict between Jews and Arabs. What swiftly emerged was a division of Palestine into a Jewish state and Arab enclaves (see Map 28.9). The Jews, who called the state they founded Israel, were victorious in a series of subsequent wars that left them in control not only of

Israel and Palestine, 1947

▨ proposed Arab State

▨ proposed Jewish State

▨ proposed international zone

— border of British mandate 1923

Hamas supporters. A series of wars from 1948 to 1974 left Israelis in occupation of lands with a large and resentful Palestinian population, many of whom, rejecting the very existence of the state of Israel, resorted to resistance by terrorism. Even peaceful demonstrations—like this one in 2005 by supporters of the radical party, Hamas—became exercises in martial discipline. Disputes over the distribution of land, water, jobs, and financial aid, and the exclusion by Israel of some Palestinian refugees from their former homes, inflamed the situation. Hamas won democratic elections—against rivals who favored accommodation with Israel—in 2006.

territory the British and the United Nations had assigned to the Arabs of Palestine, but also land that neighboring Arab states had previously occupied. In the early twenty-first century, despite intermittent signs of progress, the resulting problems remained unresolved. Israel agreed in principle to recognize a Palestinian Arab state, but its boundaries and nature remained undetermined, while guarantees for Israeli security remained usatisfactory. By choosing in effect to be the guarantor of Israel's survival, the United States, despite periodic attempts to act as an honest broker between the two sides, stoked Arab rage and alienated international opinion, especially in the Muslim world.

The economic problems of decolonized lands mounted. In the 1970s and 1980s, the value of many primary products on the world market collapsed. This was the result of two so-called revolutions: the first, known as the green revolution, oversolved the problems of famine by glutting the world with cheap grains (see Chapter 30). Simultaneously, an information revolution replaced many traditional industries and propelled the West into a postindustrial age, in which services and information replaced manufacture as the main sources of employment. An abyss opened where before there had merely been a gap in wealth between the ex-imperialists and their former subjects. Business imperialism was not easily thrown off (see Chapter 25). Even after colonies achieved political independence, their economic dependence often continued, sometimes on former colonial powers, more often on the Soviet Union or the United States—the Cold War contenders whom newly independent governments sought to play off against one another. Cuba—never formally an American colony but always smarting under the economic control of United States businesses—played the game with some success after 1959, when idealistic revolutionaries, under Fidel Castro (b. 1927), threw out a corrupt dictatorship that had enjoyed Washington's support. Castro banned foreigners from owning Cuban land, nationalized many businesses—especially those Americans owned—and established an egalitarian welfare system. The United States took both offense and fright, and Castro more or less willingly became a client of the Soviet Union, while imposing increasingly authoritarian controls on Cuba. He even served the Russians as a surrogate military force, sending troops in professed solidarity to African countries where the Soviets wanted to shore up regimes that favored them. The collapse of his Soviet ally in 1991 and the changing conditions of global trade obliged Castro to relax economic controls, but at the end of the century his system and his personal rule were still intact. Even after he handed power to his brother in 2008, Cuba remained the best—perhaps the only—example of sustained socialism in the world.

THE NEW WORLD ORDER

At the end of the Cold War, America had another opportunity to reshape the world. President Wilson's effort after World War I had failed, as had President Franklin Roosevelt's after World War II. Now the omens were better in some respects. The United States had no rival and so far exceeded other countries in power and wealth that it could set the world's agenda. America's "soft power"—the example set by the success of its democratic institutions and capitalist economy, and the appeal of

American popular culture, including movies, music, clothes, and fast food—disposed much of the rest of the world to accept American leadership and guidance.

Most of the world willingly adopted the democratic principles long associated with America, which American policy had sought to spread for most of the century. Strictly speaking, if one measures democracy by the extent of the suffrage, the only democracy in the world when the twentieth century began was New Zealand, which had had universal adult suffrage since 1893. In 1974, only 36 states could reasonably be called democracies, where the votes of the people genuinely chose and removed governments. By 2000, measured by the same standard, 139 states were democracies. By a tougher standard, including respect for the rule of law and for the civil rights of citizens in conflict with their governments, there were 86 democracies. Democratic rhetoric, at least, triumphed everywhere. Even dictatorships used it. Democracy was the only political ideology universally praised, even if governments often only honored its principles by paying them lip service.

Notable landmarks in the spread of democracy were the extinction of authoritarian government in southern Europe. Between 1974 and 1978, Greece, Portugal, and Spain all made the transition to democracy. In much of Latin America, military dictatorships seized power in the 1970s, often with the connivance of United States administrations worried about the Americas "going communist." By the 1990s, however, democracy was restored—albeit in some countries rather shakily—in almost the whole of the continent. The Philippines experienced an enduring democratic revolution in 1986, Thailand in 1992 (though the Thai military overthrew the elected prime minister in 2006, civilian rule was restored within a year.) In 1994, not long after the dissolution of the Soviet Empire, South Africa embraced democracy. This was a remarkable step by a racially privileged elite and occurred with little violence. The white parliament dissolved itself, and the outgoing elite respected the results of the first democratic elections, which brought Nelson Mandela (b. 1918) to the presidency. As he received the loyal support of the armed forces commanders, he said, "I was not unmindful of the fact that not so many years before they would not have saluted but arrested me" (see Chapter 29).

While much of the world democratized, most countries adopted what were called **human rights** into their laws. These rights included guarantees of life, personal liberty, and dignity; freedom of expression, of religion, of education, and of equality under the law; and minimal standards of nourishment, health, and housing. The Helsinki Accords of 1975, which pledged its signers to respect human rights, was particularly significant, because the Soviet Union signed it, along with most other European countries, Canada, and the United States. Dissident groups throughout the communist world were enormously encouraged. It was easier, however, to get assent in principle to the concept of human rights than to implement them, case by case, in communities of widely differing cultures. In practice, particular states, even after encoding such rights in their own laws, ignored them whenever they wished. Even the United States—which had been loud in its advocacy of human rights in other countries, and, for a while, exemplary in respecting these rights at home—found ways around its obligations in dealing with people accused of terrorist

> *"Democracy was the only political ideology universally praised, even if governments often only honored its principles by paying them lip service."*

The spread of democracy. South Africa held racially unsegregated general elections for the first time in 1994—a triumph for the policies of compromise and peaceful change advocated by Nelson Mandela, shown here casting his own vote. Mandela's African National Congress won over 60 percent of the vote and formed a coalition government with the former ruling party, the Nationalists, who had long defended white supremacy.

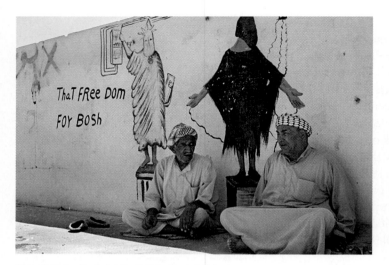

"Freedom for Bush." Graffiti in Baghdad in June 2004 satirize President George W. Bush's claim to have made war in Iraq to promote freedom. One graffito clothes the Statue of Liberty in the garb of violent U.S. racists; the other shows a tortured Iraqi. American soldiers had been caught photographing each other torturing and sexually humiliating Iraqi prisoners, including innocent noncombatants. Soon after, the U.S. government admitted that it had authorized other instances of torture beyond the jurisdiction of U.S. courts.

acts or of collaboration with the enemy during wars in Afghanistan and Iraq in the early twenty-first century. Some detainees captured in these wars were interned in the American naval base at Guantanamo Bay in Cuba, in an attempt to put them outside the protection of U.S. laws. Others, imprisoned in Iraq and Afghanistan, were subjected to torture by executive dispensation in defiance of U.S. and international law. United States authorities handed still others over to governments, such as those in Syria, Egypt, and Saudi Arabia, that routinely tortured and abused prisoners.

Democratization remained imperfect. It made little impact in some states—especially in Africa and parts of the Muslim world. Some post-Soviet republics fell into the hands of authoritarian leaders. Under Vladimir Putin, who was president from 1999 to 2008 and then prime minister, Russia itself became an authoritarian state, albeit one that preserved democratic forms and a liberal economy. In South Asia, India and Sri Lanka preserved democracy pretty constantly, despite a prolonged secessionist war by the Tamil ethnic and religious minority in Sri Lanka, while Pakistan and Bangladesh have often been under military rule. In Southeast Asia, a fault line divided nondemocratic Myanmar, Laos, Cambodia, and Vietnam from the more or less democratic states that made up the rest of the region.

In Latin America, even after the military dictatorships were dismantled, Cuba remained a dictatorship, while some new democracies seemed worryingly fragile. Elected presidents of authoritarian inclinations—Alberto Fujimori (b. 1938) in Peru, for instance, and Hugo Chávez (b. 1954) in Venezuela—showed scant respect for democratic institutions. Most disturbingly, China has continued to repress democratic opposition. However, there are signs that China might not be able to resist democracy indefinitely. The economic liberalization Deng Xiaoping launched created a new bourgeoisie, whom the government cannot exclude forever from the political arena and who are not always, or even usually, members of the Communist Party. In 1997, the British colony of Hong Kong was reincorporated into the Chinese state, with its own unfettered capitalist institutions and a measure of local democracy, under a scheme announced as "one country, two systems." Meanwhile, unrest deepened in China's outer provinces, where Tibetans and large Muslim populations remained unassimilated, unwilling to think of themselves as Chinese and resentful of Chinese rule. China, in short, despite its booming economy, is beginning to exhibit problems that the leadership might be tempted to solve by democratization.

If there was an opportunity to fashion a more democratic, more just, and more peaceful world, the United States did not take it. American leaders from the 1980s onward lacked what President George H. W. Bush (b. 1924) called "the vision thing." They made no attempt to renew efforts of the kind Wilson and Roosevelt had launched to create international institutions to preserve world peace. They dropped out of important initiatives in human rights, declining to accept the jurisdiction of an International Criminal Court. They kept aloof from efforts to establish a global environmental policy. They bypassed the United Nations when it suited them to do so. They launched military interventions and bombing raids on their own say-so against foreign targets. They exhibited what much of the world condemned as bias in their policy toward the Middle East.

The United States, in pursuit of its own national interests, often felt obliged to sponsor antidemocratic regimes, especially in the Arab world. Nor were America's own democratic credentials perfect. Two presidents—John F. Kennedy in 1960 and George W. Bush in 2000—may have come to power as a result of electoral malpractice. In 1974, Republican President Richard M. Nixon had to resign after revelations that he had been implicated in attempts to obstruct justice by subverting investigations into a break-in in 1972 at Democratic Party headquarters at the Watergate complex in Washington. Nixon's language in discussing the matter with his subordinates exposed his contempt for democracy. Campaign funding has often become as significant as policy in influencing the outcome of elections. About half the electorate has ceased to take part in the national electoral process. Presidential elections now cost billions of dollars and have been abandoned by millions of voters.

There is no question—despite the ill effects of many decisions by presidents and their advisers—that most Americans wanted America to be a benevolent superpower, and believed in the United States' traditional democratic ideals. Effectively, however, the United States had cast itself in the role of world policeman, and the American taxpayer had to pick up the tab. This situation pleased no one. But American governments proved unwilling or unable to find ways to spread the burden, share power, or provide for a future in which America would no longer have the resources to take care of the world.

Chronology: Decolonization and the Post-Cold War World	
1941–1945	Japanese occupation sets stage for postwar decolonization of Southeast Asia
1947	Indian independence and partition into India and Pakistan
1948	State of Israel established
1950s and 1960s	Decolonization of most of Africa
1956	Suez Crisis
1959	Fidel Castro takes power in Cuba
1970s	Military dictatorships take power in much of Latin America
1970s and 1980s	Value of many commodities on world market collapses
1974	36 states have a democratic franchise
1975	Helsinki Accords
1986	Democratic revolution in the Philippines
1990s	China becomes world's fastest-growing economy
1994	Nelson Mandela becomes president of South Africa
1997	Hong Kong returns to Chinese control
1999–2008	Vladimir Putin establishes authoritarian regime in Russia
2000	139 states are classifiable as democracies
2007	European Union includes 27 states

The European Union

China is the most likely successor to the United States in the role of global hegemon. Although leaders had talked of Pan-Arab or Pan-African unity, nothing meaningful had ever come of the talk or seemed likely to do so in a foreseeable future. But a chance to build loyalties across European frontiers arose from the ruins of World War II. The devastation of 1945 was a vast warning against conflict and a summons to collaboration. The collapse of European world empires threw the European states back on each other. The crisis gave institutional backbone to Europe's sagging identity. Six countries—France, West Germany, Italy, Belgium, the Netherlands, and Luxembourg—combined in the European Coal and Steel Community in 1952. The Messina Declaration in June 1955 proclaimed the goal of "a united Europe, through the development of common institutions, the progressive fusion of national economies, the creation of a common market, and the gradual harmonization of social policies." This was a new departure in history. Never before had a group of states that had often been enemies peacefully set out to construct a common future.

At every step toward those goals, Europeans dragged their feet, partly because governments were jealous of their sovereignty and partly because peoples were

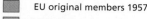

The Growth of the European Union (EU)

- EU original members 1957
- EU members by 1973
- EU members by 1986
- EU members by 1995
- EU members by 2004
- EU members by 2007
- candidate countries
- €   countries using the euro as of January 2009

protective of their national cultures and identities. The Council of Ministers that effectively ran the **European Union** was deliberately an international rather than a supranational body. Entrenched forms of protection, especially over agriculture, limited the freedom of the common market.

The economic success of the European Union complicated the problems, as the community enlarged: from the 6 original member states to 12 in 1986, 15 in 1995, and 27 in 2007 (see Map 28.10). With each enlargement, consensus became more difficult to achieve. Some countries opted out of key initiatives, including the abolition of internal border controls and the single European currency, the euro, introduced in 2002. Fundamental divisions opened between countries, typified by Britain, that wanted what the French president Charles de Gaulle (1890–1970) called "a Europe of National Fatherlands," and those that wanted a Europe "of regions" in which nation-states would wither away in favor of natural regional groupings, or a centralized European superstate.

To some extent, the adoption in the 1990s of the principle known as *subsidiarity* eased the difficulties. Borrowed from Catholic political thought, this doctrine held that decisions should always be taken at the level closest to the people whom the decisions most affected. But how many decision-making levels were needed among the local, the regional, and the pan-European? Would the traditional nation-states retain a role, and, if so, would it be subordinate to pan-European decision making? And how large should the European Union be? Reluctance to admit Muslim states—Turkey, Bosnia, and Albania—was obvious. Yet Europe needed to show that the Union could accommodate Muslims, if only because, as we shall see in the next chapter, in the closing decades of the twentieth century, Muslim minorities grew rapidly throughout Western Europe.

The big question was whether the evolving European partnership could become the "ever-closer Union" its top brass envisioned. A proposed European constitution, which represented an attempt to reconcile the conflicts between the Union and member states, was tested in a series of national referendums and parliamentary votes in 2004–2005. Each country had to endorse it for it to come into effect. Although nine countries approved the constitution, voters in France and the Netherlands rejected it by substantial margins in June 2005. A revised version of the constitution is currently being debated, but its prospects of being adopted by all 27 member states are uncertain, and it has already been rejected in a referendum by Irish voters.

In Perspective
The Anvil of War

War dominated and can almost be said to have determined global politics in the twentieth century. War strained the empires that Europeans had constructed so laboriously in the nineteenth century. In the first half of the twentieth century, those empires barely endured, and in the second half, they all collapsed. Decolonization was usually violent and economically disruptive. Much of the decolonized world, especially in Africa, was left impoverished and racked by political instability. The United States was the only country that emerged from global conflict richer and stronger.

Meanwhile, war stimulated the development of new military technologies that, by the middle of the century, had become so destructive that the world readily agreed with the judgment uttered by President John F. Kennedy in 1961. "Mankind must put an end to war, or war will put an end to mankind."

At one level, contending superpowers dominated the story of global politics in the twentieth century. At another, it was a tale of ideological conflicts, in which democracy contended with rival kinds of authoritarianism and totalitarianism.

If the great wars of the first half of the century were civil wars of Western and Eastern civilizations, the Cold War was the conflict of an increasingly globalized world—a struggle to decide what the common culture of the world would be—its shared assumptions about politics and economics. The end of the Cold War was part of a more general climax that devoured authoritarian systems and spread democracy and capitalism in their wake. Yet efforts to establish a peaceful world order failed. By the end of the century, the world depended on the only remaining superpower, the United States, to act as a global policeman. No one—especially the American taxpayer, who had to pay the check—would find this satisfactory for long. The chances increased that rivals would again contest superpower status, as the European Union began to function and as China recovered momentum, after a long period of unfulfilled potential. The prospect revived that global history would again unfold from the east as the era of Chinese disintegration and weakness—which Aleksandr Persikoff had glimpsed from his brothel in Harbin at the beginnings of the Sino-Japanese War in the 1930s—came to an end.

"The end of the Cold War was part of a more general climax that devoured authoritarian systems and spread democracy and capitalism in their wake. Yet efforts to establish a peaceful world order failed."

Chronology

1914–1918	World War I
1917	Russian Revolution begins
April 1917	United States enters World War I
1919–1920	Paris peace conference
1922	Benito Mussolini's Fascist Party seizes power in Italy
1929	United States stock market crash
1930–1931	Military seizes power across Latin America
1931	Japan invades Manchuria
1933	Nazis take power in Germany
1936–1939	Spanish Civil War
1939–1945	Nazis carry out genocide of Europe's Jews; World War II
1941	Germany invades Soviet Union; Japan attacks Pearl Harbor
August 1945	United States drops atomic bombs on Hiroshima and Nagasaki
1947	Indian independence and partition
1948	State of Israel established; Marshall Plan initiated
1949	North Atlantic Treaty Organization (NATO) formed; Soviet Union produces atomic bomb; communists take power in China
1950s and 1960s	Decolonization of most of Africa and Asia
1950–1953	Korean War
1956	Suez Crisis
1959	Fidel Castro takes power in Cuba
1961–1973	United States involvement in Vietnam War
1966	Mao launches Cultural Revolution in China
1970s	Military dictatorships in much of Latin America
1973	World oil crisis triggers global inflation
1974	36 states have democratic franchises
1985	Mikhail Gorbachev takes power in Soviet Union
1989–1991	Collapse of Soviet control of Eastern Europe and of the Soviet Union itself
1990s	China becomes world's fastest growing economy
1994	Nelson Mandela becomes president of South Africa
2000	139 states classifiable as democracies

In retrospect, the long-term significance of the war whose opening Persikoff witnessed was boundless. Dominance in East Asia and the Pacific was at stake; and over the twentieth century as a whole, this seems to have been the strategic area of greatest importance. For, as we shall see in the next chapters, during the twentieth century, the great shift of the balance of population, wealth, and power westward from Asia into European and North American hands—the dominant trend of global history in the nineteenth century—began to ease. East Asian communities began to catch up economically with Europe and even, to some extent, with America. The Pacific replaced the Atlantic as the world's foremost arena of long-range trade.

Americans, meanwhile, may have relished their country's role but did not choose it. They suffered resentment and even hatred in return. In part, this was because the United States government's exercise of global responsibilities seemed to many people to be unreasonable and unjust. On the one hand, the importance of the United States' role for the peace of the world was well illustrated in 1990, when Iraq launched a self-interested invasion of Kuwait, and American-led forces restored the status quo. Some arenas of intervention, on the other hand, seemed poorly chosen. Under President Bill Clinton (1993–2001), military action or bombing raids in Somalia, Sudan, and Serbia seemed weakly justified and ill targeted. In 2001 and 2003, President George W. Bush launched invasions of Afghanistan and Iraq that appeared, to much of the rest of the world, to have little justification in the Afghan case and no reasonable pretext at all in that of Iraq. Both adventures have been costly, and in both cases, America became committed to long-term political and military interventions, with no clear exit strategies. American power alone was evidently not enough to preserve the peace of the world indefinitely. American administrations did little to build international institutions to share the burdens or take over the task.

It was not, however, solely, or even principally, American might and muscle that made the twentieth century "the American century." The magnetism of the United States was more a matter of what political scientists came to call *soft power*: cultural influence, and the appeal of American institutions and ways of life. Nor was it only American power that made many people resent America. For every admirer of American culture, others detested or despised it. To understand the context of these reactions, we have to turn to the social and cultural history of the twentieth-century world.

PROBLEMS AND PARALLELS

1. Why can Japan's conflicts with China in the first half of the twentieth century and World Wars I and II in Europe be viewed as civil wars?

2. How did World War I weaken European colonial control? Why were President Woodrow Wilson's principles of self-determination not applied outside Europe? How successful were those principles in Europe itself?

3. Why did the United States emerge as the world's leading power after World War I? What effect did postwar disillusionment have on European society?

4. Why were conflicts over power in the 1920s and 1930s increasingly seen as ideological conflicts? What did fascism and communism have in common? Why did Hitler and Stalin sign a nonaggression pact in 1939 despite their ideological differences?

5. What effect did nuclear armaments have on world politics? How did the Cold War dominate world affairs from the late 1940s to the late 1980s? What roles did China under Mao Zedong and Cuba under Fidel Castro play during the Cold War?

6. Why did the European empires collapse so quickly after World War II? What problems did the newly independent states of Africa and Asia inherit from the colonial empires? Why was it so remarkable that Nelson Mandela became president of South Africa?

7. Why is the United States unlikely to remain the world's only superpower? Why has Europe's move toward unification since World War II been so problematic? How is China's growing economic strength likely to affect the world's economy and politics in the twenty-first century?

READ ON ▶ ▶ ▶

The opening story comes from O. A. J. Pernikoff, *Bushido: The Anatomy of Terror* (1973). Vast numbers of books are available on World War I and II. Good starting points for World War I include I. Beckett, *The Great War 1914–1918* (2001), an overview of the military, political, social, economic, and cultural aspects of the conflict; M. Gilbert, *First World War* (1996); N. Ferguson, *The Pity of War: Explaining World War I* (2000), a controversial revisionist account of the war; and P. Fussell, *The Great War and Modern Memory* (2000), a cultural history of the Western reaction to the struggle and to its legacy. Probably the best introduction to World War II is W. Murray and A. R. Millet, *A War to Be Won: Fighting the Second World War, 1937–1945* (2000). Also solid is G. Weinberg, *A World at Arms: A Global History of World War II* (1995).

I drew on F. L. Allen's *The Lords of Creation* (1996) for the background to the Depression. S. L. Engermann and R. E. Gallman, eds., *The Cambridge Economic History of the United States*, vol. 3 (1996) is searching and comprehensive.

The historiography of the Cold War has not surprisingly proven ideologically contentious. J. L. Gaddis, *The Cold War: A New History* (2005) is a reasonably balanced and well-written overview that emphasizes the relationship between the superpowers, the United States and the USSR. O. A. Westad, *The Global Cold War: Third World Interventions and the Making of Our Times* (2005), focuses instead on the global and Third World dimensions of the conflict and their complicated connections to decolonization. I found H. Thomas, *Armed Truce* (1986) helpful. A convenient introduction decolonization itself is D. Rothermund, *The Routledge Companion to Decolonization* (2006), which presents both a detailed chronology and narrative, and thematic analysis. P. Duara, *Decolonization (Rewriting Histories)* (2004) provides significant excerpts from the writings of major leaders of decolonization movements and presents the process from the perspective of the colonized. On Ethiopia see M. Meredith, *Haile Selassie's Wars* and A. Tiruneh, *The Ethiopian Revolution*.

Books on "The New World Order" tend to range from the partisan to the paranoid, but A. Slaughter, *A New World Order* (2005) is an original, if dense, reconceptualization. On the EU, see J. McCormick, *Understanding the European Union: A Concise Introduction* (3rd ed., 2005). For a broad examination of the role of war and military power in shaping world orders, see J. Black, *War and the World: Military Power and the Fate of Continents, 1450–2000* (2000).

CHAPTER 29

The Pursuit of Utopia:
Civil Society in the Twentieth Century

▲ **Women soldiers.** Though female intellectuals were prominent ideologues in the Mexican Revolution that began in 1910, revolutionaries nurtured contradictory images of women: "Marieta, don't be a flirt" was the refrain of one song about a stereotypical woman camp-follower who provides comfort for the troops, while "Adelita" was the heroine of one of the revolution's most famous anthems (and a successful stage-play), about what we would now call a female "suicide bomber." As the photograph shows, women did train as *soldaderas*—corps of guards who patrolled the ammunition dumps in the rear of the battle lines.

MEXICO

Languidly, quietly, in front of a small crowd, on September 11, 1910, a delegation from the United States unveiled a statue of George Washington—a present for the people of Mexico on the one hundredth anniversary of the start of Mexico's war of independence from Spain. On their way back to their lodgings, the delegates saw a crowd gathering near the statue of Christopher Columbus in the heart of Mexico City. They turned aside to watch what they thought would be a lavish entertainment in a city notoriously "dedicated to amusements."

Instead, they saw an antigovernment demonstration unfold, dominated by a "tall, spare, nervous woman," carrying a red silk banner, emblazoned with the insignia of a revolutionary organization called Daughters of Cuauhtemoc, after the last Aztec leader to resist the Spanish conquistadores (see Chapter 16):

> the groups carrying their beautiful floral pieces and a dozen or so banners, began to sing the national hymn. . . . Castro, chief of the mounted police, face flaming and sword raised, rode into the party . . . in a rage demanding, "Who is leader here?" There was no response and he ordered his men to disperse the crowd. . . . The mounted police rode into the party raising their swords and threatening, while a cordon of foot police . . . cleared a great circle. . . . Again the mounted police charged and broke them down; again . . . and yet again the same thing happened, but at last the little party dwindled away. The police bundled a bunch of banners into a coach and bore them off in triumph. Some of the league leaders, among them the bearer of the banner of the Daughters of Cuauhtemoc, were taken off to Belem prison.

The unfortunate flagwaver was a woman in her sixties. Dolores Jiménez was an exceptionally well-educated middle-class woman from a provincial city, noted for her journalism and poems. The declared aim of the Daughters of Cuauhtemoc was that "the women of Mexico should realize that their rights and obligations extend outside the home." As a woman who supported herself by own labor as a writer, Jiménez was in the vanguard of Mexico's women's movement, which mobilized many organizations similar to the Daughters of Cuauhtemoc, published numerous periodicals, and called for women's emancipation and enfranchisement. She was more than a feminist. She was a revolutionary firebrand who called herself a socialist, and had written a manifesto calling for the redistribution of land in favor of Mexico's poor. Her poems disclose what really mattered to her. There is no line of love, except love of freedom. She praised republicanism, the sovereignty of the people, an elected legislature, a free press.

The poems have many of the fearful features of revolutionary enthusiasm. They call on men to die for a cause and assume they will die happily. They idolize dubious heroes of the remote past. Jiménez called Mexicans "sons of Anahuac"—the mythic homeland of the Aztecs. She recalled hearing in childhood about Father Miguel Hidalgo, the poor priest who summoned his people to freedom in the rebellion of 1810 against Spain (see Chapter 21). "My ears heard it and it made my heart race." Jiménez was a romantic who associated her love of Mexico with rhapsodies on the landscape. She opposed the reelection of President Porfirio Díaz (1850–1915) partly because he was, in effect, a dictator who had exercised supreme power for more than three decades, and partly because he had shown his distaste for women who took on responsibilities outside the home.

How were the atrocities of the twentieth century related to the attempts to create ideal societies or utopias?

Why did the influence of the state first increase and then decrease in the twentieth century?

How is globalization shifting the world's patterns of wealth and power?

How has migration from former colonies and underdeveloped regions affected social change in the West?

Why did religion become more vigorous in the late twentieth century?

The celebrations the United States delegation witnessed were meant to consolidate enthusiasm for Díaz. Instead, they helped ignite a revolution. Earlier in the year, the government had gerrymandered primary election results and arrested Francisco Madero (1873–1913), the main opposition candidate for president. Madero had always claimed to advocate democracy within the law, but from prison he planned a rebellion. The independence celebrations concentrated crowds and aroused emotions. In November, Madero replied to an invitation to join a family holiday, excusing himself on the grounds that he had a revolution to lead.

Dolores Jiménez—despite repeated imprisonment—escaped to join one of the most radical and violent of the revolutionaries, Emilio Zapata (1879–1919), who led a peasant army against the landowners and the government. Although Díaz was quickly overthrown and fled the country at the end of May 1911, it was harder to find a lasting new leader or an agreed course for Mexico's future. The revolutionaries had too many causes. Nationalists hated foreign capitalists who, with Díaz's connivance, had long milked the country of resources. Provincial leaders wanted to emasculate central power. Peasants wanted to grab land or wreak vengeance on their oppressors. Anticlericals wanted to strip the church of social influence. Socialists wanted to empower workers. Self-interested warlords wanted to exploit chaos. Different ethnic constituencies—various indigenous peoples, citizens of mixed descent—wanted their share of central power or devolved government—and when they saw the chance of trading one for the other, their leaders sometimes changed their game. The country dissolved into civil war and political instability, which lasted until 1930. Ruined estates and churches, increased rates of crime, and especially of murder and rape, were among the legacies. The cause for which Jiménez hoisted her banner foundered: Mexican women did not get the vote until 1953. It was a typical twentieth-century story, of utopia ardently sought and easily lost, deflected, postponed, or abandoned.

The most disheartening aspect of the revolution was the willingness of revolutionaries to resort to violence. The ugly side of idealism showed itself early. In May 1911, when a government garrison town fell to revolutionaries, a mob leader was reportedly denouncing Chinese immigrants as government partisans and crying, "It would be best to exterminate them!" The town's self-appointed liberators massacred 250 Chinese and ransacked their property. The most terrifying paradox of the twentieth century was that all the advances of the era—in science, in technology, in the spread of education and knowledge, in the increased availability of information, and in progress toward worldwide material prosperity—did nothing to avert moral catastrophe.

The paradox does, however, make a kind of hideous, warped sense. For people who experienced the unprecedented rate of progress in the twentieth century, **utopia** seemed attainable. A world improved or perfected seemed within reach. Massacre was just one way to get there: re-creating a world without enemies. The new power of technology at the disposal of governments constituted an opportunity to reforge society for the better. The social history of the twentieth century is largely a story of utopian projects that failed, as chaos undid plans and overpowered progress. If there is a global theme in the social history of the twentieth century, this is it. Utopian ambitions inherited from the past seemed briefly realizable, before disillusionment or realism set in.

THE CONTEXT OF ATROCITIES

The twentieth century was a century of atrocities, partly because it was a century of war. War is morally brutalizing. Wartime censorship, which portrays atrocities as excesses of the other side, often conceals that fact from the public. Propaganda, ably supplemented by filmmakers, concentrates on the genuinely ennobling effects of combat—the incidents of heroism and self-sacrifice, the growth of camaraderie. The corrupting effects of war on character—the corrosion of decency, the demonizing of the foe—are omitted from the picture.

War stimulates massacres because it blinds people to their enemies' humanity. As we have seen (see Chapter 28), when the Sino-Japanese War started in 1931, the belligerent peoples were inclined to be prejudiced in each other's favor—to see themselves as fraternally linked. But as the war progressed and outrages by Japanese troops multiplied, Chinese called the Japanese "evil spirits," while Japanese called the Chinese "insects" or "pigs" or—in the case of women enslaved for military brothels—"public urinals." When they engaged in "killing practice," Japanese soldiers, according to their own later accounts, were taught to regard a Chinese victim as "something of rather less value than a dog or a cat." In the worst recorded massacre of the war, at Nanjing in 1937, John Rabe, a German resident who provided sanctuary for refugees, reported rotting corpses piled up in the streets—girls savagely raped before being shredded with bayonets or shot in the back while fleeing, babies skewered, men and women torched or hacked to death, with a ferocity Rabe found impossible to understand. The victims of the atrocities could not believe their assailants were fellow human beings. Japanese soldiers who took part in the slaughter—such as Nagatomi Hakudo, who remembered "smiling proudly as I . . . began killing people"—subsequently found their own behavior impossible to understand. If scholars' calculations are correct, 250,000 people died at Nanjing in the six to eight weeks from December 13, when the soldiers received orders to kill all prisoners of war.

Along with war, ideological and intercommunal hatreds stimulated horrifyingly inhuman behavior, which war conditions commonly made worse. During World War II (1939–1945), the Nazi regime consciously set out to exterminate groups the Nazis blamed for the ills of society: Gypsies, homosexuals, and, above all, Jews. The murder of millions of Jews, which historians have termed the **Holocaust**, was the most chilling example, because of the scale of the genocide, the systematic way in which people were killed, and the cold-blooded industrialization of the killing process. Once they had perfected the method, the killers herded Jews into death camps and drove them into sealed rooms where they gassed them to death. Pointless cruelty accompanied the Holocaust: millions enslaved, starved, and tortured in so-called scientific experiments. The weak and helpless were not spared. On the contrary, the Nazi vision of utopia demanded a world from which the weak had been gutted out and discarded.

No case of **genocide** quite matched the Nazi campaign against the Jews, but that was not for want of other attempts. After World War II, German minorities were on the receiving end of campaigns of annihilation: expelled from Czechoslovakia, the Baltic States, and Poland, massacred or exiled by the Soviet Union. At intervals across the century, massacres motivated by the desire to exterminate entire communities occurred in Turkish Armenia, in Crimea and Chechnya in the former Soviet Union, in Iraqi Kurdistan, in Rwanda and Burundi in Central Africa, in Bosnia-Herzegovina and Kosovo in the former Yugoslavia, in Darfur in southern and western Sudan, in Burma, Congo, Nigeria, and other flashpoints of ethnic tension shown on Map 29.1. Other projects for purging the

In war, atrocities breed atrocities. Chinese nationalist soldiers execute fellow countrymen accused of collaboration with the Japanese after the "Rape of Nanjing" in 1937.

"The social history of the twentieth century is largely a story of utopian projects that failed, as chaos undid plans and overpowered progress. If there is a global theme in the social history of the twentieth century, this is it."

MAP 29.1

Genocides and Atrocities, 1900–Present*

⊙ location and date with approximate number of people killed

—— political borders, 2007

The Holocaust

extent of German Reich, 1942

under German occupation, 1942

▼ concentration camp

60,000 estimated number of Jews murdered in Holocaust

percentage of total population of Jews murdered in Holocaust

—— political borders, 1939

Mass killings and "disappearances", 1975–1985
40,000

GUATEMALA
EL SALVADOR

Government-backed death squads,1979–1981
30,000

BRAZIL

Amazon Indians
500,000

Killings and "disappearances," 1973–1990
3,000

CHILE

ARGENTINA

Dirty War, 1976–1983
10,000–30,000

200 km
200 miles

NORWAY
850

FINLAND
7

SWEDEN

North Sea

Baltic Sea

ESTONIA
1,750

LATVIA
89%
85,000

LITHUANIA
87%
135,000

DENMARK
60

NETH.
80%
112,000

BELG.
48%
35,500

GERMANY
83%
180,000

POLAND
88%
2,625,000

USSR
46%
2,200,000

LUX.
95,000

FRANCE
43%
95,000

CZECHOSLOVAKIA
83%
266,500

AUSTRIA
67%
40,000

HUNGARY
50%

ROMANIA
49%
310,000

26%
11,750

YUGOSLAVIA
87%
60,000

190,000

BULGARIA
14%
7,000

ITALY

Adriatic Sea

Black Sea

N

GREECE
80%
58,500

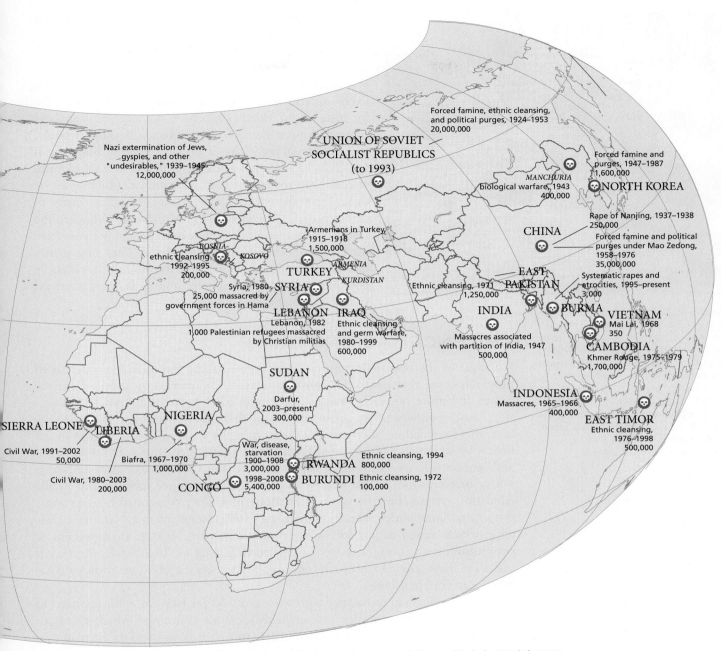

Forced famine, ethnic cleansing, and political purges, 1924–1953
20,000,000

Nazi extermination of Jews, gyspies, and other "undesirables," 1939–1945
12,000,000

UNION OF SOVIET SOCIALIST REPUBLICS
(to 1993)

MANCHURIA
biological warfare, 1943
400,000

Forced famine and purges, 1947–1987
1,600,000

NORTH KOREA

Rape of Nanjing, 1937–1938
250,000

CHINA

Forced famine and political purges under Mao Zedong, 1958–1976
35,000,000

Armenians in Turkey, 1915–1918
1,500,000

BOSNIA
ethnic cleansing 1992–1995
200,000

KOSOVO

ARMENIA

KURDISTAN

Ethnic cleansing, 1971
1,250,000

EAST PAKISTAN

Systematic rapes and atrocities, 1995–present
3,000

TURKEY

SYRIA

Syria, 1980
25,000 massacred by government forces in Hama

LEBANON
Lebanon, 1982
1,000 Palestinian refugees massacred by Christian militias

IRAQ
Ethnic cleansing and germ warfare, 1980–1999
600,000

INDIA
Massacres associated with partition of India, 1947
500,000

BURMA

VIETNAM
Mai Lai, 1968
350

CAMBODIA
Khmer Rouge, 1975–1979
1,700,000

SUDAN
Darfur, 2003–present
300,000

INDONESIA
Massacres, 1965–1966
400,000

EAST TIMOR
Ethnic cleansing, 1976–1998
500,000

SIERRA LEONE
Civil War, 1991–2002
50,000

LIBERIA
Civil War, 1980–2003
200,000

NIGERIA
Biafra, 1967–1970
1,000,000

War, disease, starvation 1900–1908
3,000,000

1998–2008
5,400,000

CONGO

RWANDA
Ethnic cleansing, 1994
800,000

BURUNDI
Ethnic cleansing, 1972
100,000

*This map does not purport to be comprehensive, but to convey the global nature of genocides and other atrocities in the twentieth century.

world of unwanted groups included the attempted extermination of political and economic communities. We can recall the ideologically driven massacres perpetrated by the dictatorships of Stalin in Russia and Mao Zedong in China, which equaled or excelled in scale anything the Nazis did, and the comparable efforts in the 1970s of Pol Pot's Khmer Rouge in Cambodia (see Chapter 28).

The history of twentieth-century atrocities showed that no level of civilization, education, or military discipline immunized people against barbarism, whenever war or fear ignited hatred and numbed compassion. During World War II, for instance, thousands of normally decent citizens of the German Reich, who prided themselves on their civilized attainments—including artists and intellectuals, who loved classical music and literature and frequented museums—took part in massacres of Jews and other alleged enemies, "deviants," and "subversives" without apparently realizing that

The Holocaust. At the Nordhausen concentration camp, the Nazis spent nothing to build and operate the gas chambers they used in other camps. The inmates at Nordhausen—catalogued as too weak or ill to be useful as slave labor—were left to starve to death. In an attempt, apparently, to leave no witnesses, guards massacred the survivors when U.S. troops approached the camp in April 1945. This photograph shows some of the more than 3,000 corpses the Americans found, but a few of the inmates were still alive.
Art Archive/Picture Desk, Inc./Kobal Collection.

they were doing anything wrong. Scientists and physicians in Germany and Japan experimented on human guinea pigs to discover more efficient methods of killing. On a lesser scale, atrocities accompanied wars, including those fought by soldiers who were raised in democracies and were relatively well educated in humane values. In the Vietnam War, for instance, in March 1968, nice, homey American boys massacred more than 300 noncombatant peasants, women, and children in the village of My Lai, under the influence of fear-induced adrenalin. During war in Iraq in 2004, pictures of American soldiers of both sexes amusing themselves by torturing and sexually abusing Iraqi prisoners, many of whom proved to be innocent noncombatants, shocked the world. The perpetrators of these outrages did not even have the excuse of being depraved by combat. They were prison guards. Like some of the Japanese in Nanjing, they actually posed for souvenir photographs, smiling as they performed vicious and degrading acts.

THE ENCROACHING STATE

For most of the twentieth century, states seemed to be the most likely agents of utopia, because they controlled most resources and exercised most power—more power and more resources than ever before in history. States did not forfeit citizens' trust, even when they abused it. For the first three-quarters or so of the century, there seemed no alternative to the state as the shaper of society. Even in the liberal West, which had inherited from the Enlightenment the doctrine of social and economic laissez-faire (see Chapter 22), the state took on ever more responsibility, for education, health, and welfare. National insurance schemes and public education systems became symbols of modernity. They consumed huge proportions of national budgets, because their costs were uncontrollable. National insurance, which aimed to pay for sickness and retirement by state management of compulsory contributions, never succeeded in paying for itself, and, wherever it was tried, new schemes sooner or later replaced it. Increasingly, taxation paid for health care and pensions.

Social policy had to balance a growing demand for freedom with the need to regulate increasingly complex and unwieldy societies. Planning—which meant, in effect, a huge surrender of individual liberty to public power and an extension of state interference into the nooks and crannies of private life—seemed an irresistible cure-all. The example of the United States, where federal initiatives helped to dispel the misery of the Great Depression of the 1930s, was encouraging. The influence of the economic thought of John Maynard Keynes (1883–1946), who argued for years for the "end of laissez-faire," was important and, for some governments, decisive (see Chapter 28).

World War II (1939–1945) also encouraged regimentation and collectivism. The war accustomed citizens to take orders, produce by command, and consume under rationing. President Franklin D. Roosevelt (1882–1945) was able to control American industry. Canada and Britain acquired command economies almost as heavily regulated as those under fascism and communism. Peace eased but did not end these conditions. In some European countries and Japan, rationing was actually stricter after the war than during it. Emergency repairs after World War II renewed government power. Everyone took it for granted that governments, with the help of agencies the victorious Allies established, would get devastated economies back to work. In most of Europe, governments nationalized major industries on which the economic infrastructure depended, such as transport, communications, and energy supply. Even states that did not adopt communism applied such measures.

Medicine and schooling illustrate best the effects of the politicization of social issues. Wherever states got involved in providing health care, the results were spectacular. Compulsory, state-funded immunization ended the rapacious diseases that had regularly killed children, including polio, measles, mumps, whooping cough, and rubella. As we shall see in the next chapter, many major killing and maiming diseases, which affected all age groups, were controlled and even eliminated, not only in rich countries, but across the world. Health education, combined with fiscal measures, changed people's habits. Smoking—a universal relaxation in the early twentieth century—became a pariah activity in many Western countries by the century's end. Many addictive stimulants and narcotics increased in popularity as they became relatively cheap—including, especially, marijuana and coca-derived substances. But governments took tough countermeasures. Toward the end of the century, publicly funded health campaigns even targeted alcoholic beverages and fatty foods, which adversely affected only a minority of consumers. Such campaigns appeared even in countries with no historic problems associated with these kinds of food and drink, including Chile and Canada, China and India.

Above all, the state got increasingly involved in paying doctors and running hospitals. Except for the United States, all rich countries acquired huge public health establishments. The results again were positive in one way. Millions of poor people were liberated from the fear of neglect. Life, for the seriously sick, ceased to be a privilege confined only to those who could pay for treatment. On the other hand, the costs of medical care spiraled out of control, and states struggled to pay the bills. Britain's National Health Service, for instance, established on a lavish scale after World War II and widely regarded as a model to follow, absorbed the biggest slice of the country's budget by the 1980s. No country was too poor to have a public health policy and at least some public funding for medical care (see Chapter 30).

Meanwhile, under the growing influence of the state, the nature of education changed. Governments' priorities for schools were concerned with solid citizenship and economic efficiency. Like democracy, education was the cure-all of a former age—a means to a dreary sort of utopia. It would transform dangerous masses into easily influenced, collaborative patriots. It would guarantee stability and sustain progress. Theorists and a few practitioners in elite institutions pursued grander projects—such as enhancing the pleasure students take in life, acquainting them with their cultural heritage, and stimulating their critical responses. For most children, these remained postponed ideals. In the twentieth century, coarser values replaced them. The noblest aims to which governments aspired were curbing unemployment, manning the technology of the future, and keeping young criminals off the streets. More people got more education at greater cost than ever, yet almost everywhere parents and employers complained about the quality of the results. In practice, out-of-school education took up the slack: universities, in-work training, and continuing-education programs that enabled people to return to college at intervals during a working life.

No part of the world was exempt from the growth of "big government," but the United States experienced the phenomenon far less than most other countries. The reasons are clear. The world wars left American territory unscarred. The American

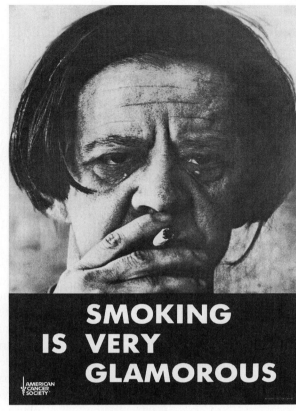

SMOKING IS VERY GLAMOROUS

AMERICAN CANCER SOCIETY

When antismoking campaigns began in the West in the 1970s, they were often privately funded and directed against the tobacco industry's own messages. Increasingly, as evidence accumulated that smoking undermined health, governments took over, combating smoking first with taxation and public health campaigns, then with outright prohibitions on smoking in public. In the mid-twentieth century, smoking was an almost universal indulgence. By the early twenty-first century in the United States, Canada, and parts of Western Europe, smokers had become a persecuted minority, forced to practice their habit furtively and in shame.

Reprinted by the permission of the American Cancer Society, Inc. All Rights Reserved.

Failed planning. As this photograph of a street in Bucharest, the capital of Romania, illustrates, the collapse of communism in Eastern Europe in 1989–1990 left grim legacies. The incompetence and rapacity of Nicolae Ceaucescu (1918–1989), Romania's communist dictator for more than 22 years, impoverished the country. Ceaucescu tore down much of Bucharest in a supposedly revolutionary program of urban planning. Unlike most of the other communist leaders in Eastern Europe, he refused to yield power peacefully. Instead, he was overthrown and executed after a brief, but bloody, civil war in December 1989. The debris from that struggle took years to clean up.

economy never suffered from the restraints on development inflicted by the division of the world into primary and secondary producers. The United States always managed to perform both functions in a big way. Americans took seriously their perception of their country as the land of the free. Although eventually, in the 1960s, the federal government began to encourage public welfare programs, especially during Democratic presidencies, and although public budgets and bureaucracies continued to grow in the United States just as they grew everywhere in the world, America remained relatively less governed than other big countries. This fact was important in "the American century" in a world that looked increasingly to the United States for models to follow.

For a while in the third quarter of the century, however, the Scandinavian countries—Sweden, Denmark, Norway, Finland, and Iceland—were more widely admired, and it appeared that the system they more or less shared would become the model for the world. Scandinavians favored liberal law-and-order policies with a welfare state and a mixed economy, heavily regulated and centrally planned. But the defects of the model soon became apparent. It created "Scandisclerosis" and "suicidal utopias." The former term referred to the way state regulation restrained business efficiency, while public ownership sapped the vigor of industry. The latter referred to the high suicide rates in "nanny states," where bureaucracy seemed to stifle individual initiative, and welfare provision cut the risk and zest out of life. Social engineering, however benevolent, could not deliver personal happiness. In the tawdry utopias modern architecture created (see Chapter 27), citizens recoiled from the dreariness of overplanned societies. People felt let down by progress and deceived by their leaders. By the 1980s, they began to lose faith in the viability of economic public sectors, as it became apparent to people all over the world that America's relatively underregulated economy was better at delivering prosperity.

Planning failed not only because human beings instinctively love liberty but also because planners' assumptions were naïve. Societies and economies are chaotic systems, where unpredictable effects disrupt planners' expectations. So the four- and five-year plans that were produced almost everywhere at some time up to the 1970s were almost everywhere discarded. In the 1980s and 1990s, governments—even those that were nominally socialist—raced to shed nationalized industries and to make peace with market forces. The perfectly planned urban projects of the 1960s, which represented the fulfillment of the ideals of rationalist architects—creating functional, egalitarian, technically proficient environments—proved practically uninhabitable. After a generation or so, they had to be demolished. At about the same time, the mixed economies and command economies favored in the postwar period were dismantled, deregulated, and restored to private enterprise. By the mid-1990s, private enterprise was responsible for more than 50 percent of output in Europe, even in formerly communist states. This was a change that swept the world. By the end of the century, only North Korea remained implacably hostile to the private sector.

This did not mean that bureaucracies ceased to grow. The balance between the public and private sector seemed impossible to get right. Whenever governments shifted responsibilities to the private sector, some communities and groups got left out of the benefits. Poverty gaps widened. Underclasses grew. Socially excluded and underprivileged communities bred crime and rebellion. More government spending had to help pay for the consequences. More state welfare agencies appeared to try to remedy the effects. Toward the end of the century, most governments faced rising crime rates and the threat of terrorism. Western govern-

Making Connections | THE ENCROACHING STATE

AREA OF CONCERN	STATE ACTIONS	CONSEQUENCES
Medicine	Compulsory state-funded immunization programs; health education; public health campaigns focusing on smoking, nutrition, drugs; hospitalization, medical care paid for by government	Control and elimination of once virulent diseases (polio, measles, mumps, rubella, smallpox, etc.); decline of smoking; increase in life expectancy; health care becomes available to poor, elderly, and previously neglected groups
Education	Public funding of education through high school and, in some countries, also for university and professional education; new emphasis on college education for more students and continuing education for adults	Higher rates of literacy; increased science and technology education leads to innovations, social transformations; unemployment declines as education increases
Welfare	Assistance for children and poor via direct payments, education, and health programs	Increased life expectancy, educational achievement, and employment rates among poor; improved standard of living
National Insurance	Financing of retirement and health care by compulsory contributions from employers, employees	Improved standard of living for elderly; drastic drop in poverty levels; better health care through specialized medical programs for elderly and disabled (e.g., Medicare in United States)

ments exploited the threat by exaggerating it. Terrorism did represent a special kind of menace, for if terrorists were to get hold of nuclear, chemical, or biological weapons, they could wreak havoc. This became one of Hollywood's favorite plots and a scenario that Western governments abused to persuade citizens to forfeit liberties. In the early twenty-first century, terrorist-induced alarmism attained new heights, thanks to an entirely exceptional terrorist success that demolished the World Trade Center towers in New York and damaged the Pentagon in Washington, D.C. This was an unrepeatable attack, achieved with minimal weaponry—using razor blades to hijack aircraft that the terrorists used, in effect, as missiles. Meanwhile, terrorism took its place alongside the hazards of modern life that demanded to be policed at the expense and inconvenience of the public—along with crime, public drunkenness, drug addiction, and other antisocial behavior.

In consequence, even after the Cold War had ended, defense and internal security demanded more funds and more personnel. Public spending accounted for 25 percent of gross domestic product (GDP) in the world's seven richest countries in 1965 and 37 percent by 2000. The encroaching state, moreover, continued to press upon civil liberties, as policemen multiplied and surveillance became more intrusive. Nor could governments shed welfare responsibilities, once they had undertaken them, without alienating voters and leaving vulnerable citizens' health or welfare exposed. Britain's costly National Health Service, for instance, became a sacred cow. Public education authorities could not discard the schools they maintained. Their only remedy for criticisms of the education system was higher

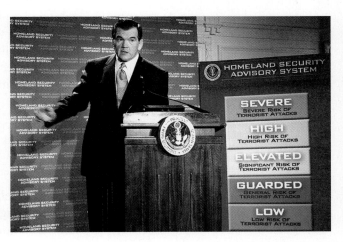

Terror alert. Former Secretary of Homeland Security Tom Ridge unveils a color-coded terrorism warning system on March 12, 2002, in Washington, D.C. Ridge said the nation was on yellow alert. The five-level system was in response to public complaints that broad terror alerts issued by the government since the September 11, 2001 attacks raised alarm without providing useful guidance. The vague categories—menacing without being informative—and the scary, angular graphics were part of the United States government's proclaimed "War on Terror," which justified the president in assuming, for an indefinite period, exceptional wartime powers of detention and surveillance that violated American traditions of civil liberties.

spending. State-funded workers' pensions became a barely affordable burden for many countries, because, as we shall see in the next chapter, life expectancy rose sharply in the late twentieth century. But somehow, governments had to find ways to pay.

UNPLANNING UTOPIA: THE TURN TOWARD INDIVIDUALISM

Nonetheless, it is undeniable that in the last quarter or so of the century, the world turned away from social and economic planning, first toward a rival kind of utopianism, represented by confidence in **individualism** and freedom, then—when that seemed to fail, too—toward a search for a third way that would deliver both prosperity and social solidarity.

Marxists' explanations for the shift are worth hearing with respect, because Marxists have a profound need to explain the forms of radicalism with which they are out of sympathy. For them, the shift was economically determined. Like all revolutions, it accompanied a transition from one means of production to another: from industrial to postindustrial economies, from the energy age to the information age. It is true that the rise of information technology (see Chapter 28) created a major new source of wealth and empowered a new class of businesspeople, distinguished by a distinctive mindset, numerate and imaginative. At about the same time, growing prosperity increased demand for service industries, which displaced manufacturing as the big money spinners in the global economy, and especially in the richest countries and communities. Individualism, therefore, according to the Marxist argument, re-arose as the ideology of a new "knowledge class," which now ran the world: the manipulators of information, who had replaced the puppeteers of production and the manipulators of the state. Or perhaps the demise of the industrial economy changed society because it also changed collective psychology. Because life seemed without purpose, no ideology seemed useful. Everyone could live for what they could get out of it—nothing more, nothing less. Frederic Jameson, the great exponent of this point of view, put it this way:

> As a service economy, we are . . . so far removed from the realities of production and work that we inhabit a dream world of artificial stimuli and televised experience: never in any previous civilization have the great metaphysical preoccupations, the fundamental questions of being and of the meaning of life, seemed so utterly pointless.

The global turn toward conservatism may also have been connected with another weighty economic factor: inflation. From the perspective of economic history, inflation was the most marked feature of the twentieth century. At times, it galloped uncontrollably, attaining rates of several thousand percent a year in Germany in 1923 and in Zimbabwe in the early twenty-first century, for example, when governments deliberately printed money in amounts that rendered the currency all but worthless. But, at historically unprecedented levels, it was a constant feature of life wherever money circulated. This fact is inseparable from the huge expansion of both resources and demand, which is part of the subject of the next chapter. If, however, one single influence drove prices upward more than anything else, it was governments' spendthrift habits with the money supply. As the number of governments grew, thanks to decolonization, and utopian projects gobbled up cash, the global money supply got out of control. The situation became intolerable in the 1970s. In October 1973, after another episode of warfare between Israel and

"Or perhaps the demise of the industrial economy changed society because it also changed collective psychology. Because life seemed without purpose, no ideology seemed useful. Everyone could live for what they could get out of it— nothing more, nothing less."

its Arab neighbors (see Chapter 28), Islamic oil-exporting countries attempted to influence American support for Israel by raising their prices. This triggered worldwide inflation on an unprecedented scale. Governments succeeded in controlling it by curtailing their ambitions, cutting expenditure, reducing borrowing, and reining in the money supply.

Deeper, longer-term influences were also at work. In part, the shift away from planning was a generational effect in the West. As the demographic consequences of the postwar baby boom began to grow, the tastes of a failed generation could be repudiated. Wartime solidarity was an emergency response for most of the societies that experienced it. It was bound to disappear into the generation gap that opened up in the 1950s and 1960s. As young people grew up without shared memories of wartime, they turned to libertarianism, existentialism, or mere self-indulgence. Youth could afford to defy parents because postwar economic recovery created plenty of well-paid work. Prosperous youth spent money in ways calculated to offend its elders and express its independence: on fashions, for instance, that were first extrovert, then psychedelic. The growth of the generation gap was measurable in the 1960s. Pop bands discarded their uniforms and grew their hair. Health statistics began to register the effects of sexual permissiveness, with epidemics of sexually transmitted diseases and cervical cancer. The contribution or response of the Catholic Church—the world's biggest and most influential Christian communion—is not often acknowledged. But in the Second Vatican Council, which convened at intervals in the 1960s, the church relaxed its rules in favor of freedom. The council licensed liturgical pluralism, showed unprecedented deference to other religions, and compromised its structures of centralized authority by elevating the role of bishops to be closer to that of the pope and the role of the laity to be closer to that of the priesthood. There could be no clearer indication that individualism was reawakening. If the church could not resist it, the state would not be able to either.

In extreme cases—and there were plenty of them in the 1960s and 1970s in the West—young rebels, alienated from the values of their elders, turned to violence. Urban guerrilla movements were never numerically strong but did wreak real havoc. They hoped that bombing, kidnapping, and shooting would spread terror, incite repression, and excite revolution. In Europe, they mounted spectacular operations against politicians, celebrities, businessmen, policemen, and service personnel, without provoking the intended reactions. They were most successful in parts of Latin America. In Argentina in the 1970s, they provoked the authorities into horrifying countermeasures, involving the disappearance of at least 15,000 victims of abduction, torture, and murder by the army and police. In Brazil, from 1969 to 1973, the government waged war against a movement that specialized in kidnapping foreign diplomats. Uruguay's almost unbroken democratic tradition was suspended from 1973 to 1985 while the army broke the urban guerrillas. Even in these countries, however, outraged youth only succeeded in provoking reaction, never in launching revolution.

Remarkably, the generation gap opened almost as wide in communist countries as in the West. The failed revolutions that marked the coming-of-age of postwar youth in 1968 came nearest to success in Paris and Prague. Student revolutionaries on one side of the Iron Curtain denounced the crisis of capitalism, while those on the other side called for a postcommunist "spring" or "thaw." In China, the ruling clique deflected youth rage into the Cultural Revolution

Hippies. May Day in Vermont, 1971. One of the paradoxes of the behavior of so-called Hippies is that they venerated nature—even to the extent of celebrating ancient pagan traditions of nature worship such as May Day—but took chemical drugs to help them perceive nature's beauties. This group, snapped by hippy photographer Peter Simon, displays some characteristic features: spaced-out, empty looks, touchy-feely intimacy, and loose-fitting clothes in bright colors reminiscent of the lurid mental images some drugs induced.

Cultural Revolution. Chinese citizens march in formation through the streets of Beijing while displaying a large portrait of Communist Party Chairman Mao Zedong (1893–1976), during the Cultural Revolution in the 1960s. The photograph is ludicrously posed, with a carefully contrived balance of workers' and peasants' costumes that seems to come straight out of a theatrical wardrobe.

(see Chapter 28). The revolutionaries' failures were part of a series of disillusioning experiences. In Russia, China, and other countries that communists had taken over, no relief followed for the sufferings of ordinary people, no end to the tyranny of small elites. In the rest of the world, capitalism was working: spreading prosperity, fomenting democracy, winning the approval of working-class voters. The left switched to soft targets: sexism, racism, elitism, the remnants of colonialism, traditional morality.

The trends of the next generation, when voters swung right, hair got shorter, fashion rebuttoned, and "moral majorities" found voice, were widely perceived as a reaction against "60s permissiveness." In reality, they represented the continuation in maturity of the projects of the young of the previous decade. Demands for personal freedom, sexual liberation, and existential self-fulfillment when one is young transform themselves naturally, when one acquires economic responsibility and family obligations, into policies of economic laissez-faire and less government. To "roll back the frontiers of the state" became the common project of those who rose to power in the West in the 1980s. Individual gratification—or, to use a widely favored euphemism, *fulfillment*—replaced broader codes of conduct and dominated many people's decision making: over whether to marry, for instance, whether to divorce, whether to procreate, how to occupy one's time.

The triumph of liberation became inseparable from sex in Western minds. The development of reliable methods of contraception, and of fairly reliable methods of protection against sexually transmitted diseases, equipped people—those who felt so inclined, at any rate—to lead undisciplined sex lives. Freedom to choose and change sexual partners proved incompatible, however, with the instinctive human tendency to feel sexual jealousy. Permissive sex subverted some of the collective loyalties on which Western society traditionally relied. Families periodically scrambled by sexual betrayal or boredom became typical of almost every Western society. Even in the small nuclear families characteristic of Western society, individualism had a dissolving effect, as family activities diminished, and family members began to eat separately and scatter for entertainment to personal video monitors, computer screens, or friendships outside the household. In the United States, fewer than one child in five was born outside wedlock in 1980. Only 20 years later, the number had risen to a third. By the end of the century, two-fifths of American marriages ended in divorce. What had once been normal—parents and children sharing the same household—became exceptional. Less than a quarter of households in the United States conformed to this pattern by the end of the century.

In the rapidly urbanizing environments of the world, family stability could not thrive as it had done in the rural communities from which the new town dwellers came. Street children crowded the streets of the developing world, becoming fodder for journalism and films, and the recruits of criminal gangs, warlords' armies, insurgents, guerrillas, and terrorists. The influence of Western lifestyles that movies, music, and broadcasting spread around the world created generation gaps everywhere. In Japan, commentators called the rootless young "new humans"—so profound was their rejection of traditional values and behavior. But the same sort of phenomenon could be observed everywhere. In the Muslim world, the young expected more freedom to choose marriage partners and careers. In South Korea and parts of Africa and the Americas, millions joined new religions and cults. Of course, every change set off reactions, and, while gaps opened between generations, chasms opened within them.

Warped Westernization? Brides and grooms standing in lines as the Unification Church weds 790 couples in a single mass ceremony in the 1970s in Seoul, South Korea. The sect, founded by Sun Myung Moon and popularly called "the Moonies," was among the most successful new religious cults of the day. Its Christian roots were, at best, remote. Moon, not Jesus, was its messiah, and his followers believed him to be divine. The Unification Church exploited the appeal of Western fashion but suppressed individualism.

COUNTERCOLONIZATION AND SOCIAL CHANGE

The world shrank. Ever-cheaper, ever-faster transport technologies meant that almost anyone could go almost anywhere. Long-range migration became possible for many of the poor of the world. The huge and growing disparities in wealth between the West and the rest of the globe drew migrants. Wars, tyrannies, and political instability drove them. In the second half of the twentieth century, the population boom in colonial and ex-colonial territories reversed one of the long-standing demographic trends of the past. The long flow of migration out of Europe into other parts of the world ended. Instead, **countercolonization** began. Birth rates in the former imperial "mother countries" declined. Labor from the rest of the world filled the gap.

It happened quickly, in step with decolonization (see Chapter 28). In 1948, the first black Jamaicans to arrive in Britain were astonished to see white men doing menial work. Immigrants to Britain from the West Indies numbered tens of thousands by 1954. Those from India reached the same number the following year, and those from Pakistan two years later. By the end of the century, Britain had more than 2 million Muslims, and France had more than 4 million. The Netherlands, with a total population of only 18 million, had nearly 1 million immigrants from its colonies and former colonies in Indonesia and the Caribbean.

Economists who tracked the growth of the sums or remittances immigrants sent home to their families—about 10 percent annually in the early twenty-first century—provided an index not only of the volume of migration and its global spread, but also its surprisingly modest economic impact. Although exact figures are disputed, in 2006, India, China, and Mexico probably each received at least $25 billion in remittances. In the former Soviet republic of Tajikistan, immigrants' remittances amounted to over a third of the national income. Most of the money went to keeping recipients fed: the transfer of cash, according to the World Bank, did little to crank up the economies of poor countries (see Map 29.2).

Countries most dependent on remittances, ca. 2007 (% of GDP)

37%	36%	32%	27%	26%	24%	24%	23%	22%
1	2	3	4	5	6	7	8	9
Tajikistan	Moldova	Tonga	Kyrgyz Republic	Honduras	Lesotho	Guyana	Lebanon	Haiti

MAP 29.2

A Shrinking World: Migration and Remittance Flows in the Early Twenty-First Century

Percentage of Noncitizen Population, ca. 2005

- greater than 40%
- 18%–40%
- 8%–17%
- 2%–7%
- less than 2%

**International migration trend since 1990
(arrow width reflects number of migrants)**

→ North and South American immigration
→ European immigration
→ Asian immigration
→ African immigration
→ Australia and Oceania immigration

Countries receiving the most remittances, ca. 2007 (US$bn)

India	27.0
China	25.7
Mexico	25.0
Philippines	17.0
France	12.5
Spain	8.9
Belgium	7.2
Germany	7.0
UK	7.0
Romania	6.8

The exchange of population was most intense, at first, between former colonies and their European mother countries, but it soon became more general, as migrants shifted from relatively poor, overpopulated parts of the world to relatively rich, underpopulated regions (see Map 29.2). Migrants from Latin America and Puerto Rico became the largest minority in the United States—over 36-million strong by the early twenty-first century. This was a form of countercolonization, since the United States had seized the territories most affected, California, Texas, and the Southwest, from Mexico during its empire-building in the nineteenth century (see Chapter 25) and had exercised informal empire over much of Latin America for most of the twentieth century. In other places, the link between imperialist pasts and present immigration patterns was barely discernible. In Italy, Spain, and Scandinavia, most of the immigrants came from outside the old imperial territories. In the Netherlands, the numbers of Moroccans and Turks equaled or exceeded those of immigrants from former Dutch colonies. In Germany, whose overseas empire had disappeared in 1918, and Switzerland, which had never had an empire, Turks formed the biggest category of guest workers. The Philippines had been an American colony until 1946, but came to supply labor—much of it illegal—for many countries in Europe and Arabia.

Immigrant community. A woman leaves a Turkish clothing shop in Berlin's Kreuzberg district, which has been called "little Istanbul." In 1961, the governments of West Germany and Turkey signed an agreement that allowed Turks to come to Germany as guest laborers, many of whom put down roots and never left. Today, Germany's Turkish community numbers over 2.5 million—the biggest minority group in the country.

Intercommunal tensions took on a new form, as communities of widely differing culture adapted to life alongside each other. One of the most remarkable changes of the late twentieth century was the way racism became socially and politically unacceptable in the West. In part, perhaps, this was another outcome of World War II. The Nazis had been racists, who regarded black people, Gypsies, and Jews, in particular, as among the "subhuman" groups suitable for exploitation or extermination. The defeat of Nazism was therefore a victory for intercommunal pluralism and coexistence. The black and Asian soldiers who fought for Britain, France, and the United States demonstrated their credentials for equality. In part, too, the decline of racism was an inevitable consequence of scientific progress. The pseudoscience that justified the racism of the nineteenth century was discredited in the twentieth.

Nevertheless, it took a long time to dismantle the legacy of racism and to convince prejudiced people to accept and respect new circumstances and new science. The United States was the critical battleground, partly because America came to lead the world in just about everything, and partly because the United States, with its huge, victimized, black minority, typified the problems. Beginning in the 1940s, African Americans fought a long series of legal cases, backed by political movements that organized demonstrations—especially those led by Martin Luther King (1929–1968)—and influenced voters, to enshrine the principal of equality in the law. Only in the 1960s, thanks to the federal courts and the administrations of Presidents John F. Kennedy (1917–1963) and Lyndon B. Johnson (1908–1973), did major breakthroughs take place. The federal government forced reluctant states to desegregate schools, outlaw whites-only privileges and facilities, and dismantle devices to stop black people's access to ballots and juries. By the end of the century, it was still not clear that efforts to redress racial inequalities had gone far enough. In 2008, the election as US president of an African immigrant's son, whose wife was a descendant of slaves, highlighted abiding problems and showed that they are reversible. Urban ghettoes and pockets of rural poverty remained.

Négritude. Aaron Douglas (1900–1979) was one of the black painters of the Harlem Renaissance of the 1920s who sought to "hurdle several generations of experience at a leap." His work is full of reminiscences of slavery, torn between pride and resentment. *Building More Stately Mansions* reminds viewers of how slaves built monuments of civilization, from ancient Egypt to modern America.

So, in consequence, did inequalities in education because public education was locally funded.

Abolition in 1961 of the "white Australia" policy, which had restricted immigration to Australia to persons of European descent, was another landmark. Migration to the country became open to people of every hue. Racial discrimination was outlawed in all European countries by the end of the century. South Africa, however, was a sticking point. Its ruling class was white, and most white South Africans, isolated from the intellectual changes that had discredited racism in most of the rest of the world, clung to an outdated conviction that black and white people should be consigned to exclusive spheres of *separate development*, a system that in practice supported white privilege. Increasingly, however, it became apparent that it was wiser for white South Africans to conserve their wealth and sacrifice their political power, rather than risk both in a protracted conflict and potentially catastrophic revolution. In the early 1990s, South Africa abandoned the policy of separate development. Black people were admitted to equality of rights, and a largely black political party assumed power peacefully, without either victimizing white South Africans or causing serious economic dislocation.

In response to unresolved tensions, people fell back on a reworked sense of their own identity. New forms of black identity were, perhaps, the most conspicuous example. Early in the twentieth century, Afro-Cuban scholars in newly independent Cuba began to treat black languages, literature, art, and religion on terms of equality with white culture. In 1906, Fernando Ortíz was interviewing black inmates in a Cuban jail. He had, as far as is known, no black ancestry himself. He was working on a thesis on the connections between race and crime. What impressed him, however, was the way the black inmates retained elements of culture—music, language, food, religion—that originated in Africa. Ortíz became an advocate of the African input to Cuba's heritage and an enthusiast for the work of black artists. Partly, thanks to his success, white advocates and imitators of black speech, music, prose, and imagery became numerous. It was relatively easy for black Cubans to feel thoroughly Cuban, especially since most people in the country had at least some black family connections. The poetry of Nicolás Guillén (1902–1989), one of the twentieth century's greatest poets, expresses this attitude. In the late 1920s, he became a leading exponent of *negrismo*—the assimilation of black influences in literature, especially his masterful use of the rhythms of black music and the street talk of black Cubans.

Coincidentally, white musicians discovered jazz, and white primitivist artists began to esteem and imitate African "tribal" art. The effect in the United States was to shake up existing black self-perceptions. During the nineteenth century, black Americans had felt Africa call to them. But the notion of returning "home" to Africa was out of favor by 1900. The senior black spokesman of the time, Booker T. Washington (1856–1915), opposed it. W. E. B. Du Bois (1868–1963), his successor, as the most influential black intellectual in the United States, was more radical than Washington. Du Bois was not content for black people simply to accept their lot and rely on education and economic improvement to raise them toward equality. He demanded social reforms. His major book, *The Souls of Black Folk*, was full of references to Africa. Du Bois was convinced that a common history connected black people throughout the world, but that history was now in the past. Black Americans had to be "both a Negro and an American." The Jamaican immigrant, Marcus Garvey, was among the black leaders who dissented. In 1916, he launched the slogan, "Africa for the black peoples of the world."

The idea that black culture embodied values superior to those of white culture was the next phase. The idea became a movement, spreading wherever black people lived—and, on its way, transforming the self-consciousness of those who were still under colonial rule or suffering under social inequalities. In French West Africa in the 1930s, Aimé Césaire and Léon Damas became brilliant spokesmen for the black self-pride they called **Négritude**. Léopold Senghor, a poet who worked alongside them and later became the first president of Senegal in 1960, defined Négritude as "the consciousness of being black, the simple recognition of fact, implying acceptance and responsibility for one's destiny as a black man, one's history and one's culture. It is the refusal to assimilate, to see oneself in the 'Other.' Rejection of the Other is affirmation of the self."

As a result, African independence movements gained strength; so did civil rights movements in countries such as South Africa and the United States, where black people were still denied equality under the law. In the late twentieth century, when those battles had been more or less won, the struggle continued against racial prejudice and remaining forms of social discrimination against black people in predominantly white countries. The black consciousness movement in the United States was a case in point, encouraging the rediscovery of African roots and even of African allegiances. "Philosophically and culturally," said the Black Muslim leader who called himself Malcolm X in 1964, "we Afro-Americans need to 'return' to Africa." Rastafarianism, a movement that identified Ethiopia as the spiritual homeland of black Americans, became popular in the same period—to the puzzlement of the Ethiopians themselves.

There was still no "master narrative" of history to rival the old, white-devised, "Eurocentric" account that almost every school curriculum taught. Black scholars had made attempts to create one, but never convincingly. Most attempts were based on obvious myths, such as the claim that black people were a lost tribe of Israel or "Nation of Islam." A more elaborate black version of global history followed, according to which Western civilization also originated in Africa and was transmitted via Egypt to ancient Greece. This seems, at best, an overstatement and oversimplification, but it is a sign of the vigor of the *Africanist* critique of our traditional picture of the world. Meanwhile, the scholarly world has come to accept that *Homo sapiens*, the species to which all of us belong, originated in Africa and that we all have a common African ancestor (see Chapter 1). These ideas have helped to justify, as well as reflect, the beginnings of a shift in the distribution of world power toward a more equitable balance, after the white, Western hegemony of the last couple of centuries.

The broader cultural impact of countercolonization was enormous. Along with the effects of accelerated economic exchange and of increased opportunities for long-range travel by Westerners, migration changed the prevailing direction of cultural exchange. By the 1990s, in Leicester—the midmost city in England—people could listen to 40 hours a week of broadcasts in Gujerati, an Indian language. In Australia, the public broadcasting services operated in 78 languages. Vietnamese, Lebanese, and North African restaurants abounded in Paris. Indian and Indonesian dishes had joined the national cuisines of Britain and the Netherlands, respectively.

Fusion religion. Students' prayers at the Nizhoni school in New Mexico are supposed to contribute to "global consciousness" and world peace by "gathering knowing from within the self." The language in which the founder expresses her views draws on Zen Buddhism, traditional Navajo spirituality, and modern Western psychology.

Chronology: Timeline of Women's Suffrage

New Zealand	1893
Australia	1902
Finland	1906
Norway	1913
Denmark, Iceland	1915
Soviet Union	1917
Canada	1918
Germany, Austria	1918
Poland, Czechoslovakia	1919
United States, Hungary	1920
Mongolia	1924
United Kingdom	1928
Turkey	1930
Spain	1931
Brazil	1932
Indonesia	1941
France	1944
Italy	1945
China, India	1949
Mexico	1953
Kenya	1963
Switzerland	1971
South Africa	1994
Kuwait	2005

But the spread of Asian influences in Westerners' tastes and thoughts also owed a lot to Western self-reevaluations. Under the weight of guilt about imperialism, postcolonial Westerners felt their own need for liberation from the legacy of the past. In the 1960s, travel to India became a compulsive fashion for Western intellectuals, along with Indian philosophy, mystical practices, music, and food. Political protesters in European and American streets in the same decade brandished copies of "little red books" containing selected thoughts of Mao Zedong. These fads waned, but Japanese, Chinese, and Indian art and thought became more important in the West for the rest of the century. Just as Western physicists looked to Daoism for help in understanding quantum mechanics (see Chapter 27), Western poets adopted the Japanese haiku form of verse. Zen became a widely revered, widely practiced intellectual tradition in the West. Buddhism, which had never attained the breadth of appeal of Christianity and Islam, began to attract converts in every clime. Black music and art, which had begun to influence the cultural mainstream in America and Europe in the earliest years of the century, captured the admiration of the white world.

The prevailing values of the late twentieth century were appropriate to a postcolonial, multicultural, pluralistic era. The fragility of life in a crowded, shrinking world and a global village encouraged or demanded multiple perspectives, as neighbors adopted or sampled each other's points of view. Hierarchies of value had to be avoided, not because they are false but because they lead to conflict. Relativism—the doctrine that each culture, and even individual, can choose appropriate norms, and therefore that no single set of norms is universally applicable (see Chapter 27)—displaced Westerners' confidence in the superiority of their own culture.

This doctrine, however, brought problems of its own. It made it hard to argue for the universality of human rights. It caused tension between minority values and mainstream culture. Festivals associated with majority religions had to be downplayed or modified to avoid offending minorities. Conflicts arose when migrants brought with them cultural practices and values that conflicted with the laws of their new homelands. In Islamic countries increasingly influenced by Sharia, or Islamic law, for instance, Westerners found that they could be prosecuted for using alcohol, or for not respecting traditional codes of dress and comportment for women. In the West, immigrants could not be allowed to continue some traditional practices, such as female circumcision, or polygamy, or the marriage of minors. "Asian values" became a slogan to justify use of the criminal law in, for example, Malaysia and Singapore, against practices the West tolerated, such as homosexuality and the recreational consumption of some drugs.

The idea that the law should treat everyone equally was so ingrained in the Western legal and philosophical tradition that it would have been unthinkable to allow people of different cultural backgrounds to be treated separately in the courts, or to be assigned separate jurisdictions, as had been usual, for instance, in the Middle Ages or under the Ottoman Empire. Most countries legislated for everyone to share the same civil rights, regardless of cultural background. Yet in practice, there were always cases of discrimination.

The status of women provoked some of the deepest difficulties. At the start of the twentieth century, no one expected uniformity in the way different cultures treated women. In the West, attention was riveted on the right to vote. In Islam, controversy centered on the rights of women in the home: to choose their husbands, for instance, or to equality with men under marriage law and in property rights. World War I (1914–1918), however, launched a profound revolution in the role of women in Western society. In practice, women were left to take command of their lives while so many men were fighting at the front. French law created the fiction of "tacit consent" to sanction women having affairs when their husbands were absent. The dead of World War I left gaps that societies were refashioned to fill. The young or old replaced the dead. Meritocracies replaced hereditary aristocracies in power. Women replaced men in the workplace. Before the war, only a few marginal countries gave women the vote. After the war, Russia, Germany, and the United States rapidly enfranchised women. So did Britain and most other Western countries, albeit with qualifications. So did Japan and Turkey.

Women had to want to break out of domesticity, but it was not necessarily in their interests to do so. Many of those who competed with men suffered for it. They had to fight discrimination. To succeed, they had either to be *superwomen*—the term became current in the 1980s for a professional or working woman who managed her life so well that she could work outside the home and also discharge the traditional roles of wife and mother within it—or accept subordination. Although legislation to equalize opportunities became normal in the West in the last quarter of the century, it was never fully effective. Many women accepted lower wages or worse contractual terms than men in corresponding jobs so that they could move in and out of work as their family responsibilities demanded. Some workplaces, especially in traditional male preserves, such as the armed forces, the police, the construction industry, and boardrooms in the industrial and financial sectors, had boyish or jock cultures, in which it was hard for women to fit and hard for men to adapt to their presence. Nevertheless, the cause of equality for women became one to which all governments and most people in the West committed, at least in theory.

In the second half of the century, Westerners expected people in other cultures to reevaluate women's roles in the same way. This did not seem an unattainable expectation. In some places outside the West, women led their countries: Israel, India, Sri Lanka, the Philippines, Nicaragua, Dominica, Argentina, Chile, Liberia, Jamaica, and even Muslim countries—Pakistan, Turkey, Indonesia, Bangladesh—all had female presidents or prime ministers between 1960 and 2008. But these were exceptional cases, and restraints on women's freedom or status remained in much of the world. China did not allow women to marry until they were 20 years old, and the growing preponderance of male over female children in China suggests that more infant girls than boys were killed or aborted. It is hard to imagine a fiercer form of discrimination than that. Opponents in Morocco and Iran interpreted government programs to establish female equality of employment and rights of freedom of marriage as infringements of parental rights and threats to the stability of home life. Female circumcision, a tradition respected in many African cultures, offended Western sensibilities. Women's educational opportunities remained restricted in much of the world outside the West, especially in rural areas. In India 87 percent of rural women were classed as illiterate at the end of the century. The corresponding figure for Bangladesh was 97 percent.

Problems associated with the status of women became acute with the ever more thorough mingling of cultures that accompanied the globe-crossing migrations of the late twentieth century. Conflicts arose over the legitimacy of arranged marriages and over the rights of divorcees. In disputes over the custody of children, for example, Western courts tended to favor mothers, Islamic courts fathers. The disputes that best illustrate the difficulty of resolving conflicts between normative laws and cultural diversity concerned the issue of appropriate dress for women and girls. In some Muslim cultures, traditions of modesty enjoined garments for women that, in various traditions, concealed most of the body and, in the most marked traditions, the whole of the face, from male eyes. To some Westerners, these rules seemed to be male-imposed infringements on female liberty—although many Muslim women freely supported them. The potential for conflict with

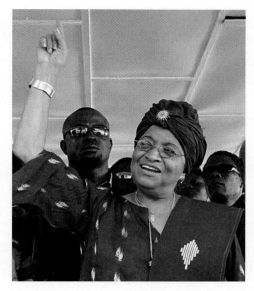

The first woman to be elected an African head of state, President Ellen Johnston-Sirleaf of Liberia, photographed in November 2005 just after her victory. Johnston gave a new twist to feminist arguments in favor of political empowerment for women by suggesting that women had special nurturing and peacemaking talents that made them more suited to leadership in the modern world than men.

> *"By the beginning of the twenty-first century, multiculturalism was beginning to look like another utopian dream, in danger of being discarded."*

Western laws arose in schools, where these traditional Muslim dress codes conflicted with school uniform regulations. In France, in the early twenty-first century, an apparently petty dispute divided society. The courts banned Muslim girls from wearing headscarves, on the rather unconvincing grounds that such scarves were religious symbols, incompatible with the hard-won secular nature of the French Republic. In the secular Turkish Republic, a dispute over the ban on headscarves for women university students threatened to bring down the government.

Such disputes raised fundamental questions about the future of the world. The new multiracial societies that were taking shape in the West posed unprecedented problems. Existing populations became prey to alarmism about the adulteration of their identities or their cultures. Debate raged over whether integration in the host society—adopting its values, language, dress, manners, food, and even, perhaps, religion—best served newly arrived immigrants; or whether **multiculturalism** could work, in which people of divergent cultures agreed on a few core values, such as allegiance to the state and deference to democracy. Both responses had their disadvantages. Integration imposed on people's freedom. Multiculturalism, according to its opponents, created ghettoes and opened dangerous gaps in mutual understanding between neighboring communities. As the number of migrants began to reach critical thresholds, most governments in the West abandoned the language of multiculturalism and began to encourage integration. Everywhere, immigration controls tightened as governments lost confidence that multiculturalism could keep the peace. The Netherlands, where people had always prided themselves on hospitality toward immigrants, introduced stringent requirements that immigrants learn Dutch and submit to citizenship tests. Britain and Germany introduced allegiance tests. By the beginning of the twenty-first century, multiculturalism was beginning to look like another utopian dream, in danger of being discarded.

Human rights provided the key test of whether universal values could thrive in a plural world. As we have seen, what was a universal right in theory could vary in practice from culture to culture, especially in connection with the treatment under the law of women, children, homosexuals, criminals, and drug users. Even in the United States, where public advocacy of human rights was as strong as anywhere, presidents seemed willing to ignore or circumvent their nominal commitment to human rights when it suited them. In 1999, the Senate acquitted President Bill Clinton of charges of attempting to subvert justice. Most of the charges against him were trivial or politically motivated. But there was little doubt that he had abused his position to prevent a fair hearing of a case of sexual harassment and discrimination that a former employee had brought against him from the time when he was Governor of Arkansas. The most flagrant instance occurred in 2002–2008, when the administration of George W. Bush licensed the torture of interrogation subjects during America's military interventions in Afghanistan and Iraq, and interned terrorism suspects in an offshore jail, to prevent them from having access to legal representation and the normal conditions of a fair trial (see Chapter 28).

The problems went even deeper. The experiences of the century made human rights a lively issue but did not by any means dispel moral confusion about the value of life. Even the most basic human rights proved impossible to guarantee universally in practice. Almost everyone, for instance, by the end of the twentieth century, paid lip service to the rights to life and to equality of respect, but these values were more honored in theory than in practice. Many countries outlawed

Opponent of multiculturalism. Pim Fortuyn (1948–2002) confronts protesters in Rotterdam during elections for the Dutch parliament. Fortuyn's Livable Netherlands Party had a distinctly anti-immigration agenda. He was assassinated by a white Dutch environmentalist in May 2002, shortly after this photo was taken. The slogan, "Stop the Dutch Haider," alludes to Jürgen Haider of Austria, another populist politician who successfully campaigned for tough immigration controls. The way Fortuyn caresses the demonstrator was part of his public image. He was a homosexual who appeared on campaigns with Moroccan boys as evidence that his opposition to immigration was not based on racial discrimination.

Rights of the unborn. Demonstrators in Lisbon, Portugal in 2007 campaign against a referendum to liberalize abortion. The slogans, which claimed to speak for the unborn, range from the religious ("I am a miracle of God") to the moral ("To kill is a crime") to the social ("Can't I go to school?"), but the most telling, perhaps, says simply, "But I want to live." Despite demonstrations such as these, more than 59 percent of those who voted in the referendum approved of loosening restrictions on abortion during the first 10 weeks of pregnancy.

capital punishment. But this did not mean that they treated human life as inviolable. In some places, the lives of some criminals continued to be regarded as dispensable, even in Japan and in many states of the United States. Many jurisdictions exempted unborn babies from the principle of inviolability of human life. The decriminalization of abortion in most of the West in the last three decades of the century served humane ends: freeing women who felt obliged to have abortions, and those who helped them, from prosecution under the law and from the agony of botched procedures administered in unsanitary conditions by untrained abortionists. But the effects were morally questionable. In 2004, the woman who had brought *Roe v. Wade*, the pro-abortion case, to the United States Supreme Court more than 30 years earlier, appealed to have the decision reversed. She had become a fervent Christian, appalled by the mass extinction of unborn lives. Euthanasia became another focus of concern over the reach of human rights. Did the moribund and the vegetative have them? Did the incurably dying have a moral right to choose to end their sufferings by assisted suicide?

GLOBALIZATION AND THE WORLD ECONOMY

Not only were cultures getting more intermingled, so were economies. **Globalization** meant the diffusion of Western, and especially American, culture throughout the world, which is a subject for the next chapter. In a more generally accepted sense, it meant the increasing economic interdependence of a world of growing trade (see Map 29.3). In the last quarter of the century, in line with the worldwide withdrawal of the state from economic regulation, businesses were able to drive a growing global economy by operating internationally with greater freedom than ever before—and to imperil global prosperity by irresponsible risk-taking, as a series of colossal failures among credit institutions in Europe and the US in 2008-9 showed.

More trade and more intercommunication promoted peace, increased prosperity, and stimulated cultural exchange. The benefits of globalization, however,

International Trade Flows, ca. 2004

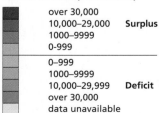

Direct investment
(arrow width reflects level of investment)

→　　from USA

→　　from Europe

→　　from Japan

Examples of countries reliant on a single export

🍌　bananas

☕　coffee

🛢　oil/petroleum

⛏　copper

Balance of trade (millions US$)

	over 30,000
	10,000–29,000　**Surplus**
	1000–9999
	0-999
	0–999
	1000–9999
	10,000–29,999　**Deficit**
	over 30,000
	data unavailable

were unevenly distributed. A relatively few vast business corporations, most of them centered in the United States, handled a disproportionate amount of the world's economic activity. Shunting their assets around the world, those businesses evaded regulation by individual governments. Powerful countries—the United States above all—were able to demand free trade where it suited them but retain protective tariffs or subsidies for businesses they favored. To some extent, globalization perpetuated the old colonial pattern of the world economy—peasants and sweated labor in poor countries supplied rich ones with cheap goods, twisting the poverty gap into a poverty spiral.

Such defects, however, could probably be fixed. Some Asian countries demonstrated that they could exploit the opportunities of the global economy, that well-run communities could break out of underdevelopment into prosperity, and that globalization—if properly managed—could make them as rich as the West.

Japan's was the exemplary case. After its defeat in 1945, Japan was ready for a makeover. No other country endured the A-bomb. But the Japanese, who live on typhoon-lashed coasts and with seismic faults that cause frequent earthquakes, are used to rebuilding after disaster. They found it more difficult, however, to cope with the psychological problems. Japanese felt the shame of defeat more deeply than people of other cultures. Never before had their country surrendered or submitted to occupation. The emperor renounced his divinity. The people disclaimed superiority over other races and meekly accepted an American formula to remake their country into a democracy.

The abandonment of militarism helped conserve investment for industry. In the 1950s, Japan's defense expenditure was less than 2 percent of its gross domestic product. Japan could now compete in trade for markets it had been unable to conquer in war. Even so, economic recovery was slow. The big corporations—which the

Americans had abolished—returned in the 1950s and 1960s. Workers, embedded in their firms, sacrificed an independent social life and became infused with corporate loyalty. This was not Western-style capitalism. But it worked. In 1960, a prime minister promised that incomes would double in 10 years. He underestimated the time span: Japan exceeded that target in 1967. In 1969, Japan overtook West Germany to become the world's second biggest national economy. In the 1970s, despite the high price of oil, Japan caught up with the average European gross national product per capita. In 1985, Japan became the world's biggest foreign investor. Growth faltered toward the end of the century, but Japan remained in the premier league of world economic powers, with the highest per capita income in the world. The outreach of the Japanese economy—building components for European manufactures, assembling complex products from parts imported from all over the world, investing in just about every country, buying banks in the United States, founding industrial plants in Europe and Africa—was typical of the time.

Other economies in Asia followed Japan toward European or North American levels of prosperity. In South Korea in the 1960s, collaboration between governments and huge corporations launched spectacular economic growth: 9 percent a year, on average, over the following three decades. The country became one of the world's major manufacturers of cars and electronic gadgets. South Koreans completed their industrialization with the highest per capita debt burden in Asia, but they demonstrated that a country could industrialize itself out of poverty. By the end of the century, Japan and South Korea together—countries with only 3 percent of the world's population—accounted for 15 percent of its income and 10 percent of its trade.

Other "tiger" economies leaped in the same direction. The mid-to-late 1960s and early 1970s were bonanza years in Southeast Asia because American military involvement in Vietnam created a huge demand for supplies, leisure facilities for troops, and all the infrastructure of a wartime baseline. Not everyone benefited. Cambodia, on Vietnam's flank, got sucked into the conflict and began a long, bloody, and destructive civil war. But other neighbors were drenched in American investment. The biggest gainers were the already industrialized or industrializing economies of Japan, South Korea, Hong Kong, and Taiwan. In the mid-1960s, Singapore followed the same path. The accelerating trade of these tiger economies generated potential for investment all around the world. Most of their surplus money, however, went on projects around the shores of the Pacific. By 1987, the United States had an annual trade deficit of $60 billion with Japan. By then, the Pacific had displaced the Atlantic as the world's major arena of commerce. Communities and investments moved around the Pacific's shores with increasing ease and freedom.

Meanwhile, Latin American countries struggled to play catch-up with the rest of the West. The game began after the global economic crisis of the 1930s, when governments in Mexico, Argentina, and Brazil saw selective industrialization as a solution to the collapse of markets for their primary produce. As these policies spread through the continent, their effects proved mixed. Native industries continued to rely on machinery imported from North America and Europe. The falling prices of basic commodities made it hard for Latin American economies to accumulate capital to reinvest in industry. Mechanization made unemployment worse. In the 1960s and 1970s, partly in response to these problems, authoritarian regimes took over most of the region. In most cases, authoritarian rule only protracted the economic disappointments, straining some countries' relations with trading partners elsewhere in the world, subjecting others to new forms of dependency on U.S. and European corporate allies and creditors. The military junta that took over Argentina in 1976, for instance, proclaimed Argentina's commitment to "the Western and Christian world" but alienated allies by brutal repression at home and military adventurism abroad.

"To some extent, globalization perpetuated the old colonial pattern of the world economy—peasants and sweated labor in poor countries supplied rich ones with cheap goods, twisting the poverty gap into a poverty spiral."

For most Latin Americans, the period was impoverishing. Between 1980 and 1987, average personal income fell in 22 countries in the region. In Peru and Argentina, people were poorer on average in 1986 than they had been in 1970. Even Mexico, which stayed ostensibly democratic and avoided the worst of the region's economic problems, only survived by incurring massive debts—and defaulting on them in 1982.

Still, the more enmeshed the global economy got, the more opportunities multiplied. More countries, more people were able to squeeze a share of the benefits. China's was the most spectacular case. The Chinese economy registered annual growth rates of nearly 10 percent in the 1990s and the early years of the twenty-first century—enough, if those rates could be sustained, to enable China's economy to overtake that of the United States as the world's biggest by 2020. By 2004, more than 400 of the world's 500 biggest companies had branches or subsidiaries in China, overwhelmingly concentrated in regions bordering the Pacific. In the last two decades of the century, India became a leading player in high-tech industries, where many multinational companies chose to locate centers of computer manufacture and telecommunications services. In the Punjab, Maharashtra, and Tamil Nadhu, India's economic growth rates toward the end of the century were comparable to China's. In the 1980s, a dose of Chicago-style economics—the doctrine, loudly advocated by economists at the University of Chicago, that low taxes and light regulation could unleash economic success—turned the Chile of the ruthless military dictator, Augusto Pinochet, into a prosperous country with a large middle class. Integration in the global economy shored up South Africa's delicate new democracy in the 1990s and helped to provide a capital-starved economy with the wealth the country needed to make a start—at least—at rebuilding after centuries of injustice. Between 1993 and 1996, U.S. investment there increased by about 50 percent, and more than 200 American firms employed some 45,000 South Africans. Brazil, meanwhile, which had already graduated from being a producer of primary products for richer economies to being a major manufacturing economy with a lively high-tech sector, achieved, in the early twenty-first century, levels of growth not far short of China's. Even some economies that remained tied to primary production generated huge profits that their governments could invest in global markets. These were oil-exporting countries with large reserves and small domestic populations to spend them on. The countries on the Arabian shore of the Persian Gulf became major players in the global economy, with investments in the industries of every continent.

Even economists who acknowledged the benefits of globalization were prey to doubts about its stability. Some systems theorists argued that the more complex the world economy grew, the more fragile it would become, because, in an interdependent system, a local failure could cause widespread disruption. The opposite happened. Early in the twentieth century, as we have seen (see Chapter 28), a local economic failure, such as the U.S. stock market crash of 1929, could plunge much of the world into depression. In the 1980s and 1990s, markets prone to panic reacted nervously to similar collapses: of major stock markets in 1987, of the British currency in 1992, of the banking system in Argentina in 1999, of the oil-pricing system and major commodity markets at irregular intervals. None of these disasters had uncontrollable repercussions. Complexity made the system robust,

Shanghai in the early twenty-first century emblemized China's promise and perils. Skyscrapers symbolized the stunning growth rates that enabled China to aim for superpower status and potentially resume its normal place as the world's richest country. The price was pollution and gaping disparities in wealth.

because multiple interconnections could bypass failures. In 2001, when terrorists destroyed the World Trade Center in New York, even the firms worst hit by the attack were back at work within days. In 2008, however, the collapse of the value of key securities in the US provoked an uncontainable global credit crisis. International collaboration mitigated the effects. But the failure of the system was so acute that electorates worldwide lost confidence in laissez-faire and clamored for a return to regulation.

CULTURE AND GLOBALIZATION

Information traveled globally with even more freedom than trade. In 1971, the world's first microprocessor appeared. Together with the fiber-optic cable, this made possible the transmission of billions of units of information along a single fiber every second. Radio transmission made virtually every item of information from every part of the world universally accessible. There were over 2.5 billion telephones in the world by the end of the century and over 500 million computers (see Figure 29.1).

The way people handled information changed. Miniaturization boosted individualism and enabled the like-minded from all over the world to form cyberspace communities. The trend was unstoppable. China, for instance, tried to control Internet access, especially after demonstrators coordinated their activities by computer in what almost turned into a revolution in 1989. But China had 30 million Internet users by 2000. Worldwide censorship became difficult—for a while. But in the early twenty-first century, major servers began to impose filters, at first to black out pornography.

People could easily drop out of the global information revolution if they wished. The surfeit of data drove some consumers into narrow-minded retreat. Some cyber communities became cyber ghettoes, in which people spent their time with minds closed to the rest of the Web. Increasing information did not necessarily increase knowledge. Wider literacy helped. By the end of the century, just about everyone in the world was familiar with writing, and probably about 85 percent of them could make at least some use of it. But most consumers used the new technology for trivial entertainments rather than self-education. Even professional intellectuals succumbed to specialization, partly in response to the proliferation of information. Students became reliant on data culled from the Internet, which changed constantly and was beyond verification. Cutting and pasting became a new form of literary activity, in which no text was stable and no work genuinely original. The ready availability of data exempted people from learning anything. **Virtual reality** excited fears of a generation of "nerds"—introverted sociopaths who communed only with their computers. In 2004, Susan Greenfield, one of the world's leading neuroscientists, predicted a future in which technology would erode individuality by replacing memory and making all experience second hand, in a "state of sensory oblivion."

Still, the Internet promoted globalization in the strongest sense of the world: the global spread of uniform culture. In reality, in a plural world, this was not a threat to cultural diversity, though people often perceived it as such. Cultural exchange crisscrossed in many directions. If there ever were to be a global culture, it would probably not replace diversity, but would rather supplement it. What people really feared was not globalization but one particular form of it: global Americanization, the triumph of American popular culture that its critics commonly called "McDonaldization" and "Coca-Colonialism" after two of the most prevalent products of American industry. Hamburgers and sodas symbolized American cultural influence, because the world associated American lifestyles with what became the nearest thing to a common culture the world possessed: consumerism.

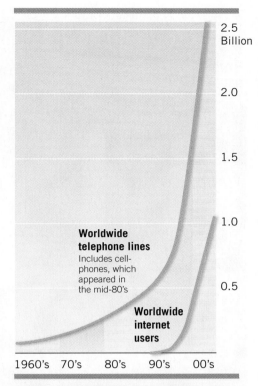

2.5 Billion

2.0

1.5

1.0

Worldwide telephone lines
Includes cell-phones, which appeared in the mid-80's

0.5

Worldwide internet users

1960's 70's 80's 90's 00's

FIGURE 29.1 TELEPHONE LINES AND INTERNET USERS WORLDWIDE CA. 1960–2000

Worldwatch Institute, www.worldwatch.org

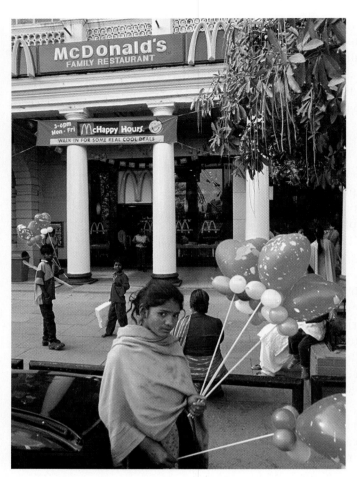

Selling dreams. Garish signs of Western economic takeover and cultural invasion deface a traditional building on a prime commercial site in New Delhi, while child workers hope to make a few pennies by selling balloons to kids rich enough to feast on the fatty carbohydrates associated (in India) with U.S. fast-food businesses.

FIGURE 29.2 NUMBER OF LANGUAGES WORLDWIDE 10,000 B.C.E. TO 2100 C.E. (PROJECTED)

The United Nations Educational, Scientific, and Cultural Organization

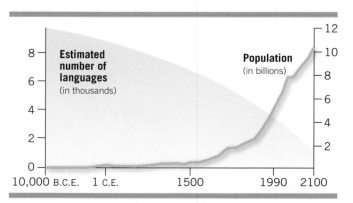

Consumerism is best defined as a system of values that puts the consumption and possession of consumer goods at or near the top of social values—as high as or higher than social obligations, spiritual fulfillment, or moral qualities. Prosperity made consumerism possible for the rich. Envy excited its appeal among the poor. The best index of the growing importance of the growth of per capita consumption, which is among the subjects of the next chapter, is its sheer scale. As we shall see, the late twentieth-century world was a battleground of consumerism against environmentalism. Consumerism nearly always won the battles. The best evidence that it was particularly strong in the United States is that Americans, on average, greatly outstripped everyone else in the world in the rate at which they consumed resources. Products that best help us measure the importance of consumerism in people's values are those that can fairly be described as a waste of money—those that only provide short-term gratification, or are actually harmful. Consumption of tobacco, alcohol, and more addictive drugs makes the case. First on grounds of morality, then—as the century wore on and morality became unfashionable—on grounds of health, governments struggled to contain these extreme forms of consumerism. Nonetheless, by 2000, the alcohol industry worldwide turned over $252 billion annually, tobacco $204 billion. The term *drugs* is harder to define, and the statistics fuzzier because the trade was illegal in most of the world. But by the most widely respected estimates, the drug trade was worth about $150 billion by the end of the century, of which drugs worth about $60 billion were consumed in the United States.

Even those who condemned American cultural influence found it hard to resist its appeal. Because American businesses dominated the major new media that controlled the worldwide transmission of culture—cinema, television, and the Internet—American images proliferated before the eyes of onlookers around the world (although by the end of the century, the Indian film industry—"Bollywood"—was shaping up as a potential rival). Often, those onlookers became admirers. The magnetism of American higher education was an important ingredient of America's soft power (Chapter 28). American universities educated a disproportionate number of the world's elites.

The most pervasive index of the global appeal of American culture was the adoption of English, in the form in which Americans speak that language, as a universal code of business, politics, science, and study. This was a major reversal in the history of culture. Languages had been diverging and multiplying for perhaps 50,000 years—probably longer than any other ingredients of culture. The spread of imperial or sacred or trading languages had sometimes displaced or extinguished other tongues. Never before, however, had a single language achieved the role of a global common tongue. Mandarin Chinese, Spanish, and Portuguese also showed some global potential. The extinction of minority languages became a conservation problem (see Figure 29.2).

SECULARISM AND THE RELIGIOUS REVIVAL

Most of the really powerful utopian visions of the twentieth century were secular—irreligious, even antireligious. Religion had to face serious challenges and sometimes ferocious persecution from hostile political ideologies. Utopians who put their faith in the state often did so in conscious revulsion from religious establishments, which had clearly failed, after what seemed a long enough period of trying, to enhance virtue or spread welfare or justice. Communists usually regarded atheism as part of their own creed and dismissed religion as "the opiate of the masses." Nazis wanted to sweep away the church, which they saw as an enfeebling influence that weakened the nation's martial virtues. Social planning relied for its appeal on a scientistic notion: that human agency alone could change societies like chemicals in a lab, and achieve predictable results, with no need for appeals to Providence or to God's grace. The world—from all these perspectives—would be better off without religion, which had caused wars, retarded science, and stifled reason with dogma. One of the most popular songs of the British rock singer, John Lennon (1940–1980), was "Imagine," in which he called on the world to reject religion in order to live in peace "for today." Religion was one of the first casualties of the skepticism that, as we saw in Chapter 27, was a major twentieth-century theme.

For most of the century, the demise of religion was widely forecast. The decline of churchgoing in the West, which lasted in America until the 1960s and still prevailed in Western Europe and Canada in the early twenty-first century, seemed to suggest that prosperity would erode faith—that Mammon would tempt worshippers away from God.

In response to secularism, however, many people with religious identities felt them more fiercely. In Egypt, for instance, the number of mosques increased nearly twice as fast as the population under the broadly secular-minded rulers of the second half of the twentieth century. The most striking case occurred in Iran, where the Shah, Muhammad Reza Pahlavi (r. 1941–1979), imposed secularization on a reluctant country in the 1960s. He claimed to be ruling people who "resembled Americans" in the "France of Asia." He ignored the Muslim clergy. He appealed to Persia's pagan past, spending—reputedly—$200 million on ceremonies re-creating the glories of the Persepolis of Darius the Great (r. 521–486 B.C.E.). He seized religious endowments without compensation to redistribute the land among peasants. He also made himself unpopular in other ways—especially by outrageously disproportionate spending on the armed services rather than on social welfare—but it was by alienating religious sensibilities that he lost his throne.

A Shiite cleric, Ayatollah Ruhollah Khomeini (1900–1989), gradually emerged as the voice of outraged Islam. Broadcasting from exile, this brilliant propagandist attracted millions of followers by his obvious incorruptibility and his unshakable self-righteousness. The Shah's regime was, he proclaimed, literally the work of the devil and must be destroyed. Khomeini (hoh-MAY-nee) called for an Islamic republic—a welfare state that would enrich all its faithful and in which all the necessities of life would be free. In 1979, he inspired a revolution. His followers filled the streets, deserted the army, and paralyzed the government by striking. The Shah went into exile. An Islamic republic dominated by Shiite clergy replaced the ancient Iranian monarchy. The success of the Iranian experiment, which followed an Islamist experiment in Pakistan in 1977, encouraged similar movements all over the Islamic world.

"The decline of churchgoing in the West, which lasted in America until the 1960s and still prevailed in Western Europe and Canada in the early twenty-first century, seemed to suggest that prosperity would erode faith—that Mammon would tempt worshippers away from God."

Revolution's patron saint. After his death in 1989 Ayatollah Ruhollah Khomeini continued to influence Iranian politics. His shrine outside Tehran became a place of pilgrimage for followers who wanted to perpetuate Islamic revolution, like the women photographed here in 2001 on the twelfth anniversary of his death. His cult helped to mobilize voters for his unusual combination of agendas—communitarian, religious, populist, and nationalist—and helped slow down and, at times, halt Iran's hesitant return to secular priorities and normal relations with the rest of the world.

Religion did decline in Western Europe and Canada. But in much of the rest of the world, faith's hold on people's hearts and minds seemed to increase—at least, to judge from attendance statistics for acts of worship. Traditional religion proved ineradicable, surviving, strengthened by persecution, after all the hostile ideologies collapsed. Far from outbidding religion, prosperity nurtured it by providing relief from materialism. That is perhaps the main reason the United States, the world's richest country, became so hospitable to religion in the late twentieth century. Yet religion never lost its appeal to the victims of poverty, for whom rewards in the next world compensated for being underprivileged here and now. That may largely explain why Christian and, to a lesser extent, Muslim propagandists found huge audiences in sub-Saharan Africa.

Traditional religions, especially Roman Catholicism, Islam, radical forms of Christianity, and Lamaist Buddhism, self-reformed successfully to confront secularism and widen their global appeal. The main challenge to traditional religions came not from atheism or secularism but from new kinds of religions. Most of these could be characterized as cults or folksy superstitions, or as personal religions concocted by individuals who did not see themselves as belonging in any particular communion but who picked and mixed from various traditions to create a menu of their own choice, like an Internet-surfing student plagiarizing a paper with the cut-and-paste facility.

Twentieth-century conditions favored cults in cities full of rootless, spiritually uneducated constituencies with excited expectations. Some fashions in belief were frankly weird. Astrology was the starting-point of the New Age movement, which, beginning in the 1960s, proclaimed the "dawning of the Age of Aquarius"—the doctrine that the astral prominence of the constellation Pisces is gradually being replaced, after about 2,000 years, with world-transforming effects. It is hard to believe that anyone could have taken such a doctrine seriously—but its success indicated how uneasy people felt at the time. Toward the end of the century, sects predicting the end of the world achieved a brief vogue—even though the year 2000 had no particular significance, since our system of numbering years is purely arbitrary. Surprisingly, skepticism favored the proliferation of weird beliefs because, as the English writer G. K. Chesterton (1874–1936) reputedly said, when people cease to believe in something, "they do not believe in nothing; they believe in anything."

The biggest growth point was the kind of religion called **fundamentalist**. It started in Protestant theology schools in Princeton, New Jersey, and Chicago in the early twentieth century in reaction to critical readings of the Bible. The idea was that the text of the Bible contains fundamental truths that cannot be questioned, either by critical inquiry or by scientific evidence. The name "fundamentalism" has been applied retrospectively to a similar doctrine, traditional in Islam, about the Quran. It can—and sometimes does—arise in the context of any religion that has a founding text or holy scripture. Karen Armstrong—one of the foremost authorities on the subject—sees fundamentalism as modern: it is scientific or pseudoscientific because it treats religion as reducible to matters of undeniable fact. Apart from the bleakness of modernity, fundamentalism's other parent is fear: fear that the end of the world is imminent, fear of *Great Satans* (Iranian clerics' term of abuse for the United States and the West in general), fear of chaos, and. above all, fear of the unfamiliar. To fundamentalists, all difference is subversive. These facts help to explain why fundamentalism arose and thrived in the modern world and has never lost its appeal. In the late twentieth century, fundamentalism in Islam and Christianity, taken together, constituted the biggest movement in the world.

All the movements we call fundamentalist are different but can be identified by the features they share: militancy, hostility to pluralism, and a determination to confuse politics with religion. Fundamentalists are self-cast as warriors against secularism. Yet, in practice, most fundamentalists are pleasant, ordinary people, who make their compromises with the wicked world and leave their religion—as most people do—at the door of their church or mosque. The militant minorities among them, meanwhile, cause trouble by declaring war on society. Some sects, with their crushing effects on individual identity, their ethic of obedience, their paranoid habits, and their campaigns of hatred or violence against the rest of the world, behave in frightening ways like the early fascist cells.

If and when they got power, fundamentalists tended to treat people of other traditions with hostility. Bahais (bah-HAIS), Christians, Sunni Muslims, and Jews all suffered discrimination and persecution in Khomeini's rigidly Shiite Iran. In Afghanistan in the 1990s, the strict Islamic Taliban regime vandalized Buddhist monuments, smashed ancient art in the country's museums, suppressed Christian worship, ordered women out of school, forced men to grow beards, and slaughtered homosexuals—of whom there were many since homosexual practice was a longstanding tradition in the country. Saudi Arabia has "religious police" who impose Wahhabism (see Chapter 21), a rigid and uncompromising form of Islam, even on non-Muslims. When a Christian fundamentalist general took power in Guatemala in 1982, the army persecuted Catholic clergy for supposedly helping Native American rebels. Where Islamic fundamentalists took power nationally or locally, they usually imposed interpretations of Islamic law that often had dire consequences for women, whose freedoms were restricted, and for people who led supposedly irregular sex lives, who were liable to be put to death. Christian fundamentalists in the United States advocated laws to ban practices they considered objectionable on religious grounds, including homosexuality, the teaching of evolution, and sex education in public schools. Religious fundamentalism rarely managed to retain power for long, or to remain unseduced by the need for political compromise, but it continued to grow as a social movement, even when its political aspirations were frustrated or diluted.

Fundamentalism was one form of the religious response to secularism. Another was to imitate the secularists—to beat them at their own game. Traditional religions could do this by showing that they could make a difference to lives in the here and now, as well as in the hereafter, by organizing social services for worshippers and aid programs for the poor of the world. New religions could try an alternative strategy. In developed countries, a lot of the new religions of the late twentieth century looked suspiciously like secularism—or even consumerism—in disguise. In South Korea, the Full Gospel Church promised its followers health and prosperity: bounding riches and bouncing bodies. In Japan, Soka Gakkai was a Buddhist form of prosperity cult that founded its own political party and spread to other consumerist societies in Europe and America. In the United States, the "next church" movement offered car-repair ministry and classes in "discovering divorce dynamics." Instead of imitating heaven, American churches increased their congregations by imitating the familiar world of trivial, middle-class lives, with coffee parties, muzak, casual clothes, and undemanding moral prescriptions. In Orange County, California, worshippers in the Crystal Cathedral of the Reverend Robert Schuller believed that business success was a mark of divine election.

> *"In the late twentieth century, fundamentalism in Islam and Christianity, taken together, constituted the biggest movement in the world."*

A CLOSER LOOK

Yoido Full Gospel Church, Seoul, Korea

At the Yoido Full Gospel Church in South Korea, where over 800,000 members of the congregation are registered, worshippers hear a gospel of prosperity, promising positive answers to prayers for health and wealth.

Many churches put choirs in uniform, but David Cho's organization also has uniforms for various ranks of church members. Uniforms suppress individuality and encourage common responses.

Giant screens are essential in a church big enough to accommodate 12,000 worshippers.

The founder, David (formerly Paul) Cho claims to have received the gospel of prosperity not from the bible or tradition, but straight from God.

The words of the familiar evangelical hymn "Nothing But the Blood of Jesus" appear on giant screens: "O precious is the flow That makes me white as snow."

The congregation remains seated through most of the service, but the mood, especially during prayer, is fervent and emotional.

Foreigners are encouraged to sit in the gallery. Services are in Korean, with English translation available over headphones.

Television cameras operate constantly.

What type of religious response to secularism is evident in the worship service depicted here?

Some new religions were essentially healing ministries—offering a form of alternative therapy for a health-obsessed age in which, in the absence of shared moral values, health was the only commonly acknowledged good. Other new religious movements of the period were more political than pontifical—striving for kingdoms of this world, of the kind Jesus disavowed. The supposedly Buddhist Aum Shinrikyo cult in Japan waged war on the rest of society. A patchily fashionable cult known as Scientology, which called itself a church, was instead classed as a political organization or as a business in many of the countries in which it operated. The **Liberation Theology** movement in Latin America was concerned with justice for the poor and oppressed, arguing that sin was not just individual moral failure but a structural feature of capitalist society. In the early twenty-first century, it was not clear how the culture wars of religions against secularism would end.

Liberation Theology. A Catholic priest holds hands with members of the Base Christian Community in Panama. Believers in Liberation Theology typically aligned themselves with left-wing, revolutionary movements, putting them in conflict with established Catholic authorities and political leaders in Latin America.

In Perspective
The Century of Paradox

Traditions had to struggle to survive the quickening pace of change, which made social and political relationships unrecognizable to successive generations and bewildering to those whose lives spanned the transformations. Science drove change, inspiring new technology, reforging the way people saw the world. The relentless growth of global population, which wars did not interrupt, increased the pressure on the world's resources. But even more than population growth, spiraling desire—consumerism, lust for abundance, impatience to enjoy the rewards of economic growth—made people exploit the planet with increasing ruthlessness.

Most of history had favored unitary states, with one religion, ethnicity, and identity. Large empires have always been multicultural, but they have usually had a dominant culture, alongside which others are, at best, tolerated. In the twentieth century, this would no longer do. The aftermath of the era of global empires, the range and intensity of migrations, the progress of ideas of racial equality, the multiplication of religions, the large-scale redrawing of state boundaries made the toleration of diversity essential to the peace of most states. Those states that rejected toleration faced traumatic periods of "ethnic cleansing." Meanwhile, democracies could only contain the intense competition of rival ideologies by embracing political pluralism—that is, the admission to the lawful political arena, on equal terms, of parties representing potentially irreconcilable views.

What was true of individual states was true of the entire world. "Shrinkage" brought peoples and cultures into unprecedented proximity. The peace and future prosperity of the world at the end of the century demanded a new global consensus in favor of pluralism, and an effort to accommodate plurality of cultures—religions, languages, ethnicities, communal identities, versions of history, value systems—on terms of equality in a single global community. The British philosopher Isaiah Berlin (1909–1997) explained how such a consensus and such an effort are possible: "There is a plurality of values which men can and do seek. . . . And the difference it

"The peace and future prosperity of the world at the end of the century demanded a new global consensus in favor of pluralism, and an effort to accommodate plurality of cultures—religions, languages, ethnicities, communal identities, versions of history, value systems—on terms of equality in a single global community."

Chronology

1933–1935	Nazi restrictions placed on German Jews
1936	Publication of John Maynard Keynes's *General Theory of Employment, Interest, and Money*
December 1937	Rape of Nanjing by Japanese troops
1939–1945	World War II
1939–1945	Holocaust
1945	International Monetary Fund (IMF) created
1950s	Japans spends 2 percent of GDP on defense
1950s and 1960s	Big corporations return to Japanese economy; generation gap emerges; civil rights movement in the United States
1960s	Second Vatican Council; Asian "tigers" begin rapid economic ascent; Cultural Revolution in China
1960–1967	Japanese incomes double
1961–1973	U.S. involvement in Vietnam War
1965	Public spending accounts for 25 percent of GDP of world's seven wealthiest nations
March 1968	My Lai massacre in Vietnam
1968	Prague Spring
1971	World's first microprocessor
1975–1979	Khmer Rouge rule in Cambodia
1979	Islamic revolution in Iran
1980s and 1990s	Governments around the world move away from nationalized economies
1980–1987	Incomes fall in most Latin American nations
1982	Mexico defaults on national debt
1985	Japan becomes world's biggest foreign investor
1989	Tiananmen Square protests in China
1990s	China's economy grows at annual rate of almost 10 percent
Late 1990s	Economies of Brazil and India grow at rapid rate
1995	World Trade Organization (WTO) created
Late twentieth century	Christian and Islamic fundamentalism on the rise; 30 million Internet users in China; public spending accounts for 37 percent of GDP of world's seven wealthiest nations; Muslim population: Britain, 2 million; France, 4 million; migrants from Latin America largest minority group in the United States
2001	Terrorist attack on United States
2008	Global financial crisis and economic recession

makes is that if a man pursues one of these values, I, who do not, am able to understand why he pursues it or what it would be like, in his circumstances, for me to be induced to pursue it. Hence the possibility of human understanding." This position differs from cultural relativism. It does not say, for instance, that all cultures can be accommodated. One might exclude Nazism, say, or cannibalism. It leaves open the possibility of peaceful argument about which culture, if any, is best. It claims, in Berlin's words, "that the multiple values are objective, part of the essence of humanity rather than arbitrary creations of men's subjective fancies." In a world where globalization made most historic communities defensive about their own cultures, it has been difficult to persuade them to coexist peacefully with the contrasting cultures of their neighbors. Still, pluralism is obviously the only practical future for a diverse world. Paradoxically, perhaps, it is the only truly uniform interest that all the world's peoples have in common.

By the end of the century, the world seemed to have tried everything. The "final solutions" and "inevitable" revolutions that extremists of right and left proposed had failed. Social planning went wrong. But the return to individualism was also disappointing. It failed to restrain the growth of government, and, rather than produce universal prosperity and social peace, it widened the poverty gap and bred terrorism and crime. Every utopia turned to ashes. The world was left looking for what some political philosophers called a "third way" between capitalism and socialism, in which freedom and order would coexist, governments would make society more equal without choking differences, and individual enterprise would thrive at the service of a wider community. These objectives were easier to state than to deliver.

It is tempting to characterize the twentieth century as a century of paradox. Frustrated hopes coincided with unprecedented progress. Uncontrolled change left much of the world mired in stagnancy. Utopias nourished moral sickness, suicide, and crime. The century of democracy was the century of dictators. The century of war was also the century of pacifism. Youth achieved more wealth and influence than ever before, but the world emerged with a vast cohort of the elderly to care for. Rule by the aged survived the empowerment of the young. Globalization broke down some states and communities but encouraged others to recover historic identities. The rise of science and secularism revived faith. Finally, as we shall see in the final chapter, the twentieth century could also be called the century of ecology. But it was peculiarly destructive of nature.

PROBLEMS AND PARALLELS

1. Why did science, technology, education, and increased prosperity fail to avert moral catastrophes in the twentieth century? How does the revolutionary career of Dolores Jiménez demonstrate this paradox?

2. Why did nation-states kill tens of millions of people in the twentieth century? Why were there so many massacres and attempts at ethnic cleansing? Why did so many states attempt to create utopias?

3. How did individualism manifest itself in both conservative and counter-conservative ways?

4. How did the demands for personal freedom, sexual liberation, and existential self-fulfillment affect family structures and the status of women in the West? Why were these trends less influential in the non-Western world?

5. How is globalization affecting economies and cultures? Why were some Asian countries so economically successful in the late twentieth century? Why was American popular culture so appealing around the world?

6. What does the term *countercolonization* mean? How did writers like W.E.B. Du Bois, Nicolás Guillén, Léopold Senghor, and Malcolm X redefine black identity in the twentieth century? Why did it take so long to dismantle the legacy of racism?

7. How did traditional and new religions respond to secularism? What features do fundamentalist movements have in common around the world? Why was the Ayatollah Ruhollah Khomeini able to establish an Islamic republic in Iran?

READ ON ▶ ▶ ▶

The opening anecdote is based on the eye-witness account of F. Starr, *Mexico and the United States* (1914). The study of wartime atrocities is ably represented by I. Chang, *The Rape of Nanjing: The Forgotten Holocaust of World War II* (1997), which shows how Nanking served as a training ground for further Japanese slaughter of civilians. *Good Man of Nanking: The Diaries of J. Rabe*, ed. by E. Wickert, translated from the German by J. E. Woods (1998), offers a first-hand account of the massacre by a German businessman who organized a refuge for Chinese civilians.

D. Bell, *The Coming of Post-Industrial Society* (1976), predicted the coming of the Information Age and the social and cultural transformations it has wrought. It should be read in conjunction with F. Jameson, *Postmodernism or the Cultural Logic of Late Capitalism* (1991), a densely written but very sophisticated analysis of postmodernism as the artistic expression of its material milieu. The same author's *Marxism and Form* (1971) remains the basic manifesto of modern Marxist cultural analysis. J. Tomlinson, *Globalization and Culture* (1999) explores similar themes from a different perspective.

A. Musallam, *From Secularism to Jihad: Sayyid Qutb and the Foundations of Radical Islamism* (2005) is an insightful examination of the founder of modern Islamic political fundamentalism. T. Madan, *Modern Myths, Locked Minds: Secularism and Fundamentalism in India* (1997) looks at the intersection of secularism, religion, and politics for India's major faiths. S. Jacoby, *Freethinkers: A History of American Secularism* (2004) examines the paradox of the secular foundations of the United States' very religiously tinged democratic culture.

N. Woods, ed., *The Political Economy of Globalization* (2000), explores key economic and political problems associated with globalization. R. Compton, *East Asian Democratization: Impact of Globalization, Culture, and Economy* (2000) uses detailed case studies of various East Asian countries to compare the political and cultural impact of globalizing economies.

CHAPTER 30

The Embattled Biosphere:
The Twentieth-Century Environment

▲ **Gathering wood.** In the Central African nation of Burkina Faso, deforestation and desertification make firewood ever harder to find. These women of Kalsaka in Yatenga Province have to walk hours from their village, two or three times a week, to gather wood.

W"Why do you travel such a long distance with this load of wood and your baby on your back?" the environmental worker asked.

"What a question!" said the woman, whose name was Rasmata. The conversation, reported in 1991, began after a long period of drought in west Burkina Faso, just south of the Sahara, on the road to the capital, Ouagadougou (wog-ah-DOO-goo). "My baby is ill. I nursed her with traditional medicine but the illness went on. . . . There is no clinic in our village—and, as we don't have any cash, I brought some wood, which I am going to sell. With the takings from the wood, I will be able to buy the modern medicine the nurse will prescribe."

"Don't you know that it is the excessive culling of trees that is causing the advance of the desert into our country?"

"What can we do? When I was a girl, there were many fruits to be gathered. We kept a third for ourselves to eat, and sold the remainder in town. . . . Now these trees are rare and you have to go a long way to find them. We used to collect firewood from trees that had died naturally. Now there aren't any. We have to go a long way, to cut living shrub and leave it to dry out for days or weeks before we can use it for our fires. It is for lack of other produce that I sell wood."

Some of Burkina Faso's problems are natural—part of the inescapable geography of the region. The Sahara has been drying and growing for thousands of years. The prevailing northeast winds powder the land beyond the desert with infertile soil. Most of the country has, on average, only a little over two inches of rain in a good year. In the last three decades of the twentieth century, droughts became routine.

Scientific interventions have improved life in some respects. For instance, in parts of the country that have rivers and fertile land, 10 percent of the population used to suffer from river blindness—sight-destroying lesions, caused by a tiny, threadlike worm that gets into the skin when black flies bite. The people could cope only by abandoning their valleys, when the disease struck, and moving to areas with poor, arid soils, until food shortages forced them to return. The internationally funded program that checked the disease in the 1980s cost less than a dollar for each person it helped.

But Burkina Faso, like neighboring countries on the desert edge, suffers from some of the most characteristic human-made environmental problems of the twenty-first-century world. Thanks, in part, to the "modern medicine" and medical technology in which Rasmata had so much faith, the population of Burkina Faso doubled to 10 million from 1975 to 1995. This medical triumph put terrible strains on the country's resources, forcing people in some areas to farm so intensively that the soil became exhausted, or in other areas, to increase their herds of livestock to unsustainable numbers. By 2000, the number of cattle in Burkina Faso was growing at a rate of 2 percent a year, and that of sheep and goats at 3 percent a year. Overgrazing is as bad for soil as overfarming. What is more, the herdsmen occupied ever more land, spreading, ahead of the advancing desert, from the north of the country into the west and center. Between 1980 and 1993, a combination of drought and overexploitation of the kind Rasmata mentioned destroyed more than 3 million acres of forest in Burkina Faso.

Well-intentioned interventions in the environment by governments and international agencies often made the problems worse. To help combat river blindness, for instance, in the mid-1970s, foreign agencies insisted on a huge resettlement program, affecting 10 percent of farmers in affected areas. By the late 1980s, it was becoming impossible to sustain many of the new settlements. To feed the increased population, farmers ceased to leave fields fallow. As a result, soils could not recover their natural fertility. The rising costs of fertilizer and insecticides hugely exceeded the increase in the value of the farmers' cotton. Families moved in ways the planners had not been able to foresee—many, for instance, in search of irrigation water, flocking to Burkina Faso's extreme southeast, where a new hydroelectric dam was being built.

Fluctuations in government policy and economic fashion could have devastating effects. New projects and development strategies came and went with bewildering speed. International agencies suspended aid if projects failed to produce quick results—three- or five-year terms were normal for funding reviews in the late twentieth century. In 1983, a military coup in Burkina Faso brought in a government the West denounced as communist. Peasants were promised the right to use any land they cleared, with terrible consequences for the remaining forests. In 2000, the government began to encourage big, supposedly efficient farms. This was contrary to the traditions of a country of small family enterprises, typically of 7 to 15 acres.

Meanwhile, international market conditions tended to impoverish these peasants, obliging them to grow cheap cash crops—mainly cotton and peanuts—for rich consumer countries, on the 20 percent or so of the land they could spare from growing their own food. From the 1980s, there was a world glut of the cheap grains the farmers were encouraged to grow to feed themselves. So they had no chance to sell their produce.

We can trace the combination of natural and human effects in the dust to which so much of the soil of Burkina Faso turned. In 1988, more than half the land in the country was officially classed as biologically degraded. By 2000, over two-thirds of the soil of the northern, central, and eastern provinces was seriously affected. All the soil in the province of Gnagna in the east had been degraded. Food economists now think that Burkina Faso can no longer support the people who live there. Since the mid-1990s, a few farmers have been able to make a good living growing expensive green beans for French supermarkets. But this route out of poverty remains impossible for peasants who are tied to the production of staples or to depleted soils.

RUSSIAN FEDERATION 143 million

UNITED KINGDOM 59 million

CANADA 31 million

UNITED STATES OF AMERICA 289 million

NORTH AMERICA

GERMANY 83 million

EUROPE

FRANCE 60 million

ITALY 57 million

SPAIN 40 million

CHINA 1,290 million

JAPAN 128 million

SOUTH KOREA 47 million

A S I A

CUBA 11 million

MEXICO 102 million

TURKEY 69 million

IRAN 72 million

VIETNAM 80 million

COLOMBIA 44 million

VENEZUELA 25 million

MOROCCO 31 million

EGYPT 70 million

PAKISTAN 149 million

INDIA 1,040 million

PHILIPPINES 79 million

PERU 27 million

BRAZIL 175 million

NIGERIA 120 million

AFRICA

BANGLADESH 143 million

SOUTH AMERICA

ARGENTINA 38 million

ETHIOPIA 66 million

TANZANIA 37 million

INDONESIA 218 million

20 million

SOUTH AFRICA 45 million

AUSTRALIA/OCEANIA

MAP 30.1

World Population, 2003

Country Area Roughly Proportional to Population

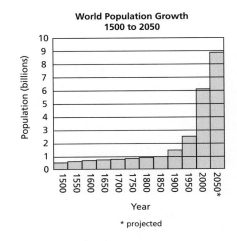

World Population Growth 1500 to 2050

Population (billions)

Year

* projected

Though Burkina Faso is particularly badly off, the problems it suffers from are global problems that can be understood and remedied—if at all—only in a global context. Take, for example, the impact of growing numbers of people. In 1900, the population of the world was 1.630 billion. In 2000, it was 6.1 billion. Global population doubled in the last 40 years of the century (the previous doubling took twice as long; the doubling before that took well over 200 years). This was not as fast as the growth rate in Burkina Faso—but it was still hard to cope with. Even before we take other factors into account, population explosion has put unprecedented pressure on the world's resources of energy, stressing and stretching our means of providing enough food and fuel to keep humankind going (see Map 30.1.)

Demand for resources, moreover, has hugely outstripped population growth. Not only does the world have more people than ever before, but they also demand, on average, vastly more food and goods and consume vastly more energy than ever before. If the population-growth figures seem astonishing by the standards of earlier periods, the output figures are even more startlingly disproportionate. Between 1900 and 1950, global output—the total value of the goods people produced—rose, at 2003 prices, from $2 trillion to $5 trillion. Between 1950 and 2000, the total soared to $39 trillion. In other words, while the population of the world less than quadrupled, output rose more than nineteenfold. In three years during the 1990s, according to a much-quoted calculation, the growth in output exceeded that of the previous 10,000 years combined.

Why did the consumption of resources leap ahead of the rise in population? It is hard to separate cause and effect. New technologies enabled twentieth-century industries to unlock new energy resources, with a consequent rise in prosperity. In the twentieth century, the world economy grew, on average, by about 1.5 percent a year—about two and a half times as fast as in the nineteenth century, when growth rates seemed dazzlingly high to those who experienced them. When prosperity leaps, people's expectations explode. Demand and supply feed off each other. The twentieth-century world got hooked on prosperity, locked

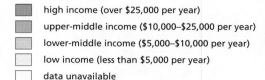

Comparative World Wealth, ca. 2008

- high income (over $25,000 per year)
- upper-middle income ($10,000–$25,000 per year)
- lower-middle income ($5,000–$10,000 per year)
- low income (less than $5,000 per year)
- data unavailable

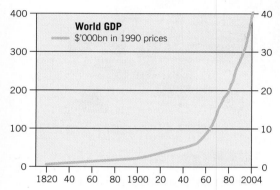

World GDP
$'000bn in 1990 prices

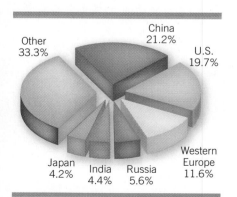

FIGURE 30.1 SHARE OF CARBON EMISSIONS, 2006

Netherlands Environmental Assessment Agency (MNP)

into dependence on economic growth (see Map 30.2). Electorates wanted more food, more goods, more energy. So governments encouraged, or at least allowed, environmental overexploitation.

The distribution of consumption suggests that overconsumption is a function of prosperity, in the same way that eating stimulates the appetite. Greed grows from growth. In 1991, an average American used up between 30 and 50 times as much copper, tin, and aluminum as a citizen of India, 43 times as much petroleum, and 184 times as much natural gas. By comparison with an average inhabitant of sub-Saharan Africa, the consumption rates of Americans or Western Europeans were several times greater even than that. Facts of these kinds are usually—and validly—cited as evidence of morally deplorable inequalities. If, however, the Indian or African were to consume as much as the Westerner, it would redress the inequality but not redeem the immorality. On the contrary, it would be an extension of bad habits.

Indeed, the effects would be worse because fast economic development always outstrips environmental restraints. China, where real average incomes virtually quadrupled in the last quarter of the twentieth century, demonstrates the possibilities and the dangers. By the mid-1990s, of the 10 cities with the most acute air-pollution problems in the world, five were in China, where pollution-related diseases were estimated to cause 1 million deaths a year—including poisoning by fluorides and arsenic that underregulated industries released into the food chain. China emitted more deadly sulfur dioxide into the atmosphere than any other country, causing acid rain to fall on much of its own land and on that of its neighbors. Overgrazing is turning the northern steppe to desert. The Gobi Desert is advancing from Central Asia toward the Yellow River valley. And desert dust from China blows across the Pacific, mixed with sulfur dioxide, over Japan and western North America. The Chinese government hardly began to tackle these problems until the late 1990s, when it tried to reduce sulfur dioxide emissions to "only" twice the amount the United Nations guidelines considered safe. In 2006, China was responsible for over a fifth of the world's carbon emissions, having overtaken even the United States—though if one takes into account China's huge population of more than 1.3 billion and need to catch up with rivals, the United States remained the world's top polluter of the atmosphere (see Figure 30.1).

The global disparities in consumption suggest a further, more worrying conclusion: Abundance is there to be exhausted. Given the chance, people gorge until, in effect, they burst or until they empty the pantry. Why people consume so much more than they need and why they have done so with unprecedented abandon in recent times are among the great, unsolved problems of human science and the great formative facts of human history. Anthropologists and philosophers have identified "spiraling desire"—an instinct, or maybe a pathology, that makes people want whatever is available, or envy whatever others have. If such a craving does exist, it could well have operated cumulatively in the twentieth century, under the impact of growing, spreading prosperity.

We can understand the problems better, though maybe not solve them, if we look first at how humans treated energy resources (food and fuel) in the twentieth century, and then at how this is connected to changes in urban and other habitats, before turning to the century's deeper environmental dangers, which are beyond human agency or human control.

The Benxi Steelworks in northern China. Satellites have identified Benxi, one of China's biggest steel production towns, as the most polluted place on Earth. Smoke billows up from smokestacks as the sun attempts to penetrate the smog.

FUEL RESOURCES

Just as steam power transformed the nineteenth-century world, so electricity and the internal combustion engine transformed the twentieth century. Electricity replaced gas for lighting and replaced steam as the power source of choice for most purposes. Fossil fuels—coal, oil, natural gas—came to be seen as the means of generating electricity rather than as direct sources of heat and light in themselves. The battery and the local generator, which was usually oil fueled, meant that the potentialities of electric power could be harnessed way beyond the industrial world. Electricity facilitated new methods of long-range communication and seemingly infinite means of managing information. In 1901, Guglielmo Marconi transmitted the first wireless telegraph message across the Atlantic. Radio waves soon linked every part of the world, communicating messages at the speed of light. In the 1960s, it became possible to engrave battery-operated computers on silicon microchips no bigger than 0.0394 of an inch in diameter. These were the most spectacular applications of electricity, but they required relatively little power. More pervasive and more effective in changing the world were the ways in which electricity penetrated everyday life: powering factories and farms, driving domestic machinery, lighting streets and interiors, propelling the engines of locomotion and transport.

The internal combustion engine came puffing and rumbling into the world in the 1890s. It could drive almost any kind of contraption from tractors to lawn mowers. Most commonly, however, it powered the motor car. Cars were rich people's toys at first, but they gradually got cheaper as they became articles of mass production. Today the world has over 600 million cars. They were socially liberating—more so, perhaps than any constitutional freedoms—because they enabled their owners to go where they liked, when they liked, as never before. But they also had lamentable effects: aggressive drivers, ugly roads, noxious fumes, raucous noise,

"Why people consume so much more than they need and why they have done so with unprecedented abandon in recent times are among the great, unsolved problems of human science and the great formative facts of human history."

Hymn to progress. In 1937, a Parisian electricity company commissioned the chic, technically innovative painter, Raoul Dufy, to decorate a gigantic canvas in celebration of the wonders of electricity. More than 180 feet long, it is still the world's largest painting. It is a hymn to progress, portraying a succession of scientists from ancient Greece onward, in a sequence of inventiveness that climaxes in electricity, symbolized as a flying spirit, zooming through the world, spreading illumination.

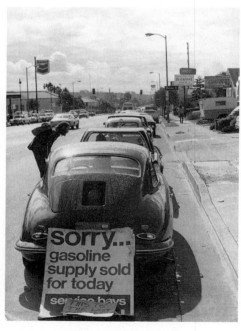

Gasoline shortage, United States, 1973. A line of parked cars ends with an ominous sign about the lack of fuel. A pedestrian bends down to the driver of one vehicle, perhaps asking if any filling stations nearby have a supply of the precious commodity. As petroleum supplies dwindle and competition for them increases, scenes like this may soon be repeated across the world.

and a huge new source of pressure on the planet's stocks of fossil fuels. Partly thanks to the internal combustion engine and partly because of oil's relative abundance, oil gradually replaced coal as the world's major source of energy, except in China. By the end of the twentieth century, oil supplied 40 percent of the world's energy, with coal and natural gas accounting in equal measure for most of the rest. Reliance on fossil fuels to supply the world's daunting energy requirements carried two major disadvantages.

First, fossil fuels are a limited resource. Exploration kept pace with demand for oil throughout the twentieth century, but people kept feeling the nagging worry that stocks would eventually run out. Competition for oil caused or exacerbated wars. Countries with major oil fields in their territories or offshore waters combined to control the price of fuel. In 1973, for instance, the Organization of Petroleum Exporting Countries (OPEC), an alliance of major oil producers, hiked the price and plunged the world into crisis. After a brief spell of energy rationing in the industrialized world and endangered revenues for the oil producers, a new era of cooperation between producers and consumers began in the 1980s. Exploitation of alternative energy sources, especially natural gas, diluted oil producers' power in the marketplace, while the producers themselves realized that they would sell a lot more oil if they stopped trying to restrain global economic growth. When price stability resumed, so did high levels of production and consumption.

The second big disadvantage of fossil fuels is that they release carbon gases into the atmosphere. In the Ice Age that began about 150,000 years ago, there were 200 parts of carbon dioxide per million in the air around the Earth. In the 1800s, the level rose to 280. Today, there are 350 parts per million (see Figure 30.2). Most of this increase is the result of human agency: the recirculation of carbon formerly locked in forests or buried underground for millions of years in the form of coal, oil, and gas. In the late twentieth century, the problem got worse because of carbon-charged gases used in refrigerators, air conditioners, and aerosol sprays—from perhaps 20,000 tons annually in 1950 to some 1.3 billion tons in 1990, when international controls finally began to take effect.

During the late twentieth century, observers grew increasingly anxious about the effects of these emissions on climate. Carbon in the atmosphere intensifies the effects of the rays of the sun, boosting temperatures, killing the plankton on which marine life depends for food, melting the edges of the ice caps, raising sea levels, and—if sustained long enough—modifying the flow of ocean currents and the pattern of the world's winds. Popular science calls this phenomenon the **greenhouse effect**. We simply do not know what the consequences would be if the world's wind and current system were to change permanently, but the periodic disasters caused by the temporary oscillations observable at intervals and recorded earlier in this book (Chapter 14) are alarming.

In view of the problems fossil fuels posed, energy consumers in the late twentieth century invested heavily in alternative sources of power. The idea of hydroelectricity was simple. As water cascades from a higher to a lower level, it can be used to turn turbines that would generate electricity. But the idea never worked in a fully satisfactory way. Hydroelectricity was available only where the right conditions of terrain and water supply favored it. It needed big rivers that could be dammed to concentrate and regulate the flow of water. Moreover, as we shall see, dams nearly always harmed agriculture.

Nor was nuclear power a fully satisfactory answer. It was the most cost-efficient form of power generation ever devised, but it, too, used an exhaustible resource—uranium—some types of which are constructed of atoms that release tremendous amounts of energy when split. Moreover, nuclear power left lethal waste products that radiated deadly agents. Apart from burying these contaminants in the ground, at the immediate cost of the space they take up and the future risk of their getting disturbed or seeping into the water table, there was no way to dispose safely of radioactive wastes.

In theory, hydrogen—the most common element on the planet—was the most promising energy source. As early as 1874, the great French master of science fiction, Jules Verne (1828–1905), imagined a hydrogen-powered world. In the 1960s, rockets were launched into outer space with motors powered by hydrogen electrons. In the early twenty-first century, the giant American automobile corporation General Motors claimed to have spent $1 billion on research into a hydrogen-driven alternative to the internal combustion engine. But hydrogen motors need frequent refueling, and business has no economic incentive to create an infrastructure of hydrogen service stations before there are hydrogen cars that will need them. It is partly a chicken-and-egg problem. There will be no mass switch to hydrogen cars until the service stations are in place, and no network of service stations will be in place until drivers have hydrogen cars.

Toward the end of the twentieth century, the search for fossil-fuel substitutes switched to what people called **renewable energy,** culled from the wind, the sun, the tides, even—potentially—the power of magnetism and the motion of the planet or even of the entire expanding universe. These remedies all posed their own problems. The sun is unreliable, and its rays are unevenly distributed around the globe. It is hard to devise turbines to harness the tides. Wind power, as exploited in the late twentieth and early twenty-first centuries, required vast numbers of ugly and intrusive windmills to generate relatively modest output. Technology to harness magnetism on a large scale has eluded researchers. Planetary and cosmic forces are, so far, beyond our grasp. Nevertheless, enough has been accomplished to demonstrate the viability of renewable solutions and to encourage further work.

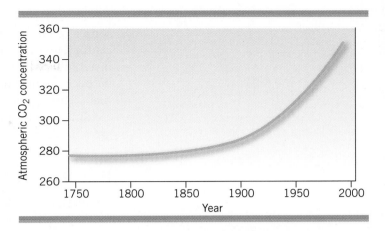

FIGURE 30.2 LEVEL OF CARBON DIOXIDE IN THE ATMOSPHERE, 1750–2000
Copyright © The Manchester Metropolitan University, 1997. Reprinted with permission.

Winds of change. Even renewable energy sources have ecological costs. Wind exploitation demands the concentrations of thousands of turbines that disfigure landscapes—as here, in the California desert—and demand maintenance.

Biofuels—oil-rich plants—presented another possible solution. Maize can be a source of ethanol for cars as well as calories for bodies. In the early twenty-first century, many countries—especially India, China, the Philippines, and Malaysia—invested heavily in jatropha, a weed formerly dismissed as useless, now prized for its oil content. So far no one has found a way to prevent commercially viable fuel-yielding plants from displacing foodstuffs, but the race is on to produce high-yielding varieties that will take up relatively little of the space the world needs to grow food.

FOOD OUTPUT

Population growth meant the world needed not only more fuel but also more food—hugely more than ever before. At the same time, dwellings, cities, and industries have taken up space that might otherwise be used to grow food. Meanwhile, the spread of deserts—*desertification*—has put more pressure on existing land. Most of this is not the result of human agency. The spread of the Sahara in Africa, for instance, has been one of the most continuous, relentless processes observable on our planet since the last Ice Age ended 20,000 years ago. People, however, have made the problem of the loss of cultivable land much worse.

In some places, for instance, in the twentieth century, as so often before—only now on a bigger scale—overexploitation wasted soils and exhausted irrigation resources. In 1932, unrestrained overfarming helped to turn much of Oklahoma and other parts of the North American west into a "Dust Bowl." In the *Grapes of Wrath*, the Nobel Prize–winning novelist, John Steinbeck (1902–1968), described the odyssey of a family of poor farmers driven from their land and forced into oppression and misery as they struggled to reach a new life in California. Marginal land all over the world became ever less productive as the result of a vicious circle of cause and effect. Farmers, like those in Burkina Faso, had to force more food from less land, while the spreading deserts edged into their fields. The result was overexploitation. Farmers had to sow new crops in fields that needed to be left fallow to recover their fertility. So soils became more exhausted, and food supplies became more precarious. Much of the world is still trapped in this cycle, especially in parts of Africa and Asia. When population growth raises food needs, farmers resort to overfarming to meet them. The result is impoverished land. Food output falls, and hunger—or nowadays, more commonly, dependence on foreign aid—spreads.

Two traditional responses to the problem of trying to get more output from less soil are irrigation and fertilization. In the twentieth century, these remedies often proved worse than the problem they were designed to cure. Take irrigation first. In the second half of the twentieth century, the proliferation of huge dams—usually combining irrigation schemes with efforts to generate hydroelectric power—made desertification worse. Dams usually have to be backed by reservoirs, which increase the extent of the surface-area of water, exposing more water to the sun. This speeds up evaporation. Meanwhile, the reservoirs absorb the water from the smaller streams and tributaries in the vicinity. This increases the salt content of the soil, because freely flowing streams no longer dilute the salt. So the dams actually leach fertility from the soil.

Yet from the 1930s, when the world's first great dams blocked the Volga River in Russia and the Colorado River in the American West, until the late 1960s, when the adverse effects of excessive damming became intolerable, dams were prestige monuments. Beloved by governments, they were showpiece projects, like the temples and pyramids of antiquity. Indeed, leaders who commissioned them often proudly compared the dams to just such ancient structures. A classic example

> "*Marginal land all over the world became ever less productive as the result of a vicious circle of cause and effect. Farmers, like those in Burkina Faso, had to force more food from less land, while the spreading deserts edged into their fields. The result was overexploitation.*"

occurred in Egypt. Built with Soviet aid during the Cold War, the Aswan Dam stretched across the Nile in the 1960s. It generated massive amounts of electricity and made it possible to regulate irrigation in Egypt with great precision. But it also trapped the silt that the Nile had carried since time immemorial to enrich Egypt's fields, shrinking the Nile delta, raising salt levels in the lower river, and choking off the flow of nutrients on which much Mediterranean marine life had formerly depended. Perhaps the single most disastrous project was the diversion in the 1950s of the two great rivers of Central Asia—the Oxus and Jaxartes (or Amu Darya and Syr Darya)—in what was then the southern Soviet Union. Soviet planners hoped to irrigate a vast plain for cotton production. Instead, they dried up the Aral, a huge inland sea, wrecked its fishing industry, and exposed deadly salt flats, from which the salt blew over the landscape, turning it barren. Although the fashion for dams declined, some monster projects continued, like dinosaurs escaping extinction. Between 1975 and 1991, Brazil and Paraguay collaborated to build a series of dams nearly five miles long across the River Paraná. The system generates more electricity than any other development in the world. In 2003, China opened an even bigger dam across the Yangtze—one of Mao Zedong's pet projects, at last brought to completion after nearly half a century of planning, debate, and construction. This Three Gorges Dam will eventually flood so much space that 2 million people will have to be resettled. At the time of its inauguration, more than two-thirds of the river waters of the world passed through dams, and China continued to plan and in some cases start work on more massive hydroelectric projects (see Figure 30.3).

Aswan High Dam. Four monstrous, cavernous hydraulic tunnels lie under the unfinished Aswan High Dam during the dam's construction in Egypt in 1964. The dam came to symbolize the ecological irresponsibility of high-cost, high-prestige hydraulic projects. It displaced population, swamped precious archaeological sites, exposed valuable water to evaporation, impoverished soils, and sped pollutants down the Nile, extinguishing much marine life in the eastern Mediterranean.

In the second half of the twentieth century, the amount of land under irrigation increased from under 247 million acres to almost 644 million acres. Today, 40 percent of the world's food is grown on irrigated land. Most irrigation water is pumped from below ground, where huge lakes and fresh water seas lie. But even this water is an exhaustible resource. The Ogallala Aquifer—a vast body of water—underlies the North American prairie. But 150,000 pumps are sucking it dry. In 1970, farmers in Kansas were told there was enough water left for a 300 years' supply. By the 1990s, the estimate had been revised to perhaps 20 or 30 years. The water table under the Sahara—where a vast inland, fresh water sea lies—falls measurably year by year. Unchecked consumption of irrigation resources in California, the Indian Punjab, the Murray-Darling river system in Australia, and the Cochabamba valley in Bolivia has had similar effects on the water table.

Fertilization, meanwhile, proved as mixed in its effects as irrigation. As we have seen (see Chapter 23), nineteenth-century agriculture relied on natural fertilizers, especially bird dung or guano. Chemical fertilizers supplied a relatively small market and seem to have had few or no ecological side effects. That changed in 1909 when Fritz Haber, a German chemist, discovered how to extract nitrogen from the atmosphere and use it to manufacture commercial fertilizer. It was like plucking food from the air. No other single invention did more to feed the growing population of the world in the second half of the century. In 1940, the world used some 4 million tons of artificial fertilizer. By 1990, it was using about 150 million

FIGURE 30.3 THE SHARE OF THE WORLD'S DAMS

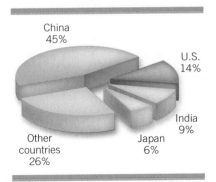

China 45%
U.S. 14%
India 9%
Japan 6%
Other countries 26%

© 2005 Pacific Institute for Studies in Development, Environment, and Security. www.pacinst.org

tons. Phosphate mining provided another source of fertilizers. Agrochemicals manufacturers found ways to double-dose the soil with chemicals to stimulate crops and kill weeds.

The practice had a startling effect on the ecosystems it touched. Many kinds of insects lost their weedy habitats. The birds, reptiles, and small mammals that fed off the insects lost their food supply. By the 1960s, the effects were so marked that Rachel Carson, a former United States' government agronomist, published her immensely influential book, *Silent Spring*, in which she predicted an America without birdsong. An ecological movement sprang up and mobilized millions of people, especially in Europe and America, to defend the environment against pollution and overexploitation. "Pollution, pollution," sang the satirist Tom Lehrer, warning listeners to beware of two things: "don't drink the water and don't breathe the air." Norman E. Borlaug, the Nobel Prize–winning agronomist who helped to develop fertilizer-friendly crops, denounced "vicious, hysterical propaganda" against agrochemicals by "scientific halfwits," but he could not stem the tide of environmentalism at a popular level. Only the resistance of governments and big business could check it.

In any case, the arguments were not as decisively imbalanced as Rachel Carson and her followers claimed. Despite the environmentalists' protests, humankind at that moment needed agrochemicals. Population growth was outstripping farmers' capacity to feed the world. Even when used together, irrigation and fertilization could not meet the growing demand for food.

In theory, the world could have gotten by in other ways. Farmers could cut down on production of less nutritious foods and increase more efficient forms of output. Beef, for instance, has tended to attract inefficient methods of production in recent times, because it commands relatively high prices. Farmers, especially in the United States, therefore tend to produce it by feeding grain to cattle. It takes on average seven units by weight of grain to fatten about one unit of beef. Humans could get 10 times as many calories from eating the grain themselves as they would get from eating the beef that ate the grain. Although beef is particularly wasteful, all livestock raising is a relatively inefficient way to use edible grain. Yet more than 70 percent of the grain grown in the United States at the end of the twentieth century, and some 40 percent of the world's grain, was devoted to animal feed.

Even more nutrition could be wrested from even less land if people were willing to live on diets of soybeans, high-lysine maize, insects, plankton, algae, and compacted edible bacteria. But by and large they are not, and in the global food market, the hungry are in any case powerless. Taste and culture are more powerful than hunger because they command more funds. Even the hungry cannot adapt to food they find tastes bad or strange, or that they cannot digest, as aid agencies have found when they have tried to make people drink milk in cultures unfamiliar with that product. Globally, the food market is geared to profit, not production. Farmers are not going to switch from more profitable to less profitable markets. Nor can they afford to do so.

As fears of global food shortages became acute early in the second half of the twentieth century, there was therefore only one way out: make plant foods more productive. Agronomists had to develop fast-growing, high-yielding, disease-resistant varieties of nutritious staples for a range of different environments. In the 1950s, research concentrated on some of the traditionally most successful and most adaptable grains, especially wheat, rice, and maize. The big breakthrough came with the adaptation of dwarf varieties of wheat from Japan and of rice from Taiwan and Indonesia. These crops were stunted in stature and so could be sprayed

"Globally, the food market is geared to profit, not production. Farmers are not going to switch from more profitable to less profitable markets. Nor can they afford to do so."

with fertilizers without toppling them. Experiments in Mexico and Washington State produced amazingly successful hybrids. By 1980, the world's average wheat yield per acre was double that of 1950. Under experimental conditions, the most successful new varieties yielded 10 times as much again as older ones. The new crops covered three-quarters of the world's grain-growing areas by the early 1990s. Meanwhile, in 1970, the United Nations' Food and Agriculture Organization reversed its predictions of widespread famine and estimated that the world could grow enough food to feed 157 billion people.

The **green revolution**—as people called it at the time—saved millions of lives. Even with the huge increase in global food output, failures of distribution contributed to many famines in the third quarter of the century. Without the new varieties the green revolution nurtured, the death toll would surely have been much higher. Nevertheless, the agronomists' successes came at a price. The new varieties were heavily dependent on chemical fertilizers and pesticides. So, as the green revolution spread, the world was—in effect—doused with poisons and pollutants. By 1985, according to the World Health Organization, pesticides had caused 1 million deaths, mostly among agricultural workers. Meanwhile, the new wonder crops crowded out traditional, local staples. The result was that peasant farmers in poor, economically deprived regions of the world produced ever-increasing quantities of cheap grains for survival and had little or no produce that they could sell at fair prices to rich consumers. Global poverty was becoming institutionalized.

Toward the end of the twentieth century, some scientists proposed to remedy the problems of the green revolution by switching to **genetically modified (GM) crops**. It became possible to modify the genes of food crops to make them resistant to insects, for example, without needing insecticides, or to deliver high yields with relatively little irrigation. The GM strategy, however, was rather like buying a rattlesnake to kill a rat—the proposed solution might be worse than the problem it was supposed to address. The new strategy might have undesirable ecological side effects of its own. Outside the United States, most governments were reluctant to encourage it, in case GM crops displaced or cross-pollinated with existing varieties and caused further losses of biodiversity (see Map 30.3). Nor would GM crops liberate farmers from reliance on chemical fertilizers.

GM technology, moreover, demanded high investment in the form of development capital. A few companies that had the power to control it dominated the market for GM seeds. With the United States government's blessing, the big bankrollers patented genes, excluded competition, and produced seed that would not reproduce naturally—in effect, compelling farmers to buy new seed every year. If widely adopted, GM would perhaps guarantee cheap food for the world for the future. But this would not necessarily be a good thing. It would condemn food producers, including most of the world's peasants, to poverty as part of a system of overproduction, depriving them—should they become dependent on GM crops—of the opportunity to specialize in supplying rare and expensive foods to rich markets. In short, GM would make the poor poorer by forcing them to buy seed to produce goods they could not sell.

Cheap food was a by-product of the success of the green revolution. In 1900, an average American family spent about 35 percent of its income on food. By 2000, the corresponding figure had fallen to less than 15 percent—and that money bought a lot more to eat. Abundance of choice grew with abundance of quantity. Big multinational companies made the most of the situation. Cheap, mass-produced foods,

Green revolution. A Dutch expert in 1969 shows Indonesian farmers how artificial fertilizer improves the growth of IR-8—the dwarf "wonder-rice" that spread around the world as a part of the "Green Revolution" of the 1960s. Increased production of grains such as this saved millions from famine, but the fertilizers and pesticides needed to grow them poisoned many of the environments in which they were used.

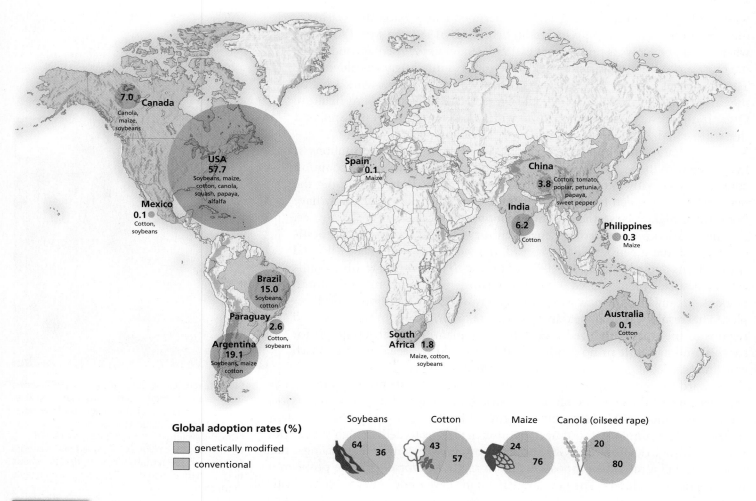

Global adoption rates (%)

◼ genetically modified
◻ conventional

Soybeans: 64 / 36
Cotton: 43 / 57
Maize: 24 / 76
Canola (oilseed rape): 20 / 80

MAP 30.3

Global distribution of genetically modified crops, 2007

By country, 2007 *(million hectares)**

⬤ percentage of global area

*Excludes countries with GM area less than 0.1m hectares

with low unit profits, could make fantastic fortunes for the companies that sold them if they marketed them on a large enough scale. The American hamburger firm McDonald's became a globally recognizable example of this sort of strategy. It began as a local no-frills drive-in restaurant in San Bernardino, California, in 1937. By the end of the twentieth century, McDonald's had tens of thousands of outlets in 120 countries. Global urbanization favored the trend. In booming cities, migrants from the countryside were cut off from the sort of food they formerly ate: painstakingly grown plant foods, freshly harvested and locally prepared. A massive switch to mass-produced food occurred in just about every major urbanizing environment in the world—not just in the industrialized West. Paradoxically, while prosperity grew and food became abundant, many people's diets deteriorated. Early in the twenty-first century, conversion of vast terrains to produce fuel crops instead of food began to change the game. Basic foodstuffs became more expensive. The effects were not encouraging. The poor in rich countries lost the benefit of cheap food. The poor in poor countries still lacked markets for their traditonal foodstuffs.

At the same time, the science of dietetics failed. In the last 40 years of the twentieth century, on dieticians' advice, Western governments promoted massive health campaigns in favor of high-carbohydrate diets, recommending bread products,

Obesity in China. Patients, all of them young, perform aerobics at the Aimi Fat Reduction Hospital in Tianjin, China in March 2005. The hospital, which attracts obese people from several Asian countries, uses acupuncture, diet, and intensive exercise to help patients shed weight.

potatoes, noodles, and rice. Cheap foods, laden with carbohydrates, especially in the form of sugar, glutted the market. In combination with the problems of distribution that urbanization created, the result was a pandemic of obesity. It started in the West, especially in the United States. In 1950, 5 percent of Americans were classified as clinically obese. By 2000, the figure had risen to over 20 percent. It then jumped to 26 per cent in 2001. Particularly alarming was the rate of increase among the young. Well over a third of under-19-year-olds qualified as obese according to the standard definition. Although the United States weighed in at the top of the fat stakes, the same trend was detectable throughout the Western world. By the end of the century, it was beginning to be noticeable in much of the rest of the globe, even in countries where obesity was virtually unknown—including China, India, South Korea, and even Japan, which, starting from a low statistical base, registered the world's steepest increase in clinical obesity in the 1990s.

Remarkably, late twentieth-century obesity was particularly a problem of the poor. This was a stunning reversal of what had been, almost universally, the pattern of the history of the world up to this time. In just about every previous period, in most societies, the rich were fat and the poor were thin. Now, it was the other way round. Formerly, abundance was a luxury. Only the rich could afford to be fat. When cheap food became abundantly available to the poor, the rich—at least, those of them who were fashion conscious—fled from fatness into dieting. In the twentieth-century West, wealth could buy you a thin physique by way of expensive "health foods," plastic surgery, personal trainers, and gym fees. The world became one in which "You can never be too rich or too thin," as Wallis Simpson (1896–1986) had said. She was a waif-thin, almost wafer-thin, socialite, whom King

Chronology: Fuel and Food

1890s	Development of internal combustion engine
1930s	World's first great dams constructed
1932	Dust Bowl emerges in central and western United States
1940–1990	Use of artificial fertilizer increases from 4 to 150 million tons
1950–1980	Wheat yields per acre double
1950–2000	Land under irrigation increases from 247 to 644 million acres
1965	Organization of Petroleum Exporting Countries (OPEC) formed
1962	Publication of Rachel Carson's *Silent Spring*
1973	OPEC oil embargo against the United States, Western Europe, and Japan
Late twentieth century	Accelerated use of genetically modified (GM) crops; search for alternative fuels intensifies
ca. 2000	600 million cars worldwide; fossil fuels account for most of world's energy consumption; carbon dioxide levels in the atmosphere reach 350 parts per million
2008	Three Gorges Dam over the Yangtze River completed

Edward VIII of Britain renounced his throne to marry in 1936. Meanwhile, the poor consoled themselves with calories in quantities they could never before afford.

The rise of obesity panicked health agencies. Yet one of the most remarkable facts about late twentieth-century obesity is how little harm it did. Most obese people managed to stay healthy and even to stay alive until a ripe old age. Nonetheless, the dramatically deadly new diseases of the period included two major killers to which the corpulent are particularly prone: heart diseases and type-II diabetes. More than 60 percent of type-II diabetes cases in America, according to a study done at Harvard University in 2001, were directly attributed to excessive weight. For the many people prone to the effect, fat in the bloodstream coated and clotted their arteries, inducing high blood pressure and causing strokes and heart attacks. A recent article in the *New England Journal of Medicine* estimates that if not reversed obesity will lower life expectancies for American children from diabetes, heart disease, and high blood pressure. If this is right, children may grow up to have shorter lives than their parents had. Life expectancy, in other words, will fall for the first time in American history. In short, twentieth-century food strategies succeeded in fighting famine and feeding the world. But they failed in just about every other important respect: overproducing abundance, increasing poverty, diminishing biodiversity, and undermining health.

> "In short, twentieth-century food strategies succeeded in fighting famine and feeding the world. But they failed in just about every other important respect. . ."

URBANIZATION

In a world in which agriculture was getting more uniform and was becoming, under the pressure of economies of scale, a vast business that huge corporations ran, it got increasingly hard to be a peasant. A few rich countries, such as Germany and France, subsidized their small farmers. In most of the rest of the world, peasants abandoned the land and followed the new roads and railway lines toward cities and a promise of prosperity that often remained unfulfilled. This was one of the most dramatic new departures ever in the way people live. For 10,000 years, most people had lived in agricultural settlements. Now centers of industrial manufacturing and services took over. Towns and cities became the normal environments for people to live in. By the end of the century, half the world lived in settlements with populations of 20,000 or more (see Map 30.4). Cities grew even in countries where agriculture remained the economically dominant way of life. In Nigeria, typically for regions struggling to escape from a role as primary producers for other people's industries, a fifth of the population lived in towns in 1963. By 1991, the proportion had shot up to a third.

Urbanization came at a high short-term cost in terms of living standards. The world hardly seemed to have learned from the degradation of urban life in the industrializing cities of the nineteenth century (see Chapter 24). Now, as urbanization spread to new regions, the same problems recurred on a greater scale. Towns grew like fungus: profusely and unhealthily. The Brazilian town of Cubatão, which sprang suddenly from the mangrove swamps at the foot of the Serra do Mar Mountains in the 1960s, typifies the horrors. Within 20 years, Cubatão became Brazil's major

The reality of pell-mell urbanization. Lagos, Nigeria, is the biggest city in sub-Saharan Africa, growing at a rate of 5 to 6 percent a year. Its population is estimated to be between 10 and 15.5 million. The photograph shows some of the results: overcrowding, gerry-building, a transport system that barely functions, unregulated trading, accumulating litter.

MAP 30.4

Population in Urban Areas, ca. 2007

(percent of total population)

▨	75 and above
▨	50–74
□	25–49
□	0–24

Urban Areas with more than 5 Million People

●   2000

◉   2015 (projected)

center for producing steel and fertilizers. In 1980, when 35 percent of infants there died before their first birthday, people who breathed toxic smog under acid rain called their hometown the "valley of death."

Cleanups eased these problems in Cubatão by the end of the century, but the pattern was continuously being repeated elsewhere. In 1980, half the world's city dwellers had no access to treated water. In effect, they had to drink and cook with raw sewage or pay a premium for bottled water. Over the twentieth century as a whole, air pollution probably killed as many people as war. Decent housing provision could not keep up with the surge of formerly rural populations to big towns. Shanties enveloped many of the great or growing cities of the world. In India in the 1990s, 1.5 million people lived on the streets of the cities, not out of poverty but simply because of the lack of housing. And though civic authorities tried to keep urban pollution under control, some effects of urbanization surprised the world and defied solutions. Nonrecyclable waste piled up. "Food deserts" emerged in towns where, with no means to grow food or store it in ways traditional in rural environments, newcomers to city life found themselves at the mercy of suppliers of the cheap, high-energy fast foods that were filling and tasted satisfying but were rarely nutritious. This is why mass obesity rapidly outgrew its origins as a disease of the newly affluent in North America and Europe, and became a worldwide urban scourge. Meanwhile, the social consequences of rapid urbanization proved hard to control. Rootless populations with unanchored loyalties bred criminal organizations and gangs and even helped to produce the private armies for the civil wars that disturbed parts of Africa, Southeast Asia, and Latin America.

By the century's end, however, there were signs that urbanization was easing. São Paulo in Brazil and Mexico City—overgrown giants with populations approaching 20 million each by some counts—began to shrink. The rise of markets for rare, traditional, artisanal, and exotic foods promised to restore the rural economy in parts of the world. Cities would certainly remain the main habitat of humans. But the trend suggested that concentrations of 100,000 to 1 million people would be normal and that mega-cities of over 10 million people would shrink.

THE CRISIS OF CONSERVATION

In the twentieth century, the human domain expanded. People took up more space and depleted more resources than ever before. One result was predictable—other species could not compete. As well as crowding out some life forms, humans blasted others into oblivion, hunting them to extinction, exterminating them with pest controls, or depriving them of their habitats or foods. By swapping plants and animals around the world—releasing invading species into unfamiliar habitats— humans condemned some native animals in affected zones to death by predation. In the 1960s, venomous Pacific snakes that had hitchhiked in the wheels of American army planes invaded Guam where they had no natural enemies and ate almost all the birds on the island within 15 years. Meanwhile, in the eastern Mediterranean, where the salt levels in the discharge from the Nile altered the ecology, new predators invaded from the Red Sea and wiped out unique local species.

Today, the world faces the loss of more species than at any time since the end of the last Ice Age. One percent of recorded species of birds and mammals has disappeared in the previous 100 years. Because of pesticides, invertebrate species, which are less well documented, are likely to have suffered far more. According to the warnings of one of the most eminent authorities, 20 percent of all invertebrate species were in imminent danger of extinction as the twentieth century drew to a close. The extinction of a species is not an isolated event. Every species is a part of the ecosystem and a link in the food chain. Every extinction threatens other species.

But how much of the disaster was really the fault of humans? Some human communities have long considered themselves to be masters or stewards of creation, or in some sense to have special responsibility for other species. So, in the twentieth century, people who became aware of the appalling rate of species extinction tended to blame humans for it. Yet in the remote past, without our aid, nature has repeatedly turned over species—eliminating some, evolving others. The Ice Age of 245 million years ago, when the Earth became a "snowball," almost wiped out all life. Sixty-five million years ago, the dinosaurs vanished. As we have seen, the extinction of many kinds of large animals followed the end of the last Ice Age, when overexploitation by human hunters may have played a part in it. To some extent, the current alarm may be a trick of the evidence. We are better informed than ever before about the state of preservation of species in the wild. We are aware of more extinctions, so we suppose more extinctions are underway. To some extent, too, the current situation is unfolding independently of human agency. Species extinction is a routine event in nature. Nonetheless, human activity undoubtedly speeded up the turnover of species during the twentieth century.

The amount of resources humans consumed left less for other species. The vigor with which farmers used pesticides and weed killers not only eliminated the species whose habitats were suppressed, but also others that fed on them. The pressure rising populations exerted on living space has probably edged many species out of existence. Half the deforestation of history happened in the twentieth century— almost all of it in tropical and wooded regions (see Map 30.5). In the last 40 years of the century, the Amazonian forests of Brazil shrank by 10 percent. In Southeast Asia, those of Thailand, Malaysia, and Borneo in Indonesia disappeared on a similar scale. By the end of the century, Africa had lost half its tropical forests, Latin Amer-

> *"The extinction of a species is not an isolated event. Every species is a part of the ecosystem and a link in the food chain. Every extinction threatens other species."*

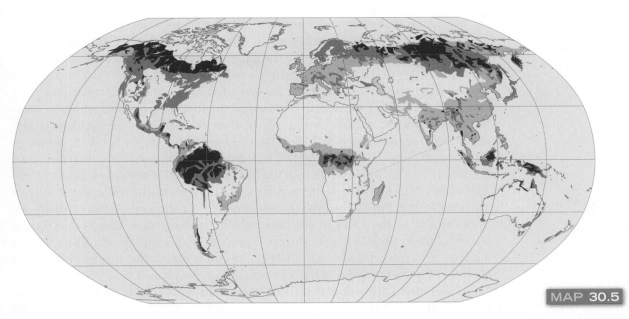

Deforestation Worldwide, ca. 2005

- ■ frontier forest
- ■ degraded forest
- ■ frontier forest 8,000 years ago

ica nearly a third. The traditional human inhabitants of these environments—foragers and seasonal farmers—survived, but their habitats shrank, and their situation grew ever more precarious. So did that of the creatures who shared their traditional homes. Environmentalists in Europe and North America—areas where felled trees had fueled economic growth for centuries—deplored the loss of forests in Asia and South America, but would not compensate peasants in the regions concerned to preserve them. In 2007, the governor of Papua in Indonesia proposed a scheme of compensation that would encourage replanting, but whether the rest of the world would be willing to invest in the scheme remains unclear.

On the other hand, the twentieth century was remarkable for the recovery of forests in temperate zones, especially in Japan and North America, and for the flowering of many movements to conserve species and habitats. People launched projects to save endangered species, or to reintroduce into particular localities species that had already disappeared from them. If more species were lost through human action than ever before, more were also saved. And if human settlement eradicated some habitats, it created others in which wildlife thrived. Every late twentieth-century town or suburban dweller has stories of possums under the couch, or racoons in the garbage, or foxes or coyotes in the shrubbery, or rabbits colonizing airports, or deer following the railway lines into the hearts of the cities or snacking on gardens. In New England, bears and mountain lions are now seen in areas where they had been absent for more than 200 years.

These successes, such as they were, happened on land. The bleakest story of environmental change and species depletion is a sea story. In the twentieth century, fish as a foodstuff leaped in popularity, like a salmon jumping the rapids. Historians debate why. In the second half of the twentieth century, after the beneficial health effects of fish oils became known (they boost nutrition, reduce cholesterol, and help prevent heart attacks), health concerns may have played a part. It is tempting to suspect that a romantic longing for wild, unfarmed food may have been influential, too. Fish is still largely a product of the hunt. Though industrial trawlers now make the catch, they still have to track the fish in the wild.

Whatever the reasons, the amount of fish that fisheries handled worldwide grew fortyfold in the twentieth century. Over that period, according to historian John McNeill, the world consumed 3 billion tons of fish. If McNeill's calculations are right, that exceeds the whole catch landed during the entire previous history of the world. Some varieties were fished to near extinction (see Map 30.6). At the end of the century, Atlantic cod stocks stood, according to common calculations, at only 10 percent of their historic average. California sardines became rarities. North Sea herrings—once a staple food in much of Europe—are now a costly treat. The Japanese sardine fishery was the most abundant in the world in the 1930s but had virtually collapsed by the mid-1990s. Off Namibia in southern Africa, fishermen caught millions of tons of sardines in the 1960s. By 1980, none were left. At the end of the century, the predicament of the Chilean sea bass, which has become a trendy dish in the United States and Western Europe, precipitated a crisis. Profit-conscious Chilean fishermen pleaded with clients to go on eating the species, while ecological enthusiasts tried to persuade restaurateurs to ban it.

If fish stocks are permanently lost, the results will be catastrophic. The use of fishmeal in fertilizers and animal feeds makes fish a vital food source for the world, way beyond the tonnage humans directly consume. But was the apparent depletion of the world's fishing stocks in the twentieth century an irreversible disaster or a temporary blip? Fish migration patterns change, and the fact that we have lost sight of traditional stocks of some species in the vastness of the ocean does not necessarily mean that they have disappeared forever. Some extraordinary cases of recuperation have been recorded. The supply of Maine lobsters, for instance, waxed and waned almost regularly during the twentieth century. Some oyster beds, once thought to have been exhausted, are now plentiful again. In the late twentieth and early twenty-first centuries, the recovery of populations of whales and harbor seals showed that marine conservation programs could work. In 2005, successful conservation policies attracted blame for an increase in the incidence of shark attacks on people in Australian waters. Fish conservation methods seem to be working for Atlantic cod and haddock. Roughly, fishermen now concentrate on each species in turn, allowing the other to recover. Sometimes, positive effects are unforeseen. Fishing for sea-urchins in New England in the late twentieth century relieved pressure on the underwater kelp forest that sea-urchins eat and lobsters inhabit: hence more lobsters.

Salvation or disaster? Fish farming is likely to supply increasing amounts of the world's protein and solve the problem of overfishing. But it creates new eco-niches for disease and threatens biodiversity. The photograph shows a fish farm in China, where aquaculture programs are among the most developed in the world.

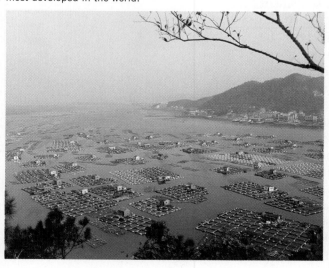

Still, many authorities have concluded that the future lay with fish farming. Fish farms produced 5 million tons of food worldwide in 1980 and 25 million tons by 2000. China accounted for more than half the total. Fish farming is an effective method of food production. Farmed salmon yield 15 times more nutrition per acre than beef cattle. The sea bass grows twice as fast under farmed conditions as in the wild. In the wild, it takes a million eggs to produce a fish. By the early twenty-first century, farmers were regularly turning 60 percent of eggs into fish. Meanwhile, techniques of fish farming improved. What was formerly a fresh water and coast-bound activity began to be possible in the deep ocean. So, despite the losses from overfishing, the world's stocks of edible fish probably were and are secure for the foreseeable future. Again, of course, we will have to pay an environmental cost. Fish farms are eco-niches for new marine plagues. Farmed species will inevitably escape into the wild and crowd out others by infection and cross-breeding.

MAP 30.6

Endangered Fisheries Worldwide, ca. 2005

- cod and cod-like fish (haddock, hake)
- flatfish (flounder, sole)
- perch-like fish (grouper, snapper, bass)

THE UNMANAGEABLE ENVIRONMENT: CLIMATE AND DISEASE

Ecological alarmism has become a trend of our times—a modern, secular form of millenarianism. We scare ourselves into expecting the apocalypse, the end of the world, or at least the end of civilization as we know it. Our fears could well come true. Civilizations have collapsed because they failed to get their relationship with the environment right. Overexploitation is a constant temptation. We still succumb to it. No period can match our own for the sheer wasteful carelessness with which we pollute our planet and consume its resources. But the ecological problems of our times do not start or stop with our self-inflicted difficulties. Bigger dangers are worrying precisely because they are not of our making. If we caused them, we could control them. But we do not cause them. They are beyond our control.

The Earth is still in its infancy. The planet has, at a reasonable guess, several billion years to go before it sizzles or freezes into lifelessness. By supposing that we could destroy our planet, we are guilty of a kind of arrogance. The Earth is hugely bigger than anything we have power to wreck. Nature will surely outlast our species. Trees that were here before humans existed will go on growing after humans have gone. So will microbes and—probably—insects, reptiles, birds, and marine species vastly older than humankind. When the planet perishes, it will be nothing to do with us. It will happen long after we are gone. And the cause will rest with cosmic forces that we are aware of but have no power to influence.

These considerations are worth bearing in mind, because if we kid ourselves into thinking that all ecological problems are our own fault, we shall be deluded into supposing that we can fix them all. It is worth remembering that we have hardly scratched the surface of the planet we inhabit. Our deepest oil wells are only thousands of feet deep. Most species have never been cataloged and are perhaps unknown. The oceans, a habitat we have not yet begun to colonize and have still done little to exploit, make up 90 percent of the planet.

So despite our self-inflicted disasters, a lot of nature still threatens us without being threatened in turn. In 2005, a hurricane devastated and drowned New Orleans, provoking President George W. Bush to acknowledge that Nature was "the world's greatest superpower." Some of the dangers prophets invoke are close to the edges of science fiction. Asteroid bombardment, for instance, is unlikely to happen,

"No period can match our own for the sheer wasteful carelessness with which we pollute our planet and consume its resources. But the ecological problems of our times do not start or stop with our self-inflicted difficulties."

Making Connections | GLOBAL ENVIRONMENTAL CHALLENGES

AREA OF HUMAN ACTIVITY		ENVIRONMENTAL AND SOCIAL EFFECTS
Fuel resources: dependence on electricity, internal combustion engine, and fossil fuels		Electricity permeates everyday life and economic activity; dependence on internal combustion engine to power transport and link suburban residential districts to cities; oil wars; increased carbon dioxide levels and global warming
Food resources: need to supply over 6 billion humans		Increased dependence on agrochemicals and large dams and irrigation projects; reliance on hybrid and genetically modified (GM) crops; depletion of fisheries; increased availability of cheap, mass-produced food leads to excess consumption of carbohydrates, fats and widespread obesity
Housing: increased urbanization/suburbanization		Widespread substandard housing and urban air, water pollution; increased nonrecyclable waste; dependence on automobiles; favorable environment for criminal organizations, gangs
Swapping plants and animals around the world to increase yields		Displacement of plant/animal species from native environments; disappearance of thousands of species of plants/animals decline in biodiversity

but the threat of it demonstrates the perplexities we face in confronting natural forces outside human control. The United States government is popularly supposed to have plans to deflect or explode an approaching asteroid with nuclear missiles, but such a defense would have unpredictable and incalculable consequences.

We face more immediate dangers. Two of the most powerful sources in nature remain barely understood and beyond our power to manage: disease-bearing microorganisms and climate. Either or both could destroy humankind with no help from us. Take climate first. For all our accumulated cunning, we cannot control climate change or reverse its effects. At best, we seem able only to edge it toward where we do not want it to go: speeding up global warming, reducing rainfall, intensifying desertification. As we have seen, for most of the period this book covers, from the waning of the last great Ice Age some 20,000 years ago, the world has been experiencing a protracted warming phase. From about the fourteenth century C.E. to about the eighteenth, warming went into temporary remission. Allowing for many ups and downs, temperatures declined slightly but significantly over much of the world (see Chapter 14). Around the mid-nineteenth century, however, warming seems to have intensified. Despite a wavering in the third quarter of the twentieth century, when falling temperatures excited prophecies of a new Ice Age, global temperatures by the turn of the millennium recovered or exceeded levels last reached some 800 years ago (see Figure 30.4). The case is urgent. In the last three decades of the twentieth century, the Arctic Ocean along the north coast of Eurasia began to turn into open sea in summer. Reports released in 2007 predicted the disappearance of 40 percent of the polar ice cap—at then prevailing rates of meltdown—by 2050. The effects will cause turmoil for the distribution of marine life, the ability of humans to live in coastal zones, the directions of winds and currents, and the temperatures of arctic waters and the land along their shores. The climate of the world will heat up even faster than before, turning wheat-growing lands in

FIGURE 30.4 GLOBAL ANNUAL AVERAGE TEMPERATURES AND PROJECTIONS, 1880–2100

© Time Inc. Reprinted by permission.

Melting Arctic ice cap. A satellite-scanned image from September, 2007, shows how the ice has retracted from the Arctic Ocean. Except where the ice touches the shore of Russian Siberia, on the left of the picture, it is now possible to sail in summer almost an entire circuit of the Arctic coasts of Europe, Asia, and the Americas.

the Midwest, for instance, back into deserts and dustbowls. The Gulf Stream will vanish from the Atlantic, making northwest Europe cold while much of the rest of the world overheats. Half the planet's inhabited islands will disappear under the sea if melted ice causes sea levels to rise by 4 to 6 inches. On the other hand, potentially vast subarctic mineral resources will become accessible to drilling—raising the prospect of international rivalry and perhaps wars to exploit them.

We do not yet know how to cope with global warming if the planet continues to heat up. Some of our efforts to deflect it seem feeble: cutting the rates of increase of carbon emissions, often by relying on trivial measures, such as recycling refrigerators (which are cooled by carbon-based gases) and banning aerosol sprays. Because of the amount of carbon already in the atmosphere, it will take a long time for current conservation efforts to register measurable effects—perhaps not before the twenty-second century. On the other hand, a new Ice Age may occur. We do not at present know how to prepare for it. The future, it seems, will be fire or ice.

Or disease will dominate it—a recurrent age of plagues (see Chapter 14). Despite the stunning achievements of medical science, humans still do not control—or even adequately understand—the microbial world in which much disease originates. The spectacular victories of the twentieth century include the defeat of some of the most terrible killing and maiming diseases doctors faced: polio, smallpox, leprosy, and a whole range of illnesses formerly responsible for heartbreaking levels of infant mortality. For a time, new treatments almost eliminated tuberculosis, though it revived in the late twentieth century. New remedies spared the lives of diabetics, though the disease is acquiring increasing numbers of victims. Improved surgery made organ transplants possible. Kidneys could be swapped, beginning in the early 1950s, and hearts transplanted, starting in 1967. The use of surgical devices to regulate the heart prolonged even more lives among those who suffered from heart disease. Medicine made a big contribution to rising life-expectancy figures. Sanitation and public health care probably made an even more spectacular difference. In privileged places, the effects were impressive. In much of Western Europe, Canada, Australia, New Zealand, and the United States, average life expectancy at the end of the century was in the mid-seventies for men and the low eighties for women. Fears multiplied of a future in which the workforce would be too small to support an increasingly elderly population and the rising costs of caring for the health of the aged. In Japan, the trend was similar, with 16 percent of the population aged over 65 in 1998. Japan, faced with the world's

"Despite the stunning achievements of medical science, humans still do not control—or even adequately understand—the microbial world in which much disease originates."

Poliomyelitis was one of the horrific new killer-diseases of the twentieth century that science managed to contain. Sanitation created an eco-niche for polio to develop. Before the twentieth century, mildly unsanitary drinking water contained tiny amounts of the virus, so people acquired immunity naturally. But after the 1920s, the disease became rampant. It paralyzed Franklin D. Roosevelt, the future U.S. president, in 1921. Most victims died through paralysis of the brain. This 1955 photograph shows mothers and children in London waiting in line with affected cheerfulness and real fear for the newly developed vaccine.

biggest increase of over-70-year-olds in the population, began to subsidize old people to resettle overseas. In China, at the end of the century, most people could expect to live into their late 60s. In India, life expectancy rose to an average of 63 years of age.

The massive increase of world population in the late twentieth century was, above all, a triumph of what we might call death control. The great population growth of the eighteenth century was probably the result of adjustments in the microbial world (see Chapter 20). That of the twentieth, by contrast, arose from human agency: medical remedies and the preventive measures of public health policy.

But scientific self-congratulation over these successes masked worrying, persistent problems. Medical advances were unfairly distributed. Life expectancy in the African countries of Benin, Burkina Faso, Burundi, and Angola, at the end of the twentieth century, remained stuck at an average in the mid-40s. In Guinea-Bissau the figure in 1998 was 42 years for men and 45 for women. In Uganda, Rwanda, and Malawi, the average for both sexes was 42 years or under. In much of the rest of sub-Saharan Africa, the situation was little better. At 112 deaths per thousand in Nigeria and 90 in Ivory Coast, sub-Saharan infant mortality rates were three or four times worse than those of most of East and Southeast Asia, and unconscionably worse than those of Western Europe (see Map 30.7).

Moreover, and inseparably, medical advances were costly. Health-care costs in America left many of the poor out of the loop. In Europe, where state-run national health services ensured a fairer distribution of benefits, taxpayers struggled to keep pace with the costs. In Britain, for instance, the National Health Service cost £400 million to run in 1951, but about £32 billion a half-century later. The cost more than doubled over the following two years, while inflation generally rose at less than 2 percent a year. By that time, public health was absorbing 6.6 percent of the nation's income. The leap in life expectancy made health-care costs worse. People lived longer, contributed less to national wealth as they got older, and consumed more of that wealth in health care. By the early 1990s, health-care costs absorbed between 7 and 10 percent of the gross domestic product of most developed countries and over 14 percent in the United States where millions had inadequate health insurance or none at all.

Furthermore, although medicine eliminated old diseases, new ones—or new forms of old ones—arose to torment humanity. The effects of pollution, drug abuse, undiscriminating sex habits, and affluence—which condemned the unwary to overindulgence and inertia—were major killers. Far more lethal, however, was the rapid evolution of viruses. Some killers, such as Ebola, Lassa fever, and the immune-destroying virus known as HIV, leaped from the eco-niches in which they had formerly been contained and began to attack humans. New forms of influenza appeared regularly, though none attained the virulence of the pandemic of 1918–1919, which claimed an estimated 30 million lives worldwide. A new strain of tuberculosis, which emerged in the late twentieth century, resists every known drug and kills half the people it infects. Bubonic plague has returned to India. New strains of cholera and malaria have emerged. Malaria cases in India rose a hundredfold to 10 million between 1965 and 1977. In sub-Saharan Africa, malaria kills 1 million children a year. Yellow fever—which had almost been eradicated by the midcentury—killed 200,000 people a year in Africa in the 1990s. Measles, a disease that immunization was expected to eradicate, was still killing 1 million people a year at the end of the century. New viruses can defeat antibiotics and other drugs, which decline in effectiveness as a result of overuse.

Life Expectancy, ca. 2007

(years)

- 70 and above
- 60–69
- 50–59
- 40–49
- less than 40

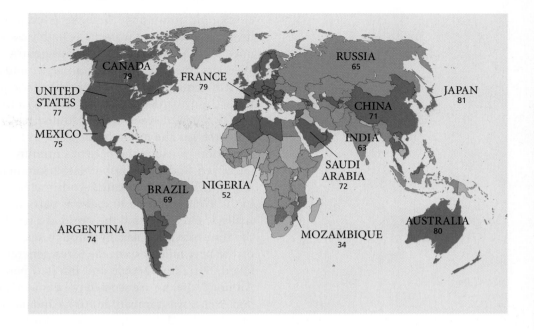

Other new diseases arose in human-made eco-niches: Legionnaire's disease, which breeds in the dampness of air-conditioning systems, was the prime example. Intensive farming created breeding conditions for salmonella in chickens and accumulated toxins in the food chain. Human-variant Creutzfeldt-Jakob Disease, or "Mad Cow disease," is a brain-killing, invariably fatal disorder, apparently caused by intensive cattle-farming methods—recycling dead sheep and cattle as fodder—and was transmitted to at least some of its victims in tainted food. Twentieth-century interventions in the environment opened many new eco-niches for disease: in over-fertilized soil, stripped of much insect life; in polluted waterways; and in the disturbed depths of the sea, where bacteria multiply in searing hot vents that humans have only lately begun to penetrate. In an increasingly interconnected world, human carriers took diseases way beyond accustomed environments. Toward the end of the century, West Nile virus from Africa turned up in New York City. A variant form of influenza from China caused widespread deaths, especially in Canada. Dengue fever from Asia has become endemic in parts of the Caribbean.

Broadly speaking, infectious diseases ceased to be major killers, though old ones constantly threatened to reemerge and new ones to develop. Chronic diseases, meanwhile, arose to replace infections as the major menace. Cancer and heart diseases grew spectacularly, especially in rich countries, without anyone knowing why. By the 1980s in the United States, one death in every four was blamed on cancer. In Britain, one death in three was ascribed to heart disease, which caused 10 million deaths a year worldwide by the end of the century. Some forms of cancer were "lifestyle diseases." Cervical cancer, for instance, was thought to be connected to sexual promiscuity or adolescent sexual intercourse, while smoking, according to medical consensus, caused lung, throat, and mouth cancers and contributed to heart disease and stroke. Obesity and its related disorders, as discussed earlier, owed their prevalence, in part, to bad eating habits. In the second half of the twentieth century, evidence began to accumulate that some medical treatments were actually contributing to the disease environment. Doctors prescribed drugs so widely that people were becoming dependent on them, while many viruses and strains of bacteria were

Bird flu. In 2005, bird flu became one in a long series of new diseases feared as the potential "next plague." Health workers culled tens of millions of poultry wherever the infection appeared. The photograph shows such an operation in progress in Turkey. Farmers lost livelihoods. Governments spent fortunes. Fear of bird flu has thus far proved exaggerated. The disease has not spread easily to humans. But mounting health scares showed growing awareness of the world's vulnerability to unfamiliar viruses.

developing immunity to them. Even where physical health improved, mental health seemed to get worse. The highly competitive capitalist societies of the developed West became prey to various neurotic disorders collectively known as stress. Worriers "medicalized" their anxieties and feelings of malaise, classifying them in their own minds as medical problems and taking them to the doctor. Medical services, already hard-pressed, became overburdened.

Two new diseases demonstrated the microbial world's destructive potential. The first was the influenza of 1918–1919, and the second, the scourge of AIDS, a condition in which the patient's immunity to all kinds of disease is progressively destroyed, and which lashed into prominence in the 1980s. AIDS started in Africa as a sexually communicated syndrome between men and women. It then broke out in the West, where, at first, it was particularly virulent among homosexuals. Eventually, it spread around the world as a result of the transfusion of infected blood or the transmission—usually through sex—of other bodily fluids. By the beginning of the new millennium, the virus generally held to be responsible for AIDS had killed 27 million people and infected perhaps as many as 80 million worldwide. Although the disease seemed to be under control in most of Europe, the Americas, and Asia, it was rampant in Africa and parts of the Caribbean, where, for a mixture of cultural and economic reasons, governments were less committed to fighting it. Toward the end of the century, doctors in South Africa reckoned that AIDS accounted for 40 percent of deaths among sexually active people (see Map 30.8). A new, more virulent, and perhaps untreatable strain seemed to be emerging in the United States early in the twenty-first century.

MAP 30.8

HIV in Africa

HIV Prevalance Rates in African Adults
(15-49 Years of Age) as of the end of 2005

- 0.0%–1.9%
- 2%–4.9%
- 5%–9.9%
- 10%–19.9%
- 20% or greater

In Perspective
The Environmental Dilemma

We can monitor the environmental transformations of the twentieth century on the map. The surface of the Earth has become a grid of routes laid out by human hands. Instead of the physical features—rivers, mountains, forests, and deserts—that used to be the markers travelers relied on, roads, rails, air routes, and shipping lanes now connect or, in their absence, isolate locations.

The results were not evenly spread across the world. On the contrary, a development gap widened between regions of growing prosperity, which produced and consumed startlingly more than other regions, and underdeveloped parts of the world, where most people got little chance to share in the increased wealth. At the century's end, the average income of people in the poorer half of the world was less than 5 percent of that of citizens of the top 20 richest countries.

In the late twentieth-century world, prosperity seemed to be the best contraceptive. In rich, industrialized communities, population growth slowed or went into reverse. Where poverty reigned, children were too valuable a resource to forego. As a result, the world's wealth gaps widened. Growing populations strained resources in the regions that could least afford to feed and care for large numbers of people, while the relative wealth of the developed world multiplied. This should not surprise anyone. Human reproduction resembles, in some respects, the production of commodities. It operates according to laws of supply and demand. Birthrates fall as income rises, because in mechanizing societies, manpower loses value and people therefore produce fewer babies. Economic progress promotes a further kind of change that also holds down population. Women's "liberation" encourages women to switch from having children to other kinds of productive activities.

Migration from poor, overpopulated areas of Africa, Asia, and Latin America into rich areas that have a shortage of labor was an inevitable consequence, with huge social, political, and cultural effects (see Chapter 29). Industrialized nations invited guest workers in, while struggling to regulate their numbers. It then proved hard to prevent the erosion of traditional cultures or the outbreak of intercommunal violence.

By the end of the century, however, there were signs that the various regions of the world were on a convergent course. In most of Latin America and Asia, population growth slowed down. Demographers began to predict that world population would peak in the early twenty-first century and then begin to fall, probably between 2020 and 2050.

On the far side of that peak in population, the world will look different. A big shift has occurred across the world in the demographic balance between old and young, north and south, east and west. While population continued to soar in Africa and the Americas, Europe was demographically stagnant by the end of the century. The population of much of Eastern Europe—especially of Russia, Latvia, and Ukraine—fell in the 1990s. Political and economic dislocation (see Chapter 28) contributed to the effect. In parts of Western Europe—Spain, Italy, and Germany—the overall population levels would also have fallen if immigrants had not helped keep the numbers up. Declining birthrates and declining male fertility—the causes of which are unknown—combined with increased life expectancy to boost the relative numbers of the elderly and inactive and reduce those of the young.

China suffered from a similar problem because the regime, alarmed at the pace of population growth, began to penalize families who chose to have more than one child. The Chinese government imposed compulsory abortions, sterilization, and

"At the century's end, the average income of people in the poorer half of the world was less than 5 percent of that of citizens of the top 20 richest countries."

"Many of the failed civilizations of the past weakened or wrecked themselves by overexploiting their environments. What are we going to do with our world? It is, so far, the only one we have to live in."

punitive fines on offenders. The result is that in the early twenty-first century China faces a population imbalance comparable to that of Europe, with a large aging population and a relative dearth of young labor. India experimented with birth control programs under government encouragement, but never imposed policies as severe as those of China. India's growth rate fell to about 2 percent a year by the end of the millennium, but it was still vigorous enough to ensure that the size of its population would continue to rank second in the world—and might even overtake China's. By the end of the century, birthrates in Thailand, Indonesia, the Indian Ocean island of Mauritius, and much of Latin America were not much higher than those in Europe. The pattern for the future looked increasingly like one of stabilizing population worldwide.

Meanwhile, in Africa and most of the Islamic world, especially the Muslim countries on the edges of the Indian subcontinent, populations were increasing rapidly. In these regions, and in parts of Latin America that are still in the early stages of a transition to European- or Japanese-style demographics, the ratios of old and young are reversed (see Figure 30.5). There are huge numbers of young people, not enough for them to do, and, typically, not enough locally produced food for them to eat.

The twentieth century was a period of intense and frequently violent competition between ideologies. Adherents of different kinds of political totalitarianisms fought wars against each other and against democracy. Religions conflicted with atheism and secularism as well as with each other. Battle lines formed around incompatible understandings of human rights and responsibilities. Economic systems collided. Whole civilizations—according to some predictions—threatened to clash. It seems surprising, on the face of it, that amid all this friction and frenzy environmentalism should have found the space to express itself and emerge, by the end of the century, as a contender to be the world's most widely shared consensus. One way to measure this is to count the increase in the number of international environmental organizations. There were 20 when World War II started in 1939 and about 40 in the late 1940s. By 1990, there were 340. Such an increase would have been impossible had the century not also witnessed unprecedented human impact on our planet. As the century wore on, the changes humans wrought—and the damage they inflicted—became glaringly visible and measurable, provoking the movement that we now usually call envi-

FIGURE 30.5 THE POPULATIONS OF JAPAN AND NIGERIA COMPARED

Reprinted with permission of the Population Reference Bureau.

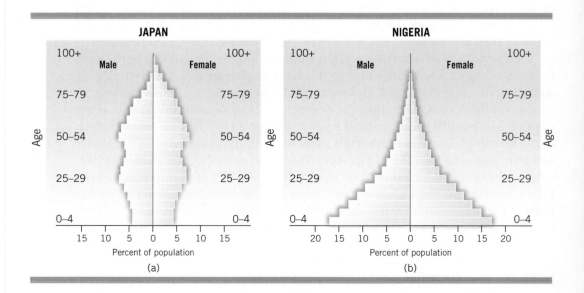

ronmentalism: a deepening and spreading conviction that humans are part of the web of the natural world; that our relationship with our environment is the inescapable framework for everything we do; and that, in consequence, care of the environment is our essential priority, whether as a self-interested strategy or as a moral or religious duty that we owe to other forms of life.

In the early twenty-first century, much of the world is experiencing growth fatigue—the feeling people have in some rich communities that we do not want a world winding into the stratosphere of spiraling desire, at ever more irresponsible levels of consumption, production, and resource depletion. Rationally, we do not need to grow richer. Instead, those of us who enjoy the privilege of relative prosperity in an unequal world need to safeguard our riches by redistributing them more fairly. The opposite argument says that capitalism works—at least it works less badly than any other economic system ever devised in the entire course of human history, because it is attuned to human nature. People are always going to want to better themselves economically. We can no more renounce the pursuit of material "happiness" than stop the world in its orbit. So it is best to try to make a virtue of this trait and find environmentally sustainable ways to increase the world's wealth and free markets to distribute it more evenly.

We can best understand the eco-history of recent times in the context of changing notions about the place of humankind in nature—the results of the new science described in Chapter 27. We know too much about our common ancestry with other animals, the limits of our peculiarities compared with other social and cultural creatures, the moral overlap between *Homo sapiens* and other species, and our ties to a complex, interconnected ecosystem, to go on thinking of humans as apart or distinct from the rest of nature. The future of our relationship with the rest of nature is best considered in the light of evidence dispersed throughout this book. Many of the failed civilizations of the past weakened or wrecked themselves by overexploiting their environments. What are we going to do with our world? It is, so far, the only one we have to live in.

Chronology

1890s	Development of internal combustion engine
1900–2000	1 percent of recorded bird and mammal species go extinct; amount of fish handled by world's fisheries increases fortyfold
1918–1919	Worldwide influenza epidemic
1930s	World's first great dams constructed
1932	Dust Bowl emerges in central and western United States
1940–1990	Use of artificial fertilizer increases from 4 to 150 million tons
1950	Global population 2.5 billion
1950–1980	Wheat yields per acre double
1950–2000	Land under irrigation increases from 247 to 644 million acres
1962	Publication of Rachel Carson's *Silent Spring*
1965	Organization of Petroleum Exporting Countries (OPEC) formed
1970	Global population 3.7 billion
1973	OPEC oil embargo against the United States, Western Europe, and Japan
1978	First known cases of AIDS
1980	50 percent of world's urban population has no access to treated drinking water
1980–2000	Fish-farm production increases from 5 to 25 million tons
1990	Global population 5.3 billion
Early 1990s	Health-care costs absorb 14 percent of GDP in the United States
Late twentieth century	Acceleration of use of genetically modified (GM) crops; search for alternative fuels intensifies
ca. 2000	50 percent of world's population lives in settlements larger than 20,000 people; world's four largest cities: Tokyo, 28 million; Mexico City, 18 million; Mumbai, 18 million; São Paulo, 17 million
ca. 2000	600 million cars worldwide; fossil fuels account for most of world's energy consumption; carbon-dioxide levels in the atmosphere reach 350 parts per million
March 28, 2001	United States pulls out of Kyoto Protocol
August 29, 2005	Hurricane Katrina ravages coast of southeastern United States
2008	Three Gorges Dam over the Yangtze River completed
2010	Global population 6.9 billion (est.)
2020	Global population 7.6 billion (est.)
2050	Forty percent of Arctic ice cap disappears (forecast)

A CLOSER LOOK

The Earth at Night

Darkness can be more revealing than daylight. Composite satellite imagery, taken over a one-year period early in the twenty-first century, shows the impact of humans on the planet.

Rich, developed regions like the United States, Europe, and Japan pulsate with light. Lights also fan out along major arteries—such as the Nile River in Egypt or the Trans-Siberian Railway in Russia.

Night fishing is visible off the coasts of Japan and Argentina, where scores of boats use bright lights to attract squid to the surface.

Natural gas burn-off is a by-product of petroleum extraction that leads to atmospheric pollution. Billions of gallons of gas go up in smoke each year.

Fires burn, either from slash-and-burn agriculture in Africa and South America, or in Australia, set off by lightning and other natural causes.

What does this photograph suggest about the world's environment and distribution of resources?

PROBLEMS AND PARALLELS

1. How has population explosion put unprecedented pressure on the world's energy resources and food supply? Why do people consume more food, goods, and energy than ever before?

2. What are the drawbacks of fossil fuels? How does the consumption of fossil fuels contribute to the greenhouse effect? What are the advantages and disadvantages of alternate sources of power?

3. How did the increased use of fertilization and irrigation in the twentieth century affect the environment? Why was Rachel Carson's book *Silent Spring* so influential? What costs were associated with the green revolution? What are the drawbacks of genetically modified crops?

4. Why has obesity increased in countries such as China, India, and Japan where it had previously been rare? Why is obesity more likely to afflict the poor than the rich in affluent Western countries?

5. How did twentieth-century urbanization affect human societies? What pressures do megacities put on the environment? Why has population growth slowed significantly in parts of the world?

6. How significant is the "crisis of conservation"? How bleak is the outlook for the environment?

7. What threats do disease and climate pose to humans in the early twenty-first century? To what extent can human beings control climate change? What are the potential consequences of the melting of the polar ice caps?

READ ON ▶ ▶ ▶

The story of Rasmata comes from O. Bennett, ed., *Greenwar: Environment and Conflict* (1991). On Burkina Faso, D. E. McMillan, *Sahel Visions: Planned Settlement and River Blindness Control in Burkina Faso* (1995) is a fascinating, personally engaged anthropologist's account of one development project. There is little else of book-length available in English, but important pamphlets include B. Paaru-Laarsen, *The Concept of Drought and Local Social and Economic Strategies in the Northern Burkina Faso*, and M. Ou draogo, *Land Tenure and Rural Development in Burkina Faso* (2002). The context is covered in M. Mortimore, *Roots in the African Dust: Sustaining the Sub-Saharan Drylands* (1998).

J. E. McNeill, *Something New under the Sun* (2001) is a superb global history of the twentieth-century environment. D. Worster, *Nature's Economy* (1985), and A. Bramwell, *Ecology in the Twentieth Century* (1989) are excellent surveys of environmentalism with contrasting arguments. F. Harris, ed., *Global Environmental Issues* (2004) is a useful and comprehensive overview. On the idea of spiraling desire, M. Girard, *Violence and the Sacred* (1979) is fundamental. D. Worster, *Dust Bowl* (1982) is an outstanding case study of degradation.

On energy, J. Twidell and T. Weir, *Renewable Energy Resources* (2005) is a good introduction to renewables. D. Yergin, *The Prize* (1993) is the classic account of oil. M. Klare, *Blood and Oil* (2004) is both scholarly and shocking. J. Rifkin, *The Hydrogen Economy* (2003) sketches the possible hydrogen-dependent future. On China, V. Smil, *China's Environmental Crisis* (1993) is perhaps the best study.

On biodiversity, K. J. Gaston and I. J. Spicer, *Biodiversity* (2004) is a sober introduction. R. Leakey and R. Lewin, *The Sixth Extinction* (1996) is vigorous, challenging, and controversial. T. M. Swanson, ed., *The Economics and Ecology of Biodiversity Decline*

(1998) is a helpful collection, which clearly demonstrates the difficulties. W. D. Ean, *With Broadax and Firebrand* (1997) narrates the destruction of the Amazonian forest. L. Lear, *Rachel Carson* (1998) is a useful life of the great environmentalist.

On food, K. Blaxter and N. Robertson, *From Dearth to Plenty* (1995) sets the context well. D. Goodman and M. J. Watts, eds., *Globalising Food* (1997) is important and wide-ranging. F. Trentmann and A. Nützenadel, eds, *Food and Globalization* (2008) and K. Kiple, *A Movable Feast* (2007) provide contrasting approaches. E. Schlosser, *Fast Food Nation* (2001) is an influential study of U. S. excess. G. Critser, *Fat Land* (2004) is journalistic and sensationalist but full of data. H. Levenstein, *Revolution at the Table* (2003) takes a longer-term view of changes in the American diet. M. Goran, *The Story of Fritz Haber* (1967) is a good biography of the pioneer of modern fertilizers.

J. Hardoy, D. Mitlin and D. Satterthwaite, *Environmental Problems in an Urbanizing World* (2001) is a good introduction to twentieth-century urbanization.

L. D. D. Harvey, *Global Warming: The Hard Science* (1999) is clear and minatory about climate. L. Garrett, *The Coming Plague* (1994) is a page-turner on disease, though much criticized for exaggerating the problems. S. Levy, *The Antibiotic Paradox* (2002) is useful for understanding the limitations of some twentieth-century therapies. A. Macfarlane, *The Savage Wars of Peace* (2003) is a wonderful study of the impact of public health policies, with special reference to Britain and Japan. I. Illich, *Limits to Medicine: The Expropriation of Health* (1999) is a classic study of the modern social history of health issues, on which L. Payer, *Medicine and Culture* (1996), and P. Starr, *The Social Transformation of American Medicine* (1984) are also important.

The World in 2015

This book has told the stories of two relationships: of human societies with each other; and of humankind with the rest of nature. Both stories are in critical phases. Just about all cultures are now in contact with each other and seem to grow more like each other, as they exchange migrant populations and mobile, instantly communicable ideas. Foraging lifeways have almost disappeared. The growth of big cities is a measure of people's displacement—in flight or by force—from traditional rural occupations. The extinction of languages and religions; the spread of common tastes, especially in food and music; and above all, perhaps, the worldwide diffusion of particular kinds of political and economic culture—representative democracy and capitalism—are signs of a world in convergence. How far will the process go? Will we generate new differences as fast as we eliminate old ones? If we get a single, global civilization, will we, like so many civilizations studied in these pages, be isolated in the universe and condemned to stagnate?

Our interactions with the planet have become more problematical than at any time since the age of plague—perhaps since the last Ice Age. Although a lot of the biosphere remains under-exploited, we now consume finite resources so fast that the sustainability of our way of life is under threat. Natural forces we seem least able to control—microbial evolution and climate change—are in a volatile phase. We have to adapt to survive.

▶ QUESTIONS

1. Compare this map with the map on pages 912–913. Why is it that many regions that were the least industrialized in 1914 will have the most people living in cities in 2015? What does this say about human history in the last 100 years?

2. Is a single, global civilization emerging in the twenty-first century? If so, does this development in any way bear similarities with what we know about the early history of the human species?

To view an interactive version of this map, as well as a video of the author describing key themes related to this Part, go to
www.myhistorylab.com

Los Angeles 14.5

Rocky Mountains

Missouri

NORTH AMERICA

Great Plains

Chicago 7.6

Toronto 5.7
St. Lawrence

Mexico City 20.4

Rio Grande

Mississippi

Appalachian Mnts

New York 17.9

CENTRAL AMERICA

ATLANTIC OCEAN

Guatemala City 5.3

Tropic of Cancer

Cape Verde

Bogotá 9.0

Guiana Highlands

PACIFIC OCEAN

Amazon Basin

Amazon

Equator

Abidjan 6.1

Lima 9.4

Andes

BRAZIL

São Paulo 21.2

Belo Horizonte 5.4

ATL OC

SOUTH AMERICA

Paraná

Rio de Janeiro 11.5

Tropic of Capricorn

Santiago 6.5

Buenos Aires 13.2

Patagonia

Antarctic

Burgeoning big cities

- Country with at least one city of five million or more residents
- Country without a city of five million or more residents
- Tokyo 27.2 — Population in millions
- Cities with populations of five million or more

Tokyo 27.2
JAPAN
Osaka 11.0
Shenyang 5.4
Seoul 9.9
Manchuria
Gobi
Beijing 11.7
Tianjin 10.3
Shanghai 13.6
Wuhan 7.8
Lena
Amur
Yenisey
Siberia
Steppes
ASIA
Chongqing 7.4
Yellow River
Yangtze
CHINA
Dhaka 12.8
Hong Kong 8.0
Manila 12.6
Philippine Islands
PACIFIC OCEAN
Moscow 8.1
Volga
London 7.5
Rhine-Ruhr North 6.6
EUROPE
Paris 9.9
Istanbul 11.4
Anatolia
Lahore 8.7
Kolkata (Calcutta) 16.7
Hanoi 5.2
Kabul 5.4
Delhi 20.9
Chittagong 6.4
Greenland
Baghdad 6.6
Euphrates
Tehran 8.2
Tigris
INDIA
Mumbai (Bombay) 22.6
Yangon (Rangoon) 6.3
Ho Chi Minh City 6.3
Mekong
Karachi 16.2
Bangkok 9.8
Cairo 11.5
Nile
Riyadh 7.5
Hyderabad 7.5
Pune 6.1
Ahmadabad 6.6
Chennai (Madras) 8.1
Sahara
Jeddah 5.2
Arabian peninsula
Surat 5.7
Bangalore 8.4
SRI LANKA
New Guinea
Lagos 16.0
AFRICA
INDONESIA
Bandung 5.3
Kinshasa 9.9
Congo
Sumatra
Jakarta 17.9
Java
INDIAN OCEAN
Seychelles
Luanda 5.1
Atlantic Ocean
Zambezi
Madagascar
Mauritius
Réunion
AUSTRALIA
Orange River
Darling River
ANTARCTICA
New Zealand

0°   30°   60°   90°   120°   150°

Abolitionism Belief that slavery and the slave trade are immoral and should be abolished.

Aborigine A member of the indigenous or earliest-known population of a region.

Aborigines Indigenous people of Australia.

Afrikaans An official language of South Africa, spoken mostly by the Boers. It is derived from seventeenth-century Dutch.

Age of Plague Term for the spread of lethal diseases from the fourteenth through the eighteenth centuries.

Ahriman The chief spirit of darkness and evil in Zoroastrianism, the enemy of Ahura Mazda.

Ahura Mazda The chief deity of Zoroastrianism, the creator of the world, the source of light, and the embodiment of good.

Al-Andalus Arabic name for the Iberian Peninsula (Spain and Portugal).

Alluvial plains Flat lands where mud from rivers or lakes renews the topsoil. If people can control the flooding that is common in such conditions, alluvial plains are excellent for settled agriculture.

Almoravids Muslim dynasty of Berber warriors that flourished from 1049 to 1145 and that established political dominance over northwest Africa and Spain.

Alternative energy Energy sources that usually produce less pollution than does the burning of fossil fuels, and are renewable in some cases.

Alternative medicine Medicines, treatments, and techniques not advocated by the mainstream medical establishment in the West.

Americanization The process by which other cultures, to a greater or lesser degree, adopt American fashions, culture, and ways of life.

Anarchists Believers in the theory that all forms of government are oppressive and undesirable and should be opposed and abolished.

Animal rights Movement that asserts that animals have fundamental rights that human beings have a moral obligation to respect.

Anti-Semitism Hostility or prejudice against Jews or Judaism.

Arthasastra Ancient Indian study of economics and politics that influenced the Emperor Asoka. The Arthasastra expresses an ideology of universal rule and emphasizes the supremacy of "the king's law" and the importance of uniform justice.

Artificial intelligence The creation of a machine or computer program that exhibits the characteristics of human intelligence.

Arts and Crafts Movement Nineteenth-century artists and intellectuals who argued that the products produced by individual craftsmen were more attractive than and morally superior to the mass, uniform goods produced by industry.

Assassins A secret order of Muslims in what is today Syria and Lebanon who terrorized and killed its opponents, both Christian and Muslim. The Assassins were active from the eleventh to the thirteenth centuries.

Atlantic Slave Trade Trade in African slaves who were bought, primarily in West Africa, by Europeans and white Americans and transported across the Atlantic, usually in horrific conditions, to satisfy the demand for labor in the plantations and mines of the Americas.

Atomic theory The theory that matter is not a continuous whole, but is composed of tiny, discrete particles.

Australopithecine (Trans.) "Southern ape-like creatures." Term used to describe prehuman species that existed before those classed under the genus *Homo*.

Axial Age A pivotal age in the history of world civilization, lasting for roughly 500 years up to the beginning of the Christian era, in which critical intellectual and cultural ideas arose in and were transmitted across the Mediterranean world, India, Iran, and East Asia.

Axial zone The densely populated central belt of world population, communication, and cultural exchange in Eurasia that stretches from Japan and China to Western Europe and North Africa.

Aztecs People of central Mexico whose civilization and empire were at their height at the time of the Spanish conquest in the early sixteenth century.

Balance of trade The relative value of goods traded between two or more nations or states. Each trading partner strives to have a favorable balance of trade, that is, to sell more to its trading partners than it buys from them.

Bantu African people sharing a common linguistic ancestry who originated in West Africa and whose early agriculture centered on the cultivation of yams and oil palms in swamplands.

Big bang theory Theory that the universe began with an explosion of almost infinitesimally compressed matter, the effects of which are still going on.

Black Death Term for a lethal disease or diseases that struck large parts of Eurasia and North Africa in the 1300s and killed millions of people.

Boers Dutch settlers and their descendents in southern Africa. The first Boers arrived in South Africa in the seventeenth century.

Bon Religion that was Buddhism's main rival in Tibet for several centuries in the late first millennium C.E.

Brahman A member of the highest, priestly caste of traditional Indian society.

British East India Company British trading company founded in 1600 that played a key role in the colonization of India. It ruled much of the subcontinent until 1857.

Bureaucratization The process by which government increasingly operates through a body of trained officials who follow a set of regular rules and procedures.

Business Imperialism Economic domination and exploitation of poorer and weaker countries by richer and stronger states.

Byzantine Empire Term for the Greek-speaking, eastern portion of the former Roman Empire, centered on Constantinople. It lasted until 1453, when it was conquered by the Ottoman Turks.

Cahokia Most spectacular existent site of Mississippi Valley Native American civilization, located near modern St. Louis.

Caliph The supreme Islamic political and religious authority, literally, the "successor" of the Prophet Muhammad.

Canyon cultures Indigenous peoples of the North American Southwest. The canyon cultures flourished beween about 850 and 1250 C.E.

Capitalism An economic system in which the means of production and distribution are privately or corporately owned.

Caste system A social system in which people's places in society, how they live and work, and with whom they can marry are determined by heredity. The Indian caste system has been intertwined with India's religious and economic systems.

Centralization The concentration of power in the hands of a central government.

Chaos theory Theory that some systems are so complex that their causes and effects are untraceable.

Chicago economics The economic theory associated with economists who taught at the University of Chicago that holds that low taxes and light government regulation will lead to economic prosperity.

Chimú Civilization centered on the Pacific coast of Peru that was conquered by the Inca in the fifteenth century.

Chinese Board of Astronomy Official department of the Chinese imperial court created in the early seventeenth century that was responsible for devising the ritual calendar.

Chinese diaspora The migration of Chinese immigrants around the world between the seventeenth and nineteenth centuries.

Chivalry The qualities idealized by the medieval European aristocracy and associated with knighthood, such as bravery, courtesy, honor, and gallantry.

Chola Expansive kingdom in southern India that had important connections with merchant communities on the coast. Chola reached its height around 1050 C.E.

Christendom Term referring to the European states in which Christianity was the dominant or only religion.

Cistercians Christian monastic order that built monasteries in places where habitation was sparse and nature hostile. Cistercians practiced a more ascetic and rigorous form of the Benedictine rule.

Citizen army The mass army the French created during the Revolution by imposing mandatory military service on the entire active adult male population. The army was created in response to the threat of invasion by an alliance of anti-Revolutionary countries in the early 1790s.

Civilizing mission The belief that imperialism and colonialism are justified because imperial powers have a duty to bring the benefits of "civilization" to, or impose them on, the "backward" people they ruled or conquered.

Clan A social group made up of a number of families that claim descent from a common ancestor and follow a hereditary chieftain.

Class struggle Conflict between competing social classes that, in Karl Marx's view, was responsible for all important historical change.

Climacteric A period of critical change in a society that is poised between different possible outcomes.

Code Napoleon Civil code promulgated by Napoleon in 1804 and spread by his armies across Europe. It still forms the basis for the legal code for many European, Latin American, and African countries.

Cold war Post–World War II rivalry between the United States and its allies and the Soviet Union and its allies. The cold war ended in 1990–1991 with the end of the Soviet Empire in Eastern Europe and the collapse of the Soviet Union itself.

Columbian Exchange Biological exchange of plants, animals, microbes, and human beings between the Americas and the rest of the world.

Commune Collective name for the citizen body of a medieval and Renaissance Italian town.

Communism A system of government in which the state plans and controls the economy, and private property and class distinctions are abolished.

Confraternities Lay Catholic charitable brotherhoods.

Confucianism Chinese doctrine founded by Confucius emphasizing learning and the fulfillment of obligations among family members, citizens, and the state.

Constitutionalism The doctrine that the state is founded on a set of fundamental laws that rulers and citizens make together and are bound to respect.

Consumerism A system of values that exalts the consumption and possession of consumer goods as both a social good and as an end in themselves.

Coolies Poor laborers from China and India who left their homelands to do hard manual and agricultural work in other parts of the world in the nineteenth and early twentieth centuries.

Copernican revolution Development of a heliocentric model of the solar system begun in 1543 by Nicholas Copernicus, a Polish churchman and astronomer.

Council of Trent A series of meetings from 1545 to 1563 to direct the response of the Roman Catholic Church to Protestantism. The council defined Catholic dogma and reformed church discipline.

Counter Reformation The Catholic effort to combat the spread of Protestantism in the sixteenth and seventeenth centuries.

Countercolonization The flow of immigrants out of former colonies to the "home countries" that used to rule them.

Country trades Commerce involving local or regional exchanges of goods from one Asian destination to another that, while often handled by European merchants, never touched Europe.

Covenant In the Bible, God's promise to the human race.

Creoles People of at least part-European descent born in the West Indies, French Louisiana, or Spanish America.

Crusades Any of the military expeditions undertaken by European Christians from the late eleventh to the thirteenth centuries to recover the Holy Land from the Muslims.

Cubism Artistic style developed by Pablo Picasso and Georges Braque in the early twentieth century, characterized by the reduction and fragmentation of natural forms into abstract, often geometric structures.

Cultural relativism The doctrine that cultures cannot be ranked in any order of merit. No culture is superior to another, and each culture must be judged on its own terms.

Cultural Revolution Campaign launched by Mao Zedong in 1965–1966 against the bureaucrats of the Chinese Communist Party. In lasted until 1976 and involved widespread disorder, violence, killings, and the persecution of intellectuals and the educated elite.

Culture Socially transmitted behavior, beliefs, institutions, and technologies that a given group of people, peoples, or animals share.

Cuneiform Mesopotamian writing system that was inscribed on clay tablets with wedge-shaped markers.

Czars (Trans.) "Caesar." Title of the emperors who ruled Russia until the revolution of 1917.

Dada An early twentieth-century European artistic and literary movement that flouted conventional and traditional aesthetic and cultural values by producing works marked by nonsense, travesty, and incongruity.

Dahomey West African slave-trading state that began to be prominent in the sixteenth century.

Daimyo Japanese feudal lord who ruled a province and was subject to the shoguns.

Daoism Chinese doctrine founded by Laozi that identified detachment from the world with the pursuit of immortality.

"Declaration of the Rights of Man and Citizen" Declaration of basic principles adopted by the French National Assembly in August 1789, at the start of the French Revolution.

Decolonization The process by which the nineteenth-century colonial empires in Asia, Africa, the Caribbean, and the Pacific were dismantled after World War II.

Deforestation The process by which trees are eliminated from an ecosystem.

Democracy Government by the people, exercised either directly or through elected representatives.

Devsirme Quota of male children supplied by Christian subjects as tribute to the Ottoman Sultan. Many of the boys were drafted into the janissaries.

Dharma In the teachings of Buddha, moral law or duty.

Diffusion The spread of a practice, belief, culture, or technology within a community or between communities.

Dirlik (Trans.) "Wealth." The term applied to provincial government in the Ottoman Empire.

Divine love God's ongoing love for and interest in human beings.

Dominicans Order of preaching friars established in 1216 by Saint Dominic.

Druze Lebanese sect that regards the caliph al-Hakim as a manifestation of God. Other Muslims regard the Druze as heretics.

Dualism Perception of the world as an arena of conflict between opposing principles of good and evil.

Dutch East India Company Dutch company founded in 1602 that enjoyed a government-granted monopoly on trade between Holland and Asia. The company eventually established a territorial empire in what is today Indonesia.

Dutch East Indies Dutch colonies in Asia centered on present-day Indonesia.

East India Trade Maritime trade between Western Europe and New England and Asia (predominantly India and China) between 1600 and 1800. Westerners paid cash for items from Asia, such as porcelain, tea, silk, cotton textiles, and spices.

Easterlies Winds coming from the east.

Ecological exchange The exchange of plants and animals between ecosystems.

Ecological imperialism Term historians use for the sweeping environmental changes European and other imperialists introduced in regions they colonized.

Ecology of civilization The interaction of people with their environment.

Economic liberalism Belief that government interference in and regulation of the economy should be kept to a minimum.

Edo Former name of Tokyo when it was the center of government for the Tokugawa shoguns.

El Niño A periodic reversal of the normal flow of Pacific currents that alters weather patterns and affects the number and location of fish in the ocean.

Elan vital The "vital force" hypothesized by the French philosopher Henri Bergson as a source of efficient causation and evolution in nature.

Empiricism The view that experience, especially of the senses, is the only source of knowledge.

Emporium trading Commerce that takes place in fixed market places or trading posts.

Enlightened despotism Reforms instituted by powerful monarchs in eighteenth-century Europe who were inspired by the principles of the Enlightenment.

Enlightenment Movement of eighteenth-century European thought championed by the *philosophes*, thinkers who held that change and reform were desirable and could be achieved by the application of reason and science. Most Enlightenment thinkers were hostile to conventional religion.

Enthusiasm "Religion" of English romantics who believed that emotion and passion were positive qualities.

Epistemology The branch of philosophy that studies the nature of knowledge.

Eugenics The theory that the human race can be improved mentally and physically by controlled selective breeding and that the state and society have a duty to encourage "superior" persons to have offspring and prevent "inferior" persons from reproducing.

Eunuchs Castrated male servants valued because they could not produce heirs or have sexual relations with women. In Byzantium, China, and the Islamic world, eunuchs could rise to high office in the state and the military.

European Union (EU) Loose economic and political federation that succeeded the European Economic Community (EEC) in 1993. It has expanded to include most of the states in Western and Eastern Europe.

Evolution Change in the genetic composition of a population over successive generations, as a result of natural selection acting on the genetic variation among individuals.

Examination system System for selecting Chinese officials and bureaucrats according to merit through a series of competitive, written examinations that, in theory, any Chinese young man could take. Success in the exams required years of intense study in classical Chinese literature. The examination system was not abolished until the early twentieth century.

Existentialism Philosophy that regards human existence as unexplainable, and stresses freedom of choice and accepting responsibility for the consequences of one's acts.

Expressionism Term describing a work of art in which forms are created primarily to evoke subjective emotions rather than to portray objective reality.

Factories Foreign trading posts in China and other parts of Asia. The chief representative of a factory was known as a "factor." Though the earliest trading posts were established by the Portuguese in the sixteenth century, the number of factories grew rapidly in the eighteenth and nineteenth centuries, with European and American merchants trading for silk, rhubarb, tea, and porcelain.

Fascism A system of government marked by centralization of authority under a dictator, stringent socioeconomic controls, and suppression of the opposition through terror and censorship.

Fatimids Muslim dynasty that ruled parts of North Africa and Egypt (909–1171).

Feminism The belief that women collectively constitute a class of society that has been historically oppressed and deserves to be set free.

Final Solution Nazi plan to murder all European Jews.

Fixed-wind systems Wind system in which the prevailing winds do not change direction for long periods of time.

Fossil fuels Fuels including peat, coal, natural gas, and oil.

Franciscans Religious order founded by Francis of Assisi in 1209 and dedicated to the virtues of humility, poverty, and charitable work among the poor.

Free trade The notion that maximum economic efficiency is achieved when barriers to trade, especially taxes on imports and exports, are eliminated.

French Revolution Political, intellectual, and social upheaval that began in France in 1789. It resulted in the overthrow of the monarchy and the establishment of a republic.

Fulani Traditional herdsmen of the Sahel in West Africa.

Fundamentalism The idea that a sacred text or texts contains fundamental truths that cannot be questioned, either by critical inquiry or by scientific evidence.

Futurism Artistic vision articulated by Emilio Filippo Marinetti in 1909. He believed that all traditional art and ideas should be repudiated, destroyed, and replaced by the new. Futurists glorified speed, technology, progress, and violence.

Gauchos Argentine cowboys.

General will Jean-Jacques Rousseau's concept of the collective will of the population. He believed that the purpose of government was to express the general will.

Genetic revolution Revolution in the understanding of human biology produced by advances in genetic research.

Genocide The systematic and planned extermination of an entire national, racial, political, or ethnic group.

Ghana A medieval West African kingdom in what are now eastern Senegal, southwest Mali, and southern Mauritania.

Global gardening The collecting in botanical gardens of plants from around the world for cultivation and study.

Globalization The process through which uniform or similar ways of life are spread across the planet.

Glyph A form of writing that uses symbolic figures that are usually engraved or incised, such as Egyptian hieroglyphics.

GM Crops that have been *genetically modified* to produce certain desired characteristics.

Golden Horde Term for Mongols who ruled much of Russia from the steppes of the lower Volga River from the thirteenth to the fifteenth centuries.

Grand Vizier The chief minister of state in the Ottoman Empire.

Greater East Asia Co-Prosperity Sphere Bloc of Asian nations under Japanese economic and political control during World War II.

Green revolution Improvements in twentieth-century agriculture that substantially increased food production by developing new strains of crops and agricultural techniques.

Greenhouse effect The increase in temperature caused by the trapping of carbon in the Earth's atmosphere.

Guardians Self-elected class of philosopher-rulers found in Plato's *Republic*.

Guomindang (GMD) Nationalist Chinese political party founded in 1912 by Sun Yat-Sen. The Guomindang took power in China in 1928 but was defeated by the Chinese Communists in 1949.

Habsburgs An Austro-German imperial family that reached the height of their power in the sixteenth century under Charles V of Spain when the Habsburgs ruled much of Europe and the Americas. The Habsburgs continued to rule a multinational empire based in Vienna until 1918.

Haj The pilgrimage to Mecca that all faithful Muslims are required to complete at least once in their lifetime if they able.

Han Dynasty that ruled China from ca. 206 B.C.E. to ca. 220 C.E. This was the period when the fundamental identity and culture of China were formed. Chinese people still refer to themselves as "Han."

Hanseatic League Founded in 1356, the Hanseatic League was a powerful network of allied ports along the North Sea and Baltic coasts that collaborated to promote trade.

Harem The quarters reserved for the female members of a Muslim household.

Herders Agriculturalists who emphasize the raising of animals, rather than plants, for food and products, such as wool and hides.

High-level equilibrium trap A situation in which an economy that is meeting high levels of demand with traditional technology finds that it has little scope to increase its output.

Hinduism Indian polytheistic religion that developed out of Brahmanism and in response to Buddhism. It remains the majority religion in India today.

Hispaniola Modern Haiti and the Dominican Republic.

Hohokam People Native American culture that flourished from about the third century B.C.E. to the mid–fifteenth century C.E. in south-central Arizona.

Holocaust Term for the murder of millions of Jews by the Nazi regime during World War II.

Holy Roman Empire A loose federation of states under an elected emperor that consisted primarily of Germany and northern Italy. It endured in various forms from 800 to 1806.

Homo erectus (Trans.) "Standing upright." Humanlike tool-using species that lived about 1.5 million years ago. At one time, Homo erectus was thought to be the first "human."

Homo ergaster (Trans.) "Workman." Humanlike species that lived 800,000 years ago and stacked the bones of its dead.

Homo habilis (Trans.) "Handy." Humanlike species that lived about 2.5 million years ago and made stone hand axes.

Homo sapiens (Trans.) "Wise." The species to which contemporary humans belong.

Human rights Notion of inherent rights that all human beings share. Based in part on the assumption that being human constitutes in itself a meaningful moral category that excludes nonhuman creatures.

Humanism Cultural and intellectual movement of the Renaissance centered on the study of the literature, art, and civilization of ancient Greece and Rome.

Hurons A Native American confederacy of eastern Canada. The Huron flourished immediately prior to contact with Europeans, but declined rapidly as a result of European diseases such as smallpox. They were allied with the French in wars against the British, the Dutch, and other Native Americans.

Husbandry The practice of cultivating crops and breeding and raising livestock; agriculture.

Ice-Age affluence Relative prosperity of Ice-Age society as the result of abundant game and wild, edible plants.

Icon A representation or picture of a Christian saint or sacred event. Icons have been traditionally venerated in the Eastern, or Orthodox Church.

Il-Khanate A branch of the Mongol Empire, centered in present-day Iran. Its rulers, the Il-Khans, converted to Islam and adopted Persian culture.

Imam A Muslim religious teacher. Also the title of Muslim political and religious rulers in Yemen and Oman.

Imperator A Latin term that originally meant an army commander under the Roman Republic and evolved into the term *emperor*.

Imperialism The policy of extending a nation's authority and influence by conquest or by establishing economic and political hegemony over other nations.

Incas Peoples of highland Peru who established an empire from northern Ecuador to central Chile before the Spanish conquest in the 1530s.

Indian National Congress Political organization created in 1885 that played a leading role in the Indian independence movement.

Indirect rule Rule by a colonial power through local elites.

Individualism Belief in the primary importance of the individual and in the virtues of self-reliance and personal independence.

Indo-European languages Language family that originated in Asia and from which most of Europe's present languages evolved.

Inductive method Method by which scientists turn individual observations and experiments into general laws.

Industrial Revolution The complex set of economic, demographic, and technological events that began in Western Europe and resulted in the advent of an industrial economy.

Industrialization The process by which an industrial economy is developed.

Information technology Technology, such as printing presses and computers, that facilitates the spread of information.

Inquisition A tribunal of the Roman Catholic Church that was charged with suppressing heresy and immorality.

Iroquois Native American confederacy based in northern New York State, originally composed of the Mohawk, Oneida, Onondaga, Cayuga, and Seneca peoples, known as the Five Nations. The confederation created a constitution sometime between the mid-1400s and the early 1600s.

Isolationism Belief that, unless directly challenged, a country should concentrate on domestic issues and avoid foreign conflicts or active participation in foreign affairs.

Jainism A way of life that arose in India designed to free the soul from evil by ascetic practices: chastity, detachment, truth, selflessness, and strict vegetarianism.

Janissaries Soldiers in an elite Ottoman infantry formation that was first organized in the fourteenth century. Originally drafted from among the sons of the sultan's Christian subjects, the janissaries had become a hereditary and militarily obsolete caste by the early nineteenth century.

Jesuits Order of regular clergy strongly committed to education, scholarship, and missionary work. Founded by Ignatius of Loyola in 1534.

Jihad Arabic word meaning "striving." Muhammad used the word to refer to the inner struggle all Muslims must wage against evil, and the real wars fought against the enemies of Islam.

Joint-stock company A business whose capital is held in transferable shares of stock by its joint owners. The Dutch East India Company, founded in 1602, was the first joint-stock company.

Kaaba The holiest place in Islam. Formerly a pagan shrine, the Kaaba is a massive cube-shaped structure in Mecca toward which Muslims turn to pray.

Keynesianism Economic policy advocated by J. M. Keynes, based on the premise that governments could adjust the distribution of wealth and regulate the functioning of the economy through taxation and public spending, without seriously weakening free enterprise or infringing freedom.

Khan A ruler of a Mongol, Tartar, or Turkish tribe.

Khedive Title held by the hereditary viceroys of Egypt in the nineteenth century. Although nominally subject to the Ottoman sultans, the khedives were, in effect, sovereign princes.

Khmer Agrarian kingdom of Cambodia, built on the wealth produced by enormous rice surpluses.

Kongo Kingdom located in west central Africa along the Congo River, founded in the fourteenth century. The Portuguese converted its rulers and elite to Catholicism in the fifteenth century.

Kulturkampf (Trans.) "The struggle for culture." Name given to the conflict between the Roman Catholic Church and the imperial German government under Chancellor Otto von Bismarck in the 1870s.

Laissez-faire An economic policy that emphasizes the minimization of government regulation and involvement in the economy.

Latin Church Dominant Christian church in Western Europe.

Latitude The angular distance north or south of the Earth's equator, measured in degrees along a meridian.

League of Nations International political organization created after World War I to resolve disputes between states peacefully and create a more just international order.

Legalism Chinese school of thought that emerged in the fourth century B.C.E. Legalists believed that morality was meaningless and that obedience to the state was the supreme good. The state thus had the right to enforce its laws under threat of the harshest penalties.

Levant The countries bordering on the eastern Mediterranean from Turkey to Egypt.

Liberation theology Religious movement in Latin America, primarily among Roman Catholics, concerned with justice for the poor and oppressed. Its adherents argue that sin is the result not just of individual moral failure but of the oppressive and exploitative way in which capitalist society is organized and functions.

Little Ice Age Protracted period of relative cold from the fourteenth to the early nineteenth centuries.

Logograms A system of writing in which stylized pictures represent a word or phrase.

Longitude An imaginary great circle on the surface of the Earth passing through the north and south poles at right angles to the equator.

Lotus Sutra The most famous of Buddhist scriptures.

Low Countries A region of northwest Europe comprising what is today Belgium, the Netherlands, and Luxembourg.

Magyars Steppeland people who invaded Eastern Europe in the tenth century and were eventually converted to Catholic Christianity. The Magyars are the majority ethnic group in present-day Hungary.

Mahayana One of the major schools of Buddhism. It emphasizes the Buddha's infinite compassion for all human beings, social concern, and universal salvation. It is the dominant branch of Buddhism in East Asia.

Mahdi A Muslim messiah, whose coming would inaugurate a cosmic struggle, preceding the end of the world.

Maize The grain that modern Americans call "corn." It was first cultivated in ancient Mesoamerica.

Mali Powerful West African state that flourished in the fourteenth century.

Malthusian Ideas inspired by Thomas Malthus's theory that population growth would always outpace growth in food supply.

Mamluks Egyptian Muslim slave army. The mamluks provided Egypt's rulers from 1390 to 1517.

Mana According to the Polynesians, a supernatural force that regulates everything in the world. For example, the mana of a net makes it catch a fish, and the mana of an herb gives it its healing powers.

Manchurian Incident Japanese invasion of Manchuria in 1931, justified by the alleged effort of the Chinese to blow up a Japanese train. In fact, Japanese agents deliberately triggered the explosion to provide a pretext for war.

Manchus A people native to Manchuria who ruled China during the Qing dynasty.

Mandarins High public officials in the Chinese Empire, usually chosen by merit after competitive written exams.

Mandate of Heaven The source of divine legitimacy for Chinese emperors. According to the mandate of heaven, emperors were chosen by the gods and retained their favor as long as the emperors acted in righteous ways. Emperors and dynasties that lost the mandate of heaven could be deposed or overthrown.

Manichaeanism A dualistic philosophy dividing the world between the two opposed principles of good and evil.

Manifest destiny Nineteenth-century belief that the United States was destined to expand across all of North America from the Atlantic to the Pacific, including Canada and Mexico.

Manila Galleons Spanish galleons that sailed each year between the Philippines and Mexico with a cargo of silk, porcelain, and other Asian luxury goods that were paid for with Mexican silver.

Maori Indigenous Polynesian people of New Zealand.

Marathas Petty Hindu princes who ruled in Maharashtra in southern India in the eighteenth century.

Maritime empires Empires based on trade and naval power that flourished in the sixteenth and seventeenth centuries.

Maroons Runaway slaves in the Americas who formed autonomous communities, and even states, between 1500 and 1800.

Marshall Plan Foreign-aid program for Western Europe after World War II, named after U.S. Secretary of State George C. Marshall.

Marxism The political and economic philosophy of Karl Marx and Friedrich Engels in which the concept of class struggle is the determining principle in social and historical change.

Material culture Concrete objects that people create.

Matrilineal A society that traces ancestry through the maternal line.

Maya Major civilization of Mesoamerica. The earliest evidence connected to Maya civilization dates from about 1000 B.C.E. Maya civilization reached its peak between 250 and 900 C.E. Maya cultural and political practices were a major influence on other Mesoamericans.

Meiji Restoration The overthrow of the Tokugawa *bakufu* in Japan in 1868 and the "restoration" of power to the imperial government under the Emperor Meiji.

Mercantilism An economic theory that emphasized close government control of the economy to maximize a country's exports and to earn as much bullion as possible.

Mesoamerica A region stretching from central Mexico to Central America. Mesoamerica was home to the Olmec, the Maya, the Aztecs, and other Native American peoples.

Messiah The anticipated savior of the Jews. Christians identified Jesus as the Messiah.

Mestizos The descendents of Europeans and Native Americans.

Microbial exchange The exchange of microbes between ecosystems.

Militarization The trend toward larger and more powerful armed forces and the organization of society and the economy to achieve that goal.

Military revolution Change in warfare in the sixteenth and seventeenth centuries that accompanied the rise of fire-power technology.

Millenarianism Belief that the end of the world is about to occur, as foretold in the biblical Book of Revelation.

Minas Gerais (Trans.) "General Mines." Region of Brazil rich in mineral resources that experienced a gold rush in the early eighteenth century.

Ming Dynasty Chinese dynasty (1368–1644) noted for its flourishing foreign trade and achievements in scholarship and the arts.

Mongols Nomadic people whose homeland was in Mongolia. In the twelfth and thirteenth centuries, they conquered most of Eurasia from China to Eastern Europe.

Monocultures The cultivation of a single dominant food crop, such as potatoes or rice. Societies that practiced monoculture were vulnerable to famine if bad weather or disease caused their single food crop to fail.

Monroe Doctrine The policy enunciated by President James Monroe in 1823 that the United States would oppose further European colonization in the Americas.

Monsoons A wind from the southwest or south that brings heavy rainfall each summer to southern Asia.

Mound agriculture Form of agriculture found in pre-Columbian North America.

Mughals Muslim dynasty founded by Babur that ruled India, at least nominally, from the mid–1500s until 1857.

Multiculturalism The belief that different cultures can coexist peacefully and equitably in a single country.

Napoleonic Wars Wars waged between France under Napoleon and its European enemies from 1799 to 1815. The fighting spilled over into the Middle East and sparked conflicts in North America and India and independence movements in the Spanish and Portuguese colonies in the Americas.

Nationalism Belief that a people who share the same language, historic experience, and sense of identity make up a nation and that every nation has the right to assert its identity, pursue its destiny, defend its rights, and be the primary focus of its people's loyalty.

Natural selection The process by which only the organisms best adapted to their environment pass on their genetic material to subsequent generations.

Nature versus nurture Debate over the relative importance of inherited characterizes and environmental factors in determining human development.

Nazis Members of the National Socialist German Workers' Party, founded in Germany in 1919 and brought to power in 1933 under Adolf Hitler.

Neanderthal (Trans.) "Neander Valley." Humanlike species, evidence for whose existence was found in the Neander River valley in northern Germany in the mid–nineteenth century. Neanderthals disappeared from the evolutionary record about 30,000 years ago.

Negritude The affirmation of the distinctive nature, quality, and validity of black culture.

Nestorianism The Christian theological doctrine that within Jesus are two distinct and separate persons, divine and human, rather than a single divine person. Orthodox Christians classed Nestorianism as a heresy, but it spread across Central Asia along the Silk Roads.

New Europes Lands in other hemispheres where the environment resembled that of Europe and where immigrants could successfully transplant a European way of life and European culture.

New Rich Rich people whose wealth was acquired in the recent past, often in industry or commerce.

New World Term Europeans applied to the Americas.

Nirvana The spiritual goal of Buddhism, when a person ends the cycle of birth and rebirth and achieves enlightenment and freedom from any attachment to material things.

Noble savage Idealized vision that some people in the West held about certain non-Europeans, especially some Native Americans and Polynesians. It was based on the notions that civilization was a corrupting force and that these peoples lived lives more in tune with nature.

Northwest Passage Water route from the Atlantic to the Pacific through the Arctic archipelago of northern Canada and along the northern coast of Alaska. For centuries, Europeans sought in vain for a more accessible route to the Pacific farther south in North America.

Obsidian Volcanic glass used to make tools, weapons, and mirrors.

Old regime Term for the social, economic, and political institutions that existed in France and the rest of Europe before the French Revolution.

Old World Term for the regions of the world—Europe, parts of Africa and Asia—that were known to Europeans before the discovery of the Americas.

Ongons Tibetan images in which spirits are thought to reside. Shamans claimed to communicate with the ongons.

OPEC The Organization of Petroleum Exporting Countries, an alliance of the world's major oil producers.

Oracle A person or group that claims to be able to have access to knowledge of the future by consulting a god. Ancient rulers often consulted oracles.

Oriental despotism Arbitrary and corrupt rule. Eighteenth-century Europeans saw it as characteristic of Asian or Islamic rulers.

Orthodox Church Dominant Christian church in the Byzantine Empire, the Balkans, and Russia.

Ottoman Empire Islamic empire based in present-day Turkey, with its capital at Istanbul. At its height in the sixteenth century, the Ottoman Empire stretched from Iraq across North Africa to the borders of Morocco and included almost all the Balkans and most of Hungary. The empire gradually declined, but endured until it was dismembered after World War I.

Pampas A vast plain of south-central South America that supports huge herds of cattle and other livestock.

Pan-African Congress A series of five meetings held between 1919 and 1945 that claimed to represent all black Africans and demanded an end to colonial rule.

Pangaea A hypothetical prehistoric supercontinent that included all the landmasses of the Earth.

Partition of India The division in 1947 along ethnic and religious lines of the British Indian Empire into two independent states: India, which was largely Hindu, and Pakistan, which was largely Muslim. The division involved widespread violence in which at least 500,000 people were killed.

Paternalism A social or economic relationship that resembles the dependency that exists between a father and his child.

Patrilineal A society that traces ancestry through the paternal line.

Philosopher's stone A substance that was believed to have the power to change base metals into gold.

Physiocrats Eighteenth-century French political economists who argued that agriculture was the foundation of any country's wealth and recommended agricultural improvements.

Plantation system System of commercial agriculture based on large landholdings, often worked by forced labor.

Polestar Bright star used for navigation.

Positivism Doctrine that asserts the undeniability of human sense perception and the power of reason to prove that what our senses perceive is true.

Pragmatism Philosophy advocated by William James that holds that the standard for evaluating the truth or validity of a theory or concept depends on how well it works and on the results that arise from holding it.

Proletariat The working class, which according to Karl Marx, would overthrow the bourgeoisie.

Protectorate A country or region that, although nominally independent and not a colony, is in fact controlled militarily, politically, and economically by a more powerful foreign state.

Protestantism The theological system of any of the churches of Western Christendom that separated from the Roman Catholic Church during the Reformation. The advent of Protestantism is usually associated with Martin Luther's break from the Catholic Church in the 1520s.

Psychoanalysis Technique developed by Sigmund Freud to treat patients suffering from emotional or psychological disorders by making them aware of their subconscious conflicts, motivations, and desires.

Public sphere Sites for the public discussion of political, social, economic, and cultural issues.

Qing dynasty Last imperial Chinese dynasty (1644–1912), founded when the Manchus, a steppeland people from Manchuria, conquered China. It was succeeded by a republic.

Quantum mechanics Mechanics based on the principle that matter and energy have the properties of both particles and waves.

Quran The sacred text of Islam dictated from God to the Prophet Muhammad by the Archangel Gabriel. Considered by Muslims to contain the final revelations of God to humanity.

Rape of Nanjing Atrocities committed by the Japanese during their occupation of the city of Nanjing, China, in 1937.

Rastafarianism A religious and political movement that began among black people in Jamaica in the 1930s. Its adherents believe that former Emperor Haile Selassie of Ethiopia (r. 1930–1974) was divine and the Messiah whose coming was foretold in the Bible.

Rationalism The doctrine that reason by itself can determine truth and solve the world's problems.

Realpolitik Political doctrine that says that the state is not subject to moral laws and has the right to do whatever safeguards it and advances its interests.

Reformation The Protestant break from the Roman Catholic Church in the sixteenth century.

Remittances Transfers of money by foreign workers to their home countries.

Renaissance Humanistic revival of classical art, architecture, literature, and learning that originated in Italy in the fourteenth century and spread throughout Europe.

Renewable energy Energy that is not derived from a finite resource such as oil or coal.

Rig Veda A collection of hymns and poems created by a sedentary people living in the area north of the Indus valley where northern India and Pakistan meet. The Rig Veda provides evidence for the theory that invaders destroyed Harappan civilization.

Romanticism Intellectual and artistic movement that arose in reaction to the Enlightenment's emphasis on reason. Romantics had a heightened interest in nature and religion, and emphasized emotion and imagination.

Rus A Slavic-Scandinavian people who created the first Russian state and converted to Orthodox Christianity.

Safavids Shiite dynasty that ruled Persia between 1501 and 1722.

Sahel A semiarid region of north Central Africa south of the Sahara Desert.

Saint Domingue A French colony on Hispaniola that flourished in the eighteenth century by cultivating sugar and coffee with slave labor. It became the modern republic of Haiti after a protracted struggle that began in the 1790s.

Samurai The hereditary Japanese feudal-military aristocracy.

Sati In Hinduism, the burning of a widow on her husband's funeral pyre.

Satyagraha (Trans.) "The force of truth." Nonviolent movement launched by Mohandas K. Gandhi, with the goal of achieving Indian independence.

Savanna A flat grassland of tropical or subtropical regions.

Scientific revolution The sweeping change in the investigation of nature and the view of the universe that took place in Europe in the sixteenth and seventeenth centuries.

Scientism The belief that science and the scientific method can explain everything in the universe and that no other form of inquiry is valid.

Scramble for Africa Late nineteenth-century competition among European powers to acquire colonies in Africa.

Sea Peoples Unknown seafaring people that contributed to the instability of the eastern Mediterranean in the twelfth century B.C.E., attacking Egypt, Palestine, Mesopotamia, Anatolia, and Syria.

Second Vatican Council Council of the Roman Catholic Church that convened at intervals in the 1960s and led to major changes in church liturgy and discipline.

Secularism Belief that religious considerations should be excluded from civil affairs or public education.

Self-determination Principle that a given people or nationality has the right to determine their own political status.

Self-strengthening Mid–nineteenth-century Chinese reform movement initiated in response to Western incursions.

Seljuks A Turkish dynasty ruling in Central and western Asia from the eleventh to the thirteenth centuries.

Serf Agricultural laborer attached to the land owned by a lord and required to perform labor in return for certain legal or customary rights. Unlike slaves, serfs could not usually be sold away from the land.

Shaman A person who acts as an intermediary between humans and spirits or gods. Such a person functions as the medium though which spirits talk to humans.

Sharia Islamic law The word *sharia* derives from the verb *shara'a*, which is connected to the concepts of "spiritual law" and "system of divine law."

Shiites Members of the most important minority tradition in the Islamic world. Shiites believe that the caliphate is the prerogative of Muhammad's nephew, Ali, and his heirs. Shiism has been the state religion in Iran since the sixteenth century.

Shinto A religion native to Japan, characterized by veneration of nature spirits and ancestors and by a lack of formal dogma.

Shogun A hereditary military ruler of Japan who exercised real power in the name of the emperor, who was usually powerless and relegated to purely ceremonial roles. The last shogun was removed from office in 1868.

Sikhism Indian religion founded by Nanak Guru in the early sixteenth century that blends elements of the Hindu and Muslim traditions.

Silk Roads Key overland trade routes that connected eastern and western Eurasia. The route first began to function in the aftermath of Alexander the Great's expansion into Central Asia at the end of the fourth century B.C.E.

Sioux A nomadic Native American people of central North America who, with the benefit of horses introduced to the Americas by the Spanish, formed a pastoralist empire in the late eighteenth and mid–nineteenth centuries.

Social Darwinism The misapplication of Darwin's biological theories to human societies, often to justify claims of racial superiority and rule by the strong over the weak.

Socialism Any of various theories or systems in which the means of producing and distributing goods is owned collectively or by a centralized government.

Socialist realism An artistic doctrine embraced by many communist and leftist regimes that the sole legitimate purpose of the arts was to glorify the ideals of the state by portraying workers, peasants, and the masses in a strictly representational, nonabstract style.

Sociobiology The study of the biological determinants of social behavior.

Solidarity Polish trade union founded in 1980 that played a key role in bringing down Poland's communist regime.

Solomids Dynasty that seized power in Ethiopia in 1270 C.E. and claimed descent from the Biblical King Solomon.

Song dynasty Dynasty (960–1279) under which China achieved one of its highest levels of culture and prosperity.

Songhay An ancient empire of West Africa in the present-day country of Mali. It reached the height of its power around 1500 C.E.

Soninke West African kingdom on the upper Niger River.

Soviet Russian term for a workers' collective.

State system Organization of early modern Europe into competing nation-states.

Steppe A vast semiarid, grass-covered plain, extending across northern Eurasia and central North America.

Stoicism Philosophy founded on the belief that nature is morally neutral and that the wise person, therefore, achieves happiness by accepting misfortune and practicing self-control.

Stranger effect The tendency some peoples have to esteem and defer to strangers.

Stream of consciousness A literary technique that presents the thoughts and feelings of a character in a novel or story as they arise in the character's mind.

Subsidiarity Doctrine that decisions should always be made at the level closest to the people whom the decisions most affect.

Suez Canal Canal linking the Mediterranean and the Red Sea. It was built by French engineers with European capital and opened in 1869.

Sufis Members of Islamic groups that cultivate mystical beliefs and practices. Sufis have often been instrumental in spreading Islam, but Muslim authorities have often distrusted them.

Sundiata Legendary hero said to have founded the kingdom of Mali in West Africa.

Sunnis Members of the dominant tradition in the Islamic world. Sunnis believe that any member of Muhammad's tribe could be designated caliph.

Surrealism Literary and artistic movement that attempts to express the workings of the subconscious.

Syllogisms A form of argument in which we can infer a necessary conclusion from two premises that prior demonstration or agreement has established to be true.

Syncretic Characterized by the reconciliation or fusion of differing systems of belief.

Taiping Rebellion Rebellion (1852–1864) against the Qing Empire that resulted in tens of millions of deaths and widespread destruction in southern China.

Tang dynasty Chinese dynasty (618–907) famous for its wealth and encouragement of the arts and literature.

Tengri "Ruler of the sky." The supreme deity of the Mongols and other steppeland peoples.

The Encyclopedia Twenty-eight volume compendium of Enlightenment thought published in French and edited by Denis Diderot. The first volume appeared in 1751.

The Mongol Peace Era in the thirteenth and fourteenth centuries when Mongol rule created order and stability in Central Asia and enabled goods and ideas to flow along the Silk Roads.

Theory of value The theory that the value of goods is not inherent, but rather determined by supply and demand.

Theravada A conservative branch of Buddhism that adheres to the nontheistic ideal of self-purification to nirvana. Theravada Buddhism emphasizes the monastic ideal and is dominant in present-day Sri Lanka and southeast Asia.

Third Rome Term Russians used for Moscow and Russian Orthodox Christianity. It expressed the belief that the Russian czars were the divinely chosen heirs of the Roman and Byzantine emperors.

Thule Inuit Indigenous Native American people who crossed the Arctic and arrived in Greenland around 1000 C.E.

Tillers Agriculturalists who emphasize the cultivation of plants for food and products, such as timber and cotton.

Tokugawa A family of shoguns that ruled Japan in the name of the emperors from 1603 to 1868.

Trading-post empires Term for the networks of imperial forts and trading posts that Europeans established in Asia in the seventeenth century.

Treasure Fleets Spanish fleets that sailed from the Caribbean each year to bring gold and silver from mines in the Americas back to Europe.

Tundra A treeless area between the ice cap and the tree line of Arctic regions.

Turks A member of any of the Turkic-speaking, nomadic peoples who originated in Central Asia. The Turks eventually converted to Islam and dominated the Middle East.

Uncertainty principle Niels Bohr and Werner Heisenberg's theory that because observers are part of every observation their findings can never be objective.

United Nations International political organization created after World War II to prevent armed conflict, settle international disputes peacefully, and provide cultural, economic, and technological aid. It was the successor to the League of Nations, which had proved to be ineffectual.

Universal love Love between all people, regardless of status, nationality, or family ties.

Upanishads The theoretical sections of the Veda (the literature of the sages of the Ganges civilization). The Upanishads were written down as early as 800 B.C.E.

Urbanization The process by which urban areas develop and expand.

Utilitarianism System of thought devised by Jeremy Bentham, based on the notion that the goal of the state was to create the greatest happiness for the greatest number of people.

Utopianism Belief in a system or ideology aimed at producing a perfect or ideal society.

Vaccination Inoculation with a vaccine to produce immunity to a particular disease.

Vernacular languages The languages that people actually spoke—as opposed to Latin—which was the language used by the Roman Catholic Church and was, for a long time, the language of scholarship, the law, and diplomacy in much of Europe.

Virtual reality A computer simulation of a real or imaginary system.

Wahhabbism Muslim sect founded by Abdul Wahhab (1703–1792), known for its strict observance of the Quran. It is the dominant form of Islam in Saudi Arabia.

Westerlies Winds coming from the west.

Westernization The process by which other cultures adopt Western styles or ways of life.

World system The system of interconnections among the world's population.

World War I Global war (1914–1918) sparked by the assassination of Archduke Francis Ferdinand of Austria by a Serb terrorist in June 1914.

World War II Global conflict that lasted from 1939 to 1945 and ended with the defeat and occupation of Fascist Italy, Nazi Germany, and Japan.

Zen A school of Mahayana Buddhism that asserts that a person can attain enlightenment through meditation, self-contemplation, and intuition.

Ziggurat A tall, tapering Mesopotamian temple. Ziggurats were the physical and cultural centers of Mesopotamian cities.

Zimbabwes Stone-built administrative centers for rulers and the elite in southern Africa. The zimbabwes flourished in the fifteenth century.

Zoroastrianism Iranian religious system founded by Zoroaster that posited a universal struggle between the forces of light (the good) and of darkness (evil).

CHAPTER 13

1. P. Jackson, ed., *The Travels of Friar Willam of Rubruck* (London, 1981), pp. 113–114.

2. R. Latham, ed., *The Travels of Marco Polo* (Harmondsworth, 1972), p. 85.

3. R. L. Davis, *Wind Against the Mountain: The Crisis of Politics and Culture in Thirteenth-Century China* (Cambridge, MA: Harvard University Asia Center, 1996), p. 62.

4. J. Fennell, *The Crisis of Medieval Russia* (Longman Publishing Group, 1983), p. 88.

CHAPTER 14

1. R. Horrox, *The Black Death* (Manchester University Press, 1994), p. 16.

2. N. Cantor, *In the Wake of the Plague* (New York: Perennial/Harper Collins, 2002), p. 199.

3. D. Hall in *Cambridge History of Southeast Asia*, ed. N. Tarling (Cambridge University Press, 1992), i. 218.

4. F. Rosenthal ed. *The Muqaddimah*, 3 vols. (New York: Pantheon Books, 1958), i, 64–65.

CHAPTER 16

1. T. Armstrong, ed., *Yermak's Campaign in Siberia* (London, 1975), pp. 38–50, 59–69, 108, 163; B. Bobrick, *East of the Sun: The Epic Conquest and Tragic History of Siberia* (London, 1993), p. 43.

CHAPTER 18

1. *Principes de la philosophie* Bk I, 8,7; Discours sur la méthode, ch 4.

CHAPTER 20

1. M.E. Itoare, ed., *The Resolution Journal of John Reinhold Forster*, 4 vols. (London, 1982), ii, 409.

CHAPTER 21

1. L. Blussé, *Strange Company* (Leiden, 1986), p. 95.

2. D. Badia, *Viajes de Ali Bey* (Madrid, 2001), p. 514.

CHAPTER 22

1. *The Figure of the Earth* (London, 1738), pp. 38–40, 77–78.

CHAPTER 23

1. J. K. Fairbank, ed., *The Cambridge History of China*, x, part I (Cambridge, 1978), p. 499.

CHAPTER 24

1. D. Northrup, ed., *Indentured Labor in the Age of Imperialism* (New York, 1995), p. 247

CHAPTER 26

1. H. S. Wilson, *Origins of West Africa Nationalism* (London, 1969), p. 167.

CHAPTER 27

1. F. Boas, *The Mind of Primitive Man* (New York, 1913), p. 113.

2. N. Chomsky, *Knowledge of Language* (Wesport, CT: 1986), p. 14.

CHAPTER 28

1. D. A. J. Pernikoff, *Bushido: The Anatomy of Terror* (1943).

CHAPTER 29

1. F. Jameson, *Marxism and Form* (Princeton, 1971), p. XVIII.

2. I. Berlin "My Intellectual Path," *New York Review of Books*, 14 May (1998); The Power of Ideas, ed. H. Hardy (Princeton, 2002), p.12.

* Page numbers in italic refer to maps and photos

I-1